PROFESSIONAL RESPONSIBILITY

A STUDENT'S GUIDE

By

Ronald D. Rotunda

*Doy & Dee Henley Chair and Distingui[...]
of Jurisprudence
Chapman University School o[...]*

and

John S. Dzienkowski

*Dean John F. Sutton, Jr. Chair in Lawyering and
the Legal Process
University of Texas School of Law*

2012–2013

The Center for Professional Responsibility

The American Bar Association

WEST®

A Thomson Reuters business

Mat #41269681

To Mark and Erica

RDR

For Judge Robert E. Keeton

JSD

*

PREFACE

Significant changes have taken place in the regulation of lawyers since the recent turn of the century. In 2002, the ABA completed a five-year project led by the Ethics 2000 Commission to modernize the Model Rules of Professional Conduct. The Commission gathered considerable comment from the legal profession and the public and redrafted many of the Rules in light of these suggestions. The ABA's adoption of the revised Model Rules in February 2002 has led to the creation of an entire new layer of regulation and legislative history on the rules that govern lawyer conduct.

The future brings us not only change but also an increase in the rate of change. Hence, the extensive February 2002 revisions were harbingers of more amendments to the Rules. In August, 2002, the ABA House of Delegates modified the Rules to reflect the work of the Commission on Multijurisdictional Practice (MJP Commission). The MJP Commission studied the practice of law across borders and developed several proposals to modernize the regulation of lawyers in a national and global society.

While these changes were going on, the corporate scandals of 2001 and 2002, paved the way for yet more change. The legal profession fell under increased and significant scrutiny when several of this country's largest corporations declared bankruptcy or disclosed involvement in significant financial crimes and frauds. The decline in confidence in the corporate stock market led Congress to hold hearings and to enact the Sarbanes Oxley Act of 2002.[1] The statute expressly directed the Securities and Exchange Commission (SEC) to implement minimum standards of professional conduct for attorneys appearing and practicing before the SEC. The adoption of new SEC regulations has had a significant impact on lawyers who represent public companies.

These events patterned the unfolding of the Watergate political scandal of the mid-1970s. During the Watergate Hearings, Congressional investigations disclosed political corruption, which led people to ask, where were the lawyers when politicians engaged in criminal and fraudulent acts? A quarter of a century later, new Congressional investigations led people to ask, where were the lawyers when the public corporations engaged in crimi-

---

[1] Sarbanes-Oxley Act of 2002, Pub. L. No. 107-204, 116 Stat. 745 (2002).

nal and fraudulent acts? In response to the Watergate scandal, the ABA lobbied successfully to require law schools to teach legal ethics. In response to the corporate scandals, the ABA formed a Task Force on Corporate Responsibility to examine the role of lawyers in the recent corporate scandals. This Task Force proposed that the ABA amend the Rules on confidentiality and on representation of clients who are entities, e.g., corporations. Hence, in August 2003, the House of Delegates adopted sweeping revisions to Rules 1.6 and 1.13. This book analyzes those revisions as well as the lawyer provisions of the Sarbanes Oxley Act of 2002.

The chapters reflect changes made to the Model Rules through March 2012 as well as the developments in the case law, literature, and regulations governing legal ethics. We not only examine and analyze the current version of the Rules but we also discuss and analyze the Rules' predecessors—the Model Code and the 1983 version of the Model Rules. We have extensively updated the text and footnotes to take into account these considerable changes in the Model Rules. We highlight the changes in the law as well as the ambiguities created by the new language. Where appropriate, we analyze the relevant ABA and state ethics opinions, case law, and scholarship. In each annual revision, we also rewrite and improve our commentary and analysis to reflect the developments in the law.

In February 2007, the ABA adopted a new Code of Judicial Conduct. We have written a new chapter 10 to reflect the new 2007 Code of Judicial Conduct. This chapter includes a comprehensive analysis and commentary on the new rules governing judicial conduct.

The 2005-2006 edition of this book witnessed the addition of Professor John Dzienkowski of the University of Texas School of Law as co-author, who can share the blame for any errors (substantive or typographical) that remain. We have proofed this book extensively, but in the nature of things some errors may still exist. Please bear in mind the words of Judge Henry de Bracton, who pleaded over 700 years ago: "I ask the reader, if he finds in this work anything superfluous or erroneous, to correct and amend it, or pass it over with eyes half closed, for to keep all in mind and err in nothing is divine rather than human."[2]

Starting with the 2005-2006 edition, we renumbered all of the chapters to reflect the organization of the Model Rules. For example, Chapter 1.5 covers Rule 1.5 on fees, and Chapter 8.3 covers Rule 8.3 on reporting lawyer misconduct. Now it is easier

---

[2] Henry De Bracton, BRACTON ON THE LAWS AND CUSTOMS OF ENGLAND 20 (Samuel Thorne translator, 1968) (circ. 1250).

to find quickly our discussion of any particular rule. This change also permits us to add Model Rules in the future without renumbering the chapters with every edition. The judicial ethics chapters now begin with Chapter 10.1.

We would like very much to express our appreciation to the staff of the ABA who helped on this project. We particularly thank Arthur Garwin, of the ABA Center for Professional Responsibility, for his careful editing and thoughtful comments. We would like to thank our respective deans for supporting our research and scholarship and our faculty assistants, Ms. Maria Sanchez and Ms. Penny Tillman. Finally, we would like to thank our parents, who made this book possible, and our children, who made it necessary.

RONALD D. ROTUNDA
JOHN S. DZIENKOWSKI

ORANGE, CALIFORNIA
AUSTIN, TEXAS
APRIL 1, 2012

*

PREFACE TO THE FIRST EDITION

Most lawyers today took a required course in Legal Ethics when they were law students, followed by a bar examination on that same subject. It was not always so. When I started teaching, my law school did not even offer the course, and the legal ethics casebooks that existed focused on the intricacies of unauthorized practice. In those days, it was easy for law students to learn the Golden Rule: "Thou shalt not lie, cheat, steal ... or advertise." The dean asked me to teach legal ethics because I was the new teacher on the block, and it was assumed that I must know something about the subject since I had just left my position as assistant majority counsel to the Senate Watergate Committee.

Times have changed. The emphasis on legal ethics began in 1974 as part of what Spiro Agnew referred to as our "post-Watergate morality." Some ridicule this movement as based on a false assumption that more study of ethics will make us more ethical. These people often think that ethics can be taught only at mother's knee.[1]

I recall a story I heard a long time ago. Two third-year law students married each other. A year later, when both had graduated, they took a belated honeymoon in Scotland. There, at a picturesque country inn, the proprietress asked how long they had been married. "It's been a year" they said. "What! A year has passed, and no wee little ones yet?" "Well," they responded, "we had to finish school." "You mean in America you have to go to school for that too?"

Well, in America, we lawyers go to school to study ethics. When I started teaching legal ethics a quarter of a century ago, one of my law school colleagues asked (not in jest), "What do you do? Teach them not to steal?" It's a little more complicated than that. Those who think of ethics as intuition are often the same people whom courts routinely disqualify because they do not appreciate the complexities of the rules of conflicts of interest. Attorneys are often their own worst lawyers. They know the law affecting their clients because it is their business to know that. But too frequently they know little about the law affecting them-

---

[1] See SPECIAL COMMISSION ON PROFESSIONALISM, ILLINOIS STATE BAR ASSOCIATION, THE BAR, THE BENCH AND PROFESSIONALISM IN ILLINOIS 8 comments (1987) ("Heard more than once was the opinion that one cannot teach another to be ethical.").

selves—the law governing lawyers. The Administrator of the Illinois Attorney Registration and Disciplinary Commission once recounted that a large percentage of lawyers pay their annual mandatory fee to support the Disciplinary Commission with checks drawn on client trust fund accounts. These attorneys apparently are unaware of the commingling rules. ("[C]ommingling is committed when a client's money is intermingled with that of his attorney and its separate identity lost so that it may be used for the attorney's personal expenses or subjected to claims of his creditors.")[2] Many lawyers today are also ignorant of recent developments regarding conflicts of interest and attorney disqualification. Some lawyers do not appreciate the distinction between a client's "confidences" and her "secrets" and do not realize that they were not supposed to volunteer either.[3] In one particular situation, a lawyer displayed his ignorance at an inopportune and inauspicious time—in the course of his deposition, when he was being sued for malpractice.

Several years ago, one of my former academic colleagues, who also practiced law, was asked whether she bought malpractice insurance, and whether it was expensive to obtain for a part-time practitioner. She responded that she did not have to buy insurance because her contract with her clients required them to waive any malpractice claims against her. Her listeners nodded knowingly until I mentioned that her standard waiver agreement violated state ethics rules, was not enforceable, and could cause her to lose her license.[4]

One need not rely on anecdotal analysis. The few existing empirical studies show that lawyers often are unaware of even basic information about the law governing lawyers.[5]

While most new entrants to the legal profession must pass a professional responsibility examination, older lawyers, who draw a disproportionate number of malpractice suits,[6] either have

---

[2] *Clark v. State Bar*, 39 Cal. 2d 161, 167-68, 246 P.2d 1, 4 (1952).

[3] *See* discussion of confidences and secrets under the Model Code and client information under the Model Rules in Chapter 1.6.

[4] ABA Model Rules of Professional Conduct, Rule 1.8(h), provides: "A lawyer shall not: (1) make an agreement prospectively limiting the lawyer's liability to a client for malpractice unless the client is independently represented in making the agreement ...." Illinois then, and now, has a similar rule derived from the ABA model. *See* Illinois Code of Professional Responsibility DR 6-102(a) (1987); ABA Model Code of Professional Responsibility DR6-102(A).

[5] *See, e.g.,* Special Project, *The Attorney-Client Privilege in Multiple Party Situations*, 8 COLUM. J. L. & SOC.PROBS. 179, 180 (1972) (reporting that its "survey revealed a general lack of awareness among attorneys as to when the attorney-client privilege will apply to inter-attorney exchanges of information").

[6] *See* COMMISSION ON PROFESSIONALISM, AMERICAN BAR ASSOCIA-

never formally studied ethics or have not kept up with the developments in the law. Many of these malpractice suits arise out of violations of professional ethics.[7]

What we call "lawyer's ethics" can be taught, and must be learned. The ethics rules are law, not merely trendy lip service. Most jurisdictions have adopted, as court rules, both the ABA's Model Rules of Professional Conduct and the ABA's Model Code of Judicial Conduct. These model rules have thus become law in the same way that the Rules of Civil Procedure have become law. These ethics rules, which impose substantive requirements on lawyers and judges, are just as complex as the rules of civil practice or the rules of evidence. Many of the ethics rules cannot be known through some sort of innate or hereditary awareness

---

TION, "...IN THE SPIRIT OF PUBLIC SERVICE:" A BLUEPRINT FOR THE REKINDLING OF LAWYER PROFESSIONALISM 24 n.*(1986), *reprinted in* 112 F.R.D. 243 (1987). *See also* Ronald D. Rotunda, *Lawyers and Professionalism: A Commentary on the Report of the American Bar Association Commission on Professionalism*,18 LOYOLA U. CHI. L. J. 1149 (1987).

[7] *See, e.g.*, William H. Gates, *The Newest Data on Lawyers' Malpractice Claims*, A.B.A. J., Apr. 1984, at 78, 80 (a significant proportion of malpractice claims arise from violations of professional responsibility, including 9.35% from failure to obtain a client's consent or to inform a client, 4.79% from failure to follow a client's instructions, and 3.39% from conflicts of interest).

In recent years, several major law firms have settled for substantial sums various malpractice claims based on ethical violations.

● New York's Rogers & Wells settled, for $40 million, a case in which it continued to represent a client after it should have known that the client was perpetrating a fraud. *After a $40M Payment, It's Not Over Yet for Rogers & Wells*, NATIONAL LAW JOURNAL, Apr. 14, 1986, at 1, col. 1.

● Baltimore's Venable, Baetjer & Howard settled, for $27 million, a lawsuit involving conflicts of interests. *Venable Agrees to $27M Accord*, NATIONAL LAW JOURNAL, May 25, 1987, at 3, col. 1.

● New York's Milberg Weiss settled, for $50 million, a malicious prosecution case brought against a lawyer. Richard Schmidt, *Milberg Weiss Agrees to Pay $50 Million to Settle Lexecon Case*, WALL STREET JOURNAL, April 14, 1999, at B17; Karen Donovan, *Milberg Weiss $50M Mistake*, NATIONAL LAW JOURNAL, April 26, 1999, at A1. The law firm, after losing a jury verdict for $45 million for malicious prosecution, settled by wiring a check for $50 million before the jury could deliberate on punitive damages.

The ramifications of ethical violations are not limited to malpractice or discipline. Restatement of the Law Governing Lawyers, Third, § 6 ("Judicial Remedies Available to Client or Nonclient for Lawyer Wrongs") (Official Draft 2000). *See, e.g.*, *United States v. Strawser*, 800 F.2d 704, 708 (7th Cir. 1986), *cert. denied*, 107 S.Ct. 1350 (1987), where the court ordered the lawyer to disgorge excessive fees under the guidelines found in both Illinois Code of Professional Responsibility DR 2-106 and Model Code of Professional Responsibility DR 2106).

Cf. In re Futuronics Corp., 655 F.2d 463, 468-71 (2d Cir. 1981), *cert. denied*, 455 U.S. 941 (1982), where the court denied a law firm over one million dollars in fees under the Bankruptcy Code because of a prohibited fee splitting arrangement and failure to comply with disclosure provisions for joint representation).

automatically infused in ordinary human beings once they are admitted to the bar. Unless a lawyer is risk-prone, he or she will need to understand the law of legal ethics.

This one volume book is intended to offer lawyers and judges an analysis of, and an initiation to, this complex topic. Few of us are, or will become, judges, but many of the issues that concern judges also concern the lawyers who practice before them, such as when a judge must disqualify herself; when a judge may be disciplined; and when judges may receive gifts and loans. Lawyers, after all, cannot give to the judge that which the judge may not receive. In addition, a lawyer cannot know when to move to disqualify a judge if the lawyer does not know when the judicial rules provide that the judge should be disqualified. Because the American Bar Association has been the undisputed leader in developing ethics rules, this book is organized around the ABA Model Rules of Professional Conduct and the ABA Model Code of Judicial Conduct, which most jurisdictions have adopted as court rules to govern lawyers and judges. Even when a jurisdiction, such as California, uses a different format, the substantive rules reflect the considerable ABA influence. In addition, the American Law Institute has recently completed its massive project, the Restatement of the Law Governing Lawyers, Third, which has been an important and helpful tool as I researched this book. Thus, this book will also examine the contributions of this new Restatement.[8]

The sources of the law of legal ethics are numerous. In addition to the ABA Model Rules and the Restatement, each jurisdiction has its own rules. There is also the case law, the commentators, and advisory ethics opinions of various bar associations as well as the opinions of the ABA Ethics Committee, which have become particularly influential. Without the use of Westlaw's computerized legal databases it would be much more difficult to access these numerous and diverse sources.

I asked others to read the manuscript for substantive comments, and I wish that I could blame them for any errors, but I cannot, though I am very thankful for all that they have done: Robert A. Creamer, Mary Devlin, Bill Freivogel, Arthur Garwin, Bob O'Malley, and Tom Morgan, to whom I am perpetually indebted for many reasons that go far beyond his willingness to read this manuscript. I am also grateful to Dean Thomas M. Mengler of the University of Illinois, for his support.

Now, a brief word about typographical errors. I ask you to bear in mind the words of Judge Henry de Bracton, who pleaded

---

[8] While the Restatement is titled, "Restatement, Third," there was no "Restatement, First," or "Restatement, Second," resulting in confusion for all but the cognoscenti.

over 700 years ago: "I ask the reader, if he finds in this work anything superfluous or erroneous, to correct and amend it, or pass it over with eyes half closed, for to keep all in mind and err in nothing is divine rather than human."[9]

I would like very much to express my appreciation to the staff of the ABA who helped me convert this manuscript to a publishable book, particularly to Jeanne P. Gray, the Director of the ABA Center for Professional Responsibility, and Arthur Garwin and Mary Devlin, also of the ABA Center for Professional Responsibility, and Ruth Woodruff, an ABA consultant. Finally, I would like to thank my parents, who made this book possible, and my children, who made it necessary.

RONALD D. ROTUNDA

February, 2001
Champaign, Ill.

*

---

[9] 2 HENRY DE BRACTON, BRACTON ON THE LAWS AND CUSTOMS OF ENGLAND 20 (Samuel Thorne translator, 1968) (circ. 1250).

Table of Contents

INTRODUCTION

I CLIENT-LAWYER RELATIONSHIPS

CHAPTER 1.1 COMPETENCE

CHAPTER 1.2 SCOPE OF REPRESENTATION AND ALLOCATION OF AUTHORITY BETWEEN CLIENT AND LAWYER

CHAPTER 1.3 DILIGENCE

CHAPTER 1.4 COMMUNICATION

CHAPTER 1.5 FEES

CHAPTER 1.6 CONFIDENTIALITY OF INFORMATION

CHAPTER 1.7 CONFLICTS OF INTEREST—CURRENT CLIENTS

CHAPTER 1.11 SPECIAL CONFLICTS OF INTEREST FOR FORMER AND CURRENT GOVERNMENT OFFICERS AND EMPLOYEES

CHAPTER 1.12 FORMER JUDGE, ARBITRATOR, MEDIATOR, OR OTHER THIRD-PARTY NEUTRAL

CHAPTER 1.13 THE ORGANIZATION AS CLIENT

CHAPTER 1.14 CLIENT WITH A DIMINISHED CAPACITY

CHAPTER 4.3 DEALING WITH UNREPRESENTED PERSONS

CHAPTER 4.4 RESPECT FOR THE RIGHTS OF THIRD PERSONS

V LAW FIRMS AND ASSOCIATIONS

CHAPTER 5.1 RESPONSIBILITIES OF A PARTNER OR SUPERVISORY LAWYER

CHAPTER 5.2 RESPONSIBILITIES OF A SUBORDINATE LAWYER

CHAPTER 5.3 THE LAWYER'S RESPONSIBILITIES REGARDING NONLAWYER ASSISTANTS

CHAPTER 5.4 PROFESSIONAL INDEPENDENCE OF A LAWYER

CHAPTER 5.5 UNAUTHORIZED PRACTICE OF LAW; MULTIJURISDICTIONAL PRACTICE OF LAW

CHAPTER 5.6 RESTRICTIONS ON THE RIGHT TO PRACTICE LAW

CHAPTER 5.7 RESPONSIBILITIES REGARDING LAW-RELATED SERVICES

VI PUBLIC SERVICE

CHAPTER 6.1 VOLUNTARY PRO BONO PUBLICO SERVICE

CHAPTER 7.6 POLITICAL CONTRIBUTIONS TO OBTAIN GOVERNMENT LEGAL ENGAGEMENTS OR APPOINTMENTS BY JUDGES

VIII MAINTAINING THE INTEGRITY OF THE PROFESSION

CHAPTER 8.1 BAR ADMISSION AND DISCIPLINARY MATTERS

CHAPTER 8.2 CHARGES AGAINST JUDICIAL AND LEGAL OFFICIALS

CHAPTER 8.3 REPORTING PROFESSIONAL MISCONDUCT

CHAPTER 8.4 MISCONDUCT

CHAPTER 8.5 DISCIPLINARY AUTHORITY AND CHOICE OF LAW

Index

INTRODUCTION

§ 1-1 AN HISTORICAL PERSPECTIVE OF THE ETHICAL RULES GOVERNING LAWYERS

§ 1-1(a) The Hoffman Resolutions

The current ABA Model Rules of Professional Conduct have a long lineage that goes back over a century and a half. In 1836, during an era when the legal profession was subject to virtually no regulation, David Hoffman, a prolific author and professor of law at the University of Maryland, published for his students fifty *"Resolutions In Regard to Professional Deportment."*[1]

Hoffman's exhortations may sound antiquated, or at least quaint, to the modern ear. He advised lawyers to let their conscience be their "sole guide" (Resolution 33), and urged lawyers to "espouse no man's cause out of envy, hatred or malice, toward his antagonist" (Resolution 2). Modern commentators have belittled his advice "lofty in aspiration and preachy in tone"— "Victorian moralizing at its worst."[2]

§ 1-1(b) Sharswood's Lectures

A generation later, in 1854, Professor (and Judge) George Sharswood, turned to the issues raised by Hoffman and published,

---

[Section 1-1]

[1]THOMAS D. MORGAN & RONALD D. ROTUNDA, PROBLEMS AND MATERIALS ON PROFESSIONAL RESPONSIBILITY 11–12 (Foundation Press, 6th ed. 1995). *See also* Russell G. Pearce, *Rediscovering the Republican Origins of the Legal Ethics Codes*, 6 GEORGETOWN J. LEGAL ETHICS 241 (1992).

[2]Geoffrey C. Hazard, *Rules of Ethics: The Drafting Task*, 36 THE RECORD OF ASSOCIATION OF THE BAR OF THE CITY OF NEW YORK 80, 81 (1981).

A Compend of Lectures on the Aims and Duties of the Profession of Law. There is no doubt that Sharswood was familiar with Hoffman's *Resolutions* and agreed with many of Hoffman's specific recommendations. But the two men differed as to the nature and extent of professional accountability. Hoffman preferred relying on the lawyer's conscience, while Sharswood embraced the external guidelines of law and the legal process.[3] The difference between the approaches of these two lawyers was probably more in degree than in kind. Sharswood was interested in looking for heroic role models but, Sharswood was more interested than Hoffman in rules that could be understood and enforced.

Sharswood's lectures greatly influenced the Alabama Bar Association, which published its "Code of Ethics" in 1887. Historians have concluded that the Alabama Code was based on Sharswood's *Essays on Professional Ethics*.[4] Alabama, in turn, paved the way for the American Bar Association to adopt its own ethics rules.[5]

§ 1-1(c) The ABA Canons of Professional Ethics

The ABA began with a very small, select membership in 1878. From its inception through 1893, its annual meetings drew only about 75 to 100 people. Then, with the beginnings of the twentieth century, the ABA membership steadily grew and its goals expanded. At first, it primarily promoted the work of the Commissioners on Uniform State Laws, civil procedure reform, bar admission, and legal education.[6] The ABA subsequently turned its attention to legal ethics and changed the legal landscape.

Although various other states followed Alabama's lead, there was no national standard or model code until August 27, 1908, when a nationwide voluntary bar association, the young Ameri-

---

[3]Maxwell Bloomfield, *David Hoffman and the Shaping of a Republican Legal Culture*, 38 MD. L. REV. 673, 687 (1979).

[4]On this question, an interesting and thorough article is, Walter Burgwyn Jones, *Canons of Professional Ethics, Their Genesis and History*, 7 NOTRE DAME LAWYER 483 (1938). Jones, like many other authorities, concluded that the Alabama Code was based on Sharswood's *Essays on Professional Ethics*, 7 NOTRE DAME LAWYER at 494.

Lawyers' rules of ethics date back to "at least thirteenth century Europe, where lawyers took oaths to abide by a list of ethics precepts." Carol Rice Andrews, *Standards of Conduct for Lawyers: An 800–Year Evolution*, 57 S.M.U. L. REV. 1385 (2004).

[5]Geoffrey C. Hazard, *Rules of Ethics: The Drafting Task*, 36 THE RECORD OF ASSOCIATION OF THE BAR OF THE CITY OF NEW YORK 81 (1981).

[6]ROSCOE POUND, THE LAWYER FROM ANTIQUITY TO MODERN TIMES: WITH PARTICULAR REFERENCE TO THE DEVELOPMENT OF BAR ASSOCIATIONS IN THE UNITED STATES 270–71 (West Pub. Co. & ABA, 1953).

can Bar Association, approved 32 Canons of Professional Ethics. These were also based on the Alabama model.[7]

The ABA initially treated its Canons of Professional Ethics as private law governing only those lawyers who chose to join the Association. For example, in 1940 it announced: "The Canons of this Association govern all its members, irrespective of the nature of their practice, and the application of the Canons is not affected by statutes or regulations governing certain activities of lawyers which may prescribe less stringent standards."[8] The ABA's remedies for violations of its rules were limited. The ABA could expel a member from its association for noncompliance with its rules, but one did need not to be admitted into the ABA in order to practice law.

Nevertheless, the impact of the ABA Canons soon extended beyond membership in the ABA. First, many states adopted the ABA Canons as positive law. If a lawyer violated the ethics rules adopted by the state supreme court, the sanction had more impact, for the lawyer could be suspended from practice or disbarred. In addition, the ABA also established an Ethics Committee to interpret its Canons by issuing opinions. These Ethics Opinions proved to be influential when courts decide issues such as disqualification, legal malpractice, and discipline.[9] Moreover, various courts cited the ABA Canons as legal authority and enforced its ethical requirements, not only in proceedings to discipline lawyers but also in other proceedings, such as hearings on

---

[7]Although the ABA Canons grew out of the Alabama experience, Sharswood's influence is clear. For example, Canon 15 of the ABA Canons of Professional Ethics (1980) includes a quotation. Canon 15 said in part:

The lawyer owes "entire devotion to the interest of the client, warm zeal in the maintenance and defense of his rights and the exertion of his utmost learning and ability."

Reprinted, in, THOMAS D. MORGAN & RONALD D. ROTUNDA, SELECTED STANDARDS ON PROFESSIONAL RESPONSIBILITY 657 (Foundation Press, 2010).

There is no attribution for this quotation in Canon 15, but it comes from GEORGE SHARSWOOD, AN ESSAY ON PROFESSIONAL ETHICS 24 (2d ed. 1860). See CHARLES W. WOLFRAM, MODERN LEGAL ETHICS 578 n.73 (West Pub. Co., 1986); Russell G. Pearce, *Rediscovering the Republican Origins of the Legal Ethics Codes*, 6 GEORGETOWN J. L. ETHICS 241 (1992).

[8]ABA Formal Opinion 203 (Nov. 23, 1940) (patent lawyer may not advertise even though the U.S. Patent Office allows certain types of advertising).

[9]The ABA Ethics Committee is now called the *Standing Committee on Ethics and Professional Responsibility*. It consists of ten members. The committee may, with the concurrence of a majority of its members, express its opinion on proper professional or judicial conduct, either on its own initiative or when requested to do so by a member of the bar or the judiciary.

motions to disqualify lawyers for engaging in conflicts of interest in violation of the Canons.[10]

Over the years, the ABA amended these Canons of Ethics to take into account the changing nature of legal practice.

§ 1-1(d) The ABA Code of Professional Responsibility

In spite of the various amendments to the Canons over a sixty year period, the canons were eventually criticized as "generalizations designed for an earlier era."[11] But it was not until 1969 that the ABA adopted a completely revised set of rules, the Code of Professional Responsibility. In keeping with the view that the CODE was "law" that governed ABA members regardless of state law, this Code (which the ABA House of Delegates approved on August 12, 1969) had an "effective date" of January 1, 1970. Until 1976, the membership form for the ABA also included a statement that the member promised to abide by the ABA CANONS OF ETHICS and, later, by the ABA CODE OF PROFESSIONAL RESPONSIBILITY.

Recall that the ABA purported to treat its Canons as private law governing those lawyers who chose to join the Association. The Antitrust Division of the Department of Justice, as well as other groups, noted serious antitrust problems when lawyers agree with each other to abide by certain purportedly "ethical" rules that restricted competition. For example, the ABA ethics rules had initially imposed serious restrictions on advertising of legal services and urged minimum fees.[12] In response to this criticism, the ABA formally acknowledged in 1978 that its Code was really only a *Model* Code.

> The Canons of Professional Ethics and the succeeding Code of Professional Responsibility have been drafted, promulgated, and amended by agencies of the American Bar Association within the context of understanding that such codes might serve only as

---

[10]*E.g., T.C. Theatre Corp. v. Warner Brothers Pictures, Inc.*, 113 F.Supp. 265, 268 & n. 4 (S.D.N.Y. 1953), citing Canon 6 of the ABA Canons of Canons of Professional Ethics.

[11]Harlan Fiske Stone, *The Public Influence of the Bar*, 48 HARV. L. REV. 1, 10 (1934).

[12]ABA Code of Professional Responsibility, EC 2-16 ("The legal profession cannot remain a viable force in fulfilling its role in our society unless its members receive adequate compensation for services rendered, and reasonable fees should be charged in appropriate cases to clients able to pay them."); EC 2-17 ("adequate compensation is necessary in order to enable the lawyer to serve his client effectively and to preserve the integrity and independence of the profession."); DR 2-101 (Publicity in General); DR 2-102 (Professional Notices, Letterheads, Offices, and Law Lists) (amended as of Feb. 17, 1976), reprinted in, THOMAS D. MORGAN & RONALD D. ROTUNDA, PROBLEMS AND MATERIALS ON PROFESSIONAL RESPONSIBILITY, at 250, 354–55 (Foundation Press, 1976).

exemplars for the proper conduct of legal practitioners but that the power of disciplinary enforcement rests with the judiciary.[13]

To emphasize this change, the ABA changed the title of its Code of Professional Responsibility to the *Model* Code of Professional Responsibility. There is no antitrust violation when the ABA, or any other organization or individual, lobbies to persuade the legislative, judicial, or executive branches of government to enact rules, because such activities are protected by the First Amendment right of petition. If the relevant government body promulgates rules, the private entity or individual who obeys a state rule that limits competition is not conspiring in restraint of trade because one does not "conspire" with the state.[14]

The ABA was quite successful in persuading state and federal courts to adopt its Model Code as law, an enacted rule of court. State courts also cited the ABA Model Code as evidence of the law even in states where it had not been officially adopted. Similarly, courts have often cited and relied on the ABA Formal and Informal Opinions interpreting the Model Code as influential evidence of the law, even though they also are not law.

§ 1-1(e) The 1983 ABA Model Rules of Professional Conduct

§ 1-1(e)(1) The Kutak Commission

Less than a decade after the ABA Model Code of Professional Responsibility was promulgated in 1969, the ABA established a Commission to create another code of ethics for the legal profession. Between 1977 and 1983, the Kutak Commission, named after its chairman, the late Robert J. Kutak, proceeded to write several drafts of a new code of conduct for lawyers. The final product completely revised the format, organization, and language of the Model Code. The 1983 Model Rules were, in part, a response to criticisms about the Model Code's focus on litigation and its three-tiered structure of canons, ethical considerations, and disciplinary rules.[15]

Over the years, the ABA has continued the format that the

---

[13]ABA Informal Opinion 1420 (June 5, 1978). *See* Thomas D. Morgan, *The Impact of Antitrust Law on the Legal Profession*, 67 FORDHAM L. REV. 415 (1998).

[14]The leading cases in this area are *Eastern R.R. Presidents Conference v. Noerr Motor Freight, Inc.*, 365 U.S. 127, 81 S.Ct. 523, 5 L.Ed.2d 464 (1961); *United Mine Workers v. Pennington*, 381 U.S. 657, 85 S.Ct. 1585, 14 L.Ed.2d 626 (1965). *See* 5

RONALD D. ROTUNDA & JOHN E. NOWAK, TREATISE ON CONSTITUTIONAL LAW: SUBSTANCE AND PROCEDURE § § 20.54 (Thomson—West, 4th ed. 2008) (6 volumes).

[15]Geoffrey C. Hazard, *Rules of Ethics: The Drafting Task*, 36 THE RECORD OF ASSOCIATION OF THE BAR OF THE CITY OF NEW YORK 77 (1981). Professor Geoffrey Hazard was the reporter and chief draftsman for the ABA Commission that drew up the

Kutak Commission first proposed in 1980. Since then, the ABA has kept the basic structure but—as we shall see—it has frequently amended various provisions in the Model Rules. At around the same time, the Roscoe Pound American Trial Lawyers Foundation was concerned that new ABA Rules would not adequately reflect the views of practicing lawyers, and would not adequately protect the interests of clients. Consequently, it asked Professor Monroe Freedman[16] to serve as Reporter for what became the American Lawyers' Code of Conduct, published as a discussion draft in 1980.[17]

The American Lawyer's Code of Conduct influenced the ABA Model Rules. In the ensuring years, the ABA has adopted at least eight important provisions from the American Lawyers' Code of Conduct. While the ABA has not formally acknowledged its pedigree, the relationship is unmistakable because the ABA usually used identical or similar language.[18]

The Kutak Commission drafted the 1983 ABA Model Rules of Professional Conduct, which the ABA House of Delegates approved in August 1983. This time, however, the ABA House of Delegates specifically defeated a motion to set an "effective" date. There is no "effective" date because the proposed law does not bind ABA members. Instead, it binds lawyers practicing in a jurisdiction where the court has adopted the ABA Rules as substantive law.

§ 1-1(e)(2) Change of Language

Normally, when one amends, changes, or redrafts a law, a change in the language used would signify the drafter's intent to change the meaning. That was not the case in the 1983 Model Rules. As one of the consultants to the ABA's Kutak Commission (which drafted the 1983 Model Rules) noted at the time, the ABA Commission often rejected the language of the Model Code not

---

ABA Model Rules.

[16]Professor Monroe H. Freedman, the former Dean at Hofstra, among other things published the first lawyers' ethics treatise, LAWYERS' ETHICS IN AN ADVERSARY SYSTEM (1975), and was the 1998 recipient of the Michael H. Franck Professional Responsibility Award to honor his lifetime of original and influential scholarship in the field of lawyers' ethics. He is the Howard Lichtenstein Distinguished Professor of Legal Ethics at Hofstra University Law School.

[17]American Lawyer's Code of Conduct (Public Discussion Draft 1980).

[18]See discussion in, Freedman, The Influence of the American Lawyer's Code of Conduct on ABA Rules and Standards, 38 HOFSTRA L. REV. 927 (2010). See also Freedman, The Influence of the American Lawyer's Code of Conduct on ABA Rules and Standards, 38 HOFSTRA L. REV. 927 (2010) at footnotes 7-14.

because of any intent to change the meaning but only because of a preference for different phraseology.[19]

§ 1-1(e)(3) The Comments

The 1983 Model Rules follow an approach similar to that which was popularized by the various Restatements published by the American Law Institute. In other words, the 1983 Model Rules place the Rule in text (often referred to as the black letter text), and then include, in official "Comments," additional material that elaborates and amplifies the Rule. The Comments are frequently understood to provide a legislative history explaining the reasons behind a rule. At other times, the Comments refer to particular examples, but, unlike the American Law Institute's Restatements of the Law, the 1983 Model Rules provide no series of hypothetical illustrations.

Although the ABA did not number the Comments to the 1983 Model Rules, some states have done so, in order to facilitate easy reference to, and citation of, a particular Comment.[20]

§ 1-1(e)(4) State Adoption of the Model Rules

By the end of 1999 over 80% of the states (and also the District of Columbia) had adopted the 1983 Model Rules, subject to various non-uniform amendments. In addition, the 1983 Model Rules have frequently been cited as evidence of the law in various court decisions, even if the jurisdiction did not formally adopt a version of the 1983 Model Rules. The 1983 ABA Model Rules have proven to be a more useful teaching tool than the Model Code.[21] Even foreign jurisdictions have looked to the ABA for leadership in the area of legal ethics.[22]

Since its adoption in 1983, the ABA has amended the 1983

---

[19]John F. Sutton, Jr., *Professional Code Becoming Controversial Rules*, 35 VIRGINIA L. WEEKLY 1, 4 col. 1 (Nov. 12, 1982).

[20]The numbers of each Comment are in brackets to indicate that they are not part of the official version of the 1983 ABA Model Rules.

[21]Ronald D. Rotunda, *Teaching Ethics Under the New Model Rules*, 14 SYLLABUS 1 (No. 3, Sept. 1983) (ABA Section on Legal Education and Admissions to the Bar).

A Note on Style and Citations. For the sake of brevity, the ABA Model Code will be referred to as the Code. The current version of the Model Rules based upon the 2002 version of the Model Rules will be referred to as

the Rules. The original version of the Model Rules passed in 1983 and amended to the year 2002, will be referred to as the 1983 Model Rules. The Disciplinary Rules of the Code will be cited as "DR," as in DR 4-101. The Ethical Considerations of the Code will be cited as "EC," as in EC 2-21. The ABA has not amended the Model Code since 1983, when it promulgated the Model Rules.

[22]*See, e.g.*, Ronald D. Rotunda, *A Czech Window on Ethics*, 18 NATIONAL LAW JOURNAL, at A15 (July 22, 1996); Ronald D. Rotunda, *Legal Ethics, The Czech Republic, and The Rule of Law*, 7 THE PROFESSIONAL LAWYER 1 (A.B.A., No. 8, 1996); Ronald D. Rotunda, *Nová pravidla profesního jednání advokátçv České republice (v komparaci s kodexy*

Model Rules numerous times. Many states have followed the lead of the ABA and adopted the amendments that the ABA House of Delegates has approved. Therefore, when studying a case or an ethics opinion in the various states, one should examine whether the decision is based upon the current version of the Model Rules or a prior version.

§ 1-1(f) The 2002 ABA Model Rules of Professional Conduct

§ 1-1(f)(1) The Ethics 2000 Commission.

In 1997, the ABA established the Commission on Evaluation of the Rules of Professional Conduct to review and update the 1983 version of the Model Rules. The Commission quickly became known as the Ethics 2000 or E2K Commission, and it was chaired by Chief Justice Norman Veasey of the Supreme Court of Delaware. Boston University Professor Nancy J. Moore was its Chief Reporter and she was assisted by George Washington Professor Thomas Morgan (1998–1999) and University of Tennessee Professor Carl Pierce. The Ethics 2000 Commission held meetings around the country, invited comments, produced drafts, and ultimately delivered a final report to the ABA House of Delegates.

The Ethics 2000 Commission made a decision that it would retain the structure of the 1983 Model Rules and simply propose amendments rather than prepare an entirely new lawyers' code of ethics. The Commission focused on examining the 1983 Rules to determine whether changes were warranted given new technology, new practices in lawyering, the need for better language or clarity, or new Supreme Court decisions. After all, the ABA had the benefit of years of study of the ALI project on the Restatement of Law Governing Lawyers and the Restatement drafts contained much groundwork on the law of lawyering in the states.

The Ethics 2000 Commission submitted its final report for consideration to the ABA House of Delegates in August 2001. The entire House of Delegates debated the report in August 2001 and in February 2002 and, after a few changes on the floor, the ABA adopted the amendment to the Model Rules at the February 2002 meeting.

§ 1-1(f)(2) Changes from the 1983 Model Rules

This book fully incorporates the 2002 and subsequent amendments adopted by the ABA House of Delegates to the Model Rules. Our chapter numbers are now organized to follow the Rule

---

USA a EU) [*The New Rules of Professional Conduct for Advocates in the Czech Republic*], 5 EMP: Evropské a mezinárodní právo 58 (Číslo 3–4, 1996).

numbers. Thus, chapter 3.4 will examine the issues raised by Rule 3.4. In each chapter that deals with a Rule, we reprint the text of the Rule and Comments. After the Rule and Comments, we have prepared a short Authors' 1983 Model Rules Comparison of the current Rule with the Rule adopted by the ABA in 1983.[23]

§ 1-1(f)(3) State Adoption of the 2002 Model Rules

The ABA has been very active in promoting the state consideration of the Model Rules for adoption. The CPR Policy Implementation Committee on Lawyer Regulation has had the responsibility for promoting the adoption of the 2002 Model Rules and the two subsequent amendments. The members of the Committee are available to the states to answer questions and to make presentations. The CPR Policy Implementation Committee has its own website that tracks the state consideration and adoption of these Rules.[24]

Arizona, Arkansas, Colorado, Connecticut, Delaware, District of Columbia, Florida, Idaho, Indiana, Iowa, Kansas, Louisiana, Maryland, Minnesota, Mississippi, Missouri, Montana, Nebraska, Nevada, New Hampshire, New Jersey, North Carolina, North Dakota, Ohio, Oklahoma, Oregon, Pennsylvania, Rhode Island, South Carolina, South Dakota, Utah, Virginia, Washington, Wisconsin, and Wyoming have amended their state codes in light of the 2002 Model Rules.[25] Despite the efforts of the ABA urging states to conform to the 2002 Model Rules in their consideration of state codes, the states have continued to adopt codes that deviate from the current ABA Model Rules. There are many reasons for the variations in the states. Some states continue to preserve local ethics rules and practices. Other states prefer the language of the Model Code or the 1983 Model Rules. Others for a variety of reasons reject the ABA's choices with respect to a particular topic. Although many reasons exist for uniformity among the states, there are benefits to experimentation in the states regarding the regulation of lawyers.

---

[23]Those who seek additional information about the Ethics 2000 project including its many drafts and legislative history should consult the Ethics 2000 website of the ABA. See http://abanet.org/cpr/ethics2K.html. See also Margaret Colgate Love, The Revised ABA Model Rules of Professional Conduct: Summary of the Work of Ethics 2000, 15 GEORGETOWN J. LEGAL ETHICS 441 (2002).

[24]See http://abanet.org/cpr/jclr/jclr_home.html.

[25]American Bar Association, Status of State Review of Professional Conduct Rules (May 29, 2007), reported at http://abanet.org/cpr/jclr/ethics_2000_status_chart.pdf. See generally Lucian T. Pera, Grading ABA Leadership on Legal Ethics Leadership: State Adoption of the Revised ABA Ethics Rules of Professional Conduct, 30 OKLAHOMA CITY U. L. REV. 637 (2005)(examining the extent to which the ABA has met its goal of achieving uniformity throughout the states).

§ 1-1(g) Amendments to the 2002 ABA Model Rules of Professional Conduct

§ 1-1(g)(1) Amendments from the Multijurisdictional Practice of Law Commission

In July 2000, the ABA formed a Commission on Multijurisdictional Practice to study the ethical and legal constraints imposed on lawyers who practice across state and country lines and to propose a coherent system for regulating such conduct that properly balances the interests of lawyers and the general public.[26] While the Multijurisdictional Practice Commission began its work, the Ethics 2000 Commission continued to propose modifications to Model Rules 5.5 (Unauthorized Practice of Law) and 8.5 (Jurisdiction). However, when the ABA House of Delegates considered the revision of the Model Rules, they deferred any consideration of those Rules until the Multijurisdictional Practice Commission had completed its work.

Given the broad topic of multijurisdictional practice, the Commission studied many facets of the problem. Their work led to several interim reports and a final report presented to the ABA House of Delegates in August 2002. The final report suggested that the ABA adopt 9 broad changes. These included:

Report 201A— Regulation of the Practice of Law by the Judiciary

Report 201B— Unauthorized Practice of Law; Multijurisdictional Practice of Law

Report 201C— Disciplinary Authority

Report 201D— Reciprocal Discipline

Report 201E— Interstate Disciplinary Enforcement

Report 201F— Pro Hac Vice Admission

Report 201G— Admission on Motion

Report 201H— Licensing of Foreign Consultants

Report 201J— Temporary Practice by Foreign Lawyers

Reports 201B and 201C form the basis for amendments that the ABA House of Delegates approved to the Model Rules 5.5 and 8.5.

§ 1-1(g)(2) Amendments from the Task Force on Corporate Responsibility

In March 2002, the president of the ABA formed a Task Force on Corporate Responsibility to "examine systemic issues relating to corporate responsibility arising out of the unexpected and traumatic bankruptcy of Enron and other Enron-like situations which have shaken confidence in the effectiveness of the gover-

---

[26]*See* American Bar Association, Commission on Multijurisdictional Practice Website, http://abanet.org/cp r/mjp-home.html.

nance and disclosure systems applicable to public companies."[27] The Task Force held public hearings and in March 2003 issued a final report with specific recommendations to the ABA House of Delegates.[28]

The Task Force's mission was not confined only to examining the role of lawyers in the corporate fraud scandals; instead, it was charged with examining all systemic issues including those involving corporate governance and the role of accountants. Thus, only part of its proposals relate to the regulation of lawyers. There are many recommendations relating to securities law, auditing law, corporate governance law, and corporate organizational theory. The changes proposed to the Model Rules, however, do attempt to place more responsibility on lawyers who represent corporations and other business entities.

Generally, the Task Force rejected the theory that lawyers for corporations should act as "gatekeepers" for the enforcement of the law.[29] However, the report advocated procedural and substantive changes for corporate attorneys. The procedural changes focused on how corporate entities should restructure lines of communication to facilitate improved communications with lawyers to ensure an entity's compliance with the law. The Task Force proposed substantive changes in Model Rule 1.13 (representing entity clients) and Model Rule 1.6 (confidentiality) to permit lawyers to disclose, in limited situations, client confidential information.[30] In August 2003, the ABA House of Delegates considered and, after much debate, adopted significant changes to these two ethics rules.

§ 1-1(g)(3) 2007 Amendments from the Standing Committee on Client Protection

After Hurricanes Katrina and Rita, lawyers from around the country sought to offer pro bono legal services to the communities and individuals affected by these natural disasters. Lawyers quickly realized that unauthorized practice of law rules posed a

---

[27]See AMERICAN BAR ASSOCIATION, REPORT OF THE AMERICAN BAR ASSOCIATION TASK FORCE ON CORPORATE RESPONSIBILITY 2 (2003).

[28]See AMERICAN BAR ASSOCIATION, REPORT OF THE AMERICAN BAR ASSOCIATION TASK FORCE ON CORPORATE RESPONSIBILITY 2-3 (2003) (chronicling activities of the Task Force).

[29]A gap clearly exists between the profession and the academic and regulatory community. National Student Marketing was viewed to establish the lawyer as gatekeeper model. See SEC v. National Student Marketing Corp., 457 F.Supp. 682 (D.D.C. 1978). See generally Reinier H. Kraakman, Gatekeepers: The Anatomy of a Third-Party Enforcement Strategy, 2 J. L. ECON. & ORG. 53 (1986). However, few in practice advocate this role for lawyers who represent corporate clients.

[30]See Larry P. Scriggins, Legal Ethics, Confidentiality, and the Organizational Client, 58 BUS. LAW. 123 (2002).

potential barrier to out-of-state lawyers who wanted to volunteer their legal services to address the myriad of problems affecting Alabama, Louisiana, Mississippi, and Texas. In particular, in Louisiana, the disaster had effectively crippled the operation of its legal system.[31] The ABA formed a Task Force on Hurricane Katrina to address the issues that such natural disasters impose upon the legal system. That Task Force quickly recommended the suspension of the application of unauthorized practice rules to enable out-of-state lawyers to assist these communities on an expedited basis.[32] The Task Force realized that the ABA should address these issues relating to a natural disaster or other emergency situation in a more systematic manner. The Task Force along with the Standing Committee on Client Protection undertook the project to draft guidelines for lawyering across state lines in an emergency situation.

In February 2007, the Standing Committee on Client Protection submitted two proposals to the ABA House of Delegates. First, the Committee drafted a Model Court Rule on Provision of Legal Services Following Determination of Major Disaster[33] and, second, it proposed amending Comment 14 to Model Rule 5.5. The House of Delegates adopted both proposals, which address the relaxation of the traditional jurisdictional limits on the practice of law during an emergency situation, such as a natural disaster, a war, or a terrorist act.

§ 1-1(g)(4) 2008 Amendments from the Section on Criminal Justice

Essentially, the effort to regulate the ethical conduct of prosecutors has focused on pretrial, trial, and appellate phases of the criminal process. However, in recent years, several public cases have illustrated that, despite the constitutional, federal, and state protections afforded to criminal defendants, the system can and does convict innocent individuals. In recent years, law schools and public interest projects have funded innocence projects to identify convicted individuals who are innocent and to attempt to exonerate them through legal proceedings. These efforts have led to proposals to establish standards for prosecutors in handling such efforts for post-conviction relief.

In 2006, the New York City Bar issued a report proposing

---

[31]See Sheryl B. Shapiro, Note, *American Bar Association's Response to Unauthorized Practice Following Katrina: Optimal or Merely Adequate,* 20 GEORGETOWN J. LEGAL ETHICS 905 (2007).

[32]See http://www.abanet.org/leade rship/2007/midyear/docs/SUMMARYO FRECOMMENDATIONS/hundredfou r.doc.

[33]This document is reprinted in Appendix M of the Lawyer's edition of this book.

amendments to the ethics rules concerning prosecutors conduct.[34] These rules addressed the responsibility of prosecutors to consider evidence of innocence presented by a convicted defendant. Eventually, these proposals were the basis for rules drafted for consideration in amendments to the New York Code of Professional Responsibility. This history served as the basis for the debate in the ABA Section on Criminal Justice and this led to an effort to amend Model Rule 3.8.[35]

In February 2008, the Section on Criminal Justice presented an amendment to Model Rule 3.8 that added two new subsections to the rule as well as several interpretive comments. This modification places a burden upon prosecutors to disclose and consider "new, credible and material evidence creating a reasonable likelihood that a convicted defendant did not commit an offense of which the defendant was convicted."[36] And, when the prosecutor has actual knowledge of "clear and convincing evidence establishing that a defendant in the prosecutor's jurisdiction was convicted of an offense that the defendant did not commit," the prosecutor has a duty to remedy the conviction.[37] These amendments are based upon the view that prosecutors are ministers of justice who owe an obligation to the system of criminal justice.

§ 1-1(g)(5) 2009 Amendments from the Standing Committee on Ethics and Professional Responsibility

Historically, when a lawyer worked on a matter in a law firm and the lawyer moved to another law firm that represented an adverse party to the client of the old firm, the imputed disqualification rule disqualified the lawyer and the new firm from continuing to represent the adverse client. In 2008, the Standing Committee on Ethics and Professional Responsibility proposed an amendment to Model Rule 1.10 that would permit the new firm to continue the representation if it implemented proper screening procedures. The proposal was postponed until the February 2009 meeting and at that time the ABA House of Delegates adopted the changes to Model Rule 1.10. New Model Rule 1.10 contains a formal exception to the imputed disqualification rule so that the new law firm may continue to represent the adverse client. Many lawyers opposed this change to imputed disqualification because

---

[34]*See* Proposed Prosecution Ethics Rules, The Committee on Professional Responsibility, 61 The Record of the Association of the Bar of the City of New York 69 (2006).

[35]http://www.abanet.org/leadershi

p/2008/midyear/sum__of__rec__docs/h undredfiveb__105B__FINAL.doc.

[36]Rule 3.8(g).

[37]Rule 3.8(h).

they believe that screening may be ineffective in limiting the effect of the conflict of interest.[38]

§ 1-1(h) Creation of the 20/20 Commission to Reexamine the Model Rules

In August 2009, Carolyn Lamm, President of the ABA, announced the formation of the ABA Commission on Ethics 20/20. This Commission was given the task of reviewing the Model Rules with a perspective of current law practice in a technologically advanced global economy. The ABA President directed the Commission to perform its work with three guiding principles: protecting the public, protecting the core values of the profession, and protecting the independence of the profession.

The Commission has identified three preliminary areas of study: "(1) issues that arise because U.S. lawyers are regulated by states but work increasingly across state and international borders; (2) issues that arise in light of current and future advances in technology that enhance virtual cross-border access; and (3) particular ethical issues raised by changing technology."[39] The ultimate goal of the three-year project is to create a set of recommendations for consideration by the ABA House of Delegates.[40] Commission 20/20 is likely to produce the future Model Rules 20/20.

As of May 2010, the 20/20 Commission had issued five Issues Papers presenting hypotheticals and questions for comment. The Papers are on the topics of (1) Choice of Law in Cross-Border Practice, (2) Client Confidentiality and Lawyers' Use of Technology, (3) Lawyers' Use of Internet Based Client Development Tools, (4) Admission by Motion, and (5) Alternative Litigation Financing. In November 2010, the Commission issued a Discussion Draft Regarding Domestic and International Outsourcing.

In February 2012, the Ethics 20/20 Commission issued final revised drafts of proposals that would be submitted to the ABA House of Delegates in August 2012. The proposals related to confidentiality issues posed by advances in technology, advertising issues related to developments in media, outsourcing of legal and nonlegal services, and jurisdictional issues of cross border law practice.

§ 1-1(i) Federal Preemption of State Law Governing the Practice of Law

Historically and traditionally, state law has governed the

---

[38]*See* Susan Martyn & James McCauley, Minority Report to ABA Report 109 (Presented to ABA House of Delegates in February 2009).

[39]*See* http://www.abanet.org/ethic

s2020/outline.pdf. This document contains a more detailed outline that will initially guide the Commission's study.

[40]*See* http://www.abanet.org/ethic s2020/.

practice of law. State courts routinely adopt ethics rules governing lawyers that are patterned after the ABA Model Rules. In addition, state statutes govern this area, such as state statutes on unauthorized law.

If the federal government—either by statute or regulation—intends to preempt state law, then federal law prevails pursuant to the supremacy clause.[41] However, as a matter of statutory construction, because of the strong tradition of state control, federal law "may not be interpreted to reach into areas of State sovereignty unless the language of the federal law compels the intrusion."[42]

For example, it is clear that federal law governing patents override state law of unauthorized practice. Thus, the Supreme Court held that Florida could not enjoin a nonlawyer registered to practice before the United States Patent Office from preparing and prosecuting patent applications in Florida, even though this constituted the "practice of law" in Florida, because of a federal statute and Patent Office regulations authorizing nonlawyers to practice before the Patent Office.[43]

Similarly, The SEC, § 307 of the Sarbanes-Oxley Act requires the SEC to promulgate rules of professional conduct for lawyers "appearing and practicing" before the SEC.[44]

However, federal law does not preempt traditional state law governing the regulation lawyers if there is no clear evidence of Congressional intent to do so. Thus, in *American Bar Association v. Federal Trade Commission*,[45] the Court held that the FTC Lacks Authority to Regulate Lawyers Under the Fair and Accurate Credit Transactions Act (FACT). The FACT Act does not contain "an 'unmistakably clear' grant of statutory authority allowing the Commission's venture into the regulation of the practice of law."[46]

---

[41]U.S. Constitution, Article VI, cl. 2 (the Supremacy Clause). *E.g.*, 2 RONALD D. ROTUNDA & JOHN E. NOWAK, TREATISE ON CONSTITUTIONAL LAW: SUBSTANCE AND PROCEDURE § § 12.1, 12.2, 12.3 (Thomson—West, 4th ed. 2008) (six volumes).

[42]*City of Abilene, Tex. v. F.C.C.*, 164 F.3d 49, 52 (D.C. Cir. 1999).

[43]*Sperry v. State of Fla. ex rel. Florida Bar*, 373 U.S. 379, 83 S. Ct. 1322, 10 L. Ed. 2d 428 (1963). *See*

§ 5.5-2(a), § 5.5-4, § 5.5-6(c), below.

[44]Section 307 of the Sarbanes-Oxley Act is titled, Rules Of Professional Responsibility For Attorneys, and is found at: § 307, 15 U.S.C.A. § 7245 (2002).

[45]*American Bar Ass'n v. F.T.C.*, 671 F. Supp. 2d 64 (D.D.C. 2009).

[46]671 F.Supp.2d 64, 73–74, 2009 WL 4289505 *6. *Accord American Bar Ass'n v. F.T.C.*, 430 F.3d 457, 471-72 (D.C. Cir. 2005).

§ 1-2 A BRIEF NOTE ON THE TERMINOLOGY OF LEGAL ETHICS

§ 1-2(a) The Distinction between Aspirational and Mandatory Duties

The "most fundamental legal skill consists of determining what kind of legal problems a situation may involve, a skill that necessarily transcends any particular specialized knowledge."[1] However, a little specialized knowledge would not hurt. The ABA Model Rules represent an important source of this specialized knowledge. In examining any problem involving legal ethics, we should first apply our traditional legal skills to the fact situation and then evaluate how the Rules deal with the problem. In certain situations, the Rules may be too vague to be useful; in other circumstance, they may be quite specific, but may appear to be bad policy. A conclusion that a Rule represents bad policy is important, because the law is not static: what the law ought to be is very relevant, because the "ought" influences the "is." The fact that law is not static is why there will be new editions of this book.[2]

That is also why the American Bar Association periodically reassesses its Model Rules. Between 1983 and 2000, the American Bar Association modified several provisions of the Rules. The ABA's creation of the Ethics 2000 Commission to reevaluate the entire Model Rules after nearly two decades of experience reflects the fact that there are institutional mechanisms for change and self-study.

The Rules not only prescribe what *must* or must not be done, but also advise what a lawyer *should* do. The predecessor to the Model Rules—the ABA Model Code of Professional Responsibility—expressed this sentiment in rules that were called "Ethical Considerations" or "EC"s. These provisions represent aspirational conduct for the lawyer.[3] As we discuss in greater detail later, the

---

[Section 1-2]

[1] Model Rules, Rule 1.1, Comment 2.

[2] For a more elaborate discussion, analysis, and research tool, *see, e.g.,* ABA/BNA, Lawyers' Manual on Professional Conduct (multi-volume loose leaf service); RICHARD UNDERWOOD & WILLIAM H. FORTUNE, TRIAL ETHICS (1988); CHARLES W. WOLFRAM, MODERN LEGAL ETHICS (1986); GEOFFREY C. HAZARD, JR. & W. WILLIAM HODES, THE LAW OF LAWYERING: A HANDBOOK ON THE MODEL RULES OF PROFESSIONAL CONDUCT (3d ed. 2010) (2 volumes); ROBERT W. HILLMAN, HILLMAN ON LAWYER MOBILITY: THE LAW AND ETHICS OF PARTNER WITHDRAWALS AND LAW FIRM BREAKUPS (Aspen Pub. 2d ed. 2010). On the ABA Model Judicial Code, *see* JEFFREY M. SHAMAN, STEVEN LUBET, & JAMES J. ALFINI, JUDICIAL CONDUCT AND ETHICS (Lexis Law Pub. 4th ed. 2007). On legal malpractice, *see* RONALD E. MALLEN & JEFFREY M. SMITH, LEGAL MALPRACTICE (Thomson/West 2011) (5 volumes).

[3] *E.g.,* if the lawyer has not regularly represented the client, the fee

ethics rules also treat some other actions as "proper;" that is, the lawyer *may* engage in such conduct, *even if* the client objects.[4]

Lawyers may only be disciplined for violating mandatory rules, even though they should strive to meet the aspirational goals. The former ABA Model Code explicitly distinguished between Ethical Considerations ("EC") and Disciplinary Rules ("DR"). The Disciplinary Rules, in contrast to the Ethical Considerations, were "mandatory in character." They stated "the minimum level of conduct below which no lawyer can fall without being subject to disciplinary action."[5] The Ethical Considerations in the ABA Model Code were presented as "aspirational" only.[6] Therefore, if conduct violated only an EC, it was not disciplinable.

Although a violation of an EC was not designed to establish a standard for discipline under the Code, courts would in some cases discipline an attorney for violating an EC.[7] However, when we look at these situations more carefully, we will see that the conduct in question fell below the minimum level of acceptable conduct and the principle could be derived from a DR, even though the particular prohibition might be expressed more clearly in the EC. Courts purporting to rely only on ECs do not always carefully and precisely explain what they are doing when they are interpreting the Model Code.

In short, one should not assume that if conduct expressly violates an EC, it does not also violate a more generally phrased DR. The ECs not only express aspirational norms; they also aid in interpreting and explaining the policies underlying a DR. "They constitute a body of principles upon which the lawyer can rely for guidance in specific situations."[8]

---

should be communicated to the client "*preferably* in writing" before or within a reasonable time after commencing the representation. Rule 1.5(b) (emphasis added).

[4]*E.g.*, Model Rule 3.2, which requires the lawyer to make reasonable efforts to expedite litigation even if the client wants delay. "Realizing financial" benefit through otherwise improper delay "is not a legitimate interest of the client." Rule 3.2, Comment 1. *Cf.* Rule 1.16(b)(3), which authorizes the lawyer to withdraw from representation (even if the client objects to withdrawal), if "a client insists upon pursuing an objective that the lawyer considers repugnant or imprudent."

[5]*See* Model Code, Preliminary Statement; DR 1-102(A)(1) (misconduct to violate a disciplinary rule).

[6]*See* Model Code, Preliminary Statement.

[7]*See Committee on Professional Ethics and Conduct of State Bar Association v. Behnke*, 276 N.W.2d 838, 840 (Iowa 1979) (violation of an EC, "standing alone," will support disciplinary action; in this case the violation was of EC 5-5).

[8]Model Code, Preliminary Statement.

Some of the ECs and DRs were also cast in terms of what the lawyer "may" do.[9] In that case the ABA Model Code gave lawyers a power to be exercised in their sound discretion. The lawyer was not required to engage in the conduct, but was authorized to do so. The client might not like the lawyer's actions and could always fire him, but the client would not be justified in accusing the lawyer of violating the ethics rules.

The ABA Model Rules of Professional Conduct continue these distinctions between what *must* be done, what *should* be done, and what *may* be done.[10] When the black letter Rules use imperatives such as "shall" or "shall not," violations are disciplinable.[11]

Finally, many of the Comments to the Model Rules use the term "should." These Comments are comparable to the ECs of the Code. If a Comment uses the term "should," it does "not add obligations to the Rules but provides guidance for practicing in compliance with the Rules."[12] Therefore, if conduct violates an explicit aspirational Comment, it also may violate a more broadly drafted Rule.[13]

§ 1-2(b) The Appearance of Impropriety

The title of Canon 9 of the Model Code of Professional Responsibility stated: "A Lawyer Should Avoid Even the Appearance of Impropriety." This "appearance" provision was a favorite of some courts, which quoted it with great frequency over the years. However, in itself, the phrase, "Appearance of Impropriety" was not a disciplinable standard. First, the titles of the Canons were not disciplinable rules themselves, but only titles of sections. They represented "axiomatic norms,"[14] rather than tests to determine when lawyers should be disciplined or disqualified. Canon 9 was titled, "The lawyer should avoid even the appearance of professional impropriety." But no disciplinary rule imposed the "appearance of impropriety" as a rule itself. In other words, the concern about the appearance of impropriety was the reason that led to the adoption of certain prophylactic rules that

---

[9]*See, e.g.*, DR 4-101(C) (when lawyer "may" reveal a client secret or confidence).

[10]Model Rules, Scope 14. *See, e.g.*, Rule 1.6(b) (when lawyer "may" reveal client information). *See also* Rule 6.1 ("A lawyer should aspire to render at least (50) hours of *pro bono publico* services per year."); Rule 1.5(b) (basis of fee should be "preferably in writing").

[11]*See* Model Rules, Scope 14. *See also* Rule 8.4(a) (misconduct to violate or attempt to violate the Model Rules).

[12]Model Rules, Scope 14.

[13]The Comments explain the Rules and provide interpretative guidance, though, of course, "the text of each Rule is authoritative." Model Rules, Scope 21.

[14]*See* Model Code, "Preliminary Statement."

banned specific conduct,[15] but the "appearance" standard was not a disciplinary rule itself.

In addition, this "appearance of impropriety" standard is indefinable unless one first defines what is an "impropriety." This "appearance of impropriety" standard may represent a reason behind a rule[16]—why, for example, some ethics rules are mechanical and absolute—but it is too vague to be a rule itself.[17]

Nonetheless, on occasion some courts have used this loose language as a standard of conduct.[18] Other courts, in contrast, warned that use of such a broad test should not substitute for analysis to demonstrate why conduct does, or does not, fit within specific disciplinary rules.[19] As the court carefully noted in *Fund of Funds, Ltd. v. Arthur Andersen & Co.*: "When dealing with ethical principles, . . . we cannot paint with broad strokes. The lines are fine and must be so marked. . . . [T]he conclusion in a particular case can be reached only after painstaking analysis of the facts and precise application of precedent."[20] The American Bar Association cautioned that if the "appearance of impropriety" language had been made a Disciplinary Rule, "it is likely that the determination of whether particular conduct violated the rule would have degenerated . . . into a determination on an instinctive, or even *ad hominem* basis."[21]

Consequently, the ABA 1983 Model Rules rejected the "appearance of impropriety" test. The Kutak Commission drafters thought that it is too loose and vague, gives no fair warning, and allows, or even encourages, instinctive judgments by disgruntled clients. Also, one cannot begin to define "appearance of impropriety" unless one first defines "impropriety," and the purported "test" does neither. The 2002 Model Rules similarly did not embrace the concept of "appearance of impropriety." The Rules, at times, impose a bright line prohibition in order to avoid an "appearance of impropriety," but that phrase, by itself, is not a test.

---

[15]DR 9-101(A), (B), & (C).

[16]*See* EC 9-3.

[17]*Procter & Gamble Co. v. Haugen*, 183 F.R.D. 571, 573 (D.Utah 1998) (emphasis added):

"The analytical approach is proper to reach a conclusion based on justifiable legal or sound policy based rationale *but not on a theory of an appearance of impropriety* or ethical restriction . . . . Ethics standards should be clear and precise so that an attorney can know beforehand what conduct is unacceptable. Applying analogy [sic] rules to impose an ethi-cal boundary should not be the standard. It does not fairly advise counsel of what is proper."

[18]*See, e.g., Kramer v. Scientific Control Corp.*, 534 F.2d 1085 (3d Cir.1976), *cert. denied*, 429 U.S. 830, 97 S.Ct. 90, 50 L.Ed.2d 94 (1976).

[19]*International Electronics Corp. v. Flanzer*, 527 F.2d 1288, 1295 (2d Cir.1975).

[20]*Fund of Funds, Ltd. v. Arthur Andersen & Co.*, 567 F.2d 225, 227 (2d Cir.1977).

[21]ABA Formal Opinion 342 (1975).

Because "impropriety" is not defined, "the term 'appearance of impropriety' is question-begging."[22] The Restatement of the Law Governing Lawyers similarly rejects this formulation.[23]

Criticisms of lawyers for alleged ethical failings have become more frequent over the years. Some of these charges are serious and well-taken, but others claim that there is an alleged conflict of interest because of an "appearance of impropriety."[24] The charge may be no more substantial than a claim that a lawyer is a friend of someone, and that the friendship causes an appearance of impropriety leading to a conflict of interest. Yet the charge, even if unsubstantial, is serious because any allegation of a conflict of interest attacks the integrity and bona fides of the person charged. As the ABA has advised, a charge of a conflict of interest "should be viewed with caution . . . for it can be misused as a technique of harassment."[25]

Charges based on allegations of an "appearance of impropriety" have increased at a rapid rate, as any search through Westlaw will demonstrate. For example, in 1999, the phrase appeared only 666 times in the Westlaw database of "all news plus wires."[26] By 2004, it appeared 1698 times, an increase of more than 250%.[27]

§ 1-2(c) The Duty of Zeal

The Model Code explicitly embraced the lawyer's obligation to provide clients with zealous representation. Canon 7 required a lawyer "to represent a client zealously within the bounds of the law." A disciplinary rule under this canon provided additional support for the notion that lawyers must represent clients with zeal. Under DR 7-101, "A lawyer shall not intentionally. . . [f]ail

---

[22]Before the 2002 revisions, the quoted language came from Rule 1.9, Comment 5. The Reporter's Notes state that this Comment was "deleted as no longer helpful to the analysis of questions arising under this Rule. *No change in substance is intended.*" (emphasis added).

[23]Restatement of the Law Governing Lawyers, Third, § 121 (Official Draft 2000), Reporter's Note to Comment *c(iv)*, at p. 259.

Some states continue to use the "appearance of impropriety" standard. *See* David Ivers, Note, *Prohibition Against Appearance of Impropriety Retained Under Model Rules of Professional Conduct*, 13 U.ARK.LITTLE ROCK L.J. 271 (1991).

[24]*E.g.* Ronald D. Rotunda, *Alleged Conflicts of Interest Because of the "Ap-*

pearance of Impropriety," 33 HOFSTRA L. REV. 1141 (2005).

[25]1983 Model Rule 1.7, Comment 15. The post–2002 version does not include this comment, for reasons of style having nothing to do with substance, though many states continue to retain this comment. *See, e.g.*, Tex. Disciplinary Rules of Professional Conduct, Rule 1.06, Comment 17.

[26]Westlaw, Allnewsplus Database (last searched Aug. 31, 2005), available at Westlaw:Allnewsplus/search: "appearance of impropriety" & da (aft 1/1/1999 & bef 12/31/1999).

[27]Westlaw, Allnewsplus Database (last searched Aug. 31, 2005), available at Westlaw:Allnewsplus/search: "appearance of impropriety" & da(aft 12/31/2003 & bef 1/11/2005).

to seek the lawful objectives of his client through reasonably available means permitted by law and the Disciplinary Rules" with certain exceptions. Those exceptions included "acceding to reasonable requests of opposing counsel which do not prejudice the rights of his client, by being punctual in fulfilling all professional commitments, by avoiding offensive tactics, or by treating with courtesy and consideration all persons involved in the legal process."[28] Lawyers were also given the right to exercise their professional judgment in "waiv[ing] or fail[ing] to assert a right or position of his client" and to "[r]efuse to aid or participate in conduct that he believes to be unlawful, even though there is some support for an argument that the conduct is legal."[29]

The Model Rules did not explicitly include a duty of zeal in the text of any rule because of a concern that "zealous" could slip into "overzealous." Several comments do refer to zeal, but one must remember in most jurisdictions that the comments are not binding. In the preamble, the drafters included the comment that "As advocate, a lawyer zealously asserts the client's position under the rules of the adversary system."[30] And, the Preamble included the reference in two additional places: (1) "[W]hen an opposing party is well represented, a lawyer can be a zealous advocate on behalf of a client and at the same time assume that justice is being done,"[31] and, (2) "These principles include the lawyer's obligation zealously to protect and pursue a client's legitimate interests, within the bounds of the law, while maintaining a professional, courteous and civil attitude toward all persons involved in the legal system."[32]

The Model Rules have reshaped the duty of zeal into the obligation of diligence and competence.[33] The framers of the Model Rules deleted the obligation of zealous representation because the term zealous often is misunderstood as overzealous.[34] Thus, although many authorities continue to talk about the lawyer's

---

[28]DR 7-101(A)(1).

[29]DR 7-101(B).

[30]Model Rules, Preamble Comment 2.

[31]Model Rules, Preamble Comment 8.

[32]Model Rules, Preamble Comment 9.

[33]Restatement of the Law Governing Lawyers, Third, § 16, Comment d (Official Draft)("The term sets forth a traditional aspiration, but it should not be misunderstood to suggest that lawyers are legally required to function with a certain emotion or style of litigating, negotiating, or counseling. For legal purposes, the term encompasses the duties of competence and diligence.").

[34]Compare *Florida Bar v. Martocci*, 791 So.2d 1074 (Fla. 2001), holding that the lawyer crossed line from *zealous* advocacy to *overzealous* disciplinable conduct by, e.g., making profane insults to opposing litigant, her family, and her counsel, making demeaning facial gestures, sticking out his tongue[!], and calling the opposing party "a nut case" and "a stupid idiot" who should "go back to Puerto Rico"); *In re Williams*, 414 N.W.2d 394 (Minn. 1987), which disciplined a

obligation of zeal, it is more useful to focus on whether the lawyer is providing competent and diligent representation within the predetermined scope of representation as agreed to by the lawyer and the client. "Zealousness" does not require lawyers "to function with a certain emotion or style of litigating, negotiating, or counseling." Instead, it merely "encompasses the duties of competence and diligence."[35]

§ 1-3 THE RESTATEMENT OF THE LAW GOVERNING LAWYERS

§ 1-3(a) Introduction

In 1986 the American Law Institute ("ALI"),[1] a prestigious group of practicing lawyers, judges, and academics, began drafting a Restatement of the Law Governing Lawyers. Unlike the ABA's Model Rules, the ALI has not proposed a code of regulations that it expects state courts to adopt as rules of court. Instead, it has drafted a series of principles, also called "black letter rules," followed by commentary and examples. Because the Restatement analyzes and systematizes the law governing the practice of law, it goes beyond the ethics rules to cover other areas that affect the practice of law, such as tort doctrines relating to malpractice, vicarious liability, the work-product doctrine, the attorney-client evidentiary privilege, the agent-principal relationship, and related areas.

The purpose of this Restatement is not only to restate what the law is but also to influence or nudge the developing case law in a particular direction. The Restatement of the Law Governing Lawyers follows in the tradition of the other Restatements that the ALI has drafted over many years. Although the ABA Model Rules greatly influence courts in adopting rules of ethics, the purpose of the ALI's Restatement is to influence courts in interpreting those ethics rules as well as other law governing lawyers and the practice of law.

§ 1-3(b) The Origin and Purpose of the American Law Institute.

When the American Law Institute ("ALI") was established in 1923, its founders included (and its membership today continues

---

lawyer for making anti-Semitic remarks to opposing counsel at a deposition. He argued that he had a right to represent his clients *zealously*. The court said, "to be zealous is not to be uncivil."414 N.W.2d 397.

[35]Restatement of the Law Governing Lawyers, Third, § 16, Comment *d* (2000).

[Section 1-3]

[1]On the American Law Institute and its special influence and role in the development of the common law, *see* PETER HAY & RONALD D. ROTUNDA, THE UNITED STATES FEDERAL SYSTEM: LEGAL INTEGRATION IN THE AMERICAN EXPERIENCE, at 324–37 (Giuffré, 1982).

to include) the most prominent members of the three predominant groups within the legal community—practicing lawyers, judges, and professors.[2] They described the ALI as an effort to clarify and bring certainty to particular fields of law.[3]

The Institute began its work by drafting a series of "restatements" of the law in a variety of subject areas, including agency, conflicts, contracts, restitution, and torts. These Restatements were originally intended to be a concise statement of the principles of law as enunciated in the thousands of cases that had been published in the states. The ALI members believed that the Restatements, authored by the most prominent legal scholars in the country, would speak with authority close to that of judicial decisions.[4] After the members of the ALI approved these Restatements, they were then published and cited by the courts.

When the ALI began to reevaluate the original Restatements in 1947, it changed the focus. The second series of Restatements did more than merely state what the law is. The ALI went further, adding comments and illustrations, and, more importantly, the Restatement Second series began to predict what the law would or *should* be in an area that was unsettled.[5]

Although the ALI has never before drafted a restatement of the law of lawyering, it titled its project, "Restatement of the Law, Third." However, there is no Restatement, Second, or Restatement, First.[6] The ALI has chosen to title its first Restatement on Lawyers the Restatement, *Third*, not out of a perverse desire to

---

[2]Ex officio members include all the Justices of the U.S. Supreme Court, the Chief Judges of the U.S. Circuit Courts of Appeals, the Chief Justices of the highest court of each state, the U.S. Attorney General and Solicitor General, the presidents of the American, National, Federal, D.C., and state bar associations, the deans of all law schools that are members of the Association of American Law Schools, and the president of that Association.

[3]GOODRICH & WALKIN, THE STORY OF THE ALI 5 (1961). The founders saw uncertainty and complexity as the major defect in American law. Nathan M. Crystal, *Codification and the Rise of the Restatement Movement*, 54 WASHINGTON L. REV. 239 (1979); N.E.H. Hull, *Restatement and Reform: A New Perspective on the Origins of the American Law Institute*, 8 LAW & HISTORY INST. 55 (1990).

[4]"A judge, a lawyer, a law teacher could then go to one source, find what the law in point was and with confidence state it to be so." GOODRICH & WALKIN, THE STORY OF THE ALI 8 (1961). *See generally* LEWIS, *History of the American Law Institute and the First Restatement of the Law, "How We Did It," in* RESTATEMENTS IN THE COURTS (1945).

[5]By 1962, the Institute also completed its work on a variety of "model" codes and uniform laws. Even when these are not enacted by the state legislatures, the authority and prestige of the ALI stands behind them as statements of what the law should be in a particular field, and courts sometimes cite these model codes as evidence of the law.

[6]There was, after all, no Napoleon II, although there was a Napoleon I and Napoleon III.

confuse lawyers and judges (though that has been a common result) but to signify that the American Law Institute is now working on a third major series of Restatements, such as the Restatement of the Law of Unfair Competition, Third, etc. Occasionally this book will refer to *tentative* drafts of the Restatement of the Law Governing Lawyers, Third, or the Proposed Official Draft or Official Draft.

§ 1-4 GAUGING THE INFLUENCE OF THE RESTATEMENT OF THE LAW GOVERNING LAWYERS

§ 1-4(a) The Statistics

It is easy to conclude that the American Bar Association's Model Code and Model Rules have been influential. The great majority of jurisdictions have adopted these ethics rules as substantive law. In contrast, it is more difficult to gauge the influence the Restatements have had in judicial decision-making, and equally difficult to predict the influence of the new RESTATEMENT OF THE LAW GOVERNING LAWYERS. One can certainly assume that this new RESTATEMENT will have influence, but one cannot easily estimate the extent of that influence.

A common way to measure the influence of academic commentary is to count the number of cases citing the commentary in question.[1] Of course, change in the law occurs at the margins, so one cannot determine the influence of the various Restatements

---

[Section 1-4]

[1]*See, e.g.,* Fred R. Shapiro, *The Most-Cited Law Review Articles Revisited,* 71 CHI-KENT L. REV. 751 (1996); Deborah J. Merritt & Melanie Putnam, *Judges and Scholars: Do Courts and Scholarly Journals Cite the Same Law Review Articles?,* 71 CHI.-KENT L. REV. 871 (1996).

The ALI keeps a running tabulation on the number of state court decisions that have cited the Restatements since the promulgation of the original Restatements beginning in 1932. As of March 1, 2004, this figure stood at 161,486. The ALI citations as a percentage of all decisions since the first Restatements were published is, of course, a figure substantially less than 5%.

Compare AMERICAN LAW INSTITUTE, "http://www.ali.org/ali/cit1.htm". The Restatement of Contracts was one of the first projects of the Institute,

and was completed in 1932. It took eleven years to complete. The number of case citations to the ALI's Principles of Corporate Governance, Model Penal Code, and the Uniform Commercial Code, also as of April 1, 1997, total 49,930. ALI 2004 Annual Report, in: "http://www.ali.org/ali/cit2.htm". The UCC accounts for over 93% of the codification citations. Codes included in the ALI's compilation of codification citations also include the Model Penal Code, the Corporate Governance Code, and the UCC.

These figures necessarily do not take into account the possibility of a decision that relies upon a prior case which in turn relied on the Restatement. In such instances, the Restatement has influenced two decisions, but may be cited in the first only. On the other hand, a judge may cite the Restatement even though it did not influence his or her decision.

in general simply by looking at absolute numbers. Leading cases are denoted "leading" because they become very influential and change the law. If the Restatement influences a case that becomes "leading," subsequent decisions may cite the leading case but not cite the relevant Restatement, thus understating the significance of the Restatement.

As with all statistical information, a number of other caveats are necessary. First of all, these figures do not reflect the influence of the Restatements in any particular jurisdiction. The Restatements may represent greater legal authority in some jurisdictions than in others. In Arizona, for example, the state supreme court has declared that the Restatements of the Law would be followed in all subsequent decisions in which Arizona law is silent, *i.e.*, unless there were legislative enactments or prior Arizona law.[2] The American Virgin Islands explicitly provides by statute that, in the absence of local laws to the contrary, the restatements of law approved by the American Law Institute provide the rules of decision in Virgin Island Courts.[3]

In contrast, other courts have specifically stated that the Restatements may not be relied upon as authority, even in those cases where a court adopts the Restatement analysis in a particular case. For example, the Oregon Supreme Court has stated that although it—

> frequently quotes sections of the Restatements of the American Law Institute, it does not literally "adopt" them. . . . In the nature of common law, such quotations in opinions are no more than shorthand expressions of the court's view that the analysis summarized in the Restatement corresponds to Oregon law applicable to the facts of the case before the court. They do not enact the exact

---

[2]*Smith v. Normart*, 51 Ariz. 134, 143, 75 P.2d 38, 42 (1938). *See also Rodriguez v. Terry*, 79 Ariz. 348, 350, 290 P.2d 248, 249 (1955); *Odekirk v. Austin*, 90 Ariz. 97, 100, 366 P.2d 80, 81 (1961). Arizona is unusual in giving the Restatements this much authority. *See* James F. Byrne, Jr., Comment, *Reevaluation of the Restatement as a Source of Law in Arizona*, 15 ARIZ. L. REV. 1021, 1021, n.4 (1973). Professor Albert Ehrenzweig has suggested that giving the Restatement this primary authority is an unconstitutional abdication of the judicial function by the state supreme court. Albert Ehrenzweig, *The Restatement as a Source of Conflict Law in Arizona*, 2 ARIZ. L. REV. 1977 (1960).

[3]1 Virgin Islands Code, Ann., § 4 states:

"APPLICATION OF COMMON LAW; RESTATEMENTS. The rules of the common law, as expressed in the restatements of the law approved by the American Law Institute, and to the extent not so expressed, as generally understood and applied in the United States, shall be the rules of decision in the courts of the Virgin Islands in cases to which they apply, in the absence of local laws to the contrary."

See, e.g, Guardian Insurance Co. v. Bain Hogg Int'l Ltd., 52 F.Supp.2d 536, 540, n. 3 (D.Virgin Islands 1999), *stay granted*, 2000 WL 34211320 (D.Virgin Islands 2000).

phrasing of the Restatement rule, complete with comments, illustrations, and caveats.[4]

The issue before the Oregon court was the relationship of Section 46 of the Restatement of Torts, concerning outrageous conduct as a cause of emotional distress, to Oregon law. The court did not refer at all to the fact that just two months prior to this decision, in a different area of tort law, the Oregon legislature *directed* the courts to use the Restatement of Torts as the basis for interpreting its newly enacted products liability legislation. Oregon enacted legislation that placed liability on a seller or lessor of a product, without regard to fault. The legislature further stated that, "[i]t is the intent of the Legislative Assembly that the rule stated in subsections (1) and (2) of this section shall be construed in accordance with the Restatement (Second) of Torts § 402A, Comments *a* to *m* (1965)."[5]

The statistics also do not reflect the Restatement's influence on the development of any particular field of law. For example, areas of the law that have traditionally been developed by judicial decision, such as contract, and torts, may be more influenced by the Restatements than other areas, where the legislatures have taken a more active role. The Restatement of Contracts accounts for approximately one-fifth of all Restatements citations, and the Restatement of Torts accounts for over 40% of the citations.[6] In contrast, some areas of the law, such as property, are largely regulated by statute. This may explain the comparatively low (3.6%) percentage of citations to the Restatement on Property.[7]

Finally, even within an area where the Restatement may have some influence, the strength of that influence is not reflected solely by the ALI compilation of citations. If the Restatements are used as the sole or main basis for a decision, as in Arizona, then they have directly influenced the development of the case law. If they are used to support a position that would have been taken regardless of the Restatements, then their authority and influence is much more difficult to measure. There are no accurate ways of quantifying degrees of influence on the development of the law. A court may use prior case law within its jurisdiction or another jurisdiction to justify a decision, but it may have really been persuaded to reach that particular conclusion because of the Restatement position.

The Restatement, Second, of Torts § 402A illustrates this point.

---

[4]*Brewer v. Erwin*, 287 Or. 435, 456, 600 P.2d 398, 410 n.12 (1979).

[5]Chapter 866, 1979 Oregon Laws 1197. *See also* 2 ALI REPORTER (No. 2) 4 (Jan. 1980).

[6]*See* ALI, ANNUAL REPORT, at http://www.ali.org/ali/cit1.htm.

[7]The extent to which the Restatement may influence a legislature in its enactments is a separate question, beyond the scope of a study of judicial decision-making.

The ALI adopted section 402A in 1964, establishing liability of sellers to consumers for defective products regardless of fault, even though only sixteen states had taken this position.[8] Many states subsequently adopted the same position, but it is impossible to determine whether a court would have adopted strict liability for consumer products regardless of the Restatement, or whether the Restatement directly led to a change in the law, or whether § 402A was important because it tilted the balance.[9] It does seem fair to assume that the Restatements may speed up (or slow down) the development in the law. Perhaps their primary influence lies not only in the persuasive logic of the Restatements themselves, but also in the fact that the ALI numbers among its members many prominent representatives of academia, the bench, and the practicing bar.

By March 27, 2011, the Restatement of the Law Governing Lawyers had been cited in 483 different state court cases and in 396 different federal cases. No other Restatement was cited less frequently.[10] But one should not make too much of the relative dearth of citations. This Restatement is relatively new; the first tentative draft was not published until April of 1988, so that we must view these statistics with caution. However, the sparse number of citations—only 879 different opinions in all state and federal courts during the course of over 20 years—do not necessarily portend clout and authority.[11]

Even this number may be too high. Consider, for example,

---

[8]See Herbert Wechsler, *Restatements and Legal Change: Problems of Policy in the Restatement Work of the American Law Institute*, 13 ST. LOUIS U.L.J. 185, 188–89 (1968).

[9]See also Alan Milner, *Restatement: Failure of a Legal Experiment*, 20 U. PITT. L. REV. 795, 799 (1959): "Merely to say that the courts have cited [the Restatement] a given number of times is simply to give credit to the efficiency of the Institute's sales-service and to overlook the fact that not only are many of the citations the last in long strings of cases inclining the same way but that, of the rest, many are just 'jumping-off' grounds for the main inquiry."

[10]The figures are from a WEST-LAW computer check. The American Law Institute states that, as of March 1, 2004, the Restatement of the Law Governing Lawyers has been cited 240 times in the state courts and 164 times

in all federal cases. [http://www.ali.org/ali/cit1.htm].

[11]In contrast, Professor Susan Martyn has suggested that the number of citations of the Restatement of the Law Governing Lawyers indicates that it is already having an impact on the development of the law. Susan Martyn, *Judicial Reliance on the Restatement (3d) of the Law Governing Lawyers*, 2 THE PROFESSIONAL LAWYER 8, 9 (ABA, No. 6, Feb. 1995), stating that "slightly more than midway through its tentative draft stage, [the Restatement] has been widely relied upon by courts to explain judicial outcomes that involve lawyer activity." However, the number of citations may not seem like a high number when compared to other Restatements or when compared to the number of cases involving lawyers over the last decade.

Professor Martyn also noted that, as of August, 1997, only 7 citations criticized the Restatement. *The*

Petrillo v. Bachenberg.[12] Both the majority and dissent cited section 73 of Restatement ("Duty of Care to Certain Non-Clients"). When both the majority and the dissent rely on the same section, it may be that, in such instances, the Restatement is not influential, just ambiguous. On the other hand, it may also show that judges in the majority and dissent believe that it is important that their views are supported by the ALI.

Even if this Restatement does not substantially change the development of the law governing lawyers, it has received much publicity in the legal press, and it therefore should affect the legal profession to the extent that it sensitizes lawyers to issues of legal ethics. In addition, the new Restatement organizes much of the law governing lawyers, and that organization may prove influential by affecting the way courts, academics, and practicing lawyers view legal ethics and think about problems involving professional responsibility.

§ 1-4(b) Significant Changes Proposed by the Restatement

To the extent that the Restatement intends to change the law (rather than clarify or restate it), the tentative evidence is ambiguous. One of the more significant proposals of the Restatement is found in section 124(2), dealing with conflicts of interest. That section, in brief, provides that a law firm is not disqualified from suing a party simply because a lawyer in that firm learned relevant confidential information about that party, while representing that party in an earlier matter (a matter that is assumed to be "substantially related" to the present matter), *if* the disqualified lawyer is screened, all parties are given notice of the screening, and "any confidential client information communicated to the personally-prohibited lawyer is *unlikely to be significant* in the subsequent matter."[13] A version of section 204(2) first appeared in Tentative Draft No. 3 (April 10, 1990). Since that time,

---

Restatement of the Law Governing Lawyers: Departures from the Model Rules, 8 THE PROFESSIONAL LAWYER 13 (ABA, No. 8, Aug. 1997), at 13, col. 2 (report of 23rd National Conference on Professional Responsibility). However, it may not be accurate to measure the Restatement's influence by noting that only a few cases criticize it; instead, it may be preferable to measure its influence by the number of decisions that state that they are changing the law because of the Restatement. If a judge does not look to the Restatement for guidance, the Restatement may not have significant influence: the fact that

a judge does not criticize the Restatement may only mean that the judge has not looked to it at all.

[12]*Petrillo v. Bachenberg*, 139 N.J. 472, 655 A.2d 1354 (N.J. 1995).

[13]Restatement of the Law Governing Lawyers, Third, § 124(2)(a) (Official Draft, 2000)(emphasis added). Section 124(2) was called section 204(2) in an earlier draft, and cited that way by the courts before the Official Draft was published. Restatement of the Law Governing Lawyers, Third, § 204(2)(a) (Proposed Final Draft No. 1, Mar. 29, 1996)(emphasis added).

while the number of reported cases raising this conflicts issue is numerous, only a few cases have ever referred to section 204(2), and they have imputed the disqualification and refused to follow the proposed new rule.[14]

Although the Reporter's Notes interpret a few trial court opinions broadly in an attempt to justify section 204(2), it should not be surprising that it has not found favor in the decisions thus far because it is quite difficult to apply. First, the trial judge ruling on the disqualification motion cannot normally decide if the prior "confidential client information" is "unlikely to be significant" in the present case unless he knows what that confidential information is. Of course, once the judge is told, the matter is no longer confidential. The lawyers opposing (or supporting) disqualification also have to know what the secret information is and why it is (or is not) significant so that they can respond to

---

[14]*Towne Development of Chandler, Inc. v. Superior Court*, 173 Ariz. 364, 369, 842 P.2d 1377, 1382 (1992) (rejecting Restatement's proposed rule); *Cardona v. General Motors Corp.*, 942 F.Supp. 968 (D.N.J.1996) (rejecting Restatement's proposed rule); *Elan Transdermal, Ltd. v. Cygnus Therapeutic Sys.*, 809 F.Supp. 1383, 1392 n.14 (N.D.Cal.1992) (same); *Roberts & Schaefer Co. v. San-Con*, 898 F.Supp. 356, 362 (S.D.W.V.1995) (finding Restatement rule not applicable).

Dieter v. Regents of the University of California, 963 F.Supp. 908, 911 (E.D.Cal.1997) cited the ABA Model Rules as well as the Restatement, but the court did not allow screening. It simply found that the attorneys, who never worked on the case while at another firm, had no confidential information. If the attorney has no confidential information, there is nothing to screen, as the court made quite clear when it stated: "Moreover, if the attorney did join a new firm, because the attorney is barred from handling the second matter, the attorney's entire firm would be barred by imputation." 963 F.Supp. 908, 911.

Decora, Inc. v. DW Wallcovering, Inc., 899 F.Supp. 132, 139 n.10 (S.D.N.Y.1995) cited the Restatement on the issue of screening; however, it also cited the ABA Rule, and a Second Circuit case—a controlling case for this district court. *Decora* then disqualified the lawyer and imputed the disqualification to the entire law firm; the court did not allow a screen. The Second Circuit case on which *Decora* relied was *Cheng v. GAF Corp.*, 631 F.2d 1052 (2d Cir.1980). *Cheng* could not have been influenced by the Restatement, as it did not even exist at the time. Moreover, *Cheng*, while referring to what it called a "Chinese Wall" and speaking of the possibility of such a screen, ended up disqualifying the individual lawyer and then imputing the disqualification to the entire law firm. The Second Circuit even ruled that the trial court had abused its discretion in not disqualifying the lawyer and the entire law firm. Another case citing the Restatement was *Marshall v. State of New York Division of State Police*, 952 F.Supp. 103, 110 (N.D.N.Y.1997). *Marshall*, like *Decora*, cited the ABA Rule, the Restatement, and various cases including *Cheng*; then, it disqualified the lawyer, imputed the disqualification to the entire law firm, and did not accept a screen.

See generally Neil W. Hamilton & Kevin R. Coan, *Are We a Profession or Merely a Business?: The Erosion of Conflicts Rules Through the Increased Use of Ethical Walls*, 27 HOFSTRA L. REV. 57 (1998).

the arguments of opposing counsel. Once the confidential information, like toothpaste, is out of the tube, it will be difficult to get it back in that tube.

Second, the judge cannot decide if the matter is "unlikely to be significant" unless he knows the full theory of the case, and that might not happen until the trial is nearly over. Lawyers deeply involved in a case often do not know the full theory until discovery is completed. Sometimes the theory of the case changes as the trial proceeds. Facts that may appear insignificant on the first day of trial take on a new complexion as more facts are presented.[15]

§ 1-4(c) Lobbying Efforts Regarding the Restatement

Although it may be too early to judge the influence of the proposed Restatement of the Law Governing Lawyers, it is clear that many lawyers and clients (what Wall Street might call the "smart money") certainly think that it will be significant. That is why the Restatement has been the subject of tremendous lobbying, rivaling the intense lobbying to which Congress is often subject.[16]

The lobbying of the insurance industry is a case in point. Consider the situation where the insurance company promises to provide a lawyer for the insured. Most courts have held that the lawyer represents the insured, not the insurer. In other words, the lawyer paid by the insurer to defend a claim owes his or her duties to the insured (the client who purchased the insurance policy) and not the insurer (who may have interests adverse to the insured). Even in a few cases where the courts may speak of the lawyer as having two clients (the insured and the insurer) the courts act as if the lawyer has only one client, the insured. Moreover, when lawyers act as if the insurer is also a client—such as when a lawyer discloses to the insurer confidential information that the insured would not want revealed to the insurer—the lawyer and insurance company have suffered the consequences.

---

[15]In the O.J. Simpson murder trial, no one would have guessed—before the trial unfolded—that a significant fact was that, years earlier, a writer researching possible TV scripts had tape recorded several interviews with Detective Mark Furman. *See* Ronald D. Rotunda, *Reporting Sensational Trials: Free Press, a Responsible Press, and Cameras in the* *Courts*, 3 COMMUNICATIONS L. & POLICY 295 (No. 2, Spring, 1998).

[16]Of course, there were important lobbying efforts in connection with the ABA's development of its 1983 Model Rules. Ted Schneyer, *Professionalism as Bar Politics: The Making of the Model Rules of Professional Conduct*, 14 LAW & SOCIAL INQUIRY 677 (1989).

In *Employers Casualty Co. v. Tilley*,[17] when the lawyer collected evidence of lack of coverage of the insured, the court held that the insurer was estopped as a matter of law from asserting a policy defense. The lawyer paid by the insurer "simply cannot take up the cudgels of the insurer against the insured." In *Lysick v. Walcom*,[18] even though the court referred to the insurer and insured as "two clients," it nonetheless made the lawyer liable for the judgment in excess of policy limits because he did not fully inform his client, the insured, about a settlement offer.

The ALI's initial Restatement draft took the standard position that the insured is the client. The insurance companies responded with intensive lobbying, even persuading a federal judge to speak with the Executive Director of the Institute.[19] Many ALI members were surprised by the intensive lobbying effort. "I was appalled," said one member, in response to the insurance lobby, because "politics and client interests are supposed to be checked at the door."[20]

§ 1-4(d) Conclusion

No book purporting to discuss the major issues of legal ethics should ignore the work of the Restatement of the Law Governing Lawyers. Even if this Restatement is not successful in persuading most courts to adopt significant changes in the law, we can expect that judges, practicing lawyers, and academics will often turn to this Restatement to examine its position on the important areas involving legal ethics. In addition, we may expect the Restatement to have a role in bringing clarity and structure to the vast and amorphous area that falls under the heading of legal ethics.

The ALI virtually completed the Official Draft in May 1998, but it was not published in final form until 2000 due to various minor and stylistic changes. The ALI renumbered many of the sections in this Official Draft. Consequently, this book will refer to the Official Draft of the ALI's Restatement of the Law Governing Lawyers unless otherwise indicated. The Restatement should prove to be a very useful tool for anyone engaging in legal research in the area of legal ethics.[21]

---

[17]*Employers Casualty Co. v. Tilley*, 496 S.W.2d 552 (Tex.1973).

[18]*Lysick v. Walcom*, 258 Cal.App.2d 136, 65 Cal.Rptr. 406 (Cal.App. 1968).

[19]Jonathan Groner, *Insurance Lobby Aims at Normally Staid ALI*, LEGAL TIMES, June 10, 1996, at 1. *See also* James Podgers, *Critics Fear*

Impact of Ethics Restatement, A.B.A. J., Oct. 1995, at 34.

[20]Jonathan Groner, *Insurance Lobby Aims at Normally Staid ALI*, LEGAL TIMES, June 10, 1996, at 1.

[21]*See* THOMAS D. MORGAN, COMPARING THE ABA MODEL RULES OF PROFESSIONAL CONDUCT WITH THE ALI RESTATEMENT (THIRD) OF THE LAW

§ 1-5 THE RELATIONSHIP OF LEGAL ETHICS WITH OTHER LAW

The history of law, said the English legal historian and commentator, F.W. Maitland, is a "seamless web."[1] This observation is equally true of the law of legal ethics. For one to write the first sentence in a book on legal ethics is to make a tear in this unity. The lawyer's ethical duty to keep the client's confidences incorporates the evidentiary attorney-client privilege, as well as the law of agency and the law governing the lawyer's work product. The lawyer's duty of competence is related to the law of tort and the tort of malpractice. The lawyer's retainer agreement with the client involves the law of contract, and takes into account that the lawyer, in entering into this contract, is a fiduciary of the client. The ethics rules in the Model Rules must also be interpreted in light of antitrust principles. And these ethics rules, such as the rules governing advertising and solicitation, must also be tested against constitutional principles, particularly those related to freedom of speech.

§ 1-6 WHAT IS A "PROFESSION"?

§ 1-6(a) Introduction

In addition to the relationship with other areas of substantive law, legal ethics is related to the interdisciplinary study of law and economics, because some of the present or past ethical violations are best understood as guild rules created by a cartel of lawyers. Thus, George Bernard Shaw cynically defined professions as "conspiracies against the laity."[1]

There is still truth in Shaw's cynicism, but just as one can be too naively optimistic, one can be too cynical as well. Legal ethics is also a branch of philosophy. "There is much more to it than

---

GOVERNING LAWYERS (ABA 2005).

[Section 1-5]

[1] Frederic W. Maitland, *Prologue to a History of English Law*, 14 L.Q.R. 13 (1898).

[Section 1-6]

[1] George Bernard Shaw, Preface to *The Doctor's Dilemma*, 9 (1911), *reprinted in* 1 BERNARD SHAW, COMPLETE PLAYS WITH PREFACES (1962). Shaw was specifically talking about medical doctors, but he made clear that his complaint that the medical profession is "a conspiracy to hide its own shortcomings," is true "of all professions." *Employers Casualty Co. v. Tilley* He also complained:

"The only evidence that can decide a case of malpractice is expert evidence: that is, the evidence of other doctors; and every doctor will allow a colleague to decimate a whole countryside sooner than violate the bond of professional etiquet[te] by giving him away."

Id. at 8.

Cf. Hizey v. Carpenter, 119 Wash.2d 251, 830 P.2d 646 (Wash. 1992), which held that a lawyer's violations of professional ethical standards—which are drafted to protect clients from the lawyer's improper actions—are *never* admissible as evidence of a lawyer's duty of care.

rules of ethics. There is a whole atmosphere of life's behavior."[2] And this atmosphere exists whether or not the constable is watching. Consequently, while commentators have accused the organized bar of being self-serving in its promotion of ethics rules,[3] the fact remains that the organized bar has also contributed substantially in developing model rules to protect clients,[4] for example, in setting up programs to enforce those rules and in developing lawyer assistance programs for lawyers who suffer from drug or alcohol abuse. While some of the rules may be self-serving, others are not, and the organized bar has sometimes fought to have the self-serving rules repealed.[5]

One cannot discuss the regulation of law without recognizing that it is a "profession." It certainly is a proud and noble profession. In the Middle Ages, it was said that there were historically four professions: the military, who professed peace; the medical doctors, who professed health; the clergy, who professed God; and lawyers, who professed justice.[6]

In modern times, it has become symbolically significant if an occupation is labeled a "profession." The word, "profession," as customarily defined and understood, evokes favorable emotions and suggests status.[7] Many occupations avidly seek to be recognized as a profession, and occupations already so acknowledged jealously guard their status as a profession.[8] An auto mechanic may have great expertise and high status within a

---

[2]John H. Wigmore, *Introduction* xxiv, *in* O. Carter, ETHICS OF THE LEGAL PROFESSION (1915).

[3]*E.g.*, Gerard Clark, *Fear and Loathing in New Orleans: The Sorry Fate of the Kutak Commission's Rules*, 17 SUFFOLK U. L. REV. 79 (1983); Steven Gillers, *What We Talked About When We Talked About Ethics: A Critical View of the Model Rules*, 46 OHIO STATE L.J. 243 (1985).

[4]The appendices to this book include some of the important model rules that the American Bar Association has developed to promote professionalism.

[5]*E.g.*, ABA COMMISSION ON PROFESSIONALISM, ". . . IN THE SPIRIT OF PUBLIC SERVICE:" A BLUEPRINT FOR THE REKINDLING OF LAWYER PROFESSIONALISM 52 & n.195 (1986), *reprinted in* 112 F.R.D. 243, 301 (1987) proposed that paralegals be licensed to perform certain relatively simple tasks (certain real estate closings, the drafting of simple wills, and selected tax services) that are performed only by licensed lawyers.

[6]Roscoe Pound included in the category of "professions," the "callings"—a word that he used—of ministry, medicine, law, and teaching. ROSCOE POUND, THE LAWYER FROM ANTIQUITY TO MODERN TIMES: WITH PARTICULAR REFERENCE TO THE DEVELOPMENT OF BAR ASSOCIATIONS IN THE UNITED STATES 5 (West Pub. Co. & ABA, 1953).

[7]*See* RONALD D. ROTUNDA, THE POLITICS OF LANGUAGE: LIBERALISM AS WORD AND SYMBOL (University of Iowa Press, 1986) on the importance of symbols and why words both reflect and mold the way we think.

[8]*E.g.*, MAGALI LARSON, THE RISE OF PROFESSIONALISM 12–15 (1977); Peter Wright, *What Is a "Profession"?*, 29 CANADIAN BAR REV. 748, 748 (1951) ("[T]he present tendency to apply 'profession' to every calling represents

group that recognizes that skill, but doctors, lawyers, pharmacists and accountants would likely not concede that even an expert mechanic is member of a learned profession.[9]

When one looks at what commentators say about "professions," it is interesting how often they agree that the rise from "occupation" to "profession" carries with it a number of supposedly necessary corollaries. Among these is the concept that it is appropriate for a profession to impose entry restrictions and to engage in other non-competitive practices, such as price fixing, peer review and the elimination or regulation of advertising. These restrictions are justified as part of the definition of "profession." The bench and bar must be careful in creating, interpreting, and applying the rules of legal ethics to guard against the tendency to assume that, because law is a "profession," that title carries with it anti-competitive baggage.[10]

Sometimes it may be useful to identify the term "profession" as relating to individuals, rather than groups. As the American Bar Association has recognized, some lawyers are professionals, and some are not.[11] On the other hand, as discussed below, lawyers as a group are different than many other people because they have fiduciary duties to their clients, duties that are not merely contractual.

A risk of labeling the practice of law or others occupations as a "profession" is that this label may then be used to justify restraints of trade that would otherwise not be accepted. History has given us various examples of legal restrictions on what certain professions rationalized and justified, and saw as inherent in, or part of, the definition of, a "profession."[12] Consider a few specific examples of the excess baggage that is typically attached to the label of "profession."

§ 1-6(b) Certification

Sociologist Daniel Bell, in his book, *The Coming of*

---

decadence in our language."); JETHRO K. LIEBERMAN, THE TYRANNY OF THE EXPERTS: HOW PROFESSIONALS ARE CLOSING THE OPEN SOCIETY 16–17 (1980).

[9]The mechanic, of course, will have a different view.

[10]*See* Thomas D. Morgan, *Toward Abandoning Organized Professionalism*, 30 HOFSTRA L. REV. 947 (2002).

[11]ABA Working Group on Civil Justice, Blueprint for Improving the Civil Justice System 12 (ABA 1992): "Professionalism lies not so much in following certain rules as in the development of personal attitudes and a manner of deportment that leads to appropriate professional relationships and courtesy in manner and creed."

[12]*See* Thomas D. Morgan, *The Evolving Concept of Professional Responsibility*, 90 HARV. L. REV. 702 (1977); Deborah L. Rhode, *Why the ABA Bothers: A Functional Perspective on Professional Codes*, 59 TEXAS L. REV. 689 (1981); Ted Schneyer, *Professionalism as Bar Politics: The Making of the Model Rules of Professional Conduct*, 14 LAW & SOCIAL INQUIRY 677 (1989).

Post-Industrial Society, defined a profession as "a learne*d* (*i.e.*, scholarly) activity" that "involves formal training, but within a broad intellectual context."[13] This, however, is merely a definition and not a theory of behavior. Purporting to clarify this description, Bell, in the very next sentence, states that, "To be within the profession *means to be* certified, formally or informally, by one's peers or by some established body with the profession."[14] Anticompetitive rules and barriers to entry, such as certification requirements, are justified—by definition.[15]

Other commentators place a similar emphasis on certification. Argyris and Schön argue in *Theory in Practice: Increasing Professional Effectiveness*,[16] that an essential element of a profession is that it is "a guild, or brotherhood of initiates, entitled to practice the special arts of the profession. . . ."[17] A "guild" or "brotherhood" may be simply another name for "cartel" or "monopoly."

Certification is also prominent in the more extensive definition by Professor Edgar H. Schein. Schein tells us that all sociologists "have agreed on the necessity to use a multiple criterion definition. . . ."[18] Schein then offers a suggested list of criteria that includes not only the service orientation of a profession

---

[13]DANIEL BELL, THE COMING OF POST-INDUSTRIAL SOCIETY 374 (1973). For more recent discussions of the professions, see S. HABER, THE QUEST FOR AUTHORITY AND HONOR IN THE AMERICAN PROFESSIONS: 1750–1900 (1991); B.A. KIMBALL, THE "TRUE PROFESSIONAL IDEAL" IN AMERICA (1992).

[14]DANIEL BELL, THE COMING OF POST-INDUSTRIAL SOCIETY 374 (1973) (emphasis added).

[15]*See* Rob Atkinson, *A Dissenter's Commentary on the Professionalism Crusade*, 74 TEXAS L. REV. 259 (1995). Professor Atkinson writes of the "apostles of professionalism" who are on a crusade:

"[T]he crusade speaks of a profession as a distinct kind of occupation characterized by such features as special education and licensing requirements; elements of nonmarket regulation, often in the hands of a occupational body rather than the state itself; and an announced ethos of public service . . . .. The second meaning that the crusade attempts to evoke when it speaks of professionalism focuses on the market failures that

create the need for professions as nonmarket means of organizing certain occupations."

Id. at 271 (footnote omitted).

[16]CHRIS ARGYRIS & DONALD A. SCHÖN, THEORY IN PRACTICE: INCREASING PROFESSIONAL EFFECTIVENESS (Jossey-Bass Pub., 1974).

[17]CHRIS ARGYRIS & DONALD A. SCHÖN, THEORY IN PRACTICE: INCREASING PROFESSIONAL EFFECTIVENESS 146 (Jossey-Bass Pub., 1974).

[18]EDGAR H. SCHEIN, PROFESSIONAL EDUCATION: SOME NEW DIRECTIONS 8 (McGraw-Hill, 1972).

Professor Schein summarizes the criteria that he believes define a profession. The professional, he writes:

(1) Is engaged in a "full time occupation;"

(2) Has "strong motivation" and a "lifetime commitment to that career;"

(3) Possesses a "specialized body of knowledge and skills acquired during a prolonged period of education and training;"

(4) Makes decisions on the basis of "general principles" or theories;

(5) Is "assumed to have a ser-

(Schein's criterion number five) but also the power to restrict entry through licensing and entry examination (his criterion number eight).[19]

Economic factors play a crucial role in this emphasis on certification and its restrictions on entry. Take, for example, the medical profession's strong control over the creation of medical schools, which effectively serves to restrict entry. I do not argue that the doctors have conspired to create a monopoly and thereby raise their incomes. Yet, in the name of a "profession," various occupations have acted *as if* they were monopolies. Thus, we are often told that standards must be raised and overcrowding must be prevented because, if "too many" people are let into a given profession, then their incomes will be lowered and the public will somehow suffer.[20]

According to this argument, the less conscientious doctors (or other professionals) will succumb to the temptation to offer inadequate services, forcing the others to go along or see their income drop below "adequate" levels. Concerns about the increasing numbers of law graduates are similar in nature. The argument boils down to the notion that professionals must be paid well to be professional.[21]

"Cut-throat," or "ruthless" competition may be appropriate for the hawkers of gadgets, it is said, but not for the professional. Why the distinction? Competition benefits the consumer of professional services, but anticompetitive behavior benefits the providers of professional services, *i.e.,* members of the profession, by increasing their incomes.[22]

Another consequence of certification is that it creates, by definition, "unauthorized practice." Under Schein's criterion number

---

vice orientation," which implies "an absence of self-interest;"

(6) Serves clients on the basis of the "objective needs of the client," which means that the professional often must "withhold moral judgments;"

(7) "Is assumed to know better what is good for the client than the client himself," and thus, even if "the client is not satisfied, the professional will, in principle, permit only his colleagues to judge his performance;"

(8) Forms professional associations that "define criteria of admission, educational standards, *licensing or other formal entry examinations*, career liens within the profession and areas of jurisdiction . . . .,"

(9) Has knowledge "assumed to be specific;" and

(10) *Ordinarily is "not allowed to advertise or seek out clients."*

Id. at 8–9 (emphasis added)

[19] *See also* CHRIS ARGYRIS & DONALD A. SCHÖN, THEORY IN PRACTICE: INCREASING PROFESSIONAL EFFECTIVENESS 146 (Jossey-Bass Pub., 1974).

[20] See discussion of "The Nimble Profession," in, LAWRENCE FRIEDMAN, A HISTORY OF AMERICAN LAW 633–39 (2d ed. 1985).

[21] *See* MILTON FRIEDMAN, CAPITALISM & FREEDOM 152 (1962).

[22] As Professor Rhode notes: "Codified standards [of ethics] can generate monetary and psychic benefits . . ..

eight, a profession is defined by its areas of jurisdiction. In all states anyone can call himself a carpenter or handyman. But in this country, only certified members of the bar can call themselves lawyers and practice law. In contrast, many continental countries are much less restrictive and allow people who are not licensed as lawyers to engage in what would be considered unauthorized practice of law in this country.[23]

Perhaps the law should be paternalistic in some cases, but not in all. If a competent adult wants a realtor or title company to prepare and fill out (at little or no cost to the lay person) a variety of forms related to a real estate transaction, why should the law interfere? The reaction of Arizona courts on this issue was typical. *State Bar v. Arizona Land Title & Trust Co.*[24] prohibited the practice. Although Realtors had engaged in such work for a long time, the court ruled that the activity involved the unauthorized practice of law, because "those acts, whether performed in court or in the law office, which lawyers customarily have carried on from day to day through the centuries must constitute 'the practice of law.' "[25]

While the Arizona decision was hardly unusual, the reaction of the state's people was not. By a vote of almost four to one, the people approved a state constitutional amendment to reverse the state supreme court. Obviously, the voters more interested in receiving customary, and apparently adequate, real estate ser-

---

What distinguishes professionals [from 'a retail grocers' association] is their relative success in packaging occupational interests as societal imperatives. In that regard, codes of ethics have proved highly useful." Deborah L. Rhode, *Why the ABA Bothers: A Functional Perspective on Professional Codes*, 59 TEXAS L. REV. 689, 690, 720 (1981). The time period that has seen an increase in the number of lawyers in recent years has also witnessed a lowering of their income. THOMAS D. MORGAN & RONALD D. ROTUNDA, PROBLEMS AND MATERIALS ON PROFESSIONAL RESPONSIBILITY 3 n. 3 (Foundation Press, 6th ed. 1995).

[23]*E.g.*, LEGAL SERVICES: A FRAMEWORK FOR THE FUTURE, *Presented to Parliament by the Lord High Chancellor, by Command of Her Majesty* (London, Her Majesty's Stationery Office, July, 1989) (discussing regulations to enable banks, building societies, and others to offer conveyancing services, to allow

trust corporations and others to prepare documents for probate, to lift barriers to the formation of certain types of partnerships, etc.); THOMAS D. MORGAN & RONALD D. ROTUNDA, PROBLEMS AND MATERIALS ON PROFESSIONAL RESPONSIBILITY 541–42 (Foundation Press, 6th ed. 1995) (discussing practice in European Union).

Unlike the situation in Europe, a licensed lawyer in the United States may be engaged in the unauthorized practice of law, *if* that lawyer is not licensed in the appropriate jurisdiction. *Symposium: Ethics and the Multijurisdictional Practice of Law*, 36 So. TEX. L. REV. 657–1197 (1995).

[24]*State Bar v. Arizona Land Title and Trust Co.*, 90 Ariz. 76, 366 P.2d 1 (Ariz.1961).

[25]366 P.2d at 9. *Contrast* Thomas D. Morgan, *The Evolving Concept of Professional Responsibility*, 90 HARV. L. REV. 702, 707–12 (1977).

vices for little or no added cost than in being protected from the realtors.[26]

§ 1-6(c) Peer Review of Incompetence

One important advantage of belonging to a profession is that it offers peer review, which provides some protection from the discipline of the marketplace. Schein notes that the achievement of "autonomy" is the "ultimate criterion of professionalization, according to most sociologists. . . ."[27] Peer review means, at least in part, that it is not the laypeople who decide whether a professional is in error. The standard is not negligence, but malpractice; therefore the decision of whether malpractice has in fact occurred must be made by peer experts.

The market may be a slow-working disciplinarian, but swift and sure punishment is hardly inherent in peer review. Peer review is an advantage for professionals,[28] although one often justified more by definition than by articulated reasons. As Bell insists, "One might say that business is called to account by its customers through the market, whereas a professional is called to account by his peers through the professional group."[29] Schein agrees, but offers, as a rationale, only a repetition of Bell's statement.[30]

There are some occupations—or more likely certain aspects of some occupations—where the review should be exercised primarily by peers. But such peer review is not justified merely by classifying an activity as "learned" or involving "formal training . . . within a broad intellectual context."[31] Although an individual may strive to be professional, an occupational group is more likely to strive to be a cartel. It is error to assume or justify special treatment for an occupation because it is called a profession. Hiding behind the label of "profession" may be monopolistic practices that do not make for sound social policy.[32]

---

[26]Ariz. Const. Art. XXVI. Real estate lawyers in Virginia are lobbying for legislation to bar anyone except lawyers from handling title searches and residential real estate closings. Susan Adams, *Backlash*, FORBES MAGAZINE, Mar. 25, 1996, at 46.

[27]EDGAR H. SCHEIN, PROFESSIONAL EDUCATION: SOME NEW DIRECTIONS 9 (McGraw-Hill, 1972).

[28]Lawrence W. Kessler, *The Unchanging Face of Legal Malpractice: How the "Captured" Regulators of the Bar Protect Attorneys*, 86 MARQUETTE L. REV. 457 (2002).

[29]DANIEL BELL, THE COMING OF POST-INDUSTRIAL SOCIETY 374 n.6 (1973).

[30]EDGAR H. SCHEIN, PROFESSIONAL EDUCATION: SOME NEW DIRECTIONS 10 (McGraw-Hill, 1972).

[31]DANIEL BELL, THE COMING OF POST-INDUSTRIAL SOCIETY 374 (1973).

[32]It is appropriate, when deciding whether a heart transplant was performed properly, or whether an airbag mechanism was repaired properly, to hear expert testimony. But deciding whether a patient should be told of the dangers of a particular surgical tech-

§ 1-6(d) An Emphasis on "Selflessness"

Another test, or definition, of "profession" asserts that professional organizations—unlike trade unions—exist primarily for the advancement of the profession (medicine, justice, or teaching), not for the advancement of the individual members. Under this definition, the professional is selfless. The professional serves the public interest and the best interest of the patient or client. Schein's criterion number five emphasizes this principle.[33] Unlike the trade unionist, the professional is not merely in a money-making trade. The professional serves others, and thereby emphasizes quality. Gaining a livelihood is incidental.[34] A professional offers a certain service and confers the same diligence and quality of service whether paid or not.[35]

---

nique, or whether an overweight oil may be used to winterize a car, should be considered either a policy matter—judged as a matter of law by the court—or simply a factual matter, to be judged by laypeople on a jury.

[33]EDGAR H. SCHEIN, PROFESSIONAL EDUCATION: SOME NEW DIRECTIONS 8 (McGraw-Hill, 1972).

[34]Cf. ROSCOE POUND, THE LAWYER FROM ANTIQUITY TO MODERN TIMES: WITH PARTICULAR REFERENCE TO THE DEVELOPMENT OF BAR ASSOCIATIONS IN THE UNITED STATES 50–51 (West Pub. Co. & ABA, 1953), who points out that in the fifth and sixth centuries in Europe, advocates studied in law schools and ceased being mere orators. Fixed fees, unauthorized practice, and other barriers to entry into the legal profession emerged.

"A certain number of advocates was fixed for each of the courts in the leading cities. Those attached to a court formed a sort of corporation. The law recognized fees and fixed the scale. Professional discipline was provided for. Thus the main lines which exist today had become established."

"In the fifth century and first quarter of the sixth legislation went forward steadily toward a well organized bar for each of the great courts. A statute of 468 prohibited the practice of advocacy by those not admitted to practice."

[35]E.g., ROSCOE POUND, THE LAWYER FROM ANTIQUITY TO MODERN TIMES: WITH PARTICULAR REFERENCE TO THE DEVELOPMENT OF BAR ASSOCIATIONS IN THE UNITED STATES 5–6 (West Pub. Co. & ABA, 1953):

"There is much more in a profession than a traditionally dignified calling. The term refers to a *group of men pursuing a learned art as a common calling in the spirit of public service*—no less a public service because it may incidentally be a means of livelihood. Pursuit of the learned art in the spirit of a public service is the primary purpose. *Gaining a livelihood is incidental*, whereas in a business or trade it is the entire purpose. Thus, if an engineer discovers a new process or invents a new mechanical device he may obtain a patent and retain for himself a profitable monopoly . . .. If a lawyer has learned something useful to the profession and so to the administration of justice through research and experience he publishes it in a legal periodical or expounds it in a paper before a bar association or in a lecture to law students. *It is not his property. He may publish it in a copyrighted book* and so have rights in the literary form in which it is expounded. But the process or method or developed principle he has worked out belongs to the world." (emphasis added)

§ 1-6(e) The Privilege to Control Competition and Limit Advertising

It is often said that professions must maintain dignity, and that both advertising and price competition are not conducive to dignity. Although the original ABA Canons of Professional Ethics of 1908 did not outlaw advertising, the Canons were eventually changed.[36] In modern times, the lawyers' professional codes outlawed undignified advertising and price competition until the U.S. Supreme Court invalidated, on First Amendment grounds, overly-broad state prohibitions on advertising.[37] Advertising restrictions that members of professional organizations agreed to abide by would not violate the First Amendment (because there is no state action), but they would still be illegal because they would violate the antitrust laws, as a conspiracy in restraint of trade.[38]

Some consider the prohibition on advertising and the maintenance of dignity to be the essence of a profession. Schein's tenth criterion certainly supports this view.[39] The Court in *Florida Bar v. Went For It, Inc.* also assumed that advertising by professionals is different than other types of commercial speech; it stated: "Speech *by professionals* obviously has many dimensions."[40] Coincidentally, however, this avoidance of price competition and limitations on advertising are also characteristics of cartels and robber barons, as well as esteemed professional organizations.[41]

To maintain the dignity of their profession, preserve quality and protect the public, auto mechanics might like to outlaw price specials, engage in price fixing and prohibit advertising of ser-

---

[36]The ABA Canons of Professional Ethics (Aug. 27, 1908) only had 32 Canons. Later, the ABA added Canons that restricted advertising. *See* Canons 40 ("Newspapers"); 43 ("Approved Law Lists"); 46 ("Notice to Local Lawyers"). The original version of Canon 27 (which is now titled, "Advertising, Direct or Indirect") was completely redrafted in 1937 to restrict severely lawyer advertising. *See* ABA Formal Opinion 276 (Sept. 20, 1947).

[37]*Bates v. State Bar*, 433 U.S. 350, 97 S.Ct. 2691, 53 L.Ed.2d 810 (1977).

[38]*Goldfarb v. Virginia State Bar*, 421 U.S. 773, 95 S.Ct. 2004, 44 L.Ed.2d 572 (1975).

[39]EDGAR H. SCHEIN, PROFESSIONAL EDUCATION: SOME NEW DIRECTIONS 8 (McGraw-Hill, 1972).

[40]515 U.S. 618, 634, 115 S.Ct. 2371, 2381, 132 L.Ed.2d 541 (1995) (emphasis added). *See* Ronald D. Rotunda, *Professionalism, Legal Advertising, and Free Speech In the Wake of Florida Bar v. Went For It, Inc.*, 49 ARK. L. REV. 703 (1997) (Symposium), reprinted in, 12 LAWYERS' LIABILITY REV. 2 (No. 10, Oct. 1998) (part I), 12 LAWYERS' LIABILITY REV. 2 (No. 11, Nov. 1998)(part II), 12 LAWYERS' LIABILITY REV. 2 (No. 12, Oct. 1998)(part III).

[41]Note, by the way, the Court's use of the phrase, "obviously." I have found that when commentators or judges use that word, it is often a signal suggesting that the statement has little logical support, but, by use of the word "obviously," the reader may not notice the problem. The statement in this footnote is obviously correct.

vices, fees and hours. But if they did these things they would break the law. Yet to maintain *their* dignity, lawyers for many years engaged in price fixing. It was not until *Goldfarb v. Virginia State Bar*[42] that the Supreme Court ruled that this practice was in violation of the antitrust laws. And, until the Supreme Court decision in *Bates v. State Bar of Arizona*,[43] state courts, using their power to promulgate rules of ethics, routinely forbade any advertising.

Advertising of legal services and price competition are related, because empirical studies have shown that advertising results in lower prices to the consumer.[44] Some people incorrectly assume that legal advertising must raise the costs to the consumer, because someone must pay for the cost of the advertising. But the empirical evidence shows that advertising *lowers* prices, so the cost must be taken out of the lawyer's profit margin.[45] This might explain why some lawyers have supported advertising restrictions. This fact may explain why many lawyers have opposed televised lawyer commercials. Television commercials lead to price wars, and no consumer of legal services has ever been wounded in a price war.

Yet, even here, it is naive to think that all lawyers support advertising restrictions because of an aversion to competition. It may be in the economic self-interest of lawyers to restrict competition by advertising, but not all lawyers parrot their economic self-interest. Life is more complicated than that. In fact, some lawyers and bar associations are selfless and altruistic.[46] Many lawyers freely give of their time in an effort to protect clients and encourage ethical behavior. In addition, the American Bar Association[47] and some state bars[48] have funded studies to demonstrate that the perceived harms of nonmisleading advertising are

---

[42]*Goldfarb v. Virginia State Bar*, 421 U.S. 773, 95 S.Ct. 2004, 44 L.Ed.2d 572 (1975).

[43]433 U.S. 350, 97 S.Ct. 2691, 53 L.Ed.2d 810 (1977).

[44]*See, e.g.*, Jesse Choper, *Consequences of Supreme Court Decisions Upholding Constitutional Right*, 83 MICH. L. REV. 1, 166–69 (1984); John R. Schroeter, *et al., Advertising and Competition in Routine Legal Service Markets: An Empirical Investigation*, 35 J. INDUS. ECON. 49 (1987).

[45]*E.g.*, Jesse Choper, *Consequences of Supreme Court Decisions Upholding Constitutional Rights*, 83 MICH. L. REV. 1, 166–69 (1984); John R. Schroeter, *et al., Advertising and*

Competition in Routine Legal Service Markets: An Empirical Investigation, 35 J. INDUS. ECON. 49 (1987).

[46]*See* Marvin E. Frankel, *Why Does Professor Abel Work at a Useless Task?*, 59 TEXAS L. REV. 723 (1981). Judge Frankel was responding to Richard Abel, *Why Does the ABA Promulgate Ethical Rules*, 59 TEXAS L. REV. 639 (1981).

[47]The ABA Commission on Advertising recommended:
"The role of the marketplace as a measure of influence on the communication of legal services should be recognized and should not be limited by overreaching or unduly restrictive policies."
ABA COMMISSION ON ADVERTIS-

overblown. The ABA's 1995 study of legal advertising goes even
further and blames lawyers' criticism of advertising for discouraging some lawyers from advertising, and thereby increasing the
stigma on members of the legal profession when they exercise
their Constitutional right to advertise.[49]

§ 1-6(f) The Importance of the Fiduciary Relationship

There is one very significant distinction among lawyers, the
green grocers, used car salespersons, new car salespersons, and
most other occupations. Lawyers are *fiduciaries* of their clients. A
fiduciary in the law is a similar to a trustee. Lawyers must act
with utmost good faith, candor, and scrupulousness in dealing
with clients. Clients have every right to expect trust from their
lawyers, who are expected to act for the benefit of their principals,
their clients. Clients have every right to expect loyalty from their
lawyers, while they do not expect loyalty from their electricians
or grocers.[50]

Much of the law of ethics is derived from, or related to, the law
of fiduciaries. An agent may not "use unfairly any information or
property which he has acquired by virtue of the agency."[51]
Lawyers, too, have the obligation to keep their clients' secrets, an
obligation that extends beyond the lawyer-client evidentiary
privilege.[52]

Similarly, the rules of conflicts of interest, discussed below, are
related to the fiduciary duties that lawyers owe their clients. Any
"agent violates his fiduciary duty to his principle if he has any

---

ING, LAWYER ADVERTISING AT THE
CROSSROADS: PROFESSIONAL POLICY
CONSIDERATIONS 149 (ABA 1995).

[48]*See* NEW YORK STATE BAR
ASSOCIATION, SPECIAL COMMITTEE ON
LAWYER ADVERTISING AND REFERRAL
SERVICES, ATTORNEY ADVERTISING
COMMITTEE REPORT, APPENDIX A, at p.
2. (Report to the House of Delegates,
Sept. 1995).

[49]ABA COMMISSION ON ADVERTIS-
ING, LAWYER ADVERTISING AT THE
CROSSROADS: PROFESSIONAL POLICY
CONSIDERATIONS 149 (ABA 1995):

"When lawyers criticize other
lawyers because they advertise, they
are advancing this stigma; this discourages other lawyers from advertising at all, thereby limiting the use of
marketing techniques and indirectly
limiting the role of the marketplace."

[50]ROSCOE POUND, THE LAWYER
FROM ANTIQUITY TO MODERN TIMES:

WITH PARTICULAR REFERENCE TO THE
DEVELOPMENT OF BAR ASSOCIATIONS IN
THE UNITED STATES 7 (West Pub. Co.
& ABA, 1953), argued:

"It must not be supposed, however, that an organized profession of
lawyers or of physicians is the same
sort of thing as a retail grocers' association or that there is no essential
difference between an organized bar
and plumbers' or lumber dealers' associations."

Eliot Freidson, a noted sociologist, scoffed at this view, claiming that
"professionals differ from trade unions
only in their sanctimoniousness." ELIOT
FREIDSON, PROFESSIONS OF MEDICINE
369 (1970).

[51]W. EDWARD SELL, AGENCY
119–20 (Foundation Press, 1975).

[52]*See* Rule 1.6, & Comment 5,
discussed below.

adverse interest in any transactions he conducts unless he has revealed his interest to the principle and the principle acquiesces."[53] And, it is hornbook law that—

> *Even where the agent's adverse interest is known to the principal*, the agent is under a duty to *disclose fully* to the principal, prior to the transaction, all the facts which he knows or should know *might* affect the judgment of the principal. Further, he has a duty *to act fairly* with the principal.[54]

We will find these ideas throughout the discussion of conflicts of interests.[55]

When the lawyer and client agree to a fee, that is a contract. But because the contract is between the client and his or her fiduciary, the ethics rules impose further requirements, such as the rule that the fee "shall be reasonable."[56]

Law is a business, and one should not ignore the fact that lawyers usually charge for their work. But one cannot understand this business and the law governing lawyers without understanding that lawyers are fiduciaries of their clients.[57]

§ 1-7 THE PUBLIC IMAGE OF LAWYERS

The popular culture often criticizes lawyers for being too tough. On the other hand, if any of us got into trouble, we probably would want a tough lawyer to represent us. The same people who are critical of "Rambo litigators" freely admit that, when they have a problem, they want a lawyer who plays hardball.[1] Let the other side be represented by Mr. Milquetoast.

Society places a dual role on lawyers—the popular culture criticizes a lawyer for being tough; that same culture also expects a lawyer simultaneously to be a friend,[2] gentle and kind.

Psychologists predict that these self-contradictory expectations

---

[53]EDWARD SELL, AGENCY 120 (Foundation Press, 1975).

[54]EDWARD SELL, AGENCY 121 (Foundation Press, 1975) (emphasis added) (footnote omitted).

[55]See discussion of Rules 1.7, 1.8, et seq. below.

[56]Rule 1.5(a). DR 2-106(A).

[57]Ronald D. Rotunda, *Teaching Ethics a Quarter of a Century After Watergate*, 51 HASTINGS L.J. 661 (2000).

[Section 1-7]

[1]William A. Brewer III & John W. Bickel II, *Etiquette of the Advocate?*, TEXAS LAWYER, March 21, 1994, at 20,

21 col. 4; James Podgers, *Public: "Shyster" OK—If He's on Your Side*, 67 A.B.A. J. 695 (1981). *See also* James A. George, *The "Rambo" Problem: Is Mandatory CLE the Way Back to Atticus?*, 62 LA. L. REV. 467 (2002); Allen K. Harris, *The Professionalism Crisis—The 'Z' Words and Other Rambo Tactics: The Conference of Chief Justices' Solution*, 53 S.C. L. REV. 549 (2002).

[2]*See* Charles Fried, *The Lawyer as Friend: The Moral Foundations of the Lawyer-Client Relation*, 85 YALE L.J. 1060 (1976); Ronald D. Rotunda, *Remembering Robert F. Drinan, S.J.*, 20 GEORGETOWN J. LEGAL ETHICS 203 (2007).

lead lawyers to be depressed, because people internalize qualities projected on them by others. As one New York Gestalt psychologist explains: "Nobody ever says they want a nice lawyer. They say, 'I want a barracuda. I want a real throat-slitter.' So lawyers have these qualities dumped on them."[3] Therefore, we may expect that some lawyers will often be depressed because they are taking on society's distaste for what they do.

These expectations comport with the experience of many lawyers. Lawyers in general, and trial lawyers in particular, lead tense lives. It is no accident that, at the July, 1995 annual meeting of the Association of Trial Lawyers of America, a two-hour crash course on stress management drew a large crowd.[4]

One need not rely on such anecdotal evidence; some scientific studies come to the same conclusion. A 1990 empirical investigation at John Hopkins University showed that severe depression is more likely to occur among lawyers than among members of 103 other occupations. A statistical analysis at Campbell University in North Carolina discovered that 11% of lawyers in that state thought of suicide at least once a month![5] Yet another study, this one measuring testosterone levels, showed high elevations of the hormone in prisoners, cold-call salespeople, the unemployed, and—no surprise here—attorneys. (Ministers and farmers, by the way, were at the low end of the scale.)[6] Other, more recent, studies dispute these findings and conclude that lawyers generally are satisfied with their work and are not discontent.[7]

Although the popular culture treats lawyers with contempt, we soon come to a different conclusion if we listen to lawyers talking about other lawyers. Very quickly a standard leitmotif emerges. Lawyers like—indeed, love—other lawyers and the law. If we put twenty lawyers in a room, they quickly would start patting each other on the back. The famous New York lawyer, Louis Nizer, for

---

[3]Amy Stevens, *Why Lawyers Are Depressed, Anxious, Bored Insomniacs*, WALL STREET JOURNAL, June 12, 1995, at B1, col. 3 & B6, col. 5 (Midwest ed.).

The way lawyers are perceived in society also influences the drafting of legal ethics codes. *See* Fred C. Zacharias, *The Image of Lawyers*, 20 GEORGETOWN J. LEGAL ETHICS 73 (2007).

[4]Richard B. Schmitt, *Trial Lawyers Take Case to the Politicians*, WALL STREET JOURNAL, July 21, 1995, at B12, col. 1 (Midwest ed.).

[5]Amy Stevens, *Why Lawyers Are Depressed, Anxious, Bored Insomniacs*, WALL STREET JOURNAL, June 12, 1995, at B1, col. 3 (Midwest ed.). *See* Marc Galanter, *Predators and Parasites: Lawyer Bashing and Civil Justice*, 28 GEORGIA L. REV. 633, 662–69 (1994).

[6]Anita Sharpe, *Spit Testing May Be Hard to Swallow In the Workplace*, WALL STREET JOURNAL, Nov. 29, 1993, at A1, A5, col.4 (Midwest ed.).

[7]John P. Heinz, Kathleen E. Hull, & Ava A. Harter, *Lawyers and Their Discontents: Findings from a Survey of the Chicago Bar*, 74 IND. L. J. 735 (1999).

example, rhapsodized that "law is truth in action. It is man's highest achievement, because it is the only weapon he has fashioned whose force rests solely on the sanctity of reason."[8] Another New York lawyer, Harrison Tweed, seconded Nizer's view. Said Tweed:

> I have a high opinion of lawyers. With all their faults, they stack up well against those in every other occupation or profession. They are better to work with or play with or fight with or drink with than most other varieties of mankind.[9]

Although lawyers may wax eloquent about the legal profession, the general public wanes.[10] Poets often capture the public mood. Life reflects art. Carl Sandburg had this to say about lawyers:

> When the lawyers are through What is there left, Bob? Can a mouse nibble at it And find enough to fasten a tooth in?

> Why is there always a secret singing When a lawyer cashes in? Why does a hearse horse snicker Hauling a lawyer away?[11]

Sandburg's perception of lawyers is hardly new.[12] Davy Crockett, the "King of the Wild Frontier," wrote in his autobiography that when he was a magistrate, his decisions were fair because he did not know "the law," but he knew about "common justice and honesty."[13] Most lay people would respond, "Amen."

The Gospel according to Luke tells us that the LORD said: "Woe to you lawyers also! You lay impossible burdens on men but will not lift a finger to lighten them . . .. Woe to you lawyers! You have taken away the key of knowledge. You yourselves have not gained access, yet you have stopped those who wished to enter."[14] Over a millennium and a half later, Shakespeare echoed this la-

---

[8]LOUIS NIZER, MY LIFE IN COURT 523 (1961).

[9]BERNARD BOTEIN, TRIAL JUDGE: THE CANDID BEHIND-THE-BENCH STORY OF JUSTICE BERNARD BOTEIN 149 (Simon & Schuster, New York 1952) (quoting Harrison Tweed).

[10]Ronald D. Rotunda, *The Legal Profession and the Public Image of Lawyers*, 23 JOURNAL OF THE LEGAL PROFESSION 51 (1999).

[11]KARL LLEWELLYN, THE BRAMBLE BUSH: OF OUR LAW AND ITS STUDY 142 (1960), quoting Carl Sandburg, *The Lawyers Know Too Much* (1951).

[12]Leonard E. Gross, *The Public Hates Lawyers: Why Should We Care?*, 29 SETON HALL L. REV. 1405 (1999). Richard H. Underwood, *The Profes-*

sional and the Liar, 87 KENT. L.J. 919 (1998–1999).

[13]DAVY CROCKETT, THE LIFE OF DAVID CROCKETT, THE ORIGINAL HUMORIST AND IRREPRESSIBLE BACKWOODSMAN: AN AUTOBIOGRAPHY 99–100 (1902):

"I was appointed one of the magistrates . . .. My judgments were never appealed from, and if they had been, they would have stuck like wax, as I gave my decisions on the principles of common justice and honesty between man and man, and relied on natural born sense, and not on law learning to guide me; for I had never read a page in a law book in all my life."

[14]Luke, ch. 11, v. 46, 52.

ment when he had one of his characters chant, "Let's kill all the lawyers."[15]

Nowadays, ethnic jokes are no longer politically correct. Jokes about disabled people similarly are no longer tolerated. But jokes about lawyers are always in good taste. Needless to say, the jokes are hardly flattering, and they reflect the view of lawyers in the popular culture.[16]

In the 1970s, Chief Justice Warren Burger became concerned that the general public saw lawyers in a bad light, that this bad public perception had increased in recent years, and that lawyers' advertising for clients, especially on television, had been a prime cause of the popular culture's attitude towards lawyers.[17] He persuaded the American Bar Association to create a special Commission to study the problem, but the Commission did not find support for Burger's hypothesis.[18]

Burger was neither alone nor original in his complaint identifying television and advertising as one of the usual suspects responsible for the public's poor view of lawyers.[19] Go to any gathering of lawyers, particularly at bar association meetings,

---

[15]WILLIAM SHAKESPEARE, HENRY VI, Part II, act 4, scene 2, line 68.

[16]*E.g.*—A client questioned a lawyer about part of the bill. "What is this $75 charge for?" asked the client. The lawyer replied: "That's when I was walking downtown, saw you on the other side of the street, crossed over to say hello, and found out that it wasn't you."

See also Arthur Garwin, *When on Mars*, 17 NOVA L. REV. 941, 942 (1993): "If upon receiving a fee from a client, a lawyer declares 'I really made a killing on this one,' the fee is unreasonable." Leonard E. Gross, *The Public Hates Lawyers: Why Should We Care?*, 29 SETON HALL L. REV. 1405 (1999): "The problem with lawyer jokes is that (1) lawyers don't think they're funny, and, (2) everyone else doesn't think they're jokes."

[17]When the Supreme Court first ruled that lawyer advertising is commercial speech protected by the First Amendment, Burger was in the dissent. *Bates v. State Bar*, 433 U.S. 350,

97 S.Ct. 2691, 53 L.Ed.2d 810 (1977).

[18]ABA COMMISSION ON PROFESSIONALISM, ". . . IN THE SPIRIT OF PUBLIC SERVICE:" A BLUEPRINT FOR THE REKINDLING OF LAWYER PROFESSIONALISM (1986), *reprinted in*, 112 F.R.D. 243 to 312 (1987). This Commission, created in response to Chief Justice Burger's concerns, ended up rejecting his analysis. The Commission acknowledged: "it seems probable that it is principally lawyers—not clients—who are concerned about the style and message of certain legal advertising." *Id.* at 27, 112 F.R.D. at 276. *See* Ronald D. Rotunda, *Lawyers and Professionalism: A Commentary on the Report of the American Bar Association Commission on Professionalism*, 18 LOYOLA UNIVERSITY OF CHICAGO L. J. 1149 (1987) (the Baker-McKenzie Foundation Lecture).

[19]Ronald D. Rotunda, *Epilogue, in* ROBERT M. JARVIS & PAUL R. JOSEPH, PRIME TIME LAW: FICTIONAL TELEVISION AS LEGAL NARRATIVE 265 (Carolina Academic Press, 1998).

and most of the armchair analysts will point the finger of guilt to televised advertisements.[20]

Bar associations also are concerned with the portrayal of lawyers on television. Both lawyers and bar groups lashed out at a Miller Brewing Company television commercial for Miller's Lite Beer. The commercial, called "Big Lawyer Roundup," featured rodeo cowboys who lassoed an overweight tax attorney and a divorce lawyer.[21]

Bar associations often believe that one of their primary missions is to improve the popular perception of lawyers. As the Florida Bar has argued, it has a "substantial" interest in "maintaining the professionalism of the members of the bar," and that the "public's perception of, and confidence in, its system of justice and those who administer it is critical to the stability of a democratic society."[22] The Bar cannot do much about the dramas or situation comedies that feature lawyers, nor can they stamp out lawyer jokes,[23] so they are left with regulating lawyers' advertisements.

The U.S. Supreme Court agreed that an important mission of the Bar is to protect the "flagging reputations of Florida lawyers. . .,"[24] and thus the majority upheld the constitutionality of a Florida rule that limited lawyers' soliciting clients. The

---

[20]*See, e.g.,* Robert D. Peltz, *Legal Advertising—Opening Pandora's Box?,* 19 STETSON L. REV. 43, 114 (1989), arguing:

"Although there are many reasons for these public image problems, advertising has *no doubt* played a great role. *It does not take a great leap of faith* to understand how television ads adversely affect the image of the profession and the ability of attorneys to act as officers of the court. . . ." (emphasis added).

Empirical studies show that legal advertising has led to the lowering of legal fees. *See, e.g.,* Jesse Choper, *Consequences of Supreme Court Decisions Upholding Constitutional Rights,* 83 MICH. L. REV. 1, 166–69 (1984); John R. Schroeter, *et al., Advertising and Competition in Routine Legal Service Markets: An Empirical Investigation,* 35 J. INDUS. ECON. 49 (1987).

[21]Randall Samborn, *Anti-Lawyer Attitude Up, But NLJ / West Poll Also Shows More People Are Using*

Attorneys, NAT'L L. J., Aug. 9, 1993, at 1, col. 1. Later, the commercial was pulled after a gunman killed nine people (including himself), and wounded six others, when he engaged in a shooting outburst at Pettit & Martin, a San Francisco law firm. *Id.*

[22]Petitioner's Brief on the Merits, at 19, in *Florida Bar v. Went for It, Inc.,* 515 U.S. 618, 115 S.Ct. 2371, 132 L.Ed.2d 541 (1995).

[23]*Cf.* Ronald D. Rotunda, *What Next? Outlawing Lawyer Jokes?,* WALL STREET JOURNAL, Aug. 8, 1995, at A12, col. 3–5 (Midwest ed.).

[24]*Florida Bar v. Went for It, Inc., 515 U.S. at 624, 115 S.Ct. at 2376.* In this case, the Court held (5 to 4) that, even though a lawyer has a constitutional right to engage in targeted mailing soliciting legal employment (not just mass mailings), Florida may ban targeted mailing by plaintiffs' attorneys for 30 days after the cause of action has occurred. The Bar argued that this cooling off period was necessary to protect the victims and the reputa-

purpose of the restriction was not to protect the public from being misled about lawyers and what they do (undignified advertisements need not be misleading), but to protect the public image of lawyers.[25]

It is true that surveys evaluating the public's opinion of lawyers usually show lawyers as ranking in admiration as slightly below insurance agents.[26] The single most significant event in the last three decades that led to a sharp decline in the public image of lawyers was Watergate, an event that occurred several years before the Supreme Court declared that lawyer advertising is a constitutional right.[27] The televised Senate Watergate Hearings showed not only that many of the Watergate conspirators were lawyers,[28] but also that the people who uncovered the scandal were lawyers, like Senator Sam Ervin, Professor Sam Dash, the

---

tion of the legal profession. Justice O'Connor wrote the majority opinion in *Went for It*.

The majority in *Went for It*, described the regulation as "an effort to protect the flagging reputations of Florida lawyers," and went on to say: "[w]e have little trouble crediting the Bar's interest as substantial." Went for It, Inc., 515 U.S. at 625, 115 S.Ct. at 2376.

Contra Leonard E. Gross, *The Public Hates Lawyers: Why Should We Care?*, 29 SETON HALL L. REV. 1405, 1459–60 (1999): "The legal profession should not be too quick to rely on the need to improve the image of lawyers as a basis for legal rules such as restrictions on lawyer advertising and solicitation."

It is true that the Bar also argued that it wished to protect the "privacy and tranquility of personal injury victims and their loved ones from intrusive, unsolicited contact by lawyers," but the Florida Rule was not well designed for that purpose because it allowed *defense* lawyers or insurance adjustors to engage in intrusive, unsolicited contact. *Id.* During the 30 day block-out period, the victims were fair game for the defense lawyers or their agents.

The Court had earlier allowed mass mailings, which are similar to newspaper flyers or handbills. *In re R.M.J.*, 455 U.S. 191, 102 S.Ct. 929,

71 L.Ed.2d 64 (1982). Once the Court allowed mass mailings, it made little sense to prohibit the mass mailing just because the computer addressed each envelope to a particular individual rather than to the "occupant." Targeted mailing is only a more efficient form of advertising than mass mailing. Ed McMahon's READERS DIGEST™ mass mailings are addressed to millions of named people. People who camp on your doorstep may not easily be avoided, but a mailing, like flyers in newspapers, can simply be discarded.

[25]*See* 6 RONALD D. ROTUNDA & JOHN E. NOWAK, TREATISE ON CONSTITUTIONAL LAW: SUBSTANCE AND PROCEDURE § 23.31 (Thomson—West, 4th ed. 2007) (6 volumes).

[26]ABA COMMISSION ON ADVERTISING, LAWYER ADVERTISING AT THE CROSSROADS: PROFESSIONAL POLICY CONSIDERATIONS 65–66 (ABA 1995) (hereinafter, "LAWYER ADVERTISING AT THE CROSSROADS").

[27]*See* BARBARA A. CURRAN, THE LEGAL NEEDS OF THE PUBLIC: A FINAL REPORT OF A NATIONAL SURVEY 232 (American Bar Foundation, 1977).

[28]Kathleen Clark, *The Legacy of Watergate for Legal Ethics Instruction*, 51 HASTINGS L.J. 673, 678–82 (2000), listing the professional discipline imposed for Watergate-related criminal conduct.

Chief Counsel of the Senate Watergate Committee, Archibald Cox and Leon Jaworski, the Watergate Special Prosecutors.

Oddly enough, the empirical evidence demonstrates that the primary way that people learn about lawyers is through watching *fictionalized* portrayals of lawyers, ranging from *Rumpole of the Bailey*[29] to *L.A. Law*.[30] When people are asked to name the lawyer whom they most admire, frequently cited names are Perry Mason and Matlock. Indeed, Matlock is more widely admired than First Lady Hillary Rodham Clinton.[31] Many people apparently think that Matlock is a real person. And because Matlock fights for justice, many of the people who watch *Matlock* think more highly of lawyers. Television sometimes increases the public's respect for lawyers.

Yet, lawyers should not expect to win popularity contests.[32] It is hardly surprising that lawyers would like to be more well-liked. So also would car mechanics, tax collectors, undertakers, medical doctors, policemen, politicians, cheerleaders, movie stars, grandparents, and just about everyone else. However, there is one important difference between lawyers and other people. Lawyers will never be widely loved as long as they are really doing their jobs.

Surveys illustrate the dilemma that lawyers face. When people are asked what they dislike most about lawyers, the top fault is that lawyers are "too interested in money," (31%); second, lawyers file "too many unnecessary lawsuits," (27%); and third, lawyers "manipulate the legal system without regard for right or wrong," (26%).[33] Now, what do people like about lawyers? For the general public, the most positive aspect of lawyers is: "Putting clients'

---

[29]*Cf.* Douglas S. Miller, *Rumpole and the Equal Opportunity Harasser (or Judge Bork's Revenge*, 20 J. LEGAL PROFESSION 165 (1995–96)).

[30]LAWYER ADVERTISING AT THE CROSSROADS, *supra*, at 66.

[31]Randall Samborn, *Who's Most Admired Lawyer?*, NAT'L L. J., Aug. 9, 1993, at 1, 20–24; LAWYER ADVERTISING AT THE CROSSROADS, *supra*, at 69.

[32]Even television does not have that much power.

[33]Randall Samborn, *Anti-Lawyer Attitude Up, But NLJ/West Poll Also Shows More People Are Using Attorneys*, NATIONAL LAW JOURNAL, Aug. 9, 1993, at 1, col. 1.

A 1986 National Law Journal survey came to similar conclusions. The top faults of lawyers were, according to the average person on the streets, that we are "too interested in money," (32%); we "manipulate the legal system without any concern for right or wrong," (22%); and we "file too many unnecessary lawsuits," (20%). *What America Really Thinks About Lawyers*, NATIONAL LAW JOURNAL, Aug. 18, 1986, at S3, *discussed in* Robert C. Post, *On the Popular Image of the Lawyer: Reflections in a Dark Glass*, 75 CALIF. L. REV. 379, 380 (1987).

interests first," (46%) and second, lawyers protect people's rights (25%).[34]

People dislike lawyers because lawyers are guns for hire who manipulate the legal system, but they like us because we fight for our clients, protect their rights, and cut through bureaucratic red tape. When we fight zealously for our client, file lawsuits, and cut through red tape we do good, but when we fight zealously for our client, file lawsuits, and manipulate the legal system, we do bad. We receive accolades and denunciations for doing the same thing.[35]

The general public may claim that they want lawyers to be less aggressive and to compromise more, but they also know that if Rosa Parks is suing because she objects to a law forcing blacks to sit at the back of the bus, the last thing she needs is a lawyer who will compromise and find her a seat in the middle of the bus.[36] Because lawyers have been instrumental in securing civil liberties for racial minorities, it should be no surprise that blacks view lawyers more favorably than do whites; 51% of blacks say that their overall impression of lawyers is "good," but only 26% of whites come to that conclusion.[37]

We should not be surprised that medical doctors rate more highly in the public opinion polls than lawyers do, because doctors simply represent the patient. There is no doctor fighting zealously for the disease. Not so for lawyers. Our legal system gives everyone their day in court, and some of these litigants are

---

[34]Randall Samborn, *Anti-Lawyer Attitude Up, But NLJ/West Poll Also Shows More People Are Using Attorneys*, NATIONAL LAW JOURNAL, Aug. 9, 1993, at 1, col. 1.

The 1986 National Law Journal survey was similar. The most admired quality of lawyers is that their top "priority is to their clients," (38%) and, second, lawyers "know how to cut through bureaucratic red tape," (31%). *What America Really Thinks About Lawyers*, NATIONAL LAW JOURNAL, Aug. 18, 1986, at S3, *discussed in* Robert C. Post, *On the Popular Image of the Lawyer: Reflections in a Dark Glass*, 75 CALIF. L. REV. 379, 380 (1987).

[35]Robert C. Post, *On the Popular Image of the Lawyer: Reflections in a Dark Glass*, 75 CALIF. L. REV. 379, 380 (1987).

[36]William Brewer & John Bickel, *Etiquette of the Advocate?*, TEXAS LAWYER 20, 21 (Mar. 21, 1994). *See also* James Podgers, *Public: "Shyster" OK—If He's on Your Side*, 67 A.B.A. J., 695–96 (1981), pointing out that members of a San Diego Focus Group who blamed lawyers for being "sue crazy," filing too many law suits, were more willing to acknowledge the need for lawyers to protect their interests.

[37]Randall Samborn, *Anti-Lawyer Attitude Up, But NLJ/West Poll Also Shows More People Are Using Attorneys*, NATIONAL LAW JOURNAL, Aug. 9, 1993, at 1, col. 1. More than 60% of whites think that lawyers have too much power and influence in society, but 22% of blacks think that lawyers have too little power and influence. *Id.*

viewed less favorably than ugly diseases. Lawyers are the messengers who are blamed for the bad message.[38]

Litigation is what economists call a zero-sum game. In order for one side to win, the other must lose. When lawyers represent clients in non-litigative matters, clients are much more positive about their experiences with lawyers.[39] However, in litigation, at least one side (often called the loser) will be unhappy. Even if the other party (often called the winner) believes that he or she has been ultimately vindicated, it is still not unusual for that party to complain that justice did not come easily but had to be fought for, summoned, and mustered. Even winners are upset because they had to hire a lawyer; justice and equity did not come knocking on the door, unbeckoned, and beg to be admitted. When winners and losers are disgruntled, their lawyers are like magnets for their complaints. These people want to see their lawyers about as much as ancient dinosaurs wanted to see giant meteors hit the earth.

Still, there is reason for some hope. Empirical studies have shown that people who use lawyers, whether in this country[40] or abroad,[41] have a higher opinion of them than people who have never used them. Familiarity can breed respect.

It is true that one of Shakespeare's characters, Dick the Butcher, says that we must "kill all the lawyers," but Dick was an unsavory character and, in context, he meant that the only way for his revolution to succeed was to kill those who represented the law.

The Khmer Rouge acted on Dick's advice. They tried to kill all the lawyers when they took over Cambodia, and one of the first things that the new Cambodian government, the post-Khmer government, did is train lawyers as a way to protect human rights. During the American military occupation of Haiti in 1994, one of the U.S. Special Forces trying to settle a dispute was quoted as saying: "When I get back to the United States, I'm

---

[38]Robert C. Post, *On the Popular Image of the Lawyer: Reflections in a Dark Glass*, 75 CALIFORNIA L. REV. 379, 388–89 (1987), carefully considers this problem.

[39]*See* BARBARA A. CURRAN, THE LEGAL NEEDS OF THE PUBLIC: A FINAL REPORT OF A NATIONAL SURVEY 262–63 (American Bar Foundation, 1977) (Clients tend to be more happy in cases involving real property matters, estate planning, and estate settlement, and least positive in cases involving torts.)

[40]BARBARA A. CURRAN, THE LEGAL NEEDS OF THE PUBLIC: THE FINAL REPORT OF A NATIONAL SURVEY 238,

passim (American Bar Foundation, 1977) (surveys showing that people who have used lawyers are more positive about them then people who have not used lawyers).

[41]Sue Farron, Margaret Llewelyn & Kath Middleton, *Public Perception of the Legal Profession: Attitudinal Surveys as a Basis for Change*, 20 J. LEGAL PROFESSION 79, 87 (1995–96): ". . . those who have no experience of legal services have a poor perception of them." But, when the "measure of satisfaction was measured for users, the scores [indicating satisfaction] increased."

probably going to hug a lawyer, because they just don't have them here."[42]

Many years ago, Justice Harry Blackmun told me that if he had his life to live over again, he would like to be a medical doctor. I found Blackmun's remarks surprising. At the time he was, after all, a U.S. Supreme Court Justice. One would think that he was at the pinnacle of his career. Why would anyone want to trade that to become a doctor? A friend, to whom I related this conversation interjected, "People often want to be doctors so that they can help people."

But lawyers help people too. Granted, unlike engineers, we construct no bridges. Unlike doctors, we mend no bones. Unlike architects we design no buildings. Unlike artists, we paint no portraits. There is little that we do that the human hand can touch. But—if we are doing our jobs properly—we take on other people's burdens, we relieve stress, we pursue justice. We enable mankind to live a more peaceful and just life. We take the veneer of civilization and we make it a little thicker.[43]

§ 1-8 THE PREAMBLE TO THE MODEL RULES OF PROFESSIONAL CONDUCT

§ 1-8(a) The Text of the ABA Model Rules Preamble

PREAMBLE: A LAWYER'S RESPONSIBILITIES

[1] A lawyer, as a member of the legal profession, is a representative of clients, an officer of the legal system and a public citizen having special responsibility for the quality of justice.

[2] As a representative of clients, a lawyer performs various functions. As advisor, a lawyer provides a client with an informed understanding of the client's legal rights and obligations and explains their practical implications. As advocate, a lawyer zealously asserts the client's position under the rules of the adversary system. As negotiator, a lawyer seeks a result advantageous to the client but consistent with requirements of honest dealings with others. As an evaluator, a lawyer acts by examining a client's legal affairs and reporting about them to the client or to others.

[3] In addition to these representational functions, a lawyer may serve as a third-party neutral, a nonrepresentational role helping the parties to resolve a dispute or

---

[42]*U.S. Unit Contends with "Voodoo Dust" Culture* (AP), THE ARIZONA DAILY-STAR, Oct. 29, 1994, at § A, p. 6, col. 3 (quoting Capt. Greg Larson). *See* Ronald D. Rotunda, *Eastern European Diary: Constitution-Building in the Former Soviet Union*, 1 THE GREEN BAG 2D SERIES 163, 173 (1998).

[43]*Cf.* MARTIN MAYER, THE LAWYERS 3 (1967).

other matter. Some of these Rules apply directly to
lawyers who are or have served as third-party neutrals.
See, e.g., Rules 1.12 and 2.4. In addition, there are Rules
that apply to lawyers who are not active in the practice of
law or to practicing lawyers even when they are acting in
a nonprofessional capacity. For example, a lawyer who
commits fraud in the conduct of a business is subject to
discipline for engaging in conduct involving dishonesty,
fraud, deceit or misrepresentation. See Rule 8.4.

[4] In all professional functions a lawyer should be
competent, prompt and diligent. A lawyer should maintain
communication with a client concerning the
representation. A lawyer should keep in confidence information relating to representation of a client except so far
as disclosure is required or permitted by the Rules of
Professional Conduct or other law.

[5] A lawyer's conduct should conform to the requirements of the law, both in professional service to clients
and in the lawyer's business and personal affairs. A lawyer
should use the law's procedures only for legitimate
purposes and not to harass or intimidate others. A lawyer
should demonstrate respect for the legal system and for
those who serve it, including judges, other lawyers and
public officials. While it is a lawyer's duty, when necessary, to challenge the rectitude of official action, it is also
a lawyer's duty to uphold legal process.

[6] As a public citizen, a lawyer should seek improvement of the law, access to the legal system, the administration of justice and the quality of service rendered by the
legal profession. As a member of a learned profession, a
lawyer should cultivate knowledge of the law beyond its
use for clients, employ that knowledge in reform of the
law and work to strengthen legal education. In addition, a
lawyer should further the public's understanding of and
confidence in the rule of law and the justice system
because legal institutions in a constitutional democracy
depend on popular participation and support to maintain
their authority. A lawyer should be mindful of deficiencies
in the administration of justice and of the fact that the
poor, and sometimes persons who are not poor, cannot afford adequate legal assistance. Therefore, all lawyers
should devote professional time and resources and use
civic influence to ensure equal access to our system of
justice for all those who because of economic or social
barriers cannot afford or secure adequate legal counsel. A
lawyer should aid the legal profession in pursuing these
objectives and should help the bar regulate itself in the
public interest.

[7] Many of a lawyer's professional responsibilities are prescribed in the Rules of Professional Conduct, as well as substantive and procedural law. However, a lawyer is also guided by personal conscience and the approbation of professional peers. A lawyer should strive to attain the highest level of skill, to improve the law and the legal profession and to exemplify the legal profession's ideals of public service.

[8] A lawyer's responsibilities as a representative of clients, an officer of the legal system and a public citizen are usually harmonious. Thus, when an opposing party is well represented, a lawyer can be a zealous advocate on behalf of a client and at the same time assume that justice is being done. So also, a lawyer can be sure that preserving client confidences ordinarily serves the public interest because people are more likely to seek legal advice, and thereby heed their legal obligations, when they know their communications will be private.

[9] In the nature of law practice, however, conflicting responsibilities are encountered. Virtually all difficult ethical problems arise from conflict between a lawyer's responsibilities to clients, to the legal system and to the lawyer's own interest in remaining an ethical person while earning a satisfactory living. The Rules of Professional Conduct often prescribe terms for resolving such conflicts. Within the framework of these Rules, however, many difficult issues of professional discretion can arise. Such issues must be resolved through the exercise of sensitive professional and moral judgment guided by the basic principles underlying the Rules. These principles include the lawyer's obligation zealously to protect and pursue a client's legitimate interests, within the bounds of the law, while maintaining a professional, courteous and civil attitude toward all persons involved in the legal system.

[10] The legal profession is largely self-governing. Although other professions also have been granted powers of self-government, the legal profession is unique in this respect because of the close relationship between the profession and the processes of government and law enforcement. This connection is manifested in the fact that ultimate authority over the legal profession is vested largely in the courts.

[11] To the extent that lawyers meet the obligations of their professional calling, the occasion for government regulation is obviated. Self-regulation also helps maintain the legal profession's independence from government domination. An independent legal profession is an impor-

tant force in preserving government under law, for abuse of legal authority is more readily challenged by a profession whose members are not dependent on government for the right to practice.

[12] The legal profession's relative autonomy carries with it special responsibilities of self-government. The profession has a responsibility to assure that its regulations are conceived in the public interest and not in furtherance of parochial or self-interested concerns of the bar. Every lawyer is responsible for observance of the Rules of Professional Conduct. A lawyer should also aid in securing their observance by other lawyers. Neglect of these responsibilities compromises the independence of the profession and the public interest which it serves.

[13] Lawyers play a vital role in the preservation of society. The fulfillment of this role requires an understanding by lawyers of their relationship to our legal system. The Rules of Professional Conduct, when properly applied, serve to define that relationship.

§ 1-8(b) The Purpose of the Preamble

Part I is titled, *Preamble: A Lawyer's Responsibilities*. It advises lawyers that they have a "special responsibility for the quality of justice."[1] It then summarizes many of the obligations of lawyers, while emphasizing the importance of lawyers to the rule of law.

The Preamble advises: "The legal profession's relative autonomy carries with it special responsibilities of self-government."[2] To a certain extent it is true that the ethics rules assume self-regulation of the legal profession, because lawyers draft the legal ethics rules, and then lawyers are involved in enforcing these rules through legal discipline. However, because the courts typically adopt the ethics rules as a rule of court, it is more precise to consider legal discipline as under the authority of the judicial branch of government.[3] The judicial branch, at the urging of the ABA, often appoints laypeople to membership on the disciplinary boards. Although lawyers are still heavily involved in the lawyer disciplinary system, the great majority of the jurisdictions have appointed at least one-third non-lawyers (*i.e.*, "public members") to the disciplinary board of the state supreme court.[4]

[Section 1-8]

[1] Preamble, Comment 1.

[2] Preamble, Comment 12.

[3] ABA REPORT OF THE COMMIS-
SION ON EVALUATION OF DISCIPLINARY

ENFORCEMENT, LAWYER REGULATION
FOR A NEW CENTURY 1 (ABA Center
for Professional Responsibility 1992).
See also id. at 1: Recommendation 1.

[4] ABA Model Rules for Lawyer
Disciplinary Enforcement, Rule 2,

§ 1-8(c) The 2002 Model Rules Changes to the Preamble

Because the Preamble sets forth the obligations of a lawyer, most of the changes in the Preamble enacted by the ABA in 2002 relate to the specific changes in roles made in the Rules. The deletion of Rule 2.2 required the removal of a reference to intermediary in the Preamble. The addition of Rule 2.4 required the addition of paragraph 3 to the Preamble.

The drafters did amend paragraph 6 to add lines about a lawyer's obligation to instill public confidence in the legal system and a lawyer's obligation to public service. They also modified paragraph 9 to provide the balance between client representation and obligations to others in the system.

§ 1-9 THE SCOPE OF THE MODEL RULES OF PROFESSIONAL CONDUCT

§ 1-9(a) The Text of the ABA Model Rules Scope

SCOPE

[14] The Rules of Professional Conduct are rules of reason. They should be interpreted with reference to the purposes of legal representation and of the law itself. Some of the Rules are imperatives, cast in the terms "shall" or "shall not." These define proper conduct for purposes of professional discipline. Others, generally cast in the term "may," are permissive and define areas under the Rules in which the lawyer has discretion to exercise professional judgment. No disciplinary action should be taken when the lawyer chooses not to act or acts within the bounds of such discretion. Other Rules define the nature of relationships between the lawyer and others. The Rules are thus partly obligatory and disciplinary and partly constitutive and descriptive in that they define a lawyer's professional role. Many of the Comments use the term "should." Comments do not add obligations to the Rules but provide guidance for practicing in compliance with the Rules.

[15] The Rules presuppose a larger legal context shaping the lawyer's role. That context includes court rules and statutes relating to matters of licensure, laws defining specific obligations of lawyers and substantive and procedural law in general. The Comments are sometimes used to alert lawyers to their responsibilities under such other law.

[16] Compliance with the Rules, as with all law in an

Commentary, at 8 (ABA, 2002). As of 1996, over two-thirds of the jurisdictions involve public members in their disciplinary structure. The ABA recommends that at least one-third of the members be nonlawyers. *Id.*

open society, depends primarily upon understanding and voluntary compliance, secondarily upon reinforcement by peer and public opinion and finally, when necessary, upon enforcement through disciplinary proceedings. The Rules do not, however, exhaust the moral and ethical considerations that should inform a lawyer, for no worthwhile human activity can be completely defined by legal rules. The Rules simply provide a framework for the ethical practice of law.

[17] Furthermore, for purposes of determining the lawyer's authority and responsibility, principles of substantive law external to these Rules determine whether a client-lawyer relationship exists. Most of the duties flowing from the client-lawyer relationship attach only after the client has requested the lawyer to render legal services and the lawyer has agreed to do so. But there are some duties, such as that of confidentiality under Rule 1.6, that attach when the lawyer agrees to consider whether a client-lawyer relationship shall be established. See Rule 1.18. Whether a client-lawyer relationship exists for any specific purpose can depend on the circumstances and may be a question of fact.

[18] Under various legal provisions, including constitutional, statutory and common law, the responsibilities of government lawyers may include authority concerning legal matters that ordinarily reposes in the client in private client-lawyer relationships. For example, a lawyer for a government agency may have authority on behalf of the government to decide upon settlement or whether to appeal from an adverse judgment. Such authority in various respects is generally vested in the attorney general and the state's attorney in state government, and their federal counterparts, and the same may be true of other government law officers. Also, lawyers under the supervision of these officers may be authorized to represent several government agencies in intragovernmental legal controversies in circumstances where a private lawyer could not represent multiple private clients. These Rules do not abrogate any such authority.

[19] Failure to comply with an obligation or prohibition imposed by a Rule is a basis for invoking the disciplinary process. The Rules presuppose that disciplinary assessment of a lawyer's conduct will be made on the basis of the facts and circumstances as they existed at the time of the conduct in question and in recognition of the fact that a lawyer often has to act upon uncertain or incomplete evidence of the situation. Moreover, the Rules presuppose

that whether or not discipline should be imposed for a violation, and the severity of a sanction, depend on all the circumstances, such as the willfulness and seriousness of the violation, extenuating factors and whether there have been previous violations.

[20] Violation of a Rule should not itself give rise to a cause of action against a lawyer nor should it create any presumption in such a case that a legal duty has been breached. In addition, violation of a Rule does not necessarily warrant any other nondisciplinary remedy, such as disqualification of a lawyer in pending litigation. The Rules are designed to provide guidance to lawyers and to provide a structure for regulating conduct through disciplinary agencies. They are not designed to be a basis for civil liability. Furthermore, the purpose of the Rules can be subverted when they are invoked by opposing parties as procedural weapons. The fact that a Rule is a just basis for a lawyer's self-assessment, or for sanctioning a lawyer under the administration of a disciplinary authority, does not imply that an antagonist in a collateral proceeding or transaction has standing to seek enforcement of the Rule. Nevertheless, since the Rules do establish standards of conduct by lawyers, a lawyer's violation of a Rule may be evidence of breach of the applicable standard of conduct.

[21] The Comment accompanying each Rule explains and illustrates the meaning and purpose of the Rule. The Preamble and this note on Scope provide general orientation. The Comments are intended as guides to interpretation, but the text of each Rule is authoritative.

§ 1-9(b) The 2002 Model Rules Changes to the Scope.

The drafters made three major changes to the Scope Note of the 2002 Rules. First, they modified old paragraph 18, now paragraph 20, about the use of the Rules to establish civil liability.[1] Second, they removed paragraph 19 about attorney-client privilege and work product.[2] Finally, they removed paragraph 20 about the lawyer's decision not to reveal confidential information under Rule 1.6.[3]

§ 1-9(c) Scope

§ 1-9(c)(1) Rules of Reason

First, the Scope section advises that the Model Rules are "rules of reason. They should be interpreted with reference to the

---

[Section 1-9]

[1] See 1983 Scope, paragraph 18.

[2] See 1983 Scope, paragraph 19.

[3] See 1983 Scope, paragraph 20.

purposes of legal representation and of the law itself."[4] The Scope note emphasizes that some of the Rules are imperatives, some are permissive, and others define the nature of the relationship between lawyers and others. "The Rules are thus partly obligatory and disciplinary and partly constitutive and descriptive in that they define a lawyer's professional role. Many of the Comments use the word 'should.' Comments do not add obligations to the Rules but provide guidance for practicing in compliance with the Rules."[5]

§ 1-9(c)(2) Reference to Other Law

The Rules do not purport to exhaust the moral and ethical considerations that any lawyer should consider in determining what action one should take, but they do provide a framework for the ethical practice of law.[6] When a state or federal court adopts the ABA Model Rules as rules of the court, those rules become law, just like the rules of civil procedure are law. However, in determining what actions to take, any lawyer must also examine *other law* outside of the Rules. For example, one may need to turn to the law of contract and agency to determine whether a lawyer-client relationship exists. Similarly, the evidentiary law of attorney-client privilege, the law of work-product privilege, the law of fiduciaries, the law of contract, the law of tort, any specific statutory provisions (particularly those dealing with the obligations and powers of government lawyers)—these are all relevant in determining the lawyer's obligations.[7]

If a lawyer fails to comply with an obligation that the jurisdiction's rules of professional conduct impose, the lawyer is subject to discipline. If the lawyer is disciplined, he or she may be suspended from the practice of law, or disbarred, or subject to a reprimand. The existence and severity of sanctions is an issue that is not discussed in the Model Rules of Professional Conduct, but is found in other law. Consequently, some jurisdictions have followed the lead of the ABA, which has developed model rules governing the procedures and sanctions for legal discipline, as well as proposals to mediate client-lawyer disputes in general and fee disputes in particular.[8]

These *other ABA Model Rules*, which are reprinted in the Appendix, should also be consulted in determining how to analyze any problem that falls within their scope.

---

[4]Scope, Comment 14.

[5]Scope, Comment 14.

[6]Scope, Comment 15.

[7]Scope, Paragraph 16, 17, 18.

[8]The ABA Standards for Imposing Lawyer Sanctions (1992). The ABA Model Rules for Lawyer Disciplinary Enforcement (2002)(procedures to govern lawyer discipline). The ABA Model Rules for Fee Arbitration (Feb. 23, 1995). The ABA Model Rules for Mediation of Client-Lawyer Disputes (Aug. 1998).

§ 1-9(c)(3) Relation of the Ethics Rules to the Law of Malpractice and Other Causes of Action

The Scope section of the 1983 Model Rules advised that a lawyer's violation of a Rule should "not give rise to a cause of action nor should it create any presumption that a legal duty has been breached."[9] The Scope was insistent that the Rules "are not designed to be a basis for civil liability," and that lawyers for parties in litigation should not use the Rules to disqualify their opponents.[10]

However, this determination that the ethics rules should not be used in malpractice cases or in disqualification motions may be likened to whistling past the graveyard. If one is concerned when crossing a graveyard at night, it does no harm to whistle, but the whistling provides no real protection either. In spite of the protestations in the Scope section, courts have often used the legal ethics rules to impose tort liability on lawyers,[11] to reverse criminal prosecutions,[12] and to disqualify lawyers.[13] As one court acknowledged, it is "common lore that the Code, though it liter-

---

[9]1983 Scope, Paragraph 18, which read in full as follows:

"[18] Violation of a Rule should not give rise to a cause of action nor should it create any presumption that a legal duty has been breached. The Rules are designed to provide guidance to lawyers and to provide a structure for regulating conduct through disciplinary agencies. They are not designed to be a basis for civil liability. Furthermore, the purpose of the Rules can be subverted when they are invoked by opposing parties as procedural weapons. The fact that a Rule is a just basis for a lawyer's self-assessment, or for sanctioning a lawyer under the administration of a disciplinary authority, does not imply that an antagonist in a collateral proceeding or transaction has standing to seek enforcement of the Rule. Accordingly, nothing in the Rules should be deemed to augment any substantive legal duty of lawyers or the extra-disciplinary consequences of violating such a duty."

[10]Scope, Paragraph 18.

[11]*See* cases discussed in, *e.g.,* Note, *The Model Rules as a Guide for Legal Malpractice,* 3 GEORGETOWN J. LEGAL ETHICS 609 (1993); Note, *The Eviden-* *tiary Use of the Ethics Code in Legal Malpractice: Erasing a Double Standard,* 109 HARV. L. REV. 1102 (1996).

There is much debate in the literature on this issue. *See* Thomas D. Morgan, *an Introduction to The Debate Over Fee Forfeitures,* 36 EMORY L.J. 755 (1987) (Symposium: Government Intrusion into the Attorney-Client Relationship); Thomas D. Morgan, *Sanctions and Remedies for Attorney Misconduct,* 19 S. ILL. U. L.J. 343 (1995); John Leubsdorf, *Legal Malpractice and Professional Responsibility,* 48 RUTGERS L. REV. 1010 (1995); Daniel L. Draisen, *The Model Rules of Professional Conduct and Their Relationship to Legal Malpractice Actions: A Practical Approach to the Use of the Rules,* 21 J. OF LEGAL PROFESSION 67 (1996–1997).

[12]*E.g., Zuck v. Alabama,* 588 F.2d 436 (5th Cir.1979), holding that there was a conflict of interest rendering a criminal trial unfair when the law firm that represented a defendant in a criminal case also represented the prosecutor sued in his personal capacity in an unrelated civil matter. The conviction must be reversed in the absence of the criminal defendant's knowing and intelligent waiver.

ally prescribes only the bases of lawyer discipline, is regularly used by courts to establish the criteria for lawyer disqualification as well."[14]

The drafters of the 2002 Rules modified this paragraph in the Scope because of the court decisions that continued to introduce the Rules as standards in malpractice and other actions. The new paragraph states:

> [20] Violation of a Rule should not itself give rise to a cause of action against a lawyer nor should it create any presumption in such a case that a legal duty has been breached. In addition, violation of a Rule does not necessarily warrant any other nondisciplinary remedy, such as disqualification of a lawyer in pending litigation. The Rules are designed to provide guidance to lawyers and to provide a structure for regulating conduct through disciplinary agencies. They are not designed to be a basis for civil liability. Furthermore, the purpose of the Rules can be subverted when they are invoked by opposing parties as procedural weapons. The fact that a Rule is a just basis for a lawyer's self-assessment, or for sanctioning a lawyer under the administration of a disciplinary authority, does not imply that an antagonist in a collateral proceeding or transaction has standing to seek enforcement of the Rule. Nevertheless, since the Rules do establish standards of conduct by lawyers, a lawyer's violation of a Rule may be evidence of breach of the applicable standard of conduct.[15]

Although this middle ground position is closer to how courts use the Rules, it is likely that courts will continue to fashion jury charges and expert reports without regard to this language.

Many states explicitly copied the ABA's 1983 Scope to the Model Rules, including the comment that the ethics rules are not meant to be enforced outside of legal discipline.[16] But, as the federal district court recognized in *Harrison v. Fisons Corp.*,[17] while the preamble to the Florida ethics rules states that they are not to be invoked as procedural weapons in litigation, courts

---

[13]*E.g., IBM v. Levin*, 579 F.2d 271 (3d Cir.1978), where the court disqualified a law firm that represented Levin in an antitrust suit against IBM while representing IBM on various labor law matters. The law firm had no continuing retainer from IBM and no specific assignment from IBM on the day that it filed the antitrust complaint against IBM, but the law firm had accepted legal assignment from IBM both before and after it had filed the antitrust complaint.

See also, e.g., Robert C. Hacker & Ronald D. Rotunda, *Attorney Conflicts of Interest*, 2 CORPORATION L. REV. 345 (1979); Ronald D. Rotunda,

Conflict Problems When Representing Members of Corporate Families, 72 NOTRE DAME L. REV. 655 (1997).

These issues are discussed in more detail below, in connection with the various Model Rules dealing with conflicts of interest.

[14]*United States v. Bullock*, 642 F.Supp. 982, 984 n. 4 (N.D.Ill.1986).

[15]2002 Rules, Scope, Paragraph 20.

[16]Model Rules, Scope, Comment 18.

[17]*Harrison v. Fisons Corp.*, 819 F.Supp. 1039, 1041 (M.D.Fla.1993).

have consistently relied on ethics codes to establish standards for ruling on claimed conflicts of interest. In fact, the Tenth Circuit instructed lawyers that the ABA Model Rules reflect the "national standard" to be used in ruling on disqualification motions.[18] Recall that these Model Rules are not law in their own right; the ABA only proposes that states adopt them.

Courts have even raised the legal ethics rules *sua sponte* and used them to disqualify lawyers.[19] Courts have also relied on these same ethics rules when they reject fee arrangements that violate them.[20] Lawyers often object to this transposition of legal ethics into the realm of disqualification motions and malpractice, but it is a natural and virtually inevitable progression.

The rules of ethics are judicially imposed court rules. It is more than a little inconsistent for a court to promulgate a rule stating that a lawyer cannot represent a particular client because to do so would violate Rule 1.6 (governing confidences and secrets) of a former client, and then allow the lawyer to appear before the court in blatant violation of the Rule—particularly when the purpose of that Rule is to protect that former client.

Similarly, it is not logical for a court to promulgate an ethics rule requiring that contingent fees be in writing[21] and then

---

[18] *Cole v. Ruidoso Municipal Schools*, 43 F.3d 1373, 1383 (10th Cir. 1994).

[19] *E.g.*, Robert C. Hacker & Ronald D. Rotunda, *Standing, Waiver, Laches, and Appealability in Attorney Disqualification Cases*, 3 CORPORATION LAW REVIEW 82 (1980).

[20] *E.g.*, *Holstein v. Grossman*, 246 Ill.App.3d 719, 186 Ill.Dec. 592, 616 N.E.2d 1224 (1993), which refused to enforce an oral fee-sharing agreement between lawyers because the client had not consented in writing, as required by the state rule based on ABA Model Rule 1.5(e)(1).

Contrast, e.g., *Shimrak v. Garcia-Mendoza*, 112 Nev. 246, 912 P.2d 822 (Nev.1996), a case of a fee dispute between a private investigator and a law firm. The law firm sought to be relieved from its contract with the investigator because the fee arrangement constituted unethical fee splitting with a lay person, so that the investigator was *in pari delicto*. The court rejected the argument, noting

that the ethics rules apply only to lawyers, not to lay investigators and that, in the court's view, not enforcing the contract would be unfair to the lay investigator.

This case did not involve an agreement between two lawyers, both of whom are bound by the ethics rules. Note also that the court's conclusion in *Shimrak* means that a court in this circumstance will enforce a contract that violates the ethics rules that are imposed by order of the court. The court's enforcement of a contract that appears to violate public policy (the policy expressed in the court rules of ethics) serves to reward lay people who contract in knowing violation of the ethics rules.

[21] Rule 1.5(c). *E.g., Estate of Pinter by Pinter v. Mc Gee*, 293 N.J.Super. 119, 679 A.2d 728 (N.J.Super.App.Div. 1996), holding that a law firm violated the ethics rule by entering into a contingent fee agreement without a written retainer signed by the firm and the client, and could *not* circumvent the rule by recovering on *quan-*

enforce an oral contract to the detriment of a party whom the Rule was drafted to protect.[22]

Courts have often applied the ethics rules in lawyer malpractice suits. Judges are hardly consistent on this question,[23] and some do state that a violation of an ethics rule does not establish malpractice.[24] On the other hand, other judges have ruled that the Rules of Professional Conduct establish the lawyer's fiduciary obligations, violation of which is malpractice.

Thus, *Rizzo v. Haines*[25] held:

---

tum meruit basis. *Accord Vaccaro v. Estate of Gorovoy*, 303 N.J.Super. 201, 207, 696 A.2d 724, 727 (App.Div.1997) (lawyers cannot benefit from their failure to comply with the requirements of Rules of Professional Conduct, Rule 1.5 by enforcing an agreement that violates that rule).

However, some authorities regard this rule as too harsh, and—while they will not enforce an oral contingent fee contract—they will allow *quantum meruit* recovery. Restatement of the Law Governing Lawyers, Third, § 39 (Official Draft 2000). In *Gagne v. Vaccaro*, 255 Conn. 390, 766 A.2d 416 (Conn. 2001), a lawyer entered into a written contingent fee agreement with his client, but it was not reduced to a writing. Then, a second lawyer replaced him and this other lawyer successfully pursued the matter and collected a contingent fee. The first lawyer wanted a fair share of the fee earned. The lack of a written agreement is not enough to deny him all fees in cases where he had acted loyally and his work had contributed to the final outcome. In those circumstances, *quantum meruit* recovery is appropriate.

[22]Restatement of the Law Governing Lawyers, Third, § 52(2)(c) (Official Draft 2000), concluding that, in a case involving the lawyer's civil liability, the trier of fact, in determining whether the lawyer violated a standard of care, may consider whether the lawyer violated an ethics rule or statute regulating the lawyer's conduct—

"to the extent that (i) the rule or statute *was designed for the protec-* tion of persons in the position of the claimant and (ii) proof of the content and construction of such a rule or statute is relevant to the claimant's claim. (emphasis added)".

[23]See Lawrence J. Latto, *The Restatement of The Law Governing Lawyers: a View From The Trenches*, 26 HOFSTRA L. REV. 697, 722–23 (1998) (footnotes omitted):

"What many, too many, courts have said about the materiality of a violation of a provision of the ethical codes to a lawyer's civil liability is, for the most part, shameful nonsense. The same holds true of the courts' comments regarding the relevance of those provisions to whether a lawyer has adequately fulfilled his duties or has performed services with adequate care. Much of this sorry state is attributable to the pernicious disclaimers in the preambles to the codes . . . .. Professor Hazard, who as Reporter for the Kutak Commission that initially produced the Model Rules might be thought to bear a share of the responsibility, dismissed these efforts to deny that the Rules had anything to do with civil liability as 'predictably futile, however, if not fatuous.' "

[24]See, e.g., *Astarte, Inc. v. Pacific Industries Systems, Inc.*, 865 F.Supp. 693 (D.Colo.1994)(Rules of Professional Conduct neither create private causes of action nor establish standards of civil liability).

[25]*Rizzo v. Haines*, 520 Pa. 484, 555 A.2d 58, 90 A.L.R.4th 1007 (Pa. 1989).

We further believe that expert testimony was not needed to detail the fiduciary obligations of an attorney who engages in financial transactions with his client, since these obligations are established by law, the Code of Professional Responsibility, and the Model Rules of Professional Conduct.[26]

Rizzo v. Haines goes so far as to say that a violation of the ABA's Model Rules—Rules proposed by the ABA but *not* yet adopted by the jurisdiction—"establishe[s]" a violation of the lawyer's obligation, so that the plaintiff does not even need expert evidence to prove a violation.[27]

Other cases do not go that far, but they do treat violation of the Rules as evidence of negligence for malpractice purposes or creating a rebuttable presumption of malpractice.[28] Some cases allow the expert witness to consider violation of an ethics rule in

---

[26]520 Pa. at 503, 555 A.2d at 67, citing Model Code of Professional Responsibility, EC 5-5, Model Rules of Professional Conduct, Rule 1.8(c).

Expert Testimony *Grimm v. Fox*, 303 Conn. 322, 33 A.3d 205 (2012). Whether plaintiff needs expert testimony to support a legal malpractice claim is a question of law, so appellate review is plenary. The normal rule is that plaintiff needs to provide expert testimony. The exception to the general rule requiring expert testimony is limited to situations where the defendant lawyer has essentially "done nothing whatsoever" to represent his or her client's interest.

Despite the court's critical language of defendants (plaintiff client's former attorneys) for violating basic rules of appellate procedure, the former client must still present expert testimony in his legal malpractice action. This expert testimony is necessary in order to establish whether the lawyer's violations of the basic rules of appellate procedure were, in fact, a breach of the requisite standard of care in the specific circumstances of the client's divorce appeal.

[27]*See also Day v. Rosenthal*, 170 Cal.App.3d 1125, 217 Cal.Rptr. 89, 102 (1985):

"The *standards governing an attorney's ethical duties are conclusively established by the Rules of Professional Conduct.* They cannot be changed by

expert testimony. If an expert testifies contrary to the Rules of Professional Conduct, the standards established by the Rules govern and the expert testimony is disregarded." [emphasis added].

[28]*E.g., Waldman v. Levine*, 544 A.2d 683 (D.C.1988) holding that an expert may rely on the ethics rules to determine negligence and the standard of care in legal malpractice cases. *Mayol v. Summers, Watson & Kimpel*, 223 Ill.App.3d 794, 166 Ill.Dec. 154, 585 N.E.2d 1176 (1992), *appeal dismissed,* 145 Ill.2d 635, 173 Ill.Dec. 6, 596 N.E.2d 630 (Ill.1992), holding that the judge may issue jury instructions that quote from the ethics rules governing lawyers just like a judge, in other negligence cases, quotes from statutes and ordinances in giving instructions:

"Juries in legal malpractice suits may properly consider standards of professional ethics pertaining to attorneys because such suits involve allegations of conduct that does not conform to minimum professional standards . . . .. Furthermore, it is well established that jury instructions may quote portions of statutes and ordinances where (1) the jury has heard evidence that defendant has violated the quoted portions of the statute or ordinance, and (2) plaintiff alleges the violation breached a duty owed to him by defendant . . . .. Like most statutes and ordinances, attorney disciplinary

evaluating the lawyer's conduct,[29] or allow the expert witness to quote from the ethics rules (but do not allow the witness to testify as to the source of the rule).[30]

One court has categorized the various approaches in the case law into four different classifications:

First, some courts hold that professional ethical standards conclusively establish the duty of care and any violation constitutes negligence per se. Second, a minority of courts finds that a professional ethical violation establishes a rebuttable presumption of legal malpractice. Third, a large majority of courts treat professional ethical standards as evidence of the common law duty of care. Finally, one court has found professional ethical standards inadmissible as evidence of an attorney's duty of care.[31]

The Restatement of the Law Governing Lawyers has adopted the third alternative: in the situation where the lawyer may be civilly liable, plaintiff's proof of a violation of the ethics rules or any statute that regulates the conduct of lawyers does not establish liability per se. However, the trier of fact may consider this violation as an aid in understanding and applying the basic principle requiring that a lawyer who owes a duty of care must exercise the competence and diligence that lawyers in similar circumstances normally exercise. If the lawyer has represented that she will exercise greater competence or diligence, then the lawyer is held to that higher standard.[32]

Thus, the Restatement of the Law Governing Lawyers has embraced what is really an unremarkable conclusion: a lawyer's violation of the ethical rules can lead to malpractice liability. As the Restatement acknowledges: *"Strictu sensu* the lawyers codes are no more than [rules enforceable through the disciplinary machinery]. Indeed, in the preambles to the codes careful efforts are made to limit the legal effect of the code provisions to that

---

rules establish minimum standards of conduct and are intended to protect the general public. For these reasons, we hold that jury instructions may quote attorney disciplinary rules in legal malpractice cases to the same extent as they may quote statutes and ordinances in instructions in other types of negligence cases."

[29]*Lazy Seven Coal Sales, Inc. v. Stone & Hinds, P.C.*, 813 S.W.2d 400 (Tenn.1991).

[30]*Hizey v. Carpenter*, 119 Wash.2d 251, 830 P.2d 646 (1992).

[31]*Allen v. Lefkoff, Duncan, Grimes & Dermer, P.C.*, 265 Ga. 374, 453 S.E.2d 719, 721 (Ga.1995) (internal case citations omitted).

Violations of ethics rules as evidence of malpractice. *E.g., Pressley v. Farley*, 579 So.2d 160 (Fla.Dist. Ct.App.1991) (rule violations not negligence per se, although admissible as some evidence of negligence).

Violations of ethics rules not admissible as evidence of malpractice. In contrast, *Hizey v. Carpenter*, 119 Wash.2d 251, 830 P.2d 646 (Wash. 1992) concluded that professional ethical standards are never admissible as evidence of a lawyer's duty of care.

[32]Restatement of the Law Governing Lawyers, Third, §§ 52(1), 2(3) (Official Draft 2000).

context. However, that effort is futile, and necessarily so."[33] The Restatement goes on to explain:

> The lawyer codes *unmistakably* help define standards of conduct relevant to civil liability claims against members of our profession.[34]

The Official Draft to the Restatement repeats these caveats and notes that general tort principles apply the regulatory standards of conduct against the members of any profession, even though the ethics codes seek to skirt the relationship between the rules governing lawyers and the lawyers' malpractice liability.[35] Thus, while the professional ethics rules are used to discipline lawyers for professional misconduct, the effect of the rules go beyond that use. Courts also use the ethics rules to disqualify lawyers because of a conflict of interest or other misconduct. As another judicial sanction in a civil case, the judge may *exclude evidence* obtained in violation of recognized standards of professional conduct.[36] Or, the court may require the lawyer to forfeit some *or all* of the lawyer's fees because of ethical lapses.[37] If the attorney's conduct is particularly egregious, the court may even impose the very harsh penalty of dismissing the pending litigation.[38] Moreover, the standards of professional conduct can

---

[33] Restatement of the Law Governing Lawyers, Third, Proposed Final Draft No. 1, at xxii (ALI, March 29, 1996).

[34] Restatement of the Law Governing Lawyers, Third, Proposed Final Draft No. 1, at xxii (ALI, March 29, 1996) (emphasis added). *See also* Restatement of the Law Governing Lawyers, Third, § 6 ("Judicial Remedies Available to Client or Nonclient for Lawyer Wrongs") (Official Draft 2000). *Cf. id.* at § 7 ("Judicial Remedies Available to Lawyer for Client Wrongs"). This text does not focus on client wrongs because the Model Rules of Professional Responsibility govern lawyers, not clients.

[35] *See* Restatement of Torts, Second, §§ 286 to 288C, § 874A. Restatement of the Law Governing Lawyers, Third, Foreword at volume 1, p. xxi (Official Draft 2000).

[36] **Exclusion of Evidence in Civil Cases.** We would expect the evidence to be excluded in a civil case, not a criminal case, where the courts

do not favor exclusion unless there is a constitutional violation.

As to exclusion in a civil case, *see, e.g., Faison v. Thornton*, 863 F.Supp. 1204 (D.Nev.1993), ruling that because the lawyers, in a civil case, committed "flagrant" violation of Nevada rule prohibiting ex parte communications with opposing party represented by counsel, it was not unfair to exclude evidence obtained during the lawyer's ex parte communications and to require those lawyers to pay the opposing parties' attorney fees of $46,599.26 as a sanction for their violation. The evidence showed that the lawyers conducted several telephone conversations and then had a five-hour meeting with the opposing party knowing that he was represented by counsel.

[37] Restatement of the Law Governing Lawyers, Third, § 37 ("Partial or Complete Forfeiture of Lawyer's Compensation") (Official Draft 2000).

[38] *Link v. Wabash Railroad Co.*, 370 U.S. 626, 82 S.Ct. 1386, 8 L.Ed.2d 734 (1962). In this case, which arose

be relevant even in the context of criminal prosecution of a lawyer.[39]

In any malpractice action, the plaintiff is typically required to prove three separate elements:

1. The employment of the attorney or other basis for duty; **2.** The failure of the attorney to exercise ordinary skill and knowledge; and **3.** That such negligence was the proximate cause of damage to the plaintiff.[40]

It will often be the case that, in order for the plaintiff to prove the failure of an attorney to exercise the ordinary skill and knowledge expected of any ethical attorney, it will be very helpful to show a violation of the Rules of Professional Conduct.[41] The plaintiff will argue that a reasonable lawyer will follow the Rules of Professional Conduct (element #2, *supra*), that a failure to follow the Rules is a failure to follow the standard of care expected of a reasonable lawyer, and that this violation was the proximate cause of harm to the plaintiff (element #3, *supra*). Even if one argues that a violation of the lawyer's obligations is not (in the words of *Rizzo v. Haines*) "established" by the Rules of Professional Conduct, a violation of the Rules will still be helpful to a plaintiff proving a malpractice case.[42]

Plaintiff, of course, still must show damages and causation resulting from the violation of any Rule that was drafted to protect the plaintiff.[43] The lawyer may have violated a Rule, such

---

out of an automobile accident, the trial court dismissed the action, *sua sponte*, for failure to prosecute, and plaintiff appealed. The Supreme Court, speaking through Justice Harlan, held that the trial judge had inherent power to dismiss without affording notice or providing an adversary hearing, and did not abuse its discretion in dismissing when plaintiff's counsel failed to appear at duly scheduled pretrial conference, in view of the excuse offered and the prior history of case. Justices Black and Douglas, and Chief Justice Warren dissented.

[39]*United States v. Bronston*, 658 F.2d 920 (2d Cir.1981), *cert. denied*, 456 U.S. 915, 102 S.Ct. 1769, 72 L.Ed.2d 174 (1982).

[40]*Rizzo v. Haines, 520 at 399, 405 A.2d at 494*, quoting RONALD MALLEN & VICTOR LEVIT, LEGAL MALPRACTICE 123 (1977).

See also, e.g., Restatement of the Law Governing Lawyers, Third, § 53 (Official Draft 2000). *Schenkel v. Monheit*, 266 Pa.Super. 396, 405 A.2d 493 (1979); *Curran v. Stradley, Ronon, Stevens & Young*, 361 Pa.Super. 17, 521 A.2d 451 (1987).

[41]Restatement of the Law Governing Lawyers, Third, § 52(2)(c) (Official Draft 2000).

[42]*E.g., Mirabito v. Liccardo*, 4 Cal.App.4th 41, 5 Cal.Rptr.2d 571 (1992), holding that an expert witness may consider the state rules of ethics in determining what the relevant standard of care is for the lawyer being sued for malpractice.

[43]Restatement of the Law Governing Lawyers, Third, §§ 53, 115 (Official Draft 2000). Restatement of the Law Governing Lawyers, Third, § 175 (Tent. Draft No. 8, March 21, 1997); Restatement of the Law Governing

as the Rule prohibiting commingling of clients' funds,[44] but if that violation did not cause the plaintiff any damage (for example, if the funds were promptly returned and any interest due on the use of the funds was promptly paid), then the lawyer is subject to professional discipline (because the lawyer did violate a disciplinary rule), but is not subject to malpractice liability (because the plaintiff suffered no damages).

§ 1-9(c)(4) The Role of Expert Testimony on the Meaning and Application of the Rules of Professional Responsibility

The Restatement explains that proof of a violation of a rule or statute regulating the conduct of lawyers "may be considered by a trier of fact *as an aid in understanding* and applying" the principle that a lawyer must exercise the competence and diligence normally exercised by lawyers in similar circumstances or has breached a fiduciary duty to a client. However, proof that the lawyer violated the rule or statute is only relevant to the extent that "(i) the rule or statute was designed for the protection of persons in the position of the claimant," and that "(ii) proof of the content and construction of such a rule or statute is relevant to the claimant's claim."[45]

Given that a lawyer's violation of the ethical rules, at the very least, may show malpractice, the next question is the extent to which a malpractice plaintiff (or a party seeking to disqualify a lawyer or succeed on another motion based on violation of the ethics rules) may use expert opinion to provide testimony to the jury or judge on the meaning of one or more of the ethics rules governing lawyers.

Lawyers, Third, § 75 (Proposed Final Draft No. 2, Apr. 6, 1998).

[44]Rule 1.15. *See* the ABA Model Rule on Financial Recordkeeping, and the ABA Model Rules for Trust Account Overdraft Notification, reprinted in Appendix A of the Lawyer's edition of this book.

[45]Restatement of the Law Governing Lawyers, Third, § 52(2)(c) (Official Draft 2000). This principle is the general tort rule, which is that sometimes, for tort purposes, the standard of conduct defined by a law or by a regulation will not be adopted. *See* Restatement of Torts, Second, § 288 (1965):

"The court will not adopt as the standard of conduct of a reasonable man the requirements of a legislative enactment or an administrative regulation whose purpose is found to be exclusively:

(a) to protect the interests of the state or any subdivision of it as such, or (b) to secure to individuals the enjoyment of rights or privileges to which they are entitled only as members of the public, or (c) to impose upon the actor the performance of a service which the state or any subdivision of it undertakes to give the public, or (d) to protect a class of persons other than the one whose interests are invaded, or (e) to protect another interest than the one invaded, or (f) to protect against other harm than that which has resulted, or (g) to protect against any other hazards than that from which the harm has resulted."

A similar question arises in the case of a lawyer who wishes to use the ethics rules as a defense to a disqualification motion or malpractice claim. The normal tort principle is that the trier of fact may consider the content and interpretation of any relevant statute or rule, including a rule of professional conduct governing lawyers, designed for the protection of persons in the position of the person relying on this rule.[46] Hence, we have the same question as to whether the lawyer may rely on expert testimony to prove that ethics rules required her to engage in action that the plaintiff now attacks.

Courts typically *require* the use of expert testimony in legal malpractice cases, unless the misconduct is so obvious that no reasonable juror could fail to understand that there has been a breach, such as, when a lawyer fails to appear in court, or does not file suit within limitations period, or fails to notify the client of his withdrawal.[47] In that limited class of cases, a party need not rely on expert testimony because the claim is "based on the common knowledge exception or violation of an explicit Rule of Professional Conduct, or a combination of both."[48]

If courts normally require expert testimony, and the lawyer's violation of the ethics rules (or the lawyer's reliance on the ethical rules as a defense to liability) is relevant, then one would expect expert testimony on the meaning of the ethics rules. That, in fact, is the general rule. However, in the case of expert testimony on the meaning of an ethics rule, a few courts argue that the question of the meaning and application of the rules governing lawyers is one of law, and thus the general rule is that the court does not accept expert testimony as to what domestic law is.[49]

Under a theory in which the meaning and application of the legal ethics rules are "law," the court—not the expert witness—should instruct the jury as to what the ethics rule in question means and how it applies in the particular case.[50] Even if the expert purports to testify about facts or opinion, the court will

---

[46]Restatement of the Law Governing Lawyers, Third, § 52(2)(c) (Official Draft 2000), at comment *f*.

[47]*Carlson v. Morton*, 229 Mont. 234, 745 P.2d 1133 (Mont.1987).

[48]Wilburn Brewer, Jr., *Expert Witness Testimony in Legal Malpractice Cases*, 45 So. Carolina L. Rev. 727, 745 (1994). This article is part of a symposium on Legal Malpractice.

[49]*See, e.g.*, Note, *Expert Legal Testimony*, 97 Harv. L. Rev. 797, 797 (1984): "it remains black-letter law

that expert legal testimony is not permissible."

Expert Testimony on Meaning of Foreign Law. Note, however, that the black letter rule is that legal experts may give their opinion as to the meaning of *foreign* law. *See, e.g.*, *Nieves-Villanueva v. Soto-Rivera*, 133 F.3d 92, 99 (1st Cir.1997).

[50]*Day v. Rosenthal*, 170 Cal.App.3d 1125, 217 Cal.Rptr. 89 (1985), *cert. denied*, 475 U.S. 1048, 106 S.Ct. 1267, 89 L.Ed.2d 576 (1986). In this case, the court used the Rules of

not allow the expert to testify about the ultimate legal conclusion; the judge alone instructs the jury as to what is the law.[51] In that situation, it follows that the litigant should not need to present expert testimony because the judge will instruct the jury as to the "law" governing the ethical obligations of the lawyer, and the judge has already ruled that he or she will now allow testimony as to meaning and application of the ethics rules, because the judge instructs as to the law.

However, that simply-stated proposition—the judge, not the expert witness, instructs the jury as to what is the law—is as many layered as an onion. Exactly what is "law" and what is "fact" in the context of the meaning and application of the rules governing the practice of law?

Ultimately, "law" is what the judge decides (even if that decision incorporates "facts"), and "fact" is what the judge instructs the jury to decide. Although this definition is certainly circlular,

---

Professional Conduct in lieu of expert testimony, but specifically held that any expert testimony contrary to the Rules was *not* admissible. 217 Cal.Rptr. at 10. The court explained that the Rules of Professional Conduct set forth a lawyer's ethical duties and expert testimony cannot change that.

See Cornell v. Wunschel, 408 N.W.2d 369, 378 (Iowa 1987), holding that expert testimony as to ethics standards is not required in this case: "our code of professional responsibility clearly sets forth the standard of disclosure. It is then the jury's duty, as in a legal malpractice case, to compare the attorney's conduct with the appropriate standard. We conclude the trial court did not err in instructing the jury on the ethical standard clearly announced in Canon 5 of our code of professional responsibility."

Fishman v. Brooks, 396 Mass. 643, 487 N.E.2d 1377, 1381–82 (Mass. 1986), stating: "Expert testimony concerning the fact of an ethical violation is not appropriate . . . .. A judge can instruct the jury (or himself) concerning the requirements of ethical rules."

In re Initial Public Offering Securities Litigation, 174 F.Supp.2d 61 (S.D.N.Y.2001). In this case, many of the defendant underwriters moved to disqualify the district judge. "In support of their motion, the moving defendants have proffered the affidavits and declarations of Professors Geoffrey Hazard and Charles Wolfram as experts in judicial ethics. For the reasons that follow, these declarations must be precluded." *Id.* at 62. The court then ruled that it would not accept expert opinion on a recusal motion because "the testimony of an expert on matters of domestic law is inadmissable for *any* purpose." *Id.* at 64.

[51]*E.g., Marx & Co., Inc. v. Diners' Club, Inc.*, 550 F.2d 505, 510 (2d Cir. 1977). *Hygh v. Jacobs*, 961 F.2d 359, 363 (2d Cir.1992); *Andrews v. Metro North Commuter R.R. Co.*, 882 F.2d 705, 708 (2d Cir.1989), holding that an engineer's testimony that defendant was negligent was an improper legal conclusion; *Weston v. Washington Metro. Area Transit Auth.*, 78 F.3d 682, 684 n. 4 (D.C.Cir.1996), holding that an "expert witness may not deliver legal conclusions on domestic law, for legal principles are outside the witness' area of expertise under Federal Rule of Evidence 702." *United States v. Feliciano*, 223 F.3d 102, 121 (2d Cir.2000), holding that, in evaluating the admissibility of expert testimony, "this Court requires the exclusion of testimony [that] states a legal conclusion."

we see its application routinely in questions involving summary judgment and other judge-jury allocation questions. Civil procedure calls such questions a "mixed question of law and fact." In a tort case, when the jurors write on the verdict sheet: "we find that the defendant was negligent," is that a statement about the law or a statement about the facts? When the trial judge overrules the jury and concludes that the defendant was not negligent, is the judge making a statement about law or fact? Similarly, in a criminal case, when the jury finds that the defendant is "guilty," it is making either a finding about a legal proposition or a finding about a factual proposition.

Courts typically say no witness, expert or otherwise, can testify about domestic law, but they may testify and give their opinion whether, on the facts as stipulated or found by a trier of fact, the legal standard as given by the court has been satisfied. Thus, the ethics expert, in opining about matters of legal ethics, will be able to testify that "yes," [or "no"], assuming that in *Jurisdiction A* the standard of care is the minimum required by the ethics rules, and assuming further that facts *X*, *Y*, and *Z* are true, it is my opinion that, all things considered, "Lawyer *L* did [or did not] measure up to that standard of care or conduct." Indeed, even courts that prohibit expert testimony on the meaning and application of the legal ethics rules in particular circumstances concede that experts may give "limited testimony on mixed questions of law and fact, but the testimony must remain focused on helping the jury or judge understand particular facts in issue and not opine on the ultimate legal conclusion."[52]

Thus the general rule is that the expert witness may testify about violation of ethics rules. The expert may testify how lawyers, in practice, apply or interpret a particular rule, what lawyers view as "reasonable" in making a conflicts check, when lawyers regard it as necessary to inform a client of a conflict, when lawyers, in practice, view a conflict as "reasonably foreseeable," and so forth. In legal malpractice cases, courts often require expert testimony and, increasingly, malpractice cases are built on ethical violations, such as conflict of interests. As one court noted:

---

[52]*In re Initial Public Offering Securities Litigation*, 174 F.Supp.2d 61 (S.D.N.Y.2001). In this case, many of the defendant underwriters moved to disqualify the district judge, who refused to disqualify himself and refused to accept expert testimony that urged his recusal. However, the court still acknowledged that experts may testify on questions of mixed law and fact.

See also In re Air Disaster at

Lockerbie, Scotland, 37 F.3d 804, 826–27 (2d Cir.1994), holding that an expert's testimony that defendants engaged in "fraud" and "deceit" was admissible because the words were used in colloquial fashion, but the statement that defendants violated federal regulations was inadmissible as a legal conclusion; *Specht v. Jensen*, 853 F.2d 805, 809–10 (10th Cir.1988) (en banc).

It is clear that there can be instances where noncompliance with the Code of Professional Responsibility does not result in malpractice. Before legal malpractice can occur, the client must have incurred damages which were directly and proximately caused by the attorney's malpractice. Because of the very nature and complexity of the Code of Professional Responsibility and the conduct of legal matters, expert testimony is required to support the allegations except in those cases which are so patently obvious as to negate this requirement.[53]

Thus, many courts allow or require expert witnesses to testify on the meaning and application of the ethics rules in a malpractice case or a disqualification motion based on alleged ethical violations. As one commentator has noted, if a court allows the introduction of the ethics rules into evidence or a jury instruction explaining the Rules, but does not allow any expert testimony, that would "permit a jury of lay persons to decide a legal malpractice case without expert testimony." This argument is particularly persuasive in "those situations explicitly governed by the Rules, such as the Rules dealing with conflicts of interest." Yet, even in other cases, and "even when the Rules are explicit, the complexity of the transaction or underlying case may be such that a lay person could not understand how a lawyer should have acted under the circumstances without expert testimony. Also, proof of a generic ethical duty, such as the duty to represent a client competently, obviously is of no more assistance to the jury than is a generic charge of the law of negligence."[54]

The general rule when the trier of fact considers either the content or construction of a statute or rule is that the expert witness, in testifying, may rely on the statute or rule in forming his or her expert opinion and—

> may testify as to its construction and application to the circumstances in question. Such a witness may rely on the usual aids to construction, such as official comments, judicial and ethics-committee opinions construing the rule or statute, and professional literature. The procedural law of the jurisdiction determines such

---

[53]*Northwestern Life Insurance Co. v. Rogers*, 61 Ohio App.3d 506, 573 N.E.2d 159, 163–64 (1989).

[54]Wilburn Brewer, Jr., *Expert Witness Testimony in Legal Malpractice Cases*, 45 So. CAROLINA L. REV. 727, 744 (1994) (footnotes omitted). *See also Cleckner v. Dale*, 719 S.W.2d 535 (Tenn.Ct.App.1986). Restatement of the Law Governing Lawyers, Third, § 52, Comment *g* (Official Draft 2000):

"Accordingly, a plaintiff alleging professional negligence or breach of fi-duciary duty ordinarily must introduce expert testimony concerning the care reasonably required in the circumstances of the case and the lawyer's failure to exercise such care. Such expert testimony is unnecessary when it would be plain to a nonlawyer or is established as a matter of law that the lawyer's acts constitute negligence (for example, when a lawyer allegedly let the statute of limitations expire or withdrew without notifying a client) or breach of fiduciary duty."

issues as the qualifications required for such a witness and whether the party calling the witness has satisfied its burden of coming forward as to the issues in question. The court may instruct the jury as to the content and construction of the statute or rule and its bearing on the issue of care, under the general principles governing jury instructions. A dispute as to whether a statute or rule may properly be considered by the trier of fact is decided by the tribunal.[55]

If the court allows expert testimony as to the meaning of the ethics rules and how lawyers typically apply and understand them in a given situation, there is the question of who is competent to testify on this issue. If the expert witness may testify on the meaning, application, and interpretation of an ethics rule, the next issue is how the court decides whether the proffered witness is qualified. Normally, the court will consider someone an expert based on his or her knowledge of the applicable rules, his or her knowledge of and contribution to the legal literature, and his or her involvement in bar activities or committees that create or interpret the professional norms.[56]

However, *Cicero v. Borg-Warner Automotive, Inc.*[57] rejected that principle. In this case, a employee who had been fired filed an age discrimination claim under a state law. The employer moved for summary judgment, which the trial court granted. The trial court then issued an order to show cause why the employee and his lawyers should not be sanctioned under Federal Rule 11. The trial court, hearing the various motions, ultimately concluded that sanctions were not warranted against the lawyers or their

---

[55]Restatement of the Law Governing Lawyers, Third, § 52, Comment *g.*

[56]*Cleckner v. Dale*, 719 S.W.2d 535 (Tenn.Ct.App.1986). In this case, plaintiffs filed a legal malpractice action against their lawyer for his conduct in a real estate transaction. The Cleckners sought to introduce expert testimony concerning the proper standard of care for lawyers representing clients in a real estate closing and whether Dale's conduct in this case met that standard. The appellate court held that the trial court erred in precluding plaintiffs from presenting expert testimony on the lawyer's standard of care. In addition, the question whether the lawyer met the appropriate standard of conduct was a question of fact; and the trial court usurped the role of the jury by assuming the role of an expert on the standard of conduct. The court bluntly stated, among other things, that: "The trial court, assuming the role of an expert, undertook to define the standard of professional conduct the jury should apply in this case. This was improper." 719 S.W.2d at 541–54.

Restatement of the Law Governing Lawyers, Third, § 52, Comment *g*: "An expert opinion of what constitutes proper conduct in the circumstances of the case may be based on the expert's own experience and judgment and on the expert's knowledge of applicable rules and statutes, of literature discussing how lawyers do or should behave, and of the conduct and belief of lawyers." (internal citations omitted).

[57]*Cicero v. Borg-Warner Automotive, Inc.*, 163 F.Supp.2d 743 (E.D. Mich.2001).

client for filing complaint or prosecuting case. However, in reaching this conclusion, the court also held that the law professor and lawyers whom the employee's lawyers retained did not qualify as experts on ethical requirements of prosecuting employment discrimination cases.

The court's reasoning in *Cicero* would likely disqualify most experts testifying on legal ethics, whether law professors or practicing lawyers. For example, the court argued that one's publication of various law review articles on ethics did not qualify him because his articles were not peer-reviewed. It is a fact of life that, for the great majority of law reviews, law students make the decision whether to accept and how to edit articles for publication.[58] The expert witness was a legal analyst on television, but those positions are also not peer reviewed. The proffered expert was a member of employment-related committees of various local bar associations, but that did not qualify him as an expert on the ethical requirements of prosecuting an employment discrimination case, for purposes of arguing that sanctions were not warranted against the plaintiff's lawyers in this employment discrimination case, because, the court said, membership on such committees did not connote expertise. The court conceded that membership in these groups implies an interest in this area of law, but it "does not necessarily connote expertise, as any attorney can select himself to be a member of these organizations." The fact that an expert witness is named in a publication listing the best lawyers in the country, was similarly insufficient to qualify him as an expert because the court in *Cicero* said, there was no evidence demonstrating who the publication's decision-makers were, their qualifications, or what criteria were used in reaching their decision. The professor had twenty years of experience practicing employment discrimination law, but that was not enough to qualify him as an expert witness according to the court, because time in service did not necessarily lead to expertise.[59]

Given its reasoning in not accepting these lawyers as expert witnesses as to what kinds of lawyer conduct constitute "reasonable" actions in the prosecution of an employment discrimination, the *Cicero* court candidly acknowledged: "The court is not certain whether there is such a thing as an 'expert' in these areas; it may well be that the only sources of 'expertise' are the courts and professional bodies charged with administering them. This issue was not raised and remains unresolved for purposes of this order."[60]

The growth potential of *Cicero* is unclear. *Cicero* is correct that

---

[58] Ronald D. Rotunda, *The Role of Law Reviews: The Extreme Centrist Position*, 62 INDIANA L.J. 1 (1986).

[59] 163 F.Supp.2d at 747–50.

[60] 163 F.Supp.2d at 747 n.3.

many law reviews are not peer-reviewed in the sense that law professors do not make the decision as to which articles to accept. However, legal ethics experts (and courts) rely on the articles that noted authorities in the field publish, so these articles are generally accepted in the field, which is more than is required in expert testimony generally.[61] Moreover, courts consistently cite and rely on law review articles as evidence of the law. Scholars in the field also rely on and cite these articles. The case law on expert testimony routinely allows experts to rely on these articles in giving their opinions.[62]

Cicero argued that "only courts and professional bodies administering legal ethics rules may be experts."[63] It is unclear, however, wonders why one would accord special expertise to members of these professional bodies given the fact that, nowadays, they often contain lay members, but not consider a lawyer who has been researching and writing about legal ethics and cited by the courts for many years.[64]

In one sense that may be true. If a person, blindfolded, throws darts at a target, he could do that for 20 years and we would not say that he has "experience," because he did not have the opportunity to learn from his mistakes or to improve through practice. But the verdict of the market place tends to value true experience. Lawyers do not practice blindfolded: a lawyer who has argued 20 cases before the U.S. Supreme Court tends to be able to charge more than one who has argued one case, just as a lawyer who has labored for 20 years in jury trial work is

---

[61]The leading case governing the court's admission of expert testimony is *Daubert v. Merrell Dow Pharmaceuticals, Inc.*, 509 U.S. 579, 113 S.Ct. 2786, 125 L.Ed.2d 469 (1993), which allows a court to accept expert testimony even if it is not "generally accepted" because "general acceptance" is not a necessary precondition to the admissibility of expert evidence. *See also Kumho Tire Co., Ltd. v. Carmichael*, 526 U.S. 137, 119 S.Ct. 1167, 143 L.Ed.2d 238 (1999). The fact that law review articles are generally accepted as authority, even by courts, should indicate that the testimony is more likely to be accepted, not less likely.

[62]*United States v. Locascio*, 6 F.3d 924, 938 (2d Cir.1993): "expert witnesses can testify to opinions based on hearsay or other inadmissible evidence if experts in the field reasonably rely on such evidence in forming their opinions. [In this case, the expert witness] was entitled to rely upon hearsay as to such matters as the structure and operating rules of organized crime families . . . , since there is little question that law enforcement agents routinely and reasonably rely upon such hearsay in the course of their duties." *United States v. Daly*, 842 F.2d 1380, 1387 (2d Cir.1988), *cert. denied*, 488 U.S. 821, 109 S.Ct. 66, 102 L.Ed.2d 43 (1988): "[I]f experts in the field reasonably rely on hearsay in forming their opinions and drawing their inferences, the expert witness may properly testify to his opinions and inferences based upon such hearsay."

[63]163 F.Supp.2d at 747 n.3.

[64]*Cicero v. Borg-Warner Automotive, Inc.*, 163 F.Supp.2d 743, 749 (E. D.Mich.2001).

considered more expert, more experienced, and more valued than a lawyer who has never tried a case. Experience counts in these other areas; should legal ethics be any different?

It may be that *Cicero* was simply adverse to the notion that there should be any expert testimony about the application, meaning, and interpretation in the legal community. If so, that is the view of the minority of cases.[65]

§ 1-9(c)(5) Fee Forfeitures

Some courts deny a lawyer part or all of her fee for ethics violations on the grounds that the client should be excused from the obligation to pay fees to a lawyer who breaches a fiduciary duty to the client. This remedy does not necessarily require plaintiff to show damages. In other words, the lawyer should not be allowed to collect a fee during the time that she was in a conflict of interest (or during the time she engaged in another ethical violation), because she should not have been representing the client at all. Sometimes this remedy is applied in conflict of interest cases.[66]

The court will impose forfeiture of all or part of the lawyer's fee as a remedy for ethics violations only in the special situation where the lawyer has engaged in a "clear and serious" violation

---

[65]Restatement of the Law Governing Lawyers, Third, § 52, Comment *g* (Official Draft 2000).

[66]*E.g., Moses v. McGarvey*, 614 P.2d 1363 (Alaska 1980), holding that former corporate lawyers who represented shareholders until they were disqualified for a conflict of interest should be denied all attorney fees.

Jeffry v. Pounds, 67 Cal.App.3d 6, 136 Cal.Rptr. 373 (Cal.Ct.App. 1977). In this case, a law firm competently represented a personal injury plaintiff, then—in the middle of his client's case—the lawyer filed a divorce case against the plaintiff on behalf of the wife of the plaintiff. The court held that the firm was not entitled to fees for the period after it took the wife's case, but was not required to forfeit the fees for the period before doing so.

City of Little Rock v. Cash, 277 Ark. 494, 644 S.W.2d 229 (Ark.1982). The court denied a fee to a lawyer who defended the city in a police misconduct suit while also suing the same city and successfully attacking its

privilege tax.

Crawford v. Logan, 656 S.W.2d 360 (Tenn.1983), holding that the court may require the lawyer to forfeit fees (totally or partially) when the lawyer violates the ethics rules. In this case, the court held that a tape recording of an interview with the woman who had allegedly engaged in adulterous relations with the lawyer's divorced client's husband came within the ambit of the disciplinary rule requiring that the lawyer, after being discharged by client, deliver to the client all "papers and property" to which the client was entitled. Therefore, the question whether the discharged lawyer's violation of the disciplinary rule should result in a forfeiture of all or part of the fee would turn on the lower court's factual determination. The supreme court remanded so that the lower court could decide whether the lawyer's ethics violation prejudiced his client in trial of the divorce action, viewed in the light of particular facts and circumstances of the case.

of her duty to her client.[67] The court should take into account several important factors—the gravity and timing of the violation; the lawyer's willfulness; the effect of the violation on the value of the lawyer's work for the client; any other threatened or actual harm to the client; and the adequacy of other remedies.[68]

If fee forfeiture occurs, it extends only to *fees*. It does not extend to disbursements that a lawyer has made on behalf of the client if the disbursement has conferred a benefit on the client.[69]

§ 1-9(c)(6) The Lawyer's Obligation to Keep Secret Information About the Client

The Scope section under the 1983 Rules made several important comments on Rule 1.6, *Confidentiality of Information*. There is no explanation why these comments were included here rather than under Rule 1.6. The drafters of the 2002 Rules did delete several of these comments, but this discussion is retained because many states continue to use this language.

First, these comments make clear that the lawyer's duty to hold client information confidential is a duty that begins when the "lawyer agrees to consider whether a client-lawyer relationship shall be established."[70] The lawyer may decide that she will not take the case (she is too busy for a case of that complexity, or the case conflicts with a trial scheduled at the same time, etc.),

---

[67]*E.g., Pringle v. La Chapelle*, 73 Cal.App.4th 1000, 87 Cal.Rptr.2d 90, 94 (Cal.App.1999), a case where the lawyer sued a corporation and its Chief Executive Officer to recover fees. The court held that even if the defendant was correct that the lawyer had violated the ethics rules relating to securing consent in cases of dual representation, this violation did not automatically result in a forfeiture of fees. The court upheld the trial court's judgment for the lawyer.

Compare Burrow v. Arce, 997 S.W.2d 229 (Tex.1999), which imposed fee forfeiture. In *Burrow*, clients filed suit against attorneys who had represented them in personal injury litigation, demanding forfeiture of all the attorney fees for alleged breaches of the lawyers' fiduciary duty, fraud, violations of the Deceptive Trade Practices Act, negligence, and breach of contract. The 11th District Court entered summary judgment for the attorneys, and the clients appealed. The *Houston Court of Appeals*, 958 S.W.2d 239, affirmed in part, and reversed and

remanded in part. Both the attorneys and the clients petitioned for review.

Justice Hecht, of the Texas Supreme Court, held that: (1) conclusory assertions in summary judgment affidavits of experienced personal injury trial lawyers that clients' settlement agreements were all fair and reasonable were insufficient to establish as a matter of law that the clients suffered no actual damages as a result of alleged misconduct by their attorneys; but (2) a client *need not prove actual damages to obtain forfeiture* of an attorney's fee due to the attorney's breach of duty to the client; and (3) additional plaintiffs were entitled to be added as parties by the amended pleadings.

[68]Restatement of the Law Governing Lawyers, Third, § 37 (Official Draft 2000).

[69]Restatement of the Law Governing Lawyers, Third, § 37, Comment *e* (Official Draft 2000).

[70]Scope, Comment 17.

but the duty imposed by Rule 1.6 exists when the lawyer "agrees to consider" whether to accept the client. This is retained in the 2002 Rules.

Second, while Rule 1.6 governs the lawyer's ethical duty to keep the client's confidences, the Rule does not govern the judicial application of the attorney-client *evidentiary* privilege, or the work-product privilege.[71] The Rule 1.6 obligation, as discussed in greater detail below, is broader than either the evidentiary privilege or the work-product privilege. A judge may determine, in enforcing a subpoena against a lawyer, that certain information is not within either the evidentiary privilege or the work-product privilege and thus the lawyer must reveal the information. But the lawyer's obligation to comply with the subpoena does not give the lawyer carte blanche to broadcast that information.

In other words, if the information is not "generally known,"[72] the lawyer should still keep it confidential and not proclaim it to the world, even though he must comply with the subpoena. For example, if the lawyer is ordered to reveal certain client information to a grand jury, he should not then tout and publicize it to the world at large, because the information has not been widely distributed and may never be know outside the grand jury room.

Iowa Supreme Court Attorney Disciplinary Board v. Marzen[73] illustrates the distinction between "generally known" and "knowable but not generally unknown." The court appointed a lawyer to represent a woman in a hospitalization commitment proceeding. He later agreed to represent her in other matters, including a dispute with her mother and a child-custody proceeding. In the course of an interview with a television news reporter, the lawyer revealed that the woman earlier sued and received a settlement from a parole officer whom she claimed had engaged in sexual misconduct. The lawyer argued he had done nothing wrong because information about the prior suit was available from public sources, but the court disagreed. However, while the information was knowable, it was not generally known, until the lawyer made it known. The ethical requirement of maintaining client confidentiality is broader than information protected by the attorney-client privilege. It appeared that the lawyer's comments were intended to defame his own client. The court imposed an indefinite suspension not to exceed six months.

Finally, the Scope acknowledges that Rule 1.6 gives the lawyer discretion to disclose information in certain circumstances. The lawyer "may reveal" client information, for example, "to prevent

---

[71]1983 Scope, Comment 19. The ABA deleted this language in 2002.

[72]*See* Rule 1.9(c)(1).

[73]*Iowa Supreme Court Attorney Disciplinary Board v. Marzen*, 779 N.W.2d 757 (Iowa 2010).

the client from committing a criminal act that the lawyer believes is likely to result in imminent death or substantial bodily harm."[74] But, the purpose of such exceptions is to give lawyers certain discretion, and the exercise of such discretion "should not be subject to reexamination," because that would be "incompatible with the general policy of promoting compliance with law through assurances that communications will be protected against disclosure."[75] This language, which was included in the 1983 Scope, was deleted in 2002.

The caveat that the 1983 Scope offered probably would not protect lawyers. Assume, for example, that a client tells his lawyer that the client is likely to kill a material witness. Rule 1.6 allows (but does not require) the lawyer to reveal that information. The 1983 Scope section advised us that the lawyer's decision not to reveal this information is a decision that should not be subject to reexamination. However, we can expect that if the client commits the murder the relatives of the deceased will sue the lawyer for failing to notify the appropriate parties when the ethics rules did not require the lawyer to remain silent. In spite of the 1983 Scope's caveat, we should not be surprised if a court holds such a lawyer liable in tort. Other professionals have been found liable,[76] and the hope expressed that the lawyer's exercise of discretion found in Rule 1.6 "should not be subject to reexamination," may be worth no more than a magnificent bequest in a pauper's will.

The Restatement of the Law Governing Lawyers considered this issue in a specific section dealing with a lawyer's duty of care to certain non-clients. One proposed subsection of that section, § 73(5), focused on a lawyer's liability to a non-client when the client threatens a crime involving imminent death or serious bodily injury. Proposed (but *not* adopted) section 73(5) proposed that a lawyer should be liable to a non-client—

when and to the extent that circumstances known to the lawyer make it clear that appropriate action by the lawyer is necessary with respect to a matter within the scope of the representation to

---

[74] Rule 1.6(b)(1).

[75] 1983 Scope, Comment 20.

[76] The leading case is *Tarasoff v. Regents of the University of California*, 17 Cal.3d 425, 431, 131 Cal.Rptr. 14, 20, 551 P.2d 334, 340 (1976), *vacating*, 13 Cal.3d 177, 118 Cal.Rptr. 129, 529 P.2d 553 (1974). In this case a psychotherapist knew of a planned murder and did not warn the victim. The court held that the psychotherapist should have warned the victim or the police or taken other necessary steps. Fail-

ure to do that stated a cause of action. *See also,* Restatement of the Law of Torts, Second, § 321.

Hawkins v. King County, 24 Wash.App. 338, 602 P.2d 361 (Wash. Ct.App.1979) involved a lawyer. The court held this lawyer not liable to a non-client victim when the lawyer (and the victim) knew that the client was dangerous, but the lawyer had no information that client planned to assault anyone.

prevent the client from committing a crime imminently threatening to cause death or serious bodily injury to an identifiable person who is unaware of the risk and the lawyer's act has facilitated the crime.[77]

In spite of the limited liability that this subsection imposed (especially in light of the requirement that the lawyer's action had to have "facilitated the crime") the Council of the American Law Institute ordered that it be deleted from the final version.[78] As the Comment (also not adopted) to this subsection notes: "Holding a lawyer liable to a victim of the client for failing to undertake such reasonable measures does not discourage any proper lawyer conduct, and can benefit the client by preventing the wrong."[79]

Lawyers should not take too much solace from the ALI's official position, because it is the position that many states have rejected. The ALI Reporter's Note advised: "As of February, 1996, the professional rules of 10 states *required* lawyers to disclose confidences when necessary to prevent a crime likely to cause death or serious bodily injury, while virtually every other state *permitted* but did not require such disclosure."[80]

§ 1-10 MODEL RULE 1.0: TERMINOLOGY

§ 1-10(a) Text of Rule 1.0

RULE 1.0: TERMINOLOGY

(a) "Belief" or "believes" denotes that the person involved actually supposed the fact in question to be true. A person's belief may be inferred from circumstances.

(b) "Confirmed in writing," when used in reference to the informed consent of a person, denotes informed consent that is given in writing by the person or a writing

---

[77]Restatement of the Law Governing Lawyers § 73(5) (Tent. Draft No. 8, Mar. 21, 1997) (footnote omitted). The footnote explains that the reason this section is placed in brackets—and not adopted by the ALI—is because the Council of the ALI in 1996, by a vote of 17-14, directed that this subsection and the accompanying Comment i "be deleted from the text tentatively approved." The Council, for the information of members, "authorized the printing of the deleted Subsection and Comment in Tentative Draft No. 8. Restatement of the Law Governing Lawyers § 73(5) (Tent. Draft No. 8, Mar. 21, 1997), at 19 n.1."

[78]*See* Restatement of the Law Governing Lawyers § 73(5) (Tent. Draft No. 8, Mar. 21, 1997), at 19 n.1.

[79]*See* Restatement of the Law Governing Lawyers § 73(5), Comment i (Tent. Draft No. 8, Mar. 21, 1997), at 31. This Comment, like § 73(5), was *not* adopted by the ALI. Restatement of the Law Governing Lawyers § 73(5) (Tent. Draft No. 8, Mar. 21, 1997), at 19 n.1.

[80]Restatement of the Law Governing Lawyers § 73(5) (Tent. Draft No. 8, Mar. 21, 1997), Reporter's Note to Comment i, at 42 (emphasis added). *See also id.* at n.4. The "Duty of Care to Certain Nonclients" is now found at Restatement of the Law Governing Lawyers, Third, § 51 (Official Draft 2000). There is no longer any subsection 51(5).

that a lawyer promptly transmits to the person confirming an oral informed consent. See paragraph (e) for the definition of "informed consent." If it is not feasible to obtain or transmit the writing at the time the person gives informed consent, then the lawyer must obtain or transmit it within a reasonable time thereafter.

(c) "Firm" or "law firm" denotes a lawyer or lawyers in a law partnership, professional corporation, sole proprietorship or other association authorized to practice law; or lawyers employed in a legal services organization or the legal department of a corporation or other organization.

(d) "Fraud" or "fraudulent" denotes conduct that is fraudulent under the substantive or procedural law of the applicable jurisdiction and has a purpose to deceive.

(e) "Informed consent" denotes the agreement by a person to a proposed course of conduct after the lawyer has communicated adequate information and explanation about the material risks of and reasonably available alternatives to the proposed course of conduct.

(f) "Knowingly," "known," or "knows" denotes actual knowledge of the fact in question. A person's knowledge may be inferred from circumstances.

(g) "Partner" denotes a member of a partnership, a shareholder in a law firm organized as a professional corporation, or a member of an association authorized to practice law.

(h) "Reasonable" or "reasonably" when used in relation to conduct by a lawyer denotes the conduct of a reasonably prudent and competent lawyer.

(i) "Reasonable belief" or "reasonably believes" when used in reference to a lawyer denotes that the lawyer believes the matter in question and that the circumstances are such that the belief is reasonable.

(j) "Reasonably should know" when used in reference to a lawyer denotes that a lawyer of reasonable prudence and competence would ascertain the matter in question.

(k) "Screened" denotes the isolation of a lawyer from any participation in a matter through the timely imposition of procedures within a firm that are reasonably adequate under the circumstances to protect information that the isolated lawyer is obligated to protect under these Rules or other law.

(*l*) "Substantial" when used in reference to degree or extent denotes a material matter of clear and weighty importance.

(m) "Tribunal" denotes a court, an arbitrator in a binding arbitration proceeding or a legislative body, administrative agency or other body acting in an adjudicative capacity. A legislative body, administrative agency or other body acts in an adjudicative capacity when a neutral official, after the presentation of evidence or legal argument by a party or parties, will render a binding legal judgment directly affecting a party's interests in a particular matter.

(n) "Writing" or "written" denotes a tangible or electronic record of a communication or representation, including handwriting, typewriting, printing, photostating, photography, audio or videorecording and e-mail. A "signed" writing includes an electronic sound, symbol or process attached to or logically associated with a writing and executed or adopted by a person with the intent to sign the writing.

Comment

Confirmed in Writing

[1] If it is not feasible to obtain or transmit a written confirmation at the time the client gives informed consent, then the lawyer must obtain or transmit it within a reasonable time thereafter. If a lawyer has obtained a client's informed consent, the lawyer may act in reliance on that consent so long as it is confirmed in writing within a reasonable time thereafter.

Firm

[2] Whether two or more lawyers constitute a firm within paragraph (c) can depend on the specific facts. For example, two practitioners who share office space and occasionally consult or assist each other ordinarily would not be regarded as constituting a firm. However, if they present themselves to the public in a way that suggests that they are a firm or conduct themselves as a firm, they should be regarded as a firm for purposes of the Rules. The terms of any formal agreement between associated lawyers are relevant in determining whether they are a firm, as is the fact that they have mutual access to information concerning the clients they serve. Furthermore, it is relevant in doubtful cases to consider the underlying purpose of the Rule that is involved. A group of lawyers could be regarded as a firm for purposes of the Rule that the same lawyer should not represent opposing parties in litigation, while it might not be so regarded for purposes of the Rule that information acquired by one lawyer is attributed to another.

[3] With respect to the law department of an organization, including the government, there is ordinarily no question that the members of the department constitute a firm within the meaning of the Rules of Professional Conduct. There can be uncertainty, however, as to the identity of the client. For example, it may not be clear whether the law department of a corporation represents a subsidiary or an affiliated corporation, as well as the corporation by

which the members of the department are directly employed. A similar question can arise concerning an unincorporated association and its local affiliates.

[4] Similar questions can also arise with respect to lawyers in legal aid and legal services organizations. Depending upon the structure of the organization, the entire organization or different components of it may constitute a firm or firms for purposes of these Rules.

Fraud

[5] When used in these Rules, the terms "fraud" or "fraudulent" refer to conduct that is characterized as such under the substantive or procedural law of the applicable jurisdiction and has a purpose to deceive. This does not include merely negligent misrepresentation or negligent failure to apprise another of relevant information. For purposes of these Rules, it is not necessary that anyone has suffered damages or relied on the misrepresentation or failure to inform.

Informed Consent

[6] Many of the Rules of Professional Conduct require the lawyer to obtain the informed consent of a client or other person (e.g., a former client or, under certain circumstances, a prospective client) before accepting or continuing representation or pursuing a course of conduct. See, e.g., Rules 1.2(c), 1.6(a) and 1.7(b). The communication necessary to obtain such consent will vary according to the Rule involved and the circumstances giving rise to the need to obtain informed consent. The lawyer must make reasonable efforts to ensure that the client or other person possesses information reasonably adequate to make an informed decision. Ordinarily, this will require communication that includes a disclosure of the facts and circumstances giving rise to the situation, any explanation reasonably necessary to inform the client or other person of the material advantages and disadvantages of the proposed course of conduct and a discussion of the client's or other person's options and alternatives. In some circumstances it may be appropriate for a lawyer to advise a client or other person to seek the advice of other counsel. A lawyer need not inform a client or other person of facts or implications already known to the client or other person; nevertheless, a lawyer who does not personally inform the client or other person assumes the risk that the client or other person is inadequately informed and the consent is invalid. In determining whether the information and explanation provided are reasonably adequate, relevant factors include whether the client or other person is experienced in legal matters generally and in making decisions of the type involved, and whether the client or other person is independently represented by other counsel in giving the consent. Normally, such persons need less information and explanation than others, and generally a client or other person who is independently represented by other counsel in giving the consent should be assumed to have given informed consent.

[7] Obtaining informed consent will usually require an affirmative response by the client or other person. In general, a lawyer may not assume consent from a client's or other person's silence. Consent

may be inferred, however, from the conduct of a client or other person who has reasonably adequate information about the matter. A number of Rules require that a person's consent be confirmed in writing. See Rules 1.7(b) and 1.9(a). For a definition of "writing" and "confirmed in writing," see paragraphs (n) and (b). Other Rules require that a client's consent be obtained in a writing signed by the client. See, e.g., Rules 1.8(a) and (g). For a definition of "signed," see paragraph (n).

Screened

[8] This definition applies to situations where screening of a personally disqualified lawyer is permitted to remove imputation of a conflict of interest under Rules 1.10, 1.11, 1.12 or 1.18.

[9] The purpose of screening is to assure the affected parties that confidential information known by the personally disqualified lawyer remains protected. The personally disqualified lawyer should acknowledge the obligation not to communicate with any of the other lawyers in the firm with respect to the matter. Similarly, other lawyers in the firm who are working on the matter should be informed that the screening is in place and that they may not communicate with the personally disqualified lawyer with respect to the matter. Additional screening measures that are appropriate for the particular matter will depend on the circumstances. To implement, reinforce and remind all affected lawyers of the presence of the screening, it may be appropriate for the firm to undertake such procedures as a written undertaking by the screened lawyer to avoid any communication with other firm personnel and any contact with any firm files or other materials relating to the matter, written notice and instructions to all other firm personnel forbidding any communication with the screened lawyer relating to the matter, denial of access by the screened lawyer to firm files or other materials relating to the matter and periodic reminders of the screen to the screened lawyer and all other firm personnel.

[10] In order to be effective, screening measures must be implemented as soon as practical after a lawyer or law firm knows or reasonably should know that there is a need for screening.

February 2009 Amendment

In February 2009, the ABA House of Delegates added a reference to Rule 1.10 in Comment 8. This change—made to the comment on screening—reflects the screening amendment to the text of Rule 1.10.

§ 1-10(b) The 2002 Model Rules Changes to Terminology

The drafters of the 2002 Model Rules made substantial changes to the Terminology section. First, they removed it from the third part of the introductory section behind the Scope and placed it in its own Rule. Rule 1.0 is the new location for all of the definitions of terms in the Terminology section. The drafters made this change to give the terms more prominence and to allow them to add Comments.[1] Second, they added ten Comments to the Terminology section. All of the text in the Comments is new. Finally, they made several changes to the terms listed in the 1983 Rules as well as the addition of several new terms.

Many of the definitions are unchanged. Rule 1.0's sections (a), (f), (h), (i), (j) and (l) have not been modified from the old Terminology section.

One major change involved the deletion of a definition of "consent after consultation" and the addition of "informed consent." The drafters changed consent after consultation throughout the Rules and Comment to read, informed consent.[2] They did not intend any new meaning; they just thought that informed consent was a more appropriate term for the interaction between lawyers and clients that leads to client consent.

Depending on the Rule and the context, the drafters have included the concepts of "a writing" and "confirmed in writing" as they relate to agreements and consents between the lawyer and the client. Rule 1.0(b) and (n) define these terms.

The drafters modified the definitions of "law firm" and "partner" to include more modern forms of practice such as partnerships, professional corporations, sole proprietorships, and legal services organizations.[3]

The drafters modified the definition of fraud to be more closely tied to the substantive laws of the particular jurisdiction, rather than to have a separate meaning in the Model Rules.[4]

There are two new terms that are introduced in the new Rule 1.0: "screened" and "tribunal." The drafters sought to define screening so that it could be used in several contexts of conflicts of interests in the Rules.[5] They also decided that the concept of a tribunal should be more clearly defined in the definitions.[6] The 1983 Rules did not contain such a definition of tribunal.

[Section 1-10]

[1] *See* Reporter's Explanation of Changes to Model Rule 1.0.

[2] Rule 1.0(e).

[3] Rule 1.0(c), (g).

[4] Rule 1.0(d).

[5] Rule 1.0(k).

[6] Rule 1.0(m). This definition includes arbitration and legislative bodies operating in an adjudicative capacity.

I. CLIENT-LAWYER RELATIONSHIPS

CHAPTER 1.1
COMPETENCE

§ 1.1–1 **Competence: the First Rule of Ethics**
§ 1.1–2 **Malpractice and Competence**

RULE 1.1: COMPETENCE

A lawyer shall provide competent representation to a client. Competent representation requires the legal knowledge, skill, thoroughness and preparation reasonably necessary for the representation.

Comment

Legal Knowledge and Skill

[1] In determining whether a lawyer employs the requisite knowledge and skill in a particular matter, relevant factors include the relative complexity and specialized nature of the matter, the lawyer's general experience, the lawyer's training and experience in the field in question, the preparation and study the lawyer is able to give the matter and whether it is feasible to refer the matter to, or associate or consult with, a lawyer of established competence in the field in question. In many instances, the required proficiency is that of a general practitioner. Expertise in a particular field of law may be required in some circumstances.

[2] A lawyer need not necessarily have special training or prior experience to handle legal problems of a type with which the lawyer is unfamiliar. A newly admitted lawyer can be as competent as a practitioner with long experience. Some important legal skills, such as the analysis of precedent, the evaluation of evidence and legal drafting, are required in all legal problems. Perhaps the most fundamental legal skill consists of determining what kind of legal problems a situation may involve, a skill that necessarily transcends any particular specialized knowledge. A lawyer can provide adequate representation in a wholly novel field through necessary study. Competent representation can also be provided through the association of a lawyer of established competence in the field in question.

[3] In an emergency a lawyer may give advice or assistance in a matter in which the lawyer does not have the skill ordinarily required where referral to or consultation or association with another lawyer would be impractical. Even in an emergency, however, assistance should be limited to that reasonably necessary in the circumstances, for ill-considered action under emergency conditions can jeopardize the client's interest.

[4] A lawyer may accept representation where the requisite level of competence can be achieved by reasonable preparation. This applies as well to a lawyer who is appointed as counsel for an unrepresented person. See also Rule 6.2.

Thoroughness and Preparation

[5] Competent handling of a particular matter includes inquiry into and analysis of the factual and legal elements of the problem, and use of methods and procedures meeting the standards of competent practitioners. It also includes adequate preparation. The required attention and preparation are determined in part by what is at stake; major litigation and complex transactions ordinarily require more extensive treatment than matters of lesser complexity and consequence. An agreement between the lawyer and the client regarding the scope of the representation may limit the matters for which the lawyer is responsible. See Rule 1.2(c).

Maintaining Competence

[6] To maintain the requisite knowledge and skill, a lawyer should keep abreast of changes in the law and its practice, engage in continuing study and education and comply with all continuing legal education requirements to which the lawyer is subject.

Authors' 1983 Model Rules Comparison

The text of the 2002 version is identical to the Rule adopted by the ABA House of Delegates in 1983.

Comments 1 to 4 are identical to the 1983 version.

In Comment 5, the drafters of the 2002 Rules added the following sentence: "An agreement between the lawyer and the client regarding the scope of the representation may limit the matters for which the lawyer is responsible. See Rule 1.2(c)." The purpose of this change was to make clear the relationship between competence and limitations on the scope of a representation. The drafters also made a few word changes in Comment 5 for stylistic and clarification purposes.

In Comment 6, the drafters added the obligation to "keep abreast of changes in the law and its practice" and the obligation to "comply with all continuing legal education requirements to which the lawyer is subject." This change identified three distinct obligations of lawyers in the context of education and preparation. The drafters deleted a sentence that referred to optional systems of peer review because this goal is aspirational rather than a requirement.

Model Code Comparison

DR 6-101(A)(1) provided that a lawyer shall not handle a matter "which he knows or should know that he is not competent to handle, without associating himself with a lawyer who is competent to handle it." DR 6-101(A)(2) requires "preparation adequate in the circumstances." Rule 1.1 more fully particularizes the elements of competence. Whereas DR 6-101(A)(3) prohibited the "[N]eglect of a legal matter," Rule 1.1 does not contain such a prohibition. Instead, Rule 1.1 affirmatively requires the lawyer to be competent.

§ 1.1–1 COMPETENCE: THE FIRST RULE OF ETHICS

It is no accident that the first Model Rule requires competence, for the drafters of the Model Rules believed that the first rule of legal ethics is competence.[1] Not only the law of malpractice but the law of ethics requires lawyers to be competent.[2] A lawyer is competent if she has "the legal knowledge, skill, thoroughness and preparation reasonably necessary for the representation."[3]

The duty of competence has three components: (1) legal knowledge, (2) skill, and (3) thoroughness and preparation.[4] In order to meet this standard, lawyers must either possess the knowledge or acquire it through study or affiliation with another lawyer to represent competently the client. Such knowledge does not need to be possessed at the outset of the client-attorney relationship, but the lawyer must reasonably believe that he can acquire it in a timely manner considering the circumstances of the representation. A competent lawyer must possess the skill needed to execute the representation of the client. Such skills include research and writing, oral advocacy and brief writing, and negotiation and drafting skills. The obligation of competence also includes the thoroughness and preparation with which a lawyer conducts the representation. This duty is in contrast to the obligation of diligence contained in Model Rule 1.2. A lawyer's failure to provide any one of these integral parts to the practice of law may constitute a breach of the obligation of competence. And, such a breach injures the client and legal system.[5]

[Section 1.1–1]

[1] In contrast, DR 1-101(A) of the ABA Model Code of Professional Responsibility dealt with character and fitness to admission to the bar. The Model Rule corresponding to that DR is Model Rule 8.1. The first section of the American Law Institute's Restatement of the Law Governing Lawyers, Third, § 1 (Official Draft 2000) is even more mundane. Section 1 simply provides that when lawyers are admitted to the bar they are subject to the "applicable law." The section of the Restatement requiring lawyers to be competent is found in § 16(2), Restatement of the Law Governing Lawyers, Third (Official Draft 2000).

[2] Rule 1.1. DR 6-101(A).

[3] Rule 1.1.

A lawyer's duty to represent a client competently and effectively does not allow a lawyer to harass another person, to violate another's legal rights, or to use means that serve no substantial purpose but to "embarrass, delay, or burden a third person. . . ." Rule 4.4. *See also* DR 7-102(A)(1); DR 7-106(C)(2); DR 7-108(D),(E).

[4] *See* ABA Center for Professional Responsibility, Annotated Model Rules of Professional Conduct 18–22 (5th ed. 2003).

[5] *See In re Nunnery, 725 N.W. 2d 613*(Wis. 2007), *noted in* 23 ABA/BNA Manual on Professional Conduct, Current Reports News 39 (Jan. 24, 2007), involving a two-month suspension for plaintiff's lawyer because he did not conduct meaningful inquiry into the veracity of suspicious documents presented to him by his client.

Reasonable lawyers can make reasonable mistakes. The lawyer is not competent when the mistake is not reasonable, and she is competent if the mistake is reasonable.[6]

§ 1.1–1(a) Experience versus Competence

The lawyer need not necessarily be *experienced* in a particular matter in order to be considered *competent* in that matter.[7] There is a first time for everything. If professional standards required a lawyer to be experienced in a matter before undertaking that matter, a lawyer would never be able to acquire the initial experience. Moreover, even a novice lawyer has training in the common denominator of all legal problems: legal method and the analysis of precedent and evidence.[8]

The lawyer need not have the necessary degree of competence prior to accepting the employment. The lawyer may properly accept the matter and then acquire the necessary competence through study and preparation in a novel area of law.[9] The Model Code added a specific caveat that this preparation should not result in "unreasonable delay or expense to his client."[10] This limitation is implicit in the requirement of the Model Rules that the preparation be "reasonable."[11]

Sometimes, the best way to acquire the necessary competence is through working with more experienced lawyers. Training and

---

The court found that Nunnery had not acted competently because he failed to reasonably inquire into the truth of his client's allegations. According to the court, the duty to act competently serves to protect both the individual client and the system of justice.

[6] *See e.g., Pincay v. Andrews*, 389 F.3d 853 (9th Cir.2004)(en banc). The court held that a lawyer's reliance on a paralegal calendaring clerk to determine the deadline to file a notice of appeal may be excusable neglect from which a court can grant relief if the subordinate miscalculates the time period. The court relied on Rule 4(a)(5), Federal Rules of Civil Procedure. "This appeal represents a lawyer's nightmare. A sophisticated law firm, with what it thought was a sophisticated system to determine and calendar filing deadlines, missed a critical one: the 30-day time period in which to file a notice of appeal under Federal Rule of Appellate Procedure 4(a)(1)(A)." The court acknowledged that nowadays, "the delegation of repetitive legal tasks

to paralegals has become a necessary fixture. Such delegation has become an integral part of the struggle to keep down the costs of legal representation . . .. We hold that delegation of the task of ascertaining the deadline was not per se inexcusable neglect." 389 F.3d 853 (9th Cir.2004).

[7] The drafters of the 2002 Model Rules added a line to the Comments to make clear that the scope of a matter will affect the competence that the lawyer will need to possess. "An agreement between the lawyer and the client regarding the scope of the representation may limit the matters for which the lawyer is responsible. *See* Rule 1.2(c)." Rule 1.1 Comment 5.

[8] Rule 1.1, Comment 2. *Cf.* EC 6-1.

[9] Rule 1.1, Comment 2. DR 6-101(A)(2). EC 6-4.

[10] EC 6-3.

[11] Rule 1.1, Comment 4. *Cf.* Rule 1.1, Comment 5.

close supervision are particularly important in developing certain skills (*e.g.*, trial practice, and negotiation). Thus, trial lawyers typically do not start trial work by handling major, complex cases all by themselves. Instead, they work with other, more experienced, lawyers. The younger lawyers—those whom the more experienced lawyers supervise—have the duty to become competent in an area before undertaking it, and the supervising lawyers, such as partners in law firms, have the responsibility to make reasonable efforts to insure that all of the lawyers in their firm or under their supervision conform to the rules of professional conduct, including the rule requiring competence.[12]

The lawyer also may establish the necessary competence by associating in the matter with another attorney (outside of the law firm) who is already competent.[13] Before the lawyer's association with someone in another law firm is proper, the client must consent to it.[14]

§ 1.1–1(b) Continuing Legal Education

The lawyer's duty to become competent includes the duty to remain competent. A lawyer has an ethical duty to engage in continuing legal education and to study in order to maintain his or her competence.[15]

Because competence is the first rule of legal ethics, the prime directive, it is proper for jurisdictions—in an effort to enhance, promote and build competence[16]—to require lawyers to attend continuing legal education classes, commonly called "CLE" or Mandatory (or Minimum) CLE ("MCLE"). Lawyers are losing their licenses for failure to attend these classes.[17] Because of the legitimate state interests in a capable and skilled bar, legal chal-

---

[12]Rule 5.1.

[13]Rule 1.1, Comment 2. DR 6-101(A)(1).

[14]Rule 1.5(e)(2); EC 2-22, 6-3. *Cf.* Rule 1.2(a). *See also* Restatement of the Law Governing Lawyers, Third, § 11 ("Fee-Splitting with Lawyers Not in Same Firm") (Official Final Draft 2000).

See Susan Martyn, *Informed Consent in the Practice of Law*, 48 Geo. Wash. L. Rev. 307 (1980).

[15]Rule 1.1, Comment 6. EC 6-2. The drafters of the 2002 Model Rules expanded the language in the Comment to include three obligations: "keep abreast of changes in the law and its practice, engage in continuing study and education and comply with

all continuing legal education requirements to which the lawyer is subject." Rule 1.1, Comment 6.

[16]*See People v. Ngo*, 14 Cal.4th 30, 36, 57 Cal.Rptr.2d 456, 460, 924 P.2d 97, 101 (1996).

[17]*E.g., In re Yamagiwa*, 97 Wash.2d 773, 650 P.2d 203 (1982) (respondent suspended for failure to comply with Continuing Legal Education (CLE) requirements; later disbarred); *In re Smith*, 189 Ariz. 144, 939 P.2d 422 (1997) (failure to comply with continuing legal education requirements warranted summary suspension).

As of 1998, 40 states had Mandatory Continuing Legal Education. N.Y. State Bar Association, Comparison of the Features of Manda-

lenges to the constitutionality of these programs are unsuccessful.[18] Lawyers must comply with the applicable continuing legal education requirements.[19]

§ 1.1-1(c) Competence in an Emergency

Because "competence" is a function of reasonableness, a different standard of competence applies in an emergency. A lawyer in such cases may give advice reasonably necessary in the circumstances "where referral to or consultation with another lawyer would be impractical."[20] However, the lawyer should limit the legal services provided to those necessary in light of the emergency circumstances. Essentially, the emergency exception to the duty of competence requires that the lawyer enter a limited engagement with the client to protect the interests of the client caused by the emergency.[21]

§ 1.1-1(d) Competence When Handling an Excessive Workload

A lawyer must provide competent and diligent representation regardless of the lawyer's workload. And, to the extent that the lawyer's workload begins to interfere with the lawyer's competent and diligent representation of existing clients, the lawyer must

---

tory Continuing Legal Education Rules in Effect as of July 1998 (1998), *at* 4–8 The ABA Web site http://www.abanet. org/cle/mclemap.html offers a map showing which states have MCLE, their specific requirements, and contact information.

[18]*See, e.g., Verner v. State of Colorado*, 533 F.Supp. 1109 (D.Colo. 1982), *aff'd*, 716 F.2d 1352 (10th Cir. 1983), holding that a Colorado rule requiring practicing attorneys and judges to complete a specified amount of continuing legal education was not irrational and therefore did not violate the substantive or procedural due process guarantees or the First Amendment or equal protection because the state has a substantial interest in regulating continuing practice of law within its borders.

In re Smith, 189 Ariz. 144, 939 P.2d 422 (1997), holding that imposition of continuing legal education requirements did not violate due process clause; that the evidence supported the finding that the attorney's ill health did not prevent him from complying with education require-

ments; and the continuing legal education rules did not violate the equal protection clause.

Warden v. State Bar of California, 21 Cal.4th 628, 982 P.2d 154, 88 Cal.Rptr.2d 283 (1999), *cert. denied*, 529 U.S. 1020, 120 S.Ct. 1422, 146 L.Ed.2d 314 (2000), reversed a Court of Appeals decision that had invalidated mandatory CLE. The Court of Appeals had argued that the exemptions to the requirement of mandatory CLE were irrational. The California Supreme Court held that statutory line drawing is not for the courts, and even though the exemptions were debatable as a matter of policy, they were not discriminatory and had sufficient rational basis to be constitutional. The MCLE exemptions for retired judges, state officers and elected officials, and law professors did not violate equal protection.

[19]Rule 1.1, Comment 6.

[20]Rule 1.1, Comment 3.

[21]*See* Restatement of the Law Governing Lawyers, Third, § 19, Comment *c* (Official Draft 2000).

begin to decline new representations and/or seek help to properly represent the lawyer's clients.

In Formal Ethics Opinion 441, the ABA addressed the ethical obligations of lawyers who represent indigent criminal defendants and who have excessive caseloads.[22] Of course, the opinion refuses to adopt a lesser standard of competence, diligence, and communication when lawyers represent indigent criminal defendants. Because lawyers owe their primary obligations to existing clients, lawyer must control their caseloads to avoid undertaking a caseload that impairs their obligations of diligence and competence.[23] And, if the work required of the existing cases becomes so burdensome that the lawyer cannot properly discharge the duties of competence and diligence, the lawyer must work to obtain help or to reduce the workload so that the lawyer can meet his or her professional responsibilities to the existing clients.[24]

Opinion 441 addresses situations in which lawyers receive their indigent clients from courts and from supervisors in public defender offices. A lawyer with an excessive caseload from court appointments may ask "the court to refrain from assigning the lawyer any new cases until such time as the lawyer's caseload has been reduced to a level that she is able to accept new cases and provide competent legal representation."[25]

A lawyer with an excessive caseload of assignments from a supervising lawyer in a public defender office must inform the supervising lawyer of the problem and seek relief. Such relief may include asking the supervisor for help with managerial responsibilities not related to the representation of clients or for help with discharging the office's duties to the existing clients. If the supervising lawyer fails to provide relief, the lawyer with the excessive caseload must go up the chain of command within the office, including up to the board of directors of the public defender institution. If such efforts fail, the lawyer may seek relief from the courts by seeking to withdraw from a sufficient number of representations to permit the lawyer to discharge her obligations to the remaining clients.[26]

---

[22]ABA Formal Opinion 441 (May 13, 2006).

[23]ABA Formal Opinion 441 (May 13, 2006). And, a lawyer should not accept new cases that require the lawyer to withdraw from existing clients.

[24]This may include filing a motion with the court to withdraw from existing cases, after properly notifying the client. ABA Formal Opinion 441, at n.15 (May 13, 2006).

[25]ABA Formal Opinion 441 (May 13, 2006).

[26]If the court refuses to allow the lawyer to withdraw from the representations, the lawyer must continue to represent the clients to the best of his

§ 1.1–2 MALPRACTICE AND COMPETENCE

§ 1.1–2(a) Waiver of Competence Not Normally Permitted

Clients can waive a lot of rights, but the ethics rules do not permit the client to waive the lawyer's duty of competence.[1]

It is sometimes said that all rules have an exception. The rule regarding competence also has an exception: sometimes a client may waive his or her right to competent representation *if* the client is separately represented at the time of the waiver decision by an independent lawyer. In general, a lawyer may not ask the client to agree to incompetent representation; however (assuming other law permits), the lawyer may make an agreement "prospectively limiting the lawyer's liability to a client for malpractice" *if* the client "is independently represented in making the agreement. . . ."[2] The rationale is easy enough to explain: if the client is independently represented in making the decision to waive malpractice liability prospectively, there is no danger of overreaching. The Model Code did not provide for this exception, but it is a logical rule and the Model Rules adopt it. This issue is discussed in more detail in connection with Rule 1.8(h).

§ 1.1–2(b) Imputed Liability for Malpractice

The restriction on the lawyer's ability to reduce his malpractice liability is limited to cases regarding his "personal malpractice."[3] Thus, a lawyer in a professional legal corporation may limit his *imputed* liability for the malpractice of his associates, *if* other law permits, *i.e.*, if a statute or regulation or provision other than the ethics rules permits the lawyer to limit his imputed liability.[4] In other words, the ethics rules, on their own, do not make it necessary for a lawyer to assume vicarious liability. Other laws, such as the law of torts or the law governing professional legal corporations, impose that liability in various circumstances.

---

ability. ABA Formal Opinion 441 (May 13, 2006).

[Section 1.1–2]

[1] Rule 1.2, Comment 5.

The Disciplinary Rules also explicitly prohibited the lawyer from attempting "to exonerate himself from or limit his liability to his client for his personal malpractice." DR 6-102(A).

[2] Rule 1.8(h).

[3] DR 6-102(A).

[4] EC 6-6. ABA Formal Opinion 96-401 (Aug. 2, 1996).

CHAPTER 1.2
SCOPE OF REPRESENTATION AND ALLOCATION OF AUTHORITY BETWEEN CLIENT AND LAWYER

RULE 1.2: SCOPE OF REPRESENTATION AND ALLOCATION OF AUTHORITY BETWEEN CLIENT AND LAWYER

(a) Subject to paragraphs (c) and (d), a lawyer shall abide by a client's decisions concerning the objectives of representation and, as required by Rule 1.4, shall consult with the client as to the means by which they are to be pursued. A lawyer may take such action on behalf of the client as is impliedly authorized to carry out the representation. A lawyer shall abide by a client's decision whether to settle a matter. In a criminal case, the lawyer shall abide by the client's decision, after consultation with the lawyer, as to a plea to be entered, whether to waive jury trial and whether the client will testify.

(b) A lawyer's representation of a client, including representation by appointment, does not constitute an endorsement of the client's political, economic, social or moral views or activities.

(c) A lawyer may limit the scope of the representation if the limitation is reasonable under the circumstances and the client gives informed consent.

(d) A lawyer shall not counsel a client to engage, or assist a client, in conduct that the lawyer knows is criminal or fraudulent, but a lawyer may discuss the legal consequences of any proposed course of conduct with a client and may counsel or assist a client to make a good faith effort to determine the validity, scope, meaning or application of the law.

Comment

Allocation of Authority between Client and Lawyer

[1] Paragraph (a) confers upon the client the ultimate authority to determine the purposes to be served by legal representation, within the limits imposed by law and the lawyer's professional obligations. The decisions specified in paragraph (a), such as whether to settle a civil matter, must also be made by the client. See Rule 1.4(a)(1) for the lawyer's duty to communicate with the client about such decisions. With respect to the means by which the client's objectives are to be pursued, the lawyer shall consult with the client as required by Rule 1.4(a)(2) and may take such action as is impliedly authorized to carry out the representation.

[2] On occasion, however, a lawyer and a client may disagree about the means to be used to accomplish the client's objectives. Clients normally defer to the special knowledge and skill of their lawyer with respect to the means to be used to accomplish their objectives, particularly with respect to technical, legal and tactical matters. Conversely, lawyers usually defer to the client regarding such questions as the expense to be incurred and concern for third persons who might be adversely affected. Because of the varied nature of the matters about which a lawyer and client might disagree and because the actions in question may implicate the interests of a tribunal or other persons, this Rule does not prescribe how such disagreements are to be resolved. Other law, however, may be applicable and should be consulted by the lawyer. The lawyer should also consult with the client and seek a mutually acceptable resolution of the disagreement. If such efforts are unavailing and the lawyer has a fundamental disagreement with the client, the lawyer may withdraw from the representation. See Rule 1.16(b)(4). Conversely, the client may resolve the disagreement by discharging the lawyer. See Rule 1.16(a)(3).

[3] At the outset of a representation, the client may authorize the lawyer to take specific action on the client's behalf without further consultation. Absent a material change in circumstances and subject to Rule 1.4, a lawyer may rely on such an advance authorization. The client may, however, revoke such authority at any time.

[4] In a case in which the client appears to be suffering diminished capacity, the lawyer's duty to abide by the client's decisions is to be guided by reference to Rule 1.14.

Independence from Client's Views or Activities

[5] Legal representation should not be denied to people who are unable to afford legal services, or whose cause is controversial or the subject of popular disapproval. By the same token, representing a client does not constitute approval of the client's views or activities.

Agreements Limiting Scope of Representation

[6] The scope of services to be provided by a lawyer may be limited by agreement with the client or by the terms under which the lawyer's services are made available to the client. When a lawyer has been retained by an insurer to represent an insured, for

example, the representation may be limited to matters related to the insurance coverage. A limited representation may be appropriate because the client has limited objectives for the representation. In addition, the terms upon which representation is undertaken may exclude specific means that might otherwise be used to accomplish the client's objectives. Such limitations may exclude actions that the client thinks are too costly or that the lawyer regards as repugnant or imprudent.

[7] Although this Rule affords the lawyer and client substantial latitude to limit the representation, the limitation must be reasonable under the circumstances. If, for example, a client's objective is limited to securing general information about the law the client needs in order to handle a common and typically uncomplicated legal problem, the lawyer and client may agree that the lawyer's services will be limited to a brief telephone consultation. Such a limitation, however, would not be reasonable if the time allotted was not sufficient to yield advice upon which the client could rely. Although an agreement for a limited representation does not exempt a lawyer from the duty to provide competent representation, the limitation is a factor to be considered when determining the legal knowledge, skill, thoroughness and preparation reasonably necessary for the representation. See Rule 1.1.

[8] All agreements concerning a lawyer's representation of a client must accord with the Rules of Professional Conduct and other law. See, e.g., Rules 1.1, 1.8 and 5.6.

Criminal, Fraudulent and Prohibited Transactions

[9] Paragraph (d) prohibits a lawyer from knowingly counseling or assisting a client to commit a crime or fraud. This prohibition, however, does not preclude the lawyer from giving an honest opinion about the actual consequences that appear likely to result from a client's conduct. Nor does the fact that a client uses advice in a course of action that is criminal or fraudulent of itself make a lawyer a party to the course of action. There is a critical distinction between presenting an analysis of legal aspects of questionable conduct and recommending the means by which a crime or fraud might be committed with impunity.

[10] When the client's course of action has already begun and is continuing, the lawyer's responsibility is especially delicate. The lawyer is required to avoid assisting the client, for example, by drafting or delivering documents that the lawyer knows are fraudulent or by suggesting how the wrongdoing might be concealed. A lawyer may not continue assisting a client in conduct that the lawyer originally supposed was legally proper but then discovers is criminal or fraudulent. The lawyer must, therefore, withdraw from the representation of the client in the matter. See Rule 1.16(a). In some cases, withdrawal alone might be insufficient. It may be necessary for the lawyer to give notice of the fact of withdrawal and to disaffirm any opinion, document, affirmation or the like. See Rule 4.1.

[11] Where the client is a fiduciary, the lawyer may be charged with special obligations in dealings with a beneficiary.

[12] Paragraph (d) applies whether or not the defrauded party is a

party to the transaction. Hence, a lawyer must not participate in a transaction to effectuate criminal or fraudulent avoidance of tax liability. Paragraph (d) does not preclude undertaking a criminal defense incident to a general retainer for legal services to a lawful enterprise. The last clause of paragraph (d) recognizes that determining the validity or interpretation of a statute or regulation may require a course of action involving disobedience of the statute or regulation or of the interpretation placed upon it by governmental authorities.

[13] If a lawyer comes to know or reasonably should know that a client expects assistance not permitted by the Rules of Professional Conduct or other law or if the lawyer intends to act contrary to the client's instructions, the lawyer must consult with the client regarding the limitations on the lawyer's conduct. See Rule 1.4(a)(5).

Authors' 1983 Model Rules Comparison

The drafters of the 2002 Rules added "and Allocation of Authority Between Client and Lawyer" to the title of Rule 1.2. Many of the changes made in the 2002 revision are elaborations of the 1983 Rule 1.2.

In Rule 1.2(a), the drafters moved the "subject to paragraph (c) and (d)" language to the beginning of the first sentence of the Rule rather than its former place at the end of the first sentence. The drafters also added a reference to Rule 1.4 and a sentence about actions by the lawyer that are impliedly authorized to carry out the representation. They believed that the lack of language about implied authority in Rule 1.2(a) was a major flaw in the manner in which lawyers operate. The drafters also edited the language about a lawyer abiding by the client's decision to accept a settlement offer to the more direct phrase, whether to "settle a matter."

The drafters made no changes to sections (b) and (d) of Rule 1.2.

In Rule 1.2(c), the drafters modified the 1983 version of this section in three ways. First, they changed "consent after consultation" to "gives informed consent." Second, they changed the word "objectives" to "scope" of the representation. The 1983 Rule improperly used the word "objectives" of the representation. Finally, the drafters added the phrase, "if the limitation is reasonable" to the text of the Rule. This had been implied through language in the Comments, but it needed to be stated in the text of the Rule.

The drafters deleted Rule 1.2(e) and moved it to Rule 1.4(a)(5) because they thought a lawyer's obligation to inform the client about limitations imposed on the lawyer's conduct by law or the Rules should be a duty of communication.

The drafters of the 2002 Rules substantially modified the Comments to Rule 1.2. *See* Reporter's Explanation of Changes to Model Rule 1.2. In Comments 1 through 4, the drafters created a new title "Allocation of Authority between Client and Lawyer" and modified old Comments 1 and 2 to fit within this category. 1983 Comment 1 is now included in new Comment 1 and 1983 Comment 2 is included in Comment 4. Comments 2 and 3 are completely new.

1983 Comment 3 is now Comment 5 and 1983 Comment 4 has been modified and included as Comment 6.

Comments 7 and 8 are new and 1983 Comments 5 though 9 are

modified and included as Comments 9 through 12. The drafters added a new Comment 13.

Model Code Comparison

[1] Paragraph (a) has no counterpart in the Disciplinary Rules of the Model Code. EC 7-7 stated: "In certain areas of legal representation not affecting the merits of the cause or substantially prejudicing the rights of a client, a lawyer is entitled to make decisions on his own. But otherwise the authority to make decisions is exclusively that of the client. . . ." EC 7-8 stated that "[I]n the final analysis, however, the . . . decision whether to forego legally available objectives or methods because of nonlegal factors is ultimately for the client. . . . In the event that the client in a nonadjudicatory matter insists upon a course of conduct that is contrary to the judgment and advice of the lawyer but not prohibited by Disciplinary Rules, the lawyer may withdraw from the employment." DR 7-101(A)(1) provided that a lawyer "shall not intentionally . . . fail to seek the lawful objectives of his client through reasonably available means permitted by law. . . . A lawyer does not violate this Disciplinary Rule, however, by . . . avoiding offensive tactics. . . ."

[2] Paragraph (b) has no counterpart in the Model Code.

[3] With regard to paragraph (c), DR 7-101(B)(1) provided that a lawyer may, "where permissible, exercise his professional judgment to waive or fail to assert a right or position of his client."

[4] With regard to paragraph (d), DR 7-102(A)(7) provided that a lawyer shall not "counsel or assist his client in conduct that the lawyer knows to be illegal or fraudulent." DR 7-102(A)(6) provided that a lawyer shall not "participate in the creation or preservation of evidence when he knows or it is obvious that the evidence is false." DR 7-106 provided that a lawyer shall not "advise his client to disregard a standing rule of a tribunal or a ruling of a tribunal . . . but he may take appropriate steps in good faith to test the validity of such rule or ruling." EC 7-5 stated that a lawyer "should never encourage or aid his client to commit criminal acts or counsel his client on how to violate the law and avoid punishment therefor."

[5] With regard to paragraph (c), DR 2-110(C)(1)(c) provided that a lawyer may withdraw from representation if a client "insists" that the lawyer engage in "conduct that is illegal or that is prohibited under the Disciplinary Rules." DR 9-101(C) provided that "a lawyer shall not state or imply that he is able to influence improperly . . . any tribunal, legislative body or public official."

§ 1.2–1 THE CREATION OF THE ATTORNEY-CLIENT RELATIONSHIP

§ 1.2–1(a) Forming the Attorney-Client Relationship

The attorney-client relationship is a special type of contract because of the fiduciary relationship between the lawyer and her client. The lawyer, who becomes the agent of the client,[1] has special responsibilities that are not imposed on the client. There are three basic ways that the attorney-client relationship may commence.

FIRST, the prospective client manifests to the lawyer the intent to retain the lawyer, who agrees to the proposal.[2]

SECOND, the prospective client manifests to the lawyer the intent to retain the lawyer and the lawyer fails to manifest a lack of intent to be so retained *under circumstances where it would be reasonable* to do so.[3]

[Section 1.2–1]

[1] Restatement of the Law Governing Lawyers, Third, §§ 14 to 19 (Official Draft 2000).

[2] Restatement of the Law Governing Lawyers, Third, § 14(1)(b) (Official Draft 2000).

Use of Expert Witnesses to Determine the Existence of an Attorney-Client Relationship. *Crystal Homes, Inc. v. Radetsky*, 895 P.2d 1179, 1182-83 (Colo. App. 1995). The earlier relationship between the corporate client and the lawyer raised the question whether a duty existed years later in a transaction unrelated to original representation. The court required expert testimony on this issue, given the facts of the case:

"A confidential relationship giving rise to fiduciary duties may be established under certain circumstances when one party has reposed special trust or justifiable confidence in the other and that confidence is invited, accepted, or undertaken by the other. However, the foundation for any confidential or fiduciary relationship asserted here was necessarily based upon the alleged attorney-client status between the parties. There is no other basis alleged for plaintiff's asserted justifiable reposition of special trust or confidence in defendant. And, the nature of any resulting special relationship and/or attendant duties arising therefrom thus would be measured against standards applicable to attorneys. Accordingly, the record supports the trial court's conclusion that an *expert opinion was required* to make a prima facie case on this theory as well." (emphasis added) (internal citations omitted).

Innes v. Howell Corp., 76 F.3d 702, 711-12 (6th Cir. 1996), on the other hand, did not require expert testimony.

"Although it is true that courts have uniformly recognized either the admissibility or necessity of expert testimony in legal malpractice actions, there is no authority to support plaintiff's contention that expert testimony is necessary to prove the existence of an attorney-client relationship. The case law makes clear that the purpose of expert testimony is to guide the jury as to the relevant standard of care in the profession, based on rules and codes of professional responsibility. The expert explains what the attorney's duties were to his client and what might constitute a breach of that duty. In other words, much like an expert in a medical malpractice case, the witness helps the jury understand a special professional standard of care that is different from the 'reasonable person' standard used in ordinary negligence cases. All of this necessarily occurs after it is settled that an existing lawyer-client relationship is in place. The expert witness does not testify as to whether the relationship has already been formed. Under Kentucky law, that is a simple question of contract formation. . . . A jury does not need an expert to tell it whether there has been mutual assent for a contract. Indeed, it would truly be unfortunate if specialized legal knowledge were required for reasonable laypersons to ascertain whether they are actually being represented by counsel."

[3] Modern interactions between consumers and professionals today pose many risks for lawyers. A law

For example, assume that the prospective client fears that his driver's license may be revoked. This person calls the lawyer's office and asks the lawyer to represent him in the revocation proceeding in 10 days. The prospective client knows that the lawyer often handles these types of cases. The lawyer's secretary tells him to mail the relevant papers concerning his case, and he does so. The secretary does not mention that the lawyer will not decide to take the case until later. The lawyer does not communicate to the prospective client until the day before the hearing, when the lawyer says that he will not take the case. The prospective client detrimentally relied on the lawyer by not seeking another lawyer when it would have been a lot easier to do so. In these circumstances, it would be reasonable for the trier of fact to conclude that an attorney-client relationship arose because the lawyer did not manifest a lack of intent to be hired by the client.[4]

THIRD, the attorney-client relationship may be formed when a

---

firm with a website needs to protect against the formation of unintended client relationships. *See* ABA Formal Op. 10-457 (Aug. 5, 2010). The law firm website needs to make it clear that no attorney-client relationship is formed until a written agreement is executed. It needs to warn the public against sending confidential information to the law firm or its lawyers. And, it needs to respond in a timely manner to inquiries from those seeking to form an attorney-client relationship.

[4]Restatement of the Law Governing Lawyers, Third, § 14(1)(b) (Official Draft 2000), and *id.* at Comment *e*, Illustration 2.

See also, e.g., Westinghouse Electric Corp. v. Kerr-McGee Corp., 580 F.2d 1311 (7th Cir.1978), *cert. denied*, 439 U.S. 955, 99 S.Ct. 353, 58 L.Ed.2d 346 (1978). In this case, lawyers for the American Petroleum Institute promised its members that information it gave to a law firm would be held confidential. Thus, each of the individual members of the American Petroleum Institute "entertained a reasonable belief that it was submitting confidential information regarding its involvement in the uranium industry to a law firm which had solicited the information upon a representation that the firm was acting in the undi-

vided interest of each company." 580 F.2d at 1320 nn. 15–17 & 1321. The court in *Westinghouse Electric* concluded that the law firm treated the lawyer for the Institute as also the lawyer for the individual members of the Institute.

In this situation, the *Westinghouse Electric* court stated: "Gulf, Kerr-McGee and Getty each entertained a reasonable belief that it was submitting *confidential information* regarding its involvement in the uranium industry to *a law firm which had solicited* the information upon a representation that the firm was acting in the *undivided* interest of *each* company." 580 F.2d at 1321 (emphasis added). The court was not treating each member of the American Petroleum Institute as a client of the law firm for all purposes. Rather, the court found that the law firm had information that was both *relevant* and *confidential*, and the law firm obtained this information after having promised to treat this information as confidential.

In *DeVaux v. American Home Assurance Co.*, 387 Mass. 814, 444 N.E.2d 355 (1983), the trier of fact could conclude that the attorney-client relationship was formed at the time the client wrote the law firm asking for help. This result was not changed by the fact that the lawyer's secretary misfiled the letter so that no lawyer

tribunal, acting within its authority, appoints a lawyer to handle a matter.[5] When a court appoints a lawyer, the target of the appointment may or may not consent to the representation. If the person consents to the court appointed representation, a traditional attorney-client relationship will arise and the obligations of the lawyer will be defined by the ethics rules. But if the person declines to be represented, a question arises as to the source for governing the relationship between the lawyer and the person who declines to be represented.

ABA Formal Opinion 07-448 addresses the question of what type of relationship is formed when the person, often a criminal defendant, declines to accept the court appointed representation.[6] The ABA holds that the source and guidance for the nature of the relationship is the court order appointing the lawyer, along with some other possible factual nuances. And, a person may accept a representation through acquiescence or implied actions. But if a person refuses to accept a representation, the ABA holds that there is no attorney-client representation. Of course, when a court appoints a lawyer as stand by counsel, the duties vary significantly from when the lawyer is appointed to conduct a full representation. "Any legal obligation owed by the lawyer to the defendant, which may be analogous to those embodied in the ethics rules, arises from the authority of the appointing tribunal and includes whatever obligations the tribunal may identify."[7]

In order for an attorney-client relationship to be formed, it is not necessary that the client pay or agree to pay any money.[8] Nor is it necessary that the client sign a written agreement.[9] Other rules governing lawyers may require that there be a written fee agreement,[10] but those rules are for the protection of the client, not the lawyer. The obligations of the lawyer and client are not symmetrical because the lawyer has fiduciary duties to the client.

§ 1.2–1(b) Rejecting Representation for the Wrong Reason

The lawyer is not like a cab driver waiting at a taxi stand. Although the cab driver must accept the next fare, the lawyer does not have to accept every client who walks through the door.

However, it can be improper for a lawyer to refuse a case for

---

ever saw it.

[5] Rule 6.2; Restatement of the Law Governing Lawyers, Third, § 14(2) (Official Draft 2000).

[6] *See* ABA Formal Op. 07-448 (Oct. 20, 2007).

[7] ABA Formal Op. 07-448 (Oct. 20, 2007).

[8] Rule 6.1(a). Restatement of the Law Governing Lawyers, Third, § 14 (Official Draft 2000), at Comment *c*.

[9] Restatement of the Law Governing Lawyers, Third, § 14 (Official Draft 2000), at Comment *c*.

[10] *See, e.g.*, Rule 1.5(b) ("preferably in writing"); Rule 1.5(c) ("contingent fee agreement shall be in writing").

the wrong reason. The Model Code made this point clearer than the Model Rules. To achieve the goal of making legal services fully available, the Code advised that a lawyer "should not lightly decline proffered employment," a principle that "requires" a lawyer to accept "his share of tendered employment which may be unattractive both to him and to the bar generally."[11] The Rules advise that a lawyer should not decline a court appointment merely because the client, or the client's cause, is unpopular[12] or because influential members of the community oppose the lawyer's involvement.[13] "*For good cause* a lawyer may seek to decline an appointment to represent a person who cannot afford to retain counsel or whose cause is unpopular."[14] The negative pregnant is that the lawyer must not otherwise decline such appointments.

In other situations, the rules governing the practice of law make it clear that the lawyer may accept certain cases. For example, a lawyer is not required to decline employment in a civil case merely because she does not believe that the case, though not frivolous, is likely to result in a decision in favor of her client. In a criminal case, she may defend the client whom she believes is guilty.[15]

In other cases, the ethics rules require the lawyer to reject employment. For example, a lawyer must refuse a case because she is too busy to give it competent attention.[16] A lawyer also must refuse a case if the client seeks to maintain a frivolous action or one brought only to harass another.[17] If the lawyer's personal feelings are so intense that her effective representation is impaired, then she must not take the case.[18] Thus, a lawyer may accept criminal defense work (a criminal rape charge) even though she believes that the client is guilty, but if her belief in her client's guilt is so strong, or she has other personal feelings that are so strong that she could not perform the work competently, she must not take the case.

§ 1.2–1(c) Representation of a Client Does Not Constitute Endorsement of the Client

A lawyer's representation of a client, including representation

---

[11] EC 2-26.

[12] Rule 6.2, Comment 1. *See also* EC 2-27.

[13] Rule 6.2, Comment 1. *See also* EC 2-28.

[14] Rule 6.2, Comment 2 (emphasis added).

[15] EC 2-29.

[16] Rule 1.1; Rule 6.2, Comment 2. EC 2-30; DR 6-101(A)(1).

[17] Rule 3.1. EC 2-30; DR 2-109(A); DR 7-102(A)(1).

[18] Rule 6.2(c) & Comment 2; EC 2-30. *See, e.g.,* Larry Cunningham, *Can a Catholic Lawyer Represent a Minor Seeking a Judicial Bypass for an Abortion? A Moral and Canon Law Analysis,* 44 CATHOLIC LEGAL STUDIES 379 (2005)(arguing that Catholics should not accept such representations).

by appointment, does not constitute an endorsement of the client's political, economic, social or moral views or activities.[19] The lawyer only represents a client in the lawyer's professional capacity. It is not necessary that the lawyer agree with, adopt, or support his or her client's views. "The obligation of loyalty to his client applies only to a lawyer in the discharge of his professional duties and implies no obligation to adopt a personal viewpoint favorable to the interests or desires of his client."[20] For instance, a lawyer who personally abhors cigarettes may still represent tobacco companies without taking up the smoking habit or defending smoking in his personal capacity, because "representing a client does not constitute approval of the client's views or activities."[21]

The Model Code specifically provided that a lawyer "may take positions on public issues and espouse legal reforms he favors without regard to the individual views of any client."[22] The general tenor of the Model Rules supports this principle. For example, the first sentence of Rule 6.4 states that a lawyer may be a director, officer, or member of a group involved in law reform activities "notwithstanding that the reform may affect the interests of a client of the lawyer." If there is no breach of loyalty when the lawyer is a member of an organization advocating law reform contrary to a client's interest—and Rule 6.4 tells us at least that much—, there should also be no breach of loyalty when the lawyer speaks out on his own behalf.[23] In both cases, the Code and Rules conclude that the benefits to clients are outweighed by the social costs that would exist if the conflicts rules were used to prohibit lawyers from exercising free speech and engaging in law reform efforts, either individually or through bar associations, legal service organizations, the A.C.L.U., and similar groups.

Granted, the client may not like the fact that the lawyer is publicly advocating law reform views contrary to the client's private interests. The client who is sufficiently upset may always fire the lawyer.[24] But the client may not properly charge that the lawyer acted unethically in taking the contrary position. This is an important distinction. If it were unethical for lawyers, in their private capacities, to engage in conduct that the client might not like, the lawyer's personal life would be severely restricted. But that is not the law; without being unethical, a lawyer representing Coca Cola can still drink Pepsi, and the criminal defense lawyer can continue to lobby the legislature for more severe crim-

---

[19]Rule 1.2(b).

[20]Rule 1.2(b). *Accord* EC 7-17.

[21]Rule 1.2, Comment 5. *See also* Rule 1.2(b).

[22]EC 7-17.

[23]*Cf.* EC 8-4.

[24]Rule 1.16(a)(3); DR 2-110(B)(4).

inal sanctions. Although the client can always fire his present lawyer and hire another lawyer, clients do not necessarily do so. The client may decide not to discharge the lawyer because good lawyers are not fungible. In other words, if one is a good enough lawyer, clients will forgive (or resign themselves to accepting) the lawyer's efforts to engage in free speech.

§ 1.2–1(d) Alleged Conflicts Between Legal Services Organizations and the Lawyer's Private Clients

For reasons of public policy, the ethics rules make it clear that it is not generally considered a conflict of interest for a lawyer to engage in pro bono activities. For example, a lawyer may participate in a legal services organization even though the legal services organization engages in actions that are adverse to the interests of the lawyer's private clients.[25]

In the typical fact situation, assume that Lawyer Alpha is a member of a private law firm and also serves as an officer, director, or member of a legal services agency. Assume that the agency represents clients who have interests adverse to the interests of the clients of Alpha. The relevant ethics rules treat the agency (but not Alpha) as having a lawyer-client relationship with its clients. Thus, as conceptual matter, Alpha is not representing the clients who are represented by the legal services organization. However, Alpha should not take part in any action or decision of the legal services organization if it would violate Alpha's duty to his private client, under Rule 1.7 (the basic ethics rule dealing with simultaneous representation of adverse interests) or if the decision or action would materially and adversely affect the client of the legal services organization.[26]

§ 1.2–1(e) Using Pro Bono Clients to Aid Private Clients

Even when the interests of the private client and the pro bono client are congruent, there still is an ethical issue if the lawyer tries to piggyback or leverage the views of the pro bono client without disclosing that he also secretly represents the private client on this issue. Or, the lawyer may be engaged in law reform activities in which he purports to have a personal belief (he is active in urging the local bar association to lobby to change a particular law) when in fact he is really representing an undisclosed, paying client.

---

[25]Model Rule 6.3, Comment 1:

"Lawyers should be encouraged to support and participate in legal service organizations. A lawyer who is an officer or a member of such an organization does not thereby have a client-lawyer relationship with persons served by the organization. However, there is potential conflict between the interests of such persons and the interests of the lawyer's clients. If the possibility of such conflict disqualified a lawyer from serving on the board of a legal services organization, the profession's involvement in such organizations would be severely curtailed."

[26]Rule 6.3(a) & (b).

The lawyer ethically should not purport to represent only a pro bono client's interests, or only her own personal interests, if she is also simultaneously representing a private client on the matter in question. If the attorney is really representing XYZ Corp., she may not pretend to be representing only her own views when advocating changes in the law or engaging in other pro bono activities. If the lawyer is representing a private client while appearing before a legislative committee and asking for law reform, the lawyer may not mislead the committee as to the true identity of the client.[27]

On the other hand, the lawyer is not disqualified from proposing law reform merely because she personally agrees with the particular law reform and her clients happen to share her personal views. Otherwise, a lawyer specializing in antitrust litigation might be regarded as disqualified from participating on a bar association committee charged with drafting proposed revisions of rules governing that subject.[28] There is no ethical requirement that law revision be in the hands of, and monopolized by, inexperienced lawyers who have never had a case in the subject matter area.

§ 1.2–2 ALLOCATION OF AUTHORITY BETWEEN CLIENT AND LAWYER

§ 1.2–2(a) The Division of Decision-Making Authority Between Lawyer and Client

In the middle of a trial, the lawyer cannot consult with her client on matters such as whether to object to a question that the other lawyer has asked on the grounds that it may violate the hearsay rules. By the time the lawyer explained the hearsay rule, its various exceptions, and the benefits and risks of presenting an objection, the opposing lawyer would have moved on to other witnesses and the particular question will have become ancient history. On the other hand, we expect that the client and not the lawyer will make the decision as to whether to plead guilty or innocent in a criminal prosecution.

The ethics rules therefore attempt to set forth basic guidelines to distinguish between those matters in which the lawyer must let the client make the decision and those in which prior client consent is unnecessary. As a general principle, the lawyer is entitled to make decisions in matters that do not affect the merits of the cause or substantially prejudice the client's rights, although, even in these cases, there may be situations where it would be prudent for the lawyer to confer with the client. In

---

[27]Rules 3.9 & 4.1(a); DR 7-106(B).   [28]Rule 6.4, Comment 1.

other situations, the client has the exclusive authority to make decisions.[1]

In general, it is the client (and not the lawyer) who has the authority to make major decisions—those affecting the merits of the case, or substantially prejudicing the client's rights. The lawyer is the agent (not the guardian) of the client, who is the principal (and not the ward of the lawyer).[2] The lawyer must abide by the "client's decisions concerning the objectives of representation. . . ."[3]

As the 1983 Rules candidly admitted, sometimes a "clear distinction . . . cannot be drawn."[4] Hence, the ethics rules use examples in an effort to illustrate the general rule and make it

---

[Section 1.2–2]

[1] Rule 1.2(a). EC 7-7. Restatement of the Law Governing Lawyers, Third, § 21 (Official Draft 2000). *See also* Restatement of the Law Governing Lawyers, Third, § 19 ("Agreements Limiting Client or Lawyer Duties") (Official Draft 2000), and § 21 ("Allocating the Authority to Decide Between Client and Lawyer"), and § 22 ("Authority Reserved to a Client"); § 23 ("Authority Reserved to a Lawyer").

[2] *See State v. Barley*, 240 N.C. 253, 81 S.E.2d 772 (1954); *Prate v. Freedman*, 583 F.2d 42, 48 (2d Cir. 1978).

[3] Rule 1.2(a).

In re Panel File No. 99-5, 607 N.W.2d 429 (Minn.2000) (per curiam) held that a lawyer's intentional failure to inform the opposing party of a settlement offer despite his client's clearly expressed wish that he do so warranted an admonition by the Lawyers Professional Responsibility Board. The client had directed the lawyer to present certain terms at a settlement conference, but the lawyer failed to do so. In fact, when the client later settled for less than the lawyer wanted to hold out for, the lawyer, said that, because the settlement was against his advice, he was no longer bound by the contingency fee contract [which would have given him $2,002.56], and instead billed the client on an hourly basis for $41,154.60. The court refused to adopt a *per se* rule that a lawyer must always offer the

settlement proposal the client directs because "an inflexible rule ignores the often extremely fluid nature of litigation and may put an attorney in the untenable position of communicating an offer that is clearly not in the client's best interest, or risk violating Rule 1.2(a)." *Id.* at 432. But, it said that in this case, the direction was so clear that the lawyer's only choice was to comply or withdraw. Justices Page and Lancaster, concurring, would have made absolute the duty to offer a client's settlement proposal.

In re Matter of Harshey, 740 N.E.2d 851 (Ind.2001) (per curiam) held that a lawyer's acceptance of a settlement offer that his client had earlier instructed him to reject warranted public reprimand. The lawyer represented a small corporation whose president was in the middle of a divorce. The lawyer had taken a contract case for the company on a contingent fee. Under the divorce decree, the president's wife would receive 45% of the net proceeds of the still-pending corporate litigation. When the lawyer told the president of a settlement offer, the president told him to turn it down. Instead, the lawyer went *ex parte* to the judge in the divorce case and got permission to settle the matter. The court reprimanded the lawyer for settling the case against a client's orders and revealing the confidential instructions to the other judge.

[4] 1983 Rule 1.2, Comment 1. This Comment was deleted from the 2002 Rules but this statement still remains

more concrete. The client decides whether or not to accept a settlement offer or to plead guilty.[5] In criminal cases, the client has the final say as to whether or not he will testify on his own behalf.[6] The client decides the *objectives* of the representation but the lawyer must consult with the client "as to the *means* by which they are pursued."[7]

The decision in *Linsk v. Linsk*[8] offers several helpful illustrations:

> [A]n attorney may refuse to call a witness even though his client desires that the witness testify; may abandon a defense he deems to be unmeritorious, may stipulate that the trial judge could view the premises, that a witness, if called, would give substantially the same testimony as a prior witness, and that the testimony of a witness in a prior trial be used in a later action; and he may waive the late filing of a complaint. On the other hand, an attorney may not, by virtue of his general authority over the conduct of the action, stipulate that his client's premises constituted an unsafe place to work where such a stipulation would dispose of the client's sole interest in the premises, nor may he stipulate to a matter that would eliminate an essential defense. He may not agree to the entry of a default judgment, or a summary judgment against his client, may not compromise his client's claim, or stipulate that only nominal damages may be awarded, and he cannot agree to an increase in the amount of the judgment against his client. Likewise, an attorney is without authority to waive findings so that no appeal can be prosecuted, or agree that a judgment may be made payable in gold coin rather than in legal tender. An attorney is also forbidden without authorization to stipulate that the opposing party's failure to comply with a statute would not be pleaded as a defense. . . .[9]

Examples of conduct that falls on one side or the other of a not-very-bright-line should not be regarded as negating all other instances. Thus, the Rules explicitly state that, in a criminal case, it is for the client to decide whether to waive a jury trial.[10] Even in a civil case, the attorney may not waive the client's jury trial right without securing the client consent, because the right to a jury is so significant.[11]

The ABA Standards Relating to the Administration of Criminal Justice, The Defense Function, generally advise that the "decisions on what witnesses to call, whether and how to conduct

---

true.

[5] Rule 1.2(a). EC 7-7.

[6] Rule 1.2(a). ABA Standards Relating to the Administration of Criminal Justice, The Defense Function, Standard 4-5.2(a)(iii).

[7] Rule 1.2(a) (emphasis added).

[8] *Linsk v. Linsk,* 70 Cal.2d 272, 74 Cal.Rptr. 544, 449 P.2d 760 (1969).

[9] 70 Cal.2d 272, 278–79, 74 Cal.Rptr. 544, 547–48, 449 P.2d 760, 763–64 (1969) (internal citations and paragraphing omitted).

[10] Rule 1.2(a).

[11] *See, e.g., Graves v. P.J. Taggares Co.,* 94 Wash.2d 298, 616 P.2d 1223 (1980).

cross-examination, what jurors to accept or strike, what trial motions should be made, and all other strategic and tactical decisions are the *exclusive province of the lawyer* after consultation with the client."[12]

However, there are important matters that fall outside of strategy or tactics. On these significant and central issues, such as the question of what plea to enter, or whether to accept a plea bargain, or waive a jury trial, to waive one's Fifth Amendment's right not to testify, or whether to appeal, the client should have the final say.[13] Similarly, the client has the final authority to decide to waive her constitutional right to speedy trial and thereby obtain a continuance.[14] Oddly enough, cases hold that the counsel has the ultimate authority to decide whether to object to the admission of evidence allegedly obtained in violation of the Fourth Amendment, even though the failure to object may result in the loss of a constitutional right.[15]

Guilty Pleas and the Insanity Defense. Notwithstanding the ethics rules that provide that it is up to the client to decide whether or not to plead guilty, there is, surprisingly, case law that says that the lawyer must plead the client not guilty by reason of insanity if that plea is available to the client. A reasonable, sane client would often choose to plead guilty instead of pleading not guilty by reason of insanity *if* the guilty plea would result in the client spending less time incarcerated than he would spend if found not guilty by reason of insanity.

Nonetheless, in *Overholser v. Lynch*,[16] the majority upheld a municipal court decision not allowing a defendant charged with

---

[12]ABA Standards Relating to the Administration of Criminal Justice, The Defense Function, Standard 4-5.2(b) (emphasis added).

[13]Rule 1.2(a). EC 7-7. ABA Standards Relating to the Administration of Criminal Justice, The Defense Function, Standard 4-5.2, Control and Direction of the Case (ABA, 1991). Restatement of the Law Governing Lawyers, Third §§ 21, 22 (Official Draft 2000).

[14]*Townsend v. Superior Court*, 15 Cal.3d 774, 126 Cal.Rptr. 251, 543 P.2d 619 (1975).

[15]*Wainwright v. Sykes*, 433 U.S. 72, 97 S.Ct. 2497, 53 L.Ed.2d 594 (1977) (Fifth Amendment, *Miranda* violation). *Henry v. Mississippi*, 379 U.S. 443, 85 S.Ct. 564, 13 L.Ed.2d 408 (1965) (Fourth Amendment, search and sei-

zure). In *Henry*, the Court characterized as "trial strategy" the defense counsel's decision not to object to the admission of certain testimony allegedly seized in violation of the Fourth Amendment.

See discussion in, 2 WAYNE R. LaFAVE & JEROLD H. ISRAEL, CRIMINAL PROCEDURE § 11.6, *"Counsel's Control over Defense Strategy"* (West Pub. Co., 2nd ed., 1984).

[16]*Overholser v. Lynch*, 288 F.2d 388 (D.C.Cir.1961), *reversed on other grounds*, 369 U.S. 705, 82 S.Ct. 1063, 8 L.Ed.2d 211 (1962).

This case was a habeas corpus proceeding testing the legality of Overholser's detention at a mental hospital. The trial judge, Joseph C. McGarraghy, ordered petitioner's release, and the hospital superintendent appealed. Judge Bastian, joined by

two violations of the D.C. bad check law to plead guilty. Lynch wrote checks in the amount of $50 each knowing that he did not have sufficient funds in his checking account to cover the amount. The trial judge had found Lynch not guilty by reason of insanity and ordered him committed to St. Elizabeth's Hospital. The D.C. Circuit agreed and held:

> [There is] almost a positive duty on the part of the trial judge not to impose a criminal sentence on a mentally ill person. In this case appellee had never before been convicted of a criminal offense and had previously served honorably as a commissioned officer in the armed forces. We suggest it would have been a plain abuse of discretion for the trial judge, in these circumstances, to allow a plea by which society would brand such a person with a criminal record. Appellee argues that the plea of guilty had been carefully considered by competent counsel and by appellee, who had been judicially declared competent to stand trial and to assist in his own defense. We think that, for the reasons stated above, this decision was one which appellee and his counsel did not have an absolute right to make.[17]

The Supreme Court, on statutory grounds, reversed and did not decide the constitutional issues presented.[18] After the Supreme Court's decision, Lynch remained at St. Elizabeth's

---

judges Miller, Prettyman, Washington, Danaher & Burger (later Chief Justice), held that, when the psychiatrist's report on defendant's competency to stand trial on a bad check charge had included a statement that the defendant's crimes were the product of specified mental disease particularly affecting financial judgment, and that the defendant required further treatment to insure against repetition of the offenses, the court properly refused to accept the plea of guilty and proceeded to trial to determine that defendant was not guilty by reason of insanity, though the defendant had been judicially declared competent to stand trial and to assist in his own defense.

Judges Fahy, Edgerton, and Bazelon dissented.

[17] 288 F.2d 388, 393.

[18] *Lynch v. Overholser*, 369 U.S. 705, 82 S.Ct. 1063, 8 L.Ed.2d 211 (1962). Justice Harlan, J., concluded that the accused (who did not claim that he had been insane when the offenses were committed and who presented no evidence to support an ac-

quittal by reason of insanity) was not properly confined in hospital for mentally ill upon finding of trial judge that he was not guilty on the ground that he was insane at time of commission of offenses. Judgment of Court of Appeals reversed and case remanded to District Court for further proceedings: "we read § 24-301(d) as applicable only to a defendant acquitted on the ground of insanity who has affirmatively relied upon a defense of insanity, and not to one, like the petitioner, who has maintained that he was mentally responsible when the alleged offense was committed." 369 U.S. at 710, 82 S.Ct. at 1067 (footnote omitted).

Justice Clark dissented: "The Court should not, as I have said, rewrite a statute merely to escape upholding it against easily parried constitutional objections. I would uphold the statute. I shall not go into details, however, since the Court does not deal with the issue. In short, petitioner has no constitutional right to choose jail confinement instead of hospitalization." Justices Frankfurter and White took no part in the decision of this case.

without any hope of an early release. There he committed suicide.[19] The ethics rules contemplate that the defendant has the right to plead guilty.

To say that the client has the right to decide whether to waive a Fifth Amendment right not to testify does not mean that the lawyer must consult with the client before objecting to, or waiving any objection to, the admission of any other testimony. While the "various rulings are not entirely consistent,"[20] constitutional objections are often on a different level than many run of the mill objections to evidence. Lawyers do not always have the same discretion to waive their client's constitutional rights as they have to waive some other rights.

Lawyers also have a right (*i.e.*, the power) to grant reasonable requests of opposing counsel that do not prejudice the client's rights. The ethics rules authorize lawyers to grant "reasonable requests regarding court procedures, settings, continuances, waiver of procedural formalities, and similar matters which do not prejudice the rights of his client."[21] For example, assume that the defendant's attorney, while preparing an Answer to the Complaint, needs more time to complete some research, so he asks the plaintiff's attorney for a one week extension in the time allowed to file the Answer. The extension would not affect the merits of the case or prejudice plaintiff. The ethics rules grant the plaintiff no right to forbid plaintiff's attorney from granting this specific request.[22] The plaintiff may hate the defendant and therefore order his lawyer to grant no extensions, no matter how reasonable they might be, but the lawyer is acting ethically when he ignores this client's particular order.[23]

Lynch v. Overholser, 369 U.S. 705, 733, 82 S.Ct. 1063, 1079.

[19] After the Court's decision, the prosecutor indicated that he would proceed with a civil commitment against Lynch. Lynch, realizing that there would be no early release, committed suicide. Richard Arens, *Due Process and the Rights of the Mentally Ill: The Strange Case of Frederick Lynch*, 13 CATHOLIC U.L. REV. 3, 27–38 (1964). *See also* David Cohn, *Offensive Use of the Insanity Defense: Imposing The Insanity Defense Over The Defendant's Objection*, 15 HASTINGS CONST. L.Q. 295 (1988).

[20] WAYNE R. LaFAVE & JEROLD H. ISRAEL, 2 CRIMINAL PROCEDURE § 11.6, at 56 (West Pub. Co., 2d ed., 1984).

[21] Rule 1.3, Comment 1; DR 7-101(A)(1). *Accord* EC 7-38. 2 WAYNE R. LaFAVE & JEROLD H. ISRAEL, CRIMINAL PROCEDURE § 11.6 (West Pub. Co., 2d ed., 1984).

[22] Rule 1.2(a) & Comment 1. Rule 1.3, Comment 1. EC 7-38.

[23] The Restatement of the Law Governing Lawyers proposes an illustration that appears to contravene this principle. It postulates a situation where Plaintiff retains Lawyer to sue Defendant:

Lawyer and Plaintiff agree that Lawyer shall be free to cooperate with Opposing Counsel concerning timing of pretrial discovery and other non-substantive matters. Subsequently, Plaintiff directs Lawyer to violate a general assurance that Lawyer had

§ 1.2–2(b) Implied Authority to Conduct the Representation

The notion that a lawyer is impliedly authorized to take action to conduct the representation has always been assumed by lawyers and clients. When a client hires a lawyer to represent her in litigation, the lawyer is impliedly authorized to take actions, such as research, drafting documents in preparation for filing, entering an appearance, responding to requests for scheduling, etc. In the 1983 Model Rules, the confidentiality provision contained in text a reference to the fact that lawyers may disclose confidential information that they are impliedly authorized to disclose to carry out the representation.[24]

The drafters to the 2002 Rules added a line to Rule 1.2(a) stating that: "A lawyer may take such action on behalf of the client as is impliedly authorized to carry out the representation."[25] The Rule and Comment encourage lawyers to consult with clients as required by Rule 1.4 so that they can understand and give input into the means that the lawyer will use to accomplish the client's

---

given to Opposing Counsel. Lawyer does not believe that Plaintiff's instruction is contrary to professional rules or other law. Lawyer is permitted to withdraw from the case if Plaintiff persists. If the tribunal refuses to permit Lawyer to withdraw, *Lawyer must comply* with Plaintiff's instruction, unless the matter is one addressed in § 23 [a Restatement section dealing with "Authority Reserved to the Lawyer."].

Restatement of the Law Governing Lawyers, Third, § 21, Illustration 1 (Official Draft 2000).

This conclusion that Lawyer should not cooperate with Opposing Counsel concerning the timing of discovery appears contrary to Rule 1.2(a). The lawyer has responsibility for technical and tactical issues. Moreover, in the illustration, "Plaintiff directs Lawyer to violate a general assurance that Lawyer had given to Opposing Counsel." For Lawyer now to ignore this general assurance would be *misleading*, because Opposing Counsel is relying on the assurance. An "assurance," after all, is a promise, a warranty, a pledge, a guarantee.

The proviso in the Restatement illustration that asserts that "Lawyer does not believe that Plaintiff's in-

struction is contrary to professional rules or other law" is an assumption that appears to be directly contrary to fact, because the professional rules— such as Rule 1.2(a) (the client chooses the objectives but the lawyer is responsible for technical and tactical issues) and Rule 8.4(c)—forbid the lawyer from being deceitful. It would be deceitful for a lawyer to violate an assurance she gave opposing counsel. (The Reporter's Note indicates that the source for this illustration is not a court decision but another illustration drawn from the Restatement of the Law of Agency, Second § 385, Comment *a*, Illustration 2 (1958). *See* Restatement of the Law Governing Lawyers, Third, § 21 (Official Draft 2000), Reporter's Note to Comment *a*, at 179.) Instead of the advice that the Restatement recommends, Lawyer should abide by the assurance that she gave to Opposing Counsel. Plaintiff can always try to fire Lawyer, but the tribunal may not allow Lawyer to withdraw from the case if that would delay the litigation.

[24] 1983 Model Rule 1.6(a).

[25] Rule 1.2(a).

objective.[26] This explicit recognition of the notion of implied authorization to act arises from the agent-principal relationship that exists in an attorney-client relationship.

§ 1.2–2(c) Disagreements Between Clients and Lawyers

The 1983 Model Rules seemed to draft a sharper distinction in the comments to Rule 1.2 about the means and objective choices in an attorney-client relationship. Under 1983 Rule 1.2(a), the client set the objectives and the lawyer chose the appropriate means. The 1983 Comment stated:

> Both lawyer and client have authority and responsibility in the objectives and means of representation. The client has ultimate authority to determine the purposes to be served by legal representation, within the limits imposed by law and the lawyer's professional obligations. Within those limits, a client also has a right to consult with the lawyer about the means to be used in pursuing those objectives. At the same time, a lawyer is not required to pursue objectives or employ means simply because a client may wish that the lawyer do so. A clear distinction between objectives and means sometimes cannot be drawn, and in many cases the client-lawyer relationship partakes of a joint undertaking. In questions of means, the lawyer should assume responsibility for technical and legal tactical issues, but should defer to the client regarding such questions as the expense to be incurred and concern for third persons who might be adversely affected.[27]

Obviously, lawyers should preferably inform clients about the means that are to be used and to arrive at some accommodation to client requests, but this language gives lawyers control over the means by which to conduct the representation.

The drafters of the 2002 Model Rules deleted this language in the Comment and instead addressed the topic of lawyer client disagreements in a separate Comment. The 2002 Comment states that in some situations, clients and lawyers will disagree about the means that the lawyer should use to accomplish the client's objectives.[28] The drafters urge clients to defer to the expertise of their lawyers, especially on "technical, legal, and tactical matters."[29] And, lawyers should defer to client's decisions when the means implicate additional expense or adverse affect on third persons. However, the Comment states: "Because of the varied nature of the matters about which a lawyer and client might disagree and because the actions in question may implicate the interests of a tribunal or other persons, this Rule does not pre-

---

[26] Rule 1.2, Comment 1.

[27] 1983 Model Rule 1.2, Comment 1.

[28] Rule 1.2, Comment 2.

[29] Rule 1.2, Comment 2.

scribe how such disagreements are to be resolved."[30] Lawyers may look to other law to find an answer and they should always seek to reach a mutual agreement with the client. Note that an unresolved dispute over the means that a lawyer should use may rise to the level of a fundamental disagreement, and may lead to permissive withdrawal under Rule 1.16(b)(4) or to a client discharge of a lawyer that requires mandatory withdrawal under Rule 1.16(a)(3).[31]

The change in position from the 1983 language to the 2002 Comment was influenced by the Restatement provisions on allocation of authority between lawyer and client.[32] The Restatement adopts the view that a lawyer's conduct in setting the means of a representation affects the client's interests, and therefore clients should have control over means as well as objectives. Thus, ideally lawyers and clients should agree on the means by which the lawyer will seek to achieve the client's objectives. And, at the outset, there should be a presumption of broad authority for the lawyer. However, if the lawyer and the client disagree as to the means, the client's choice should be honored or the lawyer should consider terminating the representation.

§ 1.2–3 THE SCOPE OF REPRESENTATION

§ 1.2–3(a) Controlling the Scope of Representation Through Contract (Including Limited Legal Services)

Because the attorney is an agent of the client, the client has a great deal of power, within the law of contract, to change the division of lawyer-client responsibility and powers.[1] For example, the client may hire the lawyer only for a limited purpose.[2] Similarly, the lawyer may ask the client's permission to forego action that the lawyer believes is unjust, even though it is otherwise in the best interest of his client.[3]

The client's and lawyer's rights to control the scope of repre-

---

[30]Rule 1.2, Comment 2.

[31]Rule 1.2, Comment 2.

[32]*See* THOMAS D. MORGAN, LAWYER LAW 189 (ABA Center on Professional Responsibility, 2005). *See also* Restatement of Law Governing Lawyers, Third, § 21 (Allocating Authority to Decide Between Lawyer and Client), § 22 (Authority Reserved to a Client). § 23 (Authority Reserved to a Lawyer) (Official Draft 2000).

[Section 1.2–3]

[1]Many law firms use retainer agreements or engagement letters at the outset of a representation. However, law firms must be careful not to include language in such contracts that can lead to contractual liability. See Richmond, Engagement Letters as a Basis for Breach of Contract Claims Against Lawyers, 27 ABA/BNA Law. Man. Prof. Conduct 171 (Mar. 16, 2011) (examining the expansion of duties owed to clients and how such agreements can lead to the application of a longer statute of limitations).

[2]Rule 1.2, Comment 6.

[3]Rule 1.2(c); Rule 1.2 Comment 6 (limitations on representation "may exclude objectives or means that the lawyer regards as repugnant or impru-

sentation may not always be controlled by the lawyer's careful drafting of the retainer agreement or engagement letter. For example, the power to draft a specific contract (or retainer) between the lawyer and client may not be used to violate the ethical codes or other law. The lawyer may not ask the client to agree to representation so limited in scope as to violate the ethics rule requiring competence. Nor may the client, by contract, surrender the right to terminate the lawyer's services or the right to settle litigation that the lawyer might wish to continue.[4]

The drafters of the 2002 Rules amended the text of Rule 1.2(c) to require that any agreement between a lawyer and a client to limit the scope of the representation must be reasonable under the circumstances. For example, if a client asks a lawyer for a will, the lawyer may explain that he can provide several levels of estate planning service to this client. The client may seek a simple will for $500 with no consideration for tax consequences, a more tailored document and a simple trust for $1,000, or a complicated estate plan with a bypass trust for $5,000.

If the client asks for the $500 representation, this request involves a limitation on the scope of the services that the lawyer will provide to the client. However, for the lawyer to offer this limited service to the client, such a limitation must be reasonable under the circumstances. If the client is wealthy enough and her economic status is complicated so that it would be unreasonable for any lawyer to draft a simple will for a client with similar wealth, the lawyer may not limit his scope of representation in that way. This limit would also implicate a breach of the lawyer's duty of competence under Rule 1.1.

But the situation may make reasonable what would be unreasonable in other circumstances. For example, if this wealthy client had no will and was leaving the country for a month vacation later in the day, the lawyer, given this time frame, may draft a simple form will with an understanding that when the client returns, the lawyer will perform the more tailored service in light of the client's wealth.

The drafters of the 2002 Rules address the topic of limited legal services and scope of representation in the Comments.[5] If a client seeks advice over the telephone so that the client can handle the simple legal matter herself, the lawyer may be able to provide such a limited legal service. However, if the situation is so complicated that it cannot be properly explained in a telephone conversation and if it requires research, the lawyer may not limit the representation in that way. To do so would allow the lawyer

---

dent."). *See also* EC 7-9.

[4] Rule 1.2, Comment 8. Cf. DR

6-102(A).

[5] *See* Rule 1.2, Comment 7.

to limit his obligations of competence by using the limited scope provision.[6]

The lawyer may unbundle her services in an effort to reduce costs for the client. In some situations, the client may not be able to afford to hire a lawyer to undertake a complete representation in even a single matter. The lawyer-client contract may specify that the lawyer will only provide narrow, "unbundled" services. For example, the lawyer might provide forms to a limited-service "client," but not accompany the client to court. When the lawyer offers a broader array of limited services to a client, he allows the client to bargain for less and thereby pay for less. Limiting the scope of representation can serve clients by making the legal system more accessible to persons who otherwise would be completely pro se.[7] When this limitation is reasonable, then the law firm can use its clearly drafted engagement letter to defend itself from the client's allegations that the firm did not provide adequate legal representation.[8]

One additional issue in jurisdictions that permit unbundled services is the question whether a client must disclose to the court the identity of the lawyer participating in draft part of the

---

[6]The Comments also refer to Rules 1.8 and 5.6 as provisions that cannot be limited through Rule 1.2's limiting the scope of representation. Rule 1.2, Comment 8. See § 6.5-4, dealing with "Unbundled Legal Services Directed at Pro Se Clients and Persons of Limited Means."

[7]See, e.g., Amendments To Rules Regulating The Florida Bar and Florida Family Law Rules of Procedure (Unbundled Legal Services), 860 So. 2d 394 (Fla. 2003). These Rules involve situations where a lawyer does not undertake a complete representation of a client in even a single matter, but rather contracts to provide narrow "unbundled" services.

Such developments are not limited to Florida; see, e.g., proposed Virginia Rule 1.2(c): "A lawyer may assist in the preparation of pleadings or other filings in court on behalf of an unrepresented person." See also Brill and Sparko, Limited Legal Services and Conflicts of Interest, 16 Geo. J. Legal Ethics 553 (2003). See also N.C. State Bar Opinion 2005-10 (Jan. 20, 2006) (examining the issues that arise when unbundled legal services are delivered through the internet), noted

in 22 ABA/BNA Manual on Professional Conduct, Current Reports News 139 (Mar. 22, 2006); Tennessee S. Ct. Board of Prof. Resp., Formal Op. 2007-F-153 (Mar. 23, 2007) (a lawyer's limited legal services to an indigent pro se litigant in drafting an initial complaint do not need to be disclosed to the court; but, additional work would need to be disclosed), noted in 23 ABA/BNA Manual on Professional Conduct, Current Reports News 196 (Apr. 18, 2007). But c.f. Hale v. U.S. Trustee, 509 F.3d 1139 (9th Cir. 2007) (attorney who provided unbundled legal services that excluded "critical and necessary services" for bankruptcy clients without obtaining the clients' proper consent was fined, lost his fee, and had restrictions placed upon his future bankruptcy practice).

[8]SCB Diversified Mun. Portfolio v. Crews & Associates, 2012 WL 13708 (E.D. La. 2012). The court held that the client signed a clearly drafted engagement letter, and this letter provided a defense to the client's allegations that the law firm did not provide adequate legal representation. E.D.La., 2012.

filing for a pro se client. On one hand, courts may wish to encourage lawyer involvement in pro se briefs;[9] on another hand, courts may wish to know the names of lawyers responsible for the content of the filing.[10]

Although the traditional rule is that only the client can settle, the client can delegate this power to the lawyer, her agent. She may properly tell her lawyer: "Use your judgment as to whether or not to accept any settlement for at least $25,000." Though the client has the sole power to accept or reject settlements, she certainly may give actual authority to the attorney to act on her behalf.

Collaborative Law Practice in the Divorce Context. The collaborative law movement seeks to influence lawyering by encouraging clients and lawyers to suspend adversarialness and instead cooperate with opposing counsel and parties to reach an agreement through a series of negotiations and mediations.[11] In a few states, the legislatures have expressly enacted collaborative law statues authorizing this form of legal representation as an alternative to traditional divorce.[12] In other states, lawyers have suggested such practice methods to their clients and have sought to implement them through a limited representation agreement with the clients.[13] In most collaborative law representations, the divorcing couples are asked to sign a four party agreement with their lawyers with details about how the lawyers and clients will conduct themselves in the divorce.[14] In most states, if the collaborative law representation breaks apart, the lawyers who represented the clients in the alternative dispute resolution method may not represent the clients in the divorce litigation. The agreement essentially limits the scope of the representation

---

[9]*See, e.g.*, Utah State Bar Ethics Advisory Op. Comm., Op. 08-01 (Apr. 8, 2008), noted in 24 Law. Man. Prof. Conduct 265 (May 28, 2008). Contra, ABA Formal Op. 07-446 (May 7, 2007). This opinion approves of nondisclosure of the lawyer's assistance to the pro se litigant.

[10]*See, e.g., Duran v. Carris*, 238 F.3d 1268 (10th Cir. 2001) (requiring disclosure of substantial assistance to a pro se client).

[11]*See* Ted Schneyer, *The Organized Bar and the Collaborative Law Movement: A Study in Professional Change*, 50 Ariz. L. Rev. 289 (2008).

[12]*See* Cal. Fam. § 2013 (West 2007); N.C. Gen Stat. § 50-70 (2006); Tex Fam. Code Ann. § 6.603 (Vernon 2005). *See also* www.collablawtexas. com.

[13]*See* Pauline H. Tessler, *Collaborative law: A New Paradigm for Divorce Lawyers*, 5 Psychol. Pub. Pol'y & L. 967 (1999); Christopher M. Fairman, *Ethics and Collaborative Lawyering: Why Put Old Hats on New Heads?*, 18 Ohio St. J. on Disp. Resol. 505 (2003).

[14]This four party agreement is often referred to as a "four way" agreement.

for the lawyers and discloses the effect of such limitations on the traditional attorney-client relationship.[15]

In 2007, a Colorado ethics opinion held that lawyers may not participate in the "four way" agreement because it creates an impermissible conflict of interest.[16] This opinion called into question the use of collaborative law practice in all jurisdictions without a state statute authorizing such legal practice.[17] In response to the Colorado opinion, the ABA issued Formal Opinion 07-447 that expressly rejected the analysis of the Colorado opinion.[18] The ABA opinion holds that with appropriate, informed consent two clients may authorize their lawyers to sign a four way agreement that includes a requirement to withdraw if the collaborative process breaks apart. Essentially, the ABA has authorized the use of collaborative law practice as a form of limited representation under Rule 1.2(c).[19]

§ 1.2–3(b) Controlling the Client-Lawyer Representation by Terminating the Lawyer's Services

The lawyer or client may also affect the extent of client control by terminating the client-lawyer relationship. In other words, the client can always fire the lawyer, who then must withdraw, even if the client seeks to terminate the lawyer for a less than noble reason.[20] For example, if the client decides to fire the lawyer because the lawyer has hired an African-American law associate, the lawyer still has no right to prevent the client from terminating the representation. The client is obviously acting improperly, for a racist reason, but the ethics rules compel the lawyer to withdraw. Other law, such as civil rights laws, might impose sanctions on the client, but the rules of ethics require the lawyer to cease the representation because the client has fired him.

The lawyer, in turn, may withdraw from further representation if the client insists on pursuing an objective that is not ille-

---

[15]Rule 1.2(c).

[16]See Colorado Bar Ass'n Ethics Op. 115 (Feb. 24, 2007). The requirement that lawyers withdraw from the representation created the conflict of interest.

[17]If the state legislature authorizes clients to use lawyers in a collaborative law practice to obtain a divorce, the ethics rules of the state may not prohibit such representations.

[18]ABA Formal Op. 07-447 (Aug. 9, 2007) ("Ethics Considerations in Collaborative Law Practice").

[19]A Missouri ethics opinion authorizes its lawyers to practice collaborative law if they obtain written informed consent from all clients and the lawyers agree to place their individual client's interests first. See Missouri Supreme Court Advisory Comm., Formal Op. 124 (Aug. 20, 2008), noted in 24 ABA/BNA Law. Man. Prof. Conduct 488 (Sept. 17, 2008).

[20]Rule 1.16(a)(3); DR 2-110(B)(4).

gal, but that "the lawyer considers repugnant or imprudent,"[21] which is discussed below, in the analysis of Rule 1.16.

The ethics rules allow the attorney and client to agree that the attorney will present all nonfrivolous issues. In addition, as a matter of constitutional law, an indigent criminal defendant can compel his appointed counsel to press a nonfrivolous appeal.[22] However, the indigent client has no constitutional right to compel his appointed counsel to present a nonfrivolous *issue* on appeal if the appointed lawyer's professional judgment is to forego certain issues.[23] For example, the lawyer may decide that presenting one argument would undercut another argument that has a greater chance of success.

§ 1.2–4 COUNSELING OR ASSISTING THE CLIENT IN CRIMINAL OR TORTIOUS CONDUCT

§ 1.2–4(a) Introduction

The client's "ultimate authority to determine the purposes to be served by legal representation"[1] is limited by other law as well as by the ethics rules. Thus, the lawyer may not "*counsel* a client to engage, *or assist* a client, in conduct that the lawyer knows is criminal or fraudulent. . . ."[2]

Unfortunately, the Rules are not as clear as we would like in defining what is meant by the words "counsel" or "assist." Obviously, the lawyer may not drive the getaway car in his client's bank robbery, but can the lawyer advise the client that the criminal penalties for robbing a state bank are less than the penalties for robbing a federal bank, or that there is no extradition for bank robbery from a particular Latin American country?

In general, we say that the lawyer cannot advise (urge, suggest, propose, counsel, exhort) the client to break the law.[3] If the client has no privilege to engage in certain conduct, lawyers have

---

[21]Rule 1.16(b)(3). *Cf.* DR 2-110(C) (1)(a); DR 7-101(B)(2).

[22]*Anders v. California*, 386 U.S. 738, 87 S.Ct. 1396, 18 L.Ed.2d 493 (1967).

[23]*Jones v. Barnes*, 463 U.S. 745, 103 S.Ct. 3308, 77 L.Ed.2d 987 (1983).

[Section 1.2–4]

[1]Rule 1.2, Comment 1.

[2]Rule 1.2(d)(emphasis added).

See ABA Formal Opinion 98-412 (Sept. 9, 1998), at 2, n.1.

Although the Rules use the term "criminal or fraudulent," the Code used the broader term "illegal or fraud-

ulent." DR 7-102(A)(7). The Code's language was more vague and could even include violation of civil law, such as tortious conduct. *See* DR 7-102(A) (7); DR 7-102(A)(6).

[3]ABA Formal Opinion 98-412 (Sept. 9, 1998), concluded that a lawyer who discovers that his client has violated a court order prohibiting or limiting the transfer of assets *must* reveal that fact to the court if that is necessary to avoid—or to correct—a lawyer's affirmative representation to the court.

If the lawyer continues to represent the client, that may constitute assisting the client's fraud on the court

no privilege to assist the client to engage in that conduct.[4] The lawyer is an agent of the client, and it is a general principle of agency law that an agent has no defense in committing a tort simply because he was acting under orders of the principal.[5] If the actions of a nonlawyer in the same circumstances would make the nonlawyer civilly liable or give the nonlawyer a defense to such liability, the same activities by a lawyer in the same circumstances generally make the lawyer liable or give that lawyer a defense. However, the lawyer is not liable for simply advising the client whether some proposed action is lawful.[6]

There are three basic exceptions to the general rule that the lawyer will be civilly liable to a nonclient for assisting the client if the client is liable. Let us turn to those three areas and then consider in more general terms the question of tortious conduct.

§ 1.2–4(b) Defamation in the Course of Litigation

FIRST, the law does give the lawyer an absolute privilege under the law of defamation to publish defamatory material about a nonclient in communications preliminary to a proceeding before a tribunal, or as a part of such a proceeding in which the lawyer participates as counsel.[7] There are several rationales for this exception to the general rule of liability. Clients should have access to the courts and imposing the risks of liability on the lawyer in this circumstance would unduly impede that access. It is not unusual for lawyers inevitably to say bad things about the adverse party, and the courts are reluctant to create another suit collateral to the first one.

---

if the client's conduct destroys the court's ability to grant effective relief to the opposing party. If the lawyer withdraws, the lawyer's obligation is not fulfilled: the lawyer must make a disclosure sufficient to warn the court not to rely on the lawyer's prior representations that the lawyer now knows are false. *Id.*

[4] Restatement of the Law Governing Lawyers, Third, § 56 & Comment *c,* ("Advising and assisting acts of client") (Official Draft 2000).

[5] Restatement of the Law of Agency, Second, § 343 (1958). If the principal is privileged to engage in certain acts, then his agent shares that privilege when acting under this command. But if the principal is not privileged, then the agent has no privilege to share.

[6] *See* Restatement of the Law Governing Lawyers, Third, § 8 ("Lawyer Criminal Offenses") (Official Draft 2000).

Useful articles on these issues include, Geoffrey C. Hazard, Jr., *How Far May a Lawyer Go in Assisting a Client in Unlawful Conduct?*, 35 MIAMI L. REV. 669 (1981); Stephen L. Pepper, *Counseling at the Limits of the Law: An Exercise in the Jurisprudence and Ethics of Lawyering*, 104 YALE L.J. 1545 (1995); Bruce A. Green, *The Criminal Regulation of Lawyers*, 67 FORDHAM L. REV. 327 (1998).

[7] Restatement of the Law Governing Lawyers, Third, § 57(1) (Official Draft 2000).

§ 1.2–4(c) Malicious Prosecution in the Course of Litigation

SECOND, the lawyer assisting a client in a civil proceeding or in initiating a criminal proceeding is not liable to the nonclient for wrongful use of civil proceedings or for malicious prosecution if the lawyer acts primarily to aid the client in obtaining a proper adjudication of the client's claim.[8] The rationale is similar to the rationale for the defamation privilege: imposing on the lawyer a risk of civil liability here would unduly impede the client's access to the courts. However, the lawyer may be guilty of abuse of process if: (1) the lawyer instituted or continued a criminal prosecution against one who is not guilty, (2) that proceeding is terminated in favor of the accused, (3) the lawyer acts with an improper motive, and (4) the lawyer has no probable cause.[9]

§ 1.2–4(d) Advising Breach of Contract

THIRD, in the case of advising a client to breach a contract, the lawyer is not liable to a nonclient for advising his client as to whether proposed client conduct is lawful or for counseling his client to break a contract in the client's interest.[10] The rationale for this privilege is different. Contracting parties need advice and assistance, and it may be difficult to determine beforehand if an arguable refusal to perform will be found to be an actionable breach of contract. Furthermore, "even an actionable breach of contract may sometimes be defensible."[11]

The lawyer—without worrying about civil liability—may not only advise but may even assist a client's breach of contract, by, for example, "sending a letter stating the client's intention not to

---

[8]Restatement of the Law Governing Lawyers, Third, § 57(2) (Official Draft 2000).

[9]See, e.g., Voytko v. Ramada Inn, 445 F.Supp. 315 (D.N.J.1978), a federal civil rights case that upheld a cause of action against a private attorney who threatened a party with criminal prosecution, and assisted in filing charges. The attorney's associate also was the prosecutor, pursuant to a law that allowed private attorneys to prosecute criminal actions. This case met the four elements of malicious prosecution: [1] a criminal proceeding that the defendant instituted or continued against the plaintiff; [2] termination of that proceeding in favor of the accused; [3] absence of probable cause for the charge; and [4] "malice (which may be inferred from lack of probable cause) or primary purpose

other than bringing the offender to justice." 415 F.Supp. at 322.

See also Richard Schmidt, Milberg Weiss Agrees to Pay $50 Million to Settle Lexecon Case, WALL STREET JOURNAL, Apr. 14, 1999, at B17 (law firm, after losing jury verdict for $45 million for malicious prosecution, settled by wiring a check for $50 million before the jury could deliberate on punitive damages); Karen Donovan, Milberg Weiss' $50M Mistake, NATIONAL L. J., Apr. 26, 1999, at A1.

[10]Restatement of the Law Governing Lawyers, Third, § 57, at Comment g, at p. 434, ("Advising or assisting client to break a contract") (Official Draft 2000).

[11]Restatement of the Law Governing Lawyers, Third, § 57, at Comment g, at p. 434 (Official Draft 2000).

perform, or by negotiating and drafting a contract, with someone else that is inconsistent with the client's other contractual obligations."[12] These same principles apply "to advising or assisting a client to interfere with a contract or prospective contract or business relationship" with a party or to interfere with a contract or relationship between two nonclients.[13]

However, this rule of nonliability in tort only applies if the lawyer acts to protect the client's interests and does not use wrongful means.[14] For example, if the lawyer acts or advises his client "for the lawyer's own benefit," so "that the client will enter contractual relations with a business in which the lawyer owns an interest," then the lawyer will be subject to liability to a *nonclient* if the lawyer's actions satisfy the other requirements of tortious interference with contracts.[15]

Although it is often said that the lawyer should give advice with a "proper purpose," one should realize that a purpose is not improper simply because the lawyer advises her client to breach the contract in order to increase the lawyer's fees or her reputation.[16] Even if the lawyer's advice is negligent or harms the client, the lawyer still is not liable to the *nonclient*, if the lawyer

---

[12]Restatement of the Law Governing Lawyers, Third, § 57, at Comment *g* (Official Draft 2000).

[13]Restatement of the Law Governing Lawyers, Third, § 57, at Comment *g*, at p. 434 (Official Draft 2000).

But see Thomas D. Morgan & Robert W. Tuttle, *Legal Representation in a Pluralist Society*, 63 Geo. Wash. L. Rev. 984, 1021 (1995). The authors, after noting that the legal privilege of advising or assisting breach of contract "does not extend to breaches of fiduciary obligations (or other intentional torts)," argue: "Where breaches of contract come closer to the fiduciary analogy, the rationale behind the privilege for advising such breaches should become correspondingly weaker." *Id.* at 1022 (footnote omitted). They conclude:

"We believe that—except in cases that belong under the fiduciary paradigm—the lawyer should explain to her client the consequences of breaching a contractual obligation, both legal and economic (*e.g.*, reputational). While explaining the consequences of breach, however, the lawyer should maintain a normative perspec-

tive of respect for the contract as a legal obligation. Breach remains a choice for the client, but it is clearly a wrongful act that—*prima facie*—the morally sensitive lawyer may not encourage and may not thereafter assist." *Id.* at 1023.

[14]Restatement of the Law of Torts, Second, §§ 770(b) & Comment *b*, & § 772(b) (1965).

[15]Restatement of the Law Governing Lawyers, Third, § 57, at Comment *g*, at 434 (Official Draft 2000).

[16]*See, e.g., Los Angeles Airways, Inc. v. Davis*, 687 F.2d 321 (9th Cir. 1982). Plaintiff sued the lawyer and business advisor of a corporation for inducing the corporation to breach a contract for the purchase of the assets of plaintiff. The trial court granted summary judgment for the defendant and the Ninth Circuit affirmed. First, the lawyer-business advisor's conduct in inducing his corporation to breach its contract for the purchase of the assets of the other corporation was privileged. And, second, this lawyer-business manager did not lose his right to claim the privilege to induce a breach of contract because he was

gives the advice with a proper purpose.[17] Of course, the lawyer would be liable to her client for her negligence, but she would not be liable to the nonclient.

§ 1.2–4(e) Torts and Deceit

In general, the lawyer is not liable to a nonclient for a client's tort unless the lawyer assisted the client by conduct that is itself tortious, or if the lawyer gave "substantial assistance" to the client knowing that the client's conduct was tortious.[18] Because misrepresentation is simply "not part of proper legal assistance," lawyers are civilly liable to nonclients for fraudulent misrepresentation, even if they engage in such deceit in the course of litigation or advice.[19] For example, if a lawyer arranges to have her client's assets transferred to her in order to defraud the creditors of the client, the lawyer will be liable to the nonclient-creditors.[20]

Furthermore, lawyers may not close their eyes to the obvious in an effort to aid their client's deceits. For example, a lawyer is liable under the federal securities laws for providing an opinion letter based on facts that the lawyer knows are false. Even if the letter explicitly states that the lawyer was basing his opinion on an assumed set of facts that the client had supplied and that the lawyer had conducted no independent investigation, the lawyer will still be liable.[21]

Because welfare programs, such as Medicaid, require that

---

motivated in part by his desire to enhance his own position with his corporation.

[17]Restatement of the Law Governing Lawyers, Third, § 57, at Comment g, at 435 (Official Draft 2000).

[18]Restatement of the Law Governing Lawyers, Third, § 55, at Comment c, at 422 (Official Draft 2000).

[19]Restatement of the Law Governing Lawyers, Third, § 56, at Comment c, at 417 (Official Draft 2000). See also Rule 4.1, Rule 8.4(c).

[20]Stochastic Decisions, Inc. v. DiDomenico, 995 F.2d 1158 (2d Cir.1993), cert. denied, 510 U.S. 945, 114 S.Ct. 385, 126 L.Ed.2d 334 (1993).

The general rule is that lawyers may engage in "legally innocuous hyperbole," but not deceit. Restatement of the Law Governing Lawyers, Third, § 56, at Comment f, at p. 423 (Official Draft 2000).

[21]Kline v. First Western Gov't Sec., Inc., 24 F.3d 480 (3d Cir.1994), cert.

denied, sub nom., Arvey, Hodes, Costello & Burman v. Kline, 513 U.S. 1032, 115 S.Ct. 613, 130 L.Ed.2d 522 (1994).

See also Newburger, Loeb & Co. v. Gross, 563 F.2d 1057 (2d Cir.1977), cert. denied, 434 U.S. 1035, 98 S.Ct. 769, 54 L.Ed.2d 782 (1978) (lawyer participated in breach of fiduciary duties clients owed to partners by making bad-faith claims and issuing false opinion letter on legal issue); McElhanon v. Hing, 151 Ariz. 386, 728 P.2d 256 (Ariz.Ct.App.1985), aff'd in part & rev'd in part on other grounds, 151 Ariz. 403, 728 P.2d 273 (Ariz.1986) (lawyer not privileged against liability for assisting client by drafting document to execute transfer in fraud of judgment creditor when lawyer had knowledge of facts and intent to defraud); Faison v. Nationwide Mortgage Corp., 839 F.2d 680 (D.C.Cir.1987), cert. denied, 488 U.S. 823, 109 S.Ct. 70, 102 L.Ed.2d 46 (1988) (lawyer liable for helping clients make a fraudulent and unlawful loan by making

participants not be too rich, there are situations where an individual will sell assets in order to qualify for the program. Legislation to prevent this[22] was quickly nicknamed the "Granny Goes to Jail Act."[23] The provision was then briefly reinforced by § 4734 of the Balanced Budget Act of 1997, which also made it a crime to take a fee for counseling someone how to manipulate assets in prohibited ways. The New York Bar Association sued to enjoin enforcement of this law.[24] The Justice Department argued that an injunction was unnecessary because it had already notified Congress it would not enforce the provision. However, the court found that the existence of the statutory prohibition was enough to cause lawyers (who take an oath to abide by the law) to engage in self-censorship. The court granted a preliminary injunction.

Subsequently, Congress enacted that the Bankruptcy Abuse Prevention and Consumer Protection Act of 2005, a section of which prohibits any "debt relief agency" from advising clients "to incur more debt in contemplation" of filing for bankruptcy. Lawyers argued that it would be unconstitutional to allow the provision to prevent them from giving truthful legal advice. *Milavetz, Gallop & Milavetz, P.A. v. United States*,[25] read the law narrowly to avoid that constitutional problem. It held that lawyers are, in fact, "debt relief agencies," but the law only prohibits them from "advising an assisted person to incur more debt when the impelling reason for the advice is the anticipation

---

and helping arrange misrepresentations); *Norman v. Brown, Todd & Heyburn*, 693 F.Supp. 1259 (D.Mass. 1988) (lawyer would be liable for substantially assisting client's fraud by providing tax-shelter opinion letter and legal assistance, when lawyer knew or should have known of fraud); *Auriemma v. Montgomery*, 860 F.2d 273 (7th Cir.1988), *cert. denied*, 492 U.S. 906, 109 S.Ct. 3215, 106 L.Ed.2d 565 (1989) (lawyer would be liable under Fair Credit Reporting Act liability for using false pretenses to obtain credit report while investigating case); *Durant Software v. Herman*, 257 Cal.Rptr. 200 (Cal.Ct.App.1989), *appeal dismissed*, 272 Cal.Rptr. 612, 795 P.2d 782 (1990) (lawyer would be liable for conspiring with judgment-debtor client to defraud creditor by conveying assets to lawyer's firm); *Kimmel v. Goland*, 51 Cal.3d 202, 271 Cal.Rptr. 191, 793 P.2d 524 (Cal.1990) (lawyer would be liable for counseling and assisting client's unlawful record-

ing of conversations); *Ackerman v. Schwartz*, 947 F.2d 841 (7th Cir.1991) (lawyer would be liable for reckless misrepresentation in tax-shelter opinion letter for client's venture); *Dutton v. Wolpoff & Abramson*, 5 F.3d 649 (3d Cir.1993) (firm liable under Fair Debt Collection Practices Act for sending a debt-collection letter found to be misleading).

[22]See the 1996 Health Insurance Portability and Accountability Act, Section 217, 42 U.S.C.A. § 1320a-7b.

[23]Michael E. Sacks, *Elder Law In*, 9 PENNSYLVANIA LAW WEEKLY 1 (No. 9, Mar. 1, 1999, 1999 WLNR 8531713).

[24]*New York State Bar Association v. Reno*, 999 F. Supp. 710 (N.D.N.Y. 1998) (court enjoins the Attorney General's enforcement of the prohibition).

[25]*Milavetz, Gallop & Milavetz, P.A. v. United States, 559 U.S.__, 130 S.Ct. 1324, 176 L.Ed.2d 79 (2010).

CLIENT CRIMINAL OR TORTIOUS CONDUCT

of bankruptcy."[26] For example, a lawyer may advise a client to buy a car on credit when doing so will let the client work, even if the debtor later files for bankruptcy, because it was the hope of enhanced financial prospects, not the anticipated filing, that was the impelling cause of incurring further debt. The Court relied on ABA Model Rule 1.2(d). In short, the requirement that the lawyer not advise an assisted person to incur more debt in contemplation of such person filing for bankruptcy does not impede "full and frank" discussions between the lawyer and client.

§ 1.2–4(f) Other Issues

Assume that the client wishes to challenge the constitutionality of a law. The best way to challenge a law that forbids picketing in front of an abortion clinic, for example, is to engage in such picketing and then raise the constitutionality of the statute in defense of the criminal charge. The Rules specifically allow advice given in order to effectuate a good faith challenge to the constitutionality of the law. The lawyer "may counsel or assist a client to make a good faith effort to determine the validity, scope, meaning or application of the law."[27]

What if the law that may be violated is constitutional, but its violation invokes a very small penalty? Assume that a county law forbids operating a department store on Sundays. A client (who wants to keep his store open because a competing store, just across the county line, remains open) asks his lawyer for advice. May the lawyer advise that the penalty for a violation is a $100 fine, but the fine is not imposed on each sale? Instead, each day of violation is treated as only one violation, so that it will make economic sense for the department store to remain open as long as the profits for that day are in excess of $100. The client may react by assuring the lawyer that he will be open for business every Sunday, because his profits are over $3,000 a day.

Has the lawyer acted unethically, or is it significant that this violation of law (unlike the advice to escape to a country with no extradition treaty with the United States) is open and notorious? A bank robbery (unlike bank embezzlement) is also open and

---

[26]559 U.S. at __, 130 S.Ct. at 1337. For example—

"[A]wareness of the possibility of bankruptcy is insufficient to trigger § 526(a)(4)'s prohibition. Instead, that provision proscribes only advice to incur more debt that is *principally motivated* by that likelihood. Thus, advice to refinance a mortgage or purchase a reliable car prior to filing because doing so will reduce the debtor's interest rates or improve his ability to repay is

not prohibited, as the promise of enhanced financial prospects, rather than the anticipated filing, is the impelling cause. Advice to incur additional debt to buy groceries, pay medical bills, or make other purchases 'reasonably necessary for the support or maintenance of the debtor or a dependent of the debtor,' § 523(a)(2)(C)(ii)(II), is similarly permissible." (emphasis added).

[27]Rule 1.2(d).

125

notorious. On the other hand, both bank robbery and embezzlement are *malum in se* (illegal under the common law, or illegal in the nature of things), while a violation of the Sunday closing laws is considered *malum prohibitum*, (not illegal unless positive law makes it illegal).[28]

In general, the ethics rules provide no easy litmus test. We know that the lawyer may present an analysis of the legal aspects of questionable conduct but may not recommend "the means by which a crime or fraud might be committed with impunity."[29] The lawyer must give her "honest opinion" about the "actual consequences" of the client's acts.[30] The fact that the client uses such advice to aid his crime or fraud "does not, of itself, make a lawyer a party to the course of action."[31] However, (assuming that the ethics rules[32] or other law do not permit or require the lawyer to reveal this client information and to engage in whistle-blowing) the lawyer must avoid furthering her client's criminal or fraudulent purposes. The lawyer therefore may not suggest, for example, how the client might conceal his illegal purpose.[33]

If the lawyer later discovers that she has been unwittingly assisting the client in conduct that the lawyer now learns is criminal or fraudulent, then the lawyer must stop assisting the client now that she has learned what is really going on. But must the lawyer resign? The 1983 Model Rules raised the issue but did not resolve it. This provision only advised the lawyer, unhelpfully, that he *may* have to withdraw.[34] The drafters of the 2002 Rules resolved this problem by requiring the lawyer to withdraw from the representation.[35] If withdrawal is not enough to stop the fraud, the lawyer must do more; he or she must file a noisy notice

---

[28]Stephen L. Pepper, *Counseling at the Limits of the Law: An Exercise in the Jurisprudence and Ethics of Lawyering*, 104 YALE L.J. 1545, 1585 (1995) discusses this distinction but concludes: "Unfortunately, the *malum in se* characterization is itself both unclear and intimately connected to personal morality, and thus subject to great dispute and difference of opinion [and] does not provide clear or rulelike guidance, although it is more determinative and helpful than either distinction alone."

[29]Rule 1.2, Comment 9. *See* EC 7-5.

[30]Rule 1.2, Comment 9. *Accord* Rule 2.1, Comment 1.

[31]Rule 1.2, Comment 9.

[32]*See* Rule 4.1(b).

[33]Rule 1.2, Comment 10.

[34]1983 Model Rule 1.2, Comment 7.

[35]Rule 1.2, Comment 10: "A lawyer may not continue assisting a client in conduct that the lawyer originally supposed was legally proper but then discovers is criminal or fraudulent. The lawyer must therefore withdraw from the representation in the matter." (emphasis added). *See also* Rule 1.16(b)(2); DR 2-110(C)(1)(b).

ABA Formal Opinion 98-412 (Sept. 9, 1998), concluded that a lawyer who discovers that his client has violated a court order prohibiting or limiting the transfer of assets *must* reveal that fact to the court if that is necessary to avoid, or to correct, a lawyer's affirmative representation to the court. The lawyer must also dis-

of withdrawal. As the Comment now clearly states: "In some cases, withdrawal alone might be insufficient. It may be necessary for the lawyer to give notice of the fact of withdrawal and to disaffirm any opinion, document, affirmation or the like."[36]

If the lawyer learns that his client or a witness on behalf of his client has presented perjured testimony or false evidence before a tribunal,[37] the ethics rules impose an obligation of candor to the court, and the lawyer's duties are set forth in Rule 3.3, discussed below.

§ 1.2–5 LAWYER ADVICE AND THE FIRST AMENDMENT

Laws restricting the arguments that lawyers present to a court may raise constitutional problems, particularly regarding the First Amendment. In some cases, the government uses its spending power to regulate the speech of the lawyers that its pays. Those issues are considered later.[1]

In other cases, the government seeks to limit the arguments of lawyers who are not government employers or otherwise receiving federal funds. The leading case is *Holder v. Humanitarian Law Project*.[2] Most of this case deals with a ban on speech of third parties who sought to support lawful activities of organiza-

---

close the client's conduct or withdraw from continued representation in the litigation if withdrawal is necessary to avoid assisting the client's fraud on the court. *Id.*

If the lawyer continues to represent the client, that may be treated as assisting the client's fraud on the court if the client's conduct destroys the court's ability to grant effective relief to the opposing party. If the lawyer withdraws, the lawyer's obligation is not fulfilled: the lawyer must make a disclosure sufficient to warn the court not to rely on the lawyer's prior representation that the lawyer now knows are false. *Id.*

[36]Rule 1.2, Comment 10 (citing Rule 4.1).

[37]*See* Rule 3.3(b)("A lawyer who represents a client in an adjudicative proceeding and who knows that a person intends to act, is engaging or has engaged in criminal or fraudulent conduct related to the proceeding shall take reasonable remedial measures, including, if necessary, disclosure to the tribunal."). *See also* Rules 3.3(a)

(3), 3.3(c). Restatement of the Law Governing Lawyers, Third, § 67, ("Using or Disclosing Information to Prevent, Rectify, or Mitigate Substantial Financial Loss") (Official Draft 2000). Remember that state ethics rules often differ for the Model Rules on this issue. *See* THOMAS D. MORGAN & RONALD D. ROTUNDA, 2002 SELECTED STANDARDS ON PROFESSIONAL RESPONSIBILITY (Foundation Press, 2002), at Appendix A, Chart of Ethics Rules on Client Confidences.

[Section 1.2–5]

[1]*See* § 6.3–2 Constitutional Limitations on the Power of the Federal Government to Use Its Spending Power to Regulate Legal Services. This section discusses cases like *Legal Services Corp. v. Velazquez*, 531 U.S. 533, 121 S. Ct. 1043, 149 L. Ed. 2d 63 (2001).

[2]*Holder v. Humanitarian Law Project*, 561 U.S. ___, 130 S. Ct. 2705, 177 L. Ed. 2d 355 (2010). Knake, Attorney Advice and the First Amendment, 68 Wash. & Lee L. Rev. 639 (2011), discusses Holder as well as

tions designated as foreign terrorist organizations. At the end of this case, the Court and the dissent briefly discussed this ban as it relates to lawyers filing amicus briefs.

In *Humanitarian Law Project*, a federal stature authorized the Secretary of State to designate groups as foreign terrorist organizations. Another federal statute imposed criminal punishment on anyone who provides "material support or resources" to a foreign terrorist organization. Plaintiffs in this case included United States citizens and domestic organizations seeking to provide support for *lawful* activities of two organizations that the Secretary of State had designated as foreign terrorist organizations. Plaintiffs sought to enjoin enforcement of the criminal ban on providing material support to such organizations. The Court rejected their claim. This law, the Court held, did not interfere with free speech, even though it barred a lot more than sending money or supplies to a terrorist group.

The free speech issue before the Court was not whether the Government may prohibit pure political speech, or may prohibit material support in the form of conduct. It is instead whether the Government may prohibit what plaintiffs wanted to do—to provide material support to the two terrorist organizations in the form of speech.

Chief Justice Roberts's majority opinion in *Humanitarian Law Project* found that that the statute punished neither mere membership in a terrorist organization nor independent advocacy aimed at promoting public sympathy for a terrorist organization. Thus, the Court had no need to question the principles protecting the freedom of association that were established in earlier cases. Hence, there was no need for the Court to "address the resolution of more difficult cases that may arise under the statute in the future."

Humanitarian Law Project ruled that the statute punished giving any type of aid to foreign terrorist organization, *including speech* that taught the organization members how to use international law or how to obtain funding for nonviolent activities of the organization. The Court subjected the statute to strict scrutiny, because it involved content-based punishment of speech. Nevertheless, the Court upheld the law, because prohibiting giving of aid to terrorist organizations is narrowly tailored to promote a government interest "of the highest order."

The majority explained that even material support meant to

---

other related cases such as, *Milavetz, Gallop & Milavetz, P.A. v. U.S.*, 130 S. Ct. 1324, 176 L. Ed. 2d 79 (2010). For a discussion of *Milavetz, see supra*, § 1.2–4(e), Torts and Deceit. See also,

5 Ronald D. Rotunda & John E. Nowak, Treatise on Constitutional Law Substance and Procedure, § 20.15(f) (5th Ed., Thomson West 2010).

promote "peaceable, lawful, conduct" can further terrorism in various ways. For example, it "frees up other resources within the organization that may be put to violent ends." It also "helps lend legitimacy to foreign terrorist groups—legitimacy that makes it easier for those groups to persist, to recruit members, and to raise funds—all of which facilitate more terrorist attacks."[3] After all, terrorist organizations do not maintain organizational firewalls that prevent commingling of support. For example. Hamas muddies the "waters between its political activism, good works, and terrorist attacks," in order to use its overt political and charitable organizations as a financial and logistical support network for its terrorist operations.[4] Money is fungible, and whatever the plaintiffs do to help the terrorist organizations frees up resources for nefarious activities. Material support of a terrorist group's *lawful* activities "facilitates the group's ability to attract 'funds,' 'financing,' and 'goods' that will further its terrorist acts."[5]

The majority also upheld punishing a person for speech promoting public acceptance of the foreign terrorist organization *if* that person spoke was done in concert with, or at the direction of, the terrorist organization. Even these forms of assistance to a foreign terrorist organization would allow that terrorist organization to save resources that it would have otherwise spent on nonviolent activities and to use those resources for terrorist activities. The Court, however, did find a "natural stopping place" for the reach of this law that bans offering aid to a foreign terrorist organization's lawful activity:

> The statute reaches only material support *coordinated* with or under the direction of a designated foreign terrorist organization. *Independent* advocacy that might be viewed as promoting the group's legitimacy is not covered.[6]

Congress drafted this statute carefully to "cover only a narrow category of speech"—speech that is "under the direction of, or in coordination with foreign groups that the speaker knows to be terrorist organizations."[7] The statute bans "training," "expert advice or assistance." For example, if plaintiffs' speech to a terrorist group "imparts a 'specific skill' or communicates advice derived from 'specialized knowledge'—for example, training on the use of international law or advice on petitioning the United Nations—then it is barred. On the other hand, plaintiffs' speech is not barred if it imparts only general or unspecialized

---

[3]*Holder v. Humanitarian Law Project*, 561 U.S. ___, 130 S. Ct. 2705, 2725, 177 L. Ed. 2d 355 (2010).

[4]561 U.S. ___, ___, 130 S.Ct. at 2725, quoting affidavits that the Government submitted.

[5]561 U.S. ___, ___, 130 S.Ct. at 2726, n.6.

[6]561 U.S. ___, ___, 130 S.Ct. at 2726.

[7]561 U.S. ___, ___, 130 S.Ct. 2723 (footnote omitted).

knowledge."[8] The speech that the law bans is specialized speech that aids known terrorism and speech that is coordinated with known terrorists.

Justice Breyer, joined by Justices Ginsburg and Sotomayor, dissented. They claimed that the statute had "no natural stopping place," illustrated by the fact that Government, in oral argument, said that the statutory ban "prohibits a lawyer hired by a designated group from filing on behalf of that group *an amicus brief* before the United Nations or even before this Court."[9] The majority would uphold this application of the statute if the lawyer would be *coordinating* with or under the direction of a designated foreign terrorist organization. The statute would not bar *independent* advocacy.

---

[8]561 U.S. ___, ___, 130 S.Ct. 2724.

[9]130 S.Ct. 2736 (Breyer, J., dissenting) (emphasis added).

CHAPTER 1.3
DILIGENCE

RULE 1.3: DILIGENCE

A lawyer shall act with reasonable diligence and promptness in representing a client

Comment

[1] A lawyer should pursue a matter on behalf of a client despite opposition, obstruction or personal inconvenience to the lawyer, and take whatever lawful and ethical measures are required to vindicate a client's cause or endeavor. A lawyer must also act with commitment and dedication to the interests of the client and with zeal in advocacy upon the client's behalf. A lawyer is not bound, however, to press for every advantage that might be realized for a client. For example, a lawyer may have authority to exercise professional discretion in determining the means by which a matter should be pursued. See Rule 1.2. The lawyer's duty to act with reasonable diligence does not require the use of offensive tactics or preclude the treating of all persons involved in the legal process with courtesy and respect.

[2] A lawyer's work load must be controlled so that each matter can be handled competently.

[3] Perhaps no professional shortcoming is more widely resented than procrastination. A client's interests often can be adversely affected by the passage of time or the change of conditions; in extreme instances, as when a lawyer overlooks a statute of limitations, the client's legal position may be destroyed. Even when the client's interests are not affected in substance, however, unreasonable delay can cause a client needless anxiety and undermine confidence in the lawyer's trustworthiness. A lawyer's duty to act with reasonable promptness, however, does not preclude the lawyer from agreeing to a reasonable request for a postponement that will not prejudice the lawyer's client.

[4] Unless the relationship is terminated as provided in Rule 1.16, a lawyer should carry through to conclusion all matters undertaken for a client. If a lawyer's employment is limited to a specific matter, the relationship terminates when the matter has been resolved. If a lawyer has served a client over a substantial period in a variety of matters, the client sometimes may assume that the lawyer will continue to serve on a continuing basis unless the lawyer gives no-

tice of withdrawal. Doubt about whether a client-lawyer relationship still exists should be clarified by the lawyer, preferably in writing, so that the client will not mistakenly suppose the lawyer is looking after the client's affairs when the lawyer has ceased to do so. For example, if a lawyer has handled a judicial or administrative proceeding that produced a result adverse to the client and the lawyer and the client have not agreed that the lawyer will handle the matter on appeal, the lawyer must consult with the client about the possibility of appeal before relinquishing responsibility for the matter. See Rule 1.4(a)(2). Whether the lawyer is obligated to prosecute the appeal for the client depends on the scope of the representation the lawyer has agreed to provide to the client. See Rule 1.2.

[5] To prevent neglect of client matters in the event of a sole practitioner's death or disability, the duty of diligence may require that each sole practitioner prepare a plan, in conformity with applicable rules, that designates another competent lawyer to review client files, notify each client of the lawyer's death or disability, and determine whether there is a need for immediate protective action. Cf. Rule 28 of the American Bar Association Model Rules for Lawyer Disciplinary Enforcement (providing for court appointment of a lawyer to inventory files and take other protective action in absence of a plan providing for another lawyer to protect the interests of the clients of a deceased or disabled lawyer).

Authors' 1983 Model Rules Comparison

The text of the 2002 version is identical to the Rule adopted by the ABA House of Delegates in 1983.

In Comment 1, the drafters of the 2002 Rules added the following sentence: "The lawyer's duty to act with reasonable diligence does not require the use of offensive tactics or preclude the treating of all persons involved in the legal process with courtesy and respect." This language was added to "provide some support for the bar's civility initiatives." Reporter's Explanation of Changes to Model Rule 1.3. The drafters also deleted a sentence about a lawyer's work load and moved it to a new Comment 2. They also made a few word changes in Comment 1 for stylistic and clarification purposes.

Comment 2 is a new one with text moved from the 1983 Comment 1. The remaining Comments were renumbered to take into account the addition of new Comment 2.

In Comment 3, the drafters of the 2002 Rules added the following sentence: "A lawyer's duty to act with reasonable promptness, however, does not preclude the lawyer from agreeing to a reasonable request for a postponement that will not prejudice the lawyer's client." The new language makes clear that lawyers may accommodate reasonable requests for postponement when there will be no prejudice to the client.

In Comment 4, the drafters clarified some language with respect to a lawyer's obligation to work on an appeal for a current client. The amendments point to both client consent after full disclosure and any prior agreements between the lawyer and the client on the scope of the representation.

Comment 5 is new and the language addresses the obligations of sole practitioners to protect their clients in case the lawyer were to die or become disabled. The drafters added this Comment to suggest that solo practitioners should consider putting into place a plan to address the possibility of death or disability and to protect those lawyer's clients in such a case.

Model Code Comparison

DR 6-101(A)(3) required that a lawyer not "neglect a legal matter entrusted to him." EC 6-4 stated that a lawyer should "give appropriate attention to his legal work." Canon 7 stated that "a lawyer should represent a client zealously within the bounds of the law." DR 7-101(A)(1) provided that a lawyer "shall not intentionally . . . fail to seek the lawful objectives of his client through reasonably available means permitted by law and the Disciplinary Rules. . . ." DR 7-101(A)(3) provided that a lawyer "shall not intentionally . . . [p]rejudice or damage his client during the course of the relationship. . . ."

§ 1.3–1 THE OBLIGATION OF REASONABLE DILIGENCE

Rule 1.3 states that lawyers should act with reasonable diligence when representing their clients. Comment 1 defines reasonable diligence to encompass both lawyer action to pursue a matter on behalf of the client and commitment and zeal to accomplish the client's objectives. The obligation that "[a] lawyer should pursue a matter on behalf of a client despite opposition, obstruction, or personal inconvenience to the lawyer" is central to the concept of a legal representation.[1] We assume that when a lawyer undertakes a representation, that lawyer will devote the resources needed to complete the job. The obligation that a lawyer "take whatever lawful and ethical measures are required to vindicate a client's cause or endeavor" encompasses the role of advocacy on behalf of a client's interests.[2]

The Comment makes clear that lawyers are not required to obtain every legal or tactical advantage for the client in the course of the representation. As stated in Rule 1.2, lawyers shall have control over the means as to how they are to conduct the representation. And, the drafters of the 2002 Rules added a line that addresses this obligation in the context of professionalism: "The duty of a lawyer to act with reasonable diligence does not require the use of offensive tactics or preclude the treating of all persons involved in the legal process with courtesy and respect."[3]

[Section 1.3–1]

[1] Rule 1.3, Comment 1.

[2] Rule 1.3, Comment 1. This Comment actually uses the terms, "zeal in advocacy" to describe this obligation.

[3] Rule 1.3, Comment 1.

§ 1.3–2 THE OBLIGATION OF REASONABLE PROMPTNESS

§ 1.3–2(a) Reasonable Promptness Under the Circumstances

When a prospective client seeks legal representation, the lawyer will assess the scope of the proposed work. The lawyer and the prospective client will discuss the facts and circumstances and, from this discussion, the lawyer will determine what constitutes reasonable promptness within which the work needs to be performed. In some cases, legal rules such as statutes of limitation will influence the lawyer's decision. In other cases, the factual circumstances such as the client's need for redress or the client's need for a contract will determine the proper time schedule. In yet other cases, the client may have a desire to obtain the legal representation on an expedited basis or a desire to proceed on a more relaxed pace. An important aspect of reasonable promptness involves lawyer disclosure of a proposed schedule for completion of the work.

The drafters of the 2002 Rules added a line to the Comments dealing with the concept of reasonable promptness under the circumstances: "A lawyer's duty to act with reasonable promptness, however, does not preclude the lawyer from agreeing to a reasonable request for a postponement that will not prejudice the lawyer's client."[1] This comment acknowledges that delays do occur and that lawyers may obtain a client's informed consent to a reasonable request for a reasonable delay. Such a delay, however, must not prejudice the client's interests in the legal representation.

The Comments also recognize that when a lawyer has accepted a representation, the client develops an expectation that the lawyer will continue to work until the completion of the matter.[2] Of course, situations will arise when the lawyer must or may withdraw from a representation. The lawyer who is withdrawing from a representation before its completion should follow the requirements of Rule 1.16. In some cases, the lawyer's work may cover different matters and may become so continuous so as to form an expectation that the lawyer will represent the client on an ongoing basis. If a lawyer seeks to terminate the attorney-client relationship in such a case, it is the burden of the lawyer to clearly delineate, preferably in writing, when and how the representation will end.[3]

In litigation and other contested matters, a situation usually arises when the dispute ends in a trial verdict or other decision

---

[Section 1.3–2]

[1]Rule 1.3, Comment 3.

[2]Rule 1.3, Comment 4.
[3]Rule 1.3, Comment 4.

and not a settlement. The lawyer and client receive the decision and are in some cases left with the choice of whether to pursue an appeal. The attorney-client agreement in the original trial may specifically address the issue of whether the lawyer will represent the client on appeal.[4] If it does not, the Comments to Rule 1.3 state that "the lawyer must consult with the client about the possibility of appeal before relinquishing responsibility for the matter."[5]

§ 1.3–2(b) The Obligation Not to Neglect a Client's Matter

Idleness is one of the seven deadly sins. It is also the devil's workshop. The ethics rules do not forbid idleness, but they do forbid procrastination. Clients often accuse lawyers of dilatoriness, procrastination, cunctation, and delay. The Model Rules acknowledge that criticism and warn that unreasonable postponements can cause "needless anxiety" to a client.[6] Thus, in addition to the lawyer's affirmative duty to engage in reasonable communication with his client,[7] the lawyer, according to the Model Code, also must not *neglect* a legal matter entrusted to him.[8] The Rules use much more affirmative language: "A lawyer shall act with reasonable diligence and promptness in representing a client."[9]

§ 1.3–2(c) Defining Neglect

"Neglect" is an important concept in the law of ethics: it means a pattern of action or inaction, or more than one instance of delay. Under the Model Code, a finding of neglect usually required proof of a pattern of behavior. If the client suffered harm because a lawyer on one occasion forgot to file an answer to a complaint in time because of inadvertence, he would be guilty of civil malpractice, but he would not be guilty of the ethical violation of neglect. "Neglect involves indifference and a *consistent failure* to carry out the obligations which the lawyer has assumed to the client or a conscious disregard for the responsibility owed to the client."[10] Neglect requires a pattern of omission.

For example, if a lawyer on one occasion fails to file a case within the statute of limitations because she does not know about the statute of limitations, she would be liable for malpractice and responsible for violating the ethical rule against incompetence,[11] but she would not be guilty of neglect because one lapse does not

---

[4] Rule 1.3, Comment 4 (citing Rule 1.2).

[5] Rule 1.3, Comment 4.

[6] Rule 1.3, Comment 2. This line was added by the drafters of the 2002 Model Rules.

[7] Rule 1.4(a).

[8] DR 6-101(A)(3).

[9] Rule 1.3. *See also* Restatement of the Law Governing Lawyers, Third, § 16(2) (Official Draft 2000).

[10] ABA Informal Opinion 1273, "Neglect"—Definition (Nov. 20, 1973).

[11] Rule 1.1.

make a pattern of activities. If she fails, in one single instance, to file a case within the statute of limitations because of inadvertence and not because of incompetence, she still would be liable for the tort of malpractice, but she would not be subject to professional discipline for "incompetence" or for "neglect" because there was no pattern of activities. There is, in short, a distinction between the lawyer's liability for the tort of malpractice versus the lawyer's risk of being subject to legal discipline (such as a bar suspension or a disbarment). Thus, sometimes, the same act may lead to both malpractice and legal discipline, or only malpractice, or only legal discipline.[12]

§ 1.3–2(d) Heavy Workload

An attorney's heavy workload does not excuse her continued neglect of legal matters committed to her.[13] It is her responsibility to control her work load so that each matter can be handled adequately.[14] Otherwise, she will be disciplined for inexcusable delay and procrastination in pursuing matters in her care.[15]

§ 1.3–3 WAIVER

In light of the fact that most of the ethics rules are for the protection of clients, generally clients can waive them if they choose. However, some rules are not subject to waiver. For example, the ethics rules do not permit the client to waive his right that his attorney act with reasonable promptness or diligence. Even the client's refusal to pay the lawyer's fee does not justify neglect. If the client deliberately ignores his obligation to pay his attorney, the attorney may withdraw from representation only after taking reasonable steps to protect her client's

---

[12]*See,e.g., In re Brown*, 967 So.2d 482 (La.2007), *noted in* 23 ABA/BNA MANUAL ON PROF. CONDUCT, Current Reports 580 (Nov. 14, 2007). In Brown, the Louisiana Supreme Court chose to reprimand, instead of suspend, a lawyer who neglected his client's personal injury case for seven years. The court noted that, while the remedy for neglect is often found in a civil action for malpractice, the clear rule violation and some prior misconduct made disciplinary sanctions appropriate.

[13]*Matter of Loomos*, 90 Wash.2d 98, 579 P.2d 350 (1978). The respondent engaged in continued neglect of probate matters entrusted to him and failed to complete the probate of an estate. The Supreme Court suspended the respondent for 30 days and said that his suspension would continue beyond the first 30 days until he made a satisfactory showing to the disciplinary board that the estate had been closed and also petitioned board for reinstatement

[14]Rule 1.3, Comment 2. *See, e.g., In re Fraser*, 83 Wash.2d 884, 523 P.2d 921 (1974).

[15]*See, e.g., In re Yates*, 78 Wash.2d 243, 473 P.2d 402 (1970) (lawyer suspended); *In re Vandercook*, 78 Wash.2d 301, 474 P.2d 106 (1970)(lawyer suspended); *In re Talbot*, 78 Wash.2d 295, 474 P.2d 88 (1970) (lawyer suspended).

interests.[1] If the matter is before a tribunal, then the lawyer may not withdraw unless the tribunal permits.[2] In any event, until the lawyer is able to withdraw in accordance with the requirements in the ethics rules, the lawyer may not neglect the client's case.[3]

§ 1.3–4 SPECIAL CIRCUMSTANCES FOR SOLE PRACTITIONERS

When a lawyer practices law alone, the possibility exists that the lawyer's clients may suffer harm when the lawyer dies or becomes disabled. If a lawyer practices without professional staff or co-counsel, the lawyer's clients may not even learn about their lawyer's death or disability until after they have suffered harm in their legal matters. Even if a lawyer uses non-lawyer personnel in practicing law, the clients who seek to transfer their matters to other lawyers may encounter problems because the non-lawyer assistants may not know the location of their documents and the lawyer's work product. And, in some cases, even a short delay in a matter could seriously prejudice the client's interests.

The drafters to the 2002 Rules added Comment 5 to Rule 1.3 to address the concept of neglect for lawyers who practice as sole practitioners. This Comment raises the prospect that Rule 1.3 may impose a duty on a sole practitioner to implement a plan to deal with that lawyer's possible death or disability so as to protect the lawyer's clients.[1] Because this language uses the word, "may" and not "must," this duty does not seem to be imposed in all cases of sole practice.[2]

We are all going to die, so in that sense, death is always foreseeable. Illness of some sort is also always foreseeable. The drafters could not have meant that the sole practitioner must also have a plan to deal with these inevitable actions because then they would have used the word "must." It is logical to assume that this duty under Comment 5 arises only in situations

---

[Section 1.3–3]

[1]Rule 1.16(b)(4) & (d). DR 2-110(A)(2) & (C)(1)(f).

[2]Rule 1.16(c). DR 2-110(A)(1).

[3]*See, e.g., In re Pines*, 26 A.D.2d 424, 275 N.Y.S.2d 122, 123 (1st Dept.1966) (per curiam) (client refusal to reimburse lawyer for expenses does not justify lawyer "in refraining from proceeding in the action for over three years. . . .").

[Section 1.3–4]

[1]The drafters of the 2002 Rules placed this Comment under Rule 1.3

because lawyers have an obligation to prevent against client neglect and the foreseeable death or disability of a lawyer may impose an obligation on the lawyer to prevent the harm resulting from the neglect. This Comment only applies to sole practitioners because, when lawyers practice in a firm, one would expect the disabled or deceased lawyer's partners to take protective action with respect to firm clients who may have time sensitive matters.

[2]Rule 1.3, Comment 5.

where it is reasonable for the lawyer to conclude that illness or the grim reaper lie before him. For example, if a sole practitioner involved in a time sensitive matter, such as complex litigation scheduled for trial in the next several months, learns she needs to have open heart surgery, it would be prudent for the lawyer "to prepare a plan . . . that designates another competent lawyer to review client files, notify each client of the lawyer's death or disability, and determine whether there is a need for immediate protective action."[3]

Any plan must comply with the Model Rules generally, thus the lawyer has to consider whether she could disclose confidential information to the outside lawyer without client consent. For example, before the lawyers "designates another competent lawyer to review client files,"[4] the lawyer should secure her client's permission in order to comply with Rule 1.6.

---

[3] Rule 1.3, Comment 5 (citing ABA Model Rule for Disciplinary Enforcement, Rule 28).

[4] Rule 1.3, Comment 5.

CHAPTER 1.4
COMMUNICATION

RULE 1.4: COMMUNICATION

(a) A lawyer shall:

(1) promptly inform the client of any decision or circumstance with respect to which the client's informed consent, as defined in Rule 1.0(e), is required by these Rules;

(2) reasonably consult with the client about the means by which the client's objectives are to be accomplished;

(3) keep the client reasonably informed about the status of the matter;

(4) promptly comply with reasonable requests for information; and

(5) consult with the client about any relevant limitation on the lawyer's conduct when the lawyer knows that the client expects assistance not permitted by the Rules of Professional Conduct or other law.

(b) A lawyer shall explain a matter to the extent reasonably necessary to permit the client to make informed decisions regarding the representation.

Comment

[1] Reasonable communication between the lawyer and the client is necessary for the client effectively to participate in the representation.

Communicating with Client

[2] If these Rules require that a particular decision about the representation be made by the client, paragraph (a)(1) requires that the lawyer promptly consult with and secure the client's consent prior to taking action unless prior discussions with the client have resolved what action the client wants the lawyer to take. For example, a lawyer who receives from opposing counsel an offer of settlement in a civil controversy or a proffered plea bargain in a criminal case must promptly inform the client of its substance unless the client has previously indicated that the proposal will be acceptable or unacceptable or has authorized the lawyer to accept or to reject the offer. See Rule 1.2(a).

[3] Paragraph (a)(2) requires the lawyer to reasonably consult with the client about the means to be used to accomplish the client's objectives. In some situations—depending on both the importance of the action under consideration and the feasibility of consulting with the client—this duty will require consultation prior to taking action. In other circumstances, such as during a trial when an immediate decision must be made, the exigency of the situation may require the lawyer to act without prior consultation. In such cases the lawyer must nonetheless act reasonably to inform the client of actions the lawyer has taken on the client's behalf. Additionally, paragraph (a)(3) requires that the lawyer keep the client reasonably informed about the status of the matter, such as significant developments affecting the timing or the substance of the representation.

[4] A lawyer's regular communication with clients will minimize the occasions on which a client will need to request information concerning the representation. When a client makes a reasonable request for information, however, paragraph (a)(4) requires prompt compliance with the request, or if a prompt response is not feasible, that the lawyer, or a member of the lawyer's staff, acknowledge receipt of the request and advise the client when a response may be expected. Client telephone calls should be promptly returned or acknowledged.

Explaining Matters

[5] The client should have sufficient information to participate intelligently in decisions concerning the objectives of the representation and the means by which they are to be pursued, to the extent the client is willing and able to do so. Adequacy of communication depends in part on the kind of advice or assistance that is involved. For example, when there is time to explain a proposal made in a negotiation, the lawyer should review all important provisions with the client before proceeding to an agreement. In litigation a lawyer should explain the general strategy and prospects of success and ordinarily should consult the client on tactics that are likely to result in significant expense or to injure or coerce others. On the other hand, a lawyer ordinarily will not be expected to describe trial or negotiation strategy in detail. The guiding principle is that the lawyer should fulfill reasonable client expectations for information consistent with the duty to act in the client's best interests, and the client's overall requirements as to the character of representation. In certain circumstances, such as when a lawyer asks a client to consent to a representation affected by a conflict of interest, the client must give informed consent, as defined in Rule 1.0(e).

[6] Ordinarily, the information to be provided is that appropriate for a client who is a comprehending and responsible adult. However, fully informing the client according to this standard may be impracticable, for example, where the client is a child or suffers from diminished capacity. See Rule 1.14. When the client is an organization or group, it is often impossible or inappropriate to inform every one of its members about its legal affairs; ordinarily, the lawyer should address communications to the appropriate officials of the organization. See Rule 1.13. Where many routine matters are

involved, a system of limited or occasional reporting may be arranged with the client.

Withholding Information

[7] In some circumstances, a lawyer may be justified in delaying transmission of information when the client would be likely to react imprudently to an immediate communication. Thus, a lawyer might withhold a psychiatric diagnosis of a client when the examining psychiatrist indicates that disclosure would harm the client. A lawyer may not withhold information to serve the lawyer's own interest or convenience or the interests or convenience of another person. Rules or court orders governing litigation may provide that information supplied to a lawyer may not be disclosed to the client. Rule 3.4(c) directs compliance with such rules or orders.

Authors' 1983 Model Rules Comparison

The 1983 Rule 1.4(a) contained two duties of communication: "A lawyer shall keep a client reasonably informed about the status of a matter and promptly comply with reasonable requests for information." The drafters of the 2002 Rules identified that the 1983 Rules discussed the obligation of communication to clients in several other Rules. Thus, they decided that all of these obligations should be pulled together and included in Rule 1.4. Reporter's Explanation of Changes to Model Rule 1.4. The drafters of the 2002 Rules under Rule 1.4(a) took the two duties of the 1983 Rules and added three additional duties to communicate under (a)(1) through (a)(5).

Comments 1 to 4 are new and explain the new more detailed focus on Rule 1.4(a).

The 1983 Comments 1 and 2 were combined into renumbered Comment 5 ("Explaining Matters"). The language has been modified to reflect the broader focus of the Rule.

Comment 6 is the 1983 Comment 3 with the one change that the last line of the old Comment was moved to the current Comment 3.

Comment 7 is the 1983 Comment 4 with one change. The drafters included a clause to the line about withholding information. The current text prohibits a lawyer from withholding information for the "interests or convenience of another person."

Model Code Comparison

Rule 1.4 has no direct counterpart in the Disciplinary Rules of the Model Code. DR 6-101(A)(3) provided that a lawyer shall not "[n]eglect a legal matter entrusted to him." DR 9-102(B)(1) provided that a lawyer shall "[p]romptly notify a client of the receipt of his funds, securities, or other properties." EC 7-8 stated that a lawyer "should exert his best efforts to insure that decisions of his client are made only after the client has been informed of relevant considerations." EC 9-2 stated that "a lawyer should fully and promptly inform his client of material developments in the matters being handled for the client."

§ 1.4–1 THE OBLIGATION TO KEEP THE CLIENT INFORMED

A fundamental assumption underlying the attorney-client relationship is that lawyers must keep their clients reasonably informed. Clients cannot effectively participate in their own representation if their lawyers do not keep their clients informed.[1] The former ABA Model Code tried to impose this obligation on lawyers with an aspirational rule by providing that the "lawyer should fully and promptly inform his client of material developments in the matters being handled for the client,"[2] and should keep his client informed of relevant considerations before the client makes decisions.[3] The Model Rules have gone further, by making clear that these requirements are not merely hortatory; to violate them is to violate a disciplinary rule.[4] The 1983 version of Rule 1.4(a) had a basic obligation for lawyers to keep their clients reasonably informed about the representation and to promptly answer their clients' reasonable requests. The current version of the Rule reaffirms this requirement.

Rule of Reason. However, the requirement of keeping the client informed is subject to a rule of reason.[5] Some clients are what lawyers call "high maintenance." Because such clients are unreasonable, the Rule places its emphasis on "reasonableness." The lawyer need "not communicate with the client as often as the client believed he should have," as long as "he kept the client adequately informed of the progress he made with each case."[6]

In fact, the lawyer may even be justified in delaying the

[Section 1.4–1]

[1] Rule 1.4, Comment 1.

[2] EC 9-2.

[3] EC 7-8.

[4] Rule 1.4(a), (b). *Accord* Restatement of the Law Governing Lawyers, Third, § 20 (Official Draft 2000). *See* Susan Martyn, *Informed Consent in the Practice of Law*, 48 GEO. WASH. L. REV. 307 (1980).

[5] *See* Rule 1.4, Comment 5.

[6] *See, e.g., In re Walker*, 293 Or. 297, 301, 647 P.2d 468, 470 (1982) (footnote omitted): "Although the accused did not communicate with the client as often as the client believed he should have, the record establishes that he kept the client adequately informed of the progress he made with each case. The record suggests delay in the accused's handling of the cases, but it does not establish neglect. There was no prejudice to the client as a result of the accused's handling the cases. The accused's handling of his client's litigation was not exemplary, but neither was it deserving of professional discipline."

In re Schoeneman, 777 A.2d 259, 264 (D.C. 2001). In this case, a lawyer had surrendered his license to practice law in Virginia in the face of pending charges that he had neglected a case and failed to keep his client informed of its progress. The D.C. court refused to accept reciprocal discipline in this case because it concluded the lawyer had not violated Rule 1.4. In this case, the client alleged that the lawyer "failed to return her telephone calls for three weeks," which the court regarded "as an allegation that Schoeneman [the lawyer] failed to keep his client reasonably informed." But the client admitted "that she and Schoeneman spoke monthly, that he traveled to Baltimore to meet her, and that she traveled to Virginia to meet him. She also states that he regularly informed her that he was continuing in his efforts to reopen her case and reach a settlement with her party opponents." The court found no Rule 1.4 violation:

transfer of information to the client if the lawyer believes the client might react imprudently.[7] The basic ethical principle is that a lawyer has the ethical obligation to keep a client "*reasonably informed*" about the status of a matter that is entrusted to her.[8]

When the client makes a specific request of his or her lawyer, the lawyer's duty is to respond promptly to the client's "reasonable" requests for information.[9] But the lawyer need not wait for the client to start the dialogue; the lawyer should also volunteer information to the client, as part of the duty of keeping the client reasonably informed.

Sometimes, when clients complain that the lawyer has "neglected" their case, they really mean that the lawyer has failed to keep them informed. If the lawyer had kept them informed, they would have known that there had been no unnecessary delay. Nonetheless, when lawyers keep their clients in the dark and unaware, without good reason, they are also violating the ethics rules.

The drafters of the 2002 Rules sought to elaborate on this fundamental obligation of lawyers to keep their clients informed.[10] They examined the entire Rules and consolidated in a new Rule 1.4(a) five specific contexts in which lawyers should provide clients with information. The following sections examine the specific duties placed on lawyers in the new Rule 1.4(a).

Insurance. Some states require that the lawyer inform the cli-

---

"An attorney need not communicate with a client as often as the client would like, as long as the attorney's conduct was reasonable under the circumstances. Schoeneman had been keeping Brice informed of the status of her case over an extended period of time. Given the nature of the matter—a long-term, complex fraud investigation coupled with extended negotiations—monthly conversations are not prima facie unreasonable. Nothing in the record points to any events or circumstances that would have required Schoeneman to communicate with Brice during the time that she was trying to reach him, or that she was not adequately informed of his efforts. We thus conclude that Brice's complaint does not allege misconduct in violation of Rule 1.4(a)." 777 A.2d at 264 (internal citation with quotation omitted).

Contrast, *In re Hallmark*, 831 A.2d 366, 374 (D.C. 2003), holding that the "respondent's failure to communicate with Ms. Patterson about the status of her case over a span of a year and a

half did not fulfill the client's reasonable expectations for information, and constituted a violation of Rule 1.4(a)."

[7] Rule 1.4, Comment 6. *Cf.* Rule 1.14.

[8] The Restatement, of the Law Governing Lawyers, Third, § 20(1) (Official Draft 2000); Restatement of the Law of Agency, Second, § 381 (1958); Restatement of the Law of Trust, Second, § 173 (1957).

[9] The Restatement, Third, of the Law Governing Lawyers, § 20(2) (Official Draft 2000).

[10] The obligation will vary depending on the capacity of the client to receive information. *See* Rule 1.4, Comment 6. If the client is under a disability, the lawyer will need to look to Rule 1.14 for guidance. If the client is an entity, Rule 1.13 establishes that the lawyer will need to communicate with its duly authorized agents.

ent as to whether the lawyer carries malpractice insurance.[11] Periodic efforts to have the ABA amend Rule 1.4 to impose an obligation to inform clients of the lawyer's insurance coverage have been unsuccessful.[12] However, on August 10, 2004, the ABA House of Delegates approved (by a close vote of 213-202) a standalone Rule on insurance disclosure, called the Model Court Rule on Insurance Disclosure.[13]

---

[11]E.g., Alaska, Ohio, and South Dakota require lawyers to advise their clients if they do not maintain a minimum measure of malpractice coverage. 18 ABA/BNA LAWYERS' MANUAL ON PROFESSIONAL CONDUCT, Current Report News 234 (April 10, 2002).

Alaska Rule 1.4(c) states: "(c) A lawyer shall inform an existing client in writing if the lawyer does not have malpractice insurance of at least $100,000 per claim and $300,000 annual aggregate and shall inform the client in writing at any time the lawyer's malpractice insurance drops below these amounts or the lawyer's malpractice insurance is terminated. A lawyer shall maintain a record of these disclosures for six years from the termination of the client's representation."

Oregon, by statute, requires members of the bar to carry malpractice insurance. O.R.S. § 9.080 (2)(a) states: "The board shall have the authority to require all active members of the state bar engaged in the private practice of law whose principal offices are in Oregon to carry professional liability insurance and shall be empowered, either by itself or in conjunction with other bar organizations, to do whatever is necessary and convenient to implement this provision, including the authority to own, organize and sponsor any insurance organization authorized under the laws of the State of Oregon and to establish a lawyer's professional liability fund."

[12]For example, the ABA Client Protection Committee, in 2002, unsuccessfully circulated a proposal to amend Rule 1.4 to require lawyers to disclose directly to their clients whether they had malpractice insur-

ance. 18 ABA/BNA LAWYERS' MANUAL ON PROFESSIONAL CONDUCT, Current Report News 233 (Apr. 10, 2002). In 2004 this Committee urged adoption of a new rule on insurance disclosure. *ABA Client Protection Committee Recommends Model Court Rule On Insurance Disclosure*, 20 ABA/BNA LAWYERS' MANUAL ON PROFESSIONAL CONDUCT, Current Report News 206 (Apr. 21, 2004). This proposed rule would have required lawyers with an active law practice to disclose on their annual registration statement whether they carry professional liability insurance.

[13]Rule ___. Insurance Disclosure [approved by the ABA House of Delegates, August 10, 2004].

A. Each lawyer admitted to the active practice of law shall certify to the [highest court of the jurisdiction] on or before [December 31 of each year]: 1) whether the lawyer is engaged in the private practice of law; 2) if engaged in the private practice of law, whether the lawyer is currently covered by professional liability insurance; 3) whether the lawyer intends to maintain insurance during the period of time the lawyer is engaged in the private practice of law; and 4) whether the lawyer is exempt from the provisions of this Rule because the lawyer is engaged in the practice of law as a full-time government lawyer or is counsel employed by an organizational client and does not represent clients outside that capacity. Each lawyer admitted to the active practice of law in this jurisdiction who reports being covered by professional liability insurance shall notify [the highest court in the jurisdiction] in writing within 30 days if the insurance policy providing coverage lapses, is no longer in effect or terminates for any reason.

B. The foregoing shall be certified by

§ 1.4–1(a) Information Necessary for Client to Make Informed Consent Decisions

Throughout the lawyer codes, the various rules provide that a lawyer must obtain a client's consent to a specific situation. In the 1983 Model Rules, this consent requirement was phrased as client "consent after consultation." In the 2002 Model Rules, the drafters changed this language to "informed consent." Thus, lawyers must now obtain the informed consent of their clients in the various contexts as imposed in the Rules.

Rule 1.4(a)(1) states that a lawyer must "promptly inform the client of any decision or circumstance with respect to which the client's informed consent, as defined in Rule 1.0(e), is required by these Rules. . . ." In other words, whenever a Rule requires that the lawyer obtain the client's informed consent, the lawyer must promptly "consult with and secure the client's consent prior to taking actions. . . ."[14] The Comment to Rule 1.4(a)(1) does go on to state that if a lawyer has previously discussed the matter with the client and obtained the client's instructions, the lawyer would not need to revisit this decision with the client.[15] However, lawyers need to be sure that there have been no material changes in the circumstances since the client made the decision. Also, this prior consent would not work in cases where the Rules require informed consent confirmed in writing or signed by the client.[16]

§ 1.4–1(b) Consultations About the Means to Accomplish Client Objectives

Under Rule 1.2, a client establishes the objectives of the representation and the lawyer is responsible for choosing the means by which accomplish these objectives. Rule 1.2(a) requires that a lawyer consult with the client about the means that should be used in the representation. Rule 1.4(a)(2) reinforces the obligation of lawyers to discuss with clients the various means that they can use to pursue the objectives of the representation.

The obligation to consult with a client about the means that

---

each lawyer admitted to the active practice of law in this jurisdiction in such form as may be prescribed by the [highest court of the jurisdiction]. The information submitted pursuant to this Rule will be made available to the public by such means as may be designated by the [highest court of the jurisdiction].

C. Any lawyer admitted to the active practice of law who fails to comply with this Rule in a timely fashion, as defined by the [highest court in the jurisdiction], may be suspended from the practice of law until such time as the lawyer complies. Supplying false information in response to this Rule shall subject the lawyer to appropriate disciplinary action.

[14] Rule 1.4, Comment 2.

[15] The Comment also cites Rule 1.2(a) dealing with client input on certain fundamental decisions.

[16] See, e.g., Rule 1.7 (requiring consent confirmed in writing in certain circumstances involving conflicts of interest); Rule 1.5(c) (requiring an agreement signed by the client in the case of a contingent fee).

should be used is defined by reasonableness and by circumstances. No one could imagine that a lawyer would need to ask clients about every choice the lawyer must make in a representation. However, at the outset of a representation and at important junctions during the matter, the lawyer has an obligation to inform the client of choices available, answer any questions that the client may have, and consider carefully the client's wishes. The Comment states that the obligation to consult will depend upon the "importance of the action under consideration and the feasibility of consulting with the client. . . ."[17] In cases where a decision needs to be made quickly, such as during trial, the lawyer cannot be expected to consult with the client before a decision is made. But the Comment states that in such a situation the lawyer should "act reasonably to inform the client of the actions the lawyer has taken."[18]

The Comments contain two paragraphs on the topic of explaining matters to clients. "The client should have sufficient information to participate intelligently in decisions concerning the objectives of the representation and the means by which they are to be pursued, to the extent the client is willing and able to do so."[19] Obviously, sophisticated clients need far less education and communication than unsophisticated clients.[20] And, the nature of the matter is very important to determine what kinds of information a client needs to be reasonably informed.[21] The Comments state it best: "The guiding principle is that the lawyer should fulfill reasonable client expectations for information consistent with the

---

[17]Rule 1.4, Comment 2.

[18]Rule 1.4, Comment 2.

[19]Rule 1.4, Comment 5.

[20]Clients who have used lawyers a lot, such as corporations involved with many transactions and litigation, understand that they are unlikely to be in daily contact with their outside lawyer except during crucial phases of the representation. In fact, such clients often expect that, in many instances, their lawyers will simply take care of the matter so that they need no longer be bothered by it. However, individual clients, particularly in the case of litigation that the clients may take personally (divorce, family disputes, or other emotional issues) often act differently. They want frequent contact with their lawyer. One of the most common complaints of this type of client is the belief that the lawyer should communicate with the client more frequently. *See, e.g.*, F. Raymond Marks & Darlene Cathcart, *Discipline Within the Legal Profession: Is It Self-Regulation?*, 1974 U. Ill. Law Forum 193, 195–217 (1974) (most common complaint of clients, over 50%, is neglect or lack of communication from their lawyers).

[21]The Comment states that in litigation the lawyer is not expected to discuss "trial or negotiation strategy in detail," but "ordinarily should consult with a client on tactics that are likely to result in significant expense or to injure or coerce others." Rule 1.4, Comment 5.

duty to act in the client's best interests, and the client's overall requirements as to the character of representation."[22]

§ 1.4–1(c) Keeping the Client Reasonably Informed About the Status of the Representation

The obligation to keep a client informed includes the duty to let a client know about important events in the course of a representation. Thus, when the lawyer has filed the complaint or scheduled depositions, the lawyer should inform the client of such events, unless a client has let the lawyer know that he or she does not want this type of information. Also, when the tribunal or third party acts, lawyers should usually inform the client about the nature of the action. This, of course, would include an obligation of informing a client about court decisions, opinions, and rulings. And, as required by Rule 1.2, a lawyer would need to inform a client about settlement offers made by an opposing party unless the lawyer and the client have previously determined how the lawyer should act when given such an offer.

§ 1.4–1(d) Reasonable Client Requests for Information

In the course of an attorney-client relationship, there will be occasions when a client attempts to contact an attorney to ask some questions.[23] Rule 1.4(a)(4) provides that lawyers "must promptly comply with reasonable requests for information." Although one would expect lawyers to understand the importance of returning phone calls and listening to clients, the inclusion of this statement in a rule makes this a disciplinable offense. Thus, lawyers must attempt to promptly respond to reasonable client requests for information. If a lawyer cannot promptly contact the client, the lawyer or a member of the lawyer's staff should establish contact with the client and inform the client when a response is likely to occur.[24]

Another important aspect of the Rule is its use of the term *reasonable* in describing client requests for information. In other words, a lawyer would not violate this Rule if the lawyer refuses to respond to unreasonable client requests for information. For example, a client who seeks information about when a court may issue its opinion on a motion may ask once or twice, but beyond that the requests may become unreasonable. In such a case, the lawyer may inform the client that he or she will contact the client when the decision is rendered. Even if a client burdens a lawyer with unreasonable requests for information, the lawyer should seek to explain to the client why the lawyer will begin to ignore the client requests.

---

[22] Rule 1.4, Comment 5.

[23] A Comment to Rule 1.4 states that such requests can be minimized when a lawyer develops a practice of regular communication with clients. Rule 1.4, Comment 4.

[24] Rule 1.4, Comment 4.

§ 1.4–1(e) Informing the Client About Limitations on Lawyer's Conduct

When a prospective or current client asks a lawyer to act in a manner that will constitute violation of the Model Rules or other law, the lawyer is obligated to inform the person about what the lawyer can and cannot do. This concept of communicating with a client has been described as informing the client about limitations on the lawyer's conduct. The limitation refers to the law or Rule that forbids a lawyer from acting or failing to act during a representation.

In the 1983 Model Rules, this concept appeared in Rule 1.2(e) under the scope of representation provision. The drafters of the 2002 Rules thought that this provision fit more precisely under Rule 1.4 because it involves a necessary communication to a client about what the lawyer is permitted to do during a representation. Thus, the provision was moved to Rule 1.4(a)(5).

Rule 1.4(a)(5) states that lawyers shall "consult with the client about any relevant limitations on the lawyer's conduct when the lawyer knows that the client expects assistance not permitted by the Rules of Professional Conduct or other law." This provision places a duty on a lawyer to warn a client about what the lawyer must do when the client expects the lawyer to act in violation of the Rules or other law. For example, if a client in a litigation matter had withheld a document that was properly subject to a discovery request, the lawyer should inform the client that the lawyer needs to turn over the document under the applicable discovery rules. Or if a client has engaged a lawyer in work that later turns out to be part of a criminal enterprise, the lawyer would need to inform the client that he or she will be withdrawing from the representation.

Rule 1.4(a)(5) continues to be tied to Rule 1.2(d); yet the drafters of the 2002 Rules did not make any reference from Rule 1.4 to Rule 1.2. When a lawyer has delineated the scope of the law for a client, and a client asks a lawyer to represent the client in a course of conduct that involves the lawyer in counseling or assisting a client in a crime or fraud, the lawyer must decline and inform the client about the relevant legal limitations on the lawyer's conduct.

§ 1.4–2 THE LIMITED RIGHT TO WITHHOLD INFORMATION FROM CLIENTS

In a Comment to Rule 1.4, the ABA addresses the controversial topic whether a lawyer has a right to withhold information from a client.[1] The Comment examines two possible situations where such lawyer conduct may be justified.

First, a lawyer may delay the disclosure of information to a client when the disclosure could reasonably be expected to harm the client. One such example noted in the Comment involves the lawyer's receipt of the results of psychiatric diagnosis.[2] Suppose a lawyer subjects the client to a psychiatric evaluation. When the doctor delivers the results to the lawyer, the doctor may tell the lawyer that disclosing the results to the client may harm the client. In such a case, a lawyer may delay disclosing the results to the client because the client may "be likely to act imprudently to an immediate communication."[3] In this situation, the lawyer may delay the disclosure until the situation is stabilized through the passage of time or until the lawyer can arrange a more appropriate meeting, perhaps with the medical professional and the client, to inform the client of the diagnosis. Second, in litigation, a court rule or order may prohibit a lawyer from disclosing certain information to the client.[4] Although such rules and orders are not commonly encountered, a court may permit a lawyer as an officer of the court to review certain information in camera.

The Comment warns lawyers that they may not withhold information from a client "to serve the lawyer's own interest or convenience or the interests or convenience of another person."[5] The sole reason for withholding the information must be the client's interests and not the interests of the lawyer or a third person. Of course, such situations are rare and should be limited to cases where disclosure is reasonably likely to cause harm to the client. The lawyer should take reasonable efforts to find, rather promptly, a situation to make the disclosure under circumstances that can minimize the harm.

[Section 1.4-2]
[1] Rule 1.4, Comment 7.
[2] Rule 1.4, Comment 7.
[3] Rule 1.4, Comment 7.

[4] Rule 1.4, Comment 7 (citing Rule 3.4(c)).

[5] Rule 1.4, Comment 7.

CHAPTER 1.5
FEES

RULE 1.5: FEES

(a) A lawyer shall not make an agreement for, charge, or collect an unreasonable fee or an unreasonable amount for expenses. The factors to be considered in determining the reasonableness of a fee include the following:

(1) the time and labor required, the novelty and difficulty of the questions involved, and the skill requisite to perform the legal service properly;

(2) the likelihood, if apparent to the client, that the acceptance of the particular employment will preclude other employment by the lawyer;

(3) the fee customarily charged in the locality for similar legal services;

(4) the amount involved and the results obtained;

(5) the time limitations imposed by the client or by the circumstances;

(6) the nature and length of the professional relationship with the client;

(7) the experience, reputation, and ability of the lawyer or lawyers performing the services; and

(8) whether the fee is fixed or contingent.

(b) The scope of the representation and the basis or rate of the fee and expenses for which the client will be responsible shall be communicated to the client, preferably in writing, before or within a reasonable time after commencing the representation, except when the lawyer will charge a regularly represented client on the same basis or rate. Any changes in the basis or rate of the fee or expenses shall also be communicated to the client.

(c) A fee may be contingent on the outcome of the matter for which the service is rendered, except in a matter in which a contingent fee is prohibited by paragraph (d) or other law. A contingent fee agreement shall be in a writing signed by the client and shall state the method by which the fee is to be determined, including the percentage or percentages that shall accrue to the lawyer in the event of settlement, trial or appeal; litigation and other expenses to be deducted from the recovery; and whether such expenses are to be deducted before or after the contingent fee is calculated. The agreement must clearly notify the client of any expenses for which the client will be liable whether or not the client is the prevailing party. Upon conclusion of a contingent fee matter, the lawyer shall provide the client with a written statement stating the outcome of the matter and, if there is a recovery, showing the remittance to the client and the method of its determination.

(d) A lawyer shall not enter into an arrangement for, charge, or collect:

(1) any fee in a domestic relations matter, the payment or amount of which is contingent upon the securing of a divorce or upon the amount of alimony or support, or property settlement in lieu thereof; or

(2) a contingent fee for representing a defendant in a criminal case.

(e) A division of a fee between lawyers who are not in the same firm may be made only if:

(1) the division is in proportion to the services performed by each lawyer or each lawyer assumes joint responsibility for the representation;

(2) the client agrees to the arrangement, including the share each lawyer will receive, and the agreement is confirmed in writing; and

(3) the total fee is reasonable.

Comment

Reasonableness of Fee and Expenses

[1] Paragraph (a) requires that lawyers charge fees that are reasonable under the circumstances. The factors specified in (1) through (8) are not exclusive. Nor will each factor be relevant in each instance. Paragraph (a) also requires that expenses for which the client will be charged must be reasonable. A lawyer may seek reimbursement for the cost of services performed in-house, such as copying, or for other expenses incurred in-house, such as telephone charges, either by charging a reasonable amount to which the client has agreed in advance or by charging an amount that reasonably reflects the cost incurred by the lawyer.

Basis or Rate of Fee

[2] When the lawyer has regularly represented a client, they ordinarily will have evolved an understanding concerning the basis or rate of the fee and the expenses for which the client will be responsible. In a new client-lawyer relationship, however, an understanding as to fees and expenses must be promptly established. Generally, it is desirable to furnish the client with at least a simple memorandum or copy of the lawyer's customary fee arrangements that states the general nature of the legal services to be provided, the basis, rate or total amount of the fee and whether and to what extent the client will be responsible for any costs, expenses or disbursements in the course of the representation. A written statement concerning the terms of the engagement reduces the possibility of misunderstanding.

[3] Contingent fees, like any other fees, are subject to the reasonableness standard of paragraph (a) of this Rule. In determining whether a particular contingent fee is reasonable, or whether it is reasonable to charge any form of contingent fee, a lawyer must consider the factors that are relevant under the circumstances. Applicable law may impose limitations on contingent fees, such as a ceiling on the percentage allowable, or may require a lawyer to offer clients an alternative basis for the fee. Applicable law also may apply to situations other than a contingent fee, for example, government regulations regarding fees in certain tax matters.

Terms of Payment

[4] A lawyer may require advance payment of a fee, but is obliged to return any unearned portion. See Rule 1.16(d). A lawyer may accept property in payment for services, such as an ownership interest in an enterprise, providing this does not involve acquisition of a proprietary interest in the cause of action or subject matter of the litigation contrary to Rule 1.8(i). However, a fee paid in property instead of money may be subject to the requirements of Rule 1.8(a) because such fees often have the essential qualities of a business transaction with the client.

[5] An agreement may not be made whose terms might induce the lawyer improperly to curtail services for the client or perform them in a way contrary to the client's interest. For example, a lawyer should not enter into an agreement whereby services are to be provided only up to a stated amount when it is foreseeable that more extensive services probably will be required, unless the situation is adequately explained to the client. Otherwise, the client might have to bargain for further assistance in the midst of a proceeding or transaction. However, it is proper to define the extent of services in light of the client's ability to pay. A lawyer should not exploit a fee arrangement based primarily on hourly charges by using wasteful procedures.

Prohibited Contingent Fees

[6] Paragraph (d) prohibits a lawyer from charging a contingent fee in a domestic relations matter when payment is contingent upon the securing of a divorce or upon the amount of alimony or support or property settlement to be obtained. This provision does not preclude a contract for a contingent fee for legal representation in

connection with the recovery of post-judgment balances due under support, alimony or other financial orders because such contracts do not implicate the same policy concerns.

Division of Fee

[7] A division of fee is a single billing to a client covering the fee of two or more lawyers who are not in the same firm. A division of fee facilitates association of more than one lawyer in a matter in which neither alone could serve the client as well, and most often is used when the fee is contingent and the division is between a referring lawyer and a trial specialist. Paragraph (e) permits the lawyers to divide a fee either on the basis of the proportion of services they render or if each lawyer assumes responsibility for the representation as a whole. In addition, the client must agree to the arrangement, including the share that each lawyer is to receive, and the agreement must be confirmed in writing. Contingent fee agreements must be in a writing signed by the client and must otherwise comply with paragraph (c) of this Rule. Joint responsibility for the representation entails financial and ethical responsibility for the representation as if the lawyers were associated in a partnership. A lawyer should only refer a matter to a lawyer whom the referring lawyer reasonably believes is competent to handle the matter. See Rule 1.1.

[8] Paragraph (e) does not prohibit or regulate division of fees to be received in the future for work done when lawyers were previously associated in a law firm.

Disputes over Fees

[9] If a procedure has been established for resolution of fee disputes, such as an arbitration or mediation procedure established by the bar, the lawyer must comply with the procedure when it is mandatory, and, even when it is voluntary, the lawyer should conscientiously consider submitting to it. Law may prescribe a procedure for determining a lawyer's fee, for example, in representation of an executor or administrator, a class or a person entitled to a reasonable fee as part of the measure of damages. The lawyer entitled to such a fee and a lawyer representing another party concerned with the fee should comply with the prescribed procedure.

Authors' 1983 Model Rules Comparison

The 1983 Rule 1.5(a) stated that a "lawyer's fee shall be reasonable." The drafters of the 2002 Rules broadened this language to prohibit lawyers from making an agreement, charging, or collecting an "unreasonable fee or an unreasonable amount for expenses." This elaboration of the reasonable fee requirement was implicit under the 1983 version. The drafters viewed the prohibition against "unreasonable expenses" as implied from the lawyer's duty to communicate to the client and her duty not to make misrepresentations to clients; however, they added explicit language to set forth this obligation very clearly.

In Rule 1.5(b), the drafters added the requirement that lawyers communicate to the client both the scope of the representation and the expenses for which a client will be responsible. This provision advises that the agreement should preferably in writing but it does not require a writing. It does not apply to regularly represented clients. The drafters also added a requirement that the lawyer must give notice to the client when the lawyer changes the basis of the fee or expenses.

In Rule 1.5(c), the drafters added a requirement that contingent fee agreements be signed by the client. They also added the following statement: "The agreement must clearly notify the client of any expenses for which the client will be liable whether or not the client is the prevailing party."

In Rule 1.5(e), the drafters remove the requirement that an agreement by two lawyers not in the same firm to assume joint responsibility be in writing, but they added to Rule 1.5(e)(2) that all agreements to share fees include information about the share each lawyer will receive and the agreement must be confirmed in writing.

Comment 1, on the reasonableness of fees and expenses, is new.

The 1983 Comment 1 is now Comment 2. The drafters added reference to reasonable expenses. They also deleted some language about whether a lawyer needs to make reference to the eight factors in Rule 1.5(e):

It is not necessary to recite all the factors that underlie the basis of the fee, but only those that are directly involved in its computation. It is sufficient, for example, to state that the basic rate is an hourly charge or a fixed amount or an estimated amount, or to identify the factors that may be taken into account in finally fixing the fee. When developments occur during the representation that render an earlier estimate substantially inaccurate, a revised estimate should be provided to the client.

Instead of this language, the drafters added language on the obligation of a lawyer to state the basis of the fee, expenses, and the general nature of legal service in a memorandum.

Comment 3 is new and makes clear that contingent fee agreements are subject to the reasonableness standard in Rule 1.5(a).

The 1983 Comment 2 is now Comment 4. The drafters removed language that stated that fees paid in property rather than money need special scrutiny because of valuation issues. Instead, they explicitly stated that such arrangements need to satisfy Rule 1.8(a) on business transactions with a client because payments in property are essentially a business transaction.

The 1983 Comment 3 is now Comment 5. The drafters moved two lines from this Comment to the new Comment 3.

Comment 6 is new and reflects the drafter's view that contingent fees may be used in post-divorce judgment divorce litigation. This position is consistent with existing practice in many states. *See* Reporter's Explanation of Changes to Model Rule 1.5.

The 1983 Comment 4 is now Comment 7 and reflects the change made in Rule 1.5(e) on referral fees. The Comment also states that referral fees that involve a contingent fee between lawyers not in the same firm must meet Rule 1.5(c).

Comment 8 is new and makes clear that Rule 1.5(e) does not address agreements among lawyers who were associated in a firm and have left and agree to share fees based upon work done while they were associated.

154

The 1983 Comment 5 is now Comment 9. The drafters added a clause stating that lawyer must participate in mandatory fee dispute resolution programs established by bar organizations and should strongly consider participating when such programs are voluntary.

Model Code Comparison

[1] DR 2-106(A) provided that a lawyer "shall not enter into an agreement for, charge, or collect an illegal or clearly excessive fee." DR 2-106(B) provided that a fee is "clearly excessive when, after a review of the facts, a lawyer of ordinary prudence would be left with a definite and firm conviction that the fee is in excess of a reasonable fee." The factors of a reasonable fee in Rule 1.5(a) are substantially identical to those listed in DR 2-106(B). EC 2-17 states that a lawyer "should not charge more than a reasonable fee. . . . "

[2] There was no counterpart to Rule 1.5(b) in the Disciplinary Rules of the Model Code. EC 2-19 stated that it is "usually beneficial to reduce to writing the understanding of the parties regarding the fee, particularly when it is contingent."

[3] There was no counterpart to paragraph (c) in the Disciplinary Rules of the Model Code. EC 2-20 provided that "[c]ontingent fee arrangements in civil cases have long been commonly accepted in the United States," but that "a lawyer generally should decline to accept employment on a contingent fee basis by one who is able to pay a reasonable fixed fee. . . . "

[4] With regard to paragraph (d), DR 2-106(C) prohibited "a contingent fee in a criminal case." EC 2-20 provided that "contingent fee arrangements in domestic relation cases are rarely justified."

[5] With regard to paragraph (e), DR 2-107(A) permitted division of fees only if: "(1) The client consents to employment of the other lawyer after a full disclosure that a division of fees will be made. (2) The division is in proportion to the services performed and responsibility assumed by each. (3) The total fee does not exceed clearly reasonable compensation. . . ." Paragraph (e) permits division without regard to the services rendered by each lawyer if they assume joint responsibility for the representation.

§ 1.5–1 FACTORS THAT DETERMINE WHETHER A FEE IS REASONABLE

§ 1.5–1(a) Introduction

In modern times, lawyers use two primary methods to determine their fees: first, the contingency fee (used primarily by plaintiffs' attorneys in personal injury actions[1]), and, second, billable hours (used by both plaintiffs' and defendants' attorneys in

---

[Section 1.5–1]

[1] Some courts have forbidden contingency fees for defense counsel. *Wunschel Law Firm, P.C. v. Clabaugh,* 291 N.W.2d 331 (Iowa 1980). On the other hand, the American Bar Association has concluded that there is no *per se* ethical objection in such cases. ABA Formal Opinion 93-373 (1993). These issues are discussed below.

all other cases, ranging from corporate advice to litigation[2]). In recent years, both types of fees have come under heavy criticism.

Because the lawyer is a fiduciary of the client, the lawyer is subject to discipline if the fees are not "reasonable."[3] The former Model Code used the term "clearly excessive,"[4] but that phrase really meant "unreasonable." It did not mean that a fee could be excessive, so as long as it was not "clearly" excessive. The Model Code itself went on to define "clearly excessive" in terms of reasonableness: "a lawyer of ordinary prudence would be left with the definite and firm conviction that the fee is in excess of a reasonable fee."[5]

The drafters of the 2002 Rules elaborated on the lawyer's obligation with respect to fees. A lawyer may not negotiate for, "charge, or collect an unreasonable fee or an unreasonable amount for expenses."[6] This language gives a more precise basis for disciplining lawyers who seek different ways to obtain excess charges from clients. "Reported cases in which lawyers are professionally disciplined or criminally prosecuted for billing abuses are disturbingly routine. Press accounts of lawyers' alleged billing and expense fraud are similarly common."[7]

Both the Model Code and the Model Rules list the same eight factors that are relevant in determining reasonableness. The ethics rules do not limit the determination of reasonableness to these eight factors, but these factors represent typical components that the lawyer may consider in setting a reasonable fee:

i.   the time and labor required, the novelty and difficulty of the questions involved, and the skill requisite to perform the legal service properly;

ii.   the likelihood, if apparent to the client, that the acceptance of the particular employment will preclude other employment by the lawyer;

---

[2]*See, e.g.,* ABA Formal Opinion 93-373 (1993); *Symposium, Legal Billing: Seeking Alternatives to the Hourly Rate,* JUDICATURE 186–202 (Jan.–Feb. 1994).

Double-Billing. On double-billing, *see also* Sonia S. Chan, *ABA Formal Opinion 93-379: Double Billing, Padding and Other Forms of Overbilling,* 9 GEORGETOWN JOURNAL OF LEGAL ETHICS 611 (1996); WILLIAM G. ROSS, THE HONEST HOUR: THE ETHICS OF TIME-BASED BILLING BY ATTORNEYS (Carolina Academic Press 1996); Kevin Hopkins, *Law Firms, Technology, and the Double-Billing Dilemma,* 12 GEORGETOWN J. LEGAL ETHICS 95 (1998).

[3]Rule 1.5(a). *See also* Restatement of the Law Governing Lawyers, Third, § 34 (Reasonable and Lawful Fees) (Official Draft 2000).

[4]DR 2-106(A).

[5]DR 2-106(B). *See also* EC 2-17 ("A lawyer should not charge more than a reasonable fee;" "adequate compensation is necessary.").

[6]Rule 1.5(a).

[7]Douglas R. Richmond, *For A Few Dollars More: The Perplexing Problems Of Unethical Billing Practices By Lawyers,* 60 S. CAROLINA L. REV. 63, 65 (2009) (footnotes omitted).

iii. the fee customarily charged in the locality for similar legal services;
iv. the amount involved and the results obtained;
v. the time limitations imposed by the client or by the circumstances;
vi. the nature and length of the professional relationship with the client;
vii. the experience, reputation, and ability of the lawyer or lawyers performing the services;
viii. whether the fee is fixed or contingent.[8]

Although a lawyer may consider factors such as how much time and labor are required, the novelty of the legal service and how much skill is needed to perform it, for many lawyers the hourly rate is the most important—or often the *sole*—factor used to determine fees.

§ 1.5–1(b) Hourly Fees

It is often said that time is money. That is certainly the truth for hourly billing. The movement from fixed fees to hourly fees began in the 1950s. Various factors, including the expansion of pretrial discovery in civil litigation, explain this shift, which was initially lauded by both clients and lawyers.[9]

If a lawyer charges by the hour, it would be unreasonable for the lawyer to bill more time than she actually spends on a matter. However, she can engage in standard practice disclosed in the retainer agreement of rounding up minimum time periods such as quarter-hours or tenths of an hour.

A lawyer basing the fee on the hours expended obviously may not engage in goldbricking, that is, employing wasteful procedures in an effort to multiply the number of billable hours.[10] Nor may the lawyer simply make up hours, that is, charge their clients for

---

[8] Rule 1.5(a); DR 2-106(B).

[9] See the careful analysis in, George B. Shepherd & Morgan Cloud, *Time and Money: Discovery Leads to Hourly Billing*, 1999 U. ILL. L. REV. 92 (1999).

[10] Rule 1.5, Comment 5. Unless there is an understanding otherwise, the lawyer should not bill separately for general overhead expenses. Restatement of the Law Governing Lawyers, Third, § 38(3)(a) (Official Draft 2000) (explaining that unless "a contract construed in the circumstances indicates otherwise," the "lawyer may not charge separately for the lawyer's general office and overhead expenses").

See Missouri v. Jenkins, 491 U.S. 274, 288 n.10, 109 S.Ct. 2463, 2472 n.10, 105 L.Ed.2d 229 (1989): "Of course, purely clerical or secretarial tasks should not be billed at a paralegal rate, regardless of who performs them." This Court also said a separate compensation award under the Civil Rights Attorney's Fees Awards Act for paralegals, law clerks, and recent law school graduates at prevailing rates was fully in accord with Act.

In re Green, 11 P.3d 1078 (Colo. 2000)(per curiam) found a fee excessive when it was based on time the *lawyer* spent faxing documents, calling the clerk's office, and other tasks that would usually be done by an as-

more hours than they actually worked, even though some empirical evidence exists indicating that some lawyers engage in this fraudulent practice.[11]

Similarly, a lawyer may not double-count hours. If the lawyer agrees to bill a client by the hour, it would violate Rule 1.5 for the lawyer to bill several clients for the same hour (*e.g.*, scheduling court appearances for two clients on the same day, spending two hours at the courthouse, and billing each client the full two hours), or for the same work product (*e.g.*, spending 15 hours preparing a research memorandum for one client, which happens to be relevant to a second client, and then billing each client the full 15 hours).

When the lawyer agrees to bill solely on the basis of time spent, one should consider the client's perspective and his expectation that the lawyer will only bill on the basis of hours actually expended. ABA Formal Opinion 93-379(1993) carefully considered these issue and reasoned that—

> A lawyer who spends four hours of time on behalf of three clients has not earned twelve billable hours. A lawyer who flies for six hours for one client, while working for five hours on behalf of another, has not earned eleven billable hours. A lawyer who is able to reuse old work product has not re-earned the hours previously billed and compensated when the work product was first generated.[12]

Sometimes when a client agrees to be billed solely on the number of hours expended, and discovers that she has lost the case, she is still presented with a big bill. The client has no right to retroactively change the manner of billing simply because, in hindsight, she wished that she had bargained differently. In other cases in which the client agrees to be billed solely on the basis of hours spent, the lawyer may be able to secure a particularly favorable result after spending fewer hours than anyone might have expected. Similarly, the lawyer may not retroactively charge for hours not actually expended. When the lawyer purports to bill only on the basis of hours expended, it is reasonable for the client to think that the lawyer will pass on any efficiency that results in fewer hours being expended. More efficient lawyers often charge

---

sistant. The court said: "charging an attorney's hourly rate for clerical services that are generally performed by a non-lawyer, and thus for which an attorney's professional skill and knowledge add no value to the service, is unreasonable as a matter of law." 11 P.3d at 1088. The court added that there is no reason or excuse for charging a client, "for one's own inefficien-

cies." 11 P.3d at 1088.

[11] Lisa G. Lerman, *Lying to Clients*, 138 U. PA. L. REV. 659, 706–20 (1990); Lisa G. Lerman, *Blue-Chip Bilking: Regulation of Billing and Expense Fraud by Lawyers*, 12 GEORGETOWN J. LEGAL ETHICS 205 (1999).

[12] ABA Formal Opinion 93-379 (Dec. 6, 1993), at 6 to 7.

more per hour. That is permissible; charging phantom hours is not.[13]

§ 1.5–1(c) After-the-Fact Analysis of Fees

If a lawyer's fee is alleged to be excessive, one or more factors may be used in determining what is an attorney's reasonable fee—what is the fair market value of his services. The court should normally look at the fee agreement as of the time that it was made, not with 20-20 hindsight.[14] If the court looked at what happened after all the facts were known, then the court is no longer examining the fee contract to see if it is reasonable; rather, the court is writing a new contract, one that the fully-informed, competent parties could not have written because those of us who are not prophets cannot act, before the fact, with 20-20 hindsight.[15]

Consider, for example, a contingent fee case where the plaintiff wins a large award. A disgruntled client, after-the-fact, can always argue that the fee is excessive because the lawyer now knows that the plaintiff has won. But, the lawyer does not know beforehand, that the client will win, nor will the lawyer know, beforehand, how much. After-the-fact, the risks inherent in a contingent fee agreement will disappear because the contingency has occurred. Thus, the court analyzes the contract as of the time it was made. At that point in time, the lawyer and client each knowingly assume different risks. The lawyer assumes the risk that the case will take a great deal of time but produce no, or a

---

[13]ABA Formal Opinion 93-379 (Dec. 6, 1993), at 7.

"[If] it turns out that the lawyer is particularly efficient in accomplishing a given result, it nonetheless will not be permissible to charge the client for more hours than were actually expended on the matter. . . . [T]he economies associated with the result must inure to the benefit of the client, not give rise to an opportunity to bill a client [for] phantom hours."

[14]In *National Credit Union Admin. Bd. v. Johnson*, 133 F.3d 1097 (8th Cir.1998), the court, in the course of holding that a lawyer is not necessarily required to refund a non-refundable retainer paid by a credit union right before it was taken over by the government, said:

"If *at that time* the NCUAB [the National Credit Union Administration Board] can establish that the fee paid

was an unreasonable one, *examined as of the date of the transfer*, then L & V [the law firm] will have to return the nonrefundable retainer, otherwise it will not."

133 F.3d at 1103 (emphasis added).

[15]As California Rule 4-200(B), Rules of Professional Conduct of the State Bar of California, *reprinted in*, THOMAS D. MORGAN & RONALD D. ROTUNDA, 1999 SELECTED STANDARDS SUPPLEMENT ON PROFESSIONAL RESPONSIBILITY 311 (Foundation Press, 1999) states:

"Unconscionability of a fee shall be determined on the basis of all the facts and circumstances *existing at the time the agreement is entered into* except where the parties contemplate that the fee will be affected by later events. . . ." (emphasis added).

very little, recovery.[16] The client, in turn, takes the risk that the case will not require that much time and produce a very handsome recovery. "Events within that range of risks, such as a high recovery, do not make unreasonable an agreement that was reasonable *when made.*"[17]

In some cases, a change in circumstances may make a fee agreement, in retrospect, unreasonable, especially if that change concerns events that were not really contemplated as part of the original bargain. For example, the court, in determining whether the fee agreement is unreasonable, may take into account later events like supervening impracticality or supervening frustration.[18] But the situations where these unknown, supervening events occur, are relatively rare.

---

[16]*See* Graham Matthew Cridland & Jacy D'Aiutolo, *When the Lawyer Owns the Client: Equity Interests as Attorney's Fees*, 15 GEORGETOWN. J. LEGAL ETHICS 759 (2002), arguing that contingent fees and the lawyer accepting payment in the form of an equity interest (stock) in the client allow the lawyer to earn what, in retrospect, seems like windfall profits. *See also,* Sharon Mary Mathew, *Stock-Based Compensation for Legal Services: Resurrecting the Ethical Dilemma*, 42 SANTA CLARA L. REV. 1227 (2002); Thomas E. Przybylski, *The Ethics of Accepting Stock in a Client as Payment for Legal Services*, 47 WAYNE L. REV. 1431 (2002).

[17]Restatement of the Law Governing Lawyers, Third, § 34 (*Reasonable and Lawful Fees*) (Official Draft 2000), at Comment *c*, "Unenforceable fee agreements," at p. 250 (emphasis added).

[18]**Supervening Frustration.** Restatement of the Law Governing Lawyers, Third, § 34 (*Reasonable and Lawful Fees*) (Official Draft 2000), at Comment *c*, "Unenforceable fee agreements," at p. 250, citing the Restatement of Contracts, Second, §§ 152 to 154, 261 to 265 (1979). For example, Restatement of Contracts, Second § 265, *Discharge by Supervening Frustration*, provides:

"Where, after a contract is made, a party's principal purpose is substantially frustrated without his fault by the occurrence of an event the non-occurrence of which was a basic assumption on which the contract was made, his remaining duties to render performance are discharged, unless the language or the circumstances indicate the contrary."

Illustration 1 to this section explains the rule:

"A and B make a contract under which B is to pay A $1,000 and is to have the use of A's window on January 10 to view a parade that has been scheduled for that day. Because of the illness of an important official, the parade is cancelled. B refuses to use the window or pay the $1,000. B's duty to pay $1,000 is discharged, and B is not liable to A for breach of contract."

Contrast Illustration 6:

"A leases a gasoline station to B. A change in traffic regulations so reduces B's business that he is unable to operate the station except at a substantial loss. B refuses to make further payments of rent. If B can still operate the station, even though at such a loss, his principal purpose of operating a gasoline station is not substantially frustrated. B's duty to pay rent is not discharged, and B is liable to A for breach of contract. The result would be the same if substantial loss were caused instead by a government regulation rationing gasoline or a termination of the franchise under which B obtained gasoline."

In determining what is reasonable, it is also certainly relevant, indeed, crucial to know if the attorney overreached the client, abused the relationship, or was not completely candid in discussing the elements of a fee or other relevant factors. For example, if the lawyer falsely told the client that lawyers in a particular area of law (*e.g.*, filing in court to change officially one's name) were charging about $100, when the standard fee was really $50, the court should find the $100 fee unreasonable because the lawyer lied to the prospective client as to the fee customarily charged in the locality for similar services. On the other hand, if Lawyer Alpha truthfully informs the prospective client that the standard rate is around $50, but that Lawyer Alpha was going to charge $100 because it is not worth his time to work on any case for less than a $100 minimum, then the client—who is fully informed—is free to accept that higher fee, which would not be unreasonable under the circumstances. Or, this client can decide to go elsewhere.

Some commentators have claimed that the nature of the lawyer's product makes rational valuation of the individual attorney's services practically impossible. Some may argue that the inability of the marketplace to value a lawyer's services means that no fee can ever be unreasonable. Or, others argue that the inability of the marketplace to value a lawyer's services means that when a claim is made that a fee is unreasonable, the factfinder should not take into account whether the fee was adequately discussed beforehand.

The case law has rejected both of these positions as painting too pessimistic a view of the ability of the market place to value services. For example, cases may arise where the client is unable to exercise the judgment that a reasonably competent adult would exercise because the lawyer may mislead the client, or take advantage of a less sophisticated client. If the lawyer is paid in property, the fee may be subject to "special scrutiny" because the lawyer may have special knowledge of the value of the property that is not disclosed to the client.[19] Courts have not found it impossible to value attorney's fees, and have found some to be excessive in the appropriate factual circumstances.[20] On the other hand, if the fee and other relevant facts and circumstances are

---

[19]Rule 1.5, Comment 4.

[20]*See, e.g.*, *The Florida Bar v. Moriber*, 314 So.2d 145 (Fla.1975) (per curiam) (even though client may have been informed of the fee of nearly $8,000 for collecting, on behalf of client, approximately $23,000 in an investor's variable payment fund, the fee was excessive because the amount to be collected had already passed to client by operation of law). *Cf. United States v. Vague*, 697 F.2d 805, 806 (7th Cir.1983) (Posner, J.), in dictum stating that even a fixed fee freely bargained by competent adults who do not complain about it may be excessive. However, in this case the court held that the district judge had exceeded

fully and fairly disclosed to a competent client, it will be difficult, if not impossible, to persuade a court to hold that such a fee is unreasonably high.

Legal Auditing of Law Firm Billing. Clients and others have turned to legal auditors to help them file objections to law firm bills, leading to the creation and rapid growth of companies that specialize in auditing legal bills. For example, Jed S. Ringel, a former litigator, started Law Audit Services in 1989, using as the corporate headquarters his maid's room in his New York City apartment. Ten years later, Law Audit Services occupied a 20,000 square foot office, employed 130 people, and audited $60,000 in legal bills on a typical business day.[21]

§ 1.5–1(d) Opportunity Costs

If a lawyer accepts one matter, that representation may well preclude him from taking other legal work. The lawyer may consider what economists call an "opportunity cost." To take one case deprives the lawyer of the opportunity to take another case. First, the lawyer only has a finite number of hours in any given period. Therefore if he takes one assignment, he may not have the time to take another one. Second, whenever a lawyer accepts one job, he creates conflicts that prevent him from accepting other work. If the client is not aware of this opportunity cost, the lawyer should tell him.[22] The issue of opportunity costs leads to the question of non-refundable retainers, discussed below.

---

his power by compelling attorney to return part of the fee.

[21]Milo Gryelin, *Crossing the Bar: If You Think Insurers are Tight, Try Being Their Lawyers*, WALL STREET JOURNAL, Feb. 9, 1999, at A1, col. 1 & A8, col. 1.

[22]Rule 1.5(a)(2); DR 2-106(B)(2). *See In re Sather*, 3 P.3d 403 (Colo. 2000), concluding that because "an attorney earns a fee only when the attorney provides a benefit or service to the client," under Colorado Rule of Professional Conduct, Rule 1.15(a) and (f), "all client funds—including engagement retainers, advance fees, flat fees, lump sum fees, etc.—must be held in trust until there is a basis on which to conclude that the attorney 'earned' the fee; otherwise, the funds must remain in the client's trust account because they are not the attorney's property." 3 P.3d at 411–12 (internal citations omitted). The court accepted the fact that "engagement retainers" may be

justified if the lawyer turns down other work or otherwise benefits the client, but the lawyer must clearly explain to the client why the fee is treated as a non-refundable retainer. The court summarized the rule:

"Engagement retainers are generally earned upon receipt and, *so long as the basis of how the attorney earns this fee is clearly explained to the client in writing*, they are the attorney's property. For other forms of advance fees, the attorney may transfer the funds to the attorney's personal or operating accounts only after earning the fees unless, within a very limited set of circumstances, the attorney and client have agreed in writing to allow the attorney to treat the unearned fees as property of the attorney. An attorney can earn fees only by providing services or conferring a benefit on the client, and the attorney must explain the nature of the services or benefit being conferred before he may treat advance funds as his own property."

3 P.3d at 412 (footnote omitted) (em-

§ 1.5–1(e) Non-Refundable Retainers

Sometimes lawyers charge a client a "non-refundable retainer." In a typical case, the retainer provides that the fee is earned when paid. The fee is payable before any work is begun and is not refundable even if the work turns out to take little time or if the client later fires the lawyer. The client is paying the lawyer for her services and also for being on call and not working for adverse parties.

Some commentators criticize non-refundable retainers[23] and courts that scrutinize them with care. For example, *Matter of Cooperman*,[24] a leading New York case, disciplined a lawyer for imposing non-refundable fees on his clients. Cooperman, in effect, told the client that once he entered an appearance in this case, he would not return any part of the fee even if the client fired him. Non-refundable fees violate the fiduciary relationship between lawyer and client, the Court of Appeals reasoned. The Court affirmed the lawyer's two-year suspension from practice.[25]

Although a non-refundable retainer does not prevent the client from firing the lawyer, it certainly makes the exercising that right more costly. Consequently, some courts often have concluded that no retainer is truly non-refundable in all cases.[26]

Courts vary in deciding whether nonrefundable retainers are

---

phasis added). The court ordered suspension for the lawyer, for various ethical violations.

[23] *See* Lester Brickman & Lawrence A. Cunningham, *Nonrefundable Retainers: Impermissible Under Fiduciary, Statutory and Contract Law*, 57 FORDHAM L. REV. 149 (1988).

[24] *Matter of Cooperman*, 83 N.Y.2d 465, 611 N.Y.S.2d 465, 633 N.E.2d 1069 (1994).

[25] *Kelly v. MD Buyline, Inc.*, 2 F.Supp.2d 420 (S.D.N.Y.1998) interpreted *Cooperman* to apply to cases involving single-case, or "special" retainers. It concluded that where the retainer is a fixed amount to be available for a defined period, a nonrefundability feature is permissible.

In re O'Farrell, 942 N.E.2d 799 (Ind. 2011), a family law practitioner charged clients a flat fee for her work. She called part of the total flat fee an "engagement retainer," which she claimed she earned upon commencement of her work on the case. In two cases, clients ended the relationship

after the lawyer began work but before she completed the case. The lawyer refused to return the engagement retainer. The flat fee agreement that informed the clients that her fee was nonrefundable even if the attorney-client relationship terminated prior to completion of the lawyer's representation violated Rule 1.5(a) prohibiting a lawyer from charging unreasonable fee. The court cited, *Matter of Cooperman*, 83 N.Y.2d 465, 611 N.Y.S.2d 465, 633 N.E.2d 1069, 1072–73 (1994).

[26] In *Federal Savings & Loan Ins. Corp. v. Angell, Holmes & Lea*, 838 F.2d 395 (9th Cir.1988), *cert. denied sub nom., Van Voorhis & Skaggs v. FSLIC*, 488 U.S. 848, 109 S.Ct. 127, 102 L.Ed.2d 100 (1988). Counsel for a savings and loan was paid a large fee which purported to be non-refundable. Three weeks later, the client was put into receivership. The FSLIC fired the lawyer and asked for return of the retainer. Because a client is always free to fire its lawyer, the firm had to return all but a reasonable fee for work done before termination.

excessive in the particular facts.[27] In some cases an attorney may incur real opportunity costs by taking a case and the attorney may make this fact clear to the client when the client retains him. Assume, for example, that a client wants her lawyer to assure her that she will set aside the month of September to try a matter. She agrees to do so for a non-refundable fee of $20,000, her typical monthly billing. She then turns down opportunities to take other litigation because it will interfere with the September trial. On August 31st the client fires the lawyer, at a time when she is unable to take the other cases that she earlier had turned down. In that case, the fee is not per se improper and a court may approve the fee as reasonable under the circumstances.[28] A law firm that includes a liquidated damages clause in a contract

---

In re Gastineau, 317 Or. 545, 857 P.2d 136 (1993), held that non-refundable flat-fee contracts are not per se improper, but they are a prohibited unreasonable fee where the lawyer does not do the necessary legal work.

Matter of Dawson, 129 N.M. 369, 8 P.3d 856, 859 (N.M. 2000) (per curiam): "a lawyer's claim that he or she charged a client a flat fee or retainer that is nonrefundable will not suffice to justify a failure to deposit unearned client funds in a trust account, a withdrawal of client funds from a trust account to pay fees that have not yet been earned, or a failure to promptly return unearned funds to a client upon termination of the representation. The Rules of Professional Conduct in this state do not permit lawyers to charge nonrefundable unearned fees."

In re Mance, 980 A.2d 1196 (D.C. 2009) held that flat fees do not become the lawyer's property—and therefore must be held in trust—until the lawyer earns them. Moreover, it is unreasonable to consider a fee "earned" before the lawyer renders any services. In other words, when a lawyer receives a flat fee, the fee is an advance of unearned fees and the property of the client until earned, unless the client provided informed consent to a different arrangement. The Court specifically agreed with *In re Sather*, 3 P.3d 403 (Colo. 2000), and added that "the client should be informed that, unless

there is agreement otherwise, the attorney must, under Rule 1.15(d), hold the flat fee in escrow until it is earned by the lawyer's provision of legal services." 980 A.2d 1196, 1207.

[27] *See, e.g., Grievance Adm'r, Attorney Grievance Com'n v. Cooper*, 757 N.W.2d 867 (Mich. 2008) (holding that a $4,000 nonrefundable retainer in a divorce action with a clearly written contract did not violate Rule 1.5).

[28] *Cf. National Credit Union Admin. Bd. v. Johnson*, 133 F.3d 1097 (8th Cir.1998), holding that a lawyer is not necessarily required to refund a non-refundable retainer paid by a credit union right before it was taken over by the government. The court said:

We simply hold as a matter of law that an insolvent debtor in a bankruptcy proceeding may pay a nonrefundable retainer to attorneys of his choice for representation if the amount paid is reasonable and is not taken from assets that the law firm either knew or should have known were secured at the time they were paid.

133 F.3d at 1103.

In re Hirschfeld, 192 Ariz. 40, 960 P.2d 640 (Ariz.1998), *cert. denied*, 525 U.S. 1122, 119 S.Ct. 904, 142 L.Ed.2d 903 (1999) held that a failure to return unearned portions of non-refundable retainers rendered the fees unreasonable and was part of the basis for the lawyer's disbarment.

On the other hand, *Bunker v. Meshbesher*, 147 F.3d 691 (8th

if the client prematurely terminates the representation essentially is implementing a minimum fee agreement. Firms may draft such clauses to apply to early termination of the relationship in a fixed fee agreement or upon the client's failure to provide adequate notice to the firm of an impending termination of the representation. The enforceability of such a clause should rely upon a facts and circumstances analysis similar to the reasonableness analysis of a nonrefundable retainer or a minimum fee.[29]

§ 1.5–1(f) Charges in the Locality

The lawyer may also consider the fees customarily charged in the locality for similar legal services.[30] It would be a violation of the antitrust laws for the bar association to discipline a lawyer because he has charged less than a minimum (or more than a maximum) fee.[31] However, the mere fact that all lawyers of similar quality charge the same, or approximately the same, fee for similar services is not in and of itself proof that lawyers conspired to fix prices. In fact, in a perfectly competitive economy, the prices for similar services tend to be about the same.

Cir.1998) upheld a non-refundable retainer. A client, charged with drug offenses, signed an agreement to pay a law firm $110,000. The contract did not state that the fee was non-refundable. The client later fired the firm and retained another lawyer who pled him guilty. The court held that the firm need not return any of the money. Although Minnesota later required non-refundable retainers to be in writing, it had not done so at the time of this case. The court upheld a jury finding of non-refundability.

Other cases approving of nonrefundable retainers under the circumstances include: *Ryan v. Butera, Beausang, Cohen & Brennan*, 193 F.3d 210 (3d Cir. 1999). In this case, a client had adopted an aggressive strategy for defense of asbestos cases against it, including filing suits against opposing counsel. To control overall costs, it retained firms at fixed fees of $1 million each, non-refundable. When the law firm had been working ten weeks for this client, the law firm demanded time to investigate before filing a suit accusing another law firm of wrongdoing. The client responded by firing the firm and demanding the return of its million dollars. The court

said the firm could keep the retainer. The fee agreement had been proposed by a sophisticated client and, while that client can terminate the relationship at any time, the law firm had performed properly and may keep its fee even though it no longer represented the client.

[29]*See McQueen, Rains & Tresch, LLP v. Citgo Petroleum Corp.*, 2008 OK 66, 195 P.3d 35 (Okla. 2008). *McQueen* involved several questions certified to the Oklahoma Supreme Court when a client terminated an attorney-client relationship that contained a liquidated clause. The client sued the law firm for $4.6 million and the Oklahoma court held that liquidated damages clauses were not per se unenforceable and that the law firm would need to meet the requirements of a nonrefundable retainer in order to make it applicable to the situation.

[30]DR 2-106(B)(3); Rule 1.5(a)(3).

[31]*Goldfarb v. Virginia State Bar*, 421 U.S. 773, 95 S.Ct. 2004, 44 L.Ed.2d 572 (1975). *See* Thomas D. Morgan, *The Impact of Antitrust Law on the Legal Profession*, 67 FORDHAM L. REV. 415 (1998)(Symposium).

§ 1.5–1(g) Price-Fixing by State Action.

Although lawyers and bar associations may not conspire to fix prices, the federal antitrust laws do not forbid the state from setting prices by state law.[32] Price-fixing by state action is exempt from the Sherman Act.[33] In other words, if a statute sets a price for legal services, a lawyer does not charge an excessive fee or conspire with the state when he or she follows the statute. The lawyer merely complies with the law. Although state-mandated fee schedules are unusual, in some cases they do exist.[34]

§ 1.5–1(h) Special Circumstances

In determining an appropriate fee, the lawyer may also take into account how much money is involved and how successful the attorney is in the particular matter.[35] It is not uncommon for a law firm and client to agree in advance to raise or lower a base hourly rate by a varying amount depending on the success of the negotiations, the size of the deal, and so forth. However, if the firm represented to the client that the fee would be based only on the number of hours worked, it would be unreasonable for the firm to retroactively change the basis of the fee.

---

[32]*Goldfarb v. Virginia State Bar*, 421 U.S. 773, 95 S.Ct. 2004, 44 L.Ed.2d 572 (1975). *Cf. FTC v. Superior Court Trial Lawyers Association*, 493 U.S. 411, 110 S.Ct. 768, 107 L.Ed.2d 851 (1990). In this case, court-appointed criminal defense lawyers who were in private practice (and not employees of the same law firm) engaged in a boycott in order to obtain higher compensation. The Court held that this boycott constituted restraint of trade in violation of the federal antitrust laws.

[33]*See, e.g., Gair v. Peck*, 6 N.Y.2d 97, 188 N.Y.S.2d 491, 160 N.E.2d 43 (1959), *cert. denied*, 361 U.S. 374, 80 S.Ct. 401, 4 L.Ed.2d 380 (1960) (maximum prices set by the court in contingent fee causes).

[34]*Bernick v. Frost*, 210 N.J.Super. 397, 400–03, 510 A.2d 56, 58–59 (N.J.Super.Ct.App.Div.1986), *cert. denied*, 105 N.J. 511, 523 A.2d 158 (1986), which noted that both New York and New Jersey have a fee schedule that applied to contingent fees in medical malpractice cases. In this case, the court applied the New Jersey fee schedule, given that there was the specific selection of New Jersey law in the fee contract; in addition, most of the work was performed there. The court did not apply the more rigorous fee schedule of New York, where the litigation occurred.

Fee Schedules and the ABA Model Rules for Mediation. The ABA Model Rules for Mediation of Client-Lawyer Disputes (Aug. 1998) create a Meditation Commission, which has the power to "establish fee schedules and oversee financial matters." Rule 2(C)(9). However, this is not the power to set fee schedules that govern lawyers generally. Instead, the Commission only has the authority to establish reasonable fees to support the program and also to waive fees in cases of hardship. "No fee should be charged a client if the charging of the fee would unduly restrict the client's access to the mediation process." Rule 2, Commentary.

[35]Rule 1.5(a)(4). DR 2-106(B)(4).

Lawyers should promptly establish the basis or rate of the fee.[36] To avoid misunderstanding the law firm should be clear. In one case, the law firm quoted specific hourly rates for services of named attorneys to a prospective client. The client then agreed in writing to pay the firm's "regular hourly rates." The court found that throughout the course of its representation, the law firm increased the hourly billing rates for its services "without notifying" the client of the changes. Moreover, the bills that the law firm sent "did not set forth the hourly rates of the attorneys or contain information from which, on their face, changes in the hourly rates could be determined." In the subsequent fee dispute, the court held that the law firm could not raise rates that the named lawyers charged without first notifying the client.[37]

The ABA advises that the Model Rules allow the lawyer and client to modify an existing fee agreement. But, the lawyer has the burden to show any modification was reasonable under the circumstances at the time of the modification. The lawyer must also show that he communicated this information to the client, who accepted this new contract. Generally, a lawyer may charge periodic, incremental increases in his regular hourly billing rates if the lawyer clearly communicates this practice to the client and the client accepts it when the lawyer-client relationship begins and these periodic increases are reasonable under the circumstances. If the lawyer seeks to modify the basic nature of a fee arrangement or significantly increase his compensation, that "ordinarily will be unreasonable," unless there are unanticipated change in circumstances.[38]

The lawyer may adjust the bill if the circumstances or the client imposes special time limitations.[39] For example, if the client asks the law firm to take on a major project with a serious time deadline, the lawyer may advise the client that the law firm will take the matter, but that the client must understand that the law firm will charge more than its usual rate because of the time constraints.[40] The client can choose to agree to this condition or seek another lawyer.

The nature and length of the relationship with the client is

---

[36] Rule 1.5, Comment 2.

[37] *Severson & Werson v. Bolinger*, 235 Cal. App. 3d 1569, 1571–1572, 1 Cal. Rptr. 2d 531, 532–533 (1st Dist. 1991). *See also, Simburg, Ketter, Sheppard & Purdy, L.L.P. v. Olshan*, 97 Wash.App. 901, 444–45, 988 P.2d 467, 471–72 (Wash.App. Div. 1,1999). Restatement Third, The Law Governing Lawyers § 18(1)(a), discussing when the lawyer makes a contract or modification beyond a reasonable time after the lawyer has begun to represent the client.

[38] ABA Formal Op.11-458 (Aug. 4, 2011). "Changing Fee Arrangements During Representation."

[39] Rule 1.5(a)(5). DR 2-106(B)(5).

[40] Restatement of the Law Governing Lawyers, Third, § 34 (Reasonable and Lawful Fees) (Official Draft 2000), at Comment *b*, p. 248.

also relevant.[41] That is, special circumstances might make a lawyer more likely to reduce a bill for an old client, or to cut a bill as a "loss leader," in an effort to encourage a new client to continue to retain the lawyer in other matters.

The lawyer may also consider his own experience, reputation, and ability.[42] Lawyers who are twice as good as other lawyers are justified in charging twice as much as the other lawyers charge. A client may always conclude that the lawyer is not twice as good, and therefore can go elsewhere for legal services.

§ 1.5–1(i) Contingent Fees: An Introduction

Another factor to consider in determining if a fee is unreasonable is whether the fee is fixed or contingent.[43] A fee that looks large in retrospect, may not appear as large if one considers that the fee was contingent and that the lawyer risked receiving nothing.[44]

§ 1.5–1(j) Fee Shifting Statutes

Cases involving fee shifting statutes should be distinguished from cases where the attorney and client bargain for a fee later challenged as excessive. In situations such as civil rights cases, the court is authorized to require the losing party to pay the attorney's fees of the prevailing party. The court in this case is applying the statute, not the ethics rules, and using that statute to impose fees on the opposing party. The party paying the fee does so because of a statute, not because of a contract. Fee shifting statutes are not like ordinary fee disputes any more than steak is like spinach, because the party paying the fee (the losing litigant) is not the party who has hired the lawyer.

Under the Civil Rights Attorney's Fee Awards Act of 1976[45] the prevailing plaintiff ordinarily should receive an attorney's fee; in contrast, the prevailing defendant may recover an attorney's fee only if the lawsuit was vexatious, frivolous, or brought to harass or embarrass the defendant. To determine what is a reasonable fee, the "critical inquiry" is generally the appropriate hourly rate multiplied by the number of hours reasonably expended on the litigation.[46]

---

[41] DR 2-106(B)(6); Rule 1.5(a)(6).

[42] DR 2-106(B)(7); Rule 1.5(a)(7).

[43] Rule 1.5(a)(8); DR 2-106(B)(8). *See also* Restatement of the Law Governing Lawyers, Third, § 35 (Official Draft 2000).

[44] This topic, contingent fees, is considered in detail later in this section in connection with Rule 1.5(d).

[45] 42 U.S.C.A. § 1988.

[46] 4 RONALD D. ROTUNDA & JOHN E. NOWAK, TREATISE ON CONSTITUTIONAL LAW: SUBSTANCE AND PROCEDURE § 19.36 (Thomson- West, 4th ed. 2008) (6 volumes).

§ 1.5–1(k) Written Fee Agreements and the Content of that Agreement

A Writing. A misunderstanding regarding fees is the most frequent cause of clients' disputes with their attorneys.[47] Consequently the Model Code prudently advised that it "is usually beneficial to reduce [the fee arrangement] to writing. . . ."[48] The Model Rules raise this recommendation to the disciplinary level, but keep the precatory language and limit it to new clients.[49] Malpractice experts also recommend that the lawyer confirm in writing the basis of the fee.[50]

The drafters of the 2002 Rules proposed that lawyers reduce all fee agreements to a writing unless the fee is *de minimus* or the lawyer regularly represents the client and the basis for the fee has not changed.[51] The ABA House of Delegates rejected this proposal because a fear exists that if the Rules require a writing and if a lawyer does not meet this requirement, the lawyer will not be able to collect the fee. The ABA House of Delegates amended Rule 1.5(b) to include a requirement that the lawyer communicate to the client the scope of the representation and the expenses for which the client will be responsible in addition to the fee. Rule 1.5(b) requires that lawyers communicate to the client any change in the basis for the fee or expenses.

As to contingent fees, discussed below, the Model Code urged

---

[47] If the lawyer enters into an oral agreement with the client and the client does not fully know or understand the fee agreement, the court will refuse to enforce the fee contract. The attorney may be able to receive compensation based upon quantum meruit. However, if the lawyer's billing entries are imprecise, the court may preclude a quantum meruit fee recovery. *See Mallin & Assoc. v. Nash Metalware, Inc.*, 849 N.Y.S.2d 752 (2008).

[48] EC 2-19.

[49] Rule 1.5(b) ("preferably in writing"). Restatement of the Law Governing Lawyers § 38 (Official Draft 2000).

Fee if there is no written or oral agreement. If the lawyer and client have neither a written fee agreement nor an oral one, then the client owes the lawyer "fair value" of the lawyer's services. Restatement of the Law Governing Lawyers, Third, § 39 (Official Draft 2000).

Fee if lawyer is discharged or withdraws. If the client fires the lawyer or the lawyer withdraws before she has completed her services, and assuming that the lawyer's discharge or withdrawal is not attributed to the lawyer's misconduct, then the lawyer may collect the fair value for her services or the ratable proportion of the compensation provided by the retainer agreement (which ever is less). However, even in these circumstances, the court will not give the lawyer the ratable proportion for her services unless the lawyer has performed severable services and imposing contractual compensation will not burden the client's ability to obtain a new lawyer. Restatement of the Law Governing Lawyers § 40(2) (Official Draft 2000).

[50] 1 RONALD E. MALLEN & JEFFREY M. SMITH, LEGAL MALPRACTICE § 2.9 (West Pub. Co. 2005 ed.).

[51] *See* Reporter's Explanation of Changes to Model Rule 1.5.

that the agreement be reduced to a writing,[52] but the Model Rules go beyond that and flatly require a writing.[53]

Are Expenses Deducted Before Or After The Fee Is Calculated? The writing required in a contingent fee representation must state how the fee is determined and whether expenses are deducted *before or after* the contingent fee is calculated.[54] Some commentators have argued that it is unethical for lawyers to have contingency fee agreements where lawyers take their contingent fee as a percentage of the total award, then subtract expenses out of the client's portion of the award.[55] Rule 1.5 does not impose this limitation.

The Non-Contingent Liability of Client for Expenses. The drafters of the 2002 Rules added a requirement that the lawyer representing a client in a contingent fee representation disclose in the writing the "expenses for which the client will be liable whether or not the client is the prevailing party." After the matter is concluded, the lawyer must also provide a detailed statement to the client.[56]

§ 1.5–1(k)(1) Price Discrimination

Both the Code and the Rules permit price discrimination. That is, the lawyer may lower a fee depending on who the client is. Because lawyers may charge less to the less wealthy, they, by necessary implication, may charge more for the same services offered to the wealthier.[57] However, no fee may be so high as to be "unreasonable," a point discussed above.

§ 1.5–2 FEE DISPUTES

§ 1.5–2(a) Interpreting the Fee Agreement

If a dispute arises involving the interpretation of the fee agreement, the court should construe the agreement as a reasonable

---

[52]EC 2-19.

[53]Rule 1.5(c).

[54]Rule 1.5(c).

[55]W. William Hodes, *Cheating Clients With The Percentage-Of-The-Gross Contingent Fee Scam*, 30 HOFSTRA L. REV. 767 (2002). It has become more common for lawyers to apply their contingency fee percentages to the gross recovery, which results in charging all litigation expenses to the client's share. Professor Brickman estimates that this practice raises actual contingency fee percentages by approximately one percent.

Lester Brickman, *Effective Hourly Rates of Contingency-Fee Lawyers: Competing Data and Non-Competitive Fees*, 81 WASH. U. L.Q. 653, 736 (2003).

[56]Rule 1.5(c). Cf. DR 2-101(B)(22) (*advertisements* of contingent fee rates must disclose whether percentages are computed before or after costs).

[57]*See, e.g.*, EC 2-24, 2-25; Rule 1.5, Comment 3 ("it is proper to define the extent of services in light of the client's ability to pay"). *Cf.* EC 2-18 (it is "commendable" for lawyer to charge less to a "brother lawyer or member of his immediate family").

person would in the circumstances of the client.[1] Lawyers should be careful when drafting their fee agreements. After all, they are drafting a document that concerns something about which they should know a lot. An old rule of interpretation states that doubtful agreements are to be construed against the drafter. "As a general proposition, the meaning of a written document, if placed in doubt, is construed against the party that wrote it, and the principle surely counts double when the drafter is a lawyer writing on his or her own account to a client. In setting fees, lawyers 'are fiduciaries who owe their clients greater duties than are owed under the general law of contracts.' "[2]

Courts tend to interpret the fee agreements in favor of clients in the event of an ambiguity because: lawyers draft the fee agreements that govern their relationship with their clients; clients have every right to trust their lawyers, who own them a fiduciary duty; lawyers are more likely to be trained in the law than their clients; and lawyers should have the experience and familiarity to know which issues have to be clarified.[3] Hence lawyers should

---

[Section 1.5–2]

[1]Restatement of the Law Governing Lawyers, Third, § 18(2) (Official Draft 2000). *See also Reiner, Reiner and Bendett PC v. Cadle Co., Conn.*, 278 Conn. 92, 897 A.2d 58 (2006), *noted in* 22 ABA/BNA MANUAL ON PROFESSIONAL CONDUCT, Current Reports News 254 (May 31, 2006). *Reiner* holds that courts must review forum selection clauses in attorney-client agreements under a reasonableness standard. If the court finds it to be unreasonable, the forum selection clause will not be enforced.

[2]*Beatty v. NP Corp.*, 31 Mass.App. Ct. 606, 612, 581 N.E.2d 1311, 1315 (1991)(internal citations omitted). *Cf.* Ronald D. Rotunda, *The New Illinois Rules of Professional Conduct: A Brief Introduction and Criticism*, 78 ILL. BAR J. 386 (1990).

[3]In *Columbus Bar Ass'n v. Brooks*, 87 Ohio St.3d 344, 721 N.E.2d 23 (1999) (per curiam), a lawyer sought to collect a one-third contingent fee and also to charge an additional hourly rate for the lawyer's secretary and paralegal. The court finds that, unless clearly agreed otherwise in writing, secretarial and legal assistant expenses are general overhead, not separately billable. Billing them in this case thus violated the fee agreement and constituted charging an unreasonable fee. For this and other matters, the court suspended the lawyer for two years, with all but six months of that suspension stayed on the condition that the lawyer reimburse the clients.

Levine v. Bayne, Snell & Krause, Ltd., 44 Tex. Sup. Ct. J. 387, 40 S.W.3d 92 (2001) involved the question of how to interpret a contingent fee agreement when the issue was the "amount" on which a contingent fee should be calculated. In this case, the Levines alleged that the Smiths were liable for defects in the Smiths' house. The Levines had agreed to pay a fee of one-third of "any amount received" from the Smiths for defects in their house. Because of these defects, the Levines had stopped making contract payments to the Smiths, so the Smiths filed a counterclaim. By the end of this litigation, the Levines had recovered about $240,000 and the Smiths had recovered about $160,000, leaving a net benefit to the Levines of about $80,000. The question was whether the Levines owed a contingent fee based on $240,000 or $80,000 based

draft their fee agreements with care, to protect their clients by giving them fair warning, and to protect themselves.[4]

§ 1.5–2(b) Suing to Collect a Fee

On an aspirational level, the Model Code advised that lawyers should not sue the client to collect a fee "unless necessary to prevent fraud or gross imposition by the client."[5] The Model Rules agree that if there is an established procedure to resolve fee disputes, such as arbitration or mediation, the "lawyer should conscientiously consider submitting to it."[6] The Restatement allows the lawyer to use any fee collection method that is not forbidden by law.[7]

Accepting Credit Cards. Many years ago, the ABA Ethics Committee concluded that it is proper for a lawyer to accept fees through credit card payment.[8] The lawyer would allow the client to use American Express, Visa, Master Card, etc., in payment of his fees and simply leave all collection problems up to the credit

---

upon the language "any amount received." The court acknowledged that the Levines had received $240,000 worth of benefit because they now owned the house free of the mortgage. Nonetheless, it ruled that the better interpretation of the words "any amount received" was to base the fee on the net, or $80,000, which reduced the Levines' liability considerably. The court said that "to impose the obligation of clarifying attorney-client contracts upon the attorney is entirely reasonable, both because of [the attorney's] greater knowledge and experience with respect to fee arrangements and because of the trust [that the] client has placed in [the attorney]." 40 S.W.3d at 95, quoting, *Cardenas v. Ramsey County*, 322 N.W.2d 191, 194 (Minn.1982)(internal quotations omitted).

[4]Lawyers who seek to protect their fee may acquire a contractual security interest in client property; however, the lawyer must meet the requirements of Rule 1.8(a) in securing the agreement. *See* ABA Formal Opinion 02-427 (May 31, 2002).

[5]EC 2-23.

[6]Rule 1.5, Comment 9. The drafters to the 2002 Rules added the clause that states if the program is mandatory, the lawyer must participate in it.

This Comment adds:

"Law may prescribe a procedure for determining a lawyer's fee, for example, in representation of an executor or administrator, a class or a person entitled to a reasonable fee as part of the measure of damages. The lawyer entitled to such a fee and a lawyer representing another party concerned with the fee should comply with the prescribed procedure."

[7]Restatement of the Law Governing Lawyers § 41 (Official Draft 2000). The Restatement also notes that the lawyer may not harass the client or use the client's confidential information if § 65 does not permit the use of that information. ABA Model Rule 1.6(b)(2) and Restatement § 65 allow the use of otherwise confidential client information to the minimum amount necessary to collect a fee.

[8]ABA Formal Opinion 338 (Nov. 16, 1974). The ABA issued Formal Opinion 338 (Nov. 16, 1974) under the Model Code, in an era before the Supreme Court gave First Amendment protections to lawyer advertising. *See Bates v. State Bar of Arizona*, 433 U.S. 350, 97 S.Ct. 2691, 53 L.Ed.2d 810 (1977); *Zauderer v. Office of Disciplinary Counsel*, 471 U.S. 626, 105 S.Ct. 2265, 85 L.Ed.2d 652 (1985).

card company. However, this earlier ethics opinion imposed some requirements (*e.g.*, no promotional materials "except possibly a small insignia"; the lawyer must secure advance approval by a bar association) that are no longer viewed as justified. Hence, over a quarter of a century later, the ABA Ethics Committee advised that, under the ABA Model Rules, lawyers may charge interest and accept credit cards as long as the advertisements are not false, fraudulent, or misleading.[9]

In any proceeding to collect a disputed fee, the lawyer, and not the client, has the burden of persuasion. The lawyer must show the existence and terms of the fee agreement.[10] The lawyer also has the burden of persuasion that the fee agreement is reasonable.[11] If the lawyer sues to collect his fee, he should not be surprised if the client counterclaims and argues that the lawyer was incompetent, the fee was unreasonable, the hours were not sufficiently documented, and so forth.

An example of a case where the court was particularly unsympathetic to a lawyer who sued to collect fees is *Lustig v. Horn*.[12] The lawyer inserted a clause [paragraph 3] in his retainer agreement that provided:

> Client agrees to pay all statements within ten (10) days after billing, that any statement remaining unpaid more than thirty (30) days will be subject to a one (1%) percent per month late charge and that *in the event of default in payment Client will pay reasonable attorney's fees and costs incurred in collecting said amount which may be due, whether by suit or arbitration* . . . . Client authorizes Attorney to withdraw from any Client funds in his possession, fees and costs which have been billed to Client. Any state-

---

[9]ABA Formal Opinion 00-420 (July 7, 2000) eliminated any limitations (other than false advertising) on making known a lawyer's acceptance of credit cards. This Opinion withdrew Formal Ethics Opinion 320 (1968), Informal Ethics Opinion 1120 (1969), Informal Ethics Opinion 1176 (1971), and Formal Ethics Opinion 338 (1974). *See* Arthur Garwin, *Bringing In the Fees: How Lawyers Collect Payment Is As Important As Setting the Price Itself*, 87 A.B.A. J. 66 (June 2001), discussing ABA Formal Opinion 00-420 (July 7, 2000).

[10]*See, e.g., Kirby v. Liska*, 214 Neb. 356, 334 N.W.2d 179 (Neb.1983) (oral fee agreement), *appeal after remand*, 217 Neb. 848, 351 N.W.2d 421 (1984).

[11]*See, e.g., Terzis v. Estate of Whalen*, 126 N.H. 88, 489 A.2d 608 (N. H.1985).

"There is much authority holding that a *lawyer has the burden* of showing the reasonableness of a fee agreement made during the representation. Some courts follow a different rule for contracts made before the representation, while others require the lawyer to show that the agreement is reasonable." Restatement of the Law Governing Lawyers § 43 (Official Draft 2000), Reporter's Note, at p. 305 (internal citations omitted) (emphasis added).

[12]*Lustig v. Horn*, 315 Ill.App.3d 319, 247 Ill.Dec. 558, 732 N.E.2d 613 (Ill.App. 1 Dist.2000).

ment not objected to in writing within thirty days from present-
ment will be deemed "accepted and approved by Client."[13]
When the lawyer sued the client for unpaid fees, the client admitted signing the agreement but denied that he owed the amount
claimed. He also said that his lawyer never explained the document to him.

Under the facts of this case, the court held that paragraph 3
was unethical and unenforceable, because a lawyer "should not
place himself in the position where he may be required to choose
between conflicting duties or where he must reconcile conflicting
interests rather than protect fully the rights of his client." The
court was troubled that the clause quoted above, paragraph 3,
"gives rise to substantial fees for vigorous prosecution of the attorney's own client." In addition, paragraph 3 might be used "to
silence a client's complaint about fees, resulting from the client's
fear of his attorney's retaliation for nonpayment of even unreasonable fees. Such a provision is not necessary to protect the attorney's interests; on the contrary, it merely serves to silence a
client should that client protest the amount billed."[14]

One should not read this case too broadly. It was significant to
the court that this client entered into this fee agreement with the
lawyer *after* the representation commenced. That time sequence,
the court announced, required the court to look at the agreement
more closely:

> "Particular attention will be given to contracts made or changed af-
> ter the relationship of attorney and client has been established. A
> presumption of undue influence arises when an attorney enters into
> a transaction with his client during the existence of the fiduciary
> relationship. As a matter of public policy, once raised, a presump-
> tion of undue influence must be rebutted by the attorney by 'clear
> and convincing' evidence."[15]

The court ruled that the lawyer may recover "reasonable fees
and costs incurred in [his] able representation of Horn," but
"Lustig's fees and costs incurred in collecting on his bills,
however, must be denied in the instant case where such a request
is premised upon a void provision of the retainer agreement."[16]

---

[13]315 Ill.App.3d at 321, 247 Ill-
.Dec. at 561, 732 N.E.2d at 616 (emphasis by the court).

[14]*Lustig v. Horn*, 315 Ill.App.3d
319, 327, 247 Ill.Dec. 558, 565, 732

N.E.2d 613, 620 (2000).

[15]315 Ill.App.3d at 327, 247
Ill. Dec. at 565, 732 N.E.2d at 620.

[16]315 Ill.App.3d at 329, 247 Ill.
Dec. at 566, 732 N.E.2d at 621.

§ 1.5–2(c) Arbitration

The ABA has developed carefully thought-out Model Rules for Fee Arbitration.[17] If the client requests arbitration, then the program makes the arbitration mandatory for the lawyer.[18] If the lawyer files a petition for arbitration, the arbitration may not proceed unless the client files a written consent within 30 days of service.[19] The burden of proof is on the lawyer to prove, by a preponderance of the evidence, that the fee is reasonable.[20] The proceedings are normally confidential, thus protecting client confidences.[21]

Some courts, following the lead of the ABA, have created fee arbitration procedures for fee disputes. Constitutional challenges to these procedures have been unsuccessful.[22] "Requiring attorneys to justify their fees in an inexpensive forum before an impartial panel is rationally related to the maintenance of the public's confidence in the legal system and to the interest in minimizing the burden on both the client and the attorney."[23] The California legislature enacted a mandatory fee arbitration act

---

[17]ABA Model Rules for Fee Arbitration (Feb. 13, 1995). In 2006, the ABA Standing Committee on Client Protection completed a comprehensive survey on fee arbitration programs in the states. Thirty-five states and fourteen counties participated in the survey. Nine charts provide detail as to the existing programs throughout this country on fee arbitration. *See* www.abanet.org/cpr/clientpro/ 2006_fee_arb_survey.html/

[18]Model Rules for Fee Arbitration, Rule 1(G)(1) & Commentary. The results of the arbitration are binding if the parties agree in writing or if no party asks for a trial de novo within 30 days after the arbitration decision has been served.

[19]Model Rules for Fee Arbitration, Rule 4(E).

[20]Model Rules for Fee Arbitration, Rule 5(O).

[21]Model Rules for Fee Arbitration, Rule 8. *Accord* ABA Model Rule 1.6(b) (2) & Comment 19. The fact that these arbitration proceedings are private does mean that the general public may not be fully informed about price gouging by a lawyer.

[22]*See, e.g., Application of LiVolsi,* 85 N.J. 576, 428 A.2d 1268 (1981) (rejecting constitutional attacks on court rule establishing attorney fee arbitration committees); *Guralnick v. Supreme Court of New Jersey,* 747 F.Supp. 1109 (D.N.J.1990) (rejecting constitutional attacks on New Jersey's compulsory attorney fee arbitration system); *Shimko v. Lobe,* 124 Ohio App.3d 336, 706 N.E.2d 354 (1997) (rejecting constitutional challenges to a rule requiring arbitration of fee disputes between lawyers from different law firms); *Nodvin v. State Bar of Georgia,* 273 Ga. 559, 544 S.E.2d 142 (2001), upholding the state's fee arbitration procedure. The court, like others, held that its authority to govern the practice of law justified its establishment of the arbitration process. Moreover, subjecting only lawyers to the process does not deny equal protection, and the fee arbitration system in practice provides notice and other required elements of due process.

[23]*Nodvin v. State Bar of Georgia,* 273 Ga. 559, 560, 544 S.E.2d 142, 145 (2001). Note, that the drafters of the 2002 Rules stated in a Comment that a lawyer must participate in a manda-

that seeks to govern dispute resolution of fee disputes between attorneys and clients.[24]

§ 1.5–2(d) Mediation

Mediation is appropriate when the dispute between lawyer and client does not allege that the lawyer engaged in misconduct or, if such an allegation is made, it only is relatively minor misconduct, sometimes called "lesser misconduct" in the jurisdiction's rules of disciplinary enforcement.[25] For mediation to be appropriate, there should be little or no injury to a client, the public, the legal system, or the profession, and there should be little likelihood that the lawyer will repeat the conduct that is the subject of mediation.[26] To fill this need, the ABA has developed Model Rules for Mediation of Client-Lawyer Disputes.[27] Mediation may be helpful in resolving disagreements involving fees, but one should realize that mediation extends to disputes that go well beyond fee issues.[28]

An allegation that a lawyer's failure to return a client's file based on a fee dispute with the client is something that may be suitable for mediation. Similar disputes that may be appropriate for mediation would include disputes involving the lawyer's release of her lien on a client's recovery in a case where a new lawyer has replaced the original lawyer, or a dispute involving

---

tory fee arbitration or mediation procedure. Rule 1.5, Comment 9.

[24]*See* Calif. Bus. & Prof. Code § 6200. *See also Aguilar v. Lerner*, 32 Cal.4th 974, 88 P.3d 24, 12 Cal.Rptr.3d 287(2004) (examining the interaction of the statute with the client's decision to file a malpractice action against the attorney).

[25]A mediation program is designed to resolve complaints referred from the jurisdiction's lawyer disciplinary agency, so such referrals should be given priority over voluntary mediations.

[26]Mediation is not suitable when the dispute involves an allegation of lawyer misconduct that, if true, would warrant a sanction restricting the lawyer's license to practice law. ABA Model Rules for Mediation of Client-Lawyer Disputes (Aug. 1998), Rule 1(C), Comment.

[27]ABA Model Rules for Mediation of Client-Lawyer Disputes (Aug. 1998).

[28]ABA Model Rules for Mediation

of Client-Lawyer Disputes (Aug. 1998), Rule 1, Commentary, explains:

"Examples of disputes that might be referred to mediation include allegations of a lawyer's failure or refusal to return a client's file based on a fee dispute with the client, release a lien on a client's recovery in a case in which the lawyer has been succeeded by another lawyer, withdraw from representation upon being discharged by the client, conclude a legal representation by preparing an essential dispositive document, such as the findings of fact and conclusions of law in a divorce or the final account in an estate, return an unearned fee or a portion of the fee, comply with his or her agreement with a medical provider on the client's behalf or communicate concerning the status of a matter.

"Other examples of situations in which the parties might agree to voluntary mediation could include allegations of a client's failure to pay or fulfill the contract, pay for costs (including future costs) or communicate with the lawyer."

the alleged failure to return an unearned portion of the fee, or an alleged failure to communicate concerning the status of a matter, or a client's alleged failure to pay for costs (including expected future costs) or to communicate with the lawyer.

Mediation sometimes may be used to complement fee arbitration proceedings. The "Client-Lawyer Mediation Commission"[29] created under the ABA Model Rules for Mediation may accept jurisdiction in a dispute in which a fee arbitration proceeding is pending but has not yet begun. The intention is to solve the dispute in a less formal way, if possible, not to refer complainants back and forth between the two programs.

§ 1.5–3 CONTINGENT FEES

§ 1.5–3(a) Introduction

The Rules impose several important requirements on contingent fees. First, all contingent fee arrangements must be in writing.[1] Previously, the Model Code merely encouraged a writing for contingent fees.[2] The drafters of the 2002 Rules added a requirement that the client in a contingent fee matter must *sign* the written agreement in order to avoid subsequent claims that the client never saw any written agreement.[3]

Writing Requirement. If the contingent fee is not in writing, the court, typically, will not enforce the oral fee agreement, for it violates Rule 1.5(c).[4] However, if the lawyer, in other respects, acted properly and did perform competently for the client, then some courts will give the lawyer *quantum meruit* recovery,[5] while some other courts refuse any recovery.[6]

---

[29]ABA Model Rules for Mediation of Client-Lawyer Disputes, Rule 1(A)(2), Rule 2.

[Section 1.5–3]

[1]*See* Rule 1.5(c).

[2]*See* EC 2-19. The Disciplinary Rules say nothing about the subject.

[3]Rule 1.5(c).

[4]*See, e.g., Vaccaro v. Estate of Gorovoy*, 303 N.J.Super. 201, 207, 696 A.2d 724, 727 (App.Div.1997) (lawyers cannot benefit from their failure to comply with the requirements of Rules of Professional Conduct, Rule 1.5 by enforcing an agreement that violates that rule).

[5]Restatement of the Law Governing Lawyers, § 39 (Official Draft 2000). In *Gagne v. Vaccaro*, 255 Conn. 390,

766 A.2d 416 (2001), a lawyer entered into a written contingent fee agreement with his client, but it was not reduced to a writing. Then, a second lawyer replaced him and this other lawyer successfully pursued the matter and collected a contingent fee. The first lawyer wanted a fair share of the fee earned. The court held that he can receive *quantum meruit* payment. The lack of a written agreement is not enough to deny him all fees in cases where he had acted loyally and his work had contributed to the final outcome. In those circumstances, *quantum meruit* recovery is appropriate.

In *Mullens v. Hansel-Henderson*, 65 P.3d 992 (Colo.2002), the agreed upon services were successfully completed but the contingent fee agreement had not been documented. Find-

The 1983 version of the Rules made it clear that the lawyer has no right to impose a contingent fee on a client who desires another arrangement: "When there is doubt whether a contingent fee is consistent with the client's best interests, the lawyer *should offer an alternative basis* for the fee and explain their implications."[7] In fact, under the Comments, the lawyer should volunteer alternative arrangements to clients if that is in the clients' best interest.[8] The contingent fee, in short, should not be for the benefit of lawyers, but for the benefit of clients who may wish to choose that type of arrangement. The lawyer is the fiduciary of the client, and the fiduciary should advise the client that an hourly arrangement is better for the client.

The drafters of the 2002 Rules eliminated this requirement. Now, the ethical obligation only requires the lawyer to offer clients an alternative basis for the fee if "applicable law" *requires* the lawyer to offer clients an alternative basis for the fee.[9] Some lawyers objected on the grounds that they prefer to take cases only if they can charge a contingent fee. The Comment removes

---

ing the proposed fees reasonable, the district court granted Mullens' fees under a *quantum meruit* theory. The court of appeals reversed, but the Colorado Supreme Court reinstated the award. "When an attorney completes the legal services for which he was retained," the Court held, "the fact that the underlying fee agreement was unenforceable does not itself preclude the attorney from being paid the reasonable value of his services. When a contract fails, equity steps in to prevent one party from taking advantage of the other." 65 P.3d at 999.

In *Slick v. Reinecker*, 154 Md.App. 312, 839 A.2d 784 (2003), Lawyer Reinecker sued Slick for breach of contract for failing to pay a contingent fee for collection of an uninsured motorist claim after an auto accident. Reinecker conceded that Slick, a friend of Reinecker's husband, had acted largely on his own in pursuit of the claim and also that Reinecker had initially agreed to assist Slick free of charge. However, Reinecker claimed that when her husband left her, her relationship with Slick changed and her work became subject to her standard contingent fee. Because Slick denied ever having agreed to pay for Reinecker's services, the lower court concluded that there was no implied-

in-fact contract. Instead, this was a "contract implied-in-law," i.e., a suit for restitution based on unjust enrichment. The court, on appeal, reversed the trial court's award of a fee to the lawyer for two reasons. First, Maryland Rule of Professional Conduct 1.5(c) prohibits a contingent fee arrangement unless it is set forth in writing. Second, in restitution, recovery should be measured by "actual gain to the defendant" and not by the market value of the services rendered by the plaintiff. Since Reinecker failed to offer proof of an increase in Slick's settlement resulting from her services, she was not entitled to any compensation.

[6]*Estate of Pinter by Pinter v. Mc Gee*, 293 N.J.Super. 119, 679 A.2d 728 (App. Div. 1996), holding that a law firm violated the ethics rule by entering into a contingent fee agreement without a written retainer signed by the firm and the client, and could *not* circumvent the rule by recovering on *quantum meruit* basis.

[7]1983 Model Rule 1.5, Comment 3 (emphasis added); cf. EC 2-20.

[8]1983 Model Rule 1.5, Comment 3.

[9]Rule 1.5, Comment 3.

the requirement that the lawyer "should offer an alternative" to
continent fees. The new Comment advises that, if the fee is reasonable, a lawyer could charge a client a contingent fee as the
only fee basis for hiring the lawyer.

One should not read too much into this Comment. The lawyer
is still the fiduciary of the client. The revised Comment 3 to Rule
1.15 makes clear that the lawyer must determine "whether it is
reasonable to charge any form of contingent fee." It may be that a
contingent fee is not in the best interest of the client, but the
lawyer only wants to accept clients if he or she can charge a
contingent fee. In that case, if a contingent fee is not in the best
interest of the client, the lawyer *must* so advise the client and
then explain that the client (or prospective client) should retain a
different lawyer, one who does not charge a contingent fee.

§ 1.5–3(b) Conflicts of Interest and Contingent Fees

Contingent fees by their nature raise potential conflicts of interest between the attorney and client.[10] For example, the client
may wish to settle litigation while the attorney would want to
press on, or vice-versa. The ethics rules attempt to reduce such
conflicts and have specific provisions—in the conflicts of interest
section—dealing with contingent fees.[11] These provisions forbid a
lawyer from acquiring a proprietary interest in the client's cause
of action or subject matter except that: (1) he may acquire a lien
to secure his fees or expenses if other law allows, and (2) he may
"contract with a client for a reasonable contingent fee in a civil
case."[12] Exception 2 validates contingent fees.

The two basic points to remember are that the lawyer cannot
ethically require the client to give up her right under Rule 1.2, to
settle litigation[13] and her right under Rule 1.16 to fire her
lawyer.[14]

For example, assume that a client ("Client") agrees to compensate her lawyer ("Lawyer") by giving him a one-fourth interest in
certain real property and mining claims. Ownership of these
properties is disputed and Lawyer defends Client (and himself as
well, to the extent that Lawyer's one-fourth interest is involved).
Then assume that Client becomes dissatisfied with Lawyer's services and tries to discharge Lawyer, who refuses to withdraw. In
this hypothetical fact situation, Lawyer has violated Rule 1.8(i)

---

[10]*See* EC 5-7.

[11]*See* Rule 1.8(i). DR 5-103(A).

[12]Rule 1.8(i). *Accord* DR 5-103(A).
See also Restatement of the Law
Governing Lawyers, Third, §§ 36, 43
(Official Draft 2000).

[13]In short, the client may not assign to the attorney his cause of action; clients cannot waive their right
to decide when to settle litigation. *See*
Rule 1.2, Comment 5. EC 7-7.

[14]Rule 1.16 (a)(3). DR 1-110(B)(4).

and Rule 1.16(a)(3) because he has refused to accept the client's discharge.[15]

§ 1.5–3(c) Common Objections Raised Against Contingent Fees

Opponents of contingency fees frequently claim that the plaintiffs' lawyers are often "over-compensated." Contingency fee lawyers dispute that claim and argue that because the lawyer only receives remuneration if the client agrees to a contingency fee and if the case is successful, the fees cannot be "too high." Clients only accept the fees if they choose to do so, and the lawyers have the risk of earning nothing.[16]

But often there is little risk of winning "nothing" because the lawyers have a diverse portfolio of cases.[17] An individual client does not have a diverse portfolio of cases, but the law firm does, so it can more easily accept a series of cases, each for a flat fee, knowing that the losses in one case are likely to be balanced by the gains in another. One commentator has charged that plaintiffs' lawyers "find that playing the litigation lottery is profitable: they bring the same dubious multimillion dollar claim before many juries in the expectation that a few random victories will more than compensate for a larger number of losses. One attorney who only handles breast implant cases boasts that he 'tell[s] everyone I've got a license to gamble.' "[18]

Moreover, in some cases involving class actions, attorneys have received very handsome fees while their clients have walked away with little. For example, in one case, the attorneys for the class action plaintiffs agreed to accept $28 million in fees while their clients would receive $14 each.[19]

Another important fact to add to the equation is that juries

---

[15]See also DR 2-110(B)(4); DR 5-103 and ABA Informal Opinion 1397 (Aug. 31, 1977).

[16]ABA Formal Opinion 94-389 (1994).

[17]See, e.g., BERT W. RAIN & JOHN E. BARRY, THE CASE FOR ABOLISHING CONTINGENT FEE ARRANGEMENTS (Washington Legal Foundation, Critical Legal Issues, Working Papers Series No. 91, Jan. 1999), at 6, n.5, noting the lawyers with a diversified portfolio of personal injury cases have little risk, with the contingent fee lawyers obtaining more than nominal settlements and awards in over 70% of their cases. See also Lester Brickman, Contingent Fees Without

Contingencies: Hamlet Without the Prince of Denmark?, 37 U.C.L.A. L. REV. 29 (1989); Richard Painter, Litigating on a Contingency: A Monopoly of Champions or a Market for Champerty?, 71 CHI.-KENT L. REV. 625 (1995).

[18]David E. Bernstein, The Breast Implant Fiasco, 87 CALIF. L. REV. 457, 492 (1999) (footnote omitted).

[19]Ralph T. King, Jr., Princely Fees, Paltry Damages Set Off Protest, WALL STREET JOURNAL, Mar. 13, 1998, at B1. See also Matthew Scully, Will Lawyers' Greed Sink the Tobacco Settlement?, WALL STREET JOURNAL, Feb. 10, 1998, at A18.

Compare Maynard Steel Casting

have meted out punitive damages with greater frequency in recent years.[20] When the jury award includes substantial punitive damages, contingency fee lawyers, in some circumstances, are compensated in a way that, if the figure were converted to an hourly rate, amounts to many thousands of dollars per hour.[21] Although it is true that the number of cases in which juries award

---

Co. v. Sheedy, 746 N.W.2d 816 (Wisc. App.2008)(holding as unreasonable a $137,000 contingent fee when the lawyer was hired after the settlement offer had been made in a class action antitrust law suit and the lawyer had devoted less than 24 hours to the case).

[20]**Punitive Damages.** Sometimes punitive damages can be so severe that their imposition violates due process. *BMW of North America, Inc. v. Gore*, 517 U.S. 559, 116 S.Ct. 1589, 134 L.Ed.2d 809 (1996). Plaintiff sued BMW because it had not disclosed to him that it had repainted part of the car. The car had been damaged, probably by acid rain. When the plaintiff discovered the repair (which cost $601), he sued BMW claiming that the nondisclosure was a form of fraud. The jury awarded the plaintiff $4,000 in compensatory damages and $4 million in punitive damages. The Court held, five to four, that the damages were so excessive as to violate due process. *See* 3 RONALD D. ROTUNDA & JOHN E. NOWAK, TREATISE ON CONSTITUTIONAL LAW: SUBSTANCE AND PROCEDURE § 17.10 (Thomson- West, 4th ed. 2008) (6 volumes).

[21]**The Tobacco Fees.** Fees in the tobacco settlements may turn out to be thousands of dollars per hour. Bradley A. Smith & Jeffrey N. Lindemann, *Legal Billing: Is the Meter Broken?*, WALL ST. J., Jan. 27, 1997, at A22, col. 3–6. *See also* Richard B. Schmitt, *Courts Whittle Down Lawyers' Fat Contingent Fees*, WALL ST. J., Jan. 28, 1998, at B1; Editorial, *Texas Tobacco*, WALL ST. J., March 19, 1998, at A18 (lawyers' fees of $2.3 billion for 18 months work). *Cf. Krause v. Rhodes*, 640 F.2d 214 (6th Cir.1981); *U.S. Steel Corp. v. Green*, 353 So.2d 86, 88 (Fla. 1977).

Arbitrators who ruled on the fees given to tobacco lawyers awarded the lawyers representing the states of Florida, Texas, and Mississippi in lawsuits against the tobacco industry $8.2 billion. The Florida attorneys received $3.43 billion, the largest attorneys' fee in history as of that point. Ann Davis, *Arbitration for $8.2 Billion in Fees in Tobacco Suit Reflects Lobbying*, WALL ST. J., Dec. 14, 1998, at B7, col. 3–4 (Midwest ed.). Ann Davis, *Cashing In on a Tobacco Bonanza*, WALL ST. J., Dec. 15, 1998, at B1 (Midwest ed.). Supporters of these payments argued that the clients bargaining for the contingent fee agreements were represented by sophisticated lawyers (typically the Attorney General of a state), and that the fees were high, even when the contingent percentages were low, because the plaintiffs' lawyers secured very high settlements. Opponents charged that the Attorneys General, who were the individuals bargaining on behalf of the states, had no personal stake and that some of them may have hoped for campaign contributions from the plaintiffs' lawyers.

The actual contingent fees that were negotiated by the states varied a fair amount. At least eight states agreed to pay their outside lawyers a 25% contingency fee. On the other hand, Illinois was able to bargain for only a 10% contingent fee. Alaska agreed to pay it outside counsel 12%. *See* Written testimony of Professor Jeffrey Harris, economics faculty of MIT, on Dec. 10, 1997, before the SUBCOMMITTEE ON COURTS AND JUDICIARY OF THE COMMITTEE OF THE JUDICIARY, U.S. House of Representatives, at 2.

The decision of various states to hire outside counsel to represent them

major punitive damages is still small (as a percentage of all cases seeking punitive damages) a personal injury lawyer with a diversified portfolio of cases is very likely to generate a handsome yearly income. For an individual defendant, the award of punitive damages may be like getting hit by lighting: it hardly ever happens to any one person in particular, but it does eventually happen to someone.[22]

Although no particular plaintiff can be assured of winning a punitive judgment, the lawyer representing a series of plaintiffs is much more likely to win a punitive award in some of the cases. Consider, for example, the woman who sued McDonald's because she spilled a hot cup of coffee on herself. She won a punitive award,[23] but earlier plaintiffs complaining of similar injuries were not so fortunate. Each lawsuit may be likened to a lottery ticket. The more tickets you have, the better chance of holding a winning ticket. The personal injury plaintiff has one ticket; the lawyer representing a lot of plaintiffs has a lot of tickets. The individual plaintiff's risk of losing is real; the lawyer's risk of losing an entire diversified portfolio of cases is statistically remote.

Another objection to contingency fees is that the fee structure

---

in the tobacco litigation is a decision to privatize a portion of the state's legal representation. If a state simply refuses to pay its legitimate bills, it is likely to find it more difficult, the next time, to hire private lawyers to represent it in other cases. Lawyers, like other professionals, may choose to engage in pro bono legal representation, but they like to be the ones that decide whether they are working for free. They are unlikely to work for free on behalf of clients who are not impoverished and who have collected billions of dollars from the tobacco industry because of the lawyers' efforts.

The states that challenged the resonableness of the contingent fees argued that the settlements came from a windfall not related to the lawyers' work. In making this argument, one factor that should be relevant is whether the state—after hiring the lawyers—changed the substantive law to aid its lawyers. A state, in this circumstance, may wish to argue that it bargained for a contingency fee in light of the adverse law that existed, and that adverse law made plaintiff's case very difficult. However, once the state legislature changed the law, the

case became substantially less difficult. Hence, a state may argue, the bargain had changed and it should not have to pay for a difficult representation when it changed the law to make the representation substantially less difficult.

The Breast Implant Litigation. For an excellent discussion of the contingent fee issues that relate to the contingency fees surrounding the breast implant litigation, see MARCIA ANGELL, SCIENCE ON TRIAL: THE CLASS OF MEDICAL EVIDENCE AND THE LAW IN THE BREAST IMPLANT CASE (W.W. Norton, 1996). An excellent review-essay of this book is, David E. Bernstein, *The Breast Implant Fiasco*, 87 CALIF. L. REV. 457 (1999).

[22]See discussion in, Ronald D. Rotunda, *Moving from Billable Hours to Fixed-Fees: Task-Based Fees and Legal Ethics*, 47 U. KANSAS L. REV. 819 (1999).

[23]*See Liebeck v. McDonald's Restaurants*, 1995 WL 360309 (D.N.M. 1994). A settlement occurred after the jury verdict. *McMahon v. Bunn-O-Matic Corp.*, 150 F.3d 651, 654 (7th Cir.1998).

encourages lawyers to take frivolous cases. The latter argument does appear, at first blush, to be counter-intuitive, because truly frivolous cases are losers. In such situations, the contingency fee lawyer should function as a gatekeeper; if the case is a likely loser, the lawyer (who only is paid if the case is successful) should be unwilling to take the case.

On the other hand, contingency fees may encourage litigation of weak (but nonfrivolous) cases involving sympathetic plaintiffs. The lawyer who takes on a portfolio of cases may be quite willing to take an individual case that is not likely to win if he or she thinks that the likelihood of all the cases being lost is small (given the fact that each severely injured plaintiff cuts a sympathetic figure when before a jury).[24]

A third major objection is that a contingent fee case places the lawyer in a conflict of interest with respect to his or her client. The lawyer may be willing to settle the case very quickly, before much work has been done, but it may not be in the best interest of the client to settle before discovery. On the other hand, as the case approaches trial, the lawyer may be more interested in not settling because, it is only by playing in the litigation lottery (by going to the jury) that the lawyer can hope to eventually hit the jackpot.[25]

Because of these objections to contingency fees, some commentators have offered various proposals to modify the contingency fee and reduce litigation. One would expect that contingency fee lawyers would not greet such proposals with a warm welcome because the proposals would likely translate into a reduction of their income. And, in fact, that is what has happened.[26]

§ 1.5–3(d) Criminal Cases

Both the Model Code and the Model Rules forbid contingent fees in criminal cases. The rationale usually given in support of

---

[24]*See* Thomas J. Miceli, *Do Contingent Fees Promote Excessive Litigation?*, 23 J. LEGAL STUDIES 211 (1994).

[25]Herbert M. Kritzler, et. al., *The Impact of Fee Arrangement on Lawyer Effort*, 19 LAW & SOCIETY REV. 251 (1985). *See generally* LESTER BRICKMAN, MICHAEL HOROWITZ & JEFFREY O'CONNELL, RETHINKING CONTINGENCY FEES (1994); Lester Brickman, *ABA Regulation of Contingency Rees: Money Talks, Ethics Walks*, 65 FORDHAM L. REV. 247 (1996), discussing ethical issues related to contingency fees.

[26]*See, e.g.,* Kevin M. Clermont & John D. Currivan, *Improving on the Contingent Fee*, 63 CORNELL L. REV. 529 (1978); Harold See, *An Alternative to the Contingent Fee*, 1984 UTAH L. REV. 485; Lester Brickman, *Contingency Fees Without Contingencies: Hamlet Without the Prince of Denmark?*, 37 U.C.L.A. L. REV. 29 (1989); LESTER BRICKMAN, MICHAEL HOROWITZ & JEFFREY O'CONNELL, RETHINKING CONTINGENCY FEES (1994); Michael Horowitz, *Making Ethics Real, Making Ethics Work: A Proposal for Contingency Fee Reform*, 44 EMORY L.J. 173 (1995).

this prohibition is the lack of a *res* out of which the fee is to be paid.[27] However, in other areas of the law, litigation may produce no *res* and yet the attorney may be paid only if successful.[28] The reason for the rule prohibiting contingent fees in criminal cases probably rests on "historical accident, arising in earlier cases during a time when all contingent fee contracts were generally regarded with great suspicion. . . ."[29] Its continuation may result from the desire of criminal defense counsel to be paid by their clients in advance; the ethical prohibition thus gives lawyers a good excuse to reject the efforts of those clients who might insist on a contingent fee if that alternative were possible. Nowadays, if the client is indigent and cannot afford to pay, the state is required to provide free appointed counsel.

It would be contrary to public policy for the state to hire a prosecutor on a contingency fee basis, i.e., the prosecutor gets paid only if he secures a criminal conviction.[30] The rationale behind this prohibition is not difficult to find: the duty of a prosecutor is to do justice, not merely to convict. The state's interest "in a criminal prosecution is not that it shall win a case, but that justice shall be done."[31]

§ 1.5–3(e) Domestic Relations Cases

The Model Code concluded that contingent fees in domestic relations matters are "rarely justified,"[32] but it did not raise this note of discouragement to the level of discipline. In contrast, the Model Rules flatly forbid fees in divorce matters contingent upon "the securing of a divorce or upon the amount of alimony or support or property settlement" achieved.[33]

The Rules do not explain the purpose of the prohibition in divorce cases, but the reason behind it is easy to understand. Public policy does not encourage divorce, and the lawyer's fee arrangements should not put the lawyer in a position where the lawyer might be encouraged to prevent any possible reconciliation of the parties: the lawyer who charged a contingent fee would

---

[27]Rule 1.5(d)(2). DR 2-106(C); EC 2-20.

[28]*See, e.g., Mills v. Electric Auto-Lite Co.*, 396 U.S. 375, 90 S.Ct. 616, 24 L.Ed.2d 593 (1970)(in a corporate derivative suit, corporation must pay plaintiff's attorney on a "benefits conferred" theory, although victory produced no *res*).

[29]CHARLES W. WOLFRAM, MODERN LEGAL ETHICS 536 (West Pub. Co. 1986).

[30]*Baca v. Padilla*, 26 N.M. 223, 190 P. 730 (1920) (contract is void and there can be no recovery on it).

[31]*Berger v. United States*, 295 U.S. 78, 88, 55 S.Ct. 629, 633, 79 L.Ed. 1314 (1935).

[32]EC 2-20.

[33]Rule 1.5(d)(1).

place himself in a conflict situation, for if he encouraged reconciliation, he could lose his fee.[34]

The lawyer, in short, may not charge a fee that is contingent on his securing a divorce. Thus, a lawyer may not charge a contingency fee for the initial securing of the amount of support, because a reconciliation would deprive the lawyer of his fee. But, he may charge a contingency fee to secure the collection of support in arrears, as the reason for the rule against contingency fees does not apply in that situation.[35] The drafters of the 2002 Rules added this exception to the Comments.[36] Similarly, the lawyer may charge a contingency fee to enforce an equitable distribution of property, though he could not ethically charge such a fee *initially* in order to secure an equitable distribution of property.[37]

Because the rule against contingency fees in domestic relations matters is based on the public policy that a lawyer should not be put in a situation where he will lose his fee if he successfully encourages reconciliation, this prohibition does not apply to cases that are not really divorce matters, even though they may involve

---

[34]*See, e.g., McCarthy v. Santangelo*, 137 Conn. 410, 78 A.2d 240 (1951). *Cf. In re Cooper*, 81 N.C.App. 27, 344 S.E.2d 27 (1986) (when property is not easily valued, the lawyer on a contingency may wish to value the property on the high side, thereby augmenting his fee, while it is in the interest of the client to minimize the value of the property).

Other Justifications for the Rule Against Contingent Fees in Divorce Matters. Sometimes courts assert other justifications. For example, some courts suggest that a client in a divorce situation is often overwrought and susceptible to the lawyer's overreaching. *Barelli v. Levin*, 144 Ind.App. 576, 247 N.E.2d 847 (1969). However, this justification is less persuasive; not all divorce clients are that susceptible, and the lawyer, as a fiduciary, is always prohibited from overreaching the client, even if the case does not involve divorce.

Some courts have argued that contingency fees in divorce matters are unethical because the court has the authority under family law statutes to award the attorney's fees. Essentially, then, there is no real risk that the client will not pay the lawyer. *Glasscock*

v. Glasscock, 304 S.C. 158, 403 S.E.2d 313 (1991). However, this rationale is not persuasive. The purpose of a contingency fee is not simply to make sure that the lawyer is paid; the law typically gives the attorney a lien on any recovery. Restatement of the Law Governing Lawyers, Third, § 43 (Official Draft 2000). Clients may also desire a contingent fee as a way of giving an added incentive to the lawyer and making sure that the client does not owe anything if there is no recovery.

[35]*See, e.g., Fletcher v. Fletcher*, 227 Ill.App.3d 194, 169 Ill.Dec. 211, 591 N.E.2d 91 (1992).

[36]Rule 1.5, Comment 6.

[37]*See, e.g.,* Maryland Committee on Professional Ethics, Opinion 97-39 (Aug. 28, 1997); Professional Ethics Commission of the Main Board of Overseers, Opinion 157 (Mar. 5, 1977).

There is one case concluding that a lawyer may not charge a contingent fee for *modifying* a support order because it treats that the same as charging a contingent fee to secure, initially, a support order. *In re Jarvis*, 254 Kan. 829, 869 P.2d 671 (1994).

family law issues. For example, this rule does not apply to paternity suits and tort actions between spouses.[38]

Sometimes lawyers seek to avoid the rule against contingency fees in divorce cases by using other types of payments that are similar to, but not exactly, contingent fees.[39] A fee that is based on the "results obtained"—*i.e.*, based on a percentage of the amount of separation that is secured—sounds like a contingency fee. If there is no divorce (a contingency), then the lawyer will not be paid. If there is a divorce, the lawyer will be paid based on the amount of support that is secured. Moreover, the policy behind the prohibition of contingency fees should apply to the "results obtained."[40] The ethics rule, after all, applies to any case where the fee is based on "the securing of a divorce or upon the amount of alimony or support or property settlement" achieved.[41] Nonetheless, some courts have upheld fees that are based on the "results obtained," while others have not.[42]

---

[38]Committee on Professional Ethics, State Bar of New York, Opinion 690 (May 13, 1977).

[39]**Minimum Fees.** Lawyers in divorce cases can ethically charge a "minimum fee" if it is understood that, if the lawyer does not complete the matter, he or she must refund any part of the fee that was not earned or is excessive. *In re Cooperman*, 187 A.D.2d 56, 591 N.Y.S.2d 855 (1993), *aff'd*, 83 N.Y.2d 465, 611 N.Y.S.2d 465, 633 N.E.2d 1069 (1994) (minimum fees are ethically proper assuming that the lawyer returns any unearned fee if the matter is not completed; the minimum fee, like all other fees, must be "reasonable"); *In re Biggs*, 318 Or. 281, 864 P.2d 1310 (1994) (nonrefundable retainer is not reasonable and "excessive," given the amount of work actually performed).

[40]A court invalidated a premium fee that was to be determined at the conclusion of the representation as too vague and uncertain to satisfy the state requirements of plain language in domestic relations cases even though the premium has to be done with the client's consent. *See Sheresky Aronson & Mayefsky, LLP v. Whitmore*, 53 A.D.3d 414, 861 N.Y.S.2d 44 (1st Dep't 2008) (clause read, "We reserve the right to discuss with you at the conclusion of your matter your payment of a reasonable additional fee to us, in excess of the actual time and disbursements, for exceptional results achieved, time expended, responsiveness accorded, or complexity involved in your case. However, no such fee will be charged to you without your consent.").

[41]Rule 1.5(d)(1).

[42]*See, e.g., Eckell v. Wilson*, 409 Pa.Super. 132, 597 A.2d 696 (1991) ("results obtained" fee upheld in divorce case as similar to a *quantum meruit* fee).

Contrast, e.g., Salerno v. Salerno, 241 N.J.Super. 536, 575 A.2d 532 (Ch.Div.1990), which found a "results obtained" fee too vague. The attorney's fee agreement between the former wife and the attorney indicated that the fee would be based on an hourly rate of $200, and also any result accomplished, the amount in controversy, and the lawyer's experience and ability. This agreement violated the rules of court by including factors that did not alert the client as to what the contemplated bill would be, did not state that the contingent portion of the fee would apply only to representation on equitable distribution, and failed to state the exact formula to be applied to the "amount

Consider the unusual decision in *Alexander v. Inman*.[43] In that case, Tennessee did *not* have an absolute ethical prohibition against contingent fees in divorce cases. The court began its analysis by noting: "contingent fee agreements are *begrudgingly permitted* in domestic relations cases."[44] That jurisdiction obviously does not follow the strict prohibition of the ABA Model Rules. The court then held that the lawyers did not violate their fiduciary duty of utmost good faith to their client when they entered into a fee agreement in a divorce matter, under which they would be paid up to 15% of client's total award. The court found that the client was financially sophisticated and admitted that she had read the agreement when she signed it, the agreement plainly set forth the possible minimum and maximum fees, and the $501,514.50 fee due under the agreement was reasonable for the quality of representation that the lawyers provided.

§ 1.5–3(f) Contingent Fees in Cases That Do Not Involve Personal Injury

Typically contingent fees often occur in personal injury litigation, but the ethics rules do not limit contingent fees to those cases. For example, it is proper for a lawyer to charge a contingent fee in an administrative agency proceeding.[45]

A commonly articulated justification of contingent fees is that they allow poorer litigants to hire competent lawyers and pay them out of the judgment won. However, the ethics rules do not limit contingent fees to such cases. In fact, they specifically allow contingent fees even though the clients are not poor. Both the Rules and the Code allow a lawyer to accept a contingent fee from a client who can afford a reasonable fixed fee.[46] Clients who can afford a fixed fee may still prefer a contingent fee because the

---

in controversy" and the result accomplished. Thus, the court ordered the former wife's attorney to remove the premium charges from the former wife's bill.

[43]*Alexander v. Inman*, 974 S.W.2d 689 (Tenn.1998).

[44]974 S.W.2d at 693 (emphasis added).

[45]EC 2–20.

[46]However, if there is doubt that a contingent fee is in the client's best interest, the lawyer should offer alternatives and explain their implications, under the 1983 version of the Model Rules. *See* Rule 1.5, Comment 3 (1983 version); *cf.* EC 2–20. The 2002 version deleted that sentence, but the principle

should be the same, derived from the lawyer's basic fiduciary duties. The lawyer should not advise the client to agree to a fee that a fully informed client would find unreasonable. If the lawyer only accepts contingency fee arrangements, the lawyer should advise the client to see a different lawyer.

The Reporter's Explanation of Changes to the ABA House of Delegates regarding the deletion of this sentence states: "The Commission proposes to delete the next to the last sentence of current Comment [3] because the statement is merely advisory, given that the requirement of offering an alternative type of fee is not stated or implied in any textual provision. If the contingent fee is reasonable, then lawyers need not offer an

contingent fee basis for compensating counsel aligns the interests of the client and the lawyer with respect to the outcome of the litigation. A contingency fee system also makes it easier for clients to budget legal expenses.

Typically, liability is not clear in a contingent fee case, but no ethical rule restricts contingent fees to that type of case. The ABA has advised that the "mere fact that liability may be clear does not, by itself, render a contingent fee inappropriate or unethical."[47] Although liability may be clear, it may be difficult to collect, and the client may wish to be assured that he need not pay until (and unless) the money is collected, and that the fee will be no more than a certain percentage of the money actually collected. The client, in short, can decide to pay for results. But if the client does not understand that liability is clear, the lawyer must explain that in order to secure knowing consent.

§ 1.5–3(g) Early Settlement Offers

The fact that a lawyer is paid a contingent fee imposes no ethical obligation to solicit an early settlement offer on behalf of the client (who may not even wish to settle). The lawyer may not have enough information about the defendant's conduct and about the claim to evaluate properly an early settlement offer.[48] Hence there is no per se ethical objection if the lawyer recommends that the client not accept an early settlement offer.

§ 1.5–3(h) Varying the Contingent Fee at Different Stages of the Case

The lawyer and client may agree that the lawyer will charge a different contingent fee rate at different stages of a matter and may increase (or decrease) the percentage taken as a fee as the amount of the recovery to the client increases. It is the last dollars of recovery, not the first, that normally require the greater effort.[49] So, if the client agrees, the lawyer may charge a higher contingent fee if the recovery becomes larger, e.g., 20% of the first $15 million, 25% of the next $15 million, and 30% of any amount over $30 million. Or, if the client agrees, the lawyer may charge a lower contingent fee for a higher recovery, e.g., 25% of the first $15 million and 20% of any amount above $15 million. There is no per se ethical objection to either type of arrangement, although other facts may make such a fee unreasonable in some instances.

---

alternative fee nor need they inform clients that other lawyers might offer an alternative."

[47] ABA Formal Opinion 94-389 (Dec. 5, 1994).

[48] ABA Formal Opinion 94-389 (Dec. 5, 1994).

[49] ABA Formal Opinion 94-389 (Dec. 5, 1994).

§ 1.5–3(i) Reverse Contingent Fees or Contingent Fees Charged by Defense Counsel in Civil Cases

Defense counsel may seek to charge the client a reverse contingent fee, that is, a fee that is inverse to the size of the plaintiff's recovery against the defendant. We do not often think of contingency fees for defense matters, but the ABA Model Rules do not preclude them. Model Rule 1.5(d) only prohibits contingent fees in divorce or criminal cases. Model Rule 1.8, another ethical rule dealing with contingent fees, also does not limit them to actions brought by plaintiffs. It simply authorizes lawyers to contract with a client "for a reasonable contingent fee in a civil case."[50] No other ethical provision prohibits contingent fees in defense cases. Commentators also agree that the ethics rules do not preclude contingent fees in defense cases.[51]

Although there is no per se objection to contingent fees charged by defense counsel in civil cases, this fee agreement is still subject to the other requirements of Rule 1.5. In other words, the fee must be reasonable and the lawyer must fully inform the client in order to secure a valid agreement to the fee arrangement. Often, the amount that plaintiff claims in a case is not readily determinable; an unliquidated tort damages complaint may claim a vague amount ("damages in excess of $1 million"). If plaintiff does not specify a liquidated dollar amount, then the negotiations between the defense lawyer and the client defendant will establish, at least initially, what should be a "fair dollar figure to attribute to plaintiff's claim."[52]

These negotiations may not be fair because the lawyer may know a lot more about the issue than what he reveals to his client. The reasonableness of the reverse contingent fee depends on the degree to which the saving from liability is reasonably ascertainable and not based on speculative factors. A plaintiff might sue the defendant for millions of dollars in punitive damages, when the lawyer knows that the realistic risk of that event occurring is remote. If the defendant in this circumstance agrees to pay defense counsel one-third of what is "saved," the reverse contingent fee could prove to be a windfall for the defense lawyer: the defense counsel may have "saved" the defendant $39 million because the plaintiff sued for $40 million and the verdict was

---

[50]ABA Model Rule 1.8(i)(2).

[51]*See, e.g.,* Note, Eric W. Lam, *Toward a Valid Defense Contingent Fee Contract: A Comparative Analysis,* 67 IOWA L. REV. 373 (1982)(discussing cases); CHARLES W. WOLFRAM, MODERN LEGAL ETHICS 533 (West Pub. Co. 1986)("There is no general prohibition against contingent fee contracts with defendants."); GEOFFREY C. HAZARD, JR. & W. WILLIAM HODES, 1 THE LAW OF LAWYERING § 1.5:401 at 118 (Prentice Hall, 2d ed., 1990)("defendant in a civil case could agree to pay a fee inversely related to the size of the plaintiff's recovery.").

[52]ABA Formal Opinion 93-373 (Apr. 16, 1993).

only for $1 million, but, in context, many people might regard that "victory" as truly hollow, and the result as not really successful. To use the plaintiff's prayer for relief in an unliquidated tort damages claim as the sole basis to calculate a reverse contingent fee is unreasonable because the claim is purely speculative in amount.[53]

When the ABA Committee on Ethics turned to this issue it reached the same conclusion. The ABA Opinion expressed concern that what it called a "reverse contingent fee" might be based on "purely speculative" factors and that the lawyer might engage in overreaching of the client, to whom the lawyer owes a fiduciary relationship. Despite this concern, the Opinion concluded that there is no *per se* objection to contingency fees for defense counsel.[54]

§ 1.5-33(j) Contingent Fees and Early Termination of the Representation

When a lawyer and client enter into a contingent fee arrangement, they contemplate and hope that the representation will end is a successful outcome which will provide compensation for the client's wrongs and the attorney's labor. Situations may arise, however, that cause a premature termination of the representation.[55] The lawyer or the client may seek to terminate the representation before the conclusion of the matter. Such cases will present the question whether the lawyer is entitled to recover costs and attorneys' fees from the client.

When the lawyer and the client mutually agree to terminate the representation, they can at that time address the issue of compensation for time expended and expenses incurred.[56] In many such cases, the representation is terminated because in the opinion of the lawyer and the client, a continued representation is not likely to result in a successful outcome. The vast majority of such cases end without any compensation or payment to the lawyer for incurred expenses.

When the lawyer ends the representation without the client's consent or without a reasonable cause, it is unlikely that the

---

[53]*Wunschel Law Firm, P.C. v. Clabaugh*, 291 N.W.2d 331, 9 A.L.R. 4th 181 (Iowa 1980).

[54]ABA Formal Opinion 93-373 (April, 16, 1993) concluded: "The Committee concludes that the Model Rules do not prohibit contingent fee arrangements for representation of defendants in civil cases based on the amount of money saved a client—provided the amount of the fee is reasonable under the circumstances, and the client has

given fully informed consent."

[55]ABA Center for Professional Responsibility, Annotated Model Rules of Professional Conduct 83–84 (ABA 6th ed. 2007).

[56]Note, this does not imply a lawyer's attempt to renegotiate the contract. A renegotiation would require that the lawyer bear a burden of justifying the modification of the agreement.

lawyer will have any claim for compensation. Rule 1.16 requires that a lawyer have good cause for permissive withdrawal from a representation.[57] If the lawyer withdraws from the representation for cause, the right to compensation will depend upon whether the cause is the result of the lawyer's conduct or the client's conduct.[58] For example, if the lawyer must withdraw because of an undiscovered conflict of interest in the lawyer's firm, the lawyer should not collect a fee from the representation. However, if the cause resulted from the client's conduct, the lawyer could seek compensation under the contingent fee contract. Most likely, such compensation would be calculated with reference to a quantum meruit standard, but in the right circumstances, the lawyer may be able to enforce the contingent fee contract.

When the client terminates the contract, the lawyer's right to compensation would depend upon whether the termination was for cause or not for cause. If the client terminated the representation because of a negligent act committed by the lawyer or because the lawyer violated one of the standards of conduct contained in the Model Rules, the lawyer would not be entitled to compensation in most cases.[59] In a limited number of cases, the lawyer may be able to make a claim for reimbursement of costs that benefit the client when the case is transferred to another lawyer.[60] And, also in a very small number of cases where lawyer cause is involved, the lawyer may be able to receive compensation based upon a quantum meruit standard. But such a standard would need to consider the cause for the termination. Also, if a client terminates a representation because of a reasonable decision that litigation is not likely to result in a successful outcome, the lawyer will not be able to receive any compensation.[61]

---

[57]See Rule 1.16(b).

[58]The situation is similar to when the client discharges the lawyer that is discussed below. The reason for the discharge will control the issue of whether compensation should be paid to the lawyer. *See Ashford v. Interstate Trucking Corp of America, Inc.*, 524 N.W.2d 500 (Minn.Ct.App.1994) (attorney had good cause to withdraw and receive quantum meruit compensation when client refused to participate in discovery).

[59]This view is consistent with the concept of fee forfeiture when the lawyer breaches an obligation to the client. *See Somuah v. Flachs*, 352 Md. 241, 721 A.2d 680 (1998)(examining client good cause for terminating the representation).

[60]When a lawyer advances costs for experts, transcripts, and other costs paid to third parties for goods and services for the benefit of the client and when such goods and services will be used by the client in pursuing the dispute, one could see an equitable argument to support the lawyer's claim to recover those costs.

[61]*See King & King, Chartered v. Harbert Int'l, Inc.*, 503 F.3d 153 (D.C. Cir. 2007)

If the client fires the lawyer for no cause whatsoever, the courts have split on how to compensate the lawyer.[62] All jurisdictions recognize the absolute right of a client to fire the attorney; but they different on how to pay the lawyer who has been fired. Some old cases provide that the lawyer will receive the benefit of his bargain and the client will be required to pay a full contingent fee, if the client ultimately has a recovery.[63] One jurisdiction apportions the highest fee the client has agreed to pay among the lawyers who have worked on the case in one proceeding.[64] The majority of the jurisdictions have followed a quantum meruit approach to compensating the lawyer for the benefit that the lawyer has provided to the client's case.[65]

Some lawyers have sought to anticipate the premature termination of a contingent fee representation by including a clause that seeks to address the situations discussed above. For example, the lawyer could include a clause that, when the client discharges

---

[62]See Lester Brickman, Setting *the Fee When the Client Discharges a Contingent Fee Attorney*, 41 EMORY L.REV. 367 (1992).

[63]*See, e.g., Mandell & Wright v. Thomas*, 441 S.W.2d 841 (Tex. 1969) (lawyer who is discharged without cause may collect a full fee).

[64]*See Saucier v. Hayes Dairy Products, Inc.*, 373 So. 102 (La.1978). *Cf. Cohen v. Grainger, Tesoriero & Bell*, 81 N.Y.2d 655, 602 N.Y.S.2d 788, 622 N.E.2d 288 (1993) (lawyer may choose either quantum meruit or a share of the second lawyer's percentage of the outcome).

DeLapaz v. SelectBuild Const., Inc., 394 Ill. App. 3d 969, 334 Ill. Dec. 496, 917 N.E.2d 93 (1st Dist. 2009). Courts have discretion to give the contingent fee award to the law firm (Touhy & Touhy) while paying the former lawyers—the by successor lawyers who are no longer with the law firm but who settled the case—only quantum meruit fees. The original contingency agreement was with the law firm of Touhy & Touhy. The trial court found that "this case was settled and dismissed with prejudice before much of the legal work that would have to be done on a case like this had been performed, and the overwhelming amount of that work had been done by attorneys and legal assistants em-

ployed by Touhy." 394 Ill.App.3d 969, 974, 334 Ill.Dec. 496, 500 917 N.E.2d 93, 97.

[65]*See Fracasse v. Brent*, 6 Cal. 3d 784, 100 Cal. Rptr. 385, 494 P.2d 9 (1972). *See also Baker v. Shapero*, 203 S.W.3d 697 (Ky. 2006). Courts generally examine the standards under Rule 1.5(a) to determine an appropriate fee under a quantum meruit standard. *See Hess v. Seeger*, 55 Or. App. 746, 641 P.2d 23 (1982) (examining skills of the attorney, results obtained, complexity of the issues, and nature of the proceedings). The Restatement uses the concept of "fair value." Restatement of the Law Governing Lawyers, Third, § 40(1) (Official Draft 2000). One key issue in the application of the quantum meruit standard is whether it should be applied immediately after the termination or only upon the successful completion of the legal matter. Some jurisdictions hold that the action by the discharged lawyer accrues immediately upon the termination. *See, e.g., Skeens v. Miller*, 331 Md. 331, 628 A.2d 185 (1993). Others hold that it only accrues upon the client's successful completion of the litigation because if the client has no recovery there would have been no fee due under the contingent fee agreement. *See, e.g. Fracasse v. Brent*, 6 Cal. 3d 784, 100 Cal. Rptr. 385, 494 P.2d 9 (1972).

the attorney without proper cause, the fee agreement is at the lawyer's option converted from a contingent fee agreement to a fixed fee agreement.[66] The enforceability of such agreements will depend upon the sophistication of the client and an application of principles of equity and public policy.

§ 1.5–4 REFERRAL FEES AND SHARING FEES

§ 1.5–4(a) Lawyers in the Same Firm

Some commentators categorize the partners in a law firm as "finders," "minders," and "grinders." The finders, also called "rainmakers," primarily bring in clients; the minders manage and supervise cases; and the grinders do most of the detail work in cases, write the briefs, research the memoranda, and so forth. Often, firms distinguish sharply among these groups in terms of pay, with the finders or rainmakers typically commanding the highest share of firm profits. Minders or grinders may even be *called* "partners" but they may not be equity partners because they may work for an annual salary and have no equity interest in the firm.[1]

If lawyers are in the same law firm, the Model Rules and the Model Code do not regulate how the lawyers divide legal fees.[2] The ethics rules simply do not concern themselves with intra-firm referrals. The rainmakers in the law firm may delegate work to, and share fees with, other lawyers in the same firm—the minders and the grinders—in any way that the law firm partnership agreement provides, without running afoul of any ethics rules relating to fee sharing.[3] However, as discussed below, the rule is quite different if the lawyers are in different law firms.

§ 1.5–4(b) Lawyers in Different Firms

Once lawyers are in different law firms, the ethics rules impose

---

[66]*Compare* JOHN S. DZIENKOWSKI & AMON BURTON, ETHICAL DILEMMAS IN THE PRACTICE OF LAW: CASE STUDIES AND PROBLEMS 364 (Thomson 2006) (providing examples of clauses to convert a contingent fee agreement to a fixed fee agreement).

[Section 1.5–4]

[1]THOMAS D. MORGAN & RONALD D. ROTUNDA, PROBLEMS AND MATERIALS ON PROFESSIONAL RESPONSIBILITY 551 (Foundation Press, 7th ed. 2000).

[2]The drafters of the 2002 Rules added a Comment to make clear that Rule 1.5(e) does not apply when a lawyer receives a future fee for work performed while the lawyers were associated with the same firm and then one of the lawyers leaves the firm. *See* Rule 1.5, Comment 8.

[3]*See, e.g., Heninger & Heninger, P.C. v. Davenport Bank & Trust Co.,* 341 N.W.2d 43, 48–49 (Iowa 1983): "The Code of Professional Responsibility does not prohibit division of a fee with a partner or associate. DR 2-107. Palmer must have known when he employed Heninger that Heninger would use his firm attorneys. For Heninger to perform all the work personally would have resulted in substantial inefficiency—use of a senior partner's time to perform functions that could be done at about half the cost by use of other attorneys in the firm."

important limitations on the power of the lawyer to shift fees from one firm to another. A division of a fee "is a single billing to a client covering the fee of two or more lawyers who are *not* in the same firm."[4] Such divisions are commonly called "referral fees" or "forwarding fees." Several rationales support the restrictions on fee splitting. If a lawyer may not handle a case because of a conflict, it is reasonable to prohibit the lawyer from receiving part of the fee.[5] In addition, historical concerns exhibit a general distaste towards commercial methods of obtaining clients.[6]

The Model Code allowed referral fees only if several conditions existed. The Model Rules also impose conditions, but with several important differences that distinguish it from the Code.

FIRST, the Model Code provided that the client had to consent to the employment of the other lawyer after "a full disclosure that a division of fees will be made."[7] The Model Rules keep this restriction—though they use slightly different language.[8] The 1983 version of Rule 1.5(e) made clear that the client did not have to be told the share each lawyer will receive. In that version of the Rule, the lawyer needed to inform the client the fact of a division but did not need to tell the client the percentage of the fee each lawyer would receive.[9]

In contrast, the Official Draft of the Restatement of the Law Governing Lawyers requires the lawyers to disclose the "terms of

---

[4]Rule 1.5, Comment 7. Restatement of the Law Governing Lawyers, Third, § 47 "Fee-Splitting with Lawyer Not in Same Firm" (Official Draft 2000).

[5]For example, if a lawyer cannot take a case because the lawyer has a conflict of interest or is likely to be an advocate witness, that lawyer should not be able to accept a referral fee for sending the case to another lawyer, even if Rule 1.5(e) is followed.

Morris & Doherty, P.C. v. Lockwood, 259 Mich.App. 38, 672 N.W.2d 884 (2003), involved. Lockwood, the referring lawyer, had become a law professor and placed her bar membership on inactive status. The law firm argued that she therefore was ineligible to receive part of an active lawyer's fee. The Michigan Court of Appeals agreed. A lawyer on inactive lawyer is a non-lawyer for purposes of Rules 1.5(e) and 5.4(a), the Court said. Forwarding a case to an-

other lawyer constitutes engaging in "law business," something inactive lawyers may not do. Thus, the Court said, the fee sharing contract was void and Professor Lockwood was entitled to nothing.

[6]Restatement of the Law Governing Lawyers, Third, § 47 (Official Draft 2000), at Comment *b*, pp. 332 to 331.

[7]DR 2-107(A)(1).

[8]Rule 1.5(e)(1).

[9]1983 Model Rule 1.5, Comment 4. *Accord*, Restatement of the Law Governing Lawyers, Third, § 59 (Proposed Final Draft No. 2, Apr. 6, 1998), at Comment *e*, p. 152: "It is not a condition of validity that the client is informed of the terms of the division." Note that the Official Draft now requires the lawyers to inform the client of the fact *and* the terms of the division. Restatement of the Law Governing Lawyers, Third, § 47(2) (Official Draft 2000).

the division."[10] However, as of 2001, only a minority of jurisdictions require that the lawyer disclose the "terms of the division."[11] Under the Restatement, if the lawyer does not make the proper disclosure and secure consent at the outset of the representation, the client may later avoid the contract unless the lawyer shows that the contract was fair and reasonable to the client.[12]

The drafters of the 2002 Rules adopted the Restatement's view that the client must be informed of the share each lawyer will receive.[13] The client must confirm this agreement in writing. If the referral agreement involves a contingent fee, the entire agreement must be in writing and the client must sign it.[14]

SECOND, both the Model Rules and the Model Code require that the total fee charged be reasonable.[15]

THIRD, both the Rules and the Code regulate the proportion of the services performed. It is with this third requirement—relating to the proportion of services performed—that the Rules and Code significantly differ. The Code required that the division of fees be made "in proportion to the services performed and the responsibilities assumed by each."[16]

For example, assume that Lawyer #1 referred a client to Lawyer #2 [who is in a different law firm], a person whom Lawyer #1 believed to be more competent to handle a particular matter. Under the Model Code, Lawyer #2 could not pay Lawyer #1 a referral fee (*e.g.*, one-third of Lawyer #2's contingent fee) because the extent of Lawyer #1's service was only to recommend Lawyer #2. The mere act of recommending Lawyer #2 does not entitle Lawyer #1 to a referral fee under the Model Code. The restrictions that the Model Code imposed did not give any financial incentive to Lawyer #1 to refer the case to Lawyer #2, even if referral is in the client's interest. However, the Code allowed Lawyer #1 to avoid the restrictions of DR 2-107(A)(2) by formally associating with Lawyer #2.[17]

Solo practitioners and practitioners in small law firms often complained that the Code discriminated against them as compared to large law firms, because the ethics rules imposed no restrictions on what might be considered "internal referrals"—intra-law firm referrals (from the "finders" to the "grinders"). The Rules seek to correct this discrimination against small law firms

---

[10]Restatement of the Law Governing Lawyers, Third, § 47(2) (Official Draft 2000).

[11]Restatement of the Law Governing Lawyers, Third, § 47(2) (Official Draft 2000), Reporter's Notes at Comment e.

[12]Restatement of the Law Govern-

ing Lawyers, Third, § 47(2) (Official Draft 2000), comment *e*, and § 18(1)(a).

[13]Rule 1.5(e)(2).

[14]Rule 1.5, Comment 7.

[15]DR 2-107(A), (B).

[16]DR 2-107(A)(2) (emphasis added).

[17]*See* DR 6-101(A)(1).

or solo practitioners, while also seeking to aid clients by *encouraging* referrals to other (more competent) lawyers.[18] Thus the Rules allow a division of fees if the client is advised and does not object to the participation of the lawyers involved, the total fee is reasonable, and the division is in "proportion to services performed by each lawyer *or* each lawyer assumes joint responsibility for the representation."[19] The 2002 Rules require that the lawyer confirm agreements based upon either division in writing to the client and inform the client about the specific share each lawyer will receive.

Some lawyers have objected to this change in the ethics rules.[20] Oddly enough, the Rules on this point merely reinstated the rule that had existed under the ABA Canons of Professional Ethics that allowed a division of fees with another lawyer "based upon a division of service *or* responsibility."[21]

If a lawyer forwards a case and accepts joint responsibility but does not meet one of the requirements of the Rule, the sanction should be a denial of the fee. If, however, the fees are shared on the basis of work performed and one aspect of Rule 1.5(e) is violated, courts may award quantum meruit to the lawyer.[22] If the law firm to whom the case is referred believes that the referring lawyer fraudulently induced it to enter into the fee-sharing arrangement, it must not sit on its rights and wait until the

---

[18]*See* Rule 1.5, Comment 7.

[19]Rule 1.5(e)(1) (emphasis added).

[20]*See, e.g.,* NATIONAL LAW JOURNAL., (Feb. 5, 1979), at p. 18 (editorial).

[21]Canon 37 (1908, as amended 1937)(emphasis added). Recall that DR 2-107(B)(2) changed this language. DR 2-107(B)(2) said that the division must be made "in proportion to the services performed *and* responsibility assumed by each." (emphasis added).

[22]*Huskinson & Brown, LLP v. Wolf,* 32 Cal.4th 453, 9 Cal.Rptr.3d 693, 84 P.3d 379 (2004), involved a medical malpractice suit referred by a law firm to Wolf in exchange for an oral agreement to receive 25% of Wolf's fee. Wolf pursued the action, but Huskinson Brown paid for a medical expert and contributed some legal services. When the client recovered a large judgment, Wolf failed to pay the referral fee. Huskinson Brown sued for breach of contract, unjust enrichment, and *quantum meruit* recovery. The trial court denied recovery for breach of contract because Rule 2-200 of the California Rules of Professional Conduct requires written consent of the client for a contract for the division of legal fees to be enforceable. However, it awarded the full 25% of the legal fees ($18,497.91) on the unjust enrichment claim, or, in the alternative, $5,800.00 in *quantum meruit* for the reasonable value of the services rendered. The court of appeal reversed, but the California Supreme Court found that Huskinson Brown was entitled to *quantum meruit* recovery. There was an expectation by both parties that Huskinson Brown's services would be compensated, and Rule 2-200 does not restrict all attorney compensation, only compensation on the basis of a division of fees.

referred case is completed. Instead, it must inform the other firm of its claim in a timely manner.[23]

§ 1.5–4(c) Joint Responsibility

The 1983 version of Rule 1.5(e) did not define in detail the meaning of *"joint responsibility."* The Comment stated that joint responsibility "entails," for that particular matter, the responsibility of a partner or supervisory lawyer as stated in Rule 5.1.[24] Rule 5.1, in turn, refers to the responsibility required of a partner or supervisory lawyer to ensure that all the lawyers in a law firm comply with the Rules of Professional Conduct.

The drafters of the 2002 Rules amended this broad definition of "joint responsibility." The Comments define joint responsibility as including both "financial and ethical responsibility for the representation as if the lawyers were associated in a partnership."[25] The language goes on to state that lawyers should only refer clients to other competent lawyers.

The reference to responsibility that would exist if the lawyers were associated in a partnership does add significant content to the definition of joint responsibility. A lawyer who receives a referral fee must seek to protect the client and to encourage refer-

---

[23]*See Ballow Brasted O'Brien & Rusin P.C. v. Logan,* 435 F.3d 235 (2d Cir. 2006). In this case, a law firm (Firm #1) representing the plaintiff in a personal injury case entered into a substitution agreement with the successor firm (Firm #2) that required Firm #2 to pay 20% of the total fees to Firm #1. After settlement, Firm #2 refused to pay, claiming that Firm #1 had induced the agreement by misrepresenting the amount of work done on the file. Firm #2 also argued that the substitution agreement violated New York DR 2–107, requiring fees to be divided in proportion to the work performed. The court held that Firm #2 had waived the claim for rescission of agreement based on fraud because it knew of the alleged misrepresentations for four years before declaring its intent to rescind the agreement. The court concluded: "Claims for rescission based on alleged fraudulent misrepresentations must be asserted in a timely manner. Having waited approximately four years to assert this very claim, Logan has failed to meet this requirement and the equities do not favor permitting the claim to pro-

ceed. As a result, he cannot be absolved from his obligations under the Agreement with BBOR, which is enforceable pursuant to New York contract law." 435 F.3d at 243.

The court also held that the agreement, which did not comply with the fee division rule, was nevertheless enforceable between parties as long as the discharged firm did some work on the file and did not refuse the request to provide more work.

Accord Alderman v. Pan Am World Airways, 169 F.3d 99, 103 (2d Cir.1999): "Under New York law, it is well established that an agreement between attorneys for division of a legal fee is valid and is enforceable in accordance with terms set forth in agreement, provided that each party actually contributed some work, labor and service toward earning of the fee and there is no claim that either refused to contribute more substantially." (internal quotation marks omitted).

[24]1983 Model Rule 1.5, Comment 4.

[25]Rule 1.5, Comment 7.

rals to competent attorneys. The assumption of joint responsibility also means the assumption of malpractice liability for the particular matter as if the lawyers were associated together. This is consistent with the standard of association under the Model Code.[26] Requiring this assumption of malpractice liability encourages the referring lawyer to pick with care the lawyer to whom the case is referred. The referring lawyer has an added incentive to pick the most competent lawyer. Recall that the first rule of legal ethics, the prime directive, is competence.[27]

The new standard under the 2002 Rules is consistent with commentators who have concluded that the requirement of "joint responsibility" in the Rule may be read "as a euphemism for assumption of joint and severable liability for legal malpractice purposes, as if the two lawyers were partners."[28] The referring lawyer is like a quasi-partner, part of an "*ad hoc* partnership or joint professional venture, for purposes of the representation in question."[29] As the Restatement concludes, the requirement of "joint responsibility" means that—

> each lawyer can be held liable in a malpractice suit *and* before the disciplinary authorities for the others' acts to the same extent as could partners in the same traditional partnership participating in the representation. Such assumption of responsibility discourages lawyers from referring clients to careless lawyers in return for a large share of the fee.[30]

In any event, a referral fee is proper under the Rules *if* Lawyer #1 assumes joint responsibility (*i.e.*, malpractice liability and the supervisory responsibility imposed by Rule 5.1) with Lawyer #2 for the particular matter, *and* the total fee is reasonable, *and* the Client is advised and does not object. The agreement must be confirmed in writing and the client needs to be informed of the share each lawyer will receive.

---

[26] DR 6-101(A)(1).

[27] Rule 1.1, Competence.

[28] CHARLES W. WOLFRAM, MODERN LEGAL ETHICS § 9.2.4 at n.9 (West Pub. Co. Practitioner's ed. 1986).

[29] 1 GEOFFREY C. HAZARD, JR. & W. WILLIAM HODES, THE LAW OF LAWYERING § 1.5:601, at 126.11 (Prentice Hall, 2nd ed., 1990).

[30] Restatement of the Law Governing Lawyers, Third, § 47 (Official Draft 2000), at Comment *d*, p. 333 (internal citation omitted) (emphasis added).

Of course, if the Rules require no more than the referring lawyer being the equivalent of a malpractice insurer, one wonders why this "insurer" must be a lawyer at all, or even an individual. Malpractice insurers need not be lawyers. They can be individuals, lay partnerships, corporations, or associations. If the only requirement is that the referring entity serves as a back-up malpractice insurer, a corporation with significant net worth would offer more protection to the client than many individual lawyers who are paid for referring cases.

§ 1.5–4(d) Comparison of Assumption of Joint Responsibility with the Sale of a Practice

A discussion of sharing fees and joint responsibility naturally raises those issues when a lawyer sells his or her law practice. Rule 1.17—which governs the sale of a law practice—does not refer to Rule 1.5(e)(1), which requires the referring lawyer to assume joint responsibility for the representation. In fact, a Comment to Rule 1.17 specifically provides that this Rule does not apply to the transfer of legal representation unrelated to the sale of a practice.[31] However, one would think, as a logical matter, that the responsibilities that a lawyer selling an entire practice must assume under Rule 1.17 should be no less than those that a referring lawyer must assume pursuant to Rule 1.5(e)(1). This view is consistent with the Comment to Rule 1.17, which notes that the seller has the obligation to exercise competence in identifying a qualified purchaser.[32] Although the seller—unlike the lawyer who refers one case—cannot exercise continuing supervision (he has, after all, left the practice), it does not appear unreasonable to make him share joint malpractice liability (as if they were partners) with the person whom he has handpicked to buy his practice. Such a rule would assure that the seller picks carefully, and it is no more onerous than the burden already imposed by Rule 1.5(e)(1).

§ 1.5–4(e) Law-Temporaries

Sometimes a law firm has a short-term need to hire lawyers for a specific project or staffing problem, or a need for a special expertise on a particular issue. In such cases, the law firm typically hires a *"temporary lawyer,"* or *"lawyer-temp"* or *"law-temp."* This type of hiring has increased appreciably in recent times. The firm may hire the law-temp either directly or use the services of a placement agency.

The law-temp is treated, for purposes of Rule 1.5(e), the same as an associate who works under the supervision of other lawyers who are associated with the law firm. Therefore, no need arises for the law firm to secure any permission or consent from the client before hiring law-temps. And, when the law firm pays the law-temp, it is not sharing a legal fee with a lawyer in a different law firm.[33] The firm does not have to reveal the compensation agreement with the law-temp any more than it would have to reveal its compensation agreement with any full-time associate

---

[31]Rule 1.17, Comment 15.
[32]Rule 1.17, Comment 11.

[33]ABA Formal Opinion 88-356 (Dec. 16, 1988), at 10.

or non-lawyer employee of the law firm, and it may even pay the law-temp a percentage of the firm's net profits.[34]

On the other hand, if the law firm does not supervise the law-temp, and the law-temp engages in independent work for a client, the law firm must secure the client's consent, because the client, by retaining the law firm, "cannot reasonably be deemed to have consented to the involvement of an independent lawyer."[35]

Surcharges and Billing Clients for the Expenses of Law-Temporaries. May the law-temporary be a profit center for the law firm? When the firm bills the client $200 for an associate, it does not give the full $200 to the associate. The associate's yearly salary (particularly in the case of a senior associate) may well be less than the total hours that the associate bills during the course of the year. The firm makes (or at least hopes to make) a profit from many of its associates. May the law firm treat law-temporaries the same way?

If the firm treats the work of the contract lawyer (law-temporary) as an expense item (that is, an expense over and above its regular fee), the ABA advises a law firm to bill the client for only what it actually paid for the contract lawyer's services. In that case, the firm may not charge the client a surcharge in billing for the services of a contract attorney that it hires to work on a case. Unless there is a specific agreement to the contrary, if the firm treats the work as an expense item (over and above its fee), the firm should bill only what it actually paid for the contract lawyer's services.

However, the ABA adds, if the contract lawyer is billed as just another lawyer whose work makes up the fee for the matter, the firm may bill the client any reasonable rate for the services just as it does for one of its associates.[36] If the law firm bills the expense of the contract lawyer's as legal fees, the client normally would expect that the law firm has supervised that work and adopted it as its own.

§ 1.5–5 HOURLY FEES

§ 1.5–5(a) Legal Audits of Hourly Fees

As mentioned above, contingent fees for plaintiff-lawyers are

---

[34]ABA Formal Opinion 88-356 (Dec. 16, 1988), at 10. The conclusion under the former Model Code is the same. ABA Formal Opinion 1140 (1979).

[35]ABA Formal Opinion 88-356 (Dec. 16, 1988), at 10.

[36]ABA Formal Opinion 00-420 (Nov. 29, 2000). *But see* Texas State Bar Professional Ethics Committee, Opinion 377 (Jan. 2007)(rejecting ABA review that law firms may mark up fees of nonfirm contract attorneys without meeting the requirements of the fee sharing rule; if the firm wishes to mark up the fees, it is essentially sharing fees with a lawyer in another firm).

quite typical in cases involving personal injury. However, in other instances, most lawyers base their charges on the hourly fee.[1] Although opponents of contingent fees sometimes favor hourly fees, one should realize that hourly fees raise their own set of problems. Clients often express concern that law firms may miscalculate hourly fees and that the hourly fee rewards law firms if they overstaff a case. Consequently, clients increasingly are auditing their lawyers' bills, and finding significant errors in the bills that their lawyers send them.[2] Law firms, in response, are auditing their own bills to catch embarrassing mistakes before the client does.[3] As legal costs continue to rise (because of higher salaries as well as the increased costs of computer support hardware and software), clients are demanding more efficient legal services.[4]

§ 1.5-5(b) Client Objections to Hourly Fees

The nature of the hourly fee may make it difficult for the client to budget legal expenses. As the Chairman of the Board of I.B.M. once lamented, the I.B.M. general counsel "is the only department head to whom we've given an unlimited budget—and he's

---

[Section 1.5-5]

[1]WILLIAM G. ROSS, THE HONEST HOUR: THE ETHICS OF TIME-BASED BILLING BY ATTORNEYS (Carolina Academic Press 1996); George B. Shepherd & Morgan Cloud, *Time and Money: Discovery Leads to Hourly Billing*, 1999 U. ILL. L. REV. 91 (1999).

[2]*See, e.g.*, Amy Stevens, *As Some Clients Grow Bill-Savvy, Others May Find They Get the Tab*, WALL STREET JOURNAL, Feb. 11, 1994, at 1–2 (Midwest ed.); Amy Stevens, *Top Chapman & Cutler Partner Chalked Up Astronomical Hours*, WALL STREET JOURNAL, May 27, 1994, at B1, col. 3–6 & B5, col. 3 (Midwest ed.)(huge number of hours billed; judge derides fee request as "blatantly, embarrassingly excessive on its face"); Darlene Ricker, *Greed, Ignorance and Overbilling*, ABA JOURNAL, Aug., 1994, at 62; Darlene Ricker, *Auditing Lawyers for a Living*, ABA JOURNAL, Aug., 1994, at 65; Paul Barrett, *Attorney Was a Critic of Law-Firm Fraud; Now He Faces Prison*, WALL STREET JOURNAL, Sept. 30, 1997, at A1, col. 6 (Midwest ed.);

Lisa G. Lerman, *Scenes from a Law Firm*, 50 RUTGERS L. REV. 2153 (1998) (part of a mini-symposium on unethical billing practices); Lisa G. Lerman, *Regulation of Unethical Billing Practices: Progress and Prospects*, 1998 THE PROFESSIONAL LAWYER 89 (ABA, 1998 Symposium Issue).

[3]*See* Erin White, *More Law Firms Are Auditing Themselves to Catch Billing Errors*, WALL STREET JOURNAL, July 14, 1998, at B6, col. 1–2 (Midwest ed.). For example, in one case where a partner charged "$285 an hour to research a basic banking and loan issue," the firm reduced the bill from $23,720 to $12,000.

[4]Edward Felsenthal, *The Practice: Not So Fast: It Only Seems Like Legal Fees Are Skyrocketing*, WALL STREET JOURNAL, May 27, 1998, at A1, col. 1 (big clients lower legal bills by "wrestling cuts in billing rates and forcing firms to work more efficiently"); Paul Barrett, *Bill Law Firms' 1997 Profits Evoke 1980s Boom Times*, WALL STREET JOURNAL, June 30, 1998, at B1, col. 5–6 (Midwest ed.).

already exceeded it."[5] However, it is not only large entities but also small businesses or members of the middle class who share the same concern, because when these small businesses and middle class citizens need a lawyer for such matters as representation in a drunk driving charge or in drafting a will, they may wish to avoid paying an hourly fee.[6] Thus, although the hourly fee is still the overwhelming method of choice when lawyers charge for their services,[7] clients and lawyers have been examining alternatives to the hourly fee.

§ 1.5–5(c) Alternative Types of Hourly Fees

Some of the most popular alternatives to a straight hourly fee include the following:[8]

- FEE LIMITS OR CAPS. In this situation, the base fee is predicated on an hourly rate but is subject to an agreed maximum. The law firm may agree not to charge more than a certain hourly rate for a maximum number of hours. Or, the law firm may impose some sort of safety valve: that is, the firm does not accept the full cost of underestimating the cost of the legal services, but it will agree not to exceed the cap without additional client review and approval.

- DISCOUNTED HOURLY RATES AND VOLUME RATES. In this situation, the firm may agree to charge reduced hourly rates to the extent that the client gives more business to the law firm. This method, like the previous one, is a modified version of the hourly rate.

- UNBUNDLED FEES. The law firm may offer the client the op-

---

[5]Quoted in, THOMAS D. MORGAN & RONALD D. ROTUNDA, PROBLEMS AND MATERIALS ON PROFESSIONAL RESPONSIBILITY 249 (Foundation Press, 6th ed. 1995).

[6]See, e.g., William G. Ross, The Ethics of Hourly Billing By Attorneys, 44 RUTGERS L. REV. 1 (1991); Ann Davis, Lug a Box, Scan Mail: Is It All Billable Time?, WALL STREET JOURNAL, Jan. 6, 1998, at B1.

[7]Gallup Poll, Billing the Time, A.B.A. J. at 72–73 (Mar. 1994).

[8]These alternatives are discussed in: ABA SECTION ON BUSINESS LAW, COMMITTEE ON LAWYER BUSINESS ETHICS, REPORT ON ALTERNATIVE BILLING ARRANGEMENTS (Revised Draft, Feb. 17, 1998).

See also Robert E. Litan & Steven C. Salop, Reforming the Lawyer-Client Relationship Through Alterna-

tive Billing Methods, 77 JUDICATURE 191 (1994); Zoe Baird, A Client's Experience with Implementing Value Billing, 77 JUDICATURE 198 (1994); Charles S. McCowan, Jr. & Esteban Herrera, Jr., Alternative Fee Arrangements: Time for Consideration, 43 LA. BAR J. 466 (1996); Geanne Rosenberg, At Law Firms, Billable Hours Give Way to "Alternative Pricing," INVESTMENT DEALERS' DIGEST, July 21, 1997, at 21; Ronald D. Rotunda, Competitive Bidding Would End "Pay-to-Play," 20 NATIONAL LAW JOURNAL A23 (June 29, 1998); Ronald D. Rotunda, Moving from Billable Hours to Fixed-Fees: Task-Based Fees and Legal Ethics, 47 U. KAN. L. REV. 1 (1999); Ronald D. Rotunda, Innovative Legal Billing, Alternatives to Billable Hours, and Ethical Hurdles, 2 JOURNAL OF THE INSTITUTE FOR THE STUDY OF LEGAL ETHICS 1701 (1999).

tion of not hiring the law firm to perform certain chores, and instead, hiring others to perform this separate, law-related work (duplicating, document indexing, messenger services). Larger corporate clients usually have in-house facilities that can perform these services more cheaply.

- VARIATIONS ON CONTINGENCY FEES. The client and lawyer may agree that the law firm will charge lower than its normal hourly fee, but then the client will pay a bonus for success in reaching particular goals or for achieving particular objectives, such as expeditious disposition of a motion or completion of a negotiation. Or, the law firm may receive a bonus in addition to the base hourly rate if a transaction closes while risking a reduction in the base hourly rate if the transaction does not close.[9]

These alternatives are often more appealing to larger corporate clients. Indeed, these clients may have their own in-house legal staff to perform the basic legal research. However, one alternative may be suitable to clients of all income levels: the fixed fee, or what is sometimes called "task-based billing."

§ 1.5–6 TASK-BASED BILLING, OR FIXED FEES

§ 1.5–6(a) Client Incentives for Fixed Fees

It may make good economic sense for a law firm to offer a client the option to pay a flat fee for its legal work. Flat fees shift the risks of the unknown—how many hours will the law firm actually have to devote to a case—from the client to the law firm. Many law firms will be able to assume this risk because the law firm has more knowledge and experience in this matter. Of

---

[9]ABA Formal Opinion 94-389 (Dec. 5, 1994) suggests the client, in a public offering, may wish to avoid paying for the law firm's services until "an identifiable fund is available from the proceeds of a public offering." This particular fee arrangement can raise special conflict of interest issues in certain circumstances where the law firm is charging for its services in connection with the offering. The ABA Section on Business Law, Committee on Lawyer Business Ethics, Report on Alternative Billing Arrangements (Revised Draft, Feb. 17, 1998), at 33, n.25, notes that unlike investment bankers, securities lawyers, "in principle, do not have an interest in the transaction of a public offering closing." In some instances "there may not be a solvent company from which to

collect a fee if the financing is not completed." *Id.*

Thus, there is a special conflict of interest when the law firm's fee is tied to the completion of a public offering that the law firm put together. *SEC v. National Student Marketing Corp.*, 457 F.Supp. 682, 691–94, 711–12 (D. D.C.1978)(lawyer, who stood to profit "handsomely" from the merging corporation where he was an officer and shareholder acted improperly when he did nothing after learning that interim financial statements were inaccurate). *See* ABA Section on Business Law, Committee on Lawyer Business Ethics, Report on Alternative Billing Arrangements (Revised Draft, Feb. 17, 1998), at 34 to 36, n.26. In re Candie's, Inc., Securities Act. Release No. 7263 (SEC Feb. 21, 1996).

course, the law firm could always refuse to work for a flat fee (but then it might find itself at a competitive disadvantage to those firms willing to assume this risk).

The law firm is also the more efficient risk-spreader because it has, in effect, a diverse portfolio of cases. A simple analogy indicates why some clients may prefer fixed fees. Assume that you wish to purchase an airline ticket from Chicago to Washington, D.C. The travel agent informs you that you will be billed at the end of the trip, and that the amount you will have to pay will be a function of various factors. For example, if airline traffic congestion causes your flight to circle the airport for an hour, that will result in an increased use of expensive fuel, so you will be billed for your pro rata cost of this "disbursement" on your behalf. If the pilot becomes ill shortly before take-off and the airline must fly in another pilot to take over the assignment, you will have to pay that expense as well. Then, of course, there can always be a wildcat strike, and you will pay for any costs associated with that too. If your flight is delayed because of engine problems and the airline is courteous enough to call you the night before, you will pay the toll charges and the cost of the time of the airline representative to contact you (billed to the nearest quarter of an hour).

The length of your flight is also an open question and that will also affect your total bill. It may normally take two and one-half hours, but sometimes it takes a little longer. You will be billed by the quarter hour for the length of the flight, so you will bear any burdens associated with delay. Of course, the flight may benefit by tail winds that shorten your flight by a quarter-hour, and then you will enjoy the reduction in your total bill by one-quarter hour, but you also know from experience that the airline seldom completes the flight in less than the allotted time, because it has no financial incentive to do so. Indeed, the more inefficient the airline is in using its resources, the more money it will collect from you.

Some clients of law firms view the lawyer's hourly billing method with the same degree of warmth and understanding that they would view a proposal by airlines to bill for flights based on a combination of hourly billing and disbursements. If airlines would propose such a billing method, many customers would not be amused. However, when clients propose fixed fees for particular legal tasks, lawyers have in their arsenal of responses a rejoinder that is foreign to the airlines: the rules of ethics.

The question whether flat, fixed fees that include the lawyer's expenses and disbursements violate the ethics rules is important because it is increasingly common for clients or lawyers to propose task-based, or fixed fee billing.[1] Some clients and law firms have made no secret of a preference for fixed fees, at least in some circumstances. In fact, some prestigious law firms have publicly announced that they are engaging in flat fee billing.[2] But, as discussed below, there is some authority that raises ethical roadblocks to this development.[3] First, let us turn to the argument that a flat-fee violates Model Rule 1.8(e).[4]

§ 1.5–6(b) Rule 1.8(e) and Fixed Fees

We live in a free country, so when a client proposes a flat fee, the law firm does not have to accept it. However, when clients have proposed fixed-fee arrangements, some lawyers have responded not by telling the client to go elsewhere; but by arguing that no lawyer may accept these fee proposals because they violate the ethical rules governing lawyers.[5] Some lawyers claim that fixed-fee arrangements may violate the ethics rules, in particular Rule 1.8, relating to the obligation of the client to assume responsibility for litigation costs. If the ethics rules (as some lawyers have argued) prohibit flat fees or task-based billing, then the law firm that does not want to engage in such billing (and is unwilling to compete with law firms offering that alternative) does not have to tell the client to shop elsewhere. The law firm need not contend with law firms that are willing to offer flat fees, because the alternative of a flat fee is nonexistent. However, the ethics rules impose no per se prohibition of fixed fees.

A basic ethical argument that some law firms advance against task-based billing is that ABA Model Rule 1.8(e) prohibits a law firm from paying or guaranteeing litigation expenses unless a client remains ultimately liable for those expenses. Otherwise, there

---

[Section 1.5–6]

[1]*See e.g.*, Amy Stevens, *Lawyers Gaze At a Future of Bills That Are Task Based*, WALL ST. J., July 1, 1994, at B6, col. 1–2 (Midwest ed.); Amy Stevens, *Frequent-Client Club Takes Flight in Trend Towards Flexible Pricing*, WALL ST. J., July 15, 1994, at B10, col. 1–2 (Midwest ed.); Andrea Gerlin, *Novel Fee Arrangements Are Slow to Take Root in U.S. Bankruptcy Cases*, WALL ST. J., July 29, 1994, at B3, col. 1–2 (Midwest ed.); Margaret A. Jacobs, *Law Partners Go to Business School For Certain Answers*, WALL ST. J., Oct. 9, 1995, at B3, col. 1–2 (Midwest ed.).

[2]Amy Stevens, *Frequent-Client Club Takes Flight in Trend Toward Flexible Pricing*, WALL ST. J., July 15,

1994, at B6, col. 1, which notes that one Chicago law firm is "offering *flat fees* and other alternative billing arrangements. So far, says partner Skip Herman, clients have 'reacted extremely well,' opting for nontraditional billing *in 75% of new matters*." (emphasis added).

[3]*See* Kentucky Advisory Ethics Opinion E-368 (1994), *reprinted in* Kentucky Bench & Bar (Fall, 1994), at 52. This opinion and related authority are discussed below.

[4]*See* Restatement of the Law Governing Lawyers, Third, § 36 (Official Draft 2000).

[5]*See* discussion below. *Cf. Topps v. Pratt & Callis, P.C.*, 206 Ill.App.3d 298, 151 Ill.Dec. 219, 564 N.E.2d 196 (1990).

would be "inadequate compensation" for the time and effort spent on the representation.[6] They argue that the law firm may bid a particular fixed amount that includes both attorneys' fees and any expenses related to the litigation. Then, if the litigation expenses are unusually high and exceed the total amount that the law firm had agreed to bill the client, the law firm's fees would be zero. That would mean that the law firm and not the client would be ultimately liable for the expenses, to the extent that the expenses exceeded the fixed fee amount.

However, ABA Model Rule 1.8 provides that the client does *not* have to be liable for any of the expenses of pending or contemplated litigation because the lawyer can agree with the client that any repayment may be "contingent on the *outcome* of the matter."[7] The term "outcome" need not necessarily mean "a complete judicial victory" or "a complete judicial loss." For example, personal injury lawyers routinely charge different contingencies depending on whether the case is settled before trial (a situation where there is no judicial determination at all), or whether the case goes to a jury verdict, or whether the case must be appealed on one or more issues, and so forth.

What a client (or law firm) who offers a fixed, flat fee for handling an entire matter is proposing is that any repayment of actual expenses (including litigation expenses)[8] be contingent on whether the expenses are less than the agreed upon flat fee, which includes both expected expenses and an expected fee.[9] This situation is not really different in kind or degree from the situation where a personal injury plaintiff's lawyer agrees with the plaintiff to take expenses out of the verdict or settlement, so that the lawyer makes no profit if the expenses exceed the amount of verdict (or the verdict gives the plaintiff nothing).[10] This arrangement does not violate Rule 1.8(e).

---

[6]*E.g.*, The Supreme Court of Ohio, Board of Commissioners on Grievances and Discipline, Ohio Opinion 97-7 (Dec. 5, 1977), *available in* 1997 WL 782951.

[7]Rule 1.8(e)(1)(emphasis added).

[8]A subsidiary benefit of a flat bill that includes all expenses is that the client does not have to worry that the expenses are incorrectly apportioned. The auditing of legal bills has become a growth industry, and these auditors have uncovered costly errors that involve simple mistakes, such as the client who was billed $8,000 for a hotel that his lawyers did not use because that hotel bill was mixed up with another hotel bill, which was erroneously sent to a different client. In another case, one partner's receipts were stapled to another lawyer's expense account. Consequently, some law firms are now engaging in internal audits before the bills are sent. Erin White, *More Law Firms Are Auditing Themselves to Catch Billing Errors*, Wall St. J., July 14, 1998, at B6, col. 1–2 (Midwest ed.). A flat-fee avoids this problem entirely.

[9]It may be the case that the total expenses of litigation turn out to exceed the proposed flat fee.

[10]In that situation then, a contingency has occurred. The repayment of

The client can always choose an hourly fee. The law firm that objects to a flat fee is not objecting to the contingency on the grounds that the total fee it will collect will be too high, but that it might be (in its view) too low. That is not an interest that the ethics rules should protect.

§ 1.5–6(c) Rationale of Model Rule 1.8(e)

§ 1.5–6(c)(1) Maintenance, Champerty, and Barratry

The conclusion that ABA Model Rule 1.8(e) should not preclude a flat fee proposal is supported by the purpose behind this rule: it exists as a modern day relative of what the common law called "maintenance," or "champerty" or "barratry."[11] *Maintenance* occurs when the lawyer improperly finances a lawsuit so as to "encourage a client to pursue lawsuits that might otherwise be forsaken."[12] The English common law objected to improperly stirring up litigation and it made maintenance a common law crime, a crime that was not abolished by statute until 1967.[13] A close kin of maintenance is *Champerty*, which occurs when one person assists a litigant in maintaining the lawsuit and, in exchange, receives from the litigant a promise to have a share in the recovery.

A kissing cousin of maintenance is *Barratry*, which involves a person who urges another to file or continue a lawsuit.[14] At com-

---

the law firm's expenses is contingent or conditional on a satisfactory outcome. If the outcome is unsatisfactory, then the expenses alone may exceed what the total flat fee was expected to be. The law firm's actual expenses of the litigation may be so large that they exceed the law firm's total bill, which included both out-of-pocket expenses and attorneys' fees. What has occurred is simply a form of contingent fee where it is the lawyer for the defendant who is being paid based on a contingency. The same thing will occur when the lawyer for the plaintiff charges a contingency fee and the outcome is unsuccessful.

[11]*See* F. MacKinnon, Contingent Fees for Legal Services: A Study of Professional Economics and Responsibilities 37–38 (1964).

[12]ABA, Annotated Model Rules of Professional Conduct 143 (ABA, 2nd ed. 1992). *Accord* Geoffrey C. Hazard, Jr. & W. William Hodes, 1 The Law of Lawyering § 1.8:602 at 274 (Aspen Law & Business, 1998, 2nd ed., with annual supplementation); Susan Lorde Martin, *Syndicated Lawsuits: Illegal Champerty or New Business Opportunity?*, 30 Am. Bus. L.J. 485, 488–89 (1992).

[13]Criminal Law Act, 1967, ch. 58, §§ 13 to 14, cited in, Charles W. Wolfram, Modern Legal Ethics § 8.13 at n. 45 (West Pub. Co. Practitioner's ed. 1986).

[14]Charles W. Wolfram, Modern Legal Ethics § 8.13 (West Pub. Co. Practitioner's ed. 1986). *See also* Katherine A. Laroe, Comment, *Much Ado About Barratry: State Regulation of Attorneys' Targeted Direct-Mail Solicitation*, 25 St. Mary's L.J. 1513, 1519–20 (1994).

mon law, a cause of action for Barratry required that the person commit three acts of instances of stirring up litigation.[15]

Modern American courts, which are not nearly as distrustful of litigation as were their common law ancestors, have withdrawn significantly from any effort to enforce these common law restrictions.[16] Rule 1.8(e) is drafted much more narrowly than its common law ancestors. Nonetheless, critics of flat fees raise the argument that the fee arrangement will improperly stir up litigation.

There is no danger of a lawyer's improper barratry, champerty, or maintenance of a client who is a defendant. As Justice Cardozo noted in the case of, *In re Gilman's Administratrix*:[17]

> The point of those [other] decisions was that the retainer of the attorney was not to attack, but to defend. He was not inciting to litigation. He was protecting the interests of a client against assaults begun or threatened.[18]

That, of course, is the situation with fixed fee arrangements. No attorney is being asked to engage in champerty or maintenance by inciting and funding a plaintiff's frivolous lawsuit against another entity. The client seeking the flat fee is often the defendant; its interests are being threatened. The defendant retains the attorney not to stir up a lawsuit, but to defend. One can hardly accuse a law firm or client of stirring up litigation when the client is a *defendant* in the law suit and would prefer to have the suit go away.

§ 1.5–6(c)(2) Loans to Clients

Model Rule 1.8(e) does place some limits on loans by attorneys to clients, but this Rule does not prohibit lawyers from agreeing to a flat fee that includes litigation expenses. Indeed, this Rule allows the lawyer to advance court costs and the expenses of litigation, repayment of which may be contingent on the outcome of the litigation.[19] To the extent that the law firm agrees to a maximum cap on expenses, it is not part of an improper effort to

---

[15]*Bailey v. Morales*, 190 F.3d 320, 322 (5th Cir.1999).

[16]*Bailey v. Morales*, 190 F.3d 320 (5th Cir.1999), holding unconstitutional a Texas statute that attempted to regulate what the court called the "cottage industry" of alleged ambulance-chasing chiropractors and others that has emerged in Texas. The statute prohibited chiropractors from soliciting employment, in person or over the telephone, from individuals who have a special need for chiropractic services arising out of a particular occurrence (*e.g.,* an accident) or a pre-existing condition (*e.g.,* arthritis). The court invalidated the law as to chiropractors because "solicitation of business by chiropractors (even barratrous solicitations) is commercial speech," and protected by the First Amendment.

[17]*In re Gilman's Administratrix*, 251 N.Y. 265, 167 N.E. 437 (1929).

[18]251 N.Y. at 269.

[19]*See also* Restatement of the Law Governing Lawyers, Third, § 36(2)(a) & Comment *c*, *Financial assistance to*

engage in champerty or maintenance. It does not prevent the client from settling the case if she wants to do so. The fee cap is not unethical because it comes with no improper strings attached.[20]

§ 1.5–6(d) Flat Fees and Alleged Conflicts of Interest

Some law firms have also objected to flat fee agreements on the grounds that they create an improper conflict of interest. The argument is that a flat fee creates the possibility that decisions regarding whether to incur a certain expense in the defense of the client will place the firm in a conflicted situation with the client.

This argument proves too much. If accepted, it would prevent any lawyer, even a plaintiff's attorney in a typical personal injury

---

a client (Official Draft 2000). The Model Code imposed the requirement that the "client remain ultimately liable for such expenses." DR 5–103(B). Consequently, some jurisdictions also require that the lawyer make sure that the client's obligation to repay these costs is unconditional unless the client is indigent. However, even in these jurisdictions there is no requirement that the lawyer sue to collect his fee. Indeed, the Model Code, as an ethical aspiration, provided that the lawyer "should *not sue* a client for a fee unless necessary to prevent fraud or gross imposition by the client." EC 2–23 (emphasis added). *Cf. Rand v. Monsanto Co.*, 926 F.2d 596 (7th Cir.1991), *appeal after remand*, 946 F.2d 897 (7th Cir.1991), which refused to apply, in a federal class action, the requirement of DR 5–103(B) making the client "ultimately liable" for litigation expenses that the lawyer advanced. This Disciplinary Rule, the court concluded, is inconsistent with Federal Rules of Civil Procedure, Rule 23. The defendants argued that the representative plaintiff in a class action must be willing to bear all the costs of the action to satisfy adequacy of representation requirement, notwithstanding local rule of professional responsibility prohibiting counsel from bearing costs of suit themselves. The court said:

"Indeed, so far as we can tell DR 5–103(B) itself serves no good purpose. The ABA has jettisoned, and the states are in the process of replacing, this relic of the rules against champerty and barratry. Monsanto does not contend that the application of DR 5–103(B) to class actions would produce any discernible benefit. We conclude that DR 5–103(B) is inconsistent with Rule 23 and therefore may not be applied to class actions. *Accord County of Suffolk v. Long Island Lighting Co.*, 710 F.Supp. 1407, 1413–15 (E.D.N.Y. 1989)."

926 F.2d at 600.

[20] *See* Note, *Guaranteeing Loans to Clients Under Minnesota's Code of Professional Responsibility*, 66 MINN. L. REV. 1091 (1982); Note, William Roger Strelow, *Loans to Client For Living Expenses*, 55 CAL. L. REV. 1419 (1967); John J. Vassen, *The Case For Allowing Lawyers to Advance Client Living Expenses*, 80 ILL. B.J. 16 (1992); Note, Michael R. Koval, *Living Expenses, Litigation Expenses, and Lending Money to Clients*, 7 GEORGETOWN. J. LEGAL ETHICS 1117 (1994); John Sahl, *Helping Clients With Living Expenses: "No Good Deed Goes Unpunished,"* 12 ABA PROFESSIONAL LAWYER 1 (Winter 2002). Professor Sahl concluded that the ABA should "adopt a more generous approach by permitting lawyers to do more to help poor clients litigate their claims. Lawyers should not be compelled, of course, to provide living expenses, but nor should they run the risk of professional discipline for humanitarian acts." *Id.* at 8.

claim, from ever agreeing that the client's reimbursement of the expenses of the litigation would be contingent on the outcome. Yet ABA Model Rule 1.8(e) specifically permits an attorney to do exactly that.[21]

One of the few cases to consider such issues extensively is *In re Oracle Securities Litigation*,[22] which rejects this conflict argument. In *Oracle*, various plaintiffs' law firms bid on the right to become class counsel. An unsuccessful bidder (the Gold firm) challenged the successful bidder (the Lowey firm) on the grounds that the Lowey firm had agreed to limit its claim for reimbursement of expenses to $325,000, and thus, the Gold firm contended, "the limitation will probably force the Lowey firm to pay for some litigation expenses out of its own pocket." The Gold firm claimed that this limitation created a conflict of interest between the Lowey firm and its client, the members of the class action, because the possibility of paying for expenses out of it own pocket "will deter the Lowey firm from incurring the expenses necessary to maximize the class' recovery."[23] The court rejected the argument that the Lowey firm violated Model Rule 1.8 or was in a conflict situation. In fact, the court found this argument to be "specious."[24]

§ 1.5–6(e) Caps on Fees But Not on Disbursements

Some lawyers argue that it would be improper for a law firm to place a cap on the reimbursements it seeks from its client because the lawyer may not know what reimbursed expenses will be necessary. For example, the law firm may have to hire an expert witness or an accounting firm, and the law firm may be reluctant to assume that cost if there is a cap on reimbursed expenses. Thus, the argument goes, there is a conflict or potential conflict of interest and therefore the ethics rules should forbid caps on ex-

---

[21]Moreover, other fee arrangements, such as a pure hourly fee agreement, raise problems that a fixed, task-based bill avoids. As the American Bar Association acknowledges, "continuous toil on or overstaffing a project for the purpose of churning out hours is also not properly considered 'earning' one's fees." ABA Formal Opinion 93-379 (Dec. 6, 1993).

Formal Opinion 93-379 deals with billing problems generally, and does not specifically discuss a fixed fee arrangement. However, footnote 4 of the Opinion does state: "Rule 1.5 clearly contemplates that there are bases for billing clients other than time expended." Later, in the text, it mentions that, if a lawyer is billing on an hourly basis, then it would be improper for that lawyer to charge a client for hours in excess of the estimated hours if "the client agreement turned the original estimate into *a cap on the fees to be charged.*" (emphasis added). This Opinion thus appears to recognize that clients and lawyers can agree to a fixed fee.

[22]*In re Oracle Securities Litigation*, 136 F.R.D. 639 (N.D.Cal.1991).

[23]136 F.R.D. at 642.

[24]136 F.R.D. at 642 (footnote omitted).

penses for which the law firm would normally seek reimbursement.

However, if a cap exists on an attorney's fees, but no cap exists on the attorney's reimbursements, a strong incentive arises for the law firm to favor the use of reimbursements and substitute those reimbursements for hourly work, thus avoiding the previously agreed upon cap on fees.[25] To some extent, non-attorney litigation expenses, such as computerized legal research, factual investigations by non-lawyers, hiring outside legal consultants (such as law professors), and so forth, are substitutes for a lawyer's hourly efforts.[26] If it is unethical for a law firm to agree to a cap on total costs (including expenses), then a law firm will favor the use of these nonattorney substitutes, which would not be subject to a cap.[27] That is why the knowledgeable client will want to preclude giving the law firm an incentive to substitute one type of billing for another. As far as the client is concerned, it is all the same money and the ability to substitute means that the fixed fee is not really fixed. That is why the client wants a fixed fee that is truly fixed.

In addition, an ethics rule that allows the client to place a cap on the lawyer's fees[28] but that also requires the lawyer to obtain full reimbursement of expenses encourages a form of cheating that is virtually impossible to police. Attorneys will be encouraged to allocate a portion of their overhead to specific litigation. All law firms have overhead: administration of the law office, secretarial services, accounting, filing, paralegal costs, library services, computer training, computerized legal research, and general clerical chores. These and other costs that must be incurred to enable the firm to operate can, under some guise, be allocated to the litigation at hand.[29] Some law firms, in fact, already specifically designate separate charges for such items as secretarial costs (approximately $45 per hour in 1995 in New

---

[25]Ronald D. Rotunda, *Innovative Legal Billing, Alternatives to Billable Hours, and Ethical Hurdles, in*, LEGAL ETHICS: ACCESS TO JUSTICE (1998) (Hofstra University School of Law Conference on Legal Ethics), *published in*, 2 JOURNAL OF THE INSTITUTE FOR THE STUDY OF LEGAL ETHICS 1701 (1999).

[26]Rule 1.8(e)(1) allows a lawyer to advance "court costs *and* expenses of litigation." (emphasis added). *Accord* Restatement of the Law Governing Lawyers, Third, § 48(2) (Proposed Final Draft No. 1, Mar. 29, 1996). Illinois Rules of Professional Conduct,

Rule 1.8(d) makes this point even clearer; it refers to litigation expenses as "including, *but not limited to*, court costs, *expenses of investigation*. . . ." (emphasis added).

[27]In re Oracle Sec. Litigation, 136 F.R.D. at 644.

[28]Surely there is nothing unethical about attorneys working for free. If lawyers can work for nothing they should be able to work subject to an agreed upon cap on their fees.

[29]*In re Oracle Sec. Litigation*, 136 F.R.D. at 644.

York firms),[30] heating and air conditioning after normal business hours, and so forth.[31] At least one firm imposed on clients a special pro rata charge for the law firm's accounting of the bill; in effect, the client must pay the law firm for the cost of accountants adding up the legal bill.

§ 1.5–6(f) Valuing Disbursements

Many law firms, whether they charge contingent fees, hourly fees, or some other type of fee, charge separately for "disbursements" that the law firm makes on behalf of the client. Charging for disbursements leads to the problem of how to value some types of "disbursements."

Some cases are easy. If the lawyer takes a $15 cab ride, the firm will bill the client for only $15. But what of other expenses that are more difficult to value? The cost of a photocopy is not merely the cost of the sheet of paper, because the machine itself has to be depreciated and serviced. And then there is the cost of the labor to use the machine.

Some firms have become quite imaginative in estimating the cost of such "disbursements." A 1995 confidential survey of 30 major New York law firms indicated that many firms charged $2 per page for an outgoing domestic fax, a 50% mark-up on Westlaw use, 25 cents per page for photocopying, and so forth.[32] A lawyer once told me that he considered the photocopy machine a "silent

---

[30]Karen Dillon, *Dumb and Dumber*, AMERICAN LAWYER, Oct., 1995, at 5, 44.

[31]The Restatement of the Law Governing Lawyers, Third, § 38(3)(a) (Official Draft 2000) states that, "[u]nless a contract construed in the circumstances indicates otherwise . . . a lawyer may not charge separately for the lawyer's general office and overhead expenses. . . . "

However, this provision does not prevent separate charges; it simply requires that the lawyer inform the client about such costs at the time that the lawyer is retained. As the Comment makes clear:

"The lawyer may, however, charge separately for such items [general office and overhead expenses such as secretarial costs and word processing] *if the client was told of the billing practice at the outset of the representation*, or was familiar with it from past experience with the lawyer or (in the case of a general billing custom in the

area) from past experiences with other lawyers. Clients sophisticated in such matters, for example, can be assumed to be familiar with the practice of lawyers in some types of representations to bill paralegal services separately from other charges."

Id. § 38, at Comment *e*.

Cf. Columbus Bar Ass'n v. Zauderer, 80 Ohio St.3d 435, 687 N.E.2d 410 (Ohio 1997), involves a lawyer who allocated expenses of the cases. Without prior agreement with his clients, he accrued many of his litigation-related expenses in a "General" category and then created a formula to assign them to individual cases. Some claimants complained, and the Bar charged him under DR 9-102(B)(3), failure to keep adequate records. The Ohio Supreme Court agreed and suspended Zauderer for a year.

[32]Karen Dillon, *Dumb and Dumber*, AMERICAN LAWYER, Oct., 1995, at 5. Other firms charged $3 per

partner." It did not speak up at meetings, took no share of the law firm profits, was no rainmaker, but it was a profit center and contributed to the bottom line like a real law partner. At the same time, the law firm could have out-sourced many of these expenses, saving their clients considerable money.[33] But then the law firm would not have benefitted by the profit from these "disbursements." The silent partner would no longer be a significant contributor to the firm's income.

In addition to these typical legal expenses, some firms feel freer than others in determining when an expense is "on behalf of" the client. It is not even exceptional for lawyers to charge clients for the snacks they eat while working on the case. In 1995, one major New York firm charged over $63 for popcorn, sodas, tea, and coffee for 15 people. At the same time, this firm could have hired an outside agency to deliver and cater these snacks for a third less.[34]

The general rule is that, just as a law firm may not charge a client for phantom hours it may not charge a client for phantom "disbursements." If the cab ride cost $10, including tip, the lawyer may not charge the client $11. If the lawyer sends a client's material to an outside photocopy service and receives a discounted rate, the lawyer must pass along that discount to the client.[35]

Sometimes the lawyer does not pay a third-party to provide a particular service. ABA Formal Opinion 93-379 advises that, unless the client and lawyer have worked out other arrangements, the lawyer may charge the client no more than the "direct cost associated with the service (*i.e.*, the actual cost of making a copy on the photocopy machine) *plus* a reasonable allocation of overhead expenses directly associated with the provision of the service (*e.g.*, the salary of a photocopy machine operator)."[36]

There are many reasonable ways to allocate these expenses. The client, of course, can always work out an arrangement with the lawyer, but in the absence of a special agreement, as long as the lawyer's method is reasonable, she has complied with her ethical obligations. The lawyer should bear in mind that the purpose of the photocopy machine is to provide a service to the client and make the lawyer's work more efficient. The photocopy machine is not supposed to be a silent partner. "The lawyer's

---

page for a fax. *Id.* at 45, col. 1.

[33]Karen Dillon, *Dumb and Dumber*, AMERICAN LAWYER, Oct., 1995, at 44

[34]Karen Dillon, *Dumb and Dumber*, AMERICAN LAWYER, Oct.,

1995, at 44 ($43 versus $63.65).

[35]ABA Formal Opinion 93-379 (Dec. 6, 1993), at 9.

[36]ABA Formal Opinion 93-379 (Dec. 6, 1993), at 9 (emphasis added).

stock in trade is the sale of legal services, not photocopy paper, tuna fish sandwiches, computer time or messenger services."[37]

Consider, for example, the cost of sending a one-page fax. The piece of paper may cost a penny and the long distance charge may be $1. Thus, the marginal cost of sending the fax may be only $1.01, since the law firm already bought the fax machine, and it is paying the secretary (or fax operator) a set monthly wage, whether he sends a fax or not. The law firm can charge only a $1.01 for the fax (the marginal, or incremental cost), or it can charge the average cost, let us say $1.50 a page to take into account other expenses, such as the depreciation of the fax machine. The key is that the "overhead" may only include costs that are directly related to the fax operation, such as the salary of the operator and the reasonable depreciation of the fax machine. The law firm may not include in the fax charge the cost of general overhead, such as the oil painting of the firm founder or, the sky box at the local stadium in order to bring the price of the fax to $5 per page plus long distance charges.[38]

---

[37]ABA Formal Opinion 93-379 (Dec. 6, 1993), at 10.

Surcharges to Clients When the Law Firm Uses a Contract Lawyer. ABA Formal Opinion 00-420 (Nov. 29, 2000), considers the situation where a lawyer hires a contract lawyer (an outside lawyer hired for a particular service, such as a temporary legal worker) for the client. If the lawyer bills the client for the use of the contract lawyer as a disbursement (an expense or a cost), then, unless the client has an understanding to the contrary, the lawyer may only charge the client the cost directly associated with the service. The lawyer may not add a surcharge. In other words, the lawyer may not normally hire the outside lawyer and bill the client for 110% of the cost of this lawyer. The lawyer normally may bill the client for only the actual costs of the outside lawyer. However, if the lawyer bills the client for the contract lawyer as fees for legal services, then the lawyer may add a surcharge (a profit) for those services (as long as the total fee is reasonable). This Formal Opinion adds that this surcharge is permissible, "whether the use and role of the contract lawyer are or are not disclosed

to the client." In short, when the lawyer bills a client for "legal services," that fee may include charges for overhead and profit.

[38]Restatement of the Law Governing Lawyers, Third, § 38(3)(a) (Official Draft 2000) agrees. *See id.*, at Comment *e*, which states that under "generally prevailing practice," the lawyer may charge the client "the actual amount of disbursements," such as "long-distance charges." The Restatement does not specifically state whether the lawyer can charge the marginal costs or the average costs of making a photocopy or sending a fax, but, in context, the Restatement would allow charging the reasonable average cost. Restatement, § 50, Reporter's Note, does cite ABA Formal Opinion 93-379 (Dec. 6, 1993), with approval, and that ABA Formal Opinion, as indicated above, does allow the law firm to charge a "reasonable allocation of overhead expenses directly associated with the service," unless the fee agreement provides otherwise. But, the lawyer may *not* charge the client for "general office and *overhead expense* such as secretarial costs and word processing" unless the client specifically agrees. Restatement, *supra*,

The clients seeking fixed fees want to avoid these special charges and any incentives for creative law firms to discover new ones. As far as clients are concerned, the money is fungible. A dollar is a dollar whether it is used for a fax or for a lawyer's salary. Placing the attorneys' fees and the expenses under one cap avoids these problems while rewarding the law firm when it makes the most efficient use of its resources. In other words, if it is more efficient for a law firm to hire an outside messenger service rather than use its own messengers, ethics rules should not encourage the law firm to do the opposite. But an ethics rule that allows the law firm to pass on the costs of the in-house service but not the outside service simply increases costs to the client.

§ 1.5–6(g) Selected Ethics Opinions Regarding Flat Fees

Notwithstanding the benefits that flat fees can confer on both clients and lawyers, only a few ethics opinions explicitly support this type of fee arrangement.[39] On the other hand, there is important authority that is substantially unsympathetic to the concept of flat fees. Consider, for example, *American Insurance Association v. Kentucky Bar Association*.[40] Various insurers objected to a Kentucky State Bar Association Advisory Ethics Opinion[41] that prohibited any lawyer from entering into a contract with any liability insurer, who hires a lawyer on behalf of the insured to defend the insured in a particular case, such as an auto accident. The proposal would have the lawyer take the defense for a set fee. The Advisory Ethics Opinion concluded that such flat fees were unethical and prohibited.

The issue then went to the Kentucky Supreme Court, which concurred. The court concluded that the flat fee would violate the state rule that corresponded to ABA Model Rule 1.7(b), prohibiting lawyers from representing a client if the lawyer's responsibilities to the client would be "materially limited" by the lawyer's responsibilities to third parties (the insurance company in this case).[42] In addition, the state bar and the state supreme court both concluded that agreeing to a set fee with the insurance

---

§ 38, at Comment *e* (emphasis added). In short, the law firm may not, without informing the client at the beginning of the representation, include general overhead expenses unrelated to the fax machine, but it may include overhead expenses that are directly related to the fax machine.

[39]Ethics opinions allowing flat fees with insurance companies (and, by analogy, with other clients) include, State Bar of Wisconsin Opinion E-83-15 (1983); Oregon State Bar Opinion 1991-98 (1991); and New Hampshire Bar Association, Formal Opinion 1990-91/5 (1991).

[40]*American Ins. Ass'n v. Kentucky Bar Ass'n*, 917 S.W.2d 568 (Ky.1996).

[41]Kentucky Advisory Ethics Opinion E-368 (1994), *reprinted in* Kentucky Bench & Bar (Fall 1994), at 52.

[42]*American Ins. Ass'n v. Kentucky Bar Ass'n*, 917 S.W.2d at 569.

company would interfere "with the lawyer's independence of professional judgment" in violation of the Kentucky rule corresponding to ABA Model Rule 1.8(f)(2).[43]

The Kentucky court's reasoning did not discuss the fact that ABA Model Rule 1.5, the main rule dealing with fees, expressly recognizes that a fee may be "fixed."[44] Instead, the court argued that a flat fee is inherently different than a retainer or a contingent fee, both of which do not constitute any violation of the ethics rules. First, the court argued that "a set fee arrangement enables the insurer to constrain counsel for the insured by, in effect, limiting the defense budget. . . ."[45] Let us consider that question.

When a client hires a lawyer for a flat fee, that practice is not really that different than when a patient hires a medical doctor for a flat fee. Patients make this choice all the time when they decide whether to join a Health Maintenance Organization (HMO). Some patients prefer to choose their doctor and not be bound by the restrictions of an HMO; other patients prefer the cost savings of joining an HMO and are willing to be bound by its restrictions. In neither case does the patient bargain for an incompetent doctor, but patients are allowed to bargain for an HMO and pay its flat fee. Clients of lawyers, like patients of medical doctors, should be allowed to join the legal equivalent of an HMO.[46] The client who agrees to pay a flat fee to the lawyer does not agree to incompetent legal representation.[47] If competent representation requires the lawyer to spend more hours than she had anticipated, she has to put in the extra hours, just as the lawyer who takes a case on a contingency must provide competent representation even if the case demands more hours of work than originally anticipated, and the contingency fee arrangement turns out not to be as lucrative as first imagined.

Even if a patient were never to join an HMO, that patient may well agree with the doctor that a particular surgery will be performed for a fixed amount. The medical insurer may make this agreement with the doctor directly. In either case, the cost of the particular surgical procedure would be fixed. And no one would one think that the doctor was acting unethically because he or she was performing the surgery for a fixed amount.

The court's argument in *American Insurance Association v.*

---

[43] 917 S.W.2d at 570.

[44] Rule 1.5(a)(8).

[45] 917 S.W.2d at 572.

[46] Rule 7.3(d) specifically allows lawyers to join the equivalent of legal HMO's (*i.e.*, prepare or group legal service plans) as long as the lawyers are not the owners or the preparer of legal service plans. The solicitation exception [discussed in Comment 8 of Rule 7.3(d)] is not relevant in this context.

[47] Rule 1.1 requires the lawyer to be competent, and that is something the client may not waive.

Kentucky Bar Association,[48] that a flat fee will allow or encourage insurers to interfere with the obligation of a lawyer to provide competent service by limiting the total amount paid to the lawyers for the insured, is counter-intuitive. It would not normally be in the interest of the insurance company to limit the defense budget in that way, because, if the lawyer does not provide an adequate defense, the insurer will have to pay the underlying judgment. The interests of the insured and insurer in presenting a competent defense are congruent in those cases where the judgment is within the policy limits, because the insurer is ultimately liable up to the policy limits.

In this sense, typical insurance policies (like automobile accident insurance) are different than medical insurance because the medical insurer only agrees to pay the doctor. In comparison, the car insurance company (unlike the medical insurer) not only pays the lawyer but also assumes liability for the underlying judgment, up to the policy limits. This difference argues in favor of allowing lawyers to charge flat fees: while the insurance company is paying the bill, its interests are more congruent with the interests of the client than are the interests of the medical insurer and the patient. If it is ethical for medical insurers to pay flat fees to medical doctors, then a fortiori it should be ethical for auto insurers to pay flat fees to lawyers. The lawyers still have the same ethical obligation to act competently while representing the insured.

In addition, any limitation that affected the obligation of the lawyer to provide competent representation would give the insured a cause of action against both the insurer and the lawyer.[49] This legal alternative is an important check to safeguard clients' rights. But this check should not obscure the more important fact that the interests of the automobile insurer and the defendant-driver are normally the same because the insurer pays the judgment and not merely the lawyer's fees.

Granted, there may be cases where the plaintiff sues for an amount in excess of the policy limits and the chances of a judgment in excess of policy limits are realistic. Yet, even in those cases—where the interests of the insurance company may differ from the interests of the insured—, the lawyer should have little incentive to give less than competent service. First, she has to worry about her own malpractice liability if she does not protect the interests of the insured. These cases (where the lawyer is liable in tort to the insured because of a conflict of interest when the lawyer wrongly protects the insurance company rather than

---

[48]*American Ins. Ass'n v. Kentucky Bar Ass'n*, 917 S.W.2d 568 (Ky.1996).

[49]This cause of action would be for breach of fiduciary duty and malpractice.

the insured) exist even when there is no flat fee.[50] Second, performing inadequately in one case is hardly the best way to persuade the insurance company to retain that lawyer in the future.

In any event, the Kentucky Court in *American Insurance Association* did not limit its reasoning to cases where the insured is realistically sued for an amount in excess of policy limits. Its primary argument was very revealing. The Kentucky court complained that a flat fee—"creates a situation whereby the attorney has an interest in the outcome of the action which conflicts with the duties owed to the client: quite simply, in easy cases, counsel will take a financial windfall; in difficult cases, counsel will take a financial loss."[51]

It is this possibility—that the lawyer will guess wrong in some cases and suffer a financial loss—that bothers the court and animates its reasoning. The court appeared to have been more concerned about the financial interests of the lawyers than of the clients. One wonders what this concern has to do with "ethics."

If the possibility that "counsel will take a financial loss" is enough to invalidate a fee arrangement, then contingent fees in personal injury cases should have been outlawed long ago. But contingency fees are permissible,[52] even though they also create a situation where counsel may "take a financial windfall" in some cases while suffering a "financial loss" in others.

Later in its opinion, the Kentucky court elaborated on this theme as it continued to show unusual solicitude and concern for the financial well-being of lawyers. The court argued that the fixed fee agreement is "ripe with potential conflicts," such as when representation of the insured "becomes more complex than anticipated, resulting in financial hardship for the attorney. . . ."[53] But it is not unethical for an attorney to suffer financial hardship when he or she guesses wrong on the outcome of a case. It periodically happens to any plaintiff-lawyer who charges a contingency fee and then loses the case. But the court's

---

[50]*See, e.g., Lysick v. Walcom*, 258 Cal.App.2d 136, 65 Cal.Rptr. 406, 28 A.L.R.3d 368 (Cal.App.1968). In this case, the lawyer became aware of a conflict of interest between the insured and insurer regarding the settlement offer that was in excess of policy limits. Because the lawyer did not protect the interests of the insured, the court found him personally liable for the amount of the judgment in excess of policy limits.

Cf., Parsons v. Continental Nat'l American Group, 113 Ariz. 223, 550

P.2d 94 (1976), holding that an insurance carrier is estopped from denying coverage under its policy when its defense is based on confidential information that it received from the lawyer for the insured, which represented the insured in the original tort action.

[51]American Ins. Ass'n v. Kentucky Bar Ass'n, 917 S.W.2d at 572.

[52]Rule 1.5(d). *See also* Model Rule 1.8(i).

[53]917 S.W.2d at 573.

repeated concern for the financial well-being of defense lawyers was not counterbalanced by any similar concern for plaintiff lawyers.

Attorneys in fact are not ethically obligated to charge any fee.[54] No ethics rule ever requires an attorney to charge any fee to represent a client. If he wants to represent his brother-in-law for free, he may do so even if the brother-in-law can afford to pay his normal hourly fee.

The Kentucky court added another argument, also based on an alleged conflict of interest: "Inherent in all of these potential conflicts is the fear that the entity paying the attorney, the insurer, and not the one to whom the attorney is obligated to defend, the insured, is controlling the legal representation."[55] Yet, once again, the court's argument proves too much. The risk that the lawyer will be more loyal to the insurer (the repeat client) and not the insured (who often is unlikely to be returning for more legal work) is a risk that is not related to the flat fee. Lawyers can be corrupted just as much by an hourly fee as by a flat fee.

Nonetheless, some other jurisdictions appear to be following the lead of the Kentucky court. The Supreme Court of Ohio's Board of Commissioners on Grievances and Discipline issued its own opinion on the propriety of a law firm agreeing to perform all or a part of an insurer's defense work for a fixed fee.[56] The Opinion candidly admitted that it is unlikely that a fixed fee would be excessive because insurance companies are not without experience and bargaining power. However, the—

> more pertinent concern is that the flat fee agreements between an attorney or law firm and a liability insurer will provide *insufficient and inadequate compensation to the attorney or law firm*. When a flat fee agreement between an attorney or law firm and a liability insurer provides insufficient compensation in regards to the time and effort spent on the representation, ethical problems emerge.[57]

Attorneys must be paid enough, this argument states, so that they will be ethical. If attorneys start to work too cheaply, they can compromise the ethics rules. This case appears to argue that the ethics rules do not merely forbid unreasonably high fees, they also prohibit unreasonably *low* fees.

---

[54] In pro bono matters, attorneys are encouraged to charge no fee or charge a reduced fee. ABA Model Rule 6.1, *Voluntary Pro Bono Publico Service* (urging 50 hours of *pro bono publico* service per year).

[55] American Ins. Ass'n v. Kentucky Bar Ass'n, 917 S.W.2d at 573.

[56] The Supreme Court of Ohio, Board of Commissioners on Grievances and Discipline, Ohio Opinion 97-7 (Dec. 5, 1977), available in 1997 WL 782951.

[57] Supreme Court of Ohio, Board of Commissioners on Grievances and Discipline, Ohio Opinion 97-7, at 3 (emphasis added).

The Ohio ethics opinion also announces that, even if the flat fee is high enough so that the attorney can ethically accept it, the attorney cannot agree to include the actual expenses in the flat fee. "In addition to paying the fixed fee, the insurer must remain ultimately liable for the actual expenses of litigation in all circumstances."[58]

This statement is, frankly, specious. If the lawyer wishes to assume the burden of paying all expenses out of the flat fee, why should the law prevent the lawyer from making that choice? The ABA Model Rules explicitly recognize that the lawyer can advance the expenses of litigation and make repayment of those costs "contingent on the outcome of the matter."[59] If the lawyer can advance expenses of litigation and agree to seek no reimbursement if the law suit is unsuccessful, should not the lawyer be able to charge a client a fixed fee and assure the client that any expenses will be deducted from the fixed fee? Plaintiffs' lawyers, in contingent fee cases, assume this risk all of the time. If the lawsuit is unsuccessful, many plaintiffs' lawyers promise their clients that they will not bill the client for expenses that would have been reimbursable if the case had been successful.[60]

Consider an ethics opinion of the Connecticut Bar Association, *Set Fee Per Case for Third Party Defense Work.*[61] An insurance company asked a law firm to perform all of its defense work in

---

[58]Supreme Court of Ohio, Board of Commissioners on Grievances and Discipline, Ohio Opinion 97-7, at 5.

[59]Rule 1.8(e)(1).

[60]One might read ABA Model Rule 1.8(e)(1) to provide that, the client must be liable for expenses of litigation at least in one circumstance: when the expenses are in excess of the flat fee and the litigation is successful. Another possible reading of this Rule requires that the lawyer cannot absorb the expenses of litigation in excess of the flat fee if the litigation is "successful." That reading is hardly compelled, because that Rule does specifically allow the lawyer to make repayment of expenses to be contingent on the outcome of the litigation. Nonetheless, even if one interprets that Rule to mean that if the defendant wins the case and the flat fee is less than the out-of-pocket expenses such as filing fees, the defense attorney must be guaranteed that he will be repaid out-of-pocket expenses. One must antici-

pate that such as case is likely to be quite rare. Nevertheless, the Ohio opinion is much broader, requiring the insurer to pay the "actual expenses of litigation in all circumstances." Supreme Court of Ohio, Board of Commissioners on Grievances and Discipline, Ohio Opinion 97-7, at 5.

See also Supreme Court of Ohio, Board of Commissioners on Grievances and Discipline, Ohio Opinion 95-2, 1995 Westlaw 813785, concluding that if a law firm enters into a flat fee agreement with an insurance company, "the expenses of litigation *must be borne by the client in addition* to the fixed flat fee. . . ." (emphasis added).

[61]Connecticut Bar Ass'n, Informal Opinion 97-20 (Sept. 24, 1997), 1997 Westlaw 700692.

Cf. West Virginia State Bar Disciplinary Board, Ethics Opinion 98-01, Mar. 26, 1998, *discussed in,* 14 ABA/BNA LAWYER'S MANUAL ON PROFESSIONAL CONDUCT, Current Reports, No. 9 (May 27, 1998), at 230–

the State of Connecticut for a flat fee per case. The law firm, rather than accepting or rejecting the proposal, asked the Connecticut Bar whether it would be unethical for a law firm to accept this proposal. If no firm could ethically accept the proposal, then no firm would be at a competitive disadvantage if it refused to consider it.

The very brief Connecticut opinion concluded that there is no per se objection to a flat fee, but then opined that the burden of proof is on the law firm if the client later complains. The flat fee arrangement would be permissible only if the law firm is able to "assure that the scope and quality of the defense is not compromised by the fee arrangement, even if the client (the insured) questions it in hindsight. . . ."[62]

It is always difficult to prove a negative. Moreover, why should the burden of proof change simply because the lawyer changes the method of computing fees? The basic rule is that, in "an action to recover damages caused by the attorney's malpractice, the plaintiff has the burden of proving every essential element of the cause of action."[63] When the fee is computed on the basis of billable hours, the law firm does not have the burden to prove that its defense was not compromised by the fee arrangement. Nor does the burden change because the plaintiff's attorney charged a contingent fee.

Admittedly, several ethics opinions and some case authority oppose flat fees, or place significant, special ethical restrictions on them. But, a careful analysis of the issue indicates these are incorrect. There is no conflict of interest that is any different in nature or degree from the inherent conflict in any fee arrangement, such as an hourly fee arrangement. Any method of paying lawyer's fees has, built into it, various inevitable conflicts. Hiring a lawyer on a flat fee arrangement no more encourages the lawyer to violate his or her ethical responsibilities than hiring the lawyer on the basis of billable hours encourages the lawyer to drag out the case, to put in unnecessary hours, to gold brick, to avoid settlement, to over-staff, or to over-research a problem.

Whether the insurance company or an individual client chooses

---

31. The Disciplinary Board said that to "guard against harm to the client, the lawyer must ensure that the fixed fee is sufficient to provide for a competent defense." A fee that is "so low" would not be "reasonable," under Rule 1.5, according the Disciplinary Board. The Board also noted that it was continuing to study flat fee issues, and it had not made a decision as to whether the flat fee is "per se" unethical, and

some flat fee arrangements "*could* violate the rules." (Emphasis in original).

[62]Connecticut Bar Ass'n, Informal Opinion 97-20 (Sept. 24, 1997), 1997 Westlaw 700692.

[63]2 Ronald E. Mallen & Jeffrey M. Smith, Legal Malpractice § 27.8 at 644 (West Pub. Co., 3rd ed. 1989) (footnote omitted).

a flat fee, the courts should intervene in cases where the lawyer has misrepresented the nature of the fee agreement or the client otherwise could not make a knowledgeable choice. The court, however, should not examine the fee arrangement using 20-20 hindsight. In retrospect, the choice may look bad or really good, but the courts should not invalidate these agreements unless the fee agreement is the product of the abuse of the lawyer's fiduciary responsibilities.

The ABA Model Rules recognize that a flat fee can include all expenses, but properly caution the lawyer to explain fully to the client what the flat fee means. A lawyer, in other words, "should not enter into an agreement whereby services are to be provided only up to a stated amount when it is foreseeable that more extensive services probably will be required, unless the situation is adequately explained to the client."[64] Lawyers, in short, can include costs in a flat fee, and should explain to their clients what this means. The law firm might state that it will pay all out-of-pocket expenses up to a certain amount. Or, it might assume all the liability for disbursements even if the disbursements are in excess of the previously agreed upon flat fee.

---

[64]Rule 1.5, Comment 5.

CHAPTER 1.6

CONFIDENTIALITY OF INFORMATION

RULE 1.6: CONFIDENTIALITY OF INFORMATION

(a) A lawyer shall not reveal information relating to the representation of a client unless the client gives informed consent, the disclosure is impliedly authorized in order to carry out the representation or the disclosure is permitted by paragraph (b).

(b) A lawyer may reveal information relating to the representation of a client to the extent the lawyer reasonably believes necessary:

(1) to prevent reasonably certain death or substantial bodily harm;

(2) to prevent the client from committing a crime or fraud that is reasonably certain to result in substantial injury to the financial interests or property of another and in furtherance of which the client has used or is using the lawyer's services;

(3) to prevent, mitigate or rectify substantial injury to the financial interests or property of another that is rea-

sonably certain to result or has resulted from the client's commission of a crime or fraud in furtherance of which the client has used the lawyer's services;

(4) to secure legal advice about the lawyer's compliance with these Rules;

(5) to establish a claim or defense on behalf of the lawyer in a controversy between the lawyer and the client, to establish a defense to a criminal charge or civil claim against the lawyer based upon conduct in which the client was involved, or to respond to allegations in any proceeding concerning the lawyer's representation of the client; or

(6) to comply with other law or a court order.

Comment

[1] This Rule governs the disclosure by a lawyer of information relating to the representation of a client during the lawyer's representation of the client. See Rule 1.18 for the lawyer's duties with respect to information provided to the lawyer by a prospective client, Rule 1.9(c)(2) for the lawyer's duty not to reveal information relating to the lawyer's prior representation of a former client and Rules 1.8(b) and 1.9(c)(1) for the lawyer's duties with respect to the use of such information to the disadvantage of clients and former clients.

[2] A fundamental principle in the client-lawyer relationship is that, in the absence of the client's informed consent, the lawyer must not reveal information relating to the representation. See Rule 1.0(e) for the definition of informed consent. This contributes to the trust that is the hallmark of the client-lawyer relationship. The client is thereby encouraged to seek legal assistance and to communicate fully and frankly with the lawyer even as to embarrassing or legally damaging subject matter. The lawyer needs this information to represent the client effectively and, if necessary, to advise the client to refrain from wrongful conduct. Almost without exception, clients come to lawyers in order to determine their rights and what is, in the complex of laws and regulations, deemed to be legal and correct. Based upon experience, lawyers know that almost all clients follow the advice given, and the law is upheld.

[3] The principle of client-lawyer confidentiality is given effect by related bodies of law: the attorney-client privilege, the work product doctrine and the rule of confidentiality established in professional ethics. The attorney-client privilege and work product doctrine apply in judicial and other proceedings in which a lawyer may be called as a witness or otherwise required to produce evidence concerning a client. The rule of client-lawyer confidentiality applies in situations other than those where evidence is sought from the lawyer through compulsion of law. The confidentiality rule, for example, applies not only to matters communicated in confidence by the client but also to all information relating to the representation, whatever its source. A lawyer may not disclose such information except as authorized or required by the Rules of Professional Conduct or other law. See also Scope.

[4] Paragraph (a) prohibits a lawyer from revealing information relating to the representation of a client. This prohibition also applies to disclosures by a lawyer that do not in themselves reveal protected information but could reasonably lead to the discovery of such information by a third person. A lawyer's use of a hypothetical to discuss issues relating to the representation is permissible so long as there is no reasonable likelihood that the listener will be able to ascertain the identity of the client or the situation involved.

Authorized Disclosure

[5] Except to the extent that the client's instructions or special circumstances limit that authority, a lawyer is impliedly authorized to make disclosures about a client when appropriate in carrying out the representation. In some situations, for example, a lawyer may be impliedly authorized to admit a fact that cannot properly be disputed or to make a disclosure that facilitates a satisfactory conclusion to a matter. Lawyers in a firm may, in the course of the firm's practice, disclose to each other information relating to a client of the firm, unless the client has instructed that particular information be confined to specified lawyers.

Disclosure Adverse to Client

[6] Although the public interest is usually best served by a strict rule requiring lawyers to preserve the confidentiality of information relating to the representation of their clients, the confidentiality rule is subject to limited exceptions. Paragraph (b)(1) recognizes the overriding value of life and physical integrity and permits disclosure reasonably necessary to prevent reasonably certain death or substantial bodily harm. Such harm is reasonably certain to occur if it will be suffered imminently or if there is a present and substantial threat that a person will suffer such harm at a later date if the lawyer fails to take action necessary to eliminate the threat. Thus, a lawyer who knows that a client has accidentally discharged toxic waste into a town's water supply may reveal this information to the authorities if there is a present and substantial risk that a person who drinks the water will contract a life-threatening or debilitating disease and the lawyer's disclosure is necessary to eliminate the threat or reduce the number of victims.

[7] Paragraph (b)(2) is a limited exception to the rule of confidentiality that permits the lawyer to reveal information to the extent necessary to enable affected persons or appropriate authorities to prevent the client from committing a crime or fraud, as defined in Rule 1.0(d), that is reasonably certain to result in substantial injury to the financial or property interests of another and in furtherance of which the client has used or is using the lawyer's services. Such a serious abuse of the client-lawyer relationship by the client forfeits the protection of this Rule. The client can, of course, prevent such disclosure by refraining from the wrongful conduct. Although paragraph (b)(2) does not require the lawyer to reveal the client's misconduct, the lawyer may not counsel or assist the client in conduct the lawyer knows is criminal or fraudulent. See Rule 1.2(d). See also Rule 1.16 with respect to the lawyer's obligation or right to withdraw from the representation of the client in such circumstances, and Rule 1.13(c), which permits the lawyer, where the cli-

ent is an organization, to reveal information relating to the representation in limited circumstances.

[8] Paragraph (b)(3) addresses the situation in which the lawyer does not learn of the client's crime or fraud until after it has been consummated. Although the client no longer has the option of preventing disclosure by refraining from the wrongful conduct, there will be situations in which the loss suffered by the affected person can be prevented, rectified or mitigated. In such situations, the lawyer may disclose information relating to the representation to the extent necessary to enable the affected persons to prevent or mitigate reasonably certain losses or to attempt to recoup their losses. Paragraph (b)(3) does not apply when a person who has committed a crime or fraud thereafter employs a lawyer for representation concerning that offense.

[9] A lawyer's confidentiality obligations do not preclude a lawyer from securing confidential legal advice about the lawyer's personal responsibility to comply with these Rules. In most situations, disclosing information to secure such advice will be impliedly authorized for the lawyer to carry out the representation. Even when the disclosure is not impliedly authorized, paragraph (b)(4) permits such disclosure because of the importance of a lawyer's compliance with the Rules of Professional Conduct.

[10] Where a legal claim or disciplinary charge alleges complicity of the lawyer in a client's conduct or other misconduct of the lawyer involving representation of the client, the lawyer may respond to the extent the lawyer reasonably believes necessary to establish a defense. The same is true with respect to a claim involving the conduct or representation of a former client. Such a charge can arise in a civil, criminal, disciplinary or other proceeding and can be based on a wrong allegedly committed by the lawyer against the client or on a wrong alleged by a third person, for example, a person claiming to have been defrauded by the lawyer and client acting together. The lawyer's right to respond arises when an assertion of such complicity has been made. Paragraph (b)(5) does not require the lawyer to await the commencement of an action or proceeding that charges such complicity, so that the defense may be established by responding directly to a third party who has made such an assertion. The right to defend also applies, of course, where a proceeding has been commenced.

[11] A lawyer entitled to a fee is permitted by paragraph (b)(5) to prove the services rendered in an action to collect it. This aspect of the rule expresses the principle that the beneficiary of a fiduciary relationship may not exploit it to the detriment of the fiduciary.

[12] Other law may require that a lawyer disclose information about a client. Whether such a law supersedes Rule 1.6 is a question of law beyond the scope of these Rules. When disclosure of information relating to the representation appears to be required by other law, the lawyer must discuss the matter with the client to the extent required by Rule 1.4. If, however, the other law supersedes this Rule and requires disclosure, paragraph (b)(6) permits the lawyer to make such disclosures as are necessary to comply with the law.

[13] A lawyer may be ordered to reveal information relating to the representation of a client by a court or by another tribunal or

governmental entity claiming authority pursuant to other law to compel the disclosure. Absent informed consent of the client to do otherwise, the lawyer should assert on behalf of the client all nonfrivolous claims that the order is not authorized by other law or that the information sought is protected against disclosure by the attorney-client privilege or other applicable law. In the event of an adverse ruling, the lawyer must consult with the client about the possibility of appeal to the extent required by Rule 1.4. Unless review is sought, however, paragraph (b)(6) permits the lawyer to comply with the court's order.

[14] Paragraph (b) permits disclosure only to the extent the lawyer reasonably believes the disclosure is necessary to accomplish one of the purposes specified. Where practicable, the lawyer should first seek to persuade the client to take suitable action to obviate the need for disclosure. In any case, a disclosure adverse to the client's interest should be no greater than the lawyer reasonably believes necessary to accomplish the purpose. If the disclosure will be made in connection with a judicial proceeding, the disclosure should be made in a manner that limits access to the information to the tribunal or other persons having a need to know it and appropriate protective orders or other arrangements should be sought by the lawyer to the fullest extent practicable.

[15] Paragraph (b) permits but does not require the disclosure of information relating to a client's representation to accomplish the purposes specified in paragraphs (b)(1) through (b)(6). In exercising the discretion conferred by this Rule, the lawyer may consider such factors as the nature of the lawyer's relationship with the client and with those who might be injured by the client, the lawyer's own involvement in the transaction and factors that may extenuate the conduct in question. A lawyer's decision not to disclose as permitted by paragraph (b) does not violate this Rule. Disclosure may be required, however, by other Rules. Some Rules require disclosure only if such disclosure would be permitted by paragraph (b). See Rules 1.2(d), 4.1(b), 8.1 and 8.3. Rule 3.3, on the other hand, requires disclosure in some circumstances regardless of whether such disclosure is permitted by this Rule. See Rule 3.3(c).

Acting Competently to Preserve Confidentiality

[16] A lawyer must act competently to safeguard information relating to the representation of a client against inadvertent or unauthorized disclosure by the lawyer or other persons who are participating in the representation of the client or who are subject to the lawyer's supervision. See Rules 1.1, 5.1 and 5.3.

[17] When transmitting a communication that includes information relating to the representation of a client, the lawyer must take reasonable precautions to prevent the information from coming into the hands of unintended recipients. This duty, however, does not require that the lawyer use special security measures if the method of communication affords a reasonable expectation of privacy. Special circumstances, however, may warrant special precautions. Factors to be considered in determining the reasonableness of the lawyer's expectation of confidentiality include the sensitivity of the information and the extent to which the privacy of the communica-

tion is protected by law or by a confidentiality agreement. A client may require the lawyer to implement special security measures not required by this Rule or may give informed consent to the use of a means of communication that would otherwise be prohibited by this Rule.

Former Client

[18] The duty of confidentiality continues after the client-lawyer relationship has terminated. See Rule 1.9(c)(2). See Rule 1.9(c)(1) for the prohibition against using such information to the disadvantage of the former client.

Authors' 1983 Model Rules Comparison

The 1983 Model Rules included only a very narrow basis for permissive disclosure of client confidences to prevent client crimes and frauds. The ABA House of Delegates explicitly rejected a Kutak Commission proposal for a broader Rule.[1]

The drafters of the 2002 Model Rules debated possible changes to Rule 1.6, and they made specific proposals on broadening permissive disclosure, but the House of Delegates again rejected any effort to expand exceptions to the confidentiality rule beyond the traditional ones contained in the 1983 version of Rule 1.6.

The drafters, in 2002, amended Rule 1.6(a) to create the new informed consent requirement as well as to clarify that disclosure may be permitted by paragraph (b).

In Rule 1.6(b), the drafters, in 2002, narrowed the lawyer's obligation to disclose to information "relating to the representation."

In Rule 1.6(b)(1), the drafters, in 2002, removed the requirement that the client be involved in a crime for permissive disclosure to arise. They also removed the word, "imminent" and replaced it with a "reasonably certain" requirement. They made these changes to expand the number of cases when a lawyer could disclose to prevent death or substantial bodily harm.

[Rule 1.6]

[1]As originally proposed by the Kutak Commission (the ABA Commission, named after its Chairman, Robert Kutak, which drafted the Model Rules of Professional Conduct), Rule 1.6 (Revised Final Draft, June 30, 1982) read as follows:

RULE 1.6 Confidentiality of Information

(a) A lawyer shall not reveal information relating to representation of a client unless the client consents after consultation, except for disclosures that are impliedly authorized in order to carry out the representation, and except as stated in paragraph (b).

(b) A lawyer may reveal such information to the extent the lawyer reasonably believes necessary:

(1) to prevent the client from committing a criminal or fraudulent act that the lawyer reasonably believes is likely to result in death or substantial bodily harm, or in substantial injury to the financial interests or property of another;

(2) to rectify the consequences of a client's criminal or fraudulent act in the furtherance of which the lawyer's services had been used;

(3) to establish a claim or defense on behalf of the lawyer in a controversy between the lawyer and the client, or to establish a defense to a criminal charge, civil claim or disciplinary complaint against the lawyer based upon conduct in which the client was involved; or

(4) to comply with other law.

The drafters, in 2002, added Rule 1.6(b)(2), but the drafters assumed that the limited disclosure that it authorizes was already implicitly authorized under the 1983 version of Rule 1.6, because lawyers should be able to seek advice from experts to assist them in complying with the Rules.

1983 Rule 1.6(b)(2) was renumbered as (b)(3) but not modified.

Rule 1.6(b)(4) deals with disclosures needed to comply with other law or a court order. The language is new but the principle is not; the drafters believed that the 1983 Rules implicitly authorized this disclosure.

The drafters deleted Comments 1, 2 & 3, which were found in the 1983 version of the Model Rules.

Comment 1 is new and describes the scope of the Rule.

Old Comment 4 is now Comment 2 with significant modification on the requirement of informed consent.

Old Comment 5 is now Comment 3 with a few word choice changes.

Old Comment 6 is deleted regarding the application of the Rule to government lawyers.

Comment 4 is new and discusses both client communications and also information relating to the representation. It contains a sentence that provides lawyers may use a hypothetical to discuss a matter with a third person so long as it preserves the confidentiality of the matter and client.

Old Comments 7 and 8 are now Comment 5 with some modification to clarify the impliedly authorized basis for disclosure.

Old Comment 9 is now Comment 6 with new language describing the disclosure to prevent bodily harms.

Old Comments 10 through 14 are deleted.

Comment 7 is new and examines the new exception under (b)(2) for disclosures to comply with the Rules.

Old Comment 18 is now Comment 8 with modifications to clarify the disclosures needed to defend or prosecute claims on behalf of the lawyer.

Old Comment 19 is now Comment 9 with significant changes to disclose information to collect a fee.

Comments 10 though 13 are new and discuss the extent of permissive disclosure under Rule 1.6(b).

Old Comments 15 and 17 are now new Comment 14.

Old Comments 20 and 21 were deleted because they were covered in new language added throughout the Comments.

Comments 15 and 16 are new and establish a standard for how lawyers are to preserve client confidentiality.

Old Comment 22 is new Comment 17 and citations to the former client Rule have been added.

Post February 2002 Amendment:

The House of Delegates, in 2002, rejected many of the proposed changes to Rule 1.6. However, the life expectancy of Rule 1.6, as the ABA House of Delegates approved it in 2002, was remarkably short. After the bankruptcy of the Enron Corporation and other scandals, discussed below, the Task Force on Corporate Responsibility made new recommendations to the ABA in August 2003. Based upon this Report, the ABA House of Delegates adopted significant amendments to Rule 1.6 at the August 2003 meeting.

In Rule 1.6, the ABA added new sections (b)(2) and (b)(3) and renumbered the old sections (b)(2) through (b)(4) to become (b)(4) though (b)(6). The added sections read as follows:

(2) to prevent the client from committing a crime or fraud that is reasonably certain to result in substantial injury to the financial interests or property of another and in furtherance of which the client has used or is using the lawyer's services;

(3) to prevent, mitigate or rectify substantial injury to the financial interests or property of another that is reasonably certain to result or has resulted from the client's commission of a crime or fraud in furtherance of which the client has used the lawyer's services;

Comments 7 and 8 are new and explain the new provisions in Rule 1.6(b)(2) and (b)(3).

2002 Comments 7 to 13 are renumbered as Comments 9 through 15.

2002 Comment 14 on withdrawal was deleted.

2002 Comments 15 through 17 are renumbered as Comments 16 through 18.

Model Code Comparison

[1] Rule 1.6 eliminates the two-pronged duty under the Model Code in favor of a single standard protecting all information about a client "relating to representation." Under DR 4-101, the requirement applied to information protected by the attorney-client privilege and to information "gained in" the professional relationship that "the client has requested be held inviolate or the disclosure of which would be embarrassing or would be likely to be detrimental to the client." EC 4-4 added that the duty differed from the evidentiary privilege in that it existed "without regard to the nature or source of information or the fact that others share the knowledge." Rule 1.6 imposes confidentiality on information relating to the representation even if it is acquired before or after the relationship existed. It does not require the client to indicate information that is to be confidential, or permit the lawyer to speculate whether particular information might be embarrassing or detrimental.

[2] Paragraph (a) permits a lawyer to disclose information where impliedly authorized to do so in order to carry out the representation. Under DR 4-101(B) and (C), a lawyer was not permitted to reveal "confidences" unless the client first consented after disclosure.

[3] Paragraph (b) redefines the exceptions to the requirement of confidentiality. Regarding paragraph (b)(1), DR 4-101(C)(3) provided that a lawyer "may reveal . . . [t]he intention of his client to commit a crime and the information necessary to prevent the crime." This option existed regardless of the seriousness of the proposed crime.

[4] With regard to paragraph (b)(2), DR 4-101(C)(4) provided that a

lawyer may reveal "[c]onfidences or secrets necessary to establish or collect his fee or to defend himself or his employers or associates against an accusation of wrongful conduct." Paragraph (b)(2) enlarges the exception to include disclosure of information relating to claims by the lawyer other than for the lawyer's fee; for example, recovery of property from the client.

§ 1.6–1 INTRODUCTION

The Origins of the Ethical Obligation. The attorney's obligation to protect a client's confidential and secret information is based in part on the rules of evidence[1]—*i.e.,* the attorney-client privilege[2] and the work product doctrine.[3] However, the obligation of confidentiality is also an ethical duty (derived from the law of agency) that is broader than the narrow contours of the evidentiary privilege. The attorney is the agent of her client, who is the principal.

Under a general rule of agency law, the agent must neither use nor disclose "information confidentially given to him by the principal or acquired by him during the course of or on account of his agency. . . ."[4] Although an attorney is certainly subject to discipline for violating the attorney-client *evidentiary* privilege,[5] he or she may also be subject to discipline for violating this ethical duty. The ethical proscription "applies not only to matters communicated in confidence by the client but also to all information relating to the representation, whatever its source."[6]

The Distinction Between the Evidentiary and the Ethical Privilege. Both the Model Code and the Model Rules offer protection much broader than the evidentiary privilege.[7] As a matter of ethics, the lawyer should not be injudicious, or

---

[Section 1.6–1]

[1] ABA Model Rule 1.6, Comment 3.

No Need for a Fee to Be Paid. Under both the Code and the Rules, it is not necessary for a fee to be charged in order for the ethical or evidentiary privilege to attach.

[2] **The Attorney-Client Evidentiary Privilege.** The Restatement of the Law Governing Lawyers, Third, extensively examines this evidentiary privilege. *See*, Restatement of the Law Governing Lawyers, Third, §§ 68 to 86 (Official Draft 2000). An analysis of the evidentiary privilege is beyond the scope of this book, which focuses on the broader ethical privilege and discusses the evidentiary privilege insofar as it relates to the ethical privilege.

[3] **The Attorney Work Product Immunity.** The Restatement of the Law Governing Lawyers, Third, extensively examines the work product doctrine. *See*, Restatement of the Law Governing Lawyers, Third, §§ 87 to 93 (Official Draft 2000). An analysis of the work product immunity is beyond the scope of this book, which focuses on the broader ethical privilege and discusses the work product immunity insofar as it relates to the ethical privilege.

[4] Restatement of the Law of Agency, Second, § 395.

[5] DR 4–101(A), (B); Rule 1.6(a).

[6] ABA Model Rule 1.6, Comment 3.

[7] *E.g. Parler & Wobber v. Miles & Stockbridge, P.C.*, 359 Md. 671, 756

231

indiscreet, or unguarded when discussing his client's affairs with people not in his law firm.[8]

Consider an example that highlights the distinction between the evidentiary and the ethical obligations: the client ("Client") asks his lawyer ("Lawyer") to represent the client in a transaction. In the course of his representation, Client asks Lawyer to solicit certain business proposals from third parties. Lawyer does so and thereby uncovers secret information from these third parties, *i.e.,* information not generally known to the world at large. Pursuant to a criminal investigation, a court later orders Lawyer to reveal this information to the grand jury on the grounds that it is not protected by the evidentiary privilege. Lawyer reveals this information in the grand jury room. Later reporters ask him: "Did you comply with the court order?" He answers: "Yes." Then they ask him: "What did you say to the grand jury?" If Lawyer responds, Lawyer will commit a disciplinary violation by revealing a client's secret.

In other words, virtually all information possessed by the attorney is *initially* within the ethical obligation established by Rule 1.6.[9] For information to be considered confidential it is not necessary that the source of the information be the client; it is only necessary that the information be "gained in the professional relationship."[10] Even though the *evidentiary privilege* does not protect this information—the judge required the lawyer to testify after ruling that the evidentiary privilege did not exist—, the *ethical obligation* still protects it. Hence, the lawyer may not broadcast the secret information. The information remains secret

---

A.2d 526 (Ct. App. 2000):

"There is a critical distinction . . . between confidentiality required by ethical rules and the evidentiary basis of the attorney-client privilege. More protection is provided to communications within the attorney-client relationship under one than the other. The confidentiality umbrella of the ethical rule encompasses 'all situations *except* where the 'evidence is sought from the lawyer through compulsion of law.' 'In the latter situation, only *the attorney-client privilege*, not the broader rule of confidentiality, protects against disclosure.' Thus, relevant evidence sought through discovery, unless protected by the attorney-client privilege, must be produced and the *ethical duty of confidence* takes a back seat to the quest for truth."

359 Md. 671, 689–90, 756 A.2d 526,

536 (internal citations omitted)(emphasis added).

[8] EC 4-2.

[9] Canon 4 of the Model Code, reaches the same result because the client's request to hold the information "inviolate" does not need to be express. It can be implied. EC 4-1, at note 1, quoting ABA Formal Opinion 250 (1943) stated that the lawyer "shall not be permitted, without the consent of his client," to reveal or disclose secret communications with the client.

[10] DR 4-101(A); Rule 1.6, Comment 3 ("also to all information relating to the representation, whatever its source").

and is not generally known, because the lawyer disclosed it only during a grand jury proceeding, a secret hearing.[11]

§ 1.6–1(a) Confidences and Secrets under the Model Code

The Model Code divided client information into two types: "confidence" and "secret."[12] A "confidence" is any information protected under the attorney-client evidentiary privilege. A "secret" is any other information that: (1) the client has requested (expressly or by implication)[13] that it be held "inviolate"; (2) disclosure would embarrass the client; or (3) disclosure would likely "be detrimental to the client."

Like the phrase "animal, vegetable, or mineral," one would think that the Model Code's three categories of information are also intended to include everything. After all, these three categories appear to cover the waterfront, including all information (whether or not communicated by the client) that would be embarrassing or detrimental to the client and all other information that the client has requested the lawyer to keep secret (even if disclosure would not be embarrassing or detrimental to the client). If the lawyer is unsure whether she can reveal the information, the prudent lawyer will simply ask the client.

It is quite clear that it was unnecessary, under Canon 4 of the ABA Model Code, that the client be the source of the information. However, the Code did not make clear whether "gained in" means "because of" the professional relationship, or the more broad, "during the course of" the professional relationship (e.g., in the course of seeking business advice, the client confides to the lawyer that the client is cheating on her husband).

The Code's language—"information gained in the professional relationship"[14]—leaves open the possibility that information is only protected when it is learned "because of" the client-attorney relationship. A broader interpretation, for example, information discovered "during the course of" the lawyer's representation of the client, would cover knowledge that the lawyer gained

---

[11]*Ex parte Taylor Coal Co., Inc.*, 401 So.2d 1, 8 (Ala. 1981):

"A substantial difference in the law is made between the attorney's ethical responsibility with reference to disclosure of confidential information and his privilege not to testify in court concerning his client's secrets. In the latter instance, the attorney can be required to testify if it is demonstrated that the attorney and client discussed the subject matter of the attorney-client relationship in the presence of a third person. However, this does not mean that the lawyer is allowed to reveal his client's secrets, even after such a disclosure in court." (internal citation omitted).

See also, e.g., Roy M. Sobelson, *Lawyers, Clients And Assurances Of Confidentiality: Lawyers Talking Without Speaking, Clients Hearing Without Listening,* 1 GEORGETOWN J. LEGAL ETHICS 703, 713–17 (1988).

[12]DR 4-101(A).

[13]EC 4-1, at note 1, *quoting* ABA Formal Opinion 250 (1943).

[14]DR 4-101(A).

fortuitously, not because of the lawyer client relationship. For example, the lawyer, in the course of a cocktail party, may have learned from her client's loquacious banker, that the client is delinquent on a major loan and may face bankruptcy. Must the lawyer keep this information secret (assuming that it is not public knowledge), or may the lawyer treat it as she would any gossip about someone to whom she owes no fiduciary duty? The Code may be open to either interpretation. In any event, the drafters of the ABA Model Rules thought that protections offered by the Code were not broad enough. Hence, they drafted new language that they intended to provide even broader protection for clients and would protect this cocktail party information.

§ 1.6–1(b) Client Information under the Model Rules

Rule 1.6 protects *all* information "relating to the representation," unless the disclosures are impliedly authorized, or fall within certain named exceptions, or have been waived by the client.[15] All information of consequence is, at least initially, offered protection.[16]

In the example considered above—during a cocktail reception the lawyer learns from her client's talkative banker that her client may be facing bankruptcy—, the lawyer is not free to pass on the cocktail chatter about her client's bankruptcy problems, as long at the information relates to her representation and is not already publicly well known.

The purpose of the broad protection of Rule 1.6 is to encourage the client to speak freely with the lawyer and to encourage the lawyer to obtain information beyond that offered by the client.[17] Needless to say, this purpose would not be furthered if a lawyer would be forced to keep information confidential after it has become a matter of general knowledge. If everyone already knows about this information, there is really nothing to keep secret. The general law of agency recognizes this exception,[18] and the Rules explicitly adopt it in Rule 1.9(c)(1), which allows a lawyer to use, to the disadvantage of a *former* client, information otherwise protected by Rule 1.6, *if* the information is "generally known."[19]

The Code did not have language that explicitly paralleled the language found in Rule 1.9(c)(1) relating to client information

---

[15]Rule 1.6(a). *See* Ronald D. Rotunda, *Monitoring the Conversations of Prisoners*, 13 THE PROFESSIONAL LAWYER 1 (No. 3, 2002).

[16]Restatement of the Law Governing Lawyers, Third, §§ 59, 60 (Official Draft 2000).

[17]EC 4–1; Rule 1.6, Comments 1, 2, 3, & 4.

[18]Restatement of the Law of Agency, Second, § 395.

[19]Even if Rule 1.6 is not applicable, a lawyer should not act to the detriment of a *present* client. It is not the Rule 1.6 duty to keep secrets that will limit the lawyer in this case; the limitation that exists in this circumstance is found in the duty of loy-

that "has become generally known." In fact EC 4-4 states that the ethical duty to protect secrets exists "without regard" to "the fact that others share the knowledge." However, in context, EC 4-4 refers to *present* clients, and assumes that the secret nature of the conversation is not lost merely because the client has shared his secret with a *few* others besides the lawyer. Such sharing, beyond a strict "need to know basis," will mean the loss of the evidentiary privilege,[20] but not the loss of the ethical privilege. However, once the information is *generally known* (even though it once was a secret), requiring the lawyer to continue to protect it would not serve the purpose of the rule.

§ 1.6–2 INADVERTENT DISCLOSURE

§ 1.6–2(a) Introduction

The client may inadvertently lose the attorney-client evidentiary privilege. For example, if the client voluntarily reveals a portion of his privileged communications, courts typically find that he may not withhold the remainder. One cannot open the door a crack; once the litigant has started to talk and divulge his privileged communications with his lawyer, he cannot slam the door shut. Some courts even find a permanent loss of the evidentiary privilege if the client *or* lawyer inadvertently discloses part of the privileged communication. They argue that one wishing to preserve the privilege "must treat the confidentiality of attorney-client communications like jewels—if not crown jewels."[1]

Lawyers must treat confidential papers with reasonable care, or the court is likely to treat the privilege as surrendered.[2]

If a court is harsh on those who inadvertently disclose matters

---

alty—a duty that extends beyond the need to protect client secrets. Rule 1.7(a), (b). DR 5-101(A).

[20]That is the standard rule of evidence governing the attorney-client privilege. *See, e.g.,* Proposed Federal Rule of Evidence 530(a)(4).

[Section 1.6–2]

[1]*In re Sealed Case,* 877 F.2d 976, 980 (D.C.Cir.1989):

"The courts will grant no greater privilege to those who assert the privilege than their own precautions warrant. We therefore agree with those courts which have held that the privilege is lost, 'even if disclosure is inadvertent.'. . . [I]f a client wishes to preserve the privilege, it must treat the confidentiality of the attorney-client communication like jewels—if

not crown jewels. Short of court-compelled disclosure, other equally extraordinary circumstances, we will not distinguish between various degrees of 'voluntariness' in waivers of the attorney-client privilege." (citations omitted).

[2]*See, e.g., S.E.C. v. Cassano,* 189 F.R.D. 83 (S.D.N.Y.1999). In the course of disclosing many documents at its office, the SEC inadvertently included a nearly 100-page draft of its "action memo" that discussed its evidence, analyzed its legal theories, and laid out the strengths and weaknesses of its case. When defense counsel saw the document, he asked the SEC for a copy. The SEC paralegal asked the responsible lawyer whether to copy it, and the lawyer (who did not ask what it was) said yes. Another 12 days

that are covered by the attorney-client privilege, that harshness is exacerbated by modern technology. With the slip of a finger, one can broadcast a fax to the wrong party or transmit an inadvertent email.

§ 1.6–2(b) The Misdirected Fax

A serious problem may result when a lawyer or another person in the lawyer's firm mistakenly faxes a document to opposing counsel instead of to the client or co-counsel. This raises a question of inadvertent disclosure and its effect on the attorney-client privilege.

Some courts have been unsympathetic to the lawyer or client who inadvertently discloses attorney-client material to the adverse party, even if the disclosure was not negligent.[3] Some courts hold, as a matter of the law, that the inadvertent disclosure waives the evidentiary privilege.[4]

In other cases, courts have ordered lawyers who receive

---

passed before the SEC discovered its mistake and tried to get the document back. The court held this bell simply could not be unrung. The court concluded that the SEC's actions in response to defense counsel's request to photocopy the memorandum were so careless as to surrender any claim that the SEC took reasonable steps to ensure its confidentiality.

In *Amgen v. Hoechst Marion Roussel, Inc.*, 190 F.R.D. 287 (D.Mass. 2000), the defense counsel inadvertently produced a box of over 3200 pages of privileged material among boxes with 70,000 pages of unprivileged material. The opinion distinguishes three ways courts have approached such situations—the "never waived" rule that requires giving the documents back, the "strict accountability" rule that treats all such situations as waivers, and a third or middle ground that looks at (1) reasonableness of precautions taken, (2) time taken to discover the error, (3) scope of the production, (4) extent of the disclosure, and (5) the interests of fairness in the situation. In this case, the defendant had not realized what had happened until the plaintiff called the situation to its attention and little could be done to avoid damage. The court treated the privilege waived,

saying it would be unjust to reward counsel's "gross negligence."

[3]*United Mine Workers v. Arch Mineral Corp.*, 145 F.R.D. 3, 6 (D.D.C. 1992). The court rejected the application of the attorney-client privilege to documents that had allegedly been misappropriated and leaked to opposing counsel. The opposing counsel, who received the documents, said that he had gained access to them only because an anonymous source sent multiple copies. Although the documents were marked, "Confidential-Attorney and Client Communication/Do not copy or further distribute," the court ruled that the privilege was lost because the other side had not taken "all possible precautions to maintain their confidentiality." 145 F.R.D. at 8–10.

[4]*In re Sealed Case*, 877 F.2d 976, 980 (D.C.Cir.1989): "Short of court-compelled disclosure, or other equally extraordinary circumstances, we will not distinguish between various degrees of 'voluntariness' in waivers of the attorney-client privilege." (footnote and internal citation omitted).

Bellsouth Advertising & Publishing Corp. v. American Business Lists, Inc., No. *1:90-CV-149-JEC*, 1992 WL 338392, at *8 (N.D.Ga.1992) (holding that inadvertent disclosure of documents constitutes a per se waiver of

attorney-client material that is inadvertently disclosed to return the documents and destroy all copies in the hands of their hands.[5]

This remedy is more likely if the lawyer and client acted reasonably with respect to treating the material covered by the evidentiary privilege. The Restatement of the Law Governing Lawyers only requires that the lawyer take "reasonable efforts" to protect client information.[6] Like the Model Rules, it recognizes that reasonable lawyers can make reasonable mistakes.[7]

This remedy—return of the documents to the original party and destruction of any remaining copies—is not difficult to implement. Moreover, this judicial relief will prevent the document in question from being introduced into evidence or used in a deposition.[8] However, it may not be possible for the lawyer to forget what he or she has read. Thus, litigants have also sought a more effective remedy by seeking to disqualify the lawyer who has received the material.

This remedy of disqualifying the lawyer is much more difficult to justify than a court order forcing the party to return the inadvertently disclosed document. First, court-ordered disqualification will not affect the situation where the client has also seen the document in question. The court cannot disqualify an adverse party who received the misdirected fax.[9]

Moreover, the remedy of disqualification would, in effect, punish Lawyer #2 (and the client of Lawyer #2) because Lawyer #1

---

the attorney-client privilege).

[5]*Resolution Trust Corp. v. First of America Bank*, 868 F.Supp. 217 (W. D.Mich.1994).

[6]Restatement of the Law Governing Lawyers, Third, § 60(1)(b) (Official Draft 2000) provides: "the lawyer *must take steps reasonable in the circumstances* to protect confidential client information against impermissible use or disclosure by the lawyer's associates or agents that may adversely affect a material interest of the client or otherwise than as instructed by the client." (emphasis added).

[7]Model Rule 1.6, Comment 17, advises lawyers to "take *reasonable* precautions to prevent the information from coming into the hands of unintended recipients. This duty, however, does not require that the lawyer use special security measures if the method of communication affords a reasonable expectation of privacy." (emphasis added).

See The Florida Bar v. Wolding, 579 So.2d 736 (Fla. 1991) (per curiam). In this case, the referee had recommended findings of guilt, admonishment, and assessment of costs in a lawyer discipline proceeding. In an original proceeding, the Supreme Court held that the lawyer's failure to lock law office files and his use of a conference room with acoustical problems did not violate the rule that prohibits revealing of information relating to representation of client.

[8]*Resolution Trust Corporation v. First of America Bank*, 868 F.Supp. 217 (W.D.Mich.1994) (although plaintiff's counsel knew what the documents said, they could not be used in evidence).

[9]*Kusch v. Ballard*, 645 So.2d 1035 (Fla.Dist.Ct.App.1994), involved a privileged document mistakenly faxed to the opposing party. The court held that the inadvertent faxing did not constitute waiver of the lawyer-client privilege but disqualification of

(or the client of Lawyer #1) turned over material that they should not have disclosed. Whether their disclosure was negligent or simply a reasonable error, the fact remains that it was the other side (Lawyer #1 or the client of Lawyer #1) that caused the problem and now the other side wants to disqualify opposing counsel because of what they (and not opposing counsel) did.

Second, even if the unintentional disclosure was not negligent,[10] the fact is that the remedy of disqualification serves to disadvantage one party because an adverse party made a mistake and the receiving party read a document that may be labeled "confidential," but was sent to him anyway. We are not speaking of a situation where a lawyer has stolen the documents or bribed someone to steal them.[11] The court may not wish to punish the sending lawyer because of his error (particularly if the error was not negligent), but neither should the court reward him by allowing his mistake to result in the disqualification of the receiving lawyer. Consequently, some courts have refused to disqualify the receiving lawyer in this situation.[12]

The ABA issued three opinions on the topic of lawyers who have received misdirected faxes. In Formal Opinion 92-368, the ABA held that when a lawyer receives a fax that has clearly been sent inadvertently by an opposing counsel, the lawyer should refrain from reviewing the materials, notify the sending lawyer, and abide by that lawyer's instructions.[13] In Formal Opinion 94-382, the ABA held that when a lawyer receives a fax or other communication that has been sent by an unauthorized source such as a whistle blower, the lawyer should either inform the adversary's lawyer and follow her instructions or refrain from using the unsolicited material until a court makes a definitive reso-

---

the innocent recipient was neither necessary nor appropriate. *See also Harold Simpson Children's Trust v. Linda Gale*, 271 Wis.2d 610, 679 N.W.2d 794 (2004) (holding that in Wisconsin a lawyer's inadvertent disclosure does not waive the attorney-client privilege).

[10]We do not, after all, require the lawyer to personally type the addresses of each envelope. The fact that a document is mailed to the wrong party does not necessarily mean that there was negligence. Reasonable people are allowed to make reasonable mistakes.

[11]*See, e.g., Lipin v. Bender*, 193 A.D.2d 424, 597 N.Y.S.2d 340 (1993).

[12]*Resolution Trust Corp. v. First America Bank*, 868 F.Supp. 217 (W.D. Mich.1994), held that disqualification of plaintiff's counsel was not warranted. "First of all, the cat is out of the bag." 868 F.Supp. at 220. The lawyer did read material, which was "clearly labeled on its face 'PRIVILEGED AND CONFIDENTIAL,'" was directed to a Senior Vice President of defendant and contained the caption of the case." 868 F.Supp. at 218. The document in question was a seven-page letter from the defendant's counsel to the defendant laying out the facts of the case to date and the defense strategy. *Id. Contrast In re Bank of America, N.A.*, 45 S.W.3d 238 (Tex. App.2001).

[13]ABA Formal Opinion 92-368 (Nov. 10, 1992).

lution of the proper disposition of the materials.[14] These ABA Formal Opinions distinguish between situations in which the fax was sent inadvertently by an attorney as a client or deliberately by a disgruntled employee.[15]

Many state bar opinions and court cases have rejected the ABA solution.[16] Of course, a lawyer may not cajole, coax or induce another lawyer to violate that other lawyer's duty of confidentiality. However, it "is not, a violation to accept the advantage of inadvertent, and even negligent, disclosure of confidential information by the other lawyer, if the effect of the other lawyer's action is to waive the right of that lawyer's client to assert confidentiality."[17]

For these reasons, the simplest solution is for the lawyer to avoid the problem by taking reasonable care to ensure that no faxes are misdirected.[18] The general trend in the law is to hold that the attorney-client privilege is not waived by inadvertent disclosure if the lawyer and client take *reasonable* precautions to guard against inadvertent disclosure.[19] What is "reasonable" depends on the circumstances, including the sensitivity of the information.[20]

The drafters of the 2002 Rules included a provision in Rule 4.4 to address the receipt of privileged documents through inadvertent disclosure.[21] Rule 4.4(b) states that if a lawyer receives a "document" relating to a representation and that lawyer knows or reasonably should know that the document was delivered

---

[14]ABA Formal Opinion 94-382 (July 5, 1994).

[15]In some cases the receiving lawyer will not know if the sender is a whistle-blower or an inattentive employee. Not all whistle-blowers announce their intention in the cover memorandum attached to the fax. But much turns on this unknown fact.

[16]*See, e.g., Aerojet-General Corp. v. Transport Indemnity Insurance*, 18 Cal.App.4th 996, 22 Cal.Rptr.2d 862 (1993), reversing the lower court and holding that even if the documents were sent inadvertently, the lawyer who received them through no wrongdoing on his part may keep them and need not inform opposing counsel.

[17]Restatement of the Law Governing Lawyers, Third, § 102, Comment *e* (Official Draft 2000), at 109.

[18]Rule 1.6, Comment 17. If the fax is misdirected, then both the receiving

lawyer and the sending lawyer have to look to their local jurisdiction to determine what happens next.

[19]*See, e.g., Transamerica Computer Co. v. IBM Corp.*, 573 F.2d 646, 652 (9th Cir.1978) (review of 17 million pages of documents with "demanding timetable" and "logistical difficulties;" held, no waiver by inadvertent disclosure). *But see Wichita Land & Cattle v. American Federal Bank*, 148 F.R.D. 456, 457–58 (D.D.C.1992) (holding that the law firm's inadvertent disclosure of two privileged documents that were among 40 boxes that were released meant a waiver of the attorney-client privilege).

[20]Restatement of the Law Governing Lawyer, Third, § 79, Comment *h* (Official Draft 2000), at p. 600.

[21]The issue of a lawyer's receipt of an inadvertent fax is discussed in more detail in Chapter 4.4.

inadvertently, the lawyer should inform the sender in a prompt manner.[22] The Rule makes clear that "document" includes "e-mail or other electronic modes of transmission subject to being read or put into readable form."[23]

Apart from the obligation to inform the sender, the text of the Rule imposes no further obligation. Comment 2 states that the Rule takes no position on the questions of privilege, whether further action is required, or whether the lawyer may read the documents.

In 2005, the ABA withdrew Formal Opinion 92–368 because of the language contained in Model Rule 4.4: "Rule 4.4(b) thus only obligates the receiving lawyer to notify the sender of the inadvertent transmission promptly. The rule does not require the receiving lawyer either to refrain from examining the materials or to abide by the instructions of the sending lawyer."[24]

We know, from the discussion above, that some courts will allow the lawyer (the first lawyer) to take advantage of the other lawyer's mistake (the second lawyer), even if the mistaken disclosure was not negligent. Other courts will only allow the first lawyer to take advantage of the second lawyer's error if that inadvertent disclosure was not negligent. Hence, it makes the most sense for the first lawyer to inform the second lawyer (which is what Comment 2 advises) and then inform the court for a ruling. If the court rules that the inadvertent disclosure did not waive the privilege, the first lawyer cannot take advantage of her opponent's mistake without fear that her client will criticize her with failure to prosecute the case zealously. If the court concluded that the inadvertent disclosure serves to waive the privilege, the first lawyer can take advantage of her opponent's mistake without worrying that she is violating any ethical rule.

§ 1.6–2(c) Lawyer's Use of Email, Cordless Phones, Wireless Web Access, and Similar Technology for Confidential and Secret Client Information

Some people have argued that law firms should not use email when transmitting information that is protected by the attorney-client privilege, or the work product privilege, or any other privilege without first securing the client's consent.[25] Wireless web access (often called Wi-Fi) may not be as secure as a phone modem

---

[22]Rule 4.4(b).

[23]Rule 4.4, Comment 2.

[24]ABA Formal Opinion 05–437 (Oct. 1, 2005).

[25]See, e.g., Iowa Bar Ass'n Opinion 1991-1 (1997), arguing that lawyers should not send any sensitive material via any type of unencrypted email without client consent.

Contra William Freivogel, Communicating With or About Clients on the Internet: Legal, Ethical, and Liability Concerns, ALAS LOSS PREVENTION JOURNAL 17 (1996). This article, written when there was hardly

hook-up or dedicated Internet cable, so that a lawyer's use of this technology may allow third parties to engage in the cyberspace equivalent of eavesdropping or snooping. Email is not secure in the same sense that a sealed letter is secure. Knowledgeable persons can, in effect, tap into email.

Yet, knowledgeable people can also tap into cordless telephones, cellular phones, and land-based phones even though it is not legal for hackers to eavesdrop on either email messages or telephones (whether cordless, land-based, digital or analogue cellular).[26] Moreover, lawyers routinely use Federal Express to send sensitive material, and Federal Express reserves the right to open the package in certain circumstances.[27] Consequently, most state ethics opinions appropriately conclude that it is reasonable for lawyers to use unencrypted email to communicate with clients, and use of email does not waive the attorney-client privilege.[28]

---

any legal authority on the issue, explained why it should be ethical for lawyers to use unencrypted email. This article was a harbinger of the conclusions that later ethical opinions reached upholding the use of unencrypted email. *See also* William Freivogel, *Internet Communications—Part II: A Larger Perspective*, ALAS Loss Prevention Journal 2 (1997); David Hricik, *Confidentiality & Privilege in High-Tech Communications*, 60 Tex. B.J. 104, 115 (1997); Karin Mika, *Of Cell Phones and Electronic Mail: Disclosure of Confidential Information under Disciplinary Rule 4-101 and Model Rule 1.6*, 13 Notre Dame J. L. Ethics & Pub. Policy 121 (1999); Louise L. Hill, *Electronic Communications And The 2002 Revisions To The Model Rules*, 16 St. John's J. Legal Comment. 529 (2002); R. Scot Hopkins & Pamela R. Reynolds, *Redefining Privacy And Security In The Electronic Communication Age: A Lawyer's Ethical Duty In The Virtual World Of The Internet*, 16 Georgetown J. Legal Ethics 675 (2003).

[26]*See* 18 U.S.C.A. §§ 2510, 2511, et seq.

[27]The standard Federal Express label lists, among its "terms and conditions," the following: "We may, at our option, open and inspect your pack-

ages before or after you give them to us to deliver." Telephone companies may also monitor telephone calls under certain limited circumstances. *See* ABA Formal Opinion 99-413 (Mar. 10, 1999), at 4.

See also N.J. Opinion 701 (Apr. 10, 2006)(generally approving law firm use of outside company servers to store client files as long as the lawyers make the company aware of the obligation of confidentiality and establish rules to ensure the protection of the files through contract, professional standards, or some other means), *noted in* 22 ABA/BNA Manual on Professional Conduct, Current Reports News 236 (May 17, 2006).

[28]*See* Illinois State Bar Association Opinion 96-10 (1997); Vermont Bar Association Opinion 97-5 (1997); South Carolina Bar Ethics Opinion 97-08 (1997); Alaska Bar Ethics Opinion 98-2 (1998); Washington, D.C. Bar Opinion 281 (1998).

ABA Formal Opinion 99-413 (Mar. 10, 1999) discusses these issues very thoroughly and concludes that lawyers may send email, including unencrypted email, over the Internet. There is a reasonable expectation of privacy because of the legal protection afforded email.

The Restatement agrees that

The client may insist that some forms of communication should not be used. In addition, in some cases, unique circumstances involving unusually sensitive, top-secret information may require increased security measures. Strong protective measures "might include the avoidance of email, just as they would warrant the avoidance of the telephone, fax, and mail."[29] In general, however, the basic rule is that the lawyer should take reasonable precautions.[30]

The ethics opinions are more divided on the issue of whether it is reasonable for lawyers to use cordless telephones, analog cellular phones, or digital cellular phones,[31] even though federal law, since 1994, now gives these phone communications the same legal protections given to land-based telephones.[32] Commentators generally conclude that one has a reasonable expectation of privacy when using cellular and similar wireless phones,[33] and ethics opinions should reach a similar conclusion in light of

---

lawyers need only take "reasonable" precautions to protect client confidences. Restatement of the Law Governing Lawyers, Third, § 60(1)(b) ("the lawyer must take reasonable steps in the circumstances to protect confidential client information") (Official Draft 2000).

See David Hricik, *E-mail and Client Confidentiality: Lawyers Worry Too Much about Transmitting Client Confidences by Internet E-mail*, 11 GEORGETOWN J. LEGAL ETHICS 459 (1998). On Internet issues in general, see, PIKE & FISCHER'S INTERNET LAW AND REGULATION (BNA, multi-volume updated service). Lawyers frequently employ third party vendors for transcription and electronic storage services, but they must require through contracts and standards that such third parties maintain client confidentiality. *See* Maine Bd. of Bar Overseers Prof'l Ethics Commission, Op. 194 (Dec. 11, 2007), *noted in* 24 ABA.BNA MANUAL ON PROF. CONDUCT, Current Reports 14 (Jan. 9, 1008).

[29]ABA Formal Opinion 99-413 (Mar. 10, 1999), at 2 (footnote omitted). On internet issues in general, see the thorough discussion in, Catherine J. Lanctot, *Attorney-Client Relation-*

ships in Cyberspace: The Peril and the Promise, 49 DUKE L.J. 147 (1999).

[30]This principle is reflected in analogous case law. *See, e.g, In re Reorganization of Electric Mutual Liability Ins. Co. (Bermuda)*, 425 Mass. 419, 681 N.E.2d 838 (1997), asked whether disclosure of a document by an anonymous source mandated a conclusion that the privilege had been waived. If the client shows that adequate protective steps were taken to preserve the confidentiality of the information, the disclosure will be presumed not to have been voluntary. *See also Abamar Housing & Development Inc. v. Lisa Daly Lady Decor Inc.*, 698 So.2d 276 (Fla.App.1997) (same).

[31]David Hricik, *E-mail and Client Confidentiality: Lawyers Worry Too Much About Transmitting Client Confidences by Internet E-mail*, 11 GEORGETOWN J. LEGAL ETHICS 459, 481 (1998).

[32]18 U.S.C.A. §§ 2510, 2511, et seq.

[33]See authorities cited in, ABA Formal Opinion 99-413 (Mar. 10, 1999), at 5 n.15.

federal legal protections.[34] However, the ABA Ethics Committee has not ruled on this specific question.[35]

The drafters of the 2002 Rules added two Comments under the heading, "Acting Competently to Preserve Confidentiality." The first Comment deals with inadvertent disclosures and the second Comment deals with transmission of confidential client information. Lawyers owe clients an obligation to take "reasonable precautions to prevent the information from coming into the hands of unintended recipients."[36] The Comment goes on to state:

> This duty, however, does not require that the lawyer use special security measures if the method of communication affords a reasonable expectation of privacy. Special circumstances, however, may warrant special precautions. Factors to be considered in determining the reasonableness of the lawyer's expectation of confidentiality include the sensitivity of the information and the extent to which the privacy of the communication is protected by law or by a confidentiality agreement.[37]

The drafters also recognize the role of client choice in the lawyer's transmission of confidential information.[38] Some clients may insist on a more secure communication while others may give informed consent to a lawyer's use of a means of communication that would be prohibited by Rule 1.6.

Company Access of Employees' E-mails. Periodically, employees sue employers over race discrimination, sex harassment, etc. In such cases, the employer often seeks access to the employee's e-mail account, so that it can see the e-mails without issuing a formal request for documents. Or, a third party may subpoena the employer for e-mails by the employee. In each case, the employee may have some expectation of privacy, such as when the e-mail account is password protected. The employer (or third party subpoenaing the employer) may argue that it should be able to see these e-mails—without respecting any privilege from the employee—because the server, on which the e-mails are stored are in the possession and control of the employer.

The cases are still sorting out this issue. The general principle should be that the e-mails are privileged if the employee had a reasonable expectation of privacy, which should normally be the case if the employee used a password-protected e-mail account. Granted, the e-mail is on the employer's possession via its server, but so is the employee's purse sitting in the locked office

---

[34]State Bar of Arizona, Advisory Opinion 95-11 (1995) has upheld the use of cordless phones.

[35]ABA Formal Opinion 99-413 (Mar. 10, 1999), at 6: "Although the Committee does not here express an opinion regarding the use of cellular or cordless telephone, ..."

[36]Rule 1.6, Comment 17.

[37]Rule 1.6, Comment 17.

[38]Rule 1.6, Comment 17.

unattended.[39] The fact that the employer can access the server and even crack the password using the wonders of its information technology experts does not mean that the material is freely available. That is particularly true if the employee is communicating with her lawyer.

In *Stengart v. Loving Care Agency, Inc.*,[40] a former employee sued her employer for alleged discrimination. The Superior Court denied her motion to require the employer to return all copies of e-mails sent by the employee to her lawyers over her work-issued laptop through employee's personal, web-based e-mail account. The employee appealed and the Appellate Division reversed. The employer took a picture of her computer's hard drive (that is, a "forensic image of the hard drive"), reviewed her internet browsing history, and read her communications to her lawyer.

The employer had a policy (in the company handbook) that the "company reserves and will exercise the right to review, audit, intercept, access, and disclose all matters on the company's media systems and services at any time, with or without notice." When the employer said "services," it may have meant "server." This policy added that e-mails and voice mail "are not to be considered private or personal to any individual employee." The employer disputed that this policy had ever been finalized. The appellate

---

[39] *Thyroff v. Nationwide Mut. Ins. Co.*, 8 N.Y.3d 283, 832 N.Y.S.2d 873, 864 N.E.2d 1272, 1278 (2007), which recognized that a computer in this context is analogous to a file cabinet for personal communications. *Thyroff* held that an employee or agent has a cause of action of conversion to intangible electronic records that are stored on a computer and are indistinguishable from printed documents.

[40] *Stengart v. Loving Care Agency, Inc.*, 408 N.J. Super. 54, 973 A.2d 390 (App. Div. 2009). *See also Curto v. Medical World Communications, Inc.*, 99 Fair Empl. Prac. Cas. (BNA) 298, 2006 WL 1318387 (E.D. N.Y. 2006).

On the other hand, another court found that an employee waived the attorney-client privilege by communicating with her attorney over her work e-mail system where the company policy clearly notified all employees that e-mails were "subject to monitoring, search or interception at any time . . . ." *Kaufman v. SunGard Inv. System*, 2006 WL 1307882 (D.N.J. 2006).

See also Alamar Ranch, LLC v. County of Boise, 2009 WL 3669741 (D. Idaho 2009). "Kirkpatrick did not attempt to protect the confidentiality of the messages by using a web-based password-protected e-mail account. She simply used her work e-mail." This court found a waiver of the attorney client privilege for some e-mails but not for others. "Kirkpatrick waived the privilege for those messages she sent from her work computer." On the other hand, "There is no evidence that the Pereidas and Gammons were aware—or should have been aware—that by copying Kirkpatrick on their e-mails to Charney they were exposing their e-mails to IHFA scrutiny. As far as the Pereidas and Gammon were concerned, they were having a confidential discussion with their attorney. The Court refuses to extend the constructive knowledge that Charney had about the monitoring of work-based e-mails to the Pereidas and Gammon—laypersons are simply not on 'high-alert' for such things as attorneys must be." 2009 WL 3669741, *4-5.

court questioned if the company's policy was clear and properly communicated, but it assumed that this policy was "in effect and applied to plaintiff at the time she sent the emails in question." Nonetheless it concluded that notwithstanding the company policy, the attorney-client privilege protects the former employee's personal e-mails to her lawyer.

The New Jersey Court broadly rejected the employer's argument that its control of its servers and its ownership of company laptops. "Property rights are no less offended when an employer examines documents stored on a computer as when an employer rifles through a folder containing an employee's private papers or reaches in and examines the contents of an employee's pockets." The Court went on to say that "even when a legitimate business purpose could support such a search, we can envision no valid precept of property law that would convert the employer's interest in determining what is in those locations with a right to own the contents of the employee's folder of private papers or the contents of his pocket." Hence, it concluded that "a breach of a company policy with regard to the use of its computers does not justify the company's claim of ownership to personal communications and information accessible there from or contained therein."[41]

When the lawyer begins to represent the employee, "as soon as practical" after there is a client-lawyer, the lawyer "typically should instruct the employee-client to avoid using a workplace device or system for sensitive or substantive communications, and perhaps for any attorney-client communications, because even seemingly ministerial communications involving matters such as scheduling can have substantive ramifications."[42]

For the lawyer representing the employer in these circumstances, the employer may have access to these emails (assum-

---

[41]*Stengart v. Loving Care Agency, Inc.*, 408 N.J. Super. 54, 69–70, 973 A.2d 390, 399 (App. Div. 2009).

See Quon v. Arch Wireless Operating Co., Inc., 529 F.3d 892, 905 (9th Cir. 2008), cert. granted, 130 S. Ct. 1011 (2009) and cert. denied, 130 S. Ct. 1011 (2009) (which held that there was a reasonable expectation of privacy in text messages stored by a service provider), *certiorari granted, sub nom., City of Ontario v. Quon*, 130 S. Ct. 1011 (2009), decided in, *City of Ontario v. Quon*, 560 U.S. __, 130 S.Ct. 2619, 177 L.Ed.2d 216 (2010), holding that a city's review of a police officer's text messages was reasonable under the circumstances, and thus did not violate Fourth Amendment. The Court specifically noted that people do not lose Fourth Amendment rights merely because they work for the government instead of a private employer; however, special needs, beyond the normal need for law enforcement, "make the warrant and probable-cause requirement impracticable for government employers." 560 U.S. at __, 130 S.Ct. at 2628.

[42]ABA Formal Op. 11-459 (Aug. 4, 2011), "Duty to Protect the Confidentiality of E-mail Communications with One's Client."

ing, again, that there is no hacking and that the employer has not violated any express or implied promise of confidentiality). If there is a court rule, or statute, labor agreement, or something else that creates a reasonable expectation of privacy that requires the employer (or the employer's lawyer) to notify the employee (the opposing litigant or prospective opposing litigant), then the lawyer should follow those rules.

If the law governing potential disclosure is "unclear," then Rule 1.6(b)(6) allows the employer's lawyer to disclose to the opposing litigant that the employer has retrieved the employee's attorney-client e-mail communications "to the extent the lawyer reasonably believes it is necessary to do so to comply with the relevant law." If the law governing "potential disclosure is unclear, the lawyer need not risk violating a legal or ethical obligation"[43]

Assuming that it is clear that the employer may have legitimate access to the employee's email, then the lawyer's duty is different. Under those circumstances, "neither Rule 4.4(b) nor any other Rule requires the employer's lawyer to notify opposing counsel of the receipt of the communications."[44]

Using an E-mail Provider that Engages in Data-Mining

Some law firms and lawyers use services like Google's Gmail instead of using their own servers. Often, companies like Google engage extensive data mining for advertising purposes. Google says that no person sees individual data. The general rule is that a lawyer may use an e-mail service provider that conducts computer scans of e-mails to generate computer advertising, if no human beings (other than the sender and recipient) review the e-mails.[45]

§ 1.6–2(d) Disclosure of Confidences Contained in Metadata

Increasingly, lawyers exchange electronic files with opposing counsel in litigation and non-litigation matters. Such files may contain confidential information, called "metadata" that is hidden in the coding of the electronic file. Metadata may include deleted text, information about the person who made the changes to the document, the date and time of the changes, and other informa-

---

[43] ABA Formal Op. 11-460 (Aug. 4, 2011), "Duty when Lawyer Receives Copies of a Third Party's E-mail Communications with Counsel."

[44] ABA Formal Op. 11-460 (Aug. 4, 2011), "Duty when Lawyer Receives Copies of a Third Party's E-mail Communications with Counsel."

[45] N/Y. Ethics Opinion 820, 2008 WL 788413 (N.Y. State Bar Association. Committee on Professional Ethics) (Feb. 8, 2008).

tion that could provide an opposing party with valuable confidential information.[46]

One view of the metadata issue places a burden upon the transmitting lawyer to take reasonable care so that they do not inadvertently disclose confidential information to the opposing side.[47] Not all information contained in metadata is confidential client information. But, to the extent that metadata contains confidential client information, a New York Bar Opinion requires that lawyers exercise reasonable care not to disclose confidential client information, and such care may require that the lawyer keep up with technological advances to "clean" the metadata from the electronic file.[48]

Another view of the metadata issue is to prohibit the receiving lawyer from "mining" or using technology to pull confidential information from the electronic file.[49] This view relies upon the authorities addressing the case of an inadvertent fax.[50] However, some attorneys complain that they should have a right to examine a file for metadata, just as they could examine a paper document for fingerprints.[51] And, one could argue that scrubbing

---

[46]Sometimes the other party may find this metadata of great interest, because, e.g., a redlined change may suggest how much more the opposing party is willing to pay for a settlement. Or, the date that someone created a document may be important for discovery purposes.

[47]See David Hricik & Robert R. Jueneman, *The Transmission and Receipt of Invisible Confidential Information*, 15 THE PROFESSIONAL LAWYER 18 (2004).

[48]N.Y. State Bar Opinion 782 (Dec. 8, 2004).

[49]N.Y. State Bar Opinion 749 (2003).

For an opinion that had no clear conclusion, see Pennsylvania Bar Association Committee on Legal Ethics and Professional Responsibility, Formal Opinion Number 2007-500 (2007), 2007 WL 5314341. It concluded that:

"under the Pennsylvania Rules of Professional Conduct, each attorney *must determine for himself or herself whether to utilize the metadata* contained in documents and other electronic files

based upon the lawyer's judgment and the particular factual situation. This determination should be based upon the nature of the information received, how and from whom the information was received, attorney-client privilege and work product rules, and common sense, reciprocity and professional courtesy. Although the waiver of the attorney-client privilege with respect to privileged and confidential materials is a matter for judicial determination, the Committee believes that the inadvertent transmissions of such materials should not constitute a waiver of the privilege, except in the case of extreme carelessness or indifference." 2007 WL 5314341, *7.

[50]A New York County Ethics Opinion relied upon the authorities in the inadvertent fax area to hold that lawyers should not search or use metadata from an opponent's electronic communications unless the lawyers have made a contrary agreement. See N.Y. County Lawyers' Ass'n Comm. On Prof. Ethics, Op. 738 (Mar. 24, 2008).

[51]Jessica M. Walker, *Not So Evident*, MIAMI DAILY BUS. REV. (Apr. 17, 2006).

metadata from a file could subject the lawyer to a claim of obstruction of justice.

A lawyer who sends an electronic file of a contract or settlement document to opposing counsel does not intend to disclose confidential information contained in the metadata. Thus, the disclosure of metadata in such a case is similar to the inadvertently sent fax.

ABA Formal Opinion 06–442 also addressed the lawyer's use of metadata. It concluded that the Model Rules do not prohibit lawyers from discovering and using metadata found in documents that other lawyers transmit to them, even though the other lawyer may not know that the electronic version of the document contains metadata.[52] Model Rule 4.4(b) supports this conclusion, although the ABA Opinion specifically declined to decide whether metadata contained in a received document should be considered "inadvertent" and thus subject to the requirement of Rule 4.4(b).

As in the case of the inadvertent fax, other law may also regulate whether a lawyer may use metadata in a judicial proceeding. Lawyers who receive documents containing metadata will need to examine the facts of their situation to determine whether they have an obligation to inform the sending lawyer under Rule 4.4(b).

The Opinion advised that lawyers who do not wish to give metadata to their opponents should avoid creating the metadata in the first place (e.g., by not using the redlining function in a word processing program, or by not embedding comments in a document). They may also fax the document or only provide a hard copy. Or, the lawyers can use computer software programs to scrub metadata from a document before they email it to their opponents. It is the duty of the lawyer to "safeguard information relating to the representation."[53]

Sometimes a document has forensic interest. In that case, ABA Formal Opinion 06–442 advised, in footnote 13: "Of course, when responding to discovery, a lawyer must not alter a document when it would be unlawful or unethical to do so, e.g., Rule 3.4(a)."

Some lawyers strongly object to looking at metadata and

---

[52]ABA Formal Opinion 06–442 (Aug. 5, 2006).

A Pennsylvania Ethics Opinion similarly leaves it up to individual lawyers on whether they should use the information contained in metadata, however, it did list a number of factors that lawyers should consider in making such a decision, including: the judgment of the lawyer; particular facts of the situation; the lawyer's view of his obligation to the client; the nature of the information received; how and from the information was received; and common sense, reciprocity, and professional courtesy. *See* Pa. Bar. Ass'n Comm. on Legal Ethics and Prof. Responsibility, Formal Op. 2007-500 (2007).

[53]Rule 1.6, Comment 16, quoted in ABA Formal Opinion 06–442.

compare using it to rummaging about the opponent's garbage.[54] On the other hand, there are analogues in the nondigital world to metadata. Attorneys routinely mine data found in the analog version of digital documents, which computer people call "hard copy."

For example, consider the case where there is a dispute between a former client and his former lawyer (let us call him Alpha) on legal fees. Alpha claims that he kept careful contemporaneous records of his time, and his handwritten time-records support him. No one would be surprised if the lawyer representing the former client (let us call this lawyer Beta) would subpoena these time records. And, it would hardly be surprising if Beta hired an expert to examine the time records to determine if the lawyer created the records over the course of a year or all on the same day (based on how the ink seeped through the page).

Mining a digital document is really no different from mining an analog document. The lawyer may use an ink specialist in one case versus a computer specialist in the other. Neither case involves sneaking into the opponent's briefcase or rummaging through his garbage.

When a lawyer requests the production of computer files or hard drives in discovery, and the electronic files contain metadata that provides confidential information about changes made by the client, such information is not inadvertent disclosure. And, scrubbing of such data may subject a client or lawyer to discovery abuse and obstruction of justice penalties.[55]

§ 1.6–2(e) A Lawyer's Obligations When the Lawyer Discovers that a Client Confidence Has Been Disclosed

Model Rule 1.6 establishes the duty of the lawyer to protect client confidential information and the circumstances under which the lawyer may disclose such information. What are a lawyer's obligations when the lawyer discovers that someone in the law firm has disclosed a client's confidences? The lawyer may discover that another lawyer or employee has intentionally disclosed the information to an outside party, such as a conversation with a

---

[54]*See* David Hricik, *Mining for Embedded Data: Is it Ethical to Take Intentional Advantage of Other People's Failures?*, 8 N.C.J.L. & TECH 231 (2007) (arguing that it requires active, deliberate steps to reveal the usually invisible confidential information embedded in an electronic document and it borders on dishonesty). *See also* Ariz. State Bar Comm. on the Rules of Prof'l Conduct, Op. 07–03 (Nov. 2007) (holding that lawyers should not examine electronic communications for the purpose of mining the metadata and that lawyers who discover metadata that reveals confidential information must inform the sender), noted in 23 ABA/BNA MANUAL ON PROFESSIONAL CONDUCT, Current Reports 641 (Dec. 26, 2007).

[55]ABA Formal Opinion 06–442 (Aug. 5, 2006)("Of course, when responding to discovery, a lawyer must not alter a document when it would be unlawful or unethical to do so, e.g., Rule 3.4(a).").

friend or news reporter. Or, the lawyer may discover that the information has been disclosed inadvertently, such as in the case of metadata or an inadvertently sent fax.

Although there is not much authority on this issue, the proper analysis points to one conclusion. The lawyer as agent for the client principal has an obligation to protect confidential client information. If a lawyer discovers that someone in the firm has intentionally or inadvertently disclosed confidential information, Model Rule 5.1(b)(2) directs the lawyer to take reasonable remedial measures to protect client interests. Such measures may include asserting the client's attorney-client privilege on the disclosed information and possibly seeking court protection of the disclosed information. If the confidential information was disclosed as a result of a crime, such as the theft of a law firm laptop or a network security breach, the lawyer may need to inform the authorities. If the disclosure of the confidential information involves another lawyer's misconduct, the lawyer may need to comply with Model Rule 8.3's duty to disclose misconduct to the appropriate authority.

The ultimate question is whether the lawyer owes a duty to the client to inform the client that confidential information has been disclosed. Several authorities point to an affirmative answer. A lawyer owes fiduciary duties to the client, and the obligation of full candor to the client requires that the lawyer disclose the breach to the client.[56] Rule 1.4(a)(3) instructs the lawyer to keep the client reasonably informed about the status of a matter. Clients may be able to mitigate the harm caused by the breach, but such mitigation can only occur if they have knowledge of the breach of confidentiality. A lawyer has an obligation to inform clients about the lawyer's negligent acts, and a breach of the duty of confidentiality would seem to fall within the policy of such disclosure.[57]

§ 1.6–3 LAWYERS CONSULTING WITH OTHER LAWYERS IN DIFFERENT LAW FIRMS, WHEN THEY ARE NOT ASSOCIATED IN A MATTER

Lawyers in the same law firm may routinely discuss with each other confidential matters involving a client. This is the default rule that applies even if the client hired Lawyer #1 and never

---

[56] *See Burrow v. Arce*, 997 S.W.2d 229, 240 (Tex.1999).

[57] *See* RONALD E. MALLEN & JEFFREY M. SMITH, LEGAL MALPRACTICE 2007 EDITION 437 (2007) ("A duty of disclosure exists when the attorney's representation continues, and the client's interests can be adversely affected by nondisclosure.").

expected that Lawyer #1 would discuss a question with Lawyer #2.[1]

In addition, with the client's express permission, the lawyer in one firm may associate with a lawyer in a different firm in order to handle a particular matter.[2] Often, this association occurs when the lawyer in another law firm has special expertise to bring to a matter. In this case as well, the default rule is that the lawyers in the two different law firms may freely consult with each other about the client confidences related to that case.

A third type of consulting is a little different because the lawyer consults with another lawyer in a different firm but he does not secure the explicit consent of the client before doing so. Consider the case when Lawyer #1 seeks legal advice from Lawyer #2, because that second lawyer has a special expertise or a more detached judgment on the issue because he is in a different law firm. Sometimes, Lawyer #1 may consult Lawyer #2 on an ethics question to determine if a special action is required.[3] The 1983 Model Rules did not expressly address this disclosure; however, a standard of practice developed for such consultations.

In all cases, Lawyer #1 must be careful not to jeopardize or compromise the duty of confidentiality owed to his client when consulting with Lawyer #2. For example, Lawyer #1 should avoid consulting with a lawyer who is likely to be representing the adverse party. The prudent lawyer should obtain assurances of confidentiality and an agreement that the consulted lawyer will not engage in adverse representation. Lawyer #1 may ask general legal questions, speak in hypotheticals, and avoid discussing specific facts that would identify the client to Lawyer #2. Lawyer #1 is impliedly authorized to disclose some information in this context if the disclosure does not compromise the attorney-client privilege and if it is not otherwise detrimental to the client.

The ABA Ethics Opinion[4] on this issue has concluded that there is no Attorney-Client relationship between Lawyer #2 (the consulted lawyer) and the client of Lawyer #1, but Lawyer #2 may either "expressly or impliedly" agree to respect the confidentiality of the information that was disclosed. Unless there is an express or implied agreement that the consulted lawyer will not undertake representation adverse to the client of the consulting lawyer, the consulted lawyer may undertake such representation; in these circumstances, the consulted lawyer has no duty of

---

[Section 1.6–3]

[1]Rule 1.6, Comment 5.

[2]Rule 1.1, Comment 2; Rule 1.5(e); DR 6-101(A)(1).

[3]Drew L. Kershen, *The Ethics of Ethics Consultation*, 6 THE PROFESSIONAL LAWYER 1 (ABA, No. 3, May, 1995).

[4]ABA Formal Opinion 98-411 (Aug. 30, 1998).

confidentiality under Rule 1.6 and no conflict of interest under Rule 1.7.[5]

The drafters of the 2002 Rules sought to clarify this disclosure for purposes of consulting another lawyer in the context of complying with the ethics rules. Rule 1.6(b)(4) allows a lawyer to disclose confidential information to the extent necessary "to secure legal advice about the lawyer's compliance with these Rules."[6] The Comments state that such disclosure probably falls under the impliedly authorized exception; however, if it does not, the importance of complying with the ethics rules justifies an express exception.[7]

§ 1.6–4 THE PROSPECTIVE CLIENT

To protect legitimate client expectations, the ethics rules protect not only confidential information that the lawyer learned from her clients, but also secret information that she learned from a *prospective* client who sought to (but did not) retain her.[1] This ethical principle is derived from the fact that the information from the prospective client is also privileged.

The 1983 version of Model Rule 1.6 did not make this point explicitly, but it acknowledged it in the Preamble of the Model Rules.[2] In addition, a 1990 ABA Formal Opinion[3] concluded that Model Rule 1.6 protects information from a would-be client seeking representation, even though the lawyer does not undertake representation of, or perform legal work for, the would-be client.[4]

Protecting the confidences of the prospective client who does not retain the lawyer imposes an opportunity cost on any lawyer interviewing a prospective client because that lawyer may later be disqualified from representing the opponent of the would-be client. Consequently, ABA Formal Opinion 90-358[5] suggested several ways for the law firm to limit these costs.

First, the law firm dealing with the prospective client may institute procedures to identify as early as possible conflicts of prospective clients. In addition, the firm may take steps to limit

---

[5] These issues are thoroughly discussed in ABA Formal Opinion 98-411 (Aug. 30, 1998).

[6] Rule 1.6(b)(4).

[7] Rule 1.6, Comment 9.

[Section 1.6–4]

[1] EC 4-1.

[2] ABA Model Rules, Preamble, Scope, 17: "But there are some duties, such as that of confidentiality under Rule 1.6, that attach when the lawyer agrees to consider whether a client-lawyer relationship shall be established."

[3] ABA Formal Opinion 90-358 (Sept. 13, 1990). As discussed below, this ABA Formal Opinion suggests steps a firm should take to minimize the risk of future disqualification.

[4] *See also* Restatement of the Law Governing Lawyers § 15 ("Lawyer's Duties to Prospective Client") (Official Draft 2000).

[5] ABA Formal Opinion 90-358 (Sept. 13, 1990).

information obtained at the initial interview to the information necessary to check for conflicts. The firm may also obtain from the prospective client waivers of confidentiality for disclosures at the initial interview.

ABA Formal Opinion 90-358 also advised that some courts might accept the law firm's screening of the lawyer who learned confidential information "where the information disclosed by the would-be client is not extensive or sensitive. . . ."[6] The 1983 Model Rules themselves, however, did not provide for screening of the disqualified lawyer, except in the case of the movement of a lawyer between government and private practice.[7] Consequently, this ethics opinion must mean only that the prospective client can agree to accept screening and waive a right that it could otherwise exercise.[8]

---

[6]ABA Formal Opinion 90-358 (Sept. 13, 1990).

[7]*See* 1983 Model Rule 1.11; 1983 Model Rule 1.10, Comment 5 (pointing out that different policy considerations justify screening in that situation that do not justify screening when lawyers move from one private firm to another).

[8]In contrast, Restatement of the Law Governing Lawyers, Third, § 204(2)(a) (Proposed Final Draft No. 1, Mar. 29, 1996) proposed to allow screening without client consent. Section 204(2) states:

"(2) Imputation specified in § 203 does not restrict an affiliated lawyer with respect to a former-client conflict under § 213, when there is no reasonably apparent risk that confidential information of the former client will be used with material adverse effect on the former client because:

"(a) any confidential client information communicated to the personally-prohibited lawyer is unlikely to be significant in the subsequent matter;

"(b) the personally-prohibited lawyer is subject to screening measures adequate to eliminate involvement by that lawyer in the representation; and

"(c) timely and adequate notice of the screening has been provided to all affected clients."

Later, the Comment makes clear that—

"If the requirements of either Subsection (2) or (3) are met, imputation is removed and *consent to the representation by the former client is not required*. The required screening measures must be imposed in the subsequent representation at the time the conflict is discovered or reasonably should have been discovered, and they must be of sufficient scope, continuity, and duration to assure that there will be no material risk to confidential client information."

Restatement of the Law Governing Lawyers, Third, § 204(2)(a) (Proposed Final Draft No. 1, Mar. 29, 1996), Comment *d*.

The Restatement imposes on the lawyer or firm seeking to remove imputation "the burden of persuasion that there is no reasonable prospect that confidential information of the former client will be used with material adverse effect on the former client. Significance of the information is determined by its probable utility in the later representation, including such factors as the following: (1) whether the value of the information as proof or for tactical purposes is peripheral or tenuous; (2) whether the information in most material respects is now publicly known; (3) whether the information was of only temporary significance; (4) the scope of the second

Under the 1983 Model Rules, if the prospective client—when informed of these alternatives—decides that it did not want to waive any rights, that it did not want to accept a screen, and so forth, then the law firm knows about the type of client with which it is dealing, and it may decide not to proceed further (because of the opportunity costs that this prospective client imposes if it does not eventually choose the law firm to represent it), or it may decide to accept the preconditions that the prospective client imposes. In that case, the firm, with its eyes wide open, has made the choice to accept these opportunity costs.[9]

The drafters of the 2002 Model Rules sought to address a lawyer's obligation of confidentiality to prospective clients in a more explicit manner. In addition, the drafters realized that the 1983 version of the Rules did not have any explicit Rule dealing with a *prospective* client. One would have to cull the basic principles by reading various sections of different Rules as well as the relevant Ethics Opinions.

Consequently they drafted Rule 1.18, which deals explicitly with a lawyer's duties to a prospective client. Rule 1.18(b) gives

---

representation; and (5) the duration and degree of responsibility of the personally-prohibited lawyer in the earlier representation." *Id.*

The significance of this proposal may depend on how narrowly one defines "is unlikely to be significant in the subsequent matter." One problem is that a court may not be able to determine "significance" without knowing what the information is, and—once the information is revealed—the confidential information is no longer confidential because the judge knows it. For example, the information known by the lawyer may show that his former client was guilty of laches. Once the judge is told this information, the judge will rule that the information is really material and therefore the screen will not work. But the judge will know of the laches problem and thus may, *sua sponte*, dismiss on grounds of laches. The statement in the Comment that one determines the significance of the relevant information by considering if that information "in most material respects is now publicly know," certainly says that, even if the information is *not* publicly known in one *material* respect, there still can be screening.

[9]The Restatement of the Law Governing Lawyers, Third, § 132, Comment g(i) (Official Draft 2000), offers similar counsel. It also provides that, even if the lawyer obtains confidential information from the former prospective client in the course of the initial interview, if the information is not "extensive and sensitive," the lawyer should not be barred by that information from representing the other adverse clients who might benefit from use of the information. That is, the lawyer should be *trusted* not to use this adverse information.

Restatement of the Law Governing Lawyers, Third, § 15(2) (Official Draft 2000) continues this proposal. It provides that a lawyer is disqualified from representing a client with interests materially adverse to the prospective client if the matter is the same or substantially related, but this disqualification exists "only" when the lawyer has confidential information "that could be significantly harmful to the prospective client in the matter" *and* either the affected and prospective client waive their rights *or* this personally-prohibited lawyer is screened. Id. § 15(2)(a)(ii).

former prospective clients all the rights of former clients under Rule 1.9 with respect to the obligation of confidentiality. Furthermore, the drafters decided that they would permit screening of the lawyer who acquired the information from the prospective client if the "lawyer who received the information took reasonable measures to avoid exposure to more disqualifying information than was reasonably necessary to determine whether to represent the prospective client . . . ."[10]

Rule 1.18 seeks to mitigate the harsh result that a duty of confidentiality and loyalty to a prospective client could prevent the firm from representing other adverse parties in the future. The decision to treat prospective clients who retain the lawyer the same as former clients for the purposes of confidentiality and the decision to permit screening in situations where the lawyer is careful to limit the information obtained properly balances the competing interests at stake.

§ 1.6–5 THE FORMER CLIENT

§ 1.6–5(a) When the Former Client Is Still Living

When a client becomes a *former* client, the lawyer's obligation to preserve the former client's confidences and secrets does not end.[1] In fact, the primary rationale behind the Rule that places important restrictions on the ability of a lawyer to sue or take a position adverse to a former client arises from the need to protect confidences or secrets of the former client that are relevant, *i.e.*, material, to the present representation.[2]

§ 1.6–5(b) When the Client Has Died

Normally, one would assume that the attorney-client privilege should survive the client's death. And in most cases, this result regarding the privilege is not controversial. But, circumstances may arise that question whether this result should have some exceptions. For example, may a lawyer reveal that her client has

---

[10]Rule 1.18(d). Of course, the screening must be timely, remove the disqualified lawyer from participating in the matter, and not apportion any fee to the disqualified lawyer. And, the law firm must provide notice to the prospective client. Rule 1.18(d)(1), (2).

[Section 1.6–5]

[1]EC 4-6. *See also* Rule 1.9.

[2]Rule 1.9(b)(2), (c)(2). *See also* Rule 1.9, Comments 6 to 7.

See also Sealed Party v. Sealed Party, S.D. Tex., Civ. No. H–04–2229, 2006 WL 1207732 (May 4, 2006), *noted*

in 22 ABA/BNA MANUAL ON PROFESSIONAL CONDUCT, Current Reports News 250 (May 31, 2006). *Sealed Party* found that a lawyer breached his duty of confidentiality to a former client by issuing a press release about a settlement without obtaining his former client's consent. This press release violated the confidentiality clause of the settlement and disclosed confidential views of the client. The court refused to award damages or a disgorgement of the fee because the client failed to prove injury resulting from the disclosure.

confessed to a crime for which an innocent person is about to be punished? In that circumstance, the lawyer's silence will cause a grave injustice. If the client is deceased, the lawyer's disclosure of the client's secret will not place the client in jeopardy. But it certainly may call into question the history and memory of the character of the former client.

This question is the subject of much debate.[3] The lawyer's silence in such a case may permit a grave injustice to be done, as illustrated in *State v. Macumber*.[4] *Macumber* held that the trial judge in a murder case had properly excluded testimony by two attorneys that a third person, now deceased, had confessed to them that he had killed the people whom the state is charging the defendant with murdering. This third person confessed to the two attorneys who had represented him when he was tried in federal court for an unrelated murder. The state court ruled that the attorney-client privilege prevented this disclosure. The dissent argued that when this third person died and therefore the chance of his prosecution for other crimes ended, any purported privilege was merely a matter of property interest, which should not prevail over the constitutional right of the accused to introduce reliable hearsay declarations evidencing his innocence.

An early draft of the proposed Restatement of the Law, Third, of the Law Governing Lawyers offered an illustration based on (and agreeing with) *Macumber*.[5] At the May, 1989 annual meeting of the American Law Institute, several members objected to this illustration as "grotesque," "revolting," and "disgusting." It is not right, they said, that a lawyer may reveal privileged information in a fee dispute but not to prevent an innocent person from going to jail. By the lopsided vote of 164 to 65, the ALI members voted to strike the illustration. The ALI thus rejected the rule espoused in the *Macumber* decision.

A comment in the final version of the Restatement now criticizes the *Macumber* result. The Restatement acknowledges that strict limitation on the exception of the attorney-client privilege to ongoing or future crimes "would prohibit a lawyer from testifying that a client confessed to a crime for which an innocent person is on trial."[6] The United Kingdom, for example, recognizes an

---

[3]*See, e.g.*, CHARLES W. WOLFRAM, MODERN LEGAL ETHICS 673 (West Pub. Co. 1986).

[4]*State v. Macumber*, 112 Ariz. 569, 544 P.2d 1084 (1976).

[5]Restatement of the Law Govern-

ing Lawyers, Third, § 132, Illustration 4 (Tentative Draft No. 2, Apr. 7, 1989)

[6]Restatement of the Law Governing Lawyers, Third, § 82, Comment *e* (Official Draft 2000).

exception to the attorney-client privilege when it would result in the conviction of an innocent person.[7]

The Restatement's Comment concludes: "At least in capital cases, the argument for extending the exception (*i.e.*, not applying the attorney-client privilege to exclude otherwise admissible evidence) seems compelling."[8] However, if one is persuaded by the United Kingdom rule, it makes little sense to limit it to capital cases, as the Restatement suggests. A penalty of capital punishment is very permanent, to be sure, but 20 years or life imprisonment is also permanent. Under the Restatement position, the law should tell the defendant: if you were sentenced to death, you could have the evidence that would exonerate you, but because you are only sentenced to life imprisonment, you must be deprived of such evidence, even in the case where the person being protected (the guilty party, who had confessed to his lawyer) has died, so that the law can no longer bring him to justice.

Under the 2002 Rules, an argument exists that a lawyer may be able to disclose information of a deceased client if the wrongfully accused person was threatened with reasonably certain death or substantial bodily harm. The drafters of the 2002 Rules amended Rule 1.6(b)(1) to permit a lawyer to disclose confidential client information even if the client is not engaged in a current or future crime.[9] And, since Rule 1.9 specifically notes that a lawyer may be permitted or required to make a disclosure against former clients if the other Rules permit or require a lawyer to do so, *Macumber* may be resolved differently if the client is threatened with the reasonably certain punishment of the death penalty.[10]

Although the academic commentary[11] and the American Law Institute rejected the result in *Macumber* as unfair, the U.S.

---

[7]*Regina v. Barton*, [1973] W.L.R. 115 (Cr. Ct.), holding that the solicitor must produce any document otherwise admissible to prove that the defendant was innocent of the charged criminal offense, notwithstanding the attorney-client privilege. *Regina v. Ataou*, [1988] 2 W.L.R. 1147 (C.A.), holding that the trial judge may refuse to apply the attorney-client privilege to an attempt by the accused to cross examine a prosecution witness about conversations the witness had with his solicitor exonerating the accused. A leading English treatise, M. HOWARD, P. CRANCE, & D. HOCHBERG, PHIPSON ON EVIDENCE 500 (14th ed. 1990) concludes that the attorney-client privilege does not apply in the circumstance where it would prevent the accused from calling evidence that might lead to his acquittal on criminal charges. *See also* Restatement of the Law Governing Lawyers, Third, § 82, Reporter's Note at Comment *e* (Official Draft 2000).

[8]Restatement of the Law Governing Lawyers, Third, § 82, Comment *e* (Official Draft 2000).

[9]Rule 1.6(b)(1) states that a lawyer may reveal confidential client information to the extent that the lawyer reasonably believes necessary "to prevent reasonably certain death or substantial bodily harm. . . ."

[10]Rule 1.9(c)(2).

[11]2 CHRISTOPHER B. MUELLER & LAIRD C. KIRKPATRICK, FEDERAL EVIDENCE (2nd ed. 1994) § 199, p. 380:

Supreme Court was not persuaded, as demonstrated by its divided decision in *Swidler & Berlin v. United States*.[12] This celebrated case tested whether the Office of Independent Counsel could subpoena notes of conversations between Vincent Foster (then a White House aide) and his lawyer shortly before Mr. Foster's suicide. The Independent Counsel sought these notes as part of a criminal investigation of President and Mrs. Clinton.

In the D.C. Circuit, Judges Williams and Wald had analyzed the precedent and found that, while cases often say the attorney-client privilege survives death, it is usually said in the context of finding an exception to the rule to assist in construction of a will. Thus, they concluded, it is reasonable to make another exception for communications significant to a criminal prosecution since the client's own criminal liability obviously expires when he does. Further, the Court held, post-death reputation is not sufficiently important to most people to make them not be candid with their lawyer even if the privilege would not survive their death.[13]

In the closing days of the term, the Supreme Court reversed, six to three.[14] Chief Justice Rehnquist, for the Court, argued: "Knowing that communications will remain confidential even after death encourages the client to communicate fully and frankly with counsel. While the fear of disclosure, and the consequent withholding of information from counsel, may be reduced if disclosure is limited to posthumous disclosure in a criminal context, it seems unreasonable to assume that it vanishes altogether. Clients may be concerned about reputation, civil liability, or possible harm to friends or family. Posthumous disclosure of such communications may be as feared as disclosure during the client's lifetime."[15]

Justice O'Connor, joined by Justices Scalia and Thomas, dissented. She argued: "In my view, a criminal defendant's right to exculpatory evidence or a compelling law enforcement need for information may, where the testimony is not available from other

---

"[I]f a deceased client has confessed to criminal acts that are later charged to another, surely the latter's need for evidence sometimes outweighs the interest in preserving the confidences." Terminating the privilege upon the client's death "could not to any substantial degree lessen the encouragement for free disclosure which is [its] purpose." 1 J. Strong, McCORMICK ON EVIDENCE § 94, at 350 (West Pub. Co. 4th ed. 1992).

[12] *Swidler & Berlin v. United States*, 524 U.S. 399, 118 S.Ct. 2081, 141 L.Ed.2d 379 (1998).

[13] *In re Sealed Case*, 124 F.3d 230 (D.C.Cir.1997). Judge Tatel dissented.

[14] *Swidler & Berlin v. United States*, 524 U.S. 399, 118 S.Ct. 2081, 141 L.Ed.2d 379 (1998).

[15] 524 U.S. at 400, 118 S.Ct. at 2083.

sources, override a client's posthumous interest in confidentiality."[16]

Note that if Vince Foster were alive, the prosecutor could give him immunity from prosecution, thus forcing him to testify, notwithstanding any concern that his forced testimony would adversely affect his reputation, civil liability, or the civil or criminal liability of his friends and family. Mr. Foster's death gave him the functional equivalent of immunity from prosecution. But the Supreme Court refused to accept this argument.

§ 1.6–6 CO-PLAINTIFFS OR CO-DEFENDANTS OF A CLIENT: CONFIDENTIAL DUTIES OWED TO PERSONS OTHER THAN CLIENTS OR FORMER CLIENTS

Under the law of agency, an agent of a principal (*e.g.*, the lawyer-agent for a client-principal) may not reveal information about a third party *if* the principal [*i.e.*, the client] has a fiduciary obligation to keep that information confidential. The lawyer is not an agent of the third party, but she may be a *subagent* of the client, who has a fiduciary obligation to keep information confidential.[1] The lawyer's fiduciary duty comes from the law of agency, not the law of ethics, because the Model Rules impose no

---

[16]Swidler & Berlin v. United States, 524 U.S. at 410, 118 S.Ct. at 2088.

Cf. Matter of John Doe Grand Jury Investigation, 408 Mass. 480, 562 N.E.2d 69 (1990). Prosecutors strongly suspected that Charles Stuart had been responsible for the deaths of Carol and Christopher Stuart. Charles Stuart had talked with his lawyer for two hours on the day before his death, and the prosecutor surmised that he had admitted the crime to the lawyer. If so, the state could both stop looking for a suspect for the murders and be sure not to charge someone else for them. The court held, however, that the privilege did not end with Charles' death and no amount of interest in knowing the truth could justify making the lawyer talk.

[Section 1.6–6]

[1]**Subagents.** Restatement of the Law of Agency, Second (1958), § 5, Comment *d*, at p. 24:

"A subagent performing acts which the appointing agent has authorized him to perform in accordance with an authorization from the principal is an agent of the principal . . .. Furthermore, the subagent stands in a fiduciary relation to the principal and *is subject to all the liability of an agent to the principal* except liability dependent upon the existence of a contractual relation between them." (emphasis added)(internal references omitted).

See also Restatement of the Law of Agency, Second (1958), § 428, comment *a*: "[O]ne who agrees with the agent to act for the principal in a transaction becomes a subagent, and owes to the principal *all the duties of a fiduciary* to a beneficiary." (emphasis added). The subagent acts in a dual capacity, both as agent and as principal. For an extensive discussion, see *Stortroen v. Beneficial Finance Co.*, 736 P.2d 391 (Colo.1987) (in a multiple listing real estate transaction involving residential property, selling broker or sales person, in absence of written agreement creating different agency relationship, is agent of listing broker and subagent of vendor).

Co-Agent. A subagent is differ-

special ethical duties that the lawyer owes to these third parties who are not clients, former clients, or prospective clients of the lawyer.[2]

In a typical fact pattern, a lawyer (Lawyer) represents one client (Client) who is sued, along with other co-defendants. Each of the other defendants is separately represented, and they decide to cooperate with each other because their interests are aligned. For example, the co-defendants may set up a joint defense consortium.[3] Even though Lawyer becomes privy to confidences discussed by the other members or lawyers in this consortium, it is clear that Lawyer is not representing any of these other co-defendants.

It is because of the existence of this joint defense consortium that Client (under the law of agency) assumes certain fiduciary duties to the other co-defendants. *If* Client, under the law of agency, assumes a fiduciary duty to third parties to keep certain information confidential, then Lawyer (who is the sub-agent of Client) may not reveal information about these third parties that Client has an obligation to keep confidential.[4] This duty does not come from the Model Rules but from the law of agency.[5]

Let us consider the example of the joint defense consortium further. If Lawyer, in the course of representing his client (*e.g.*,

---

ent than a co-agent. A subagent is acting in a dual capacity; he or she is an agent (of one principal) and a principal (of a different agent). In contrast, a *co-agent* situation exists when two agents both act for the same principal. J. DENNIS HYNES, AGENCY AND PARTNERSHIP (Michie Co., 4th ed. 1994). For example, a lawyer may be the agent of the client, and that client may be the agent of a third party. The lawyer would not be the agent of the third party but the client would be an agent of the third party and owe fiduciary duties to that third party. The law of agency may impose certain obligations on the lawyer, who is an agent of the client, who is an agent of a third party.

[2] ABA Formal Opinion 95-395 (July 24, 1995).

[3] *See* Amy Foote, Note, *Joint Defense Agreements in Criminal Prosecutions: Tactical and Ethical Implications*, 12 GEORGETOWN J. LEGAL ETHICS 377 (1999).

[4] Restatement of the Law Governing Lawyers, Third, (Official Draft 2000), § 132, comment *g(ii)*. *See, id.* at p. 385:

"A lawyer who learns confidential information from a person represented by another lawyer pursuant to a common-interest sharing arrangement is precluded from a later representation adverse to the former sharing person when information *actually shared* by that person with the lawyer or the lawyer's client is material and relevant to the later matter. Such a threatened use of shared information is inconsistent with the undertaking of confidentiality that is part of such an arrangement." (emphasis added) (internal references omitted).

[5] For a discussion and analysis of subagency, see *Stortroen v. Beneficial Finance Co.*, 736 P.2d 391 (Colo.1987). In this case, there was a multiple listing real estate transaction involving residential property. The court held that "in a multiple listing real estate transaction involving residential property the selling broker or salesperson, in the absence of a written agreement creating a different agency relation-

Company #1) acquires confidential information about other members of the joint defense agreement (*e.g.*, Company #2, Company #3, etc.), Rule 1.6 imposes on the lawyer a duty to his client, Company #1, to keep this information confidential. Even if this information came from other companies, it is still information "relating to the representation" and thus protected under Rule 1.6, because of the duty that the lawyer owes Company #1. Company #1 may waive its rights and consent to the lawyer using this information.

Although Rule 1.6 imposes on Lawyer a duty owed to Company #1, it imposes on this lawyer no duty to the *other* companies, who were never his clients, prospective clients, or former clients. Consequently, if Company #1 waives its rights under Rule 1.6, the ABA Ethics Committee has concluded that the *ethics rules* do not bar the lawyer from taking on a related representation that is adverse to one of the *other* companies, because doing so no longer violates any rights owed to Company #1.[6]

Although the Model Rules do not prevent the lawyer from suing Company #2 (*if* Lawyer's former client, Company #1, waives any rights it may have under Rule 1.6), the *law of agency does impose a restriction*. In the example we have been discussing, Company #1 [the client] was the agent of the co-defendants in the defense consortium, the members of which shared confidential information. The lawyer for Company #1 is therefore a subagent of this client who, in turn, was the agent of the co-defendants. Consequently, the lawyer has a fiduciary obligation to other members of this defense consortium[7]—and a court may disqualify the lawyer because of the law of agency, but *not* because of the

---

ship, is an agent of the listing broker and, as such, is within a chain of agency to the seller." Id. at 393. This agent was the subagent of the vendor. The vendor's counterproposal delivered to the subagent-selling broker for submission to the purchaser became a binding contract when the subagent-selling broker received notice of its signed acceptance by the purchasers. That court explained:

"A subagent is 'a person appointed by an agent empowered to do so, to perform functions undertaken by the agent for the principal, but for whose conduct the agent agrees with the principal to be primarily responsible.' A subagent is the agent of both the appointing agent and the principal. Notice to an agent given in the course of a transaction which is within the scope of the agency is notice to the principal. So too, notice to a subagent who is under a duty to communicate the notice to the agent is effective to the same extent as if notice had been given to the agent."

736 P.2d at 395–96 (internal citations omitted).

[6]ABA Formal Opinion 95-395 (July 24, 1995). *Accord* Restatement of the Law Governing Lawyers, Third, (Proposed Final Draft No. 1, Mar. 29, 1996), § 213, comment g(ii), ("Person about whom lawyer learned confidential information while representing former client"), at 718 to 720.

[7]Restatement of the Law of Agency, Second, §§ 5, 396, 428 (1958).

law of ethics.[8] While the ethics rules often incorporate duties from other law, such as the law of agency or the law of evidence, the Model Rules do not incorporate this particular duty.[9]

The cases do not always articulate the distinction between the fiduciary duties of a subagent and a lawyer as carefully as they might. But this difference or variation between the fiduciary duties of a subagent and a lawyer is more than theoretical. General agency law does not normally impute a restriction (or a disqualification) to other persons. Hence, if the lawyer's relationship to a particular party is not that of lawyer-client, but rather nonclient and subagent-principal, the law governing subagents would not require imputation.[10]

This subagency principle extends beyond joint defense agreements. For example, assume that Lawyer represents Hospital in several cases and, because of that representation, has access to Patient's medical records. Thus lawyer learns confidential information about Patient (*e.g.*, that Patient has an addiction to a controlled substance) even though Patient was not a party to

---

[8]ABA Formal Opinion 95-395 (July 24, 1995) & n.3.

See, e.g., Wilson P. Abraham Const. Corp. v. Armco Steel Corp., 559 F.2d 250 (5th Cir.1977) (lawyer must be disqualified because of the shared confidences in such a common defense); *Trone v. Smith*, 621 F.2d 994 (9th Cir.1980); *Kevlik v. Goldstein*, 724 F.2d 844 (1st Cir.1984) (same).

United States v. Henke, 222 F.3d 633 (9th Cir.2000), involved a joint defense agreement in which one of the participants became a government witness. Lawyers for the other defendants moved to withdraw, arguing that they were limited in their ability to cross-examine that witness because he had disclosed information they had an obligation to protect. The Ninth Circuit agreed that the situation presented a conflict requiring reversal of the convictions. The court said:

"Just as an attorney would not be allowed to proceed against his former client in a cause of action substantially related to the matters in which he previously represented that client, an attorney should also not be allowed to proceed against a co-defendant of a former client wherein the subject matter of the present controversy is substantially related to the matters in which the attorney was previously involved, and wherein confidential exchanges of information took place between the various co-defendants in preparation of a joint defense."

222 F.3d 633, 637, *quoting, Wilson P. Abraham Const. Corp. v. Armco Steel Corp.*, 559 F.2d 250, 253 (5th Cir.1977).

[9]ABA Formal Opinion 95-395 (July 24, 1995).

If the lawyer sells this information to third parties (or simply reveals it), the lawyer is still subject to Rule 1.6, which prevents the lawyer from "reveal[ing] information relating to the representation of a client" unless various exceptions apply. The information, even if secured from third parties, is still related to the client's representation. The client, however, may waive her rights. In addition, the lawyer may have duties under the law of agency. *See* Restatement of the Law of Agency, Second, §§ 5, 241, 396.

[10]Restatement of the Law Governing Lawyers, § 132, Comment *g(ii)*, ("Duties to a person about whom a lawyer learned confidential information while representing a former client"), at p. 384.

the earlier case. Now, Lawyer represents another party in a suit where Patient will be an adverse witness. It would be useful for Lawyer to be able to cross-examine Patient about his addiction and thus undermine his credibility. However, under the law of agency: "Lawyer may not reveal information about Patient that Hospital has an obligation to keep confidential."[11]

§ 1.6–6(a) Imputation to Other Lawyers in the Firm

If a lawyer is disqualified under the rules of ethics, those rules often impute that disqualification to other lawyers in the same firm.[12] However, in this case, the lawyer is disqualified under the law of agency because he is a subagent. Agency law does not normally impute disqualification. So, if the lawyer is disqualified, that disqualification would not prevent other lawyers in the same firm from engaging in the representation that was forbidden to the first lawyer.[13]

Special circumstances, however, may impute the disqualification to the entire law firm. In *National Medical Enterprises, Inc.*

---

[11]Restatement of the Law Governing Lawyers, Third, (Official Draft 2000), § 132, comment *g(ii)*, Illustration 7, at p. 384.

The relevant parties may waive their rights; for example, Patient may consent to Lawyer using the information against him (highly unlikely), or the new client may consent to Lawyer not using this information to attack the credibility of Patient on the witness stand.

Still, it will be very difficult for the new client to waive his rights without knowing the substance of the information that his lawyer cannot use against Patient. How can one knowingly waive a right without fully knowing what it is that one is asked to waive? The Restatement acknowledges this difficulty: "However if, *without violating the obligation* to Patient, Lawyer can *adequately reveal* to Plaintiff the nature of the conflict of interest and the likely effect of restricted cross examination, Lawyer may represent Plaintiff with Plaintiff's *informed* consent." Restatement of the Law Governing Lawyers, Third, (Official Draft 2000), § 132, comment *g(ii)*, at pp. 384 to 385 (emphasis added).

[12]*See* Rule 1.10, discussed below.

[13]**Subagency and Imputation.** As Restatement of the Law Governing Lawyers, Third, (Official Draft 2000), § 132, comment *g(ii)*, at 384 to 385, explains, the lawyer who is privy to the confidential information (confidential under the law of agency, not necessarily confidential under the law of ethics) should be screened from the other lawyers in the firm. Although the Model Rules do not provide for a screen (except in the special case involving government lawyers (Rule 1.11), the lawyer in this case is not being disqualified under the law of ethics. It is the law of agency that would impose a screen). *See also* Restatement of the Law of Agency, Second (1958), § 428, comment *a*. In short:

"An important difference between general agency law and the law governing lawyers is that general agency law does not normally impute a restriction to other persons. Thus, when a lawyer's relationship to a third person is not that of lawyer-client but that, for example, of subagent-principal, imputation might not be required under the law governing subagents."

Restatement of the Law Governing Lawyers, Third, (Official Draft 2000), § 132, comment *g(ii)*, at p. 384.

v. Godbey,[14] a lawyer represented a hospital administrator as a possible defendant in a criminal health care fraud investigation. The other potential co-defendants in the action had separate counsel, but a joint defense agreement was signed by all of the potential defendants and their counsel. The government brought its investigation to a close and the representation of all defendants came to a natural conclusion. A plaintiff approached the law firm that had represented the hospital administrator and sought to sue the hospital, not the individuals in a civil suit. The hospital and the former client brought a motion to disqualify the lawyer and law firm because it had entered into a joint defense agreement with the hospital. The Texas Supreme Court disqualified the lawyer and the law firm on both motions. The hospital's motion was granted because it was a party to a joint defense agreement.[15] The former client's motion was granted because of the potential risk that suing the co-defendant to the law firm may expose its former client to a reopening of the government's criminal investigation.[16] If this decision is read broadly, lawyers may owe duties to parties to a joint defense or joint plaintiff's agreement not to use confidential information against them in future litigation. A narrow reading, however, would focus on the potential criminal exposure in the case and the fact that there is no statute of limitations on reopening the government's case against the former client.

§ 1.6–7 THE LAW FIRM'S SUPERVISORY RESPONSIBILITIES OVER ITS AGENTS REGARDING ATTORNEY-CLIENT CONFIDENCES

§ 1.6–7(a) Confidences with Lawyers within the Same Firm

A client who hires a law firm often only deals with a few

---

[14]*National Medical Enterprises, Inc. v. Godbey*, 924 S.W.2d 123 (Tex. 1996).

[15]The opinion contains some broad language about the fiduciary duties owed to signatories to a joint defense agreement. "[W]e hold that an attorney's knowledge of non-client confidential information that he has promised to preserve is imputed to the other lawyers in the firm." 924 S.W.2d 132. After this decision, law firms have modified joint defense agreements in Texas to include an advanced consent to future lawsuits and use of confidential information outside of the action

that is described in the joint defense agreement.

[16]The court used a very interesting analogy: "The chances of being struck by lightening are slight, but not slight enough, given the consequences, to risk standing under a tree in a thunderstorm. Cronin [the former client] is not likely to be struck by lightening in the pending case, even though he is in the midst of a severe thunderstorm, but he is entitled to object to being forced by his former lawyer to stand under a tree while the storm rages on." 924 S.W.2d at 133.

lawyers in a firm, but the client really hires the firm to represent the client's interests. Partners and associates regularly discuss with each other the affairs of their clients and seek from each other advice regarding client matters.[1] The expectation and existence of such intrafirm communication is one of the primary reasons for the rule regarding imputation of attorney disqualifications.[2]

Consequently, unless the client otherwise directs, a lawyer may disclose to other lawyers in the firm information protected by Model Rule 1.6.[3]

§ 1.6–7(b) Nonlawyer Employees of the Law Firm

Lawyers employ nonlawyer employees to enable them to efficiently deliver legal services to clients.[4] Thus, it is reasonable for lawyers to disclose client confidences to nonlawyer employees, such as secretaries, investigators, and paralegals. These employees should treat this client information as confidentially as the lawyers treat it.[5] However, the Model Rules have no jurisdiction over these nonlawyer employees.[6] Thus, the ethics rules impose a requirement that the lawyers in the firm reasonably supervise these employees. It is part of a lawyer's professional responsibility to exercise reasonable care to prevent her employees or associates from violating the obligation regarding client confidences or secrets.[7]

A lawyer who fails in her duty of supervision violates these ethics rules even though no secrets are in fact disclosed because the ethics violation is the failure to supervise. Similarly, a lawyer who adequately supervises has fulfilled her obligation, even though the employee nonetheless improperly discloses a client secret or confidence.

The lawyer may give "limited information from his files to an outside agency" for accounting or other legitimate purposes if the lawyer exercises due care in selecting the agency.[8] However, the

---

[Section 1.6–7]

[1] Rule 1.6, Comment 5; EC 4-2.

[2] *See* Rule 1.10, Comment 2.

[3] *See* Rule 1.6, Comment 5; EC 4-2.

[4] "In the modern world of legal practice, the delegation of repetitive legal tasks to paralegals has become a necessary fixture. Such delegation has become an integral part of the struggle to keep down the costs of legal representation. Moreover, the delegation of such tasks to specialized, well-educated nonlawyers may well ensure greater accuracy in meeting deadlines than a practice of having each lawyer in a large firm calculate each filing deadline anew." *Pincay v. Andrews*, 389 F.3d 853 (9th Cir.2004) (en banc).

[5] LAURA L. MORRISON & GINA M. DeCIANI, LEGAL ETHICS FOR PARALEGALS AND THE LAW OFFICE 129–64 (West Pub. Co. 1995).

[6] *See* Rule 5.3, Comment 1.

[7] Rule 5.3; DR 4-101(D); EC 4-5.

[8] EC 4-3; Rule 5.3, Comment 1

lawyer may not transfer this information if the client chooses to forbid it.[9]

§ 1.6–8 ENTITY CLIENTS AND THE ATTORNEY–CLIENT PRIVILEGE

All clients, whether they are natural persons or entities created under the law, may claim an attorney-client privilege as to communications between them and their lawyers made in furtherance of obtaining legal services. However—as a matter of federal or state evidence law—the scope of the privilege and its exceptions may differ when an entity client is involved. It is also often more difficult to define how the privilege applies because incorporeal entities act only through their corporeal agents. The following discussion examines selected issues in the context of the attorney-client privilege as it applies to government and corporate clients.

§ 1.6–8(a) The Government as Client and the Attorney-Client Privilege

The obligations imposed by Model Rule 1.6 apply not only to lawyers in private practice, but also to attorneys for the government and lawyers for any other entity, such as a corporation, or an association.[1]

The attorney-client privilege and the duty to protect confidences exist for government lawyers because the Government has the same interests in protecting its confidentiality, securing candid

---

(referring to "independent contractors").

ABA Formal Opinion 95-393 (Apr. 24, 1995) concludes that a government lawyer may disclose to a nonlawyer supervisor information relating to representation if this disclosure helps carry out the client's representation. If it is not used for that purpose, the lawyer can disclose it only if the client expressly consents, after consultation with his lawyer. If there is no consent, the lawyer may disclose data (*e.g.*, demographic information) from the client's files only in a way that does not identify the client or compromise the confidentiality of any particular client's data or permit the data to be traced back to that client.

[9]EC 4-3. *Cf.* Rule 1.6, Comment 5.

[Section 1.6–8]

[1]1983 Model Rule 1.6, Comments 6 & 16. Note this language was deleted as not needed because the concept of confidentiality to a government client is well established.

In addition, Rule 1.11(b) protects a third party, but not the government client itself, from the use of confidential government information against it by a former government lawyer. Rule 1.9(c) protects the government itself from its former lawyer using confidential information against it. ABA Formal Opinion 97-409 (Aug. 2, 1997), at 8 to 9 n.7.

advice, and preparing for litigation.[2] The Restatement of the Law Governing Lawyers, explains that the "rationale for the [attorney-client] privilege is that confidentiality enhances the value of client-lawyer communications and hence the efficacy of legal services."[3] Later, it emphasizes that the "attorney-client privilege extends to a communication of a governmental organization" as it would to a private organization.[4] The attorney-client privilege "aids government entities and employees in obtaining legal advice founded on a complete and accurate factual picture."[5]

When the Supreme Court promulgated the Federal Rules of Evidence in 1972, it included nine specific categories of privileges, one of which is an attorney-client privilege. Proposed Federal Rule 503 defined the privilege to encompass public officers and public entities within its definition of "client."[6] Although Congress did not adopt Proposed Rule 503, courts and commentators have treated that proposed rule as a reflection and restatement of federal common law principles.[7]

Hence, Model Rule 1.6—reflecting this background—imposes on government lawyers the same obligations as private lawyers

---

[2]*E.g., Vogel v. Gruaz*, 110 U.S. 311, 4 S.Ct. 12, 28 L.Ed 158 (1884) held that a communication made to an Illinois state's attorney by a prospective was privileged. The lawyer's duty was to "commence and prosecute" all criminal prosecutions. In this case, a person asked the lawyer whether the facts communicated make out a case of larceny for a criminal prosecution. This information, the Court said, is an absolutely privileged communication, and cannot, in a suit against that person to recover damages for speaking words charging larceny, be testified to by the state's attorney, even though there is evidence of the person speaking the same words to persons other than the Government attorney. *In Re: A Witness Before the Special Grand Jury*, 288 F.3d 289, 291 (7th Cir.2002): "[B]oth parties here concede that, at least in the civil and regulatory context, the government is entitled to the same attorney-client privilege as any other client."

[3]Restatement of the Law Governing Lawyers, Third, § 68 Comment *c* (2000).

[4]Restatement of the Law Governing Lawyers, Third, § 74.

[5]Restatement, § 74, at Comment b.

[6]Proposed Fed. R. Evidence 503(a)(1), in 56 F.R.D. 183, 235 (1972). The official Commentary accompanying the proposed rule explained that the "definition of 'client' includes governmental bodies." 56 F.R.D. at 236.

[7]*E.g., In re Grand Jury Subpoena Duces Tecum*, 112 F.3d 910, 915 (8th Cir.1997), explaining that Proposed Rule 503 is " 'a useful starting place' for an examination of the federal common law of attorney-client privilege."

In *United States v. Mackey*, 405 F.Supp. 854, 858 (E.D.N.Y.1975), Judge Weinstein added: "The specific Rules on privilege promulgated by the Supreme Court are reflective of 'reason and experience.' They are the culmination of three drafts prepared by an Advisory Committee consisting of judges, practicing lawyers and academicians." *Accord* 3 JACK B. WEINSTEIN & MARGARET A. BERGER, WEINSTEIN'S FEDERAL EVIDENCE, § 503.02, at 503–10 (2d ed.1997): "[Proposed Rule 503] restates, rather than modifies, the common-law lawyer-client privilege. Thus, it has considerable utility as a guide to the federal com-

to comply with the confidentiality obligations. This Model Rule applies not only to lawyers in private practice, but also to attorneys for any entity, such as a union, a partnership, a corporation, an unincorporated entity, or a government agency.[8]

The general principle is that government lawyers have an attorney-client privilege with their client, but the client is the "government," and not a particular governmental official. The government attorney may assert the attorney-client privilege to third parties, but he or she may not validly assert it when it is the government itself that is seeking the information.[9] Thus, a government lawyer cannot refuse to divulge information relevant to a criminal investigation on the grounds that another government official confided in her, because the government lawyer represents the government, not any official in his or her personal capacity. In short, a government lawyer may not assert the government attorney-client privilege against the government.[10]

Standard rules of attorney-client privilege, corporate law, and legal ethics all conclude that lawyers for an entity represent the incorporeal entity, not any individual employee. For example, if control of the corporation changes, the corporation, speaking through new management, can require that its former attorneys disclose to it otherwise privileged information. The corporation, not the deposed CEO, controls the privilege.[11] If the CEO (or an aide to, or the spouse of, the CEO) gives incriminating or other relevant information to the general counsel of the corporation,

---

mon law."

[8]1983 Model Rule 1.6, Comments 6 & 16. The ABA eventually deleted this language as unnecessary because the concept of confidentiality to a government client is now well-established.

In addition, Rule 1.11(b) protects a third party, but not the government client itself, from the use of confidential government information against it by a former government lawyer. Rule 1.9(c) protects the government itself from its former lawyer using confidential information against it. ABA Formal Opinion 97–409 (Aug. 2, 1997), at 8–9 n.7.

[9]Ronald D. Rotunda, *Lips Unlocked: Attorney-Client Privilege and the Government Lawyer*, 20 LEGAL TIMES 21–22, 28 (June 30, 1997).

[10]Ronald D. Rotunda, *White House Counsel and the Attorney-Client Privi-*

lege, 1 PROFESSIONAL RESPONSIBILITY, LEGAL ETHICS, AND LEGAL EDUCATION NEWS 1 (Federalist Society, No. 3, 1997).

[11]The privilege does not belong to the individual agents of the corporation seeking the legal advice; instead, privilege belongs to the corporation, because the corporation is the client. *CFTC v. Weintraub*, 471 U.S. 343, 349, 105 S.Ct. 1986, 85 L.Ed.2d 372 (1985): "[W]hen control of a corporation passes to new management, the authority to assert and waive the corporation's attorney-client privilege passes as well. . . . Displaced managers may not assert the privilege over the wishes of current managers, even as to statements that the former might have made to counsel concerning matters within the scope of their corporate duties." *See also Dexia Credit Local v. Rogan*, 231 F.R.D. 268, 277 (N.D. Ill. 2004).

the general counsel cannot keep that information from the corporation. If the board of directors requires the corporation's lawyer to disclose certain information to the authorities, the lawyers must disclose it.

With respect to lawyers, the general principle is similar. Government lawyers have an attorney-client privilege with their client, which is the "government" or an agency of the government, but not a particular official. For example, the assistant U.S. Attorney represents the Department of Justice and not the U.S. Attorney in his personal capacity. The government attorney may assert the attorney-client privilege to third parties, but he or she may not validly assert it when it is the government itself that is seeking the information. For example, the government may issue a subpoena in a criminal investigation. Thus, a government lawyer cannot refuse to divulge to a grand jury information that is subpoenaed and relevant to a criminal investigation simply because another government official confided in her. The government lawyer represents the government, not any official in his or her personal capacity. In short, a government lawyer may not assert the government attorney-client privilege against the government, because the government lawyer works for the government as an incorporeal entity. The lawyer does not work for any particular public official.

The main decisions in this area are from the Eighth,[12] D.C.,[13] Seventh,[14] and Second Circuits.[15] The first two involve President Clinton, and they both come to this same conclusion. The third disagrees with the first two and adopts a *broader* view of the attorney-client privilege. The fourth decision recognizes an even *broader* view than the third decision.

In re Grand Jury Subpoena Duces Tecum,[16] from the Eighth Circuit, held that, even if a governmental attorney-client privilege exists in other contexts, "the White House may not use the privilege to withhold potentially relevant information from a

---

[12]*In re Grand Jury Subpoena Duces Tecum,* 112 F.3d 910 (8th Cir.1997), *cert. denied, sub nom. Office of President v. Office of Independent Counsel,* 521 U.S. 1105, 117 S.Ct. 2482, 138 L.Ed.2d 991 (1997), held that, even if a governmental attorney-client privilege exists in other contexts, "the White House may not use the privilege to withhold potentially relevant information from a federal grand jury." 112 F.3d at 915.

[13]*In re Lindsey,* 158 F.3d 1263 (D.C.Cir.1998), *cert. denied, sub nom.,*

Office of President v. Office of Independent Counsel, 525 U.S. 996, 119 S.Ct. 466, 142 L.Ed.2d 418 (1998).

[14]*In re Witness Before the Special Grand Jury 2000–2,* 288 F.3d 289 (7th Cir. 2002).

[15]*In re Grand Jury Investigation,* 399 F.3d 527 (2d Cir. 2005).

[16]112 F.3d 910 (8th Cir.1997), *cert. denied, sub nom., Office of President v. Office of Independent Counsel,* 521 U.S. 1105, 117 S.Ct. 2482, 138 L.Ed.2d 991 (1997).

federal grand jury."[17] This case involved ongoing investigative proceedings before a federal grand jury, which was investigating the relationship of President Clinton and his wife with a savings and loan association and land development corporation.

The Office of Independent Counsel (OIC) moved to compel production of documents subpoenaed by the grand jury. The court agreed with the OIC, holding that: (1) the appeal involved a justiciable matter and was properly before it; (2) as a matter of first impression, the White House could not invoke any form of governmental attorney-client privilege to withhold potentially relevant information from a grand jury because the White House cannot be indicted; (3) no "common interest" existed between the President's wife in her personal capacity and the White House justifying invocation of the common-interest doctrine to extend the attorney-client privilege to conversations involving the President's wife, her personal attorney, and attorneys representing the White House; (4) Hillary Rodham Clinton's reasonable belief that conversations at issue were confidential was irrelevant to the determination of the applicability of the attorney-client privilege; (5) the work product doctrine did not shield the documents generated by the White House attorneys from being produced in response to subpoena; (6) the anticipation of Congressional hearings concerning the matter under investigation did not bring these documents within protection of the work product doctrine; and (7) the denial of the attorney-client privilege and work product doctrine was retroactively applicable to the case at bar.

President Clinton and the White House based their position on the argument that Ms. Clinton was a White House official, albeit an unpaid one. If the First Lady is a government official, she is an unusual one, for she is neither elected nor appointed. She would be the only executive branch official who cannot be impeached, although the Constitution provides that "all civil Officers of the United States" are subject to impeachment.[18] It is true that she has a budget, but the former presidents have federal budgets too. The Eighth Circuit held that lawyers in the White House do not have a governmental attorney-client privilege to withhold relevant information from the Independent Counsel (who stands in the shoes of the Attorney General), in light a federal stature that requires reporting of wrongdoing.[19]

In other words, the Eighth Circuit agreed that the Government

---

[17] 112 F.3d at 915.

[18] U.S. Constitution, Article II, § 4.

[19] 28 U.S.C.A. § 535(b), provides:

"Any information, allegation, or complaint received in a department or agency of the executive branch of the Government relating to violations of

has an attorney-client privilege, citing the Restatement of the Law Governing Lawyers, but then held, in the circumstances of this case, that privilege did not apply because the government was investigating wrongdoing.

The next major decision is *In re Lindsey*.[20] In this case, the D.C. Circuit held that: Bruce Lindsey, the Deputy White House Counsel to President Clinton, could not validly assert the government attorney-client privilege to avoid responding to a grand jury, if he possessed information relating to possible criminal violations. The government attorneys may not rely on the government attorney-client privilege to shield information related to criminal misconduct from disclosure to a grand jury.

Information that the Deputy White House Counsel learned when acting as an intermediary between President Clinton and his private counsel was protected by the President's personal attorney-client privilege, the court held, but the intermediary doctrine did *not* apply to instances where the Deputy White House Counsel consulted with the President's private counsel on litigation strategy. The Deputy White House Counsel could not rely on any "common interest" doctrine nor the President's personal attorney-client privilege to withhold information about possible criminal misconduct obtained in conferring with the President and his private counsel on matters of overlapping concern to the President personally and in his official capacity.

The third major decision is *In re Witness Before the Special Grand Jury 2000–2*.[21] The case involved conversations between Roger Bickel, then-Chief Legal Counsel to Illinois Secretary of State (and later Governor) George Ryan. Ryan consulted with Bickel on both official and non-official matters when he was Secretary of State and later, when Ryan was Governor of Illinois. Meanwhile, federal prosecutors had begun investigating the Secretary of State's office for evidence of an alleged bribery scheme, and the grand jury hearing the bribery case subpoenaed Bickel. Bickel and Governor Ryan resisted the subpoena, arguing that Bickel's conversations in the Secretary of State's office were privileged, but the Seventh Circuit disagreed and ordered Bickel to testify.

The court, like the prior decisions, simply refused to use the attorney-client privilege to prevent the federal grand jury from investigating criminal wrong-doing:

The central question on this appeal is whether a state govern-

---

Title 18 involving Government officers and employees shall be expeditiously reported to the Attorney General by the head of the department or agency."

[20]158 F.3d 1263 (D.C.Cir.1998),

cert. denied, sub nom., Office of President v. Office of Independent Counsel, 525 U.S. 996, 119 S.Ct. 466, 142 L.Ed.2d 418 (1998).

[21]288 F.3d 289 (7th Cir. 2002).

ment lawyer may refuse, on the basis of the attorney-client privilege, to disclose communications with a state officeholder *when faced with a grand jury subpoena*. The district court found that in the context of a federal criminal investigation, no such government attorney-client privilege existed. We agree with this determination, and therefore affirm.[22]

The Seventh Circuit, in short, accepted the attorney-client privilege for government lawyers in the civil or regulatory context, but not in the grand jury or criminal context. "While we recognize the need for full and frank communication between government officials, we are more persuaded by the serious arguments against extending the attorney-client privilege to protect communications between government lawyers and the public officials they serve *when criminal proceedings are at issue*."[23]

Another decision in this litany of cases is *In re Grand Jury Investigation*,[24] from the Second Circuit. This court rejected the holdings of these other Circuits that government officials may not use the attorney-client privilege to protect discussions of *personal* legal problems with government lawyers from grand jury subpoenas. The case involved former Connecticut Governor John Rowland who became the target of a federal investigation into bribery charges. When a grand jury subpoenaed Rowland's former chief legal counsel, Anne George, to compel her testimony, she admitted to having numerous conversations with Rowland on the topic of bribery, but invoked the attorney-client privilege as to the content of the discussions. The District Court entered an order compelling George's testimony. In doing so, it distinguished the government attorney-client privilege in the grand jury context, stating that "unlike a private lawyer's duty of loyalty to an individual client, a government lawyer's duty" lies with both the client and the public. The Office of the Governor and Rowland appealed.

A panel of the Second Circuit rejected the Government's assertion that George's loyalty to the Governor "must yield to her loyalty to the public, to whom she owes ultimate allegiance." Citing a Connecticut statute that specifically recognizes the government attorney-client privilege in any legal proceeding, the court said that the statute highlights the fact that "the public interest is not nearly as obvious as the Government suggests." In upholding George's privilege claim, the court argued: "the traditional rationale for the privilege applies with special force in the government context," where there is a vital public interest for high state officials "to receive and act upon the best possible legal advice."

---

[22]*In re Witness Before Special Grand Jury 2000–2*, 288 F.3d 289, 290 (7th Cir. 2002).

[23]*Id.* at 293 (emphasis added).

[24]399 F.3d 527 (2d Cir. 2005).

The prior cases accepted the attorney-client privilege and work-product doctrine for government lawyers except in the case of a federal grand jury investigation of criminal activity. This case accepts the attorney-client privilege even in that circumstance. The Second Circuit did rely on a state statute, but that statute should not trump federal law, given the Supremacy Clause.

In the civil litigation context, the Second Circuit addressed the issue of first impression of whether the attorney-client privilege protects emails between a government lawyer with no policy making authority and a public official seeking to assess the legality of a policy and a consideration of alternatives.[25] The court held that such emails were privileged even if other matters are discussed within the emails. The *In re County of Erie* case involved a challenge to a county sheriff policy of subjecting those placed in detention facilities to an invasive strip search. The plaintiffs sought discovery of emails between government lawyers and public officials discussing the strip search policy. In upholding the privilege, the court held, "When a lawyer has been asked to assess compliance with a legal obligation, the lawyer's recommendation of a policy that complies (or better complies) with the legal obligation-or that advocates and promotes compliance, or oversees implementation of compliance measures-is legal advice. Public officials who craft policies that may directly implicate the legal rights or responsibilities of the public should be 'encouraged to seek out and receive fully informed legal advice' in the course of formulating such policies."[26]

§ 1.6–8(b) The Corporation as Client and the Attorney–Client Privilege

For the last fifty years, the courts and commentators have had disparate views on the definition and scope of the attorney-client evidentiary privilege for the corporate client.[27] Until the Supreme Court's decision in *Upjohn v. United States*,[28] in 1981 courts used two approaches for the corporate attorney-client privilege. Many courts adopted a control group test that limited the privilege to communications to corporate counsel from those individuals who had authority to control or participate in the corporation's legal affairs.[29] This narrow view did not protect communications made to lawyers from outside the control group even if the corporation anticipated litigation. Other courts focused on the subject matter

---

[25]*See In re County of Erie*, 473 F.3d 413 (2d Cir. 2007).

[26]*Id.* at 422.

[27]*See generally* KENNETH S. BROUN, MCCORMICK ON EVIDENCE § 87.1 (6th ed. 2006).

[28]*Upjohn v. United States*, 449 U.S. 383, 101 S.Ct. 677, 66 L.Ed.2d 584 (1981).

[29]*See City of Philadelphia v. Westinghouse Electric Corp.*, 210 F.Supp. 483 (E.D.Pa. 1962).

of the communications.[30] If the individuals made the communications for the specific purpose of securing legal advice for the corporation, the attorney-client privilege protected them.

In *Upjohn*, the Supreme Court rejected, for purposes of federal law, the control group test. Instead, it adopted a broader, more flexible approach in applying the attorney-client privilege to corporate clients.[31] The Court viewed the purpose of the privilege to protect communication from corporate agents to the entity's attorneys to obtain legal advice.[32] The opinion analyzed the corporate communications at issue in *Upjohn* and found them to fall within the privilege because they were "(1) . . . communicated for the express purposes of securing legal advice for the corporation, (2) . . . relate[d] to the specific corporate duties of the communicating employee, and (3) . . . treated as confidential within the corporation itself."[33]

---

[30]*See, e.g., Harper Row Publishers, Inc. v. Decker*, 423 F.2d 487 (7th Cir. 1970), *aff'd by an equally divided court*, 400 U.S. 348, 91 S.Ct. 479, 27 L.Ed.2d 433 (1971).

[31]449 U.S. 383, 101 S.Ct. 677, 66 L.Ed.2d 584 (1981) ("Middle-level-and indeed lower-level-employees can, by actions within the scope of their employment, embroil the corporation in serious legal difficulties, and it is only natural that these employees would have the relevant information needed by corporate counsel if he is adequately to advise the client with respect to such actual or potential difficulties."). The *Upjohn* case involved a company that learned from the auditors that certain of its divisions may have made illegal payments to foreign governments in violations of the law. The general counsel met with outside counsel and they decided to conduct an internal investigation of the possible illegal payments. The general counsel prepared a confidential questionnaire directed at the various lower level employees to learn about the extent of any illegal payments so as to create a legal response to the possible problem. After the company's self disclosure to the SEC and IRS, the IRS issued a summons seeking to compel production of the answers to the questionnaires and other information discovered in the internal investigation.

[32]449 U.S. at 392, 101 S.Ct. at 684:

"The narrow scope given the attorney-client privilege by the court below not only makes it difficult for corporate attorneys to formulate sound advice when their client is faced with a specific legal problem but also threatens to limit the valuable efforts of corporate counsel to ensure their client's compliance with the law."

[33]KENNETH S. BROUN, McCORMICK ON EVIDENCE § 87.1, at 393 (6th ed. 2006). Professor Bradley Wendel has identified up to twelve possible elements of the *Upjohn* test:

"The communications were (1) made by the Upjohn employees (2) to counsel for Upjohn (3) acting as such (4) at the direction of corporate superiors (5) in order to secure legal advice from counsel. (6) The information was not available from upper-echelon management, (7) concerned matters within the scope of the employees' corporate duties, (8) and was given by the employees with an awareness that they were being questioned for the purposes of the corporation obtaining advice. (9) The communication identified the general counsel as the author of the documents, and (10) were accompanied by a statement of policy respecting the payments and the company's willing-

Many state courts have followed the *Upjohn* definition of the privilege. However, other states have formulated their own approaches to the corporate privilege.[34]

In many jurisdictions, corporate clients may not assert the attorney-client privilege in shareholder derivative litigation because both the plaintiff shareholders and the defendant corporation are purporting to act in the interests of the entity. Thus, many jurisdictions have followed the decision in *Garner v. Wolfinbarger*,[35] which gives a qualified attorney client privilege to the corporate management, but permits the plaintiffs to pierce this privilege upon a showing of good cause. And, in some cases, courts have applied this analysis in cases outside the context of shareholder derivative litigation.[36]

Despite the existence of a corporate attorney-client privilege, several corporate and entity clients have chosen not to assert their privilege when the entity is under a criminal investigation.[37] The question to what extent this decision is truly "voluntarily" is the subject of much dispute. The origin of entity waiver of the privilege comes from the 1991 United States Sentencing Guidelines that awarded organizations charged with a crime with a lower culpability score if they cooperated with government authorities, including a full disclosure of the known facts.[38]

Subsequently, the Holder Memorandum reinforced this view. In the Holder Memorandum, then Deputy Attorney General Eric Holder provided guidelines for deciding whether to charge a corporate entity with a crime.[39] One of those guidelines specifically included whether the corporation "accepted responsibility"

---

ness to comply with the law. Finally, (11) the communications were considered highly confidential when made and (12) have been kept confidential by the company."

W. BRADLEY WENDEL, PROFESSIONAL RESPONSIBILITY: EXAMPLES AND EXPLANATIONS 158–59 (2d ed. 2007).

[34]*See, e.g., Samaritan Foundation v. Goodfarb*, 176 Ariz. 497, 862 P.2d 870 (Az. 1993); *National Tank Co., v. Brotherton*, 851 S.W.2d 193 (Tex. 1993); *State v. Ogle*, 297 Or. 84, 682 P.2d 267 (Or. 1984).

[35]430 F.2d 1093 (5th Cir. 1970), *cert. denied sub nom. Garner v. First American Life Ins. Co.*, 401 U.S. 974, 91 S.Ct. 1191, 28 L.Ed.2d 323 (1971). *See* RESTATEMENT, THE LAW GOVERNING LAWYERS, Third § 85 (ALI 2000).

[36]KENNETH S. BROUN, MCCORMICK ON EVIDENCE § 87.1, at 395 (6th ed. 2006).

[37]*See* Amon Burton & John S. Dzienkowski, *Reexamining the Role of In-House Lawyers After the Conviction of Arthur Andersen*, in ENRON: CORPORATE FIASCOS AND THEIR IMPLICATIONS 689 (Nancy B. Rapoport & Bala G. Dharan, ed. 2004) (Arthur Andersen waived its attorney-client privilege in order to cooperate with the government investigation).

[38]UNITED STATES SENTENCING GUIDELINES MANUAL ch. 8 (1991) (chapter on Sentencing of Organizations).

[39]Memorandum from the Deputy Attorney General, Eric Holder, to All

for its actions and "cooperated" with full disclosure, including a waiver of the attorney-client privilege.[40]

In 2003, when Enron and the other major corporate scandals began to come to light, then Deputy Attorney General Larry Thompson issued the Thompson Memorandum, which largely adopted the views of the Holder Memorandum with respect to waiver of the attorney-client privilege.[41] The Thompson Memorandum did encourage a closer scrutiny of corporate cooperation with the criminal investigation and a focus on whether the corporate actors were concealing any information from the government. In 2004, the United States Sentencing Guidelines were amended to further promote corporate waiver of the attorney-client privilege.[42] One additional Justice Department memorandum encouraged the districts of the department to establish written review processes to "ensure appropriate prosecutorial discretion."[43]

Many groups, including the American Bar Association criticized the Justice Department's efforts to pressure corporations to waive the attorney-client privilege and release confidential data as a prerequisite to obtaining government leniency in charging the corporation with a crime and in the sentencing process.[44]

This public criticism led to two changes. The United States Sentencing Commission modified its guidelines to return to the 1991 language that does not explicitly refer to the waiver of the

Component Heads and United States Attorneys (June 16, 1999), *available at* http://www.usdoj.gov/ criminal/ fraud/ policy/ Chargingcorps.html.

[40]Memorandum from the Deputy Attorney General, Eric Holder, to All Component Heads and United States Attorneys II.A (June 16, 1999). Note the Holder memorandum did place some limits on requests for waiver of the attorney-client privilege. "This waiver should ordinarily be limited to the factual internal investigation and any contemporaneous advice given to the corporation concerning the conduct at issue. Except in unusual circumstances, prosecutors should not seek a waiver with respect to communications and work product related to advice concerning the government's criminal investigation." *Id.* At VI.B. n.2.

[41]Memorandum from the Deputy Attorney General, Larry D. Thompson, to Heads of Department Components

and United States Attorneys (Jan. 20, 2003) *available at* http:// www.usdoj.gov/dag/cftf/ corporate_guidelines.htm.

[42]United States Sentencing Guidelines Manual § 8C2.5(g), 8C2.5 comment n.12 (2004) ("Waiver of attorney-client privilege and of work product protections is not a prerequisite to a reduction in culpability score . . . unless such waiver is necessary in order to provide timely and thorough disclosure of all pertinent information known to the organization.).

[43]Memorandum from Acting Deputy Attorney General, Robert D. McCallum, to Heads of Department Components and United States Attorneys (Oct. 21, 2005).

[44]ABA Task Force on the Attorney–Client Privilege, *Report of the American Bar Association's Task Force on the Attorney Client Privilege*, 60 BUS. LAW. 1029 (2005).

attorney-client privilege.[45] And, Deputy Attorney General Paul McNulty issued the McNulty Memorandum, which removed some of the explicit language of waiving the attorney-client privilege and refocused the government's decision to charge a corporation on cooperation rather than solely upon disclosure.[46] Furthermore, the McNulty Memorandum included specific guidelines on how and when federal prosecutors should seek to obtain waiver of the attorney-client privilege.[47] Opponents claimed that the changes insufficiently protected the importance of the attorney-client privilege.

In 2008, then-Deputy Attorney General Mark Filip issued what became known as the "Filip Guidelines." This memorandum substantially softened the pressure upon corporations to waive the attorney-client privilege. The focus of the government decision on whether to grant credit is based upon the entity's timely disclosure of information rather than the specific waiver of the privilege. The Guidelines prohibit government pressure to waive "core" attorney-client communications or work product that contains such information. Undoubtedly, corporations are still under pressure to cooperate and disclose information, but the focus of government negotiations is no longer on broad waivers of the privilege.

§ 1.6–9 THE OBLIGATION OF CONFIDENTIALITY TO MULTIPLE CLIENTS IN THE SAME MATTER

When a lawyer represents multiple clients in a common matter, it is understood that one risk the lawyer must disclose to the parties before accepting the representation involves the joint client exception to the attorney-client privilege.[1] Under the joint client exception, the privilege does not attach between joint clients. In litigation between joint clients, any one of them may ask the lawyer to testify or to produce communications from any one of the other clients. Because any one of the joint clients may waive

---

[45]UNITED STATES SENTENCING GUIDELINES MANUAL § 8C2.5 comment n.12. (2006).

[46]Memorandum from the Deputy Attorney General, Paul J. McNulty, to Heads of Department Components and United States Attorneys (Dec. 12, 2006), *available at* http:// www.usdoj.gov/dag/speech/2006/ mcnulty_memo.pdf.

[47]Memorandum from the Deputy Attorney General, Paul J. McNulty, to Heads of Department Components and United States Attorneys (Dec. 12, 2006), *available at* http://

www.usdoj.gov/dag/speech/2006/ mcnulty_memo.pdf. This Memorandum lists factors that the Government should consider before asking for a waiver of the attorney-client privilege as well as different standards of waiver for different categories of corporate confidential information.

[Section 1.6–9]

[1]Rule 1.7, Comment 30. F.A. Gosset, J., quoting this Ethics Treatise in, *White Cap Const. Supply, Inc. v. Tighton Fastener and Supply Corp.*, 2010 WL 3259355, *8 (D. Neb. 2010).

the privilege, a risk exists that in third party litigation against the joint clients, the third party may initiate settlement negotiations in civil cases or plea-bargaining in criminal cases that include a request that one of the joint clients waive the privilege.

The conflicts of interest rule also requires that a lawyer inform the parties of any confidentiality issues that may arise in a multiple client representation so that they can properly assess whether they would like only one lawyer to represent them in the common matter.[2] Essentially, the lawyer should inform the prospective clients that if they have anything to hide or to keep confidential, they should have separate representation. If such information is mentioned in front of the other parties, the other parties will learn the confidence, and then through the joint client exception to the privilege they can use it against the person revealing the confidence. If the parties seek to tell the lawyer a secret in confidence, that creates a difficult ethics problem.

In theory, a lawyer for multiple clients in a common representation owes each client an obligation of confidentiality, but the duty of loyalty owed to each client prohibits the lawyer from keeping the confidence unless special circumstances exist. The contours of this obligation were somewhat unstated in the 1983 Model Rules; but all lawyers knew these issues were present in multiple client representations.[3] The drafters of the 2002 Rules address them more explicitly in the Comments to Rule 1.7.

When a lawyer explains this to a group of prospective clients who seek to hire the lawyer in a common representation, the lawyer should "advise each client that information will be shared and that the lawyer will have to withdraw if one client decides that some matter material to the representation shall be kept from the other."[4]

Although the presumption of shared confidences should be the default rule for most multiple client representations, there will be a limited number of situations where it is reasonable for the parties to agree not to share with each other the information the lawyer will receive. Consider, for example, a situation involving trade secrets that the multiple clients would like to disclose to the lawyer but keep confidential from each other. Each of the parties, with proper consent, can keep the trade secrets confidential from each other when those parties hire one lawyer to create a joint venture.[5]

The Restatement provides more guidance on the topic of confidentiality among multiple clients in a common

<hr>

[2] Rule 1.7, Comment 30.
[3] 1983 Model Rule 2.2.
[4] Rule 1.7, Comment 31.

[5] Rule 1.7, Comment 31. Of course, such an agreement is more likely to be appropriate between so-

representation. The Restatement agrees with the position that confidential information should generally be shared, but that in special cases, the clients may agree not to share confidential information.[6] If the parties do not have any agreement on this issue, there are only a scant number of judicial decisions on this problem. If one of the clients provides confidential information to the lawyer and the client asks the lawyer not to share this with the other co-clients, this may raise issues of competence (Rule 1.1), communication (Rule 1.4), and conflicts of interest (Rule 1.7). Situations will clearly arise in which the lawyer's inability to share the information with the opposing side will require that the lawyer withdraw from the representation. The Restatement provides that "[i]n the course of withdrawal, the lawyer has discretion to warn the affected co-client that a matter seriously and adversely affecting that person's interests has come to light, which the other co-client refuses to permit the lawyer to disclose."[7]

The Restatement also warns that, even if the parties had agreed to allow the lawyer to keep information confidential, the lawyer may determine that "the uninformed co-client would not have agreed to nondisclosure had that co-client been aware of the nature of the adverse information."[8] In such a case, the lawyer must withdraw from the representation if the client who possesses the confidential information will not share it with the co-client. The area of confidentiality among multiple clients is an important one, and the Restatement provides significant guidance.[9]

In 2008, the ABA finally addressed the concept of confidential-

---

phisticated parties and when a valid business reason exists for not sharing the information.

[6]Restatement of the Law Governing Lawyers, Third, (Official Draft 2000), § 60, comment *l* (suggesting that proprietary or financial information is the type of information that clients could agree not to share).

[7]Restatement of the Law Governing Lawyers, Third, (Official Draft 2000), § 60, comment *l*.

[8]Restatement of the Law Governing Lawyers, Third, (Official Draft 2000), § 60, comment *l*.

[9]The Restatement gives 3 illustrations:

2. Lawyer has been retained by Husband and Wife to prepare wills pursuant to an arrangement under which each spouse agrees to leave most of their property to the other (compare § 130, Comment c, Illustrations 1–3). Shortly after the wills are executed, Husband (unknown to Wife) asks Lawyer to prepare an inter vivos trust for an illegitimate child whose existence Husband has kept secret from Wife for many years and about whom Husband had not previously informed Lawyer. Husband states that Wife would be distraught at learning of Husband's infidelity and of Husband's years of silence and that disclosure of the information could destroy their marriage. Husband directs Lawyer not to inform Wife. The inter vivos trust that Husband proposes to create would not materially affect Wife's own estate plan or her expected receipt of property under Husband's will, because Husband proposes to use property designated in Husband's will for a personally favored charity. In view of the lack of material effect on Wife, Lawyer may assist Husband to establish and fund

ity when a lawyer represents multiple clients in ABA Formal Opinion 08-450.[10] Although this Opinion is written in the context of an insurance company hiring one lawyer to represent an employee and an employer who are defendants in a lawsuit, this Formal Opinion tries to offer a broader articulation of how lawyers should address confidentiality issues among multiple clients. That is a problem, though, because the example it uses is an insurance situation where there is a latent coverage dispute *if* the lawyer shares all information shared with everyone. Or, the insurance hypothetical may involve a claim of bad faith denial of coverage. Those situations offer obvious and brutal conflicts of interest if the lawyer represents—or treats as a client—the insured *and* the insurer. In such cases, the lawyer may continue without informed consent; indeed, the situation probably does not allow for consent because the conflicts are so basic. The normal rule is that the lawyer represents the insured; the insurer is not the client but is merely paying the bills, as Rule 5.4(c) explicitly provides. Interestingly, Formal Opinion 08-450 never even cites Rule 5.4(c).

Essentially, ABA Formal Opinion 08-450 requires that a lawyer

---

the inter vivos trust and refrain from disclosing Husband's information to Wife.

3. Same facts as Illustration 2, except that Husband's proposed inter vivos trust would significantly deplete Husband's estate, to Wife's material detriment and in frustration of the Spouses' intended testamentary arrangements. If Husband refuses to inform Wife or to permit Lawyer to do so, Lawyer must withdraw from representing both Husband and Wife. In the light of all relevant circumstances, Lawyer may exercise discretion whether to inform Wife either that circumstances, which Lawyer has been asked not to reveal, indicate that she should revoke her recent will or to inform Wife of some or all the details of the information that Husband has recently provided so that Wife may protect her interests. Alternatively, Lawyer may inform Wife only that Lawyer is withdrawing because Husband will not permit disclosure of relevant information.

4. Lawyer represents both A and B in forming a business. Before the business is completely formed, A discloses to Lawyer that he has been convicted of defrauding business associates on two recent occasions. The circumstances of the communication from A are such that Lawyer reasonably infers

that A believes that B is unaware of that information and does not want it provided to B. Lawyer reasonably believes that B would call off the arrangement with A if B were made aware of the information. Lawyer must first attempt to persuade A either to inform B directly or to permit Lawyer to inform B of the information. Failing that, Lawyer must withdraw from representing both A and B. In doing so, Lawyer has discretion to warn B that Lawyer has learned in confidence information indicating that B is at significant risk in carrying through with the business arrangement, but that A will not permit Lawyer to disclose that information to B. On the other hand, even if the circumstances do not warrant invoking § 67, Lawyer has the further discretion to inform B of the specific nature of A's communication to B if Lawyer reasonably believes this necessary to protect B's interests in view of the immediacy and magnitude of the threat that Lawyer perceives posed to B.

Restatement of the Law Governing Lawyers, Third, (Official Draft 2000), § 60, comment *l*, illustrations 2, 3, 4.

[10]*See* ABA Formal Ethics Opinion 08-450 (Apr. 9, 2008).

protect each client's confidential information whether or not the lawyer is representing the clients together or separately. This is the default position in all representations. Thus, at the outset of a multiple client representation, the lawyer may choose to discuss several options that require the express consent of the clients. At that time, the lawyer must discuss the scope of representation of each client and the lawyer's obligations of confidentiality to each client. To the extent that the representation requires the consent of the clients to the conflict (or potential conflict) of interest, the lawyer must address the clients' expectations as to confidentiality in order for the consent to be informed. If a lawyer represents three plaintiffs or defendants in the same matter, and each plaintiff (or defendant) wants to have full Rule 1.6 confidentiality rights as against each co-client, then the lawyer cannot take that case from the beginning.

The insurance situation is not a multiple client representation. The ABA Formal Opinion assumes (without explanation) that it is. In a typical multiple client situation, the lawyer learns confidential information from one client that the other clients would like to acquire but the disclosure of that information would harm the client who disclosed the information. The ABA Opinion advises that the lawyer may not disclose such information to the other clients unless an exception to Model Rule 1.6 permits disclosure or unless the clients have made an express agreement that such information may be shared. "Whether any agreement made before the lawyer understands the facts giving rise to the conflict may satisfy 'informed consent' (which presumes appreciation of 'adequate information' about those facts) is highly doubtful."[11]

However, that does not seem to be what Rule 1.7, Comment 18 provides. It advises, quite sensibly: "When representation of multiple clients in a single matter is undertaken, the information [necessary for informed consent] must include the implications of the common representation, including possible effects on loyalty, *confidentiality, and the attorney client privilege and the advantages and risks involved.*" (emphasis added). That is the Rule, and that is what lawyers should do at the outset, for foreseeable conflicts. As for the unforeseeable? Well, we cannot see it by definition. At the point when it is on the horizon and we can see it, then we simply follow the advice of Rule 1.7, Comment 18.

Thus, ABA Formal Opinion seems to foreclose default rules on sharing of confidential information among multiple clients at the outset of the representation. That is surprising. It appears to set a high contemporaneous requirement of informed consent on

---

[11]*Id.*

specific sharing of information, and it rejects the concept of implied authorization in this setting.[12] Of course, the lawyer may share information if the circumstances meet one of the exceptions in Rule 1.6. Absent informed consent or an exception, ABA Formal Opinion 08-450 appears to prohibit a lawyer from sharing the information; the lawyer, instead, would need to withdraw from the client with whom the information may not be shared.[13]

As noted above, ABA Opinion 08-450 is written in the context of a lawyer hired by one insurance company to represent the employee and the employer in a tort action where a coverage issue or other conflict develops. It posits an employee who may inform a lawyer about facts that could bring his conduct out of the scope of his employment and thus not covered by the insurance policy or by his employer.

It is puzzling why the ABA used the insurance insured relationship as the model multiple client factual setting because the triangular relationship involving lawyers, insurance companies, and insured is a complex one with many issues ultimately resolved on a state-by-state basis. It is also puzzling why the ABA Formal Opinion, without explanation, extrapolates to a generality from this unusual circumstance. Perhaps the drafters of this ABA Formal Opinion unintentionally illustrate the problems with advisory opinions: the advice is general and may not be applicable to specific facts. That is why federal courts are limited to "cases and controversies."

When a lawyer represents multiple clients in transactional issues, the lawyer may encounter dozens of issues technically covered by Rule 1.6, where the lawyer or a client may share some level of potential adversity to one or more of the clients.[14] This ABA Formal Opinion may be read to require that the lawyer stop and obtain informed consent on every instance before the confidential information may be used or disclosed. The ABA's view seems to make much sense in the specific insurance context that was the focus of this Opinion, but it seems to be unwieldy in the transactions setting. The better approach would seem to permit lawyers to set default rules for clients at the outset of the

---

[12]This Opinion states that implied authorization can never be used when disclosure is adverse to the client. *Id.*

[13]In some situations, the lawyer will need to withdraw from all of the clients because the lawyer cannot adequately represent them in light of the information that was received during the representation.

[14]This Opinion treats client disclosures identical to information discovered during the representation by the lawyer. When a lawyer is working on a matter for multiple clients to a business venture and a third person informs the lawyer that the promoter client is under audit by the IRS, why does this information belong to the promoter client? Did the lawyer not discover it while working for the promoter and the investors?

representation. As Rule 1.7, Comment 30 advises: "With regard to the attorney-client privilege, the prevailing rule is that, as between commonly represented clients, the privilege does not attach."

§ 1.6–10 SPECIFIC PROHIBITIONS ON REVEALING OR USING CLIENT SECRETS

In general the lawyer must not reveal or use a client confidence or secret unless certain exceptions are applicable. These exceptions, found in the Model Rules, the Model Code, or other law, are discussed more fully below.

§ 1.6–10(a) Using Client Information to the Disadvantage of the Client

Both the Rules and the Code forbid using client secrets or confidences to the disadvantage of the client.[1] This prohibition applies equally to protect a former client, *if* the information has not become generally known.[2]

Note that a lawyer may violate this rule of confidentiality even if she does not disclose the information to anyone. She can violate this rule by *using* the information to the client's detriment. If the agent is allowed to use confidential information against the principal, that would tend to harm the freedom of communication that should exist between principal and agent. For example, assume that a Lawyer learned (in confidence) that Client is planning to renew the lease on the building that Client now uses. Lawyer then secretly visits Lessor and obtains the lease on Lawyer's own account but does not tell Lessor any Client information. Lawyer plans to raise the rent because she learned, in confidence, that this location is more important to Client than Lessor suspects. Lawyer has committed a disciplinable violation.[3] She has not revealed the secret information to anyone, but she has certainly *used* it.

§ 1.6–10(b) Using, But Not Revealing, Client Information Even If the Client Suffers No Detriment

Unless the client consents, the lawyer may not use a client confidence or secret for the lawyer's own advantage (or a third person's advantage). Under the Model Code, this rule is applicable whether or not the client suffers detriment.[4]

[Section 1.6–10]

[1] Rule 1.8(b); DR 4–101(B)(2).

[2] Rule 1.9(c)(1). *See* EC 4–6.

[3] *Cf.* Restatement of the Law of Agency, Second (1958), at § 395 & Illustration 1, which states that the agent "may be required to hold this lease as constructive trustee" for the principal.

[4] DR 4–101(B)(3).

This prohibition on the use of client information is an old one.[5] It also reflects basic principles of agency law. No agent, whether a lawyer or not, may use the principal's secret information to the agent's advantage even if there is no detriment to the principal and the use of the information does not require revealing it.[6] The remedy in the law of agency for this breach of trust is that the agent must turn over any profits to the principal. For example, where "a corporation has decided to operate an enterprise at a place where land values will be increased because of such operation, a corporate officer who takes advantage of his special knowledge to buy land in the vicinity is accountable for the profits he makes, *even though such purchases have no adverse effect upon the enterprise.*"[7] This rule is not applicable if the "information is a matter of general knowledge."[8] The value of this confidential or secret information belongs to the client. The lawyer may not sell it or use it to the lawyer's own advantage unless the client consents.

The Model Rules, surprisingly, have *no* section corresponding to DR 4-101(B)(3). Moreover, a Comment to Rule 1.8 seems to negate the possibility that the Rules could be interpreted to incorporate the principle of DR 4-101(B)(3).[9] This Comment states: "Use of information relating to the representation to the disadvantage of the client violates the lawyer's duty of loyalty. . . . For example, if a lawyer learns that a client intends to purchase and develop several parcels of land, the lawyer may not use that information to purchase one of the parcels in competition with the client or to recommend that another client make such a purchase. The Rule does not prohibit uses *that do not disadvantage the client.*"[10] The negative implication is that there is no ethical problem if the lawyer's purchase of the land and use of the client's "insider" information does not harm the client.

The Model Code would impose discipline on a lawyer who acquired the property under the conditions stated in this Comment to Rule 1.8, even without the condition stated in italics. Even if a jurisdiction were to adopt the Rules instead of the Code,

[5]*See* ABA Canons of Professional Ethics, Canon 11 (1908), and Canon 37 (1908), as amended. *See, e.g., Healy v. Gray*, 184 Iowa 111, 119, 168 N.W. 222, 225 (1918): "[A]n attorney will not be permitted to make use of knowledge, or information, acquired by him through his professional relations with his client, or in the conduct of his client's business to his own advantage or profit."

[6]Restatement of the Law of Agency, Second, § 388, and Comment c (1958).

[7]Restatement of the Law of Agency, Second, § 388, at Comment c. See also *Id.* at § 395, Comment e (emphasis added) (1958).

[8]Restatement of the Law of Agency, Second, § 395 (1958).

[9]Rule 1.8, Comment 5.

[10]Rule 1.8, Comment 5 (emphasis added).

a lawyer who used client information for the lawyer's advantage would have to turn over to the client any profits made, pursuant to the common law of agency. Thus, a lawyer who turns to this section of the Model Rules for a safe harbor will find (when a court, applying the law of agency, orders him to account to the client for any profits made) that this harbor is heavily mined. The lawyer may not use "on his own account" confidential information acquired from a former client.[11] However, this lawyer would not be subject to discipline under the Model Rules.

The Restatement of the Law Governing Lawyers initially followed the view of the Model Rules and did not forbid the lawyer from using confidential client information for personal enrichment as long as the client did not suffer detriment.[12] However, the final version of the Restatement rejects that view and now prohibits a lawyer's self-dealing in confidential information, regardless of the lack of risk of prejudice to the client.[13] If the lawyer does engage in such self-dealing, the client can force the lawyer to disgorge any profits. The Restatement takes no position on the question of discipline and points out that the various states disciplinary rules differ as to whether this self-dealing also constitutes a disciplinary violation.[14]

§ 1.6–11 CLIENT WAIVER

§ 1.6–11(a) Explicit Waiver

Clients may always waive their confidentiality rights. If the lawyer wants the client to consent to waive rights to confidentiality, this consent is effective only if the lawyer makes a full disclosure to the client.[1] In order for the consent to be effective,

---

[11]Restatement of the Law of Agency, Second § 395, 396(b), (c) (1958).

[12]Ronald D. Rotunda, *Proposed Restatement of the Law Governing Lawyers* (Sept. 7, 1990), *reprinted in,* 136 FEDERAL RULES DECISIONS 236, 266 to 271 (1991).

[13]Restatement of the Law Governing Lawyers, Third, § 60(2) (Official Draft 2000).

[14]Restatement of the Law Governing Lawyers, Third, § 60(2) (Official Draft 2000), at Comment *j*, at p. 467.

[Section 1.6–11]

[1]Rule 1.6(a), 1.8(b); DR 4-101(B) (3), (C)(1). *See also* Restatement of the Law Governing Lawyers, Third, § 62 (Official Draft 2000); Robert C. Hacker & Ronald D. Rotunda, *Waiver of Attorney-Client Privilege*, 2 CORP. L. REV. 250 (1979).

the lawyer must communicate to the client enough information to permit the client to appreciate the significance of the waiver.[2]

§ 1.6–11(b) Implied Waiver

The Code did not explicitly provide for implied consent, but its definition of "secret" is consistent with, and perhaps assumes, this possibility. In effect, DR 4-101(A) provides that the lawyer may reveal client information if: (1) it is not protected as an evidentiary privilege; (2) the client does not specifically request confidential treatment; (3) the information would not be embarrassing; *and* (4) the information is not likely to be detrimental.

The Rules explicitly recognize an implied consent, narrowly defined as disclosures "impliedly authorized in order to carry out the representation."[3] For example, the lawyer may disclose information in order to satisfactorily conclude a negotiation, or the lawyer in litigation may admit a fact that "cannot properly be disputed."[4]

§ 1.6–12 REVEALING CLIENT INFORMATION

§ 1.6–12(a) When Required or Permitted By Other Ethics Rules

Other provisions of the ethics rules may permit or require disclosure in certain situations. The lawyer should follow these other, more specific sections when they are applicable.[1] For example, other ethics rules, discussed elsewhere, require a lawyer to reveal client perjury.[2]

§ 1.6–12(a)(1) Disclosures to Secure Legal Advice About the Lawyer's Compliance with Ethics Rules

When a lawyer or law firm faces an ethical dilemma, may the lawyer or law firm consult with an outside lawyer who is an expert in an effort to properly comply with the Model Rules or other law? The 1983 Model Rules did not have an explicit provision authorizing such disclosure, but most lawyers believed that such disclosures were permitted under Rule 1.6. A contrary result would require lawyers to ask clients for consent to disclose information and would give clients too much control over whether expert advice could be sought to address ethics issues.

---

[2]*See* Rule 1.0(e).

[3]Rule 1.6(a). *See also* Restatement of the Law Governing Lawyers, Third, § 61 (Official Draft 2000).

[4]Rule 1.6, Comment 5.

[Section 1.6–12]

[1]Rule 1.6, Comment 20 refers to Rules 2.2, 2.3, 3.3, and 4.1. *See also*

DR 4-101(C)(2).

[2]*See* Rule 3.3(a)(4) & (b), and DR 7-102(B).

The drafters of the 2002 Model Rules addressed this issue in Rule 1.6(b)(4). This provision authorized disclosure to the extent they are necessary "to secure legal advice about the lawyer's compliance with these Rules."[3] The client does not need to be informed about the consultation or the substance of the advice given by the expert. The policy underlying the exception to confidentiality is clear: lawyers should have the right to consult with experts to help them with compliance of the rules of ethics.

§ 1.6-12(a)(2) Disclosure of Conflicts Information When Lawyers Move Between Law Firms

The conflicts of interest rules impose obligations upon lawyers who switch firms and the firms who choose to hire these migratory lawyers. The lawyer who changes firms owes duties to her former clients under Model Rule 1.9. And, the lawyer's new law firm is required to protect existing clients under Model Rules 1.7 and 1.10. In particular, the amendment in February 2009 authorizing the screening of migratory lawyers illustrates the importance of a receiving law firm to manage the conflicts that may arise when a new lawyer is brought into the firm.[4]

The circumstances of lawyers who change firms can vary significantly. Some lawyer moves are made voluntarily. Others are the result of the law firm discharging the lawyer from employment. Lawyers who migrate may be partners or associates with a varying level of involvement in the former law firm's client matters. What is clear is that law firms interested in hiring lawyers who have worked for another firm must carefully examine the actual and potential conflicts of interest that arise when the new lawyer joins the firm. Some firms may make the employment decision first and then worry about managing the conflicts of interest issues. Other firms may withhold the decision to employ pending a careful examination of the conflicts that may arise when a new lawyer joins the firm.

Under the confidentiality provisions of the Model Code and the Model Rules, it would seem that migratory lawyers could not disclose confidential client information to new firms in order to help them comply with the conflicts of interest rules.[5] The type of information that law firms would need to examine ranges from client identity to scope of the representation to confidences about strategy in publicly filed matters and in matters not within the public records.[6] Some authorities relied upon the impliedly au-

---

[3]Rule 1.6(b)(4).

[4]Rule 1.10(a).

[5]*See generally* Tremblay, *Migrating Lawyers and the Ethics of Conflicts*

Checking, 19 GEORGETOWN J. LEGAL ETHICS 489 (2006).

[6]*See* Wald, *Lawyer Mobility and Legal Ethics: Resolving the Tension*

thorized language of Rule 1.6 to permit such disclosures.[7] Others regarded confidentiality as not covering information needed to perform a conflict check.[8] Still others suggested that law firms use an outside intermediary to examine the information so as to limit its use to the conflicts analysis.[9] In light of the common practice of switching firms, law firms needed more precise guidance as to what they could do to comply with the conflicts of interest rules.

ABA Formal Opinion 09-455 examines the disclosure issues that arise when a law firm seeks to comply with conflicts of interest rules when hiring a migrating lawyer.[10] Using a "rule of reason" approach to the Model Rules, the ABA Formal Opinion authorizes disclosures of basic information to allow firms and lawyers to comply with the law of conflicts of interest. Such an approach is needed to comply with Rules 1.7, 1.9, and 1.10 as well as to allow lawyers to move from one firm to another. The Opinion warns that such disclosures should not be greater than what is reasonably necessary to identify and address the conflict. Lawyers and law firms disclosing confidential information must seek to preserve their attorney-client privilege and must avoid "otherwise prejudic[ing] a client or former client."[11] Also, such basic information should only be disclosed if a conflicts analysis is "reasonably necessary" under the circumstances. In other words, the potential move by the lawyer has moved past a preliminary stage to one involving substantive discussions. If the analysis of the conflicts problem requires detailed information, the law firm should attempt to obtain the information from other sources or obtain the consent of the affected clients. The Formal Ethics Opinion addresses the suggestion that the law firm use an intermediary to examine the confidential information apart from the firm to determine how the conflict should be resolved. "This approach should not compromise any privilege nor frustrate the reasonable expectations of a client."[12] And, the Opinion warns that such a procedure should not be used if the client has prohibited the firm from disclosing the information. But, the Opinion seems to mildly approve this approach as possibly fitting under Rule 1.6(b)(4)'s "advice of counsel" to conform to the rules of ethics.

Between Confidentiality Requirements and Contemporary Lawyers' Career Paths, 31 J. Legal Prof. 199 (2007).

[7]ABA Formal Opinion 98-411 (Aug. 30, 1998).

[8]See Boston Bar Association Ethics Comm., Opinion 2004-1 (2005).

[9]Tremblay, *Migrating Lawyers and the Ethics of Conflicts Checking*, 19 Georgetown J. Legal Ethics 489, 544-45 (2006) (describing a "middle counsel" approach).

[10]ABA Formal Opinion 09-455 (Oct. 8, 2009).

[11]ABA Formal Opinion 09-455, at 5 (Oct. 8, 2009).

[12]ABA Formal Opinion 09-455, at 5 (Oct. 8, 2009).

Lawyers and law firms seeking to comply with the conflicts of interest rules in a migratory lawyer situation must be careful in how they handle confidential client information. ABA Formal Opinion 09-455 gives some comfort, but it is not binding in the states and it contains many warnings for law firms seeking access to confidential information of a former client. When lawyers switch firms, tensions may arise that accentuate hostile behavior by the individuals involved. And, claims of breach of confidentiality can become central to the situation.

§ 1.6–12(b) When Required By Other Law or Court Order

The Model Code had an explicit provision allowing lawyers to reveal secret information when "required by law or court order."[13] The Proposed Final Draft of the 1983 Model Rules had a provision similar to the Model Code. This provision provided that the lawyer may reveal confidential, secret client information to "comply with other law."[14] Oddly enough, the ABA House of Delegates explicitly deleted this provision from the 1983 version of Rule 1.6, but language in the 1983 Comment made the same point.[15]

The drafters of the 2002 Model Rules added new section (b)(6)

---

[13]DR 4-101(C)(2). *Cf.*, DR 7-102(A)(3); DR 7-102(B)(2). *See Matter of Kerr*, 86 Wash.2d 655, 662 n. 2, 548 P.2d 297, 301 n. 2 (1976).

Technically, the language in the Code should state, when required by "*other* law" or court order. The Model Code is not law, of course, but it is a proposal that becomes law when the local court enacts it by court rule to govern lawyers. It becomes law, in the same way that the rules of civil procedure or the rules of evidence become law.

[14]Kutak Commission, proposed Model Rule 1.6(b)(4), *reprinted in*, THOMAS D. MORGAN & RONALD D. ROTUNDA, 1999 SELECTED STANDARDS ON PROFESSIONAL RESPONSIBILITY 18 n. * (Foundation Press, 1999).

[15]*See* 1983 Model Rule 1.6, Comment 21. *See also* Restatement of the Law Governing Lawyers, Third, § 63 (Official Draft 2000).

Congressional Subpoenas. Washington, D.C. Bar Ethics Committee, Opinion 288, *Compliance with Subpoena from Congressional Subcommittee to Produce Lawyer's Files Containing Client Confidences or Secrets.* (adopted Oct. 20, 1998, Issued, Feb. 16, 1999). This Opinion advises that if a Congressional subcommittee orders a lawyer to turn over client documents notwithstanding the attorney-client privilege, the lawyer may do so because the turnover is then "required by law:"

"In response to a Congressional subcommittee's subpoena for a lawyer's files pertaining to the representation of a current or former client and containing confidences or secrets that the client does not wish to disclose, the lawyer has a professional responsibility to seek to quash or limit the subpoena on all available, legitimate grounds to protect confidential documents and client secrets. If, thereafter, the Congressional subcommittee overrules these objections, orders production of the documents and threatens to hold the lawyer in contempt absent compliance with the subpoena, then, in the absence of a judicial order forbidding the production, the lawyer is permitted, but not required, by the D.C. Rules of Professional Conduct to produce the subpoenaed documents. A

that permits, but does not require, a lawyer to disclose confidential information to comply with "other law or a court order."[16] They did not intend this as a change in prior law; the drafters sought to move this into text instead of leaving it as a reference in the Comments.[17]

If the disclosure is permitted or required under federal law, such as Sarbanes Oxley, the federal law would preempt the application of a contrary state rule.[18] If disclosure is permitted or required under state law, such as a child abuse reporting statute, one would think that the state policy promoting disclosure would override a general confidentiality rule. But, given the exception under Rule 1.6(b)(6), such analysis is not needed.

If a court orders the lawyer to reveal information that the lawyer thinks is protected by the attorney-client privilege, the lawyer *may* reveal the information, or the lawyer may challenge any court order requiring his testimony. However, there is no ethical requirement that the lawyer *must* first suffer contempt before revealing client information in response to a court order. The lawyer may simply comply with the order and reveal the client confidences rather than violate the order and challenge the contempt.[19] The 1983 version of the Model Rules, unlike the Model Code, did not make it explicit that the lawyer need not challenge the judge's order, but the principle was implied. A Comment stated that the lawyer must comply with the "final orders of a court or other tribunal. . . ."[20] If the lawyer did not appeal the tribunal's order, it becomes final and, hence, must be obeyed.

The drafters of the 2002 Model Rules added new language to the Comments to address the proper response of a lawyer when a court issues an order to disclose confidential information. The lawyer should inform the client and then either obtain her

---

directive of a Congressional subcommittee accompanied by a threat of fines and imprisonment pursuant to federal criminal law satisfies the standard of 'required by law' as that phrase is used in D.C. Rule of Professional Conduct 1.6(d)(2)(A)."

[16]Rule 1.6(b)(6). This provision was originally enacted as Rule 1.6(b)(4); however, it was renumbered to reflect the amendments to Rule 1.6 in 2003.

[17]*See* Reporter's Explanation of Changes to Model Rule 1.6.

[18]*See* N.C. State Bar Opinion 2005–9 (Jan. 20, 2006) (stating that the lawyers may disclose information to the SEC under Sarbanes Oxley despite a state ethics rule that would forbid disclosure), *noted in* 22 ABA/ BNA MANUAL ON PROFESSIONAL CONDUCT, Current Reports News 105 (Mar. 8, 2006).

[19]*See* DR 4-101(C)(2), providing that the lawyer "*may* reveal" client information when "required" by court order. *Cf., e.g., Dike v. Dike*, 75 Wash.2d 1, 14–15, 448 P.2d 490, 498–499 (1968) (because it was proper for the lawyer to challenge the lower court order, the contempt order against the lawyer is vacated).

[20]Rule 1.6, Comment 20.

informed consent to comply with the disclosure or secure her authority to challenge the court's decision:

> Absent informed consent of the client to do otherwise, the lawyer should assert on behalf of the client all nonfrivolous claims that the order is not authorized by other law or that the information sought is protected against disclosure by the attorney-client privilege or other applicable law. In the event of an adverse ruling, the lawyer must consult with the client about the possibility of appeal to the extent required by Rule 1.4.[21]

If the lawyer does not appeal the decision of the court, Rule 1.6(b) says that the lawyer *may* comply, but the court order will say that the lawyer *must* comply with the court order.[22]

Lawyers may only use legal process to lawfully challenge the ruling.[23] The lawyer may make a good faith effort to determine the validity of the court's application of the law.[24] But the lawyer may not "knowingly disobey an obligation under the rules of a tribunal except for an *open refusal* based on an assertion that no valid obligation exists."[25] In short, the lawyer may challenge the court order or obey it; she does not have the choice of ignoring it.[26]

In any event, although courts will uphold valid claims of the attorney-client evidentiary privilege, they will not protect what the Model Code called client "secrets," because "secrets" are a concept in the law of ethics;[27] secrets are not protected as an evidentiary privilege.

The drafters of the 2002 Rules also addressed the lawyer who has decided to comply with a court order to disclose confidential information. The lawyer should take precaution to only disclose what the court has ordered to be disclosed and to take such measures as may be used in the particular circumstances to

---

[21]Rule 1.6, Comment 13.

[22]The ABA's removal of the "must comply" language with respect to final orders that have not been appealed does not make sense. Lawyers must comply with valid court orders to disclose information. *See* Rule 1.2; Rule 3.4(c); Rule 8.3(c).

[23]On the other hand, the lawyer should not counsel his or her client to violate the lawful processes and disobey a court order. *See, e.g.*, Restatement of the Law Governing Lawyers, Third § 94 & Comment *d* (Violation of Court Order) and the Reporter Notes (Official Draft 2000), at 8, 15, 17.

[24]Rule 1.2(d). The last clause of this section "recognizes that determin-

ing the validity or interpretation of a statute or regulation may require a course of action involving disobedience of the statute or regulation or of the interpretation placed upon it by government authorities." Rule 1.2, Comment 12.

[25]Rule 3.4(d)(emphasis added).

[26]If a court orders a lawyer to reveal information, then the lawyer must comply, even though the lawyer thinks that the court is in error. The lawyer can seek to appeal, but ultimately, the ethics rules give the lawyers no comfort if they seek to ignore court orders.

[27]Rule 1.6, Comment 5; DR 4-101(A).

protect further disclosure and use of the information.[28] In some cases, it may be possible to disclose the information in camera or

[28]Rule 1.6, Comment 14.

See also ABA Formal Opinion 10-456 (July 14, 2010), concluding that if the defendant, in a criminal case, raises a claim of ineffective counsel, the defense counsel may defend himself. However, if the prosecutor asks the defense counsel for the defendant's criminal file, the defense counsel should raise all nonfrivolous defenses to that disclosure.

Interlocutory Appeals. *Mohawk Industries, Inc. v. Carpenter,* ___ U.S. ___, 130 S.Ct. 599, 175 L.Ed.2d 458 (2009), decided the important practical question of when a party may take an interlocutory appeal of an order requiring disclosure of a communication arguably protected by the attorney-client privilege.

A former company employee sued a company claiming that it fired him for reporting to the company that it was employing illegal immigrants. After his initial report to the company, the employee claimed that company lawyers allegedly coerced him to recant his statements. When he refused, he claimed the company fired him. At the same time, in a class action filed against the company for allegedly driving down wages by hiring illegal immigrants, the plaintiffs moved for an evidentiary hearing regarding the employee's allegations. The company responded by claiming the employee had fabricated the allegations, and that it fired the employee because he attempted to have the company hire an illegal immigrant in violation of federal law. The employee moved to compel the company to produce information about his meeting with the company's attorney and its decision to fire him. The district court held that information privileged, but also held the company waived the privilege by its representations in the class action suit. It ordered the company to produce the requested information. The

Eleventh Circuit dismissed an appeal from the order because it was not an immediately reviewable collateral order, and it refused to issue a writ of mandamus.

The Supreme Court held that an order is only immediately reviewable under the collateral order doctrine if it "(1) conclusively determines the disputed question; (2) resolves an important issue completely separate from the merits of the action; and (3) is effectively unreviewable on appeal from a final judgment," citing the leading case in this area, *Cohen v. Beneficial Industrial Loan Corp.*, 337 U.S. 541, 69 S.Ct. 1221, 93 L.Ed. 1528 (1949). This test focuses on the entire class of claims, and not the individualized order in a particular case. Under the test, the company failed the third prong because orders that are adverse to the attorney-client privilege can be reviewed following a final judgment. On appeal, a court could find an order regarding the privilege erroneous, vacate the judgment, and remand for a new trial that excludes the "privileged material and its fruits" of the improperly admitted evidence.

The Court asserted that the risk that a trial court may order disclosure likely will not reduce the incentives for lawyers and clients to communicate fully under the anticipated benefit of a broad attorney-client privilege. A litigant facing an injurious or novel privilege ruling may seek certification of the order for interlocutory appeal, seek a writ of mandamus, or refuse to comply, thereby allowing the trial court to impose sanctions or hold the party in contempt so as to permit postjudgment review of the order. Even if the damage done to some litigants was "only imperfectly reparable" upon review of a final judgment, the Court concluded that it is inappropriate to make disclosure orders immediately appealable as of right.

under a protective order. If this is possible, the lawyer should attempt to narrow the disclosure requested by the court.

§ 1.6–12(b)(1) "Or Other Tribunal"

Note that Comment 13 to Rule 1.6 makes clear that the lawyer may comply with an order of a court "or other tribunal."[29] An arbitrator in a private arbitration is a "tribunal" for purposes of the Model Rules.[30]

Treating an "arbitration" as a "tribunal" fits within the purpose of the ethics rules. As one court pointed out:

> An arbitrator . . . has the power to issue subpoenas, compel the production of relevant documentary evidence, administer oaths and affirmations, determine the law and facts of the case, and generally exercise the powers of a court in the management and conduct of the hearing.

> Moreover, in an effort to offset rising litigation costs and overcrowded dockets, arbitration has become an integral part of the New Jersey judicial system. Less formal and less costly than litigation, arbitration is now mandated in certain automobile negligence and personal injury actions. The effectiveness of arbitration as an alternative to formal litigation clearly would be undermined if counsel did not deal candidly with arbitrators.[31]

§ 1.6–12(c) Revealing Information to Collect a Fee

The lawyer may reveal client confidences or secrets if necessary in order to establish or collect the lawyer's fee.[32] The purpose of this exception is to prevent the client, who is the "beneficiary of a fiduciary relationship," from exploiting that relationship to the detriment of the lawyer-fiduciary.[33]

For example, the client ought not be excused from a contractual obligation to pay a fee solely because the lawyer could not prove (unless he revealed a client confidence or secret) that services were in fact performed.[34] The lawyer in this case would be revealing confidences in order to establish that it was appropriate to perform the work for the client and that the work was, in fact, done.

---

[29] Rule 1.6, Comment 13.

[30] Rule 1.0(m) (definition of a tribunal).

See also In the Matter of Forrest, 158 N.J. 428, 730 A.2d 340 (1999) (per curiam), holding that a lawyer violated the disciplinary rule requiring disclosure of material facts to a tribunal, when the lawyer withheld the fact of the client's death from the arbitrator in a personal injury action. The court cited Rule 3.3(a)(5). For misconduct, including the failure to disclose a material fact to the tribunal, the court imposed a six-month suspension from the practice of law.

[31] *In the Matter of Forrest*, 158 N.J. 428, 435, 730 A.2d 340, 344 (1999) (per curiam) (internal citations omitted).

[32] Rule 1.6(b)(5); DR 4-101(C)(4). *See also* Restatement of the Law Governing Lawyers, Third, § 65 (Official Draft 2000).

[33] Rule 1.6, Comment 11.

[34] *See Cannon v. United States Acoustics Corp.*, 532 F.2d 1118, 1120 (7th Cir.1976) (per curiam).

Similarly, the lawyer may use client confidences to secure or collect the fee. In *Nakasian v. Incontrade, Inc.*[35] the lawyer secured an attachment on the client's property. He only knew about the existence and location of this property—secret bank account—because of what his client had earlier told him in confidence. It was proper for the lawyer to use this client confidence in order to collect his fee.[36]

This right to use confidences or secrets does not create a right to blackmail the client. The lawyer may not state to the client: "Pay the fee or I will reveal to your employer your income tax problems." The lawyer may only exercise the right to reveal client information to the extent that it is reasonably *necessary* to establish or collect the fee. There must not be any extortion or unnecessary disclosure.[37]

§ 1.6–12(d) Responding to Allegations of Wrongful Conduct

It is well established that a lawyer is justified in disclosing client information if necessary to respond to a client's accusation of wrongful conduct.[38] Originally, the ABA ethics rules limited this exception to the case where the "lawyer is accused *by his client*. . . ."[39] When the ABA adopted the Model Code of Professional Responsibility in 1969, it had no such limitation. The Model Code allows the lawyer to reveal client information "if nec-

---

[35]*Nakasian v. Incontrade, Inc.*, 409 F.Supp. 1220, 1224 (S.D.N.Y.1976) (lawyer, in effort to collect fee, may use client confidences to procure attachment order against client property).

[36]*Accord* ABA Formal Opinion 250 (June 26, 1943).

[37]*See* Rule 1.6, Comment 10.

In re Disciplinary Proceeding Against Boelter, 139 Wash.2d 81, 985 P.2d 328 (1999), suspended a lawyer for six months because of his threats to reveal confidential client information in order to collect a fee. The lawyer had told the client:

"You should understand that if we are forced to file suit, you forgo the attorney-client privilege and I would be forced to reveal that you lied on your statements to the IRS and to the bank as to your financial condition. This would entail disclosure of the tapes of our conversations about your hidden assets. There is a federal statute 18 U.S.C. § 1001 which provides for up to one year in jail for such

perjury. The choice is yours."

139 Wash.2d at 85, 985 P.2d at 331. The court said that Boelter later admitted that "his implication that Withey had violated 18 U.S.C. § 1001 was not researched. He characterized the letter, however, as being the product of *concern* for Withey, and not any desire to scare him into making payment." 139 Wash.2d at 92, 985 P.2d at 335. (emphasis in original). The court agreed that fair warning about the firm's limited ability to disclose confidential information is permissible, but the "tape" was a fabrication and the fees claimed were excessive. The court upheld the lawyer's six-month suspension.

[38]*See* ABA Formal Opinion 202 (May 25, 1940), relying on Canons of Professional Ethics, Canon 37 (ABA, 1908, as amended).

[39]ABA Canons of Professional Ethics, Canon 37(emphasis added) (ABA, 1908, as amended).

essary" to respond to anyone's "accusation of wrongful conduct," though the lawyer should disclose only that which is "necessary" to establish a defense to the charge.[40] It is not necessary that the accuser brings any formal proceedings or actually files any lawsuit against the lawyer.[41]

Originally the drafters of the 1983 Model Rules proposed to limit this right of disclosure to cases where the client and the lawyer were involved in a lawsuit or where the lawyer had to use the client information to establish a defense to a civil or criminal claim based on conduct in which the client was involved. However, the Rules now agree with the Code in this regard, though the wording is different.[42]

Although Rule 1.6 uses words such as "criminal charge," "civil claim," or "allegations in any proceeding,"[43] it is not necessary that the accuser initiate any formal proceedings before the lawyer may reveal client information. Indeed, the accuser may be someone other than the client. The Comment is quite clear on this point: "The lawyer's right to respond [to allegations of wrongful conduct] arises when an assertion of such complicity has been made. Paragraph (b)(5) *does not require the lawyer to await the commencement of an action* or a proceeding so that the defense may be established by responding *directly to a third party* who had made such an assertion."[44]

Under the 1983 Model Rules, a Comment stated that if it does not prejudice the lawyer's ability to establish a defense and if it is practicable to do so, "the lawyer should advise the client of the third party's assertion and request that the client respond appropriately."[45] However, the client cannot prevent the lawyer from establishing the lawyer's innocence. The drafters of the 2002 Rules deleted this language, but they stated that no change in law was intended. Instead, they point to the Comment that says where practicable the lawyer should give the client a chance to remove the need for the lawyer's disclosure.[46] This Comment is not as explicit as the one under the 1983 Rules, but it would be prudent practice for a lawyer to inform the client that the lawyer plans to make a disclosure of confidential client information in order to defend himself.

For example, assume that a newspaper editorial accuses

---

[40]DR 4-101(C)(4).

[41]*See, e.g., Meyerhofer v. Empire Fire & Marine Ins. Co.*, 497 F.2d 1190, 1194–95 (2d Cir.1974), *cert. denied*, 419 U.S. 998, 95 S.Ct. 314, 42 L.Ed.2d 272 (1974).

[42]*See* Rule 1.6(b)(5).

[43]Rule 1.6(b)(5).

[44]Rule 1.6, Comment 10 (emphasis added). *See also* Restatement of the Law Governing Lawyers, Third, § 64 (Official Draft 2000).

[45]1983 Model Rule 1.6, Comment 17.

[46]*See* Reporter's Explanation of Changes to Model Rule 1.6.

Lawyer of having won an acquittal in an important criminal case years ago by suborning her client's perjury. Lawyer responds by writing a letter to the newspaper revealing that her client had intentionally kept Lawyer in the dark about the perjury and that Lawyer never learned of it until years after the acquittal, when the client confessed to Lawyer on his deathbed. Assume further that the client, at that time, also told Lawyer never to reveal the perjury; then Client died. Lawyer also states that an associate in her office who was present during the conversation in question confirms her version. Under both the Code and the Rules, Lawyer's disclosures are not disciplinable in these circumstances.

In summary, the Model Rules make clear that, first, the lawyer need not wait until a proceeding has been brought challenging the lawyer's conduct. Second, the client need not be the person making the charge. And, third, the lawyer can respond directly to a third person making the charge. Similarly, the case law[47] and commentators[48] agree with the Model Rules in allowing a lawyer to disclose what otherwise would be client secrets in order for the lawyer to make a preemptive defense on his own behalf.

Granted, some commentators criticize this important exception in the Model Rules on the grounds that lawyers placed it in there for self-serving reasons: to protect themselves. My reaction is like the police commissioner in Rick's Bar: "I am shocked, shocked, to find gambling going on in Casablanca." We should also realize that this rule makes lawyers more willing to take cases because it does not allow the client to use the ethics rules to make it more difficult for lawyers to prove that they are entitled to collect lawfully earned fees.

---

[47]See, e.g., In re National Mortgage Equity Corp. Litigation, 120 F.R.D. 687 (C.D.Cal.1988); In re Friend, 411 F.Supp. 776 (S.D.N.Y.1975).

[48]See, e.g., ABA, ANNOTATED MODEL RULES, (ABA, 5th ed., 2003), at 98, pointing out that the charges regarding the lawyer's conduct can be brought by a third person, and "the lawyer need not await commencement of an action or proceeding before responding in self-defense."

1 GEOFFREY C. HAZARD & W. WILLIAM HODES, THE LAW OF LAWYERING (2nd ed. 1998), § 1.6:306, at p. 176.2: "If even an innocent lawyer must wait until criminal or civil charges are actually filed, he may suffer severe and unwarranted loss of reputation, not to mention time and money, before achieving vindication . . . .. For these reasons, the Comment to Rule 1.6 opts for a reading that clearly goes beyond traditional and purely passive self-defense." [footnote omitted].

CHARLES W. WOLFRAM, MODERN LEGAL ETHICS 309 (West, 1986): "A lawyer can disclose confidential information to defend against charges of improper lawyer conduct made by third parties."

§ 1.6–12(e) When the Client Intends to Commit a Future Crime

§ 1.6–12(e)(1) Introduction

A basic principle of agency law is that the agent is under no duty to keep secret any information that the principal is about to commit a crime:

> An agent is privileged to reveal information confidentially acquired by him in the course of his agency in the protection of a superior interest of himself or a third person. Thus, if the confidential information is to the effect that the principal is committing or about to commit a crime, the agent is under no duty not to reveal it.
>
> However, an attorney employed to represent a client in a criminal proceeding has no duty to reveal that the client has confessed his guilt.[49]

The Code codified this common law rule (and the distinction it draws between confessions of past crimes and intentions to commit future ones). Thus the Code provided that the lawyer "may reveal" the client's intention "to commit a crime" as well as the information necessary to prevent it.[50]

The Code did not distinguish between types of crimes—violation of a trivial offense versus premeditated murder—nor did the rule offer any guidelines to cabin the lawyer's exercise of discretion. We were only told that the attorney "may" reveal this information. However, a pre-Code ABA Formal Opinion, in considering the Canons of Professional Ethics, stated that if "the facts in the attorney's possession indicate beyond reasonable doubt that a crime will be committed," then disclosure of confidences is required.[51] The Code quoted this portion of the Formal Opinion in the footnotes,[52] and, consequently, this Disciplinary Rule may be interpreted to adopt the test of the Formal Opinion. Thus, DR 4-103(C)(3) appears to permit a lawyer to reveal the client's intention to commit a crime and probably requires such disclosure if the lawyer knows, beyond a reasonable doubt, that the client will commit the crime.[53]

An early version of the 1983 Model Rules made some effort to draw useful distinctions not present in the Code. First, this early draft *required* the lawyer to reveal client information if "necessary to prevent the client from committing an act that would

---

[49]Restatement of the Law of Agency, Second, § 395, Comment *f* (1958).

[50]DR 4-101(C)(3).

[51]ABA Formal Opinion 314 (Apr. 27, 1965).

[52]DR 4-101(C)(3) n.16.

[53]Ronald D. Rotunda, *Book Review of Freedman's "Lawyers' Ethics in An Adversary System,"* 89 HARVARD L. REV. 62 (1976); Ronald D. Rotunda, *When the Client Lies: Unhelpful Guidelines from the ABA*, 1 CORPORATION L. REV. 34 (1978).

result in death or serious bodily harm to another person. . . ."[54] This mandatory disclosure proposal reflected already existing tort law.[55]

The next draft of the proposed 1983 Rules eliminated this mandatory disclosure proposal, but allowed disclosure in order "to prevent the client from committing a criminal or fraudulent act that the lawyer believes is likely to result in death or substantial bodily harm, or substantial injury to the financial interests or property of another;" or "to rectify the consequences of a client's criminal or fraudulent act in the commission of which the lawyer's services had been used."[56] This draft drew some interesting distinctions involving, first, crimes or frauds causing serious harm and, second, circumstances where the lawyer learns that his services had unwittingly been used (actually, misused) by the client.

The final version of the 1983 Model Rules was significantly more protective of client information than either its predecessors or the Code. Essentially, it permitted a lawyer to disclose information necessary to prevent a client from committing a crime involving imminent death or substantial bodily harm. Lawyers were not given any discretion to disclose confidential information to prevent financial crimes or frauds by a client.

The drafters of the 2002 Rules sought to both expand the basis for disclosure when bodily harm is involved and to provide discretion for lawyers who wanted permissive disclosure to prevent financial crimes or frauds. The ABA House of Delegates rejected this change to Rule 1.6 relating to prevention of financial crimes or frauds. In 2003, the ABA adopted an amendment to Rule 1.6 that was very similar to the Rule rejected one year earlier.

§ 1.6–12(e)(2) Preventing Death or Substantial Bodily Harm

The 1983 Version of Rule 1.6. When the ABA House of Delegates approved Rule 1.6 in 1983, it contained no mandatory rule requiring disclosure. With respect to the fraud or crime issue, it only permitted disclosure to prevent the client "from com-

---

[54]Draft Model Rule 1.7(b) (ABA Discussion Draft, Jan. 30, 1980).

[55]*See, e.g., Tarasoff v. Regents of the University of California,* 17 Cal.3d 425, 131 Cal.Rptr. 14, 551 P.2d 334 (1976) (when psychotherapist knew of his patient's planned murder, the psychotherapist was liable in tort when he did not take steps reasonably necessary under the circumstances, such as notifying the police or the victim).

[56]Proposed Final Draft of Model Rules, Rule 1.6(b)(2), (3) (May 30, 1981), reprinted in Thomas D. Morgan & Ronald D. Rotunda, 1980 Selected Standards Supplement 113 (Foundation Press, 1980).

mitting a criminal act that the lawyer believes is likely to result in *imminent death or substantial bodily* harm."[57]

This requirement that the bodily harm be "substantial" means that harm must be serious, involving life-threatening injuries or illnesses, "and the consequences of events such as imprisonment for a substantial period and child sexual abuse. It also includes a client's threat of suicide,"[58] if suicide is a crime under the law of the jurisdiction.

The requirement in the 1983 Rule that the death be "imminent" suggested that the death must come within a short amount of time. Most jurisdictions did not follow the lead of the ABA on this issue and they gave the lawyer more discretion to reveal client confidences.[59] The Restatement of the Law Governing Lawyers also recommended a different test, concluding that the lawyer may use or disclose confidential client information if the lawyer reasonably believes that disclosure is necessary to prevent "*reasonably certain* death or serious bodily harm."[60] Assume, for example, that a client's environmental law violation—the release of toxic substances into the city's water supply—may cause death to the elderly in the city. In this situation, the death would be "reasonably certain" but not "imminent." The Restatement would authorize disclosure.[61]

The Restatement and Preventing Death or Substantial Bodily Harm. The Restatement authorizes the lawyer to reveal client confidences "to prevent reasonably certain death or serious bodily harm," even when the lawyer learns of the information

---

[57] 1983 Model Rule 1.6(b)(1) (emphasis added).

[58] Restatement of the Law Governing Lawyers, Third, § 66 (Official Draft 2000), at Comment *c*, pp. 498 to 499.

[59] Restatement of the Law Governing Lawyers, Third, § 66 (Official Draft 2000), Reporter's Note to Comment *c*, at p. 147. THOMAS D. MORGAN & RONALD D. ROTUNDA, 2002 SELECTED STANDARDS ON PROFESSIONAL RESPONSIBILITY (Foundation Press, 2002), following the ABA Model Rules, at appendix A, *Ethics Rules on Client Confidences*.

E.g., State v. Hansen, 122 Wash.2d 712, 721, 862 P.2d 117, 122 (1993). "We hold that attorneys, as officers of the court, have a duty to warn of true threats to harm members of the judiciary communicated to them by

clients or by third parties." In this case, the defendant made a threat against a judge during the defendant's conversation with an attorney whom he was attempting to retain. The threat was not protected by attorney-client privilege.

[60] Restatement of the Law Governing Lawyers, Third, § 61(1) (Official Draft 2000).

[61] Restatement of the Law Governing Lawyers, Third, § 66 (Official Draft 2000), Comment *c* & Illustration 3. The Restatement's illustration postulates that the death or serious bodily harm will occur "within a short period," that the client refuses to take corrective action, and a warning to the city will permit the authorities to remove or lessen the threat.

because of a non-criminal act of the client.[62] In this circumstance, the client's action is neither a crime nor a fraud. No state explicitly allows this exception,[63] but the Restatement reasonably concludes that because of the importance of human life no state would discipline a lawyer who acted in such a situation.

The Restatement also does not require that the death be "imminent." Instead, the lawyer *may* disclose if disclosure is "to prevent *reasonably certain* death *or* serious bodily harm."[64]

For example, assume a case where the plaintiff is suing the defendant for personal injuries arising out of an alleged tort. The defense lawyer has the plaintiff examined by a medical doctor who advises the defense lawyer that the plaintiff has a life-threatening and undiagnosed aortal aneurism, which can be repaired through surgery if the plaintiff were to know about it. The defendant might not permit the defense lawyer to reveal that information because of the risk that plaintiff may claim additional damages after the corrective surgery. Nonetheless, the defense lawyer *may* warn the plaintiff.[65]

---

[62]Restatement of the Law Governing Lawyers, Third, § 66 (Official Draft 2000), Comment b.

[63]Restatement of the Law Governing Lawyers, Third, § 66 (Official Draft 2000), Reporter's Note to Comment b, at p. 502.

[64]Restatement of the Law Governing Lawyers, Third, § 66 (Official Draft 2000), Comment b (emphasis added).

[65]Restatement of the Law Governing Lawyers, Third, § 66 (Official Draft 2000), Comment b, Illustration 1, which is based on *Spaulding v. Zimmerman*, 263 Minn. 346, 116 N.W.2d 704 (1962).

In *Spaulding v. Zimmerman*, 263 Minn. 346, 116 N.W.2d 704 (1962), the court set aside a prior order approving a tort settlement for a minor because the lawyer for the defendant did not disclose what he knew about the seriousness of the plaintiff's injury. At the time the court approved settlement on behalf of the minor for injuries sustained, neither the court, nor the minor nor his counsel nor his medical attendants were aware that the minor was suffering from an aorta aneurysm that might have resulted from the accident. However, the defen-dants and their counsel were aware that such situation existed and they did not disclose it to the court, even though this aneurysm was life-threatening: "The seriousness of this disability is indicated by Dr. Hannah's report indicating the imminent danger of death therefrom." 263 Minn. 346, 353, 116 N.W.2d 704, 710. The appellate court ruled that the lower court had not abused its discretion in setting aside such settlement, even though "no canon of ethics or legal obligation may have required them to inform plaintiff or his counsel with respect thereto, or to advise the court therein" of the aneurysm. 263 Minn. 346, 353–54, 116 N.W.2d 704, 710.

Note, in this case, that there was no evidence that the lawyer even tried to persuade the client to allow disclosure. The *Spaulding case* has generated substantial academic criticism. *See* Roger C. Cramton & Lori P. Knowles, *Professional Secrecy and Its Exceptions: Spaulding v. Zimmerman Revisited*, 83 MINN. L. REV. 63 (1998); Shelly Stucky Watson, *Keeping Secrets that Harm Others: Medical Standards Illuminate Lawyer's Dilemma*, 71 NEB. L. REV. 1123 (1992); Marc L. Sands, *The Attorney's Affirmative Duty to*

Rule 1.6 after the 2002 Revisions. The drafters of the 2002 Rules made several significant changes to the section permitting disclosure to prevent death or bodily harm. First, they deleted the language relating to a client "crime." Now, the lawyer may disclose information that she otherwise would have to keep secret under Rule 1.6 if necessary "to prevent reasonably certain death or substantial bodily harm."[66] By removing the need to have a client crime, a client suicide will always fit within the rule, even if the state does not treat suicide as a crime.

In addition, it is no longer necessary that the death be "imminent." The Rules follow the Restatement and only require that the death be "reasonably certain" or that there be "substantial bodily harm." The drafters removed the word "imminent" that had modified "death" or "bodily harm." There is no reason why a lingering but reasonably certain death should trigger a different disclosure power. Moreover, crimes, such as environmental crimes, involve future harm that is likely to result after the passage of time.[67] Hence, after the 2002 amendment, permissive disclosure applies to a larger category of cases involving reasonably certain death or substantial bodily harm.

In the example discussed in footnote 54 of this section involving the aneurysm,[68] the former Rule 1.6 did not allow permissive disclosure because the client had not engaged in a crime. Under the 2002 version of Rule 1.6, the lawyer may disclose the information necessary to prevent reasonably certain death or bodily harm.

Warn Foreseeable Victims of a Client's Intended Violent Assault, 21 TORT & INS. L.J. 355 (1986); Davalene Cooper, *The Ethical Rules Lack Ethics: Tort Liability When a Lawyer Fails to Warn a Third Party of a Client's Threat to Cause Serious Physical Harm or Death*, 36 IDAHO L. REV. 479 (2000).

At the time the court decided *Spaulding*, the medical ethical guidelines were not as clear as they are today. A current Opinion of the Council on Ethical and Judicial Affairs of the American Medical Association states that a limited patient-physician relationship exists when the doctor is an examining physician for purposes of an expert opinion. *See* AMA, E-10.03. This relationship requires that the doctor inform the patient about "important health information or abnormalities that he or she discovers dur-

ing the course of the examination." In line with this view, *Stanley v. McCarver*, 208 Ariz. 219, 92 P.3d 849 (2004), held that a physician hired to be an expert owed a duty of disclosure to the threatened person. The Arizona Supreme Court held that: (1) as a matter of first impression, a radiologist owed a duty of reasonable care to the person, even in the absence of an doctor-patient relationship, and (2) whether the duty requires the doctor to report directly to patient was a question was fact.

[66]Rule 1.6(b)(1).

[67]Rule 1.6, Comment 6 (providing example of dumping of toxic waste into a drinking system).

[68]*Spaulding v. Zimmerman*, 263 Minn. 346, 116 N.W.2d 704 (1962).

§ 1.6–12(e)(3) Preventing Crimes and Frauds Involving Substantial Financial Injury

Before 2003, the ABA had several opportunities to adopt a provision that gave lawyers discretion to disclose confidential information to prevent financial crimes or frauds. In 1983, the Kutak Commission had proposed such a rule to the House of Delegates. In 1991, the ABA House of Delegates had another opportunity to adopt permissive disclosure for financial crimes and frauds. But the House declined the opportunity both times.

The drafters of the 2002 Rules gave the House a third opportunity. They proposed a new section of Rule 1.6 to allow lawyers to disclose confidential information necessary to prevent financial crimes or frauds. Again, the ABA rejected the proposal. The ABA sought to maintain the lawyer's obligation of confidentiality as a core value of lawyering. Apart from the ability to disclose to prevent bodily harm or death to a person, the ABA did not want to create a spectrum of possible disclosures.

They were also concerned that "may disclose" would become "must disclose" when lawyers factored in tort liability exposure under a new Rule. In other words, if a lawyer *may* disclose, but chooses not to disclose, and a disgruntled investor sued the lawyer for failure to disclose, the lawyer may not be able to rely on her ethical obligation not to disclose because it would have permitted disclosure. Hence, for tort purposes, "may" might become "must."[69]

The fourth time was the charm. In March 2002, the president of the ABA formed a Task Force on Corporate Responsibility to "examine systemic issues relating to corporate responsibility arising out of the unexpected and traumatic bankruptcy of Enron and other Enron-like situations which have shaken confidence in the effectiveness of the governance and disclosure systems applicable to public companies."[70] The Task Force held public hearings and in March 2003 issued a final report with specific recommendations to the ABA House of Delegates.[71] The Task Force proposed an amendment to Rule 1.6 to permit a lawyer to disclose information to prevent a crime or fraud likely to result in substantial injury to a third person. The ABA adopted this amendment to the 2002 Rules in August 2003.

---

[69]*See e.g., State v. Hansen*, 122 Wash.2d 712, 721, 862 P.2d 117, 122 (1993), a criminal prosecution: "We hold that attorneys, as officers of the court, *have a duty to warn of true threats* to harm members of the judiciary communicated to them by clients or by third parties." (emphasis added).

[70]*See* American Bar Association, Report of the American Bar Association Task Force on Corporate Responsibility 2 (2003).

[71]American Bar Association, Report of the American Bar Association Task Force on Corporate Responsibility 2 to 3 (2003).

The new Rule 1.6(b)(2) was drafted in response to the Enron bankruptcy and related scandals,[72] as well as pressure from the Securities and Exchange Commission.[73] It provides that a lawyer may disclose confidential client information "to prevent the client from committing a crime or fraud . . . reasonably certain to result in substantial injury to the financial interests or property of another and in furtherance of which the client has used or is using the lawyer's services."[74]

The ABA limited disclosure to financial crimes or frauds involving substantial injury.[75] It also limited permissive disclosure to situations in which the client used the lawyer's services as part

---

[72]*E.g. In re Enron Corp. Securities, Derivative & ERISA Litigation*, 235 F.Supp.2d 549 (S.D.Tex. 2002); *SEC v. WorldCom, Inc.*, Litigation Release No. 17866, 2002 WL 31662699 (Nov. 26, 2002); *SEC v. HealthSouth Corp. & Richard M. Scrushy*, 2003 WL 31393469, Litigation Release No. 18044 (Mar. 20, 2003).

   Fred C. Zacharias, *Lawyers as* Gatekeepers, 41 San Diego L. Rev. 1387 (2004); John C. Coffee, Jr., *Understanding Enron: "It's About the Gatekeepers, Stupid,"* 57 Bus. Lawyer 1403 (2002); Roger C. Cramton, *Enron and the Corporate Lawyer: A Primer on Legal and Ethical Issues*, 58 Bus. Lawyer 143 (2002); Lisa H. Nicholson, *A Hobson's Choice for Securities Lawyers in the Post-Enron Environment: Striking a Balance Between the Obligation of Client Loyalty and Market Gatekeeper*, 16 Georgetown J. Legal Ethics 91 (2002).

[73]ABA, Report of the American Bar Association Task Force on Corporate Responsibility 7-8 (2003) (footnotes omitted):

   "In response to concern that existing rules of professional conduct did not sufficiently direct the lawyer for the corporation to report illegal conduct to the corporation's board of directors, Congress adopted Section 307 of the Sarbanes-Oxley Act of 2002, requiring the SEC to promulgate rules of professional conduct for lawyers 'appearing and practicing' before the SEC. In specified circumstances, those rules will require lawyers to report to the highest levels of corporate authority material violations of the securities

laws and other failures of legal compliance. The SEC adopted these rules (the 'Part 205 Rules') on January 29, 2003, and has proposed additional rules of conduct that in some circumstances would require a lawyer to withdraw as counsel and to have that withdrawal reported outside the company by the lawyer or, alternatively, by the company. In describing these proposed rules, the SEC noted with approval this Task Force's Preliminary Report, and its Chairman at the same time indicated that further rulemaking would be influenced by action taken by the ABA."

[74]Rule 1.6(b)(2).

[75]**Sarbanes-Oxley Act of 2002, § 307.** Section 307 of the Sarbanes-Oxley Act is titled, Rules Of Professional Responsibility For Attorneys, and is found at: § 307, 15 U.S.C.A. § 7245 (2002). This section provides, in part: "Not later than 180 days after July 30, 2002, the Commission shall issue rules, in the public interest and for the protection of investors, setting forth minimum standards of professional conduct for attorneys appearing and practicing before the Commission in any way in the representation of issuers." The standards for attorney conduct that the SEC adopted pursuant to this section are codified in 17 C.F.R. § 205.3. These issues are discussed in greater detail in connection with Rule 1.13.

   Federal Preemption of State Laws that Regulate Law Practice. The Sarbanes-Oxley Act of 2002, § 307 preempts on contrary state law. However, federal law preempts state law

of this crime or fraud. The lawyer's right to disclose is based upon the client's breach of an obligation to the lawyer not to use the lawyer's services in such a manner.[76]

§ 1.6–12(e)(4) Preventing a Fraud on the Entity

In August 2003, the ABA also adopted a significant revision to Rule 1.13, relating to representing entities as clients.[77] The ABA based this revision on the report of the Task Force on Corporate Responsibility. On the substantive rules that govern lawyer conduct, the Task Force recommended, and the ABA adopted, four changes to Model Rule 1.13, which are discussed in more detail in the chapter focusing on Rule 1.13.

First, it modified Model Rule 1.13 to apply an objective standard to the issue of when a lawyer should go "up the ladder" or chain of command within the entity. Instead of requiring a lawyer to act only when she "knows" about material injury to the entity, the lawyer must act when she "knows facts from which a reasonable lawyer, under the circumstances, would conclude that" the entity may be subjected to material harm.[78]

Second, the ABA requires that the lawyer take a more active involvement in moving "up the ladder" in the entity to make sure that the highest authority in the entity really knows what is

---

governing attorney regulation only if there is evidence of clear Congressional intent to do so. Thus, in *American Bar Ass'n v. F.T.C.*, 671 F. Supp. 2d 64 (D.D.C. 2009), the Court held that the FTC Lacks Authority to Regulate Lawyers Under the Fair and Accurate Credit Transactions Act (FACT). The FACT Act does not contain "an 'unmistakably clear' grant of statutory authority allowing the Commission's venture into the regulation of the practice of law." 671 F.Supp.2d 64, 73–74, 2009 WL 4289505 *6. *Accord American Bar Ass'n v. F.T.C.*, 430 F.3d 457, 471-72 (D.C. Cir. 2005).

The Sarbanes-Oxley Act, Pub. L. No. 107-204, 116 Stat. 745, § 101 is codified in scattered sections of 11, 15, 18, 28, and 29 U.S.C.A.

See Richard W. Painter & Jennifer E. Duggan, *Lawyer Disclosure of Corporate Fraud: Establishing a Firm Foundation*, 50 SMU L. Rev. 225 (1996); Richard W. Painter, *Rules Lawyers Play By*, 76 N.Y.U. L. Rev. 665, 719 (2001); John Paul Lucci, *Enron—The Bankruptcy Heard Around The World And The International*

Ricochet Of Sarbanes-Oxley, 67 Alb. L. Rev. 211 (2003); Richard W. Painter, *Convergence And Competition In Rules Governing Lawyers And Auditors*, 29 J. Corp. L. 397 (2004).

[76]*In re Lane*, 889 A.2d 3 (N.H. 2005) rejected a six-month suspension and found no bad conduct for a lawyer accused of disclosing confidential client information in order to prevent the client-executor from defrauding his mother. The court said that the lawyer proved a reasonable belief that he needed to provide the surviving child's lawyer with evidence of a previously undisclosed life insurance policy in order to prevent criminal activity by the executor.

Rule 1.6, Comment 7.

[77]Rule 1.13.

[78]American Bar Association, Report of the American Bar Association Task Force on Corporate Responsibility 82 (2003). *See also* Rule 1.13, Comment 3: "As defined in Rule 1.0(f), knowledge can be inferred from circumstances, and a lawyer cannot ignore the obvious."

happening. Unless the lawyer reasonably believes that it is simply not necessary in the best interest of the entity, she "*shall* refer the matter to higher authority in the organization, including, if warranted by the circumstances to the *highest authority*" that other law determines can act on behalf of the organization.[79]

Third, if the entity fires the lawyer and the lawyer "reasonably believes" that the client fired her because she fulfilled her responsibilities under Rule 1.13 (b) or (c)—both of which deal with situations, for example, where an organization is engaged in action, intends to act or refuses to act in a matter related to the representation that is a violation of a legal obligation to the organization—or the lawyer withdraws from representation in order to fulfill her duties or rights under Rules 1.13(b) or 1.13(c), then the lawyer "*shall* proceed as the lawyer reasonably believes necessary" to make sure the organization's highest authority knows of the lawyer's discharge or withdrawal.[80] The lawyer, in short, must inform the highest authority about the fact that the lawyer has withdrawn or has been fired.[81]

Finally, the ABA modified Rule 1.13 to permit a lawyer to disclose confidential information when corporate action or inaction would involve a clear violation of the law that is reasonably likely to result in substantial injury to the entity.[82] This right of disclosure overrides the Rule 1.6 obligation of confidentiality.[83]

§ 1.6–12(e)(5) Preventing Client Fraud on the Tribunal

The former Model Code, the 1983 Model Rules, and the Model Rules after the major revisions of 2002 all require a lawyer not to permit a client to commit a fraud on the tribunal.[84] However, the exact nature of what the lawyer must do when the client has committed the fraud has changed over time. Also, the former Code did not speak with the same clarity as the present Model Rules.[85]

It is now clear that when the lawyer discovers that a client is

---

[79] Rule 1.13(b)(emphasis added).

[80] Rule 1.13(e) (emphasis added).

[81] American Bar Association, Report of the American Bar Association Task Force on Corporate Responsibility 83-84 (2003).

[82] American Bar Association, Report of the American Bar Association Task Force on Corporate Responsibility 83 (2003).

[83] Under the conditions outlined in Rule 1.13, "the lawyer may reveal information relating to the representation whether or not Rule 1.6 permits

such disclosure, but only if and to the extent the lawyer reasonably believes necessary to prevent substantial injury to the organization." Rule 1.13(c).

[84] DR 7-102; Rule 3.3.

[85] *See, e.g.,* Ronald D. Rotunda, *When the Client Lies: Unhelpful Guidelines from the ABA,* 1 CORPORATION LAW REVIEW 34 (1978); Ronald D. Rotunda, *Teaching Ethics Under the New Model Rules,* 14 SYLLABUS 1 (No. 3, Sept. 1983) (ABA Section on Legal Education and Admissions to the Bar).

committing or has committed a fraud on the tribunal, the lawyer must take action to correct it. The lawyer should try to persuade or cajole the client to correct the fraud, but if that fails, a lawyer must disclose the fraud to the court to correct it. This obligation exists whether or not that Rule 1.6 permits disclosure.[86]

§ 1.6–12(e)(6) Proposed Client Wrongdoing and a Noisy Notice of Withdrawal

Both the Rules and the Code agree that if the client will use a lawyer's services to further the client's "criminal or fraudulent conduct," then the lawyer must withdraw.[87] In some circumstances, a lawyer's withdrawal from representation may amount to a disclosure of client confidences or secrets. For example, if a lawyer withdraws in such a manner as to suggest that the client intends to commit fraud, then the lawyer will have disclosed information detrimental to the client. In 1965, before the ABA adopted the Model Code, an ABA Formal Opinion[88] recognized that in some instances "the very act of disassociation would have the effect of violating Canon 37."[89] That is no longer the rule; the current ethics rules require the lawyer to prevent or undo the client's fraud, notwithstanding Rule 1.6.[90]

Different considerations will apply if perjured testimony or false evidence has been offered before a *tribunal*, a topic considered later.[91]

If a lawyer withdraws from representation of a client, the Model Code did not specifically address whether the lawyer may formally inform third parties that the lawyer is no longer in the case. None of the early drafts of the Model Rules talked of filing a *Notice of Withdrawal*. However, the final version of the 1983 Model Rules contained a Comment on this new concept, created for the first time by those Rules.

The Model Rules, *prior to* the 2003 revisions, authorized a lawyer to file this *Notice of Withdrawal* even though its issuance may be a warning that the client is up to no good. The lawyer

---

[86]Rule 3.3.

[87]DR 2-110(B)(2); DR 7-102(A)(7); Rule 1.6, Comment 7; Rule 1.16(a)(1).

[88]ABA Formal Opinion 314 (Apr. 27, 1965).

[89]Canon 37 of the ABA Canons of Professional Ethics (1908, as amended) is the predecessor to DR 4-101 of the Model Code.

[90]*See* Rule 1.2, Comments 9 to 13; Rule 1.6, Comment 7; Rule 1.16, Comments 2 & 7.

[91]*See* Model Rule 3.3, discussed below. Rule 3.3(c): "The duties stated in paragraphs (a) and (b) continue to the conclusion of the proceeding, and apply even if compliance requires disclosure of information otherwise protected by Rule 1.6."

See also ABA Formal Opinion 87-353 (Apr. 20, 1987) ("Lawyer's Responsibilities With Relation to Client Perjury"), also discussed below.

may not blow the whistle; he or she may wave a red flag.[92] The relevant Comment provided:

> After withdrawal the lawyer is required to refrain from making disclosure of the client's confidences, except as otherwise provided in Rule 1.6. Neither this Rule nor Rule 1.8(b) nor Rule 1.16(d) prevents the lawyer from giving notice of the fact of withdrawal and the lawyer may also withdraw or disaffirm any opinion, document, affirmation, or the like.[93]

Rule 1.8(b), referred to in this Comment, provides that the lawyer shall not use client information to the disadvantage of the client, unless the client consents. Rule 1.16(d) states that, after withdrawal, the lawyer must take reasonable steps to protect a client's interests. Neither of these Rules, nor Rule 1.6 itself, limited the power to withdraw discussed in Rule 1.6. Hence, the lawyer may engage in a "noisy withdrawal."[94]

Note also that this Comment did not purport to limit to whom the *Notice of Withdrawal* may be sent. The lawyer could send this *Notice* to third parties, not merely the opposing side.

Consider this hypothetical. Assume that Lawyer learns, on the eve of closing, that the limited partnership agreement that Lawyer has prepared for her Client is a criminal fraud under the federal securities laws. Lawyer confronts Client, who states that he will go through with the deal and if Lawyer does not like it, Lawyer can resign. Lawyer then resigns, in compliance with what the ethics rules require.[95] But, under the Model Rules, *prior to the 2003 revisions*, she may do more than simply leave her position, accept the client's behavior, and silently slip away. Lawyer may also send a *Notice of Withdrawal* to the other side and to the

---

[92]*See* Ronald D. Rotunda, *The Notice of Withdrawal and the New Model Rules of Professional Conduct: Blowing the Whistle and Waiving the Red Flag*, 63 OR. L. REV. 455 (1984), *reprinted in*, 1985 CRIMINAL LAW REVIEW 533, and *excerpted in* 34 LAW REVIEW DIGEST 14 (Mar./Apr. 1985).

[93]Rule 1.6, former Comment 15 (deleted by the 2003 revisions).

[94]ABA Formal Opinion 98-412 (Sept. 9, 1998), concluded that a lawyer who discovers that his client has violated a court order prohibiting or limiting the transfer of assets *must* reveal that fact to the court if that is necessary to avoid, or to correct, a lawyer's affirmative representation to the court. The lawyer must also disclose the client's conduct or withdraw from continued representation in the litigation if withdrawal is necessary to avoid assisting the client's fraud on the court.

If the lawyer continues to represent the client, that may constitute assisting the client's fraud on the court if the client's conduct destroys the court's ability to grant effective relief to the opposing party. If the lawyer simply withdraws, the lawyer's obligation is not fulfilled: the lawyer must make a disclosure sufficient enough to warn the court not to rely on the lawyer's prior representations that the lawyer now knows are false. *Id.*

[95]Rule 1.16(a)(1); DR 2-110(B)(2).

Securities & Exchange Commission.[96] She may not describe exactly why she is withdrawing, but the other lawyers should be sufficiently warned that something is afoot.

The client could not preclude the lawyer from filing a noisy withdrawal by firing the lawyer first. "Whenever circumstances exist that would otherwise require a lawyer to withdraw, disaffirmance [of the lawyer's work product] may be in order even if the client fires her before she has a chance to do so."[97]

However, ABA Formal Opinion 92-366 advised that, if the fraud is already completed and the lawyer knows or reasonably believes that the client does not intend to make further fraudulent use of the lawyer's services, the lawyer may (but is not required to) withdraw. But she may *not* file a noisy withdrawal.[98] A lawyer should take this advice at her peril.[99] Lawyers have a greater obligation than merely considering what to do next; those who sit on their hands in such a situation may find that the courts are less understanding than this ABA opinion.[100]

After the 2003 revisions to Rule 1.6, the power and obligation

---

[96]Under the Model Code DR 4-101(C)(3), the lawyer could reveal this information.

[97]ABA Formal Opinion 92-366 (Aug. 8, 1992). This ABA Formal Opinion assumes that a lawyer for a small manufacturing firm has given an opinion that its client's accounts receivable represent legal obligations of the purchasers of the goods. Now, the lawyer finds that many of the accounts are fictional and that the client is in financial trouble. The opinion says that under Model Rule 1.6, the lawyer must withdraw from all future dealings involving this loan, and must disavow the prior opinion. Otherwise, the lawyer would be "assisting" the client to get future extensions of credit, for example.

[98]ABA Formal Opinion 92-366 (Aug. 8, 1992). This Opinion includes a vigorous dissent.

[99]*See SEC v. National Student Marketing Corp.*, 457 F.Supp. 682, 713 (D.D.C.1978), an SEC proceeding challenging the behavior of lawyers and others in a situation involving a failure to disclose. The lawyers "were required to speak out at the closing concerning the obvious materiality of the information." Their "silence was

not only a breach of this duty to speak, but in addition lent the appearance of legitimacy to the closing."

[100]**Bank Examiners.** ABA Formal Opinion 93-375 (1993) dealt with a lawyer's obligation to disclose adverse information in the context of a bank examination. The Opinion (which had no dissents) argued that the lawyer may not lie to the bank examiners, but the lawyer is not affirmatively obliged to warn about problems at the bank or otherwise reveal client confidences. If the lawyer reasonably believes the bank is engaged in fraud, however, the lawyer must take steps to avoid assisting it to do so, including, in some cases, withdrawing from the representation.

The Opinion also considered the situation where the bank official, against the lawyer's advice and *in the lawyer's presence*, makes knowingly false statements to bank examiners. The Opinion advises the lawyer "at the first *private* opportunity, to urge the client to correct the falsehood" and consider what actions may be required under Rule 1.13 because the Bank, an organization, is the client. However, this Opinion advises—

"*unless the lawyer knew in advance* that the client intended to make

of the lawyer dealing with the client who has involved the lawyer in fraud is much greater. The new Rule 1.6(b) now adds two new subsections that provide:

> A lawyer may reveal information relating to the representation of a client to the extent the lawyer reasonably believes necessary. . . .
>
> (2) to prevent the client from committing a crime or fraud that is reasonably certain to result in substantial injury to the financial interests or property of another and in furtherance of which the client has used or is using the lawyer's services;
>
> (3) to prevent, mitigate or rectify substantial injury to the financial interests or property of another that is reasonably certain to result or has resulted from the client's commission of a crime or fraud in furtherance of which the client has used the lawyer's services.[101]

Consider the hypothetical considered above, where that Lawyer learns, on the eve of closing, that the limited partnership agreement that Lawyer has prepared for her Client is a criminal fraud under the federal securities laws. If the client insists on continuing the fraud, the lawyer may simply reveal it.[102]

This addition of Rule 1.6(b)(3) does not signal the end of a "notice of withdrawal." Granted, Rule 1.6 and its Comments no longer mention the concept. However, Rule 1.2(d) requires that the lawyer must not assist a client in engaging in conduct the lawyer

---

such a misrepresentation, she herself at this point cannot be said to be a party to it and has violated no ethical duty. We therefore *see no reason*, in this context, *why the lawyer should be required to do anything* that would signal to the bank examiners her disapproval of the client's course of conduct. She is not required to jump to her feet. . . . [S]he is not required to make a 'noisy withdrawal' that would effectively disaffirm her involvement to date." Formal Opinion 93-375, at 8 (emphasis added).

If the client does not rectify his fraud and "refuses to correct his lie," the lawyer "*may* be required to *consider* whether or not to terminate the representation." The lawyer should "not come to any subsequent meetings with the [bank] examiners if she knows that the client intends to persist in the deception" because her silent presence might make her a party to her client's fraud. Formal Opinion 93-375, at 8 (emphasis added).

Moreover, the factual predicate

in ABA Formal Opinion 93-375, at 8—"*unless the lawyer knew in advance* that the client intended to make such a misrepresentation"—encourages a lawyer to be ignorant. If she expects that her client will continue its fraud in the meeting with bank examiners— certainly a reasonable expectation unless the client, like Saul on the road to Damascus, undergoes an instant religious conversion—she should tell her client, "do not tell me in advance that you will do that which anyone would expect you to do, because then I will have ethical obligations that will interfere with your effort to defraud the bank examiners."

[101] Rule 1.6(b)(3).

[102] The 2003 revisions to Rule 1.6, are substantially similar to the Restatement of the Law Governing Lawyers § 67 (Official Draft 2000): "Using Or Disclosing Information To Prevent, Rectify, Or Mitigate Substantial Financial Loss."

knows is criminal or fraudulent. A comment to that Rule then provides:

> When the client's course of action has already begun and is continuing, the lawyer's responsibility is especially delicate. The lawyer is required to avoid assisting the client, for example, by drafting or delivering documents that the lawyer knows are fraudulent or by suggesting how the wrongdoing might be concealed. A lawyer may not continue assisting a client in conduct that the lawyer originally supposed was legally proper but then discovers is criminal or fraudulent. The lawyer must, therefore, withdraw from the representation of the client in the matter. See Rule 1.16(a). In some cases, withdrawal alone might be insufficient. It may be necessary for the lawyer to *give notice of the fact of withdrawal and to disaffirm any opinion, document, affirmation or the like.* See Rule 4.1.[103]

Rule 4.1 also refers to a "Notice of Withdrawal" in a roundabout way. First, Rule 4.1(b) provides that the lawyer may not "fail to disclose a material fact to a third person when disclosure is necessary to avoid assisting a criminal or fraudulent act by a client, unless disclosure is prohibited by Rule 1.6." The obvious question is what a lawyer should do if she finds herself in a position where she must not "fail to disclose" information to a third person to avoid assisting a client's criminal or fraudulent act, but Rule 1.6 prohibits disclosure.

Rule 4.1 resolves this dilemma by turning to a "notice of withdrawal." The Comment advises:

> Ordinarily, a lawyer can avoid assisting a client's crime or fraud by withdrawing from the representation. Sometimes it may be necessary for the lawyer to give *notice of the fact of withdrawal* and to disaffirm an opinion, document, affirmation or the like. In extreme cases, substantive law may require a lawyer to disclose information relating to the representation to avoid being deemed to have assisted the client's crime or fraud. If the lawyer can avoid assisting a client's crime or fraud only by disclosing this information, then under paragraph (b) the lawyer is required to do so, unless the disclosure is prohibited by Rule 1.6.[104]

Rule 4.1 recognizes that in special circumstances other law ("substantive law") will sometimes require the lawyer to disclose client confidences. In other cases, the lawyer's withdrawal will be enough to fulfill her professional obligations. In between these poles, there are cases where "it may be necessary for the lawyer to give *notice of the fact of withdrawal* and to disaffirm an opinion, document, affirmation or the like." This form of signalling or flag-

---

[103]Rule 1.2, Comment 10 (emphasis added).

[104]Rule 4.1, Comment 3 (emphasis added).

ging is the way the Rules have balanced the competing interests.[105]

Hence, the new Rule 1.6 broadens considerably the lawyer's power to disclose client information otherwise protected by Rule 1.6. However, the Rule does not impose the duty to disclose, although other law may do so.[106] The lawyer retains the power to file a noisy notice of withdrawal in cases contemplated by Rules 1.2 and 4.1. In addition, because that Rule is written to give the lawyer a discretionary instead of a mandatory duty ("*may* reveal information. . ."), the lawyer may choose to file a noisy notice of withdrawal instead of making a disclosure in cases within the disclosure provisions of Rule 1.6(b).

The noisy notice may be a form of conduct that involves communication. A noisy withdrawal serves to signal to the knowledgeable observer that something is amiss. But the Rules allow this form of communication notwithstanding the general confidentiality provisions of Rule 1.6 because the purpose of the noisy withdrawal is to signal something important to the outside world. It a compromise between blowing the whistle and silently slipping away. When there are circumstances where the lawyer cannot speak up, he can still waive a red flag.

§ 1.6–12(f) Client Involved in a Past Crime or Fraud Where Lawyers Services Were Used

§ 1.6–12(f)(1) Introduction

The Model Code did not have any provision that permitted lawyers to disclose information about a *past* crime or fraud. The 1983 Model Rules focused on future crimes involving imminent death or substantial bodily harm. The ABA House of Delegates in 1983 had rejected a Kutak Commission recommendation that a lawyer may disclose "to rectify the consequences of a client's criminal or fraudulent act in the furtherance of which the lawyer's financial services have been used."[107] The ABA rejected a similar proposal that came before the House of Delegates in 1991.[108] Normally, when clients turn to lawyers to help them with *past* acts, they expect that the attorney client privilege as well as the ethical restraints of Rule 1.6 will seal the lawyer's lips.

---

[105]Geoffrey C. Hazard, Jr., *Rectification Of Client Fraud: Death And Revival Of A Professional Norm*, 33 EMORY L.J. 271, 304 (1984): "What the ABA has done is loudly to proclaim that a lawyer may not blow the whistle, but quietly to affirm that he may wave a flag." (footnote omitted).

[106]*Tarasoff v. Regents of the University of California*, 17 Cal.3d 425, 131 Cal.Rptr. 14, 551 P.2d 334 (1976), discussed below.

[107]PROFESSIONAL RESPONSIBILITY: STANDARDS, RULES & STATUTES, 2004–2005 EDITION, at 229 (John Dzienkowski, ed. 2004).

[108]*See* PROFESSIONAL RESPONSIBILITY: STANDARDS, RULES & STATUTES, 2004–2005 EDITION, at 228 (John Dzienkowski, ed. 2004).

The drafters of the 2002 Rules proposed a new disclosure provision under Rule 1.6(b) that was very similar to the Kutak Commission's proposal in the 1980s. The ABA House of Delegates once again rejected the effort to broaden permissive disclosure under Rule 1.6. However, in 2003, the pressures of SEC rulemaking and the corporate scandals of Enron, Worldcom,[109] and Tyco led the ABA to adopt the exception related to *past crimes* in the narrow case where the client has misused the lawyer's services to perpetrate the fraud.

Rule 1.6(b)(3) allows the lawyer to reveal information otherwise protected by Rule 1.6 in order "to prevent, mitigate or rectify substantial injury to the financial interests or property of another that is reasonably certain to result or has resulted from the client's commission of a crime or fraud in furtherance of which the client has used the lawyer's services." In other words, if the client has misused the lawyer's services to commit a fraud, and the lawyer discovers this fact, the lawyer may disclose to rectify the damage. This exception is discussed below.

§ 1.6–12(f)(2) Offering False Evidence and Rule 3.3

The Rules have always had a provision that requires a lawyer to take appropriate measures when he has submitted evidence to a tribunal and has later learned that the evidence was false when submitted. This provision under the Candor to the Court Rule involves a client use of a lawyer's services to perpetuate a crime or fraud and it involves disclosure to correct the past crime or fraud.

If the lawyer has offered material evidence and later learns of its falsity, under the Rules the lawyer "must take reasonable remedial measures."[110] This duty applies "even if compliance requires disclosure of information otherwise protected" by the confidentiality requirements of Rule 1.6.[111] Similarly, the lawyer's duty continues "to the conclusion of the proceeding" even though "compliance requires disclosure of information otherwise protected by Rule 1.6."[112]

A "noisy withdrawal" might not be sufficient to undo the fraud's impact on the case. For example, the opposing party might drop the case or settle it in reliance on the false deposition, in spite of the lawyer's noisy withdrawal. Consequently, "[d]irect disclosure under Rule 3.3, to the opposing party or if need be to the court, may prove to be the only reasonable remedial measure in the client fraud situations most likely to be encountered in pretrial

---

[109]*E.g., SEC v. WorldCom, Inc.,* 2002 WL 31662699 Litigation Release No. 17866 (Nov. 26, 2002).

[110]Rule 3.3(a)(3).

[111]*See* discussion under Rule 3.3(c), below. *See also Jones v. Clinton,* 36 F.Supp.2d 1118 (E.D.Ark.1999).

[112]Rule 3.3(c).

proceedings."[113] This issue is discussed in detail in connection with Rule 3.3.

§ 1.6–12(f)(3) Preventing, Rectifying, or Mitigating Substantial Financial Harm Resulting from a Past Crime or Fraud

In March 2002, the president of the ABA formed a Task Force on Corporate Responsibility to "examine systemic issues relating to corporate responsibility arising out of the unexpected and traumatic bankruptcy of Enron and other Enron-like situations which have shaken confidence in the effectiveness of the governance and disclosure systems applicable to public companies."[114] The Task Force held public hearings and in March 2003 issued a final report with specific recommendations to the ABA House of Delegates.[115] The Task Force presented its recommendations to the ABA at its annual meeting in August 2003.

The Task Force did not confine its mission to examining the role of lawyers in the corporate fraud scandals; instead, it examined all systemic issues including those involving corporate governance and the role of accountants. Thus, only some of its proposals relate to the regulation of lawyers. There are many recommendations relating to securities law, auditing law, corporate governance law, and corporate organizational theory. The changes proposed to the Model Rules, however, attempted to place more responsibility on lawyers who represent corporations and other business entities.

The Task Force recommended, among other things, to amend Rule 1.6 to permit disclosure by a lawyer:

> to prevent, mitigate or rectify substantial injury to the financial interests or property of another that is reasonably certain to result or has resulted from the client's commission of a crime or fraud in furtherance of which the client has used the lawyer's services;[116]

As mentioned above, other groups had presented similar proposals to the ABA House of Delegates, which had voted them down repeatedly. This time, the House accepted the recommendations.

This exception to confidentiality seeks to permit a lawyer to take action after the criminal or fraudulent behavior has taken place but before its effects are over, in the case where the lawyer's disclosure can prevent, rectify, or mitigate substantial loss to the

---

[113]ABA Formal Opinion 93-376 (Aug. 6, 1993).

[114]*See* American Bar Association, Report of the American Bar Association Task Force on Corporate Responsibility 2 (2003).

[115]American Bar Association, Report of the American Bar Association Task Force on Corporate Responsibility 2-3 (2003). *See* Rule 1.6(b)(3).

[116]American Bar Association, Report of the American Bar Association Task Force on Corporate Responsibility 77 (2003).

third person.[117] For example, if the client has committed a past crime relating to lying on loan documents and the bank has not paid out all of the loan proceeds, a disclosure by the client's lawyer could mitigate the financial loss.

There are limits to how broadly one may interpret the terms, "mitigate" or "rectify." Consider the case where the client, using the services of a lawyer (Lawyer #1), completes a loan application that, unknown to the lawyer, is fraudulent. Let us assume that the bank discovers the fraud and hires its lawyer to sue the client. The client then hires a new lawyer (Lawyer #2) to represent him. The new lawyer may *not* disclose the client's fraud because Rule 1.6(b)(3) is simply inapplicable. Comment 8 makes that clear when it advises that Rule 1.6(b)(3) "does not apply when a person who has committed a crime or fraud thereafter employs a lawyer for representation concerning that offense."

But, can Lawyer #1 reveal the fraud? The lawyer's disclosure will serve to "rectify substantial injury to the financial interests or property of another that . . . has resulted from the client's commission of a crime or fraud in furtherance of which the client has used the lawyer's services." Is this disclosure justified solely because Lawyer #1's disclosure will rectify the client's fraud? Assume further the client has not yet spent the proceeds of the fraudulent loan, or that the client has the money to return the moneys expended. In light of the context that the ABA adopted these provisions after the Enron scandals, one would expect a significant push towards disclosure. The most natural reading of this section authorizes the lawyer to disclose.

§ 1.6–12(g) The Crime-Fraud Exception to the Attorney-Client Privilege

The Model Rules create the ethical duty to keep client confidences. However, there is also the narrower evidentiary attorney-client privilege. One should distinguish between the lawyer's limited right to disclose *future* actions under Rule 1.6(b)(1), and the loss of the evidentiary attorney-client privilege because of *past* actions, under the crime-fraud exception.

A litigant may claim that the opposing party's conduct has been fraudulent or criminal. A client may not claim the evidentiary privilege of the communications with the lawyer that were in furtherance of the criminal or fraudulent transaction.[118] It is not necessary for the lawyer to have known that he or she was

---

[117]Rule 1.6, Comment 8.

[118]*See In re Grand Jury Investigation*, 445 F.3d 266 (3d Cir. 2006), *noted in* 22 ABA/BNA MANUAL ON PROFESSIONAL CONDUCT, Current Reports News 208 (May 3, 2006). This case involved a client who sought legal advice regarding a criminal investigation. The attorney informed the client about a grand jury subpoena that had

part of a criminal or fraudulent transaction. For example, if the client secures the lawyer's services in order to file a perjurious affidavit, the client's conversations with the lawyer with respect to this affidavit are not privileged, *even if the lawyer did not know* at the time that the client was committing perjury.[119]

The party opposing the privilege based on the crime-fraud exception has the burden of producing evidence that, if unexplained, is prima facie evidence of the existence of the exception. Then, the burden of persuasion shifts to the party asserting the privilege to give a reasonable explanation of the conduct or of the communication. If the court does not accept the explanation, then the privilege is lost. The court uses the preponderance of the evidence standard in weighing the evidence and the rebuttal evidence.[120]

§ 1.6–12(h) Tort Liability and the Lawyer's Discretion to Reveal Client Information

Although Rule 1.6(b)(1) gives the lawyer discretion to reveal client information to prevent death or bodily harm, the drafters of the 1983 Model Rules viewed this discretion as absolute and

---

been issued and that it covered email communications. There was no evidence that the client took action to prevent the deletion of these messages. And, the court found that the client's failure to stop deletion of emails triggered the crime-fraud exception to the attorney-client privilege. The attorney had no knowledge of the client's criminal plan to destroy evidence.

[119] *In Re Sealed Case*, 162 F.3d 670, 674 333 U.S.App.D.C. 245, 248 (D.C.Cir. Decided, May 26, 1998, unsealed, Dec. 1, 1998) ("After reviewing the government's *in camera* submission, the court found that 'Ms. Lewinsky consulted Mr. Carter for the purpose of committing perjury and obstructing justice and used the material he prepared for her for the purpose of committing perjury and obstructing justice'.").

United States v. Zolin, 491 U.S. 554, 575, 109 S.Ct. 2619, 2632, 105 L.Ed.2d 469 (1989), held that "the threshold showing to obtain *in camera* review may be met by using any relevant evidence, lawfully obtained, that has not been adjudicated to be privileged."

[120] *See, e.g., Haines v. Liggett Group, Inc.*, 975 F.2d 81 (3d Cir.1992); *The American Tobacco Co. v. Florida*, 697 So.2d 1249, 1256 (4th Dist.Fla. 1997).

In *Frease v. Glazer*, 330 Or. 364, 4 P.3d 56 (2000), a woman wanted her husband's lawyer's files after the husband had fled with their son, presumably taking him to Iran. The husband had hired the lawyer after the wife had previously hidden the son, and the wife argued that the lawyer had been hired as part of the illegal plan to flee the country. The court found that the husband's flight alone did not waive the attorney-client privilege; the court will not grant *in camera* review on the basis of the crime-fraud exception because the wife did not present sufficient evidence to support a reasonable belief that *in camera* review may yield evidence establishing the exception's applicability.

not subject to review by the disciplinary authority or the courts.[121] The drafters of the 2002 Rules rephrased this discretion to make it consistent with the change on whether a violation of a Rule can serve as evidence of a breach of a standard.[122] The Comments to Rule 1.6 state that section (b) does not require disclosure and therefore a lawyer's failure to disclose is not a violation of this provision.[123] The drafters cited to several other Rules that require disclosure. A lawyer may violate one of those other provisions.[124] But the drafters of the 2002 Rules sought to retain significant discretion in the provision protecting client confidentiality.

One wonders if the judiciary will recognize the purported nonreviewable discretion, in light of court decisions like *Tarasoff v. Regents of the University of California*.[125] In *Tarasoff*, a psychotherapist knew of a planned murder and did not warn the victim. The court held that a cause of action in tort existed.

> When a therapist determines, or pursuant to the standards of the profession should determine, that his patient presents a serious danger of violence to another, he incurs an obligation to use reasonable care to protect the intended victim against such danger. The discharge of this duty may require the therapist to take one or more of various steps, depending upon the nature of the case. Thus it may call for him to warn the intended victim or others likely to apprise the victim of the danger, to notify the police, or to take whatever other steps are reasonably necessary under the circumstances.[126]

Given decisions like *Tarasoff*, the efforts of the ABA House of Delegates to grant lawyers unreviewable discretion may well be unsuccessful, at least in a tort case with the right set of facts.[127] The Rules do admit that other law may mandate disclosure and

---

[121]1983 Model Rule 1.6, Comment 13: "A lawyer's decision not to take preventive action permitted by paragraph (b)(1) does not violate this Rule." *See also* 1983 Model Rule, "Scope," 20: "The lawyer's exercise of discretion not to disclose information under Rule 1.6 should not be subject to reexamination."

[122]*See* Rule, Scope 20.

[123]Rule 1.6, Comment 15.

[124]Rule 1.6, Comment 15 (citing to Rule 3.3 as overriding 1.6(b)). New Rule 1.13 also overrides Rule 1.6.

[125]*Tarasoff v. Regents of the University of California*, 17 Cal.3d

425, 131 Cal.Rptr. 14, 551 P.2d 334 (1976).

[126]17 Cal.3d at 431, 131 Cal.Rptr. at 20, 551 P.2d at 340.

[127]The Restatement also concludes that the lawyer's decision to reveal or not reveal should be unreviewable. Restatement of the Law Governing Lawyers, Third, § 66(e) (Official Draft 2000). *See also id.* at Comment g: "Subsequent re-examination of the reasonableness of a lawyer's action in the light of later developments would be unwarranted; reasonableness of the lawyer's belief at the time and under the circumstances in which the lawyer acts is alone controlling."

thereby supersede Rule 1.6.[128] *Tarasoff*, a tort case involving the privileges of the medical profession, represents other law that the courts are likely to apply to lawyers. The courts should normally respect the lawyer's discretion,[129] but there may be cases where that discretion is abused. It is quite typical for courts to hold that "discretion" does not mean "unreviewable discretion."

---

[128]*See* Rule 1.6, Comment 20.

[129]*Hawkins v. King County, Dep't of Rehabilitative Services*, 24 Wash.App. 338, 602 P.2d 361 (Wash. 1979), dismissed a case against a lawyer seeking to hold a lawyer liable in tort for not revealing a client's intentions, but the court did so on narrow grounds. The court said, first, there is a common-law duty of a lawyer to volunteer certain information about his client to a court considering pretrial release, but this duty must be limited to situations where the information gained convinces the lawyer that his client intends to commit a crime or inflict injury upon unknowing third persons. In this case, where the potential victims of the client (*i.e.*, his mother and sister) already knew that the client might be dangerous and that he had been released from confinement, there was no duty on the part of his lawyer to warn the client's mother of the risk of which she was already fully cognizant. In addition, the lawyer received no information that the client planned to assault anyone but only that he was mentally ill and likely to be dangerous to himself and others.

CHAPTER 1.7
CONFLICTS OF INTEREST—CURRENT CLIENTS

RULE 1.7: CONFLICT OF INTEREST: CURRENT CLIENTS

(a) Except as provided in paragraph (b), a lawyer shall not represent a client if the representation involves a concurrent conflict of interest. A concurrent conflict of interest exists if:

(1) the representation of one client will be directly adverse to another client; or

(2) there is a significant risk that the representation of one or more clients will be materially limited by the lawyer's responsibilities to another client, a former client or a third person or by a personal interest of the lawyer.

(b) Notwithstanding the existence of a concurrent conflict of interest under paragraph (a), a lawyer may represent a client if:

(1) the lawyer reasonably believes that the lawyer will be able to provide competent and diligent representation to each affected client;

(2) the representation is not prohibited by law;

(3) the representation does not involve the assertion of a claim by one client against another client represented by the lawyer in the same litigation or other proceeding before a tribunal; and

(4) each affected client gives informed consent, confirmed in writing.

Comment

General Principles

[1] Loyalty and independent judgment are essential elements in the lawyer's relationship to a client. Concurrent conflicts of interest can arise from the lawyer's responsibilities to another client, a former client or a third person or from the lawyer's own interests. For specific Rules regarding certain concurrent conflicts of interest, see Rule 1.8. For former client conflicts of interest, see Rule 1.9. For conflicts of interest involving prospective clients, see Rule 1.18. For definitions of "informed consent" and "confirmed in writing," see Rule 1.0(e) and (b).

[2] Resolution of a conflict of interest problem under this Rule requires the lawyer to: 1) clearly identify the client or clients; 2) determine whether a conflict of interest exists; 3) decide whether the representation may be undertaken despite the existence of a conflict, i.e., whether the conflict is consentable; and 4) if so, consult with the clients affected under paragraph (a) and obtain their informed consent, confirmed in writing. The clients affected under paragraph (a) include both of the clients referred to in paragraph (a)(1) and the one or more clients whose representation might be materially limited under paragraph (a)(2).

[3] A conflict of interest may exist before representation is undertaken, in which event the representation must be declined, unless the lawyer obtains the informed consent of each client under the conditions of paragraph (b). To determine whether a conflict of interest exists, a lawyer should adopt reasonable procedures, appropriate for the size and type of firm and practice, to determine in both litigation and non-litigation matters the persons and issues involved. See also Comment to Rule 5.1. Ignorance caused by a failure to institute such procedures will not excuse a lawyer's violation of this Rule. As to whether a client-lawyer relationship exists or, having once been established, is continuing, see Comment to Rule 1.3 and Scope.

[4] If a conflict arises after representation has been undertaken, the lawyer ordinarily must withdraw from the representation, unless the lawyer has obtained the informed consent of the client under the conditions of paragraph (b). See Rule 1.16. Where more than one client is involved, whether the lawyer may continue to represent any of the clients is determined both by the lawyer's ability to comply with duties owed to the former client and by the lawyer's ability to represent adequately the remaining client or clients, given the lawyer's duties to the former client. See Rule 1.9. See also Comments [5] and [29].

[5] Unforeseeable developments, such as changes in corporate and other organizational affiliations or the addition or realignment of parties in litigation, might create conflicts in the midst of a representation, as when a company sued by the lawyer on behalf of one client is bought by another client represented by the lawyer in an unrelated matter. Depending on the circumstances, the lawyer may have the option to withdraw from one of the representations in order to avoid the conflict. The lawyer must seek court approval where necessary and take steps to minimize harm to the clients. See Rule

1.16. The lawyer must continue to protect the confidences of the client from whose representation the lawyer has withdrawn. See Rule 1.9(c).

Identifying Conflicts of Interest: Directly Adverse

[6] Loyalty to a current client prohibits undertaking representation directly adverse to that client without that client's informed consent. Thus, absent consent, a lawyer may not act as an advocate in one matter against a person the lawyer represents in some other matter, even when the matters are wholly unrelated. The client as to whom the representation is directly adverse is likely to feel betrayed, and the resulting damage to the client-lawyer relationship is likely to impair the lawyer's ability to represent the client effectively. In addition, the client on whose behalf the adverse representation is undertaken reasonably may fear that the lawyer will pursue that client's case less effectively out of deference to the other client, i.e., that the representation may be materially limited by the lawyer's interest in retaining the current client. Similarly, a directly adverse conflict may arise when a lawyer is required to cross-examine a client who appears as a witness in a lawsuit involving another client, as when the testimony will be damaging to the client who is represented in the lawsuit. On the other hand, simultaneous representation in unrelated matters of clients whose interests are only economically adverse, such as representation of competing economic enterprises in unrelated litigation, does not ordinarily constitute a conflict of interest and thus may not require consent of the respective clients.

[7] Directly adverse conflicts can also arise in transactional matters. For example, if a lawyer is asked to represent the seller of a business in negotiations with a buyer represented by the lawyer, not in the same transaction but in another, unrelated matter, the lawyer could not undertake the representation without the informed consent of each client.

Identifying Conflicts of Interest: Material Limitation

[8] Even where there is no direct adverseness, a conflict of interest exists if there is a significant risk that a lawyer's ability to consider, recommend or carry out an appropriate course of action for the client will be materially limited as a result of the lawyer's other responsibilities or interests. For example, a lawyer asked to represent several individuals seeking to form a joint venture is likely to be materially limited in the lawyer's ability to recommend or advocate all possible positions that each might take because of the lawyer's duty of loyalty to the others. The conflict in effect forecloses alternatives that would otherwise be available to the client. The mere possibility of subsequent harm does not itself require disclosure and consent. The critical questions are the likelihood that a difference in interests will eventuate and, if it does, whether it will materially interfere with the lawyer's independent professional judgment in considering alternatives or foreclose courses of action that reasonably should be pursued on behalf of the client.

Lawyer's Responsibilities to Former Clients and Other Third Persons

[9] In addition to conflicts with other current clients, a lawyer's

duties of loyalty and independence may be materially limited by responsibilities to former clients under Rule 1.9 or by the lawyer's responsibilities to other persons, such as fiduciary duties arising from a lawyer's service as a trustee, executor or corporate director.

Personal Interest Conflicts

[10] The lawyer's own interests should not be permitted to have an adverse effect on representation of a client. For example, if the probity of a lawyer's own conduct in a transaction is in serious question, it may be difficult or impossible for the lawyer to give a client detached advice. Similarly, when a lawyer has discussions concerning possible employment with an opponent of the lawyer's client, or with a law firm representing the opponent, such discussions could materially limit the lawyer's representation of the client. In addition, a lawyer may not allow related business interests to affect representation, for example, by referring clients to an enterprise in which the lawyer has an undisclosed financial interest. See Rule 1.8 for specific Rules pertaining to a number of personal interest conflicts, including business transactions with clients. See also Rule 1.10 (personal interest conflicts under Rule 1.7 ordinarily are not imputed to other lawyers in a law firm).

[11] When lawyers representing different clients in the same matter or in substantially related matters are closely related by blood or marriage, there may be a significant risk that client confidences will be revealed and that the lawyer's family relationship will interfere with both loyalty and independent professional judgment. As a result, each client is entitled to know of the existence and implications of the relationship between the lawyers before the lawyer agrees to undertake the representation. Thus, a lawyer related to another lawyer, e.g., as parent, child, sibling or spouse, ordinarily may not represent a client in a matter where that lawyer is representing another party, unless each client gives informed consent. The disqualification arising from a close family relationship is personal and ordinarily is not imputed to members of firms with whom the lawyers are associated. See Rule 1.10.

[12] A lawyer is prohibited from engaging in sexual relationships with a client unless the sexual relationship predates the formation of the client-lawyer relationship. See Rule 1.8(j).

Interest of Person Paying for a Lawyer's Service

[13] A lawyer may be paid from a source other than the client, including a co-client, if the client is informed of that fact and consents and the arrangement does not compromise the lawyer's duty of loyalty or independent judgment to the client. See Rule 1.8(f). If acceptance of the payment from any other source presents a significant risk that the lawyer's representation of the client will be materially limited by the lawyer's own interest in accommodating the person paying the lawyer's fee or by the lawyer's responsibilities to a payer who is also a co-client, then the lawyer must comply with the requirements of paragraph (b) before accepting the representation, including determining whether the conflict is consentable and, if so, that the client has adequate information about the material risks of the representation.

Prohibited Representations

[14] Ordinarily, clients may consent to representation notwithstand-

ing a conflict. However, as indicated in paragraph (b), some conflicts are nonconsentable, meaning that the lawyer involved cannot properly ask for such agreement or provide representation on the basis of the client's consent. When the lawyer is representing more than one client, the question of consentability must be resolved as to each client.

[15] Consentability is typically determined by considering whether the interests of the clients will be adequately protected if the clients are permitted to give their informed consent to representation burdened by a conflict of interest. Thus, under paragraph (b)(1), representation is prohibited if in the circumstances the lawyer cannot reasonably conclude that the lawyer will be able to provide competent and diligent representation. See Rule 1.1 (competence) and Rule 1.3 (diligence).

[16] Paragraph (b)(2) describes conflicts that are nonconsentable because the representation is prohibited by applicable law. For example, in some states substantive law provides that the same lawyer may not represent more than one defendant in a capital case, even with the consent of the clients, and under federal criminal statutes certain representations by a former government lawyer are prohibited, despite the informed consent of the former client. In addition, decisional law in some states limits the ability of a governmental client, such as a municipality, to consent to a conflict of interest.

[17] Paragraph (b)(3) describes conflicts that are nonconsentable because of the institutional interest in vigorous development of each client's position when the clients are aligned directly against each other in the same litigation or other proceeding before a tribunal. Whether clients are aligned directly against each other within the meaning of this paragraph requires examination of the context of the proceeding. Although this paragraph does not preclude a lawyer's multiple representation of adverse parties to a mediation (because mediation is not a proceeding before a "tribunal" under Rule 1.0(m)), such representation may be precluded by paragraph (b)(1).

Informed Consent

[18] Informed consent requires that each affected client be aware of the relevant circumstances and of the material and reasonably foreseeable ways that the conflict could have adverse effects on the interests of that client. See Rule 1.0(e) (informed consent). The information required depends on the nature of the conflict and the nature of the risks involved. When representation of multiple clients in a single matter is undertaken, the information must include the implications of the common representation, including possible effects on loyalty, confidentiality and the attorney-client privilege and the advantages and risks involved. See Comments [30] and [31] (effect of common representation on confidentiality).

[19] Under some circumstances it may be impossible to make the disclosure necessary to obtain consent. For example, when the lawyer represents different clients in related matters and one of the clients refuses to consent to the disclosure necessary to permit the other client to make an informed decision, the lawyer cannot

properly ask the latter to consent. In some cases the alternative to common representation can be that each party may have to obtain separate representation with the possibility of incurring additional costs. These costs, along with the benefits of securing separate representation, are factors that may be considered by the affected client in determining whether common representation is in the client's interests.

Consent Confirmed in Writing

[20] Paragraph (b) requires the lawyer to obtain the informed consent of the client, confirmed in writing. Such a writing may consist of a document executed by the client or one that the lawyer promptly records and transmits to the client following an oral consent. See Rule 1.0(b). See also Rule 1.0(n) (writing includes electronic transmission). If it is not feasible to obtain or transmit the writing at the time the client gives informed consent, then the lawyer must obtain or transmit it within a reasonable time thereafter. See Rule 1.0(b). The requirement of a writing does not supplant the need in most cases for the lawyer to talk with the client, to explain the risks and advantages, if any, of representation burdened with a conflict of interest, as well as reasonably available alternatives, and to afford the client a reasonable opportunity to consider the risks and alternatives and to raise questions and concerns. Rather, the writing is required in order to impress upon clients the seriousness of the decision the client is being asked to make and to avoid disputes or ambiguities that might later occur in the absence of a writing.

Revoking Consent

[21] A client who has given consent to a conflict may revoke the consent and, like any other client, may terminate the lawyer's representation at any time. Whether revoking consent to the client's own representation precludes the lawyer from continuing to represent other clients depends on the circumstances, including the nature of the conflict, whether the client revoked consent because of a material change in circumstances, the reasonable expectations of the other clients and whether material detriment to the other clients or the lawyer would result.

Consent to Future Conflict

[22] Whether a lawyer may properly request a client to waive conflicts that might arise in the future is subject to the test of paragraph (b). The effectiveness of such waivers is generally determined by the extent to which the client reasonably understands the material risks that the waiver entails. The more comprehensive the explanation of the types of future representations that might arise and the actual and reasonably foreseeable adverse consequences of those representations, the greater the likelihood that the client will have the requisite understanding. Thus, if the client agrees to consent to a particular type of conflict with which the client is already familiar, then the consent ordinarily will be effective with regard to that type of conflict. If the consent is general and open-ended, then the consent ordinarily will be ineffective, because it is not reasonably likely that the client will have

understood the material risks involved. On the other hand, if the client is an experienced user of the legal services involved and is reasonably informed regarding the risk that a conflict may arise, such consent is more likely to be effective, particularly if, e.g., the client is independently represented by other counsel in giving consent and the consent is limited to future conflicts unrelated to the subject of the representation. In any case, advance consent cannot be effective if the circumstances that materialize in the future are such as would make the conflict nonconsentable under paragraph (b).

Conflicts in Litigation

[23] Paragraph (b)(3) prohibits representation of opposing parties in the same litigation, regardless of the clients' consent. On the other hand, simultaneous representation of parties whose interests in litigation may conflict, such as coplaintiffs or codefendants, is governed by paragraph (a)(2). A conflict may exist by reason of substantial discrepancy in the parties' testimony, incompatibility in positions in relation to an opposing party or the fact that there are substantially different possibilities of settlement of the claims or liabilities in question. Such conflicts can arise in criminal cases as well as civil. The potential for conflict of interest in representing multiple defendants in a criminal case is so grave that ordinarily a lawyer should decline to represent more than one codefendant. On the other hand, common representation of persons having similar interests in civil litigation is proper if the requirements of paragraph (b) are met.

[24] Ordinarily a lawyer may take inconsistent legal positions in different tribunals at different times on behalf of different clients. The mere fact that advocating a legal position on behalf of one client might create precedent adverse to the interests of a client represented by the lawyer in an unrelated matter does not create a conflict of interest. A conflict of interest exists, however, if there is a significant risk that a lawyer's action on behalf of one client will materially limit the lawyer's effectiveness in representing another client in a different case; for example, when a decision favoring one client will create a precedent likely to seriously weaken the position taken on behalf of the other client. Factors relevant in determining whether the clients need to be advised of the risk include: where the cases are pending, whether the issue is substantive or procedural, the temporal relationship between the matters, the significance of the issue to the immediate and long-term interests of the clients involved and the clients' reasonable expectations in retaining the lawyer. If there is significant risk of material limitation, then absent informed consent of the affected clients, the lawyer must refuse one of the representations or withdraw from one or both matters.

[25] When a lawyer represents or seeks to represent a class of plaintiffs or defendants in a class-action lawsuit, unnamed members of the class are ordinarily not considered to be clients of the lawyer for purposes of applying paragraph (a)(1) of this Rule. Thus, the lawyer does not typically need to get the consent of such a person before representing a client suing the person in an unrelated matter. Similarly, a lawyer seeking to represent an opponent in a

class action does not typically need the consent of an unnamed member of the class whom the lawyer represents in an unrelated matter.

Nonlitigation Conflicts

[26] Conflicts of interest under paragraphs (a)(1) and (a)(2) arise in contexts other than litigation. For a discussion of directly adverse conflicts in transactional matters, see Comment [7]. Relevant factors in determining whether there is significant potential for material limitation include the duration and intimacy of the lawyer's relationship with the client or clients involved, the functions being performed by the lawyer, the likelihood that disagreements will arise and the likely prejudice to the client from the conflict. The question is often one of proximity and degree. See Comment [8].

[27] For example, conflict questions may arise in estate planning and estate administration. A lawyer may be called upon to prepare wills for several family members, such as husband and wife, and, depending upon the circumstances, a conflict of interest may be present. In estate administration the identity of the client may be unclear under the law of a particular jurisdiction. Under one view, the client is the fiduciary; under another view the client is the estate or trust, including its beneficiaries. In order to comply with conflict of interest rules, the lawyer should make clear the lawyer's relationship to the parties involved.

[28] Whether a conflict is consentable depends on the circumstances. For example, a lawyer may not represent multiple parties to a negotiation whose interests are fundamentally antagonistic to each other, but common representation is permissible where the clients are generally aligned in interest even though there is some difference in interest among them. Thus, a lawyer may seek to establish or adjust a relationship between clients on an amicable and mutually advantageous basis; for example, in helping to organize a business in which two or more clients are entrepreneurs, working out the financial reorganization of an enterprise in which two or more clients have an interest or arranging a property distribution in settlement of an estate. The lawyer seeks to resolve potentially adverse interests by developing the parties' mutual interests. Otherwise, each party might have to obtain separate representation, with the possibility of incurring additional cost, complication or even litigation. Given these and other relevant factors, the clients may prefer that the lawyer act for all of them.

Special Considerations in Common Representation

[29] In considering whether to represent multiple clients in the same matter, a lawyer should be mindful that if the common representation fails because the potentially adverse interests cannot be reconciled, the result can be additional cost, embarrassment and recrimination. Ordinarily, the lawyer will be forced to withdraw from representing all of the clients if the common representation fails. In some situations, the risk of failure is so great that multiple representation is plainly impossible. For example, a lawyer cannot undertake common representation of clients where contentious litigation or negotiations between them are imminent or contemplated. Moreover, because the lawyer is required to be impartial between

325

commonly represented clients, representation of multiple clients is improper when it is unlikely that impartiality can be maintained. Generally, if the relationship between the parties has already assumed antagonism, the possibility that the clients' interests can be adequately served by common representation is not very good. Other relevant factors are whether the lawyer subsequently will represent both parties on a continuing basis and whether the situation involves creating or terminating a relationship between the parties.

[30] A particularly important factor in determining the appropriateness of common representation is the effect on client-lawyer confidentiality and the attorney-client privilege. With regard to the attorney-client privilege, the prevailing rule is that, as between commonly represented clients, the privilege does not attach. Hence, it must be assumed that if litigation eventuates between the clients, the privilege will not protect any such communications, and the clients should be so advised.

[31] As to the duty of confidentiality, continued common representation will almost certainly be inadequate if one client asks the lawyer not to disclose to the other client information relevant to the common representation. This is so because the lawyer has an equal duty of loyalty to each client, and each client has the right to be informed of anything bearing on the representation that might affect that client's interests and the right to expect that the lawyer will use that information to that client's benefit. See Rule 1.4. The lawyer should, at the outset of the common representation and as part of the process of obtaining each client's informed consent, advise each client that information will be shared and that the lawyer will have to withdraw if one client decides that some matter material to the representation should be kept from the other. In limited circumstances, it may be appropriate for the lawyer to proceed with the representation when the clients have agreed, after being properly informed, that the lawyer will keep certain information confidential. For example, the lawyer may reasonably conclude that failure to disclose one client's trade secrets to another client will not adversely affect representation involving a joint venture between the clients and agree to keep that information confidential with the informed consent of both clients.

[32] When seeking to establish or adjust a relationship between clients, the lawyer should make clear that the lawyer's role is not that of partisanship normally expected in other circumstances and, thus, that the clients may be required to assume greater responsibility for decisions than when each client is separately represented. Any limitations on the scope of the representation made necessary as a result of the common representation should be fully explained to the clients at the outset of the representation. See Rule 1.2(c).

[33] Subject to the above limitations, each client in the common representation has the right to loyal and diligent representation and the protection of Rule 1.9 concerning the obligations to a former client. The client also has the right to discharge the lawyer as stated in Rule 1.16.

Organizational Clients

[34] A lawyer who represents a corporation or other organization

does not, by virtue of that representation, necessarily represent any constituent or affiliated organization, such as a parent or subsidiary. See Rule 1.13(a). Thus, the lawyer for an organization is not barred from accepting representation adverse to an affiliate in an unrelated matter, unless the circumstances are such that the affiliate should also be considered a client of the lawyer, there is an understanding between the lawyer and the organizational client that the lawyer will avoid representation adverse to the client's affiliates, or the lawyer's obligations to either the organizational client or the new client are likely to limit materially the lawyer's representation of the other client.

[35] A lawyer for a corporation or other organization who is also a member of its board of directors should determine whether the responsibilities of the two roles may conflict. The lawyer may be called on to advise the corporation in matters involving actions of the directors. Consideration should be given to the frequency with which such situations may arise, the potential intensity of the conflict, the effect of the lawyer's resignation from the board and the possibility of the corporation's obtaining legal advice from another lawyer in such situations. If there is material risk that the dual role will compromise the lawyer's independence of professional judgment, the lawyer should not serve as a director or should cease to act as the corporation's lawyer when conflicts of interest arise. The lawyer should advise the other members of the board that in some circumstances matters discussed at board meetings while the lawyer is present in the capacity of director might not be protected by the attorney-client privilege and that conflict of interest considerations might require the lawyer's recusal as a director or might require the lawyer and the lawyer's firm to decline representation of the corporation in a matter.

Authors' 1983 Model Rules Comparison[1]

The drafters of the 2002 Rules substantially amended the text and Comments of Rule 1.7 for purposes of clarity; however, the analysis and result in conflicts cases is similar under the both versions of this Rule.

The drafters changed the title of the Rule from "Conflicts of Interest: General Rule" to "Conflicts of Interests: Current Clients."

The 1983 version of Rule 1.7 dealt with what it called "directly adverse" conflicts under paragraph (a) and "materially limited" conflicts under paragraph (b). Under each of those provisions, the 1983 spelled out a two step approach to solving the conflict. Rule 1.7 read as follows:

[Rule 1.7]

[1]In 1987, the ABA added the following sentence to Comment 1 of the 1983 Rules: "The lawyer should adopt reasonable procedures, appropriate for the size and type of firm and practice, to determine in both litigation and non-litigation matters the parties and issues involved and to determine whether there are actual or potential conflicts of interest." The remainder of paragraph 1 in the original version of this Comment now appears in the current paragraph 2.

RULE 1.7 Conflict of Interest: General Rule

(a) A lawyer shall not represent a client if the representation of that client will be directly adverse to another client, unless:

(1) the lawyer reasonably believes the representation will not adversely affect the relationship with the other client; and

(2) each client consents after consultation.

(b) A lawyer shall not represent a client if the representation of that client may be materially limited by the lawyer's responsibilities to another client or to a third person, or by the lawyer's own interests, unless:

(1) the lawyer reasonably believes the representation will not be adversely affected; and

(2) the client consents after consultation. When representation of multiple clients in a single matter is undertaken, the consultation shall include explanation of the implications of the common representation and the advantages and risks involved.

The drafters of the 2002 Rules thought the conflicts should be spelled out first and the solution should be spelled out second. Thus, the current paragraph (a) provides information about two present client conflicts and paragraph (b) provides information about how they may be solved, if at all.

In Comment 1, the drafters amended the language to explain that loyalty and independent judgment are the cornerstones of conflicts law.

Comment 2 is new and sets forth a method for approaching conflicts of interests.

In Comment 3, the drafters amended the language slightly to more forcefully explain when conflicts may arise.

The drafters renumbered old Comment 2 as Comment 4 and amended it to reflect the "informed consent" language.

Comment 5 is new and examines how unforeseen changes in facts may create conflicts.

The drafters renumbered old Comment 3 as Comment 6 and elaborated the analysis of "directly adverse" conflicts.

Comment 7 is new and examines directly adverse conflicts in transactional matters.

The drafters renumbered old Comment 4 as Comment 8; it examines materially limited conflicts.

Comment 9 is new and examines the link between Rule 1.7 and Rule 1.9.

The drafters renumbered old Comment 6 as Comment 10; it continues to examine personal interest conflicts.

Comments 11 and 12 are new and further elaborate on personal interest conflicts.

The drafters renumbered old Comment 10 as Comment 13 and amended it to more generally address conflicts created when a third party pays for the legal services of another.

The drafters renumbered old Comment 5 as Comment 14 and amended it to refocus the discussion to examine the issue of consent. It explains that some conflicts are nonconsentable.

Comments 15 to 17 are new and continue to discuss the issue of consent in Rule 1.7.

Comments 18 to 19 are new and examine the requirement of informed consent.

Comment 20 is new and discusses the confirmed in writing requirement.

Comment 21 is new and discusses the issue of whether consent may be revoked.

Comment 22 is new and discusses the issue of consent to future conflicts.

The drafters renumbered old Comment 7 as Comment 23; it discusses conflicts in litigation.

Old Comments 8 and 9 were deleted.

Comments 24 to 25 are new and continue to discuss litigation conflicts.

The drafters renumbered old Comments 11 to 13 as Comments 26 to 28 and amended them to discuss conflicts in nonlitigation situations.

Comments 29 to 33 are new and examine conflicts in multiple client representations. Much of this language was moved from the Comments to the 1983 version of Rule 2.2 after it was deleted.

Comment 34 is new and examines conflicts when a lawyer represents an entity client.

The drafters renumbered old Comment 13 as Comment 35; they added the last line and a clause to urge lawyers to withdraw when conflicts arise with respect to an organizational client.

Old Comment 15 was deleted.

Model Code Comparison

[1] DR 5-101(A) provided that "[e]xcept with the consent of his client after full disclosure, a lawyer shall not accept employment if the exercise of his professional judgment on behalf of the client will be or reasonably may be affected by his own financial, business, property, or personal interests." DR 5-105(A) provided that a lawyer "shall decline proffered employment if the exercise of his independent professional judgment in behalf of a client will be or is likely to be adversely affected by the acceptance of the proffered employment, or if it would be likely to involve him in representing differing interests, except to the extent permitted under DR 5-105(C)." DR 5-105(C) provided that "a lawyer may represent multiple clients if it is obvious that he can adequately represent the interest of each and if each consents to the representation after full disclosure of the possible effect of such representation on the exercise of his independent professional judgment on behalf of each." DR 5-107(B) provided that a lawyer "shall not permit a person who recommends, employs, or pays him to render legal services for another to direct or regulate his professional judgment in rendering such services."

[2] Rule 1.7 clarifies DR 5-105(A) by requiring that, when the lawyer's other interests are involved, not only must the client consent after consultation but also that, independent of such consent, the representation reasonably appears not to be adversely affected by the lawyer's other interests. This requirement appears

to be the intended meaning of the provision in DR 5-105(C) that "it is obvious that he can adequately represent" the client, and was implicit in EC 5-2, which stated that a lawyer "should not accept proffered employment if his personal interests or desires will, or there is a reasonable probability that they will, affect adversely the advice to be given or services to be rendered the prospective client."

§ 1.7–1 INTRODUCTION[1]

§ 1.7–1(a) The Basic Rationale

The rules governing conflict of interest derive, in large part, from the need to protect client confidences and secrets and the need to assure clients that they have their lawyer's loyalty.[2] The rules are found, primarily, in Rules 1.7 through 1.13 of the ABA Model Rules and in Canon 5 of the ABA Model Code.[3]

One of the lawyer's primary duties is to protect the client's secret or confidential information. This duty survives the client-lawyer relationship, and even applies to conversations with prospective clients. For example, if a lawyer simultaneously represents Client A and Client B (or now represents Client B and previously represented Client A), a conflict may develop because the lawyer may know secret information about Client A (the present, or former, client) and this information would be relevant, material, or useful to Client B, whom the lawyer is representing in a related case.[4] If the lawyer does not reveal the information to B, the lawyer would be violating her duty of loyalty to B because she would not be representing B vigorously. But, if the lawyer

---

[Section 1.7–1]

[1] Attorneys who are researching conflicts of interest issues should consult www.freivogelonconflicts.com, a website devoted to a sophisticated commentary on the law of conflicts of interest. William Freivogel includes some in depth analysis of some of the basics of conflicts law as well as a discussion of new cases and authorities.

[2] See *Developments in the Law—Conflicts of Interest in the Legal Profession*, 94 HARV. L. REV. 1244, 1252–60 (1981) (examining the instrumental (harm to the client) and intrinsic (loyalty to the client) justifications underlying the conflicts of interest rules).

[3] See also Restatement of the Law Governing Lawyers, Third, §§ 121 to 135 (Official Draft 2000). The basic rule regarding personal interest conflicts of interest is § 125, "A Lawyer's Personal Interest Affecting Representation of Client." The sections that correspond to Rule 1.7 are § 128, "Representing Parties with Conflicting Interests in Litigation," § 129, "Conflicts of Interest in Criminal Litigation," and § 130, "Multiple Representation in Non-Litigated Matter."

[4] **Related Cases.** Assume that a lawyer represents Client A (an all-news radio station or a newspaper) and the lawyer also represents Client B (a local celebrity). Client A may want to know all the gossip about Client B, but the lawyer who represents both Clients A and B is not in a conflict. It is not a conflict for the lawyer to keep the secrets of Client B from Client A because the representations involve unrelated matters. However, the lawyer cannot represent Client B in a defamation suit against Client A.

does reveal this information to *B,* then lawyer would be violating her duty to *A* to keep *A*'s secrets.

In the example just given, the conflict derives from the fact that the lawyer either divulges the secrets of one client (or a former client), or fails to represent vigorously the other client. However, conflicts of interest can arise even if there is no breach of client secrets. For example, assume that a lawyer for Client *D* is paid by the insurer of Client *D.* The insurer instructs the lawyer (who is defending *D,* the insured, in a tort suit) not to dispute Plaintiff's charge that *D*'s tortious conduct was really intentional. If the jury believes that *D* acted intentionally, the insurer will not be liable because the policy does not cover intentional torts. If the lawyer follows the insurer's instructions, she will be violating her duty of loyalty to *D,* her client.

Complaints about attorneys' conflicts of interest have a long pedigree. The London Ordinance of 1280 forbade attorneys from engaging in various conflicts, such as taking "money from both parties in any action." The penalty was suspension for three years. In the case where an attorney takes money, "and then leaves his client, and leagues himself with the other party," the penalty was that the attorney "shall render double [apparently, return twice his fee to the client] and he shall not be heard in that case."[5] About a decade later, a tome attacking attorneys specifically complained about attorneys taking fees "from both sides in one cause."[6] There is nothing new under the sun.

Given these policies and rationales behind the rubric of conflict of interests, the rules distinguish between various types of conflicts. There might be a conflict between the client and the lawyer's business or personal interests; or between the client and another present or former client; or between the client and a person or group who may be paying for the client's legal assistance. This chapter will analyze and discuss these categories of conflicts.

§ 1.7–1(b) Comparing Rule 1.7(a)(1) and Rule 1.7(b)(2)

The 1983 version of Rule 1.7 contained two provisions: (1) Rule 1.7(a) dealt with what it called "directly adverse" conflicts; and

---

[5]Jonathan Rose, *The Ambidextrous Lawyer: Conflict of Interest and the Medieval and Early Modern Legal Profession,* 7 U. CHI. LAW SCHOOL ROUNDTABLE: A JOURNAL OF INTERDISCIPLINARY LEGAL STUDIES 137, 146-47 & n.48 (2000). This article provides a very thorough and interesting discussion and analysis of the relevant history.

[6]Quoted in, Jonathan Rose, *The Ambidextrous Lawyer: Conflict of Interest and the Medieval and Early Modern Legal Profession,* 7 U. CHI. LAW SCHOOL ROUNDTABLE: A JOURNAL OF INTERDISCIPLINARY LEGAL STUDIES 137, 139 & n.11 (2000).

(2) Rule 1.7(b) dealt with "materially limited" conflicts.[7] Under each paragraph, the drafters of the 1983 rules provided a two-step approach to resolve the conflict.

The drafters of the 2002 Rules restructured Rule 1.7 to put both tests in Rule 1.7(a) and to provide the means by which to resolve all present client conflicts in Rule 1.7(b). The 1983 structure was confusing. Now, all present client conflicts should be covered in one provision. Also, all present client conflicts are now resolved with one test. While language of the 1983 and the 2002 version of Rule 1.7 are similar, the structure is definitely improved. The drafters also added twenty Comments to this Rule in order to improve our understanding of textual language. The following analysis will focus primarily on the Rule 1.7 as it has been amended.

Rule 1.7(a)(1) must cover situations that are different than Rule 1.7(a)(2), or there would be no need for separate subsections of this Rule. The problem is that the language that the two subsections use is hardly self-defining. Rule 1.7(a)(1) prohibits a lawyer representing a client if that representation "will be *directly* adverse to another client." Rule 1.7(a)(2) also prohibits a representation if there is a significant risk that the representation "will be *materially limited* by the lawyer's responsibilities to another client, a former client, or a third person or by a personal interest of the lawyer."[8] This Rule offers no test to distinguish "*directly* adverse" from "*materially limited*." The Comments, however, offer some guidance.

The prohibition against direct adverse conflicts is grounded in the obligation of loyalty to current clients. A current client expects that their lawyer will not take another representation that is

---

[7]Rule 1.7, Conflict of Interest: General Rule, provides:

"(a) A lawyer shall not represent a client if the representation of that client will be directly adverse to another, unless:

"(1) the lawyer reasonably believes the representation will not adversely affect the relationship with the other client; and

"(2) each client consents after consultation.

"(b) A lawyer shall not represent a client if the representation of that client may be materially limited by the lawyer's responsibilities to another client or to a third person, or by the lawyer's own interests, unless:

"(1) the lawyer reasonably believes the representation will not be adversely affected; and

"(2) the client consents after consultation. When representation of multiple clients in a single matter is undertaken, the consultation shall include explanation of the implications of the common representation and the advantages and risks involved."

[8]Rule 1.7 (emphasis added). *See also* Rule 1.7, Comments 6, 8; DR 5-105(A).

directly adverse to the representation of the current client.[9] The most fundamental example of clients who are directly adverse to each other involves the situation where one lawyer or law firm represents the plaintiff and the defendant in the same action.

Lawyers, by training, think it is preposterous for the same firm to represent both sides in the very same action. However, in some professions such as accounting, firms can create company focused teams representing different clients seeking a competitive license or bid, if the firm screened each team from the other.

The long tradition of the legal profession is otherwise. We start with the principle that the client hires the "firm" and not just a particular lawyer in the firm. In the legal profession, despite the hired gun model of advocacy, it is a "directly adverse" conflict if one law firm is on both sides of the same case. A variation of this situation arises when a law firm represents multiple plaintiffs or defendants and one of them seeks to sue the others (via a cross claim) in the matter in which the law firm is involved. This situation also creates what the rules call a "directly adverse" conflict of interest.

The Rule tries to define "directly adverse" by example. A "directly adverse conflict" arises when a lawyer, representing Client Alpha in litigation, cross examines a witness who happens to be Client Beta in a different matter, if the cross examination may elicit damaging information involving Client Beta.[10] A law firm that sues a present client even on an unrelated matter is also involved in a directly adverse conflict.[11] For example, if a law firm currently represents an oil company on tax matters, a directly adverse conflict arises if the firm represents a different client suing the oil company on an environmental oil spill.

This example arises in *litigation* against the oil company client, but a "directly adverse" conflict is not limited to litigation. There is also a "directly adverse" conflict if Law Firm #1 negotiates, on behalf of a buyer, the sale of a property where the seller is also a client of the firm. This conflict is "directly adverse" even if the seller has retained a different law firm (Law Firm #2) for

---

[9] Rule 1.7, Comment 6.

[10] Rule 1.7, Comment 6. ABA Formal Ethics Opinion 92-367 (Oct. 16, 1992), *Lawyer Examining A Client As An Adverse Witness, Or Conducting Third Party Discovery Of The Client*, advises that a lawyer who, in the course of representing a client examines another client as an adverse witness in a matter—even though the other matter is unrelated to the lawyer's representation of the other client—or conducts third party discovery of the client in such a matter, will likely face a conflict that is disqualifying in the absence of appropriate client consent. Any such disqualification is imputed to other lawyers in the lawyer's firm.

[11] Rule 1.7, Comment 6.

the negotiations because the seller is also the client of Law Firm #1.[12]

The problem with using a vague phrase like "directly adverse" is that law firms represent clients that compete with each other in the business world. When a firm helps one client, it may hurt another client, knowingly or unknowingly. The law firm that aids a water utility in raising its rates hurts all the firm's other clients who use water.[13] The law firm that represents the local Ford car dealer in buying some real estate may also represent the local Mercedes dealer in a contract matter. The representations and the clients have nothing to do with each other, but the clients are competitors in the business world.

Law firms may be very cognizant of the businesses and products of all of their clients or they may know little outside of the scope of representation of their client's business affairs. Obviously, if "directly adverse" meant any economic competition, conflicts would exist in every boutique firm and large firm. Thus, the Comments to Rule 1.7 advise that "simultaneous representation in unrelated matters of clients whose interests are only economically adverse, such as representation of competing economic enterprises in unrelated litigation, does not ordinarily constitute a conflict of interest and thus may not require consent of the respective clients."[14]

This interpretation is necessary to keep the conflicts of interest rules workable and focused on the serious problems. Legitimate client expectations do not extend to believing that a law firm will not represent the client's competitors in unrelated matters. The dry cleaner who hires a lawyer to handle a property tax dispute is not surprised that his lawyer may also represent a local grocery store or another dry cleaner in a different property tax dispute. Indeed, the reason the dry cleaner hires the lawyer is because of her expertise in property tax matters.

Besides "directly adverse" conflicts, there are "materially limited" conflicts. Materially limited conflicts are focused on client harm and thus they tend to be easier to define. If one would assume that a lawyer without a conflict would provide a baseline of conduct in a typical representation, a lawyer with a materially limited conflict is torn between providing the baseline and some lesser representation because of some other set of obligations.

---

[12] Rule 1.7, Comment 7.

[13] ABA Formal Opinion 05-434 (Dec. 8, 2004), at n. 8:

> where a lawyer may have represented two clients in unrelated matters and both clients were in competition to sell foods to a third party, the representation of one of those clients in negotiat-

ing a sale to a third party would not constitute a violation of Rule 1.7(a).

[14] Rule 1.7, Comment 6. How one can identify the extraordinary cases where this does create a conflict is difficult to state.

This type of conflict implicates situations that create "a significant risk that a lawyer's ability to consider, recommend, carry out an appropriate course of conduct" is limited by the other obligations.[15] Those obligations may lie to another current client, a former client, a third person, the law firm's self interests, or to the personal interests of a specific lawyer.

The application of the "materially limited" conflicts rule to current clients may involve current clients whom the law firm represents in separate actions, or current clients whom the law firm represents in the same lawsuit or negotiation.[16] For example, assume a law firm represents plaintiffs in a class action against various banks in a state, and the firm recommends that these clients should not add Bank A to the list of defendants. There may be legitimate reasons not to add Bank A (adding that bank may affect venue), but if Bank A is a current client of the firm, that situation creates a materially limited conflict with respect to the plaintiff clients. Would a lawyer without that Bank A as a client make the same recommendation to the clients?

In addition, the "materially limited" test applies when a law firm represents multiple plaintiffs or multiple defendants in litigation or multiple clients forming a partnership or resolving a dispute. For example, the lawyer who represents several people forming a new business venture must make sure that there is no significant risk that the lawyer's responsibilities to one of these people does not materially limit his responsibilities to the other clients.

Materially limited conflicts arise in an incalculable number of ways. Lawyers may owe an obligation to another client and thus may downplay the work of one client for another. They may choose to put effort into current client matters based upon profitability while leaving other clients in the lurch. Lawyers may have obligations to relatives, to individuals with whom they are seeking employment, or to their own financial interests because of investments or ownership of a business. The key inquiry is whether a "significant risk" exists that the representation of one client will suffer because of the lawyer's obligations to self or others. The "mere possibility" of subsequent harm does not trigger Rule 1.7(a)(2).[17]

Conflicts of interest analysis is very fact specific and it is difficult to generalize one approach for all conflicts. It is accurate to say that usually conflicts are absent one minute and present the next minute. In many cases, conflicts arise as potentially present

---

[15]Rule 1.7, Comment 8. The significant risk language was added to the text of the Rule by the drafters of the 2002 Rules.

[16]See Rule 1.7(b), Comment 8; DR 5-105(B), (C).

[17]Rule 1.7, Comment 8.

and some facts may change to accentuate them or remove them. The potential conflict may become an actual conflict and thus covered by Rule 1.7. The drafters of the 2002 Rules chose not to use the terms actual and potential although they are clearly implicated in the tests. The directly adverse test seems to require actual adversity to trigger Rule 1.7(b)(1). On the other hand, materially limited conflicts arise when a significant risk exists that the representation of the client will be materially limited. The term, "significant risk" is less than actually present but more than merely potential. The Comments seem to focus on the "likelihood that a difference in interests will eventuate and, if it does, whether it will materially interfere with the lawyer's independent professional judgment in considering alternatives or foreclose courts of action that should be pursued on behalf of the client."[18] Lawyers need to focus on the potentiality of materially limited conflicts of interest.

§ 1.7-1(c) Solving Current Client Conflicts

The 1983 version of the Rules had a two step approach for current conflicts of interest. The drafters of the 2002 Rules put all requirements for solving a current client conflict into Rule 1.7(b). This provision has four inquiries:

FIRST, the lawyer must make an independent determination that the lawyer can provide competent and diligent representation to all of the affected clients. The 1983 version had a different formulation of this inquiry. It required the lawyer to "reasonably believe that the representation would not be adversely affected."[19] Although the ABA used this standard for almost twenty years, it was a difficult one to apply.[20] The inquiry into competent and diligent representation is far easier to apply and more appropriate.

SECOND, the lawyer must examine whether some other law prohibits the lawyer from accepting the representation.[21] Obviously, this invites courts and legislatures into making law that prohibits certain types of conflicts of interest and lawyers and clients must abide by these legally mandated disqualifications.

THIRD, the drafters codified a category of nonconsentable conflicts by requiring that the lawyer not represent one client

---

[18]Rule 1.7, Comment 8.

[19]1983 Model Rule 1.7(a)(1), (b)(1).

[20]In the vast majority of conflicts cases, it was not really possible to state that there would be no adverse effect. One could say that the effect was tolerable or one that should be left to a client's consent. Some states and courts transformed the "not adversely affect the representation" test into whether a reasonable lawyer would recommend to a client that they consent to the conflict.

[21]Rule 1.7(b)(2).

against another client "in the same litigation or other proceedings before a tribunal."[22]

FINALLY, each affected client must give the lawyer "informed consent, confirmed in writing."[23]

Essentially, this four-part test can be summarized as follows. Lawyers may never represent plaintiff and defendant or parties that oppose each other in litigation or before a tribunal. Lawyers must abide by law that would disqualify them from representing clients involved in a conflict.

Apart from these two situations, the lawyer is left with a two part test similar to the one used under the 1983 Rules. First, the lawyer must make an independent determination that the lawyer can competently and diligently represent each affected client. And, each affected client must give informed consent confirmed in writing to the lawyer. These restrictions apply whether the lawyer represents multiple parties, whether or not the parties are in litigation. For example, in the case of, *In re Botimer*,[24] the Court suspended a lawyer for six months because he represented feuding family members representing multiple clients without obtaining informed consent in writing to the joint representation. When a dispute arose among the family members, the lawyer then violated confidentiality rule by revealing confidences.

Bear in mind that the client may be able to waive the conflict, but some conflicts are not waiveable. When a conflicts rule is designed to protect only the client, little reason exists to prohibit a lawyer from engaging in the representation when a competent and informed client desires to waive that protection. In contrast, if the conflicts rule is designed to protect a systemic interest—an interest of the system of justice—client waiver should be ineffective.

Rule 1.7, unlike some Rules,[25] allows a client waiver, but—in order for that waiver to be effective—the lawyer must reasonably believe that he or she can provide competent and diligent repre-

---

[22]Rule 1.7(b)(3).

[23]Rule 1.7(b)(4).

[24]*In re Disciplinary Proceeding Against Botimer*, 166 Wash. 2d 759, 214 P.3d 133 (2009). A controversy arose when one client (James) would not recognize that the other clients (family members Ruth and/or Jan) had an ownership stake in a nursing home that James ran. Both brothers disagreed as to the extent of each one's stock ownership. Botimer assisted Jan and Ruth in negotiations with James regarding potential solutions. Botimer did not obtain conflict waivers in the course of his assistance of the various members of the Reinking family. Further, he did not discuss the advantages and disadvantages of joint representation. Botimer did not use a written client engagement agreement or any other method to obtain consent in writing to the conflict.

[25]For example, Rule 1.8(d), governing the lawyer's securing of media or literary rights, does not provide for a waiver, while other rules, *e.g.*, Rules 1.8(f), (g), allow a client's knowing consent.

sentation to the affected clients despite (1) the presence of clients who are directly adverse to each other or (2) the presence of a situation implicating conflicting obligations to the interests of clients or others.[26] In order for the lawyer to act reasonably, the lawyer must institute reasonable conflicts procedures so that lawyers in the firm know if they are representing clients with adverse or potentially adverse interests. The lawyer should not benefit from ignorance: if the lawyer does not know that there are clients with adverse positions because there are no reasonable conflicts procedures, then the lawyer has not complied with Rule 1.7.[27]

On the issue of informed consent, confirmed in writing, it is now clear that the lawyer must explain to the clients the relevant circumstances that created the conflict and the manner in which the conflict can affect the clients in the future.[28] Of course, lawyers must only discuss material and foreseeable effects. They can only discuss "foreseeable" conflicts by definition, because a reasonable lawyer cannot discuss what one cannot foresee. Yet, prudence requires that lawyers should err on the side of disclosure. If the conflict arises because of a potential multiple client representation, the prospective clients must know the risks

---

[26] Rule 1.7(b)(1).

[27] **Conflicts Checks within a Law Firm.** *See* Rule 1.7, Comment 3. The lawyer's belief that there is no conflict must be reasonable and in good faith; on this point, the commentators are in agreement. *See, e.g.,* Restatement of the Law Governing Lawyers, Third, § 121, comment *c(iv)* (Official Draft 2000); RONALD E. MALLEN & JEFFREY M. SMITH, LEGAL MALPRACTICE § 12.10 (West Pub. Co. 3d ed. 1989); 1 GEOFFREY C. HAZARD, JR. & W. WILLIAM HODES, THE LAW OF LAWYERING: A HANDBOOK ON THE MODEL RULES OF PROFESSIONAL CONDUCT § 10.7 (Prentice Hall 3d ed. 2001)(with annual supplementation). Lawyers who do not institute reasonable conflicts procedures to ferret out conflicts and potential conflicts would be acting contrary to the ethics requirement discussed in Rule 1.7, Comment 3.

Comparing Rule 1.7's "Reasonable" Requirement and Rule 1.10's "Knowing" Requirement. Rule 1.7, Comment 3, refers to the "lawyer" adopting reasonable conflict checking procedure. But, the lawyer may be a lowly associate in a large law firm. The "law firm" is the entity that really establishes the conflicts checking procedures. Consider the situation where Lawyer A (a partner in the law firm) cannot take a case because of a conflict under Rule 1.7. This law firm does not have a reasonable conflicts checking procedure and so the case is assigned to Lawyer B (another partner) and Lawyer C (an associate). Lawyer C is disqualified because Lawyer A's conflict is imputed to him, pursuant to Rule 1.10(a). But, Rule 1.10(a)—unlike Rule 1.7—has a "knowing" requirement: while Lawyers A, B, and C are associated in the same law firm, "none of them shall *knowingly* represent a client when any one of them practicing alone would be prohibited . . .." The responsibility of the associate, Lawyer C, should be a function based on Rule 1.10 and Rule 5.2, dealing with the responsibilities of a subordinate lawyer. And the liability of Lawyer B (the other partner) should be a function of Rule 1.10 and Rule 5.1, dealing with the responsibilities of a partner or supervisory lawyer.

[28] Rule 1.7, Comment 18.

and benefits of having one lawyer represent them before they enter into the representation.[29] Clients considering a multiple client representation are entitled to consider the costs of having separate lawyers in determining whether to consent.[30]

If the lawyer cannot disclose all of the information because some or all of it is confidential and the lawyer cannot obtain the consent to share the information, the lawyer may not seek to obtain the clients' consent to the conflict.[31] The inability of the lawyer to provide full information to the clients prevents the clients from giving informed consent. Clients cannot consent to a *knowing* waiver of the conflict because the lawyer does not give him all the necessary information.

The requirement that the lawyer provide a client with a confirmation of the consent *in writing* is designed to impress upon the client the seriousness of the conflict of interest.[32]

The requirement of a writing does not necessarily excuse the lawyer from talking to the client. A writing is not the only means by which to inform the client of the risks and circumstances necessary to give informed consent. The preferred method of obtaining consent is first to have a conversation with the client explaining the conflict and answering questions. Then the lawyer should follow up any oral consent with a writing at or shortly after the client gives informed consent. Thus, the client may execute a written consent or, after giving oral consent, can receive a writing from the lawyer confirming that the client has provided consent to the conflict of interest.

With respect to the different types of conflicts, we will consider why the client may desire to waive and under what circumstances that waiver will be effective. But first we turn to a related issue, the question of implied waiver.

§ 1.7–1(d) Implied Waiver

The ethics rules do not provide for an "implied" waiver by the client. In fact, the ethics rule set out an explicit procedure for a waiver. The client should be able to rely on the lawyer, on whom the Rules place the obligation to secure an informed consent.[33]

However, in cases not involving lawyer discipline, a court, in some instances, may conclude—in deciding whether to disqualify a lawyer—that the lawyer has not complied with Rule 1.7, that the client has not consented to the conflict, that the lawyer has not secured a valid waiver from client, and that the client has not voluntarily relinquished a known right, but the court will never-

---

[29] Rule 1.7, Comment 18.
[30] Rule 1.7, Comment 19.
[31] Rule 1.7, Comment 19.

[32] Rule 1.7, Comment 20, "Consent Confirmed in Writing."
[33] Rule 1.7(b)(3).

theless go on to find that there has been an *implied* waiver.[34] For example, the court might argue that the party waited too long to bring its motion.[35]

Courts typically do not describe the source of this "implied" waiver. It certainly does not come from Rule 1.7. A waiver is a voluntary relinquishment of a known right. If the party raising the conflict has played fast and loose with the court (for example, by making a calculation not to raise a conflict until later, so that the disqualification will impose a greater financial burden on the other party), then it is not difficult to understand why the court would react negatively and find what should more properly be called a "forfeiture," but what the court may erroneously call an implied waiver. Courts should not allow lawyers and their clients to plant error in the record.[36]

It is a different story when the party does not raise a conflict simply because it did not know about the relevant facts until later. If the lawyers do not secure a valid consent from their client, the burden should be on the lawyers to give promptly to the client the information needed to effectuate a valid waiver.

The Rules of Professional Conduct govern lawyers, not clients; and clients—when dealing with their lawyers—should be able to trust their lawyers and not assume that they are making a pact with the devil. It is the duty of the lawyer (when seeking to secure a waiver from a client or former client) to candidlly tell the client the relevant facts, *and* bring home to the client the significance of those facts. The client may know certain facts (*e.g.,* "I trusted my lawyer with confidential information and now she is representing another party against me"), but the client may not know the

---

[34]*See, e.g., Conoco v. Baskin,* 803 S.W.2d 416, 420 (Tex.App.El Paso, 1991, no writ).

[35]*Cox v. American Cast Iron Pipe Co.,* 847 F.2d 725, 730 (11th Cir.1988). The court concluded that any alleged need to "prevent the appearance of impropriety" did not require the disqualification of counsel in Title VII action. The lawyer had formed a law firm with another lawyer who had represented the defendant in the action five years before but was not currently participating in the action, the issue of disqualification was not raised until shortly before trial, the action had been pending for 14 years, and plaintiffs' current counsel had represented them for four years.

See also, e.g., Redd v. Shell Oil

Co., 518 F.2d 311, 316 (10th Cir.1975); *Trust Corp. v. Piper Aircraft Corp.,* 701 F.2d 85, 87–88 (9th Cir.1983); *Glover v. Libman,* 578 F.Supp. 748, 760 (N.D.Ga.1983); *Cox v. American Cast Iron Pipe Co.,* 847 F.2d 725, 729 (11th Cir.1988).

[36]*Redd v. Shell Oil Co.,* 518 F.2d 311 (10th Cir.1975); *Central Milk Producers Co-op. v. Sentry Food Stores,* 573 F.2d 988 (8th Cir.1978).

"A litigant may not delay filing a motion to disqualify in order to use the motion later as a tool to deprive his opponent of counsel of his choice after substantial preparation of the case has been completed." *Jackson v. J.C. Penney Co.,* 521 F.Supp. 1032, 1034–35 (N.D.Ga.1981), relying on ABA Model Code, Canons 4, 5, & 9.

significance of those facts (*i.e.,* that the lawyer must disqualify herself unless the client voluntarily relinquishes the right not to risk having confidential information used against her).[37]

§ 1.7–1(e) Imputation or Vicarious Disqualification

Both the ABA Model Rules and the ABA Model Code sometimes *impute* one lawyer's disqualifying conflict to all of the other lawyers in the same firm. Some cases refer to this concept as vicarious disqualification. The Rules and the Code often differ as to when a conflict is imputed, in part because the Rules reflect the modern practice of law. The drafters were able to deal with specific problem areas that the old Model Code did not anticipate.

Because imputation applies even when the law firm is very large, with branch offices in many states, the firm must adopt reasonable procedures, appropriate for the size and type of firm and practice, to determine whether there are actual or potential conflicts in both litigation and nonlitigation matters.[38]

Given today's law practice, all lawyers should have a computerized conflicts system that contains information about former and current clients of the law firm. Because such systems have flaws in input and search, the computer system should be backed up by a manual system. Lawyers and nonlawyers should receive a list of potential cases and have an opportunity to report an actual or potential conflict of interest.

§ 1.7–1(f) Consequences of a Conflict of Interest

A violation of the conflicts of interest rules may have several implications. In litigation, the most common consequence is that the opposing party will seek to disqualify the law firm with the conflict from continuing to represent the client. Lawyers often file such motions on behalf of a party who has standing to minimize the effect of the conflict on the merits of the litigation and to obtain the strategic benefit of delay and harassment of the opposing side.[39] If the conflict is such that it "taints" the fact finding process or fairness of the trial, the court should grant the motion.[40] For example, if the conflict occurs because the conflicted lawyer is privy to the confidential information of his former client, and this

---

[37]Ronald D. Rotunda, *Legal Ethics*, 45 SOUTHWESTERN L.J. 2035, 2037–38 (1992).

[38]Rule 1.7, Comment 3.

[39]Courts often require that only a party who has standing may raise a conflict of interest in a motion to disqualify. *See* ABA CENTER FOR PROFESSIONAL RESPONSIBILITY, ANNOTATED MODEL RULES OF PROFESSIONAL CONDUCT 122–23 (ABA 6th ed. 2007),

citing e.g., In re Yarn Processing Patent Validity Litigation, 530 F.2d 83 (5th Cir. 1976); *FMC Technologies, Inc. v. Edwards*, 420 F. Supp. 2d 1153 (W.D. Wash. 2006).

[40]*Board of Ed. of City of New York v. Nyquist*, 590 F.2d 1241 (2d Cir. 1979). See also Douglas R. Richmond, *The Rude Question of Standing in Attorney Disqualification Disputes*, 25 AM. J. TRIAL ADVOCACY 17 (2001).

information would be relevant to the lawyer's representation of a new client against the former client, the conflict will taint the fact finding process. If the conflicted lawyer may reduce the vigor of his representation or pull his punches on behalf of Client #1 because he is simultaneously representing Client #2 in another matter, the conflict will taint the fact finding process.[41]

However, if the alleged ethical violation does not affect the fact finding process or the fairness of the trial, then the court should leave any enforcement of the alleged violation to the other fora for remedying conflicts of interest. For example, a claim by a defendant that plaintiff's lawyer improperly solicited the plaintiff will not taint the fact-finding process.[42] By drawing this distinction between alleged ethics violations that taint the fact finding process and alleged ethics violations that do not, the court will make it less likely that counsel will be able to use a disqualification motion as a "technique of harassment."[43]

Courts usually require motions to disqualify to be made on a timely basis. Delay by one of the parties is often considered to waive the right to move for disqualification. Of course, courts consider the effect of the disqualification on the schedule of the case as well as on the fairness to the party who will need to seek new counsel. Depending on the tribunal, decisions of a court to disqualify counsel may or may not be appealable. In federal court, the trial courts decision to disqualify or not disqualify counsel is

---

[41]Restatement of the Law Governing Lawyers, Third, § 6 (Official Draft 2000), Comment i, explains:

"Disqualification draws on the inherent power of courts to regulate the conduct of lawyers . . . as well as the related inherent power of judges to regulate the course of proceedings before them . . .. Disqualification, where appropriate, ensures that the case is well presented in court, that confidential information of present or former clients is not misused, and that a client's substantial interest in a lawyer's loyalty is protected." [internal citations omitted].

[42]See Lefrak v. Arabian American Oil Co., 527 F.2d 1136 (2d Cir. 1975).

[43]Rule 1.7, Comment 15. See, e.g., Universal City Studios, Inc. v. Reimerdes, 98 F. Supp. 2d 449 (S.D. N.Y. 2000), which involved an effort to preven defendants from posting a computer program on their web site that

would defeat plaintiffs' encryption protection of its DVDs. One of the defendants' law firms represented on of the plaintiffs (Time Warner) in a completely different action involving the Harry Potter books. Time Warner moved to disqualify that firm, which responded by basically telling Time Warner to fire it if it was unhappy. The court agreed that the law firm was in a conflict and could not avoid it by firing the client. The court also found the firm's conduct to be improper, but it still refused to disqualify it. First, the trial was only two months away, so the motion was untimely. Second, Time Warner knew about the conflict for almost a month before it bothered to raise it with the law firm it sought to disqualify. Time Warner's motion seemed "tactically motivated," the court said, and it would not be prejudiced by the court's refusal to disqualify. 98 F.Supp.2d 455.

generally not considered appealable.[44] In the state courts, the jurisdictions differ on the appealability issue.[45]

A lawyer's involvement with a conflict of interest may subject the lawyer to claim of a breach of duty to the client. A conflict of interest may serve as a basis for a breach of fiduciary duty that may require a forfeiture of all or part of the lawyer's attorney's fee.[46] Or it may serve as the basis of a malpractice action allowing the client to recover damages. Furthermore, a conflict of interest may subject the lawyer to state bar discipline.

§ 1.7-1(g) Strategic Disqualification Motions

Some people argue that lawyers should not make strategic disqualification motions—motions where the primary motive of the movant is to impose costs on the adversary. Initially, the ABA Model Rules acknowledged that position, when an older version said that a charge of a conflict of interest "should be viewed with caution . . . for it can be misused as a technique of harassment."[47] The post–2002 version does not include this comment, though some states continue to retain it.[48]

A motion to disqualify is either frivolous or not. If it is frivolous, the court should obviously reject it. If it is not frivolous, the court should rule on the merits without regard to the motive of the movant. When a lawyer objects to hearsay, no judge ever says, "Aha, a hearsay objection—I might rule differently if the lawyer might be making this for tactical reasons"? No party makes any motion that it regards as strategically disadvantageous or tactically unwise. Conflict motions and disqualification motions are no different than evidentiary motions.

§ 1.7-2 SIMULTANEOUS REPRESENTATION OF ADVERSE MULTIPLE CLIENTS IN RELATED MATTERS

§ 1.7-2(a) Introduction

It is common for lawyers to represent two or more clients in the same matter. For example, the lawyer may be asked to represent several clients in setting up a small corporation, or a

---

[44]*See Richardson-Merrell, Inc. v. Koller*, 472 U.S. 424, 105 S. Ct. 2757, 86 L. Ed. 2d 340 (1985)(denying appeal for order granting motion to disqualify); *Firestone Tire & Rubber Co. v. Risjord*, 449 U.S. 368, 101 S. Ct. 669, 66 L. Ed. 2d 571 (1981) (denying appeal for order denying motion to disqualify).

[45]William Freivogel, FREIVOGEL ON CONFLICTS (Mar. 2008), at http://www.freivogelonconflicts.com/new_pag

e43.htm (surveying different state holdings on appealability of disqualification orders).

[46]*See Burrow v. Arce*, 997 S.W.2d 229 (Tex. 1999).

[47]1983 ABA Model Rule 1.7, Comment 15.

[48]*E.g.*, Tex. Disciplinary Rules of Professional Conduct, Rule 1.06, Comment 17.

husband and wife in a real estate closing, or the driver and owner-passenger of a car when both are sued for injuries arising out of an automobile accident.

It is often in the best interest of clients to share the same lawyer. Such an arrangement reduces legal fees and saves time. Public policy does not require two different lawyers if one will suffice. A cost to the system of legal representation arises if the courts are too quick to prohibit legal representation because of unrealistic dangers of a conflict of interests. Consequently, the mere possibility of conflict does not itself preclude the representation.[1] On the other hand, such an arrangement does create the potential for conflict, so the lawyer must "weigh carefully the possibility that his judgment may be impaired or his loyalty divided if he accepts or continues the employment."[2]

§ 1.7–2(b) Litigation versus Counseling

The potential of conflict when representing multiple clients exists whether the representation involves litigation or counseling. However, disqualification is more likely in litigation than in counseling. First, in litigation the lawyer acts primarily as an advocate, while, in counseling, the lawyer is giving advice and the advocacy role is more muted.[3] Moreover, in litigation, the court can disqualify the lawyer, but when lawyers represent their clients in counseling, no judge is present to rule on disqualification, so the only realistic remedy is either discipline before the bar discipline authorities or damages for malpractice if a client is disgruntled enough to sue his former lawyer. Consequently, there is more case law dealing with conflicts of interest in litigation.

As a general rule, a "lawyer should never represent *in litigation* multiple clients with differing interests; and there are few situations in which he would be justified in representing *in litigation* multiple clients with potentially differing interests."[4]

The 2002 version of the Rules make clear that the lawyer may

[Section 1.7–2]

[1]Rule 1.7, Comments 29 to 33.

[2]EC 5-15. *See* Steven Lubet, *There Are No Scriveners Here*, 84 IOWA L. REV. 341 (1999).

[3]Rules 2.1, 3.1. *Cf.* EC 7-4, 7-5.

[4]EC 5-15 (emphasis added).

In *United States v. Gellene*, 182 F.3d 578 (7th Cir.1999), a lawyer's failure to disclose a conflict of interest was also a crime. Gellene, a partner in the New York firm of Milbank, Tweed, Hadley & McCloy, represented the debtor in a Chapter 11 bankruptcy. He was required to swear to a declaration identifying the firm's connection to all other parties in interest, but he failed to disclose that the firm also represented the senior secured creditor. He admitted bad judgment but denied a fraudulent intent. The jury found otherwise. Gellene was sentenced to 15 months in the penitentiary and paid a $15,000 fine, the sentence having been increased because Gellene, as a lawyer, had abused a "position of trust." *See also* Charles W. Wolfram, *The Boiling Pot Of Lawyer Conflicts In Bankruptcy*, 18 MISS. C. L. REV. 383 (1998).

not represent both Client *A* and *B* in the case of *A v. B*.[5] Rule 1.7(a)(1) speaks to the situation where the representation of a client is "*directly adverse*" to another client. Rule 1.7(b)(3) prohibits representation of opposing parties in litigation.[6] If a lawyer represents multiple clients in litigation who are all on the same side—all co-plaintiffs, or all co-defendants—Rule 1.7(a)(2) is applicable and (according to the Comments), Rule 1.7(a)(1) may also apply.[7] Rule 1.7(a)(1), dealing with a "directly adverse" conflict, applies if conflict exists among the multiple clients.

Of course, in almost every case, multiple clients are *potentially* adverse to each other whether it is in the settlement opportunities, their prospective testimony, or potential cross claims. However, the mere potentiality is not enough to trigger Rule 1.7(b); the potentiality must create a "significant risk." Reasonable lawyers, in other words, are not liable for not foreseeing what is beyond the horizon.

§ 1.7–2(c) Waiver in the Litigation Context

The conflict illustrated by the case of *A v. B*—where the lawyer represents both *A* and *B* who are suing each other—is so great that it would not even be cured by consent.[8] The conflict is so serious that the ABA has prohibited it in Rule 1.7.[9] In other words, the Rules do not allow the parties to waive such a conflict because the systemic interest—the interest in the system of justice—requires that lawyers not represent opposing parties before a tribunal.

In the 1983 version of the Rule, the Comments made it clear that some conflicts are nonconsentable because the adverse relationship is too great. Hence, a lawyer could not represent adverse parties in litigation even if all parties consented.[10] In the case of *A v. B*, a lawyer could not reasonably conclude that he or she could adequately represent both *A* and *B*. Therefore, *A* and *B*'s

---

[5]*See* Rule 1.7(a). *See, e.g., Jedwabny v. Philadelphia Transportation Co.*, 390 Pa. 231, 135 A.2d 252 (1957), *cert. denied*, 355 U.S. 966, 78 S.Ct. 557, 2 L.Ed.2d 541 (1958), holding that the same lawyer cannot represent both the plaintiff and defendant in the same case, even with the consent of both parties. *See also Sapienza v. New York News*, 481 F.Supp. 676 (S.D.N.Y.1979).

[6]Rule 1.7(b)(3).

[7]*See* Rule 1.7, Comment 2.

[8]Rule 1.7(b)(3). *Jedwabny v. Philadelphia Transportation Co.*, 390 Pa. 231, 135 A.2d 252 (1957), *cert.*

denied, 355 U.S. 966, 78 S.Ct. 557, 2 L.Ed.2d 541 (1958).

[9]Rule 1.7(a)(1) & Rule 1.7(b)(3) (proving for no waiver of this conflict) & Comment 6.

[10]To reach this result, one required a multi-step analysis of Rule 1.7 as it existed in the 1983 version. First, before a lawyer could represent clients who were "directly adverse" to each other, the lawyer had to obtain each client's consent. However, that consent was ineffective, "when a disinterested lawyer would conclude that the client should not agree to the representation under the circumstances, the lawyer involved cannot properly

consent, even though made after full disclosure, would not waive the conflict.[11] The systemic interest in the fair administration of justice would prevail and normally prevent the clients from agreeing to this representation.[12]

§ 1.7–2(d) Multiple Client Representation in the Nonlitigation Context

The 1983 version of the Model Rules contained language in Rule 1.7(b) concerning the representation of multiple clients and the manner in which the lawyer should proceed. The 1983 Model Rules also included Rule 2.2 (the lawyer as intermediary), which purported to address situations where lawyers represent two or more clients with potentially conflicting interests. The existence of these two rules created significant confusion whether lawyers needed to meet the conditions of Rule 1.7(b) or Rule 2.2 or both when examining the conflicts that arise when a lawyer represents multiple clients in a nonlitigation setting.

The drafters of the 2002 Rules deleted Rule 2.2 and instead moved most of the Comments with amendment to Rule 1.7.[13]

It is now clear that Rule 1.7 does not absolutely prohibit a lawyer from representing adverse parties outside of the litigation context. Lawyers may consider representing multiple parties seeking to resolve a dispute over partnership assets *if* the lawyer secures an adequate waiver. In fact, in some cases, a lawyer

---

ask for such agreement or provide representation on the basis of the client's consent." 1983 Model Rule 1.7(a)(1). *See also* 1983 Model Rule 1.7, Comment 5. The Model Code required that it must be "obvious" that the lawyer can adequately represent the interest of each client. DR 5-105(C). A "*dis*interested" lawyer is not an "*un*interested" lawyer; rather, the Rule refers to a lawyer who is not encumbered or constrained by the conflict that the conflicted lawyer faces. The 1983 version of the Rules intended that clients A and B, in the case of A v. B, could not consent because a "disinterested lawyer would conclude that the client should not agree to the representation under the circumstances."

See also Ariz. State Bar Comm. on the Rules of Prof'l Conduct, Op. 07-04 (Nov. 2007), *noted in* 23 ABA/BNA Manual on Prof. Conduct 620 (Dec. 12, 2007) (examining factors in conflicts that may make the situation nonconsentable for the involved clients).

[11] *See, e.g., Jedwabny v. Philadelphia Transportation Co.*, 390 Pa. 231, 135 A.2d 252 (1957), *cert. denied*, 355 U.S. 966, 78 S.Ct. 557, 2 L.Ed.2d 541 (1958).

[12] On the other hand, there may be cases that are denominated "litigation," but are really uncontested. If two parties are involved in an uncontested divorce. For example, they may be able to agree to have one lawyer represent both of them, this may be possible, where the lawyer's job is simply to draw up the papers and put into writing the divorce settlement, of which the two parties fully understand the consequences and to which they agreed. However, many lawyers would be unwilling to take such a case because of the risk that one of the parties will later become disgruntled and sue.

[13] Rule 1.7, Comments 29 to 33.

could consider representing a buyer and seller of real estate.[14] However, in order to accept the representation of adverse interest outside of a tribunal, the lawyer would need to examine the remaining tests under Rule 1.7(b). First, the lawyer would need to make an independent determination that the lawyer could competently and diligently represent each of the clients in the matter.[15] Second, the lawyer would need to determine that the conflict was not governed by other law.[16] Finally, the lawyer would need to obtain the client's informed consent.[17]

One must read the Comments to fully appreciate what a lawyer must do before accepting the representation of multiple clients. Obviously, using one lawyer to represent multiple parties has significant benefits in many cases. The cost of representation is likely to be reduced. The contentious behavior similarly is likely to be minimized. And, if the parties have made all of their own choices, the lawyer can simply verify their decisions and memorialize the agreement. Such representations can occur in forming a transaction or resolving a dispute. They typically arise among partners forming and operating businesses or between husbands and wives in the management of their assets and legal positions.

All potential clients to a multiple client representation must be informed of the risks and benefits of the representation. The risks obviously include the possibility of failure—at which time, one or more parties can suffer "additional cost, embarrassment, and recrimination."[18] In most cases, the lawyer will need to withdraw from all of the parties because the lawyer will not be able to meet Rule 1.7's conflict of interest inquiry. When the possibility of failure is great, lawyers should not take multiple client representations even if the clients would consent. Also, a lawyer with prior obligations to one or more of the clients to a multiple client representation should be mindful of obligations to those persons and obligations to others not to be biased.

Of all of the disclosures that lawyers must make to potential clients to a multiple client representation, the most important is the explanation of the effect of the common representation on confidentiality.[19] One aspect of this disclosure is to inform the persons that any party to a joint representation can waive the attorney-client privilege. Another aspect of the effect on confiden-

---

[14]*But see* Restatement of Law Governing Lawyers, Third, § 122(2) (Official Draft 2000) (providing two illustrations where multiple client representation in a buyer seller transaction would be inappropriate because of the conflict of interest).

[15]Rule 1.7(b)(1).

[16]Rule 1.7(b)(2).

[17]Rule 1.7(b)(4).

[18]Rule 1.7, Comment 29.

[19]Rule 1.7, Comment 30.

tiality is the need to tell the prospective clients that if they have something to protect from the others, they need to have a separate lawyer to represent their interests. A lawyer in a multiple client representation has equal loyalty to each client and thus cannot, in the majority of cases, properly discharge this obligation and keep information confidential against others.[20] In fact, a lawyer should inform the prospective clients of the ground rules on confidentiality. In most multiple client representations, the clients should be informed that all information will be shared with all of the clients.[21] It is possible to have a rule of limited or no sharing, but that would need to be done with sophisticated clients with a valid business reason for keeping the information confidential from the other person.

The final disclosure to the clients needs to focus on how one lawyer can properly represent multiple clients in the specific facts of the case.[22] If the parties expect special help, this cannot be accomplished with one lawyer. If the parties are unequal in bargaining power, the lawyer should not become involved in the multiple client representation. However, if the lawyer believes that the parties are capable of making their own decisions, the lawyer still needs to explain that one lawyer representing multiple parties prevents the lawyer from advocating for any one client's interests. Thus, the representation is clearly different. The clients are foregoing the vigorous representation that would attach when they have their own lawyers and instead they are placing their collective interest in an agreement.

Over the years, multiple client representation has become more risky, and in a country with commonplace malpractice suits, some lawyers are refusing to offer the service. These lawyers find the wealthier client and urge that client to let them represent only one client. The other parties to the transaction will need separate counsel or they may go unrepresented. The risk of malpractice is too great because lawyers cannot possibly anticipate all of the problems that can arise in a multiple client representation. Some of the more serious problems have arisen in the representation of buyer and seller of real estate.[23] However, all multiple client representations, even those of representing husband and wife have potential risks for lawyers.

---

[20]Rule 1.7, Comment 31.

[21]Rule 1.7, Comment 31.

[22]Rule 1.7, Comment 32.

[23]*See In re Lanza*, 65 N.J. 347, 322 A.2d 445 (1974) (reprimand). In this case, a lawyer was asked by the seller to represent both the buyer and the seller in the sale of a house transaction. The lawyer described conflict and obtained full consent from the parties. During the transaction, it became clear that the buyer lacked $5,000 in cash to close the deal. The buyer suggested that he write a post dated check for the amount. The seller seemed fine with this resolution and the lawyer largely stayed out of the negotiations. The lawyer completed the transaction and after the buyer

§ 1.7–3 SIMULTANEOUSLY REPRESENTING ADVERSE CLIENTS IN UNRELATED MATTERS

§ 1.7–3(a) Introduction

Clearly, as the previous section explained, the lawyer may not represent Clients *A* and *B* in the case of *A v. B,* because the lawyer would be representing adverse parties in the same matter. However, it is also the basic rule that a lawyer may not sue *A* on behalf of *B,* while simultaneously representing *A* in another, *completely unrelated* matter.[1]

For example, assume that Lawyer represents Wife in a divorce suit against Husband while simultaneously representing Husband, who is seeking to collect on his worker's compensation claim.[2] Although the two cases—the divorce and the worker's compensation claim—are completely unrelated and create no danger of any use of confidences in one case that would or could be useful or relevant in the other case, the lawyer who accepts the Wife's divorce is engaged in a breach of the lawyer's duty of loyalty against the Husband.[3]

When an attorney represents one client in a suit against another, some adverse effect on the lawyer's exercise of independent judgment on behalf of a client may arise because of the lawyer's

---

moved in, the buyer complained that the basement leaked. He cancelled the post dated check.

See *Baldasare v. Butler,* 254 N.J.Super. 502, 604 A.2d 112 (1992) (malpractice suit). In this case, a lawyer represents buyer and seller in a real estate deal. The buyers could not complete their financing and thus they needed to extend the option period. In the meantime, unbeknownst to the sellers the property had appreciated by $1,400,000. The lawyer was generally aware of the increased value and a specific deal to buy the property at a much higher price, yet he did not inform the buyers. He drafted the extension of the option period, and the buyers did in fact purchase the property. The property was quickly resold for a gain and the sellers sued the lawyer for malpractice. *See also Simpson v. James,* 903 F.2d 372 (5th Cir.1990) (malpractice suit).

[Section 1.7–3]

[1]On this issue, see Thomas D. Morgan, *Suing a Current Client,* 9 GEORGETOWN J. LEGAL ETHICS 1157 (1996); Thomas D. Morgan, *Suing a Current Client,* 1 J. INSTITUTE FOR STUDY LEGAL ETHICS 87 (1996); Brian J. Redding, Redding, *Suing a Current Client: A Response to Professor Morgan,* 10 GEORGETOWN J. LEGAL ETHICS 487 (1997).

The Texas version of the Model Rules permits a law firm to sue a present client on an unrelated matter as long as the case does not involve an allegation of fraud against the client. *See* Tex. Disciplinary Rule 1.06, Comment 11; *In re Southwestern Bell Yellow Pages, Inc.,* 141 S.W.3d 229 (Tex. App. San Antonio 2004). The Fifth Circuit rejected the application of this rule in federal district courts despite the fact that the federal court had adopted the Texas Disciplinary Rules as governing rules of ethical conduct. *See In re Dresser Industries, Inc.,* 972 F.2d 540 (5th Cir. 1992).

[2]*Memphis & Shelby County Bar Ass'n v. Sanderson,* 52 Tenn.App. 684, 378 S.W.2d 173 (1963) (lawyer disbarred).

[3]Rule 1.7, Comment 6.

adversarial posture towards that client in another matter.[4] For example, in the attorney's effort to please his long-standing client, there may be a diminution in the rigor of his representation of the client in the matter where he is suing the long-standing client.[5] The lawyer might not—or it might appear that he might not—fight as vigorously for one of his clients as he otherwise would.[6]

Along similar lines, consider *Zuck v. Alabama*,[7] where a law firm represented a defendant in a criminal case while it also represented the prosecutor who was being sued in his personal capacity in an unrelated civil matter. The court held that this constituted an actual conflict of interest rendering the criminal trial unfair in the absence of the criminal defendant's knowing and intelligent waiver. The law firm in this case would be subject to divided loyalties.[8] The lawyer for the criminal defendant might be less likely to assert prosecutorial misconduct and attack the good faith of the prosecutor (arguments that malign the prosecutor personally), if the same firm simultaneously represents the prosecutor in his personal capacity.

---

[4]*I.B.M. Corp. v. Levin*, 579 F.2d 271 (3d Cir.1978).

[5]579 F.2d at 280.

[6]*See* ABA Formal Opinion 05–435 (Dec. 8, 2004) (simultaneous representation of liability insurer named in litigation and a client against the insured of the same liability insurance company is not automatically considered a directly adverse conflict under Rule 1.7(a)(1), without additional facts that would accentuate the conflict). The Opinion states that economic adversity alone is not sufficient to create a directly adverse conflict. Other factors, such as whether the lawyer will need to cross examine representatives of the liability insurance company, may accentuate the adversity. A conflict may arise under Rule 1.7(a)(2) if the lawyer believes that there is a significant risk that one or both representations may be materially limited.

[7]*Zuck v. Alabama*, 588 F.2d 436 (5th Cir.1979).

[8]Other courts have argued that *Zuck* is no longer good law on the constitutional due process issue. *United States v. Mett*, 65 F.3d 1531 (9th Cir.1995), *cert. denied*, 519 U.S. 870, 117 S.Ct. 185, 136 L.Ed.2d 124 (1996), stating:

"The *Cuyler* standard serves to distinguish this case from the pre-*Cuyler* case principally relied on by petitioners, *Zuck v. Alabama*, 588 F.2d 436 (5th Cir.1979), *cert. denied*, 444 U.S. 833, 100 S.Ct. 63, 62 L.Ed.2d 42 (1979). There, the defendants' law firm also represented the prosecutor in a civil matter. The Fifth Circuit in *Zuck* found that any 'actual' conflict—and thus the conflict at issue in that case—renders a trial 'fundamentally unfair' and is a *per se* due process violation. *Id.* at 438–39. This holding is, of course, contrary to *Cuyler's* requirement that the defendant show that the conflict had an adverse effect on the lawyer's performance."

65 F.3d at 1534 n.2.

Mett held that the defendants were not denied effective assistance of counsel even though the defense lawyer had been engaged in a prior representation of a prosecuting attorney on a DWI charge. In *Mett*, the court noted: "All parties appear to have waived any possible conflict orally and Cassiday [the defense counsel] assumed the representation. Nothing was put in writing, and the district court was not informed." 65 F.3d at 1533.

When the Simultaneous Representation of Conflicting Interests Is Manufactured. A court typically will disqualify a law firm in the case of Plaintiff v. Defendant if it is representing Plaintiff in that suit while simultaneously representing—in unrelated matters that may or may not involve litigation—Defendant. The reason the court disqualifies is not because of the risk that the law firm will breach confidence, for we can assume that there are no relevant confidences to breach and that the cases are completely unrelated. The court disqualifies because of a breach of loyalty. The lawyer should not be suing a current client, as the Second Circuit said long ago: "we think it would be questionable conduct for an attorney to participate in any lawsuit against his own client without the knowledge and consent of all concerned. . . . [T]he maintenance of public confidence in the bar requires an attorney to decline employment adverse to his client, even though the nature of such employment is wholly unrelated to that of his existing representation."[9]

The rule prohibiting a lawyer from suing a current client is designed to prevent an "actual or apparent conflict in loyalties or diminution in the vigor of his representation."[10] It is not designed to disqualify the lawyer because one of his clients has manufactured the conflict. This principle is illustrated in *Sumitomo v. J.P. Morgan & Co.*[11]

In *Sumitomo*, the law firm of Paul, Weiss, Rifkind, Wharton & Garrison ("Paul Weiss") represented Sumitomo in investigating an employee who was responsible for losses from copper trading and who later confessed to unauthorized copper trading. Later, Sumitomo received demands for payment from banks with respect to transactions of which it was unaware. Eventually, various law suits were filed alleging liability for Sumitomo's $2.6 billion loss from copper-trading transactions. Sumitomo retained Paul Weiss to represent it before regulatory and law enforcement authorities investigating the copper trading and to defend it in any litigation arising from this copper trading.

When Paul Weiss discovered that several of its clients were among Sumitomo's potential adversaries, Paul Weiss advised

---

[9]*Cinema 5, Ltd. v. Cinerama, Inc.*, 528 F.2d 1384, 1386–87, 1976-1 Trade Cases ¶ 60,698 (2d Cir.1976). *See also Matter of Kelly*, 23 N.Y.2d 368, 376, 296 N.Y.S.2d 937, 943, 244 N.E.2d 456, 460 (1968), which emphasized the importance of loyalty: " 'with rare and conditional exceptions'; the lawyer may not place himself in a position where a conflicting interest may, even inadvertently, affect, or give the appearance of affecting, the obligations of the professional relationship."

[10]*Cinema 5, Ltd. v. Cinerama, Inc.*, 528 F.2d at 1387.

[11]*Sumitomo v. J.P. Morgan & Co.*, 2000 WL 145747 (S.D.N.Y.2000). *See also Mercedes v. Blue*, 2001 WL 527477, 1 (S.D.N.Y.2001), which discussed *Sumitomo* and denied defendants' application to disqualify plaintiffs' counsel or appoint a guardian *ad litem*.

Sumitomo that it could not evaluate potential claims against those clients or otherwise represent Sumitomo in connection with any future litigation with those clients. Accordingly, when Ocean View (a Paul Weiss client) sued Sumitomo in June 1998 in the Southern District of New York, and Ocean View refused to waive Paul Weiss' conflict of interests, Paul Weiss advised Sumitomo that it should retain separate counsel.

Later, Sumitomo asked Paul Weiss to seek a waiver from Chase Manhattan Bank (another current Paul Weiss client) to permit Paul Weiss to evaluate Sumitomo's potential claims against Chase and to discuss any valid claims with Chase before Sumitomo commenced litigation. Chase refused, so Sumitomo hired separate counsel, which sued Chase. Sumitomo also hired Paul Weiss to sue J. P. Morgan (a non-Paul Weiss client) and Paul Weiss did so.

Thus, we had two separate law suits with Sumitomo represented by two different law firms, so Paul Weiss was not in a position where it was representing Sumitomo while simultaneously suing Chase. Then Chase moved to consolidate, for pretrial discovery purposes, the J.P. Morgan and Chase cases, and—given that the cases were consolidated—Chase moved to disqualify Paul Weiss because (Chase argued) Paul Weiss was now an adversary to Chase, a current client (in unrelated matters).

The court granted the pretrial discovery consolidation but refused to disqualify Paul Weiss even though Chase was a client of Paul Weiss. Chase raised no argument that Paul Weiss might be privy to relevant confidences. Indeed, "Chase's attorneys acknowledged that use of confidential information in violation of Canon 4 was not in issue."[12] The conflict, if it existed, was based on an alleged breach of loyalty, not any alleged breach of confidences. And, this alleged conflict occurred *only* because Chase moved to consolidate the two different law suits.

The court refused to disqualify Paul Weiss. "Chase is a huge financial institution," the court said. It is not an individual that would feel a betrayal of trust. Furthermore, there is no reason to believe Paul Weiss would go easy on Chase out of a desire to keep its good will: "Indeed, the fact that Chase had made this motion demonstrated that Chase does not believe that Paul Weiss will not vigorously represent Sumitomo."[13]

Most importantly, this is not a case of a law firm suing its current client. Paul Weiss was not representing Sumitomo against Chase. A different law firm was suing Chase, and the alleged conflict could not have occurred if Chase had not successfully moved to consolidate the two cases, for purposes of pre-trial

---

[12] 2000 WL 145747, *3 n. 3.   [13] 2000 WL 145747, *4.

discovery only. Paul Weiss will not be in a position where it will be adverse to Chase. Paul Weiss may use information that the other firm secured from Chase during discovery, but Chase could hardly argue that information is "secret" when it has disclosed it to an adversary in the course of discovery.

> Here, Paul Weiss is not representing Sumitomo against Chase in this litigation in violation of DR 5-105. Instead, Paul Weiss is representing Sumitomo against Morgan, a non-client, while [a different law firm] is representing Sumitomo against Chase, Paul Weiss' current client in an unrelated matter. Thus, the per se rule against simultaneous representation articulated in *Cinema 5* and other decisions does not require the Court to disqualify Paul Weiss.[14]

There is thus no reason to disqualify Paul Weiss.

§ 1.7–3(b) Waiver and Simultaneous Adverse Representation

In the case where the lawyer is suing *A* on behalf of *B,* while simultaneously representing *A* in another, *completely unrelated* matter, it is unclear whether client consent is ever effective to allow such dual representation. Although the lawyer is not representing opposing parties in the same case, there is authority that the duty of loyalty precludes effective consent. Under this authority, consent is not normally effective in curing such a conflict.

In 1934, an ABA ethics opinion took this strict view of conflicts and concluded that an attorney who represents an insurance company in worker's compensation cases may not accept employment from a former general agent who is suing that same insurance company, even if the insurance company does not object.[15] The Opinion expressly stated that, although it "assume[d] that the insurance company has expressed no objection" to the lawyer's representation against the insurance company, "that does not relieve lawyer *A* from his obligation to accept no employment from a new client in a case where fidelity to the new client may require examination of the motives and the good faith of the insurance company by which he has been and is employed in numerous other cases *and whose patronage he desires to continue.*"[16]

The ineffectiveness of client consent is illustrated by *Matter of Kelly v. Greason.*[17] Two lawyers, Kelly and Whalen, were in a law partnership. Whalen was then employed as an insurance ad-

---

[14]2000 WL 145747, *4.

[15]ABA Formal Opinion 112 (May 10, 1934).

[16]ABA Formal Opinion 112 (May 10, 1934) (emphasis added). *See also*

HENRY DRINKER, LEGAL ETHICS 111 (1953).

[17]*Matter of Kelly v. Greason*, 23 N.Y.2d 368, 374–79, 296 N.Y.S.2d 937, 942–46, 244 N.E.2d 456, 459–62

juster for the Nationwide Insurance Co. Whalen had no access to any Nationwide files other than those of claims assigned to him. Nonetheless, the firm handled some claims against Nationwide.

There was no proof that any of the Nationwide settlements were unreasonable or unfair to either the insurance carrier or the claimants. Nor was there any prejudice to any of Nationwide's claimants by the partnership's failure to bring a negligence liability claim against the carrier. Nonetheless, the court held that "it was, prima facie, evidence of professional misconduct for the partnership to represent claimants, whether assureds of Nationwide or not, in their claims against the carrier, while at the same time Whalen was also the carrier's employee."[18] The court's broad dictum found that discipline was appropriate unless, and *perhaps even if*, consent had been obtained from *both* clients after full disclosure.

The purpose of this rule restricting the simultaneous representation of adverse parties is to protect the systemic interest in the fair administration of justice as well as to protect the clients' interest in loyalty. A "lawyer ordinarily may not act as advocate against a person the lawyer represents in some other matter, even if it is wholly unrelated."[19] Thus there is a substantial question whether, even "with consent in such circumstances the attorney may profit from breach of the duty of loyalty."[20] On the other hand, others may argue that whatever the problem is, there is no breach of loyalty if the parties give their informed consent. The clients' freely-given consent waives the loyalty issue.

The drafters of the 2002 Rules make a distinction between cases where the directly adverse conflict is completely loyalty based and situations where a directly adverse conflict may have materially limited implications. Where the matters are totally unrelated and the only interest of the client is an expectation that the lawyer will not sue a present client, the Rules seem to approve of consent.[21] However, in some cases, the betrayal of a lawyer who now seeks to represent an adverse party may lead to an impairment of the relationship. Also, it may lead to a feeling that the lawyer may be less effective on behalf of the client out of deference to the other client. In such cases, consent is more problematic.[22]

However, in some cases consent may not be freely-given. If the lawyer, in effect, tells the client—"I am representing this other

---

(1968).

[18] 23 N.Y.2d at 376, 296 N.Y.S.2d at 944, 244 N.E.2d at 461.

[19] Rule 1.7, Comment 6.

[20] Lawrence S. Fordham, *There are Substantial Limitations on Representation of Clients in Litigation Which are Not Obvious in the Code of Professional Responsibility*, 33 THE BUS. LAWYER 1193, 1204 (1978).

[21] Rule 1.7, Comment 6.

[22] Rule 1.7, Comment 6.

client who is suing you; if you do not like that, you can take your business elsewhere"—the lawyer is seeking to profit (by taking the other representation) by his breach of loyalty. He cannot drop the disfavored client like a hot potato.[23]

§ 1.7–3(c) Competing Economic Enterprises

There are limits on the application of the rules prohibiting the simultaneous representation of adverse interests. It depends on how strictly one defines the word "adverse." If a lawyer represents a large business entity, he or she may ordinarily represent another economic enterprise in a matter that is unrelated, even though one enterprise is competing with the other.

For example, let us assume that a lawyer is representing both A and B in two separate and unrelated matters, such as the situation where the lawyer represents a major auto company on a securities matter while representing another, competing major auto company on a different, unrelated securities matter. Although A and B generally compete with each other, the lawyer is not suing either A or B. Nor is the lawyer giving legal advice to A that is to be used against B (or vice versa). Nor is there any violation of client confidences or secrets. In the words of the Model Rules, A and B are only "generally adverse" because they are merely competing economic enterprises; they are not "*directly* adverse."[24]

Similarly, a law firm may represent a water utility in raising its rates even though that representation hurts all the firm's

---

[23]*See, e.g.,* Ronald D. Rotunda, *One Potato, Two Potato, Three Potato, Four,* 14 LEGAL TIMES 23 (Aug. 12, 1991).

[24]Rule 1.7, Comment 6 (emphasis added).

The 1983 version of Rule 1.7 contained a Comment dealing with a lawyer who represents general competitors in unrelated litigation. Its intent may have been to reach the same conclusion that one reaches under Comment 6 of the 2002 version of the Model Rules. Former Comment 8 stated that: "there are circumstances in which a lawyer may act as advocate against a client. For example, a lawyer representing an enterprise with diverse operations may accept employment *as an advocate against the enterprise* in an unrelated matter *if* doing so will *not* adversely affect the lawyer's relationship with the enterprise or conduct of the suit and if both clients consent upon consultation." 1983 Model Rule 1.7, Comment 8 (emphasis added). No black letter rule in the model rules explicitly authorized this action. The Model Code nowhere approved of a lawyer suing a present client, whether or not the client is a large enterprise. *See, e.g., IBM Corp. v. Levin,* 579 F.2d 271 (3d Cir.1978). The circumstance hypothesized by Comment 8 assumed fact situations that would be few and far between. First, this Comment required that both clients consent after consultation. And, second, the lawyer must conclude that this dual representation—advocating in one case against the very enterprise that the lawyer represents in another matter—would not affect the lawyer's relationship with the client against whom he is now advocating. The drafters of the 2002 Rules decided to delete this Comment as confusing while creating the new Comment 6, which does deal with generally competing economic enterprises.

other clients who use water. The law firm that represents the local Ford car dealer in buying some real estate may also represent the local Mercedes dealer in a contract matter. The representations and the clients have nothing to do with each other, even though the clients are competitors in the business world.[25]

Although a law firm may represent competitors who compete against each other for third party business, the law firm may not become involved in a scheme to divert one client's business to another present client.[26] Such conduct may subject the firm to a claim of breach of fiduciary duty and the injured client may seek disgorgement of fees paid to the firm as a remedy for the law firm's conduct.[27]

In contrast, if the lawyer were suing Client A on behalf of Client B in one matter, the lawyer should not be able simultaneously to represent Client A, on a different matter, even if the two matters are completely unrelated.[28] As part of the duty of loyalty, a lawyer may not sue a present client without knowing consent.

§ 1.7–3(d) Negotiations

A lawyer, while acting as an advocate for one party, cannot represent the opposite side in negotiation.[29] However, a lawyer may represent several parties on the *same side* of a negotiation even though there is some difference among them.[30]

Many good business reasons exist why several clients involved in a business transaction may all wish to use the same lawyer.[31] Multiple lawyers are expensive, and may needlessly exacerbate or create discord or disagreements. The multiple parties often share a common goal, and a single lawyer may help them reach it more quickly. Thus there are good policy reasons why the law should not treat this situation as a prohibited conflict not subject

---

[25]*See* § 1.7-3(c), *infra* (conflicts in representing competing economic enterprises).

[26]*See Ulico Casualty Co. v. Wilson, Elser, Moskowitz, Edelman & Dicker,* 16 Misc. 3d 105, 843 N.Y.S. 2d 749 (N.Y. Supp. 2007), *noted in* 23 ABA/BNA MANUAL ON PROFESSIONAL CONDUCT, Current Reports News 192 (Apr. 18, 2007).

[27]*See Ulico Casualty Co. v. Wilson, Elser, Moskowitz, Edelman & Dicker,* 16 Misc. 3d 105, 843 N.Y.S. 2d 749 (N.Y. Supp. 2007), *noted in* 23 ABA/BNA MANUAL ON PROFESSIONAL CONDUCT, Current Reports News 192 (Apr. 18, 2007).

[28]Robert C. Hacker & Ronald D.

Rotunda, *Attorney Conflicts of Interest,* 2 CORPORATION LAW REVIEW 345 (1979). *See, e.g., I.B.M. Corp. v. Levin,* 579 F.2d 271 (3d Cir.1978).

[29]A lawyer "may not represent multiple parties to a negotiation whose interests are fundamentally antagonistic to each other, but common representation is permissible where clients are generally aligned in interest even though there is some difference of interest among them." Rule 1.7, Comment 28. *See also* DR 5-105(A), EC 5-15.

[30]*See* Rule 1.7(a)(2).

[31]Steven Lubet, *There Are No Scriveners Here,* 84 IOWA L. REV. 341, 350 (1999).

to waiver. The law should not require two lawyers where one will do.

Nonetheless, the empirical evidence shows that a leading source of malpractice liability for lawyers is the situation where they represent multiple clients in the same business transaction.[32] Consequently, prudent lawyers should approach such situations with care, and be sure to secure the necessary consents if representation of any client "may be materially limited by the lawyer's responsibilities to another client . . .."[33] And, when it is necessary to secure consent, the lawyers make sure that they secure knowing consent from each of their multiple clients. The lawyer must bring home to the clients the significance of what is going on.[34]

If a lawyer does seek to be a part of a situation involving fundamentally antagonistic multiple parties in negotiation, he should do so as an *intermediator*, not as an advocate.[35]

§ 1.7-3(e) Using Conflicts Counsel for Discrete Matters to Avoid Disqualification

§ 1.7-3(e)(1) Introduction

As discussed above, a general principle of legal ethics is that a law firm may not represent a client who is suing someone who is also a client of the law firm (1) even though the two matters are unrelated, (2) a different law firm represents the client in that law suit, and (3) there is no risk that the lawyer would violate the confidences of any client. Other ethics rules can magnify the significance of this rule by imputing the disqualification of every lawyer in the law firm to every other lawyer in the same firm. Courts enforce these rules by disqualifying the offending law firm.

---

[32]*See, e.g.,* Brian Redding, *Conflicts of Interest in Business Transactions: A Serious Problem That Is Getting Worse*, ALAS Loss Prevention Journal, Sept., 1994, at 2.

[33]Rule 1.7(a)(2).

[34]Rule 1.7(b)(4) & Comments 18 to 19. *See also* Rule 1.7, Comments 29 to 33.

Lawyer As Amanuensis. Sometimes the clients will hire the lawyer as a mere scrivener, an amanuensis, an expensive typist whose only job is to translate the agreement into the appropriate legalese. The existence of a potential conflict is substantially reduced if the lawyer is not hired to help create the deal, but only to write

it down, scribe-like. Jonathan R. Macey & Geoffrey P. Miller, *An Economic Analysis of Conflict of Interest Regulations*, 82 Iowa L. Rev. 965, 999 (1997).

However, the lawyer first has to determine if he or she is hired in an amanuensis situation. As Steven Lubet, *There Are No Scriveners Here*, 84 Iowa L. Rev. 341, 350 (1999), points out (in a criticism of part of the Macey and Miller article, *supra*), a lawyer may act "as a mere scrivener, but the choice should be the client's and it should never fall below the 'consent threshold' as defined by Macey and Miller." *Id.* at 346 (footnote omitted).

[35]*See* Rule 1.7, Comment 28.

In some cases, law firms can often avoid disqualification by using "conflicts counsel," *i.e.*, the client retains a new lawyer from a different law firm to handle a discrete, severable matter—the matter that created the conflict. Although the cases—typically in the area of discovery and bankruptcy—often do not discuss the rationale for using conflicts counsel, their instincts are correct: using conflicts counsel in certain situations mitigates the burden of disqualification while protecting the underlying reasons behind disqualification.

Let us consider the basic scenario. Law Firm represents Client #1, which finds itself adverse to Client #2. Law Firm represents Client #2 in other, unrelated matters, but another law firm represents Client #2 in the particular matter that leads to the adversity. For example, Law Firm represents Client #1 in a patent dispute with Client #2, and that same Law Firm represents Client #2 in a real estate dispute with a third party. Client #1 and Client #2 are both clients of Law Firm, which must therefore disqualify itself (if the clients do not waive the conflict). That is the standard rule. But there is coda or addendum to this basic scenario.

Assume that Law Firm is representing Client #1 in a matter but only a portion of that matter is adverse to Client #2. Assume further that this portion of the matter that involves Client #2 is discrete and separable from the rest of the matter. For example, in the course of representing Client #1 (in a case adverse to a third party), the Law Firm may decide that it is necessary to depose or cross examine Client #2. Client #2 is not a party to this lawsuit but would be an adverse witness. The question is whether Law Firm can avoid disqualification if Client #1 hires separate counsel to represent it in this discrete portion of the case. The conflicts rules do not talk about dividing cases into discrete, severable parts, but that does not mean that severability is a bad idea.

Disqualifying counsel places burdens on the judicial system, for there is typically delay when the party has to hire another law firm to handle the matter. In addition, disqualification places burdens on the party, who is not able to retain counsel of choice. Disqualification also imposes financial costs on the client who must reeducate the new lawyer who replaces the old one. If there are good reasons to disqualify counsel, then we accept the burdens that disqualification imposes. But there should be good reasons. If the legal system can respect the client's legitimate expectation of loyalty without disqualifying the law firm, then disqualification becomes unnecessary and expensive.[36]

If a way exists to protect to protect a client's legitimate expectation of loyalty without disqualifying the law firm, then the law should disfavor disqualification because it would impose burdens without the compensating benefits. In a few lower courts and unpublished decisions, an emerging case law implements what courts often call "conflicts counsel."[37] This new counsel would represent the client on a discrete, easily severable matter. The courts do not always label what they are doing, and often do not discuss why they are doing it. Yet, a few courts sometimes allow law firms to use "conflicts counsel" to comply with the ethics rules while protecting a client's expectation of loyalty and reducing (rather than exacerbating) litigation costs. Other courts do not even talk about the issue.

§ 1.7-3(e)(2) Adverse Witnesses and Discovery

One situation that invites the use of conflict counsel involves the case where the lawyer on behalf of one client cross-examines a present client as an adverse witness. Assume that a lawyer ("Law Firm #1") represents Client #1 in a matter. Law Firm #1, in the course of litigation, cross examines another individual, Client #2 (who is another client of the same firm) as an adverse witness. Because Client #2 is a material witness, Law Firm #1 will ordinarily face a disqualifying conflict of interest unless there is appropriate client consent, even if the law firm's representation of Client #1 is completely unrelated to the law firm's representation of Client #2.

The general rule is that this situation is a conflict that disqualifies the lawyer.[38] This general rule is certainly justified. There is a risk that the lawyer may have secret information that he could use in cross-examining his client, even if the cases are unrelated. The lawyer may know, for example, that the witness will become extremely nervous and embarrassed if asked about his medication, so that the witness will look like she is lying even though she is telling the truth.[39] Yet, even if there is no risk of a loss of confidentiality there is a risk of a breach of loyalty. The lawyer's

---

[36]Justice Beth Baker, quoting Treatise in, *Krutzfeldt Ranch, LLC v. Pinnacle Bank*, 2012 MT 15, 2012 WL 273311, *9 (Mont. 2012).

[37]These issues are also considered in, Rotunda, *Resolving Client Conflicts by Hiring "Conflicts Counsel,"* 62 HASTINGS L. J. 677 (2011).

[38]Rule 1.7, Comment 6; ABA Formal Opinion 92-367 (Oct. 16, 1992).

See discussion and case citations in, § 1.7-6(c) (Examining a Present Client as Adverse Witness) (ABA-West, 2009).

[39]*Chugach Electric Association v. United States District Court*, 370 F.2d 441 (9th Cir. 1966), *cert. denied*, 389 U.S. 820 (1967).

pecuniary interest in possible future business from Client #2 may cause him to avoid vigorous cross-examination that might embarrass or offend the witness. If the lawyer does engage in vigorous cross examination, that witness will feel betrayed because his own lawyer is the one who is challenging his recollection.

Yet, there is an alternative that avoids disqualification without compromising the legitimate expectations of either client. The Rules of Professional Conduct allow a lawyer to limit the scope of the representation if the limitation if reasonable under the circumstances and the client gives informed consent.[40] In our witness scenario, if the lawyer, in representing Client #1, learns that she may have to depose and cross examine Client #2, the lawyer can agree with Client #1 that her representation will not include a discrete and separable issue—the questioning of Client #2. Client #1 would hire another law firm to handles this discrete matter. If Client #1 agrees to that limitation, Client #2 could not force the disqualification of the Law Firm, because the Law Firm will not be adverse to Client #2, even if Client #2 does not consent.

Over 30 years ago—before the ABA Model Rules even existed—Judge (later Justice) Stevens suggested this approach in *United States v. Jeffers*.[41] This case may be the first case to use what I call a "conflicts counsel." Stevens acknowledged that "ethical considerations inhibited" the lawyer's ability "to interrogate the witness thoroughly, or his willingness to permit another member of his firm to do so," but then said, without any discussion, that the lawyer should have "made an offer to have some other lawyer retained for this limited purpose . . . ."[42]

While he offered no reasons to support his suggestion, what he proposed is not merely formalistic. Client #1 would not (and could not) consent to any limitation that it believed would cause its lawyer to act incompetently. Client #1 simply hires two law firms, Law Firm #1 would be responsible for most of the case and the other (the "conflicts counsel") would be responsible for cross-examining the witness. Client #2 does not want Law Firm #1 (its lawyer on other matters) to use secrets against him or be disloyal to him, but Law Firm #1 will not be doing that. It will not handle anything dealing with this discrete matter—the cross-examination of Client #2. Because Law Firm #1 has nothing to do with this discrete matter, it will not be disloyal to Client #2.

---

[40]Rule 1.2(c). *See also* RESTATEMENT OF THE LAW GOVERNING LAWYERS, Third (ALI 2000), at § 121.

[41]*United States v. Jeffers*, 520 F.2d 1256 (7th Cir, 1975) (Stevens, J., later Justice Stevens).

[42]520 F.2d 1256, 1266. *United States v. Agosto*, 675 F.2d 965, 974 & n.7 (8th Cir. 1982), approved of using what it called "back-up" counsel to avoid the conflict in criminal cases, citing *Jeffers* and Tague, *Multiple Representation and Conflicts of Interest in Criminal Cases*, 67 GEORGETOWN L.J. 1075, 1115 (1979).

Remember, that Client #2 is not a party in the case involving Client #1; it is just a witness. Client #2 will have its own lawyer representing it,[43] and the lawyer examining Client #2 will not be Law Firm #1 but a different lawyer not at all connected with Law Firm #1.

A related issue deals with discovery. A lawyer who represents Client #1 may well have to conduct third party discovery of Client #2. That also raises a conflict even if the lawyer is searching for documents and does not expect to cross-examine his client.[44] The trial judge might also join multiple cases for purposes of discovery only, or for all purposes, because of efficiency, and consistency. The lawyer for one client may find that he is engaged in discovery of another client, who is separately represented in the matter.

An unpublished case that focuses on this issue is *Sumitomo Corp v. J.P. Morgan & Co., Inc.*[45] The Paul Weiss law firm was representing Sumitomo in investigating an employee who was responsible for losses from copper trading. Later, Sumitomo received demands for payment from over 40 banks with respect to transactions of which it was unaware. Paul Weiss realized that it represented some of those banks. Hence, it told Sumitomo that—with respect to those banks who were Paul Weiss client—it could not evaluate the claim or litigate the bank claim on Sumitomo's behalf. In other cases where the banks were not clients, Paul Weiss would represent Sumitomo. Thus, Paul Weiss represented Sumitomo in filing suit against J.P. Morgan.

But, Paul Weiss could not represent Sumitomo in its suit against Chase Manhattan (Chase), because Chase was a Paul Weiss client in other matters. Paul Weiss sought a limited waiver from Chase to permit Paul Weiss to evaluate Sumitomo's potential claims against Chase and to discuss any valid claims with Chase before Sumitomo commenced litigation. Chase refused. So, Sumitomo retained a different law firm to represent

---

[43]The courts will not impute to the conflicts counsel the knowledge that Law Firm has. *Akerly v. Red Barn System, Inc.*, 551 F.2d 539 (3d Cir.1977) (refusing to disqualify main counsel following the disqualification of his local counsel); *American Can Co. v. Citrus Feed Co.*, 436 F.2d 1125 (5th Cir.1971) (reversing trial court order imputing local counsel's disqualification to a cocounsel firm serving as trial counsel). *See also* ABA Formal Opinion 92-367 (Oct. 16, 1992), which approved of the *Jeffers* proposal of using conflicts counsel.

[44]ABA Formal Opinion 92-367 (Oct. 16, 1992) noted that it will "frequently be the case that a lawyer's taking discovery, whether testimonial or documentary, on behalf of one client, of a third party who is also a client, will present such direct adverseness, so as to be disqualifying under Rule 1.7(a)."

[45]*Sumitomo Corp v. J.P. Morgan & Co., Inc.*, 2000 WL 145747 (S.D.N.Y.2000).

it in evaluating that claim and filing a separate suit against Chase.

Paul Weiss continued to represent Chase in other matters, and but not in the case that Sumitomo brought against Chase. Thus, there were two cases (*Sumitomo v. J.P. Morgan* and *Sumitomo v. Chase*), and Paul Weiss was involved in only the first one. At that point, we have two separate lawsuits. However, the judge, at Chase's request, consolidated these two cases for pretrial discovery.[46] Thus, the two cases became one. Then, Chase moved to disqualify Paul Weiss from representing Sumitomo and suing J.P. Morgan because the two cases had become one.[47]

The Court rejected the motion and refused to disqualify Paul Weiss. There was no conflict because Sumitomo had employed special conflicts counsel:

> Paul Weiss is not representing Sumitomo against Chase in this litigation in violation of [New York Code] DR 5-105. Instead, Paul Weiss is representing Sumitomo against Morgan, a non-client, while [a different law firm] Kronish Lieb is representing Sumitomo against Chase, Paul Weiss' current client in an unrelated matter. Thus, the *per se* rule against simultaneous representation articulated in *Cinema 5* and other decisions does not require the Court to disqualify Paul Weiss.[48]

Again, the court does not explain its reasoning or offer any further detail, but its conclusion is sound. This second law firm, Kronish Lieb, became the conflicts counsel—the lawyer that the client retains to avoid a disqualification of the client's other lawyer.

The court's rule protects the interests of both clients. First, there is Sumitomo. Sumitomo surely did not believe that Paul Weiss would not represent its interests vigorously out of a desire to please its other client Chase. If it had, it would not have hired Paul Weiss.

Chase, the other client, had two interests worth protecting. First, it had its interest in client confidentiality. Kronish Lieb, a different law firm, is representing Paul Weiss in the case served to protect Chase's interest in confidentiality, because Kronish Lieb was never a lawyer for Chase and was not privy to its

---

[46] 2000 WL 145747 at *1, n.1.

[47] 2000 WL 145747 at *2: "Chase moved for disqualification of Paul Weiss, advancing two arguments. First, . . . upon consolidation of the Morgan action and the Chase action, disqualification is appropriate because . . . Paul Weiss' representation of Sumitomo would involve Paul Weiss representing one client who was suing another client in a consolidated action. Second, Chase contended that even if the cases were not consolidated, disqualification is warranted because although Chase was not a party to the litigation in which Paul Weiss was representing Sumitomo, Paul Weiss' representation would adversely affect Chase."

[48] 2000 WL 145747, *4.

secrets. However, one might argue that Paul Weiss could violate its ethical duties and leak secret information to Kronish Lieb. That argument, if accepted, may prove too much: if Paul Weiss wanted to violate its duties of confidentiality, it need not be counsel of record in the J.P. Morgan matter to do that.

On the other hand, telling Chase that there are other ways for Paul Weiss to act improperly is cold comfort. More significantly, the court explained, Paul Weiss did not have any relevant privileged information concerning Chase obtained through its prior representation of Chase. The lack of relevant confidential information is pivotal: Paul Weiss could not be giving Sumitomo an unfair advantage by using confidential information from Chase because it had no such information.[49] Chase did not have an interest in confidentiality. It only had an interest in loyalty; that it, it had an interest that its own lawyer not be adverse to it.

The judge's ruling protected that second interest—that Chase has a right to expect loyalty from its lawyer, Paul Weiss. Chase had every right to expect Paul Weiss not to represent a party against it, but Paul Weiss was not doing that. Paul Weiss was representing Sumitomo against other banks, but not against Chase. Sumitomo hired a separate law firm to bring that case. And, to make the point that the issues were clearly severable consider the following: the only reason the two cases were treated as one is the court consolidated them for convenience (at the request of Chase).[50] In *Sumitomo*, for example, there were suits against dozens of banks and the new counsel simply handled one discrete law suit against Chase.

Of course, Sumitomo has the expense of hiring Paul Weiss, and the additional expense of hiring Kronish Lieb. But Sumitomo was not complaining; only Case was complaining. Still, because of that problem, when a law firm plans to divide the case in this way, it should document what it is doing very clearly so that the client understands it is paying for separate counsel because of a problem the law firm has, not a problem inherent in the client's

---

[49] 2000 WL 145747, *3.

[50] *See also* District of Columbia Bar Legal Ethics Committee, Opinion 343 (Feb. 2008), http://www.dcbar.org/for__lawyers/ethics/legal__ethics/opinions/opinion343.cfm. It concluded that a lawyer may limit the scope of an engagement to a discrete legal issue or stage in litigation to avoid a client conflict. By "agreeing only to represent a client as to a discrete legal issue or with respect to a discrete stage in the litigation, a lawyer may be able to limit the scope of the representation such that the new matter is not substantially related to the prior matter. Restrictions on the scope of the representation that effectively ensure that there is no substantial risk that confidential factual information as would normally have been obtained in the prior representation would be useful or relevant to advance the client's position in the new matter may, under certain circumstances, be sufficient to avoid a conflict of interest."

case. Sumitomo could certainly replace Paul Weiss entirely, but that is now what it wanted to do, and the court correctly allowed the alternative that Sumitomo chose.

§ 1.7-3(e)(3) Bankruptcy and Conflicts Counsel

Bankruptcy offers another opportunity for the use of conflicts counsel to lessen the costs of litigation. The economic cycle of boom and bust is an inevitable byproduct of capitalism. And matching the cycle is countercyclical behavior, for anyone engaged in economic activity, including lawyers. While many law firms are laying off[51] partners and associates in some areas of the law, other areas are booming. Bankruptcy is one such area.

Lawyers representing the bankrupt business operate with the happy knowledge that their fees are more secure than the most secured creditor. The bankruptcy judge is supposed to make sure of that.[52] While the lawyer's fees are certain, we know by the iron law of mathematics that every dollar that goes to the lawyer is one less dollar to pay to a creditor.[53] Hence, the law should not impose rules that unnecessarily increase lawyer's fees. That would hurt creditors.

Costs associated with hiring new counsel are certainly justified when disqualification serves important purposes. Typically, the disqualification protects a client's legitimate expectations of client loyalty and client confidences.[54] However, it is incorrect to think that ethics is like money, more is better than less. The economists would tell us that more is better than less at zero cost. So it is with professional responsibility. More is better than less, unless the costs are more than the benefits.[55]

One circumstance where the costs do not justify the disqualifi-

---

[51]"Laying off" is the common term used in the news reports, and we use although it is a misnomer. Lawyers are not like members of the pipefitters union; we do not expect the law firms to call back its laid-off partners when the economy improves.

[52]The judge must approve fee awards, which may be contested. On occasion, a judge will independently view the amount requested as too high and reject the request. The relevant statute authorizes the bankruptcy court, "on its own motion" to "award compensation that is less than the amount of compensation that is requested." 11 U.S.C.A. § 330(a)(2). *E.g., In re Recycling Industries, Inc.,* 243 B.R. 396, 35 Bankr. Ct. Dec. 136 (Bankr. D. Colo. 2000) (billing for work

of summer associates was excessive as to time spent and as to hourly rate).

[53]Rapoport, *Rethinking Fees in Chapter 11 Bankruptcy Cases,* 5 J. Bus. & Tech. Law 263 (2010): "there's significant overstaffing and duplication of effort—especially in the larger bankruptcy cases. What's worse is that there's no easy way to pinpoint just where the overstaffing is occurring in each case and no easy way to tell when the duplication of effort is necessary to represent the clients' interests and when it's just simple 'me, too' makework.'" (footnote omitted).

[54]§§ 1.6, 1.8, 1.9, 1.10.

[55]For example, the American Bar Association, in February 2009 amended its rules regarding imputed disqualification because it found that

cation in bankruptcy is when the firm that is the subject of the disqualification motion has not violated any legitimate client expectation of loyalty or confidence.

Let us focus on a primary issue of legal ethics related to conflicts of interest and bankruptcy representation. There are various scenarios and they can be complex. But, in each one, a law firm ("Law Firm") represents a party ("Party # 1") in connection with a bankruptcy. Party #2 is an unsecured or secured creditor of the estate or a prospective lender to the estate. Party #2 is also a client of Law Firm, but Law Firm represents Party #2 only in unrelated matters, that is, matters that do not involve the bankruptcy litigation. Party #2 uses a different law firm in the bankruptcy litigation—not an uncommon occurrence when major corporations hire various law firms to represent it on different matters.

There are four major variations, all of which raise possible conflicts of issues under the ABA Model Rules of Professional Conduct—

- Law Firm is the attorney for the debtor or trustee in a U.S. bankruptcy.
- Law Firm is the attorney for a Creditors' Committee in a U.S. bankruptcy.
- A member of Law Firm is the trustee of a liquidating trust created because of a U.S. bankruptcy, or a plan administrator under a plan of reorganization.
- Law Firm represents one creditor in its claims against the bankruptcy estate, while other law firms represent other creditors. One or more of these other creditors are also clients of Law Firm in unrelated matters.

In each situation, Party #2 is an unsecured or secured creditor of the estate or a prospective lender to the estate. And, in each of these situations, Law Firm would not be taking positions adverse to Party #2 (its client in unrelated matters) because, in each case, a different law firm (Law Firm #2) would be representing the debtor or trustee in a U.S. bankruptcy, or the Creditors' Committee in a U.S. bankruptcy, etc.

In other words, Law Firm represents Party #1 in various matters. Sometimes, the interests of Party #1 may conflict with the interests of Party #2. In those cases, Law Firm does *not* represent Party #1. Instead, Law Firm #2 represents Party #1 in the portion of the matter or negotiation that is adverse to Party #2.

The question is whether Law Firm may ethically represent

---

the costs outweighed the benefits. One can certainly dispute the weighing of the competing interests, but the important point is that all the parties concerned recognized that they must weigh the costs and benefits. § 1.10-44, "2009 Screening Amendments to Rule 1.10(a)."

Party #1 (its client) provided that Law Firm #2 represents Party #1 in any situation where Party #1 has an interest adverse to Party #2 (a client of Law Firm in unrelated matters). Law Firm will not assist Law Firm #2 in these matters. In that way, Law Firm will never be in a position where it is adverse to a current client.

In addition to the ethics rules, which courts routinely enforce by disqualifying the law firm, there is also the issue of the propriety of this representation under the bankruptcy laws. If Congress enacts a law (such as a bankruptcy law) that prohibits a representation for reasons that Congress deems sufficient, the ethics rules (which are rules of the court) do not override the legislative determination. Obviously, state and federal courts must follow valid federal statutes, even if those statutes are inconsistent with state ethics rules.[56]

Bankruptcy law incorporates, to some extent, the law of ethics.[57] If there is an ethical violation, the courts are more likely to find a bankruptcy prohibition, and if there is no violation of the ethics rules, the bankruptcy court is more likely to find no violation of the bankruptcy rules.[58] Hence, it is doubly important to determine if there is a conflict under the ethics rules governing lawyers.

As discussed above, one's first view of the basic law governing disqualification is that there is a conflict of interests in each of these various scenarios. But, if one looks more closely, a law firm can avoid the disqualification if it uses what we may call a "conflicts counsel" in the situations discussed. In those circumstances, public policy, legitimate client expectations, and the

---

[56]E.g., *Sperry v. Florida ex rel. Florida Bar*, 373 U.S. 379, 83 S.Ct. 1322, 10 L.Ed.2d 428 (1963). Although state ethics rules did not allow nonlawyers to appear before various agencies, including the Patent Court, federal law did allow nonlawyers to appear before the Patent Court. Because of the federal law authorizing an appearance, by a nonlawyer, *Sperry* held that the Supremacy Clause overrode state rules to the contrary. 1 RONALD D. ROTUNDA & JOHN E. NOWAK, TREATISE ON CONSTITUTIONAL LAW: SUBSTANCE AND PROCEDURE §§ 3.1-3.3 (Thomson/West 4th ed. 2007) (6 volume treatise).

[57]E.g., *In re GHR Energy Corp.*, 60 B.R. 52, 61 (Bkrtcy.S.D.Tex.1985), stating that in deciding "whether the McCabe/Gordon firm, by hiring Christie, holds an interest adverse to the estate [for bankruptcy law purposes],

the Court has looked for guidance to the Code of Professional Responsibility." *In re Caldor, Inc.*, 193 B.R. 165, 178 (S.D.N.Y. 1996): "Courts look to the Code of Professional Responsibility in analyzing conflicts under the Bankruptcy Code." *In re Enron Corp.*, 2002 WL 32034346, *12 (Bankr. Ct. S.D.N.Y. 2002), *affirmed*, 2003 WL 223455 (S.D.N.Y. 2003) (quoting *Caldor* with approval).

[58]E.g., *In re Enron Corp.*, 2003 WL 223455 *9 (S.D.N.Y. 2003):

This Court concurs with the bankruptcy court that, having found both that Milbank is not involved in any matter in which it has an adverse interest and that the use of conflicts counsel and ethical walls are appropriate, there is no basis for a violation of the Code of Professional Responsibility.

emerging case law indicate that there is no valid conflict of interest.

In several cases, the bankruptcy courts have noted the use of conflicts counsel, and apparently approved of the idea, though they often do not discuss the rationale.[59]

Daido Steel Co., Ltd. v. Official Committee of Unsecured Creditors[60] is one such case. The official committee of unsecured creditors in a Chapter 11 case filed an application with the bankruptcy court for permission to continue to retain their attorney, who also represented the purchaser of debtor's assets on matters not related to bankruptcy proceedings. Daido, the single largest creditor, objected because of a conflict of interest. The Brouse & McDowell law firm ("B&M") represented the Committee. Later, Hamlin Holding, Inc. ("HHI") entered into negotiations with the debtors to purchase substantially all of their assets. B&M also represented HHI, but on matters unrelated to the bankruptcy. Separate counsel represented HHI. The court found that a statute[61] did not prohibit representation of the committee by the law firm that also represented the purchaser of debtor's assets on matters unrelated to bankruptcy. The court specifically did not consider the legal ethics issues,[62] although it did find that the law firm did not have an "adverse interest" within the meaning of the relevant bankruptcy statute.[63]

In re Rockaway Bedding, Inc.[64] also approved of using conflicts counsel to avoid the conflict. However, that case did consider the ethics rules. *Rockaway Bedding* found no violation of either the bankruptcy law or the ethics rules governing the practice of law. It also used the term "conflicts counsel." Again, it offered little in the way of discussing the rationale.

The law firm in question, Duane Morris LLP, "agreed not to assert any claim of fraud, misrepresentation or dishonest conduct against PNC Bank in connection with the Debtors' Chapter 11

---

[59]Bankruptcy cases that acknowledged the use of "conflicts counsel," typically without discussion, include *In re Global Crossing Ltd.*, 295 B.R. 726, 728 (Bankr. S.D.N.Y. 2003); *In re Winn-Dixie Stores, Inc.*, 326 B.R. 853, 855 (Bankr. M.D. Fla. 2005); *In re Mirant Corp.*, 354 B.R. 113, 149 (Bankr. N.D. Tex. 2006); *In re Adelphia Communications Corp.*, 359 B.R. 54, 55 (Bankr. S.D.N.Y. 2006); *In re Calpine Corp.*, 377 B.R. 808, 810 (Bankr. S.D.N.Y. 2007); *In re Delta Air Lines, Inc.*, 370 B.R. 552, 553 (Bankr. S.D.N.Y. 2007); *In re Rockaway Bedding, Inc.*, 2007 WL 1461319, *2,

*4 (Bankr. D.N.J. 2007); *In re Bayou Group, LLC*, 362 B.R. 624, 639 (Bankr. S.D.N.Y. 2007). As discussed below, the law does not limit the use of "conflicts counsel" to bankruptcy cases.

[60]*Daido Steel Co., Ltd. v. Official Committee of Unsecured Creditors*, 178 B.R. 129 (N.D. Ohio 1995).

[61]11 U.S.C.A. § 1103(b).

[62]178 B.R. 129, 132.

[63]11 U.S.C.A. § 1103(b).

[64]*In re Rockaway Bedding, Inc.*, 2007 WL 1461319 (Bkrtcy. D.N.J. 2007).

proceedings." If a claim should arise, Duane Morris LLP offered to "to retain separate conflicts counsel to pursue such claims or allow the Official Committee of Unsecured Creditors to assert such claims on the Debtors' behalf. In the event that a dispute arises between the Debtors and Mr. Potamkin, counsel other than Duane Morris LLP will represent all parties." "Matters relating to misrepresentations and fraud are carved out of the waiver and will be assigned to either conflicts counsel or the Official Committee of Unsecured Creditors to prosecute on the Debtors' behalf." Given this arrangement, the court found no conflict. "Given the prophylactic provisions in place, this Court also believes that Duane Morris LLP's representation is in accordance with New Jersey Rule of Professional Conduct 1.7."[65]

In re Enron[66] similarly found no violation of the bankruptcy law or legal ethics. A creditor (Exco) moved to disqualify a law firm (Milbank, Tweed) from representing the unsecured creditors' committee in Enron's Chapter 11 cases. Milbank argued that it was not simultaneously representing the Committee and any other party in this chapter 11 case with an interest adverse to the bankruptcy estate. The client hired separate counsel for that. The Court agreed and used the term "conflicts counsel."[67]

Two of the members of the official committee of the unsecured creditors were significant clients of Milbank. Milbank also represented numerous other creditors on matters unrelated to the Enron bankruptcy case. Another committee member, a surety, was a plaintiff in a lawsuit alleging that the two committee members who were alleged clients of Milbank conspired with others to defraud the surety. Prior to the filing of the Chapter 11 bankruptcy, Milbank represented entities who had arranged for a billion dollar structured finance offering on behalf of a debtor affiliate. This offering included issuance of the debtor's stock and an agreement to sell that stock. In the five years prior to the Chapter 11 filing, Milbank represented several of the debtors in 125 transactions, and collected almost $18 million in legal fees. And, finally, the debtors had paid nearly a half-million dollars in fees to Milbank during the preference period. Milbank did not voluntarily repay the preference, but it did agree not to defend a preference action and abide by the findings of a court-appointed

---

[65]2007 WL 1461319, *2, *4, & *5 (Footnote omitted).

[66]*In re Enron*, 2002 WL 32034346, *10 (Bankr. S.D.N.Y. 2002).

[67]*In re Enron*, 2002 WL 32034346, *11: "There is no basis in this record to question the adequacy of this procedure or the internal ethical walls established at Milbank. Conflicts counsel, limited engagement agreements, and ethical walls have been acceptable procedures to address conflict of interests issues."

examiner.[68] Still, there was no conflict because on all relevant issues, Milbank used a separate conflicts counsel. The creditors' committee used this second law firm, the conflicts counsel, to handle matters that Milbank or its clients on other matters might have a conflict of interests.[69]

Consider another scenario, where Law Firm represents one creditor in its claims against the bankruptcy estate, while other law firms represent other creditors. One or more of these other creditors are also clients of Law Firm in unrelated matters. The ABA Model Rules of Professional Conduct[70] do not regard this situation as raising what it calls "directly adverse" conflicts. The Comments do not really offer any litmus test to determine what is "direct" versus "indirect," but the ABA does give a few examples. If a lawyer represents clients who are competing economic enterprises in unrelated litigation, that "does not ordinarily constitute a conflict of interest and thus may not require consent of the respective clients."[71] In other words, a law firm may represent a water utility in its efforts to raise its rates although that representation, if successful, disadvantages all the Law Firm's other clients who use water.[72] Or, the law firm may represent the local Toyota car dealer in buying some real estate while simultaneously representing the local Mercedes dealer in a contract matter. "The representations and the clients have nothing to do with each other, even though the clients are competitors in the business world."[73]

In the same sense, the creditors are all competitors for the assets of the estate, but that does not mean that they will be suing each other. Law Firm will be representing its client, while other creditors will have their own counsel to represent their interests. There is no disqualifying conflict merely because members of a Creditors Committee assert claims in differing amounts and subject to differing potential setoffs.[74]

---

[68]Richman, *Mega-Case Conflict Issues: Enron Committee Counsel*, 21-SEP AM. BANKR. INST. J. 20 (2002).

[69]The District Court approved this resolution of the issue. *In re Enron (Exco Resources, Inc. v. Milbank, Tweed, Hadley & McCloy LLP)*, 2003 WL 223455 (S.D.N.Y. 2003).

[70]Rule 1.7.

[71]Rule 1.7, Comment 6.

[72]§ 1.7–3(c), *supra*.

[73]§ 1.7–3(c), *supra* (footnote omitted).

[74]*In re Rusty Jones, Inc.*, 107 B.R. 161 (Bankr. N.D.Ill.1989) concluded, on the facts of that case, that the law firm may represent both the creditors' committee and individual creditors unless there is a showing of actual conflict of interest. The Court added:

"Individual members of this Creditors Committee assert claims in differing amounts and subject to differing potential setoffs. However, that does not create an adverse interest which would prohibit one counsel from representing individual members of the committee and also the committee as a

Thus, *In re National Liquidators, Inc.*[75] held that concurrent representation of unsecured creditors' committee and individual unsecured creditors is permissible unless there is an actual dispute:

> It simply exceeds rational bounds to rule that an adverse interest exists merely because a committee member's or a creditor's transactions with the debtor will be investigated, or because a remote, speculative, hypothetical possibility exists that, in the future, the estate or the Committee may dispute the creditor's claim or bring a cause of action against the creditor.[76]

However, there may be other cases where one creditor takes an adverse action against another creditor in the same matter. If there is an actual dispute, then there should be a conflict. As *National Liquidators* explained:

> [S]ection 1103(b)'s bar to attorney representation includes a requirement that there exist some allegation or evidence suggesting the likelihood of some actual dispute, strife, discord, or difference between the committee and its constituent or member. The Court is not establishing a high threshold. For example, should any evidence suggest the existence of possible challenges to a creditor's claim, the existence of a possible recovery action against the creditor, or the existence of any possible dispute between a committee and one of its constituents or members, then a disqualifying adverse interest exists under the Bankruptcy Code. Undoubtedly, actual disputes or actual allegations of the need for a recovery action engender adverse interests. Speculation and hypothesizing, however, will not carry the day.[77]

An impermissible conflict would exist if the lawyer who had previously represented Chapter 11 debtors-in-possession was now defending fraudulent transfer claims against the corporation. The lawyer learned confidential information disclosed during his prior representation. The lawyer was "in a position to take advantage of information previously revealed to him by the debtors as debtors-in-possession in an effort to frustrate and hinder the duties of the trustee and former debtors-in-possession to administer the bankruptcy estate for the benefit of all creditors therein."[78] The fraudulent transfer claims that the lawyer was attempting to defend were the same fraudulent transfer claims

---

whole when all members of the committee share claims of a similar nature. In short, no adverse interests have been demonstrated here between individual members of the Committee represented by Hinshaw and the Committee as a whole." 107 B.R. 161, 165.

[75]*In re National Liquidators, Inc.*, 182 B.R. 186 (S.D. Ohio 1995).

[76]182 B.R. 186, 192.

[77]182 B.R. 186, 192-93 (internal citation omitted), citing *Badami v. K.E. Joy*, 175 B.R. 303 (Bankr. D.Neb. 1994).

[78]*Badami v. K.E. Joy*, 175 B.R. 303, 305 (Bankr. D.Neb.1994).

that the Chapter 11 debtors-in-possession were obligated to assert prior to the conversion to Chapter 11.[79]

Consider these various cases. Law Firm is the attorney for the debtor or trustee in a U.S. bankruptcy. Or, Law Firm is the attorney for a Creditors' Committee in a U.S. bankruptcy. Or, a member of Law Firm is the trustee of a liquidating trust created because of a U.S. bankruptcy.[80] Or, Law Firm is the attorney for a debtor or trustee in a pending U.S. bankruptcy proceeding where there is a proposed Debtor in Possession (DIP) financing.

In each of these cases, there should be no conflict of interest when a law firm uses conflicts counsel in the situations discussed here. Law Firm may ethically represent Party #1 (its client) provided that conflicts counsel (Law Firm #2) represents Party #1 in any situation where Party #1 has an interest adverse to Party #2, who is also a current client of Law Firm on unrelated matters. Law Firm, of course, will not assist Law Firm #2 in these matters.

By using conflicts counsel, Law Firm will never be in a position where it is adverse to a current client. Law Firm will not be representing a bankruptcy client against a current client of Law Firm, in violation of ABA Model Rule 1.7. Instead, Law Firm will be representing the bankruptcy client against various nonclients, while conflicts counsel will be representing the bankruptcy client against any current client of Law Firm in unrelated matters. Thus, the *per se* rule against simultaneous representation articulated in *Cinema 5*[81] and other decisions does not require the Court to disqualify Law Firm.[82]

§ 1.7-3(e)(4) Public Defenders and Conflicts Counsel.

We find evidence that some public defenders are using "conflicts counsel" to take care of cases where the public defender's office

---

[79]"This interest and duty to prosecute claims against K.E. Joy P.C. on behalf of the estate is adverse to the interest of K.E. Joy P.C. in retaining funds transferred to it by the debtors." 75 B.R. 303, 305.

[80]In such a case, the debtor or trustee, on the advice of the Law Firm attorney, will retain counsel to represent the interests of the debtor or trustee. The Law Firm attorney will not retain the Law Firm in any case in which it would be adverse to a current client of Law Firm. It is not wrong for a lawyer to recommend that

an individual or entity retain counsel to vindicate its interests. In fact, that it was the ethics rules provide. ABA Model Rule 4.3: "The lawyer shall not give advice to an unrepresented person [the debtor or trustee], other than the advice to secure counsel." *Accord*, DR 7-104(A)(2), § 1200.35(a)(2).

[81]*Cinema 5 Ltd. v. Cinerama, Inc.*, 528 F.2d 1384, 1386 (2d Cir. 1976).

[82]See the similar language in *Sumitomo Corp. v. J. P. Morgan & Co., Inc.*, 2000 WL 145747, *4 (S.D.N.Y. 2000).

cannot represent a criminal defendant. For example, Humboldt County, California has created a "conflict counsel."[83]

While the use of conflicts counsel in this situation is generally, under the radar screen of court decisions, it has not escaped the attention of private criminal defense lawyers who are objecting to the potential loss of business.[84]

§ 1.7-3(e)(5) Conclusion

Conflicts routinely arise in cases involving cross examination, discovery, and bankruptcy, but its use need not be limited to these areas. There are other matters where the use of "conflicts counsel" will protect the legitimate interests of the various clients without imposing unnecessary expenses on the parties. For example, an issue on appeal may come up for the first time, and it will raise a conflict for the lawyer. Rather than disqualifying the law firm from all work on the matter, the court may approve of conflicts counsel if the particular issue is severable.[85]

Prospective litigation is another area where conflicts counsel will be useful. Let us say that a Client has a distribution contract with a manufacturer. It is certainly foreseeable that disputes may arise under this contract. Let us assume that the Law Firm represents Client in connection with this distribution contract, while simultaneously representing the Manufacturer in a local real-estate matter completely unrelated to the Client's business. Client and Lawyer should be able to agree between themselves that the Law Firm will not represent Client if there is any dispute

[83]*See* http://co.humboldt.ca.us/con fcsel/ (accessed Aug. 10, 2010).

[84]See report in, http://pdstuff.apu blicdefender.com/2007/09/18/lawyers-a t-war-over-conflict-counsel/ (accessed Aug. 10, 2010), noting that the Florida Association of Criminal Defense Lawyers has urged Florida's Attorney General to block a law that establishes five Regional Conflict Counsels, who will act as public defenders for indigent criminal defendants when the regular Public Defender has a conflict.

[85]*Buysse v. Baumann-Furrie & Co.*, 448 N.W.2d 865, 869 (Minn.1989). The lawyer permissibly withdrew from preparing a portion of appellate brief, thus avoiding a conflict. The Court ruled that it would not require the lawyer for the judgment creditors to withdraw. However, the Court said, conflicts counsel should have filed a separate brief rather than merely take responsibility for a portion of one brief.

That would serve to highlight the severability of the issue. The Court explained that the work of the conflicts counsel on appeal "was limited to representation of the judgment creditors in the determination of the coverage question." On appeal, the original counsel and the conflicts counsel filed a joint brief "in which there is no discernible line of demarcation between insurance coverage issues and other issues involved in this litigation." The Court said that "the lawyers in question confined their activities on appeal to their respective spheres of representation," but went on to say that "*separate briefs would have been a more fitting way to carry out the undertaking* to separate representation on the coverage issues from representation on all other issues." 448 N.W.2d 865, 869 (Minn.1989) (emphasis added).

with the Manufacturer. Client would use a separate conflicts counsel if that eventuality occurs.

This agreement eliminates the potential conflict without imposing the opportunity cost of Law Firm refusing to represent Client merely because of the possibility of the conflict. This agreement would not require the Manufacture's consent. In the event of a lawsuit, conflicts counsel would represent Client while Manufacturer would retain its own counsel. But Law Firm could continue to represent Client and Manufacturer on unrelated issues.[86]

The use of conflicts counsel need not be limited to litigation. It may be also appropriate in negotiations in multiparty business. Law firms, of course, cannot use this procedure as a sham, where the otherwise-conflicted firm becomes a behind-the-scenes manager of the matter that it has undertaken not to pursue. And the firm itself may not take actions that hurt the law firm's other client. But with those caveats, the presence of one or two areas of conflict that can be severed would mean that the law will not disqualify the lawyer altogether.[87] In all such cases, a law firm would be limiting the scope of its representation to avoid conflict with a current or former client (Party #2), if the client whose representation the law firm limits (Party #1) will consent after full disclosure and if that limitation does not so restrict representation as to render it incompetent.

Careful lawyers should also consider asking their clients to waive, in advance, any objection to using conflicts counsel to handle issues that are discrete and severable and do not involve risk of misusing the client's confidences. Clients, in other words, may waive in futuro breaches of loyalty if the lawyer uses conflicts counsel to handle a discrete matter. But, we would not reasonably expect clients to waive, in futuro, beaches of confidentiality because one cannot know now the significance in the future of the breach of confidentiality.

Prior client agreement should be necessary for the court to allow use of conflict counsel to resolve a conflict. However, that at a

---

[86]The RESTATEMENT OF THE LAW GOVERNING LAWYERS supports the use of "conflicts counsel," but it does not use this term. Instead, it speaks of the law firm limiting the scope of its engagement. *"Such an agreement would not require the consent of Manufacturer."* The RESTATEMENT OF THE LAW GOVERNING LAWYERS, Third (ALI 2000), at § 121, Comment c(iii), Illustration 4 (emphasis added).

[87]Association of the Bar of the City of New York Committee on Professional and Judicial Ethics, FORMAL OPINION 2001-3 (2001), addressed this issue, cited *Sumitomo* with approval, and approved of using conflicts counsel. The Opinion said that it was appropriate for another firm to bring the case against the client that the principal firm cannot bring. The case is discussed in, ABA/BNA LAWYERS' MANUAL ON PROFESSIONAL CONDUCT, Current Report, Ethics Opinions, vol. 17, p. 455 (Aug. 1, 2001), *reprinted in,* Westlaw, 1295 PLI/Corp 1191.

minimum, lawyers and clients should be permitted to agree in advance that conflict counsel will be used, and that this agreement should be enforceable. They should also be able to make a commitment in advance as to what types of matters or parts of matters are discrete and severable such that use of conflict counsel makes sense. Alternatively, clients who do not like using the conflict counsel approach should be permitted to agree in advance with their lawyers not to use this approach. Then the lawyers know the real opportunity cost of representing a client who objects to using conflicts counsel.

Conflicts counsel is a useful tool to ameliorate the costs of disqualifying a law firm while protecting legitimate client interests in confidentiality and loyalty. A few cases—typically unreported and conclusory—embrace this technique but do not discuss its rationale. This Comment explains the justification. In addition, courts should codify what the lower courts and unreported decisions are doing by adopting a rule regularizing the procedure so that its use will not be happenstance. In those cases where the matter causing the conflict is severable and distinct and the risks of loss of confidentiality are minuscule, the courts should allow conflicts counsel.

§ 1.7–4 SECURING INFORMED CONSENT

§ 1.7–4(a) Full Disclosure

Before a lawyer may represent clients who are—or are reasonably likely to be—in conflict with each other, the lawyer must secure each client's informed consent. In order for this consent to be knowing, the lawyer must give each client "full disclosure."[1] In some cases, however, such "full disclosure" may require disclosure of confidences or secrets that the lawyer may not reveal under Model Rule 1.6.[2] In such situations the lawyer cannot secure adequate consent from Client *A* without violating his or her duty to keep confidential the secrets of Client *B*. When the lawyer cannot secure adequate consent without violating his duty to keep confidential the secrets and confidences of each client, that lawyer may not take on such representation.[3]

Full disclosure requires the lawyer to reveal all the facts, legal

---

[Section 1.7–4]

[1]*See* Rule 1.7(b)(4) & Comment 18; Rule 1.0(e) (definition of "informed consent"); DR 5-105(C).

[2]*See* GEOFFREY HAZARD, ETHICS IN THE PRACTICE OF LAW 24, 76 (Yale Univ. Press 1978). The analogous provision of the Model Code is Canon 4.

[3]*See* Rule 1.7, Comment 19.

Lettley v. State, 358 Md. 26, 746 A.2d 392 (2000). Trial counsel represented two clients, one of whom was a defendant in a murder case. The other client told the lawyer that he—not the current defendant—had committed the crime. The lawyer asked to withdraw, reasoning that she could neither reveal who had made this confession nor effectively represent the current

implications, possible effects, and other circumstances relating to the proposed representation. The lawyer must bring home to the client, in a way that the client can understand, the significance of what is said. A client's "mere knowledge of the existence of his attorney's other representation does not alone constitute full disclosure."[4]

§ 1.7–4(b) Prospective Waivers of a Conflict

If a client can waive a conflict, he may choose to waive his objections prospectively, *if* the prospective waiver meets all the requirements for waiving a present conflict of interest. The lawyer relying on this prospective waiver must show that the waiver reasonably contemplated the future conflict so that the client's consent is a knowing consent, that is, it is reasonably viewed as fully informed when he gave it. The lawyer must give the client the information in such a way that the client will appreciate the significance of the waiver that is being sought.[5]

The 1983 version of the Model Rules did not have a specific section dealing with advance waivers or waivers *in futuro*. However, the case law and various ethics opinions concluded that the client does have the power to agree to waive a conflict in advance.[6] The drafters of the 2002 Rules codified this law and added a new Comment that acknowledges that clients normally have the power to waive a conflict in advance, or *in futuro*.

In order to be effective, an advanced waiver or waiver *in futuro*

---

client without using the information, such as by seeking to show that the other person looked like the defendant. The lawyer told the trial judge: "I don't feel that I can represent him to the fullest of my ability because in order to represent him fully I would basically have to roll over on another client using information that was told to me in confidence at a time when I represented that person." 358 Md. 26, 30, 746 A.2d 392, 394. The trial judge, surprisingly, refused to let the lawyer withdraw because, the judge argued, no new lawyer would have known the information and thus could not have provided better representation. The Maryland Supreme Court reversed. The problem is divided loyalties: defense counsel would feel constrained in such things as cross-examination. To effectively represent one client, she would implicate the other. This conflict was serious enough to constitute ineffective assistance of counsel, permitting the defendant a new trial.

[4]*Financial General Bankshares, Inc. v. Metzger*, 523 F.Supp. 744, 771 (D.D.C.1981), *vacated*, 680 F.2d 768 (D.C.Cir.1982).

[5]Rule 1.7, Comment 22. *See* Richard W. Painter, *Advance Waiver of Conflicts*, 13 GEORGETOWN J. LEGAL ETHICS 289, 327 (2000); Lawrence J. Fox, *All's OK Between Consenting Adults: Enlightened Rule on Privacy, Obscene Rule on Ethics*, 29 HOFSTRA L. REV. 701 (2001); Jonathan J. Lerner, *Honoring Choice By Consenting Adults: Prospective Conflict Waivers As A Mature Solution To Ethical Gamesmanship—A Response To Mr. Fox*, 29 HOFSTRA L. REV. 971 (2001).

[6]*See* ABA Formal Opinion 93–372 (Apr. 10, 1993). Note, the ABA withdrew this opinion in 2005 to reflect the new language in the Comments to Rule 1.7 about prospective consents to conflicts of interests. *See* ABA Formal Opinion 05–436 (May 11, 2005).

must meet the test of Rule 1.7(b).[7] The key factor to determine if an advance waiver is effective is whether the lawyer can properly explain to the client all of the material risks associated with the future conflict.[8] There are a number of factors that are important in determining the effectiveness of any advanced consent. These include the comprehensiveness of the information provided to the client, the sophistication and experience of the client with respect to such conflicts, and the extent to which the actual conflict that arises in the future matches the information provided to the client and agreed upon in the advance consent.[9]

However, a prospective waiver does not extend to disclosure or use of client confidences against the client, unless the client very explicitly agrees to such disclosure or use.[10] In other words, a client may waive, prospectively, a conflict based on loyalty, but it may not normally waive, prospectively, a conflict based on breach of confidences, because at the time of the prospective waiver a client cannot normally know what those confidences might be or what their significance might be.[11]

In Formal Opinion 05–436, the ABA made a few subtle changes to the language in Comment 22 of Rule 1.7.[12] First, it clarified that the term "waiver" in the phrase, "prospective waiver" means the same as informed consent as used in Rule 1.7 and throughout the Model Rules. Second, it interpreted the language that a consent to a future conflict is more likely to be effective if it is limited to a future conflict "unrelated to the subject matter of the representation." The ABA opinion states:

We are of the opinion, therefore, that the term "unrelated to" as

---

[7] Rule 1.7, Comment 22.

[8] A federal district court invalidated a broad waiver to future conflicts of interest of a corporate client as not satisfying a "truly informed consent" standard. *See* 24 ABA/BNA Law. Man. Prof. Conduct 427 (Aug. 8, 2008), *citing Celgene v. KV Pharmaceutical Co.*, Civ. No. 07-4819 (D.N.J. 2008) (unpublished).

[9] Rule 1.7, Comment 22. The Comment specifically mentions that general, open ended consents are far less likely to be effective than more specific, tailored consent to the anticipated future conflict.

[10] ABA Formal Opinion 05–436 (May 11, 2005). D.C. Bar, Opinion 309, *Advance Waivers of Conflicts of Interest* (Dec. 2001), at footnote 10, explaining that waivers permitting the use or disclosure of confidential information

may not be implied from waivers of conflicts of interest. "Because of their considerable potential for mischief, waivers of confidentiality require particular scrutiny and may be invalid even when granted by sophisticated clients with counsel (in-house or outside) independent of the lawyer seeking the waiver."

[11] *Westinghouse Electric Corp. v. Gulf Oil Corp.*, 588 F.2d 221, 229 (7th Cir.1978). "Disqualification based on the potential for abuse of confidential information, however, involves different considerations which preclude the effectiveness of consent, particularly a vague, general consent given or implied prior to the threat of disclosure or adverse litigation." *Id.*

[12] ABA Formal Opinion 05–436 (May 11, 2005).

used in Comment [22] should be read as meaning not "substantially related to," as that term is used in Rule 1.9 and its Comment [3], i.e., that the future matters as to which the client's consent to the lawyer's conflicting representation is sought do not involve the same transaction or legal dispute that is the subject of the lawyer's present representation of the consenting client, and are not of such a nature that the disclosure or use by the lawyer of information relating to the representation of the consenting client would materially advance the position of the future clients.[13]

This interpretation is consistent with the view that the focus of the conflicts rules is to protect client confidential information.

For example, assume that a Corporation [Corporation #1] located in Los Angeles hires the local office of a national law firm to negotiate and draft a lease on a Los Angeles building. The law firm asks Corporation #1 to waive any objections to the Chicago office of that law firm representing a Chicago bank [Corporation #2] in negotiating mortgages on Chicago property, even if the mortgagor happens to be another, separate division of Corporation #1. Corporation #1 may waive, prospectively, its objections to this possible conflict of loyalties.[14]

This prospective waiver would not normally include a waiver of confidences. Assume that the law firm later learns certain secrets about Corporation #1 that would be relevant to its negotiation of the mortgage of its subsidiary [e.g., its dire need to obtain a mortgage and its willingness to pay a higher than normal interest rate because of internal plans]. The prospective consent to the representation would not normally include consent to the adverse use of confidential information. At the time Corporation #1 consented to the prospective waiver, it did not (and could not) know that the law firm would later learn information—about Corporation's willingness to pay a higher rate of interest—that would become significant to the later negotiations.

Suppose that a large client ("Alpha") who gives a little business to a lot of different firms asks the law firm to represent it in a specific matter. Later, the law firm may ask Alpha for permission to withdraw from representing Alpha in any given manner and then ask for permission to represent a new client in matters where there would be no danger of any revelation of Alpha's confidences or secrets. One should not be surprised if Alpha refuses consent. Indeed, it may be the case that one reason that Alpha retained a large number of extremely capable firms is to preempt possible adversaries from hiring those firms.

---

[13] ABA Formal Opinion 05–436 (May 11, 2005).

[14] The law firm must also secure consent from the party (Corporation #2) it is representing in the negotia-tions, because that party should know that the law firm is representing Corporation #1 on other matters, a fact that may compromise the law firm's undivided loyalty towards Corporation #2.

What law firms should do, if they wish to reduce such opportunity costs, is to ask for consent *before* accepting Alpha's initial retention. The courts will not accept open-ended waivers[15] to future conflicts, just as courts do not routinely accept the parking garage's sign purporting to affirm that "parking in this lot signifies your consent to waive any and all tort damages." But carefully-drawn waivers should meet judicial approval if well-informed clients agree to them, where the firm brings home to the new client the significance of what is waived and what is consented to, and where the client is not asked to waive, in the future, its confidences or secrets before it can know the significance of these confidences or secrets.

In short, some conflicts are common and familiar to the client, and the client may wish to waive these conflicts in advance. If the lawyer fully informs her client of any risk that the client might thus face, the client may waive such conflicts in advance.[16] If the circumstances or the reasonable expectations that formed the basis of the client's consent materially change, the lawyer must bring these new factors to the attention of the client and secure new consent.[17]

§ 1.7–5 THE HOT POTATO DOCTRINE

In general, if a law firm finds itself simultaneously representing two adverse clients in two different law suits, it may not avoid the problem simply by dropping the disfavored client like a "hot potato."[1] Absent special circumstances,[2] if the parties do not

---

[15]"Disqualification based on the potential for abuse of confidential information, however, involves different considerations which preclude the effectiveness of consent, *particularly a vague, general consent* given or implied prior to the threat of disclosure or adverse litigation." *Westinghouse Electric Corp. v. Gulf Oil Corp.*, 588 F.2d 221, 229 (7th Cir.1978) (emphasis added). *See also* Rule 1.7, Comment 22.

[16]Restatement of the Law Governing Lawyers, Third, § 122, at Comment *d*, at 268 to 270 (Official Draft 2000).

See also N.Y.City Bar Opinion 2006–1 (Feb. 17, 2006) (extensive discussion of advance waivers and sample forms for blanket waivers and substantially related waivers), *noted in* 22 ABA/BNA MANUAL ON PROFES-

SIONAL CONDUCT, Current Reports News 165 (Apr. 5, 2006). This opinion goes beyond the limitations found in Comment 22 to Rule 1.7, by permitting certain waivers in substantially related transactions matters.

[17]*Worldspan, L.P. v. The Sabre Group Holdings, Inc.*, 5 F.Supp.2d 1356 (N.D.Ga.1998).

[Section 1.7–5]

[1]*See, e.g.*, Ronald D. Rotunda, *One Potato, Two Potato, Three Potato, Four*, 14 LEGAL TIMES 23 (Aug. 12, 1991).

[2]The court in *Pennwalt Corp. v. Plough, Inc.*, 85 F.R.D. 264 (D.Del. 1980), applied the "hot potato" doctrine but did not require disqualification because the conflict arose from a client merger and was therefore inadvertent. The court also found that given the timing of the conflict it was

consent to the conflict, the law firm must withdraw from representing both parties in the two cases.[3]

The basic conflicts rule, of course, is that a lawyer may not sue Client A on behalf of Client B while simultaneously representing A, even in a completely unrelated matter. This rule exists in a world where law firms are ever-changing. When law firms undergo metamorphoses by merger or acquisition—and sometimes when they just stand still—, their client list may contain two clients who are directly adverse to each other. Some law firms erroneously conclude that the firm should pick one of the clients to continue representing and withdraw from representing the other. However, the general rule is that, if the firm withdraws from further representation of Client A, it still may not ethically represent Client B.

This is what is often called the "hot potato" problem. The general rule is that one cannot drop a client like a hot potato. From the image of the kitchen comes the rule that binds the modern law firm.

The "hot potato" phrase probably derives from *Picker International Inc. v. Varian Associates Inc.*[4] In that case, a large national law firm merged with a smaller firm based in Chicago. When client lists were compared, it turned out that the merging firms were representing opponents in current litigation and that the new firm was thus in the position of suing a client. (The larger firm was suing B on behalf of A, its longtime client; the smaller firm (now part of the larger law firm) was representing B in various matters, but not in the case of A v. B.)

The newly merged firm sought to withdraw from representing

---

highly unlikely that the conflict involved a misuse of confidential information or adverse effect on the representation. *See also Gould Inc. v. Mitsui Mining & Smelting Co.*, 738 F.Supp. 1121 (N.D.Ohio 1990) (client acquisition and merger created conflict therefore court applies "less mechanical approach" to "balance the various interests"): *Pioneer-Standard Electronics, Inc. v. Cap Gemini America, Inc.*, 2002 WL 553460 (N.D.Ohio 2002) (disqualification not required because conflict created by merger did not implicate confidential information or other prejudice through continued representation). *But see GATX/Airlog Co. v. Evergreen Int'l Airlines*, 8 F.Supp.2d 1182 (N.D.Cal.1998) (law firm should have anticipated that bank client with beneficial interest in assets of another

firm client could have a dispute involving the financing transaction).

[3]*Picker Int'l, Inc. v. Varian Assoc., Inc.*, 670 F.Supp. 1363 (N.D.Ohio 1987), aff'd, 869 F.2d 578 (Fed.Cir.1989). *See also, e.g., Pioneer-Standard Electronics, Inc. v. Cap Gemini America, Inc.*, 2002 WL 553460, *2 (N.D.Ohio 2002): "Shearman's termination of its relationship with Pioneer is ineffective because Shearman terminated its attorney-client relationship with Pioneer only after it was asked to represent Cap Gemini in this litigation and Pioneer refused to waive the conflict."

[4]*Picker Int'l Inc. v. Varian Associates Inc.*, 670 F.Supp. 1363 (N.D.Ohio 1987), aff'd, 869 F.2d 578 (Fed.Cir. 1989).

the smaller firm's client and to continue representing the longtime client of the larger firm. The federal trial court held that the firm could not do that without the consent of all affected clients. Failing such consent, the new firm had to withdraw in the case of *A v. B* from representing both parties: "A firm may not drop a client like a hot potato, especially if it is in order to keep a far more lucrative client."[5] From such colorful images the law of conflicts develops.

The general principles that the *Picker* court articulated are not unusual, but the particular case was, and the trial court's strict application of the conflict rules was hardly self-evident. While the large firm was representing Client *A* in a suit against Client *B*, none of the lawyers (from either the new or the old law firms) had ever been involved in that particular litigation on behalf of *B*.

Moreover, assume that the rearrangement of the law firms followed a different order. Assume first that the smaller firm had first disbanded and then withdrawn from further representation of *B*, on the grounds that the law firm no longer existed. Then, assume that the larger firm hired all (or most) of the lawyers from the now-disbanded smaller firm. In that situation, it could be said that the larger firm never had *B* as a client. Hence there never was a client to drop.

The court in *Picker* did not buy that argument. Nor did it buy the argument that the representation of Client *A* should be allowed to go forward because the larger firm did not merge with the smaller firm in order to drop the smaller client. None of the lawyers ever had any intent to impose any extra costs on the smaller client, and there was never any danger of a breach of Client *B*'s confidences. The court was similarly unmoved by the contention that a strict hot potato rule reduces lawyer mobility and impedes efficient restructuring in the legal profession.

Although some courts have been sensitive to such arguments in other contexts, the case law before and after *Picker* remains unsympathetic in this context.[6] Courts generally follow the principle articulated in *Picker* even if they do not adopt the hot potato metaphor.

Hot potatoes not only burn law firms that have restructured; they can be hard for any firm to handle. The issue has also become more important in this era of transient client loyalties. Say a potential client comes along with interests adverse to an existing client. The firm views the new business favorably and

---

[5] 670 F.Supp. at 1365.

[6] *See, e.g., Cinema 5, Ltd. v. Cinerama, Inc.*, 528 F.2d 1384 (2d Cir. 1976); *Harte Biltmore Ltd. v. First Pa. Bank N.A.*, 655 F.Supp. 419 (S.D.Fla. 1987).

wants to withdraw from further representation of its preexisting client in order to free itself to work for the newcomer. The firm wants to convert the preexisting client to a former client, and then accept the new client.

Courts do not view preemptive withdrawal favorably, and typically treat this situation as a hot potato because the law firm drops the preexisting client with the specific intent of taking on the new client.[7] Consequently, many clients impose an opportunity cost on the firm, measured by the new clients that the firm cannot accept while representing the original client. The cost is magnified because the firm may not remove it by the simple expedient of "firing" the current client to accept a new one.

When there is a question of whether the client is really a "former" client, the courts tend to resolve the facts against the law firm if it is reasonable for the client to think that it is a continuing client.[8] Consequently, law firms should seriously consider sending out letters of disengagement, so that the client and the law firm know where they stand.[9]

Another problem is created by the ripple effect caused when a major client—Client Alpha—passes out a small amount of business to a large number of firms. Ethics rules impose on the firms a prohibition, first, against suing Alpha and, second, against withdrawing from representing Alpha in order to accept a client adverse to Alpha. This problem is well-illustrated by *Boardwalk Properties Inc. v. BPHC Acquisition Inc.*[10] New York developer Donald Trump was one of the third-party defendants in Boardwalk Properties. In a ruling from the bench, the judge noted that the law firm subject to disqualification—

> was not Trump's only law firm—and I am troubled somewhat by the notion, for example, that the Trump organization retained a lot of law firms and potentially disqualified a lot of law firms . . . .. No active law firm in this area (when I say this area, I'm talking about

---

[7]*See, e.g., Unified Sewerage Agency v. Jelco, Inc.,* 646 F.2d 1339, 1345 n. 4 (9th Cir.1981).

[8]*See, e.g., Shearing v. Allergan, Inc.,* 1994 WL 396139 (D.Nev.1994), where the client had not retained the law firm for more than a year, but the relationship had not formally ended, and the preexisting client had been a client of the law firm for 13 years. The court treated the preexisting client as a present client and applied the hot potato rule.

[9]But it should be obvious that many law firms do not send out letters of *dis*engagement because they do not like to turn down business that may be coming down the road. Hope springs eternal. Rather than tell a client that the law firm now considers it a former client who should go elsewhere for legal work, the firm would like to leave the door open.

[10]*Boardwalk Properties Inc. v. BPHC Acquisition Inc.,* Docket No. ATL-C-000051-89E (Superior Court of New Jersey, Chancery Division, Atlantic County 1989).

New Jersey and Pennsylvania and New York, all of which have law firms that get actively involved in litigation here in some way or another), all those law firms know that Donald Trump and the organizations of which he's a part are very active. They get involved in a lot of cases, and [the firms] know that when they choose to represent that type of an organization there are certain upsides and certain downsides. One of the upsides is a nice client; one of the downsides is you're not going to be able to take cases against that client. And the answer isn't that I'll represent them until it looks better that I sue them, and then I won't represent them.[11]

The lawyer cannot avoid the hot potato rule by withdrawing in order to represent another client.[12] On the other hand, this state of affairs should suggest the appropriateness of advance consent. Both the client and the lawyer will know where they stand. The lawyer can accept a client waiver without worrying that the client "retained a lot of law firms and potentially disqualified a lot of law firms."[13] And the client can assure the lawyer that this representation will not impose unnecessary opportunity costs on the law firm.

In any event, for purposes of the hot potato rule, a preexisting client is treated as a former client if the withdrawal occurs at the time that the client and the lawyer contemplated the end of the representation: the client is "former" because the lawyer has completed the discrete assignment. Or, the client is "former" because the client has discharged the lawyer (other than a discharge for cause arising out of the lawyer's improper representation, because a lawyer-fiduciary should not benefit from a violation of his fiduciary obligations).[14] Or, the client is "former" because another ground exists justifying the lawyer's mandatory or permissive withdrawal. The important point, the touchstone, is that the lawyer, in converting a preexisting client into a former client for purposes of the hot potato rule, "is not motivated *primarily* by a desire to represent the new client."[15]

The authorities have recognized one exception to the hot potato

---

[11]Docket No. ATL-C-000051-89E (Superior Court of New Jersey, Chancery Division, Atlantic County 1989).

[12]Restatement of the Law Governing Lawyers, Third, § 213, Reporter's Notes to Comment c, at 724 (Proposed Final Draft No. 1, Mar. 29, 1996).

[13]*Boardwalk Properties Inc. v. BPHC Acquisition Inc.*, Docket No. ATL-C-000051-89E (Superior Court of New Jersey, Chancery Division, Atlantic County 1989).

[14]For a case considering a "reverse hot potato," see *Coke v. Equity Residential Properties Trust*, 440 Mass. 511, 800 N.E.2d 280 (2003). A client moved to disqualify a law firm and lost the motion and the client appealed. During the appeal, the client discharged the law firm and the court held that the termination rendered the appeal moot and the law firm was free to continue its case against the client.

[15]Restatement of the Law Governing Lawyers, Third, § 213, at Comment c, at 711 (Proposed Final Draft No. 1, Mar. 29, 1996) (emphasis added). The Reporter's Notes used the phrase, "solely," but the official Com-

rule, referred to as the "thrust upon" exception.[16] In some cases, a court expressly permits a law firm to drop one client and keep another client when a conflict has arisen due to no fault of the law firm. In such a case, the law firm accepted both clients at a time when there was no conflict. And some external unforeseen event, such as a corporate reorganization, merger, takeover, or an unforeseeable addition or realignment of the parties to the litigation, is the source of the new conflict of interest.[17] Because the law firm was not the source of the conflict and because it could not have foreseen the event creating the conflict, courts excuse the conflict as one that has been "thrust upon" the firm.

The legal profession is changing dramatically, creating new factual situations that were unheard of a few years ago. Though some lawyers may think less about loyalty than they should, and new factual contexts create more complex scenarios, the ethical standards that govern these scenarios still have loyalty as their touchstone. Movers and shakers should be mindful.

§ 1.7–6 SPECIAL PROBLEM AREAS

§ 1.7–6(a) Estate Planning and Representing Fiduciaries

Rule 1.7 recognizes that special problems may occur in the course of estate planning and estate administration.[1] Although the problems may be special, the rules are not. In other words, the Model Rules make no special exception for lawyers engaged in estate planning.[2]

Confidences and Conflicts: Who is the Client? There are several basic conflicts issues to which every estate lawyer must

---

ment states that the lawyer "is not motivated *primarily* by a desire to represent the new client." Restatement of the Law Governing Lawyers, Third, § 213, at Comment *c*, at 711 (Proposed Final Draft No. 1, Mar. 29, 1996) (emphasis added). "Primarily" is the better test, because people may have many motives for their behavior and it is difficult to prove a negative (that the lawyer did not consider another motive). But, if the lawyer was not motivated "primarily" by the desire to represent another client, then the "but-for" motive, what really animated the lawyer, is not improper.

[16]See William Freivogel, Freivogel on Conflicts, Hot Potato Doctrine (Mar. 2008), http://freivogelonconflicts.com/new__page__25.htm (citing cases relying upon the thrust upon exception).

[17]Rule 1.7, Comment 5 (giving examples of unforeseen events that can create a conflict of interest).

[Section 1.7–6]

[1]Rule 1.7, Comment 27.

[2]ABA Formal Opinion 94-380 (May 9, 1994), *Counseling a Fiduciary,* considered the situation where lawyers represent the fiduciary in a trust or estate matter. The question before the ABA Ethics Committee was whether there are exceptions to the Model Rules that apply only to lawyers practicing in this area. The Committee said: "We find no such exceptions." It added: "The fact that the fiduciary has obligations to the beneficiaries of the trust or estate does not in itself either expand or limit the lawyer's obligations to the fiduciary client under the Model Rules, nor impose on the lawyer

be sensitive. First, several family members, such as the husband and wife, may call on the same lawyer to prepare wills. Or a family member who expects to become a potential beneficiary may hire the lawyer to draft a will for the elderly relative.[3] The lawyer must make sure that there are no conflicts among these family members and that there are no secrets that one member has that he or she does not want revealed to other members. For example, assume that the husband wants to leave money to his illegitimate son but does not want his wife to know that he has an illegitimate offspring and that he is providing for him in his will. The wife, in turn, wants to know exactly how her husband's will is drafted. If the husband and wife use the same lawyer to draft the will, the lawyer has a conflict because the same lawyer cannot keep a secret on behalf of one client while keeping that information secret from the other client.

However, according to ABA Formal Opinion 04–434, a lawyer may represent a testator who seeks to disinherit a beneficiary that the lawyer represents on an unrelated matter.[4] The Opinion relies heavily on the concept that, unless a contract or law provides otherwise, testators are completely free to dispose of their assets in any way they so desire. And, it states that instruments disinheriting a beneficiary are simple and straightforward. Despite this general view that these two representations are not directly adverse, the Opinion does discuss situations where a conflict may arise:

> The issue becomes more complicated if the testator asks for the lawyer's advice as to whether the beneficiary should be disinherited, or if the lawyer initiates such advice, either as a matter of the lawyer's usual practice in dealing with such matters, or because the lawyer believes that such advice is, in the circumstances, in the testator's interest. By advising the testator whether, rather than how, to disinherit the beneficiary, the lawyer has raised the level of

obligations toward the beneficiaries that the lawyer would not have toward other third parties. Specifically, the lawyer's obligation to preserve the client's confidences under Rule 1.6 is not altered by the circumstance that the client is a fiduciary."

One should bear in mind that this Opinion has certain self-declared limitations:

"We address in this opinion the circumstances of a lawyer who has undertaken to *represent only the fiduciary*, and *not the beneficiaries* of the estate or trust for which the fiduciary has responsibility. We do not, therefore, deal with the conflict of interest issues that may arise when a lawyer undertakes simultaneously to represent both fiduciary and beneficiary with regard to the same subject matter. Of course, other conflict of interest issues under Model Rules 1.7 and 1.9 may arise if the lawyer previously represented or currently represents a beneficiary about other matters." *Id.* (footnote omitted) (emphasis added).

[3]*See* ABA Formal Opinion 02-428 (Aug. 9, 2002) ("Drafting Will on Recommendation of Potential Beneficiary Who Also is a Client").

[4]ABA Formal Opinion 04–434 (Dec. 8, 2004).

the engagement from the purely ministerial to a situation in which the lawyer must exercise judgment and discretion on behalf of the testator. . . .

Problems also can arise in situations where the lawyer has represented both the testator and other family members in connection with family estate planning. If proceeding as the testator has directed violates previously agreed-upon family estate planning objectives, the lawyer must consider her responsibilities to other family members who have been her clients for family estate planning.

If, for instance, a family has made its estate plans on the shared assumption (never reduced to an enforceable agreement) that the testator has provided for a disabled family member, thus relieving the others of that burden, then the lawyer may conclude that, in light of her responsibilities to her other clients, she cannot in good conscience implement the testator's intended disinheritance of that disabled family member, especially if the testator refuses to permit the lawyer to reveal the disinheritance.[5]

Lawyers should probably avoid representing both the testator and the beneficiary when the testator seeks to disinherit the beneficiary.

Other conflicts may arise whenever the lawyer represents multiple clients, such as representing the trustee and the beneficiary with respect to the same matter. Conflicts may arise when a lawyer accepts a position as a personal representative or trustee named in a will or trust the lawyer prepared for the client.[6]

A typical ethics issue is determining exactly who the client in estate administration is. In some jurisdictions, the client is the fiduciary. In other jurisdictions, the client is the estate or trust, including its beneficiaries. The majority view,[7] which the ABA Model Rules adopts,[8] is that the lawyer who represents a fiduciary does not also represent the beneficiaries.[9]

For example, a law firm that drafted a will did not have a

---

[5]ABA Formal Opinion 04–434(Dec. 8, 2004)(footnotes omitted).

[6]See ABA Formal Opinion 02-426 (May 31, 2002) (providing guidance when a lawyer serves as a fiduciary for a trust or estate that the lawyer prepared).

[7]Succession of Wallace, 574 So.2d 348 (La.1991). This case held that a statute providing that the executor of the decedent's estate may discharge the lawyer designated in the testator's will "only for just cause," impermissibly conflicts with the disciplinary rule promulgated by the state supreme court, which provides that a lawyer

representing a client in any manner is required to withdraw from employment if the client discharges him.

[8]The ABA Model Rules adopt the majority rule. ABA Formal Opinion 94-380 (May 9, 1994), advises the lawyer to make clear his or her relationship to the parties.

[9]Does a law firm who represents a bank trust department in its capacity as executor of the decedent's estate have client obligations to the bank on unrelated matters? See William Freivogel, FREIVOGEL ON CONFLICTS, Bank/Trust Departments, in http://frei vogelonconflicts.com/new__page__42.h

conflict of interest in later representing both an executor and a beneficiary of that will against another beneficiary. That is because the executor and a beneficiary have aligned interests and the other beneficiary is not a client.[10]

In some cases the identity of the client may be unclear under the law of a particular jurisdiction. If the identity of the client is unclear under the law, the lawyer should "make clear the relationship to the parties involved."[11]

When the Client Is a Fiduciary. The law of the particular jurisdiction may impose certain obligations on the fiduciary. In the view of the ABA Ethics Committee, the fact that the law may impose duties on the fiduciary towards the beneficiary does not serve to impose parallel obligations on the lawyer for the fiduciary.[12] The lawyer, under Rule 1.6, must keep confidential information relating to her client. Although there is case law to the contrary, the ABA Ethics Committee stated: "Disclosure of client confidences is not impliedly authorized simply because the client owes duties to third parties . . .. *Rule 1.6 does not authorize* the disclosure of information on the basis that *the lawyer knows that the fiduciary is committing or will commit a criminal or fraudulent act.*"[13]

However, after the ABA's 2003 amendments to Rule 1.6, a lawyer may have discretion to disclose confidential information to prevent substantial harm to a third person where the lawyer's

---

tm (Mar. 2008). Freivogel notes that the case authority seems to hold that this presents a conflict, but the Commentary on the ABA Model Rules of the American College of Trust and Estate Counsel takes the opposite view:

A lawyer who is asked to represent a corporate fiduciary in connection with a fiduciary estate should consider discussing with the fiduciary the extent to which the representation might preclude the lawyer from representing an adverse party in an unrelated matter. In the absence of a contrary agreement, a lawyer who represents a corporate fiduciary in connection with the administration of a fiduciary estate should not be treated as representing the fiduciary generally for purposes of applying Rule 1.7 with regard to a wholly unrelated matter. In particular, the representation of a corporate fiduciary in a representative capacity should not preclude the lawyer from representing an adverse party in connection with a wholly unrelated mat-

ter, such as a real estate transaction or labor negotiation or another estate or trust administration.

http://www.actec.org/pubInfoArk/comm/mrpc17.html.

[10]*Baker Manock & Jensen v. Superior Court,* 175 Cal. App. 4th 1414, 96 Cal. Rptr. 3d 785 (5th Dist. 2009).

[11]ABA Formal Opinion 94-380, *quoting* Rule 1.7, Comment 13 (now Comment 27).

[12]ABA Formal Opinion 94-380, at 3.

[13]ABA Formal Opinion 94-380, at 4 (emphasis added). The ABA Ethics Committee admitted that "some jurisdictions have lessened the protection of client confidence in order to provide greater protection to the interests of third parties," but the Model Rules furnish no additional exceptions to Rule 1.6's prohibition on disclosure.

services are being used.[14] Or the lawyer may be able to disclose confidential information to rectify or mitigate a past crime or fraud involving substantial financial harm to a third person where the lawyer's services were used.[15]

However, under the position that ABA Formal Opinion 94–380 embraces, if the lawyer knows that her client (the fiduciary) is defrauding the beneficiaries, the lawyer may withdraw. She will be even required to withdraw if her services are being used by the client in his fraudulent conduct.[16] Then, under the 1983 version of the Model Rules, if the lawyer withdraws, she can file a noisy notice of withdrawal and give it to the beneficiaries.[17]

The Restatement explicitly rejects ABA Formal Opinion 94–380, and offers more protection to these non-clients.[18] The Restatement follows the case law that holds that a lawyer owes a duty of care to certain non-clients in some circumstances.[19] The Restatement concluded that the lawyer owes a duty of care to a

---

[14]Rule 1.6(b)(2).

[15]Rule 1.6(b)(3).

[16]1983 Model Rule 1.6, Comment 15; Rule 1.16(a)(1). ABA Formal Opinion 94–380 (May 9, 1994), at 5.

[17]1983 Model Rule 1.6, Comment 16 (now deleted).

[18]Restatement of the Law Governing Lawyers, § 73(4) and Comment *h* (Tentative Draft No. 8, Mar. 21, 1997).

[19]*Fickett v. Superior Court*, 27 Ariz.App. 793, 558 P.2d 988 (1976). The conservator of an incompetent's estate sued the former guardian and the lawyers for the former guardian, alleging that the lawyer was negligent in failing to discover that the guardian had embarked upon a scheme of misappropriation, conversion, and improper investment. The court held that there was a cause of action against a lawyer for failure to use care in detecting and preventing the conservator's misappropriation of the assets of an incompetent person. The fact issue, whether the lawyer knew or should have known that the guardian was acting adversely to the ward's interests, precluded summary judgment. An unreported decision specifically declined to follow *Fickett*: *Great American Insurance Company v. Perry*, 1994 WL 101991 (Minn.App.1994), *reviewed denied*, May 17, 1994.

Jenkins v. Wheeler, 69 N.C.App. 140, 316 S.E.2d 354, 61 A.L.R.4th 605 (1984), *review denied*, 311 N.C. 758, 321 S.E.2d 136 (1984). The court held that the lawyer owed the heir a duty to use reasonable care in representing her mother's estate, and therefore the heir had standing to sue the lawyer in tort. In addition, allegations that the lawyer failed to list a wrongful death action as an asset of estate, that he gave wrongful legal advice to administratrix, and that he continued the representation of conflicting interests, sufficiently alleged malpractice on attorney's part. The court also held that this malpractice claim was not barred by the heir's contributory negligence.

Charleson v. Hardesty, 108 Nev. 878, 839 P.2d 1303 (1992), held that the lawyer for the trustee owed fiduciary duties to beneficiaries. The court therefore reversed and remanded for further proceedings.

In re Wyatt's Case, 159 N.H. 285, 982 A.2d 396 (2009). The New Hampshire Supreme Court suspended a lawyer for two years because he violated the conflict of interest rules by representing a ward and the ward's conservator, and acting adversely to the ward by aiding others to seek a guardianship over him. The lawyer violated conflicts of interest by representing the ward with respect to a voluntary conservatorship of ward's es-

non-client when and to the extent that (1) the client is a trustee, guardian, executor, or fiduciary acting primarily to perform similar functions for the non-client; and (2) the circumstances make it "clear" that the lawyer "knows" that he must take certain action within the scope of the representation to prevent or to rectify the client's breach of fiduciary duty to the non-client if (i) the breach is a crime or fraud or (ii) the lawyer assisted or is assisting the breach; (iii) it is not reasonable for the non-client to protect his own rights; and (iv) imposition of this duty on the lawyer will not "significantly impair" the lawyer's obligations to his client.[20]

Consider this example, where the Restatement and a reasonable body of case law would impose liability on the lawyer:

> Lawyer represents Client in Client's capacity as trustee of an express trust for the benefit of Beneficiary. Client tells Lawyer that Client proposes to transfer trust funds into Client's own account, in circumstances that would constitute embezzlement. Lawyer informs Client that the transfer would be criminal, but Client nevertheless makes the transfer, as Lawyer then knows. Lawyer takes no steps to prevent or rectify the consequences, for example by warning Beneficiary or informing the court to which Client as trustee must make an annual accounting. The jurisdiction's professional rules do not forbid such disclosures. Client likewise makes no disclosure. The funds are lost, to the harm of Beneficiary. Lawyer is subject to liability to Beneficiary under this Section.[21]

A similar ethical issue is presented in the situation when the client is a person (a trustee) with fiduciary obligations to someone else. If the trustee consults the lawyer, should a beneficiary of the trust be entitled to know what transpired in the discussion?

ABA Formal Opinion 94–380[22] advised that ordinarily the answer is no. In its view, a trustee or other fiduciary is entitled to consult a lawyer and Rule 1.6 provides no exception where persons with fiduciary duties are involved.

In *Wells Fargo Bank, N.A. v. Superior Court*,[23] the beneficiaries alleged that a trustee had engaged in misconduct in the adminis-

---

tate while concurrently representing the conservator, where there was no evidence that attorney considered and reasonably concluded that concurrent representation of the ward and the conservator would not adversely affect either client, or that the clients knowingly consented after consultation. After ending his representation of the ward, the lawyer also violated the former client conflicts rule by continuing to pursue the guardianship.

[20]Restatement of the Law Governing Lawyers, Third, § 51(4) (Official Draft 2000).

[21]Restatement of the Law Governing Lawyers, Third, § 51 (Official Draft 2000), Comment *h*, Illustration 5 (internal cross-reference omitted).

[22]ABA Formal Opinion 94–380 (May 9, 1994).

[23]*Wells Fargo Bank, N.A. v. Superior Court*, 22 Cal.4th 201, 91

tration of the trust. They argued that a trustee has a duty of candor to beneficiaries and must let them see all documents relating to administration of the trust. The trustee answered that everyone is entitled to get confidential legal advice, even trustees. The court ruled that the beneficiaries had no right to see trustee-attorney communications about administration of the trust. The lawyer for the trustee is not the lawyer for the beneficiaries. The trustee may have duties to the beneficiaries, but the lawyer does not. The court held, in short, that: (1) there is no authority for requiring a trustee to produce communications protected by the attorney-client privilege, regardless of whether communications dealt with trust administration or allegations of misconduct, and (2) the beneficiaries could not discover the work product of the co-trustee's counsel.

In contrast, the Restatement of the Law Governing Lawyers concludes that the beneficiary can get access to communications between a trustee and a lawyer where (1) the trustee is charged with a breach of fiduciary duty, (2) the communication is relevant to the claimed breach, and (3) the lawyer was retained to advise the trustee concerning the administration of the trust (as opposed to being hired later to defend the trustee).[24] Other cases support the Restatement position and the distinction it draws between the trustee retaining the lawyer for advice concerning the administration of the trust (not protected) instead of the trustee hiring the lawyer to defend the trustee (protected).[25]

§ 1.7–6(b) Lawyer Hired as Expert Witness

A law firm or party may hire a lawyer as an expert witness, typically in a legal malpractice case. The testifying expert witness is like any non-lawyer expert witness. He or she is hired to present expert testimony to aid the trier of fact. If one is hired as a lawyer, then one has the duty to advance a client's objectives diligently. But that duty is inconsistent with the duty of a testifying expert, whose duty is to assist the trier of fact in determin-

---

Cal.Rptr.2d 716, 990 P.2d 591 (2000).

[24] Restatement (Third) The Law Governing Lawyers § 84, "Fiduciary-Lawyer Communications" (Official Draft 2000).

[25] *Amatuzio v. Gandalf Sys. Corp.*, 932 F.Supp. 113, 117 (D.N.J.1996), holding: "Where the client seeking to maintain the veil of secrecy is other than an individual acting in his own right, the law has recognized certain exceptions to the duty of confidentiality. These exceptions generally arise where the putative client owes a duty, particularly a fiduciary duty, to the adverse party seeking disclosure. Thus, a beneficiary of a trust may be able to force disclosures of communications between the trustee and his attorney on matters relating to the administration of the trust. Obviously the trustee owes a strong duty to the beneficiary, and the attorney-client privilege should not be used as a shield when the performance of that duty is called into question." *Id.* (citing the Restatement).

ing, for example, the standards of the legal community in a particular factual context, or the law in a foreign jurisdiction.[26]

Because the lawyer is not hired as a lawyer or an advocate, the lawyer has no client-lawyer relationship with the law firm or the litigant ("Litigant").[27] However, the lawyer may also be representing another party ("Client") as an advocate. Rule 1.7(a) applies to the lawyer's representation of a client who is adverse to the interests of a party for whom the lawyer is testifying as an expert witness. The lawyer does not represent the Litigant, but does have a client-lawyer relationship with (and a duty to protect the confidences and secrets of) the Client.

Normally, we would not expect that either engagement would affect the other. However, if the lawyer's duty (under the law of agency) to protect the confidences of the Litigant would "materially limit" her duties to her Client under Rule 1.7(a)(2), then the lawyer is in a conflict, which is imputed to all the other lawyers in her firm pursuant to Rule 1.10.[28]

After the lawyer-expert witness terminates her engagement for Litigant, Rule 1.9 (governing conflicts involving a former client) does not preclude her from representing a party in a case adverse to Litigant because she was never Litigant's lawyer. However, she may have duties under other law[29] to keep certain information about Litigant confidential. If that duty exists and would materially limit her representation of the new client in a matter adverse to Litigant, then she would be disqualified by Rule 1.7,[30]

---

[26]If the other law firm hires a lawyer as a nontestifying expert consultant, rather than as a testifying expert witness, then this lawyer's role is really as co-counsel.

[27]Philadelphia Bar Ass'n, Professional Guidance Committee, Opinion 88-34 (1988) (lawyer may serve as testifying expert for one party while simultaneously serving as testifying expert for the opponent of that party in a different, unrelated suit, because the lawyer is not retained as a lawyer); Standing Committee on Legal Ethics, Virginia State Bar, Opinion 1884 (1989) (lawyer may file affidavit as an expert for both the plaintiff and the defendant on different issues in the same litigation, because the lawyer is acting solely in the capacity of an expert witness); Ethics Committee, State Bar of South Dakota, Opinion 91-92 (1992) (an insurance company

who hires lawyer to be a testifying expert witness is not the client of that lawyer).

[28]ABA Formal Opinion 97-407 (May 13, 1997).

[29]**Subagents.** For example, the former expert witness may have a duty under the law of agency, as a subagent, or she may have assumed such a duty by contract. ABA Formal Opinion 97-407 (May 13, 1997) at 9 n.9. *See also* Restatement of the Law of Agency, Second (1958), § 428, Comment *a*. A subagent acts in a dual capacity; the person is both an agent (acting on behalf of one principal) and a principal (who has an agent acting on his own behalf). *Cf. Conforti & Eisele, Inc. v. Division of Building Construction*, 170 N.J.Super. 64, 405 A.2d 487 (1979).

[30]ABA Formal Opinion 97-407 (May 13, 1997) at 11 to 12.

not by Rule 1.9. Her disqualification would then be imputed to law firm pursuant to Rule 1.10.

§ 1.7–6(c) Examining a Present Client as Adverse Witness

Assume that a lawyer (Attorney Alpha) represents Client A in a matter. Alpha, in the course of litigation, examines another individual, Client B (who is another client of the same firm), as an adverse witness. Or, Alpha conducts discovery of Client B as an adverse witness. In either case, if Client B is a material witness, Alpha will ordinarily face a conflict of interest that is disqualifying unless there is appropriate client consent. The conflict exists even if the law firm's representation of Client A is unrelated to the law firm's representation of Client B, because, when the lawyer cross-examines his own client as an adverse witness, or conducting third party discovery against one's own client. This situation is likely—

> (1) to pit the duty of loyalty to each client against the duty of loyalty to the other; (2) to risk breaching the duty of confidentiality to the client-witness; and (3) to present a tension between the lawyer's own pecuniary interest in continued employment by the client-witness and the lawyer's ability to effectively represent the litigation client. The first two of these hazards are likely to present a direct adverseness of interest falling within Rule 1.7(a)[(1)]; all three may constitute material limitations on the lawyer's representation, so as to come under Rule . . . [1.7(a)(2)].[31]

Obviously, if Attorney Alpha does possess secret information that would be useful in attacking the veracity of Client B, then there is a conflict because of Rule 1.6(a). If Attorney Alpha possesses this relevant secret information, Attorney Alpha cannot use it to cross-examine Mr. B even if Mr. B is no longer a present client but only a former one, because the duty to keep client confidences outlasts the client-lawyer relationship.[32] If there is no relevant secret, there is no problem in cross-examining the former client or engaging in conduct adverse to him because the duty of loyalty protects a present client, not a former one.[33]

As to present clients, even if there is no breach of confidence,

---

[31]ABA Formal Opinion 92-367 (Oct. 16, 1992). The Committee added:

"[I]f there is a continuing relationship between lawyer and client, even if the lawyer is not on a retainer, and even if no active matters are being handled, the strict provisions governing conflicts in simultaneous representations, in Rule 1.7, rather than the more permissive former-client provisions, in Rule 1.9, are likely to apply." (footnote omitted).

See also Rule 1.7, Comment 6.

[32]Rule 1.6, Comment 18; Rule 1.9(b).

[33]McCarthy v. John T. Henderson, Inc., 246 N.J.Super. 225, 587 A.2d 280 (App.Div.1991), refusing to disqualify a lawyer now opposing a former client where the lawyer's knowledge aided him in negotiating with his former client. See also Richardson v. State, 183 P.3d 15 (Kan. Ct. App. 2008), Judge Leben citing this discussion in the Le-

there still is a breach of loyalty. Attorney Alpha may hold back and be more reserved in his cross-examination of Client *B* because of his loyalty to Client *B* and his pecuniary interest in continued representation of Client *B*.[34] Attorney Alpha may find it difficult to attack the credibility of Client *B* in one proceeding while defending his credibility in the other proceeding.[35]

The law firm should decline the new representation if it does not secure appropriate consent. If the conflict arises or becomes foreseeable only after both representations are underway, withdrawal from one of the cases may be possible, but if the clients oppose the lawyer's withdrawal, the hot potato rule may limit this alternative. If the lawyer does seek to withdraw, he should consider the priority in time of the commencement of the representations as well as the balance of equities in terms of the prejudice arising from the withdrawal.[36] Alternatively, it may be possible for the client to retain another lawyer solely for the purpose of examining the client of the principal lawyer.[37]

Consider this example. Shortly before trial, Plaintiff's trial attorney died. Plaintiff therefore asks Lawyer to represent him in a malpractice case, where Doctor will be an expert witness on behalf of Defendant. However, Lawyer already represents Doctor as client on various unrelated matters (such as drafting a will and drafting a lease on some property that the doctor owns). Cross-examining Doctor as an adversary's expert witness "will almost inescapably be a direct adverseness under Rule 1.7(a)[(1)]," precluding representation, unless (1) both clients consent, and (2) Lawyer reasonably believes that her cross examination of Doctor and her relationship with both clients will not be affected. If her belief is not reasonable, even consent will not cure the conflict. Normally, Lawyer cannot competently cross examine Doctor without challenging Doctor's qualifications and credibility.[38]

GAL ETHICS treatise.

[34]*See, e.g., State v. Reis*, 4 Haw.App. 327, 666 P.2d 612 (1983), holding that a criminal defense lawyer may not simultaneously represent adverse witness.

[35]Bar Association of Nassau County, N.Y., Committee on Professional Ethics, Opinion 86-46 (1986).

[36]ABA Formal Opinion 92-367 (Oct. 16, 1992) at 8.

[37]*United States v. Jeffers*, 520 F.2d 1256, 1266 (7th Cir.1975), *cert.* *denied*, 423 U.S. 1066, 96 S.Ct. 805, 46 L.Ed.2d 656 (1976) suggests this alternative, though it was not the issue before the court. Then Judge (later Justice) John Paul Stevens, on the Seventh Circuit, said: "there is nothing in the record suggesting any reason why he [the lawyer] could not have made an offer to have some other lawyer retained for this limited purpose. . . ."

[38]ABA Formal Opinion 92-367 (Oct. 16, 1992).

§ 1.7–6(d) Multiple Representation in Criminal Cases: The Role of the Court in Ensuring Constitutionally Adequate Representation

§ 1.7–6(d)(1) Conflicts of Defense Attorneys and Claims of Ineffective Assistance of Counsel

If a party in civil litigation waives a conflict, the court may sometimes raise a conflicts issue *sua sponte*, but it often does not interfere.[39] In criminal cases, the balance of equities is different because the court wants to make sure that the public interest in fair prosecutions is protected and that the criminal defendant has had adequate representation of counsel, a right guaranteed by the Sixth Amendment.[40]

In some cases, a defendant will raise a claim that his counsel's multiple representation results in a conflict of interest that deprives the defendant of his Sixth Amendment right of effective assistance of counsel. In other cases, the prosecution will challenge the defense counsel's multiple representation because the prosecutor has an interest in securing valid convictions, that is, convictions that are consistent with the Sixth Amendment. If a court finds that a defense counsel's representation of multiple interests has created a constitutionally inadequate representation, then the court will overturn the conviction. Reversals of criminal convictions to enforce conflicts rules are not an everyday occurrence, but they can hardly be called a unique event.

The leading case dealing with general claims of ineffective assistance of counsel is *Strickland v. Washington*.[41] The Court created a high hurdle for the criminal defendant. To justify a

---

[39] Robert C. Hacker & Ronald D. Rotunda, *Standing, Waiver, Laches, and Appealability in Attorney Disqualification Cases*, 3 CORPORATION L. REV. 82 (1980).

[40] In *Wheat v. United States*, 486 U.S. 153, 108 S.Ct. 1692, 100 L.Ed.2d 140 (1988), the Supreme Court held (5 to 4) that the district court was within its discretion in rejecting defendant's waiver of his right to conflict-free counsel and in refusing to permit defendant's proposed substitution of attorneys. Two days before trial, defendant asked to be represented by the lawyer who was representing others charged in a series of cases against an alleged drug conspiracy. The government objected on the grounds that defendants in some cases would be witnesses in others. If the same lawyer represented them all, he would be restricted in his cross-examination of his clients when they were witnesses and would lay the predicate for a later claim of ineffective assistance of counsel. "Not only the interest of a criminal defendant but the institutional interest in the rendition of just verdicts in criminal cases may be jeopardized by unregulated multiple representation." *But see Ryan v. Eighth Judicial Dist. Court ex rel. County of Clark*, 168 P.3d 703 (Nev. 2007) (permitting husband and wife charged with murder to consent to multiple client representation once they were given the opportunity to consult with independent counsel before signing the waiver).

[41] *Strickland v. Washington*, 466 U.S. 668, 104 S.Ct. 2052, 80 L.Ed.2d 674 (1984).

reversal, the defendant must show that his lawyer's acts or omissions are "outside the wide range of professionally competent assistance" and the ineffectiveness must cause "actual prejudice." "It is not enough for the defendant to show that the errors had some conceivable effect on the outcome of the proceedings."[42]

---

[42]466 U.S. at 691, 104 S.Ct. at 2067.

Filing Criminal Appeals. In *Roe v. Flores-Ortega*, 528 U.S. 470, 120 S.Ct. 1029, 145 L.Ed.2d 985 (2000), the criminal defendant, who had pled guilty to second-degree murder, sought habeas corpus relief, alleging that his defense counsel had been ineffective in failing to file notice of appeal. The Supreme Court held that counsel's failure to file notice of appeal without defendant's consent is not per se deficient. The defendant had pled guilty to second-degree murder and, when he was sentenced, he was told he had 60 days to appeal. The public defender made a note to file the appeal but then failed to do so. The defendant's later efforts to do so were rejected as untimely but, on habeas corpus, the Ninth Circuit found the failure to file had been without the defendant's consent and thus constituted ineffective assistance of counsel. The Supreme Court held that *Strickland v. Washington* standards governed. Under the "objective standard of reasonableness" element of *Strickland*, there is no automatic obligation to appeal, the Court said, but—

"counsel has a constitutionally-imposed duty to consult with the defendant about an appeal when there is reason to think either (1) that a rational defendant would want to appeal (for example, because there are nonfrivolous grounds for appeal), or (2) that this particular defendant reasonably demonstrated to counsel that he was interested in appealing. In making this determination, courts must take into account all the information counsel knew or should have known." 528 U.S. 470, 480, 120 S.Ct. 1029, 1036.

After a guilty plea, an appeal may be less likely, but the court must ask, for example, whether the defendant was denied the bargained-for sentence. Under the "prejudice" element of *Strickland*, the defendant must show that, but for the lawyer's conduct, he would have appealed. Justices Souter, Stevens, Breyer & Ginsburg concurred but said a failure of counsel to consult with the defendant about an appeal will "almost always" be ineffective assistance.

Mitigating Factors. In *Glover v. United States*, 531 U.S. 198, 121 S.Ct. 696, 148 L.Ed.2d 604 (2001), *on remand*, 13 Fed.Appx. 353, 2001 WL 435078 (7th Cir. 2001) (Not selected for publication in the Federal Reporter, NO. 98-4021), 149 F.Supp.2d 371 (N.D.Ill.2001) (granting post-conviction release) the Supreme Court upheld the claim of inadequate assistance of counsel as a remedy for lawyer negligence. The criminal defendant, convicted of labor racketeering, money laundering, and tax evasion, filed a motion to correct his sentence, contending that his counsel's failure to argue for grouping of certain offenses under the Sentencing Guidelines constituted ineffective assistance of counsel. Counsel's failure to get charges "grouped" increased the defendant's sentence by 6 to 21 months. The Seventh Circuit had refused to find inadequate assistance because it considered the sentence increase so small as not to constitute "prejudice" under *Strickland*, but the Supreme Court rejected that analysis. Even a 6 month additional sentence must be taken into account in making the overall judgment of whether the lawyer's assistance was inadequate. "[A]ny amount of actual jail time has Sixth Amendment significance." 531 U.S. 198, 199,

Strickland does not end the discussion, because the Supreme Court earlier created a special principle in the context of conflicts of interest in *Holloway v. Arkansas*.[43] The Court held that a criminal conviction must be reversed if a trial judge requires joint representation in a criminal case after a defendant's timely objection. The joint representation is presumed prejudicial. "Joint representation of conflicting interests is suspect because of what it tends to prevent the attorney from doing."

The *Holloway* Court recognized that a conflict may "prevent an attorney from challenging the admission of evidence prejudicial to one client but perhaps favorable to another, or from arguing at the sentencing hearing the relative involvement and culpability of his clients in order to minimize the culpability of one by emphasizing that of another." In addition, the defense lawyer's joint representation of multiple parties may have precluded him from exploring possible plea negotiations, or from considering the possibility of an agreement to testify for the prosecution in exchange for a lesser charge or for a favorable sentencing recommendation.

In *Holloway* the defendant had made a timely objection to the multiple representation. In contrast, in *Cuyler v. Sullivan*[44] no party lodged any timely objection to multiple representations. *Cuyler* promulgated a new rule for that situation. If there is no objection, then, absent special circumstances, the trial court may assume that multiple representations do not result in a conflict or that the clients knowingly accept such risk of a conflict. However, if the court knows, or reasonably should know, that a particular conflict of interest exists, it must initiate an inquiry into the propriety of multiple representation.

Thus, under *Cuyler*, in order to establish a Sixth Amendment violation from multiple representation, a defendant who raised no objection at trial must demonstrate that an actual conflict of interest adversely affected the adequacy of his lawyer's performance; it is not necessary for the defendant also to demonstrate

---

121 S.Ct. 696, 698.

   Cone v. Bell, 243 F.3d 961 (6th Cir.2001), held that it was ineffective assistance of counsel at the sentencing phase for trial counsel in a death penalty case to put on no mitigating evidence and to waive final argument "because counsel feared the prosecutor might make a 'devastating' argument" even though "counsel had plenty of mitigating evidence at his fingertips; yet he failed to present it at the sentencing phase." *Id.* at 979. The court responded to this argument by asking,

"How much more devastating for the petitioner could the prosecutor's 'devastating' argument have been than the death sentence the petitioner got without such argument?" 243 F.3d at 979.

   [43]*Holloway v. Arkansas*, 435 U.S. 475, 98 S.Ct. 1173, 55 L.Ed.2d 426 (1978) (as to state court proceedings). *See also Glasser v. U.S.*, 315 U.S. 60, 62 S. Ct. 457, 86 L. Ed. 680 (1942) (as to federal court proceedings).

   [44]*Cuyler v. Sullivan*, 446 U.S. 335, 100 S.Ct. 1708, 64 L.Ed.2d 333 (1980).

prejudice. The fact that the same lawyer represents multiple defendants does not create a violation under the Sixth Amendment unless it gives rise to an actual conflict of interest. The mere possibility of a conflict of interest arising from multiple representations is not sufficient to impugn a criminal conviction.[45]

---

[45]*Burger v. Kemp*, 483 U.S. 776, 107 S.Ct. 3114, 97 L.Ed.2d 638 (1987), *rehearing denied*, 483 U.S. 1056, 108 S.Ct. 32, 97 L.Ed.2d 820 (1987). One lawyer represented one defendant while his law partner represented the co-defendant in a separate proceeding. The Court (5 to 4) explained that *Holloway* had rejected a *per se* approach and required a showing that the conflict had an adverse effect on the lawyer's performance. The Court will *presume prejudice* "only if the defendant demonstrates that counsel 'actively represented conflicting interests' and that 'an actual conflict of interest adversely affected his lawyer's performance.'" 483 U.S. at 783, 107 S.Ct. at 3120 (citations omitted). The two partners did talk about trial strategy, but there were separate trials, reducing any incentive for one lawyer to change tactics for the benefit of the other client. There was no argument that any conflict prevented counsel from negotiating a plea bargain because the prosecutor refused to bargain. And, even if there were an actual conflict of interest, the majority concluded that it did not harm the lawyer's advocacy.

Post-*Cuyler cases* where the court has found that the conflict has caused an adverse effect on the lawyer's representation of the client before the court or in negotiations with the government include:

United States v. Hearst, 638 F.2d 1190, 1193 (9th Cir.1980), *cert. denied*, 451 U.S. 938, 101 S.Ct. 2018, 68 L.Ed.2d 325 (1981) (failure to seek continuance, failure to seek change of venue, and failure to put client on the stand).

Brown v. United States, 665 F.2d 271, 272 (9th Cir.1982) (inadequate cross-examination).

United States v. Allen, 831 F.2d 1487, 1496–97 (9th Cir.1987), *cert. denied*, 487 U.S. 1237, 108 S.Ct. 2907, 101 L.Ed.2d 939 (1988) (misrepresenting the relative culpability of codefendants).

Oliver v. Wainwright, 782 F.2d 1521, 1524–25 (11th Cir.), *cert. denied*, 479 U.S. 914, 107 S.Ct. 313, 93 L.Ed.2d 287 (1986). In order to show that an "actual conflict" hindered the lawyer's performance, the criminal defendant must make a factual showing of inconsistent interests or point to "specific instances in the record" to suggest an actual impairment of his or her interests. "Thus, an alleged conflict of interest is not significant unless the alternative defense or strategy suggested is plausible." 782 F.2d at 1525.

Fitzpatrick v. McCormick, 869 F.2d 1247, 1252–54 (9th Cir.1989) (failure to present exculpatory evidence), *cert. denied*, 493 U.S. 872, 110 S.Ct. 203, 107 L.Ed.2d 156 (1989).

United States v. Miskinis, 966 F.2d 1263, 1268 (9th Cir.1992) (failure to put on certain defenses and witnesses).

Sanders v. Ratelle, 21 F.3d 1446, 1453–55 (9th Cir.1994), where the lawyer failed to interview a key potential witness and advised the witness to invoke the Fifth Amendment at the client's trial.

Freund v. Butterworth, 165 F.3d 839 (11th Cir.1999) (en banc), *cert. denied*, 528 U.S. 817, 120 S.Ct. 57, 145 L.Ed.2d 50 (1999), holding that the defendant need not prove the actual revelation of confidential information during prior representation in order to show an actual conflict; that the issue of whether the lawyer's prior representation is substantially and particularly related to subsequent represen-

In 2006, the Supreme Court addressed an ineffective assistance of counsel claim in a case in which a judge had erroneously denied pro hac vice admission to the defendant's lawyer.[46] The Court held that an "erroneous deprivation of the criminal defendant's counsel of choice" required reversal of the conviction without a showing of prejudice or ineffectiveness.[47] The Court also classified the error as "structural" and therefore it was not "harmless error." This opinion broadened the reach of ineffective assistance of counsel protection to include the defendant's choice of counsel.

Representation by Disbarred Lawyer. *United States v. Stevens*[48] did not find *per se* ineffective assistance when the defendant's appointed lawyer was disbarred a week *before* trial. Neither the defendant, nor the lawyer, nor the court, nor the government knew that information before the trial. In that case, the lawyer at least fulfilled the substantive requirements for admission to the bar. He was a lawyer, but not a lawyer admitted to practice at the time.

Similarly, *United States v. Mouzin*[49] held that there is no *per se* ineffective assistance of counsel because the defense lawyer was disbarred *during* trial—for conduct not related to the case. The trial judge did not commit error by allowing the lawyer to

---

tation is a mixed question of law and fact that is not subject to presumption of correctness accorded state court findings of fact on appeal in habeas corpus case; and the prior representations did not give rise to actual conflict of interest.

See generally Nancy J. Moore, *Conflicts of Interest in the Simultaneous Representation of Multiple Clients: a Proposed Solution to the Current Confusion and Controversy*, 61 TEX. L. REV. 211 (1982); Karen Covey, *The Right to Counsel of One's Choice: Joint Representation of Criminal*, 58 NOTRE DAME L. REV. 793 (1983); WAYNE R. LAFAVE & JEROLD H. ISRAEL, CRIMINAL PROCEDURE § 11.9 (West, 2d ed. 1992); Restatement of the Law Governing Lawyers, Third § 210 (Proposed Final Draft No. 1, Mar. 29, 1996).

[46]*See United States v. Gonzalez–Lopez*, 548 U.S. 140, 126 S.Ct. 2557, 165 L.Ed.2d 409 (2006).

[47]The Court stated: "Where the right to be assisted by counsel of one's choice is wrongly denied, therefore, it is unnecessary to conduct an ineffectiveness or prejudice inquiry to es-

tablish a Sixth Amendment violation. Deprivation of the right is 'complete' when the defendant is erroneously prevented from being represented by the lawyer he wants, regardless of the quality of the representation he received. To argue otherwise is to confuse the right to counsel of choice-which is the right to a particular lawyer regardless of comparative effectiveness-with the right to effective counsel-which imposes a baseline requirement of competence on whatever lawyer is chosen or appointed." 126 S.Ct. at 2563.

[48]*United States v. Stevens*, 978 F.2d 565 (10th Cir. 1992).

[49]*United States v. Mouzin*, 785 F.2d 682, 696-98 (9th Cir.1986), *cert. denied, sub nom.*, Carvajal v United States, 479 U.S. 985, 107 S.Ct. 574, 93 L.Ed.2d 577 (1986). *United States v. Watson*, 479 F.3d 607, 610 (8th Cir.2007) held that there was no *per se* ineffectiveness of counsel in a case where the lawyer was a trained and qualified attorney, but with technical licensing problems.

continue representation to end of case. Even the failure of the trial judge to inform the defendant of his lawyer's disbarment during trial did not render the defendant's conviction invalid, where the lawyer retained the ability to render effective assistance of counsel at trial.

In contrast, *United States v. Bergman*,[50] involved a purported lawyer who was not a lawyer at all. In reality, he was an ex-convict who had never taken the bar, never attended law school, and never graduated from college. He represented the criminal defendant at a competency hearing. In those circumstances, the court held that there was *per se* ineffective assistance of counsel because the so-called "lawyer" never trained as counsel at all. There is *per se* ineffectiveness if someone who has not been admitted to any bar based on his failure to ever meet the substantive requirements for the practice of law represents a criminal defendant, unbeknownst to him.

Assertion of Ineffective Assistance of Counsel. When a criminal defendant claims that his lawyer provided constitutionally ineffective assistance of counsel, that claim ordinarily waives the attorney-client privilege with respect to communications relevant to that contention.[51]

However that waiver does not necessarily extend to the lawyer's Rule 1.6 ethical obligation not to disclose information relating to the representation, advises ABA Formal Opinion 10-456.[52] In other words, the ethical obligation is broader than the evidentiary privilege. This ABA Opinion advises that if the prosecutor asked the defense counsel for the defendant's file, defense counsel should raise all nonfrivolous defenses to that disclosure. The court may require the defense lawyer to testify in response to the defendant's charges, but until ordered to do so, the lawyer must remain silent. Some believe that a claim of ineffective assistance falls within the "self-defense" exception of Rule 1.6(b)(5), but Formal Opinion 10-456 argues that this exception only applies where a response from the lawyer is objectively necessary. "[I]t will be extremely difficult for defense counsel to conclude that there is a reasonable need in self-defense to disclose client confidences to the prosecutor outside any court-supervised setting." As Rule 1.6, Comment 14 advises, Rule 1.6(b)

---

[50]*United States v. Bergman*, 599 F.3d 1142 (10th Cir. 2010). *See also Solina v. United States*, 709 F.2d 160 (2d Cir.1983).

[51]Restatement Third, The Law Governing Lawyers § 80(1)(b), Comment c.

[52]ABA Formal Opinion 10-456 (July 14, 2010).

"permits disclosure only to the extent the lawyer reasonably believes necessary to accomplish one of the purposes specified."[53]

§ 1.7–6(d)(2) Conflicts When Private Attorneys Have Criminal Prosecution Powers

In *Young v. United States ex rel. Vuitton et Fils S.A.*,[54] the Court held that a federal court may appoint a special private prosecutor to prosecute out-of-court contempt, because of the special, unique nature of the offense. "The ability to punish disobedience to judicial orders is regarded as essential in ensuring that the Judiciary has a means to vindicate its own authority without complete dependence on other branches. . . . Courts cannot be at the mercy of another branch in deciding whether such proceedings should be initiated."[55]

If a court is faced with a criminal contempt, it should ordinarily first request the government prosecutor to prosecute. Because the judiciary cannot be completely dependent on the Executive Branch, if the U.S. Attorney or other government-employed attorney denies the request, the court should then appoint a "private prosecutor."[56]

However, if the court is forced to appoint a "private prosecutor," the court should not appoint to that position an attorney who is counsel for an interested party in the underlying civil litigation because to do so would place the private prosecutor in an improper conflict of interest position.[57] The private prosecutor should be disinterested and not owe any loyalty to a private client. In a criminal contempt action the prosecutor (even if court-appointed) represents the Government or the People, not the private party who is the beneficiary of the court order that may have been violated. Prosecutors, who wield the power to prosecute criminally must be guided solely by their sense of public

---

[53]E.g., *Dixon v. State Bar*, 32 Cal.3d 728, 187 Cal. Rptr. 30, 653 P.2d 321, 325 (1982), which sanctioned a lawyer for disclosing gratuitously a former client's confidence in response to the former client's motion to enjoin the lawyer from harassing her.

[54]*Young v. United States ex rel. Vuitton et Fils S.A.*, 481 U.S. 787, 107 S.Ct. 2124, 95 L.Ed.2d 740 (1987). *Cf. McCann v. New York Stock Exchange*, 80 F.2d 211, 214 (2d Cir.1935), *cert. denied* 299 U.S. 603, 57 S.Ct. 233, 81 L.Ed. 444 (1936). *See* 2 RONALD D. ROTUNDA & JOHN E. NOWAK, TREATISE ON CONSTITUTIONAL LAW: SUBSTANCE AND PROCEDURE § 9.6 (Thomson- West,

4th ed. 2007) (6 volumes).

[55]481 U.S. at 795, 107 S.Ct. at 2131. Congress may reasonably regulate such judicial power, but Congress cannot abrogate or render inoperative for all practical purposes the *inherent* power of courts to deal with contempt of court. *Michaelson v. United States ex rel. Chicago, St. P., M. & O. Ry. Co.*, 266 U.S. 42, 65–66, 45 S.Ct. 18, 19–20, 69 L.Ed. 162 (1924).

[56]481 U.S. at 801–04, 107 S.Ct. at 2134.

[57]481 U.S. at 802, 107 S.Ct. at 2135–41.

responsibility for the attainment of justice, and not by any sense of loyalty or duty to private clients.

Thus, it is a leitmotif of the criminal law of ethics that the sovereign wins whenever justice is done.[58] The twofold duty of the prosecutor is to assure that the guilty shall not escape, but also that the innocent shall not suffer. The prime directive is not to convict but to seek justice. There are conflicts of interest if a private attorney has control of, or prosecutes, a criminal case.[59] That is why, for example, prosecutors may not be paid contingent fees (with the fee contingent on securing conviction).[60]

---

[58]The case law supporting this principle includes, *e.g., Brady v. Maryland,* 373 U.S. 83, 87, 83 S.Ct. 1194, 1196, 10 L.Ed.2d 215 (1963) ("Society wins not only when the guilty are convicted, but when criminal trials are fair."); *Berger v. United States,* 295 U.S. 78, 88, 55 S.Ct. 629, 633, 79 L.Ed. 1314 (1935) ("The United States Attorney is the representative not of an ordinary party to a controversy, but of a sovereignty whose obligation to govern impartially is as compelling as its obligation to govern at all; and whose interest, therefore, in a criminal prosecution is not that it shall win a case, but that justice shall be done . . .. He may prosecute with earnestness and vigor—indeed, he should do so. But, while he may strike hard blows, he is not at liberty to strike foul ones. It is as much his duty to refrain from improper methods calculated to produce a wrongful conviction as it is to use every legitimate means to bring about a just one."). *Yuba Natural Resources, Inc. v. United States,* 821 F.2d 638, 639 (Fed.Cir.1987).

The Commentators agree. *See, e.g.,* ABA Project on Standards for Criminal Justice, Advisory Committee on the Prosecution and Defense Functions, Standards Relating to the Prosecution Function and the Defense Function §§ 1.1(c) (1971) ("the duty of the prosecutor is to seek justice, not merely to Convict"); Model Rule 3.8, Comment 1 ("A prosecutor has the responsibility of a minister of justice and not simply that of an advocate. This responsibility carries with it specific obligations to see . . . that guilt is decided upon the basis of sufficient evidence."); Model Code, EC 7-13 (1981) ("The responsibility of a public prosecutor differs from that of the usual advocate; his duty is to seek justice, not merely to convict . . . ."); Professional Responsibility: Report of the Joint Conference, 44 A.B.A.J. 1159, 1218 (1958) ("The public prosecutor must recall that he occupies a dual role, being obligated, on the one hand, to furnish [an] adversary element . . . but being possessed, on the other, of important governmental powers that are pledged to the accomplishment of one objective only, that of impartial justice."); *Developments in the Law—Conflicts of Interest in the Legal Profession,* 94 HARV. L. REV. 1244, 1417 (1981) (" 'justice' of the case . . . is supposedly the principal, if not only, concern of the prosecutor").

[59]Fred Zacharias, *Structuring the Ethics of Prosecutorial Trial Practice: Can Prosecutors Do Justice,* 44 VAND. L.REV. 45, 45 (1991): the ethics rules "treat prosecutors as advocates," but also as "ministers" having an ethical duty to "do justice." John D. Bessler, *The Public Interest and the Unconstitutionality of Private Prosecutors,* 47 ARK. L. REV. 511, 515 (1994).

[60]*Cf., e.g., People ex rel. Clancy v. Superior Court (Ebel),* 39 Cal.3d 740, 218 Cal.Rptr. 24, 705 P.2d 347 (1985) (contingency fee for prosecutor improper), *cert. denied, sub nom., City of Corona v. Superior Court,* 479 U.S. 848, 107 S.Ct. 170, 93 L.Ed.2d 108 (1986).

Consider *State of Tennessee v. Culbreath.*[61] A private anti-obscenity organization asked a private lawyer who was experienced in prosecuting obscenity cases to contact the local prosecutor's office to discuss local decency issues. The prosecutor asked him to assist in the investigation and prosecution of cases but said the state could only pay his expenses. They agreed that the private organization could pay for his time. Then, both civil and criminal charges were filed against sexually-oriented businesses. The court held that the prosecutor's office must be disqualified. A prosecutor is supposed to exercise discretion. In this situation, the private lawyer had such a duty of loyalty to the private organization that he could not fairly exercise prosecutorial discretion. Thus, the court dismissed the indictments of the defendants.[62]

Victims may certainly cooperate with prosecutors. That should not be a problem so long as private interests do not control or improperly affect the prosecutor's discretionary choices.[63] The criminal prosecutor works for the public interest, not for private interests.

§ 1.7–6(d)(3) Release-Dismissal Agreements: Conflicts When Prosecutors Dismiss Criminal Charges in Exchange for Criminal Defendants Dropping Civil Rights Claims

Sometimes prosecutors believe that they should voluntarily dismiss a criminal case. In this situation, they also want assurance that the criminal suspect will not file false arrest or civil rights suits against the arresting officer, or the police generally, the investigators, the prosecutors, or third parties. In these cases, the prosecutor asked the criminal defendant to sign what is often called a release-dismissal agreement. This written agreement typically provides that the prosecutor will either dismiss the

---

[61]*State of Tennessee v. Culbreath,* 30 S.W.3d 309 (Tenn.2000).

[62]*People v. Eubanks,* 14 Cal.4th 580, 14 Cal.4th 1282D, 59 Cal.Rptr.2d 200, 927 P.2d 310 (1996), as modified on denial of rehearing (Feb. 26, 1997). The court held that the district attorney's conflict of interest did not warrant disqualification from criminal prosecution unless it was so grave as to render fair treatment of defendant unlikely; victim's financial assistance to prosecutor could, but did not necessarily, create conflict of interest warranting disqualification. Under circumstances of the case, disqualification was warranted.

[63]*Commonwealth v. Ellis,* 429 Mass. 362, 708 N.E.2d 644 (1999). The court held, under the facts, the state laws providing for insurance company underwriting of insurance fraud investigations and prosecutions and for referral of such cases to the Attorney General's office by an Insurance Fraud Bureau (IFB) financed by insurers did not compromise the disinterestedness of prosecutors so as to violate due process principles. The statutory scheme did not permit insurers to control the system by withdrawing financial support; it did not operate for the financial benefit of insurers; and it did not give the IFB control over prosecutorial discretion.

charges against the defendant or will place the defendant on probation; in exchange the defendant releases any claims against the police, the municipality, etc., for any alleged harm caused by, or during, the arrest of the defendant.[64]

If the prosecutor acts reasonably, in the interest of justice, and in good faith, courts will not normally prohibit what may be characterized as a form of plea bargaining. Release-dismissal agreements are not per se unenforceable. Of course, for this plea bargain to work, the prosecutor should reasonably believe that he has probable cause for the criminal charges that he agrees to drop–the prosecutor should not have engaged in prosecutorial misconduct or trumped up charges.[65]

---

[64]Seth F. Kreimer, *Releases, Redress, And Police Misconduct: Reflections On Agreements To Waive Civil Rights Actions In Exchange For Dismissal Of Criminal Charges*, 136 U. PA. L. REV. 851 (1988).

[65]*Town of Newton v. Rumery*, 480 U.S. 386, 107 S.Ct. 1187, 94 L.Ed.2d 405(1987). Plaintiff brought suit under 42 U.S.C.A. § 1983, alleging that a town and its officers violated his constitutional rights by arresting him, defaming him, and imprisoning him falsely. The trial court dismissed the suit on the ground that plaintiff had released his right to file a civil rights action in return for a prosecutor's dismissal of criminal charges against him. The Third Circuit reversed, but the U.S. Supreme Court reversed the Third Circuit and remanded. The Supreme Court held that, first, there is no *per se* rule invalidating release-dismissal agreements; a criminal defendant may release his right to file a civil rights action in return for a prosecutor's dismissal of pending criminal charges. Second, a release-dismissal agreement is enforceable if the defendant voluntarily entered into it and the prosecutor had a legitimate reason to make the agreement that was directly related to his prosecutorial responsibilities and was independent of his discretion to bring criminal charges.

Cain v. Darby Borough, 7 F.3d 377, 139 A.L.R. Fed. 677, 680 (3rd Cir.

1993), *cert. denied, Darby Borough v. Cain*, 510 U.S. 1195, 114 S.Ct. 1303, 127 L.Ed.2d 655 (1994). The Third Circuit held that a release-dismissal agreement executed by defendant pursuant to a blanket policy that all defendants participating in the Accelerated Rehabilitative Disposition program had to release their civil rights claims did not service public interest and could not be enforced.

Davis v. Ort, 42 F.Supp.2d 465 (D.N.J.1999), *affirmed*, 203 F.3d 816 (3rd Cir.1999). The plaintiff in this case had pled guilty in municipal court to charges including driving while intoxicated. He later brought a civil rights action against the arresting police officer, alleging that the officer used excessive force against him. Officer moved for summary judgment on grounds that claimant's plea agreement precluded suit. The court held that: (1) the claimant voluntarily had entered a plea agreement in which he released a right to bring a civil action against the arresting officer in exchange for a reduction of charges against him; (2) the agreement objectively served the public interest of obviating the government's burden of defending against a marginal claim; and (3) the evidence supported a finding that prosecutor's proffered public interest reasons for offering plea agreement were his actual reasons for seeking release.

Consider *Hoines v. Barney's Club, Inc.*[66] Employees of defendant had arrested plaintiff on a charge of disturbing the peace and incarcerated him in county jail for approximately two hours before being released on $25 bail. The plaintiff then told the assistant district attorney that he wanted to file a criminal complaint against the defendants, but the district attorney responded that he would oppose that because he believed that probable cause had existed for plaintiff's arrest. The district attorney then stated he would be inclined to dismiss the charge against plaintiff if plaintiff would sign a release of all claims against other parties involved in the arrest, including the County of Douglas and the State of Nevada. The prosecutor later said that he believed that there was probable cause for plaintiff's arrest, but that it would be unfair to fail to provide protection to the concerned parties against a civil action for false arrest, and that therefore his recommendation of dismissal was conditioned on plaintiff's execution of a release.[67]

Plaintiff signed the release and later filed a civil suit in California against the defendants, alleging assault, battery, false imprisonment, malicious prosecution, and intentional infliction of

---

[66] *Hoines v. Barney's Club, Inc.*, 28 Cal.3d 603, 170 Cal.Rptr. 42, 620 P.2d 628 (1980).

See also, e.g., *Dziuma v. Korvettes*, 61 A.D.2d 677, 679, 403 N.Y.S.2d 269, 270 (1978): "a defendant in a criminal action may knowingly, voluntarily and intelligently offer a release or relinquishment of civil remedies during plea bargaining negotiations."

Horne v. Pane, 514 F.Supp. 551 (S.D.N.Y.1981), denied summary judgment for the defendant. The plaintiff had signed an agreement after charges against him for assault and disorderly conduct were adjourned in contemplation of a dismissal. This agreement said that the plaintiff would hold defendant and all other uniformed court personnel and the city harmless and agree not to pursue any civil remedy for events in question. The court held that this agreement did not operate to preclude the plaintiff from thereafter filing a civil complaint against defendant for alleged deprivation of constitutional rights under color of state law when the defendant allegedly abused plaintiff on account of his race and allegedly subjected plaintiff to unlawful assault and battery. The *Horne* court simply announced: "It seems to us beyond question that a criminal defendant forced to choose between being prosecuted on criminal charges on the one hand, and not being prosecuted but giving up certain constitutionally guaranteed civil rights on the other, cannot as a matter of law make an uncoerced choice." Horne v. Pane, 514 F.Supp. at 552. This is an unusually broad holding, but remember, it was decided six years prior to *Town of Newton v. Rumery*, 480 U.S. 386, 107 S.Ct. 1187, 94 L.Ed.2d 405 (1987).

[67] ABA Formal Opinion 92-363 (July 6, 1992), applying the Model Rules, said that a lawyer *may* use the possibility of bringing criminal charges in negotiations in a civil case if both the civil case and criminal violation are well founded in fact and law and if the threat would not constitute extortion under state law. The lawyer may even agree not to file criminal charges as an element of settling a civil claim if that agreement would not violate some provision of law that required reporting of crimes.

emotional distress. The defendants (Nevada corporations) responded, as an affirmative defense, that plaintiff had, for consideration, released defendants from all claims asserted in the complaint. Plaintiff argued that the release should be void on grounds of public policy. The court disagreed with plaintiff and upheld the release.

The court held, first, that the dismissal of a charge of disturbing the peace in exchange for plaintiff's release of defendants from civil liability did not contravene public policy as expressed in a statute providing punishment for the common-law crime of compounding a crime. Second, the practice of discharging misdemeanants on condition of a release of civil liabilities or stipulation of probable cause for arrest does not contravene public policy when the prosecutor acts in interest of justice.[68]

Release-dismissal agreements serve important purposes, yet, courts should exercise caution and not automatically give blanket approvals to such agreements, for empirical evidence concludes that many prosecutors disapprove of them, and some prosecutors use the agreements primarily as a means of routinely eliminating civil rights claims and accommodating police and municipal claims departments.[69]

---

[68] *Cf. MacDonald v. Musick*, 425 F.2d 373, 375–76 (9th Cir.1970), *cert. denied*, 400 U.S. 852, 91 S.Ct. 54, 27 L.Ed.2d 90 (1970), was a habeas corpus proceeding. The Ninth Circuit found a violation of DR 7-105(A) when a prosecutor offered to dismiss criminal charges against the criminal defendant *if* that defendant would then agree that the police had probable cause for his arrest. When the defendant refused to give up his possible civil suit against the police department, the prosecutor amended the criminal complaint to include an additional charge. The court argued that the prosecutor violated DR 7-105(A), in part because of his special duties under DR 7-103(A).

Hoines distinguished *MacDonald*. That case involved improper motivations and coercive tactics. "The Ninth Circuit deemed the prosecutor's improper motivations to constitute coercive tactics denying due process of law." *Hoines v. Barney's Club, Inc.*, 28 Cal.3d 603, 608, 170 Cal.Rptr. 42, 45, 620 P.2d 628, 631. The Ninth Circuit certainly was hostile to the prosecutor's motivation. In *MacDonald*, the jury found that the civil rights plaintiff (former criminal defendant) was guilty of resisting arrest. Therefore there had to be probable cause on that charge. In *Hoines* the prosecutor engaged in no coercive conduct.

In *MacDonald*, the civil rights plaintiff *never* signed a release of his civil claims. As *Hoines* pointed out: "In MacDonald no release or its equivalent was in issue as the accused in that case elected to be prosecuted." *Hoines v. Barney's Club, Inc.*, 28 Cal.3d 603, 608, 170 Cal.Rptr. 42, 45, 620 P.2d 628, 631 (footnote omitted).

[69] Seth F. Kreimer, *Releases, Redress, and Police Misconduct: Reflections on Agreements to Waive Civil Rights Actions in Exchange for Dismissal of Criminal Charges*, 136 U. PA. L. REV. 851, 853 (1988).

§ 1.7–6(e) Representing Government Entities and Private Clients Simultaneously

Sometimes the government retains a private law firm to represent it on a particular matter. That law firm also continues to represent private clients, some of whom may take positions adverse to the government. For example, the lawyer may represent a private party suing the state in the court of claims to recover on a contract, while defending the state before the court of claims in a personal injury tort on state-leased land.[70] The question is when should the ethics rules treat this situation as a conflict.

The general principle is that the lawyer must first determine if the client is the government as a whole or a smaller entity, such as a particular agency or department.[71] Initially, the identity of the client for conflicts purposes is established by agreement between the lawyer and the client when the client (in this case, the government official authorized to speak for the client) retains the lawyer. If there is no express agreement, one should look at the reasonable expectations of the client, such as how the government entity is funded, how it is legally defined, and whether it has independent legal authority on the matter for which it hired the lawyer.

If the two government agencies or departments are treated as one and the same client, then there is a simultaneous representation of conflicting interests, and the lawyer would be representing one client (the private client) while simultaneously opposing her own client in violation of Rule 1.7(a)(1). If two government agencies or departments are treated as different entities, then the lawyer will not be opposing her client. She will be representing one client (the private client) while opposing a government entity that is not her client. However, the lawyer must still decide if her representation of the government entity will be adversely

---

[70]These facts, but not the analysis, come from *Aerojet Properties, Inc. v. State of New York*, 138 A.D.2d 39, 530 N.Y.S.2d 624 (1988). The court used a different analysis in deciding the case. In a very brief opinion, it allowed the private lawyer to represent a plaintiff suing the state to recover unpaid rent on property that the state office of general services leased. Simultaneously, the lawyer defended the state in a personal injury matter relating to state-owned land. Both cases were heard in the court of claims, but

the two cases were unrelated to each other and there was no real potential for the disclosure of confidential information. On this basis, the court held that the law firm would not be disqualified as counsel for a claimant in Court of Claims because the firm also represented the State in a unrelated lawsuit.

[71]This issue is explained in more detail in connection with the examination of Rule 1.13, the Organization as Client.

affected—or, "materially limited" in the words of Rule 1.7(a)(2)—because of the relationship between the two government entities.[72]

If it is materially limited, she must disclose the situation and obtain valid consent from both her private client and the government client.[73]

§ 1.7–6(f) Job Negotiations Between Lawyer for One Party and Adverse Party or Lawyer for Adverse Party

Rule 1.12(b) governs a lawyer's employment negotiations with any person involved as a party or lawyer for a party in any matter in which the lawyer is substantially participating as an arbitrator or other adjudicative officer. This Rule also governs job searches by law clerks of judges.

In contrast, no special Model Rule deals exclusively with the situation where a lawyer employed in one law firm explores employment opportunities with a law firm representing an adverse party (or with that adverse party directly). However, the drafters of the 2002 Rules added a line to the Comments that a lawyer who negotiates for employment with an opposing party or the party's lawyer could raise a materially limited conflict.[74] Lawyers are much more mobile in today's world. There was a time when a lawyer joined a firm and it was expected to be like marriage, a life commitment. Now, when a lawyer joins a firm, it is more like modern marriage, frequently ending in divorce and remarriage.

ABA Formal Opinion 96-400[75] carefully examined this issue and concluded that discussions involving a change in employment should be considered under Rule 1.7(b) as something that may "materially" limit the lawyer's representation of a client. On the other hand, if the lawyer is not merely exploring a change in employment but actually moving from one firm to another that he has been opposing in litigation, that situation is already squarely governed by Rule 1.9(a), with any disqualification under that rule imputed to all lawyers in the new firm under Rule 1.10.

The general rule is that a lawyer in one law firm negotiating for employment with another firm that represents a client with interests adverse to the interests of a client of the first law firm

---

[72]These issues are explored in ABA Formal Opinion 97-405 (Apr. 19, 1997), which is discussed more fully in connection with Model Rule 1.13, the Organization as Client.

[73]Formal Opinion 97-405 (Apr. 19, 1997) analogized the situation to where a lawyer represents a corporate subsidiary in one case while representing another client with a matter adverse to a subsidiary of the same corporation. *See* ABA Formal Opinion 95-390 (Jan. 25, 1995).

[74]Rule 1.7, Comment 10.

[75]ABA Formal Opinion 96-400 (Jan. 24, 1996). Restatement of the Law Governing Lawyers, Third, § 125 & Comment *d*, (*Lawyer seeking employment with opposing party or law firm*) (Official Draft 2000).

must take appropriate steps to protect client interests. These steps include consulting with the client or a supervisory lawyer before the point when such negotiations are reasonably likely to interfere materially with the lawyer's professional judgment, and withdrawing from further representation.[76]

ABA Formal Opinion 96-400 realistically recognizes that an unreciprocated expression of interest from either side is not sufficient to trigger a disclosure requirement. However, where the interest is "concrete, communicated and mutual," any situations that would present a Rule 1.9 problem if the job transfer were actually made would require disclosure to, and consent of, affected clients or (with client consent) withdrawal from one or more of the matters.

Even when job negotiations are in the exploratory stage, there *may* be a conflict, if the exploration is sufficiently concrete. When a lawyer is exploring job prospects with an opposing law firm, her judgment may be affected by her desire to "curry favor with, or at least not antagonize, the prospective employer."[77] For example, the lawyer may be reluctant to file a motion for sanctions against the lawyer in the morning if she is meeting with him that afternoon to discuss switching law firms.[78]

There are two factors that affect what the lawyer should do and when he should do it. First, what is the nature of the lawyer's role in representing the client? Second, what is the extent to which the lawyer's interest in the possible job is concrete, communicated, and reciprocated?

With respect to the first issue, the ABA Ethics Committee reasoned that the risk that a lawyer's job discussions will adversely affect his judgment is greater when the lawyer has an active role in representing a client. A low-level associate may only be engaged in legal research on a case, and not at all involved in the strategic planning. Even a lawyer in charge of the case may not have an active role to play at the moment, for

---

[76]In *Stanley v. Richmond*, 35 Cal.App.4th 1070, 41 Cal.Rptr.2d 768 (1995), two lawyers were discussing the merger of their practices at the same time they represented opposing parties in a divorce. There were prolonged negotiations over how to divide the husband's retirement fund and how to dispose of the house. The lawyers allegedly recognized that it would be helpful to them to settle the case so the merger could take place. The court concluded, after discussing the complicated fact situation, that plaintiff established enough of a prima facie case of malpractice to require a new trial.

[77]ABA Formal Opinion 96-400 (Jan. 24, 1996), at p. 3.

[78]*See, e.g., McCafferty v. Musat*, 817 P.2d 1039 (Colo.App.1990). In this case, the court found a lawyer liable in malpractice when he recommended that his client accept a low settlement offer *before* the lawyer had conducted adequate discovery but *after* the opposing law firm had offered a job to this lawyer, a job that this lawyer had solicited.

example, if he is awaiting a ruling after the appellate briefs have been filed and the case has already been argued.[79]

It is also important that the lawyer's interest in the other firm is concrete and has been communicated. Some lawyers may read advertisements, speak casually with their friends in other law firms, or have only general discussions with other firms "The Committee does not suggest that such thoughts or conduct, without more, give rise to an obligation to consult and seek consent of a represented client."[80] However, if "discussion of employment has become concrete and the interest in such employment is mutual, the lawyer must promptly inform the client."[81]

Moreover, if a lawyer is interested in another firm, but that firm does not reciprocate the interest, there is no duty to inform the client and seek consent, because it is unlikely that a rejected overture from another firm will materially influence that lawyer's judgment in a way that will adversely affect his representation of his client. Similarly, if the lawyer receives an unsolicited offer from the opposing firm or party, but promptly rejects it, there is no need to consult with the client and secure consent.

There does come a time when the job negotiations are concrete, the discussions have occurred, and the interest is mutual. Then the lawyer must consult with the client "at the earliest point that a client's interest could be prejudiced." If a lawyer has "an active and material role in representing a client in litigation," he "must consult and obtain the consent of that client, ordinarily before he participates in a substantive discussion of his experience, clients or business potential or the terms of an association with an opposing firm."[82]

Note that one issue is whether the lawyer has "an active and material role in representing a client in litigation." Sometimes the lawyer has a role in the case, and it may even be a major role, but it may still be the case that the lawyer does not normally contact the client directly. If the lawyer does not have the principal relationship with the client—and that would be true for most associates and some partners—the job-seeking lawyer does not have to call the client out of the blue. Instead, he simply has

---

[79]ABA Formal Opinion 96–400 (Jan. 24, 1996) at 6 & n.9.

[80]ABA Formal Opinion 96–400 (Jan. 24, 1996), at 5.

[81]Restatement of the Law Governing Lawyers, Third, § 125 & Comment d (Official Draft 2000), at p. 314.

Failure to Secure Client Consent. If there is no effective client consent, "the lawyer must terminate all further discussions concerning the employment, or withdraw from representing the client." Restatement of the Law Governing Lawyers, Third, § 206 & Comment d (Proposed Final Draft No. 1, Mar. 29, 1996), at p. 628. Accord, Restatement of the Law Governing Lawyers, Third, § 125, Comment d (Official Draft 2000).

[82]ABA Formal Opinion 96–400 (Jan. 24, 1996), at 6 (footnote omitted).

to inform his supervisor or the partner who is the principal contact-person with the client. That person will then decide what to do, such as seeking client consent or moving the lawyer to a different matter and a different client.

Imputation. There is the question of *imputation*. If the job-seeking lawyer is moved to a different client because of job-seeking negotiations with the opposing law firm, he is no longer representing that client and thus has avoided a problem under Rule 1.7(a)(2). But, as the ABA Ethics Committee in 1996 candidly acknowledged, the literal reading of Rule 1.10 would appear to impute to the other lawyers of the firm the disqualification of the job-seeking lawyer "even after he himself had withdrawn from the matter." But that broad imputation rule would severely limit lawyer mobility and not serve any important client interest. "Accordingly, we will not infer that the drafters of Rule 1.10 intended it to apply so broadly."[83]

While this conclusion did appear to violate the plain language of Rule 1.10 as it existed prior to the 2002 revisions, the Ethics Committee's determination was reasonable. The conflict that the job-hunting lawyer has is a very personal one. It simply is not reasonable to believe that the fact that the lawyer may be interested in leaving the firm and may join an opposing firm will diminish the zeal of the remaining law firm members in representing the client.[84]

The present Model Rules take care of this imputation problem explicitly. There is a Comment that makes clear that this type of conflict is "personal," and that such "personal interest conflicts under Rule 1.7 ordinarily are not imputed to other lawyers in a law firm."[85]

The Firm Hiring the Job-Seeking Lawyer. The ethical obligations involving the job-seeking lawyer are a little different when viewed from the perspective of the law firm that may be hiring that lawyer from the other law firm. If Rule 1.9(a) disqualifies the job-seeking lawyer from switching sides and if Rule 1.10 imputes that disqualification to other members of the law firm, then the law firm hiring the job-seeking lawyer must consult

---

[83]ABA Formal Opinion 96-400, at 8. *See also id.* at 9: "In sum, the Rule . . . [1.7(a)(2)] conflict that the negotiating lawyer would have if he continued to work on the matter while pursuing such discussions need not, through Rule 1.10, be imputed to others in the firm."

[84]Although the negotiating lawyer's conflict of interest is not imputed to other lawyers in his firm, those other lawyers must evaluate whether they may themselves have a conflict by virtue of their own interest in their colleague's negotiations.

[85]Rule 1.7, Comment 10.

with the client and seek consent.[86] The law firm should initiate this consultation with the client at the time that the law firm's interest in hiring the lawyer becomes "sufficiently intense" that it raises a question that this interest "may materially limit the firm's on-going representation of its client."[87]

§ 1.7–6(g) Related Lawyers Representing Adverse Parties

A situation may arise where a lawyer represents a client who is suing or otherwise taking a position directly adverse to another party who is, in turn, represented by a relative of the first lawyer. Assume, for example, that Lawyer A represents P who is suing D. Lawyer B represents D. Conflicts of interest may arise if Lawyers A and B—although each are practicing law in different firms—are married to each other, or related as parent, child, or sibling.

The Model Code had no explicit provision dealing with this issue. An ABA Formal Opinion,[88] interpreting the Code, found no *per se* disqualification with the husband/wife relationship, but otherwise offered little concrete guidance. It did state, however, that if one spouse is disqualified under DR 5-105(A) (which is the basic Code provision dealing with conflicts of interest), the entire firm is disqualified under DR 5-105(D).

The 1983 version of the Model Rules had an explicit provision regarding such relationships. Rule 1.8(i) prohibited Lawyer A from representing Client P if Lawyer B is the spouse, parent, child, or sibling representing Client D, and P and D are "directly adverse" to each other, unless the client consents.[89] However, this prohibition is *not imputed* to the other members of either A's or B's firm.[90] For example, under the 1983 Rules [*see* former Rule 1.8(i)], a husband could not represent a plaintiff while his wife represents the defendant (unless each client knowingly consents). But the husband's law firm could represent plaintiff while the wife or the wife's law firm represents defendant. In other words, the conflict of either spouse is not imputed to the other lawyers in the same firm.

This no-imputation rule is the same under the 2002 Model Rules. However, the drafters of the 2002 Rules moved the material under Rule 1.8(i) to the Comments under Rule 1.7(a)(2). They argued that this topic was originally placed in Rule 1.8 in order to avoid imputing this type of conflict to the other members of the law firm. Because Rule 1.10(a) now includes an exception to

---

[86]ABA Formal Opinion 96-400, at 10 to 11, citing Rule 1.4 and Rule 1.7(b) [which is now 1.7(a)(2)].

[87]ABA Formal Opinion 96-400, at p. 10.

[88]ABA Formal Opinion 340 (Sept. 23, 1975).

[89]Rule 1.8(i).

[90]*See* Rule 1.10.

imputation for personal interest conflicts under Rule 1.7, and because Rule 1.8(k) has a special imputation rule that imputes to the firm only the special conflicts rules of Rule 1.8(a) through (i), the drafters concluded that they should move the rule dealing with spousal conflicts to the Comments under Rule 1.7.[91]

The drafters of the 2002 Rules also thought the 1983 version of Rule 1.8(i) [the spousal conflict rule] was underinclusive, because it only covered specific related individuals and not other relationships that may raise a conflict of interest,[92] and also overinclusive, because it permitted simple consent even if the conflict seriously limited the representation. The intent of the drafters, by placing the conflict under Rule 1.7, is to make the analysis more flexible and focused on how the factual situation materially limits the representation of the client.

Lawyers need to monitor blood and marital relationships of lawyers who represent parties opposing each other.[93] Lawyers who are either related to each other or live together and who are on opposite sides of a case must take special care that they do not inadvertently disclose confidential information that may harm their client. Phone messages on the home voice mail machine might disclose a strategic weakness in a case. A lawyer should not carelessly leave on the kitchen table a memorandum discussing the client's willingness to increase the offer in settlement. If the other lawyer—who lives in the house or who is a frequent guest—sees that information, the damage will be hard to undo.

Lawyers who are related or very close to each other might also permit the relationship to interfere with loyalty and independent judgment to their clients. If lawyers will be taking opposite sides of cases that are substantially related to each other, and if these lawyers are closely related by blood or marriage, they must "reveal the existence and the implications of the relationship between the lawyers before the lawyer agrees to undertake the representation."[94] The Comments echo the same test as existed in the old Rule 1.8(i) that lawyers who are related as parent, child, sibling, or spouse to a lawyer representing a party adverse to the client should obtain both clients' consent before each lawyer can personally represent the clients. However, this conflict is not imputed to other members of the firm, which is the topic to which we now turn.

Imputation. Ordinarily such conflicts are not imputed to the firm because they are personal interest conflicts. However, they

---

[91]*See* Reporter's Explanation of Changes to Model Rule 1.8.

[92]*See* Reporter's Explanation of Changes to Model Rule 1.8.

[93]*See* Rule 1.7, Comment 11.

[94]Rule 1.7, Comment 11.

may be imputed if the conflict presents a material risk of limiting the representation of the client.[95]

If the conflicts were automatically imputed, there would be serious difficulties in particular for families where both spouses are lawyers. The Rules are quite happy to impose a strict imputation rule to protect legitimate interests of the client but not when the interests are less clear and the burdens on the lawyers are great. In this case, the interests to the client can be met without imposing an automatic imputation rule. And, if such a rule were imposed, it would create problems for any large firm that wanted to hire a spouse of a lawyer working at another large firm. The ethics rules have never imposed such an imputation rule[96] and the present rules continue that tradition.

§ 1.7–6(h) When a Lawyer's Client Is Another Lawyer, While Both Lawyers Represent Other Clients Whose Interests Are Adverse

Lawyers, like other people, can also be clients. Lawyers sometimes hire other lawyers to represent them. A lawyer may be involved in a divorce, or decide to adopt a child, or buy a house, or sue a contractor. Sometimes, if the law firm is big enough, the lawyer may ask another lawyer in the same firm to handle the matter. But sometimes the lawyer retains a lawyer from a different law firm. We would not be surprised if a lawyer practicing in a law firm that specializes in patent law hires a lawyer in a different law firm to represent him in drafting a will or handling a divorce. When a lawyer represents another lawyer, or a lawyer is a client of another lawyer, and these lawyers are in different law firms, there are ethical ramifications that the lawyers must consider.[97]

§ 1.7–6(h)(1) Litigation: When A Lawyer Retains Another Lawyer

First, let us consider the situation when the legal representation involves litigation. When a *lawyer retains another lawyer from a different law firm to represent him* in a legal matter, there is the possibility of a conflict of interests if the two lawyers simultaneously represent clients who are adverse to each other. For example, Lawyer #1 (Mary) represents Plaintiff (and Lawyer

---

[95]*See* Rule 1.10(a).

[96]ABA Formal Opinion 340 (Sept. 23, 1975).

[97]See the discussion in ABA Formal Opinion 97-406 (Apr. 19, 1997) ("Lawyer as Lawyer For or Client of Another Lawyer"). The ABA Ethics Committee concluded that this poten- tial conflict should normally be ana- lyzed under Rule 1.7(b), not Rule 1.7(a). *See generally* Steven C. Krane, *When Lawyers Represent Their Adversaries: Conflicts of Interests Arising Out of the Lawyer-Lawyer Relationship*, 23 HOFSTRA L.REV. 791 (1995).

#2 (John) represents Defendant) in the case of *P vs. D*, while Lawyer #1 (Mary) also represents Lawyer #2 (John) who is personally seeking a divorce in the case of *Lawyer #2 [John] v. Wife*.

These issues are normally analyzed under Rule 1.7(a)(2) because when two lawyers are adverse to each other in litigation, they are not attacking each other personally. However, these conflicts issues are also analyzed under Rule 1.7(a)(1) if a lawyer is in a situation where she attacks the credibility or integrity of the other lawyer, who—by hypothesis—is also her client in a different matter. In that case, the lawyer representing the other lawyer is "directly adverse" under Rule 1.7(a)(1), because she is attacking the integrity of her own client.[98] There is the risk that she may temper her advocacy on behalf of her client in the case (because the opposing lawyer is also her client, whom she does not wish to alienate and whose continued patronage she wants).

In determining whether the relationship between Lawyer Mary and Lawyer John may "materially" limit the relationship between the two lawyers, the ABA Ethics Committee recommends that the lawyers consider relevant factors such as the relative importance of the matter to Lawyer John (the represented lawyer), the relative size of the fee to Lawyer Mary (the representing lawyer), the relative importance of the matter to Lawyer Mary and Lawyer John and to the other clients of these lawyers, the sensitivity of the matter, the similarity and relationship, if any, between the matters, and the nature of the relationship of the lawyers to each other and their clients.[99]

In any case involving litigation (whether criminal or civil), there is also the possibility of a conflict for a reason that is peculiar to litigation: the existence of the client-lawyer relationship may affect the judgment of either lawyer as to whether to move for sanctions against the adversary counsel (who is either the client of, or lawyer for, the lawyer moving for sanctions).[100] Lawyer

---

[98] ABA Formal Opinion 97-406, at 3 n.4. *Cf.* ABA Formal Opinion 92-367 (Oct. 16, 1992) ("Lawyer Examining a Client as an Adverse Witness, or Conducting Third Party Discovery of the Client").

[99] ABA Formal Opinion 97-406, at 3.

[100] *Cf. Zuck v. Alabama*, 588 F.2d 436 (5th Cir. 1979), where the same law firm simultaneously represented a defendant in a criminal case and the prosecutor who was being sued in his personal capacity in an unrelated civil matter. There was an actual conflict of interest rendering the criminal trial unfair in the absence of the criminal defendant's knowing and intelligent waiver. The law firm in this case would be subject to divided loyalties. The law firm representing the criminal defendant may be less likely to assert prosecutorial misconduct and attack the good faith of the prosecutor (arguments that malign the prosecutor personally) because the same law firm would then be attacking its client, the

Mary will be naturally reluctant to move for sanctions against Lawyer John if Lawyer John is also the client of Lawyer Mary.

Pursuant to Rule 1.7(a)(2), if a lawyer's representation of a client "may be materially limited" by her representation of another client (in this case, Lawyer #2, who is also the lawyer representing a client adverse to Lawyer #1), or by the "lawyer's own interest" (Lawyer #2's interest may be affected by the fact that Lawyer #2 is represented by Lawyer #1), then the lawyer is disqualified under Rule 1.7(a)(2) unless the two provisos of that Rule are met: (1) the lawyer reasonably believes that the representation will not be adversely affected, and (2) the client knowingly consents after consultation.[101]

In some cases, the client cannot knowingly consent because the represented lawyer (Lawyer #2) does not allow Lawyer #1 to make a full disclosure. For instance, Lawyer #2 may not want the other party to know that she has hired Lawyer #1 for a delicate matter—to represent Lawyer #2 in a lawyer disciplinary proceeding, or a sealed arbitration proceeding regarding alleged malpractice. If the lawyer cannot make this full disclosure to her, then she cannot properly ask for a consent and waiver.[102]

§ 1.7–6(h)(2) Imputation in Litigation

If Lawyer #1 is disqualified under Rule 1.7(b) in this situation from representing Lawyer #2, this disqualification is imputed to all the other lawyers in the firm pursuant to Rule 1.10. That

---

prosecutor.

[101]ABA Formal Opinion 97-406, which discusses this problem of a lawyer in the role as lawyer for (or client of) another lawyer, agrees with this analysis but then adds an unusual statement: "However, neither lawyer nor his or her own third-party client may compel the opposing lawyer to decline, or to withdraw from, a representation of a third-party client that the opposing lawyer has concluded is permissible under the analysis above." Formal Opinion 97-406 (Apr. 19, 1997), at p. 4.

This ABA Formal Opinion cites no authority for this proposition. If there is a potential conflict under Rule 1.7, then the lawyer may not accept or continue a representation unless she "reasonably believes" that her representation will not be affected *and* the client consents after a full disclosure. If the client does not consent, the requirements of Rule 1.7 are simply

not satisfied.

For example, if Client #1 of Lawyer #1 is told that Lawyer #1 wishes to represent Lawyer #2 (who represents an adversary of Client #1) and Client #1 does not consent to this conflict, then Lawyer #1 cannot agree to represent Lawyer #2.

If Lawyer #1 already represents Lawyer #2 as a client, and then asks Lawyer #2 for permission to accept representation of prospective Client #1 (who will be adverse to a client of Lawyer #2), and Lawyer #2 refuses to give consent, then Lawyer #1 cannot accept prospective Client #1. Lawyer #1 cannot drop Lawyer #2 like a hot potato because of Lawyer #1's desire to represent prospective Client #1. In that case, Lawyer #2 "may compel the opposing lawyer to decline" representation of a third party. The "hot potato doctrine" is discussed earlier in this section.

[102]Rule 1.7, Comment 14.

means that, whenever a lawyer in a law firm represents a lawyer in a different law firm, the representation imposes an opportunity cost on the entire law firm. If any lawyer in a law firm is representing Lawyer #2, that law firm must secure consent from each of its clients who have a position adverse to any client that Lawyer #2 is then representing.[103]

§ 1.7–6(h)(3) Comparing Litigation to Non-Litigation

Now, let us turn to matters not involving litigation. The analysis in this case is different if Lawyer #1's representation of Lawyer #2 (two lawyers in different law firms) does not involve litigation. One must also distinguish between the representing lawyer (Lawyer #1) and the represented lawyer (Lawyer #2).

ABA Formal Opinion 97-406 does not explicitly draw any distinctions based on whether or not the matter involves litigation. However, all the examples that this opinion offers as to when it would be improper for Lawyer #2 to represent a client in a matter adverse to a client represented by Lawyer #1 (his personal lawyer), and where Lawyer #2's disqualification should be imputed to all other lawyers in Lawyer #2's law firm involve litigation:

> There may also be circumstances in which the represented lawyer's *personal interest* is so substantial, or so entwined with the interest of other lawyers in his firm that Rule 1.10(a) must apply. This may be true, for example, when a lawyer is represented in a matter that relates to legal work, licensure or professional reputation.[104]

Moreover, in litigation, there is always the risk that there will be an attack on the lawyer's professional reputation, not only because of the risk of sanctions (a risk that is often bandied about even though the statistical chances are small), but also because there is an adverse effect on a lawyer's reputation if she loses the case badly. Hence, the problem of a potential conflict when Lawyer #1 represents Lawyer #2 while representing another party who is adverse to the interests of Lawyer #2 is always greater when the situation involves litigation.

§ 1.7–6(h)(4) Imputation in Non-Litigation

Consider the situation where Lawyer #1 represents Lawyer #2 in a personal matter, such as the sale of Lawyer #2's house or the drafting of a will for Lawyer #2. Rule 1.7 governs this case because the representing lawyer (Lawyer #1) has all the responsibilities toward Lawyer #2 that he has towards any other client. Consequently, any conflicts that might exist under Rule 1.7 are

---

[103]This imputation is logical, given the language of the Rules. However, the Rules could be drafted to treat this conflict as personal to the lawyer and not imputed to other members of the same law firm.

[104]ABA Formal Opinion 97-406 (Apr. 19, 1997), at 7.

imputed to all the other lawyers in that law firm pursuant to Rule 1.10. The duties one has to a client are shared by all lawyers in the same firm.

In this scenario, the represented lawyer (Lawyer #2) is not acting in her capacity as a lawyer when she is being represented. She is a client of Lawyer #1, not a lawyer with fiduciary responsibilities toward Lawyer #1. Lawyer #2 (the represented lawyer) should not personally represent a client adverse to a client of Lawyer #1 if her personal interests or personal friendship might compromise her duty of loyalty towards her client. However, that personal interest should not be imputed to other lawyers in her law firm. If other lawyers in Lawyer #2's firm know of the fact that she is represented by Lawyer #1, they are not disqualified unless their personal interests or personal friendship might compromise their duty of loyalty towards their clients.[105]

This position was adopted by the drafters of the 2002 Rules in Rule 1.10(a). Personal interest conflicts normally are not imputed to the lawyers in the firm unless a material risk exists that the conflict will somehow limit the representation of the client.

§ 1.7–6(h)(5) Disclosure to Client

A member of the ABA Ethics Committee, Lawrence J. Fox, filed a concurrence to ABA Formal Opinion 97-406 that contains useful advice to every prudent lawyer. He explained that he differed with his colleagues because he believed that—

> there are situations in which the lawyer concludes that there is no material limitation and, nonetheless, the lawyer is *required*, not simply well-advised, to inform the client of this fact. . . . I can imagine (without stretching my imagination) a large category of cases where the fact of the lawyer's representing the opposing lawyer does not trigger the requirements of Rule 1.7(b) (now Rule 1.7(a)(2)), but does trigger an obligation to disclose.[106]

This disclosure obligation is triggered by Rule 1.4(b), which

---

[105]ABA Formal Opinion 97-406 comes to this same conclusion but does not adopt this analysis. Instead, it states: "It is unreasonable to assume, as a literal application of Rule 1.10(a) would require, that all lawyers in the firm share the personal reservations that may lead one lawyer in the firm to conclude that she cannot be an effective advocate for a third party client against a lawyer who also represents her. In many cases a lawyer's colleagues may be unaware of her personal legal matter, or who is handling it, and there seems to be no good reason to charge them with this knowl-edge." ABA Formal Opinion 97-406, at 7.

However, as a member of the Ethics Committee, Lawrence J. Fox, noted in his special concurrence, the majority's common sense exception to imputation requirement of Rule 1.10 "is not found in the Rule . . .. It is my view that our obligation is to interpret rules, not craft legislative exceptions to them through the opinion-writing process." *Id.* at 10 (Lawrence J. Fox, concurring).

[106]ABA Formal Opinion 97-406 (Apr. 19, 1997), at p. 9 (emphasis in original) (Lawrence J. Fox, concur-

requires a lawyer to explain a matter to the extent reasonably necessary to make informed decisions regarding the representation. The lawyer must "inform the client that the lawyer is either representing or being represented by the lawyer on the other side."[107]

The prudent lawyer will disclose. However, for the reasons explained above, this duty should not be imputed to other lawyers in the same firm. In other words, the disclosure obligation should exist so that the client will know that his lawyer is represented by (or is representing) the other side's lawyer.

§ 1.7–6(i) Personal Interests of a Lawyer That May Be Idiosyncratic

Consider the prospective client who asks a lawyer (Lawyer Alpha) to sue Dr. Smith for medical malpractice. Alpha happens to know Dr. Smith, who is her good friend and neighbor, and consequently she does not want to take the case. Alpha should not take the case if she believes that her close personal friendship will adversely interfere with her own interests.[108] In addition, she may not wish to take the case simply because she does not want to create a sore point with her neighbor. While a lawyer may think that one should not take lawsuits personally (it's just business), the neighbor may have a less enlightened view of the process if he is the defendant and his neighbor is representing the plaintiff.

Alpha may not want to sue her neighbor because he is her neighbor and she feels that there is a conflict. But should that conflict be imputed to everyone else in the law firm? What if the neighbor is not a good friend, but Alpha, the next door neighbor, just thinks that it is bad policy for her to sue her neighbor because neighborly relations may materially limit her representation? Again, Alpha can always turn down the case, but what if another lawyer in the firm (Beta) wants to accept the representation? Should Alpha's personal disqualification be imputed to Beta and others in Alpha's law firm?

What if Alpha is only a low-level, junior associate and will exercise no influence over the case? She may not want to represent a certain client (*e.g.*, her neighbor, or a company promoting gun sales, or an accused rapist), and the depth of her feelings may be such that she is in a conflict within the meaning of Rule 1.7. But must the entire law firm be disqualified by imputation in this situation, pursuant to Rule 1.10(a), which imputes any

---

ring).

[107]ABA Formal Opinion 97-406, at p. 9.

[108]Rule 1.7(a)(2). Justice Leben, J.,

citing this Ethics Treatise in, *Kebert v. State*, 222 P.3d 564 (Table), 2010 WL 198509, *3 (Kan.App. 2010).

disqualification under Rule 1.7(a)(2), unless the client knowingly waives the conflict after consultation?

The 1983 version of the Model Rules indicated that the conflict based on depth of a lawyer's personal feelings, under Rule 1.7(a)(2), is automatically imputed to the entire firm. That, after all, is what the language of Rule 1.10(a) actually says.

Occasionally the news reports that some associates at a large New York or Washington, DC law firm are protesting the firm's decision to represent a particular client (for instance, a foreign country that often sponsors terrorism or a Swiss bank that does not want to pay reparations for its wartime actions). The law firm typically does not require any lawyer to work on these cases, but the partners in that firm would likely be surprised to learn that the depth of feeling that would disqualify even one lawyer under Rule 1.7(a)(2) is (apparently) automatically imputed to all lawyer in that firm. In other words, the feelings and beliefs of even one associate may cause the entire law firm to be disqualified in the matter.

The ABA Ethics Committee has not considered this issue, but in two other opinions raising different issues it has been willing to conclude that the imputation requirements in general, and Rule 1.10 in particular, should not be read too literally.[109] Yet, that may offer little comfort to a lawyer who would like more certainty, particularly inasmuch as the Reporters of the Restatement of the Law Governing Lawyers concluded that Rule 1.10 does in fact impute the disqualification in this circumstance to the entire law firm.[110]

It is clear that a lawyer shall not represent a client if the lawyer is unable to render effective representation because doing so would be incompatible with the lawyer's personal beliefs.[111] What

---

[109] ABA Formal Opinion 96-400 (Jan. 24, 1996) ("Job Negotiations with Adverse Firm or Party"); ABA Formal Opinion 97-406 (Apr. 19, 1997) ("Lawyer as Lawyer For or Client of Another Lawyer").

[110] The Reporter's Notes to Comment g state: "Conflicts produced by the personal interests of a lawyer are imputed to persons affiliated with the lawyer by DR 5-105(D) of the ABA Model Code of Professional Responsibility and Rule 1.10(a) of the ABA Model Rules of Professional Con-

duct." Restatement of the Law Governing Lawyers, Third (Proposed Final Draft No. 1, Mar. 29, 1996), at 637.

[111] See Restatement of the Law Governing Lawyers, Third, (Official Draft 2000), at § 125, pp. 317-318 (Comment g) points out that the— "personal interests of a lawyer may be idiosyncratic or otherwise of such a kind that it is improbable that affiliated lawyers would be impaired in their representation of clients due to such interests."

is less clear is whether that personal belief should be imputed to the other members of the law firm who do not share it.[112]

The drafters of the 2002 Rules solved this problem by putting in a clause into Rule 1.10(a) that does not automatically impute to the law firm the personal interest conflicts of one of its lawyers. If the personal interest conflict poses no significant material risk of limiting the representation of the client by the remaining lawyers, the conflict is not imputed to the firm.

Hence, if a lawyer should not accept a case because of his individualistic, unique, or highly personal reservations or beliefs, that lawyer is ethically disqualified from taking the case. However, that lawyer's disqualification should not normally be imputed to the law firm. As long as the disqualified lawyer has nothing further to do with the case, this personal disqualification should not be imputed to other lawyers in her law firm because, unlike the conflicts treated in Rule 1.7, it is very unlikely that affiliated lawyers will be affected by the individualistic, idiosyncratic beliefs of this lawyer. On the other hand, if it is reasonable to believe that the individually disqualified lawyer will adversely *affect* the representation by other lawyers in the law firm, then this situation is different and the disqualification should be imputed to the law firm. In that setting, the individually disqualified lawyer's removal from the case has not removed her ability to affect it.

§ 1.7–6(j) Lawyers as Members of Unions

When a law firm employs personnel, it is, in general, subject to the same laws as other employers, such as laws forbidding discrimination on the basis of race or sex,[113] or age,[114] or fraud.[115] Similarly, bar associations may not promulgate minimum fee

---

[112]Restatement of the Law Governing Lawyers, Third, § 125 (Official Draft 2000) treats the lawyer's personal interest affecting the representation of the client as a conflict that is imputed, but then, in Comment g, states that the idiosyncratic conflicts should not be imputed.

[113]*See, e.g., Hishon v. King & Spalding*, 467 U.S. 69, 104 S.Ct. 2229, 81 L.Ed.2d 59 (1984), which held that Congressional statutes prohibiting race and sex discrimination could validly be applied to law firm decisions regarding employment and partnership practices. In response to the law firm's argument that application of the antidiscrimination law would restrict its freedom of expression and associa-

tion, the Court stated "respondent has not shown how its ability to fulfill such a function would be inhibited by a requirement that it consider petitioner for partnership on her merits. Moreover, as we have held in another context, '[i]nvidious private discrimination may be characterized as a form of exercising freedom of association protected by the First Amendment, but it has never been accorded affirmative constitutional protections.' " *citing, Norwood v. Harrison*, 413 U.S. 455, 470, 93 S.Ct. 2804, 2813, 37 L.Ed.2d 723 (1973); *Hishon*, 467 U.S. at 78, 104 S.Ct. at 2235. *See also Lucido v. Cravath, Swaine & Moore*, 425 F.Supp. 123 (S.D.N.Y.1977), a case involving relations and ethnic discrimination in assigning work to an associate and in

schedules under the antitrust laws,[116] and lawyers may not join in conspiracies in an effort to obtain higher compensation.[117] However, the situation may be more complex when the ethics rules coexist with generally applicable laws regulating unions and collective bargaining.

Consider the case where lawyer-employees join a union, which represents all employees in collective bargaining with the employer, who is also the client. In these circumstances, a third-party (the union) is in posture that is adversarial to the client (typically a government agency or perhaps a corporation). The negotiations with the union typically involve the terms and conditions of employment, including discipline, discharge, work assignments, hours, and so forth. Legal ethics may also govern these issues.

The client may wish to assign work to its lawyers based on the employer's view of each lawyer's expertise, but the union contract, governing matters such as the conditions of work, may impose different work rules, such as assigning work based on seniority. The employer wishes to maintain a confidential relationship with its lawyers, and may believe this relationship is threatened by its lawyers' relationship with the union, which bargains on their behalf and may demand to know about matters that the employer wants to keep confidential. The union may go on strike, while the employer desires its lawyers to represent it zealously in promptly defending a particular suit. Or, the employer may want a particular lawyer-employee to work over the weekend to prepare for a major case or complete a project, but the employee may have a right to refuse overtime or take a vacation according to the union contract. Or, the lawyers (who are also union members) end up suing their own client, the employer, and thus appear to place themselves in a situation that compromises their general duty of loyalty to their client.[118]

promotion.

[114]*Breckinridge v. Bristol-Myers Co.*, 624 F.Supp. 79 (S.D.Ind.1985) (discharged house counsel has cause of action for age discrimination).

[115]*Stewart v. Jackson & Nash*, 976 F.2d 86 (2d Cir.1992) (cause of action of lawyer alleging that law firm engaged in fraud in inducing him to join the firm).

[116]*Goldfarb v. Virginia State Bar*, 421 U.S. 773, 95 S.Ct. 2004, 44 L.Ed.2d 572 (1975).

[117]*F.T.C. v. Superior Court Trial Lawyers Ass'n*, 493 U.S. 411, 110 S.Ct. 768, 107 L.Ed.2d 851 (1990), holding that the federal antitrust laws forbid individual lawyers who are not employed by the same law firm from engaging in concerted action to withhold services to raise their compensation.

[118]*See, e.g., Anderson v. Eaton*, 211 Cal. 113, 116, 293 P. 788, 789 (1930): "It is . . . an attorney's duty to protect his client in every possible way, and it is a violation of that duty for him to

The Model Code[119] and an ABA Informal Opinion[120] briefly referred to this issue. They imposed no *per se* prohibition, but concluded that there may be problems and warn the lawyers to be free of outside influences.

The ABA Model Rules do not discuss this issue directly, though Rule 1.7(a)(2) warns lawyers that they violate the ethics rules if their representation of a client is "materially limited" by the lawyers' obligations "to a third person."

The Restatement of the Law Governing Lawyers acknowledges that those who employ lawyers are subject to the generally applicable law governing anti-discrimination legislation, laws against unjustified discharge, and labor relations. However, it "remains to be decided whether some such laws, for example, the National Labor Relations Act, are subject to implied qualifications that accommodate the professional obligations of lawyers."[121]

Only a few cases discuss this issue.[122] In one opinion, the court concluded that a state statute (which did not exclude manage-

---

assume a position adverse or antagonistic to his client without the latter's free and intelligent consent . . .. By virtue of this rule an attorney is precluded from assuming any relation which would prevent him from devoting his entire energies to his client's interests."

[119] EC 5-13 provides:

"A lawyer should not maintain membership in, *or be influenced by any organization of employees that undertakes to prescribe, direct, or suggest when or how he should fulfill his professional obligations to a person or organization that employs him as a lawyer.* Although *it is not necessarily improper* for a lawyer employed by a corporation or similar entity to be a member of an organization of employees, he should be vigilant to safeguard his fidelity as a lawyer to his employee, free from outside influences." (emphasis added).

[120] ABA Informal Opinion 1325 (Mar. 31, 1975), found no *per se* rule against a group of lawyers, all hired by a single employer, joining a union. These lawyers could not, however, strike if that would lead to the neglect or sabotage of the employer-client's legal affairs. But, "in some situations participation in a strike might be no more disruptive of the performance of

legal work than taking a two week vacation might be."

This position evolved from earlier opinions that initially were less sympathetic to union membership. ABA Informal Opinion 917 (Jan. 25, 1966), deciding that U.S. government lawyers cannot join a union under the ethics rules. ABA Informal Opinion 986 (July 3, 1967), ruling that, generally, the ethics rules do not allow lawyers to join unions because of the resulting conflict with the lawyers' duty to their client; however, lawyers who work for a single employer may join a union but they could not strike or divulge confidences or engage in any other ethical violations.

[121] Restatement of the Law Governing Lawyers, Third, § 56, Comment *k* (Official Draft 2000).

In a series of cases in 1977, the N.L.R.B. asserted such jurisdiction. *Foley, Hoag & Eliot*, 229 N.L.R.B. 456 (1977); *Wayne County Neighborhood Legal Services, Inc.*, 229 N.L.R.B. 1023 (1977); *Camden Regional Legal Services, Inc.*, 231 N.L.R.B. 224 (1977).

[122] **Illinois.** *Salaried Employees of North America v. Illinois Local Labor Relations Board*, 202 Ill.App.3d 1013, 148 Ill.Dec. 329, 560 N.E.2d 926 (1990)

ment or confidential employees from its coverage) allows government employees who are lawyers to unionize,[123] but the county
government (which was the governmental entity bargaining with
the union) would be free to rearrange assignments within the
county counsel's office to make sure that "it receives the legal
representation in which it has full confidence."[124] Once the union
employees announced their intention to sue, the trial court acted

---

(unique organization and division of responsibilities within the law department supported the labor board's conclusion that the lawyers within the City of Chicago's law department are "managerial" and thus excluded from collective bargaining under state law).

California. *Santa Clara County Counsel Attorneys Ass'n v. Woodside*, 7 Cal.4th 525, 28 Cal.Rptr.2d 617, 869 P.2d 1142 (1994) (discussed in the text).

Florida. *State Employees Attorneys Guild, FPD, NUHHCE, AFSCME, AFL-CIO v. State of Florida*, 653 So.2d 487 (Fla.App. 1st Dist.1995). In this case, the union appealed an order that dismissed the union's petition to be certified as bargaining agent for state-employed lawyers. The District Court of Appeals declined to address the issue of whether a state statute that excluded state attorneys from the definition of "public employee" for purposes of the right to engage in collective bargaining violated a Florida State Constitutional provision guaranteeing bargaining rights. The court then affirmed without prejudice to the union's right to bring a declaratory judgment action in circuit court.

After further litigation, the union won the right to unionize lawyers who were employees of the State of Florida. *Chiles v. State Employees Attorneys Guild*, 734 So.2d 1030 (Fla.1999) (No. 93,665). The Florida Supreme Court held unconstitutional a Florida law that, in effect, provided: "Those persons who by virtue of their positions of employment are regulated by the Florida Supreme Court," are prohibited from engaging in collective bargaining with their government employer. 734 So.2d at 1031. The state supreme court said:

"We hold that this prohibition is unconstitutional under article I, section 6 of the Florida Constitution because the State has failed to prove the requisite necessity for a wholesale ban on collective bargaining by government lawyers. In so holding, we emphasize that lawyers exercising their constitutional right to bargain collectively may not violate the Rules Regulating The Florida Bar and must give unqualified deference to the traditional duty of loyalty that a lawyer owes to a client." 734 So.2d at 1031.

This opinion clears the way for collective bargaining by the State Employees Attorneys' Guild.

[123] *Santa Clara County Counsel Attorneys Ass'n v. Woodside*, 7 Cal.4th 525, 28 Cal.Rptr.2d 617, 869 P.2d 1142 (1994). The lawyer would be subject to discipline if she "violates actual disciplinary rules, most particularly rules pertaining to the attorney's duty to represent the client faithfully, competently, and confidentially . . . .. An attorney, in pursuing rights of self-representation, may not use delaying tactics in handling existing litigation or other matters of representation for the purpose of gaining advantage in a dispute over salary and fringe benefits." 7 Cal.4th at 552, 28 Cal.Rptr.2d at 632, 869 P.2d at 1157.

[124] 7 Cal.4th at 532, 28 Cal.Rptr.2d at 619, 869 P.2d at 1144. Justice Panelli filed a dissenting opinion: "The majority concludes that, at least in this case, an attorney's interest in suing a present client takes precedence over the client's right to discharge an attorney who no longer enjoys the client's full trust and confidence." 7 Cal.4th at 558, 28 Cal.Rptr.2d at 636, 869 P.2d at 1162.

properly in upholding the right of the county to exclude these lawyers from confidential meetings.

The county could not lawfully punish the lawyers for unionizing and filing suit against the county (their client), because the statute protects the union members in these circumstances. However—

> there is no reason why the County should not be accorded great flexibility in reorganizing the County Counsel's office to respond to the lawsuit. This may include, as the trial court below suggested, the reassignment of Association members to matters of representation outside the field of labor relations. Nothing in the [state statute] prohibits the Board and its members from asserting their rights, as clients, to refuse representation from the Association attorneys on any given matter, and to make use of non-Association attorneys or outside counsel in sensitive matters, so long as such reassignment is done nonpunitively. By allowing the County this flexibility, the trial court properly balanced the County's need for obtaining representation in which it has full confidence with the Attorneys' statutory employment rights.[125]

§ 1.7–6(k) Lawyers Representing Entities and Other Organizations

When the lawyer represents an entity, such as a corporation, union, or a governmental unit, she owes her allegiance to the incorporeal entity and not to a stockholder, director, officer, employee, representative, or other person connected with the entity.[126] This issue is discussed below, in connection with Rule 1.13.

§ 1.7–6(l) The Lawyer as Director of the Corporate Client

If a law firm does a substantial amount of work for a particular corporate client, it is not uncommon for one of the partners of the firm also to be a member of the corporation's board of directors. This dual role invites potential conflicts. For example, the lawyer on the board may be a witness to certain events and then may be asked to be both a prospective witness and an advocate in litigation.[127] The client may be confused as to when the lawyer is giving business advice (in her capacity as a director) or legal

---

[125] 7 Cal.4th at 557, 28 Cal.Rptr.2d at 635–36, 869 P.2d at 1160–61.

[126] Rule 1.13. *See also* ABA Model Code, EC 5–18. Problems relating to representation of an organization—corporations, partnerships, trade associations, etc.—are discussed below in connection with the analysis of Model Rule 1.13.

[127] *See* Restatement of the Law Governing Lawyers, Third, § 135 (Official Draft 2000), Comments *d* & *e*.

The famous New York lawyer, Paul Cravath advised:

> in most cases the client is best advised by a lawyer who maintains an objective point of view and that such objectivity may be impeded by any

423

advice (in her capacity as counsel).[128] If the corporation is sued, the lawyer who is also a director is more likely to find herself a named defendant.[129]

For these reasons, at least one major legal malpractice insurer discourages lawyers from serving on boards of public companies and excludes from its malpractice coverage those lawyers who hold top board positions, such as chairman or vice chairman.[130]

Granted, some corporations like to have their outside counsel sit in on board meetings. However, one does not have to be a member of the board in order to sit in on its meetings. The corporation need only invite its counsel to attend. And, it is also true that some lawyers like to be members of the board. For one thing, it makes it less likely that their corporate client will wander off and decide to retain a different law firm to represent it.

The Model Code had no specific language dealing with the situation of the lawyer serving simultaneously as a director of, and the lawyer to, the corporate client. The Rules acknowledge the issue, do not impose a *per se* prohibition on the dual role, and offer little concrete guidance except to advise that the lawyer should not wear these two hats if "there is a material risk that the dual

---

financial interest in the clients' business or any participation in its management. Accordingly, he made it the policy of the firm that neither its partners nor its associates should hold equity securities of any client, or serve as a director of a corporate client, or have a financial interest, direct or indirect, in any transaction in which the firm was acting as counsel. Occasionally, more frequently in recent years, clients have insisted upon exceptions permitting partners to occupy directorships and own qualifying equity securities, but the exceptions have been few.

2 R.T. Swaine, THE CRAVATH FIRM AND ITS PREDECESSORS: 1819–1948 (1948), at pp. 9–10.

This issue has often been discussed in the literature, with the great majority of commentators warning of the risks inherent in the situation where the lawyer is simultaneously representing the corporate client and is acting as a director of the corporate client. *See, e.g.,* Lefkowitz, *The Attorney-Client Relationship and the Corporation,* 26 RECORD OF THE ASS'N OF THE BAR OF THE CITY OF NEW YORK 697 (No.8, Nov.1971); Report on the

Commission on Professionalism, *In the Spirit of Public Service: A Blueprint for Rekindling of Lawyer Professionalism,* reprinted in, 112 F.R.D. 243, 280-281 (1986); Monroe Freedman, *You CAN Do It, But You Shouldn't,* AMERICAN LAWYER (Dec. 1992), at 43; Susan R. Martyn, *Lawyers as Directors: Who Serves and Why?,* THE PROFESSIONAL LAWYER, 1966 SYMPOSIUM ISSUE (ABA Center for Professional Responsibility) THE LAWYER AS DIRECTOR OF A CLIENT, ABA Section on Business Law (ABA, Aug. 4, 1997).

[128] N.Y. State Bar Ass'n, Committee on Professional Ethics, Opinion 589 (1988), 1988 WL 236147.

[129] ABA Formal Opinion 98-410 (Feb. 27, 1998), at 3 n.4.

[130] *See* WALL ST. J., Dec. 31, 1993, at 12, col. 1–2 (Midwest ed.).

See also Continental Cas. Co. v. Smith, 243 F. Supp.2d 576 (E.D.La. 2003) (upholding insurance company claim that it was not required to defend malpractice action against a lawyer who also held a position an as an officer in the company client).

role will compromise the lawyer's independence of professional judgment."[131]

ABA Formal Opinion 98-410[132] offers useful warnings that the prudent lawyer should heed. The lawyer should make sure the client understands that: (1) the legal counsel and director have different responsibilities,[133] (2) in some cases discussions with the lawyer in her role as a director will not be covered by the client-lawyer privilege,[134] and (3) the lawyer may have to disqualify herself or refuse to undertake a representation because of a conflict of interest.

The Restatement of the Law Governing Lawyers also does not propose any *per se* prohibition. It concludes that the requirement that a lawyer representing a corporation must represent the "entity" means that the duty of a lawyer for the corporation "is generally consistent with the duties of a director or officer."[135] However, if the obligations or personal interests of the lawyer as a director are "materially adverse" to the obligations or personal interests of the lawyer as corporate counsel, then the lawyer must withdraw from representation unless the corporate client consents to the representation.[136]

For example, there may be a conflict if both the corporation

---

[131]Rule 1.7, Comment 35.

[132]ABA Formal Opinion 98-410 (Feb. 27, 1998).

[133]**Response to Auditor's Request for Information.** The *Statement of Policy Regarding Lawyers' Responses to Auditors' Request for Information*, 31 BUSINESS LAWYER (No. 3, Apr. 1975), is the basic discussion of the lawyer's duty, as lawyer, to respond to auditors' requests. The standard disclaimer provides that the lawyer's response is limited to matters involving "substantive attention by the lawyer in the form of legal consultation. . . ."

However, if the lawyer responding to this request is also a director, "the law firm should expand the disclaimer to exclude any information the law firm's lawyer-director may have as a director." ABA Formal Opinion 98-410 (Feb. 27, 1998), at 7 n.15.

[134]A particularly harsh case is, *Federal Savings & Loan Ins. Corp. v. Fielding*, 343 F.Supp. 537, 546 (D.Nev. 1972). When the lawyer became a corporate director, the court said:

"When the attorney and the client get in bed together as business partners, their relationship is a business relationship, not a professional one, and their confidences are business confidences unprotected by a professional privilege."

See, e.g., SEC v. Gulf & Western Industries, Inc., 518 F.Supp. 675 (D.D. C.1981), holding that when the outside counsel was also a corporate director and officer, the communications with the corporation were not privileged because of the lawyer's multiple roles. *United States v. Wilson*, 798 F.2d 509, 513 (1st Cir. 1986), holding that the client-lawyer privilege did not apply because the lawyer was really offering business advice.

[135]Restatement of the Law Governing Lawyers, Third, § 135, Comment *d*, at 418 (Official Draft 2000).

[136]Restatement of the Law Governing Lawyers, Third, § 135, Comment *d*, at 418 (Official Draft 2000). If the lawyer is disqualified, this disqualification is imputed to the other lawyers in her law firm. *Id.* at 756.

and the lawyer-director are defendants in the same lawsuit, so that the court may rule that the lawyer-director may not represent the corporation.[137] Another conflict would arise if a former lawyer-director had served on the board of a hospital extensively evaluating and approving certain policies. In this case, both that former lawyer-director and his law firm would later be disqualified from representing the plaintiff in a medical malpractice case against that hospital involving policies that the lawyer-director had earlier approved and implemented.[138]

The 1983 version of the Model Rules included one Comment on this topic.[139] The language required lawyers to examine the manner in which the two roles—lawyer and director—may conflict. If in his capacity as a board member, the lawyer is called upon to make judgments where his firm is providing the advice, a conflict of interest will arise. The board member lawyer should give consideration to resigning or obtaining an independent legal opinion.

The drafters of the 2002 Rules added a clause that reinforces the notion that a lawyer-director may need to withdraw from one or both of the matters.[140] They also advised that lawyers who are considering joining a board of directors should disclose to the

---

[137]*Harrison v. Keystone Coca-Cola Bottling Co.*, 428 F.Supp. 149 (M.D. Pa.1977). In this case, the court ruled that the director-lawyer's "intimate connection with Keystone, both as Director and co-defendant render it highly unlikely that he will be able to try this case with the degree of detachment required by the code of Professional Responsibility, and that he must therefore be disqualified." *Id.* However, the court allowed this director-lawyer to be personally represented by his law partner (who was also his son). *See also Cottonwood Estates, Inc. v. Paradise Builders, Inc.*, 128 Ariz. 99, 624 P.2d 296, 301–02 (1981) (holding that lawyer who also was an officer for the client could not represent the client as an advocate when lawyer was likely to be called as a key witness).

[138]*Berry v. Saline Memorial Hospital*, 322 Ark. 182, 907 S.W.2d 736 (1995), held that a lawyer owed the hospital a duty not to take a case adverse to the hospital based on confidential information gained while he was director. There was a conflict of

interest requiring the law firm's disqualification because the firm could not represent a patient in an action necessarily involving issues related to the very policies that the lawyer-director had approved and implemented. The lawyer, as a member of the hospital board of governors, was privy to confidential and privileged information about the hospital's quality assurance activities and the peer reviews conducted by the medical staff. "He was not employed as the hospital's attorney, but he was asked questions by board members because of his profession." Berry, 322 Ark. at 184, 902 S.W.2d at 738. Shortly after he left the board, another lawyer in the firm sought to represent the plaintiff in a malpractice action against the hospital.

[139]1983 Model Rule 14.

[140]Rule 1.7, Comment 35. *See also* Susanna M. Kim, *Dual Identities and Dueling Obligations: Preserving Independence in Corporate Representation*, 68 TENN. L. REV. 179 (2001) (discouraging lawyers from simultaneously serving as directors of their

entity the risks to the attorney-client privilege when the lawyer director is present in a board meeting. In addition, the lawyer must warn the entity that the lawyer might have to withdraw or recuse himself in some situations.[141]

§ 1.7–6(m) Private Attorneys on the Board of Legal Services Organizations

An attorney in a private law firm may also be a member, officer, or director of a legal services organization engaged in pro bono activities, including lawsuits against private parties represented by the attorney's private firm. Such a situation may raise a conflict.[142] There is, however, no *per se* prohibition.[143] If there were a blanket ban, it would be difficult for lawyers to volunteer their pro bono services. As a matter of public policy, it is helpful if private practitioners serve on the boards of legal service organizations to help deliver legal services to the indigent.

In general, the lawyer should not participate in a particular action or decision of the legal services organization if doing so would involve a conflict under the general conflict provisions of Rule 1.7.[144] The lawyer also should not participate in a particular decision or action of the legal services organization if doing so would have a "material adverse effect" on the representation of a client of the legal services organization when that client's interests are adverse to the interests of a client of the lawyer.[145]

§ 1.7–6(n) The Insured and the Insurer

§ 1.7–6(n)(1) Introduction

The insurer, in a typical liability insurance policy (*e.g.,* automobile coverage), agrees to pay any liability within the policy limits and to provide a lawyer to defend the insured.[146] The insured, in turn, agrees to cooperate. Ordinarily, the insured and

---

clients and noting that accountants as professionals are barred by their own code of ethics from serving as directors on the boards of their corporate clients); Patrick W. Straub, *ABA Task Force Misses the Mark: Attorneys Should Not Be Discouraged from Serving on Their Corporate Clients' Board of Directors*, 25 DEL. J. CORP. L. 261 (2000) (encouraging lawyers to simultaneously serve as directors of their clients).

[141] Rule 1.7, Comment 35.

[142] Rule 6.3.

[143] Restatement of the Law Governing Lawyers, Third, § 135, Comment *e*, at 419 (Official Draft 2000):

"In general, if there is a risk that the lawyer-director's performance of functions as a director [of the legal services organization] with respect to a particular decision would materially and adversely affect the lawyer's representation of private clients, the lawyer may not participate in that decision without the informed consent of affected clients."

[144] Rule 6.3(a).

[145] Rule 6.3(b).

[146] *See* Rule 1.8(f), the ethical rule governing when a lawyer representing a client accepts compensation from one other than his client (*i.e.,* the insurance company). Rule 1.8(f) is discussed

the insurer have a "community of interest,"[147] because both wish to defend vigorously against the claim brought by plaintiff. However, conflicts may arise when the suit is for more than the policy limits and the insured is more anxious than the insurer to settle for an amount less than those limits. Or, the insurer and the insured disagree as to whether the claim is covered by the policy. Or, the insurer may wish to spend less on lawyers' fees to defend the lawsuit than the insured prefers.[148]

The Model Code acknowledged these potential conflicts, but otherwise gave little concrete guidance, noting simply that "[t]ypically recurring situations involving potentially differing interests" include cases where the lawyer represents "an insured and his insurer."[149] The 1983 Model Rules went further in warning that when "an insurer and its insured have conflicting interests in a matter arising from a liability insurance agreement, and the insurer is required to provide special counsel for the insured," then this arrangement "should assure the special counsel's professional independence."[150] The drafters to the 2002 Rules deleted this language and instead stated: "If acceptance of the payment from any other source presents a significant risk that the lawyer's representation of the client will be materially limited by the lawyer's own interest in accommodating the person paying the lawyer's fee or by the lawyer's responsibilities to a payer who is also a co-client, then the lawyer must comply with the requirements of paragraph (b) before accepting the representation, including determining whether the conflict is consentable and, if so, that the client has adequate information about the material risks of the representation."[151]

The case law is not entirely consistent, but the trend is to consider the lawyer in such cases to owe the duty of loyalty to the insured. Rather than treating such a lawyer as representing only the insurer,[152] or representing both the insured and the insurer,[153] much of the case law treats the insured as "the client," and the

---

below.

[147]See ABA Formal Opinion 282 (May 27, 1950).

[148]A thoughtful article on these ethical issues is, Thomas D. Morgan, *What Insurance Scholars Should Know About Professional Responsibility*, 4 CONN. INS. L.J. 1 (1997–1998). This article is part of a Symposium on Liability Insurance Conflicts and Professional Responsibility.

[149]EC 5-17.

[150]1983 Model Rule 1.7, Comment 10.

[151]Rule 1.7, Comment 13.

[152]ABA Formal Opinion 96-403 (Aug. 2, 1996), at 2 n.2, specifies that it does "not address the lawyer's duties to the insured if the insured is not a client." That statement—"if the insured is not a client"—is, frankly, difficult to understand. The lawyer will be filing a notice of appearance in court on behalf of the insured, not the insurer. (Granted, a state, like Louisiana, may allow the plaintiff in the tort case to sue the insurance company directly. But, such direct actions against insurance companies are un-

insurer as a third party who pays for the lawyer and has certain contractual rights by agreement with the insured.[154] At a minimum, if the lawyer was proceeding along the lines of representing two clients, the lawyer would have an obligation to inform the insured and obtain that person's informed consent.[155]

The insurer is no stranger to the relationship between the lawyer and the insured because the contract between the insured and insurer gives the insurer certain significant rights. That contract will govern when the insured has authorized the insurer

---

usual.) In the very great majority of cases, the lawyer files an appearance on behalf of the insured. Hence, if the lawyer, who is in court speaking on behalf of the insured, is not representing the insured, then the judge and the insured will wonder why the lawyer filed a notice of appearance purporting to represent the insured.

Cf. ABA Formal Opinion 05–435 (Dec. 8, 2004) (simultaneous representation of liability insurer named in litigation and a client against the insured of the same liability insurance company is not automatically considered a directly adverse conflict under Rule 1.7, without additional facts that would accentuate the conflict).

[153]See *Nevada Yellow Cab Corp. v. Eighth Judicial Dist. Court ex rel. County of Clark*, 152 P.3d 737, 742 (Nev. 2007)(holding that, in the absence of a conflict of interest, the lawyer represents both the insured and the insurance company).

[154]A leading article (by a lawyer who, at the time, represented a malpractice carrier), concluded that the lawyer only represents the insured. *See* Robert O'Malley, *Ethics Principles for the Insurer, the Insured and Defense Counsel: the Eternal Triangle Reformed*, 66 TULANE L. REV. 511 (1991).

The main articles arguing that the lawyer represents both the insurer and the insured include, *e.g.*, Charles Silver, *Does Insurance Defense Counsel Represent the Company or the Insured?*, 72 TEXAS L. REV. 1583 (1994); Charles Silver & Michael Sean Quinn, *Wrong*

Turns on the Three Way Street: Dispelling Nonsense About Insurance Defense Lawyers, 5 COVERAGE 1 (Nov./Dec. 1995); Charles Silver & Michael Sean Quinn, *Are Liability Carriers Second-Class Clients? No, But They May Be Soon—A Call to Arms Against the Restatement (Third) of the Law Governing Lawyers*, 6 COVERAGE 21 (Mar./Apr. 1996). *See also* Charles Silver & Kent Syverud, *The Professional Responsibilities of Insurance Defense Lawyers*, 45 DUKE L.J. 255 (1995); and Brooke Wunnicke, *The Eternal Triangle: Standards of Ethical Representation by the Insurance Defense Lawyer*, FOR DEF., Feb. 1989, at 7. For a reaction to this position, *see*, Thomas D. Morgan & Charles W. Wolfram, *Insurance Defense Lawyers and the Restatement: A Reply to Professors Silver and Quinn*, 6 COVERAGE 8 (Jan./Feb. 1996).

[155]See *Amendment to Rules Regulating the Florida Bar re: Rules of Professional Conduct*, 838 So.2d 1140 (Fla.2003). Part (e) of Rule 4-1.7 Conflict of Interest, for example, says that "a lawyer has a duty to ascertain whether the lawyer will be representing both the insurer and the insured as clients, or only the insured, and to inform both the insured and the insurer regarding the scope of the representation." The comments to the rule add that this unique tripartite relationship creates ambiguity as to whom the lawyer represents; the desire of this rule is to minimize confusion and inconsistent expectations that may arise.

to settle within policy limits, as well as various other matters.[156] The lawyer then should follow the contract (except to the extent that it violates the Rules).[157]

Both the Model Rules[158] and Model Code[159] provide support for this view that the lawyer represents only one client, the insured.[160] Both establish that, if another person pays the lawyer to render legal services for another, the lawyer may not permit that other person to interfere with the lawyer's professional judgment.

The Restatement of the Law Governing Lawyers approaches the issue more directly. Its evaluation of the case law concludes:

> It is clear in an insurance situation that a lawyer designated to defend the insured has a client-lawyer relationship with the insured. The insurer is not, simply by the fact that it designates the lawyer, a client of the lawyer.[161]

The insurance carrier has legitimate interests, for example, to know the progress of the defense, to evaluate if a particular defense expense is cost-effective, and to sue for malpractice if the lawyer for the insured is incompetent. The insurer does not have to be called a "client" to have any of these rights.[162] As one leading academic has concluded: "When thinking about the tripartite

---

[156]As the court said in *Moritz v. Medical Protective Co.*, 428 F.Supp. 865, 871 (W.D.Wis.1977): "when the insured elects to tender to the insurer the defense of a claim against him or her, he or she consents to having the insurer choose the lawyer who is to defend the claim; and the insurer is entitled to control the defense by taking charge of the incidents of the defense including the supervising of the litigation."

[157]ABA Formal Opinion 96–403 (Aug. 2, 1996) states that the lawyer hired by the insurer to represent the insured may represent the insured alone, or (with appropriate disclosures and consultation) may represent both the insured and the insurer for all, or some, of the matter in controversy. However, it concludes that so long as the insured is a client, it is the Rules of Professional Conduct and not the insurance contract that governs the lawyer's obligations to the insured.

[158]Rule 1.8(f)(2).

[159]DR 5–107(B).

[160]*See also* Rule 1.7, Comment 13; Rule 5.4(c).

[161]Restatement of the Law Governing Lawyers, Third, § 134, Comment *f* ("Representing insured") (Official Draft 2000). Even if the insurance contract states that the lawyer represents the insurer, the Comment explicitly warns: "The insurer is not, by the fact of designation alone, a client of the lawyer."

When there are differences or conflicts between the interests of the insurer and insured (*e.g.*, when there is a question whether the claim is within the coverage of the policy, or when there is a claim in excess of policy limits), the lawyer's duty of loyalty is not to the insurer.

ABA Formal Opinion 96–403 (Aug. 2, 1996), at note 2 acknowledges that "the prevailing view appears to be that the lawyer represents both the insured and the insurer, at least for some purposes."

[162]See the thorough discussion of these issues in, Thomas D. Morgan, *What Insurance Scholars Should Know About Professional Responsibility*, 4 CONN. INS. L.J. 1 (1997–1998). Professor Morgan concludes that the answer to the question of whether the insurer

relationship between the insured, the insurance company and lawyer," the "lawyer who acts as if only the insured has the status of client will be least likely to go wrong."[163]

Let us now compare several typical fact situations, all of which are specific examples of a more general issue: the insurer-insured case is a well-known archetype, related to other, less-litigated, instances where one person or entity pays a lawyer to represent another, such as when parents pay a lawyer to represent their son who is charged with possession of an illegal substance, or when a legal aid office pays a lawyer to represent an indigent client.

§ 1.7–6(n)(2) Failure to Notify the Insured about Possible Settlements—When the Insured Wants to Settle

Consider the example where the insured is more anxious to settle than the insurer. For instance, in one case, the plaintiff offered to settle for $12,500 when the policy limit was $10,000. The defendant (the insured) was willing to add the additional $2,500. The insurer initially authorized settlement of $9,500. However, the lawyer for the insured did not relay to the insured this relevant settlement information, did not seek an extra $2,500 from the insurer, and did not inform the insured that the settlement offer was rejected. Lawyers have the basic ethical duty to keep their clients (in this case, the insured) reasonably informed about the matter and explain what is going on.[164]

The lawyer did not keep his client (the insured) informed about

---

is a second client of the lawyer is less significant than it might at first appear. "Indeed, calling the insurance carrier a second client would carry with it few of the benefits its proponents imagine and hope, and it would routinely create the potential for conflicts of interest." *Id.* at 7–8. He adds, "more often than not, the one-client approach gives all parties better guidance on how to handle concrete issues as they arise in a case." *Id.* at 9.

For example, the insured can sue the lawyer for malpractice under a theory of "equitable subrogation." *Atlanta Int'l Ins. Co. v. Bell*, 438 Mich. 512, 475 N.W.2d 294 (Mich.1991). The insurance company wants progress reports, and it can stay informed about the status of the matter because Rule 1.6, Comment 7 explicitly states that a lawyer is "impliedly authorized to make disclosures about a client when appropriate to carrying out the representation . . . ." At least one court has disagreed with the theory of "equitable subrogation." *See Pine Island Farmers Coop v. Erstad & Riemer, P.A.*, 649 N.W.2d 444 (Minn. 2002)(holding that insurer may not sue attorney because no attorney-client relationship exists). *Compare Paradigm Ins. Co. v. Langerman Law Offices, P.A.*, 200 Ariz. 146, 24 P.3d 593, 599–600 (2001) (citing Restatement of Law Governing Lawyers, Third, § 51(3), court holds that lawyer may still owe a duty to the nonclient insurance company).

[163]Thomas D. Morgan, *What Insurance Scholars Should Know About Professional Responsibility*, 4 CONN. INS. L.J. 1, 16 (1997–1998); Thomas D. Morgan, *Whose Lawyer Are You Anyway?*, 23 WM. MITCHELL L. REV. 11 (1997).

[164]Rule 1.4 ("Communication").

the settlement offer and related information. The case went to trial, and the verdict was for $225,000. The lawyer had acted as if his sole duty as to settlement was to the insurer. Thus, this lawyer found himself personally liable for the judgment in excess of policy limits.[165]

§ 1.7–6(n)(3) Failure to Notify the Insured about Possible Settlements—When the Insured Does Not Want to Settle: Professional Liability Policies

In some cases it is the insurer who is more anxious to settle than the insured. Under standard insurance law, an insurance company is free to exercise its own judgment as to whether to enter into a settlement within policy limits. The general rule is that unless there is an express policy provision to the contrary, the insurer may settle a case despite the insured's request that it not do so.[166]

However, professional malpractice policies are sometimes written differently than the garden variety automobile policy. The professional wants to protect her reputation and avoid any implication that she was incompetent. Thus, the insured may want the insurer to fight, not settle. Consequently, it is common for professional liability policies to contain a settlement clause that grants the insured the right to refuse to consent to a settlement. Such policies typically also have an express limitation on the insurer's liability if there is a judgment in excess of

---

[165]*Lysick v. Walcom*, 258 Cal.App.2d 136, 65 Cal.Rptr. 406 (1968).

When remedy sought is not damages. We often assume, when the insurance company settles a claim for the defendant, that the remedy sought is damages and that there is no need for the insured to be involved if he is not paying any of those damages. But the settlement may not be a monetary settlement. Assume, for example, a dispute involving title to land. The plaintiff sues the defendant over where the lot line is supposed to be. The title insurance company for the defendant offers to settle the dispute by transferring the disputed land from the defendant to the plaintiff. The insured-defendant is normally the one to sign the deed. The signature of the claims agent is not what the plaintiff wants or needs. The need for this remedy highlights the simple fact that the insured is involved in the settlement. The insured, by contract, may autho-

rize, in advance, the insurance company to settle a case for an amount within the policy. But if the settlement requires the insured to do something (sign a deed) and the insured has not already authorized the insurer to be his or her agent with the power of attorney, the insurance company will have to secure the insured's signature. The basic principle is that lawyers have the ethical duty to keep their clients reasonably informed.

[166]ALAN D. WINDT, INSURANCE CLAIMS AND DISPUTES; REPRESENTATION OF INSURANCE COMPANIES AND INSUREDS 191 (1982).

Mitchum v. Hudgens, 533 So.2d 194 (Ala.1988) (the insurance contract may give the insurer the right to settle a malpractice case within the policy limits, even over the objection of the insured). *See also Feliberty v. Damon*, 72 N.Y.2d 112, 531 N.Y.S.2d 778, 527 N.E.2d 261 (1988).

the policy coverage.[167] Obviously, if the insured retains a right to prevent a settlement, the lawyer must keep the insured informed so that she can exercise her rights under the insurance contract.

Even if the insurer has a right to settle, that does not necessary mean that the lawyer has a right to refuse to inform the insured about what is going on, *if* the insured makes clear that he wants to know. Even if the insured has no right to veto a settlement, if the insured informs the lawyer that he wants to know about any decision regarding settlement before it is final, the lawyer should inform the insured. That, at least, is the holding in *Rogers v. Robson, Masters, Ryan, Brumund and Belom.*[168]

The plaintiff in *Rogers* was a doctor who had an insurance policy that provided that the insurer did *not* have to secure the written consent of the insured before the insurer made settlement of any claim or suit. The doctor was sued for medical malpractice and the lawyers assigned by the insurer to defend the case negotiated a settlement with the victim. The insurer accepted the settlement, paid $1,250, and the lawyers effected dismissal of the action. The doctor had "repeatedly informed" one of the law partners that he would not consent to settlement and the doctor was never advised that the insurer intended to settle.

The defendants in *Rogers* argued that "they did not breach an independent duty owed to plaintiff; that because the insurer was authorized to settle the malpractice litigation without plaintiff's consent, no conflict of interest arose between the parties to the insurance contract . . .."[169] However, the Illinois Supreme Court disagreed. It held that these facts gave rise to a cause of action. Although the court treated the lawyer as representing both the insured and the insurer,[170] the court held that the insured—

> was entitled to a full disclosure of the intent to settle the litigation without his consent and contrary to his express instructions. Defendants' duty to make such disclosure stemmed from their attorney-client relationship with plaintiff and was not affected by the extent of the insurer's authority to settle without plaintiff's consent . . . .. Nor need we reach the question whether plaintiff can prove damages which are the proximate result of the breach of the

---

[167]ALAN D. WINDT, INSURANCE CLAIMS AND DISPUTES; REPRESENTATION OF INSURANCE COMPANIES AND INSUREDS 191 n.22. (1982).

[168]*Rogers v. Robson, Masters, Ryan, Brumund & Belom,* 81 Ill.2d 201, 40 Ill.Dec. 816, 407 N.E.2d 47 (1980).

[169]81 Ill.2d 201, 204, 40 Ill.Dec. 816, 817, 407 N.E.2d 47, 48.

[170]"Although defendants were employed by the insurer, plaintiff, as well as the insurer, was their client, and was entitled to a full disclosure of the intent to settle the litigation without his consent and contrary to his express instructions." Rogers, 81 Ill.2d 201, 205, 40 Ill.Dec. 816, 818, 407 N.E.2d 47, 49 (internal citations omitted).

duty to make a full disclosure of the conflict between the defendants' two clients.[171]

The court did not explain what damages, if any, Dr. Rogers suffered. Moreover, if the lawyer had informed Dr. Rogers of the insurance company's intent to settle, Dr. Rogers could not have stopped that settlement because he had not purchased the type of coverage that allowed him to prevent the insurance company from settling. However, if the lawyers had told Dr. Rogers that which he insisted he be told, Dr. Rogers could have waived the protections of his insurance policy, released the insurance company, and hired his own lawyer to defend the lawsuit instead of settling it.[172] The lawyer's failure to keep Dr. Rogers informed, after he made it very clear that he wanted to be informed, gave rise to a cause of action against his lawyers. Dr. Rogers, on remand, would then have to prove damages.

§ 1.7–6(n)(4) Disputes about Policy Coverage and Respecting the Insured's Confidences

Traditionally, the insurer's duty to defend the insured and its duty to pay a damage award are separate duties. In other words, a policy may provide coverage of defense costs even though the insurer may have a valid defense against paying the ultimate judgment rendered against the insured. When there is a dispute between the insured and the insurer as to the extent of the policy coverage, the insurer frequently provides a defense to the insured under a "reservation of rights." The insurer, although providing the defense for the insured, usually announces that it is not waiving any defenses it may have under the policy against bearing the ultimate liability. Because defense of the plaintiff's claim and the gathering of evidence as to policy coverage may go on simultaneously for some period, the usual rule is that two different lawyers must be involved, one to give the insurer an opinion on policy defenses or policy coverage and one to defend the insured.

Disputes about policy coverage are, initially, an issue under insurance law. However, these disputes frequently are connected with charges of a violation of legal ethics. In the typical case, the insured complains that the lawyer purporting to represent the insured (a lawyer who, after all, files a notice of appearance on

---

[171] 81 Ill.2d 201, 205–06, 40 Ill.Dec. 816, 818, 407 N.E.2d 47, 49.

[172] Thus, ABA Formal Opinion 96-403 (Aug. 2, 1996) explains that if the lawyer knows that the insured objects to a settlement, the lawyer may not settle the claim at the direction of the insurer without notifying the insured and giving him an opportunity to reject the insurer's offered defense and assume the responsibility of his own defense at his own expense. This notice to the insured should also serve to bring home the possibility that he will be assuming the substantive liability.

behalf of the insured) is really working against the insured and on behalf of the insurer, in violation of his duty of loyalty and his duty to protect client secrets.

The lawyer's obligation to the insured requires that she respect the insured's confidences. Thus a "lawyer may not defend the insured and at the same time investigate the failure of the insured to give timely notice of the accident involved as required by the insurance policy. Nor may counsel reveal to the insurer the insured's confidential disclosure indicating that his earlier version of the accident is untrue, or that the case is not covered by the insurance policy."[173]

Needless to say, the lawyer for the insured must not mislead the insured as to what is happening.[174] In *Allstate Insurance Co. v. Keller*,[175] for example, the attorneys assigned to represent the insured deposed the insured to gather evidence that he was not the driver of the vehicle at the time of the accident. They did not explain to the insured that the purpose of the deposition was to strengthen the insurer's claim of lack of coverage. The court agreed that the insured's initial false statements that he was the driver were a breach of the cooperation clause, but it held the defense was waived. After the insured's assigned attorneys "became aware of a conflict of interest" between their client, the insured, and their employer, the insurer, the attorney had to disclose "this information or its significance" to the insured. Failure to deal with this conflict in a way that assured the insured had loyal, independent representation resulted in loss of the policy defense.

In *Employers Casualty Company v. Tilley*,[176] the insured claimed that his failure to report an accident promptly, as the policy required, was because he had not known about the accident until he was sued. A lawyer was assigned to defend him, pursuant to a reservation of the company's rights. While the lawyer was preparing the defense, however, he was also gather-

---

[173]Robert Aronson, *Conflict of Interest Problems of the Private Practitioner*, in PROFESSIONAL RESPONSIBILITY: A GUIDE FOR ATTORNEYS 91, 104 (ABA 1978).

[174]*Cf.* Rule 1.13(f); Rule 4.3.

[175]*Allstate Ins. Co. v. Keller*, 17 Ill.App.2d 44, 149 N.E.2d 482 (Ill.App. 1958).

[176]*Employers Cas. Co. v. Tilley*, 496 S.W.2d 552 (Tex.1973).

Parsons v. Continental National American Group, 113 Ariz. 223, 550 P.2d 94 (1976), involved a case where

an attorney, hired by the insurer to represent the insured, used the "confidential relationship between an attorney and client" [*i.e.*, the insured] to gather information about the insured in order to deny coverage under the policy. Parsons, 113 Ariz. at 228, 550 P.2d at 99. The remedy for this type of misconduct has bite. The court ruled that this misconduct conduct "constitutes a waiver of any policy defense, and the insurance company is estopped as a matter of law from disclaiming any coverage under the exclusionary clause in the policy."

ing evidence of when Tilley or his employees first knew of the accident. "An attorney employed by an insurer to represent the insured simply cannot take up the cudgels of the insurer against the insured," the Court said. The insured was found to have been prejudiced by the lawyer's dual role, so the insurer was "estopped as a matter of law" from asserting its policy defense.[177]

Another aspect of confidentiality relates to the insurer's efforts to contain costs. Insurance company will want to prevent the lawyer from spending unnecessarily. Whether the expenses are really unnecessary (or whether the limits impair the lawyer's ability to act competently) is discussed in the next section. The issue here is when the lawyer may share this information with the insurer without violating the lawyer's obligation to protect the confidentiality and secrets of the insured. For example, the insurance company may demand that the insured's lawyer submit billing records to outside auditors.

ABA Formal Opinion 01-421[178] informs us that the lawyer may disclose information to the insurance company itself, if the lawyer reasonably believes it will advance the interest of the insured, *i.e.*, by helping the insurance company to decide when to settle, to assure the insurer that all is being handled properly, etc. The lawyer certainly should have no problem giving the insurer information such as billing records of a general nature or information that is publicly known, such as the lawyer's court appearances. The insurer will already know some other information because the insured will have forwarded it to the insurer to facilitate the defense, such as the insured's medical information. This Opinion advises that, while this information may be subject to Rule 1.6(a) as confidential client information, "its disclosure to the insurer nonetheless would be authorized impliedly either to comply with the insurance contract or to carry out the representation, or both."

Yet, the ABA Opinion warns, there are ethical limits on the lawyer's ability to keep the insured fully informed. There will be "rare situations" where the lawyer's disclosure to the insurer of confidential information will adversely affect a "material interest" of the "client-insured." In those cases, the lawyer may not disclose such confidential information without first "obtaining the informed consent of the client-insured."[179] Similarly, unless the client consents, the lawyer also "may not disclose information that may reveal the client's motives or other sensitive insights, nor disclose information to third party auditors . . . .."

---

[177]*See also Montanez v. Irizarry-Rodriguez*, 273 N.J.Super. 276, 641 A.2d 1079 (N.J.Super.App.1994) (lawyer for insured may not impeach the insured's story when the insured testifies).

[178]ABA Formal Opinion 01-421 (Feb. 16, 2001).

[179]ABA Formal Opinion 01-421 (Feb. 16, 2001), footnote 26 omitted, citing Restatement of the Law Governing Lawyers, Third, §§ 61 and 60(1)(a)

In order to secure the necessary consent, the lawyer must inform the client of the "client's obligation"[180] under the insurance contract (including the obligation to cooperate with the insurer). The lawyer must also explain that the insured's "failure to agree to disclosure could risk loss of insurance coverage." And, the lawyer should advise the client that disclosure of information to a "third-party auditor, a vendor with whom the lawyer has no employment or direct contractual relationship, may not be deemed essential to the representation and may, therefore, result in a waiver—albeit unintended—of the privilege. Therefore, since such disclosures always involve the *risk* of loss of privilege, the lawyer must obtain the insured's informed consent before sending bills with such information to a third party hired by the insurer to audit the bills."[181]

This position by the ABA does not end the dispute. *United States v. Legal Services for New York City*[182] enforced two administrative subpoenas from the inspector general's office of the Legal Services Corporation for similar information from legal aid organizations. The LSC was concerned that organizations were overstating the number of cases handled, so it required data by case number, subject matter and client names. Because "only privileged materials may be withheld from a response to the subpoenas; because the attorney-client privilege is not properly invoked by respondents' blanket objection; and because the [Office of the Inspector General of the Legal Services Corporation's] proposal to erect an administrative 'screen' to safeguard the names is not unreasonable," the court said it would enforce the subpoenas.[183] In addition, the statutory audit authority trumps state ethics rules and any requirement of confidentiality.

§ 1.7–6(n)(5) Disputes as to the Amount of Resources Used to Defend the Insured

Disputes sometimes arise between the insurer (who is paying the lawyers' fee and the other expenses of defending the law suit) and the insured as to how many resources should be employed in defending the suit. The insurance contract, to which the insured

---

(Official Draft 2000).

[180]This reference to the insured as a "client" is an acknowledgment by the ABA Formal Opinion that the insured is the lawyer's client. Even though this Formal Opinion states that it is not deciding whether the lawyer represents the insured, the insurer or both, the Opinion is based on the assumption that the lawyer, at the very least, represents the insured as a client. This result should not be startling, for the lawyer typically enters a court appearance for the insured.

[181]ABA Formal Opinion 01–421 (Feb. 16, 2001) (emphasis in original), footnotes 28–30 omitted.

[182]*United States v. Legal Services for New York City*, 100 F.Supp.2d 42 (D.D.C.2000), *affirmed*, 249 F.3d 1077, 346 U.S.App.D.C. 83, 50 Fed.R.Serv.3d 740 (D.C.Cir.2001).

[183]100 F.Supp.2d at 43.

consents, requires the insured to cooperate with the insurer, which retains certain rights to control the defense and the litigation strategy.[184]

However, the lawyer may not accept the insurance company's direction as to litigation strategy if so doing would result in the lawyer performing incompetently. The first rule of legal ethics is competence,[185] and the insurance contract does not override the law of legal ethics.[186]

Consider this example from the American Law Institute's Restatement of the Law Governing Lawyers. The Insurer agrees, by contract, to insure Policyholder and provide a defense. Plaintiff then sues Policyholder for claims that are within the policy and within the monetary limits of the policy. Insurer retains Lawyer to defend the action. Now—

> Lawyer believes that doubling the number of depositions taken, at a cost of $5,000, would somewhat increase Policyholder's chances of prevailing and Lawyer so informs Insurer and Policyholder. If the insurance contract confers authority on Insurer to make such decisions about expense of defense, and Lawyer *reasonably believes* that the additional depositions can be forgone without violating the duty of competent representation owed by Lawyer to Policyholder, Lawyer may comply with Insurer's direction that taking [these further] depositions would not be worth the cost.[187]

Based on these facts, this conclusion is certainly correct. The insured may agree by contract to authorize the insurer to exercise this kind of discretion, and the lawyer should accept this decision. If the client were not insured so that the client herself issued this direction—that no additional depositions should be taken—the lawyer would have to follow that instruction. The client/insured may authorize the insurer to act on her behalf. But the lawyer may not accept this direction from the insurer *if* that means that the lawyer is performing incompetent service.[188]

---

[184]*See, e.g., Crum v. Anchor Cas. Co.*, 264 Minn. 378, 119 N.W.2d 703 (Minn.1963); *Buchanan v. Buchanan*, 99 Cal.App.3d 587, 160 Cal.Rptr. 577 (Cal.App.1979).

[185]Rule 1.1.

[186]ABA Formal Opinion 96-403 (Aug. 2, 1996).

[187]Restatement of the Law Governing Lawyers, Third, § 134, Illustration 5, at p. 409 (internal citation omitted) (emphasis added) (Official Draft 2000).

[188]ABA Formal Opinion 01-421 (Feb. 16, 2001), which acknowledges that insurance companies "have a legitimate interest in lawyer billing practices and in controlling expenses." However, the lawyer may comply with insurance company litigation guidelines only where they do not "materially" impair the lawyer's own independent professional judgment on behalf of the client, or "result in his inability to provide competent representation to the insured." If the insurer insists on imposing these limits, and the insured refuses to consent to the limited representation, then the lawyer must either withdraw from the case or continue to represent the insurer with-

§ 1.7–6(*o*) Positional Conflicts

§ 1.7–6(*o*)(1) Introduction

A lawyer may represent Client *A*—in the case of *A vs. X*—seeking a particular legal result on one lawsuit (e.g., that the statute of limitations for tort should be tolled until the malpractice could reasonably have been discovered) and, at the same time, represent Client *B* in a completely different matter—the case of *Z vs. B*—raising the same general legal question. However, may the lawyer, on behalf of *B*, defend the contrary legal position?[189]

§ 1.7–6(*o*)(2) The Model Code Compared to the Model Rules

The Model Code had no specific rule prohibiting a lawyer from taking different positions in different cases. Client *A* (or Client *B*) may object, but whether the lawyer responds to these objections

---

out compensation.

This Opinion *explicitly* did not purport to decide whether the lawyer represents the insured, the insurer, or both. Instead, it relied on Rule 5.4(c), which provides in part that a lawyer "shall not permit a person who recommends, employs or pays a lawyer to render legal services *for another* to direct or regulate the lawyer's professional judgment in rendering . . . legal services." (emphasis added). However, that Rule assumes the other person is a client, so the Opinion had to be rejecting the view that the lawyer *only* represents the insurance company. Indeed, the Opinion itself later refers to the insured as the "client-insured." So, at a minimum, the insured is a client.

See also In the Matter of the Rules of Professional Conduct and Insurer Imposed Billing Rules and Procedures, 299 Mont. 321, 2 P.3d 806 (2000). In this case, defense counsel appointed by insurers to represent their insureds brought an original proceeding for declaratory relief. The issue was whether insurer-imposed billing and practice rules violated the Rules of Professional Conduct. The Montana Supreme Court held that (1) the insured is the *sole* client of defense counsel appointed by the insurer, and thus, the insurer is not a co-client of

defense counsel; (2) the insurers' prior-approval requirements violated the Rules of Professional Conduct by fundamentally interfering with defense counsels' exercise of their independent judgment and their duty to give undivided loyalty to insureds; and (3) the disclosures, to insurers' third-party auditors, of detailed descriptions of professional services rendered by defense counsel required the contemporaneous, fully informed consent of insureds. The court entered declaratory judgment. *See*, Eugene R. Anderson, *Insurance Companies Expose Insurance Industry Crooked Lawyers*, 11 COVERAGE 20 (ABA, No. 2, March/April 2001), discussing this case. *Contrast*, Lloyd E. Williams, Jr. & David E. Morgans, *Challenges to File Handling and Billing Guidelines*, FOR THE DEFENSE, June 2000, at 8.

[189]*See* John S. Dzienkowski, *Positional Conflicts Of Interest*, 71 TEXAS L. REV. 457 (1993); Ester F. Lardent, *Positional Conflicts In The Pro Bono Context: Ethical Considerations And Market Forces*, 67 FORDHAM L. REV. 2279 (1999); Noreen L. Slank, *Positional Conflicts: Is It Ethical To Simultaneously Represent Clients With Opposing Legal Positions?*, 81 MICH. B.J. 15, 18 (May 2002).

is a business question, not an ethical one. The Code only explicitly referred to positional conflicts in the pro bono context, and in that situation specifically allowed positional conflicts.[190]

The 1983 Model Rules, in contrast, raised a question about this practice but provided virtually no guidance in answering it. Comment 9 to Rule 1.7 allowed lawyers to advocate antagonistic positions on the same legal question in different cases "unless representation of either client would be adversely affected." Thus, says this Comment, it normally is proper to assert different positions "in cases pending in different trial courts, but it *may* be improper to do so in cases pending at the *same time* in an [the same?] appellate court."[191]

§ 1.7–6(*o*)(3) The Restatement

The American Law Institute's Restatement of the Law Governing Lawyers[192] accepts the notion of positional conflicts, but the conclusions in two illustrations it presents read like an *ipse dixit*. Illustration 5 allows an attorney to represent Client A and Client B in two separate cases brought in two different federal district courts, where the lawyer will seek to introduce certain evidence in one trial and argue against its admissibility in the other trial. Even though "there is some possibility" that the court's ruling in one case might be published and cited as authority in the other proceeding, the lawyer "may proceed with both representations *without obtaining the consent* of the clients involved."[193]

With Illustration 6, the American Law Institute contrasts Illustration 5. The facts are the same as in Illustration 5, except both cases are now before the U.S. Supreme Court, which will decide the common evidentiary question. This Illustration concludes that now there is a conflict and it is so great that "even the informed consent of both Client A and Client B would be insufficient to" remove the conflict and permit the lawyer to argue

---

[190]*See* EC 7-17 (lawyer may advocate law reform contrary to interest or desires of client). *Cf.* EC 8-1. *See also* Fed.R.Civ.P., Rule 8(e)(2) (inconsistent pleadings in same case allowed).

[191]1983 Model Rule 1.7, Comment 9 (emphasis added).

[192]In an earlier version, the Restatement of the Law Governing Lawyers, Third, § 209, Illustration 5 (Tentative Draft No. 4, Apr. 10, 1991), Illustration 5 in draft version used the phrase, "substantial possibility." In the Official Draft, this Illustration used the phrase, "some possibility." Restatement of the Law Governing Lawyers, Third, § 128, Illustrations 5 and 6 (Official Draft 2000), at pp. 343-44.

The Official Draft uses the language quoted in the text. Restatement of the Law Governing Lawyers, Third, § 128, Illustrations 5 & 6 (Official Draft 2000), at pp. 343-44.

[193]Restatement of the Law Governing Lawyers, Third, § 128, Illustrations 5 and 6 (Official Draft 2000) (emphasis added).

both cases before the Supreme Court.[194] Perhaps Clients *A* and *B* (when told of the conflict in Illustration 6) might be surprised to know that Illustration 5 advised their common lawyer that he had *no* obligation to tell them when he *first planted* the seed of the conflict in Illustration 5.

Any disqualification based on positional conflicts is magnified by the fact that positional conflicts are addressed in Rule 1.7,[195] and Rule 1.10 imputes all of Rule 1.7.[196] Nowadays, when it is not unusual for firms to have hundreds of members scattered among various cities, there may well be positional conflicts, like those discussed in Illustration 5, going on all the time. A California State Bar Formal Opinion concluded that a lawyer may ethically represent two clients who are not directly adverse to one another even if the lawyer would be arguing opposite sides of the same legal question before the same judge: positional conflicts are "common and prolific in our adversarial system of justice, [and] every time an attorney argues a point of law, it is probable that other clients will then or later be adversely affected."[197] It would be difficult for a conflicts check even to uncover these positional conflicts because legal arguments change all the time, even within the same case. The California Opinion concluded that even if "there is a substantial likelihood that one or both clients will be prejudiced by the representation, the attorney is not acting unethically by continuing the representation." Moreover, even "if the attorney chooses not to disclose the two representations the attorney does not violate his or her duty of loyalty to the client."[198]

§ 1.7-6(*o*)(4) Formal Opinion 93-377

The leading ABA Formal Opinion on this issue[199] specifically rejects the distinction articulated in 1983 Model Rule 1.7, Comment 9, between appellate and trial courts. It acknowledges that Comment 9 espouses this distinction, but it concludes that this Comment merely recognizes, "but does not resolve," the issue.

ABA Formal Opinion 93-377 presumes that the issue on which conflicting positions would be taken is an issue of substantive law, rather than an issue of discovery, or procedural or evidentiary law. This opinion argues that procedural, discovery and evidentiary issues "almost invariably turn on their particular facts,

---

[194]In an earlier version, in the Restatement of the Law Governing Lawyers, Third, § 209, Illustration 6 (Tentative Draft No. 4, April 10, 1991) uses the more tentative phrase, "is likely that;" in the Official Draft, § 128, Illustration 6 uses the phrase, "would be insufficient."

[195]Rule 1.7, Comment 9.

[196]Rule 1.10(a).

[197]California State Bar Formal Opinion 1989-108.

[198]California State Bar Formal Opinion 1989-108.

[199]ABA Formal Opinion 93-377 (Oct. 16, 1993).

and it is therefore rare that such issues will give rise to the type of conflict problem that is the subject of this Opinion." Whether that factual assertion is correct is a matter of some dispute. Recall that the American Law Institute's example of a positional conflict involved an evidentiary question.

In any event, this ABA Formal Opinion concludes that, if a lawyer is asked to advocate a position on a *substantive* legal issue that is directly contrary to the position that the lawyer (or any other lawyer in the same firm) is urging in a different and unrelated matter in the *same jurisdiction*, then there is the possibility of a positional conflict. Consequently, the lawyer should refuse to accept the second representation (or withdraw from the first representation if withdrawal is "otherwise permissible") if there is a "substantial risk" that the lawyer's advocacy on behalf of one client will create a legal precedent that, "even if not binding," is "likely materially to undercut the legal position being urged on behalf of the other client." However, the law firm can continue with both representations if both clients consent after full disclosure.[200]

There are no litmus tests in this area. The ABA Formal Opinion offers some important factors to consider. For example, if the two matters are being litigated in different jurisdictions *and* there is no substantial risk that either representation will be adversely affected by the other, the lawyer may proceed with both representations. In determining whether there is this substantial risk, the lawyer should consider, for example, whether the issue is one of federal law, where one federal judge will respectfully consider the decision of another federal judge even if they are not in the same district or state; whether the issue is so important that its determination is likely to affect the ultimate outcome of the case; and whether the firm might de-emphasize certain arguments in order to avoid affecting the other case.[201]

The client—who may not like the fact that the lawyer is publicly advocating law reform positions that are contrary to the client's private interests—can always fire the lawyer,[202] but that does not mean that the lawyer acted unethically in taking a contrary position. In practice, of course, the client may choose not to discharge the lawyer because lawyers are not fungible. If you are a good enough lawyer, your clients will resign themselves to the fact that you take principled positions advocating law reform.

Positional conflicts may occur when a lawyer takes a legal position in one case (evidence should be excluded under the hearsay

---

[200]ABA Formal Opinion 93-377 (Oct. 16, 1993).

[201]ABA Formal Opinion 93-377 (Oct. 16, 1993). *See generally* John S.

Dzienkowski, *Positional Conflicts of Interest*, 71 TEXAS L. REV. 457 (1993).

[202]Rule 1.16(a)(3); DR 2-110(B)(4).

rule; the statute of limitations should be tolled because of the defendant's concealment) that is contrary to a legal position that the lawyer takes in another case. The same lawyer (or the same law firm) is taking conflicting legal positions on an issue of law that is relatively abstract.

These types of "conflicts" are difficult to deal with because lawyers take conflicting legal positions all of time.[203] They sometimes take conflicting legal positions in the same case. Moreover, it is difficult to insert these constantly changing legal positions into the conflicts database of any large firm, particularly one that has offices in different cities.

Consequently, courts are not quick to disqualify simply because a client objects to a legal argument that its law firm makes in a case to which that client is not a party. As one court said, in brushing aside a disqualification motion claiming a conflict: "one can understand that Chase's in-house counsel might be unhappy that a law firm which represents it in some matters was taking a position in litigation involving another client that, if adopted, would prejudice an argument that Chase was advancing in a separate case, that does not mean that the law firm is violating a confidence of its client or engaging in unethical conduct."[204]

§ 1.7–6(*o*)(5) 2002 Model Rules

The drafters added a Comment specifically dealing with positional conflicts of interests.[205] It advised that, generally, it is not a conflict for a lawyer to take adverse legal positions for different clients in different tribunals at different times. The mere creation of adverse precedent is not enough. The focus of the conflict must be on how the positional conflict materially injures another client of the lawyer. If a significant risk exists that a lawyer's litigation position will materially limit the lawyer's liti-

---

[203]For a criticism of classifying positional conflicts as conflicts of interest, see Helen A. Anderson, Legal Doubletalk and the Concern with Positional Conflicts: "A Foolish Consistency,"? 111 PENN. STATE L. REV. 1 (2006). This article argues that:

"a legal positional conflict is not a true conflict of interest, and should not be the subject of an ethical prohibition. Because of the incentives it creates, a rule against positional conflicts gives greater control to wealthy clients over the availability of legal services without significantly protecting the rights of poor or middle income clients. Business conflicts already exert significant pressure on lawyers; too much concern with potential positional conflicts only increases that pressure."

"This article also argues that eliminating an ethical prohibition against positional conflicts could mitigate much of the credibility concerns raised by contradictory legal arguments. But even if the profession fully endorsed the ethic of independence and eliminated a rule against positional conflicts, some credibility problems would inevitably remain. Thus, while there should be no rule against positional conflicts, a court should respect an appointed attorney's decision to withdraw because of credibility concerns." *Id.* at 5.

[204]*Sumitomo v. J.P. Morgan & Co.*, 2000 WL 145747 *4 (S.D.N.Y.2000).

[205]Rule 1.7, Comment 24.

gation of another matter for another client, the lawyer has identified a conflict of interest.

The Comment goes on to list several factors that the lawyer should consider in determining if there is a positional conflict: "where the cases are pending, whether the issue is substantive or procedural, the temporal relationship between the matters, the significance of the issue to the immediate and long term interests of the clients involved, and the clients' reasonable expectations in retaining the lawyer."[206] If a conflict arises so that a significant risk exists that the representation of one or more clients may be materially limited, the lawyer must satisfy Rule 1.7(b).

§ 1.7–6(o)(6) Comparing the Taking of Adverse Legal Positions with the Taking of Adverse Factual Positions

A different type of conflict occurs when lawyers take conflicting positions in two different cases regarding a particular item of property, the same res, the same facts. This type of conflict is much easier to deal with, because the conflict is more obvious.

Consider *Fiandaca v. Cunningham*,[207] where New Hampshire Legal Assistance (NHLA) represented women prisoners objecting to overcrowding. The state, in response, offered to move some of the prisoners to another facility that was being used as a hospital for the mentally retarded. NHLA (which also represented the retarded persons in that hospital) objected to the state's offer because it would adversely affect their other clients, the mentally retarded. The First Circuit held that NHLA was in a conflict when it urged declining a settlement for one client because that settlement would adversely affect clients in a different case. Hence, the trial court should not have certified New Hampshire Legal Assistance as the class counsel.

Fiandaca is not a case of conflicting abstract legal positions because the lawyers were taking conflicting positions regarding the same piece of property, the hospital. However, one can draw from *Fiandaca* a legal principle that is useful in analyzing all positional conflicts: is the lawyer (and, by imputed disqualification, the law firm) likely to modify, soft-pedal, temper, or adjust arguments in one case in order to benefit the other client?

§ 1.7–6(p) Patent Cases

Andrew Corporation v. Beverly Manufacturing Co.[208] held that a merged law firm violated the conflict of interest rules by writing patent opinion letters for one client that were adverse to interests of another client without first obtaining consent from

---

[206]Rule 1.7, Comment 24.

[207]*Fiandaca v. Cunningham*, 827 F.2d 825 (1st Cir.1987).

[208]415 F.Supp.2d 919 (N.D.Ill. 2006) (Holderman, J.).

both clients. The case began when plaintiff Andrew Corporation ("Andrew"), alleged that defendant Beverly Manufacturing Company ("Beverly") infringed three of Andrew's patents. Andrew also alleged that Beverly's infringement was "willful." Beverly wanted to use three opinion letters that its lawyers from the law firm of Barnes & Thornburg ("B & K") had given it to defend against Andrew's allegations of willful infringement.

B & T's letters to its client, Beverly Manufacturing, concluded that Beverly's products did not infringe three patents held by Andrew Corporation. However, Andrew was a client of B & T in patent litigation when that B & T wrote these letters. Other lawyers represented Beverly in this case. Andrew moved to disqualify B & T in this case and also to exclude these letters from evidence. Beverly intended to use these letters to avoid a finding of willful patent infringement. B & T's letters were directly adverse to its client, Andrew. The court granted Andrew's motion, permitted no one from B & T to testify or otherwise participate in the case, and excluded the letters as evidence on the willfulness issue. The court said it was irrelevant that the law firm was unaware of the clients' adverse interests at time of the merger, that no single lawyer at the firm worked for both clients, or that the lawyers in question did not discuss their concurrent representation.

The court concluded:

> in the absence of valid consents by both Andrew and Beverly waiving the conflict after full disclosure to each, Barnes & Thornburg's only competent legal opinion in July and August 2003 to Beverly consistent with the Code of Professional Conduct was to refrain from expressing any opinion. Therefore, as a matter of law, this court holds that the July and August 2003 opinion letters were not issued by competent opinion counsel. The only remedy available to enforce adherence to the Rules of Professional Conduct is, to the extent possible, place the parties in the position they would have been in had counsel acted competently in accordance with the Rules of Professional Conduct. Consequently, it appears that to be fair and to uphold the integrity of the profession, no opinion letter by Barnes & Thornburg while laboring under the unwaived conflict of interest, should be used in any manner in this case.[209]

---

[209] *Andrew Corp. v. Beverly Mfg. Co.*, 415 F.Supp.2d at 928. *See also* Virginia State Bar Standing Committee on Legal Ethics, Op. 1774 (2/13/03), *discussed in* ABA/BNA Lawyers' Manual on Professional Conduct, Current Report, Ethics Opinions, March 12, 2003. This ethics opinion concluded that a conflict arose when a lawyer in a firm prepared a validity opinion for Client A regarding a patent that Client A sought to invalidate when the patent in question was held by Client B, another current client of the law firm.

CHAPTER 1.8

CONFLICT OF INTEREST—SPECIFIC RULES

RULE 1.8: CONFLICT OF INTEREST: CURRENT CLIENTS: SPECIFIC RULES

(a) A lawyer shall not enter into a business transaction with a client or knowingly acquire an ownership, possessory, security or other pecuniary interest adverse to a client unless:

(1) the transaction and terms on which the lawyer acquires the interest are fair and reasonable to the client and are fully disclosed and transmitted in writing in a manner that can be reasonably understood by the client;

(2) the client is advised in writing of the desirability of seeking and is given a reasonable opportunity to seek the advice of independent legal counsel on the transaction; and

(3) the client gives informed consent, in a writing signed by the client, to the essential terms of the transaction and the lawyer's role in the transaction, including whether the lawyer is representing the client in the transaction.

(b) A lawyer shall not use information relating to representation of a client to the disadvantage of the client unless the client gives informed consent, except as permitted or required by these Rules.

(c) A lawyer shall not solicit any substantial gift from a client, including a testamentary gift, or prepare on behalf of a client an instrument giving the lawyer or a person related to the lawyer any substantial gift unless the lawyer or other recipient of the gift is related to the client. For purposes of this paragraph, related persons include a spouse, child, grandchild, parent, grandparent or other relative or individual with whom the lawyer or the client maintains a close, familial relationship.

(d) Prior to the conclusion of representation of a client, a lawyer shall not make or negotiate an agreement giving the lawyer literary or media rights to a portrayal or account based in substantial part on information relating to the representation.

(e) A lawyer shall not provide financial assistance to a client in connection with pending or contemplated litigation, except that:

(1) a lawyer may advance court costs and expenses of litigation, the repayment of which may be contingent on the outcome of the matter; and

(2) a lawyer representing an indigent client may pay court costs and expenses of litigation on behalf of the client.

(f) A lawyer shall not accept compensation for representing a client from one other than the client unless:

(1) the client gives informed consent;

(2) there is no interference with the lawyer's independence of professional judgment or with the client-lawyer relationship; and

(3) information relating to representation of a client is protected as required by Rule 1.6.

(g) A lawyer who represents two or more clients shall not participate in making an aggregate settlement of the claims of or against the clients, or in a criminal case an aggregated agreement as to guilty or nolo contendere pleas, unless each client gives informed consent, in a writing signed by the client. The lawyer's disclosure shall include the existence and nature of all the claims or pleas involved and of the participation of each person in the settlement.

(h) A lawyer shall not:

(1) make an agreement prospectively limiting the

lawyer's liability to a client for malpractice unless the client is independently represented in making the agreement; or

(2) settle a claim or potential claim for such liability with an unrepresented client or former client unless that person is advised in writing of the desirability of seeking and is given a reasonable opportunity to seek the advice of independent legal counsel in connection therewith.

(i) A lawyer shall not acquire a proprietary interest in the cause of action or subject matter of litigation the lawyer is conducting for a client, except that the lawyer may:

(1) acquire a lien authorized by law to secure the lawyer's fee or expenses; and

(2) contract with a client for a reasonable contingent fee in a civil case.

(j) A lawyer shall not have sexual relations with a client unless a consensual sexual relationship existed between them when the client-lawyer relationship commenced.

(k) While lawyers are associated in a firm, a prohibition in the foregoing paragraphs (a) through (i) that applies to any one of them shall apply to all of them.

Comment

Business Transactions Between Client and Lawyer

[1] A lawyer's legal skill and training, together with the relationship of trust and confidence between lawyer and client, create the possibility of overreaching when the lawyer participates in a business, property or financial transaction with a client, for example, a loan or sales transaction or a lawyer investment on behalf of a client. The requirements of paragraph (a) must be met even when the transaction is not closely related to the subject matter of the representation, as when a lawyer drafting a will for a client learns that the client needs money for unrelated expenses and offers to make a loan to the client. The Rule applies to lawyers engaged in the sale of goods or services related to the practice of law, for example, the sale of title insurance or investment services to existing clients of the lawyer's legal practice. See Rule 5.7. It also applies to lawyers purchasing property from estates they represent. It does not apply to ordinary fee arrangements between client and lawyer, which are governed by Rule 1.5, although its requirements must be met when the lawyer accepts an interest in the client's business or other nonmonetary property as payment of all or part of a fee. In addition, the Rule does not apply to standard commercial transactions between the lawyer and the client for products or services that the client generally markets to others, for example, banking or brokerage services, medical services, products manufactured or distributed by the client, and utilities' services. In such transac-

tions, the lawyer has no advantage in dealing with the client, and the restrictions in paragraph (a) are unnecessary and impracticable.

[2] Paragraph (a)(1) requires that the transaction itself be fair to the client and that its essential terms be communicated to the client, in writing, in a manner that can be reasonably understood. Paragraph (a)(2) requires that the client also be advised, in writing, of the desirability of seeking the advice of independent legal counsel. It also requires that the client be given a reasonable opportunity to obtain such advice. Paragraph (a)(3) requires that the lawyer obtain the client's informed consent, in a writing signed by the client, both to the essential terms of the transaction and to the lawyer's role. When necessary, the lawyer should discuss both the material risks of the proposed transaction, including any risk presented by the lawyer's involvement, and the existence of reasonably available alternatives and should explain why the advice of independent legal counsel is desirable. See Rule 1.0(e) (definition of informed consent).

[3] The risk to a client is greatest when the client expects the lawyer to represent the client in the transaction itself or when the lawyer's financial interest otherwise poses a significant risk that the lawyer's representation of the client will be materially limited by the lawyer's financial interest in the transaction. Here the lawyer's role requires that the lawyer must comply, not only with the requirements of paragraph (a), but also with the requirements of Rule 1.7. Under that Rule, the lawyer must disclose the risks associated with the lawyer's dual role as both legal adviser and participant in the transaction, such as the risk that the lawyer will structure the transaction or give legal advice in a way that favors the lawyer's interests at the expense of the client. Moreover, the lawyer must obtain the client's informed consent. In some cases, the lawyer's interest may be such that Rule 1.7 will preclude the lawyer from seeking the client's consent to the transaction.

[4] If the client is independently represented in the transaction, paragraph (a)(2) of this Rule is inapplicable, and the paragraph (a)(1) requirement for full disclosure is satisfied either by a written disclosure by the lawyer involved in the transaction or by the client's independent counsel. The fact that the client was independently represented in the transaction is relevant in determining whether the agreement was fair and reasonable to the client as paragraph (a)(1) further requires.

Use of Information Related to Representation

[5] Use of information relating to the representation to the disadvantage of the client violates the lawyer's duty of loyalty. Paragraph (b) applies when the information is used to benefit either the lawyer or a third person, such as another client or business associate of the lawyer. For example, if a lawyer learns that a client intends to purchase and develop several parcels of land, the lawyer may not use that information to purchase one of the parcels in competition with the client or to recommend that another client make such a purchase. The Rule does not prohibit uses that do not disadvantage the client. For example, a lawyer who learns a government agency's interpretation of trade legislation during the representation of one

client may properly use that information to benefit other clients. Paragraph (b) prohibits disadvantageous use of client information unless the client gives informed consent, except as permitted or required by these Rules. See Rules 1.2(d), 1.6, 1.9(c), 3.3, 4.1(b), 8.1 and 8.3.

Gifts to Lawyers

[6] A lawyer may accept a gift from a client, if the transaction meets general standards of fairness. For example, a simple gift such as a present given at a holiday or as a token of appreciation is permitted. If a client offers the lawyer a more substantial gift, paragraph (c) does not prohibit the lawyer from accepting it, although such a gift may be voidable by the client under the doctrine of undue influence, which treats client gifts as presumptively fraudulent. In any event, due to concerns about overreaching and imposition on clients, a lawyer may not suggest that a substantial gift be made to the lawyer or for the lawyer's benefit, except where the lawyer is related to the client as set forth in paragraph (c).

[7] If effectuation of a substantial gift requires preparing a legal instrument such as a will or conveyance, the client should have the detached advice that another lawyer can provide. The sole exception to this Rule is where the client is a relative of the donee.

[8] This Rule does not prohibit a lawyer from seeking to have the lawyer or a partner or associate of the lawyer named as executor of the client's estate or to another potentially lucrative fiduciary position. Nevertheless, such appointments will be subject to the general conflict of interest provision in Rule 1.7 when there is a significant risk that the lawyer's interest in obtaining the appointment will materially limit the lawyer's independent professional judgment in advising the client concerning the choice of an executor or other fiduciary. In obtaining the client's informed consent to the conflict, the lawyer should advise the client concerning the nature and extent of the lawyer's financial interest in the appointment, as well as the availability of alternative candidates for the position.

Literary Rights

[9] An agreement by which a lawyer acquires literary or media rights concerning the conduct of the representation creates a conflict between the interests of the client and the personal interests of the lawyer. Measures suitable in the representation of the client may detract from the publication value of an account of the representation. Paragraph (d) does not prohibit a lawyer representing a client in a transaction concerning literary property from agreeing that the lawyer's fee shall consist of a share in ownership in the property, if the arrangement conforms to Rule 1.5 and paragraphs (a) and (i).

Financial Assistance

[10] Lawyers may not subsidize lawsuits or administrative proceedings brought on behalf of their clients, including making or guaranteeing loans to their clients for living expenses, because to do so would encourage clients to pursue lawsuits that might not otherwise be brought and because such assistance gives lawyers too great a financial stake in the litigation. These dangers do not war-

rant a prohibition on a lawyer lending a client court costs and litigation expenses, including the expenses of medical examination and the costs of obtaining and presenting evidence, because these advances are virtually indistinguishable from contingent fees and help ensure access to the courts. Similarly, an exception allowing lawyers representing indigent clients to pay court costs and litigation expenses regardless of whether these funds will be repaid is warranted.

Person Paying for a Lawyer's Services

[11] Lawyers are frequently asked to represent a client under circumstances in which a third person will compensate the lawyer, in whole or in part. The third person might be a relative or friend, an indemnitor (such as a liability insurance company) or a co-client (such as a corporation sued along with one or more of its employees). Because third-party payers frequently have interests that differ from those of the client, including interests in minimizing the amount spent on the representation and in learning how the representation is progressing, lawyers are prohibited from accepting or continuing such representations unless the lawyer determines that there will be no interference with the lawyer's independent professional judgment and there is informed consent from the client. See also Rule 5.4(c) (prohibiting interference with a lawyer's professional judgment by one who recommends, employs or pays the lawyer to render legal services for another).

[12] Sometimes, it will be sufficient for the lawyer to obtain the client's informed consent regarding the fact of the payment and the identity of the third-party payer. If, however, the fee arrangement creates a conflict of interest for the lawyer, then the lawyer must comply with Rule. 1.7. The lawyer must also conform to the requirements of Rule 1.6 concerning confidentiality. Under Rule 1.7(a), a conflict of interest exists if there is significant risk that the lawyer's representation of the client will be materially limited by the lawyer's own interest in the fee arrangement or by the lawyer's responsibilities to the third-party payer (for example, when the third-party payer is a co-client). Under Rule 1.7(b), the lawyer may accept or continue the representation with the informed consent of each affected client, unless the conflict is nonconsentable under that paragraph. Under Rule 1.7(b), the informed consent must be confirmed in writing.

Aggregate Settlements

[13] Differences in willingness to make or accept an offer of settlement are among the risks of common representation of multiple clients by a single lawyer. Under Rule 1.7, this is one of the risks that should be discussed before undertaking the representation, as part of the process of obtaining the clients' informed consent. In addition, Rule 1.2(a) protects each client's right to have the final say in deciding whether to accept or reject an offer of settlement and in deciding whether to enter a guilty or nolo contendere plea in a criminal case. The rule stated in this paragraph is a corollary of both these Rules and provides that, before any settlement offer or plea bargain is made or accepted on behalf of multiple clients, the lawyer must inform each of them about all the material terms of

the settlement, including what the other clients will receive or pay if the settlement or plea offer is accepted. See also Rule 1.0(e) (definition of informed consent). Lawyers representing a class of plaintiffs or defendants, or those proceeding derivatively, may not have a full client-lawyer relationship with each member of the class; nevertheless, such lawyers must comply with applicable rules regulating notification of class members and other procedural requirements designed to ensure adequate protection of the entire class.

Limiting Liability and Settling Malpractice Claims

[14] Agreements prospectively limiting a lawyer's liability for malpractice are prohibited unless the client is independently represented in making the agreement because they are likely to undermine competent and diligent representation. Also, many clients are unable to evaluate the desirability of making such an agreement before a dispute has arisen, particularly if they are then represented by the lawyer seeking the agreement. This paragraph does not, however, prohibit a lawyer from entering into an agreement with the client to arbitrate legal malpractice claims, provided such agreements are enforceable and the client is fully informed of the scope and effect of the agreement. Nor does this paragraph limit the ability of lawyers to practice in the form of a limited-liability entity, where permitted by law, provided that each lawyer remains personally liable to the client for his or her own conduct and the firm complies with any conditions required by law, such as provisions requiring client notification or maintenance of adequate liability insurance. Nor does it prohibit an agreement in accordance with Rule 1.2 that defines the scope of the representation, although a definition of scope that makes the obligations of representation illusory will amount to an attempt to limit liability.

[15] Agreements settling a claim or a potential claim for malpractice are not prohibited by this Rule. Nevertheless, in view of the danger that a lawyer will take unfair advantage of an unrepresented client or former client, the lawyer must first advise such a person in writing of the appropriateness of independent representation in connection with such a settlement. In addition, the lawyer must give the client or former client a reasonable opportunity to find and consult independent counsel.

Acquiring Proprietary Interest in Litigation

[16] Paragraph (i) states the traditional general rule that lawyers are prohibited from acquiring a proprietary interest in litigation. Like paragraph (e), the general rule has its basis in common law champerty and maintenance and is designed to avoid giving the lawyer too great an interest in the representation. In addition, when the lawyer acquires an ownership interest in the subject of the representation, it will be more difficult for a client to discharge the lawyer if the client so desires. The Rule is subject to specific exceptions developed in decisional law and continued in these Rules. The exception for certain advances of the costs of litigation is set forth in paragraph (e). In addition, paragraph (i) sets forth exceptions for liens authorized by law to secure the lawyer's fees or expenses and contracts for reasonable contingent fees. The law of

each jurisdiction determines which liens are authorized by law. These may include liens granted by statute, liens originating in common law and liens acquired by contract with the client. When a lawyer acquires by contract a security interest in property other than that recovered through the lawyer's efforts in the litigation, such an acquisition is a business or financial transaction with a client and is governed by the requirements of paragraph (a). Contracts for contingent fees in civil cases are governed by Rule 1.5.

Client-Lawyer Sexual Relationships

[17] The relationship between lawyer and client is a fiduciary one in which the lawyer occupies the highest position of trust and confidence. The relationship is almost always unequal; thus, a sexual relationship between lawyer and client can involve unfair exploitation of the lawyer's fiduciary role, in violation of the lawyer's basic ethical obligation not to use the trust of the client to the client's disadvantage. In addition, such a relationship presents a significant danger that, because of the lawyer's emotional involvement, the lawyer will be unable to represent the client without impairment of the exercise of independent professional judgment. Moreover, a blurred line between the professional and personal relationships may make it difficult to predict to what extent client confidences will be protected by the attorney-client evidentiary privilege, since client confidences are protected by privilege only when they are imparted in the context of the client-lawyer relationship. Because of the significant danger of harm to client interests and because the client's own emotional involvement renders it unlikely that the client could give adequate informed consent, this Rule prohibits the lawyer from having sexual relations with a client regardless of whether the relationship is consensual and regardless of the absence of prejudice to the client.

[18] Sexual relationships that predate the client-lawyer relationship are not prohibited. Issues relating to the exploitation of the fiduciary relationship and client dependency are diminished when the sexual relationship existed prior to the commencement of the client-lawyer relationship. However, before proceeding with the representation in these circumstances, the lawyer should consider whether the lawyer's ability to represent the client will be materially limited by the relationship. See Rule 1.7(a)(2).

[19] When the client is an organization, paragraph (j) of this Rule prohibits a lawyer for the organization (whether inside counsel or outside counsel) from having a sexual relationship with a constituent of the organization who supervises, directs or regularly consults with that lawyer concerning the organization's legal matters.

Imputation of Prohibitions

[20] Under paragraph (k), a prohibition on conduct by an individual lawyer in paragraphs (a) through (i) also applies to all lawyers associated in a firm with the personally prohibited lawyer. For example, one lawyer in a firm may not enter into a business transaction with a client of another member of the firm without complying with paragraph (a), even if the first lawyer is not personally involved in the representation of the client. The prohibition set forth in paragraph (j) is personal and is not applied to associated lawyers.

Authors' 1983 Model Rules Comparison

The 1983 Rule 1.8 was entitled "Conflict of Interest: Prohibited Transactions." The drafters of the 2002 Model Rules changed this to "Conflict of Interest: Specific Rules" to reflect the fact that most of the provisions under Rule 1.8 did not prohibit the transaction completely, they simply provided detailed guidance for many transactions.

In Rule 1.8(a) on business transactions with a client, the drafters added a clause to paragraph (a)(2) requiring the lawyer to advise the client about the desirability of seeking an independent lawyer in writing. They also added detail to paragraph (a)(3) to the requirement of client consent. The new provision requires a lawyer to obtain the client's informed consent in writing and the writing must contain the essential terms of the transaction and the lawyer's role in the transaction. The lawyer must inform the client in the consent whether the lawyer is representing the client in the transaction.

In Rule 1.8(b), the drafters modified the text to require informed consent instead of consent after consultation and they deleted specific references to Rules 1.6 and 3.3 and replaced it with a more general requirement to comply with the Rules.

In Rule 1.8(c), the drafters added a specific prohibition on solicitation of substantial gifts. They also deleted the specific categories of relatives of the lawyer who may not receive a gift or bequest and added a line at the end of paragraph (c) defining more broadly the persons who may not receive gifts from the lawyer's clients. Several other word changes were made in this Rule.

Rule 1.8(d) and Rule 1.8(e) were not amended.

In Rule 1.8(f)(1), the drafters replaced "consent after consultation" with "informed consent."

In Rule 1.8(g), the drafters replaced "consent after consultation" with "informed consent, in a writing signed by the client." They also made some minor word changes including dividing a sentence into two sentences.

In Rule 1.8(h), the drafters subdivided the text into subsections (1) and (2) and with respect to Rule 1.8(h)(1) on prospective limitations on liability, they removed the requirement that it be permitted by law. On the topic of setting past liability, the drafters added "potential claims" to the Rule 1.8(h)(2) and they clarified that lawyers must advise an unrepresented client or former client of the desirability of seeking and is given an opportunity to seek the advice of an independent lawyer.

The drafters deleted Rule 1.8(i) on related lawyers representing opposing parties and moved this topic under Rule 1.7 (general conflicts of interest).

The drafters renumbered Rule 1.8(j) as (i) and made a slight word change.

The drafters added new Rule 1.8(j) on sex with clients and new Rule 1.8(k) on imputing Rule 1.8 conflicts to other lawyers in the law firm.

In the Comments, the drafters added the word, "Business" to the title, "Transactions Between Client and Lawyer."

Comment 1 was substantially modified to explain the basis for Rule 1.8(a) and the scope of the application of the Rule.

Comments 2, 3, and 4 are all new and explain in detail how to apply Rule 1.8(a) to client lawyer business transactions.

Comment 5 is new and explains Rule 1.8(b) on lawyer use of client information.

The drafter broke up old Comment 2 into new Comments 6 and 7 and made a few changes to reflect the changes made to Rule 1.8(c).

Comment 8 is new and explains the application of Rule 1.8(c) to the situation where a lawyer seeks to have a lawyer in the firm named as a executor of an estate.

Old Comment 3 is now new Comment 9 with a minor reference change.

Comment 10 is new and discusses the policies underlying Rule 1.8(e) on financial assistance to clients.

Old Comment 4 was completely deleted.

Comments 11, 12, and 13 are new and examine the application of Rules 1.8(f) and (g).

Old Comments 5 and 6 were completely deleted.

Comments 14 and 15 are new and designed to explain the application of Rule 1.8(h).

Old Comment 6 was renumbered as Comment 16 and substantially amended.

Comments 17 to 20 are new and discuss the two new provisions, Rule 1.8(j) and Rule 1.8(k).

Model Code Comparison

[1] With regard to paragraph (a), DR 5-104(A) provided that a lawyer "shall not enter into a business transaction with a client if they have differing interests therein and if the client expects the lawyer to exercise his professional judgment therein for the protection of the client, unless the client has consented after full disclosure." EC 5-3 stated that a lawyer "should not seek to persuade his client to permit him to invest in an undertaking of his client nor make improper use of his professional relationship to influence his client to invest in an enterprise in which the lawyer is interested."

[2] With regard to paragraph (b), DR 4-101(B)(3) provided that a lawyer should not use "a confidence or secret of his client for the advantage of himself, or of a third person, unless the client consents after full disclosure."

[3] There was no counterpart to paragraph (c) in the Disciplinary Rules of the Model Code. EC 5-5 stated that a lawyer "should not suggest to his client that a gift be made to himself or for his benefit. If a lawyer accepts a gift from his client, he is peculiarly susceptible to the charge that he unduly influenced or overreached the client. If a client voluntarily offers to make a gift to his lawyer, the lawyer may accept the gift, but before doing so, he should urge that the client secure disinterested advice from an independent, competent person who is cognizant of all the circumstances. Other than in exceptional circumstances, a lawyer should insist that an instru-

ment in which his client desires to name him beneficially be prepared by another lawyer selected by the client."

[4] Paragraph (d) is substantially similar to DR 5-104(B), but refers to "literary or media" rights, a more generally inclusive term than "publication" rights.

[5] Paragraph (e)(1) is similar to DR 5-103(B), but eliminates the requirement that "the client remains ultimately liable for such expenses."

[6] Paragraph (e)(2) has no counterpart in the Model Code.

[7] Paragraph (f) is substantially identical to DR 5-107(A)(1).

[8] Paragraph (g) is substantially identical to DR 5-106.

[9] The first clause of paragraph (h) is similar to DR 6-102(A). There was no counterpart in the Model Code to the second clause of paragraph (h).

[10] Paragraph (i) has no counterpart in the Model Code.

[11] Paragraph (j) is substantially identical to DR 5-103(A).

§ 1.8–1 INTRODUCTION

Rule 1.8 considers various specific conflicts issues, all grouped together in one rule with several subsections. Rule 1.8 recognizes and implements the general principle that lawyers are fiduciaries of their clients, but these fiduciaries may also be involved in business dealings and other relationships with their clients.

The 1983 version of Rule 1.8 was entitled, "Prohibited Transactions." The drafters of the 2002 Model Rules changed this to "Specific Rules" to reflect the renaming of Rule 1.7 as a general conflicts rule. It also reflects the view that most of the provisions of Rule 1.8 do not completely prohibit the transactions.

The 1983 version of Rule 1.8 contained a provision specifically dealing with the conflict created when related lawyers representing opposing parties to a contested matter.[1] This conflict arises in litigation and other contested matters with opposing parties. The drafters of the 2002 Rules deleted Rule 1.8(i) and moved this discussion into the Comments of Rule 1.7.

§ 1.8–2 RULE 1.8(a)—BUSINESS TRANSACTIONS WITH A CURRENT CLIENT

§ 1.8–2(a) Business Dealings with the Client

The lawyer may be involved in business dealings with others that may affect the lawyer's ability to represent the client. There is a conflict if these interests are significant and material enough to affect the lawyer's judgment.[1] The lawyer in such cases should not accept the case unless he or she reasonably believes that the

---

[Section 1.8–1]

[1] 1983 Model Rule 1.8(i).

[Section 1.8–2]

[1] Restatement of the Law Govern-

representation will not be adversely affected and the client consents.[2]

If the lawyer deals with the client in a business transaction, the lawyer may overreach the client, who may be relying on the lawyer's independent legal judgment. The Code and the Rules attempt to deal with this problem in slightly different ways.

The Model Code forbids business relations with the client, unless the client consents after full disclosure, if two conditions exist: (1) the lawyer and client have differing interests, and (2) the client expects the lawyer to exercise his or her legal judgment for the protection of the client.[3] On the aspirational level, the Model Code also provides that lawyers should not "seek to persuade" their clients to permit them to invest in the client's business or undertaking.[4] Even if the lawyer's efforts at persuasion are unsuccessful, he has violated this ethical aspiration by attempting to persuade the client.

In contrast, the Model Rules do not focus on the client's expectation that the lawyer will exercise professional judgment on behalf of the client. Rather, they allow client business dealings with the lawyer if: (1) the transaction is fair and reasonable to the client; (2) the terms of the transaction are given to the client *in writing* in clear language so that the client can understand them; (3) the client is advised in writing and given a reasonable opportunity to consult another lawyer (whether or not the client actually exercises that opportunity);[5] and (4) the client consents *in a writing*.[6] Rule 1.8 does not specifically forbid the lawyer from seeking to invest in the client's enterprise.

It is not the duty of the client, even if sophisticated, to recognize the conflict. Rather it is the duty of the lawyer to bring the matter to the client's attention and explain the significance of what is happening in a way that the client can understand.[7] If the lawyer represents a client in a transaction, and also receives

---

ing Lawyers, Third, § 126 (Official Draft 2000).

[2] Rule 1.7(b); DR 5-101(A).

[3] DR 5-104(A).

[4] EC 5-3.

[5] *Petit-Clair v. Nelson*, 344 N.J.Super. 538, 543, 782 A.2d 960, 963 (N.J.Super.A.D.2001). A lawyer sued to foreclose on a mortgage that the corporations' president and secretary had given on their personal residence to secure the payment of attorney fees for the lawyer's representation of the corporations. The trial court found the mortgage was invalid, and the appel-late division affirmed because the "plaintiff's failure to comply with the mandatory dictate of [Rules of Professional Conduct] 1.8(a), the making of the mortgage in plaintiff's favor was unreasonable and unfair to defendants."

[6] Rule 1.8(a).

[7] *Committee on Professional Ethics and Conduct v. Mershon*, 316 N.W.2d 895 (Iowa 1982).

Accounts Receivables. ABA Formal Opinion 00-416 (Apr. 7, 2000) addressed the specialized question of whether a lawyer may purchase a client's accounts receivables. The

a personal benefit in addition to the client's fee, then the lawyer's ethical obligation is "not always fulfilled by merely disclosing" the lawyer's personal stake, explaining the potential consequences, and obtaining consent. The lawyer must ensure that the transaction is fair and reasonable. In other words, a lawyer cannot obtain a "good deal" from a current client. The best way to comply with this requirement is to obtain an independent appraisal to determine whether the transaction is fair and reasonable. And, the lawyer "must always ensure that his or her personal interest does not interfere with the unfettered exercise of professional judgment the client is entitled to expect under the circumstances. The best way to achieve this, of course, is to see that the client has independent advice."[8]

Opinion advises that the lawyer may do that in a transaction that meets the requirements of Rule 1.8(a). If the lawyer may have to sue the client's debtors to collect the accounts, however, Rules 1.7 and 1.9 may come into play as well because of the possibility of conflicts of interest. For example, the lawyer might pursue the client's collection efforts with lessened ardor in the hopes of persuading the client to sell the uncollected debt to the lawyer at an artificially reduced price.

[8]*Matter of Breen*, 171 Ariz. 250, 254, 830 P.2d 462, 466 (1992).

Tortious Interference with Contract. In general, a lawyer is not subject to liability to a third party simply because he advised his client to breach a contract with that third party. *See, e.g., Brown Mackie College v. Graham*, 981 F.2d 1149 (10th Cir.1992) (lawyer who advised students to withdraw from school not liable to the school). In fact, the lawyer is not liable to the third party even if his advice to his own client was negligent. Thus, in *Beatie v. DeLong*, 164 A.D.2d 104, 561 N.Y.S.2d 448(1990), the court held that a lawyer was not liable to a non-client because the lawyer had *negligently* advised a client that the client's contingent fee contract with another lawyer—the non-client—was not valid. Of course, a lawyer can be liable to his own client for giving negligent advice. However, in this case, the non-client was suing

and the court found no liability to the non-client for the negligent advice given to the client. In general the lawyer would be liable to his own client for negligence, but not to the third party to whom he does not owe a duty.

The situation changes when the lawyer's advice to the client is affected by the lawyer's own personal financial interests. Thus, cases have held that a lawyer who advised the client to breach a sales contract so that the lawyer could himself purchase the property was liable to the third party for tortious interference with contract. *Duggin v. Adams*, 234 Va. 221, 360 S.E.2d 832 (Va.1987). *See* Jenna Green, *Suit Targets 3 Swidler Lawyers*, LEGAL TIMES, Feb. 22, 1999, at 9, noting that three lawyers at a Washington, D.C. law firm are "accused of illegally forming a company to steal away the contract for the administration of Liberia's maritime registry—a program of critical importance for the coastal country's economy." The law firm was representing Liberia in a suit it filed against the International Trust Co. of Liberia (ITC) disputing a contract it had with Liberia. ITC claimed that it had a valid contract with Liberia and the lawyers representing Liberia did not disclose that they had a "substantial commercial interest in the failure of those very negotiations."

In another instance, the lawyer advised the client to breach his contract with the non-client in order to punish that non-client (who had re-

The Comments clarify the application of Rule 1.8(a). A lawyer must comply with this Rule even when the topic of the legal representation is not in any way related to the business transaction.[9] It applies to tailor made transactions between lawyers and clients such as loans or sales of real estate.[10] Rule 1.8(a) also applies when the lawyer offers to sell a client law related services.[11] However, the provision does not govern routine transactions between a lawyer and a client when the transactions were offered on the same terms as the general public. In other words, if the lawyer uses a client business to buy groceries on the same terms as the general public, Rule 1.8(a) does not apply. The provisions also do not apply when the client has hired another lawyer in another firm to represent him in the transaction with the lawyer.

The drafters of the 2002 Model Rules require that a lawyer make clear in a writing whether or not the lawyer is representing the client in the business transaction.[12] If the lawyer is not representing the client in the business transaction, then the lawyer is dealing with a current client, but an unrepresented person for purposes of the deal. One would assume that most lawyers will choose not to represent the client in the business transaction because of the increased liability to the lawyer.

§ 1.8–2(a)(1) Investing in the Client

Rule 1.5 allows a lawyer to accept property in exchange for services, such as "an ownership interest in an enterprise . . .."[13] The last few years of the twentieth century saw a tremendous surge in the stock market, particularly in the stock of so-called "dot.com" companies. What goes up must come down, and during the years 2000 and 2001, many of these stocks tumbled (with the NASDAQ Composite losing about 60% of its value from it peak). With the burst of the Internet bubble in 2000 and 2001, stock in Internet companies became less beguiling and captivating and their charms were easier to resist.

But when the stock market was soaring, various law firms—particularly those based on the West Coast and serving high technology start-up companies headquartered in Silicon Valley—sought to invest in their clients and receive, for example, stock,

---

fused to pay the lawyer's fee in another matter). *Miller v. St. Charles Condominium Ass'n*, 141 Ill.App.3d 834, 96 Ill.Dec. 311, 491 N.E.2d 125 (1986).

[9] Rule 1.8, Comment 1.

[10] In *Liggett v. Young*, 877 N.E.2d 178 (Ind. 2007), the court addressed the ethical issues of a lawyer who entered into a home construction contract with his client, a builder. A viola-

tion of Rule 1.8(a) did not create per se liability, but a client may sue the attorney for breach of common law duties. The court left open the question of the "standard commercial transaction" exception to Rule 1.8(a).

[11] Rule 5.7.

[12] Rule 1.8(a)(3).

[13] Rule 1.5, Comment 4.

options, warrants, in lieu or all or part of the law firm's fee.[14] Some firms refused to trade fees for stock; they invested cash in client ventures. Some law firms profited handsomely during this period, *if* they were lucky enough to sell the stock before the collapse of the stock market starting towards the end of 2000 and continuing until approximately 2004. Realistic investors know that the stock market goes down as well as up, and it is a lot less fun when the market plunges.

Although some lawyers seek equity participation in their clients, many clients favor this development. When clients pay lawyers in "stock," or "warrants," etc., they ease their cash flow problems by using another "currency" to buy legal services. Those lawyers who are "risk-preferrers" or "risk-takers" increase their utility by giving them a chance to buy into the client with their own "currency," legal services. This should lead to the market for legal services becoming more competitive (because the clients and lawyers offer more products), and more efficient (because there is a better allocation of risk). The general society should also benefit because the greater variety of payment methods allows a broader ranger of legal services to be made more affordable to a broader ranger of clients.[15]

Although good economic reasons exist why both some clients and some lawyers favor this development, there are still ethical risks. The Model Rules of Professional Conduct do not impose any *per se* prohibition preventing a lawyer from acquiring an ownership interest in a client, either in lieu of a cash fee for providing legal services or as an investment opportunity in connection with such services. However, this arrangement can lead to ethics problems. ABA Formal Opinion 00-418[16] analyzes the basic issues that arise when a lawyer takes stock in lieu of a cash fee. First, the fee is still subject to the bedrock, elementary ethics rule that the total fee must still be reasonable.

ABA Formal Opinion 00-418 also makes clear that Rule 1.8(a) applies to such arrangements, and if the lawyers trade legal services for stock, they must in addition satisfy Rule 1.5(a)'s requirement that the total fee be reasonable. The stock should be valued

---

[14]*See* John S. Dzienkowski & Robert J. Peroni, *The Decline in Lawyer Independence: Lawyer Equity Investments in Clients*, 81 TEXAS L. REV. 405 (2002); Gwyneth E. McAlpine, Comment, *Getting a Piece of the Action: Should Lawyers Be Allowed to Invest in Their Clients' Stock?*, 47 U.C.L.A. L. REV. 549 (1999); Debra Baker, *Who Wants to be a Millionaire?*, 86 A.B.A. J., Feb. 2000, at pp. 36, 37; Cameron

Stracher, *Beyond Billable Hours*, WALL STREET JOURNAL, Feb. 12, 2001, at p. A26.

[15]Jason M. Klein, *No Fool for a Client: the Finance and Incentives Behind Stock-based Compensation for Corporate Attorneys*, 1999 COLUM. BUS. L. REV. 329, 362 (1999).

[16]ABA Formal Opinion 00-418 (July 7, 2000).

at the time it is acquired and the "reasonableness" should be determined at that time.[17] The agreement between the lawyer and the corporate entity should also specify what the lawyer is to do for that fee. The lawyer, pursuant to Rule 1.7(b), should take care to avoid conflicts between the client's interests and the lawyer's own personal economic interests as an owner. The lawyer must also make sure that, pursuant to Rule 2.1, he is exercising independent judgment in advising the client concerning legal matters.

Finally, the Opinion cautions that lawyers should be aware that this fee arrangement may lead to conflicts of interest. For example, there may be problems under Rule 1.8(j) if the company's only asset is a cause of action, or under Rule 1.7(b) if the stock is or becomes a major asset of the lawyer.

The Opinion warns lawyers, that pursuant to Rule 1.8(a)(3), the lawyer must give the client a reasonable opportunity to seek the advice of an independent counsel in the transaction and the client must consent to the transaction in writing. But then it states: "Although it is better practice to set forth all the salient features of the transaction in a written document, compliance with Rule 1.8(a) does not require reiteration of details that the client already knows from other sources."[18]

One should be aware that an oral agreement is not worth the paper on which it is printed, so that the lawyer takes risks when he or she relies on oral waivers of "details." The obligation of the lawyer is to disclose to the client what is happening in a way that brings home to the client the significance of the information communicated. Written statements of these details serve to bring home to the client the significance of the waiver, and that protects both the lawyer and the client. The Formal Opinion recognizes this fact of life by adding, just after the previously quoted

---

[17]*Holmes v. Loveless*, 122 Wash. App. 470, 94 P.3d 338 (Div. 1 2004) (law firm agreed to discount its billing in exchange for a 5% share of the revenue of a real estate project; court opined that reasonableness may need to be examined over the course of the agreement).

[18]ABA Formal Opinion 00-418 (July 7, 2000) states:

Although it is better practice to set forth all the salient features of the transaction in a written document, compliance with Rule 1.8(a) does not require reiteration of details that the client already knows from other sources. Indeed, too much detail may tend to distract attention from the material terms. Nonetheless, the lawyer bears the risk of omitting a term that seems unimportant at the time, but later becomes significant because she has the burden of showing reasonable compliance with Rule 1.8(a)(1). A good faith effort to explain in understandable language the important features of the particular arrangement and its material consequences as far as reasonably can be ascertained at the time of the stock acquisition should satisfy the full disclosure requirements of Rule 1.8(a).

ABA Formal Opinion 00-418 (July 7, 2000) (footnote omitted).

461

sentence, the following phrase: "the lawyer bears the risk of omitting a term that seems unimportant at the time."[19]

Despite the ABA's endorsement of lawyer equity investments in clients, lawyers should proceed on such ventures with great care.[20] A law firm should have a formalized policy on dealing with investments in clients. Unsupervised investments by individual lawyers pose risks of insider trading and a direct effect on the judgment of the lawyer performing the work for the client. Some firms place such investments in a separate investment partnership and remove the decision to sell the stock from the lawyers who work on the client's matter.

Ongoing legal representations tend to pose the greatest conflicts of interest because lawyers are asked to provide independent judgment on matters that could have an immediate affect on the stock price. Clients should certainly be free to reject efforts by law firms to invest in their clients if they so choose. Undoubtedly, the presence of a law firm investment enhances the risk of malpractice actions when malpractice plaintiff seeks to argue that the law firm should have taken an action, but was unwilling to do so because that action might have a short term adverse effect on the value of the stock.

§ 1.8–2(b) Acquiring an Interest Adverse to a Client

Rule 1.8(a) prohibits a lawyer from knowingly acquiring "an ownership, possessory, security, or other pecuniary interest adverse to a client" unless the lawyer meets the requirements examined above in the context of business transactions with a client.[21]

For example, unless a lawyer met the requirements of Rule 1.8(a), he could not purchase a mortgage from a bank where the borrower was a current client of the lawyer. To do so would place the lawyer's interest in collecting on the loan in conflict with the

---

[19]*Passante v. McWilliam*, 53 Cal.App.4th 1240, 1248, 62 Cal.Rptr.2d 298, 302 (1997), holding that a lawyer for a corporation should be denied recovery of $32 million for stock of the corporation that its board previously had authorized to be issued to him in connection with his legal services because the lawyer failed to advise board to consult independent counsel about the transaction. This case emphasizes that, "even though an equity billing arrangement may be fair and reasonable in substance to a client, courts are willing to impose penalties on law firms that do not comply with procedural requirements in order to create the proper incentives for compliance by other law firms." Poonam Puri, *Taking Stock of Taking Stock*, 87 CORNELL L. REV. 99, 138 (2001).

[20]For a comprehensive examination of the problems created by lawyer equity investments in clients, see John S. Dzienkowski & Robert J. Peroni, *The Decline in Lawyer Independence: Lawyer Equity Investments in Clients*, 81 TEXAS L. REV. 405 (2002).

[21]Rule 1.8(a).

client who is obligated to repay the loan.[22] On the other hand, if the lawyer met the three requirements of 1.8(a), the lawyer's purchase of the mortgage loan from the bank would be permissible.

§ 1.8–3 RULE 1.8(b)—USING CLIENT INFORMATION

In general, a lawyer may not use client secrets or confidences to the disadvantage of her client.[1] This prohibition applies equally to protect a former client *if* the information has not become generally known.[2]

Note that a lawyer violates this rule of confidentiality even if the lawyer does not disclose the information to anyone. What is relevant is that she *uses* the information to the client's detriment. If the agent is allowed to use confidential information for purposes that cause injury to the principal, that would tend to harm the freedom of communication that should exist between principal and agent. It also violates the fiduciary duties that a lawyer owes to her client.

For example, assume that Lawyer Alpha learned, in confidence, that Client is planning to buy certain farm land in order to build a new shopping center. Lawyer then secretly visits the farmer and buys this land, but does not reveal to the farmer any of Client's secret information. Lawyer plans to raise the price in reselling the land to Client because she learned, in confidence from Client, that this location is more important to Client than the farmer suspects. Lawyer has violated her obligations under Rule 1.6 and Rule 1.8(a).[3]

The Model Code provided that the lawyer may not *use* a client

---

[22] A similar conflict of interest arises when a lawyer is involved with the finance company that loans money to the client for litigation fees. Utah State Bar Ethics Advisory Opinion Comm. Op. 06–03 (Dec. 8, 2006), *noted in* ABA/BNA MANUAL ON PROFESSIONAL CONDUCT, Current Reports News 15 (Jan. 24, 2007), deemed highly improper an arrangement whereby a client might receive a loan from a company capitalized and owned by the lawyer's relatives and managed by the lawyer himself. The lawyer's duty to his client would be incompatible with his duties to the finance company and his loyalties to his relatives. The committee also disapproved of the lawyer personally taking out a loan, the repayment of which would be calculated based on whether and how

much the lawyer recovered on a contingent fee basis.

[Section 1.8–3]

[1] Rule 1.8(b); DR 4-101(B)(2).

[2] Rule 1.9(c)(1). *See* EC 4-6.

[3] Rule 1.8(a) & Comment 1; DR 4-101(B)(1),(2).

This principle reflects the basic duties that any agent owes to his principal. *Chalupiak v. Stahlman*, 368 Pa. 83, 87–91, 81 A.2d 577, 580–81 (1951). Restatement of the Law of Agency, Second (1958), § 395, states: "Unless otherwise agreed, an agent is subject to a duty to the principal not to use . . . information . . . acquired by him during the course of or on account of his agency * * * to the injury of the principal, on his own account . . . although such information does

confidence or secret for the lawyer's own advantage (or to advantage a third person), unless the client consents. Without such consent, the lawyer violates the Model Code even though the lawyer does not *reveal* the secret information. This prohibition is applicable whether or not the client suffers economic harm.[4]

This prohibition on the use of client information is an old one.[5] It reflects the basic agency rule that no agent (whether or not a lawyer) may use the principal's secret information to the agent's advantage even if there is no detriment to the principal and even if using the information does not require revealing it.[6]

Under the law of agency, if the agent uses confidential information of the principal for personal gain, then the agent must turn over to the principal any profits. For example, if a "corporation has decided to operate an enterprise at a place where land values will be increased because of such operation, a corporate officer who takes advantage of his special knowledge to buy land in the vicinity is accountable for the profits he makes, *even though such purchases have no adverse effect upon the enterprise.*"[7] This rule is not applicable if the "information is a matter of general knowledge."[8]

The theory behind the Model Code—and the law of agency that the Code reflects—is that this confidential or secret information belongs to the client. The lawyer may not sell it or use it to the lawyer's own advantage unless the client consents.

The Rules have no section that corresponds to the Model Code, DR 4-101(B)(3). Moreover, the Comment to Rule 1.8(b) appears to negate the possibility that the Rules could be interpreted to incorporate DR 4-101(B)(3). That Comment provides: "Use of information relating to the representation *to the disadvantage of the* client violated the lawyer's duty of loyalty." However, the very next sentence says: "Paragraph (b) applies when the information is used to benefit either the lawyer or a third person, such

---

not relate to the transaction in which he is then employed. . . ."

   [4]DR 4-101(B)(3).

   [5]*See* ABA Canons of Professional Ethics, Canon 11 (1908), and Canon 37 (1908), as amended.

   See, e.g. Healy v. Gray, 184 Iowa 111, 119, 168 N.W. 222, 225 (1918): "[A]n attorney will not be permitted to make use of knowledge, or information, acquired by him through his professional relations with his client, or in the conduct of his client's busi-

ness to his own advantage or profit."

   [6]Restatement of the Law of Agency, Second (1958), § 388, and Comment c. *See also* W. Edward Sell, Agency §§ 132–33 (Foundation Press, 1975).

   [7]Restatement of the Law of Agency, Second (1958), § 388, at Comment c. *See also id.* at § 395, Comment *e* (emphasis added).

   [8]Restatement of the Law of Agency, Second (1958), § 388, at § 395.

as another client or business associate of the lawyer."[9] That second sentence, if read alone, appears to place a broad prohibition on the lawyer. The next sentence gives the following example: "For example, if a lawyer learns that a client intends to purchase and develop several parcels of land, the lawyer may not use that information to purchase one of the parcels *in competition with the client* or to recommend that another client make such a purchase. The Rule does not prohibit uses that do not disadvantage the client."[10] The negative implication is that there is no ethical problem if the lawyer's purchase of the land and use of the client's "insider" information does not harm the client. The next sentence appears to affirm that negative implication because it says: "The Rule *does not* prohibit uses that do not disadvantage the client."[11]

The Model Code forbade the conduct described in this Comment even without the condition stated in italics (*"to the disadvantage of the client"*). In addition, even if a jurisdiction that adopts this provision of the Model Rules, a lawyer who used client information for the lawyer's advantage would still have to account to the client for any profits made, under the general law of agency. Thus, a lawyer who relies on this Comment of the Model Rules for a safe harbor will find (when a court, pursuant to the law of agency, orders an accounting to the client for any profits made) that this harbor is heavily mined.[12] The lawyer may not use, "on his own account," confidential information acquired from a former client.[13]

If the lawyer uses his client's inside information in the course

---

[9] Rule 1.8, Comment 5 (emphasis added). Prior to the 2002 revisions, Comment 5 had read: "Paragraph (b) prohibits *disadvantageous* use of client information, unless a client gives informed consent. . . . " (emphasis added).

[10] Rule 1.8, Comment 5 (emphasis added).

[11] Rule 1.8, Comment 5 (emphasis added).

[12] Ronald D. Rotunda, *Judicial Conference—Second Circuit: RICO and the Proposed Restatement of the Law Governing Lawyers*, (Sept. 7, 1990), 136 Federal Rules Decisions 236, 266 to 271 (1991).

[13] Restatement of the Law of Agency, Second (1958), § 395, 396(b), (c). *See also* Robert C. Hacker & Ronald D. Rotunda, *Corporate Confidences and the Duty to Refrain from Insider Trading*, 6 CORPORATION L. REV. 53 (1983).

Initially, the Restatement of the Law Governing Lawyers, Third, § 111(1) (Tent.Draft No. 3, 1990), followed the Model Rules. However, the final draft of the Restatement of the Law Governing Lawyers, Third, § 60(2) (Official Draft 2000) provides that, unless the client consents, "a lawyer who uses confidential information of a client for the lawyer's pecuniary gain other than in the practice of law must account to the client for any profits made." So now the Restatement of Agency and the Restatement of the Law Governing Lawyers are consistent.

The Comments to § 60 explain: "The lawyer codes [on ethics] differ over whether such self-enriching use or disclosure constitutes a disciplinary violation in the absence of prejudice to the client." Restatement of the Law

of buying or selling stock, he will find that he is subject to criminal prosecution. *United States v. O'Hagan*[14] makes that clear. As the Supreme Court held, a lawyer is subject to Rule 10b-5 liability for trading on inside information obtained while his firm was representing a client. The SEC prosecuted the lawyer criminally for securities fraud under the so-called "misappropriation theory," *i.e.*, he defrauded both his law firm and its client, persons to whom he owed a fiduciary duty, by taking their information and using it to benefit himself. The Supreme Court upheld the application of the misappropriation theory to Rule 10b-5 cases and rejected any claim that there is no "fiduciary duty" owed. The lawyer's use of the information is inherently "deceptive," and the fraud is "consummated" when the information is used "in connection with the purchase or sale of [a] security."[15]

Thus, in this situation, the lawyer would be liable under the law of agency, and would be subject to discipline under the Model Code. If the matter involved insider trading of stocks he would also be subject to criminal liability. If the lawyer sought refuge in Model Rule 1.8(b), he would be sadly disappointed. But, he should be able to argue that he should not be subject to discipline under the Model Rules because he did not "reveal" the "information" to third parties and did not use it "to the disadvantage of his client."[16]

§ 1.8–4 RULE 1.8(c)—ACCEPTING GIFTS FROM CLIENTS

Because of the danger that the lawyer may overreach the client and abuse the fiduciary relationship, lawyers should observe several important ethical restrictions when accepting client gifts. Some gifts do not involve the drafting of any instruments. In contrast, a gift given by a will demands that a legal instrument be drafted. A typical case involving no legal instrument occurs when the client, happy with the lawyer's work, decides to give a gift, which may be nominal (a basket of fruit) or substantial (e.g., a large amount of cash in addition to the agreed upon fee, or an expensive gold watch).

Governing Lawyers, Third, § 60(2) (Official Draft 2000), at Comment *j*.

[14]*United States v. O'Hagan*, 521 U.S. 642, 117 S.Ct. 2199, 138 L.Ed.2d 724 (1997). In this case, Dorsey & Whitney in Minneapolis was retained by Grand Metropolitan PLC (Grand Met), a London corporation, in an plan to acquire Pillsbury, a large publicly-traded company. O'Hagan, a Dorsey & Whitney partner not working on the matter, purchased call option contracts and shares of Pillsbury stock on the open market. When Grand Met announced its takeover plans, Pillsbury stock rose from $39 to $60 and O'Hagan made over $4.3 million.

[15]*See* 521 U.S. at 643–44, 117 S.Ct. at 2203.

[16]Ronald D. Rotunda, *Proposed Restatement of the Law Governing Lawyers* (Sept. 7, 1990), *reprinted in*, 136 FEDERAL RULES DECISIONS 236, 266 to 271 (1991).

The old Model Code had no disciplinary rule dealing with such cases. On the aspirational level, the Code recommended that the lawyer should, before accepting the gift, advise the client to secure "disinterested advice from an independent competent person who is cognizant of all the circumstances."[1] This other person need not be a lawyer. The client need not secure such advice but the lawyer should urge that course of action. Under EC 5-5, this review by a third person should take place regardless of whether the gift is substantial or nominal. If the transfer of the gift requires an instrument, such as a will, the Code provided—on the ethical rather than disciplinable level—that another lawyer should prepare the instrument except in undefined "exceptional circumstances."[2]

Because the Model Code drew no distinction between substantial and nominal gifts, it went too far by regulating client gifts that are trivial. In contrast, the Rule 1.8(c) restrictions, prior to the 2002 revisions, did not go far enough, for they did not purport to regulate at all any client gifts that do not require the lawyer to prepare an instrument.[3]

The drafters of the 2002 Model Rules cured this problem. The new Rule 1.8(c) continues the restrictions on preparing an instrument. In addition, it now includes a clause that prohibits a lawyer from *soliciting* a substantial gift from a client.[4] Prior to this amendment, if a lawyer solicited a substantial gift that did not require a legal instrument, the Rule theoretically did not regulate such behavior. Therefore, under the 2002 version of Rule 1.8(c), a lawyer may not ask a client to give the lawyer a bonus to recognize the client's extra-appreciation of the lawyer's work. The client can come with this idea on his own, but the lawyer may not put a sign on the desk that says that tipping is gratefully acknowledged.

If the gift is substantial, *and* if its delivery requires that a legal instrument be drafted, then the lawyer may not draft the instrument.[5] The client should secure "detached advice" from an-

---

[Section 1.8–4]

[1] EC 5-5.

[2] EC 5-5.

[3] Rule 1.8(c), *prior to* the 2002 revisions, stated: "A lawyer shall not prepare an instrument giving the lawyer or a person related to the lawyer as parent, child, sibling, or spouse any substantial gift including a testamentary gift, except where the client is related to the donee."

[4] Rule 1.8(c).

[5] In *Attorney Grievance Commission of Maryland v. Stein*, 373 Md. 531, 819 A.2d 372 (2003), the attorney violated Maryland's Rule 1.8(c) when he drafted a will for his client providing a substantial gift to himself. The issue before the court was the appropriate sanction. The court imposed an indefinite suspension upon Stein, stating "[w]e consider a violation of Rule 1.8(c) to be most serious." 819

other lawyer.[6] The client may not use another lawyer in the disqualified lawyer's firm. Instead, an independent lawyer in another law firm should draft the instrument.[7]

The lawyer in the other firm who drafts the instrument must act as a lawyer and explain the ramifications to the client, including the fact that the client does not owe any obligation to the lawyer to make any gift. If the disqualified lawyer prepared all of the papers and sent them to another lawyer in another firm to give to the client without giving any legal advice, the client would later be able to attack the outside lawyer's independent by arguing that he did not act as an independent lawyer, just a scrivener.

If the gift is substantial but does not require an instrument, and if the lawyer does not solicit it, then the text of Rule 1.8(c) is inapplicable. However the Comment adopts a "general standards of fairness" test.[8] "A lawyer may accept a gift from a client, if the transaction meets general standards of fairness."[9]

The Comment goes on to acknowledge that Rule 1.8(c) may not prohibit the lawyer from taking the gift, but it warns that agency and fiduciary duty law presumptively treat client gifts as fraudulent. Such law also places the burden on the lawyer to demonstrate the fairness of the transaction. The failure to meet the burden often leads courts to find a gift voidable by the client on the grounds of the doctrine of undue influence.

If a lawyer cannot accept or solicit a substantial gift for herself, then the lawyer may not solicit the gift for persons related to her as "spouse, child, grandchild, parent, grandparent, or other relatives or individuals with whom the lawyer or the client maintains a close, familial relationship."[10] This prohibition is necessary to prevent lawyers from getting around the Rule by structuring client gifts to related persons: some people launder money; others launder bequests.

Two exceptions exist to Rule 1.8(c). This Rule does not apply when the lawyer is related to the client under the definition of re-

---

A.2d at 379. However, the majority declined to impose a further sanction of requiring Stein to disclaim his interest in his deceased client's estate. The majority believed there was no precedent for such a sanction. It acknowledged that there may be the potential for a "cost/benefit analysis" leading to a lawyer's violation of the rule, but it found there was no evidence that Stein had engaged in such an analysis. The dissent was troubled by the failure to implement "the one sanction that, more than any other, will assure that the Rule is followed." *Id.* at 381. "If lawyers know that a violation of the Rule will bring them no financial gain, they will have no incentive to violate the Rule, and that, above all else, is what will protect the public." *Id.* at 382.

[6] Rule 1.8, Comment 2.

[7] Rule 1.8(k).

[8] Rule 1.8, Comment 6. *See also* Restatement of the Law Governing Lawyers, Third, § 127 ("A Client Gift to Lawyer") (Official Draft 2000).

[9] Rule 1.8, Comment 6.

[10] Rule 1.8(c).

lationship used above. This exception makes sense because lawyers and family members should be free to provide and accept legal work and argue for their views on disposition of property. Of course, other law may affect the validity of such documents or transfers. For example, if a lawyer related to the client drafts a will giving the lawyer a disproportionate percentage of the assets, wills and estates law may provide a challenge for such a representation between family members.

A second exception is contained in the Comments. The drafters to the 2002 Model Rules added language that announces that Rule 1.8(c) should not be interpreted to prohibit a lawyer from seeking to be appointed as executor of the client's assets or a similar lucrative fiduciary position.[11] Such conflicts are handled under the general conflicts of interests (Rule 1.7). Rule 1.8(c) does not impose a *per se* ban.[12]

§ 1.8–5 RULE 1.8(d)—PUBLICATION RIGHTS

Consider the situation where the lawyer negotiates with the client for publication rights to a particular matter before that matter has ended and while the lawyer is still in the employ of the client. There is a danger that the lawyer, in bargaining with the client, may overreach. For example, the client, needing the lawyer's services, may feel pressured to waive the attorney-client privilege, so that the attorney can later write a more interesting book. Also, the lawyer, in his representation of the client, may be consciously or unconsciously influenced to "enhance the value of his publication rights to the prejudice of his client."[1]

The Code prohibited the lawyer from acquiring from the client an interest in publication rights relating to the subject matter "[p]rior to the conclusion of all aspects of the matter giving rise to his employment. . . ."[2] Out of an overabundance of caution, this also forbids acquiring such rights if the matter giving rise to the employment still continues, even though another lawyer now

---

[11]Rule 1.8, Comment 8.

[12]Comment 8 states that the lawyer seeking such an appointment for himself or for others in the firm must inform the client about the wishes and the consequences. Also, the client needs to give informed consent to the lawyer or related lawyer as serving as a fiduciary.

[Section 1.8–5]

[1]EC 5-4. *Accord* Rule 1.8, Comment 3.

[2]DR 5-104(B).

represents the client and the first lawyer's employment regarding that matter has ended.[3]

The Rules, in contrast, only prohibit acquiring such rights "[p]rior to the conclusion of representation of a client. . . ."[4] Once the representation has ended, the lawyer has no special powers or advantages in negotiating any publication rights from her former client. The lawyer would be in no better bargaining position than any other person who wanted to write a book on the client's legal adventures.

Rule 1.8(d), like its predecessor, DR 5–104(B), exists not simply to protect the client but also to protect the interest of the judicial system in competent representation. If a lawyer decides to forego a certain motion because it would reduce the publicity value of the media rights, it is not only the criminal defendant who is hurt, but also the system of justice. Even if the defendant wishes to waive rights, and even if the defendant is competent and informed enough to do so, the system of justice has an interest in making sure that innocent people are not falsely convicted. Therefore, neither the Code nor the Rules provide for client waiver of these restrictions.

However, some jurisdictions take a different view of the issue. California (ignoring the systemic interests and basing its decision on the California Rules—which in this respect are not modeled on the Code or Rules) does allow for client waiver.[5]

If the lawyer represented the client in a criminal matter and the representation is completed, the lawyer, before negotiating for portrayal rights with a former client, must consider the Second Circuit decision of *In re Von Bulow*.[6] This decision examined the effect on the attorney-client privilege of a former client's consent to permit a lawyer to author a book on the subject of the representation. The court held that such consent does amount to a limited waiver of the privilege. Therefore, a victim or the victim's family may use some of the information contained in a lawyer's book to establish civil liability against the former client.

After *In re Von Bulow*, lawyers must assess the risk that portrayal rights may waive some or all of the privilege and therefore expose the client to enhanced civil liability based upon the same facts as the lawyer's criminal representation. At a min-

---

[3]EC 5-4.

[4]Rule 1.8(d). The Code referred to "publication rights," but the Rules use a term that the drafters thought more expansive—"literary or media rights." *Compare* DR 5-104(A), *with* Rule 1.8(d); *see* Code Comparison 5. *See also* Restatement of the Law Governing Lawyers § 36(3) (Official Draft 2000).

[5]*See, e.g., Maxwell v. Superior Court of Los Angeles County*, 30 Cal.3d 606, 180 Cal.Rptr. 177, 639 P.2d 248 (1982).

[6]*In re Von Bulow*, 828 F.2d 94 (2d Cir.1987).

imum, the lawyer needs to disclose such risk to the former client. In some cases, the increased risk may be so great that the lawyer should refrain from seeking portrayal rights from the client.[7]

If the lawyer represents the client in a dispute or other transaction concerning literary property, *e.g.*, a copyright claim, the lawyer may contract for a reasonable contingent fee, that is, a reasonable share of the ownership of the literary property, assuming no other rules are violated. The prohibition on publication rights is not meant to cover this situation.[8] This situation does not raise the problem that Rule 1.8(d) was intended to solve. The lawyer is simply seeking a percentage of the res, or recovery. In some cases, the recovery may be a parcel of land. In other cases, it may be a sum of money. In a case involving a copyright dispute, it may be the value of the royalty. This type of contingent fee does not violate Rule 1.8(d).[9]

§ 1.8–6 RULE 1.8(e)—FINANCIAL ADVANCES TO THE CLIENT

Expenses of Litigation. When representing a client in a matter involving litigation, the lawyer may not provide financial assistance to the client, but may advance or guarantee the expenses of litigation, such as the expenses of a medical examination.[1]

Originally, the ethics rules placed several important limitations on financial advances. The Model Code had a specific requirement that the client must remain "ultimately liable" for

---

[7]In the O.J. Simpson case, many of the lawyers on O.J.'s "Dream Team" authored books on the criminal trial; however, their books state that none of the information in the book is based upon confidential information provided by O.J. the former client. Instead, the book is based upon public information contained in the record. This approach seeks to prevent a court from holding that O.J. waived some or all of his privilege in consenting to a former lawyer's portrayal rights based upon the criminal representation.

[8]Rule 1.8, Comment 3. *See also* Restatement of the Law Governing Lawyers § 36(3) (Official Draft 2000).

[9]It does not violate Rule 1.8(j), because Rule 1.8(j)(2) specifically allows a contract for a reasonable contingent fee in a civil case, even though that is a proprietary interest in the

cause of action or subject matter of the litigation.

[Section 1.8–6]

[1]Rule 1.8(e). Restatement of the Law Governing Lawyers, Third, §§ 36(1), (2) (Official Draft 2000).

Of course, a fee agreement that does not violate Rule 1.8(d) might violate other rules, such as the prohibition against excessive fees. While the trend in the law is to allow lawyers flexibility to advance and/or pay for court costs, a few commentators have unsuccessfully urged very strict restrictions. Wendy Watrous, *Lawyer or Loan Shark? Rule 1.8(e) Of Louisiana's Rules Of Professional Conduct Blurs the Line*, 48 Loyola L. Rev. 117, 118 (2002): "This comment argues that Rule 1.8(e) should be rewritten to prohibit attorneys from lending money to clients for any reason whatsoever

471

these expenses,[2] but also advised (inconsistently) that the lawyer should not normally sue to collect his fee except to prevent fraud or gross imposition,[3] and that lawyers should charge the less fortunate clients a smaller fee or no fee.[4]

The Rules are more straightforward on this point and better reflect what lawyers do in practice. The Rules eliminate the requirement of client reimbursement and also allow the lawyer to pay directly an indigent's litigation expenses and court costs without the client remaining ultimately liable.[5]

Rule 1.8(e) states that lawyers may not provide financial assistance to a client other than advancing litigation expenses and court costs. Litigation expenses include costs expended for experts, studies on how the accident occurred, medical expenses to determine the extent of a plaintiffs' injury, and costs to transport the client to the place of trial. Court costs include court filing fees and transcript costs. A lawyer may not advance or pay a client's living or general medical expenses because these expenses are not within the permitted court costs and expenses of litigation category.

If the client is not indigent, the lawyer must incorporate such advances in the fee agreement and provide that they be repaid out of the proceeds of recovery.[6] If the client is indigent, the lawyer may simply pay such expenses and not make them recoverable from any proceeds of the litigation.

Loans. In some cases, the client's injuries prevent her from earning sufficient monies to support a family. Consider, for example, the situation where the client is threatened with eviction from an apartment, and she lacks the funds necessary to pay basic sustenance expenses for her family. Assume, moreover, that the client had an excellent chance of prevailing in the personal injury action because of the defendant's liability. In such a situation, some lawyers turned to Rule 1.8(a) to provide a loan to the client; they hoped to satisfy the business transaction Rule as a way to get around the prohibition of Rule 1.8(e). The 2002 revisions to the Rule prohibit that loan. The drafters of the 2002

---

because, as time has shown, anything less than a complete ban on loans from attorneys to clients offers too much potential for abuse by unscrupulous lawyers."

See also La. R. Prof. Conduct, Rule 1.8(e) (adopted Jan. 5, 2006) (providing detailed guidelines on financial assistance to clients), *noted in* 22 ABA/BNA MANUAL ON PROFESSIONAL CONDUCT, Current Reports News 20 (Jan. 11, 2006).

[2] DR 5-103(B).

[3] EC 2-23.

[4] EC 2-16

[5] Rule 1.8(e)(1), (2).

[6] Rule 1.5(c) specifies that in contingent fee agreements lawyers must directly address whether such litigation expenses advanced by a lawyer are paid before or after deducting the attorneys' fees.

Rules wanted to eliminate that loophole. They made clear that Rule 1.8(e) prohibits "making or guaranteeing loans for living expenses, because to do so would encourage clients to pursue lawsuits that might not otherwise be brought and because such assistance gives lawyers too great a financial stake in the litigation."[7]

Bail. While bail is an expense of litigation, the Rules do not give the lawyer carte blanche authority to advance bail funds to the client. In the case where the lawyer represents a defendant, there are the limits to the lawyer's ability to arrange for, or post, bail for a client if the lawyer represents the client in that matter. While an ABA Formal Opinion concludes that there is no per se prohibition against posting such a bond, it suggests that, in all but a few unusual circumstances, such action is prohibited because the lawyer's personal interest in recovering the advanced amount would "create a significant risk that her representation of the client would be materially limited" and thus would violate Model Rule 1.7(a).[8]

Rule 1.7(b) would permit continued representation even in the face of a conflict between the personal interests of a lawyer and the interests of a client *if* the client gives informed consent. However, "[i]n all but the rarest of circumstances" the unique conditions of incarceration generally imply that the client's acquiescence will not be significantly genuine and voluntary to qualify as "informed consent" under Rule 1.7(b). The Opinion then listed possible circumstances where posting a bond may be permissible, including where: (1) the amount involved is negligible, (2) the lawyer is a friend of the family of the client who can expect indemnification from the family, or (3) situations such as civil

---

[7]Rule 1.8, Comment 10.

May a lawyer arrange a loan for a client with an independent loan company? See Maine Board of Bar Overseers Professional Ethics Comm'n, Op. 191, (Dec. 21, 2006), *noted in* ABA/BNA MANUAL ON PROFESSIONAL CONDUCT, Current Reports News 16 (Jan. 24, 2007). Opinion 191 refused to issue a definitive ethical decision on lawyers helping their clients obtain litigation loans from a company that takes a cut of the recovery in personal injury cases. The commission cautioned: this arrangement would have to satisfy the Maine criminal champerty statute, but even if the loans are criminally legal, the lawyer should evaluate the arrangement for conflicts of interest, confidentiality

breaches, and interests adverse to the client. *See generally* Julia M. McLaughlin, *Litigation Funding: Charting a Legal and Ethical Course*, 31 VT. L. REV. 615 (2007).

[8]ABA Formal Opinion 03-432 (2004).

For an example of an unusual conflict of interest created by the lawyer arranging for bail, see the case of *Mississippi Commission on Judicial Performance v. Atkinson*, 645 So.2d 1331 (Miss.1994). The court imposed a public reprimand on a lawyer who set the accused's bail while the lawyer was serving as municipal judge; the lawyer then sought to reduce his client's bail while acting as a practicing attorney representing the accused.

rights cases where it is likely that no one else will post bond on behalf of the criminal defendant.

§ 1.8–7 RULE 1.8(f)—ACCEPTING COMPENSATION FROM NON-CLIENTS

Third-Party Payers. Sometimes a third party may offer to pay the lawyer to represent the client. Parents may pay a lawyer to represent their son who is charged with a crime. Or, an employer may pay a lawyer to represent an employee who is sued for matters within the scope of employment.

Not surprisingly, third parties who offer to pay for another person's legal expenses often have interests that differ from the interests of the represented client.[1] Thus, Rule 1.8(f) addresses the conflicts of interest and the lawyer's duty to prevent third party payors from interfering in the representation of the client.

Basic Principles. If someone other than the client pays for the client's legal services, the lawyer's obligations are still to the client. The lawyer may not allow this third party (who is paying for the services or who recommended the lawyer) to interfere with the lawyer's professional judgment.[2] The lawyer must make sure that the client knows about, and consents to, the third party compensating the lawyer.[3] This arrangement must also respect the client's right to confidentiality.[4]

Insurance and Rule 1.8. Insurance companies often fit within the contours of Rule 1.8(f). The insurance company will pay the lawyer to represent the insured. Sometimes this arrangement leads to questions of alleged conflict of interests. This conflicts issue is discussed above, under the analysis of Rule 1.7.

In some instances, the fee agreement between the lawyer and the third party creates a conflict of interest between the third party and the client. For example, if the agreement permits the third party from discontinuing payment for the representation upon the occurrence of certain events, the conflict is governed by

---

[Section 1.8–7]

[1] Rule 1.8, Comment 11.

[2] Rule 5.4(c); DR 5-107(B). *Cf.* Rule 1.8(f). *See* ABA Formal Opinion 02-428 (Aug. 9, 2002) ("Drafting Will on Recommendation of a Potential Beneficiary Who Also is a Client").

[3] Rule 1.8(f)(2); DR 5-107(A)(1).

[4] Rule 1.8(f)(3). The third party payer may want to know matters about the client that are confidential. The lawyer may not reveal this information, even though the third party is paying the lawyer, unless the client consents. Clients may always waive their confidentiality rights, this waiver is effective only if the lawyer makes a full disclosure to the client. Rule 1.6(a), 1.8(b). DR 4-101(B)(3), (C)(1).

In order for the consent to be effective, the lawyer must communicate to the client enough information to permit the client to appreciate the significance of the waiver. *E.g.*, Restatement of the Law Governing Lawyers, Third, § 134 ("Compensation or Direction by a Third Person") (Official Draft 2000).

Rule 1.7.[5] The lawyer must examine the effect of the conflict to determine whether the lawyer can provide competent and diligent representation and obtain the client's consent.

§ 1.8–8 RULE 1.8(g)—AGGREGATE SETTLEMENTS

The lawyer, on behalf of her multiple clients, may negotiate an aggregate settlement of the civil claims, or an agreement of guilty or nolo contendere pleas covering multiple clients in a criminal case.[1] In such cases, however, each client must consent after consultation, which must include "disclosure of the existence and nature of all the claims involved and of the participation of each person in the settlement."[2] The drafters of the 2002 Model Rules added the requirement that such consent needs to be in a writing signed by the client.

Assume, for example, that Attorney Alpha represents 18 individual plaintiffs who entered into a prior agreement that majority rule would govern acceptance of a settlement. Defendant offered $155,000 for distribution to the group, which voted 13-5 to accept it. Notwithstanding the prior agreement, plaintiffs have a right to agree or refuse to agree once the settlement was made known to them.[3] Alpha obviously must disclose the settlement offer to each of his clients, and any of them can reject it.[4]

Rule 1.8(g) does not define the term, "aggregate settlement,"

---

[5]Rule 1.8, Comment 12.

[Section 1.8–8]

[1]Of course, there are very few situations where one lawyer represents multiple criminal defendants (persons, not entities) because of the inherent conflicts of interest that arise when one lawyer represents multiple clients in a criminal case.

[2]Rule 1.8(g). *Accord* DR 5-106(A).

[3]*Hayes v. Eagle-Picher Industries, Inc.*, 513 F.2d 892 (10th Cir.1975).

[4]**Fee Forfeiture as a Remedy.** In special situations, the court may require a lawyer to forfeit part or all of her fee as a remedy for ethics violations, if the lawyer has engaged in a "clear and serious" violation of her duty to her client. The court should take into account the gravity and timing of the violation, the lawyer's willfulness, the effect of the violation on the value of the lawyer's work for the client, any other threatened or actual harm to the client, and the adequacy of other remedies. Restatement of the Law Governing Lawyers, Third, § 37 (Official Draft 2000).

In connection with an alleged violation of the aggregate settlement principle in Rule 1.8(g), the Texas Supreme Court held out the possibility that fee forfeiture would be an appropriate remedy. In *Burrow v. Arce*, 997 S.W.2d 229 (Tex.1999), the Texas Supreme Court held that a lawyer "who breaches his fiduciary duty to his client may be required to forfeit all or part of his fee, irrespective of whether the breach caused the client actual damages." *Id.* at 232. The amount of the fee forfeited is a question for the court, not a jury. The court then reversed the lower court only insofar as it affirmed defendants' summary judgment based on affidavits the court found to be conclusory.

Turning to the allegation that the lawyers reached an aggregate settlement in violation of Rule 1.08(f) of the Texas Disciplinary Rules of Professional Conduct, the court noted that the lawyers subject to this rule

thus there has been some ambiguity as to when the rule applies. ABA Ethics Opinion 06–438 defines "aggregate settlement" as occurring when "when two or more clients who are represented by the same lawyer together resolve their claims or defenses or pleas. It is not necessary that all of the lawyer's clients facing criminal charges, having claims against the same parties, or having defenses against the same claims, participate in the matter's resolution for it to be an aggregate settlement or aggregated agreement. The rule applies when any two or more clients consent to have their matters resolved together."[5] This definition adopts an expansive view of aggregate settlement—essentially requiring compliance with Rule 1.8 whenever a lawyer is negotiating on behalf of multiple clients in resolving jointly any aspect of the clients' case.

The purpose of the aggregate settlement rule is to require that all lawyers representing multiple clients in an aggregate settlement provide each client with sufficient information to allow the client to decide whether to accept the settlement.[6] Such basic information must include the settlement offered to the other clients. Note that if the opposing party makes a settlement offer to only one of the lawyer's clients at a time, the aggregate settlement rule does not apply. However, such information may need to be shared with the other clients under Rule 1.7 because the lawyer's failure to do so materially limits the lawyer's representation of the client who does not have information about settlement offers made to other clients of the lawyer.

Rule 1.8(g) does not specifically describe the type of information that the lawyer must provide to the client to satisfy disclosure to the multiple clients. It states, "The lawyer's

---

argued that it "is too vague and impractical for any violation to warrant forfeiture of an attorney's fee. The lower courts did not find it necessary to address this argument, and given the difficult considerations involved, we believe it to be imprudent for us to decide the matter in the first instance without a full airing below. Even were we to address it, we could not render judgment for the Attorneys without considering whether the other alleged disciplinary rules violations might also justify forfeiture, an issue barely mentioned in all the parties' briefing. All these issues must be considered by the district court on remand." *Id.* at 246 (footnotes omitted).

[5]ABA Formal Opinion 06–438

(Feb. 10, 2006).

[6]Some commentators have argued that the aggregate settlement rule may impose costs on clients because it limits the flexibility that lawyers could exercise to obtain the largest possible settlement for all of their clients. *See* Charles Silver & Lynn Baker, *Mass Lawsuits and the Aggregate Settlement Rule*, 32 WAKE FOREST L. REV. 733 (1997); Charles Silver & Lynn Baker, *I Cut, You Choose: the Role of Plaintiffs' Counsel in Allocating Settlement Proceeds*, 84 VA. L. REV. 1541 (1998). *But see* Nancy J. Moore, *The Case Against Changing the Aggregate Settlement Rules in Mass Tort Lawsuits*, 41 S. TEX. L. REV. 149 (1999).

disclosure shall include the existence and nature of all of the claims or pleas involved and of the participation of each person in the settlement."[7] Thus, some lawyers believed that the disclosure could be general in nature describing the broad contours of the settlements received by the other clients. ABA Opinion 06–438 rejects this view and provides specific guidance as to what the lawyer must disclose:

> In order to ensure a valid and informed consent to an aggregate settlement or aggregated agreement, Rule 1.8(g) requires a lawyer to disclose, at a minimum, the following information to the clients for whom or to whom the settlement or agreement proposal is made:
>
> • The total amount of the aggregate settlement or the result of the aggregated agreement.
>
> • The existence and nature of all of the claims, defenses, or pleas involved in the aggregate settlement or aggregated agreement.
>
> • The details of every other client's participation in the aggregate settlement or aggregated agreement, whether it be their settlement contributions, their settlement receipts, the resolution of their criminal charges, or any other contribution or receipt of something of value as a result of the aggregate resolution. For example, if one client is favored over the other(s) by receiving non-monetary remuneration, that fact must be disclosed to the other client(s).
>
> • The total fees and costs to be paid to the lawyer as a result of the aggregate settlement, if the lawyer's fees and/or costs will be paid, in whole or in part, from the proceeds of the settlement or by an opposing party or parties.
>
> • The method by which costs (including costs already paid by the lawyer as well as costs to be paid out of the settlement proceeds) are to be apportioned among them.
>
> These detailed disclosures must be made in the context of a specific offer or demand. Accordingly, the informed consent required by the rule generally cannot be obtained in advance of the formulation of such an offer or demand.[8]

The requirement of a detailed disclosure is justified on the ground that the clients need to have this information to make an informed decision on whether to accept the settlement and to counteract the conflict of interest that results in an aggregate settlement offer.

The aggregate settlement rule does not resolve several issues. First, does the Rule apply to class action settlements? The drafters of the 2002 Model Rules made the following observation: "Lawyers representing a class of plaintiffs or defendants, or those proceeding derivatively, may not have a full client-lawyer relationship with each member of the class; nevertheless, such

---

[7]Rule 1.8(g).   (Feb. 10, 2006).

[8]ABA Formal Opinion 06–438

lawyers must comply with applicable rules regulating notification of class members and other procedural requirements designed to ensure adequate protection of the entire class."[9] This statement seems to say that if the lawyer has an attorney-client relationship with two or more individuals, the aggregate settlement rule would apply. However, one would assume in most class actions, the court will insist on controlling communications to the class.

Second, the Rule and its Comments do not make clear whether clients may waive the application of the Rule.[10] Some lawyers would like to obtain from their clients authority to advocate for the largest possible settlement and specific authority to accept it without subsequent authorization or authority to accept it by majority vote of the plaintiffs without needing to divide the settlement among the plaintiffs.[11] Once the settlement is agreed upon, the proceeds could be divided by the lawyer or a third party expert or through some procedure established by the lawyer. One argument for waiver of the Rule is that by removing the requirement that the lawyer disclose to each client the settlement given to the other clients, it gives the lawyer flexibility to negotiate the settlement. By settling for a large dollar amount instead of specific amounts for each client, the clients with the weaker cases may be paid more under such a system. These questions implicate concerns about the right to control settlement under Rule 1.2(a), the right to place reasonable limits on the representation under Rule 1.2(c), and whether disclosure requirements may be waived by clients.

Finally, some personal injury lawyers with multiple clients have sought to satisfy the aggregate settlement rule through a point system for allocating dollars for injuries sustained by the clients. The lawyers hire a doctor to assess points for each possible injury. Each plaintiff will agree to the point schedule and that the lawyer will seek to obtain a settlement of all claims in one dollar amount. Once the monies are obtained, they will be disbursed by giving a plaintiff his or points as the numerator over a denominator of all of the points allocated to all plaintiffs.

---

[9] Rule 1.8, Comment 13.

[10] As noted above, ABA Formal Opinion 06–438 states that the disclosure to the multiple clients must be done in the context of a specific offer and not in advance; therefore, it would seem to foreclose a waiver of the rule or prospective agreement on how to divide the settlement funds among the clients. It also cites with approval cases that hold that a majority vote approach to accepting a settlement violate Rule 1.8(g). *See* ABA Formal Opinion 06–438, at n.9 (Feb. 10, 2006).

[11] In corporate law, for example, parties can bind themselves through the use of a voting trust or voting agreement. *See* James D. Cox & Thomas Lee Hazen, Cox & Hazen on Corporations (2d ed. 2003)(examining statutory and judicial law on the use and abuse of voting trusts and agreements).

It is uncertain whether such a system for allocating the proceeds satisfies Rule 1.9(g).

§ 1.8–9 RULE 1.8(h)—LIMITING THE LAWYER'S LIABILITY FOR MALPRACTICE

§ 1.8–9(a) Prospective Limitations of Liability

§ 1.8–9(a)(1) Introduction

The lawyer may not require the client to enter into an agreement *prospectively* limiting the lawyer's liability to that client for malpractice.[1] The Code did not explicitly use the word "prospectively," but that must have been its intent.[2] Otherwise, if the former client sued the lawyer for malpractice, the former client (who now is separately represented by new counsel) could not settle with, and release, the first lawyer regarding that claim.

§ 1.8–9(a)(2) Limiting Malpractice Liability by Agreement

The Rules at one point forbade the lawyer from asking the client to agree to incompetent representation.[3] However, elsewhere the 1983 Model Rules made it clear that, if "permitted by law," the lawyer may make an agreement "prospectively limiting the lawyer's liability to a client for malpractice" *if* the client "is independently represented in making the agreement. . . ."[4] The rationale behind this principle is that there is no risk that the first lawyer will be able to overreach the client if a second lawyer independently represents the client in making the decision to waive malpractice liability prospectively. The Comment appropriately

---

[Section 1.8–9]

[1]Rule 1.8(h). DR 6-102(A).

[2]*Cf.* Rule 1.8, Code Comparison 10. The language of DR 6-102(A), because of a drafting error, was not explicitly limited to *prospective* attempts, *i.e.*, attempts before the malpractice actually occurs, but such a limitation must be read into it. Otherwise it would forbid the lawyer from agreeing to a settlement offer in which the client suing for malpractice released his claim. Model Rule 1.8(h) is drafted more clearly and avoids this problem.

[3]Rule 1.2, Comment 5 of the 1983 Model Rules.

[4]Rule 1.8(h). *See also* Restatement of the Law Governing Lawyers, Third, § 54 (Official Draft 2000). The clause, found in the 1983 version of Rule 1.8(h)—"unless permitted by law"—should not be read to require that other law specifically and independently *authorize* and empower this waiver. In the former Soviet Union, the general rule was that the citizen could not do something unless a law specifically allowed it. In the United States, in contrast, any citizen can do whatever he or she wishes, as long as a valid, constitutional law does not prohibit that action. *See* Ronald D. Rotunda, *Interpreting an Unwritten Constitution*, 12 HARVARD J.L. & PUB. POLICY 15 (1989). Thus, unless a state or federal law forbids such a waiver, a lawyer should be able to make an agreement "prospectively limiting the lawyer's liability to a client for malpractice" if the client "is independently represented in making the agreement."

notes that it is often difficult for clients to evaluate whether they should make such an agreement before the dispute arises with the lawyer.[5]

The drafters of the 2002 Model Rules deleted the "as permitted by law" language from Rule 1.8(h).[6] They studied the issue and determined that no jurisdiction has a statute or court decision prohibiting the prospective limitation on a lawyer's liability to a client. In light of this finding, the drafters believed that this language served no useful purpose in light of the fact that the default rule in the United States is that people may legally do whatever the law does not forbid.[7] We do not need a law or rule to authorize us to do something that no law or rule prohibits.

At first, it may be difficult to imagine situations where a lawyer would send a client down the street to another attorney in a different law firm solely for the purposes of securing advice so that the client can waive malpractice liability. One might think that, as a practical matter, it will be the unusual case where an individual will hire a second lawyer to represent him in negotiating an employment agreement with his first lawyer under which the second lawyer advises the client to waive his first lawyer's malpractice liability prospectively. In such cases, once the client visits the second lawyer, we should not be surprised if the second lawyer advises the client that no reason exists for waiving malpractice: the client need only hire the second lawyer to perform the task and this second lawyer will not waive his malpractice liability.

However, the typical case to which this rule applies would probably not involve individual clients. Rather, it would involve corporations represented by their own inside counsel. When the

---

[5]Rule 1.8, Comment 14.

Some clauses in the lawyer's fee agreement may constitute a violation of the rule on limiting a lawyer's liability to a client. *See Iowa Sup. Ct. Disc. Bd. v. Powell, 726 N.W.2d 397 (Iowa 2007), noted in* 23 ABA/BNA MANUAL ON PROFESSIONAL CONDUCT, Current Reports News 65 (Feb. 7, 2007). The Iowa Supreme Court declared that two provisions in the lawyer's fee agreement were unethical attempts to limit his liability: (1) Client waives any negligence claims and fee disputes if he does not raise them within ten days of receiving a monthly invoice, and (2) Client agrees to indemnify Powell for all expenses and legal fees relating to collection of fees.

[6]The phrase, "unless permitted by law" was added during the debate on this Rule in 1983 in the House of Delegates. Another commentator has argued that this phrase, in "literal terms" serves to ban all exoneration agreements. 1 GEOFFREY C. HAZARD, JR. & W. WILLIAM HODES, THE LAW OF LAWYERING: A HANDBOOK ON THE MODEL RULES OF PROFESSIONAL CONDUCT § 12.18 (Aspen Law & Business, 3d ed. 2001). That may have been the intent of one or more sponsors, but it is not what the phrase says. The phrase simply does not say "unless other law *specifically authorizes*."

[7]*See* Reporter's Explanation of Changes to Model Rule 1.8.

inside counsel hires outside counsel on behalf of the corporation, the corporation might find it reasonable to waive malpractice liability in some instances. Rule 1.8(h) would allow that prospective waiver because the client (the corporation) is separately represented by its own inside counsel. This rule is a modification of the general principle of Rule 1.1, that a client cannot waive competence.[8]

Thus Rule 1.8(h) does have a very practical application because it allows a corporation to control its legal costs when retaining outside counsel. The corporation, for example, may wish to hire the outside counsel to perform a specific, limited task, such as drafting a particular contract. The outside lawyer may argue that he has to perform an extensive overview of the problem and independently evaluate the tax implications before he can be certain that the contract can competently be written in that limited way. The corporation, to place a specific cap on its legal costs, can assure the lawyer that he should only perform that specific legal task and not be worried about malpractice liability for not investigating the tax implications of the contract.

Or, the corporation may hire the outside lawyer and retain her to draft a contract based on certain legal research that the corporation's in-house counsel has already prepared. The outside lawyer may be concerned that she should not rely on legal research that was prepared by someone whom she does not know and who did not work under her supervision. Once again the in-house counsel can allay her fears by advising the corporation to waive any malpractice claims it has against the outside lawyer for relying on the legal research prepared by the corporation's in-house legal staff. That way, the corporation can more easily control its legal costs.[9]

§ 1.8–9(a)(3) Limited Liability Partnership Agreement

The Limited Liability Company (LLC) is a form of law firm or-

---

[8]For an analysis of when limited performance is appropriate, see Fred C. Zacharias, *Limited Performance Agreements: Should Clients Get What They Pay For?*, 11 GEORGETOWN J. LEGAL ETHICS 915 (1998). *See also* David A. Hyman & Charles Silver, *And Such Small Portions: Limited Performance Agreements and the Cost/Quality/Access Trade-Off*, 11 GEORGETOWN J. LEGAL ETHICS 959 (1998); Fred C. Zacharias, *Reply to Hyman and Silver: Clients Should Not Get Less Than They Deserve*, 11 GEORGETOWN J. LEGAL ETHICS 981 (1998).

[9]However, the corporation could not waive any malpractice claims it had against its in-house legal staff unless the corporation were represented by separate counsel in advising it to exercise such a waiver. Needless to say, as a practical matter, the corporation is normally extremely unlikely to sue its own in-house counsel for malpractice, but the failure to sue would be a function of the corporation's business judgment, not a function of any restriction in the Model Rules of Professional Conduct.

ganization that immunizes lawyers from vicarious liability for the malpractice of others in their firm. Some jurisdictions allow lawyers to practice in the form of LLCs, professional corporations, or other similar business forms that limit vicarious tort liability.

The Model Code had a provision (not found in the Rules) that allowed a lawyer in a professional legal corporation to limit her imputed liability for her associates' malpractice, *if* other law permits.[10] This rule only applied if the law firm was organized as a professional legal corporation. This requirement raises questions of interpretation. Is the requirement that other law permit mean that no other law forbids this arrangement, or that there is another law that specifically allows this arrangement? Typically, we can do whatever the law does not prohibit. We do not need a law that makes clear that we are allowed to walk on the sidewalk, cross the street, eat when we feel like eating, etc. We are permitted to do anything that the law does not forbid.

The Rules avoid these issues because they do not involve themselves in this level of detail, do not impose special rules on professional legal corporations, and place no ethical hurdles in the way of lawyers who set up their business form in this way. Model Rule 1.8(h) (on limiting liability for one's own malpractice) does not require vicarious liability, and no other Model Rule requires a lawyer to assume liability for his or her partner's malpractice. The ethics rules, in short, do not require lawyers to be vicariously liable for the torts of their partners.[11]

Although state tort law may exempt lawyers from vicarious liability for the torts of their partners or subordinate lawyers, the ethics rules that require lawyers to exercise appropriate supervision still apply,[12] so a lawyer may be subject to discipline for failure to supervise even though he or she is not subject to tort liability.[13]

If the law firm is set up in a form to limit vicarious liability, plaintiffs often strive to find direct liability when vicarious liability is unavailable. An interesting example is *Sanders, Bruin,*

---

[10]EC 6-6.

[11]ABA Formal Opinion 96-401 (Aug. 2, 1996). The drafters of the 2002 Model Rules added a sentence in the Comments that Rule 1.8(h) does not apply to lawyers who form an LLP under state law. The drafters stated that: "Nor does this paragraph limit the ability of lawyers to practice in the form of a limited-liability entity, where permitted by law, provided that each lawyer remains personally liable to the client for his or her own conduct and the firm complies with any conditions required by law, such as provisions requiring client notification or maintenance of adequate liability insurance." Rule 1.8, Comment 14.

[12]Rules 5.1 and 5.3 on the duty to supervise and Rule 5.4 on participation of non-lawyers in the partnership all apply to LLCs.

[13]ABA Formal Opinion 96-401 (Aug. 2, 1996).

Coll & Worley, P.A. v. McKay Oil Corp.[14] Plaintiff used the ethics rules to create individual liability. An LLC voted to terminate representation of a client six weeks before a major arbitration, allegedly because of illness of the partner who was to handle the litigation. The client considered the termination to be malpractice, and the question was whether liability was limited to the firm's assets or could be asserted against each shareholder in the LLC. The court held each liable. Although shareholders in an LLC cannot be held vicariously liable, in this case liability was imposed because of each shareholder's individual act of voting.

§ 1.8–9(a)(4) Arbitration Agreements of Malpractice Claims

The general rule is that arbitration agreements are not in conflict with the prohibition on advance waivers of malpractice liability.[15] The arbitration agreement simply provides a different forum to determine if there is liability and, if there is, what the remedy should be.[16] Arbitration goes to remedy, not liability. Thus, a lawyer dealing with a new client may insert an arbitration clause into the retainer agreement without violating any fiduciary obligations.[17] The lawyer may even insert a mandatory arbitration clause in the retainer agreement when the arbitration covers malpractice and other non-fee complaints.[18] However, before a law firm includes an arbitration clause in the retainer

---

[14]*Sanders, Bruin, Coll & Worley, P.A. v. McKay Oil Corp.*, 123 N.M. 457, 943 P.2d 104 (1997).

[15]**Arbitration Agreements.** *See, e.g., Masurovsky v. Green,* 687 A.2d 198 (D.C.App.1996), accepts arbitration agreements and held that an agreement to arbitrate a malpractice claim is to be interpreted first by the court, not the arbitrator. The drafters to the 2002 Rules included this statement in the Comments: "This paragraph does not, however, prohibit a lawyer from entering into an agreement with the client to arbitrate legal malpractice claims, provided such agreements are enforceable and the client is fully informed of the scope and effect of the agreement." Rule 1.8, Comment 14.

See also David Hricik, *Lawyer-Client Arbitration Agreements*, E-ETHICS, Vol. I, No. 2, http://www.hricik.com/eethics/1.2.html (examining the ethical issues in lawyer-client arbitration agreements).

[16]A forum selection clause choosing state court as the tribunal to hear the malpractice cases against the firm is enforceable. *See Ginter ex rel. Ballard v. Belcher, Prendergast & Laporte,* 536 F.3d 439 (5th Cir. 2008).

[17]California State Bar Standing Committee on Professional Responsibility and Conduct, Formal Opinion 1989-116. The committee said that the lawyer has a fiduciary duty to fully explain to his clients the arbitration provision and its legal consequences.

[18]*Haynes v. Kuder,* 591 A.2d 1286 (D.C.App.1991). *See* ABA Formal Opinion 02-425 (Feb. 20, 2002) (approving a lawyer-client agreement to submit to all disputes to mandatory, binding arbitration); Texas State Bar Prof. Ethics Comm., Op. 586 (Oct. 2008) (permitting mandatory arbitration of malpractice claims but requiring fairness in the terms of the agreement and full disclosure of the benefits and risks of arbitration). *But see* John S.

agreement, the firm should contact its malpractice insurance carrier to determine whether such a clause may affect the coverage of the policy.[19]

The ABA has developed Model Rules for Fee Arbitration.[20] These Rules provide that proceedings are normally confidential, thus protecting client confidences.[21] If the client requests arbitration, then the program makes the arbitration mandatory for the lawyer.[22] If the lawyer petitions for arbitration, it does not proceed unless the client files a written consent within 30 days of service.[23]

Dzienkowski, *Legal Malpractice and the Multistate Law Firm: Supervision of Multistate Offices; Firms as Limited Liability Partnerships; and Predispute Agreements to Arbitrate Client Malpractice Claims,* 36 S. Tex. L. Rev. 967, 990–991 (1995) (arguing that legal profession should prohibit law firms from imposing "take it or leave it" mandatory and binding predispute arbitration clauses in the case of unsophisticated clients).

[19]*See* William Freivogel, *Arbitration of Malpractice Claims,* FREIVOGEL ON CONFLICTS (Mar. 2008), at http://web.me.com/billfreivogel/Freivogel/Freivogel_on_Conflicts.html (stating that malpractice insurance carriers may not wish to be bound by an arbitration clause and may provide a defense to the policy coverage).

[20]ABA Model Rules for Fee Arbitration (Feb. 13, 1995).

[21]Model Rules for Fee Arbitration, Rule 8. *Accord* ABA Model Rules of Professional Conduct, Rule 1.6(b)(2) & Comment 19.

[22]Model Rules for Fee Arbitration, Rule 1(G)(1) & Commentary. The results of the arbitration are binding if the parties agree in writing or if no party asks for a trial de novo with 30 days after the arbitration decision has been served.

Constitutionality of Rules That Impose Client-Initiated Arbitration on the Lawyer. Lawyers have objected, without success, to those state rules that make arbitra-

tion mandatory for the lawyer but not for the client.

Anderson v. Elliott, 555 A.2d 1042 (Me.), *cert. denied,* 493 U.S. 978, 110 S.Ct. 504, 107 L.Ed.2d 507 (1989), upheld the Maine requirement that lawyers submit to client-initiated mandatory arbitration of fee claims. The lawyer had argued that arbitration denied him his constitutional right to a jury trial, but the court held that the right must be read in the context of the court's supervisory power over attorneys.

Guralnick v. New Jersey Supreme Court, 747 F.Supp. 1109 (D. N.J.1990), rejected lawyers' arguments that a New Jersey system of fee arbitration that only a client may initiate unconstitutionally denied them due process, violated their Thirteenth Amendment rights, and violated the antitrust laws.

A. Fred Miller, P.C. v. Purvis, 921 P.2d 610 (Alaska 1996), examined mandatory fee arbitration and held that the lack of judicial review of an arbitration award did not constitute a denial of due process. The court agreed that judicial review on the merits would be desirable to have in an arbitration process, but the lack of it does not violate the Constitution. Part of the purpose of arbitration is to achieve a quick, binding review of a dispute. Judicial review would impose a burden on clients that the Constitution does not require.

[23]Model Rules for Fee Arbitration, Rule 4(E).

Under these Model Rules, the lawyer has the burden to prove, by a preponderance of the evidence, that the fee is reasonable.[24]

§ 1.8–9(b) Subsequent Limitations of Liability

§ 1.8–9(b)(1) Introduction

Let us say that a client or former client ("Disgruntled Client") has a malpractice claim against his own attorney ("Attorney"). If Disgruntled Client is not represented by independent counsel regarding that malpractice claim,[25] then Rule 1.8(h) also requires Attorney (who is being charged with malpractice) to advise Disgruntled Client that independent representation is appropriate before settlement.

Model Rule 1.8(h) takes into account several important concerns. It allows the Attorney to settle the claim, it does not require the Disgruntled Client to retain another lawyer, and it protects the less sophisticated client by requiring the Attorney to advise the Disgruntled Client in writing that independent legal representation on this issue is appropriate. The advice should be clear enough to bring home to Disgruntled Client the significance of the decision not to secure independent legal representation. And, the lawyer must give the client a reasonable opportunity to seek independent counsel.[26]

As a further protection for the Disgruntled Client thinking of settling a malpractice claim, the Rules require that the lawyer's advice regarding the appropriateness of independent representation must be "in writing." The ABA Section on General Practice recommended this requirement and the ABA Commission accepted it without opposition.[27] A writing is not only a record less fallible than one's memory, it also serves to bring home to the recipient the significance of the situation.

There is no counterpart in the Model Code for this procedure.[28] In essence, under the Model Code, Disgruntled Client is either a former client who is representing himself *pro se*, or he is a present client with no *independent* representation on his malpractice claim.

§ 1.8–9(b)(2) Settling Fee Disputes and Malpractice Countersuits

In some cases, when a lawyer sues a client for unpaid fees, the

---

[24]Model Rules for Fee Arbitration, Rule 5(O).

[25]If Disgruntled Client is represented by his or her *new* lawyer in the lawsuit against the first lawyer, that raises no special conflicts problems. The new lawyer simply negotiates or tries the suit against the first lawyer.

[26]This explicit statement was added by the drafters of the 2002 Rules.

[27]*See* The Legislative History of the Model Rules of Professional Conduct 60 to 64 (ABA, Center for Professional Responsibility 1987).

[28]*See* Rule 1.8(h) & Model Code Comparison 5. *Compare* DR 6–102(A).

client countersues with a malpractice claim. The lawyer can ethically settle the fee claim and at the same time insist upon a waiver of what is often seen as a frivolous malpractice charge, *if* the client is advised that independent counsel should be obtained prior to negotiating such a settlement or release. A client simply threatening such a countersuit may not ever consult with a new lawyer, but that is his decision.

The lawyer may not condition the fee settlement on a client's agreement not to file a disciplinary charge.[29] That surely violates the lawyer's fiduciary obligation.

§ 1.8–10 RULE 1.8(i)—ACQUIRING A PROPRIETY INTEREST IN THE CLIENT'S CAUSE OF ACTION

Rule 1.8(i) limits the lawyer's ability to acquire a propriety interest in a client's cause of action or the subject of the litigation. A lawyer may not become a co-client by purchasing an ownership interest in a cause of action. Such prohibitions existed in the common law crimes of champerty and maintenance.[1] When a lawyer owns a piece of the litigation, that lawyer has a significant conflict of interest with the client. In some cases, lawyers will want to pursue their interests far beyond where the client would stop. In other cases, the ownership interest in the underlying cause of action will inhibit a client's desire to fire the lawyer. The lawyer who acquires a financial interest in litigation creates the risk that he will not exercise independent professional judgment for his client.[2]

However, two important exceptions serve to limit substantially this restriction.[3] First, lawyers may use liens to secure their fees or expenses. Second, lawyers may contract with their clients for contingent fees in civil cases.

§ 1.8–10(a) Liens

First, let us turn to liens. Subsection (i) recognizes the lawyer's right—offered by other law—to secure her fee or expenses by lien.[4] There are two basic types of liens, RETAINING LIENS and CHARGING LIENS.

Most states allow a lawyer a RETAINING LIEN, which gives the lawyer a possessory interest in the client's papers and funds in

---

[29]D.C. Bar Ethics Opinion 260 (Oct. 18, 1995).

[Section 1.8–10]

[1]Rule 1.8, Comment 16.

[2]Perretta, J., citing Treatise in *McLaughlin v. Amirsaleh*, 65 Mass.App.Ct. 873, 844 N.E.2d 1105, 1113 (Mass. App. Ct. 2006).

[3]Restatement of the Law Governing Lawyers § 36(1) (Official Draft 2000).

[4]A lawyer may also protect a fee by acquiring a contractual security interest in client property. Lawyers may take security to protect a fee earned or to be earned. *See* ABA Informal Opinion 593 (Oct. 25, 1962).

the lawyer's possession. She can use this lien to secure payment of her fee.[5] In other words, the lawyer will not return papers and other property of her client that the lawyer possesses if the client has not paid the lawyer. That is the rule in the majority of jurisdictions and in the Restatement of the Law of Agency, Second,[6] and the Restatement of Security.[7]

On the other hand, the Restatement of the Law Governing Lawyers adopts the minority view.[8] The position it embraces is that the lawyer should not acquire a nonconsensual lien on property in the lawyer's possession or recovered by the client through the lawyer's efforts. The client and lawyer may agree that the lawyer should have a security interest in the client's property. Otherwise, the Restatement does not recognize any retaining liens on client property, except as provided by statute.[9] It argues that the lawyer's use of the client's papers against the client is at war with the lawyer's fiduciary responsibility to the client.[10]

If the client does not pay the lawyer for her work in preparing

---

In 2002, the ABA issued Formal Opinion 02-427 to clarify that Rule 1.8(i) permits a lawyer to acquire a contractual lien when the subject matter of the representation is litigation as long as the lien satisfies state law. ABA Formal Opinion 02-427 (May 31, 2002). If the lawyer acquires a lien on property other than the subject matter of the litigation, the lawyer must also satisfy Rule 1.8(a).

[5]**Retaining Lien.** There are exceptions to the scope of this retaining lien. First, if the lawyer loses possession, she loses the lien. Moreover, the lien does not apply to property that the client gives the lawyer merely for safekeeping. *Akers v. Akers*, 233 Minn. 133, 46 N.W.2d 87 (1951).

There are other exceptions as well. *See, e.g., Pomerantz v. Schandler*, 704 F.2d 681 (2d Cir.1983) (per curiam), holding that if the client in a criminal case has an urgent need of the papers to defend his case, and this client does not have the funds to pay his lawyer, the court, in its discretion, can order the papers to be turned over to the client. But, in general, the "attorney's lien cannot be disregarded merely because the pressure it is supposed to exert becomes effective." 704 F.2d at 683. *People v. Altvater*, 78 Misc.2d 24, 355 N.Y.S.2d 736 (1974)

(in murder case, first lawyer may retain the originals but the second lawyer can make copies).

Resolution Trust Corp. v. Elman, 949 F.2d 624 (2d Cir.1991), held that the lawyer for a failed bank cannot move to the head of the creditors' line but must file claim with the Resolution Trust Corporation. *F.D.I.C. v. Shain, Schaffer & Rafanello*, 944 F.2d 129 (3d Cir.1991).

[6]Restatement of the Law of Agency, Second (1958), § 464.

[7]Restatement of Security, § 62(b).

[8]Restatement of the Law Governing Lawyers, Third, § 43 (Official Draft 2000), at Comment *b*, pp. 307 to 308. *See generally* John Leubsdorf, *Against Lawyer Retaining Liens*, 72 FORDHAM L. REV. 849 (2004).

[9]Restatement of the Law Governing Lawyers, Third, § 43 (Official Draft 2000), at Comment *a*, pp. 306 to 307.

[10]In *Sage Realty Corp. v. Proskauer Rose Goetz & Mendelsohn L.L.P.*, 91 N.Y.2d 30, 666 N.Y.S.2d 985, 689 N.E.2d 879 (N.Y.1997), a client who had paid over a million dollars in fees in a large financing transaction decided to switch lawyers. It asked the Proskauer law firm for its file, now totaling so many volumes that the index alone ran 58 pages. The

particular documents, then the Restatement does allow a lawyer to retain these "unpaid-for documents." However, even here, the "lawyer may not retain unpaid-for documents when doing so will unreasonably harm the client."[11]

Most states also allow a lawyer a CHARGING LIEN. This lien is non-possessory. It gives the lawyer—who gives notice to the person paying the settlement or judgment—a right to have any recovery in the case applied to the payment of her fees. After the lawyer has given her notice, the person or entity paying the amount in settlement or judgment is liable for the lawyer's fees if that person pays the amount directly to the lawyer's client. Typically, the check is made out to both the lawyer and client, so both the lawyer and the party (or insurer) paying the amount are protected.[12]

The Restatement does not have the same problem with charging liens as it does with retaining liens, because it argues these liens do not have the same coercive effects of a retaining lien. Unless a statutory scheme provides otherwise, the Restatement articulates two requirements for a valid charging lien.

First, the client must agree in writing to the charging lien. This requirement makes the lien consensual. It also serves to give the client notice that the lawyer can receive part of any recovery. The lien agreement need not use the word "lien," but it should be clear that the lawyer is entitled to a part of any recovery to pay her fee.[13] Lawyers will make this writing part of their standard fee agreements.

Second, the third party against whom the lien will be enforced "must have been afforded notice of the lien as required by law."[14] The Restatement does not specify that the lawyer furnish this notice, but we should expect that the lawyer will be the one to do it, since clients have little incentive to do so.

§ 1.8–10(b) Contingent Fees

Subsection (2) of Rule 1.8(i) validates contingent fees. It

---

firm turned over the closing documents, client-supplied papers and correspondence with third parties, but not its own internal work product. The New York Court of Appeals, citing the Restatement of the Law Governing Lawyers, held that the client is presumptively entitled to all its papers, except for limited exceptions such as documents intended only for internal law firm use. However, the law firm may normally charge the client for the function of assembling and delivering the documents to the client.

[11] Restatement of the Law Governing Lawyers, Third, § 43 (Official Draft 2000), at Comment c, p. 308.

[12] See e.g., Hafter v. Farkas, 498 F.2d 587 (2d Cir.1974).

[13] Restatement of the Law Governing Lawyers, Third, § 43 (Official Draft 2000), at Comment e. See also id. at § 45(2).

[14] Restatement of the Law Governing Lawyers, Third, § 43 (Official Draft 2000), at Comment e.

provides that the lawyer "shall not acquire a propriety interest in the cause of action" *except* that the lawyer may "contract with a client for a reasonable contingent fee in a civil case."

At first it appears that Rule 1.8(i)(2) is an exception that is so broad that it swallows up the prohibitory language of Rule 1.8(i). While little of Rule 1.8(i) is left, it still exists. Taken together, these two provisions mean that a lawyer can acquire a proprietary interest in the cause of action or subject matter of litigation (that is what a contingent fee is, after all), but the lawyer's interest in the case cannot be that of a co-plaintiff. In other words, the client may not assign to the attorney part of his cause of action in a way that would allow the lawyer to prevent settlement. The client cannot waive his right to decide when to settle litigation.[15]

For example, assume that Client agrees to compensate Lawyer by giving her a one-fourth interest in certain real property and mining claims. Ownership of these properties is disputed and Lawyer defends Client (and Lawyer herself as well, to the extent that the Lawyer's one-fourth interest is involved). Client becomes dissatisfied with Lawyer's services and tries to discharge Lawyer, who refuses to leave. Lawyer has violated the ethics rules[16] because she has refused to accept the client's discharge.[17]

One ethics opinion[18] argues that a lawyer who prosecutes a patent application may not take an interest in the patent as security for payment of the fee. Because a patent application is technically "litigation," the Opinion asserted that this arrangement would necessarily constitute taking an interest in the subject matter of litigation. However, this argument ignores the effect of the exception authorized by Rule 1.8(j)(2). The lawyer may take a contingent fee in a patent case. The fee may be excessive under Rule 1.5(a), but Rule 1.8(j)(2) does not prohibit it.

§ 1.8–11 RULE 1.8(j)—SEXUAL RELATIONS WITH CLIENTS

Lawyers who take unfair advantage of their clients violate their fiduciary obligations. There is a violation of the lawyer's fiduciary obligations if the lawyer unfairly exploits the fiduciary relationship, or, during the course of the representation, enters into a sexual relationship with the client that impairs the

---

[15]Rule 1.2, Comment 5; EC 7-7.

See In re Lewis, 266 Ga. 61, 463 S.E.2d 862 (1995). The court suspended the lawyer for 18 months because he required the client, in the contingent fee agreement, to give the lawyer blanket authority to settle the suit. The client always has the right to decide on settlement, the court said,

and a contingent fee agreement cannot be used as the vehicle to waive that right.

[16]Rule 1.8(i), Rule 1.16, Comment 4; DR 2-110(B)(4), and DR 5-103.

[17]ABA Informal Opinion 1397 (Aug. 31, 1977).

[18]D.C. Bar Opinion 95 (1988).

lawyer's ability to act competently. The client's consent may not avoid the ethical problem because the lawyer's potential undue influence and the client's emotional vulnerability serve to vitiate meaningful consent.[1]

Neither the 1983 Model Rules nor the Model Code had special rules that deal *explicitly* with the issue of a lawyer's sexual relations with a client, but the principles can easily be derived from the basic fiduciary rules that already form the foundations of the rules governing conflicts of interest. The drafters of the 2002 Model Rules believed that there should be an explicit Rule, so they added a new paragraph (j).

Rule 1.8(j) prohibits a lawyer from having a sexual relationship with a client unless such a consensual relationship existed *prior to* the beginning of the attorney-client relationship.[2] This Rule offers a bright line on whether lawyers may have such a relationship with clients during the representation. As the ABA Ethics Committee has noted, the roles of "lover and lawyer" are potentially conflicting, and run afoul of the ethics rules for several reasons. First, there is: (1) a potential abuse of the fiduciary relationship between that lawyer and a vulnerable client,[3] (2) a loss of emotional distance between the client and lawyer, which

---

[Section 1.8–11]

[1]ABA Formal Opinion 92-356 (July 6, 1992), at 8. *Cf.* Rule 1.14(a) (client under an emotional impairment). This issue is a frequent topic in the law reviews. *E.g.,* L. Mischler, *Reconciling Rapture, Representation, and Responsibility: An Argument Against Per Se Bans on Attorney-Client Sex,* 10 GEORGETOWN J. LEGAL ETHICS 209 (1997); Chesley Payne, *An Overview of Sexual Harassment in the Attorney-Client Relationship as Interpreted Under the ABA Rules of Professional Conduct,* 26 J. LEGAL PROF. 249 (2002); Florence Vincent, *Regulating Intimacy of Lawyers: Why is it Needed and How Should it Be Approached?,* 33 U. TOLEDO L. REV. 645 (2002). Malinda L. Seymore, *Attorney-Client Sex: a Feminist Critique of the Absence of Regulation,* 15 Yale J.L. & Feminism 175 (2003) argues, surprisingly: "Lawyers, in most jurisdictions, can have sex with their clients without violating a standard of professional responsibility."

Emotionally Fragile Client. When the disciplinary authorities seek to impose discipline, they should consider, as an aggravating factor, the lawyer's knowledge of the emotional vulnerability of the victim. ABA Standards for Imposing Lawyer Sanctions, § 9.22(h) (1986, as amended).

See, e.g., *In re Berg,* 264 Kan. 254, 955 P.2d 1240 (1998), ruled that a lawyer's *initiation* of a sexual relationship with an emotionally fragile client violated the fiduciary relationship between lawyer and client and required the disbarment of the lawyer even in the absence of notice provided by a specific rule.

[2]The Comments specifically state that the Rule applies to lawyers for corporations and prohibits them from having a sexual relationship with a "constituent of the organization who supervises, directs or regularly consults with that lawyer concerning the organization's legal matters." Rule 1.8, Comment 19.

[3]*See, e.g., Case of Drucker,* 133 N.H. 326, 577 A.2d 1198 (1990), which involved a lawyer who knew his client was under psychiatric care and emo-

can adversely affect the lawyer's need for her objective, detached professional judgment, (3) potential conflicts of interest between the lawyer and client, and (4) a confusion between which communications are made in a professional relationship and which are personal.[4]

When the sexual relationship *predates* the professional relationship, exploitation of the fiduciary duties and the possibility of client dependency are diminished,[5] because the lawyer has not abused the preexisting fiduciary relationship to begin the affair.[6] On the other hand, if the lawyer and other person begin an affair, there seldom is any reason why the other person—who has decided that he needs a lawyer—must pick the lawyer with whom he is having an affair.

When there is a romantic relationship that *predates* the lawyer-client relationship, Rule 1.8(j) does not come into play, but there is still the possibility that the lawyer will run afoul of the general rules dealing with conflicts of interest. Medical doctors do not treat family members because of a concern that there is the potential for impaired judgment and lack of objectivity. This same lack of detachment may apply to the lawyer who is romantically involved with the client, even though the romantic relationship existed prior to the establishment of a lawyer-client relationship. If there is a reasonable possibility that the romantic connection will impair the legal representation of the client, or the client harmed by the continuation of the sexual relationship,

---

tionally fragile. The lawyer initiated the affair, and then ended it, but the client had fallen in love with him. Her husband also found her diary describing her feelings, a revelation that made her divorce more stressful. The court found that the lawyer had taken advantage of his client and suspended him for two years.

[4]ABA Formal Opinion 92-356 (July 6, 1992).

[5]Rule 1.8, Comment 18. *See also, Attorney Grievance Commission of Maryland v. Culver*, 381 Md. 241, 849 A.2d 423 (Ct. App. 2004). The court found that the lawyer's sexual intercourse and contact with client while representing her in a divorce case violated the conflict of interest rule, was criminal conduct of adultery reflecting adversely on his fitness to practice law, and was prejudicial to administration of justice. This lawyer made threats to the client that, if she did not cooperate with him and accede

to his sexual demands, he would deliberately sabotage her case so that she would lose custody of her children, and the sexual conduct was exploitative and coercive and was not consensual. For these reasons and others, the court disbarred the lawyer.

[6]ABA Formal Opinion 92-364 (July 6, 1992), at 1, n.1.

See Matter of Lewis, 262 Ga. 37, 415 S.E.2d 173 (1992), which involved a lawyer who had a sexual relationship with the client while representing her in a child custody proceeding. Not only were issues of differential power and impaired judgment presented, but the fact of the relationship could affect whether the mother got custody of the children. Three justices voted for disbarment but the lawyer was only suspended, perhaps because lawyer and client had been lovers before the professional relationship began.

the attorney should not undertake, or should withdraw from, the legal representation. Although the Rules do not impose a per se prohibition, a Comment properly advises that, "before proceeding with the representation in these circumstances, the lawyer should consider whether the lawyer's ability to represent the client will be materially limited by the relationship."[7]

The cautious lawyer who is romantically involved with a *prospective* client should also consider a simple fact: the prospective client can always hire a different lawyer. Romantic partners are not fungible, but—although we do not like to admit it—lawyers usually are. The lawyer can avoid potential problems simply by having the "prospective client/romantic interest" hire a different lawyer.

Hence, several states have adopted rules or statutes that restrict or limit sex between lawyers and their clients.[8] The cautious lawyer should take that fact into consideration when the romantic interest asked for legal advice.

In addition, lawyers assume a risk of malpractice based on the romantic involvement. Thus, a Rhode Island jury awarded a client $25,000 compensatory and $250,000 punitive damages for malpractice because of her sexual relationship with her lawyer. She testified that the lawyer handling her divorce forced her to have sex by threatening to work actively to lose custody of her child. The court did not require the client to prove that there was any adverse result in the underlying legal work done for her. She was awarded custody, alimony, child support, and 60% of the marital assets.[9]

If the lawyer is involved in a sexual dalliance during the course

---

[7]Rule 1.8, Comment 18.

[8]*See, e.g.,* Calif. Bus. & Prof. Code, §§ 6106.7 to 6106.8; Calif. Rules of Prof. Conduct, Rule 3-120.

[9]*Lawyer Liable for Coerced Sex,* ABA Journal, Feb. 1993, at 24. *See* Howard Brill, *Sex with the Client: Ten Reasons to Say "No!,"* 33 SANTA CLARA L. REV. 651 (1993).

Vallinoto v. DiSandro, 688 A.2d 830 (R.I.1997), on the other hand, found that sex with a client was not malpractice. The client, who wanted a divorce, was an alien married to an American. The court found that the lawyer performed an excellent job in the representation, obtaining for his client custody of her child, significant child support, and 60% of the marital assets. However, they had an intimate relationship since early in the representation. The lawyer said it was consensual; the client said he told her she would be deported if he stopped representing her, and thus she felt compelled to continue the relationship until she got her divorce. It was only later when she married another man that she decided to sue her former lawyer. The Rhode Island court was unsympathetic with the client's charges, saying she was well-educated, had money of her own, and could have ended the representation and the affair at any time. One justice dissented; the conduct may not have been professional negligence, he said, but it was certainly a breach of fiduciary duty that should have supported the jury's finding of malpractice.

of litigation, there is, in addition, the risk of a reversal because the relationship may result in a conflict of interests, particularly in criminal cases.[10]

Of course, besides the risk of malpractice and reversal, there is the risk of professional discipline. In *Tante v. Herring*,[11] for example, a woman consulted a lawyer for help in collecting a social security disability claim. The lawyer helped her obtain a favorable award, but when he learned of the woman's impaired emotional and mental functioning, he persuaded her to have an affair with him. He infected her with two strains of venereal disease and she in turn infected her husband. Both husband and wife were permitted to recover from the lawyer for breach of fiduciary duty. The lawyer was also suspended from practice for 18 months.[12]

---

[10]*See, e.g., Commonwealth v. Croken*, 432 Mass. 266, 733 N.E.2d 1005 (2000). The appointed defense counsel was in a "close relationship" with an assistant district attorney who later became his wife. The court found no "actual" conflict requiring automatic reversal of the conviction, but it found that defense counsel should have disclosed the relationship to his client and obtained informed consent. The court remanded for an evidentiary hearing into the adequacy of the defense.

In contrast, consider *Hernandez v. State*, 750 So.2d 50 (Fla.App.1999) (motion on rehearing en banc), [previously reported at: 745 So. 2d 391, and withdrawn from the bound volume], which involved a lawyer who had an affair with the client's wife. A panel of the court originally concluded this state of affairs constituted per se ineffective assistance of counsel because the lawyer could not truly want the defendant acquitted so that he could return home. The full court, however, disagreed, because the conflict of interest was only "potential," not actual. The possible effect on the defense due to the affair was simply "informed speculation." In fact, the jury acquitted the defendant of the most serious charge against him, and the defendant's "unqualified endorsement" of the results that the same lawyer achieved in a concurrent Federal prosecution also undercut defendant's argument.

[11]*Tante v. Herring*, 264 Ga. 694, 453 S.E.2d 686 (1994).

[12]*Matter of Tante*, 264 Ga. 692, 453 S.E.2d 688 (1994), *reconsideration denied* (Dec. 2, 1994). *See also In the Matter of Patrick Anene Egbune*, 971 P.2d 1065 (Colo.1999), *cert. denied*, 526 U.S. 1115, 119 S.Ct. 1762, 143 L.Ed.2d 793 (1999) (improper sexual harassment of unwilling client; lawyer suspended for one year and one day).

The State of Illinois has witnessed a series of cases that appear to have come full circle. The first court opinion on this question, an intermediate appellate court, was hostile to the claims of sexual harassment. *Suppressed v. Suppressed*, 206 Ill.App.3d 918, 151 Ill.Dec. 830, 565 N.E.2d 101 (1990), involved a divorce client who testified that her lawyer twice took her to an apartment where he had her inhale something that disoriented her and then had sexual relations with her. She filed a discipline charge, but the Illinois disciplinary authorities did not impose discipline. The court also dismissed a malpractice action that alleged breach of fiduciary duty. This lower court agreed that this client felt coerced into sex, but that was not enough for he court, which said that the client only suffered emotional harm, not a "quantifiable" injury.

§ 1.8–12 RULE 1.8(k)—IMPUTATION OF RULE 1.8 CONFLICTS TO OTHER LAWYERS IN THE LAW FIRM

The drafters of the 2002 Rules added a new paragraph (k) to address imputation issues with respect to provisions 1.8(a) through (j). The drafters decided to impute all of the Rule 1.8 conflicts to other lawyers in the law firm, *except* Rule 1.8(j) on sexual relationships with clients.[1] The reason for excluding the

---

Doe v. Roe and Roe & Roe Ltd., 289 Ill.App.3d 116, 224 Ill.Dec. 325, 681 N.E.2d 640 (1997), rejected much of the reasoning in *Suppressed*, and held that a lawyer in a divorce case who coerces the client into a sexual relationship breaches a fiduciary duty to the client and that emotional distress may be considered as an element of damages.

In re Rinella, 175 Ill.2d 504, 222 Ill.Dec. 375, 677 N.E.2d 909 (1997), *cert. denied*, 522 U.S. 951, 118 S.Ct. 371, 139 L.Ed.2d 288 (1997), decided by the Illinois Supreme Court, involved various clients who alleged that their lawyer had pressured them into sexual relationships. The disciplinary authorities sought discipline. Even though no disciplinary rule deals specifically with the conduct, the Illinois Supreme Court held that it constituted a conflict of interest because the women believed they had to submit to get quality legal representation. The conduct was also "prejudicial to the administration of justice." The court suspended the lawyer.

In *Kling v. Landry*, 292 Ill.App.3d 329, 226 Ill.Dec. 684, 686 N.E.2d 33 (1997), the court held that the client's claims were sufficient to state a case for intentional battery, but rejected a negligence claim. The court evaluated prior Illinois law and concluded:

"We agree that an attorney breaches his fiduciary duty to his client by exploiting his position as an attorney to gain sexual favors. We believe that such a breach arises where the attorney: (1) makes his legal representation contingent upon sexual involvement; (2) compromises the

client's legal interests as a result of the sexual involvement; or (3) uses information, obtained in the course of representing a client which suggests that the client might be unusually vulnerable to a suggestion of sexual involvement, to seduce the client. *Doe, 289 Ill.App.3d at 129*, 224 Ill.Dec. 325, 681 N.E.2d 640. We caution, however, that sexual intercourse between two consenting adults is not, of itself, actionable conduct. *Hertel v. Sullivan*, 261 Ill.App.3d 156, 160, 198 Ill.Dec. 574, 633 N.E.2d 36 (1994). Moreover, we note that the nature of the attorney-client relationship is to provide legal services rather than to improve a client's mental or emotional well-being. *See Suppressed, 206 Ill.App.3d at 923–24*, 151 Ill.Dec. 830, 565 N.E.2d 101. In the instant case, unlike *Doe*, there have been no allegations that the defendant made his legal representation contingent upon the plaintiff's sexual involvement or that he compromised the plaintiff's legal interests as a result of the sexual involvement."

292 Ill.App.3d 329, 337, 226 Ill.Dec. 684, 690–91, 686 N.E.2d 33, 39–40.

[Section 1.8–12]

[1]*See also* Restatement (Third) of the Law Governing Lawyers § 16 Comment *e* (Official Draft 2000): "A lawyer may not obtain unfair contracts or gifts (see §§ 126 & 127) or enter a sexual relationship with a client when that would undermine the client's case, abuse the client's dependence on the lawyer, or create risk to the lawyer's independent judgment, for example when the lawyer represents the client in divorce proceedings (*see also,*

provision dealing with sex with clients from the general imputation is the simple fact that this rule addresses a personal conflict, not a systemic one.

Lawyer Alpha should not engage in consensual sexual relations with client unless the romantic relationship predated the lawyer-client relationship. However, Lawyer Alpha may send the client to another lawyer in Alpha's firm to handle the matter. Rule 1.8(k) does not impute Alpha's disqualification to other lawyers in Alpha's firm.

---

e.g., § 41 (abusive fee-collection methods). *See generally* Restatement Second, Agency §§ 387 to 398)."

CHAPTER 1.9
DUTIES TO FORMER CLIENTS

RULE 1.9: DUTIES TO FORMER CLIENTS

(a) A lawyer who has formerly represented a client in a matter shall not thereafter represent another person in the same or a substantially related matter in which that person's interests are materially adverse to the interests of the former client unless the former client gives informed consent, confirmed in writing.

(b) A lawyer shall not knowingly represent a person in the same or a substantially related matter in which a firm with which the lawyer formerly was associated had previously represented a client

(1) whose interests are materially adverse to that person; and

(2) about whom the lawyer had acquired information protected by Rules 1.6 and 1.9(c) that is material to the matter;

unless the former client gives informed consent, confirmed in writing.

(c) A lawyer who has formerly represented a client in a matter or whose present or former firm has formerly represented a client in a matter shall not thereafter:

(1) use information relating to the representation to the disadvantage of the former client except as these Rules would permit or require with respect to a client, or when the information has become generally known; or

(2) reveal information relating to the representation except as these Rules would permit or require with respect to a client.

496

Comment

[1] After termination of a client-lawyer relationship, a lawyer has certain continuing duties with respect to confidentiality and conflicts of interest and thus may not represent another client except in conformity with this Rule. Under this Rule, for example, a lawyer could not properly seek to rescind on behalf of a new client a contract drafted on behalf of the former client. So also a lawyer who has prosecuted an accused person could not properly represent the accused in a subsequent civil action against the government concerning the same transaction. Nor could a lawyer who has represented multiple clients in a matter represent one of the clients against the others in the same or a substantially related matter after a dispute arose among the clients in that matter, unless all affected clients give informed consent. See Comment [9]. Current and former government lawyers must comply with this Rule to the extent required by Rule 1.11.

[2] The scope of a "matter" for purposes of this Rule depends on the facts of a particular situation or transaction. The lawyer's involvement in a matter can also be a question of degree. When a lawyer has been directly involved in a specific transaction, subsequent representation of other clients with materially adverse interests in that transaction clearly is prohibited. On the other hand, a lawyer who recurrently handled a type of problem for a former client is not precluded from later representing another client in a factually distinct problem of that type even though the subsequent representation involves a position adverse to the prior client. Similar considerations can apply to the reassignment of military lawyers between defense and prosecution functions within the same military jurisdictions. The underlying question is whether the lawyer was so involved in the matter that the subsequent representation can be justly regarded as a changing of sides in the matter in question.

[3] Matters are "substantially related" for purposes of this Rule if they involve the same transaction or legal dispute or if there otherwise is a substantial risk that confidential factual information as would normally have been obtained in the prior representation would materially advance the client's position in the subsequent matter. For example, a lawyer who has represented a businessperson and learned extensive private financial information about that person may not then represent that person's spouse in seeking a divorce. Similarly, a lawyer who has previously represented a client in securing environmental permits to build a shopping center would be precluded from representing neighbors seeking to oppose rezoning of the property on the basis of environmental considerations; however, the lawyer would not be precluded, on the grounds of substantial relationship, from defending a tenant of the completed shopping center in resisting eviction for nonpayment of rent. Information that has been disclosed to the public or to other parties adverse to the former client ordinarily will not be disqualifying. Information acquired in a prior representation may have been rendered obsolete by the passage of time, a circumstance that may be relevant in determining whether two representations are substantially related. In the case of an organizational client, general knowledge of the client's policies and practices ordinarily will

not preclude a subsequent representation; on the other hand, knowledge of specific facts gained in a prior representation that are relevant to the matter in question ordinarily will preclude such a representation. A former client is not required to reveal the confidential information learned by the lawyer in order to establish a substantial risk that the lawyer has confidential information to use in the subsequent matter. A conclusion about the possession of such information may be based on the nature of the services the lawyer provided the former client and information that would in ordinary practice be learned by a lawyer providing such services.

Lawyers Moving Between Firms

[4] When lawyers have been associated within a firm but then end their association, the question of whether a lawyer should undertake representation is more complicated. There are several competing considerations. First, the client previously represented by the former firm must be reasonably assured that the principle of loyalty to the client is not compromised. Second, the rule should not be so broadly cast as to preclude other persons from having reasonable choice of legal counsel. Third, the rule should not unreasonably hamper lawyers from forming new associations and taking on new clients after having left a previous association. In this connection, it should be recognized that today many lawyers practice in firms, that many lawyers to some degree limit their practice to one field or another, and that many move from one association to another several times in their careers. If the concept of imputation were applied with unqualified rigor, the result would be radical curtailment of the opportunity of lawyers to move from one practice setting to another and of the opportunity of clients to change counsel.

[5] Paragraph (b) operates to disqualify the lawyer only when the lawyer involved has actual knowledge of information protected by Rules 1.6 and 1.9(c). Thus, if a lawyer while with one firm acquired no knowledge or information relating to a particular client of the firm, and that lawyer later joined another firm, neither the lawyer individually nor the second firm is disqualified from representing another client in the same or a related matter even though the interests of the two clients conflict. See Rule 1.10(b) for the restrictions on a firm once a lawyer has terminated association with the firm.

[6] Application of paragraph (b) depends on a situation's particular facts, aided by inferences, deductions or working presumptions that reasonably may be made about the way in which lawyers work together. A lawyer may have general access to files of all clients of a law firm and may regularly participate in discussions of their affairs; it should be inferred that such a lawyer in fact is privy to all information about all the firm's clients. In contrast, another lawyer may have access to the files of only a limited number of clients and participate in discussions of the affairs of no other clients; in the absence of information to the contrary, it should be inferred that such a lawyer in fact is privy to information about the clients actually served but not those of other clients. In such an inquiry, the burden of proof should rest upon the firm whose disqualification is sought.

[7] Independent of the question of disqualification of a firm, a lawyer

changing professional association has a continuing duty to preserve confidentiality of information about a client formerly represented. See Rules 1.6 and 1.9(c).

[8] Paragraph (c) provides that information acquired by the lawyer in the course of representing a client may not subsequently be used or revealed by the lawyer to the disadvantage of the client. However, the fact that a lawyer has once served a client does not preclude the lawyer from using generally known information about that client when later representing another client.

[9] The provisions of this Rule are for the protection of former clients and can be waived if the client gives informed consent, which consent must be confirmed in writing under paragraphs (a) and (b). See Rule 1.0(e). With regard to the effectiveness of an advance waiver, see Comment [22] to Rule 1.7. With regard to disqualification of a firm with which a lawyer is or was formerly associated, see Rule 1.10.

Authors' 1983 Model Rules Comparison

The following represents Model Rule 1.9 as it was adopted in 1983:

A Lawyer who has formerly represented a client in a matter shall not thereafter:

(a) Represent another person in the same or a substantially related matter in which that person's interests are materially adverse to the interests of the former client unless the former client consents after consultation; or

(b) Use information relating to the representation to the disadvantage of the former client except as Rule 1.6 would permit with respect to a client or when the information has become generally known.

In 1989, the ABA amended Model Rule 1.9 by moving some of the text in original 1983 version of Model Rule 1.10(b) into Rule 1.9(b). The original Rule 1.9(b) was moved to Model Rule 1.9(c). The impetus behind this change was to clarify an overlap between Model Rule 1.9 and 1.10 and to address the question of duties to former clients when a lawyer changes firms and did not represent the former client but may have acquired confidential information about a former client of the old firm. At that time, the corresponding comments were moved without significant amendment.

The drafters of the 2002 Model Rules changed the title of Rule 1.9 from "Conflict of Interests: Former Clients" to "Duties to Former Clients" to reflect that this provision also addresses obligations of confidentiality to former clients.

In Rule 1.9(a) and Rule 1.9(b), the drafters modified the "consent after consultation" requirement to read, "informed consent, confirmed in writing."

In Rule 1.9(c), the drafters removed specific references to Rules 1.6 and Rule 3.3 in paragraph (c)(1) and (c)(2) and replaced them with a more general reference to compliance with the Rules.

In Comment 1, the drafters amended the language to explain the coverage of the Rule. They also added the last sentence to address obligations to former multiple clients not to represent one of the clients against the others in the same or related matter without consent.

In Comment 2, the drafters made minor word changes to the language.

Comment 3 is new and addresses the definition of substantially related.

Old Comment 3 was renumbered as new Comment 4 without amendment.

Old Comments 4 and 5 were deleted. Comment 5 examined the relationship of Rule 1.9 to the old standard of appearance of impropriety. The Comment read as follows:

> [5] The other rubric formerly used for dealing with disqualification is the appearance of impropriety proscribed in Canon 9 of the ABA Model Code of Professional Responsibility. This rubric has a two fold problem. First, the appearance of impropriety can be taken to include any new client-lawyer relationship that might make a former client feel anxious. If that meaning were adopted, disqualification would become little more than a question of subjective judgment by the former client. Second, since "impropriety" is undefined, the term "appearance of impropriety" is question-begging. It therefore has to be recognized that the problem of disqualification cannot be properly resolved either by simple analogy to a lawyer practicing alone or by the very general concept of appearance of impropriety.

The drafters deleted this Comment because in their opinion this language is no longer helpful in examining Rule 1.9. *See* Reporter's Explanation of Changes to Model Rule 1.9.

Old Comment 8 was renumbered as Comment 5 with minor changes.

Old Comment 9 was renumbered as Comment 6 with two significant changes. The two lines were deleted on the topic of preserving confidential information. A last line was added addressing the burden of proof issue.

Old Comments 7 and 10 were deleted.

Old Comments 9 and 11 were renumbered as Comments 7 and 8 with minor changes.

Old Comment 12 was renumbered as Comment 9 with changes to the references and scope.

Model Code Comparison[1]

[1] There was no counterpart to this Rule in the Disciplinary Rules of the Model Code. Representation adverse to a former client was sometimes dealt with under the rubric of Canon 9 of the Model Code, which provided: "A lawyer should avoid even the appearance of impropriety." Also applicable were EC 4-6 which stated that the

---

[Rule 1.9]

[1]When ABA modified Model Rule 1.9 in 1989, it did not change the text of the Model Code Comparison. Thus, the current Model Code Comparison only refers to the Model Rule 1.9 as originally enacted. To understand the amended Model Rule 1.9, one must read the following text quoted from the Code Comparison to Model Rule 1.10: "DR 5-105(D) provided that '[i]f a lawyer is required to decline or to withdraw from employment under a Disciplinary Rule, no partner, or associate, or any other lawyer affiliated with him or his firm, may accept or continue such employment.' "

"obligation of a lawyer to preserve the confidences and secrets of his client continues after the termination of his employment" and Canon 5 which stated that "[a] lawyer should exercise independent professional judgment on behalf of a client."

[2] The provision in paragraph (a) for waiver by the former client is similar to DR 5-105(C).

[3] The exception in the last clause of paragraph (c)(1) permits a lawyer to use information relating to a former client that is in the "public domain," a use that was also not prohibited by the Model Code, which protected only "confidences and secrets." Since the scope of paragraph (a) is much broader than "confidences and secrets," it is necessary to define when a lawyer may make use of information about a client after the client-lawyer relationship has terminated.

§ 1.9–1 WHEN A LAWYER JOINS A FIRM

§ 1.9–1(a) An Introductory Caveat on the Distinction Between Rule 1.9 and Rule 1.10

Rule 1.9 governs conflicts that arise out of the fact that a lawyer previously represented one client and is now representing a different client in a matter that is adverse to his former client. Rule 1.9 governs the situation where the lawyer is *personally* disqualified, *i.e.*, individually disqualified. The basic principle of Rule 1.9 is that, unless there is a proper waiver by the client, a lawyer should be disqualified from taking a matter adverse to his former client if the lawyer acquired confidential client information from the former client that is material to the new representation.

In addition, Rule 1.9 disqualifies the lawyer if he now represents a person in a matter that is "the same or substantially related,"[1] to the past representation of another client, and the new client's interests are materially adverse to the interests of the former client. The lawyer, for example, may not switch sides, by defending the criminal defendant at trial and then arguing the appeal on behalf of the state, or drafting a will for the deceased and then seeking to break the will on behalf of a disgruntled heir.

Although Rule 1.9 deals with personal disqualifications, Rule 1.10, discussed below, deals with *imputed* disqualification. If one lawyer in a law firm is disqualified, not every other lawyer in the same firm is automatically disqualified. Some disqualifications are imputed and others are not. Rule 1.10 lays out the basic rule regarding imputation. For example, the Rule 1.8(k) imputes most of the provisions of 1.8, but not the sexual relations with a client rule. Rule 1.11 governs imputation in the government lawyer conflict area. But, Rule 1.10 does not impute that disqualification

---

[Section 1.9–1]

[1] Rule 1.9(a).

to other members of the law firm. However, Rule 1.10 does impute to all members of a law firm any of the disqualifications of Rule 1.9.[2]

The discussion of Rule 1.9 will focus on when a particular lawyer ("Lawyer X") is disqualified. Lawyer X may be disqualified because he has actual confidential knowledge about the former client that is material to the present situation.[3]

As long as Lawyer X is with that law firm, the law firm is also disqualified, because of Rule 1.10(a), which governs imputation of conflicts of interest. If Lawyer X (by hypothesis, the only person who has the confidential knowledge) leaves that law firm, then Lawyer X is still disqualified (because of Rule 1.0), but X's former law firm is no longer disqualified, because the only reason the original law firm was disqualified is because of the knowledge of Lawyer X and he is no longer there.[4] Thus, when examining a problem under Rule 1.9, we should keep in mind that we must also examine it under Rule 1.10 to determine the extent of the imputation. Now, let us turn to Rule 1.9.

§ 1.9–1(b) The Obligation of Loyalty to Former Clients

§ 1.9–1(b)(1) Introduction

Rule 1.9(a) and Rule 1.9(b) govern the extent to which a lawyer who joins a new firm carries with him any disqualifications from the old firm.[5]

§ 1.9–1(b)(2) The Prohibition Against Representing New Clients Against Former Clients on the Same or Substantially Related Matters

Rule 1.9(a) is fairly straight forward. If a lawyer used to represent a client in a particular matter but no longer does so, that

---

[2]"While lawyers are associated in a firm, none of them shall knowingly represent a client when any one of them practicing alone would be prohibited from doing so by Rules 1.7 or 1.9." Rule 1.10(a).

[3]Rule 1.7(a)(2).

[4]Rule 1.10(b). It is Rule 1.10 and not Rule 1.7 that advises us that the firm is no longer disqualified because Lawyer X (the lawyer who "infected" the law firm with his personal knowledge) is no longer there. When he left the law firm, no person retained actual knowledge about the representation to impute to the other members of the law firm.

[5]See also Restatement of the Law Governing Lawyers, Third, § 132

("Representation Adverse to Interest of a Former Client") (Official Draft 2000). Rule 1.11 governs the conflicts of interest obligations of a former government lawyer, not Rules 1.9(a) & (b). ABA Formal Opinion 97-409 (Aug. 2, 1997). But the drafters of the 2002 Rules imposed Rule 1.9 on current government lawyers. Rule 1.11(d)(1). However, the ABA Formal Opinion 97-409 concludes that a former government lawyer is subject to Rule 1.9(c), which protects the government by not allowing its former lawyers to use confidential or secret government information to the disadvantage of the government. Id. The drafters of the 2002 Rules adopted this view in Rule 1.11(a)(1).

lawyer is still disqualified from representing a new client in that same matter if that new client has interests "materially adverse" to the former client.[6] The lawyer, in short, may not switch sides.[7] The lawyer also may not take a matter adverse to the former client if that matter is "*substantially related*" to the former matter.

For example, let us assume that Lawyer, while a member of Firm #1, was one of the lawyers who represented Plaintiff in the case of *Plaintiff versus Defendant*. Now Lawyer leaves Firm #1 and moves to Firm #2. Firm #2 happens to represent Defendant in the case of *Plaintiff versus Defendant*. Lawyer is disqualified from switching sides. Because he used to represent Plaintiff, he now cannot represent Defendant in the very same case.

Even if the cases are not exactly the same, the lawyer will be disqualified if the new matter is "substantially related" to the former matter. It is to that topic we now turn.

§ 1.9–1(b)(3) The *T.C. Theatre Corp. Case* and the Substantial Relationship Test

The standard developed to determine conflicts in subsequent representation cases was initially a judicial rule, incorporated into the Model Code only by inference in Canons 4, 5, and 9. Judge Weinfeld developed the basic test in the leading case of *T.C. Theatre Corp. v. Warner Brothers Pictures, Inc.*:[8]

> [T]he former client need show no more than that the matters embraced within the pending suit wherein his former attorney appears on behalf of his adversary are *substantially related* to the matters or cause of action wherein the attorney previously represented him, the former client. The Court will assume that during the course of the former representation confidences were disclosed to the attorney bearing on the subject matter of the representation. It will not inquire into their nature and extent. Only in this manner can the lawyer's duty of absolute fidelity be enforced and the spirit of the rule relating to privileged communications be maintained.[9]

---

[6]A client may switch sides by settling a matter and subsequently the law firm's obligation to the settling client may prevent the firm from representing a non-settling co-defendant. *See FMC Technologies, Inc. v. Edwards*, 420 F.Supp.2d 1153 (W.D.Wash. 2006), *noted in* 22 ABA/BNA MANUAL ON PROFESSIONAL CONDUCT, Current Reports News 161 (Apr. 5, 2006).

[7]*See Schaefer v. General Elec. Co.*, 102 Fair Empl. Prac. Cas. (BNA) 1332, 90 Empl. Prac. Dec. (CCH) P 43079, 2008 WL 649189 (D. Conn. 2008), *quoting Treatise.*

[8]*T.C. Theatre Corp. v. Warner Brothers Pictures, Inc.*, 113 F.Supp. 265, 268–69 (S.D.N.Y.1953). Bruce A. Markell, J., in, *In re North American Deed Co.*, 334 B.R. 443 (D. Nev. 2005), *citing* LEGAL ETHICS TREATISE.

[9]113 F.Supp. at 268–69 (emphasis added).

Judge Weinfeld's "substantial relationship" test for subsequent representation cases has been quoted, relied on, cited, and followed by a host of other court decisions.[10]

The Rules, unlike the Code, have an explicit section dealing with this problem. Rule 1.9 recognizes two interests that must be protected: (1) loyalty and (2) client confidences.

As a matter of client loyalty, whether or not the lawyer, in the case of *A vs. B*, learned from Client *A* secret or confidential information, that particular lawyer cannot now "switch sides" in the same matter and represent Client *B*.[11] "Thus, a lawyer could not properly seek to rescind on behalf of a new client a contract [that this lawyer had] drafted on behalf of the former client."[12]

If the matter is not exactly the same, the lawyer still may not "switch sides" if the matters are "substantially related."[13] Whether the matters are so related is a question of degree. If the lawyer is involved in a "specific transaction" as opposed to a "recurrently handled type of problem," then the switching of sides is a direct breach of loyalty, and a conflict exists in the subsequent representation. In contrast, if the matter was a "recurrently handled type of problem," the lawyer may represent a new client "in a wholly distinct problem of that [general] type even though the subsequent representation involves a position adverse to the prior client."[14]

The drafters of the 2002 Rules added a Comment defining substantially related. It first begins by stating "substantially related" includes the "same transaction or legal dispute" or "if there otherwise is a substantial risk that confidential factual information as would normally have been obtained in the prior representation would materially advance the client's position in the subsequent matter."[15] The Comment goes on to state that

> Information that has been disclosed to the public or to other parties adverse to the former client ordinarily will not be disqualifying. Information acquired in a prior representation may have been rendered obsolete by the passage of time, a circumstance that may be relevant in determining whether two representations are substantially related. In the case of an organizational client, general knowledge of the client's policies and practices ordinarily will not preclude a subsequent representation; on the other hand, *knowl-*

---

[10]*See, e.g., Emle Industries, Inc. v. Patentex, Inc.*, 478 F.2d 562, 570–71 (2d Cir.1973); *Schloetter v. Railoc of Indiana, Inc.*, 546 F.2d 706, 710–11 (7th Cir.1976).

[11]Rule 1.9(a), & Comments 1, 2, 8. *See Schaefer v. General Elec. Co.*, 102 Fair Empl. Prac. Cas. (BNA) 1332, 90 Empl. Prac. Dec. (CCH) P 43079,

2008 WL 649189 (D. Conn. 2008), *quoting Treatise.*

[12]Rule 1.9, Comment 1.

[13]*T.C. Theatre Corp. v. Warner Brothers Pictures, Inc.*, 113 F.Supp. 265 (S.D.N.Y.1953); Rule 1.9(a).

[14]Rule 1.9, Comment 2.

[15]Rule 1.9, Comment 3.

edge of specific facts gained in a prior representation that are *relevant to the matter* in question ordinarily will preclude such a representation.[16]
The italicized reference to knowledge about client policies and practices is sometimes referred to as the playbook information.[17] The lawyer may not reveal it.

Consider this example: Lawyer "L" has represented several banks over the years. However, a year ago he resigned from representing any of these banks when he changed law firms. He still practices in the same locality. He now plans to defend a debtor in a collection matter. L no longer has any banker clients, and the new collection suit is a matter *unrelated* to his previous employment. In this case, his former clients may not prevent the new representation. In fact, "L need not obtain the consent of his former clients nor even inform them of his plan."[18] On the other hand, if the matters were related, *i.e.*, if "L" had relevant confidential information, then he is disqualified.

The Rules and the Code also prohibit the lawyer from using confidential or secret information acquired from the former client on behalf of a new client. The case law, interpreting the Model Code, reached this result by having the definition of "substantial relationship" turn on "the possibility, or appearance thereof, that confidential information might have been given to the attorney in relation to the subsequent matter in which disqualification is sought."[19] Rule 1.9(c)(1) reaches this same result more directly, by providing that the lawyer may not "use information relating to the representation to the disadvantage of the former client. . . ."[20]

The courts have split on their interpretation of substantially

---

[16]Rule 1.9, Comment 3 (emphasis added).

[17]**Knowledge of Client Playbook and the Substantial Relationship Test.** *See Maritrans GP, Inc. v. Pepper Hamilton & Sheetz*, 529 Pa. 241, 602 A.2d 1277 (1992). The highest court in Pennsylvania granted injunctive relief to prevent the law firm from representing a competitor in negotiations with the competitor's labor union because the firm possessed confidential playbook information. The Court stated: "whether a law firm can later represent competitors of its former client is a matter that must be decided from case to case and depends on a number of factors. One factor is the extent to which the fiduciary was involved in its client's affairs."

But see Ex parte Regions Bank, 914 So. 2d 843 (Ala. 2005)(rejecting playbook knowledge as a basis to create a substantial relationship).

[18]GEOFFREY C. HAZARD & W. WILLIAM HODES, THE LAW OF LAWYERING: A HANDBOOK ON THE MODEL RULES OF PROFESSIONAL CONDUCT 184–85 (Prentice Hall, 1985).

[19]*Westinghouse Electric Corp. v. Gulf Oil Corp.*, 588 F.2d 221, 224 (7th Cir.1978).

[20]*See also* Rule 1.9(b)(2). ABA Ethics Opinion 95-395 (July 24, 1995), asked whether a lawyer who had once represented one member of a joint insurance-defense consortium may now take on a related representation against one of the other insurer-members. The Committee concluded

related into three broad groups: information specific inquiries, objective matter inquiries, and loyalty inquiries. Many state courts focus on determining whether the law firm possesses confidential information from the former client in applying the substantially related test.[21] The Seventh Circuit has adopted an objective matter test that is designed to save judicial resources. Judges need only to look at the matters of the first and second representation and ask objectively whether it is likely that in the matter of the representation of the former client the firm would learn information that would help matters for the new client.[22] The Fifth Circuit has defined substantially related to include a

---

that relevant confidential information learned from the prior client clearly could not be disclosed, and the lawyer could not act contrary to the interest of his own former client. If the lawyer knows no relevant confidences, and if the new case is not contrary to the interests of the prior client, or if the prior client waives its rights, then the lawyer can take the case. Thus there is no per se prohibition, but the new client should know these limitations and any implications they may have for the lawyer's role in the present case. For case authority concurring with ABA Ethics Opinion 95-395, see *Clean Investments, LLC v. DiSanto*, 489 F. Supp. 2d 100 (D. Me. 2007); *GTE North, Inc. v. Apache Products Co.*, 914 F. Supp. 1575 (N.D. Ill. 1996).

[21]*See, e.g., In re Brandsness*, 299 Or. 420, 702 P.2d 1098 (1985)(based on a slightly different version of the former client rule but focused on confidential information acquired in the representation of the former client); *In re Estate of Wright*, 377 Ill. App. 3d 800, 317 Ill. Dec. 194, 881 N.E.2d 362 (2d Dist. 2007)(focusing on confidential information in holding that law firm that represented mother in financial transaction with son cannot later represent son against mother's estate in dispute over the same transaction); *NCNB Texas National Bank v. Coker*, 765 S.W.2d 398 (Tex. 1989)(The Texas Supreme Court held that "the severity of the remedy requested requires the movant to establish a preponderance of the facts indicating a substantial relation between the two representa-

tions." In particular, the movant must show that "the factual matter involved were so related to the facts in the pending litigation that it creates a genuine threat that confidences revealed to his former counsel will be divulged to his present adversary." If this is met, "the moving party is entitled to a conclusive presumption that confidences and secrets were imparted to the former attorney."). *See also* Charles W. Wolfram, *Former-Client Conflicts*, 10 GEORGETOWN J. LEGAL ETHICS 677 (1997)("Loyalty considerations should have no separate role in extending the substantial relationship standard beyond the area defined by confidentiality considerations.")

[22]*See Analytica v. NPD Research*, 708 F.2d 1263 (7th Cir.1983). Judge Posner uses an objective test: "if the lawyers could have obtained confidential information in the first representation that would be relevant to the second" the lawyers are disqualified:

The "substantial relationship" test has its problems, but conducting a factual inquiry into every case into whether confidences had actually been revealed would not be a satisfactory alternative, particularly in a case such as this where the issue is not just whether they had been revealed, but whether they will be revealed during a pending litigation. Apart from the difficulty of taking evidence on the question without compromising the confidences themselves, the only witnesses would be the very lawyers whose firm was sought to be disqualified . . . and their interest not only in retaining a client but in denying a serious breach of professional ethics might outweigh any

loyalty based test focused on client expectations.[23] However, the problem with loyalty and client expectations involves its predictability and definition.[24] When does loyalty to former clients begin and end? Does it vary with the fees paid to the law firm? And, do sophisticated (or cynical) clients have different expectations of loyalty than unsophisticated (less suspicious) clients?

The drafters of the 2002 Rules clearly exhibited a preference for a confidential information test, but they did not foreclose the use of the other tests that the Seventh and Fifth Circuits articulated. The confidential information test has its problems, particularly the fact that the parties in the second case are focusing on information learned about the former client in the first representation. Disclosure of such information is damaging to the former client and thus the Model Rules state that "A former client is not required to reveal confidential information learned by the lawyer in order to establish a substantial risk that the lawyer has confidential information to use in the subsequent matter."[25] Normally, one would think that percolation of different interpretations of "substantially related" will lead to better ethics rules in the long run. However, when a different rule exists in the same state but completely dependent upon whether the case is tried in federal or state court, this results in anomalous results for the citizens of the state.

The Special Situation of the Accommodation Client. Some authorities relax the application of the former client rule

---

felt obligation "to come clean." While "appearances of impropriety" as a principle of professional responsibility invites and maybe has undergone uncritical expansion because of its vague and open-ended character, in this case it has meaning and weight. For a law firm to represent one client today, and the client's adversary tomorrow in a closely related matter, creates an unsavory appearance of conflict of interest that is difficult to dispel in the eyes of the lay public—or for that matter the bench and the bar—by the filing of affidavits, difficult to verify objectively, denying that improper communication has taken place or will take place between the lawyers in the firm handling the two sides.

[23]See In re American Airlines, 972 F.2d 605 (5th Cir.1992):

A party seeking to disqualify counsel under the substantial relationship test need not prove that the past and the present matters are so similar that a lawyer's continued involvement threatens to taint the trial. Rather, the former client must demonstrate that the two matters are substantially related . . .. [W]e adhere to our precedents in refusing to reduce the concerns underlying the substantial relationship test to a client's interests in preserving his confidential information. The second fundamental concern protected by the test is not the public interest in lawyers avoiding "even the appearance of impropriety," but the client's interests in the loyalty of his attorney.

[24]See Ted Schneyer, *Nostalgia in the Fifth Circuit: Holding the Line on Litigation Conflicts Through Federal Common Law*, 16 REVIEW OF LITIGATION 537 (1997).

[25]Rule 1.9, Comment 3. Some courts use presumptions to address this problem. *See, e.g., NCNB Texas National Bank v. Coker*, 765 S.W.2d 398 (Tex. 1989).

507

and its substantial relationship test when the lawyer has represented an accommodation client in the past.[26] Such a representation presumes the representation of a primary client under a normal attorney-client relationship and at the same time the representation of a accommodation client who is somehow related to the primary client. For example, the lawyer agrees to represent the corporate entity and at the same time agrees to represent an employee as an accommodation in order to save costs. The accommodation client is not viewed as triggering the traditional aspects of the attorney-client relationship. Therefore, in the agreement with the accommodation client, the lawyer could contractually retain the right to withdraw from the accommodation client and continue to represent the primary client.

The Restatement offers support for such a treatment of accommodation clients by classifying them as parties who are accepting a limited representation with an advanced consent to permit the lawyer to continue representing the primary client in the same matter when the lawyer withdraws from the accommodation client.[27] Although some support exists in a few cases for recognizing accommodation clients,[28] the concept is not found in Model Rule 1.9 and the authorities that have interpreted this rule.[29] Clearly, corporate lawyers who represent the entity as well as its officers and employees have an incentive to enter into accommodation client contracts with the officer and employee parties who may not be paying the legal fees and whose conduct may be covered by the entity's insurance policy.

§ 1.9–1(b)(4) Former Client Conflicts When Lawyers Switch Firms

Rule 1.9(b) is a little more complicated than Rule 1.9(a). It provides that if the lawyer was associated with a former law firm, and the firm has previously represented the client in a matter, the lawyer may not ethically represent a new client with interests adverse to the client of the former firm *if* the lawyer

---

[26]*See* William Freivogel, FREIVOGEL ON CONFLICTS, Former Client Conflicts: Accommodation Clients (Mar. 2008) in http://freivogelonconflicts.com/new_page_34.htm#"Accommodation%20Client; Douglas R. Richmond, *Accommodation Clients*, 35 AKRON L. REV. 59 (2001).

[27]Restatement of Law Governing Lawyers, Third, § 132, Comment i (Official Draft 2000).

[28]See, e.g., *Allegaert v. Perot*, 565 F.2d 246, 250 (2d Cir. 1977). The court stated, "Because [the accommodation client] necessarily knew that information given to Weil, Goshal, and Leva, Hawes would certainly be conveyed to their primary clients in view of the realignment agreement, the substantial relationship test is inapposite."

[29]*See* ABA CENTER FOR PROFESSIONAL RESPONSIBILITY, ANNOTATED MODEL RULES OF PROFESSIONAL Conduct 158 (6th ed. 2007) (citing *Exterior Systems, Inc. v. Noble Composites, Inc.*, 175 F. Supp. 2d 1112 (N.D. Ind. 2001).

had acquired secret information about this former client, *i.e.*, information protected by Rules 1.6 or 1.9(c).[30]

In cases that are under either Rule 1.9(b) or Rule 1.9(c), the former client may decide to waive the disqualification, thus allowing the law firm to continue the representation. In order to understand these two subsections, let us turn to several examples.

Assume that lawyer Alpha is a member of Firm *#1*. Firm *#1* represents Client *P* in a suit against Client *D*. Alpha herself was not involved in any representation of Client *P*, and Alpha has not acquired any secret or confidential information from Client *P* that is relevant to Client *D*. Alpha now leaves Firm #1 and joins Firm #2, which represents Client *D*.

Note that *P*'s and *D*'s interests are materially adverse to each other *and* Firm #2 (Alpha's new firm) is representing *D* in a matter that is the same as (or substantially related to) the matter in which Firm #1 (Alpha's old firm) is representing *P*. Nonetheless, both Firm #2 and Alpha may properly represent *D* against *P* because Alpha acquired from Client *P* no material information protected by Rules 1.6 or 1.9(b). This same result would be reached either under Rule 1.9(b) or under the prior case law.[31]

Consider a similar hypothetical. Lawyer Gamma is a member

---

[30]*See, e.g.*, ABA Formal Opinion 99-415 (Sept. 8, 1999). *See generally* Amon Burton, *Migratory Lawyers and Imputed Conflicts of Interest*, 16 REVIEW OF LITIGATION 665 (1997); Paul R. Tremblay, *Migrating Lawyers and the Ethics of Conflict Checking*, 19 GEORGETOWN J. LEGAL ETHICS 489 (2006).

[31]*See, e.g., Silver Chrysler Plymouth, Inc. v. Chrysler Motors Corp.*, 518 F.2d 751, 757 (2d Cir.1975) (a client cannot "reasonably expect to foreclose either all lawyers formerly at the firm or even those who have represented it on unrelated matters from subsequently representing an opposing party").

Representation Adverse to an Organization by Its Former In-house Lawyer. A similar analysis applies when in-house corporate counsel or in-house lawyer for any other organization leaves and joins a law firm or another organization. *See, e.g., PGE v. Duncan Weinberg, Miller & Pembroke, P.C.*, 162 Or.App. 265, 986 P.2d 35 (1999). This question is also analyzed under Rule 1.9. In general, the former in-house lawyer is not precluded by the ethics rules from taking a case adverse to his or her former employer (just as any lawyer may take a case adverse to a former client) if the former counsel has no relevant, material confidences.

ABA Formal Opinion 99-415 (Sept. 8, 1999) considers this precise question and concludes:

"A former in-house lawyer may, without obtaining consent from the former client, represent a client in a matter that is materially adverse to the lawyer's former employer unless during the course of the lawyer's employment by the organization either the lawyer *personally* had represented the employer in the same matter or in a substantially related matter or another member of the organization's legal department had done so *and* the *former in-house lawyer had acquired protected information material* to the new matter.

"The fact that the lawyer had represented his former employer in similar types of matters or that the lawyer had gained a general knowledge of the strategies, policies, or

of the firm of Alpha & Beta. Alpha represents *P* in the case of *P vs. D*. Gamma, while with the law firm of Alpha & Beta, did not work on the case of *P vs. D* and acquired no knowledge relating to client *P*. Gamma then leaves the firm and joins another firm, the "second firm." "[N]either the lawyer [Gamma] individually nor the second firm is disqualified from representing another client in the same or a related manner even though the interests of the two clients conflict."[32]

Now assume the same facts in the previous hypothetical except that Alpha *personally* worked for *P* in the case of *P v. D* while Alpha was with Firm #1. Alpha did not acquire any material client secrets or confidences, but she did work on that particular case. For example, she filed an appearance in court and asked for a continuance. By hypothesis, there is no need to protect the former client's secrets or confidences.

The Model Code did not directly deal with this issue. However, it may be the case that neither Alpha nor Firm #2 (Alpha's new firm) could represent *D*. Alpha is personally disqualified because she personally represented *P*, and commentators suggested that it would be improper for her now to switch sides.[33] Because Alpha's disqualification is personal to her (not imputed to her),

---

personnel of the former employer is not sufficient by itself to establish a substantial relationship between the current matter and matters in the legal department at the organization for purposes of Rule 1.9(a). Moreover, general supervisory responsibility such as that exercised by the head of a legal department ordinarily is not by itself sufficient to establish that a lawyer represented his former employer in a particular matter even if it is the same as or substantially related to a matter at the new firm.

"The Committee nevertheless is of the opinion that an in-house lawyer may, in the course of his employment as in-house counsel, gain such sensitive information concerning matters in which the legal department represented the organization that is material to the subsequent representation as to be disqualified from subsequent representation under Rules 1.9(a) or 1.9(b) or prohibited from disclosing that information under Rule 1.9(c)."

For example, simply because the name of the former in-house law-yer routinely appears on court pleadings does not mean that the former lawyer is automatically excluded from later representing the adverse party, as ABA Formal Opinion 99-415 notes:

"[I]f the name of the general counsel appears on all pleadings filed by the organization as a matter of general policy, the matter is relatively small or routine, and the legal department is large, the general counsel may not have any familiarity with the matter and should not be viewed as having represented the organization in connection with it unless the rules of practice of the jurisdiction require a contrary conclusion. However, if a matter involved significant litigation and the name of the in-house lawyer appeared on the pleadings, it may be presumed that the lawyer represented the organization in that matter."

ABA Formal Opinion 99-415 (text at footnote 9, which is omitted; footnote 9 states that the presumption should be rebuttable).

[32] Rule 1.9, Comment 9.

[33] *See, e.g.*, HENRY DRINKER, LEGAL ETHICS 115 (1953).

her disqualification is imputed to all the lawyers in her new firm, Firm #2.[34]

The Model Rules are clearer. Unless the former client consents, Alpha is *personally* disqualified. Rule 1.9(a) provides that if Alpha formerly represented a client in a matter, she may not thereafter represent another person in the same or a substantially related matter, if that other person's interest is materially adverse to the interest of the former client (unless, or course, the former client consents).[35]

§ 1.9–1(b)(5) Using Client Information for the Lawyer's Personal Benefit

Both the Code and the Rules forbid using client secrets or confidences to the disadvantage of the client.[36] This prohibition applies equally to protect a former client, *unless* the information has become generally known.[37] "As a general matter, whether there is a 'representation' under Rule 1.9(a) depends upon whether a lawyer received client confidences material to the subsequent representation."[38]

Note that a lawyer violates this rule of confidentiality even if the lawyer does not disclose the information to anyone. What is relevant is that she *uses* the information to the client's detriment.[39] If the agent is allowed to use confidential information for purposes that cause injury to the principal, that would tend to harm the freedom of communication that should exist between principal and agent. For example, Lawyer learned, in confidence, that Client is planning to renew the lease on the building that Client now uses. Lawyer then secretly visits Lessor and obtains the lease on Lawyer's own account but does not tell Lessor any Client information. Lawyer plans to raise the rent because she learned, in confidence, that this location is more important to Client than Lessor suspects. Lawyer has committed a disciplinable violation.[40]

Unless the client consents, the lawyer may not use a client confidence or secret for the lawyer's own advantage (or a third

---

[34]*See* DR 5-105(D).

[35]*See also* Rule 1.9, Comment 2 ("When a lawyer has been directly involved in a specific transaction, subsequent representation of other clients with materially adverse interests clearly is prohibited.").

[36]Rule 1.9(c); Rule 1.8(b). DR 4-101(B)(2).

[37]Rule 1.9(c)(1). *See* EC 4-6.

[38]ABA Formal Opinion 97-409 (Aug. 2, 1977), at 9 n.8.

[39]Rule 1.9(c)(1) ("use the information . . . or when the information has become generally known").

[40]*Cf.* Restatement of the Law of Agency, Second, § 395 & Illustration 1, which states that the agent "may be required to hold this lease as constructive trustee" for the principal.

person's advantage). Under the Model Code, this rule is applicable whether or not the client suffers detriment.[41]

This prohibition on the use of client information is an old one.[42] It also reflects basic principles of agency law. No agent, whether or not a lawyer, may use the principal's secret information to the agent's advantage even if there is no detriment to the principal and even if using the information does not require revealing it.[43] The remedy in the law of agency for this breach of trust is that the agent must turn over any profits to the principal. For example, where "a corporation has decided to operate an enterprise at a place where land values will be increased because of such operation, a corporate officer who takes advantage of his special knowledge to buy land in the vicinity is accountable for the profits he makes, *even though such purchases have no adverse effect upon the enterprise.*"[44] This rule is not applicable if the "information is a matter of general knowledge."[45]

The theory behind the Model Code—and the law of agency that the Code reflects—is that this confidential or secret information belongs to the client. The lawyer may not sell it or use it to the lawyer's own advantage unless the client consents.

The Model Rules, surprisingly, have *no* section corresponding to DR 4-101(B)(3). Moreover, Rule 1.8, Comment 5 seems to negate the possibility that the Rules could be interpreted to incorporate the principle of DR 4-101(B)(3). That Comment says: "Use of information relating to the representation *to the disadvantage of the client* violates the lawyer's duty of loyalty . . .. The Rule does not prohibit uses that do not *disadvantage* the client."[46] The negative implication is that there is no ethical problem if the lawyer's use of the client's "insider" information does not harm the client.

The conduct described in Rule 1.8, Comment 5 is improper under the Code even without the condition stated in italics. Similarly, even if a jurisdiction would adopt the Rules instead of the Code, under the general law of agency a lawyer who used client information for the lawyer's advantage must account to the

[41]DR 4-101(B)(3).

[42]*See* ABA Canons of Professional Ethics, Canon 11 (1908), and Canon 37 (1908), as amended. *See, e.g., Healy v. Gray*, 184 Iowa 111, 119, 168 N.W. 222, 225 (1918): "[A]n attorney will not be permitted to make use of knowledge, or information, acquired by him through his professional relations with his client, or in the conduct of his client's business to his own advantage or profit."

[43]Restatement of the Law of Agency, Second, § 388, and Comment c.

[44]Restatement of the Law of Agency, Second, § 388, at Comment c. See also id. at § 395, Comment *e* (emphasis added).

[45]Restatement of the Law of Agency, Second, § 388, & § 395.

[46]Rule 1.8, Comment 5 (emphasis added).

client for any profits made. The lawyer who turns to this section of the Model Rules for comfort (when a court, pursuant to the law of agency, orders him to account to the client for any profits made) will find no solace. The lawyer may not use "on his own account" confidential information acquired from a former client.[47] However, it would appear that the Model Rules may not subject a lawyer to discipline for his misuse of client information.[48]

§ 1.9–1(b)(6) A Lawyer's Right to Engage in Activity or Express a Personal Viewpoint not in Accordance with a Client's Interests

A lawyer may express a personal viewpoint that is adverse to the interest of a former client (or even a present client in a pending matter) as long as the lawyer does not compromise the client confidences and the lawyer's zealous representation of the client.[49] Thus, the Model Rules provide that lawyers, in general, may

---

[47]Restatement of the Law of Agency, Second, § 395, 396(b), (c).

The Restatement of the Law Governing Lawyers, Third, § 60 (Official Draft 2000), also does not adopt the Model Rules on this issue. Section 112, titled, *Lawyer's Duty to Safeguard Confidential Client Information* provides:

"(1) Except as provided in §§ 61–67, during and after representation of a client:

"(a) the lawyer may not use or disclose confidential client information as defined in § 59 if there is a reasonable prospect that doing so will adversely affect a material interest of the client or if the client has instructed the lawyer not to use or disclose such information;

"(b) the lawyer must take steps reasonable in the circumstances to protect confidential client information against impermissible use or disclosure by the lawyer's associates or agents that may adversely affect a material interest of the client or otherwise than as instructed by the client.

"(2) Except as stated in § 62, a lawyer who uses confidential information of a client for the lawyer's pecuniary gain other than in the practice of law must account to the client for any profits made."

Comment j states that the purpose of subsection (2) is to prohibit a "lawyer from using or disclosing confidential client information for the lawyer's personal enrichment, *regardless of lack of risk of prejudice to the affected client.*" *Id.* at Comment *j*, at p. 467. This Comment also states that the "lawyer codes differ over whether such self-enriching use or disclosure constitutes a disciplinary violation in the absence of prejudice to the client." *Id.*

[48]Ronald D. Rotunda, *Judicial Conference—Second Circuit: RICO and the Proposed Restatement of the Law Governing Lawyers* (Sept. 7, 1990), *reprinted in*, 136 FEDERAL RULES DECISIONS 236, 266 to 271 (1991). On the other hand, Model Rule jurisdictions have disciplined lawyers for using secret client information, even in the absence of detriment to the client. *In re Guidone*, 139 N.J. 272, 653 A.2d 1127 (1994).

[49]Association of the Bar of the City of New York, Committee on Professional and Judicial Ethics, Formal Op. 1997-3 (Mar.1997), 1997 WL 1724483.

advocate law reform even though that reform may affect the interests of a client.[50] Ethics opinions have long provided:

> The obligation of loyalty to the client applies only to a lawyer in the discharge of professional duties and implies no obligation to adopt a personal viewpoint favorable to the interests or desires of the client. While a lawyer must act always with circumspection in order that the lawyer's conduct will not adversely affect the rights of a client in a matter the lawyer is then handling, the lawyer may take positions on public issues and espouse legal reforms favored by the lawyer without regard to the individual views of any client.[51]

This principle has a constitutional dimension, because lawyers do not forfeit their rights of free speech when they represent clients.[52] A related principle of ethics fortifies this constitutional principle— the lawyer's advocacy for a client does not imply that the lawyer is advocating her own personal views:

> In general, a lawyer may publicly take personal positions on controversial issues without regard to whether the positions are consistent with those of some or all of the lawyer's clients. Consent of the lawyer's clients is not required. Lawyers usually represent many clients, and professional detachment is one of the qualities a lawyer brings to each client.[53]

However, the right of free speech does not override the duty to keep a client's confidences. When the lawyer discusses public issues, he may not use a client's confidential information.[54] For

---

[50]ABA Model Rules 1.2(b), 6.3, 6.4.

[51]Association of the Bar of the City of New York, Committee on Professional and Judicial Ethics, Formal Op. 1997-3 (Mar.1997), 1997 WL 1724483, *2.

Joe v. Two Thiry Nine Joint Venture, 47 Tex. Sup. Ct. J. 1058, 145 S.W. 3d 150 (2004). Client sued its lawyer and the lawyer's law for malpractice and breach of fiduciary duty after the lawyer (who was also a member of the city council) voted in favor of a construction moratorium when that vote was adverse to his client. Among other things, the Court ruled that the lawyer and law firm owed no duty to inform their client of the city council meeting where the lawyer voted in favor of the moratorium. While a lawyer owes to his client a duty to inform the client of matters material to the representation, this duty to inform does not extend to matters beyond the scope of the representation.

[52]*Johnston v. Koppes*, 850 F.2d 594, 596–97 (9th Cir. 1988) held that the public employer may not sanction a lawyer for her private-policy positions that she advocated:

> Loyalty to a client requires subordination of a lawyer's personal interests when acting in a professional capacity. But loyalty to a client does not require extinguishment of a lawyer's deepest convictions; and there are occasions where exercise of these convictions- even an exercise debatable in professional terms-is protected by the Constitution.

[53]Restatement Third, The Law Governing Lawyers § 125, Comment e.

[54]Restatement Third, The Law Governing Lawyers § 125, Comment e (internal citation omitted).

example, consider *Oasis West Realty, LLC v. Goldman.*[55] In this case, the former client (Oasis) sued its former lawyer (Goldman) and his law firm for breach of fiduciary duty, professional negligence, and breach of contract, claiming use of confidential information from its former client. The court held that plaintiff stated a cause of action.

In 2004, Oasis, in an effort to redevelop real estate it owned in Beverly Hills, hired Goldman and his law firm because Goldman was heavily involved in Beverly Hills politics and homeowners' matters. Plaintiff believed Goldman could assist in securing approval for the project. Defendants represented Oasis for a little over a year, and then the representation ended.

In 2008, Goldman became involved in a campaign to prevent the same redevelopment project by soliciting about 20 signatures on a referendum petition to overturn the Beverly Hills City Council's approval of the project. Goldman also attended a city council meeting and unsuccessfully spoke against enforcement of a requirement that persons soliciting signatures for a referendum petition carry the full text of the resolution.

Despite Goldman's efforts, the voters upheld the city council's approval by a narrow margin. Oasis then filed a complaint for breach of fiduciary duty, professional negligence, and breach of contract against Goldman and his law firm, seeking over $4 million in damages. The Court of Appeals dismissed that suit, arguing that Goldman was exercising his right of petition and free speech. The California Supreme Court refused to dismiss the suit and sent the case back for a trial because Oasis alleged it had "revealed confidences to Mr. Goldman, which it reasonably believed would remain forever inviolate."

Goldman insisted that he never "disclosed any confidential information acquired during the representation of Oasis to anyone, and did not believe that he disclosed to anyone that he had ever represented Oasis in connection with the Hilton project." Oasis did not offer direct evidence that Goldman relied on confidential information in formulating his opposition or in designing his plea to his neighbors to join him in opposing the project, but the Court said, at this stage, the proper inquiry "is whether the plaintiff proffers sufficient evidence for such an inference."[56] That is true here.

The ethics rules required Goldman to disclose to Oasis "any personal relationship or interest that he knew or reasonably should have known could substantially affect the exercise of his

---

[55]*Oasis West Realty, LLC v. Goldman*, 51 Cal. 4th 811, 124 Cal. Rptr. 3d 256, 250 P.3d 1115 (2011).

[56]*Oasis West Realty, LLC v.* *Goldman*, 51 Cal. 4th 811, 823, 124 Cal. Rptr. 3d 256, 250 P.3d 1115, 1123 (2011).

professional judgment—but never did so." Hence, it is "reasonable to infer that Goldman's opposition to the project developed over the course of the representation, fueled by the confidential information he gleaned during it."[57] For example, while representing the real estate developer, the lawyer may discover that "city officials are particularly concerned about the parking and traffic impacts of a proposed development, or that an identifiable population demographic is especially disposed to oppose the proposed development."[58] He could then "use this information to campaign (quite effectively, one would imagine) against the precise project the attorney had previously been paid to promote."[59]

§ 1.9–2 LAWYER HIRED AS EXPERT WITNESS

A law firm or party may hire a lawyer as an expert witness, typically in a legal malpractice case to assist the trier of fact in determining, for example, the standards of the legal community in a particular factual context, or to prove foreign law. The testifying expert witness is like any non-lawyer expert witness. She is hired to present expert testimony to aid the trier of fact, a duty that is inconsistent with the duty of a lawyer, which is to advance a client's objectives diligently.[1]

Because the lawyer is not hired as an advocate, the lawyer has no attorney-client relationship with the law firm or the litigant (hereinafter, "Litigant"). Therefore, after the termination of her engagement as an expert witness for Litigant, Rule 1.9 does not preclude her from representing a party in a case adverse to Litigant because she was never Litigant's lawyer. However, she may have duties under other law[2] to keep certain information about Litigant confidential, and if that duty to keep the Litigant's information confidential would materially limit her representation of

---

[57]*Oasis West Realty, LLC v. Goldman*, 51 Cal. 4th 811, 822, 124 Cal. Rptr. 3d 256, 264, 250 P.3d 1115, 1122 (2011).

[58]*Oasis West Realty, LLC v. Goldman*, 51 Cal. 4th 811, 823, 124 Cal. Rptr. 3d 256, 265, 250 P.3d 1115, 1122 (2011).

[59]*Oasis West Realty, LLC v. Goldman*, 51 Cal. 4th 811, 823, 124 Cal. Rptr. 3d 256, 265, 250 P.3d 1115 (2011).

[Section 1.9–2]

[1]If a law firm hires a lawyer as a nontestifying expert consultant, then the lawyer's role is comparable to that of a co-counsel, not a testifying expert witness.

[2]For example, the former expert witness may have a duty under the law of agency, as a subagent, or she may have assumed it by contract. ABA Formal Opinion 97-407 (May 13, 1997) at 9 n.9.

Steven Lubet, Expert Testimony: A Guide for Expert Witnesses and the Lawyers Who Examine Them 175–77 (National Institute for Trial Advocacy, 1998) explains the different concerns at play here. First, "expert witnesses should assume that all of their communications, with either the client or retaining counsel, may be subject to disclosure through the process of discovery." However, even "in the absence of a separate ethical duty, principles of agency law require that an expert take

the new client in a matter adverse to Litigant, she would be disqualified by Rule 1.7.[3] Her disqualification would be then imputed to law firm pursuant to Rule 1.10.

§ 1.9–3 INFORMATION GENERALLY KNOWN

The protection offered a former client's confidences has some limits, otherwise a lawyer could seldom represent a new client against a former client. If the reason to protect the confidence is no longer applicable, then the protection is lost. Thus it is not disqualifying if a lawyer had access to *general information concerning the personality of a client,* which is always helpful in later suits against that client. . . ."[1] Most lawyers "who have represented organizational clients will inevitably have general

---

reasonable steps to safeguard client confidences and refrain from using confidential information for self-enrichment or other purposes." Thus, "[t]he law of agency imposes an obligation to refrain from exploiting a client's confidences for the benefit of another. Thus, an expert should not accept conflicting engagements, either concurrently or successively, that are factually related, since this could risk misuse or exploitation of a client's confidences." (footnotes omitted).

See Restatement of the Law of Agency, Second (1958), § 428, comment *a.*

Cf. Conforti & Eisele, Inc. v. Division of Building Construction, 170 N.J.Super. 64, 405 A.2d 487 (1979).

[3]ABA Formal Opinion 97-407 (May 13, 1997), at 11 to 12.

[Section 1.9–3]

[1]*Unified Sewerage Agency of Washington County, Oregon v. Jelco Inc.,* 646 F.2d 1339, 1351 (9th Cir. 1981), which refused to disqualify a law firm even though it had earlier gained "information and insights from Jelco about such things as Jelco's institutional attitudes towards negotiation and settlement and Jelco's method of doing business." The law firm "did not have access to any specific information that would help [it] prevail against Jelco. . . . " The court also found that the party seeking disqualification had earlier consented and thus waived its rights.

But see Chugach Electric Association v. United States District Court, 370 F.2d 441 (9th Cir.1966), *cert. denied,* 389 U.S. 820, 88 S.Ct. 40, 19 L.Ed.2d 71 (1967). The lawyer was general counsel and later consultant to Chugach. The Board of Directors of the Company was divided on many issues and when a minority of the Board gained control and became a majority, the lawyer resigned. The lawyer later represented the trustee in bankruptcy of a coal company and sued Chugach claiming an antitrust conspiracy because of alleged agreements and overt acts occurring after the attorney severed any connection with Chugach. The court disqualified the lawyer. "The problem here is not limited to the question whether [the lawyer] was connected with petitioner as its counsel at the time agreements were reached and overt acts taken, but includes the question whether, as attorney, he was in a position to acquire knowledge casting light on the purpose of later acts and agreements . . .. A likelihood here exists which cannot be disregarded that [the lawyer's] knowledge of private matters gained in confidence would provide him with greater insight and understanding of the significance of subsequent events in an antitrust context and offer a promising source of discovery." *Id.* at 443.

Chugach includes language that can be interpreted to be an unusually broad view of what constitutes confidential client information—"greater

517

information about the inner workings of the client," but that information is not normally or necessarily disqualifying under Rule 1.9.[2]

Similarly, there is no need to protect client information if that information has become "generally known;"[3] or if the former client consents to the subsequent representation[4]; or if the other exceptions to the normal rule protecting client confidences are applicable.[5]

§ 1.9–4 IMPUTING KNOWLEDGE THAT IS ONLY IMPUTED AND NOT ACTUAL

Rule 1.9(b), together with Rule 1.10(b), provide there is no need to limit the practice of a lawyer because of client secrets when the lawyer has no actual (but only imputed) knowledge of those secrets. Thus, if Lawyer A leaves *Firm X* (which represents *Client #1*) and then joins *Firm Y*, Lawyer A is not precluded from representing *Client #2*, even though Client #2's interests are materially adverse to *Client #1*, *if* Lawyer A never acquired any confidential or secret information about *Client #1* while Lawyer A was a member of *Firm X*.[1] Otherwise, Lawyer A would be a peculiar form of a Typhoid Mary, someone who does not have any disease herself (she has no actual knowledge) but is still a carrier, who is able to infect any firm she joined with knowledge that she never actually had, because she only has "imputed" knowledge (*i.e.*, knowledge that was attributed to her while she was with her original firm). The general principle is that the law of ethics does not impute to other lawyers the knowledge of Lawyer #1 if Lawyer #1's knowledge is only imputed and not actual.

§ 1.9–5 BURDEN OF PROOF

The application of Rule 1.9(b) and similar rules often turns on the question of whether a lawyer had acquired material client information protected as client confidences or secrets. "In such an inquiry, the burden of proof should rest upon the firm whose disqualification is sought."[1]

However, the fact that the firm must demonstrate that it is *not* the depository of client information that is relevant and secret does not mean that the burden can never be met. It is always difficult to prove a negative, and courts have consequently recog-

---

insight and understanding of the significance of subsequent events." 370 F.2d at 443. Such a broad view does not reflect the more carefully crafted view of many subsequent cases.

[2]ABA Formal Opinion 97-409 (Aug. 2, 1997), at 15 n. 17.

[3]Rule 1.9(c)(1).

[4]Rule 1.9(a).

[5]Rule 1.6; DR 4-101(C).

[Section 1.9–4]

[1]*See* Rule 1.10(b).

[Section 1.9–5]

[1]Rule 1.9, Comment 6.

nized that, particularly in these cases, the standard for proof should not be "unattainably high."[2]

§ 1.9–6 WAIVER

§ 1.9–6(a) Introduction

Because Rule 1.9 seeks to protect the former client, that former client may waive its benefits. This principle predates the enactment of the Model Rules. As the court stated in the case of, *In re Yarn Processing Patent Validity Litigation:*[1]

> A former client may consent to the employment of the attorney by an adverse party even where the former client is involved in the case as a party. [T]his might typically occur where the former client realizes that any prior disclosures will not prejudice him in the new case. Such consent will prevent the disqualification of the attorney even in a criminal case.[2]

§ 1.9–6(b) Rule 1.9(a) and Rule 1.9(b)

Rules 1.9 (a) and 1.9(b) allow the former client to waive the conflict of interest. In both cases, if there is a conflict under these rules, an otherwise disqualified lawyer may represent a new client against the former client *if* "the former client gives informed consent, confirmed in writing."[3]

The word "informed consent" is a term of art. It means more than merely "talk." The lawyer "informs" his client when he "has communicated adequate information and explanation about the material risks of and reasonably available alternatives to the proposed course of conduct."[4] In other words, the lawyer must bring home to the client not only the relevant facts and the relevant law but also the significance of those facts and the law.[5]

---

[2]*Laskey Bros. of W. Va., Inc. v. Warner Bros. Pictures, Inc.*, 224 F.2d 824, 827 (2d Cir.1955). *See Gas-A-Tron of Arizona v. Union Oil Co. of California*, 534 F.2d 1322, 1325 (9th Cir.1976) (per curiam), *cert. denied*, 429 U.S. 861, 97 S.Ct. 164, 50 L.Ed.2d 139 (1976): "[W]e are convinced that any initial inference of impropriety that arose from [Lawyer *B*'s] potential physical access to the files of Exxon and Shell and from his association with lawyers who did know confidential information about them was dispelled by evidence that he saw none of the files other than those relating to the cases assigned to him heretofore described and that he heard no confidences about Exxon and Shell from the lawyers with whom he was earlier associated." Rebuttal by attorney affidavit may also be allowed. *Silver Chrysler Plymouth, Inc. v. Chrysler Motors Corp.*, 518 F.2d 751, 756 (2d Cir.1975).

[Section 1.9–6]

[1]*In re Yarn Processing Patent Validity Litigation*, 530 F.2d 83 (5th Cir.1976).

[2]530 F.2d 83, 89. *See also Cox v. American Cast Iron Pipe Co.*, 847 F.2d 725, 729 (11th Cir.1988).

[3]Rule 1.9(a); Rule 1.9(b).

[4]Model Rules, Terminology [2], "Consult" or "Consultation."

[5]Restatement of the Law Governing Lawyers, Third, § 122(2) (Official

Once the lawyer has fully informed the former client of the relevant information, then, the former client may waive his rights.[6]

§ 1.9–6(c) Rule 1.9(c)

Rule 1.9(c)(1) at first appears not to allow a waiver. The provision makes no direct reference to a waiver. It simply states that the lawyer who has formerly represented a client may not *use* information to the disadvantage of the former client unless one of the factors exists. First, the lawyer can use information to the disadvantage of the former client if the information has become "generally known."[7] In that case there are no longer any secrets to protect. Second, the lawyer can use this information about the former client if "these Rules" permit or require the lawyer to reveal it. There is no reference to a waiver. However, Rule 1.6 itself allows the client to waive,[8] so Rule 1.9(c) should also be read to incorporate a waiver element.

Similarly, Rule 1.9(c)(2) makes no direct reference to a waiver. It prohibits a lawyer from *revealing* client information unless "these Rules" permit or require it.[9] The same reasoning that applies to Rule 1.9(c)(1) applies to Rule 1.9(c)(2). Thus, this Rule also should allow a waiver by its incorporation of the elements of Rule 1.6.

§ 1.9–6(d) Implied Waiver

In some cases, a court may conclude that the lawyer has not complied with Rule 1.9, that the client has not consented to the conflict, that the lawyer has not secured a valid waiver from client, *and* that the client has not voluntarily relinquished a known right. But the court may then go on to find that there has been an *implied* waiver.[10] For example, the court might argue that the party waited too long to bring its motion after learning certain facts.

Courts typically do not identify the source of this "implied"

Draft 2000).

[6]*See, e.g., United States v. Valdez*, 149 F.R.D. 223 (D.Utah 1993), where the court refused to disqualify a lawyer for various reasons, including waiver.

[7]Rule 1.9(c)(1).

[8]Rule 1.6(a).

[9]*In re Lane*, 889 A.2d 3 (N.H. 2005) rejected a six-month suspension and cleared a lawyer accused of disclosing confidential client information in order to prevent the client-executor from defrauding his mother. The court said that the lawyer proved a reasonable belief that he needed to provide the surviving child's lawyer with evidence of a previously undisclosed life insurance policy in order to prevent criminal activity by the executor. The court went on to say that, as a matter of first impression, the lawyer had the burden to prove (by a preponderance of the evidence) an exception to Rule 1.9(c)(1) allowing the lawyer to use information relating to the representation to the disadvantage of former client.

[10]*See, e.g., Conoco v. Baskin*, 803 S.W.2d 416, 420 (Tex.App.El Paso, 1991, no writ).

waiver. It does not come from the Rules of Professional Conduct.[11] If the party raising the conflict has played fast and loose with the court (for example, by making a calculation not to raise a conflict until later, so that the disqualification will impose a greater financial burden on the other party), then it is not difficult to understand why the court would react negatively and find what should more properly be called a *"forfeiture,"* but what the court may erroneously call an "implied waiver." Courts should not allow lawyers and their clients to plant error in the record.[12]

On the other hand, it is a different story when the party does not raise a conflict simply because it did not know about the significance of the relevant facts until later. If the lawyers do not secure a valid consent from their client, the burden should be on the lawyers to give promptly to the client the information needed to effectuate a valid waiver. That means that the former client should know both the relevant facts and the significance of those facts. Only then does the former client know that he should consult with the new lawyer.

The client should not have to approach his lawyer with the same anxiousness or trepidations that one would have when asked to sign a pact with the devil. Clients—who are not expected to know the ethics rules governing their lawyers—presume that they can trust their lawyers and former lawyers. It is the lawyer's responsibility, when trying to secure a waiver from a client or former client, to disclose candidly to the client the relevant facts and bring home to the client the significance of those facts.[13] Although the client may be aware of certain facts ("I trusted my lawyer with confidential information and now she is no longer representing me but another party"), the client may not know the significance of those facts (that the lawyer must disqualify herself unless the client voluntarily relinquishes a known right).[14]

§ 1.9–6(e) Prospective Waivers of a Conflict

If a former client may waive a conflict, he or she should also be able to waive its objections prospectively, *if* the prospective waiver meets all the requirements required when the former client grants consent to a present conflict of interest. The lawyer rely-

---

[11]*Cf., Snyderburn v. Bantock*, 625 So.2d 7 (Fla.Dist.App.1993).

[12]"A motion to disqualify should be made with reasonable promptness after a party discovers the facts which lead to the motion. A litigant may not delay filing a motion to disqualify in order to use the motion later as a tool to deprive his opponent of counsel of his choice after substantial prepara-

tion of the case has been completed." *Jackson v. J.C. Penney Co.*, 521 F.Supp. 1032, 1034–35 (N.D.Ga.1981) (internal citations omitted).

[13]After all, the Rules of Professional Conduct governs lawyers, not clients.

[14]Ronald D. Rotunda, *Legal Ethics*, 45 SOUTHWESTERN L.J. 2035, 2037–38 (1992).

ing on this prospective waiver must show that it "reasonably contemplated" the future conflict so that the client's consent is reasonably viewed as fully informed when it was given.[15] In other words, the lawyer must give the client (or former client) the information in a way that this client or former client will appreciate the significance of the waiver that is being sought.

As one court explained in the course of analyzing the validity of a prospective waiver:

> Looking only at the original letter itself, the Court finds that its very language is ambiguous. The phrase "will not be precluded from representing clients who may have interests adverse to WORLDSPAN so long as (1) such adverse matter" does not necessarily or even impliedly foreshadow future directly adverse litigation. It is the opinion of this Court that future directly adverse litigation against one's present client is a matter of such an entirely different quality and exponentially greater magnitude, and so unusual given the position of trust existing between lawyer and client, that any document intended to grant standing consent for the lawyer to litigate against his own client must identify that *possibility, if not in plain language, at least by irresistible inference including reference to specific parties, the circumstances under which such adverse representation would be undertaken, and all relevant like information.*[16]

For example, when the client initially retains the lawyer, the lawyer may propose that the client agree to waive any future rights it may have under Rule 1.9 to prevent the lawyer from taking a matter that is adverse to the former client when that matter is the "same or substantially related" to the former matter. While a client or former client can always waive its rights—as Rules 1.9(a) & (b) provide—it is much harder to find a valid waiver when the waiver concerns a future waiver that encompasses disclosure or use of client confidences against the client, un-

---

[15]*See Worldspan, L.P. v. The Sabre Group Holdings, Inc.*, 5 F.Supp.2d 1356 (N.D.Ga.1998), holding that a prospective conflicts waiver was inadequate because it did not reference the future, directly-adverse litigation. In addition:

"While the significant lapse of time, and, indeed, an apparent on-again, off-again, series of representations in the interval, would seem to make it most difficult for a consent that may have been thoroughly informed in 1992 to be informed in 1998, in view of the pace of change in the world, and indeed in the airline and computer industries, it is not impossible, but, as one court has said, 'such standing consent must by necessity be exceedingly explicit.' *Florida Ins. Guaranty Assn., Inc. v. Carey Canada*, 749 F.Supp. 255, 260 (S.D.Fla.1990)." 5 F.Supp.2d at 1358.

[16]*Worldspan, L.P. v. The Sabre Group Holdings, Inc.*, 5 F.Supp.2d 1356, 1359–60 (N.D.Ga.1998) (emphasis added).

See Richard W. Painter, *Advance Waiver of Conflicts*, 13 GEORGETOWN J. LEGAL ETHICS 289 (2000) for a careful analysis of this issue.

less the client very explicitly agreed to such disclosure or use.[17]
In other words, a client may waive, prospectively, a conflict based
on loyalty, but it may not normally waive, prospectively, a conflict
based on breach of confidences, because a client cannot normally
know at the time of the prospective waiver what those confidences
might be or their relevance and significance. A client's (or a former client's) prospective consent to his lawyer's representation of
another client with adverse interests "does not amount to consent
to breach of confidential disclosure or the use of that information
against the consenting party. . . ."[18] Clients endowed with
ordinary business sense and experience would not normally agree
to such remarkably prejudicial arrangements, because it is
"unworthy of credence" to believe that a former client would "willingly and freely consent" to give to his adversary the "weapons
with which to contest, and, possibly defeat, his valuable rights.
. . ."[19]

A prospective waiver would not normally include a prospective
waiver of *confidences*. For example, if the law firm learned certain
secrets about its Former Client that would be relevant to its
negotiation on behalf of its Current Client in negotiations adverse
to Former Client, then Former Client's consent to the future
adverse representation would not normally include consent to the
adverse use of confidential information. At the time that Former
Client consented to the waiver, it would not normally know that
the law firm would later use information that would be relevant
to the negotiations.

Lawyers and clients will be able to agree, by contract, when it
is mutually beneficial for the client to engage in an advance
waiver of conflicts if the courts create rules that clarify when the
courts will enforce these advance waivers. Courts "should
uniformly enforce such waivers in cases where the client giving
the waiver was independently represented by counsel at the time
the waiver was given. Courts should also encourage clarity in
advance waivers by construing ambiguous provisions against the
lawyer that received the waiver. A waiver, however, should not
have to specify the particular conflict involved in order to be upheld as unambiguous. If enforced uniformly, advance waivers of

---

[17] *See* ABA Formal Opinion 05–
372 (May 11, 2005), *superseding* ABA
Formal Opinion 93-372 (Apr. 16,
1993).

[18] *Westinghouse Electric Corp. v.
Gulf Oil Corp.*, 588 F.2d 221, 229 (7th
Cir.1978).

[19] 588 F.2d at 228–29.

conflicts will help lawyers and clients alike avoid unnecessary and expensive ex-post litigation over disqualification."[20]

§ 1.9–6(f) Clients and Lawyers Who Deliberately Create Conflicts

Some clients deliberately hire many firms to work on various aspects of their legal business. Whether or not the clients intend to deliberately create conflicts by spreading their work around, the inevitable result is that the lawyer who accepts such work suffers an opportunity cost: the lawyer accepts this small amount of business from a client in the hopes of securing more business in the future; increased employment may not come to pass, but the lawyer is disqualified from accepting work that would be adverse to his present client, and he cannot drop the client like a hot potato if other work comes along.[21] The law firm does not have to accept this new business, but does it with eyes open, recognizing that it may mean more business from the client down the road. The lawyer can protect himself by refusing to accept the representation or by asking for a prospective waiver of a conflict in the appropriate circumstances.

It is common practice for some clients, particularly very large ones, to employ different law firms. By spreading the work around, they can compare quality and expenses. Just as law firms do not want to be captive to a single client, a client may not want to be captive to a single law firm. This practice does not normally raise any ethical issues.

The situation is different if the lawyer consults an adversary lawyer for the deliberate purpose of creating a conflict.[22] The first lawyer who consults in bad faith for the purposes of creating a conflict of interest is really misleading the second lawyer. The first lawyer is using the conflict of interest rules as a sword, to impose an unneeded restriction, instead of using it as a shield to protect legitimate expectations of loyalty and confidentiality.

The same problem can exist if the knowledgeable client

---

[20]Richard W. Painter, *Advance Waiver of Conflicts*, 13 GEORGETOWN J. LEGAL ETHICS 289, 328–29 (2000).

[21]*See* Chapter 1.7–5, supra. *See also* Ronald D. Rotunda, *One Potato, Two Potato, Three Potato, Four*, 14 LEGAL TIMES 23 (Aug. 12, 1991) for a discussion of the "hot potato" rule.

[22]ABA Formal Opinion 98-411 (August 30, 1998), *Ethical Issues In Lawyer-To-Lawyer Consultation* advises, at footnote 8: "consultation *for the deliberate purpose of disqualifying potential adversaries* would violate Rule 8.4(c), which prohibits conduct involving dishonesty, fraud, deceit or misrepresentation, and possibly Rule 8.4(d), which prohibits conduct prejudicial to the administration of justice."

For a discussion of clients who in bad faith use the ethics rules as a sword to disqualify lawyers, see, Ronald D. Rotunda, *Law, Lawyers and Managers, in* THE ETHICS OF CORPORATE CONDUCT (Clarence Walton, ed. 1977) (published by Prentice-Hall, Inc., for the American Assembly of Columbia University).

pretends to think about hiring a lawyer but the prospective hiring is not really in good faith—the client really wants to disqualify the law firm and prevent it from representing an adversary. A law firm, for example, may have developed a nationwide practice in representing large corporations in takeover battles. An unscrupulous client may wish to consult this law firm, not really with the bona fide intention of hiring the firm but simply to preemptively disqualify that firm from representing the adversary.

Virginia Ethics Opinion 1794[23] advises that if "someone poses as a prospective client and shares confidences with a lawyer with the secret intention of creating a conflict of interest, the lawyer does not owe that person any duty of confidentiality and is free to represent the person's opponent in the matter discussed during the consultation."

To the same effect is an Indiana Ethics Opinion,[24] which concludes a lawyer is not within ethical bounds "if he (or she) refers an existing client to another lawyer, with the main intention of creating a conflict on the part of the second lawyer. . . ." The fact situation this Opinion had in mind was that of a lawyer who limits his practice to domestic relations eventually discovers that other lawyers have referred their clients to him for consultations, because they intend to disqualify him from representing their clients' spouses.

The Opinion acknowledged that there is no ethical rule directly on point, but it reasoned from vague statements in the Preamble and also from Rule 4.4(a), which provides that in representing a client, "a lawyer shall not use means that have no substantial purpose other than to embarrass, delay, or burden a third person . . . ." In this case, there is no substantial purpose of the lawyer's action other than to burden the opposing lawyer by creating a purported conflict.

If a party seeks to disqualify the opposing lawyer, and that lawyer establishes that the party was acting in bad faith to deliberately create a conflict (the party was hiring the law firm solely to create a conflict), the court should not grant the disqualification motion because granting the motion does not fur-

---

[23]Virginia Ethics Opinion 1794 (June 30, 2004), ABA/BNA Lawyers' Manual on Professional Conduct, at 1201:8705. This opinion goes on to warn: "In the normal situation, however, an initial consultation does give rise to a duty of confidentiality that precludes the latter representation. A general disclaimer stating that the initial consultation does not create a lawyer-client relationship is ineffective to eliminate the duty of confidentiality. To be effective, the disclaimer must clearly demonstrate the prospective client's informed consent to the use of confidential information."

[24]Indiana State Bar Ass'n Ethics Opinion 2 (2000), *reprinted in* RES GESTAE (June 2000), at 31–32.

ther legitimate client expectations. In light of these ethics opinions, the court should treat bad faith behavior as a waiver of disqualification rights that would otherwise exist.

CHAPTER 1.10

CONFLICTS OF INTEREST—IMPUTED DISQUALIFICATION

RULE 1.10: IMPUTATION OF CONFLICTS OF INTEREST: GENERAL RULE

(a) While lawyers are associated in a firm, none of them shall knowingly represent a client when any one of them practicing alone would be prohibited from doing so by Rules 1.7 or 1.9, unless

(1) the prohibition is based upon a personal interest of the disqualified lawyer and does not present a significant risk of materially limiting the representation of the client by the remaining lawyers in the firm; or

(2) the prohibition is based upon Rule 1.9(a), or (b), and arises out of the disqualified lawyer's association with a prior firm, and

(i) the disqualified lawyer is timely screened from any participation in the matter and is apportioned no part of the fee therefrom;

(ii) written notice is promptly given to any affected former client to enable the former client to ascertain compliance with the provisions of this Rule, which shall include a description of the screening procedures employed; a statement of the firm's and of the screened lawyer's compliance with these Rules; a statement that

527

review may be available before a tribunal; and an agreement by the firm to respond promptly to any written inquiries or objections by the former client about the screening procedures; and

(iii) certifications of compliance with these Rules and with the screening procedures are provided to the former client by the screened lawyer and by a partner of the firm, at reasonable intervals upon the former client's written request and upon termination of the screening procedures.

(b) When a lawyer has terminated an association with a firm, the firm is not prohibited from thereafter representing a person with interests materially adverse to those of a client represented by the formerly associated lawyer and not currently represented by the firm, unless:

(1) the matter is the same or substantially related to that in which the formerly associated lawyer represented the client; and

(2) any lawyer remaining in the firm has information protected by Rules 1.6 and 1.9(c) that is material to the matter.

(c) A disqualification prescribed by this rule may be waived by the affected client under the conditions stated in Rule 1.7.

(d) The disqualification of lawyers associated in a firm with former or current government lawyers is governed by Rule 1.11.

Comment

Definition of "Firm"

[1] For purposes of the Rules of Professional Conduct, the term "firm" denotes lawyers in a law partnership, professional corporation, sole proprietorship or other association authorized to practice law; or lawyers employed in a legal services organization or the legal department of a corporation or other organization. See Rule 1.0(c). Whether two or more lawyers constitute a firm within this definition can depend on the specific facts. See Rule 1.0, Comments [2] to [4].

Principles of Imputed Disqualification

[2] The rule of imputed disqualification stated in paragraph (a) gives effect to the principle of loyalty to the client as it applies to lawyers who practice in a law firm. Such situations can be considered from the premise that a firm of lawyers is essentially one lawyer for purposes of the rules governing loyalty to the client, or from the premise that each lawyer is vicariously bound by the obligation of loyalty owed by each lawyer with whom the lawyer is associated. Paragraph (a) operates only among the lawyers currently associated in a firm. When a lawyer moves from one firm to another, the situation is governed by Rules 1.9(b) and 1.10(b).

[3] The rule in paragraph (a) does not prohibit representation where neither questions of client loyalty nor protection of confidential information are presented. Where one lawyer in a firm could not effectively represent a given client because of strong political beliefs, for example, but that lawyer will do no work on the case and the personal beliefs of the lawyer will not materially limit the representation by others in the firm, the firm should not be disqualified. On the other hand, if an opposing party in a case were owned by a lawyer in the law firm, and others in the firm would be materially limited in pursuing the matter because of loyalty to that lawyer, the personal disqualification of the lawyer would be imputed to all others in the firm.

[4] The rule in paragraph (a) also does not prohibit representation by others in the law firm where the person prohibited from involvement in a matter is a nonlawyer, such as a paralegal or legal secretary. Nor does paragraph (a) prohibit representation if the lawyer is prohibited from acting because of events before the person became a lawyer, for example, work that the person did while a law student. Such persons, however, ordinarily must be screened from any personal participation in the matter to avoid communication to others in the firm of confidential information that both the nonlawyers and the firm have a legal duty to protect. See Rules 1.0(k) and 5.3.

[5] Rule 1.10(b) operates to permit a law firm, under certain circumstances, to represent a person with interests directly adverse to those of a client represented by a lawyer who formerly was associated with the firm. The Rule applies regardless of when the formerly associated lawyer represented the client. However, the law firm may not represent a person with interests adverse to those of a present client of the firm, which would violate Rule 1.7. Moreover, the firm may not represent the person where the matter is the same or substantially related to that in which the formerly associated lawyer represented the client and any other lawyer currently in the firm has material information protected by Rules 1.6 and 1.9(c).

[6] Rule 1.10(c) removes imputation with the informed consent of the affected client or former client under the conditions stated in Rule 1.7. The conditions stated in Rule 1.7 require the lawyer to determine that the representation is not prohibited by Rule 1.7(b) and that each affected client or former client has given informed consent to the representation, confirmed in writing. In some cases, the risk may be so severe that the conflict may not be cured by client consent. For a discussion of the effectiveness of client waivers of conflicts that might arise in the future, see Rule 1.7, Comment [22]. For a definition of informed consent, see Rule 1.0(e).

[7] Rule 1.10(a)(2) similarly removes the imputation otherwise required by Rule 1.10(a), but unlike section (c), it does so without requiring that there be informed consent by the former client. Instead, it requires that the procedures laid out in sections (a)(2)(i) to (iii) be followed. A description of effective screening mechanisms appears in Rule 1.0(k). Lawyers should be aware, however, that, even where screening mechanisms have been adopted, tribunals may consider additional factors in ruling upon motions to disqualify a lawyer from pending litigation.

[8] Paragraph (a)(2)(i) does not prohibit the screened lawyer from receiving a salary or partnership share established by prior independent agreement, but that lawyer may not receive compensation directly related to the matter in which the lawyer is disqualified.

[9] The notice required by paragraph (a)(2)(ii) generally should include a description of the screened lawyer's prior representation and be given as soon as practicable after the need for screening becomes apparent. It also should include a statement by the screened lawyer and the firm that the client's material confidential information has not been disclosed or used in violation of the Rules. The notice is intended to enable the former client to evaluate and comment upon the effectiveness of the screening procedures.

[10] The certifications required by paragraph (a)(2)(iii) give the former client assurance that the client's material confidential information has not been disclosed or used inappropriately, either prior to timely implementation of a screen or thereafter. If compliance cannot be certified, the certificate must describe the failure to comply.

[11] Where a lawyer has joined a private firm after having represented the government, imputation is governed by Rule 1.11(b) and (c), not this Rule. Under Rule 1.11(d), where a lawyer represents the government after having served clients in private practice, nongovernmental employment or in another government agency, former-client conflicts are not imputed to government lawyers associated with the individually disqualified lawyer.

[12] Where a lawyer is prohibited from engaging in certain transactions under Rule 1.8, paragraph (k) of that Rule, and not this Rule, determines whether that prohibition also applies to other lawyers associated in a firm with the personally prohibited lawyer.

Authors' 1983 Model Rules Comparison

The 1983 version of Rule 1.10 dealt with imputed disqualification and lawyers switching firms.

In 1989, the ABA amended Model Rule 1.10 to remove original Rule 1.10(b) and move it to Model Rule 1.9(b). The ABA thus renumbered original Model Rule 1.10(c) and 1.10(d) as new Model Rule 1.10(b) and 1.10(c). The impetus behind this change was to clarify an overlap between Model Rule 1.9 and 1.10 and to address the question of duties to former clients when a lawyer changes firms and did not represent the former client but may have acquired confidential information about a former client of the old firm. Also, the ABA added the words "and, not currently represented by the firm" to current Model Rule 1.10(b). This was added to clarify the problem that when a lawyer leaves a firm, Model Rule 1.7's general prohibition of a directly adverse conflict still applies to the situation. The 1983 version of Model Rule 1.10 is reproduced below:

(a) While lawyers are associated in a firm, none of them shall knowingly represent a client when any one of them practicing alone would be prohibited from doing so by Rules 1.7, 1.8(c), 1.9 or 2.2.

(b) When a lawyer becomes associated with a firm, the firm may not knowingly represent a person in the same or a substantially related matter in which that lawyer, or a firm with which the lawyer was associated, had previously represented a client whose interests are materially adverse to that person and about whom the lawyer had acquired information protected by Rules 1.6 and 1.9(b) that is material to the matter.

(c) When a lawyer has terminated an association with a firm, the firm is not prohibited from thereafter representing a person with interests materially adverse to those of a client represented by the formerly associated lawyer unless:

(1) the matter is the same or substantially related to that in which the formerly associated lawyer represented the client; and

(2) any lawyer remaining in the firm has information protected by Rules 1.6 and 1.9(b) that is material to the matter.

(d) A disqualification prescribed by this rule may be waived by the affected client under the conditions stated in Rule 1.7.

When the ABA amended Model Rule 1.10 in 1989, it moved several paragraphs of comments from Model Rule 1.10 to Model Rule 1.9.

The drafters of the 2002 Model Rules changed the title of the Rule from "Imputed Disqualification" to "Imputation of Conflicts of Interests."

In Rule 1.10(a), the drafters deleted a reference to 1.8(c) and 2.2 and added the following clause: "unless the prohibition is based on a personal interest of the prohibited lawyer and does not present a significant risk of materially limiting the representation of the client by the remaining lawyers in the firm." This new clause removes imputation in certain situations when one of the lawyers in the firm is disqualified by virtue of a personal conflict of interest.

The drafters did not amend Rules 1.10(b) and (c).

Rule 1.10(d) is new and states that this Rule does not govern disqualification of a law firm when the conflict results from a lawyer's role as a current or former government lawyer. Those conflicts are governed by Rule 1.11.

In Comment 1, the drafters added language to the first line to define more completely the term, "firm." They added a reference to Rule 1.0(c) and its Comments and deleted several sentences at the end of Comment 1.

Comments 2, 3, and 5 were deleted.

Old Comment 6 was renumbered as Comment 2 without change.

Comments 3 and 4 are new and cover the application of Rule 1.10(a).

Old Comment 7 was not changed but was renumbered as Comment 5.

Comment 6 is new and covered the application of Rule 1.10(c).

Old Comment 4 was renumbered as Comment 7 and substantially amended to reflect the new Rule 1.10(d).

Comment 8 is new and explains that imputation issues under Rule 1.8 conflicts are governed under Rule 1.8(k) and not Rule 1.10.

Post February 2002 Amendment

At the February 2008 meeting of the ABA, the House of Delegates considered and passed an amendment to Rule 1.10 to permit screening.

The drafters took 1.10(a) and made the last line into (a)(1) and added (a)(2) to implement screening.

The drafters added new comments 7-10 and renumbered old 7 and 8 to become new 11 and 12.

At the August 2009 Meeting of the ABA, the House of Delegates adopted a housekeeping modification to Model Rule 1.10 to clarify ambiguous language adopted in 2009. The amendments changed the word "prohibited" to "disqualified" in Rule 1.10(a)(1) and added the following clause to Rule 1.10(a)(2): "and arises out of the disqualified lawyer's association with a prior firm."

Model Code Comparison

DR 5-105(D) provided that "[i]f a lawyer is required to decline or to withdraw from employment under a Disciplinary Rule, no partner, or associate, or any other lawyer affiliated with him or his firm, may accept or continue such employment."

§ 1.10–1 VICARIOUS DISQUALIFICATION AND AN INTRODUCTION TO RULE 1.10: IMPUTING ONE'S LAWYER CONFLICTS OF INTEREST TO OTHER LAWYERS

§ 1.10–1(a) Introduction

It has long been the general rule in disqualification cases that if "a lawyer is required to decline employment or to withdraw from employment, no partner or associate, or any other lawyer affiliated with him or his firm may accept or continue such employment."[1] One attorney's disqualification is imputed to all lawyers in the firm.[2] The imputation crosses practice areas and all of the offices of the law firm even when information is not shared on a routine basis. And, if the lawyer actually disqualified as to a particular case moves to a new firm, his disqualification is normally imputed to all the lawyers of the new firm.[3]

Model Rule 1.10 sets forth the general rule for imputed disqualification. It is more narrowly drafted than DR 5-105(D). For the most part, it reflects the rule as it has actually been interpreted by the case law. Model Rule 1.10, unlike the broader

---

[Section 1.10–1]

[1]DR 5-105(D). Originally, DR 5-105(D) imputed only the disqualification of DR 5-105(A), (B), & (C). In 1975 the ABA amended the rule so that it was extended to impute a disqualification under any Disciplinary Rule. *See* Thomas D. Morgan, *Appropriate Limits on Participation by a Former Agency Official in Matters Before an Agency*, 1980 DUKE L. J. 1, 15 (1980).

[2]*See, e.g., Consolidated Theatres v. Warner Brothers, Circuit Management Corp.*, 216 F.2d 920 (2d Cir. 1954).

[3]*Id.* The Code itself provided no explicit exceptions to this general rule, but in practice it has been interpreted to allow various exceptions. *See, e.g.*, ABA Formal Opinion 342 (Nov. 24, 1975)(dealing with the former government attorney).

language found in the ABA Model Code, is a good restatement of the case law.[4]

When a client employs a lawyer in a law firm to perform legal services on behalf of the client, the legal profession presumes that the lawyer has an obligation to use all of the resources of the firm in the representation. We assume that lawyers within a firm generally share confidential information with each other. In many law firms, partner or shareholder lawyers share firm profits. The concept of imputed disqualification is based upon the notion that clients expect all of the lawyers in the firm to owe a duty of loyalty to them and that economic incentives would push them to use the information contained within the files of the firm, possibly imposing costs on the client.

The drafters of the Model Code and the Model Rules have been reluctant to implement the concept of screening to lawyers in a private law firm as a general matter. The practice of screening is defined as preventing the disqualified lawyer from obtaining profits from the matter that created the conflict, limiting the disqualified lawyer's access to the files of the matter that created the disqualified lawyer, and limiting the communications between the disqualified lawyer and the other lawyers in the firm on the matter that created the conflict.

In the 1983 Model Rules, the ABA permitted screening in the government lawyer conflict context under Rule 1.11. In the 2002 Model Rules, the drafters sought to expand the use of screening when a disqualified lawyer joins a new firm. The ABA House of Delegates rejected this new proposed paragraph. The 2002 Rules added screening in Rule 1.18 when the disqualified lawyer interviews a prospective client and makes sure to only receive information needed to decide whether the accept the representation. In 2009, the ABA amended Rule 1.10(a) to allow limited screening when a lawyer moves from one private law firm to another. This issue is discussed in § 1.10-4(a).

§ 1.10-1(b) Limited Applicability to Personal Interest Conflicts of One Lawyer in a Firm

The drafters of the 2002 Model Rules added a clause to the end of paragraph (a) that removes the imputation of a personal conflict of one lawyer to the other members of the firm if the conflict "does not present a significant risk of materially limiting the representation of the client by the remaining lawyers in the

---

[4]*See also* Restatement of the Law Governing Lawyers, Third, § 123 ("Imputation of Conflict of Interest to Affiliated Lawyer"), § 124 ("Removing Imputation") (Official Draft 2000).

firm."[5] This raises the question, what are personal interest conflicts?

Let us consider two examples. First, assume a lawyer in the firm holds such a strong personal belief against a client that the lawyer cannot competently represent that client. The client may sell tobacco products and our hypothetical lawyer is so opposed to tobacco that he cannot represent that client. Hence, the ethics rules prevent that lawyer from representing that client. The other lawyers are free to represent that client as long as the disqualified lawyer does not work on the case.[6] Note that Rule 1.10 and its Comment do not require that the firm disclose the conflict to the client, just that they follow Rule 1.10(a).

For a second example, assume that a lawyer in the firm holds a significant ownership interest adverse to the interests of a firm client. The lawyer may not represent that client. In addition, the other lawyers in the firm may be materially limited from pursuing the client's interest out of loyalty to the lawyer. Rule 1.10 would disqualify the firm from representing the client.[7] This second example is not a personal interest conflict.

Personal interest conflicts do not arise from situations covered by Rule 1.8. Rule 1.10 makes clear that the application of the imputed disqualification in the context of that provision is governed by Rule 1.8(k).[8]

However, the Comments to Rule 1.7 discuss a new category of "personal interest" conflicts.[9] These conflicts are created by the lawyer's own interests, such as the lawyer's personal business interests or employment interests.[10] Another category includes lawyers who are related to each other by blood or marriage who are asked to represent opposing parties to litigation or a transaction.[11] If the lawyer is disqualified because of his or her relation to the opposing lawyer, the firm should not be disqualified under Rule 1.10(a). There may also be conflicts arising from a sexual relationship one lawyer has with a client. Rule 1.8(k) deals with conflict and also does not impute it to other lawyers in the firm.

§ 1.10–1(c) Inapplicability of Rule 1.10 to Government Lawyers and Former Government Lawyers

The disqualification principles of Rule 1.10 are more extensive

---

[5] Rule 1.10(a).

[6] Rule 1.10, Comment 3.

[7] Rule 1.10, Comment 3.

[8] Rule 1.10, Comment 8.

[9] Rule 1.7, Comments 10 to 12.

[10] Rule 1.7, Comment 10. A specific example is provided—a lawyer who interviews for employment with an opposing party or law firm. Note that the Comment goes on to reference business transactions with a client and Rule 1.8, but as stated above, the personal interest conflict exception of Rule 1.10(a) does not apply to 1.8 conflicts.

[11] Rule 1.7, Comment 11.

than those provided by Rule 1.11 ("Successive Government and Private Employment"). Although Rule 1.10, in general, imputes to all lawyers in the law firm the disqualification of one lawyer in that law firm, this rule does not apply to a former private practitioner who is now in government service.[12] For example, Model Rule 1.10 does not allow a screen to cure the imputed conflict in some circumstances where Model Rule 1.11 would specifically allow the use of a screen.

The government is subject to different protections because of what public policy views as the special governmental interest in recruiting lawyers who will not be unduly burdened in seeking later private employment because of their former affiliation with the government. Similarly, because of the government's unusually broad legal relationships, it should not be unduly hampered when it recruits a lawyer from the private sector.[13] Other policy reasons also justify this distinction between lawyers in government versus lawyers in private practice. The partners and associates in private law firms and similar private associations of lawyers have an economic incentive to work for the economic good of the entire partnership. The lawyer for the government has no similar financial incentive.

§ 1.10–2 WAIVER AND SCREENING UNDER THE 2002 VERSION OF THE MODEL RULES

§ 1.10–2(a) Waiver

Any affected client protected by the principles of Rule 1.10 may waive its protections *if* each client gives informed consent, confirmed in writing, and each lawyer involved reasonably believes that he or she will be able to provide competent and diligent representation.[1] Thus, a waiver is not effective unless: first, all parties knowingly consent after consultation; and second, the conflict is such that it can be waived ("the lawyer reasonably believes").

§ 1.10–2(b) Screening

When a client hires a private law firm, it is generally understood that the client expects to benefit from the expertise of the various lawyers in that firm. The client expects loyalty and confidentiality from the entire law firm. Though a client may only deal with a few lawyers in a firm, the client really hires the firm. Partners and associates regularly discuss with each other the affairs of their clients and seek from each other advice regarding

---

[12]*See* Rule 1.10, Comment 7.

[13]Rule 1.11, Comment 4.

[Section 1.10–2]

[1]Rule 1.10(c).

client affairs.[2] Such intra-firm communication is one of the reasons for the rule regarding imputation of attorney disqualifications.[3]

Thus, if a lawyer is disqualified, and this disqualification is imputed to other members of the firm, the original version of Rule 1.10 did not provide for screening as a method of curing the disqualification. Rule 1.10 (unlike Rule 1.11) nowhere refers to a screen.[4] In the 2002 Rules, the drafters continued screening in Rule 1.11 (government lawyers), Rule 1.12 (former judge or other adjudicative officer), and Rule 1.18 (lawyer interviewing a prospective client).

Although the language of the Model Rules was clear, a few cases suggested that a screen may be sufficient to remove the imputation of the disqualification even in jurisdictions that have adopted Rule 1.10. Sometimes this suggestion is dictum, or the court is faced with a peculiar set of facts.[5] Some courts permit the law firm to overcome a presumption of shared confidences by implementing a screen and offering attorney affidavits and electronic audits tracking access to the files.[6]

A client could waive his entire protections under Rule 1.10, or he could decide to waive on the condition that the law firm institute a screen—or what is sometimes called creating a

---

[2] Rule 1.6, Comment 8; EC 4-2.

[3] *See* Rule 1.10, Comment 1.

[4] *See* ABA Formal Opinion 98-411 (Aug. 30, 1998), at 9 n. 13. In the 1983 Rules, Comment 5 to Rule 1.10 emphasized the obvious, that this failure was not inadvertent: screening "is not allowed under Rule 1.10." The drafters deleted this language, but there is no mistake that Rule 1.10 does not embrace screening.

[5] *See, e.g., Nemours Foundation v. Gilbane, Aetna, Federal Ins. Co.*, 632 F.Supp. 418 (D.Del.1986)(referring to a "cone of silence" and to Rule 1.11(a), which allows screening for the former *government* attorney). *See also* ABA Formal Opinion 90-358 (Sept. 13, 1990) at n.12 (noting that some cases have referred to screening in cases not involving the former government attorney).

Lennartson v. Anoka-Hennepin Independent School District No. 11, 662 N.W.2d 125 (Minn. 2003), rejects screening of a lawyer who was actively involved in representing the plaintiff before moving to the firm representing the defendant in a matter. Rather than follow ABA Model Rule 1.10, the Minnesota Court applied its own Rule, Minn. R. Prof. Conduct 1.10(b), which follows section 124 of Restatement, Third, The Law Governing Lawyers. The Minnesota Rule permits screening only where the "information [learned at the first firm] is unlikely to be significant in the matter." In this case, the lawyer had reviewed the plaintiff's whole file in preparation for conducting a key deposition. The Court refused to let someone with that much information be screened. It disqualified her new firm.

[6] *See Arista Records LLC v. Lime Group LLC*, 2011 WL 672254 (S.D.N.Y. 2011) (Judge Kimba Wood denied a motion to disqualify even when the law firm used a substandard screen because the firm had rebutted the presumption of shared confidences.)

"Chinese Wall"—around the affected attorney.[7] But Rule 1.10 by itself did not approve or validate a screening device and, in fact, does not allow the use of a screen as a device to cure a conflict. Thus, some firms sought to offer screening as a way of obtaining a client's consent to permit the remaining lawyers in the firm to take the representation. However, as discussed in § 1.10–4, since 2009, Model Rule 1.10(a)(2) allows a screen in limited circumstances.

§ 1.10–3 THE RESTATEMENT PROPOSAL REGARDING SCREENING OF LAWYERS MOVING FROM ONE PRIVATE LAW FIRM TO ANOTHER PRIVATE LAW FIRM

The Restatement, Third, of the Law Governing Lawyers has suggested a narrow role for screening.[1] Section 124 is entitled, "Removing Imputation." That section, in brief, provides that a law firm is not disqualified from suing a party simply because a lawyer in that firm learned relevant confidential information about that party, when representing that party in an earlier matter (a matter that is assumed to be "substantially related" to the present matter), *if* the disqualified lawyer is screened, all parties are given notice of the screening, and "any confidential client information communicated to the personally prohibited lawyer is *unlikely to be significant* in the subsequent matter."[2]

A version of section 204(2) first appeared in 1990.[3] Thus far, only a few cases have ever referred to section 204(2), and they have imputed the disqualification and refused to follow the

---

[7]*See, e.g., State ex rel. Freezer Services, Inc. v. Mullen*, 235 Neb. 981, 458 N.W.2d 245 (Neb.1990) (not allowing screening of lawyer because of conflict created when two law firms merged); *Lansing-Delaware Water District v. Oak Lane Park, Inc.*, 248 Kan. 563, 808 P.2d 1369 (Kan.1991); *United States v. Davis*, 780 F.Supp. 21 (D.D.C.1991).

[Section 1.10–3]

[1]Restatement of the Law Governing Lawyers, Third, § 124(2) (Official Draft 2000).

[2]Restatement of the Law Governing Lawyers, Third, § 124(2)(a) (Official Draft 2000)(emphasis added).

[3]Restatement of the Law Governing Lawyers, Third, § 204(2) (Tentative Draft No. 3 (Apr. 10, 1990)).

proposed new rule.[4] This proposal to allow screening has not fared well in the case law.[5]

---

[4]*Towne Development of Chandler, Inc. v. Superior Court*, 173 Ariz. 364, 369, 842 P.2d 1377, 1382 (1992) (rejecting Restatement's proposed rule); *Cardona v. General Motors Corp.*, 942 F.Supp. 968 (D.N.J.1996) (rejecting Restatement's proposed rule); *Elan Transdermal, Ltd. v. Cygnus Therapeutic Systems*, 809 F.Supp. 1383, 1392 n. 14 (N.D.Cal.1992) (same); *Roberts and Schaefer Co. v. San-Con*, 898 F.Supp. 356, 362 (S.D.W. Va.1995) (finding Restatement rule not applicable).

Dieter v. Regents of the University of California, 963 F.Supp. 908, 911 (E.D.Cal.1997) cited the ABA Model Rules as well as the Restatement, but the court did not allow screening. It simply found that the attorneys, who never worked on the case while at another firm, had no confidential information. If the attorney has no confidential information, there is nothing to screen, as the court made quite clear when it stated: "Moreover, if the attorney did join a new firm, because the attorney is barred from handling the second matter, the attorney's entire firm would be barred by imputation." 963 F.Supp. 908, 911.

Decora, Inc. v. DW Wallcovering, Inc., 899 F.Supp. 132, 139 n. 10 (S.D.N.Y.1995) cited the Restatement on the issue of screening; however, it also cited the ABA Rule, and a Second Circuit case—a controlling case for this district court. *Decora* then disqualified the lawyer and imputed the disqualification to the entire law firm; the court did not allow a screen. The Second Circuit case on which *Decora* relied was *Cheng v. GAF Corp.*, 631 F.2d 1052 (2d Cir.1980). *Cheng* obviously was not influenced by the Restatement, which did not even exist at the time. Moreover, *Cheng*, while referring to what it called a "Chinese Wall" and speaking of the possibility of such a screen, ended up disqualifying the individual lawyer and then imputing the disqualification to the entire law firm. The Second Circuit even ruled that the trial court had abused its discretion in not disqualifying the lawyer and the entire law firm.

Another case citing the Restatement was *Marshall v. State of New York Division of State Police*, 952 F.Supp. 103, 110 (N.D.N.Y.1997). *Marshall*, like *Decora*, cited the ABA Rule, the Restatement, and various cases including *Cheng*; then, it disqualified the lawyer, imputed the disqualification to the entire law firm, and did not accept a screen.

See also Kassis v. Teacher's Insurance and Annuity Association, 93 N.Y.2d 611, 695 N.Y.S.2d 515, 717 N.E.2d 674 (1999) (holding that a law firm should be disqualified from representing the defendants because it hired a former associate of another law firm who, while employed at that other law firm, had represented the plaintiffs. The court ordered disqualification even though the new firm had screened the lawyer in question. "Defendants' conclusory averments that the lawyer did not acquire such confidences during the prior representation failed to rebut the presumption as a matter of law. The erection of a 'Chinese Wall' in this case, therefore, was inconsequential." 93 N.Y.2d at 619, 695 N.Y.S.2d at 520, 717 N.E.2d at 679).

[5]William Freivogel's excellent website provides a state-by-state review of the authorities on screening a lawyer who switches law firms. *See* WILLIAM FREIVOGEL, FREIVOGEL ON CONFLICTS, Changing Firms (Mar. 2008), in http://freivogelonconflicts.com/new_page_13.htm.

Note, the concept of screening has been adopted in the ethics codes of a few jurisdictions and applies as a standard in disciplinary cases. *See* ABA CENTER FOR PROFESSIONAL RESPONSIBILITY, ANNOTATED MODEL RULES OF PROFESSIONAL CONDUCT 192

Several reasons may account for this fact. A trial judge ruling on the disqualification motion cannot normally decide if the prior "confidential client information" is "unlikely to be significant" in the present case unless he knows what that confidential information is. Of course, once the judge is told, the matter is no longer confidential. The lawyers opposing (or supporting) disqualification also have to know what the secret information is, and why it is (or is not) significant so that they can respond to the arguments of opposing counsel.

In addition, a judge cannot determine if the matter is "unlikely to be significant" unless he knows the full theory of the case, and that might not happen until the trial is nearly over. Even lawyers deeply involved in a case often do not know the full theory until discovery is completed. In addition, the theory of the case may change as the trial proceeds. Facts that may appear insignificant on the first day of trial take on a new complexion as the facts are presented.

When the Restatement uses the phrase, "is *unlikely to be significant* in the subsequent matter,"[6] it is possible to interpret that language to mean, "is irrelevant or immaterial to the subsequent matter." If that is what this section means, it means very little, because Rule 1.9(b), dealing with the former client, already allows a lawyer to represent a party adverse to a former client if the confidential information about the former client is immaterial to the matter. The Restatement language contemplates that the individual lawyer would be screened from the rest of the lawyers in the law firm, and any of these other lawyers could handle the case. But, if the lawyer's information is truly immaterial, as Rule 1.9 requires, then even the individual lawyer could handle the matter, because there is nothing from which to screen him: the information is immaterial.

The drafters to the 2002 Model Rules proposed a new paragraph (c) based upon the Restatement section 124:

(c) When a lawyer becomes associated with a firm, no lawyer associated in the firm shall knowingly represent a person in a matter in which that lawyer is disqualified under Rule 1.9 unless:

(1) the personally disqualified lawyer is timely screened from any participation in the matter and is apportioned no part of the fee therefrom; and

(2) written notice is promptly given to any affected former client to enable it to ascertain compliance with the provisions of this Rule.

The drafters believed that such a rule properly balanced the obligations to the former client with the rights of new clients to

---

(ABA, 5th ed. 2003).

[6]Restatement of the Law Govern-

ing Lawyers, Third, § 124(2)(a) (Official Draft 2000)(emphasis added).

choose counsel and not face disqualification when lawyers switch firms.[7] The ABA House of Delegates rejected this proposed draft of a new paragraph.[8]

Although the Restatement has had a limited influence on the judicial opinions examining the issue of imputation, the states have begun to adopt versions of Rule 1.10 that expressly permit screening in some circumstances to avoid disqualification when a lawyer has switched firms.[9] A study of state positions on screening finds that by 2007 almost half of the states permit some form of screening in this circumstance.[10] Some states have modified their version of Rule 1.10 to permit screening of a lawyer who moves to a new firm to avoid the disqualification of the firm.[11] Other states have adopted a more limited role for screening when the lawyer changes firms, for example, permitting screening only when the lawyer's role at the former firm was limited or not one of lead counsel or when that lawyer did not acquire significant or material information related to the new representation.[12] This trend balances the need to allow lawyer mobility with the need to protect the client's confidential information.

---

[7]*See* Reporter's Explanation of Changes to Model Rule 1.10.

[8]*See* ABA CENTER FOR PROFESSIONAL RESPONSIBILITY, ANNOTATED MODEL RULES OF PROFESSIONAL CONDUCT 192 (5th ed. 2003).

[9]*See* Joan C. Rogers, *Analysis and Perspective: Screening Gains Acceptance as Method to Avoid Vicarious Disqualification*, 23 ABA/BNA MANUAL ON PROF. CONDUCT 647 (Dec. 26, 2007).

[10]*See* Thomas D. Morgan & Ronald D. Rotunda, 2008 SELECTED STANDARDS ON PROFESSIONAL RESPONSIBILITY 168–173 (2008) (reproducing ALAS Chart on Lateral Lawyer Screening).

[11]These states include: Delaware, Kentucky, Maryland, Montana, Michigan, North Carolina, Oregon, Pennsylvania, Rhode Island, Utah and Washington. 23 ABA/BNA MANUAL ON PROF. CONDUCT 647 (Dec. 26, 2007). For example, Pennsylvania has adopted the following provision in their version of Rule 1.10:

(b) When a lawyer becomes associated with a firm, the firm may not knowingly represent a person in the same or a substantially related matter in which that lawyer, or a firm with which the lawyer was associated, had previously represented a client whose interests are materially adverse to that person and about whom the lawyer had acquired information protected by Rules 1.6 and 1.9(c) that is material to the matter unless:

(1) the disqualified lawyer is screened from any participation in the matter and is apportioned no part of the fee therefrom; and

(2) written notice is promptly given to the appropriate client to enable it to ascertain compliance with the provisions of this rule.

Pa. Rules of Prof. Conduct, Rule 1.10(b).

[12]These states include Arizona, Indiana, Massachusetts, Minnesota, Nevada. New Jersey, North Dakota, Ohio, Tennessee, and Wisconsin. See Thomas D. Morgan & Ronald D. Rotunda, 2008 SELECTED STANDARDS ON PROFESSIONAL RESPONSIBILITY 168–173 (2008)

§ 1.10-4 2009 SCREENING AMENDMENTS TO RULE 1.10(a)

At the August 2008 meeting of the ABA, the House of Delegates considered, yet again, a screening amendment. By one vote the issue was postponed indefinitely. But, "indefinitely," did not mean forever. The supporters rescheduled the issue for the February 2009 meeting; there were two proposals on the floor.[1] The ABA Standing Committee on Ethics and Professional Responsibility put forward a broad proposal to allow screening without client consent. The ABA Section of Litigation proposed screening in a narrower class of cases.[2] Both proposals sought to address the issue of a lawyer who moves from one law firm to another law firm, in the situation where the firms are on opposite sides of the same case and the lawyer worked on the case in the first law firm. Under the 2002 version of Rule 1.10, the second firm is disqualified when it hires the lawyer from the first firm who carries with him the confidences about his former client. Under the proposed screening changes, the second law firm would be permitted to screen the migratory lawyer and thus avoid disqualification. The screening proposals would make lawyer mobility easier, while risking client confidences.

After a heated debate, the House of Delegates adopted a modification of Rule 1.10(a) that would allow law firms to use screening to avoid imputed disqualification. The language is based upon the Ethics Standing Committee draft and not the Section of Litigation draft. Under the Rule as the House of Delegates adopted it, a law firm can avoid imputation of a conflict based upon Rule 1.9(a) or (b) by timely screening the affected lawyer from participating in the case and from being apportioned nor part of the profits from the matter from which he is screened.

The ABA imposed additional burdens on the law firm in an effort to try to allay the concerns of lawyers that screening is not effective. To make sure that the screen is opaque and not translucent, the second law firm (the law firm that hires the lawyer) must provide prompt and detailed notice of the screening to the affected former client. By "former client" we mean the former client of the screened-lawyer; this former client was never the client of the new law firm that hired the screened-lawyer.

This second law firm must also inform the former client that this former client may seek review of the screening in court and that the law firm will respond promptly to any inquiries made by

---

[Section 1.10-4]

[1]*See* 25 ABA/BNA Law. Man. Prof. Conduct 37 (Jan. 29, 2009).

[2]The Section of Litigation proposal would only permit screening if the migratory lawyer "had neither substantial involvement nor material information relating to the matter." *Id.*

the former client.[3] The law firm that is instituting the screen must at regular intervals provide this former client with a certification of the screening procedures and also must inform the former client if such screening is no longer in place.[4]

After the adoption of the Rule 1.10 amendment, some observers noted that the language of new Rule 1.10 was far broader than that which its drafters intended.[5] In other words, the ABA House of Delegates debated this Rule as a limited screening amendment for migratory lawyers who change firms, *not* as a general screening rule for all former client conflicts. But the language of the Rule and Comment did not limit screening to the migratory lawyer situation. The ethics lawyers in the ABA submitted the ambiguity issue for possible correction to the ABA Rules and Calendar Committee for a housekeeping amendment. But the Committee declined to make any change to the language adopted by the House of Delegates.

In 2009, several committees of the ABA supported a housekeeping amendment that would correct the ambiguity in amended Rule 1.10.[6] The House of Delegates approved this amendment that makes clear that the screening provision is only intended to apply to the migratory lawyer situation.

§ 1.10–5 SCREENING NON-LAWYERS WHO MOVE FROM ONE LAW FIRM TO ANOTHER

The case law generally allows screening of nonlawyers, such as paralegals or secretaries, who move from one law firm to another. The cases reason that the job mobility of these nonlawyers would be severely affected if their knowledge were automatically

---

[3]The text of the rule and the comment contemplates that the former client could ask the court to impose additional requirements if a belief exists that the proposed screening mechanism is not adequate in a particular case.

[4]New Comment 10 explains the additional detail and information must confirm that the affected lawyer has not disclosed confidences to the law firm at any time so that the screen is working to place a barrier between the affected lawyer and the lawyers performing the work for the adverse client.

[5]*See* http://www.legalethicsforu m.com/blog/2009/03/drafting-error-in-n ew-model-rule-110.html.

[6]The amendment read as follows:

(a) While lawyers are associated in a firm, none of them shall knowingly represent a client when any one of them practicing alone would be prohibited from doing so by Rules 1.7 or 1.9, unless

(1) the prohibition is based upon a personal interest of the ~~prohibited~~ disqualified lawyer and does not present a significant risk of materially limiting the representation of the client by the remaining lawyers in the firm; or

(2) the prohibition is based upon Rule 1.9(a) or (b), and arises out of the disqualified lawyer's association with a prior firm, and . . .

imputed to all lawyers in the new firm. The law should not impose such a heavy burden if the needs of the rules of ethics do not require it. Nonlawyers, unlike lawyers, may not fully appreciate or remember the significance of knowledge that they may have picked up in the prior law firm. Whether or not one finds this rationale persuasive, the fact remains that the case law does not disqualify a law firm if the new law firm carefully screens the nonlawyer who had been exposed to relevant secrets while working in the prior law firm.[1] This view is supported by the Restate-

---

[Section 1.10–5]

[1]*See, e.g., Herron v. Jones*, 276 Ark. 493, 637 S.W.2d 569 (Ark.1982) (no imputation of knowledge of legal secretary so long as the secretary was "walled off" from work on the case for the new firm).

In re Complex Asbestos Litigation, 232 Cal.App.3d 572, 283 Cal.Rptr. 732 (Cal.App.1991) (paralegal now working for plaintiffs' law firm had worked for a defendants' law firm on asbestos cases and there was a real danger of misuse of defense secrets; law firm disqualified because paralegal not screened).

State ex rel. Creighton University v. Hickman, 245 Neb. 247, 512 N.W.2d 374 (Neb.1994) may be an aberrational case. It certainly involved unusual facts. A woman had worked for the law firm representing the defendant during law school and later as a lawyer. Indeed, she had worked on this very case. Later, she was *disbarred* and went to work for an agency that placed temporary workers in litigation support. The law firm representing the plaintiff hired her as a paralegal in this case, in ignorance of her prior involvement in the case. She kept secret from the new law firm the fact that she had graduated from law school and was disbarred. The court held that a "bright line" test was required, and, in order to protect defendant's confidential information, the court disqualified plaintiff's law firm in spite of the fact that it had been misled about her prior employment history. This "paralegal" had not been screened because she kept from

the law firm the knowledge that would have alerted that firm to screen her.

Ciaffone v. Eighth Judicial District Court, 113 Nev. 1165, 945 P.2d 950 (Nev.1997) (legal secretary, while a temporary worker, worked for two months at law firm representing defendant; later, the law firm representing plaintiff hired her permanently, but she was not screened even though there was a realistic risk of misuse of secrets; the court ordered disqualification of the law firm).

City of Apopka v. All Corners, Inc., 701 So.2d 641 (Fla.App.1997) (legal secretary who moved from one law firm to another carrying with her secrets; the law firm was not disqualified because it carefully screened her).

In re American Home Products Corp., 985 S.W.2d 68 (Tex.1998) involved a law firm that had hired a legal assistant who had worked on the other side of a matter, for counsel for one of the defendants in the Norplant litigation. She billed 72.5 hours interviewing potential witnesses, meeting with counsel, investigating plaintiffs, and writing memoranda about how witnesses might be used. After counsel for one of the plaintiffs hired her, the defendant moved to disqualify that firm. While it was not improper to hire an opposing firm's legal assistant, it was improper not to screen her. In fact, she was assigned to work on the very case that she had researched for the other side. The Texas Supreme Court ordered disqualification. Plaintiffs' co-counsel was not also automatically disqualified, but might have been if co-counsel had jointly prepared the case for trial or otherwise could be

ment and by an Informal Ethics Opinion.[2] However, there are a minority of jurisdictions that seem to reject screening in the nonlawyer context.[3]

The drafters of the 2002 Model Rules added a Comment that adopts the position taken in these cases.[4] Rule 1.10 does not impute to the lawyers confidential information obtained by nonlawyer employees when they occupied another job. It also does not impute information obtained by a lawyer in the firm while they worked in another employment as a nonlawyer, including in the position of a law clerk. The Comment states that the lawyers in the firm should normally screen such nonlawyers and lawyers from participating in the matter related to their prior employment.[5] This is needed to prevent the lawyers in the firm from obtaining information from the nonlawyers and to prevent the nonlawyers from obtaining information that could make its way back to the prior employer.

§ 1.10–6 DEFINING THE "FIRM"

§ 1.10–6(a) Introduction

Rule 1.10 applies to lawyers associated together in a law "firm," a term intended to encompass not only private law firms but also corporate legal departments and legal service organizations.[1] Because the purpose of this rule is to protect client confidences and client loyalty,[2] the definition of "firm" may vary. The 1983 Model Rules contained much of this definitional material in the Comments to Rule 1.10. The drafters of the 2002 Model Rules moved this language to Rule 1.0(c) and its Comments.[3]

Consider the way the law treats a legal aid office with offices in several locations compared to the differing treatment of a law firm that has officers in several cities. Although "firm" includes a legal aid office, it does not necessarily include lawyers employed in separate units of the same legal aid organization.[4] Even if the public defender lawyers are in the same office, the need to protect

---

presumed to have shared the legal assistant's tainted information.

[2]See Restatement of Law Governing Lawyers, Third, § 123 (Official Draft 2000), Comment f; ABA Informal Opinion 88-1526 (June 22, 1988).

[3]William Freivogel's excellent conflicts website provides a comprehensive list of the authorities that seem to reject screening in the nonlawyer changing law firms context. See WILLIAM FREIVOGEL, FREIVOGEL ON CONFLICTS, Changing Firms (Mar. 2008) in http://freivogelonconflicts.co m/new__page__13.htm (citing among other cases, *Zimmerman v. Mahaska Bottling Co.*, 270 Kan. 810, 19 P.3d 784 (2001)).

[4]Rule 1.10, Comment 4.

[5]Rule 1.10, Comment 4.

[Section 1.10–6]

[1]See Rule 1.0(c).

[2]Rule 1.10, Comment 1.

[3]Rule 1.0(c) & Rule 1.0, Comment 2 to 4.

[4]Rule 1.0, Comment 4.

confidences of clients is lessened because the lawyers do not have the same financial incentives that lawyers in a private law firm would have to talk about the case.[5] The various branches of a private law firm would be treated as the same "firm" for conflicts purposes because the lawyers do have the same financial incentives to collaborate with each other on firm business.

The definition of "firm" for this purpose may also include co-counsel who are not members of the same firm but who are representing the same party *if* co-counsel have exchanged confidential information.[6]

In determining whether two or more lawyers should be treated as a "firm," it is relevant to know if the lawyers have mutual access to information concerning the clients that they serve. Thus, courts have not always disqualified an entire prosecutor's office; they have not treated the government prosecutor's office as one "firm" if care has been taken to make sure that the personally disqualified lawyer with the confidential information is screened from the other lawyers.[7]

---

[5]*United States v. Reynoso*, 6 F.Supp.2d 269 (S.D.N.Y.1998). The Federal Defender Division of the Legal Aid Society assigned a lawyer (Lawyer #1) to represent the defendant. Four years earlier, another lawyer (Lawyer #2), while in private practice and now also in the Federal Defender Division, had represented Vasquez, a defendant in his criminal trial. Vasquez was now a potential government witness against Reynosa. The court conceded that Lawyer #2 would personally be disqualified from cross-examining his former client about the very matter that was the subject of the former representation. However, the court rejected the government's argument that Lawyer #2's disqualification should be imputed to Lawyer #1. The court refused to impute disqualification within the entire Federal Defender Division because the lawyers had no common financial interest in the cases, they did not talk about the cases, and the files in the earlier case had been sent to storage. The Federal Defender Division should not be treated as a private law firm.

[6]*See, e.g., Fund of Funds, Inc. v. Arthur Andersen & Co.*, 567 F.2d 225, 235 (2d Cir. 1977)(relationship between co-counsel disqualified both lawyers). *But see, e.g., Smith v. Whatcott*, 774 F.2d 1032 (10th Cir. 1985); *Frazier v. Superior Court*, 118 Cal. Rptr.2d 129 (Cal.App.2002); *Brown v. Eighth Judicial Dist. Court ex rel. County of Clark*, 116 Nev. 1200, 14 P.3d 1266 (2000).

[7]In *State ex rel. Romley v. Superior Court*, 184 Ariz. 223, 908 P.2d 37 (Ariz.App.1995), a new assistant prosecutor, while in private practice, had worked for varying periods on cases still pending. He clearly was disqualified from now working on these cases for the government, but the question was whether the whole Maricopa County prosecutor's office was disqualified. The prosecutor had screened the new lawyer and the court found that he would have no reason to risk a career by violating the arrangement. Thus, imputed disqualification was not required. *See* Model Rule 1.11(c)(1).

Similarly a "law firm" may include lawyers who only share office space but who imply to the public that they are a partnership.[8] Because these lawyers act *as if* they are partners, application of Rule 1.10 is necessary to protect client expectations of loyalty.[9]

§ 1.10–6(b) Lawyers Currently Associated in a Firm

Rule 1.10(a) is the basic imputation rule for lawyers *while* they are currently associated in the same firm. This Rule states that only the disqualification principles of certain Rules[10] are imputed to all the other lawyers. In addition, if there is imputation, it exists only while these other lawyers are currently associated in the same firm as the disqualified lawyer.

Rule 1.10(a), unlike DR 5–105(D), does *not* impute to all the lawyers in the firm the disqualification of all the other lawyers in the firm. Rather it imputes only those disqualifications specifically mentioned. Rule 1.10(a) imputes all of Rule 1.7 and Rule 1.9. It does not impute the disqualifications imposed by any other Rule. However, given the fact that Rule 1.10(a) imputes *all* of Rule 1.7, that general imputation of Rule 1.7 may carry within its wake much of Rule 1.8. One would have to look at the specific factual circumstances. In other words, the fact that a Rule 1.10(a) does not provide for automatic imputation of a disqualification of the subsections of Rule 1.8 [other than Rule 1.8(c)] does not mean that there might not be imputation of any of those subsections under the provisions of Rule 1.7, given the appropriate facts.

Moreover, Rule 1.10(a) is not at all applicable to situations where one lawyer—either the one with the actual disqualification, or another lawyer with the imputed disqualification—leaves the first firm and joins another. Rule 1.10(b) and Rule 1.9 govern those situations.

For example, assume Client asks Lawyer A to draft a will giving Lawyer A's son a large sum of money. Lawyer A says: "I cannot draft this instrument, but my partner B can do it." Lawyers A and B have violated Rule 1.10(a) because they are practicing law in the same firm, as a single entity.

In contrast, now assume that Lawyer A leaves the firm and joins a different law firm. When Client makes the same request, Lawyer A says: "I cannot draft the will but my good friend and former law partner, Lawyer B can." Lawyers A and B have not violated Rule 1.10(a) because they are no longer currently associated in the same law firm.

---

[8] Rule 1.0, Comment 2.

[9] *See, e.g.,* ABA Formal Opinion 94–388 (Dec. 4, 1994) ("Relationships Among Law Firms").

But compare DR 2–102(D) (lawyers may not hold themselves out as partners "unless they are in fact partners."); Rule 7.5(d) (same).

[10] Rule 1.7 ("Conflict of Interest: General Rule"); Rule 1.9 ("Conflict of Interest: Former Client").

§ 1.10–6(c) Lawyer Temps or Temporaries

A law firm may hire temporary lawyers (or "law-temps") for a specific project expected to last for only a limited period of time, or to meet a short-term staffing need, or to supply a special proficiency on a particular problem. The firm may hire the temporary lawyer either directly or use the services of a placement agency. This lawyer may work on a single matter or on several different matters in the same firm. In addition, he may work part-time for one law firm while simultaneously working on other matters for other firms.

The use of temporary lawyers raises standard conflicts of interest issues that occur whenever a law firm hires a lawyer who then moves to another law firm. Thus, ABA Formal Opinion 88-356[11] analyzed conflicts issues related to temporary lawyers and concluded that Rules 1.7 and 1.9 should govern. For example, a temporary lawyer, under Rule 1.7, may not personally work simultaneously on matters for clients of different firms if the representation of each is directly adverse to each other. If a temporary lawyer works on a particular matter for a client, that temporary lawyer—just like any other lawyer whose relationship with the law firm is expected to be longer—"represents" that client for purposes of Rule 1.7 and Rule 1.9.

The more difficult question is whether temporary lawyers are "associated" in a firm for purposes of the imputed disqualification sections of Rule 1.10.

The ethics rules should protect legitimate client expectations, but it is also true that an overly broad disqualification rule would impose significant costs on the law-temp, resulting in a "radical curtailment of the opportunity to move from one practice setting to another and of the opportunity of clients to change counsel."[12] A legitimate client expectation, and a prime purpose of the imputation rules in this context (where the law-temp is not in the partnership track and has no special loyalty to any particular law firm) is to protect client confidences and secrets.

Consequently, the ABA Opinion concluded that the answer must be determined by a functional analysis of the facts and circumstances involved:

> Ultimately, whether a temporary lawyer is treated as being "associated with a firm" while working on a matter for the firm depends on whether the nature of the relationship is such that the temporary lawyer has access to information relating to the representation of firm clients other than the client on whose matters the lawyer is working and the consequent risk of improper disclosure or misuse

---

[11]ABA Formal Opinion 88-356 (Dec. 16, 1988).

[12]ABA Formal Opinion 88-356 (Dec. 16, 1988), at 5.

of information relating to representation of other clients of the firm.[13]

For example, if the law-temp works on only a single matter for a particular law firm, and does not have access to information relevant to the representation of the law firm's other clients, then the law-temp should not be treated as "associated" with the law firm for purposes of Rule 1.10.[14] The law-temp and the law firm in this case are treated as two separate and independent law firms who temporarily join forces and collaborate on a particular project or case.

On the other hand, if the law-temp worked for several clients while being assigned to the law firm, and appeared to have had access to secret and confidential information of other clients of that law firm, the law-temp will be treated as "associated" with the law firm for purposes of the imputation rule, unless the law firm is able to demonstrate, "through accurate records or otherwise," that the law-temp "had access to information relating to the representation only of certain other clients."[15]

§ 1.10–6(d) The "Of Counsel" Relationship

Sometimes a lawyer not in a law firm will work on a brief with that law firm and then be designated "of counsel" on that brief. When this term, "of counsel," is used in a circumstance like this one, to signify only that there is a relationship for a particular case, the designation does not imply any imputed disqualification under Rule 1.10.[16]

In other circumstances, a law firm will use the "of counsel" designation—or similar ones, such as "special counsel," "tax counsel," "senior counsel," etc.—in its general announcements, letterheads, office signs, and so forth. The person so designated is neither a "partner" (with the shared liability and managerial responsibility that is implied by the term "partner" or "principal"), nor is the person an "associate" (a junior non-partner). The "of counsel" may be a lawyer who is retired from the firm but still works on occasion on a particular project, or a retired judge who has associated with the firm and may work part time, or a probationary partner-to-be. The designation that a lawyer is "of counsel" to a firm "typically describes a lawyer having a close,

---

[13]ABA Formal Opinion 88-356 (Dec. 16, 1988), at 6.

[14]Rule 1.10(a) refers to lawyers "associated" in a single law firm. Rule 1.10(b) governs lawyers who have "terminated an association" with a law firm.

[15]ABA Formal Opinion 88-356 (Dec. 16, 1988), at 6.

[16]ABA Formal Opinion 90-357 (May 10, 1990).

continuing relationship with the firm, but who does not share directly in the firm's profits."[17]

In legal circles, the use of the "of counsel" appellation in such circumstances implies to the world that there is some sort of on-going, general relationship.[18] Consequently, because of this continuing relationship, the "of counsel" lawyer is treated as "associated" for purposes of imputed disqualifications. If one lawyer is "of counsel" to two different law firms, that lawyer and both law firms are treated as one firm for purposes of imputed disqualification.[19]

§ 1.10–7 VICARIOUS OR IMPUTED DISQUALIFICATION

§ 1.10–7(a) Rule 1.10(a): Vicarious Disqualification When Lawyers Leave a Law Firm

A basic principle of the Model Rules is that: *Imputed knowledge is not thereafter imputed to another lawyer.* Let us assume, for example, that Lawyer #1 represents Client P in a matter—*P v. D.* In that situation, the conflicts rules provide that no lawyer in the firm in which Lawyer #1 works is allowed to represent D, because all of Lawyer #1's knowledge about Client P is imputed to every other lawyer in the same firm.[1] Such a representation would breach Lawyer #1's duty to P. Similarly, no member of #1's firm could represent D because of the firm's duty of loyalty to P.[2] The Rules do not articulate these principles in this exact language; this is a fair reading.

Assume now that Lawyer #2 (a partner or associate in Lawyer #1's firm) leaves that firm and joins another firm to represent D. Lawyer #2's representation of D against P does not breach P's expectation of loyalty from Lawyer #1 or Lawyer #1's firm. Neither Lawyer #1 nor any lawyer in Lawyer #1's law firm is adverse to P. If the duty of loyalty would prevent Lawyer #2 [who is now in a different law firm] from litigating against P, then no lawyer

---

[17]Thomas D. Morgan, *Conflicts of Interest And The New Forms of Professional Associations*, 39 S. TEX. L. REV. 215, 219 (1998) (footnote omitted). Historically, this term, "of counsel" was an honorific title, "given to lawyers upon their retirement to suggest the wisdom they had attained and upon which the firm might sometime call, but not to imply any active role in the firm. Increasingly, however, the term is being applied to persons with a continuing role in a practice who are too experienced to be designated 'associates,' but whom the firm is unwilling to grant—or who choose not to seek-an equity position in the partner-

ship." 39 S. TEX. L. REV. at 225 (footnotes omitted).

[18]DR 2-102(A)(4) stated: "A lawyer may be designated 'Of Counsel' on a letterhead if he has a continuing relationship with a lawyer or law firm, other than as a partner or associate." The Model Rules do not use the term "Of Counsel."

[19]ABA Formal Opinion 90-357 (May 10, 1990).

[Section 1.10–7]

[1]Rule 1.7(a).

[2]Rule 1.10(a) & Comment 2.

could ever represent a client against a former client, yet we know the rule is otherwise.[3]

On the other hand, if Lawyer #2 had personally acquired confidential knowledge about P that would be helpful to D, then Lawyer #2's representation of D would be improper because it would violate Lawyer #2's duty under Rule 1.6 to safeguard client information.[4]

If Lawyer #2 did not *personally* represent Client P *and* did not acquire any material secrets or confidences from Client P, neither Lawyer #2 nor Lawyer #2's new firm should be disqualified from representing Client D.[5] Otherwise mobility of the legal profession would be severely restricted, a burden not justified by any need to protect client loyalty or client information, neither one of which, by hypothesis, exists.

Moreover, if the law imputed Lawyer #2's imputed knowledge to #2's new firm, then the imputed disqualification could exist *ad infinitum*. For example, Lawyer #3 (Lawyer #2's new partner) leaves that firm and joins yet another law firm: if Lawyer #2's imputed disqualification were imputed to Lawyer #3, is Lawyer #3's doubly-imputed knowledge also imputed to the lawyers in Lawyer #3's new firm? The general rule is no. "[N]ew partners of a vicariously disqualified partner, to whom knowledge has been imputed during a former partnership, are not necessarily disqualified: they need only show that the vicariously disqualified partner's knowledge was imputed, not actual."[6]

§ 1.10–7(b) Rule 1.10(b): Vicarious Disqualification When a Lawyer Leaves a Law Firm

Rule 1.10(b) governs the extent to which Firm #1 is still disqualified from handling a matter when Lawyer Alpha (the cause of the initial disqualification) has left Firm #1. Basically Rule 1.10(b) states that, once Lawyer Alpha leaves Firm #1, Firm #1 may then represent clients materially adverse to Firm #1's former clients who had been represented by Alpha when she was with Firm #1, unless: the matter involved is the same as (or substantially related to) the matter in which Alpha (the formerly associated lawyer) had represented the client *and* any of the lawyers still with Firm #1 have knowledge of the former client's material secrets or confidences.[7]

In other words, assume that Lawyer Alpha was the only lawyer in Firm #1 who handled all of a client's affairs ("Client #1"); when Alpha left Firm #1 she took with her both her Client #1, and all

---

[3]*See* Rule 1.9.

[4]Rule 1.9(b).

[5]Rule 1.9(b) & Comment 7.

[6]*American Can Co. v. Citrus Feed*

Co., 436 F.2d 1125, 1129 (5th Cir. 1971).

[7]The client's material secrets or confidences refer to client information protected by Rules 1.6 or 1.9(c).

confidential information relating to Client *#1*. If those are the facts, then there is no need to preclude Firm *#1* from taking matters adverse to that Client *#1* (the law firm's *former* client). Firm *#1* would not be breaching any loyalty it owes to Client *#1* (Lawyer Alpha's Client), because Client *#1* is no longer a present client of Firm *#1* but a former one. And Firm *#1* would not be violating any obligations it has to keep secret any confidential information relating to the firm's former client, because the only person who has that information is Lawyer Alpha, and she is no longer with the law firm.

Similarly, if Lawyer Alpha and several other lawyers in Firm *#1* had knowledge of Client *#1*'s confidences, but all of these lawyers have now left the firm (*e.g.* when Lawyer Alpha left the firm, she took these other lawyers with her), then Law Firm *#1* may represent clients adverse to Client *#1*, the former client.

Assume that Lawyer Alpha, a member of Firm *#1*, represents Client *D* on various matters. Client *D* gives Alpha confidential information relating to a patent. Alpha did not relate any of the confidential information regarding the patent to any member of Firm *#1*. Then Alpha leaves Firm *#1*, takes Client *D* with him, and moves to Firm *#2*. Subsequently Client *P* asks Firm *#1* to represent it in a patent infringement action against *D*. Alpha and Firm *#2* represent *D* in this patent suit. Firm *#1* may properly represent *P*.[8]

§ 1.10–7(c) Burden of Proof

The application of Rule 1.10 and similar rules often turns on the question whether a lawyer had acquired material client information protected as client confidences or secrets. "In such an inquiry, the burden of proof should rest upon the firm whose disqualification is sought."[9]

The law firm thus has the burden of demonstrating that it is *not* the depository of material, protected client information. It is often difficult to prove a negative, but, in this case, that does not mean that the burden can never be met. The standard for proof should not be "unattainably high . . . particularly where . . . the attorney must prove a negative."[10] The lawyers can simply testify that they were not privy to the information. The party seeking

---

[8]*Novo Terapeutisk Laboratorium A/S v. Baxter Travenol Laboratories, Inc.*, 607 F.2d 186 (7th Cir.1979) (*en banc*). *Accord* Rule 1.10, Comment 7.

[9]Rule 1.9, Comment 6.

[10]*Laskey Bros. of W. Va., Inc. v. Warner Bros. Pictures, Inc.*, 224 F.2d 824, 827 (2d Cir.1955). *See Gas-A-Tron of Arizona v. Union Oil Co. of Califor-*

nia, 534 F.2d 1322, 1325 (9th Cir.1976) (per curiam), *cert. denied*, 429 U.S. 861, 97 S.Ct. 164, 50 L.Ed.2d 139 (1976):

"[W]e are convinced that any initial inference of impropriety that arose from [Lawyer *B*'s] potential physical access to the files of Exxon and Shell and from his association with lawyers who did know confiden-

disqualification may not be comforted by this testimony, for he or she may think that the lawyers might just fabricate.

§ 1.10–8 SANCTIONS

§ 1.10–8(a) Discipline

If an attorney is involved in a conflict of interest, he or she is subject to at least three sanctions. First, the lawyer may be subject to discipline. The disciplinary authorities may suspend, reprimand, or conceivably disbar the lawyer. Discipline is independent of other remedies; the decision of a court to refuse to disqualify a lawyer does not preclude discipline, because the judge may conclude that the conflict of interest did not affect or taint the fact-finding process.

In practice, discipline is not the most frequently used sanction, because private parties seek, and the courts often impose, other remedies. These remedies should apply to disqualifications under Rules 1.7, 1.8, 1.9, 1.10, 1.11, and 1.12.

§ 1.10–8(b) Malpractice

If an attorney violates one of the disciplinable rules relating to conflicts of interest, and if that violation causes damage to the client, the lawyer may also be liable for damages for the tort of malpractice.[1]

§ 1.10–8(c) Loss of Fees

Attorneys involved in conflicts may also lose their fees. Judge Learned Hand noted in *Silbiger v. Prudence Bonds Corp.*[2] "[B]y the beginning of the Seventeenth Century it had become a common-place that an attorney must not represent opposed interests; and the usual consequence has been that he is disbarred from receiving any fee from either, no matter how successful his labors."[3]

---

tial information about them was dispelled by evidence that he saw none of the files other than those relating to the cases assigned to him heretofore described and that he heard no confidences about Exxon and Shell from the lawyers with whom he was earlier associated."

The court may allow rebuttal by attorney affidavit. *Silver Chrysler Plymouth, Inc. v. Chrysler Motors Corp.*, 518 F.2d 751, 756 (2d Cir.1975).

[Section 1.10–8]

[1] *See, e.g., Arlinghaus v. Ritenour*, 622 F.2d 629 (2d Cir.1980).

[2] *Silbiger v. Prudence Bonds Corp.*, 180 F.2d 917 (2d Cir.1950).

[3] 180 F.2d 917, 920 (2d Cir.1950) (footnotes omitted).

See also City of Little Rock v. Cash, 277 Ark. 494, 644 S.W.2d 229 (Ark.1982). The court denied a fee to a lawyer who defended the city in a police misconduct suit while also suing the same city and successfully attacking its privilege tax. *See also Hendry v. Pelland*, 73 F.3d 397, 401 (D.C. Cir. 1996)(holding that plaintiff seeking forfeiture of attorneys' fee need only prove violation of am ethics rule and not actual harm).

For example, in *Dewey v. R. J. Reynolds Tobacco Co.*,[4] the plaintiffs' law firm hired a lawyer from the defendant's firm. The court held that this lawyer's prior representation of a tobacco company disqualified him from representing plaintiff in this tobacco liability suit. However, the court denied the defendant's motion to disqualify the plaintiff's law firm because that would hurt the plaintiff who was not at fault. Instead, the court ordered the plaintiffs' firm to continue but for no fee! The plaintiff law firm, the court said, "will be entitled to a fee for services performed up to the date of this opinion, calculated on any reasonable basis (one geared to an hourly charge comes immediately to mind, but there may be others). So much of the balance as would ordinarily be included in that firm's fee will be retained by plaintiff."[5]

In many bankruptcy cases, courts require law firms to forfeit fees for not disclosing a conflict. Thus, *In re Congoleum Corp.*[6] held fee forfeiture was appropriate when a law firm failed to disclose all its relationships to the various parties when the debtor retained it as a "special insurance counsel." There was actual conflict of interest and the law firm's lack of disinterestedness indicated that retention of law firm was contrary to the section of the Bankruptcy Code governing the employment of professional persons. On remand, the trial judge denied the firm $13 million in legal fees for failing to disclose conflicts of interest while doing bankruptcy work for Congoleum Corp.[7]

---

[4] 109 N.J. 201, 536 A.2d 243 (1988).

[5] 109 N.J. 201, 220, 536 A.2d 243, 252 (1988)

[6] 426 F.3d 675 (3d Cir. 2005).

[7] "Conflicts Cost Firm in Congoleum Case $13 Million in Fees," 183 New Jersey L.J. 429 (Feb. 13, 2006): "U.S. Bankruptcy Judge Kathryn Ferguson, supervising Congoleum's Chapter 11 reorganization, found that if Gilbert Heintz & Randolph had come clean about the conflicts, she wouldn't have approved the firm's retention as special insurance counsel in January 2004."

Bankruptcy Cases. 11 U.S.C. A. § 328(c) authorizes the bankruptcy court to deny compensation to lawyers acting contrary to 11 U.S.C.A. § 327(a), which will occur if the counsel for the debtor or creditor's committee is not "disinterested" or has an "interest adverse to the estate."

See also In re Jore Corp., 298 B.R. 703 (D. Mont. 2003), which held that a law firm's violation of its disclosure obligations, in failing to disclose limitation on DIP lender's waiver of conflict of interest, was not a mere de minimis failure. The court ordered a disgorgement of fees ($1.6 million), but it did allow the firm to be reimbursed for expenses that it incurred in complying with bankruptcy court's case management order.

In re Leslie Fay Companies Inc., 175 B.R. 525 (Bankr.S.D.N.Y. 1994), which held that counsel's failure to disclose potential conflicts that might have impaired its investigation into fraud by debtor's upper management warranted monetary sanction in amount of cost of investigating counsel's performance (over $800,000), but

§ 1.10–8(d) Disqualification

Disqualification has become a frequent remedy for conflicts of interest that occur in the course of litigation. The court may disqualify the attorney from further representation in that litigation, *if* the conflict is such that it may "taint" the fact-finding process.[8]

§ 1.10–8(d)(1) Tactical Use of Conflicts Motions

It is often charged that lawyers use disqualification motions to secure tactical advantage. The ethics rules advise that attorneys should not use motions to disqualify opposing counsel as a "technique of harassment."[9] However, this admonition really relies on a lawyer's self-restraint. If the disqualification motion is valid, a court should grant it. If the disqualification motion is invalid, the court should deny it. As long as the motion is not frivolous, there is little a court can or should do to prevent the disqualification motion from being made.

One thing the court should not do is refuse to grant a proper motion for disqualification. The Model Rules of Professional Conduct are rules that lawyers must follow because the local court has enacted them as a rule of court. They are law, just like the Rules of Civil Procedure or the Rules of Evidence are law. In addition, they are the court's own rules. For the court to announce that it will allow a lawyer to appear before it and repre-

---

not disqualification in the circumstances of this case.

[8]*Compare Board of Education of City of New York v. Nyquist*, 590 F.2d 1241 (2d Cir.1979) (no disqualification when only claim is possible "appearance of impropriety" and "no claim that the trial will be tainted . . ."), *with Ceramco, Inc. v. Lee Pharmaceuticals*, 510 F.2d 268, 271 (2d Cir.1975) ("the courts have not only the supervisory power but the duty and responsibility to disqualify counsel for unethical conduct prejudicial to his adversaries.").

Thus, improper attorney solicitation of clients may merit discipline, but should not merit disqualification because it does not *taint* or prejudice the fact finding process. *Fisher Studio, Inc. v. Loew's Inc.*, 232 F.2d 199, 204 (2d Cir.1956), *cert. denied*, 352 U.S. 836, 77 S.Ct. 56, 1 L.Ed.2d 55 (1956).

The Second Circuit, in *Nyquist*, developed this taint test, but other jurisdictions might create different standards.

Appearance of Impropriety. The Model Rules do not use the vague, "appearance of impropriety" test in determining whether a conflict exists. The Restatement of the Law Governing Lawyers similarly rejects this formulation. Restatement of the Law Governing Lawyers, Third, § 5, Reporter's Note to Comment *c(iv)* (Official Draft 2000).

One cannot define the "appearance of impropriety" unless one first defines "impropriety," but the phrase defines neither word. This phrase is therefore not really a test but an invitation for *ad hoc* or *ad hominen* decision-making. The "appearance of impropriety" may be a reason why a particular rule is drafted the way it is, it may explain why the rule has a blanket-prohibition, but it is not a rule itself.

[9]1983 Model Rule 1.7, Comment 35.

sent a client in defiance of the court's own rules when that appearance will taint the trial is incongruous, to say the least.

The courts do not preclude disqualification motions by applying overly strict notions of standing and laches. Similarly, they do not easily *imply* client waiver of attorney conflicts.[10] The client can always "waive" in the sense of voluntarily relinquishing a known right, but that is different than implying a waiver that the client never intended.

§ 1.10–8(d)(2) Appealability

When parties litigate attorney disqualification in the course of litigation, the question arises as to when adverse trial rulings (either granting or denying disqualification) are appealable prior to the conclusion of the main case. State and federal rules sometimes differ on this question.[11]

In the federal system, the Supreme Court has ruled that in a civil case a trial court decision denying or granting disqualification is not appealable as a final decision.[12]

Since 1981, in *Firestone Tire & Rubber Co. v. Risjord*,[13] the Supreme Court has held that denials of motions to disqualify are not interlocutory orders and not appealable as of right in civil cases. Subsequent courts have expanded that ruling so that neither the grant nor the denial of a motion to disqualify is now appealable as of right in either civil or criminal cases.[14] Many state courts have followed the federal lead and also reject the notion of a right to appeal on this issue.

§ 1.10–8(d)(3) Mandamus as an Alternative to the Lack of Appealability of Conflicts Motions

Mandamus is still a remedy for parties who claim that the lower court's disqualification was in error, though mandamus is

---

[10]Robert C. Hacker & Ronald D. Rotunda, *Standing, Waiver, Laches and Appealability in Attorney Disqualification Cases*, 3 CORP.L.REV. 82 (1980).

[11]For a discussion of the early law, see Robert Hacker & Ronald D. Rotunda, *Standing, Waiver, Laches, and Appealability in Attorney Disqualification Cases*, 3 CORPORATION L. REV. 82 (1980).

[12]*Firestone Tire & Rubber Co. v. Risjord*, 449 U.S. 368, 101 S.Ct. 669, 66 L.Ed.2d 571 (1981) (under 28 U.S.C.A. § 1291, order denying disqualification motion not immediately appealable); *Richardson-Merrell, Inc. v. Koller*, 472 U.S. 424, 105 S.Ct. 2757,

86 L.Ed.2d 340 (1985) (order granting disqualification motion not immediately appealable).

[13]*Firestone Tire & Rubber Co. v. Risjord*, 449 U.S. 368, 101 S.Ct. 669, 66 L.Ed.2d 571 (1981).

[14]*Flanagan v. United States*, 465 U.S. 259, 104 S.Ct. 1051, 79 L.Ed.2d 288 (1984) (no appeal of grant of disqualification motion in criminal cases); *Richardson-Merrell, Inc. v. Koller*, 472 U.S. 424, 105 S.Ct. 2757, 86 L.Ed.2d 340 (1985) (no appeal of grant of a motion to disqualify in civil case); *United States v. White*, 743 F.2d 488 (7th Cir. 1984)(no appeal of denial of motion to disqualify in criminal case).

an extraordinary writ and thus a procedurally difficult remedy.[15] At least one federal court has ruled that mandamus is an appropriate remedy if the trial court applied an incorrect legal rule, though the appellate court will continue to defer to the trial judge on issues of fact.[16] But in most instances there is no longer any appeal as of right because the trial court granted, or refused to grant, a disqualification motion.

§ 1.10–8(d)(4) Dearth of Appellate Conflicts Precedents

The consequence of the dearth of appellate court rulings since *Risjord* has led to what might be called the death of binding precedent in attorney disqualification cases. In the pre-*Risjord* era, there were many disqualification motions, and lower federal courts found themselves reversed with some regularity. A body of law was developing, and—because the Courts of Appeal were developing it—there were various bright lines and clear tests emerging to guide the lower courts in disqualification motions. A lower court that made up its own rules would be promptly reversed.

In the post-*Risjord* era, trial court judges have almost carte blanche to disqualify, or not to disqualify, as they see fit. Although the U.S. Supreme Court is properly concerned about a conflict among the circuits, and will typically grant review to resolve such a conflict, a conflict among the district courts in attorney disqualification cases is now standard operating procedure. *Risjord* and the cases in its wake have not reduced the number of disqualification motions, but they have reduced the uniformity in the case law by preventing appeals.[17]

Consider *Stratagem Development Corp. v. Heron International*

---

[15]**Mandamus.** A few courts of appeal have agreed to review lower court decisions using the extraordinary writ of mandamus. *Matter of Sandahl*, 980 F.2d 1118 (7th Cir.1992); *In re American Airlines, Inc.*, 972 F.2d 605 (5th Cir.1992), *cert. denied*, 507 U.S. 912, 113 S.Ct. 1262, 122 L.Ed.2d 659 (1993).

[16]*Matter of Sandahl*, 980 F.2d 1118 (7th Cir.1992).

[17]*See, e.g., SWS Financial Fund A v. Salomon Brothers Inc.*, 790 F.Supp. 1392 (N.D.Ill.1992) (Duff, J.). The law firm had filed suit against the defendant for alleged violation of commodities regulations and the antitrust laws. The defendant was a *current* cli-

ent of the firm's with respect to issues of compliance with commodities trading regulations. The court denied the defendant's motion to disqualify the firm. Judge B.B. Duff said that he wanted to avoid creating an incentive for companies to give several law firms small pieces of business so as to disqualify them later, although there was no evidence that had happened in this case. The ethics rules of the Northern District of Illinois (which are identical to the ABA Model Rules on this issue) prohibit a law firm from suing a current client, even if the matters are unrelated. Rule 1.7, & Comment 3, Rules of Professional Conduct, Northern District of Illinois. But, the trial judge's ruling was not appealable.

N.V.,[18] a case that ruled that lawyers cannot be adverse to affiliates of their corporate clients. *Stratagem* argued that lawyers who represent trade associations cannot be adverse to members of the trade association, even those these members are not the clients of the law firm, have never been represented by the law firm, and may never be represented by the law firm.[19]

Stratagem was a case decided in the Southern District of New York. Nearly a decade earlier, the Second Circuit, which has jurisdiction over the Southern District, rejected the principle later adopted in *Stratagem*. The Second Circuit, in fact, specifically stated, for example, that a "law firm that represents the American Bar Association need not decline to represent a client injured by an automobile driven by a member of the ABA."[20] In short, lawyers who represent the ABA or a trade association may be adverse to members of the ABA or the trade association.

But the trial court in *Stratagem* could gloss over past precedent in its own circuit because there was no appeal as of right. What happened in *Stratagem* is not unusual. There appears to be an increasing lack of uniformity, by the number of judges who create new rules and new exceptions, all in a context where there is unlikely ever to be any appellate decision to end the confusion and conflicts in the trial level.

This development—the dearth of precedent—is significant, because it gives greater prerogative and freedom to a judge faced with a motion to disqualify a law firm. In the meantime, law firms and their clients are subjected to expensive litigation, with little hope for appeal as of right. There tends to be broad, unreviewable discretion, rather than brighter lines and clearer tests so that firms know what to do. A rule that says that the judge may, or may not, disqualify only after "sift[ing]" through "all the facts and circumstances"[21] gives little guidance to law firms and clients who, understandably, would like to know what

---

[18]*Stratagem Development Corp. v. Heron International N.V.*, 756 F.Supp. 789 (S.D.N.Y.1991).

[19]*Stratagem*, 756 F.Supp. at 792.

[20]*Glueck v. Jonathan Logan, Inc.*, 653 F.2d 746, 749 (2d Cir.1981). *Stratagem*, oddly enough, cited the *trial* court in *Glueck* in support of its broad rule. *See*, 756 F.Supp. at 792, *citing Glueck v. Jonathan Logan, Inc.*, 512 F.Supp. 223, 227 (S.D.N.Y.1981), *aff'd on different grounds*, 653 F.2d 746 (2d Cir.1981).

Stratagem, 756 F.Supp. at 792, also relied on *Rosman v. Shapiro*, 653

F.Supp. 1441 (S.D.N.Y.1987), which it described as a case where the law firm was disqualified because it represented a closely held corporation in which plaintiff and defendant each held 50% of the stock. In *Rosman*, the trial court found no relevant confidences, but it specifically ruled that the disqualified law firm had actually entered into an attorney client relationship with both Rosman and Shapiro. *Rosman*, 653 F.Supp. at 1445. The *Rosman* trial court did not use any broad parent/subsidiary theory.

[21]*See, e.g., Pennwalt Corp. v. Plough, Inc.*, 85 F.R.D. 264, 269 (D.

the rules are so that they can obey them before a disqualification motion is ever filed. It is all right to "weigh the interests" only if the courts first calibrate the scales and inform us how the weight of the different interests is determined.

Lawyers who are very ethical do not want to go near the line that demarcates ethical behavior from unethical behavior. Lawyers who are disqualified lose their clients for that particular case, and—depending on the client's reactions—perhaps in others as well. In addition, ethical lawyers are reluctant to risk soiling their reputation with the adverse publicity of a disqualification order.

Thus, the vague test for a conflict rule, and the unreviewability of the courts' orders involving disqualification are two factors that serve to give a competitive advantage to the less ethical lawyer, the more risk prone lawyer, and the lawyer who is willing to play the lower court lottery. Such lawyers care less about their reputation, and the risk of being disqualified is tempered by the reality that the lawyer who turns down business because of possible disqualification will lose the client for sure, but the lawyer who takes the case might not be disqualified.

Vague rules mean that judges may not disqualify when they should. Vague standards also give a competitive advantage to lawyers who are willing to go to the edge of the line (and occasionally cross it). We live in a world where law firms that are anxious to avoid conflicts of interest find themselves handicapped and penalized compared to ethically-challenged law firms that are willing to go up to, and occasionally cross, a vague ethics line.

Del.1980).

CHAPTER 1.11
SPECIAL CONFLICTS OF INTEREST FOR FORMER AND CURRENT GOVERNMENT OFFICERS AND EMPLOYEES

RULE 1.11: SPECIAL CONFLICTS OF INTEREST FOR FORMER AND CURRENT GOVERNMENT OFFICERS AND EMPLOYEES

(a) Except as law may otherwise expressly permit, a lawyer who has formerly served as a public officer or employee of the government:

(1) is subject to Rule 1.9(c); and

(2) shall not otherwise represent a client in connection with a matter in which the lawyer participated personally and substantially as a public officer or employee, unless the appropriate government agency gives its informed consent, confirmed in writing, to the representation.

(b) When a lawyer is disqualified from representation under paragraph (a), no lawyer in a firm with which that lawyer is associated may knowingly undertake or continue representation in such a matter unless:

(1) the disqualified lawyer is timely screened from any participation in the matter and is apportioned no part of the fee therefrom; and

(2) written notice is promptly given to the appropriate government agency to enable it to ascertain compliance with the provisions of this rule.

(c) Except as law may otherwise expressly permit, a lawyer having information that the lawyer knows is confidential government information about a person acquired when the lawyer was a public officer or employee, may not represent a private client whose interests are adverse to that person in a matter in which the information could be used to the material disadvantage of that person. As used in this Rule, the term "confidential government information" means information that has been obtained under governmental authority and which, at the time this Rule is applied, the government is prohibited by law from disclosing to the public or has a legal privilege not to disclose and which is not otherwise available to the public. A firm with which that lawyer is associated may undertake or continue representation in the matter only if the disqualified lawyer is timely screened from any participation in the matter and is apportioned no part of the fee therefrom.

(d) Except as law may otherwise expressly permit, a lawyer currently serving as a public officer or employee:

(1) is subject to Rules 1.7 and 1.9; and

(2) shall not:

(i) participate in a matter in which the lawyer participated personally and substantially while in private practice or nongovernmental employment, unless the appropriate government agency gives its informed consent, confirmed in writing; or

(ii) negotiate for private employment with any person who is involved as a party or as lawyer for a party in a matter in which the lawyer is participating personally and substantially, except that a lawyer serving as a law clerk to a judge, other adjudicative officer or arbitrator may negotiate for private employment as permitted by Rule 1.12(b) and subject to the conditions stated in Rule 1.12(b).

(e) As used in this Rule, the term "matter" includes:

(1) any judicial or other proceeding, application, request for a ruling or other determination, contract, claim, controversy, investigation, charge, accusation, arrest or other particular matter involving a specific party or parties, and

(2) any other matter covered by the conflict of interest rules of the appropriate government agency.

Comment

[1] A lawyer who has served or is currently serving as a public officer or employee is personally subject to the Rules of Professional Conduct, including the prohibition against concurrent conflicts of interest stated in Rule 1.7. In addition, such a lawyer may be subject to statutes and government regulations regarding conflict of interest. Such statutes and regulations may circumscribe the extent to which the government agency may give consent under this Rule. See Rule 1.0(e) for the definition of informed consent.

[2] Paragraphs (a)(1), (a)(2) and (d)(1) restate the obligations of an individual lawyer who has served or is currently serving as an officer or employee of the government toward a former government or private client. Rule 1.10 is not applicable to the conflicts of interest addressed by this Rule. Rather, paragraph (b) sets forth a special imputation rule for former government lawyers that provides for screening and notice. Because of the special problems raised by imputation within a government agency, paragraph (d) does not impute the conflicts of a lawyer currently serving as an officer or employee of the government to other associated government officers or employees, although ordinarily it will be prudent to screen such lawyers.

[3] Paragraphs (a)(2) and (d)(2) apply regardless of whether a lawyer is adverse to a former client and are thus designed not only to protect the former client, but also to prevent a lawyer from exploiting public office for the advantage of another client. For example, a lawyer who has pursued a claim on behalf of the government may not pursue the same claim on behalf of a later private client after the lawyer has left government service, except when authorized to do so by the government agency under paragraph (a). Similarly, a lawyer who has pursued a claim on behalf of a private client may not pursue the claim on behalf of the government, except when authorized to do so by paragraph (d). As with paragraphs (a)(1) and (d)(1), Rule 1.10 is not applicable to the conflicts of interest addressed by these paragraphs.

[4] This Rule represents a balancing of interests. On the one hand, where the successive clients are a government agency and another client, public or private, the risk exists that power or discretion vested in that agency might be used for the special benefit of the other client. A lawyer should not be in a position where benefit to the other client might affect performance of the lawyer's professional functions on behalf of the government. Also, unfair advantage could accrue to the other client by reason of access to confidential government information about the client's adversary obtainable only through the lawyer's government service. On the other hand, the rules governing lawyers presently or formerly employed by a government agency should not be so restrictive as to inhibit transfer of employment to and from the government. The government has a legitimate need to attract qualified lawyers as well as to maintain high ethical standards. Thus a former government lawyer is disqualified only from particular matters in which the lawyer participated personally and substantially. The provisions for screening and waiver in paragraph (b) are necessary to prevent the disqualification rule from imposing too severe a deterrent against entering public service. The limitation of disqualification in paragraphs (a)(2) and (d)(2) to matters involving a specific party or parties, rather than extending disqualification to all substantive issues on which the lawyer worked, serves a similar function.

[5] When a lawyer has been employed by one government agency and then moves to a second government agency, it may be appropriate to treat that second agency as another client for purposes of this Rule, as when a lawyer is employed by a city and subsequently is employed by a federal agency. However, because the conflict of

interest is governed by paragraph (d), the latter agency is not
required to screen the lawyer as paragraph (b) requires a law firm
to do. The question of whether two government agencies should be
regarded as the same or different clients for conflict of interest
purposes is beyond the scope of these Rules. See Rule 1.13 Comment [6].

[6] Paragraphs (b) and (c) contemplate a screening arrangement.
See Rule 1.0(k) (requirements for screening procedures). These
paragraphs do not prohibit a lawyer from receiving a salary or
partnership share established by prior independent agreement, but
that lawyer may not receive compensation directly relating the
lawyer's compensation to the fee in the matter in which the lawyer
is disqualified.

[7] Notice, including a description of the screened lawyer's prior
representation and of the screening procedures employed, generally
should be given as soon as practicable after the need for screening
becomes apparent.

[8] Paragraph (c) operates only when the lawyer in question has
knowledge of the information, which means actual knowledge; it
does not operate with respect to information that merely could be
imputed to the lawyer.

[9] Paragraphs (a) and (d) do not prohibit a lawyer from jointly
representing a private party and a government agency when doing
so is permitted by Rule 1.7 and is not otherwise prohibited by law.

[10] For purposes of paragraph (e) of this Rule, a "matter" may
continue in another form. In determining whether two particular
matters are the same, the lawyer should consider the extent to
which the matters involve the same basic facts, the same or related
parties, and the time elapsed.

Authors' 1983 Model Rules Comparison

The drafters of the 2002 Model Rules made significant changes to
Rule 1.11.

The 1983 version of this Rule was titled, "Successive Government
and Private Employment," and the drafters changed it to "Special
Conflicts of Interest for Former and Current Government Officers
and Employees."

In Rule 1.11(a), which deals with conflicts with a former government lawyer, the drafters made it clear that this Rule and Rule
1.9(c) govern the former government lawyer. They added a clause
in subsection (a) that this provision governs not only former government lawyers but all lawyers who were former public officers or
government employees. The drafters broke this provision into two
requirements. First, (a)(1), makes former government lawyers
subject to Rule 1.9(c) on use and disclosure of confidential
information. This point had been a subject of debate under the 1983
Model Rules. Second, (a)(1) imposes a new "informed consent,
confirmed in writing" standard.

In Rule 1.11(b), the drafters addressed imputed disqualification
more precisely by making it clear that when a lawyer is disqualified, the other lawyers in the law firm are also disqualified unless
the affected lawyer is screened from the representation. They added

the word, "timely," to reflect the need to examine loans early in the process.

The drafter moved Rule 1.11(b) of the 1983 version to Rule 1.11(c). The drafters also moved the long definition of confidential government information from the 1983 Rule 1.11(e) to paragraph (b) and they added a requirement of "timely" screening.

In Rule 1.11(d), the drafters clarified that current government employees are governed by Rules 1.7 and 1.9. The revised rule explains that when a conflict arises between the current government employment and the former private employment, the lawyer needs to obtain informed consent from the appropriate government agency. *See* Rule 1.11(d)(2)(i).

The 1983 version of Rule 1.11(d) was renumbered so it is now Rule 1.11(e).

The drafters deleted old Comment 1.

Old Comment 2 was renumbered as Comment 1 and amended to clarify the focus of this Rule.

Comments 2 and 3 are new and explain the operation of Rule 1.11(a) and the policies underlying the obligations to the government as a former client.

Old Comment 3 was renumbered as Comment 4 and modified to explain the balancing of interests when lawyers move in and out of government.

Old Comment 4 was renumbered as Comment 5 and amended to clarify obligations when lawyers move from one government client to another.

Old Comment 4 was renumbered as Comment 6 and amended slightly to clarify screening.

Comment 7 is new and explains the notice requirement under Rule 1.11

Old Comments 7 and 8 are renumbered as Comments 8 and 9 with only a change in reference to the proper paragraph of the Rule.

Old Comment 9 is deleted.

Comment 10 is new and examines the notion when a "matter" may continue in another form. The Comment explains: "In determining whether two particular matters are the same, the lawyer should consider the extent to which the matters involve the same basic facts, the same or related parties, and the time elapsed"

Model Code Comparison

[1] Paragraph (a) is similar to DR 9-101(B), except that the latter used the terms "in which he had substantial responsibility while he was a public employee."

[2] Paragraphs (b), (c), (d) and (e) have no counterparts in the Model Code.

§ 1.11-1 THE REVOLVING DOOR

Model Rule 1.10 is the basic rule dealing with imputing the conflicts of one lawyer in a law firm to other lawyers in the same firm. However, that Rule defines "firm" as including lawyers "in a law partnership, professional corporation, sole proprietorship or other association authorized to practice law; or lawyers employed in a legal services organization or in the legal department of a corporation or other organization."[1] There are, in short, special rules dealing with a lawyer who leaves the government to join a private law firm or a lawyer who leaves a private sector position to join the government. Those rules are found in Model Rule 1.11.[2]

Model Rule 1.11 deals with what is often called the "revolving door" of lawyers who move between private practice and government service. The goal of the ethics rules in this area is to limit potential abuses—*e.g.*, the risk of improper use of confidential government information or the risk that the government lawyer might use that position to benefit a future private employer—without unduly restricting the ability of the government to attract lawyers.[3]

The ethics rules acknowledge that there are public benefits, within limits, to having the door between government service and private practice revolve. If lawyers who worked for the government could not leave for private practice, or the conflicts rules governing their leaving were too strict, it would be more difficult for the government to recruit lawyers. Strict imputation rules would also limit the choices available to clients. The ethics rules will take away from a client the right to choose a particular lawyer, if there is a good reason to limit that choice. But if the reasons are insufficiently weighty, the rules are reluctant to limit the client's private choice.

In addition, because of the government's unusually broad legal relationships, it does not wish to be unduly hampered when it recruits a lawyer from the private sector.[4] If a lawyer who started working for the government knew that the conflicts rules were so strict that it would be difficult for the lawyer to return to private practice and engage in legal work in an area related to his or her governmental service, that lawyer would be more reluctant to shift to government service because the road to government service was a one-way street.

[Section 1.11–1]

[1] Rule 1.10, Comment 1.

[2] Rule 1.10(d). *See also* Restatement of the Law Governing Lawyers, Third, § 97 ("Representing the Governmental Client") (Official Draft 2000), and Restatement of the Law Governing Lawyers, Third, § 133 ("A Former Government Lawyer or Officer") (Official Draft 2000).

[3] *See* Rule 1.11, Comment 4.

[4] *See* Rule 1.11, Comment 4. *See, e.g.* Thomas D. Morgan, *Appropriate Limits on Participation by a Former Agency Official in Matters Before an Agency*, 1980 DUKE L.J., 1 (1980); Thomas D. Morgan, *Screening the Disqualified Lawyer: The Wrong Solution to the Wrong Problem*, 10 U. ARKANSAS (LITTLE ROCK) L.J. 37 (1987); Ronald D. Rotunda, *Ethical Problems in Federal Agency Hiring of Private Attorneys*, 1 GEORGETOWN J. LEGAL ETHICS 85 (1987).

The revolving door is (if we may mix metaphors) a two-way street. There is a public interest in encouraging private lawyers to engage in public service and in having public lawyers enter the private sector. Lawyers in private practice who earlier had served in the government have the experience that helps them understand both the substance and rationale of government policy. These former government lawyers, when they move to the private sector, carry with them some of the attitudes of law enforcement. The knowledge and experience of these former government lawyers might encourage their clients to comply with the law.

Thus, Rule 1.11 "protects three government functions, those of client, recruiter of able employees, and law enforcer."[5]

§ 1.11–2 THE HISTORICAL DEVELOPMENT OF THE ETHICS RULES GOVERNING THE REVOLVING DOOR

Prior to the ABA's approval of the Model Rules, no general provision of the Model Code dealt with the issue of lawyers moving in and out of government. Instead, the case law and the ethics opinions derived the ethics rules from more general provisions in the Model Code. The basic provision of the Model Code is DR 9-101(B): "A lawyer shall not accept *private* employment in a *matter* in which he had *substantial responsibility* while he was a *public employee.*"[1]

The meaning of these italicized words was very important given the breadth of this rule when read in connection with DR 5-105(D). That is because DR 5-105(D) imputed every disqualification of DR 9-101(B) to every other lawyer in the private firm where the former government lawyer practiced.

The seminal ABA Formal Opinion dealing with the Revolving Door under the Model Rules is ABA Formal Opinion 342.[2] This Formal Opinion evolved into Model Rule 1.11, and it addressed several issues that remain important under Model Rule 1.11.

Rule 1.11(a) is in many respects substantially similar to DR 9-101(B), as ABA Formal Opinion 342[3] interpreted that rule. However, the Model Rule is more specific and drafted more carefully. Also, it adds several additional, distinct requirements. Consequently, this section will analyze Model Rule 1.11 while

---

[5]Restatement of the Law Governing Lawyers, Third, § 133. Comment *b* (Official Draft 2000).

[Section 1.11–2]

[1]DR 9-101(B)(emphasis added).

[2]ABA Formal Opinion 342 (Nov. 24, 1975). *See also* ABA Formal Opinion 97-409 (Aug. 2, 1997), discussed below, which elaborates on ABA Formal Opinion 342 as it examines Model Rule 1.11.

[3]ABA Formal Opinion 97-409 (Aug. 2, 1997).

incorporating the learning of Formal Opinion 342 as well as pointing out the additional, specific requirements of Rule 1.11.

§ 1.11–3 THE GOVERNMENT LAWYER MOVING INTO PRIVATE PRACTICE

§ 1.11–3(a) Private Employment

First, in analyzing the revolving door between government
work and private employment, let us consider the concept of
"private employment." ABA Formal Opinion 342 explains that
"private employment" means work "as a private practitioner." If
a lawyer remains in private practice and accepts, as one of her
clients, a government agency, that lawyer is accepting *private*
employment from the government agency.[1] In this case, the
lawyer in private practice would have various clients, one of
which is a government agency.

Even if the lawyer represents the government agency on a
contingent fee arrangement,[2] like the private lawyers who
represented various state and local governments in suing tobacco
companies or gun manufacturers, the lawyer remains in private
practice while representing various private clients, including one
or more governments or governmental agencies.[3]

The 1983 Model Rules adopted this distinction and elaborated
on it. Thus, if "the client is an agency of one government, that
agency should be treated as a private client for purposes of this
Rule if the lawyer thereafter represents an agency of another
government, as when a lawyer represents a city and subsequently
is employed by a federal agency."[4] In this case, the lawyer
represents various clients, and two of those clients are different

---

[Section 1.11–3]

[1] *See, e.g.*, ABA Formal Opinion
342 (Nov. 24, 1975). Paul R. Cherry,
Magistrate Judge, in *Ramos v. Pabey*,
2005 WL 2240036 (N.D. Ind. 2005), at
p. *12, *citing* LEGAL ETHICS TREATISE.

[2] *General Motors Corp. v. City of
New York*, 501 F.2d 639 (2d Cir.1974)
(private lawyer accepts contingent fee
case from New York City).

[3] **The Distinction Between
Representing the Government and
Being Paid by the Government.**
The mere fact that the government is
paying a lawyer does not mean that
the lawyer works on behalf of the
government. For example, public defenders do not work on behalf of the
government when they represent criminal defendants. The defendant whom

the public defender represents is the
client; the government is merely paying for the services.

In many instances, the public
defender is a full-time employee of the
government, rather than a lawyer in
private practice who represents the defendant because the judge assigns the
case to him. That change does not affect the result that even a full-time
government employee does not represent the government in this situation.
See, e.g., Restatement of the Law
Governing Lawyers § 97. Comment *c*,
at pp. 46 to 47 (Official Draft 2000).

[4] Rule 1.11, Comment 4 (1983
version of Model Rules). The hypothetical situation discussed in this Comment is similar to the facts of *General
Motors Corp. v. City of New York*, 501
F.2d 639 (2d Cir.1974), except in that

government agencies. Public policy would not favor the lawyer using and leveraging, on behalf of her law firm, the secret information that she learned while representing one client (a city) to aid a different client, even if that different client is another government agency of a different branch of government.

The drafters of the 2002 Model Rules reworded the title and the coverage of the Rule to obviate the need for the Comment quoted above, which was therefore deleted.[5] Rule 1.11 covers conflicts of former and current government officers and employees. Rule 1.11(a) addresses conflicts related to "a lawyer who has formerly served as a public officer or employee of the government."[6] The result is the same under both the 1983 and 2002 version of the Model Rules; Rule 1.11 covers government officials and employees and not a lawyer representing the government as a client.

A lawyer may be a full time employee of a government agency. Therefore, she is not representing this agency "as a private practitioner." For example, assume that the lawyer represents one government agency as a full time employee. Then, another government agency recruits her to change jobs. The rules do not treat this situation as a case where the lawyer is representing the agency "as a private practitioner."[7] Because she is a salaried, full time employee, there is no realistic danger that a lawyer will abuse her government office for private gain merely because she moves from one salaried government position to another salaried government position. The basic purpose of Rule 1.11 is not likely to be offended by this type of mobility.[8]

The drafters of the 2002 Model Rules also added a requirement that lawyers who move from government to private practice must comply with Rule 1.9(c), relating to the use and disclosure of client information.

§ 1.11–3(b) "Matter"

The term "matter" refers to "a discrete and isolatable transac-

---

case the lawyer (who earlier had been a full-time employee of the federal government) entered private practice and then represented the city of New York.

See also Restatement of the Law Governing Lawyers § 97, Comment *c*, at pp. 46 to 47 (Official Draft 2000).

[5]Rule 1.11, Comment 4 (1983 version of Model Rules) said that if "the client is an agency of one government, that agency should be treated as a private client for purposes of this Rule if the lawyer thereafter represents an agency of another government, as when a lawyer represents a city and subsequently is employed by a federal agency."

[6]Rule 1.11(a).

[7]Rule 1.11(c) protects government confidences when the lawyer moves from government employment to "private" employment.

[8]Rule 1.11, Comment 4.

tion or set of transactions between identifiable parties."[9] If two situations involve the same parties and the same facts, they very likely will be considered the "same matter."[10] Model Rule 1.11(e)

---

[9]ABA Formal Opinion 342 (Nov. 24, 1975).

[10]Restatement of the Law Governing Lawyers, Third, § 133, ("A Former Government Lawyer Or Officer"), Comment e ("Definition of a 'matter.' ") (Official Draft 2000). A "matter" is:

"often defined as a judicial or other proceeding, application, request for a ruling or other determination, contract, claim, controversy, investigation, charge, accusation, arrest, or other particular matter involving a specific party or parties. Drafting of a statute or regulation of general applicability is not included under that definition, nor is work on a case of the same type (but not the same parties) as the one in which the lawyer seeks to be involved."

Not the "Same" Matter. *Committee for Washington's Riverfront Parks v. Thompson*, 451 A.2d 1177 (D.C.1982), holding that there was not the same "matter" simply because a former lawyer in the Department of the Interior was on a task force that approved guidelines for the development of the Georgetown waterfront area. Later, he represented private clients that considered a specific design proposal.

Laker Airways Ltd. v. Pan American World Airways, 103 F.R.D. 22, 39 Fed.R.Serv.2d 1043 (D.D.C. 1984). A "matter" does not include a lawyer's rule-making and policy-making activities unless the activity is narrow in scope and is confined to specified issues and identifiable parties such that it may be properly characterized as "quasi-judicial" in nature. In this case, a Justice Department lawyer worked on overseas air travel antitrust issues and also wrote recommendation as to whether the Government should allow Laker Airways to fly an Atlantic route. The court did not require disqualification. However, "the Disciplinary Rule would bar counsel from representing a private party in a

regulatory or rule-making proceeding when he previously participated as a government attorney *in the same proceeding*. Such a practice of 'switching sides' is the primary target of the Rule." *Laker Airways Ltd.*, 103 F.R.D. 22, 34 n.40 (emphasis in original).

The "Same" Matter. *Securities Investor Protection Corp. v. Vigman*, 587 F.Supp. 1358 (C.D.Cal.1984), holding that there was the very "same matter" when the court disqualified former lawyers for the SEC who represented a private plaintiff in a securities fraud case, because they earlier represented the government in a civil securities suit that involved stock manipulations, and the later private suit involved that "precise subject." There was a "discrete series of transactions involving a specific situation and specific parties." 587 F.Supp. at 1366.

United States v. Philip Morris Inc., 312 F.Supp.2d 27 (D.D.C. 2004), disqualified a former justice department lawyer from participation in defending certain cases involving tobacco companies. The lawyer had worked 28 years for the DOJ. He had worked on an FDA rulemaking asserting the FDA's right to regulate tobacco and worked on the litigation seeking to defend that rule. He also worked on an analysis of the Master Settlement Agreement between the tobacco industry and the states and wrote a memorandum on obtaining access to internal tobacco company documents. After his retirement, Sherman & Sterling hired him. In this motion to disqualify Sherman & Sterling, Judge Kessler found that the work the lawyer did on the earlier FDA cases constituted a "matter" and that work done on the rule-making was closely related to it. Applying D.C. Rule 1.11, the Court concluded the lawyer learned confidential government information that could be relevant to the current litigation and she ordered Sherman & Sterling

is intended to codify the discussion in ABA Formal Opinion 342 of the definition of "matter."[11]

For example, assume that a lawyer ("Lawyer A") represents Government in suing Widget, Inc. for a strip-mining violation. Then, Lawyer A leaves the Government and represents Widget, Inc. in its defense of this suit. Or, assume that this same Lawyer A, who used to represent the Government against Widget, now represents a class action plaintiff suing Widget for pollution damage growing out of the same facts. These law suits involve the same "matter."[12]

In contrast, consider the case where Lawyer is a counsel for a congressional committee. Lawyer helps the committee draft a new law governing the coal industry and establishing requirements for returning the land back to its natural form after strip mining. He then leaves the congressional committee and begins work for Coal Co., Inc. involving the same point of *law*. The two situations are not the same "matter" because there is no discrete transaction between identifiable parties in a particular situation. Drafting a law for the government, or drafting general agency regulations, or engaging in policy making does not disqualify a lawyer from later private employment involving the same point of law.[13]

Similarly, Rule 1.11 does not disqualify a lawyer who worked for a government claims administration agency from later representing private parties who have claims before the agency, except in connection with particular claims that she "personally" handled while she was a government employee for that agency.[14]

A "matter" may continue in another form. In deciding whether

---

disqualified.

[11]ABA Formal Opinion 97-409 (Aug. 2, 1997), at 6, n.5.

[12]*See, e.g., United States v. Ta*, 938 F.Supp. 762 (D.Utah 1996), holding that a private lawyer who, while a government prosecutor, assigned a lawyer to try the criminal case against defendant and discussed the charges in that case with the trial prosecutor is disqualified from representing the defendant in that same criminal case. *See also State ex rel. Jefferson County Bd. of Zoning Appeals v. Wilkes*, 221 W. Va. 432, 655 S.E.2d 178 (2007), *noted in* 23 ABA/BNA MANUAL ON PROF. CONDUCT 611 (Dec. 12, 2007) holding that former assistant county attorney who had represented the county zoning board against the devel-

oper's original application for a special use permit could not subsequently represent the developer in a second application to expand the size of the proposed development.

[13]*See, e.g., National Bonded Warehouse Association, Inc. v. United States*, 718 F.Supp. 967 (Ct. International Trade 1989), holding that an attorney who formerly worked for the Customs Service and developed agency regulations may later represent plaintiffs challenging the validity of those regulations. *See also* ABA Formal Opinion 97-409 (Aug. 2, 1997).

[14]ABA Formal Opinion 97-409 (Aug. 2, 1997). These issues are carefully considered in Thomas D. Morgan, *Appropriate Limits on Participation by a Former Agency Official in Matters*

two particular matters are really the same "matter," the lawyer "should consider the extent to which the matters involve the same basic facts, the same or related parties, and the time elapsed."[15]

For example, "a discrete series of transactions involving a specific situation and specific parties" in a 1973 civil action is "part and parcel of a subsequent, broader allegation of widespread securities fraud and racketeering in the case" before the court, which was filed in 1983. The 1983 complaint alleged that defendants conspired to manipulate the price of securities. The court held that the two cases were the same "matter." The former SEC lawyers are representing the plaintiff in the 1983 case "in connection with a matter" that the SEC had prosecuted in the 1973 civil action.[16]

§ 1.11–3(c) Personal and Substantial Responsibility

A government lawyer does not have "substantial responsibility" over a matter if he only gives perfunctory approval or disapproval. The lawyer should have "had such a heavy responsibility for the matter in question that it is likely he became personally and substantially involved in the investigative or deliberative processes regarding that matter."[17]

Before an Agency, 1980 DUKE L.J. 1 (1980).

[15]Rule 1.11, Comment 10.

[16]*Securities Investor Protection Corp. v. Vigman*, 587 F.Supp. 1358, 1366 (D.C.Cal.1984).

[17]ABA Formal Opinion 342 (Nov. 24, 1975). *See, e.g., In re Abraham D. Sofaer*, 728 A.2d 625 (D.C.App.1999). In this case, the court held that the violation of Rule 1.11(a) governing acceptance of other employment following work as a public officer or employee warranted an informal admonition. The lawyer, the court said, violated Rule 1.11(a) by undertaking to represent the government of Libya in connection with criminal and civil disputes and litigation arising from the 1988 bombing of Pan American Flight 103 over Lockerbie, Scotland, because this lawyer, while serving as Legal Advisor (functionally General Counsel) for the State Department, had taken part "personally and substantially" in the U.S. Government's investigation of the bombing

and in related diplomatic and legal activities. After leaving government, Libya retained Sofaer at a fee of $250,000 per month to represent it in connection with civil and criminal litigation arising out of that incident.

Sofaer argued that his involvement in the matter while at the State Department had not been "personal and substantial," and indeed, that while he was there, suspicion was substantially focused on other possible perpetrators. Amici curiae supporting Mr. Sofaer contended that, if Sofaer were found guilty, no lawyer could safely move in and out of government. The *Sofaer* court found that Sofaer's involvement was "personal and substantial" and that his violation of Rule 1.11 was clear. The court ruled that the disciplinary rule that prohibits a lawyer from accepting other employment in connection with a matter that is the same as, or substantially related to, the matter in which the lawyer took part as public officer or employee bars participation in overlapping government and private matters if it is rea-

What is "personal" and "substantial" for purposes of Rule 1.11[18] is a narrower concept than the term "represented," as used in Rule 1.9, so that Rule 1.9(a) and Rule 1.9(c) more readily disqualify a private lawyer moving from one private firm to another than Rule 1.11 will disqualify a private lawyer moving from the government to a private law firm.[19] For example, if a government lawyer merely entered an appearance on behalf of a government official, he has "represented" the government, but he was not participating "personally and substantially" for purposes of Rule 1.11.[20]

§ 1.11–3(d) Public Employee

The term, "public employee," encompasses every capacity in which the government employs the lawyer. It is not necessary that the government employ the government official in his capacity as a lawyer. The government employee might be a policy adviser to the President, or the administrative head of an agency.[21] The lawyer may be a policy adviser to the Governor and, in that capacity, negotiates for the state government's purchase of a compute system. The policy adviser, when she leaves the government, may not represent the computer contractor in a dispute arising under the contract that she had negotiated.[22]

---

sonable to infer that the lawyer may have received information during the first representation that might be useful to the second. The actual receipt of information, and hence disclosure of it, is immaterial. His activities warranted informal admonition by bar counsel.

[18]Rule 1.11(a) and Rule 1.11(d) both refer to situations where a lawyer "participated personally and substantially." This same test—"personally and substantially"—is also used in Rule 1.12(a) & (b), discussed below.

[19]ABA Formal Opinion 97-409 (Aug. 2, 1997), at 8 & n. 8.

[20]ABA Formal Opinion 97-409 (Aug. 2, 1997), at 8 & n. 8, *citing Violet v. Brown*, 9 Vet. App. 530 (Vet.App. 1996).

Contra Telos, Inc. v. Hawaiian Telephone Co., 397 F.Supp. 1314 (D.Hawai'i 1975), holding that a lawyer is involved "personally and substantially" merely by signing a complaint in a case. Professor Morgan criticizes this decision, pointing out its logical problem: "unless it appears that the signer could have prevented the complaint or knows some secret about the strength of the government's case, disqualification does not seem to serve any real governmental interest." Thomas D. Morgan, *Appropriate Limits on Participation by a Former Agency Official in Matters Before an Agency*, 1980 DUKE L.J. 1, 63 n.261 (1980).

[21]ABA Formal Opinion 342 (Nov. 24, 1975).

[22]Restatement of the Law Governing Lawyers, Third, § 133, ("A Former Government Lawyer Or Officer"), Comment c, illustration 1 (Official Draft 2000).

Model Rule 1.11 still governs because it covers all cases where the government employed the lawyer "as a public officer or employee."[23]

§ 1.11–3(e) Imputation, Waiver, and Screening

§ 1.11–3(e)(1) Imputation

Model Rule 1.11[24] and ABA Formal Opinion 342 both conclude that there is no pressing public need to automatically impute to a law firm the disqualification of a former government lawyer. An inflexible imputation rule is costly because it restricts government recruitment and limits a client's choice of lawyers.[25] The benefits do not justify imposing this cost when the screening will remove the ability of the former government lawyer to share confidential information. Because the balance of interests is different, the Rules do not provide for screening when conflicts are imputed to lawyers who are not former government lawyers.[26]

Thus, in spite of the broad language of DR 5-105(D), ABA Formal Opinion 342 concluded that the former government lawyer's disqualification is not imputed to the other lawyers in his new firm *if* the former government lawyer is "screened, to the satisfaction of the government agency concerned, from participation in the work and compensation of the firm on any matter over which as a public employee he had substantial responsibility."

Model Rule 1.11 explicitly codifies this result[27] and adds several important elaborations.

If a lawyer participated "personally and substantially" as a public officer or employee, that lawyer is *personally* disqualified from representing a private client in connection with that matter, unless the government agency consents, *i.e.,* waives the conflict.[28] However, this lawyer's personal disqualification—assuming the agency does not consent to the representation—is not imputed to

---

[23]Rule 1.11(a), (b), and (c)(1) all use this same phrase.

[24]Rule 1.11, Comment 3.

[25]This is an empirical question. At the time that Formal Opinion 343 was drafted, in 1975, many lawyers were choosing private practice over government work. In the late 1990's, it appears that government work was more popular.

[26]Rule 1.10(d) makes clear: "The disqualification of lawyers associated in a firm with former or current *government* lawyers is governed by Rule 1.11." (emphasis added). *See also SK Handtool Corp. v. Dresser Industries, Inc.*, 246 Ill.App.3d 979, 989, 619

N.E.2d 1282, 1288, 189 Ill.Dec. 233, 239 (1993): "[T]he proposed ABA Rules and the ABA House of Delegates both rejected the concept of screening for non-government attorneys" *citing* Ronald D. Rotunda, *The New Rules of Professional Conduct: A Brief Introduction and Comment,* 78 ILL. B.J. 386, 390 (1990); ABA Commission on Evaluation of Professional Standards, Model Rules of Professional Conduct, Rule 1.10 (1984).

[27]Rule 1.11(a)(1) ("the disqualified lawyer is screened"); Rule 1.11(b) ("if the disqualified lawyer is screened").

[28]Rule 1.11(a).

the entire law firm, as the second sentence of Rule 1.11(a) makes clear, if, *and only if,* the disqualified lawyer is "screened" from any participation in the matter and is apportioned no part of the fee from this particular matter.[29]

§ 1.11–3(e)(2) Prompt Notification

In order to make sure that this screen is effective and opaque, and not transparent or translucent, the law firm that is screening a disqualified lawyer must "promptly" notify the governmental agency in writing, so that it may assure itself that the firm has complied with the requirements of this rule.[30]

"Promptly" means "as soon as practicable after the need for screening becomes apparent."[31] While the lawyer must notify the government agency, there is *no* requirement that any notice be given to any adverse *private party* to enable it to ascertain that there has been compliance with this Rule.[32]

§ 1.11–3(e)(3) Waiver

ABA Formal Opinion 342 spoke of the need to permit "the one protected by DR 9-101(B) to waive" its protection. The Formal Opinion, interpreting the Model Code, dealt with the imputed disqualification problem by allowing the governmental agency to "waive" the disqualification if the personally disqualified lawyer were screened from participation in a particular matter. Hence, the question arises as to whether a government agency may unreasonably refuse to "waive," *e.g.*, to withhold its waiver only for tactical reasons. Case law under the Model Code concluded that the government may not refuse to waive if the refusal is not reasonable.[33] In effect, the "waiver" was a fiction: the agency must waive if there is adequate screening.

The Model Rules avoid this issue and the need to create a legal fiction simply by not requiring any government consent as to screening. The government must receive notice so that it can ascertain that the screening is effective. However, it has no power to withhold its consent to a proper screening.

The only time that consent enters into the picture is when the former government lawyer wants to be able *personally* to represent a private client in a matter in which he had earlier participated, personally and substantially, as a government

---

[29]Rule 1.11 (a)(1), (2). *See, e.g., In re Abraham D. Sofaer*, 728 A.2d 625 (D.C.App.1999) (violation of disciplinary rule governing acceptance of other employment following work as public officer or employee warranted informal admonition by bar counsel.)

[30]Rule 1.11(a)(2).

[31]Rule 1.11, Comment 7.

[32]*Compare* Rule 1.11(c), *with* Rule 1.11(a)(2).

[33]*See Kesselhaut v. United States*, 555 F.2d 791, 794 (Ct.Cl.1977) (per curiam) (government's unjustified withholding of consent to a screening not binding on the court).

official. In that case, the former governmental lawyer does need consent from the government.[34] But this consent is a true consent: the government, just like a private client, may withhold it.

§ 1.11–3(e)(4) Apportionment of the Fee

The screened lawyer must be "apportioned no part of the fee" from the disqualifying matter.[35] This provision is less restrictive than it first appears, and is less restrictive than ABA Formal Opinion 342 because Comment 6 to Rule 1.11 explicitly allows the screened lawyer to receive "a salary or partnership share established by prior independent agreement." The Rule only prohibits "*directly* relating the attorney's compensation to the fee" in the disqualifying matter.[36]

It thus appears that the lawyer can continue to receive his or her basic partnership draw (*e.g.* .5% of the partnership profits) even though that percentage will include money from all the cases of the law firm, including the case in which the personally disqualified governmental lawyer was screened. The law firm is not required to offer the personally disqualified governmental lawyer .5% of all partnership profits minus any profits from the case in which the lawyer had been screened. However, the law firm may not single out this one case and offer the disqualified lawyer a percentage of that case.[37]

§ 1.11–3(f) Preemption by Other Law

Rule 1.11 expressly incorporates the requirements of other law, such as a special statute or rule regulating conflicts of interest by lawyers working for (or who had worked for) the government. The first subsection of this Rule,[38] as well as the Comments, emphasize that the requirements of this Rule do not apply if these other laws "expressly permit" a conflict that Rule 1.11 would prohibit, or if these other laws prevent the government consenting to a conflict that would otherwise be disqualifying.[39] In other words, if this other law does not preempt Rule 1.11, then Rule 1.11 operates in addition to that other law.

§ 1.11–3(g) Confidential Governmental Information

Rule 1.11(b) has a special provision regarding confidential government information. "Confidential government information" is defined as information obtained pursuant to government

---

[34]Rule 1.11(a)[first sentence].

[35]Rule 1.11(a)(1).

[36]Rules 1.11, Comment 6 (emphasis added).

[37]Rule 1.11, Comment 6 states explicitly that Rule 1.11(a)(1) & Rule 1.11(b) "do *not* prevent a lawyer from receiving a salary *or partnership share* established by *prior* independent agreement." (emphasis added).

[38]Rule 1.11(a).

[39]Rule 1.11(a) & Comment 1.

authority and not available to the public.[40] The former government attorney cannot use such confidential information about a person to the "material disadvantage of that person."[41] This special restriction on the former government lawyer is not imputed to other members of the firm if the former government lawyer is screened from the matter in question and is apportioned no part of the fee from that matter.

The word "person" in Rule 1.11(c) refers to third parties, not the government. If the former government lawyer opposes an adverse third party after leaving government service, Rule 1.11(c) serves to protect that third party by not allowing the former government lawyer to use confidential government information about that person against that person. While Rule 1.11(c) protects adverse third parties, it does not prohibit the former government lawyer from using the confidential government information against the government client.[42]

That does not mean that the former government lawyer is free to use confidential government information against her former employer, because Rule 1.9(d) prohibits the former government lawyer from using information relating to her government representation adversely to her former government client.[43] Thus, a former government lawyer may normally represent a private party challenging generally applicable agency regulations that the former government lawyer personally helped draft, because drafting those regulations is not a "matter" under Rule 1.11. However, that former government lawyer is still subject to Rule 1.9(c), and thus forbidden from using nonpublic confidential information relating to her earlier representation of the government. If her representation of her private client would require her to use this nonpublic government information, she would not be able to represent her private client because of Rule 1.9(c), but her firm could take the case as long as she was screened.[44]

§ 1.11–3(h) Negotiating for Private Employment

The lawyer in government service must not negotiate for private employment with a party who is involved in a matter in

---

[40]Rule 1.11(c).

[41]Rule 1.11(c).

[42]ABA Formal Opinion 97-409 (Aug. 2, 1997), at 7 to 8, n.7.

[43]Formal Opinion 97-409 (Aug. 2, 1997). Rule 1.9(c) is the only portion of Rule 1.9 that applies to the former government lawyer. The conflict of interest provisions that regulate the former government lawyer are found in Rule 1.11, not Rule 1.9(a) or Rule 1.9(b). *Id.*

[44]Formal Opinion 97-409 (Aug. 2, 1997), at 16.

which the government lawyer is then participating personally and substantially.[45]

§ 1.11–3(h)(1) Judicial Law Clerks

Law clerks seeking private employment are treated differently than other former government lawyers. A special rule provides that the law clerk may negotiate for employment with a party or lawyer even though the law clerk is personally and substantially involved in the matter, but the law clerk must first notify the judge.[46] Even though Model Rule 1.11 permits the lawyer law clerk to continue to work on the matter after notifying the judge, most judges will assign the matter to another law clerk. Some state courts have very specific rules about law clerks negotiating or accepting compensation from law firms.[47]

§ 1.11–4 THE PRIVATE LAWYER MOVING INTO GOVERNMENT PRACTICE

Just as lawyers may move from government service to private practice, a lawyer in private practice may move to government service. Rule 1.11(d) is the basic rule governing this situation.

§ 1.11–4(a) The Basic Conflicts Prohibition

The elemental conflict rule is that a lawyer now working for the government may not participate in a matter if she, while in private practice, personally and substantially participated in that matter. The rationale for this rule was easy to understand. If the lawyer had participated "personally and substantially" while in private practice, she is likely to have learned confidential information from the private client, and she should not be in a position where she can use that information to the detriment of the former client. She also should not switch sides in that same matter by now working for the government in a position adverse to her former private client. Moreover, she should not use her position while in public service to give special, inappropriate benefits to her former private client.

The 1983 Model Rules stated that a lawyer who personally and substantially worked on a matter while in private practice may work on the government matter if other law imposes on that governmental lawyer [*i.e.* the government lawyer formerly in private practice] a nondelegable duty to act.[1] This provision provides a rather unexplained exception to this prohibition. It states that a lawyer may participate in a matter *even though* she

---

[45]Rule 1.11(d)(2).

[46]Rule 1.12(b).

[47]*See* Code of Conduct for Law Clerks and Staff Attorneys of the Supreme Court of Texas. http://www.sup reme.courts.state.tx.us/rules/pdf/clk-co nduct-atty.pdf.

[Section 1.11–4]

[1]1983 Model Rule 1.11(c)(1). *See also* ABA Standards Relating to the

had participated in it "personally and substantially while in private practice or nongovernment employment" *if* the applicable law provides that the government lawyer has a nondelegable duty to act in the matter.[2] The comments give no example to illustrate this provision. Presumably it means that if a statute requires a particular government official to act on a matter, that statute overrides Rule 1.11(c)(1) if the statute does not allow the official to withdraw from the matter even though this official, while in private practice, was "personally and substantially" on the same matter.

The drafters of the 2002 Rules deleted this language and instead substituted an exception to the disqualification if the "appropriate government agency give its informed consent, confirmed in writing."[3] Presumably, a government agency could balance the impact of the government lawyer's work on the matter while in private practice with the current posture of the case and the effect of the conflict of interest on the government position. Clearly, one would not expect this exception to be used often, but at least the mechanism is in place for possible consent.

The Model Rules have always been clear that Rule 1.11 governs a government lawyer's conflicts with work that lawyer did while in private practice. However, some confusion exists about whether a government lawyer had obligations under Rule 1.7 or Rule 1.9 in analyzing the situation. In other situations, Rules 1.7 and 1.9 were more restrictive than Rule 1.11 and in other situations, the opposite was true. The drafters of the 2002 Model Rules decided to impose Rule 1.7 and Rule 1.9 duties on all government lawyers who previously worked in private practice.

For example, under Rule 1.7, a government lawyer may have multiple government clients and this may create a conflict of interest under Rule 1.7(a)(2).[4] A government lawyer may have a personal conflict because of investments or personal or familial relationships with lawyers representing opposing sides. Rule

---

Administration of Justice, Standard 3-1.3 (c), "Conflict of Interest" (ABA, 3rd ed. 1992).

[2] 1983 Model Rule 1.11(c)(1).

[3] Rule 1.11(d)(2)(i). The Reporter's Notes specifically state that the informed consent of the government agency may include situations where "under applicable law no one is, or by lawful delegation may be, authorized to act in the lawyer's stead in the matter." Reporter's Explanation of Changes to Model Rule 1.11.

[4] One could easily imagine a situation in which a government lawyer represents the Environmental Protection Agency and the Department of Defense as defendant in litigation seeking to impose an environmental impact statement obligation in a particular military site. May the plaintiff raise the conflict of one government lawyer representing both governmental clients? If the Attorney General asserts the position that such conflicts are matters reserved for the executive branch, should a court seek to insure that the lawyers have followed Rule 1.7?

1.11(d)(1) makes it clear that Rule 1.7 applies to the conduct of government lawyers. Also, under Rule 1.9, a government lawyer may owe specific duties to a former private client. Some of those duties arise in the context of the same or substantially related matters, but others relate to use and disclosure of confidential information of a former client. Again, Rule 1.11(d)(1) makes clear that the government lawyer must follow Rule 1.9.

§ 1.11–4(b) Imputation

In the case of the private lawyer moving into government service, the benefits related to imputed disqualification are not considered significant enough to justify the burdens associated with it. Consequently, the disqualification imposed on the former private practitioner now in government service is not imputed to any other lawyers within the government.[5]

The burdens are certainly severe. To impute disqualification would place a tremendous cost on the government. If the rule imputed disqualification to all the other lawyers in the particular agency or department, like the Department of Justice, it would often be hard for the government to hire a lawyer from private practice because so many other government lawyers would then be disqualified by imputation.[6]

Moreover, the reward structure in the government is different than the reward structure of private firms, where the disqualification of a lawyer moving from one firm to another is automatically imputed.[7] For example, consider the case of the government lawyer formerly in private practice who knows confidences and secrets of her former client. This lawyer, now working for the government, obviously cannot ethically reveal her former client's secrets to her new colleagues.[8] But, her knowledge of these secrets is not imputed to her new colleagues because there is less incentive for her to breach the screen that walls her off on this matter from her colleagues. A salaried government lawyer does not have

---

[5]*See* Rule 1.10(d) (stating that government lawyer conflicts are governed solely by Rule 1.11). Rule 1.11, in turn, does not impute the disqualification on the former private practitioners. In fact, the former private lawyer is not herself disqualified if the appropriate government agency gives informed consent, confirmed in writing. Rule 1.11(d)(2)(i).

[6]Rule 1.11, Comment 3: "The provisions for screening and waiver are necessary to prevent the disqualification rule from imposing too severe a deterrent against entering public service." The requirements of Rule 1.11(b) do "not operate with respect to information that merely could be imputed to the lawyer." Rule 1.11, Comment 7.

[7]On the imputed disqualification of private lawyers moving from one private firm to another, see the discussion of Rule 1.10, above.

[8]*See* Canon 4; Rule 1.6.

the financial interest in the success of departmental representation that is inherent in private practice.[9]

Furthermore, in criminal cases, the duty of a government lawyer is different than the ethical duty of a private lawyer. "The duty of the prosecutor is to seek justice, not merely to convict."[10] The sovereign wins whenever justice is done.

Although the government lawyer's disqualification is not imputed to her colleagues, she should still be screened from participation in the particular matter.[11] Since the government official cannot use the confidential information she acquired while in private practice,[12] she must not participate in any government matter that would require her to use this confidential information. The drafters of the 2002 Model Rules did not make the screening of the government lawyer mandatory under Rule 1.11(d). The comment says that "ordinarily it would be prudent to screen such lawyers."[13] The Reporter's notes expressly state that they do require screening because in some cases it would be impractical for the government to do so.[14] The better approach would have been to impose screening unless it is impractical instead of leaving the idea that some lesser effort would suffice.

---

[9]ABA Formal Opinion 342 (Nov. 25, 1975).

[10]ABA Standards Relating to the Administration of Justice, Standard 3-1.2(c), "The Function of the Prosecutor," (3rd ed. 1992).

[11]ABA Formal Opinion 342 (Nov. 25, 1975).

[12]Rule 1.11(d). *See also* Rule 1.6; Rule 1.8(b); Rule 1.6, Comment 18: "The duty of confidentiality continues after the client-lawyer relationship has terminated."

[13]Rule 1.11, Comment 2.

[14]Reporter's Explanation of Changes to Model Rule 1.11.

CHAPTER 1.12
FORMER JUDGE, ARBITRATOR, MEDIATOR, OR OTHER THIRD-PARTY NEUTRAL

RULE 1.12: FORMER JUDGE, ARBITRATOR, MEDIATOR OR OTHER THIRD-PARTY NEUTRAL

(a) Except as stated in paragraph (d), a lawyer shall not represent anyone in connection with a matter in which the lawyer participated personally and substantially as a judge or other adjudicative officer or law clerk to such a person or as an arbitrator, mediator or other third-party neutral, unless all parties to the proceeding give informed consent, confirmed in writing.

(b) A lawyer shall not negotiate for employment with any person who is involved as a party or as lawyer for a party in a matter in which the lawyer is participating personally and substantially as a judge or other adjudicative officer or as an arbitrator, mediator or other third-party neutral. A lawyer serving as a law clerk to a judge or other adjudicative officer may negotiate for employment with a party or lawyer involved in a matter in which the clerk is participating personally and substantially, but only after the lawyer has notified the judge or other adjudicative officer.

(c) If a lawyer is disqualified by paragraph (a), no lawyer in a firm with which that lawyer is associated may knowingly undertake or continue representation in the matter unless:

(1) the disqualified lawyer is timely screened from any participation in the matter and is apportioned no part of the fee therefrom; and

(2) written notice is promptly given to the parties and any appropriate tribunal to enable them to ascertain compliance with the provisions of this rule.

(d) An arbitrator selected as a partisan of a party in a multimember arbitration panel is not prohibited from subsequently representing that party.

Comment

[1] This Rule generally parallels Rule 1.11. The term "personally and substantially" signifies that a judge who was a member of a multimember court, and thereafter left judicial office to practice law, is not prohibited from representing a client in a matter pending in the court, but in which the former judge did not participate. So also the fact that a former judge exercised administrative responsibility in a court does not prevent the former judge from acting as a lawyer in a matter where the judge had previously exercised remote or incidental administrative responsibility that did not affect the merits. Compare the Comment to Rule 1.11. The term "adjudicative officer" includes such officials as judges pro tempore, referees, special masters, hearing officers and other parajudicial officers, and also lawyers who serve as part-time judges. Paragraphs C(2), D(2) and E(2) of the Application Section of the Model Code of Judicial Conduct provide that a part-time judge, judge pro tempore or retired judge recalled to active service, shall not "act as a lawyer in a proceeding in which the judge has served as a judge or in any other proceeding related thereto." Although phrased differently from this Rule, those Rules correspond in meaning.

[2] Like former judges, lawyers who have served as arbitrators, mediators or other third-party neutrals may be asked to represent a client in a matter in which the lawyer participated personally and substantially. This Rule forbids such representation unless all of the parties to the proceedings give their informed consent, confirmed in writing. See Rule 1.0(e) and (b). Other law or codes of ethics governing third-party neutrals may impose more stringent standards of personal or imputed disqualification. See Rule 2.4.

[3] Although lawyers who serve as third-party neutrals do not have information concerning the parties that is protected under Rule 1.6, they typically owe the parties an obligation of confidentiality under law or codes of ethics governing third-party neutrals. Thus, paragraph (c) provides that conflicts of the personally disqualified lawyer will be imputed to other lawyers in a law firm unless the conditions of this paragraph are met.

[4] Requirements for screening procedures are stated in Rule 1.0(k). Paragraph (c)(1) does not prohibit the screened lawyer from receiving a salary or partnership share established by prior independent agreement, but that lawyer may not receive compensation directly related to the matter in which the lawyer is disqualified.

[5] Notice, including a description of the screened lawyer's prior representation and of the screening procedures employed, generally should be given as soon as practicable after the need for screening becomes apparent.

Authors' 1983 Model Rules Comparison

The drafters of the 2002 Rules added "Mediator or Other Third-Party Neutral" to the title of this Rule.

In Rule 1.12(a), the drafters removed arbitrator from one part of the sentence and later in the sentence added "or as an arbitrator, mediator or other third-party neutral." They also added "give informed" to modify consent and "confirmed in writing."

In Rule 1.12(b), the drafters added "mediator or other third party neutral" to the scope of this section.

In Rule 1.12(c)(1), the drafters added the word, "timely" to modify the word "screened." In Rule 1.12(c)(2), they added "parties" to the target of any notice that should be given.

Comment 1 was not modified.

Comment 2 to 5 are new and they elaborate on the addition of mediators and other third-party neutrals to the Rule as well as the operation of screening and notice in general.

Model Code Comparison

[1] Paragraph (a) is substantially similar to DR 9-101(A), which provided that a lawyer "shall not accept private employment in a matter upon the merits of which he has acted in a judicial capacity." Paragraph (a) differs, however, in that it is broader in scope and states more specifically the persons to whom it applies. There was no counterpart in the Model Code to paragraphs (b), (c) or (d).

[2] With regard to arbitrators, EC 5-20 stated that "a lawyer [who] has undertaken to act as an impartial arbitrator or mediator, . . . should not thereafter represent in the dispute any of the parties involved." DR 9-101(A) did not permit a waiver of the disqualification applied to former judges by consent of the parties. However, DR 5-105(C) was similar in effect and could be construed to permit waiver.

§ 1.12–1 DISQUALIFICATION OF FORMER JUDGES— THE GENERAL RULE

The ABA Model Code of Judicial Conduct applies to sitting judges.[1] For the ethical restrictions of former judges, one turns primarily to ABA Model Rule 1.12. A *former judge* may not accept private employment in a matter if she acted in a judicial capacity, on the merits of that case.[2] Rule 1.12 essentially extends the principles of Rule 1.11 (conflicts involving former government lawyers) to judges and other adjudicatory officials.

§ 1.12–1(a) Judge's Law Clerk

If the judge's *law clerk* "personally and substantially" participated with the judge on the case, then the law clerk is also dis-

---

[Section 1.12–1]

[1]The ABA Model Code of Judicial Conduct is discussed below. See also § 10.3–24(b), "Recusal Issues When a Judge is Considered for Another Position."

[2]DR 9-101(A); Rule 1.12(a) ("participated personally and substantially").

This disqualification rule ap-plies not only to judges but to other persons who have acted in a "judicial capacity," such as a hearing officer, special master, or referee. Rule 1.12(a), Comment 1. *Powers v. State Dept. of Social Welfare*, 208 Kan. 605, 493 P.2d 590 (1972) (DR 9-101(A) applies to referee in social welfare department). *See also* EC 5-20 (impartial mediator or arbitrator).

qualified from later representing anyone in the same matter.[3] The judge's law clerk may, however, negotiate for employment with a party or attorney who is involved in a matter—even though the clerk is participating personally and substantially on that matter—so long as the clerk notifies the judge.[4]

An interesting decision where the court disqualified a lawyer because she was a former law clerk is *Monument Builders of Pennsylvania, Inc. v. Catholic Cemeteries Association, Inc.*[5] In this case an association of independent cemetery monument builders and dealers brought suit alleging breach of settlement agreements in an antitrust class action against various cemeteries and cemetery associations. The defendants moved to disqualify plaintiffs counsel, and the District Court agreed. First, the former law clerk was practicing in Pennsylvania, and thus was subject to the Pennsylvania rules, which governed all members of the bar. In addition, she was subject to other ethical restrictions because she was a former law clerk in that district.

Monument Builders held that Rule 1.12 of the Pennsylvania Rules of Professional Conduct disqualified the former law clerk of a judge (this judge had presided over an antitrust class action) from representing the plaintiff in a subsequent action alleging a breach of the settlement agreements reached in first suit. Second, the Code of Conduct for Law Clerks (1994 ed.) and the Code of Conduct for Judicial Employees (1996 ed.) are legally authoritative and binding on law clerks even after they leave the judges' employment. These Codes required law clerks to "avoid impropriety and the appearance of impropriety." Thus, they also disqualified the former law clerk in these circumstances.

Note that the court disqualified the former law *clerk*. The court did not disqualify the judge. A party cannot force a judge who has handled a case to recuse himself because the opposing law firm hired the judge's former law clerk. "Any other conclusion would promote the hiring of associates merely to disqualify a judge, a policy no judicial system can tolerate."[6]

§ 1.12–1(b) Partisan Arbitrators

A *partisan arbitrator*—i.e., the partisan member of a multimem-

---

[3]Rule 1.12(a). *Cf.* ABA Formal Opinion 96-400 (Jan. 24, 1996), "Job Negotiations with Adverse Firm or Party."

[4]Rule 1.12(b).

[5]*Monument Builders of Pennsylvania, Inc. v. The Catholic Cemeteries Association, Inc.*, 1999-2 Trade Cases P 72727, 190 F.R.D. 164 (E.D.Pa.1999).

[6]*Comparato v. Schait*, 362 N.J.Super. 113, 119, 827 A.2d 306, 310 (N.J.Super.A.D.2003), *appeal denied*, 178 N.J. 248, 837 A.2d 1091 (2003). *See also Hunt v. American Bank & Trust Co.*, 783 F.2d 1011, 1016 (11th Cir.1986): "If a clerk has a possible conflict of interest it is the clerk, not the judge, who must be disqualified."

Hamid v. Price Waterhouse, 51 F.3d 1411, 1415–17 (9th Cir.1995),

ber arbitration panel[7]—is not disqualified from later representing a party to the arbitration because that type of arbitrator did not serve, in that matter, as an impartial decision-maker.[8] Rule 1.12 does not purport to govern partisan arbitrators.

§ 1.12–1(c) Distinction Between Mediators and Adjudicators

§ 1.12–1(c)(1) The 1983 Version of Rule 1.12

The 1983 Model Rules made a distinction between third parties who render a decision for the parties and other individual parties involved in alternative dispute resolution. Rule 1.12 applied to judges and arbitrators but did not apply to mediators and other third party neutrals. The purpose underlying this distinction was that lawyers who participate in adjudicating a dispute occupy an official government function and receive information through official processes. Judges and arbitrators should not represent the parties in the same matters in which they participated; however, their law firms should be able to represent one of the parties if the law firms properly screen the lawyer adjudicator. Rule 1.12 also sought to encourage lawyers to become judges and arbitrators and a broad imputed disqualification principle would discourage law firms from hiring former judges and arbitrators.

Mediators and other third party neutrals do not render a decision. They simply facilitate the resolution of disputes through mediation and other tactics. The drafters of the 1983 Rules analogized the mediation function to be closer to intermediation rather than adjudication. Therefore, they drafted Rule 1.12 so it did not apply to mediators or other persons involved in facilitative actions in alternative dispute resolution. The following decision illustrates the treatment of mediators under this view.

Cho v. Superior Court[9] illustrates, by analogy, the distinction between judges and arbitrators, who are governed by Rule 1.12,

---

holding that a trial judge did not have to recuse herself even though the judge's clerk was an associate of the firm before joining the judge's chambers and the former firm represented the parties in an action before the court. The clerk did not know his former firm represented clients in the matter and the firm did not appear for any parties; the clerk did not return to firm after clerkship; and the lawsuit involved a very large number of defendants.

[7]Some arbitration agreements provide that each party is required to select a partisan arbitrator and the two party selected arbitrators select a third neutral arbitrator. This tripartite panel will hear the dispute and render a decision. Some parties select a lawyer to serves as a partisan arbitrator. Rule 1.12(d) states that it does not apply to disqualify the lawyer or the law firm in subsequent representations.

[8]Rule 1.12(d).

[9]*Cho v. Superior Court*, 39 Cal.App.4th 113, 45 Cal.Rptr.2d 863 (1995).

and intermediators, who are governed by Rule 2.2. In *Cho*, a judge presided over settlement discussions in another incarnation of this case. Then, he left the bench and became "of counsel" to the defendant's firm. Judge Cho was *not* an intermediary because he did not represent any party while he was a judge. He was a settlement judge, not representing any party, rather than an intermediary, who represents two or more parties.

While Judge Cho had attempted to mediate the dispute, he had received confidential information from the plaintiff. The court disqualified his entire law firm although the former judge said that he now remembers none of this. If he had been an intermediary under Rule 2.2, he still would have been disqualified. The court observed: "[A]lthough mediators function in some ways as neutral coordinators of dispute resolution, they also assume the role of a confidant, and it is that aspect of their role that distinguishes them from adjudicators."[10] Although screening under Rule 1.12 is proper for former adjudicators who only see what each side shows the other, it is not proper for former mediators.

§ 1.12–1(c)(2) Rule 1.12 after the 2002 Revisions

The drafters of the 2002 Rules studied this distinction drawn between arbitrators and mediators and concluded that that the focus on adjudication was misplaced. They believed that mediators and other third-party neutrals are closer in function to third parties seeking to resolve disputes. The drafters examined the issue of how these different third parties handle confidential information:

> The Commission determined that mediators and other third-party neutrals should be treated in the same manner because 1) there is typically less confidential information obtained in these proceedings than when the lawyer represents clients in a client-lawyer relationship and 2) although the third-party neutral usually owes a duty of confidentiality to the parties, it is not the same duty of confidentiality owed under Rule 1.6. The Commission also heard testimony that third-party neutrals do not share information with other lawyers in the firm in the same way that lawyers representing clients do.[11]

The drafters also believed that the 1983 position on mediators and third-party neutrals might discourage lawyers from serving in that function because of the broad view of conflict disqualification.

Rule 1.12, as revised, now disqualifies any lawyer who

---

[10] The court was quoting *Poly Software International, Inc. v. Su*, 880 F.Supp. 1487 (D.Utah.1995). The court held that both the former judge and law firm that hired him had to be disqualified from representing the litigant in an action in which the former judge received *ex parte* confidences during settlement conferences.

[11] Reporter's Explanation of Changes to Model Rule 1.12.

participated personally and substantially as a judge, other adjudicative officer, arbitrator, mediator, or third party neutral unless all parties in a proceeding give informed consent, confirmed in writing.[12] The drafters borrowed the term "personally and substantially" from Rule 1.11. This test—"personally and substantially"—is intended to limit disqualifications to cases in which the lawyer adjudicator or facilitator worked on the merits, rather than cases in the same court before other judges or cases in which the lawyer worked on a scheduling issue.[13] Once arbitrators and other facilitators are included in the Rule, their conflict is not automatically imputed to the law firm in which they practice, if they satisfy the requirements of 1.12(c), described in § 1.12-2.[14]

§ 1.12–1(d) Waiver

The purpose of the general rule requiring disqualification of the former judge is to protect the parties. Consequently, they may knowingly waive this protection.[15]

§ 1.12–2 IMPUTATION AND SCREENING

The disqualification of the former judge, arbitrator, or mediator is *not* imputed to any other lawyer in the former official's new law firm if two conditions exist: first, the former judge, arbitrator, or mediator is screened from the disqualifying matter and apportioned no part of the fee from it;[1] second, the law firm promptly gives written notice to the appropriate tribunal so that it can determine that the screening is adequate.[2] This screening and notice provision parallels the rule regarding the former govern-

---

[12]The Comment to this Rule states that "[T]he term 'adjudicative officer' includes such officials as judges pro tempore, referees, special masters, hearing officers and other parajudicial officers, and also lawyers who serve as part-time judges." Rule 1.12, Comment 1.

[13]Rule 1.12, Comment 1.

[14]*See* Va. State Bar Opinion 1826 (Mar. 28, 2006) (examining conflicts created for two partners in a law firm who owned a separate mediation firm), *noted in* 22 ABA/BNA MANUAL ON PROFESSIONAL CONDUCT, Current Reports News 187 (Apr. 19, 2006).

[15]Rule 1.12(a). *Cf.* Model Code of Judicial Conduct, Canon 3F (1990),

which provides for waiver of certain disqualifications by a sitting judge.

[Section 1.12–2]

[1]Rule 1.12(c)(1). The Comment states that this provision "does not prohibit the screened lawyer from receiving a salary or partnership share established by prior independent agreement, but that lawyer may not receive compensation directed related to the matter in which the lawyer is disqualified."

[2]Rule 1.12(c). The Comment states that the law firm should provide notice to all concerned "as soon as practicable after the need for screening becomes apparent." Rule 1.12, Comment 5.

ment lawyer.[3]

---

[3]*See* Rule 1.11(a).

CHAPTER 1.13
THE ORGANIZATION AS CLIENT

RULE 1.13: ORGANIZATION AS CLIENT

(a) A lawyer employed or retained by an organization represents the organization acting through its duly authorized constituents.

(b) If a lawyer for an organization knows that an officer, employee or other person associated with the organization is engaged in action, intends to act or refuses to act in a matter related to the representation that is a violation of a legal obligation to the organization, or a violation of law that reasonably might be imputed to the organization, and that is likely to result in substantial injury to the organization, then the lawyer shall proceed as is reasonably necessary in the best interest of the organization. Unless the lawyer reasonably believes that it is not necessary in the best interest of the organization to do so, the lawyer shall refer the matter to higher authority in the organization, including, if warranted by the circumstances, to the highest authority that can act on behalf of the organization as determined by applicable law.

(c) Except as provided in paragraph (d), if

(1) despite the lawyer's efforts in accordance with paragraph (b) the highest authority that can act on behalf of the organization insists upon or fails to address in a timely and appropriate manner an action or a refusal to act, that is clearly a violation of law, and

(2) the lawyer reasonably believes that the violation is reasonably certain to result in substantial injury to the organization,

then the lawyer may reveal information relating to the

representation whether or not Rule 1.6 permits such disclosure, but only if and to the extent the lawyer reasonably believes necessary to prevent substantial injury to the organization.

(d) Paragraph (c) shall not apply with respect to information relating to a lawyer's representation of an organization to investigate an alleged violation of law, or to defend the organization or an officer, employee or other constituent associated with the organization against a claim arising out of an alleged violation of law.

(e) A lawyer who reasonably believes that he or she has been discharged because of the lawyer's actions taken pursuant to paragraphs (b) or (c), or who withdraws under circumstances that require or permit the lawyer to take action under either of those paragraphs, shall proceed as the lawyer reasonably believes necessary to assure that the organization's highest authority is informed of the lawyer's discharge or withdrawal.

(f) In dealing with an organization's directors, officers, employees, members, shareholders or other constituents, a lawyer shall explain the identity of the client when the lawyer knows or reasonably should know that the organization's interests are adverse to those of the constituents with whom the lawyer is dealing.

(g) A lawyer representing an organization may also represent any of its directors, officers, employees, members, shareholders or other constituents, subject to the provisions of Rule 1.7. If the organization's consent to the dual representation is required by Rule 1.7, the consent shall be given by an appropriate official of the organization other than the individual who is to be represented, or by the shareholders.

Comment

The Entity as the Client

[1] An organizational client is a legal entity, but it cannot act except through its officers, directors, employees, shareholders and other constituents. Officers, directors, employees and shareholders are the constituents of the corporate organizational client. The duties defined in this Comment apply equally to unincorporated associations. "Other constituents" as used in this Comment means the positions equivalent to officers, directors, employees and shareholders held by persons acting for organizational clients that are not corporations.

[2] When one of the constituents of an organizational client communicates with the organization's lawyer in that person's organizational capacity, the communication is protected by Rule 1.6. Thus, by way of example, if an organizational client requests its lawyer to

investigate allegations of wrongdoing, interviews made in the course
of that investigation between the lawyer and the client's employees
or other constituents are covered by Rule 1.6. This does not mean,
however, that constituents of an organizational client are the clients
of the lawyer. The lawyer may not disclose to such constituents information relating to the representation except for disclosures
explicitly or impliedly authorized by the organizational client in order to carry out the representation or as otherwise permitted by
Rule 1.6.

[3] When constituents of the organization make decisions for it, the
decisions ordinarily must be accepted by the lawyer even if their
utility or prudence is doubtful. Decisions concerning policy and
operations, including ones entailing serious risk, are not as such in
the lawyer's province. Paragraph (b) makes clear, however, that
when the lawyer knows that the organization is likely to be
substantially injured by action of an officer or other constituent
that violates a legal obligation to the organization or is in violation
of law that might be imputed to the organization, the lawyer must
proceed as is reasonably necessary in the best interest of the
organization. As defined in Rule 1.0(f), knowledge can be inferred
from circumstances, and a lawyer cannot ignore the obvious.

[4] In determining how to proceed under paragraph (b), the lawyer
should give due consideration to the seriousness of the violation
and its consequences, the responsibility in the organization and the
apparent motivation of the person involved, the policies of the organization concerning such matters, and any other relevant
considerations. Ordinarily, referral to a higher authority would be
necessary. In some circumstances, however, it may be appropriate
for the lawyer to ask the constituent to reconsider the matter; for
example, if the circumstances involve a constituent's innocent misunderstanding of law and subsequent acceptance of the lawyer's
advice, the lawyer may reasonably conclude that the best interest
of the organization does not require that the matter be referred to
higher authority. If a constituent persists in conduct contrary to the
lawyer's advice, it will be necessary for the lawyer to take steps to
have the matter reviewed by a higher authority in the organization.
If the matter is of sufficient seriousness and importance or urgency
to the organization, referral to higher authority in the organization
may be necessary even if the lawyer has not communicated with
the constituent. Any measures taken should, to the extent
practicable, minimize the risk of revealing information relating to
the representation to persons outside the organization. Even in circumstances where a lawyer is not obligated by Rule 1.13 to proceed,
a lawyer may bring to the attention of an organizational client,
including its highest authority, matters that the lawyer reasonably
believes to be of sufficient importance to warrant doing so in the
best interest of the organization.

[5] Paragraph (b) also makes clear that when it is reasonably necessary to enable the organization to address the matter in a timely
and appropriate manner, the lawyer must refer the matter to higher
authority, including, if warranted by the circumstances, the highest
authority that can act on behalf of the organization under applicable
law. The organization's highest authority to whom a matter may be

referred ordinarily will be the board of directors or similar governing body. However, applicable law may prescribe that under certain conditions the highest authority reposes elsewhere, for example, in the independent directors of a corporation.

[6] The authority and responsibility provided in this Rule are concurrent with the authority and responsibility provided in other Rules. In particular, this Rule does not limit or expand the lawyer's responsibility under Rules 1.8, 1.16, 3.3 or 4.1. Paragraph (c) of this Rule supplements Rule 1.6(b) by providing an additional basis upon which the lawyer may reveal information relating to the representation, but does not modify, restrict, or limit the provisions of Rule 1.6(b)(1) to (6). Under paragraph (c) the lawyer may reveal such information only when the organization's highest authority insists upon or fails to address threatened or ongoing action that is clearly a violation of law, and then only to the extent the lawyer reasonably believes necessary to prevent reasonably certain substantial injury to the organization. It is not necessary that the lawyer's services be used in furtherance of the violation, but it is required that the matter be related to the lawyer's representation of the organization. If the lawyer's services are being used by an organization to further a crime or fraud by the organization, Rules 1.6(b)(2) and 1.6(b)(3) may permit the lawyer to disclose confidential information. In such circumstances Rule 1.2(d) may also be applicable, in which event, withdrawal from the representation under Rule 1.16(a)(1) may be required.

Relation to Other Rules

[7] Paragraph (d) makes clear that the authority of a lawyer to disclose information relating to a representation in circumstances described in paragraph (c) does not apply with respect to information relating to a lawyer's engagement by an organization to investigate an alleged violation of law or to defend the organization or an officer, employee or other person associated with the organization against a claim arising out of an alleged violation of law. This is necessary in order to enable organizational clients to enjoy the full benefits of legal counsel in conducting an investigation or defending against a claim.

[8] A lawyer who reasonably believes that he or she has been discharged because of the lawyer's actions taken pursuant to paragraph (b) or (c), or who withdraws in circumstances that require or permit the lawyer to take action under either of these paragraphs, must proceed as the lawyer reasonably believes necessary to assure that the organization's highest authority is informed of the lawyer's discharge or withdrawal.

Government Agency

[9] The duty defined in this Rule applies to governmental organizations. Defining precisely the identity of the client and prescribing the resulting obligations of such lawyers may be more difficult in the government context and is a matter beyond the scope of these Rules. See Scope [18]. Although in some circumstances the client may be a specific agency, it may also be a branch of government, such as the executive branch, or the government as a whole. For example, if the action or failure to act involves the head of a

bureau, either the department of which the bureau is a part or the relevant branch of government may be the client for purposes of this Rule. Moreover, in a matter involving the conduct of government officials, a government lawyer may have authority under applicable law to question such conduct more extensively than that of a lawyer for a private organization in similar circumstances. Thus, when the client is a governmental organization, a different balance may be appropriate between maintaining confidentiality and assuring that the wrongful act is prevented or rectified, for public business is involved. In addition, duties of lawyers employed by the government or lawyers in military service may be defined by statutes and regulation. This Rule does not limit that authority. See Scope.

Clarifying the Lawyer's Role

[10] There are times when the organization's interest may be or become adverse to those of one or more of its constituents. In such circumstances the lawyer should advise any constituent, whose interest the lawyer finds adverse to that of the organization of the conflict or potential conflict of interest, that the lawyer cannot represent such constituent, and that such person may wish to obtain independent representation. Care must be taken to assure that the individual understands that, when there is such adversity of interest, the lawyer for the organization cannot provide legal representation for that constituent individual, and that discussions between the lawyer for the organization and the individual may not be privileged.

[11] Whether such a warning should be given by the lawyer for the organization to any constituent individual may turn on the facts of each case.

Dual Representation

[12] Paragraph (g) recognizes that a lawyer for an organization may also represent a principal officer or major shareholder.

Derivative Actions

[13] Under generally prevailing law, the shareholders or members of a corporation may bring suit to compel the directors to perform their legal obligations in the supervision of the organization. Members of unincorporated associations have essentially the same right. Such an action may be brought nominally by the organization, but usually is, in fact, a legal controversy over management of the organization.

[14] The question can arise whether counsel for the organization may defend such an action. The proposition that the organization is the lawyer's client does not alone resolve the issue. Most derivative actions are a normal incident of an organization's affairs, to be defended by the organization's lawyer like any other suit. However, if the claim involves serious charges of wrongdoing by those in control of the organization, a conflict may arise between the lawyer's duty to the organization and the lawyer's relationship with the board. In those circumstances, Rule 1.7 governs who should represent the directors and the organization.

Authors' 1983 Model Rules Comparison

The drafters of the 2002 Model Rules did not make many changes to Rule 1.13.

In Rule 1.13(b)(1), the drafters added the word "for" before the word "reconsideration." In Rule 1.13(b)(3), they changed the word "in" to "on."

In Rule 1.13(d), the drafters changed the terms "it is apparent" to the words, "the lawyer knows or reasonably should know."

In Comments 1 to 3, the drafters did not make any changes.

In Comment 4, the drafters amended the language to remove a reference to "in extreme cases" to note that ordinarily the lawyer may refer matters to the board.

In Comment 5, the drafters made a minor change to refer to the Rules in general rather than one rule.

In Comment 6, the drafters clarified the identity of the government client and made a Comment that some decisions about government representation are beyond the scope of the Rule.

In Comments 7 to 11, the drafters did not make any changes.

Post February 2002 Amendment:

The Task Force on Corporate Responsibility made its final recommendations to the ABA in August 2003. Based upon this Report, the ABA House of Delegates adopted significant amendments to Rule 1.13 at the August meeting.

The ABA amended Rule 1.13(b) and Rule 1.13(c) to clarify the role of the lawyer in a situation in which someone was acting in a way that was likely to cause substantial injury to the entity.

The ABA added new sections (d) and (e) to address the new role of the lawyer in sections (b) and (c). Rule 1.13(d) provides that sections (b) and (c) do not apply when a lawyer is hired to defend an entity against allegations of a violation of the law. Rule 1.13(e) addresses the lawyer's duty to seek to inform the highest authority that can act on behalf of an entity when the lawyer has been discharged because of the actions taken under (b) and (c).

The ABA renumbered the 2002 versions of sections (d) and (e) to become (f) and (g) without amendment.

In Comments 1 to 2, the ABA made no changes.

In Comment 3, the ABA deleted a large portion of the language dealing with measures that a lawyer may take to try to convince the agents of an entity to act in accordance with the law. This Comment now provides background information for the next two comments.

Comment 4 is new and contains the language on how a lawyer is to proceed under Rule 1.13(b) when someone insists on action that is likely to cause substantial injury to the entity client.

The drafters renumbered old Comment 4 as Comment 5 and added several lines clarifying the need to provide notice within the entity to the highest authority that can act on behalf of the entity.

The drafters renumbered old Comment 5 as Comment 6 and added several lines explaining the relationship of the new disclosure provision in Rule 1.13(c) to Rules 1.6 and 1.16.

Comment 7 is new and addresses the new Rule 1.13(d).

Comment 8 is new and addresses the new Rule 1.13(e).

The drafters renumbered Comments 6 to 11 to become 9 to 14 with one minor change in Comment 12 dealing with a reference to the renumbered text.

Model Code Comparison

There was no counterpart to this Rule in the Disciplinary Rules of the Model Code. EC 5-18 stated that a "lawyer employed or retained by a corporation or similar entity owes his allegiance to the entity and not to a stockholder, director, officer, employee, representative, or other person connected with the entity. In advising the entity, a lawyer should keep paramount its interests and his professional judgment should not be influenced by the personal desires of any person or organization. Occasionally, a lawyer for an entity is requested by a stockholder, director, officer, employee, representative, or other person connected with the entity to represent him in an individual capacity; in such case the lawyer may serve the individual only if the lawyer is convinced that differing interests are not present." EC 5-24 stated that although a lawyer "may be employed by a business corporation with non-lawyers serving as directors or officers, and they necessarily have the right to make decisions of business policy, a lawyer must decline to accept direction of his professional judgment from any layman." DR 5-107(B) provided that a lawyer "shall not permit a person who . . . employs . . . him to render legal services for another to direct or regulate his professional judgment in rendering such legal services."[1]

[Rule 1.13]

[1]As originally proposed by the Kutak Commission, Rule 1.13 (Revised Final Draft, June 30, 1982) read as follows:

(a) A lawyer employed or retained to represent an organization represents the organization as distinct from its directors, officers, employees, members, shareholders or other constituents.

(b) If a lawyer for an organization knows that an officer, employee or other person associated with the organization is engaged in action, intends to act or refuses to act in a matter related to the representation that is a violation of a legal obligation to the organization, or a violation of law which reasonably might be imputed to the organization, and is likely to result in substantial injury to the organization, the lawyer shall proceed as is reasonably necessary in the best interest of the organization. In determining how to proceed, the lawyer shall give due consideration to the seriousness of the violation and its consequences, the scope and nature of the lawyer's representation, the responsibility in the organization and the apparent motivation of the person involved, the policies of the organization concerning such matters and any other relevant considerations. Any measures taken shall be designed to minimize disruption of the organization and the risk of revealing information relating to the representation to persons outside the organization. Such measures may include among others:

(1) asking reconsideration of the matter;

(2) advising that a separate legal opinion on the matter be sought for presentation to appropriate authority in the organization; and

(3) referring the matter to higher authority in the organization, including,

§ 1.13–1 REPRESENTING CORPORATIONS AND OTHER ENTITIES

§ 1.13–1(a) Introduction

The Approach of the ABA Model Code. The former ABA Model Code accepted the general principle that a lawyer employed or retained by a corporation or similar entity "owes his allegiance to the entity and not to a stockholder, director, officer, employee, representative, or other person connected with the entity."[1] The entity may be, for example, a corporation, union, a partnership or a governmental agency.

Unfortunately, the Model Code did not elaborate. It offered little in the way of concrete guidance in applying this entity theory of ethics. We know the lawyer owes his or her allegiance to the incorporeal entity, but the vague standard of EC 5-18 did not advise us how to determine what this incorporeal entity really wants. Incorporeal beings have no mouth and do not necessarily speak clearly.

The most specific guidance was found in EC 5-24, which stated that the lawyer should make legal judgments but defer to the business judgment of the agents of the entity. Directors and officers "necessarily have the right to make decisions of business policy," but a lawyer "must decline to accept direction of his professional judgment from any layman." Yet, the people who often speak for the entity (the Chairman of the Board, the union

---

if warranted by the seriousness of the matter, referral to the highest authority that can act in behalf of the organization as determined by applicable law.

(c) When the organization's highest authority insists upon action, or refuses to take action, that is clearly a violation of a legal obligation to the organization, or a violation of law which reasonably might be imputed to the organization, and is likely to result in substantial injury to the organization, the lawyer may take further remedial action that the lawyer reasonably believes to be in the best interest of the organization. Such action may include revealing information otherwise protected by Rule 1.6 only if the lawyer reasonably believes that:

(1) the highest authority in the organization has acted to further the personal or financial interests of members of that authority which are in conflict with the interest of the organization; and

(2) revealing the information is neces-

sary in the best interest of the organization.

(d) In dealing with an organization's directors, officers, employees, members, shareholders or other constituents, a lawyer shall explain the identity of the client when the lawyer believes that such explanation is necessary to avoid misunderstandings on their part.

(e) A lawyer representing an organization may also represent any of its directors, officers, employees, members, shareholders or other constituents, subject to the provisions of Rule 1.7. If the organization's consent to the dual representation is required by Rule 1.7, the consent shall be given by an appropriate official of the organization other than the individual who is to be represented or by the shareholders.

[Section 1.13–1]

[1] EC 5-18.

595

president, the various partners in a partnership) are lay people, not lawyers. Hence, even this specific guidance was not as helpful as it might first appear.

The Model Rules. The Model Rules, in particular Model Rule 1.13(b) & (c), embrace the entity theory, but they offer a more a more useful analytical tool than the bare bones of EC 5-18.[2] Thus, Rule 1.13 provides that the lawyer "employed or retained by an organization *represents the organization* acting through its duly authorized constituents."[3] Although the language of the Model Rules is slightly different from the Model Code, no suggestion arises that the drafters intended any substantial change in the new language.[4] However, Rule 1.13 then goes beyond the Model Code by elaborating on this entity theory and offering more concrete guidance.[5]

The lawyer represents the "entity," but this legal entity can only act through its officers and other duly authorized agents.[6] The entity theory offers no Rosetta Stone to solve all corporate conflicts problems, but it does provide some solutions. If a competitor sues a corporate client alleging an antitrust violation, it is easy to conclude that the corporate lawyer does not represent a shareholder of the defendant who is also a shareholder of plaintiff. Rather, the lawyer represents the corporation as an entity.[7]

But what of other, more difficult cases—where the shareholders of the corporation sue derivatively, alleging that the directors have not performed their legal obligations? Or, consider the case where the lawyer for a corporation is asked to defend it from a

---

[2]Ronald D. Rotunda & Robert C. Hacker, *Representing the Corporate Client and the Proposed Rules of Professional Conduct*, 6 CORP. L. REV. 269.

[3]Rule 1.13(a)(emphasis added). *Cf.* DR 5-107(B). *See also* Restatement of the Law Governing Lawyers, Third, § 96 (Official Draft 2000).

[4]*See* Rule 1.13, Code Comparison 1.

A Note on the Changes in Language Between the ABA Model Code and the ABA Model Rules. Normally, if the drafters of a new law used different language when redrafting a statute or rule, that change would typically indicate that they meant to alter the meaning. If they did not intend to change the meaning, why would they modify the language? However, this standard principle in inter-

preting legislation does not apply to the reformulated language of the ABA Model Rules. Often times the Commission, which drafted the Rules, rejected the language of the Model Code because of a preference for different phraseology, not because of any intent to change the meaning. John Sutton, *Professional Code Becoming Controversial Rules*, 35 VIRGINIA L. WEEKLY 1, 4 col. 1 (Nov. 12, 1982).

[5]*See also* Restatement of the Law Governing Lawyers, Third, § 131 ("Conflicts of Interest in Representing an Organization") (Official Draft 2000).

[6]*See* Rule 1.13(a) & Comment 1.

[7]*See* Ronald D. Rotunda, *Law, Lawyers, and Managers, in* THE ETHICS OF CORPORATE CONDUCT, 127, 129 (Clarence Walton, ed., Prentice-Hall, Inc., 1977).

hostile takeover, which may be in the best economic interests of the shareholders. Or, consider the ethical obligations of a corporate lawyer who discovers that one of the officers is violating a law (*e.g.*, engaging in price-fixing). This violation would be imputed to the entity, but it "benefits" the corporation *if* the corporation is not caught.

That is where the Model Rules provide a clearer road map. It is to that road map that we now turn. In 2002, the ABA House of Delegates approved various revisions to Rule 1.13, in an effort to make the roadmap clearer. Those changes were short-lived because, in August, 2003, the House of Delegates approved even more substantial changes to Rule 1.6 and 1.13, in response to various corporate scandals including the bankruptcy of Enron Corporation. This chapter discusses Rule 1.13 in light of its various changes. The end result is a roadmap that seeks to navigate between Scylla and Charybdis, between the risk of aiding and abetting client fraud and the danger of violating client confidences.

§ 1.13–1(b) Corporate and Non-Corporate Organizations Treated Similarly

We normally think of a corporation as an "entity." In contrast, the Uniform Partnership Act, drafted in 1914, treats partnerships as "aggregates." The modern trend in partnership law is to treat partnerships as entities.[8] For purposes of partnership law, it is relevant whether a partnership is an aggregate or an entity. However, this distinction is *not* relevant for purposes of the law of ethics. Rule 1.13 intends to cover all organizations.

Whatever local corporate law or partnership law or agency law intends, those rules do not apply to the law of ethics. The tests and requirements of Rule 1.13 apply equally to unincorporated associations as well as corporations.[9]

The ethics rules treat corporate and non-corporate organizations similarly. It matters not that other law treats an organization as an aggregate or an entity. Rule 1.13 is the general template for all organizations, no matter how other law characterizes them. Corporations, unions, trade associations, general and limited partnerships, government agencies—they are all "enti-

---

[8]Although the UPA is still law in many states, about half of the states now have adopted the Revised Uniform Partnership Act (RUPA), which treats a partnership as an "entity." *See* Donald J. Weidner & John W. Larson, *The Revised Uniform Partnership Act: The Reporters' Overview*, 49 Bus. Law. 1 (1993); J. Dennis Hynes, Agency, Partnership and the LLC: The Law of Unincorporated Enterprises 544, 556–57 (Lexis Law Publishing, 5th ed. 1998).

[9]Rule 1.13, Comment 1. The title of Rule 1.13 makes the point as well. The title is not the "Corporation as Client," it is, the "Organization as Client."

ties" for purposes of the ethics rules governing the practice of law.

§ 1.13–1(c) Outside and In-House Counsel Representing the Entity

Rule 1.13 applies equally to outside lawyers and in-house counsel. Both inside and outside lawyers represent the entity as client acting through its duly authorized constituents.[10] If an agent of the corporation acts or intends to act in a manner that is likely to impose substantial injury on the entity, Rule 1.13 imposes duties on outside and in-house lawyers.[11] If some person associated with the entity misunderstands the lawyer's role in the representation of the entity, it is the duty of the lawyer, whether outside or in-house, to clarify the misunderstanding.[12] The bottom line is that the Rules assume that lawyers who are employees of the client still must exercise independent judgment in representing the entity.

In general, there are some very important practical differences between in-house counsel and outside counsel. First, in-house lawyers have only one client (and, in some cases, affiliates of that one client) and thus their livelihood depends upon the continued representation of the client in a manner acceptable to the individuals who control and manage the client. The fact that the in-house corporate lawyer has only one client serves to reduce conflicts because in-house lawyers do not often encounter the potential for conflicts with other current and future clients because they have only one client, the organization. But the fact that a lawyer has only one client makes it economically more difficult for the lawyer to terminate his relationship.

Outside lawyers and law firms have many clients and typically make efforts to ensure that their practices are diversified.[13] The economic pressure on an individual's ability to earn a living in a job clearly creates the potential to influence behavior.[14] On the other hand, while a law firm has many clients, a partner within that firm may represent only a few clients. A partner may draw

---

[10]Rule 1.13(a). On the ethical obligations of inside and outside counsel, see Ronald D. Rotunda, *Law, Lawyers and Managers*, in, THE ETHICS OF CORPORATE CONDUCT (Clarence Walton, ed. 1977) (published by Prentice-Hall, Inc., Englewood Cliffs, N.J., for the American Assembly of Columbia University).

[11]Rule 1.13(b).

[12]Rule 1.13(f).

[13]The need for outside law firms to diversify has been pointed out in the context of client fraud in the past. *See* PHILIP B. HEYMANN & LANCE LIEBMAN, THE SOCIAL RESPONSIBILITIES OF LAWYERS 186 (Foundation Press 1988) (discussing the OPM Leasing case and the fact that the Singer Hutner law firm had relied upon OPM for 60% of its billings during the period of time from 1976–1980).

[14]Sarbanes-Oxley Act of 2002, Pub. L. No. 107-204, § 406, 116 Stat. 745 (2002) (requiring a company to have a code of ethics).

much of his livelihood from one corporate client. That corporation's fees may amount to only one or two percent of the law firm's annual billings, but it may constitute eighty percent of one partner's billings.

Second, the in-house lawyer is an employee of the organization. This statement has several implications. In-house lawyers receive all their compensation from one client, and nonlawyers within the organization monitor their conduct. If a law firm fires a client, the firm does not lose pension rights. If an inside counsel leaves a corporation, he or she may suffer substantially more economic loss in the form of forfeiture of pension benefits.

In addition, the officers and managers of the organization may view the in-house lawyer differently from the outside lawyers. The officers and managers often consider their in-house lawyers to be "team players" and not like outside counsel, whose time and loyalties are shared by many other clients, some of whom might even be the client's competitors.

In-house lawyers may be more often expected to make business as well as legal decisions. During the dot.com boom years, the compensation of an in-house lawyer often included options to acquire shares of stock in the corporation and thus the lawyer might have had a more direct financial stake in the stock price of the client organization.[15] The corporation could also compensate outside counsel by options, but this form of compensation is less typical for outside counsel.

In a sense, in-house lawyers represent an exception to the principle that only lawyers should be allowed to control the practice of law. The legal profession has long accepted the notion that lawyers could join a corporation as employees (rather than as independent contractors) and continue to deliver legal services.[16] The lay client (who are the corporate officers) direct the lawyer-employees. On the other hand, we should not make too much of this argument, for when lawyers are members of a

---

[15]*See* Nancy J. Moore, *Conflicts of Interest for In-House Counsel: Issues Emerging from the Expanding Role of the Attorney-Employee*, 39 S. Tex. L. Rev. 497, 539 (1998); Jodi Brandenburg & David Coher, *Going for the Gold: Equity Stakes in Corporate Clients*, 14 Georgetown J. Legal Ethics 1179, 1189–91 (2001); John S. Dzienkowski & Robert J. Peroni, *The Decline in Lawyer Independence: Lawyer Equity Investments in Clients*, 81 Texas L. Rev. 405, 516–19 (2002) (examining the propriety of the prac-

tice of in-house lawyers receiving stock in the corporation); Susan Saab Fortney & Jett Hanna, *Fortifying a Law Firm's Ethical Infrastructure: Avoiding Legal Malpractice Claims Based on Conflicts of Interest*, 33 St. Mary's L.J. 669, 704–13 (2002).

[16]*See* John S. Dzienkowski & Robert J. Peroni, *Multidisciplinary Practice and the American Legal Profession: A Market Approach to Regulating the Delivery of Legal Services in the Twenty-First Century*, 69 Fordham L. Rev. 83 (2000).

law firm, those lawyer still works for their various lay clients. Ultimately, the client directs the lawyer who accepts that direction unless it violates the ethics rules.

State ethics opinions have authorized a corporation to charge its subsidiary for legal services that its in-house counsel provides to the subsidiary.[17] In the debate over multidisciplinary practice of law, some members of the legal profession unsuccessfully argued that lawyers employed by corporations (or lawyers employed by partnerships in the case of the accounting firms who had members who were also lawyers admitted to the bar) should be permitted to practice law on behalf of the clients of the corporate employer.[18]

Other important practical differences exist between in-house and outside counsel. Interpersonal relationships may affect how professionals interact with clients. When a lawyer works in the same office, walks the halls, and interacts with the constituents of an organization every day (and develops personal and social friendships with the managers of a business entity), those interpersonal relationships can influence the legal representation.

In-house lawyers typically have much more information about the client than do the outside lawyers. They have access to business and legal information, as well as informal sources of information about the individuals who run the organization. This knowledge presents a unique opportunity to influence the corporate decision-makers, including officers, employees, and directors, to avoid a risk of substantial injury to the client. On the other hand, they may be less detached from the client's constituents. When the lawyer deals with the organization's constituents, such as its officers, employees, or members, the lawyer should explain that the lawyer is representing the organization, not the officer, employee, etc., if it is necessary to clarify the lawyer's role.[19] Both inside and outside counsel have this obligation, but it may be more likely that it is necessary for the inside counsel to clarify his role if he is involved in more of the day-to-day activities of the officers, employees, etc.

Of course, outside lawyers could find themselves the identical situation. We are talking about differences in degree rather than differences in kind.

Notwithstanding these practical differences, the ethics rules

---

[17]*See e.g.*, Michael D. Morrison & James R. Old, Jr., *Economics, Exigencies and Ethics: Whose Choice? Emerging Trends and Issues in Texas Insurance Defense Practice*, 53 Baylor L. Rev. 349, 400 (2001) (discussing Tex. Comm. On Professional Ethics, Opinion 531, 62 Tex. B.J. 1123 (1999)).

[18]*See* Charles W. Wolfram, *In-house MDPs?*, National L.J., Mar. 6, 2000, at B6.

[19]Rule 1.13(g) & Comment 10 & 11.

impose the same burdens and obligations on inside and outside counsel. Prior to the 2002 revisions, Rule 1.13(b)(2) advised the lawyer to seek "a separate legal opinion" if he is trying to determine how to proceed when he learns that an officer, employee, etc. may be acting in a way that is detrimental to the organization. The inside counsel could simply ask outside counsel to review the matter. The revised Rule 1.13(b)(2) no longer has that language. Instead, it simply says that the lawyer "shall proceed as is reasonably necessary in the best interests of the organization." In proceeding, he may have to refer the matter, if warranted, "to the highest authority that can act on behalf of the organization."[20]

However, it still makes good sense for the inside lawyer to seek the advice of the outside lawyer in a matter that is unclear. If the outside lawyer comes to a different conclusion than the inside counsel, the inside lawyer may rethink his original conclusion, particularly if the outside counsel's advice appears to be detached.

§ 1.13–2 PROTECTING THE INTERESTS OF THE ENTITY CLIENT

§ 1.13–2(a) A Lawyer's Duty to Prevent "Substantial" Harm to the Entity

The Model Rules have always imposed an obligation on a lawyer for an entity to prevent substantial harm to the organization. Two situations under Rule 1.13(b) trigger the obligation for the lawyer to act: the lawyer knows that "an officer, employee, or other person associated with the organization is engaged in action, intends to act or refuses to act in a matter related to the representation (1) that is a violation of a legal obligation to the entity, or (2) a violation of law that might be reasonably imputed to the organization" and (3) is likely to result in substantial injury to the client.[1]

Conduct that constitutes a violation of a legal obligation to the organization includes the failure to follow corporate procedures, theft of corporate property or opportunities, and damage to corporate interests. Conduct that involves a violation of a law that others may reasonably impute to the corporation involves

---

[20]Rule 1.13(b).

[Section 1.13–2]

[1]Rule 1.13(b). It is unclear whether the clause—"is likely to result in substantial injury to the organization"—modifies both clauses [1] and [2] or only clause [2]. In other words, must the agent's violation of a legal obligation to the entity result in substantial injury, or is the amount of injury relevant only if the agent's legal violation might be imputed to the entity? The language of Rule 1.13(b) does not number the clauses and grammatically allows either interpretation. *See* Robert C. Hacker & Ronald D. Rotunda, *Representing the Corporate Client and the Proposed Rules of Professional Conduct,* 6 CORP. L. REV. 269 (1983).

the many federal and state laws directed at corporations. Some of those laws require disclosure to permit agencies to regulate corporate behavior. Other laws involve self reporting of transactions for tax purposes. Essentially, both types of conduct by agents or related persons of a corporation may subject the entity to substantial harm.

Rule 1.13(b) does not require a lawyer to take action for all harm that may potentially result to the client. The Rule requires action when the conduct of others is "likely to result in *substantial injury* to the organization."[2] With corporations, a major source of injury involves the financial interests of the entity.

Even after the 2002 revisions, it is unclear whether the requirement of "substantial injury to the organization" means substantial "if discovered," or substantial "assuming that it is discovered." For example, let us consider a situation where the corporate lawyer discovers that one of the officers of the corporation is engaging in price-fixing on behalf of the corporation. Assume that if the agent's criminal actions are discovered, the violation of law will be imputed to the corporation and will result in substantial treble damages. This criminal law violation would be imputed to the entity, but this violation increases corporate profits and thus may be considered to "benefit" the corporation *if* the corporation is not caught. If the criminal violation is not disclosed, the corporation will reap substantial profits from price-fixing.

It is unclear how Rule 1.13(b) is intended to apply in this situation. It makes more sense to interpret this Rule to mean "substantial" *assuming* that the crime is discovered. An alternative interpretation—which the sentence structure does not grammatically disallow—would reward constituents of the entity if they were successful in hiding wrongful activity, and thus encouraging lawyers to hear and see no evil. That type of behavior is contrary to the premise of Rule 1.13 that the organization's lawyers should find out what the entity wants so that he or she can act in its best interests. The attorney cannot make that determination unless she first discovers what is going on. If, for example, the entity really "wants" to commit a crime (*e.g.*, price-fixing) then the attorney may resign pursuant to Rule 1.16 or take other action pursuant to other applicable rules.

Hence, it makes sense to interpret the language to mean "substantial," assuming that the crime is discovered (and assuming that the crime is serious, rather than a technical violation).

The Rules do not obligate the lawyer to take the uncomfortable role of a whistleblower simply if the lawyer discovers that an employee may be submitting reimbursements for minor personal

---

[2]Rule 1.13(b)(emphasis added).

expenses. Rule 1.13(b) requires that the there must be a "violation of a legal obligation to the organization, or a violation of law that might reasonably be imputed to the organization, *and* that is likely to result in *substantial injury to the organization.*"[3]

However, a lawyer's knowledge about minor reimbursement irregularities may be evidence of greater problems with the reimbursement procedure. Depending on other circumstances, the lawyer may need to consider more than the magnitude of the financial loss.

In interpreting what is "substantial," it is more reasonable to treat "substantial" in some sort of absolute rather than comparative sense. Ten million dollars is substantial in an absolute sense, while it may amount to less than one percent of the sales of many large corporations. Ten million dollars to the Federal Government is a pittance, if considered as a percentage of the yearly budget or the accumulated national debt. It is still, however, not a small sum: it represents the total tax receipts the Government collects from a blue collar worker and his hundred closest friends over the next twenty years.

In the recent corporate frauds involving the use of "off book" transactions and special purpose entities, the corporate actors were involved with fraudulent transactions that were minor dollar amounts compared to the entire asset of the firm ($10 million in fraud versus $1 billion in assets). Such transactions violated disclosure requirements on financial statements and often involved the filing of false reports. Also, amounts add up. If the lawyer can turn a blind eye to a $10 million fraud in one year, does he keep the eye covered the next year as well? And if others join the fraud, does the lawyer add up the amounts or consider them as if they were all divorced from each other even though the problem is systemic?

Hence, despite an argument that a dollar amount may be immaterial to the assets of the firm, the character of the acts and the consequences of serious state and federal securities violations clearly brought the transactions within the standard of "likely to result in substantial injury to the organization."[4]

If the violation of law imputed to the organization is a crime, but the criminal penalties are relatively minor, is the violation "substantial" simply because it is a crime? Some jurisdictions treat speeding tickets as criminal. Does Rule Rule 1.13 really require the lawyer to treat such crimes as serious enough to mandate whistle-blowing. One would think not.

Some commentators have argued that "[c]riminal matters must

---

[3]Rule 1.13(b)(emphasis added).   [4]Rule 1.13(b).

normally be considered *per se* 'substantial'"[5] and thus the lawyer would have no choice but to demand reconsideration of the matter or to take it to a higher authority within the organization. If the highest authority refuses to comply with the law, the lawyer should consider withdrawal under Rule 1.16. In contrast, if the penalty is *civil* and relatively minor, the action that the corporation should take is a "judgment call, and should be left in the hands of those empowered to make such judgments for the organization."[6]

Neither the Comments nor the black letter of Rule 1.13 define "substantial" to mean all crimes. Elsewhere the Rules do not define all crime as equally bad. Rule 8.4(b) states that it is misconduct for a lawyer to engage in a crime only if it reflects adversely on the lawyer's fitness or trustworthiness.

There still is the question of whether the penalty—assuming the violation is discovered—is substantial. Some violations, though technically denominated as criminal, may result in very minor penalties that reflect society's toleration. A hardware store may violate a Sunday closing law (a so-called blue law), but the jurisdiction might provide that the criminal fine is only $20 per violation and each day that the store is open is counted as only one violation. In that circumstance, whether the law calls this penalty a civil fine or a criminal fine, its imposition might result in no substantial injury to the entity.

The purpose of Rule 1.13 is to impose a special duty on a lawyer who knows that someone affiliated with the entity client is acting in such a way that is likely to directly or indirectly cause *substantial* harm to the entity client. The reason why the Model Rules have placed this duty on lawyers for organizational clients (and not on lawyers for non-organization clients) is that organizational clients can only act through their duly authorized constituents. Because the entity's decisions are made by nonclient actors,[7] the Rules require the lawyer to monitor those choices when they

---

[5]*See* 1 GEOFFREY C. HAZARD & W. WILLIAM HODES, THE LAW OF LAWYERING: A HANDBOOK ON THE MODEL RULES OF PROFESSIONAL CONDUCT § 17.11 (Aspen Publishers, 3d ed. 2001) (with annual supplementation).

[6]*See* 1 GEOFFREY C. HAZARD & W. WILLIAM HODES, THE LAW OF LAWYERING: A HANDBOOK ON THE MODEL RULES OF PROFESSIONAL CONDUCT § 17.11 (Aspen Publishers, 3rd ed. 2001) (with annual supplementation).

[7]The Comments state: "When constituents of the organization make decisions for it, the decisions ordinarily must be accepted by the lawyer even if their utility or prudence is doubtful. Decisions concerning policy and operations, including ones entailing serious risk, are not as such in the lawyer's province. . . . [But] when the lawyer knows that the organization is likely to be substantially injured by action of an officer or other constituent that violates a legal obligation to the organization or is in violation of law," the lawyer must take action. Model Rule 1.13, Comment 3.

threaten to impose substantial injury to a client that is an organization.

Another way of looking at the matter is to think of the issue from the perspective of identifying what the client really wants. If the client were an individual, it is easy for the lawyer to know what his client desires. He just asks the client. But an organization has no mouth; it is an incorporeal entity that can only speak through its agents. These agents may not always have the best interests of the client as heart. Hence, the Rules place an obligation on the lawyer to know what the client really wants. To do that, the lawyer must exhaust his internal remedies by going up the corporate ladder or the organizational ladder to find out what the corporation wants. That obligation does not exist when the matters involved are insubstantial. In those cases, the lawyer can rely on the business judgment and the good faith of the nonlawyer agents of the organization.

But, when the matter is substantial enough, the lawyer has to do more than follow directions of an agent who, hypothetically, may be looting the organization. The lawyer must exhaust his internal remedies, and it is to that issue we now turn.

§ 1.13–2(b) Exhaustion of Internal Remedies Under the 2002 Model Rules

Under 2002 version of Rule 1.13(b), a lawyer who represents an entity and obtains knowledge that a person is acting or is intends to act in a manner "that is a violation of a legal obligation to the organization, or a violation of law that might be imputed to the organization," must act in the "best interests" of the client.[8] How does one define "best interest of the organization?" The action that a lawyer for an entity should take depends upon many variables.[9]

The text of Rule 1.13 seems to limit the lawyer's obligation to act only to cases in which the misconduct of constituent is connected "to a matter related to the representation" by the lawyer.[10] In other words, if the lawyer for the organization represents the client in a narrow matter, the obligation only arises with respect to constituent action related to the matter and not other matters generally. There is no general obligation for a lawyer to be an officious meddler.

For example, when an entity retains a law firm for all of its legal work, the lawyers always have a Rule 1.13(b) obligation to

---

[8] 2002 Model Rule 1.13(b).

[9] 2002 Model Rule 1.13(b) (emphasis added). *See generally* George C. Harris, *Taking the Entity Theory Seriously: Lawyer Liability for Failure to Prevent Harm to Organizational Clients Through Disclosure of Constituent Wrongdoing*, 11 GEORGETOWN J. LEGAL ETHICS 597 (1998).

[10] 2002 Model Rule 1.13(b).

prevent harm to the entity client. Also, lawyers who serve as general counsel by the very definition of their position have legal responsibility for all of the legal affairs of the entity and therefore must take action to prevent harm to the client.[11] Because this Rule sets forth disciplinary standards for lawyers, a breach of fiduciary claim may lie against a lawyer who works in a narrow area but has knowledge of constituent action that is likely to cause harm to the client.

However, if the outside lawyer represents the entity in tax matters, the lawyer does not have an obligation to take action when constituents act in the environmental area in such a way that could cause substantial harm to the client.

The 2002 version of Rule 1.13(b) provided that the lawyer should examine the following factors to determine how to proceed: (1) "the seriousness of the violation and its consequences," (2) "the responsibility in the organization and the apparent motivation of the person involved," (3) "the policies of the organization concerning such matters," and (4) "other relevant considerations."[12]

The first two factors define the circumstances surrounding the action of the constituent. Serious breaches of obligations to the client or violations of the law require different action than trivial

---

[11]As stated above, the drafters of this Rule applied it equally to in-house and outside counsel. The general counsel of a corporation is customarily responsible for all legal matters affecting the entity. Thus, it would be difficult to argue that the scope of representation should alleviate a general counsel's obligation to the client. Similarly, subordinate lawyers who report to the general counsel should fall under the ambit of this broad rule. It is the general counsel's responsibility to establish procedures to ensure that the ethics rules are followed in all aspects of lawyering provided to the client. Thus, when a lawyer in a legal department discovers a situation that threatens injury to the client, that lawyer should be obligated to bring this situation to the attention of those other members of the legal department who are responsible for the matter. The officers and directors of a corporation should demand that their general counsel establish such systems for monitoring the legal problems of the client. In house lawyers do not have an excuse that the matter is beyond the scope of their representation.

In-house lawyers are likely to possess much more information about the officers and directors and the motivation underlying their decisions. In-house lawyers typically have more information about a corporate agent's past conduct (or they should be able to obtain it more readily than would outside counsel). Further, in-house lawyers should know the organizational structure of the corporation. So moving a sensitive decision up the ladder should be—at least in theory— easier because the in-house lawyers should know who within the entity has the authority or power to act quickly to change any conduct that threatens the welfare of entity. Further, based upon their past experience, in-house lawyers can work to change internal policies of the entity to prevent similar recurrences.

[12]2002 Model Rule 1.13. Note the ABA moved this language into the Comments in 2003. See 2003 Model Rule 1.13, Comment 4.

wrongs. The consequences of the breach or violation of the law are very important in shaping a lawyer's response. The third factor asks the lawyer whether the organization has policies in effect to control or report such constituent action. If so, the lawyer should consider using them.

The last factor, "other relevant circumstances," provides flexibility to the lawyer. The lawyer should consider whether the constituent's action is past, present, or future. Some situations provide little time for action, thus the lawyer must act more expeditiously. Other situations offer a more relaxed approach to addressing the problem. A key factor is whether the lawyer's legal services have been used by the entity to engage in the harmful conduct. If so, the lawyer may have obligations under other Rules or other law.[13]

The drafters of the 2002 Rules only made one minor amendment to 1983 Rule 1.13(b). They decided that to retain the structure of internal exhaustion of remedies for lawyers who sought to remedy potential harm to the organization client. The 2002 Rule 1.13(b) first stated that "Any measures taken shall be designed to minimize disruption of the organization and the risk of revealing information relating to the representation to persons outside the organization."[14] This was consistent with the 2002 version of Rule 1.6 and the view that disclosures outside the organization could impose a disproportionate harm on the entity compared with the benefits that disclosure would bring.

The 2002 version of Rule 1.13(b) listed three possible actions that a lawyer should take when attempting to prevent harm to the entity. The lawyer should consider:

(1) asking for reconsideration of the matter;

(2) advising that a separate legal opinion on the matter be sought for presentation to appropriate authority in the organization; and

(3) referring the matter to higher authority in the organization, including, if warranted by the seriousness of the matter, referral to the highest authority that can act on behalf of the organization as determined by applicable law.[15]

Ultimately, the Rule stated that if the lawyer approached the highest authority that can act on behalf of the corporation and that person still insists to act in a manner that is a clear violation of the law and likely to result in substantial injury to the or-

---

[13]*See* Rule 1.2(d), Rule 1.4(a)(5), Rule 1.6, Rule 3.3, or Rule 4.1.

[14]2002 Model Rule 1.13(b).

[15]2002 Model Rule 1.13(b). "Clear justification should exist for seeking review over the head of the constituent normally responsible for it." 2002 Model Rule 1.13, Comment 4. The highest authority of a corporation is typically the Board of Directors. In non-corporate entities (such as partnerships, unions, trade associations, etc.) the highest authority might be another group.

ganization client, the lawyer may withdraw following the requirements of Rule 1.16.[16]

The 1983 and 2002 versions of Rule 1.13 embraced the role of the lawyer to work within an organization to convince the agents to act in such a way to avoid violating the law and avoid exposing the entity to substantial harm.[17] If the efforts failed, the lawyer was given discretion to withdraw. The ABA has in Rule 1.16 used withdrawal as a means of solving ethics problems, thus lawyers could distance themselves from directors and officers who continued to insist on a course of conduct likely to result in substantial harm to the organization client.

The withdrawal option has different consequences for outside and in-house counsel. Withdrawal has consequences to an in-house lawyer quite different from lawyers in private law firms. If an in-house lawyer withdraws, he no longer has *any* client. Moreover, he no longer has a job or monthly income. Outside lawyers, on the other hand, can withdraw from representing one client and still retain their other clients. And law firms that have a diversified client base can withdraw from representing one client and not be adversely affected from a financial standpoint. The bottom line is that an in-house lawyer who has one client and who faces the prospect of having to withdraw is asked to sacrifice a career to maintain the ethical norm.

The 2002 version of Rule 1.13 does offer in-house counsel one avenue to fulfill their ethical responsibilities—reliance on the opinion of outside counsel. When in-house lawyers are confronted with a situation that may materially injure the client, they often ask management to obtain a legal opinion from outside independent counsel. In fact, this avenue is expressly endorsed by the 2002 version of Rule 1.13. The implication is that the Rule contemplates an in-house attorney using outside attorneys to bolster the in-house lawyer's position that the corporation's management should choose another course of conduct. In corporate scandals, however, in-house lawyers have often relied upon outside law firms that had conflicts of interest, which had the scope of their investigation limited, or which ultimately gave opinions that stated that the conduct in question was not illegal.

In-house lawyers should be aware that reliance on an outside

---

[16]2002 Model Rule 1.13(c). Again, this subsection is ambiguous as to whether the requirement of "likely to result in substantial injury" means likely "only if revealed" or likely "assuming that it is discovered."

[17]Some commentators have referred to this as "internal whistleblow-ing." DEBORAH L. RHODE, PROFESSIONAL RESPONSIBILITY: ETHICS BY THE PERVASIVE METHOD 280–82 (Aspen 1998). See also, Richard W. Painter, *Toward A Market For Lawyer Disclosure Services: In Search Of Optimal Whistleblowing Rules*, 63 GEO. WASH. L. REV. 221 (1995).

legal opinion to circumvent the in-house lawyer's obligations is not an automatic release of liability. In-house lawyers have significant input into choosing the outside law firm for an independent outside opinion and how the legal questions are framed to those outside lawyers. An in-house lawyer who selects a firm that has no experience in the issue's subject matter, or a lawyer who may have a conflict or bias on the merits of the opinion has denied the client the opportunity of a truly independent opinion.[18] Of course, if the in-house general counsel is currently a partner in the outside law firm,[19] using that firm does not provide an independent legal opinion.[20] An in-house lawyer who fails to fully inform the outside counsel of all factual information similarly renders worthless any opinion provided. Additionally, even if outside counsel provides an opinion that the conduct is not improper, in-house counsel still needs to make an independent determination whether the conduct is a violation of the law or an obligation to the client that would be likely to cause material injury to the client. If the in-house lawyer believes that an injury is likely, the outside opinion does not relieve the lawyer from making the concerns known to the highest authorities within the entity. If, despite the lawyer's efforts to effect a change in corporate policy, the highest authority insists on pursing the course of conduct that could materially injure the corporation, the lawyer may withdraw. However, the lawyer is instructed by the Model Rules to "minimize disruption of the organization and the risk of revealing information to persons outside the organization."[21]

Of course, lawyers needed to interpret this Rule in light of the general confidentiality rule in the jurisdiction, as well as the

---

[18]Many in-house lawyers are hired from the outside firm used by the corporation. In some cases, the personal relationships that the in-house lawyers have developed with the outside firm may threaten the independence of the legal opinion. That may be accentuated if the conduct in question relates to other advice or work that the outside firm has done for the client.

[19]This dual employment situation was more common several decades ago; however, there still are situations where clients ask an outside law firm lawyer to serve as general counsel of the corporation. *Cf.* John K. Wells, *Multiple Directorships: The Fiduciary Duties and Conflicts of Interests that* *Arise When One Individual Serves More Than One Corporation*, 33 J. Marshall L. Rev. 561, 565 (2000) (Individuals commonly serve on three, four, or five corporate boards.)

[20]In Simpson Thatcher's representation of Global Crossing, there is some indication that the firm had placed one of its partners into the corporation to act as its general counsel. That practice, which was common in the oil industry, raises many ethical and liability concerns and should not be done except in the most unusual of circumstances. *See* Joseph Menn, *Global Crossing Case Figure Not Questioned*, L.A. Times, Feb. 22, 2002, pt. 3, at 1.

[21]2002 Model Rule 1.13(b).

federal and state statutes applicable to the matter in question. These sources of professional standards or statutory law may permit or require disclosure depending upon the circumstances once the constituents of the entity have made clear the action that will be taken.[22] Many states permit lawyers to disclose ongoing financial crimes or frauds.[23] Additionally, federal and state statutes impose disclosure requirements upon entities and responsible parties for matters involving the public interest. Issues involving environmental, food and drug, endangered species, and toxic waste often have corresponding disclosure requirements. However, in the absence of such ethical rules or statutes permitting or requiring disclosure, in-house counsel is not permitted to breach client confidentiality to persons outside the entity.

§ 1.13–2(c) Sarbanes-Oxley and the SEC Rules on Lawyer Responsibility.[24]

Following the recent corporate scandals and the staggering financial losses incurred by investors, Congress could not ignore the loss of investor confidence in the securities markets and the growing awareness of systemic deficiencies in corporate responsibility and the governance of public companies. These deficiencies encompassed not only inaction by the boards of directors of these companies, but the contribution of various professional groups such as attorneys, accountants, and investment banking firms that assisted these companies in structuring and facilitating fraudulent transactions.[25] Even a representative of the American Bar Association acknowledged that attorneys representing and advising corporate clients bear some share of the blame for this failure of the corporate governance system.[26]

In response to this crisis, Congress passed the Sarbanes-Oxley Act of 2002 ("Sarbanes-Oxley"), which was signed into law on

---

[22]Once that determination is made, the lawyer then is governed by the other Rules. In other words, Rule 1.13 is in addition to and does not replace other Rules, such as Rule 1.6 (Confidentiality); Rule 1.8 (Conflicts); Rule 1.16 (Withdrawal); Rule 3.3 (Candor Towards the Tribunal); or Rule 4.1 (Truthfulness to Others).

[23]For example, the Texas Disciplinary Rules authorize a lawyer to "reveal confidential information . . . [w]hen the lawyer has reason to believe it is necessary to do so in order to prevent the client from committing a criminal or fraudulent act." Tex. Disciplinary R. Prof. Conduct R. 1.05(c) (7) (1995).

[24]This discussion is based on Amon Burton & John S. Dzienkowski, *Reexamining the Role of In-House Lawyers After the Conviction of Arthur Anderson*, in ENRON, CORPORATE FIASCOS AND THEIR IMPLICATIONS 689–762 (Nancy B. Rapoport & Bala G. Dharan eds., Foundation Press, 2004).

[25]Richard Painter, *Convergence and Competition in Rules Governing Lawyers and Auditors*, 29 J. CORP. L. 397 (2004).

[26]In a press release issued in July 2002 by the American Bar Association regarding the ABA's Task Force on Corporate Responsibility, President Robert Hirshon of the ABA stated that

July 30, 2002.[27] § 307 of Sarbanes-Oxley mandated that the SEC establish minimum standards of professional conduct for attorneys appearing and practicing before the SEC.[28] It expressly provided that the SEC adopt rules requiring a lawyer to report evidence of a material violation of the securities laws or of a breach of fiduciary duty or similar violation to the chief legal counsel or executive officer of a public company. Moreover, if the chief legal counsel or chief executive officer failed to respond appropriately within a reasonable period of time, then the reporting lawyer must report the evidence of misconduct up the corporate ladder to a committee composed of independent members of the board of directors or the entire board of directors.

The SEC adopted attorney conduct rules implementing Section 307 (the "SEC Rules") of Sarbanes-Oxley in late January 2003.[29] These rules represent an attempt by the SEC to balance the public interest in protecting investors from fraud while preserving client-attorney relationships and maintaining client confidential information. The SEC Rules established institutional procedures outlining the process by which in-house and outside attorneys are to report evidence of any material misconduct up the corporate ladder. The SEC Rules also imposed substantial obligations on the chief legal officer (normally the in-house general

---

"[corporate] counsel have in too many instances fallen short of providing active, informed and independent stewardship." ABA Press Release, "ABA Corporate Responsibility Task Force Recommends New Corporate Governance Standards, Lawyer Ethics Rules" dated July 24, 2002. Likewise the SEC's Proposed Rule: Implementation of Standards of Professional Conduct for Attorneys Release Nos. 33-8186; 34-47282; IC-25920; File No. S7-45-02, January 29, 2003 available at http://www.sec.gov/rules/proposed/33-8186.htm, stated that: "Indeed the Cheek Report Release [the Preliminary Report of the American Bar Association Task Force on Corporate Responsibility dated July 16, 2002] concluded that 'the system of corporate governance at many public companies has failed dramatically.' Moreover, the Cheek Report acknowledges that attorneys representing and advising corporate clients bear some share of the blame for this failure."

[27]Sarbanes-Oxley Act of 2002, 15 U.S.C. § 7201 et. al. Pub. L. No.

107-204, 116 Stat. 745 (2002). *See generally* Roger C. Cramton, George M. Cohen & Susan P. Koniak, *The Legal and Ethical Duties after Sarbanes-Oxley*, 49 Villanova L. Rev. 725 (2004); Thomas D. Morgan, *Sarbanes-Oxley, A Complication, Not a Contribution in the Effort to Improve a Corporate Lawyer's Professional Conduct*, 17 Georgetown J. Legal Ethics 1 (2003).

[28]Sarbanes-Oxley Act of 2002, § 307, 15 U.S.C. § 7245 (2002).

[29]Securities and Exchange Commission, Final Rule: Implementation of Standards of Professional Conduct for Attorneys, Release Nos. 33-8185; 34-47276, *available at* http://www.sec.gov/rules/final/33-8185.htm, 17 C.F.R. Part 205, 68 Fed. Reg. 6296. *See generally* Stephanie R.E. Patterson, *Professional Responsibility and Liability in a Post-Enron World: Section 307 of the Sarbanes-Oxley Act: Eroding the Legal Profession's system of Self-Governance?*, 7 N.C. Banking Inst. 155 (Apr. 2003).

counsel) of a public company to investigate any reports of corporate misconduct.[30]

Reporting "up the ladder" under the SEC Rules means that any credible evidence of a material violation of law must be reported by either an in-house or outside lawyer (specifically including a subordinate lawyer[31] and his or her supervising lawyer[32]) for the entity to the chief legal officer or chief executive officer of the entity. The chief legal officer is then required to conduct an investigation and, unless he or she reasonably believes that no material violation has occurred, is ongoing or is about to occur, the chief legal officer must take action to cause the company to adopt remedial measures to stop the wrongdoing or prevent any material violations that have not yet occurred.[33] If the reporting lawyer does not reasonably believe that an appropriate response has been made, then he is obligated to report the evidence to a committee of independent members of the board of directors or to the entire board of directors.[34] As an alternative, if a public company has created a qualified legal compliance committee ("QLCC") consisting of independent directors not employed by the company, then a lawyer can report any evidence of misconduct to the QLCC.[35]

The concept of reporting "up the ladder" within an organization is not new. Most state lawyer ethics rules already include an "up the ladder" reporting requirement based on Model Rule 1.13.[36] However, Model Rule 1.13 and comparable state rules contain only general principles and provide that the lawyer for an entity simply must "proceed as is reasonably necessary" in the best interests of the client if the lawyer knows that an officer or employee is engaged in conduct harmful to the entity.[37] These lawyer ethics rules do not *require* an attorney to report corporate misconduct to a higher authority within the organization; they merely suggest it as an option.[38] The recent wave of corporate scandals that wiped out billions of shareholders' equity in public companies and undermined investor confidence in United States securities markets put to rest any illusions that existing lawyer ethics rules such as ABA Model Rule 1.13 can realistically be expected to address and prevent client fraud.

---

[30]17 C.F.R. § 205.3(b)(2), 68 Fed. Reg. 6321. The chief legal officer may refer a report of a material violation to a previously established qualified legal compliance committee pursuant to § 205.3(c)(2).

[31]17 C.F.R. § 205.5, 68 Fed. Reg. 6323.

[32]17 C.F.R. § 205.4, 68 Fed. Reg. 6323.

[33]17 C.F.R. § 205.3(b)(2), 68 Fed. Reg. 6321.

[34]17 C.F.R. § 205.3(b)(3), 68 Fed. Reg. 6321.

[35]17 C.F.R. at § 205.3(c), 68 Fed. Reg. 6322.

[36]2002 Model Rule 1.13.

[37]2002 Model Rule 1.13(b) (emphasis added).

[38]2002 Model Rule 1.13(b)(2).

The SEC Rules apply to all attorneys, whether in-house or outside counsel, who appear and practice before the SEC in representing public companies on securities related matters. The term "appearing and practicing" includes: transacting business with the SEC; representing an issuer in a SEC administrative proceeding or investigation; providing securities law advice regarding the preparing, or participating in preparing, documents that the attorney has notice will be filed with, or incorporated into, a filing for the issuer with the SEC; or advising an issuer regarding SEC filings, including whether information must be disclosed or filed or incorporated into documents that will be filed with the SEC.[39]

The scope of what misconduct must be reported "up the ladder" is quite broad. An attorney subject to the SEC Rules who *becomes aware of* evidence of a material violation by the entity or any of its officers, directors, employees or agents is required to report any evidence of a material violation of federal or state securities laws, or a material breach of a fiduciary or similar duty existing under state or federal laws.[40] The fact that Sarbanes-Oxley included a breach of "fiduciary or similar duty" substantially expanded the scope of misconduct covered under the SEC Rules.

This language, however, presents two questions. What level of knowledge is required to constitute awareness of credible evidence, and what constitutes material evidence? The SEC's interpretive discussion that accompanied issuance of the SEC Rules makes it clear that an attorney's obligation to report evidence of a material violation is based on an objective standard, not the attorney's subjective beliefs.[41] The threshold of knowledge required to invoke the reporting obligation requires only that evidence of material wrongdoing be "reasonably likely."[42] This is in contrast to the standard under Model Rule 1.13 and most state ethics rules which require actual knowledge of a material violation. Under the SEC Rules, a material violation must be more than a mere possibility, but it need not be "more likely than not."[43]

The SEC Rules provide a safety valve that permits a lawyer to disclose confidential information to the SEC relating to a repre-

[39]Securities and Exchange Commission, Final Rule: Implementation of Standards of Professional Conduct for Attorneys, 17 C.F.R. Part 205.2(a), 68 Fed. Reg. 6297, available at http://www.sec.gov/rules/final/33–8185.htm.

[40]17 C.F.R. at § 205.2(i).

[41]Securities and Exchange Commission, Final Rule: Implementation of Standards of Professional Conduct for Attorneys, 17 C.F.R. Part 205, 68 Fed. Reg. 6296, 6323.

[42]17 C.F.R. at § 205.2(e), 62 Fed. Reg. 6301.

[43]Securities and Exchange Commission, Final Rule: Implementation of Standards of Professional Conduct for Attorneys, 17 C.F.R. Part 205.2(e), 68 Fed. Reg. 6302.

sentation, even without the client's consent.[44] This is available to a lawyer if he reasonably believes that public disclosure is necessary to prevent a public company from committing a material violation likely to cause substantial injury to the financial interest of the issuer or investors, or to prevent fraud upon the SEC or perjury in an investigative or administrative proceeding, or to rectify a material violation in furtherance of which the attorney's services had been used and which caused or may cause a substantial injury to the issuer or investors.

The most controversial provision in the rules initially proposed by the SEC required lawyers under certain circumstances to make a "noisy withdrawal" by notifying the SEC if they terminated their representation of a public company which had failed to make an appropriate response to a report of a material violation of law. This provision was not included in the SEC Rules issued in January 2003, but rather was deferred by the SEC pursuant to a separate Proposing Release issued on January 29, 2003[45] requesting additional public comments.

The new SEC Release proposed adding a new section 2.05.3(d) to the SEC Rules that would address the situation in which a lawyer reasonably believes a public company has made either no response within a reasonable time or had not made an appropriate response to reported evidence of a material violation. Because withdrawing from a representation of a company has substantially different consequences to in-house attorneys, section 205.3(d) would treat outside retained attorneys and in-house attorneys differently.[46]

If an outside, retained attorney does not receive an appropriate response, or no response within a reasonable time, the outside attorney must withdraw from the representation and, within one business day, give written notice to the SEC of the attorney's withdrawal, indicating that the withdrawal was based on professional considerations.[47] Furthermore, the outside attorney must promptly disaffirm to the SEC "any opinion, document, affirmation, representation, characterization, or the like in a document filed with or submitted to the SEC that the attorney prepared or assisted in preparing and that the attorney reasonably believes is or may be materially false or misleading."[48]

Under the same circumstances, an in-house counsel who failed

---

[44]17 C.F.R. § 205.3(c)(2), 68 Fed. Reg. 6321.

[45]Securities and Exchange Commission, Proposed Rule: Implementation of Standards of Professional Conduct for Attorneys, Release Nos. 33-8186; 34-47282; IC-25920; File No. S7-45-02, January 29, 2003, available at http://www.sec.gov/rules/propo sed/33-8186.htm, 67 Fed. Reg. 71,669.

[46]SEC Proposed Rule at 71,688.

[47]SEC Proposed Rule at 71,688.

[48]SEC Proposed Rules at 71,688.

to receive an appropriate response would need only notify the SEC within one business day that he or she intends to disaffirm any such similar document and promptly disaffirm to the SEC such document. The chief legal officer must then inform any new attorney who is retained or employed to replace the in-house attorney that the withdrawal was based on professional considerations.[49] The in-house attorney would not be required to resign his employment with the company. This is an acknowledgment of the reality that in-house attorneys effectively have only one client and requiring them to withdraw means forcing them to quit a job and have no income. Hence, requiring an in-house to resign would impede disclosure of wrongdoing, which is the opposite of what the SEC Rules seek to accomplish.

Instead of requiring the lawyer or law firm to make a noisy withdrawal, the SEC submitted an alternative proposal for public comment that would require the issuer or public company to report to the SEC in the event it receives a lawyer's notice of withdrawal for failure to receive an appropriate response.[50]

§ 1.13–2(d) Responding to Enron, Tyco, and Worldcom: The Report of the Task Force on Corporate Responsibility.[51]

In March 2002, the president of the ABA formed a Task Force on Corporate Responsibility to "examine systemic issues relating to corporate responsibility arising out of the unexpected and traumatic bankruptcy of Enron and other Enron-like situations which have shaken confidence in the effectiveness of the governance and disclosure systems applicable to public companies."[52] The Task Force held public hearings and in March 2003 issued a final report with specific recommendations to the ABA House of Delegates.[53] The ABA adopted these recommendations at its annual meeting in August 2003.

The Task Force's mission was not confined to examining the role of lawyers in the corporate fraud scandals; instead, its mandate was to examine all systemic issues including those involving corporate governance and the role of accountants. Thus, only part of its proposals relate to the regulation of lawyers. The

---

[49]SEC Proposed Rule at 71,689.

[50]SEC Proposed Rule at 71,684.

[51]This discussion is based on Amon Burton & John S. Dzienkowski, *Reexamining the Role of In-House Lawyers After the Conviction of Arthur Anderson,* in ENRON, CORPORATE FIASCOS AND THEIR IMPLICATIONS 689–762 (Nancy B. Rapoport & Bala G. Dharan eds., Foundation Press,

2004).

[52]*See* American Bar Association, Report of the American Bar Association Task Force on Corporate Responsibility 2 (2003) [hereinafter ABA CORPORATE RESPONSIBILITY TASK FORCE REPORT].

[53]*See* ABA Corporate Responsibility Task Force Report at 2 to 3 (chronicling activities of the Task Force).

Report makes many recommendations relating to securities law, auditing law, corporate governance law, and corporate organizational theory. The changes proposed to the Model Rules, however, do place more responsibility on lawyers who represent corporations and other business entities.

Generally, the Task Force rejected the theory that lawyers for corporations should act as "gatekeepers" for the enforcement of the law.[54] However, the Report advocates procedural and substantive changes for corporate attorneys. The procedural changes focused on how corporate entities should restructure lines of communication to facilitate improved communications with lawyers to ensure an entity's compliance with the law. The proposed substantive changes in the ethics rules clarify issues regarding Rule 1.13 and more importantly they advocate changing the confidentiality rule (Rule 1.6) to permit lawyers to disclose, in limited situations, client confidential information which would make the Model Rules more consistent with the confidentiality rules in a majority of the states.[55]

On the issue of corporate structure, the Task Force focused on the manner in which communications with in-house and outside lawyers could be improved with officers and directors that govern the corporation:

> First, the board of directors should establish a practice of regular, executive session meetings between the general counsel and a committee of independent directors. Second, each retention of outside counsel to the corporation, should establish two things at the outside of the engagement: (1) a direct line of communication between outside counsel and the corporation's general counsel; and (2) the understanding that outside counsel are obligated to apprise the general counsel, through that direct line of communication, of material violations or potential violations of law by the corporation

---

[54]A gap clearly exists between the profession and the academic and regulatory community. National Student Marketing was viewed to establish the lawyer as gatekeeper model. *See SEC v. National Student Marketing Corp.*, 457 F.Supp. 682 (D.D.C.1978). *See generally* Reinier H. Kraakman, *Gatekeepers: The Anatomy of a Third-Party Enforcement Strategy*, 2 J. L. ECON. & ORG. 53 (1986). However, few in practice advocate this role for lawyers who represent corporate clients. *See also Report of the New York City Bar Association Task Force on the Lawyer's Role in Corporate Governance—*

November 2006, 62 BUS. LAW. 427 (2007)(detailing recommendations of the N.Y. City Bar Association on the lawyer's role in corporate governance and rejecting the suggestion that lawyers become gatekeepers).

[55]*See* Richard W. Painter & Jennifer E. Duggan, *Lawyer Disclosure Of Corporate Fraud: Establishing A Firm Foundation*, 50 S.M.U. L. REV. 225 (1996); Larry P. Scriggins, *Legal Ethics, Confidentiality, and the Organizational Client*, 58 BUS. LAW. 123 (2002).

or of material violations or potential violations of duties to the corporation.[56]

These recommendations were designed to remove impediments to frequent and frank communication between lawyers and corporate directors. Frequent meetings between independent directors and in-house counsel will foster interpersonal relationships, trust, and frankness necessary to implement an effective "up the ladder" strategy. The requirement that outside counsel establish a line of communication with in-house counsel is designed to give the outside lawyers access to a person with similar obligations to the entity-the in-house counsel-who may be able to implement corporate compliance with the law.

On the substantive rules that govern lawyer conduct, the Task Force recommended four changes to Model Rule 1.13. First, Model Rule 1.13, should be modified to apply an objective standard to the issue of when a lawyer should go "up the ladder." Instead of just requiring lawyer action when a lawyer "knows" about material injury to the entity, the lawyer would need to act when that lawyer "knows facts from which a reasonable lawyer, under the circumstances, would conclude that" the entity may be subjected to material harm.[57] Second, the Task Force recommends that the rule be changed to require more active "up the ladder" involvement by a lawyer for the entity. Third, when a lawyer withdraws from a representation or is fired by the client, the lawyer may inform the highest authority about the fact that the lawyer has withdrawn or has been fired.[58] Finally, the Task Force recommends that the rule be modified to permit a lawyer to disclose confidential information when corporate action or inaction would involve a clear violation of the law that is reasonably likely to result in substantial injury to the entity.[59]

The Task Force recommendations also included a suggestion that Model Rule 1.6 on confidentiality be modified to permit disclosure by a lawyer in two circumstances:

(2) to prevent the client from committing a crime or fraud that is reasonably certain to result in substantial injury to the financial interests or property of another and in furtherance of which the client has used or is using the lawyer's services;

(3) to prevent, mitigate or rectify substantial injury to the financial interests or property of another that is reasonably certain to result

---

[56]ABA Corporate Responsibility Task Force Report at 36 (footnotes omitted).

[57]ABA Corporate Responsibility Task Force Report at 82.

[58]ABA Corporate Responsibility Task Force Report at 83 to 84.

[59]ABA Corporate Responsibility Task Force Report at 83.

or has resulted from the client's commission of a crime or fraud in furtherance of which the client has used the lawyer's services;[60]

The ABA adopted these suggestions in August 2003 despite the fact that the ABA House of Delegates had repeatedly rejected similar proposals in the past.

§ 1.13–2(e) Exhaustion of Internal Remedies and Permissive Disclosure Under the 2003 Amendments to Rule 1.13.

Based upon the Report of the Corporate Task Force, the ABA House of Delegates amended Rule 1.13 in August 2003. It is widely believed that the ABA moved to adopt the amendments to Rule 1.13 and Rule 1.6 to forestall the SEC's consideration and adoption of the proposed mandatory noisy withdrawal regulations. Some members of the ABA House of Delegates objected to the federalization of ethics rules and other members objected to the notion of mandatory disclosure to a governmental agency.

Basically, the ABA left the structure of the 2002 Rule largely intact; however, they specifically amended the obligations of a lawyer to prevent constituents from acting in such a way to impose substantial harm on the entity.

Rule 1.13 still authorizes the lawyer to exhaust the internal remedies of the organization to determine what it really wants. Rule 1.13 still imposes on the lawyer a duty to go up the corporate ladder to protect the organization from being defrauded or from defrauding others. The Rule also allows the lawyer to engage in permissive disclosure outside of the entity *if* the highest authority refuses to act in a way to address the constituent's actions that are likely to cause substantial harm to the entity.

The ABA made five specific changes while keeping some important ethical standards. The new Rule 1.13(b) begins with the same language advising a lawyer that she has new duties if she knows that an agent or constituent who acts in violation of an obligation to the entity or who will violate legal standards that may be imputed to the entity and such behavior is likely to cause substantial harm.

The Rule continues to require that "the lawyer shall proceed as is reasonably necessary in the best interests of the organization."[61] However, the first change refers to what specific actions a lawyer should take. The ABA removed from Rule 1.13(b) details about how a lawyer should go about seeking to change the view of agents of the entity about the past, present, or future conduct that is likely to cause substantial injury to the entity client. The guidance still exists but it is now in the Comments, which advise the lawyer to ask for a separate legal opinion or reconsideration

---

[60]ABA Corporate Responsibility Task Force Report at 77.

[61]Rule 1.13(b).

of the matter.[62] The drafters probably sought to focus the black letter language in the Rule on one option. The Comments include details on how to implement that one option.

The second change is that after requiring that lawyers act in the best interests of the organization the Rule adds a new, mandatory duty:

> Unless the lawyer reasonably believes that it is not necessary in the best interest of the organization to do so, the lawyer *shall refer* the matter to higher authority in the organization, including, if warranted by the circumstances, to the highest authority that can act on behalf of the organization as determined by applicable law.[63]

This provision requires the lawyer to go "up the corporate ladder" to determine what the organization really wants. The organization has internal remedies: if the lawyer first exhausts those internal remedies it may not be necessary for the lawyer to take other actions. Thus, under the 2003 Rules, lawyers must inform individuals in the chain of authority who can influence the decisions of the person who is acting contrary to the best interests of the organization. This change reinforces the requirement of internal exhaustion of remedies.

The third change in Rule 1.13 is that the ABA removed the permissive *withdrawal* language and substituted permissive *disclosure* outside of the entity. This change is clearly the most significant and a modification in the ABA's position on disclosing financial crimes or frauds. Under the modified Rule 1.13(c), if the lawyer's efforts to go up the chain of command have failed and if "the lawyer reasonably believes that the violation is reasonably certain to result in substantial injury to the organization, *then* the lawyer *may reveal* information relating to the representation. . . ."[64]

When a lawyer seeks to disclose information to prevent the harm to the client, the lawyer should engage in such disclosure only to the extent he reasonably believes it is necessary to prevent substantial injury to the client.[65] The Rule does not authorize *carte blanche* disclosure. However, Rule 1.13 permits disclosure whether or not Rule 1.6 permits disclosure to protect the organizational client.[66]

For non-organizational clients, Rule 1.16 is where the lawyer turns to determine if he may engage in permissive disclosure of client confidences. For organizational clients, the lawyer may disclose if either Rule 1.13 or Rule 1.6 authorize disclosure. In that sense, Rule 1.16 grants organizational clients less protection of

---

[62]Rule 1.13, Comment 4.

[63]Rule 1.13(b) (emphasis added).

[64]Rule 1.13(c)(2) (emphasis

added).

[65]Rule 1.13(c)(2).

[66]Rule 1.13(c)(2).

confidential information than it provides to non-organizational clients. That is the legacy of corporate frauds like Enron.

The fourth modification is that the 2003 revisions now make it quite clear that the lawyer's obligation to exhaust internal remedies and to engage in permissive disclosure does not apply to matters when the organization hires the lawyer specifically to investigate or defend a corporation on wrongdoing or a violation of the law. For example, if the SEC charges a corporation with fraud, and the corporation hires a lawyer to represent it, that lawyer has no right to disclose the fraud to the SEC. She was not involved in the fraud; she is representing the client who is fighting a matter on which she did not participate.

Rule 1.13(d) limits the application of permissive disclosure under Rule 1.13(c) for matters in which a lawyer has been specifically hired to represent the entity in an investigation or defense.[67] Otherwise, when a corporation is subject to a government investigation or a defendant in litigation, the lawyer hired to defend the entity in an adversarial proceeding may have obligations to disclose information that are contrary to the purpose of the representation. Note that this provision does not alleviate the lawyer from Rule 1.13(b) obligations of internal exhaustion of remedies. So if in the course of the representation the agents of the entity begin to act in a way that triggers Rule 1.13(b) obligations, the lawyer must act in the best interests of the entity and refer the matter to higher authority.

The fifth change in the 2003 revisions governs a lawyer who has been fired or who has withdrawn in the midst of performing duties under Rule 1.13(b) or (c). When a lawyer complies with the "up the ladder" procedures in an effort to prevent the entity from incurring substantial injury, the organization may not be pleased and it may fire the lawyer. Alternatively, Rule 1.16 may require the lawyer to withdraw.

The discharge of an organization's lawyer presents a difficult problem. On one hand, the discharged lawyer must cease to provide legal services to the client. However, the individuals who run the entity may not be aware why the lawyer was fired. If the organization's leaders knew what was really going on, they might act differently.

Rule 1.13(e) deals with this issue. It obligates ("shall proceed") the lawyer to contact the highest authority that can act on behalf of the entity client. If a lawyer reasonably believes that he or she was fired because of an attempt to comply with Rule 1.13(b) and (c), the lawyer "shall proceed as the lawyer reasonably believes necessary" to assure that the highest authority knows that the

---

[67]Rule 1.13(d).

lawyer was terminated.[68] The lawyer must attempt to inform the highest authority that can act on behalf of the entity why the organization has chosen to discharge the lawyer or why she felt forced to withdraw.

§ 1.13–2(f) Applying the Current Rule 1.13 to Prevent "Substantial" Harm to the Client.

All lawyers who represent entities whether they are public or private, for profit or not for profit, or corporate or non-corporate must follow Rule 1.13. Rule 1.13(b) requires that a lawyer for an organizational client protect the client from employees, officers, agents, and constituents that have acted, are acting, or plan to act in such a way that imposes substantial risk of harm to the client. The obligation to protect applies to matters within the scope of work that the lawyer is performing for the entity. Such harm may result from the agent acting in breach of a violation to the entity or in violation of a civil or criminal law that could reasonably be imputed to the entity. The lawyer only has an obligation to prevent reasonably likely risk of substantial harm to the entity client, not all harms.

Under Rule 1.13(b), the lawyer shall proceed as is in the best interests of the client. Unless such action is not necessary, the lawyer shall refer the matter to higher authority in the organization. In some cases, the lawyer first should talk with the agent or constituent and inform them of the lawyer's position about the wrongful conduct. For example, "if the circumstances involve a constituent's innocent misunderstanding of the law and subsequent acceptance of the lawyer's advice," the lawyer does not need to inform higher authority.[69]

If the constituent refuses to follow the lawyer's advice, the lawyer should consider referring the matter to higher authority. The drafters of the Rules stated that in a serious case of likely substantial harm to the entity, the lawyer does not need to inform the constituent.[70] The circumstances may even warrant that the lawyer refer the matter to the highest authority that can act on behalf of the organization client. The reason that the Rule refers to the "highest authority" instead of saying the "Board of Directors" is that the Rule applies to all organizations, not merely large corporations. In closed corporations or unions or partnerships, etc., state law may provide that another group or individual is the "highest authority." In the case of a public corporation, the highest authority is the board of directors. In the case of a government, the highest authority may the head of the agency or a committee chair.

---

[68] Rule 1.13(e). Note that *other law* may require disclosure if the client has fired the lawyer.

[69] Rule 1.13, Comment 4.

[70] Rule 1.13, Comment 4.

The Rule makes clear that the lawyer uses common sense ("proceed as is reasonably necessary") in deciding who best to proceed. She may consider the time needed to act in deciding whether to begin at the lower levels of the organizational structure or to proceed to the highest authority that can act.[71] She should look, for example, at the motivations of the people involved, the seriousness of the violation, the way the organization has treated the matter in the past, or the views of other lawyers who know about the matter.[72]

Revealing Information Outside the Organization. If the lawyer's efforts fail to convince the highest authority that can act on behalf of the corporation[73] and if "the lawyer reasonably believes that the violation is reasonably certain to result in substantial injury" to the client, then the lawyer may reveal information the lawyer believes is necessary to prevent substantial injury to the entity.[74]

The Rule is open ended and does not specify to whom the lawyer should reveal the information. However, it is designed to permit lawyers to attempt to prevent harm to organizational clients when their constituents act in such a way to expose the clients to likely risks or substantial harm. Hence, if the matter involves securities fraud, the lawyer might reveal the information to the SEC.

If a lawyer is fired while attempting to discharge such an obligation under Rule 1.13(b) or (c), then Rule 1.13(e) requires the lawyer to attempt to inform the highest authority that he or she was discharged when attempting to address a situation involving substantial harm to the entity.

Applicability of Other Ethics Rules. Rule 1.13 is an important ethics rule, but it is not the only ethics rule that applies when a lawyer represents a client involved in a crime or fraud. If the conduct involves litigation before a tribunal, the lawyer may be permitted or required to disclose under Rule 3.3. If the action of the constituent involves nonlitigation, the lawyer may be permitted to disclose under Rule 1.6. Thus, if the entity client used the lawyer's services to perpetuate a crime or fraud likely to result in substantial financial harm to a third person, the lawyer may disclose to prevent the crime or fraud under Rule 1.6(b)(2) or to rectify or mitigate a past crime under Rule 1.6(b)(3). If the lawyer were directly involved in a client fraud against a third person, Rule 4.1(b) may make such disclosure mandatory.

---

[71]Rule 1.13, Comment 5.

[72]Rule 1.13, Comments 4, 5.

[73]The Rule is written so that the lawyer does not need to wait for the highest authority to make a decision. If the highest authority fails to ad- dress the matter in a timely and appropriate way, the lawyer can proceed to disclose information under the Rule. *See* Rule 1.13(c)(1).

[74]Rule 1.13(c).

Most of the authorities posit corporate actors as refusing to comply with the law rather than active participation in a crime or fraud as the lawyer considers her professional responsibilities. When the entity's directors, officers, or employees are engaged in a current or future crime or fraud, the in-house lawyer must not counsel or assist those agents.[75] One ethics opinion holds that an in-house lawyer who knows that the chief executive office intends to destroy or conceal papers that are subject to an outstanding discovery order in pending litigation must refuse to hand those documents to the corporate officer.[76] The opinion follows the standard guidance of rule 1.13 in dissuading agents from engaging in conduct that is likely to harm the entity and asking for reconsideration. Is also reaffirms the obligation of a litigator under Rule 3.4(a) not to assist another in the unlawful "obstruction of another party's access to evidence." The opinion views the lawyer as having an important role in protecting the interests of the entity client.

Applicability of Other Law. Other law will also inform the lawyer's conduct. In the case of public companies, the federal and state securities laws would apply and could override Rule 1.13. In the case of regulated industries such as banking, specific federal statutes govern the conduct of corporations. And, more recently in the tax area, Congress and the Treasury have implemented several penalties directed at lawyers who represent corporations.

The enactment of Sarbanes-Oxley and its regulations and the new Rule 1.13 and Rule 1.6 are a direct result of the corporate scandals in the 1990s and 2000s. Rule 1.13 applies in addition to, and not in lieu of, Sarbanes-Oxley.

Sarbanes-Oxley is the legacy of major corporate scandals. Enron as an entity hid losses and generated gains through the use of special purpose entities while failing to properly disclose to the market its conduct. Worldcom reported a gain when it had a substantial loss through a rather basic accounting entry fraudulent scheme. Tyco suffered losses due to alleged corporate looting by its officers and employees without full disclosure to the market.

Will the new statutes and ethics norms prevent such corporate scandals? It is often difficult to tell in advance whether the new view of lawyers as gatekeepers may provide incentive for lawyers to withdraw earlier in representations or to disclose to persons outside of the entity clients.[77] These new laws certainly increase the risks of law practice. Occupations with no problems tend not

---

[75]See Rule 1.2(d).

[76]See Michigan State Bar Comm. on Prof & Judicial Ethics, Informal Op. RI-345 (Oct. 24, 2008), noted in 24 ABA/BNA Law.Man. Prof. Conduct 618 (Nov. 26, 2008).

[77]See Fred Zacharias, Lawyers as Gatekeepers, 41 SAN DIEGO L. REV.

to pay as well as more risky occupations. Perhaps the resulting malpractice liability that arises from these scandals will impose a greater incentive on lawyers to police their clients. Only time will tell.

§ 1.13–3 ACTUAL OR APPARENT REPRESENTATION OF THE ORGANIZATION AND ONE OR MORE OF ITS CONSTITUENTS

§ 1.13–3(a) Whom the Lawyer Represents.

Occasionally the lawyer representing the organization also will have a relationship with the entity's employees, who may believe that the lawyer also represents their interests. The lawyer should clarify his role and must explain the identity of the client if it is apparent that the organization's interests are adverse to those people with whom the lawyer is dealing.[1]

The lawyers do not have any obligation to give *Miranda* warnings—"anything you say can and will be used against you"—but lawyers do have the obligation to clear up confusion as to whom they represent when the lawyer reasonably should know that the confusion exists.[2]

§ 1.13–3(b) Fiduciary Duties Owed to Shareholders in Closely Held Entities.

In *Fassihi v. Sommers, Schwartz, Silver, Schwartz & Tyler, P.C.*,[3] the president and 50% shareholder asked the corporate lawyer to oust the vice president and 50% shareholder from the closely held entity.[4] The lawyer performed the tasks that led to a dissolution of the entity, but he did so without notifying the vice president and 50% shareholder. Notice and a meeting were required under the corporate by-laws. The ousted shareholder sued the lawyer on a theory that the lawyer owed him a fiduciary duty and the lawyer's conduct violated this duty. A Michigan Court of Appeals held that even though no attorney-client relationship existed between the lawyer and the shareholder, the lawyer may have owed the shareholder a fiduciary duty:

> A fiduciary relationship arises when one reposes faith, confidence, and trust in another's judgment and advice. Where a confidence has

---

1387 (2005) (arging that lawyers have always been and will continue to be gatekeepers regarding client misconduct and fraud).

[Section 1.13–3]

[1] Rule 1.13(f). See DR 7-104(A). Restatement Third, The Law Governing Lawyers § 103(2).

[2] See § 1.13(d), infra, on *Upjohn* warnings.

[3] *Fassihi v. Sommers, Schwartz, Silver, Schwartz & Tyler, P.C.*, 107 Mich.App. 509, 309 N.W.2d 645 (1981).

[4] See Rossman, *The Descendants of Fassihi: A Comparative Analysis of Recent Cases Addressing the Fiduciary Claims of Disgruntled Stakeholders Against Attorney's Representing Closely-Held Entities*, 38 IND. L. REV. 177 (2005).

been betrayed by the party in the position of influence, this betrayal is actionable, and the origin of the confidence is immaterial . . . . Furthermore, whether there exists a confidential relationship apart from a well defined fiduciary category is a question of fact . . . .

Instances in which the corporation attorney's stand in a fiduciary relationship to individual shareholders are obviously more likely to arise where the number of shareholders is small. In such cases it is not really a matter of the courts piercing the corporate entity. Instead, the corporate attorney's, because of their close interaction with a shareholder or shareholders, simply stand in confidential relationships in respect to both the corporation and individual shareholders.[5]

Although other jurisdictions have not adopted *Fassihi*'s view that a lawyer for a closely held entity may owe fiduciary duties to individual shareholders simply because the corporation is closely held. However, the case illustrates the point that, when representing closely held entities, lawyers often have direct contact with individual agents of the entity and therefore may assume some duties to them because of the risk that the agent thinks that the lawyer also represents the interests of the agent.[6] Still, the facts of *Fassihi* are relatively unique.

§ 1.13-3(c) Representing the Organization and One or More of Its Constituents.

The lawyer may represent both the organization and one or more of its constituents if the normal requirements of informed consent are met, and the potential conflict can be waived.[7] The person who should give consent on behalf of the organization should be an "appropriate" person representing the organization "other than the individual who is to be represented, or [it may be given] by the shareholders."[8] For example, the shareholders may give consent in a close corporation.

One might have to turn to other law, such as corporate law, to determine who that official is, such as the President, or Chairperson of the Board of Directors, or the entire Board.

---

[5]107 Mich. App. at 514-17, 309 N.W.2d at 648-49.

[6]For a detailed analysis of the cases that hold for and against establishment of a duty to the shareholders or constituents in the closely held entity context, see William Freivogel, FREIVOGEL ON CONFLICTS, Corporations (Including Close Corporations) (Mar. 2008), in http://freivogelonconflicts.com/new__page__18.htm. Many of the cases holding for a duty to an individual involve unique facts and do not establish a general duty to constituents of a closely held entity.

[7]*See* Rules 1.13(g); 1.7; DR 5-105(C).

[8]Rule 1.13(g).

§ 1.13-3(d) *Upjohn* Warnings

In *Upjohn v. United States*,[9] the U.S. Supreme Court rejected the "control group" test to determine who, in the organization, has the attorney-client privilege. Under the "control group" test, the court limited the evidentiary privilege to communications between corporate counsel and those individuals who had authority to control or participate in the corporation's legal affairs. Instead, *Upjohn* held that the evidential privilege applies to communications made by corporate employees to counsel for the corporation acting at the direction of corporate superiors in order to secure legal advice from its counsel. When the employees were aware that they were being questioned so that the corporation could obtain legal advice, the attorney-client privilege protecting these communications against compelled disclosure was consistent with the underlying purposes of the attorney-client privilege, were protected against compelled disclosure.[10]

As mentioned above, corporate counsel does not have to provide *Miranda* warnings to the corporate employees that they interview,[11] but they do have to explain the identity of the client when the lawyer should know that interests of the corporation are adverse to the interests of the employee.[12] These warnings are often called *Corporate Miranda Warnings* or *Upjohn Warnings*:

> Such warnings make clear that the corporate lawyers do not represent the individual employee; that anything said by the employee to the lawyers will be protected by the company's attorney-client privilege subject to waiver of the privilege in the sole discretion of the company; and that the individual may wish to consult with his own attorney if he has any concerns about his own potential legal exposure.[13]

In the typical scenario, the corporation's lawyer interviews employees about an issue. The corporation later decides to waive any attorney-client privilege it possesses with respect to these communications and turn them over to the Government, as part of effort to persuade the Government that it is co-operating with a currently pending investigation. The employee then seeks to suppress this evidence on the grounds that the employee's own attorney-client privilege prevents disclosure.

---

[9] *Upjohn v. United States*, 449 U.S. 383, 101 S.Ct. 677, 66 L.Ed.2d 584 (1981). See discussion in § 1.6-8(b) The Corporation as Client and the Attorney-Client Privilege.

[10] 449 U.S. at 394-95, 101 S.Ct. at 685.

[11] *See* § 1.13-3(a), *supra*.

[12] Rule 1.13(f).

[13] *United States v. Ruehle*, 583 F.3d 600, 604 n.3 (9th Cir. 2009).

For example, *United States v. International Brotherhood of Teamsters.*[14] This case involved Jere Nash, a campaign manager for the Carey for his reelection to the Presidency of the Teamsters. Nash sought to prevent the Carey Campaign from making disclosures to the Government, arguing that he was entitled to a personal claim of attorney-client privilege with regard to these conversations.

> Nash was told that his comments to the CW & S attorney's would be reported to Carey, and that Nash was cautioned not to disclose the substance of the meeting to individuals outside of the Carey Campaign, since this could destroy the "privileged" nature of the conversation. The CW & S attorney's understood these references to "privilege" to mean the privilege belonging to the Carey Campaign, rather than to Nash individually, but there was *never an explicit discussion between CW & S and Nash as to whose "privilege" was involved or whose prerogative it would be to waive it.*[15]

The court concluded that Nash could not plead the privilege because he had "neither sought nor received legal advice from" the entity's lawyers on "personal matters." Consequently, he may not prevent the election campaign from disclosing his conversations with the corporate counsel "corporate matters by asserting a personal claim of privilege."[16]

The application of *Upjohn Warnings* was central to the decision in *United States v. Ruehle.*[17] This was a criminal case. The Government prosecuted the chief financial officer (CFO) of Broadcom and other defendants for charges arising from the corporation's stock option granting practices. The law firm of Irell & Manella represented Broadcom. William Ruehle, Broadcom's CFO, was clearly a possible target of the investigation. Irell concurrently represented Ruehle personally in a different matter. Irell lawyers interviewed Ruehle about Broadcom's stock option practices. According to the trial judge, the Irell lawyers (without Ruehle's knowledge or consent) gave Broadcom a copy of the report of their Ruehle interview. Broadcom, in turn, instructed Irell to give a copy of this report to the FBI in order to show the Government that Broadcom was co-operative.

After Ruehle learned about these he events, he claimed that his attorney-client privilege protected his interviews from being turned over. The trial court argued that the apparent candor with which the Irell lawyers discussed the case with Ruehle reasonably led him to believe that the Irell lawyers represented him in this case as well. The appellate court accepted the trial court's

---

[14] *United States v. International Brotherhood of Teamsters*, 119 F.3d 210, 217 (2d Cir. 1997).

[15] 119 F.3d at 213 (emphasis added).

[16] 119 F.3d at 216.

[17] *United States v. Ruehle*, 583 F.3d 600 (9th Cir. 2009).

finding that there was no evidence that the lawyers gave Ruehle an oral warning to the contrary. The Irell attorney's testified that they provided Ruehle a so-called *Upjohn* or *corporate Miranda warning.* Yet, Irell lawyers neither took notes nor created any writing that memorialized their conversation on this issue in writing.[18] The trial concluded that the Irell lawyers breached their duty of loyalty to Ruehle. In addition to suppressing government use of the Ruehle statements, the court referred the Irell lawyers to the State Bar of California for discipline.

Nonetheless, when Government filed an interlocutory appeal, the Ninth Circuit reversed. Ruehle argued that "clear breaches of professional duties warrant suppression in a criminal prosecution." The Court rejected "this novel argument. . . ."[19] On the other hand, if the information is really privileged as a evidentiary matter, the courts will not allow it to be used. But that is different than suppressing information that is not privileged on the alternative theory that the lawyer violated the state ethics rules in securing that information. "[M]aterial protected by the attorney-client privilege may come to light as a result of counsel's breach of a duty of confidentiality. But it is the protected nature of the information that is material, not the ethical violation by counsel."[20]

The Court of Appeals then turned the issue of whether Ruehle's statements were privileged. It concluded that CFO knew that his statements to the lawyer were made for the purpose of disclosing the information to the outside auditors and thus he knew or should know that they were not made in confidence. "At no point did the topic of the civil securities lawsuits arise as it might relate to Ruehle personally. Nor did Ruehle ever indicate to the lawyers that he was seeking legal advice in his individual capacity."[21] The CFO admitted he understood the fruits of attorney's inquiries would be disclosed to accounting firm in order to convince the independent auditors of the integrity of corporation's financial statements or to take appropriate accounting measures to rectify any misleading reports.[22] Since the CFO knew that the lawyers were going to disclose the information to the auditors, he knew it was not privileged, even if he did not know

---

[18]583 F.3d at 604 n.3.

[19]583 F.3d at 613 (footnote omitted).

United States v. Lowery, 166 F.3d 1119, 1124 (11th Cir.1999), holding that a "state rule of professional conduct cannot provide an adequate basis for a federal court to suppress evidence that is otherwise admissible."

United States v. Keen, 508 F.2d 986, 989 (9th Cir.1974), holding that evidence "obtained in violation of neither the Constitution nor federal law is admissible in federal courts, even though obtained in violation of state law."

[20]583 F.3d at 813.

[21]583 F.3d at 604.

[22]583 F.3d at 610-11.

that the lawyers were also going to disclose the information to the Government.

A special Task Force of the White Collar Committee of the American Bar Association's Section on Criminal Justice advised the following Upjohn warning, as a matter of best practices:

I am a lawyer for or from Corporation A. I represent only Corporation A, and I do not represent you personally.

I am conducting this interview to gather facts in order to provide legal advice for Corporation A. This interview is part of an investigation to determine the facts and circumstances of X in order to advise Corporation A how best to proceed.

Your communications with me are protected by the attorney-client privilege. But the attorney-client privilege belongs solely to Corporation A, not you. That means that Corporation A alone may elect to waive the attorney-client privilege and reveal our discussion to third parties. Corporation A alone may decide to waive the privilege and disclose this discussion to such third parties as federal or state agencies, at its sole discretion, and without notifying you.

In order for this discussion to be subject to the privilege, it must be kept in confidence. In other words, with the exception of your own attorney, you may not disclose the substance of this interview to any third party, including other employees or anyone outside of the company. You may discuss the facts of what happened but you may not discuss this discussion.

Do you have any questions?

Are you willing to proceed?[23]

First, the lawyers should provide these *Upjohn* warnings to the employee or agent of the corporation *before* they conduct the interview. Second, the lawyers should *orally* advise the employee or agent of the *Upjohn* warnings, and should also prepare a writ-

---

[23]ABA WCCC Working Group, *Upjohn Warnings*: Recommended Best Practices When Corporate Counsel Interacts with Corporate Employees (July 17, 2009), at 3, http://meetings.a banet.org/webupload/commupload/CR 301000/newsletterpubs/ABAUpjohnTa skForceReport.pdf (accessed Mar. 11, 2011).

See In re Grand Jury Subpoena: Under Seal, 415 F.3d 333, 340 (4th Cir. 2005):

our opinion should not be read as an implicit acceptance of the watered-down "*Upjohn* warnings" the investigating attorney's gave the appellants. It is a potential legal and ethical mine field. Had the investigating attorney's, in fact, entered into an attorney-client relationship with appellants, as their statements to the appellants professed they could, they would not have been free to waive the appellants' privilege when a conflict arose. It should have seemed obvious that they could not have jettisoned one client in favor of another. Rather, they would have had to withdraw from all representation and to maintain all confidences. Indeed, the court would be hard pressed to identify how investigating counsel could robustly investigate and report to management or the board of directors of a publicly-traded corporation with the necessary candor if counsel were constrained by ethical obligations to individual employees. However, because we agree with the district court that the appellants never entered into an attorney-client relationship with the investigating attorney's, they averted these troubling issues.

ten statement to ensure that the lawyers give the same warnings in each interview. Finally, the lawyers should make a *written* record that they have provided warnings through, at minimum, handwritten notes or the creation of a contemporaneous memorandum of the interview.[24]

§ 1.13–4 REPRESENTING PARTNERSHIPS

The partnership laws of some states treat partnerships as "aggregates" while others may treat partnerships as "entities." The ethical rules do not rely on this distinction. Although distinctions between entities and aggregates may well be appropriate for purposes of partnership or tort law, they do not fit well with the purposes behind legal ethics. For example, if the default rule[1] were that a lawyer for a partnership treats the partnership as an aggregate for ethics purposes and thus represents each of the members of a partnership, then that lawyer would be in a conflict whenever a partner of the partnership sued the partnership, because the lawyer for the partnership would automatically be treated as representing the partnership and each of its members, such as the partner who is suing the partnership.

Consequently, Rule 1.13 explicitly provides that it applies equally to unincorporated associations,[2] which is what partnerships are. A partnership has distinct legal rights and duties. It can enter into contracts, and sue in its own name. It may have objectives that are different than those of some of its members. The lawyer is the agent of the partnership, and may even repre-

---

[24]ABA WCCC Working Group, *Upjohn Warnings*: Recommended Best Practices When Corporate Counsel Interacts With Corporate Employees (July 17, 2009), at 3, http://meetings.abanet.org/webupload/commupload/CR301000/newsletterpubs/ABAUpjohnTaskForceReport.pdf (accessed Mar. 11, 2011).

[Section 1.13–4]

[1]**Factual Determination.** It may be the case that a lawyer represents a partnership and all of its partners in a matter. We are talking here of the default rule: what happens if the lawyer does *not state or imply* to the partners that he is representing their interests? *See* Restatement of the Law Governing Lawyers, Third, § 14 & Comment *f* (Official Draft 2000).

Compare Hopper v. Frank, 16 F.3d 92 (5th Cir.1994), concluding that on the facts before it, there was no evidence that the business partners who hired an attorney to represent the limited partnership in sale of limited partnership interests also represented individual partners, *with Margulies v. Upchurch*, 696 P.2d 1195 (Utah 1985), holding that the law firm's representation of a limited partnership in commercial litigation gave rise to and implied attorney-client relationship or fiduciary duty with respect to the individual partners, who reasonably believed that the law firm was acting for their individual interests as well as those of the partnership, and who stood to be either benefitted or harmed by the outcome of the commercial litigation. The court then disqualified the lawyers.

[2]Rule 1.13, Comment 2.

sent the partnership in a dispute with one or more of the individual partners.[3]

In general, the lawyer representing a partnership "represents the entity rather than the individual partners *unless the specific circumstances show otherwise.*"[4] In determining whether an attorney-client relationship exists between the partnership lawyer and one or more of its partners, one would look at factors such as whether the lawyer led the individual partner into believing that the lawyer assumed a duty of representing the individual partner; whether the individual partner was individually represented when the partnership was created; and whether evidence existed that the individual partner relied on the lawyer as his or her separate counsel.[5]

Note that the analysis of the identity of the client may be somewhat more complicated when the lawyer is representing a limited partnership. The ABA in Formal Opinion 92–361 refused to apply the same rule to general partnerships and limited partnerships.[6] The courts have also varied on their treatment of duties to the passive investors, the limited partners.[7] The lawyer's engagement letter with a limited partnership could have significant effect on the identity of the client.

§ 1.13–5 REPRESENTING TRADE ASSOCIATIONS

A lawyer who represents a trade association (*e.g.*, the Raisin Farmers Association, the Dental Assistants Association, or the National Rifle Association), normally represents that "entity," and not the individual members of the trade association. The lawyer, for example, can ethically represent the American Bar Association while simultaneously representing an automobile accident victim who is suing an ABA member (a lawyer) for a car wreck.[1] Rule 1.13 treats a trade association as an entity, with the lawyer representing that entity and not the constituent members

---

[3]*See e.g., Responsible Citizens v. Superior Court*, 16 Cal.App.4th 1717, 1730–31, 20 Cal.Rptr.2d 756, 764 (1993); *Kapelus v. State Bar*, 44 Cal.3d 179, 242 Cal.Rptr. 196, 745 P.2d 917 (1987).

[4]ABA Formal Opinion 91–361 (July 12, 1991) (emphasis added).

[5]ABA Formal Opinion 91–361 (July 12, 1991).

[6]ABA Formal Opinion 91–361, n.1 (July 12, 1991).

[7]See William Freivogel, Freivogel on Conflicts, Limited Partnerships (Mar. 2008), in http://freivogelonconfli cts.com/new__page__7.htm (citing the authorities on both sides).

[Section 1.13–5]

[1]ABA Formal Opinion 92–365 (July 6, 1992).

Greate Bay Hotel & Casino, Inc. t/a Sands Hotel & Casino v. The City of Atlantic City, 264 N.J.Super. 213, 624 A.2d 102 (1993). In that case a casino was a member of a business association. It moved to disqualify a law firm representing a lessee who was intervening in an action brought by that casino to have the city acquire land for its benefit, on the grounds that the law firm's representation of

of the entity, even though the trade association would not exist but for the financial contribution and membership of its individual members.

Yet, if the lawyer or the trade association leads the members of the trade association to believe that the lawyer represents the members of the trade association,[2] the courts may treat the lawyer as if that dual representation exits. Consider *Westinghouse Electric Corp. v. Kerr-McGee Corp.*[3]

The law firm of Kirkland & Ellis filed an antitrust action on behalf of its client, Westinghouse, against various corporations alleging price-fixing violations in the uranium industry. Meanwhile, a trade association, the American Petroleum Institute ("API"), had hired Kirkland to oppose legislative proposals introduced in Congress that would require energy companies to divest uranium companies that they owned. As luck would have it, on the very same day that Kirkland's Chicago office (representing Westinghouse) filed this antitrust suit, Kirkland's Washington, D.C. office (representing API) released a report that advocated the opposite assertion and argued that there already was existing competition in the oil-uranium industry. API was not a defendant in the antitrust suit, but three members of API were defendants.

In connection with the API representation, individual members of API had given confidential information on their uranium assets to Kirkland & Ellis' Washington office, in order to aid that law firm in opposing the threatened legislation. But the lawyers for API had promised the API members that this information would be held confidential. In this case, each of the individual members of API "entertained a reasonable belief that it was submitting confidential information regarding its involvement in

---

business trust of which casino and others were members was impermissible. The Superior Court held that the business trust was an "organization," and that the law firm could represent that organization while representing other clients whose interests were adverse to the interests of the individual members of the business trust. The lawyer for an unincorporated business trust did not, because of that representation, automatically represent the individual members of that trust, so that the lawyer could represent an opponent of an individual member of that trust.

Contra Stratagem Development Corp. v. Heron International N.V., 756 F.Supp. 789 (S.D.N.Y.1991), which argued that if a law firm represented a trade association, it could not represent any other client in an unrelated law suit brought against any member of the trade association. 756 F.Supp. at 792, citing *Glueck v. Jonathan Logan, Inc.*, 512 F.Supp. 223, 227 (S.D.N.Y.), *aff'd on different grounds*, 653 F.2d 746 (2d Cir.1981).

[2] *See* Rule 1.13(f).

[3] *Westinghouse Electric Corp. v. Kerr-McGee Corp.*, 580 F.2d 1311 (7th Cir.1978), *cert. denied*, 439 U.S. 955, 99 S.Ct. 353, 58 L.Ed.2d 346 (1978). *See also Westinghouse Electric Corp. v. Gulf Oil Corp.*, 588 F.2d 221 (7th Cir. 1978).

the uranium industry to a law firm which had solicited the information upon a representation that the firm was acting in the undivided interest of each company."[4] The lawyers for API had assured the individual members that the confidential information secured from each member would not be released either to the general public or to the other members of API. Yet, this information was now in the hands of a law firm that was suing the trade association member from whom it had obtained the information after giving a promise of confidentiality.[5]

The court disqualified Kirkland & Ellis, but not because it simultaneously represented the trade association of which Kerr-McGee was a member. The court did not disqualify the law firm on any broad theory that lawyers for a trade association automatically must treat as clients each of the trade association's members. Rather, the law firm must treat these trade association members as if they were clients because the law firm used its representation of the trade association to acquire confidential information under a promise of confidentiality; this information was relevant to the law suit, and the firm must keep its promise.[6] The court, in effect, concluded that the law firm must be disqualified because it may not use information relating to the representation to disadvantage one from whom it had acquired that information under a promise of confidentiality. The law firm's prior work for one defendant was sufficiently related to issues raised in antitrust litigation to require the firm's disqualification as counsel for plaintiff.[7]

The court never ruled that the law firm had breached its duty

---

[4]580 F.2d at 1320 nn. 15–17 & 1321. *See also* Restatement of the Law Governing Lawyers § 14 (Official Draft 2000), and *id.* at Reporter's Note at p. 134.

[5]**Putative Client's Reasonable Belief.** D.C. Bar Legal Ethics Committee, Opinion 305 (2001), concludes that if a lawyer represents a trade association as an entity, that does not create an attorney-client relationship between the lawyer and members of the association. However, there are circumstances in which representing a client adverse to a member of the association might create a conflict of interest. If the member reasonably believes that it is being individually represented by the lawyer, the member is, regardless of an express agreement, a *de facto* client of the lawyer. Factors one should examine when

inquiring what is a member's reasonable belief include whether the member disclosed confidential information to the association's lawyer, whether the member had separate representation, whether the lawyer had ever previously represented the member individually, and whether the member reasonably relied on the lawyer's representation of his individual interest.

[6]"Gulf, Kerr-McGee and Getty each entertained a reasonable belief that it was submitting *confidential information* regarding its involvement in the uranium industry to *a law firm which had solicited* the information upon a representation that the firm was acting in the *undivided* interest of *each* company." 580 F.2d at 1321 (emphasis added).

[7]*Cf.* ABA Ethics Opinion 95-395 (July 24, 1995). This Opinion consid-

to keep information confidential. But, if the law firm has this information, it is disqualified because of the normal rule that does not allow a law firm to sue a former client if it acquired confidential information that is relevant to the present suit. Kerr McGee was not a former client or a present client, but it was treated as if it were protected by that principle because of the promise of confidentiality on which it relied.

It did not matter that the lawyers with the knowledge related to one representation might be screened from the lawyers working on the other matter in a different city. The court did not accept the view that a large law firm, with offices geographically separate, is under a different set of ethical rules: the law firm cannot avoid the rules that impute disqualification by creating—in the words of that opinion—a "Chinese Wall" around some lawyers to wall them off from confidences known by other lawyers in the firm.[8]

Later, ABA Formal Opinion 92-365[9] came to a similar conclusion. A law firm that represents a trade association ordinarily may file an unrelated action against a member of the association with whom the lawyer has formed no attorney-client relationship unless the representation would impair the lawyer's representation of the association itself. This result supports the view that *Westinghouse* is a case about enforcing promises of confidentiality, not giving client-like status to individual members of associations in all circumstances.[10]

---

ered the question whether a lawyer who had once represented one member of a joint insurance-defense consortium is *per se* prohibited from taking on a related representation against one of the other insurer-members. It concluded that if the lawyer knows no relevant confidences, and if the new case is not contrary to the interests of the prior client, or if the prior client waives its rights, then the lawyer can take the case. Thus there is no *per se* prohibition, but the new client should be told these facts and any implications that they may have for the lawyer's role in the present case. Moreover, the Opinion noted, fiduciary responsibilities under the law of agency impose limits on the lawyer's ability to use or reveal secret information learned from other members of the consortium.

[8] "Though Kirkland asserted, and the district court agreed, that it constructed a 'Chinese Wall' between 8–14 Chicago-based attorneys working for Westinghouse and the 6 D.C.-based attorneys working for [API]. . . ." 580 F.2d at 1320.

[9] ABA Formal Opinion 92-365 (July 6, 1992).

[10] In *United States v. ASCAP*, 129 F.Supp.2d 327 (S.D.N.Y.2001), a composer claimed that ASCAP had failed to pay him royalties he was due for the use of music he had composed. ASCAP's regular in-side and out-side counsel defended the suit, and the composer moved to disqualify them, arguing that he was a member of ASCAP and thus that ASCAP's lawyers represented him as well. Even though ASCAP is an unincorporated association, it is an "organization"

§ 1.13-6 DERIVATIVE SUITS

In a derivative suit, the shareholders sue on behalf of the corporation, which is unwilling to sue. In such cases the corporation may be aligned as a defendant and the other defendants may include corporate officers or directors. May the corporate counsel also defend these other corporate constituents against the claims of the corporate shareholders, or does the lawyer's representation of both the corporation and corporate officers and directors constitute an improper conflict of interests with the corporation? For example, if the shareholder/plaintiffs are successful, the individual defendants may have to pay a money judgment to the corporation. The corporate-defendant then is like a reluctant plaintiff; it benefits from the lawsuit brought against it and the other defendants.

A typical case opposing joint representation is *Cannon v. United States Acoustics Corp.*,[1] which the Seventh Circuit affirmed on this point.[2] *Cannon* was decided under the Model Code, but its analysis is still relevant under the Model Rules. *Cannon* relied on two ethical considerations of the Model Code[3] in concluding that, "in a derivative suit the better course is for the corporation to be represented by *independent* counsel from the outset; even though [existing] counsel believes in good faith that no conflict exists."[4] This new counsel should then advise the corporation as to the role that it should play in the litigation.[5]

The Model Rules reject any *per se* rule regarding derivative

---

represented as an "entity." The court held the ASCAP lawyers do not represent the members personally and thus the court denied disqualification.

[Section 1.13-6]

[1] *Cannon v. United States Acoustics Corp.*, 398 F.Supp. 209 (N.D.Ill.1975), *aff'd in part, rev'd in part*, 532 F.2d 1118 (7th Cir.1976) (per curiam).

[2] 532 F.2d 1118 (7th Cir.1976) (per curiam), *affirming this ground and reversing other grounds*, 398 F.Supp. 209 (N.D.Ill.1975).

See also Hicks v. Edwards, 75 Wash.App. 156, 876 P.2d 953 (Wash. App. Div. 2, 1994), *review denied*, 125 Wash.2d 1015, 890 P.2d 20 (1995) (Table No. 62100-4), citing *Cannon* with approval. In this case, a minority shareholder brought a derivative suit alleging that the majority shareholders had diverted the corporation's

money to their own use. The Superior Court disqualified the corporation's lawyer from representing both the corporation and its majority shareholders and then imposed sanctions upon the lawyer for failing to investigate conflict issue prior to commencing dual representation. The lawyer appealed the imposition of sanctions, and the Court of Appeals held that the lawyer's conduct in arguing that he could represent both corporation and majority shareholders was not "baseless," so sanctions were improper.

[3] EC 5-15, EC 5-18.

[4] 398 F.Supp. at 219–20 (emphasis added). *See also* Note, *Independent Representation for Corporate Defendants in Derivative Suits*, 74 YALE L.J. 524 (1965).

[5] 398 F.Supp. at 219–20.

See also Rowen v. LeMars Mutual Ins. Co. of Iowa, 230 N.W.2d

suits. They recognize the ethical issue but offer little concrete guidance. The Rules only provide that, if the claim "involves serious charges of wrongdoing by those in control of the organization," then a conflict "may arise," and then the general standards of Rule 1.7 should govern "who should represent the directors and the organization."[6]

§ 1.13–7 CORPORATE FAMILY ISSUES

§ 1.13–7(a) Introduction

Should separate corporations that are affiliated with each other (as parent/subsidiary, or as sister corporations) be treated the same for purposes of determining whether the lawyer representing one corporation has a conflict of interest if she takes a case adverse to another corporation in the same corporate family?[1]

In the typical fact situation, Corporation X, a client of "Law Firm," asks it to file suit against Corporation A. Corporation A is not a client of Law Firm, but Corporation B is, and Corporation A is a subsidiary of Corporation B. Corporation B may wholly-own Corporation A, or may own a major stake in Corporation A. May Law Firm sue Corporation A while simultaneously representing its parent, Corporation B, on an unrelated matter? Or, assume that Law Firm does not represent Corporation B but does represent Corporation C. Then, may Law Firm sue Corporation A while simultaneously representing Corporation C, when both Corporations A and C are subsidiaries of Corporation B?

Law Firm, of course, may not represent a client in one matter while suing it in another, even though the two matters are unrelated.[2] Should the parent and subsidiary (Corporations A and B), or the two sister corporations (Corporations A and C) be

---

905, 914–15 (Iowa 1975), citing various cases and then stating: "It is also well established that a potential conflict of interest exists when the same law firm attempts to represent the nominal corporate defendant in a derivative action while at the same time representing the corporate insiders accused of wrongdoing."

See also, e.g., Frank v. Ducy, 1986 WL 1964 (N.D.Ill.1986), noting that "Courts have been increasingly reluctant to permit a single lawyer or law firm to represent both a corporation and the individual directors in shareholder's derivative actions."

Tydings v. Berk Enterprises, 80 Md.App. 634, 565 A.2d 390, 393 (1989), citing the ABA Model Rules and stating: "Representation of a corporation as an entity and the majority of its directors, individually, creates a possible conflict of interest for the attorney, particularly where the corporation's interests are adverse to those of the directors."

[6]Rule 1.13, Comment 13.

[Section 1.13–7]

[1]*See* William Freivogel, FREIVOGEL ON CONFLICTS, Corporate Families (Mar. 2008), in http://freivogelonconflicts.com/new__page__6.htm (examining the ethics and judicial opinions on this question).

[2]Rule 1.7(a)(1) & Comment 1.

treated as one client, or does the Law Firm represent only "the entity," that is, Corporation *B*?[3]

Some cases have assumed, without extensive analysis, that representing a corporation in one matter while undertaking a representation directly adverse to an affiliate of that corporation, such as a parent corporation, subsidiary, or sister corporation, is normally an improper conflict of interest.[4] However, that assumption does not follow from the entity theory of representation, which states that the lawyer for an entity, such as a corporation, represents that entity and not its shareholders (and the shareholders might be one or more other corporations that own most or all of its stock).

The law in this area is not entirely clear. In general, when confronted with the corporate family issues and the possibility of conflicts, the lawyer should consider various factors. The lawyer should evaluate how separate the corporate entities really are. Are corporate formalities really observed? To what extent are the two entities really run separately? What is the nature of the charges that Corporation *X* has filed against Corporation *A*? For example, does Corporation *X*'s lawsuit allege fraud or criminal conduct by Corporation *A*? Are the personnel with whom the lawyer must deal the same people? It would be difficult for the lawyer, on day one, to call the general counsel of Parent Corporation, loyally advise her about the latest strategies on behalf of Subsidiary, and then, on day two, call the same general counsel and engage in tough negotiations on behalf of another client suing Parent Corporation in a RICO action.[5]

A law firm should not undertake a representation adverse to

---

[3]*See* Ronald D. Rotunda, *Sister Act: Conflicts of Interest with Sister Corporations, in* LEGAL ETHICS: THE CORE ISSUES (1996) (Hofstra University School of Law Conference on Legal Ethics), 1 JOURNAL OF THE INSTITUTE FOR THE STUDY OF LEGAL ETHICS 215 (1996); Ronald D. Rotunda, *Conflict Problems When Representing Members of Corporate Families*, 72 NOTRE DAME LAW REVIEW 655 (1997); Richard W. Painter, *Contracting Around Conflicts In A Family Representation: Louis Brandeis and the Warren Trust*, 8 U. CHI. L. SCHOOL ROUNDTABLE 353 (2001).

[4]*See, e.g., Gen-Cor, LLC v. Buckeye Corrugated, Inc.*, 111 F. Supp. 2d 1049 (S.D. Ind. 2000); *Stratagem Development Corp. v. Heron Intern. N.V.*, 756 F. Supp. 789, 792 (S.D. N.Y.

1991); *Pennwalt Corp. v. Plough, Inc.*, 85 F.R.D. 264 (D. Del. 1980).

[5]*See Teradyne, Inc. v. Hewlett-Packard Co.*, 20 U.S.P.Q.2d (BNA) 1143, 1991 WL 239940 (N.D.Cal.1991). *Teradyne* disqualified the law firm, looked carefully at the facts, and was impressed that counsel for the subsidiary was hired by and supervised by the legal department of the parent corporation. The court cited Formal Opinion No. 1989-113 of the State Bar of California's Standing Committee on Professional Responsibility and Conduct (July 6, 1990).

Contrast *Reuben H. Donnelley Corp. v. Sprint Publishing and Advertising, Inc.*, 1996 WL 99902 (N. D.Ill.1996). In a thoughtful opinion, Judge Wayne Andersen refused to disqualify a law firm in a corporate

Corporation *A* (which is affiliated with Corporation *B*, a corporate client of the law firm), if that adverse matter is the same as, or substantially related to, the matter on which the law firm represents Corporation *B*. The reason for this restriction is that clients can decide to waive, in advance, the lawyer's duty of loyalty, but courts will look with suspicion on a waiver, *in advance*, of the lawyer's duty to preserve confidences.[6] If the adverse matter is the same or substantially related to the matter on which the law firm presently represents the client entity, or if the law firm has learned confidences from the corporate client that are relevant to the case brought against the affiliate of the corporate client, the obligation to preserve the confidences owed to the corporate client preclude the representation.[7]

§ 1.13–7(b) The Entity Theory

One should not automatically treat the members of a corporate family (e.g. parent and subsidiaries) as alter egos of each other. Those who argue that the lawyer for a corporation automatically represents (or should be treated as representing) each of the affiliated corporations (the wholly-owned subsidiaries of the corporations, or the parent corporation, or the sister corporations), fail to consider the implications of Rule 1.13, which states that the lawyer for an organization, such as a corporation, does not represent the constituent members of the organization, such as its shareholders (*i.e.*, the parent corporation) but rather represents the organization as an entity. That is not to say that there might still be a conflict, under Rule 1.7 or under another Rule, but the decision to come to that conclusion requires careful analysis. In the law governing corporations, this concept is called "piercing the corporate veil." One should not reflexively and

---

family situation. There was one general counsel for two subsidiaries, however, this particular individual did not personally retain the law firm that he now sought to disqualify and was not actively managing the litigation in question.

[6]*See* ABA Formal Opinion 93-372, Waivers of Future Conflicts of Interest (Apr. 16, 1993)("courts are very reluctant to conclude from a prospective waiver an agreement by the client to waive rights of confidentiality").

[7]**Material Confidential Information.** The facts in *Morrison Knudsen Corporation v. Hancock, Rothert & Bunshoft*, 69 Cal.App.4th 223, 81 Cal.Rptr.2d 425 (Cal.App. 1999), required disqualification because confidential information could be compromised. The plaintiff water district hired a law firm to pursue claims against defendant contractor. This law firm was also working for the insurance company for the defendant's parent corporation to monitor the work of the defense counsel actually representing the defendant's parent. The court found this relationship more attenuated than usual. Nonetheless, the law firm as "monitoring counsel" had access to confidential information about the parent's litigating strategies that could be relevant in a case like this one. While the parent and subsidiary did not meet the "alter ego" test used in ABA Opinion 95-390, they had a "unity of interests" sufficient to make disqualification appropriate.

instinctively pierce the corporate veil for conflicts purposes without further analysis.

The case where one corporation is the subsidiary of one or more other corporations is merely a situation where the shareholder of the corporation happens to be another corporation. But the client should normally be thought to be the entity, not the shareholders, even if the shareholders are corporations. Thus, a Comment warns that "the organization's interest may be or become adverse to those of one or more of its constituents." In such cases, the lawyer should advise the constituent that "the lawyer cannot represent such constituent. . . ."[8] The lawyer, however, can continue to represent the corporation. Rule 1.13 does not accept the view that a law firm is in a *per se* conflict whenever it advances a position that is adverse to a constituent element (a corporate affiliate) of one of its clients.

Various state and local bar ethics opinions have focused on these corporate family ethical issues, and they are not of one mind. For example, one ethics opinion concludes that a lawyer who represents a parent corporation also may represent a party with interests adverse to a subsidiary of the parent corporation in an unrelated matter *if*: (1) the lawyer does not have access to confidential information adverse to the subsidiary, (2) there is no attorney-client relationship between the attorney and subsidiary, and (3) the parent corporation's interests are not materially affected by action against the subsidiary.[9]

Yet another ethics opinion[10] concludes that a lawyer may undertake representation adverse to a wholly owned subsidiary of the existing corporate client so long as the parent corporation is not the alter ego of the subsidiary and the subsidiary has not revealed confidential information to the lawyer with the expectation that it would not be used adversely to the subsidiary. This Opinion advises: "The percentage of ownership of stock, while a factor to consider, is by no means itself determinative."[11]

The leading ABA ethics opinion on this issue is ABA Formal

---

[8]Rule 1.13, Comment 10.

[9]New York County Lawyers' Association, Committee on Professional Ethics, Opinion 684 (July 8, 1991).

[10]California State Bar Standing Committee on Professional Responsibility and Conduct, Formal Opinion 1989-113 (July 6, 1990).

Apex Oil Co. v. Wickland Oil Co., 1995 WL 293944 (E.D.Cal.1995), decided after the ABA promulgated Formal Opinion 95-390 (Jan. 25, 1995), rejects its reasoning in favor of a much more specific, and narrow, approach. The court held that a parent and subsidiary would be considered the same client for purposes of the conflict of interest rules only if the two entities were true *alter egos*.

[11]California State Bar Standing Committee on Professional Responsibility and Conduct, Formal Opinion 1989-113 (July 6, 1990).

Opinion 95-390.[12] The ABA Ethics Committee spent several years considering this controversial opinion, which was finally issued over several dissents. This Formal Opinion concluded that the Model Rules do not prohibit a law firm from representing a party adverse to a corporation (without consent) merely because the law firm represents, in an unrelated matter, another corporation that is affiliated (*e.g.*, as parent, subsidiary, sister corporation) with the adverse corporation. However, there may be circumstances in a particular case where it is reasonable to treat the affiliate as a client, either generally, or for purposes of client conflicts. Yet even in such cases, the ABA Formal Opinion advised that a "lawyer who has no reason to know that his potential adversary is an affiliate of his client will not necessarily violate Rule 1.7 by accepting the new representation without his client's consent."[13]

ABA Formal Opinion 95-390 focused on several different fact patterns to illuminate the principles that it was advancing. First, there is no general, per se rule that prevents a lawyer from representing, in an unrelated matter, another corporation affiliated with the adverse corporation.[14] Nonetheless, instances arise where the law of ethics should treat the situation as a conflict— where the nature of the lawyer's dealings with the affiliates of the corporate client are such that they all become clients or should be treated as if they were all clients of the same lawyer.

One example would be where the lawyer works for the corporate parent on a stock issue intended to benefit all subsidiaries and collects confidential information from all of them. Another situation is where the lawyer's relationship with the corporate affiliate may lead that affiliate to reasonably believe that it is a client of the lawyer, as when the lawyer for a subsidiary was hired by, and reports directly to, an officer or general counsel of the parent. The relationship between the corporate client and the affiliate may be such that the lawyer must regard the affiliate as its client, where one corporation is the alter ego of the other.[15]

To preclude the law firm from representing a client (*e.g.*, Client Beta) adverse to Corporation **A2** merely because the law firm

---

[12]ABA Formal Opinion 95-390 (Jan. 25, 1995). *Cf.* ABA Formal Opinion 97-405 (Apr. 19, 1997), titled, "Conflicts in Representing Government Entities."

[13]ABA Formal Opinion 95-390 (Jan. 25, 1995).

[14]*E.g.*, as parent, subsidiary, or sister corporation.

[15]**Dissenting Opinions to ABA Formal Opinion 95-390.** The eloquent dissents to ABA Formal Opinion 95-390 argued that it is sophistry to think of Corporations **A1** and **A2** as separate entities, because affiliated corporations have a financial relationship with each other. Corporate "families are financially totally interdependent," and the "location of a

also represents Corporation **A1** in an unrelated matter serves to deprive Client Beta of its choice of its own counsel. The law sometimes does that, but it does not do so cavalierly. The reason must be sufficiently weighty. The reason in this case cannot be to protect the confidential information of Corporation **A1** (because, by hypothesis, we have assumed that the law firm knows no rele-

---

corporate family's losses are totally irrelevant to the impact on the bottom line." *See* Lawrence J. Fox, dissenting. The distinction between different parts of the same corporation and different corporations in a corporate family "exalts form over substance." *See* Richard L. Amster, dissenting ("an elevation of form over substance"); Lawrence J. Fox, dissenting ("exalts form over substance").

Analogy to Representation of an Insured. The dissenters' emphasis on "the bottom line" is misplaced. The dissenters are correct that whatever happens financially to a corporation in the corporate family will affect "the bottom line" but that cannot be the test for determining who is the lawyer's client and to whom the lawyer owes a duty of loyalty. *Cf. Board of Education v. Nyquist*, 590 F.2d 1241, 1247 (2d Cir.1979). Let us assume what should be a clear case of financial interdependence: Corporation **A1** (the parent) agrees to pay the legal bills of the counsel for Corporation **A2**. That arrangement is similar to the typical insurance relationship, where the insurer pays the legal fees of the lawyer for the insured. A corporation (or private individual) buys an insurance policy that obligates the insurer to pay the damage award, if any, and also to pay the costs of defense.

What happens to the insured affects the bottom line of the insurance corporation. Although the insurance corporation pays the lawyer's fees, the lawyer's ethical obligation is to the insured, not to the insurer. The insurer merely pays the bills of the lawyer and any judgment to the plaintiff, up to the policy limits. Yet, these financial obligations confer on the insurer no right to control the profes-

sional judgment of the lawyer for the insured. Rule 1.8(f). Even though the insurance company's payment of legal fees affects the "bottom line," *Stratagem Development Corp. v. Heron International N.V.*, 756 F.Supp. 789, 792 (S.D.N.Y.1991), of the insurer, the basic rule is that the lawyer represents the insured, not the insurer. *See, e.g., Allstate Insurance Co. v. Keller*, 17 Ill.App.2d 44, 149 N.E.2d 482 (Ill.App. 1958); *Employers Casualty Co. v. Tilley*, 496 S.W.2d 552 (Tex.1973). Restatement of the Law Governing Lawyers, Third, § 134, Comments *c* & *f* (Official Draft 2000). There is no logical reason why the various members of corporate families should automatically be treated as *one* entity for ethical purposes, while the insurer and the insured are automatically recognized as *separate* entities.

Analogy to Partnerships and Trade Associations. Two earlier ABA Formal Opinions apply the entity theory to partnerships and trade associations: ABA Formal Opinion 91-361, "Representation of a Partnership" (July 12, 1991); ABA Formal Opinion 92-365, "Trade Associations as Clients" (July 6, 1992). Partners who are members of either a limited or general partnership, and members of a trade association also have financial relationships with each other, just like affiliated corporations have financial relationships with each other. The two ABA Formal Opinions on partnerships and trade associations did not conclude that the lawyer for a partnership or for a trade association should normally be treated as the lawyer for all the members of the partnership or a trade association, even if what affects a member affects the bottom line of the client, or vice versa.

vant confidential information),[16] nor is the reason to protect the law firm's loyalty towards Corporation **A1**. The law firm, after all, is not suing Corporation **A1**. It is adverse to Corporation **A2**, and that corporation is merely the shareholder of Corporation **A1**.

§ 1.13–7(c) Situations Where the Courts Should "Pierce the Corporate Veil" for Conflicts Purposes

The separate legal existence of corporations is something that the law continually recognizes. The reason why corporations create corporate families is because the law confers various substantive benefits on corporate entities that are created and treated as separate entities. It is not a matter of mere form devoid of substance. In corporate law, courts may pierce the corporate veil but they do not do so casually.[17] Corporate law normally treats each corporation as a separate, incorporeal entity. Various rules determine the relatively rare circumstances that allow a court to pierce the corporate veil, thereby circumventing a fundamental legal principle of corporate law. Courts may disregard the corporate entity only in certain cases, when necessary to avoid misuse of the law of incorporation, such as when a subsidiary is undercapitalized.[18]

In ethics as in corporate law, if one is to pierce the corporate veil for the purpose of deciding a disqualification issue, one should determine when public policy demands a piercing. A similar analysis should apply to disqualification issues. Model Rule 1.7 invites such an analysis.

Rule 1.7(a)(1) disqualifies a lawyer who represents one client "directly adverse to another client," unless the lawyer reasonably believes that her representation will not be adversely affected and that she can secure the consent of both clients.[19] Model Rule 1.7(a)(2) similarly disqualifies if the attorney's representation of the plaintiff against one corporation might be compromised or, in the words of that rule, "materially limited" by her obligations to a sister corporation, unless first, each client gives informed con-

---

[16]If there were relevant confidences, then Rule 1.6 and Rule 1.7, Comment 5 would preclude the representation.

[17]HARRY G. HENN, HANDBOOK OF THE LAW OF CORPORATIONS § 148 (2d ed. 1970); LARRY E. RIBSTEIN & PETER V. LETSOU, BUSINESS ASSOCIATIONS § 3.05(E)(1996).

[18]*Bucyrus-Erie Co. v. General Products Corp.*, 643 F.2d 413 (6th Cir. 1981); *Lucas v. Texas Industries, Inc.*, 696 S.W.2d 372 (Tex.1984) (though parent was not held liable, the court stated that it might pierce the corporate veil and hold the parent company liable if the subsidiary was not reasonably capitalized in light of the nature and risk of its business); *St. Paul Fire and Marine Ins. Co. v. PepsiCo, Inc.*, 884 F.2d 688 (2d Cir. 1989).

[19]ABA Model Rule 1.7(a)(2) & Comment 6.

sent,[20] and second, the lawyer reasonably believes that she can provide "competent and diligent representation."[21]

Another situation involves the case where the failure to disqualify the law firm would interfere with or taint the results of the litigation. Consider *Gould, Inc. v. Mitsui Mining & Smelting Co.*[22] In that case, the Law Firm represented plaintiff Gould suing various defendants, including Pechiney, alleging unfair competition. Pechiney moved to disqualify the Law Firm because the Law Firm also represented (in unrelated patent matters) IG Technologies, a wholly-owned subsidiary of Pechiney. The court noted that, the Law Firm "has made no effort to obtain the consent of Gould or Pechiney, nor did it ever attempt to notify them of this conflict of interest."[23] But the court still refused disqualification as a remedy because—

> *First*, there has been no demonstration that Pechiney has been prejudiced in any way by [the Law Firm's] representation of Gould. Confidential Pechiney information has not passed to Gould as a result of [the Law Firm's] representation of IGT, which is unrelated to the instant case. *Second*, disqualifying [the Law Firm] from representing Gould would not only cost Gould a great deal of time and money, in retaining new counsel, it would significantly delay the progress of this case.... *Finally*, the conflict was created by Pechiney's acquisition of IGT several years after the instant case was commenced, not by any affirmative act of [the Law Firm]. In short, *the integrity of the judicial process in this case has not been threatened by the conflict.*[24]

This test, whether the alleged conflict has threatened "the integrity of the judicial process," appears to be a strict one, signifying that there should be very few parent/subsidiary cases where disqualification is an appropriate remedy.

An example where a threat to the integrity of the judicial process would occur is the situation where the lawyer, while representing Corporation **A1**, learned client secrets that would be

---

[20]Rule 1.7(a)(2).

[21]Rule 1.7(b)(1). *See Pennwalt Corp. v. Plough, Inc.*, 85 F.R.D. 264 (D.Del.1980), where the court noted that a conflict involving the affiliated corporations would develop because the two sister corporations were being reorganized so that they would be in the same division, with the Chief Executive Office of that division sitting on both boards of directors. The legal departments also were being consolidated so that there would be one legal department under the active supervision of the same attorney. 85 F.R.D. at 272. Though the court refused to disqualify for other reasons (the alleged conflict had been "thrust upon" the law firm by the merger activities of the corporation now seeking to disqualify the law firm), the existence of similar personnel is relevant.

[22]*Gould, Inc. v. Mitsui Mining & Smelting Co.*, 738 F.Supp. 1121 (N.D.Ohio 1990).

[23]738 F.Supp. at 1126.

[24]738 F.Supp. at 1126–27 (emphasis added). The court appears to have found an implied waiver after balancing the equities.

relevant in the case against Corporation **A2**. In that case, the representation would taint the judicial process because the lawyer learned relevant confidences that would be used to her advantage without the consent of Corporation **A2**.[25]

If a corporation is a member of the same corporate family, the lawyer—who represents a sister corporation or a subsidiary or a parent—should determine how separate the corporate entities really are, whether the two entities are really run separately and whether corporate formalities are observed. In addition, the nature of the charges that Corporation *X* has filed against Corporation *A* [a member of the corporate family of ABC] may be relevant. For example, if Corporation *X*'s lawsuit alleges that Corporation *A* has engaged in fraud or criminal conduct, that may implicate the entire corporate family in a way that a dispute involving adverse possession would not.[26]

It is also relevant to determine if the personnel with whom the lawyer must deal are the same people. Do the different members of the corporate family use the same in-house counsel? It would be difficult for the lawyer, on day one, to call the general counsel of Parent Corporation, loyally advise her about the latest strategies on behalf of Subsidiary, and then, on day two, call the same general counsel and engage in tough negotiations on behalf of another client suing Parent Corporation in a RICO action.[27]

For example, consider *GSI Commerce Solutions, Inc. v.*

---

[25]*Westinghouse Electric Corp. v. Kerr-McGee Corp.*, 580 F.2d 1311, 1321 (7th Cir.1978), *cert. denied*, 439 U.S. 955, 99 S.Ct. 353, 58 L.Ed.2d 346 (1978).

[26]*See Teradyne, Inc. v. Hewlett-Packard Co.*, 20 U.S.P.Q.2d (BNA) 1143, 1991 WL 239940 (N.D.Cal.1991). *Teradyne* disqualified the law firm, looked carefully at the facts, and was impressed that counsel for the subsidiary was hired by and supervised by the legal department of the parent corporation.

Contrast Reuben H. Donnelley Corp. v. Sprint Publishing and Advertising, Inc., 1996 WL 99902 (N. D.Ill.1996), which refused to disqualify a law firm in a corporate family situation. While there was one general counsel for two subsidiaries, this particular individual did not personally retain the law firm that he now sought to disqualify and was not actively managing the litigation in question.

[27]*Travelers Indemnity Co. v. Gerling Global Reinsurance Corp.*, 2000 WL 1159260 (S.D.N.Y.2000). Gerling and non-party Gerling Global Reinsurance Company of America ("GGRCA") are both subsidiaries of Gerling AG. A law firm, LeBoeuf Lamb, represented GGRCA in two active matters relating to reinsurance of environmental claims; it also acted as its outside counsel with respect to reinsurance regulatory issues. In the current matter, LeBoeuf Lamb was representing Travelers against Gerling, while it was simultaneously representing GGRCA, Gerling's sister corporation, in at least two active matters, and was its primary outside counsel for reinsurance regulatory advice.

The court acknowledged that law firms are not *per se* barred from representing one part of a corporate family and suing another. However, in this case, although Gerling and GGRCA are separate legal entities,

Babycenter,[28] which upheld the trial court's disqualification of a law firm. The law firm simultaneously represented a parent company (Johnson & Johnson) on various matters, while representing a party adverse to one of Johnson & Johnson's wholly-owned subsidiaries. The litigation involved a matter unrelated to the law firm's representation of Johnson & Johnson. The district court did not abuse its discretion in granting the disqualification motion that the subsidiary filed because the operational relationship between the two companies was close and thus the representation reasonably could diminish "the level of confidence and trust in counsel" held by Johnson & Johnson.

In determining whether the parent company and its subsidiary are effectively one entity for conflict-of-interest purposes, the court looked at (1) the entities' financial interdependence and (2) the operational commonality across multiple departments (e.g. accounting, audit, cash management, employee benefits, finance, human resources, information technology, insurance, payroll, and travel services and systems). The court emphasized that both entities relied on the same in-house legal department to handle their legal affairs. This counsel was involved in the underlying dispute since it first arose, including mediation efforts and obtaining outside counsel for the subsidiary. This combination of these factors called for disqualification of the firm.[29]

Another situation occurs when the lawyer suing the corporation affiliated with a corporate client is asking for declaratory or injunctive relief that would impose restrictions on the corporate client itself. In such a case, the court, for ethical purposes, should, in effect, pierce the corporate veil and impose disqualification.

---

these sister companies shared common offices, a common computer system, and human resource and payroll departments and corporate services staff. They also had significantly overlapping senior management. The court was concerned that LeBoeuf attorneys "will no doubt continue to advise GGRCA management regarding ongoing litigation, while at the same time other LeBoeuf attorneys may be preparing to depose these same individuals, in their capacity as Gerling management, for the prosecution of this case." 2000 WL 1159260, *6. The court granted Gerling's motion to disqualify the law firm in this case and the underlying arbitration.

[28]*GSI Commerce Solutions, Inc. v. Babycenter, LLC*, 618 F.3d 204 (2d Cir. 2010). The court relied on ABA Formal Opinion 95-390 and Model Rule 1.7, Comment 34.

[29]*Discotrade Ltd. v. Wyeth–Ayerst International Inc.*, 200 F.Supp.2d 355 (S.D.N.Y.2002). The court disqualified Dorsey & Whitney from representing a plaintiff because it also represented the defendant's sister corporation in unrelated matters. All of the directors of the sister companies were the same; they shared the same president, computer system, and financial management; the same in-house legal department served them all.

Cases such as these are discussed in Rotunda, *Conflict Problems When Representing Members of Corporate Families*, 72 NOTRE DAME L. REV. 655 (1997).

For example, in *Hilton v. Barnett Banks, Inc.*,[30] the law firm for Hilton sued Barnett Banks while representing a subsidiary of Barnett Banks. Hilton's law firm did not name its client-affiliate as a party, but it did ask for injunctive relief against "all affiliates" of Barnett Banks. Hence, the court treated the affiliate as a *de facto* party and disqualified the law firm. The affiliated client was not (or soon would not be) a mere bystander to this particular lawsuit.

Law firms and corporate clients can avoid problems by clarifying, in the initial retention agreement, the extent to which the client consents to adverse representation against an affiliate of the corporate client.[31] The initial engagement letter could always state that some or all members of the corporate family should be treated as a single entity, or as separate entities.[32] If a law firm's decision to represent a particular corporation means that it must forego the opportunity to represent a whole host of other clients, the corporate client can easily inform that law firm, which should know that it is making a decision that will impose heavy opportunity costs. Clients, as well, should think through whether it is worthwhile to impose this opportunity cost on the law firm.

Because the law is unclear in this area, it is also useful for law firms to ask their corporate clients about parent-subsidiary information and include that information in their conflict of interest databases, so that they will be aware of the risks of conflicts issues.[33]

Just as outside law firms must address the problems of corporate family conflicts, in-house lawyers must deal with these issues when representing different corporate entities. A New

---

[30] *Hilton v. Barnett Banks, Inc.*, 1994 WL 776971 (M.D.Fla.1994).

[31] See Assoc. of Bar of City of New York Comm. on Prof. & Jud. Ethics, N.Y. City Ethics Op. 2007-3. Opinion 2007-3 examines the factors that law firms should consider when analyzing an intra corporate family conflict of interest. The opinion states that firms should consider addressing such problems in the engagement letter and with an advance consent arrangement.

[32] The new corporate client who is a member of a corporate family should know better than the law firm the contours of that family and how the client wants to be treated for conflicts purposes.

[33] One should realize that the law firm may not know, and may have no reasonable means of knowing, who are all the members of a corporate family that is constantly changing over the years. The law firm may not be able to predict, and will also have no way to prevent, a future merger or corporate reorganization. *See Gould, Inc. v. Mitsui Mining & Smelting Co.*, 738 F.Supp. 1121, 1125–26 (N.D.Ohio 1990); *Pennwalt Corp. v. Plough, Inc.*, 85 F.R.D. 264, 266 (D.Del.1980). ABA Formal Opinion 95-390 recognizes this problem and opines that a "lawyer who has no reason to know that his potential adversary is an affiliate of his client will not necessarily violate Rule 1.7 by accepting the new representation without his client's consent." ABA Formal Opinion 95–390 (Jan. 25, 1995).

York City Bar Ethics Opinion provides significant guidance to corporate legal departments.[34] Many corporations have a parent corporation in-house department and legal departments spread throughout the subsidiaries. In such cases, the conflicts of the parent corporation are imputed to the subsidiaries and vice versa. The Opinion addresses two common situations in large corporations. When the corporation has wholly owned subsidiaries, the parent's interests govern those of the subsidiary. This single entity and interest result is mandated by corporate law. However, when subsidiaries are not wholly owned or when a corporation controls, but does not completely own, an entity or venture, conflicts between the parent corporation and the related entity are analyzed as if the corporate actors were separate entities. Thus, a corporation's legal or working control does not resolve the conflicts problem because a part of the related entity is owned by others. The Opinion suggests that in-house lawyers use outside counsel to evaluate conflicts and propose solutions. And, such solutions may include advance waivers and limited scope representations.

The ethics issues involved in the corporate family situation are somewhat analogous to the case where a lawyer, in a private law firm, represents—as one of its clients—the government or a government agency. To that issue we now turn.

§ 1.13–7(d) Representing Government Entities While Simultaneously Representing Private Parties

§ 1.13–7(d)(1) Introduction

Sometimes the government hires a private law firm to represent it on some matters. That law firm may simultaneously represent private clients, some of whom may develop interests that are adverse to the government. There may be a government statute or regulation that controls this situation, and, if so, one must first turn to it.[35] The statute may provide that the government automatically waives certain conflicts. Of course, the lawyer still must obtain a knowing waiver from the private client.

Assuming that there is no valid relevant statute that mandates a different result or procedure, and that Rule 1.11 does not com-

---

[34]See N.Y. City Bar Assoc. Comm. on Prof. & Judicial Ethics, Formal Op. 2008-2 (Sept. 2008), noted in 24 ABA/BNA Law. Man. Prof. Conduct 542 (Oct. 15, 2008).

[35]Rule 1.13, Comment 9: "Duties of lawyers employed by the govern-ment or lawyers in military service may be defined by statutes or regulations. Therefore, defining precisely the identity of the client and prescribing the resulting obligations of such lawyers may be more difficult in the government context."

mand a different result,[36] then one must turn to the ethics rules. If there is a simultaneous representation of adverse interests, then Rule 1.7 applies, and the law firm is in a conflict.[37]

§ 1.13–7(e) Is the Client the "Entire Government" or a Specific Agency?

This basic question—who is the client?—is hardly a new one. The twist in the facts occurs when there is a question as to who is the government client. Is it the *entire* "government" as an entity, or is it just a certain agency or a particular department?

Consider *People v. Crawford Distributing Co., Inc.*[38] Illinois law allows the Attorney General to hire private lawyers who act as assistant attorneys general and represent the state in various types of litigation. In this case, beer distributors convicted of fixing prices argued on appeal that their convictions were tainted because the lawyers who represented the defendants were in a firm in which at least one member was a special assistant attorney general for non-antitrust civil proceedings. If the client is "the government," or "the entire government," then there is a simultaneous representation of conflicting interests. That is the first question to which the court turned.

The majority found no conflict, because the court defined the client as an entity much narrower than "the government." The court engaged in a functional analysis of the interests as stake. It reasoned: "If [a person] whose authority does not include criminal cases takes on the representation of a person charged in a criminal proceeding in which the Attorney General is involved, that attorney is not placed in a position . . . where he might have to cross-examine and impeach his own clients. Neither is he placed in a position . . . where his civil clients stand to gain by the conviction of the individual he represents in the criminal case."[39] The special Assistant Attorney General for a limited type

---

[36] Rule 1.11, "Special Conflicts of Interest for Former and Current Government Officers and Employees," allows the creation of a screen between the lawyer and other lawyers, thus limiting the strictness of the normal imputation requirements of Rule 1.10.

[37] *See Perillo v. Johnson*, 79 F.3d 441, 447 (5th Cir. 1996), holding that an "actual" conflict of interest exists when a lawyer represents two clients whose interests in the outcome of a matter are different.

Waiver. Note that sometimes, as discussed under Rule 1.7, the eth-

ics rules may not allow this conflict to be waived by the clients, even if all of them are fully informed.

[38] *People v. Crawford Distributing Co., Inc.*, 65 Ill.App.3d 790, 22 Ill.Dec. 525, 382 N.E.2d 1223 (1978), *aff'd*, 78 Ill.2d 70, 34 Ill.Dec. 296, 397 N.E.2d 1362 (1979).

[39] 65 Ill.App.3d 790, at 795, 22 Ill.Dec. 525, at 530, 382 N.E.2d 1223, at 1228.

The dissent argued, however, "[i]t is most doubtful that an attorney retained by a private client to do tax work . . . could properly undertake to

of civil cases owes no duty to the Attorney General in criminal matters, so there is no conflict.[40]

Model Rule 1.13 treats the government as an "organization," for purposes of this Rule. A Comment states quite specifically: "The duty defined in this Rule applies to governmental organizations."[41] However, this Comment then states, almost in an off-hand manner: "Although in some circumstances the client may be a specific agency, it is *generally* the government as a whole."[42]

The ABA Committee on Ethics, in Formal Opinion 97-405, rejects this comment as simply not "dispositive."[43] It proposed a functional analysis similar to the functional analysis of *People v. Crawford Distributing Co., Inc.*,[44] discussed above.

First, the lawyer must determine if the client is the government as a whole or a smaller entity, such as a particular agency or department. Initially, the identity of the client for conflicts

---

sue that client in a personal injury case. The fact that an appointee is retained for a special category of practice does not alter the nature of an attorney-client relationship which establishes the commitment of the attorney to the interests of that client." 65 Ill.App.3d 790, at 804, 22 Ill.Dec. 525, at 536, 382 N.E.2d 1223, at 1234 (dissenting opinion).

[40]*See also Aerojet Properties, Inc. v. State of New York*, 138 A.D.2d 39, 530 N.Y.S.2d 624 (1988). In this case, the court found no conflict when a lawyer represented a claimant seeking unpaid rent against the state before the Court of Claims, while simultaneously defending the state before the Court of Claims in a personal injury matter. "Given the multitudinous nature of the State's activities, even the appearance of impropriety seems de minimis here." 138 A.D.2d at 41, 530 N.Y.S.2d at 625.

State of Minnesota v. Philip Morris, Inc., 1998 WL 257214 (2d Dist.1994) (unpublished). Several firms representing the defendants were also representing state agencies in various unrelated matters. The judge denied the state's motions to disqualify those firms, because "the representation of their respective state agencies does not adversely affect" the state. In a later opinion the court ruled

on various discovery issues. *State of Minnesota v. Philip Morris Inc.*, 1998 WL 257214 (D.Minn.1998).

[41]Rule 1.13, Comment 9.

[42]Rule 1.13, Comment 9 (emphasis added).

[43]ABA Formal Opinion 97-405 (Apr. 19, 1997), at 8, n.5. The ABA Ethics Committee added this thought, *id.* at 9, n.5: "We note that the D.C. Bar opinion appears to have been similarly unpersuaded that the narrower definition of the government client contained in D.C. Rule 1.6(i) ('the client of the government lawyer is the agency that employs the lawyer') should also apply in the conflicts context. *See* D.C. Bar, Legal Ethics Comm. Opinion 268 at n. 6."

Although the ABA Ethics Committee concluded that the client is not generally the "government as a whole," the Committee was more divided on the issue of whether a lawyer representing one member of the corporate family should be treated as representing the corporate family as a whole. ABA Formal Opinion 95-390 (Jan. 25, 1995).

[44]*People v. Crawford Distributing Co., Inc.*, 65 Ill.App.3d 790, 22 Ill.Dec. 525, 382 N.E.2d 1223 (1978), *aff'd*, 78 Ill.2d 70, 34 Ill.Dec. 296, 397 N.E.2d 1362 (1979).

purposes is established by agreement between the lawyer and the client when the client (in this case, the government official authorized to speak for the client) retains the lawyer.[45] The agreement with the government as to the scope of employment and the definition of the government "client" is not allowed to frustrate the reasonable expectations of the private client, who expects a conflict-free representation. Lawyers and the government client cannot prevent the private client from asserting a conflict by the simple expedient of agreeing to an unusually narrow and artificial definition of the "government client." On the other hand, the agreement should prevent the government client from later arguing that the definition of the government "client" should be retroactively enlarged.

If no express agreement exists, then the ABA Formal Opinion advises that one should look at the reasonable expectations of the government client, such as how the government entity is funded, how it is legally defined, and whether it has independent legal authority on the matter for which it hired the lawyer.[46]

This ABA recommendation makes sense. One can think of many cases where it would be unnatural to treat the government client as the government as a whole. One obvious example is the case where one branch of "the government as a whole" has a dispute with another branch of "the government," as when Congress and the President dispute the constitutionality of a legislative veto. Each branch will have its own counsel, neither of whom will be representing the "government as a whole."

§ 1.13–7(f) Disclosure to Private Clients When Lawyers Are Representing Government Agencies

ABA Formal Opinion 97-405 offers a useful caution and warn-

---

[45]ABA Formal Opinion 97-405 (Apr.19, 1997), relying on Rule 1.2, and ABA Formal Opinion 95-390 (Jan. 25, 1995), which states that a corporate client, when retaining a lawyer, may specify whether the "corporate client expects some or all of its affiliates to be treated as clients for purposes of Rule 1.7."

[46]*Brown & Williamson v. Pataki*, 152 F.Supp.2d 276 (S.D.N.Y.2001), refused to disqualify Covington & Burling for representing New York state's welfare department in efforts to obtain federal funding while simultaneously representing clients who were suing the state in *Brown & Williamson v. Pataki*. In the *Brown & Williamson v. Pataki* case, the firm

was trying to overturn the prohibition of selling cigarettes to New York residents by mail order. The court acknowledges that determining who the client was in a case involving the government was a difficult matter, and the agency signing the contract with the firm is not controlling. Nor could the whole state executive branch be deemed the client. There was no relationship between this case and what the firm did for the state in other matters; for example, the firm would not cross-examine people it was advising in other matters, and the issues in the two cases were different. Thus, the court refused to disqualify the law firm.

ing about the lawyer's need for full disclosure to his private clients who may have interests adverse to the government entity that is related to the specific government entity that the lawyer is also representing:

> *Only if* the two government entities are not considered the same client, and if there is otherwise no basis for the lawyer to conclude that either representation would be "materially limited" by the other, or by other relevant consideration (such as the lawyer's personal interests), would the lawyer have no obligation under the Model Rules to tell either client about the other or seek the permission of either or both to represent them simultaneously.[47]

If the two government agencies are treated as one and the same client, the lawyer would be representing one client (the private client) while simultaneously opposing her own client in violation of Rule 1.7(a)(1). If the two government entities are not treated as one for purposes of legal ethics, then the lawyer will not be opposing her client. She will be representing one client (the private client) while opposing a government entity that is not her client. However, the lawyer must still decide if the representation of her client will be adversely affected—or, "materially limited" in the words of Rule 1.7(a)(2)—because of the relationship between the two government entities.[48] A key issue is whether the lawyer will be pulling her punches on behalf of the private client while representing the particular government agency.[49]

The situation where a lawyer represents one government entity while representing a private client with adverse interests is analogous to the situation where a lawyer represents a subsidiary of a corporate family. "The same functional analysis that might lead to a finding of 'material limitation' where two representations involve corporate subsidiaries is applicable where two representations involve different subdivisions of the same government."[50] If the lawyer is representing one client in a way that will have an adverse effect on "either the 'financial well-being or programmatic purposes' of the" other client, then the lawyer "must seek the consent of the affected client."[51] To make this decision, the attorney should consider factors such as the "relative importance of

---

[47]ABA Formal Opinion 97-405 (Apr.19, 1997), at 5 (emphasis added).

[48]These issues are explored in, ABA Formal Opinion 97-405 (Apr.19, 1997).

[49]If the lawyer's representation is "materially limited," she must disclose the situation and obtain valid consent from both her private client and the government client. Formal Opinion 97-405 (Apr.19, 1997).

[50]ABA Formal Opinion 97-405 (Apr.19, 1997), at 11.

[51]ABA Formal Opinion 97-405 (Apr.19, 1997), at 12.

the representation to the respective clients or to their lawyers and the directness of the adverseness between them."[52]

The test is a bit vague, as the ABA Ethics Committee concedes. It warns us that "common sense is occasionally useful in determining when client consent to a conflict must be obtained, [but] it is rarely sufficient to answer the ethical questions presented under the Model Rules."[53]

---

[52]ABA Formal Opinion 97-405 (Apr.19, 1997), at 12. "There *may* be situations in which a lawyer's representation of the government on an important issue of public policy so identifies her with an official public position that she would be effectively compromised in her ability convincingly to oppose any part of the government on behalf of a private client, even in an entirely unrelated matter." *Id.* (emphasis added). This Opinion offers no concrete example to illustrate this statement.

[53]ABA Formal Opinion 97-405 (Apr.19, 1997), at 6.

CHAPTER 1.14
CLIENT WITH A DIMINISHED CAPACITY

RULE 1.14: CLIENT WITH DIMINISHED CAPACITY

(a) When a client's capacity to make adequately considered decisions in connection with a representation is diminished, whether because of minority, mental impairment or for some other reason, the lawyer shall, as far as reasonably possible, maintain a normal client-lawyer relationship with the client.

(b) When the lawyer reasonably believes that the client has diminished capacity, is at risk of substantial physical, financial or other harm unless action is taken and cannot adequately act in the client's own interest, the lawyer may take reasonably necessary protective action, including consulting with individuals or entities that have the ability to take action to protect the client and, in appropriate cases, seeking the appointment of a guardian ad litem, conservator or guardian.

(c) Information relating to the representation of a client with diminished capacity is protected by Rule 1.6. When taking protective action pursuant to paragraph (b), the lawyer is impliedly authorized under Rule 1.6(a) to reveal information about the client, but only to the extent reasonably necessary to protect the client's interests.

Comment

[1] The normal client-lawyer relationship is based on the assumption that the client, when properly advised and assisted, is capable of making decisions about important matters. When the client is a minor or suffers from a diminished mental capacity, however, maintaining the ordinary client-lawyer relationship may not be possible in all respects. In particular, a severely incapacitated person may have no power to make legally binding decisions. Nevertheless, a client with diminished capacity often has the ability to understand, deliberate upon, and reach conclusions about matters affecting the client's own well-being. For example, children as young

as five or six years of age, and certainly those of ten or twelve, are regarded as having opinions that are entitled to weight in legal proceedings concerning their custody. So also, it is recognized that some persons of advanced age can be quite capable of handling routine financial matters while needing special legal protection concerning major transactions.

[2] The fact that a client suffers a disability does not diminish the lawyer's obligation to treat the client with attention and respect. Even if the person has a legal representative, the lawyer should as far as possible accord the represented person the status of client, particularly in maintaining communication.

[3] The client may wish to have family members or other persons participate in discussions with the lawyer. When necessary to assist in the representation, the presence of such persons generally does not affect the applicability of the attorney-client evidentiary privilege. Nevertheless, the lawyer must keep the client's interests foremost and, except for protective action authorized under paragraph (b), must look to the client, and not family members, to make decisions on the client's behalf.

[4] If a legal representative has already been appointed for the client, the lawyer should ordinarily look to the representative for decisions on behalf of the client. In matters involving a minor, whether the lawyer should look to the parents as natural guardians may depend on the type of proceeding or matter in which the lawyer is representing the minor. If the lawyer represents the guardian as distinct from the ward, and is aware that the guardian is acting adversely to the ward's interest, the lawyer may have an obligation to prevent or rectify the guardian's misconduct. See Rule 1.2(d).

Taking Protective Action

[5] If a lawyer reasonably believes that a client is at risk of substantial physical, financial or other harm unless action is taken, and that a normal client-lawyer relationship cannot be maintained as provided in paragraph (a) because the client lacks sufficient capacity to communicate or to make adequately considered decisions in connection with the representation, then paragraph (b) permits the lawyer to take protective measures deemed necessary. Such measures could include: consulting with family members, using a reconsideration period to permit clarification or improvement of circumstances, using voluntary surrogate decisionmaking tools such as durable powers of attorney or consulting with support groups, professional services, adult-protective agencies or other individuals or entities that have the ability to protect the client. In taking any protective action, the lawyer should be guided by such factors as the wishes and values of the client to the extent known, the client's best interests and the goals of intruding into the client's decisionmaking autonomy to the least extent feasible, maximizing client capacities and respecting the client's family and social connections.

[6] In determining the extent of the client's diminished capacity, the lawyer should consider and balance such factors as: the client's ability to articulate reasoning leading to a decision, variability of state of mind and ability to appreciate consequences of a decision;

the substantive fairness of a decision; and the consistency of a decision with the known long-term commitments and values of the client. In appropriate circumstances, the lawyer may seek guidance from an appropriate diagnostician.

[7] If a legal representative has not been appointed, the lawyer should consider whether appointment of a guardian ad litem, conservator or guardian is necessary to protect the client's interests. Thus, if a client with diminished capacity has substantial property that should be sold for the client's benefit, effective completion of the transaction may require appointment of a legal representative. In addition, rules of procedure in litigation sometimes provide that minors or persons with diminished capacity must be represented by a guardian or next friend if they do not have a general guardian. In many circumstances, however, appointment of a legal representative may be more expensive or traumatic for the client than circumstances in fact require. Evaluation of such circumstances is a matter entrusted to the professional judgment of the lawyer. In considering alternatives, however, the lawyer should be aware of any law that requires the lawyer to advocate the least restrictive action on behalf of the client.

Disclosure of the Client's Condition

[8] Disclosure of the client's diminished capacity could adversely affect the client's interests. For example, raising the question of diminished capacity could, in some circumstances, lead to proceedings for involuntary commitment. Information relating to the representation is protected by Rule 1.6. Therefore, unless authorized to do so, the lawyer may not disclose such information. When taking protective action pursuant to paragraph (b), the lawyer is impliedly authorized to make the necessary disclosures, even when the client directs the lawyer to the contrary. Nevertheless, given the risks of disclosure, paragraph (c) limits what the lawyer may disclose in consulting with other individuals or entities or seeking the appointment of a legal representative. At the very least, the lawyer should determine whether it is likely that the person or entity consulted with will act adversely to the client's interests before discussing matters related to the client. The lawyer's position in such cases is an unavoidably difficult one.

Emergency Legal Assistance

[9] In an emergency where the health, safety or a financial interest of a person with seriously diminished capacity is threatened with imminent and irreparable harm, a lawyer may take legal action on behalf of such a person even though the person is unable to establish a client-lawyer relationship or to make or express considered judgments about the matter, when the person or another acting in good faith on that person's behalf has consulted with the lawyer. Even in such an emergency, however, the lawyer should not act unless the lawyer reasonably believes that the person has no other lawyer, agent or other representative available. The lawyer should take legal action on behalf of the person only to the extent reasonably necessary to maintain the status quo or otherwise avoid imminent and irreparable harm. A lawyer who undertakes to represent a person in such an exigent situation has the same duties under these Rules as the lawyer would with respect to a client.

[10] A lawyer who acts on behalf of a person with seriously diminished capacity in an emergency should keep the confidences of the person as if dealing with a client, disclosing them only to the extent necessary to accomplish the intended protective action. The lawyer should disclose to any tribunal involved and to any other counsel involved the nature of his or her relationship with the person. The lawyer should take steps to regularize the relationship or implement other protective solutions as soon as possible. Normally, a lawyer would not seek compensation for such emergency actions taken.

Authors' 1983 Model Rules Comparison

The 1983 Model Rules contained Rule 1.14 and it was entitled, Client Under a Disability. In 1997, the ABA adopted two new Comments. Comments 6 and 7 addressed the issue of dealing with a prospective client who is under a disability in an emergency situation.

The drafters of the 2002 Model Rules made several changes to this Rule beginning with the title. The new title is "Client With Diminished Capacity."

In Rule 1.14(a), the drafters changed the words, "ability" to "capacity," "impaired" to "diminished," and "disability" to "impairment." These changes were consistent with the slight refocus of the Rule on to the client's capacity. *See* Reporter's Explanation of Changes to Model Rule 1.14.

In Rule 1.14(b), the drafters significantly reworded the standard for a lawyer's ability to take protective action if a client can no longer act in his or her interest. The old Rule 1.14(b) stated, "A lawyer may seek the appointment of a guardian or take other protective action with respect to a client, only when the lawyer reasonably believes that the client cannot adequately act in the client's own interest." The new language offers the lawyer who seeks to take protective action options that are less intrusive than appointing a guardian. The drafters also sought to limit action only to those situations when the client is at risk of substantial injury.

Rule 1.14(c) is new and offers the lawyer guidance as to how this Rule interacts with Rule 1.6.

In Comment 1, the drafters made several word changes, mostly adding the words "diminished capacity" to describe the new focus of the Rule. They deleted the following line: "Furthermore, to an increasing extent the law recognizes intermediate degrees of competence."

In Comment 2, the drafters deleted the following line: "If the person has no guardian or legal representative, the lawyer often must act as de facto guardian." They also made a verb tense change in the last sentence.

Comment 3 is new and examines the possibility of involving the client's family in this decision.

Old Comments 3 and 4 are combined to new Comment 4. The language about appointing a guardian has been removed from this Comment and placed into Comments 5, 6, and 7. A new sentence about looking to the parents as natural guardians has been added.

The drafters added new Comments 5, 6, and 7 under the topic "Taking Protective Action." Comment 5 explores an entire series of options that a lawyer could take. Comment 6 offers guidance as to a lawyer's evaluation of the extent of a client's capacity. Comment 7 offers guidance as to appointing a legal guardian for the client.

Old Comment 5 is now new Comment 8, but the drafters have deleted the first line of the old Comment and added four sentences near the end of the Comment. The new language interprets the interaction of this Rule with Rule 1.6 on confidentiality.

Old Comments 6 and 7 have been renumbered as new Comments 9 and 10. The drafters removed the old term, "disabled" and have replaced it with the phrase "seriously diminished capacity."

Model Code Comparison

There was no counterpart to this Rule in the Disciplinary Rules of the Model Code. EC 7-11 stated that the "responsibilities of a lawyer may vary according to the intelligence, experience, mental condition or age of a client. . . . Examples include the representation of an illiterate or an incompetent." EC 7-12 stated that "[a]ny mental or physical condition of a client that renders him incapable of making a considered judgment on his own behalf casts additional responsibilities upon his lawyer. Where an incompetent is acting through a guardian or other legal representative, a lawyer must look to such representative for those decisions which are normally the prerogative of the client to make. If a client under disability has no legal representative, his lawyer may be compelled in court proceedings to make decisions on behalf of the client. If the client is capable of understanding the matter in question or of contributing to the advancement of his interests, regardless of whether he is legally disqualified from performing certain acts, the lawyer should obtain from him all possible aid. If the disability of a client and the lack of a legal representative compel the lawyer to make decisions for his client, the lawyer should consider all circumstances then prevailing and act with care to safeguard and advance the interests of his client. But obviously a lawyer cannot perform any act or make any decision which the law requires his client to perform or make, either acting for himself if competent, or by a duly constituted representative if legally incompetent."

§ 1.14–1 DEALING WITH A CLIENT WITH A DIMINISHED CAPACITY

A client's youth may impair his ability to render a considered judgment, or the client may be an adult (or child) who is under a mental disability, so that he does not appreciate the full significance of what is going on.[1] When the diminished capacity results from mental impairment, the lawyer must make an assessment

---

[Section 1.14–1]

[1] *See, e.g., Quesnell v. State,* 83 Wash.2d 224, 517 P.2d 568 (1973) involved a civil commitment proceeding. The court held that the guardian ad litem could not waive the client/ patient's right to a jury trial court without the knowing consent of the patient, and that it was error to conduct the commitment proceedings without a jury after the patient attempted to invoke that right. "The

of the client's mental capacity. Comment 6 lists a number of factors that a lawyer should consider when making this assessment: "the client's ability of articulate reasoning leading to a decision, variability of state of mind and ability to appreciate consequences of a decision; the substantive fairness of a decision; and the consistency of a decision with the known, long-term commitments and values of the client."[2] The authorities seem to authorize a lawyer to seek assistance from a diagnostician or from the client's family members,[3] however, the lawyer needs to be careful not to violate the obligation of confidentiality to the client.[4] Of course, in some cases, such as a criminal defendant client's decision not to oppose execution, a lawyer may have difficulty in assessing a client's mental capacity and may wish to override a client's wishes because of the belief that the client's choices are not rational.[5]

In dealing with a client with a diminished capacity, the lawyer should endeavor, insofar as possible, to maintain a normal client-lawyer relationship.[6] Even if the client is under a legal disability, he or she might still be capable of understanding the matter, and the lawyer should therefore consult with the client. There are "intermediate degrees of competence."[7] Rule 1.14 deals with these issues. It does not give the lawyer carte blanche to impose on the client the lawyer's personal view of what is in the client's best interest. Rather, Rule 1.14 authorizes the lawyer to engage in a

---

rights of the involuntarily held mental patient can never be fully protected unless he is represented by a lawyer who carefully tests each element of the case presented against his allegedly mentally ill client." 83 Wash.2d 224, 237, 517 P.2d 568, 576.

In re M.R., 135 N.J. 155, 638 A.2d 1274 (N.J.1994) involved a case where the client had Down's Syndrome. The lawyer was instructed to follow the client's instructions and argue for her positions unless they unreasonably risked harm to her welfare or unless her positions were "absurd."

[2] Rule 1.14, Comment 6.

[3] *See* Rule 1.14, Comment 6; ABA Formal Op. 96-404 (1996).

[4] Rule 1.14, Comment 8.

[5] *See* J.C. Oleson, *Swilling Hemlock: The Legal Ethics of Defending a Client Who Wishes to Volunteer for Execution*, 63 WASH. & LEE L.REV. 147 (2006) (criticizing the guidance

provided by Rule 1.14 and suggesting that lawyer should consider rejecting client's wishes to volunteer for execution).

[6] Rule 1.14; EC 7-12. Restatement of the Law Governing Lawyers, Third, § 24 ("A Client with Diminished Capacity") (Official Draft 2000).

[7] 1983 Model Rule 1.14, Comment 1. EC 7-12 advises that the lawyer should obtain "all possible aid" from the client if he or she is capable of understanding the matter in question, even if the client is legally disqualified from performing certain acts.

Criminal Cases. These issues often arise in a civil context, such as when the client makes a will or disposes of property. But they may also arise in a criminal context. *See, e.g.,* Josephine Ross, *Autonomy Versus a Client's Best Interests: The Defense Lawyer's Dilemma When Mentally Ill Clients Seek to Control Their Defense*, 35 AM. CRIM. L. REV. 1343–86 (1998).

limited intervention when the client's mental incapacity is such that he or she cannot adequately protect his or her own interests.[8]

Rule 1.14(a)'s obligation to maintain as reasonable an attorney-client relationship as possible clearly focuses on two obligations of a lawyer. A lawyer owes an obligation to keep a client informed under Rule 1.4. This obligation includes giving the client information necessary to make adequately informed decisions. A lawyer has an obligation under Rule 1.2 to consult with the client as to the means that the lawyer will use to meet the client's objectives. This obligation implicitly requires that the lawyer determine the client's objectives after consultation with the client.

§ 1.14–2 TAKING ACTION NECESSARY TO PROTECT THE CLIENT WITH A DIMINISHED CAPACITY

The 1983 Model Rules adoption of Rule 1.14 represented a bold move for the ABA. This provision authorized a lawyer to act to protect a client's interests without the client's consent when the lawyer "reasonably believes that the client cannot adequately act in the client's own interest."[1] Such protective action includes seeking the appointment of a guardian for the client. The lawyer, in such cases, should take into account that it may be traumatic or expensive for the client if such a legal representative is appointed.[2]

Of course, a lawyer should always seek to obtain the client's consent to allow the lawyer to take protective action for a client with a diminished capacity. If despite such efforts, the client does not respond or is not capable of making a decision, the lawyer may take protective action.

The drafters of the 2002 Model Rules elaborated significantly upon the lawyer who seeks to take protective action on behalf of the client. First, the text of the Rule now requires that the lawyer only take action when the client with a diminished capacity "is at risk of substantial physical, financial, or other harm unless ac-

---

[8]Daniel L. Bray & Michael D. Ensley, *Dealing with the Mentally Incapacitated Client: The Ethics Issues Facing the Attorney*, 33 FAMILY L. QUARTERLY 329, 330 (Summer 1999). The authors argue that the key to Rule 1.14 "lies in the interpretation of the 'other protective action.' [Rule 1.14(b)]" This language "does not give the lawyer an open-ended license to substitute her judgment for the client's. Rather,

the lawyer must only act when absolutely necessary to do so." *Id.* at 348.

[Section 1.14–2]

[1]1983 Model Rule 1.14(b).

[2]Rule 1.14, Comment 4. *Cf.* Rule 1.4, Comment 4 (lawyer may withhold client's psychiatric diagnosis if the "examining psychiatrist indicates that disclosure would harm the client").

tion is taken."[3] The diminished capacity must be such that the client "lacks sufficient capacity to communicate or to make adequately considered decisions . . .,"[4] then the lawyer may take protective action.

Second, Rule 1.14(b) offers lawyers examples of less intrusive protective action than appointment of a conservator or guardian such as involving other individuals or entities to help the client. The Comment offers the following guidance:

> Such measures could include: consulting with family members, using a reconsideration period to permit clarification or improvement of circumstances, using voluntary surrogate decisionmaking tools such as durable powers of attorney or consulting with support groups, professional services, adult-protective agencies or other individuals or entities that have the ability to protect the client. In taking any protective action, the lawyer should be guided by such factors as the wishes and values of the client to the extent known, the client's best interests and the goals of intruding into the client's decisionmaking autonomy to the least extent feasible, maximizing client capacities and respecting the client's family and social connections.[5]

The decision to seek appointment of a guardian is a serious one and should be guided by other legal principles in the law of guardianship and the lawyer's judgment.[6]

Finally, the drafters of the 2002 Rules placed into the text of Rule 1.14 a provision explicitly dealing with confidentiality. Rule 1.14(c) states that any information possessed by the lawyer about the client's capacity is confidential information protected by Rule 1.6. The text makes it clear that when a lawyer takes protective action under Rule 1.14(b), "the lawyer is impliedly authorized under Rule 1.6(a) to reveal information about the client, but only to the extent reasonably necessary to protect the client's interests."[7] The Comment states that this implied authorization even overrides a client directive to the contrary.[8] The drafters give lawyers the right to disclose confidential information but they state: "At the very least, the lawyer should determine whether it is likely that the person or entity consulted with will act adversely to the client's interests before discussing matters related to the client."[9]

Under the 1983 Model Rules, it was unclear whether a lawyer could act to take protective actions when the client had expressly told the lawyer not to take such action. The 2002 version of Rule

---

[3]Rule 1.14(b).

[4]Rule 1.14(b). New Comment 6 provides guidance as to how a lawyer should make this determination and offers the option of seeking help from an appropriate diagnostician.

[5]Rule 1.14, Comment 5.

[6]Rule 1.14, Comment 7.

[7]Rule 1.14(c).

[8]Rule 1.14, Comment 8.

[9]Rule 1.14, Comment 8.

1.14 seems to answer this question. One comment offers the following weighing of factors:

> In taking any protective action, the lawyer should be guided by such factors as the wishes and values of the client to the extent known, the client's best interests and the goals of intruding into the client's decisionmaking autonomy to the least extent feasible, maximizing client capacities and respecting the client's family and social connections.[10]

Another comment explicitly states that a lawyer could override a client's wish as to disclosure of confidential information.[11]

If one believes that a client has a severely diminished capacity, then the decisions and wishes of that client may not have the force of a person's true will. In other words, the very reason why a lawyer may take protective action is to protect the client from substantial injury. If the client says, do not inform anyone else, and yet the client is still likely to suffer substantial injury, that choice may be overridden by a lawyer serving the client's best interests. This Rule therefore provides for overriding Rule 1.2's mandate on allocation of authority because of a client's diminished capacity.

ABA Formal Opinion 96-404[12] attempts to deal with the problems of clients who have become legally incompetent to handle their own affairs. If the client is in fact incompetent, the Opinion acknowledges, Rule 1.14's admonition to try to "maintain a normal client-lawyer relationship" with the client is not realistic. Indeed, in some states, the agency relationship between lawyer and client may be dissolved because of the client-principal's incompetence.[13] Further, lawyer withdrawal in such circumstances may be a solution that is impossible without "material adverse effect" on the client's interests.

This Formal Opinion thus counsels that a lawyer should take the "least restrictive action under the circumstances;" appointment of a guardian should not be chosen "if other, less drastic, solutions are available." Further, even if a guardian is needed for some purposes, something less than a general guardianship

---

[10]Rule 1.14, Comment 5.

[11]Rule 1.14, Comment 8.

[12]ABA Formal Opinion 96-404 (Aug. 2, 1996).

[13]Oddly enough, Rule 1.16, Comment 6 appears to come to an opposite conclusion. It states: "If the client is mentally incompetent, the client may *lack the legal capacity to discharge* the lawyer, and in any event the discharge may be seriously adverse to the client's interests." (emphasis added).

See also Hawkins v. Principi, 2004 WL 396064, *2 (Vet.App.,2004): "Model Rule 1.14 does not provide for the termination of the attorney-client relationship because of diminished capacity; rather, that Model Rule suggests that counsel should maintain that relationship as normally as possible." Note: this opinion will not be published in a printed volume. The disposition will appear in a reporter table.

should be sought if possible. Although the lawyer may file the petition for guardianship, it must be because the lawyer concludes it is necessary, not because someone else (such as a family member) requests it. Finally, if the lawyer is asked to recommend a guardian, any expectation the lawyer may have of future employment by the guardian must be disclosed to the appointing court, as must any different preference for a guardian that the client might have expressed.

In an "extreme case" the lawyer may even initiate proceedings for a conservatorship or similar protection for the client.[14] If the lawyer takes this route, then the lawyer is "impliedly authorized"—under Rule 1.6(a)—to make the necessary disclosures for the client's best interests.[15] For example, the lawyer may need to consult a medical doctor.

§ 1.14–3 EMERGENCY LEGAL SERVICES FOR PERSONS WITH A DIMINISHED CAPACITY

In 1997, the ABA added two Comments to Rule 1.14 dealing with Emergency Legal Assistance. These Comments address several issues that arise when a person with a diminished capacity seeks legal services on an emergency basis from a lawyer.

First, a person with a diminished capacity may seek to engage a lawyer in an emergency situation, but they may be unable to establish an attorney-client relationship or make judgments about the matter. Rule 1.14 permits the lawyer to take action even though an attorney-client relationship has not been clearly established as long as it is an emergency situation.[1] Before a lawyer may take such action, the lawyer needs to "reasonably believe that the person has no other lawyer, agent or other representative available."[2] Also, the lawyer may only take such action that is "reasonably necessary to maintain the status quo or otherwise avoid imminent or irreparable harm."[3]

Second, when a lawyer undertakes emergency legal services for a person with a diminished capacity who is unable to establish an attorney-client relationship, the Rules require that the lawyer has the same ethical duties to that person that he would owe to a

---

[14]Rule 1.16, Comment 6; Rule 1.14(b).

[15]ABA Formal Opinion 89-1530 (1989). Not all authority agrees with this ABA ethics opinion. For example, Opinion 1989-112 (1989) of the State Bar of California, Committee on Professional Responsibility and Conduct, concluded that the lawyer may *not* reveal client confidences to the court and family members even when the lawyer believes that the client is in-

competent. *Accord* Illinois State Bar Ass'n, Committee on Professional Ethics, Opinion 89-12 (1990); Michigan Bar Committee on Professional and Judicial Ethics, Opinion CI-882 (1983).

[Section 1.14–3]

[1]*See* Rule 1.14, Comment 9.

[2]Rule 1.14, Comment 9.

[3]Rule 1.14, Comment 9.

client.[4] In particular, the lawyer must keep information relation to the emergency legal services confidential, except to the extent necessary to protect the person. When appearing before a tribunal, the lawyer must inform the tribunal of the nature of the relationship with the person.[5] The lawyer should as soon as possible seek to form an attorney-client relationship or implement other protective measures.

The Comments suggest dealing with Emergency Legal Assistance that lawyers would not normally seek to charge the person for work performed under these circumstances.[6] However, even though there is technically no "contract"—because the individual does not have the capacity to contract—the common law allows this person with diminished capacity to consent to legal representation, and it also provides that this person is *liable to pay counsel*, under the doctrine of "necessaries."[7] If the lawyer should not charge a reasonable fee for services rendered although the law of contracts states that he can charge, there will be less incentive for the lawyer to step up to the plate and play the role of a Good Samaritan.

The Comments on "Emergency Legal Assistance" address the responsibility of a lawyer to a nonclient, but a person whose health, safety or a financial interest is threatened with imminent and irreparable harm. When a person's capacity is seriously diminished, a lawyer should be able to act even though the person cannot form an attorney-client relationship. These Comments balance the rights of unrepresented persons with that of the lawyer to take protective action for such a person. It would not make sense to prohibit a lawyer from taking such action.

---

[4]Rule 1.14, Comment 9.

[5]Rule 1.14, Comment 10.

[6]Rule 1.14, Comment 10.

[7]**Necessaries.** "Persons having no capacity or limited capacity to contract are often liable for necessaries furnished to them or to their wives or children. Though often treated as contractual, such liabilities are quasi-contractual: the liability is measured by the value of the necessaries rather than by the terms of the promise." Restatement (Second) of the Law of Contracts, § 12, Comment *f* (1981).

CHAPTER 1.15
SAFEKEEPING PROPERTY

RULE 1.15: SAFEKEEPING PROPERTY

(a) A lawyer shall hold property of clients or third persons that is in a lawyer's possession in connection with a representation separate from the lawyer's own property. Funds shall be kept in a separate account maintained in the state where the lawyer's office is situated, or elsewhere with the consent of the client or third person. Other property shall be identified as such and appropriately safeguarded. Complete records of such account funds and other property shall be kept by the lawyer and shall be preserved for a period of [five years] after termination of the representation.

(b) A lawyer may deposit the lawyer's own funds in a client trust account for the sole purpose of paying bank service charges on that account, but only in an amount necessary for that purpose.

(c) A lawyer shall deposit into a client trust account legal fees and expenses that have been paid in advance, to be withdrawn by the lawyer only as fees are earned or expenses incurred.

(d) Upon receiving funds or other property in which a client or third person has an interest, a lawyer shall promptly notify the client or third person. Except as stated in this rule or otherwise permitted by law or by agreement with the client, a lawyer shall promptly deliver to the client or third person any funds or other property that the client or third person is entitled to receive and, upon request by the client or third person, shall promptly render a full accounting regarding such property.

(e) When in the course of representation a lawyer is in possession of property in which two or more persons (one

of whom may be the lawyer) claim interests, the property shall be kept separate by the lawyer until the dispute is resolved. The lawyer shall promptly distribute all portions of the property as to which the interests are not in dispute.

Comment

[1] A lawyer should hold property of others with the care required of a professional fiduciary. Securities should be kept in a safe deposit box, except when some other form of safekeeping is warranted by special circumstances. All property that is the property of clients or third persons, including prospective clients, must be kept separate from the lawyer's business and personal property and, if monies, in one or more trust accounts. Separate trust accounts may be warranted when administering estate monies or acting in similar fiduciary capacities. A lawyer should maintain on a current basis books and records in accordance with generally accepted accounting practice and comply with any recordkeeping rules established by law or court order. See, e.g., ABA Model Financial Recordkeeping Rule.

[2] While normally it is impermissible to commingle the lawyer's own funds with client funds, paragraph (b) provides that it is permissible when necessary to pay bank service charges on that account. Accurate records must be kept regarding which part of the funds are the lawyer's.

[3] Lawyers often receive funds from which the lawyer's fee will be paid. The lawyer is not required to remit to the client funds that the lawyer reasonably believes represent fees owed. However, a lawyer may not hold funds to coerce a client into accepting the lawyer's contention. The disputed portion of the funds must be kept in a trust account and the lawyer should suggest means for prompt resolution of the dispute, such as arbitration. The undisputed portion of the funds shall be promptly distributed.

[4] Paragraph (e) also recognizes that third parties may have lawful claims against specific funds or other property in a lawyer's custody, such as a client's creditor who has a lien on funds recovered in a personal injury action. A lawyer may have a duty under applicable law to protect such third-party claims against wrongful interference by the client. In such cases, when the third-party claim is not frivolous under applicable law, the lawyer must refuse to surrender the property to the client until the claims are resolved. A lawyer should not unilaterally assume to arbitrate a dispute between the client and the third party, but, when there are substantial grounds for dispute as to the person entitled to the funds, the lawyer may file an action to have a court resolve the dispute.

[5] The obligations of a lawyer under this Rule are independent of those arising from activity other than rendering legal services. For example, a lawyer who serves only as an escrow agent is governed by the applicable law relating to fiduciaries even though the lawyer does not render legal services in the transaction and is not governed by this Rule.

[6] A lawyers' fund for client protection provides a means through the collective efforts of the bar to reimburse persons who have lost

money or property as a result of dishonest conduct of a lawyer. Where such a fund has been established, a lawyer must participate where it is mandatory, and, even when it is voluntary, the lawyer should participate.

Authors' 1983 Model Rules Comparison

The drafters of the 2002 Rules added a new section (b) permitting lawyers to place firm funds in a client trust account to the extent such funds are needed to cover bank service charges.

The drafters added new section (c) requiring that lawyers place unearned fees and advance expense deposits in a client trust account.

The 1983 Rule 1.15(b) was renumbered to section (d) and not amended.

The 1983 Rule 1.15(c) was renumbered to section (e) and slightly amended. The drafters made clear that disputes may take place between the lawyer and the client or the client and a third person. They also added the last line that requires prompt payment of any monies not in dispute.

In Comment 1, the drafters added prospective clients to those whose property must be kept in a separate account. They also added the last line to the Comment that requires lawyers to follow current basis accounting in accordance with generally accepted accounting practice and local law. The drafters included a citation to the ABA Model Financial Recordkeeping Rule.

Comment 2 is new and explains new Rule 1.15(b).

The 1983 Comment 2 is renumbered as Comment 3. The drafters amended the language to address advance payment of fees.

The 1983 Comment 3 is renumbered as Comment 4. The drafters substantially amended this Comment to make clear that when a third party has a valid legal right, such as a lien, against client funds, the lawyer must keep the funds until the dispute is resolved. The drafters recognized in the last line in the Comment that in some cases the lawyer may need to file an action to resolve the third party dispute before the funds are released. *See* Reporter's Explanation of Changes to Model Rule 1.15.

The 1983 Comment 4 is renumbered as Comment 5. The drafters added the word, "only" to describe escrow agent and reaffirmed that such conduct is "not governed by this Rule."

The 1983 Comment 5 is renumbered as Comment 6. The drafters changed the reference from "client security fund" to "lawyers' fund for client protection," and they modified the language to require lawyer participation when a jurisdiction makes it a mandatory fund. The new language also states that a lawyer should participate when the jurisdiction makes it voluntary.

Model Code Comparison

[1] With regard to paragraph (a), DR 9-102(A) provided that "funds of clients" are to be kept in an identifiable bank account in the state in which the lawyer's office is situated. DR 9-102(B)(2) provided that a lawyer shall "identify and label securities and properties of a client . . . and place them in . . . safekeeping. . . ." DR 9-102(B)(3) required that a lawyer "[m]aintain complete records of all funds, se-

curities, and other properties of a client. . . . ." Paragraph (a) extends these requirements to property of a third person that is in the lawyer's possession in connection with the representation.

[2] Paragraph (b) is substantially similar to DR 9-102(B)(1), (3) and (4).

[3] Paragraph (c) is similar to DR 9-102(A)(2), except that the requirement regarding disputes applies to property concerning which an interest is claimed by a third person as well as by a client.

§ 1.15–1 ESTABLISHING TRUST FUND ACCOUNTS

A lawyer who receives funds of property belonging to a client or third person owes that party duties with respect to the funds or property. These obligations arise from the fiduciary duties that agents owe their principals to protect property belonging to another. In some jurisdictions, the duties have been informed by trust law holding that a lawyer who holds property of another acts as a trustee for a beneficiary.

Given that lawyers routinely receive funds and property of clients and third persons, the ABA has codified those duties in Model Rule 1.15. Lawyers must keep client funds in a trust account and must never commingle those funds with the personal or business accounts of the lawyer. Property other than funds must be appropriately safeguarded and must similarly be identified as belonging to another person. Lawyers must promptly notify clients and third persons when they receive their funds or property and must promptly deliver such funds or property unless other arrangements are made. All transactions must be properly documented in accounting books or logs and must be kept current. And, lawyers must provide an accounting when requested by the client or third person. All lawyers and law firms must establish proper accounting procedures to implement Model Rule 1.15. And, they must properly supervise non-lawyer employees in discharging these responsibilities.[1]

§ 1.15–1(a) What Must Be Kept in Trust

The requirements of the Model Code and the Model Rules are substantially similar, but some interesting differences arise in the details. Under both provisions, the lawyer must keep separate, identifiable accounts of client funds. The law firm may not commingle the firm's (or lawyer's) own funds with these client funds.[2] For example, a law firm must not pay its debts by drawing a check on a client's trust fund account. The firm first should withdraw from that account any amount to which it is entitled.

[Section 1.15–1]

[1] *See Florida Bar v. Jerry Arthur Riggs, Sr., 944 So.2d 167 (Fla. Sup. Ct. 2006)* (court upholds a a three-year suspension of practice for a lawyer who turned over bookkeeping duties to an employee and who then failed to supervise that employee).

[2] Rule 1.15(a). DR 9-102(A).

The firm then should place that amount in the firm's own account and draw a check on its own account.[3] The lawyer may not even temporarily borrow client funds, even if the client suffers no injury and, after the fact, assents to the lawyer's conduct. Such borrowing is really conversion.

The trust fund rule prohibits commingling client funds with the lawyer's funds. The client's funds must be segregated from the lawyer's funds.[4] In addition to money and other such property, the lawyer "must take reasonable steps" to safeguard documents that the lawyer possesses that relate to her representation of a client or former client.[5]

The lawyer must also put into trust account the property that belongs to a non-client when the lawyer receives that property in the course of representing the client.[6] In other words, the lawyer must place in the trust account property, such as the deed of the client's spouse, or property that the lawyer received in his capacity as an executor, escrow agent, etc., "unless that capacity is unrelated to a representation."[7] This particular provision follows present practice.[8]

The Model Code *exempted* from the trust fund requirement any

---

[3]*See Matter of Rabb*, 73 N.J. 272, 374 A.2d 461 (1977).

[4]*See, e.g., In re Chase Ingersoll*, 186 Ill.2d 163, 237 Ill.Dec. 760, 710 N.E.2d 390 (1999)[Docket No. 85127] (respondent disbarred for, among other things, depositing [on five occasions over a three month period] less than $2,000 of his personal funds into two client trust fund accounts at two different banks).

[5]Restatement of the Law Governing Lawyers, Third, § 46(1) (Official Draft 2000).

See, e.g., Florida Bar v. Carlton, 366 So.2d 406 (Fla.1978) (per curiam). The lawyer was disciplined for various reasons, including: "Respondent did fail and neglect to place the insurance policies of Chapman in a safe deposit box or other place of safekeeping to maintain them and, furthermore, was unable to render an account as to the whereabouts of the insurance policy properties of his client." 366 So.2d at 408.

Attorney Grievance Commission of Maryland v. Pollack, 289 Md. 603, 425 A.2d 1352 (App.1981), holding that the lawyer's "failure to record

deed covering transfer of property, failure to disclose to purchasers or referring attorney that deed could not be located for a period of three months, and failure to take any action to protect clients during such period warrants suspension for an indefinite term without prejudice to right to file motion 60 days after date of order seeking termination."

[6]Rule 1.15(a).

[7]Restatement of the Law Governing Lawyers, Third, § 44 (Official Draft 2000), Comment *b*.

See also, e.g., In re Young, 111 Ill.2d 98, 94 Ill.Dec. 767, 488 N.E.2d 1014 (1986). The clients hired the lawyer to represent them in the sale of their home. The lawyer agreed to hold over $3,200 in escrow until his clients' title was cleared. The purchaser presented the lawyer with a check to cover this amount, but the lawyer failed to put it in a trust account. Instead he put it in his personal business account. Because of various extenuating circumstances, the court agreed to sanction the lawyer with only a censure.

[8]*See, e.g., Matter of Lurie*, 113

client funds paid as *advances for costs and expenses*.[9] The drafters of the Model Code offered no policy justification to support this exception, and thus the Rules do not continue it. These funds are now subject to the trust fund requirement. The drafters of the 2002 Rules made this explicit in Rule 1.15(c).

The legislative history of the 1983 Model Rules stated that the requirement of Rule 1.15(a), on safekeeping property, did not apply the trust fund rule to prepaid legal fees: "Paragraph (a) does not apply to unearned prepaid legal fees, but any unearned amounts must be returned to the client at the termination of the lawyer's services under Rule 1.16."[10] The apparent rationale was that these unearned, prepaid fees were not client funds; they were the lawyer's funds. The lawyer should deposit his funds in his own account. When the lawyer completes his services, he must return all prepaid fees that have not been earned,[11] but under the 1983 Rules there was no requirement that, in the interim, these prepaid fees be separately maintained.[12]

The drafters of the 2002 Rules changed this result in Rule 1.15(c) by adding a requirement that advanced fees also need to be held in the client trust account. The drafters noted that the loss of advance fees by clients represents the largest categories of claims in state client protection funds.[13] The old rule was a little unusual, because it resulted in the lawyer collecting legal fees before they were earned. One can say that the fees are "prepaid," and earned when paid, but that is simply not true: the fees are not earned if any "unearned amounts must be returned to the client." Under Rule 1.15(c), lawyers must keep both advance fees and expenses in the trust account until they are earned or incurred.

The trust account requirement was so strict that at all times only client funds could be kept in the account. Therefore, if the lawyer earned fees, the lawyer would send a statement to the client and would need to withdraw the earned fees within a reasonable time (assuming that the client did not object to the lawyer's earned fees). For example, a lawyer could not continue to leave earned legal fees in the client trust account for months at a time

---

Ariz. 95, 546 P.2d 1126 (1976).

[9] DR 9-102(A).

[10] *See* Reporter's "Legal Background" to Rule 1.15 *reprinted in* THOMAS D. MORGAN & RONALD D. ROTUNDA, 1983 SELECTED STANDARDS SUPPLEMENT 210 (Foundation Press, 1983). This "Legal Background" refers to Rule 1.15(a), the language of which was not changed between this draft and its approval by the ABA.

[11] *See* Rule 1.16(d) ("refunding any advance payment of fee that has not been earned.").

[12] The Code is unclear as to the status of prepaid, unearned legal fees, and the states differ, with some requiring trust fund treatment and some not.

[13] *See* Reporter's Explanation of Changes to Model Rule 1.15.

because this practice constitutes commingling of funds. So serious is this issue that the ABA in 2002 adopted a new Rule 1.15(b) that permits a lawyer to add the lawyer's own funds to the trust account to cover bank expenses. But the lawyer may only add what is necessary to cover those expenses and no more than this amount.

In addition to these requirements, the trust fund bank account should be maintained in the state where the law office is, unless the client consents to a different place.[14]

§ 1.15–1(b) Safekeeping

The lawyer must safeguard the client's property. For example, the client's securities should be kept in a safe or safe deposit box, unless circumstances dictate a different form of safekeeping. All property that belongs to clients or third persons must be kept separate from the lawyer's business and personal property, and tangible property should be identified as belonging to the client. Client money must be placed in one or more trust accounts. When the lawyer administers estate monies or acts in a similar fiduciary capacity, separate trust accounts may be warranted.[15]

If the lawyer keeps physical property of the client instead of financial assets like cash, stocks, or bonds, the lawyer must still safeguard that property. For example, in *The Florida Bar v. Grosso*,[16] the lawyer's client was sentenced to probation, so he could not have any guns. The lawyer, agreeing to keep the client's gun collection for him, put the guns in his garage. However, Florida weather is very humid and the lawyer did not safeguard this property properly. When the lawyer returned the guns a year later, they were rusty and pitted and parts were missing. The court suspended the lawyer for 90 days.

§ 1.15–1(c) Recordkeeping

The lawyer must maintain "complete records" of all client property and "render appropriate accounts to his client regarding them."[17] To this requirement originally found in the Model Code, the Model Rules added a requirement that these records be kept for a given number of years (the Rules recommend five years) after the legal representation has ended.[18]

---

[14] Rule 1.15(a); DR 9-102(B)(2).

[15] Rule 1.15, Comment 1; Restatement of the Law Governing Lawyers, Third, § 44 (Official Draft 2000). *See also Attorney Grievance Commission v. Boehm*, 293 Md. 476, 446 A.2d 52,

53 n.2 (1982).

[16] *The Florida Bar v. Grosso*, 760 So.2d 940 (Fla.2000).

[17] Rule 1.15(a), (b); DR 9-102(B) (3).

[18] Rule 1.15(a).

The law firm must identify other client property as such, and safeguard it appropriately.[19] As an illustration of this principle, assume that Client gives Lawyer bearer bonds for safe-keeping while Client is in Europe on an extended vacation. Lawyer then places these bonds in the office safe, but does not identify them as belonging to Client. In this situation, Lawyer has committed a disciplinable violation because of the imprecise record keeping.

Beyond these basic principles, the Model Rules do not give further guidance on what should be the most prudent (or, at the very least, the minimal) standards for financial recordkeeping. Based on a study of existing court rules, the ABA has codified what is the Model Rule on Financial Recordkeeping.[20] This Model Rule—which is *not* part of the ABA Model Rules on Professional Conduct—makes clear, for example, that only a lawyer admitted to practice in the relevant jurisdiction (and therefore subject to discipline in that jurisdiction) may be an authorized signatory on the account, and that withdrawals must be made only by bank transfer or by a check payable to a named payee, not "to cash."[21]

§ 1.15-1(d) The Duty of Prompt Notice and Delivery

When the lawyer receives funds belonging in a trust fund account, the lawyer must promptly notify the client, or third party.[22] The lawyer must then "promptly pay or deliver" to the client any trust funds or property that the client requests and to which the client is entitled.[23] The Model Rules do not explicitly adopt the requirement of a "request" by a client or third party.[24]

Lawyers may be tempted to delay notice and/or delivery of funds if the client may be unsophisticated or vulnerable to mismanaging the monies. In such a case, a lawyer could make an agreement in advance that the lawyer will hold the funds until the client completes a money management course. However, in the absence of such an agreement, the lawyer may not withhold notice or payment even if it is in the best interests of the client.

If the matter involves a contingent fee, the lawyer must render a written accounting to the client that states "the outcome of the matter, and if there is a recovery, showing the remittance to the client and the method of its determination."[25] If the matter does

---

[19]Rule 1.15(a); DR 9-102(B)(2)

[20]**Model Rule on Financial Recordkeeping.** The ABA House of Delegates adopted the Model Rule on Financial Recordkeeping on February 9, 1993. This Rule, reprinted in Appendix B of the Lawyer's edition of this book, offers detailed recommendations that go beyond the bare bones of Rule 1.15 of the Model Rules of Professional Conduct.

[21]Model Rule on Financial Recordkeeping, at B(1),(3).

[22]Rule 1.15(b); DR 9-102(B)(1).

[23]DR 9-102(B)(4).

[24]*See* Rule 1.15(b).

[25]Rule 1.5(c).

not involve a contingent fee, the lawyer must provide an accounting upon request by the client.[26]

§ 1.15–1(e) Disputes Regarding Trust Fund Property

Occasionally the client and lawyer may have a dispute regarding trust fund property. For example, the settlement check for $90,000 may be deposited in the client account, and the lawyer would like to withdraw the agreed upon fee of one-third plus the amount to cover disbursements. But the client may claim that less than a third is owed to the lawyer, perhaps because of a dispute regarding whether one-third was reasonable under the circumstances, or because of a disagreement over disbursements.

The lawyer may not withdraw the *disputed portion* of the money until the dispute is resolved.[27] On the other hand, the lawyer must promptly distribute the undisputed portion to the client and withdraw for himself the undisputed portion of the funds from the trust fund account when they are due.[28] The lawyer may not coerce the client to give up his claim by refusing to deliver to the client the money that is undisputedly the client's.[29] And, the client may not withhold the undisputed portion of the lawyer's fee for similar leverage.

Rule 1.15(e) also applied to disputes between the client and another third person or entity. For example, a client in a personal injury case may have agreed to pay the hospital bill when the client receives a recovery in the personal injury case. If the hospital learns about the client's recovery in the litigation, they may call or write to the lawyer asking that the lawyer pay the hospital directly. Rule 1.15(e) requires that a lawyer keep disputed funds in a separate account and the Comment states that the lawyer may need to file a suit to resolve the dispute.[30] However, when should a lawyer keep such funds and when are such funds properly disputed?

If a lawyer receives a letter from a hospital, a lawyer could always ask a client whether the client wishes to pay the hospital bill directly. If the hospital has obtained a valid lien under state law on the proceeds from any recovery and the hospital has

---

[26]Rule 1.15(d).

[27]Rule 1.15(e); DR 9-102(A)(2).

[28]*See* California State Bar Standing Comm. on Professional Responsibility and Conduct, Formal Op. 2006–171, *noted in* 22 ABA/BNA MANUAL ON PROFESSIONAL CONDUCT, Current Reports News 532 (Nov. 1, 2006). This opinion declared that once a lawyer has withdrawn her fee and disbursed the remainder to the client in compliance with the fee agreement and the

ethics rules, a client dispute of the fee does not obligate the attorney to replace settlement funds. At the moment of a proper withdrawal, the money loses its "trust" status and becomes personal property of the lawyer, despite later client protests about the fee.

[29]*See also* Restatement of the Law Governing Lawyers, Third, §§ 45, 46 (Official Draft 2000).

[30]Rule 1.15, Comment 4.

provided verification to the lawyer of this lien,[31] then the lawyer must withhold the funds for the hospital.[32] If the client disputes the lien or the amount, the lawyer must hold only the disputed amount in a separate account until it is resolved. If the hospital does not have a valid lien under state law on the funds, the lawyer must release the funds promptly to the client.

Some might ask why a lawyer should become a payor of client funds to hospitals, doctors, and others. Such organizations have lobbied for the strengthening of third party lien laws. Also, in many cases, lawyers become involved in negotiating reductions of medical bills and in exchange for concession, the health care providers request that the client give them a lien in proceeds from the litigation.

§ 1.15–2 MODEL RULE FOR PAYEE NOTIFICATION

When insurance carriers pay liability claims pursuant to settlement or verdict, the insurance carriers typically pay the settlement proceeds to the litigant's lawyer of record, usually by check or draft payable jointly to the claimant and the claimant's lawyer. That way, the lawyer can protect his or her lien in the proceeds.[1] Because the insurance carrier typically does not notify the claimant when it makes payment to the claimant's lawyer, a dishonest lawyer can steal the client's portion of this payment, by forging the client's signature.[2] The dishonest lawyer can even settle the claim without notifying his client. This gap in the process permits dishonest practices to interfere with the settlement and payment of insurance claims.

Experience has shown that these problems are substantially reduced in states that adopt the ABA Model Rule for Payee

---

[31]Although this varies from jurisdiction to jurisdiction, many states require a written and signed document that has the client directing the lawyer to pay the hospital directly out of the proceeds of any recovery. If the lawyer has actual knowledge that the nonclient has a lawful claim to the client funds, such as a statutory subrogation right, a judicial lien, a court order, or a valid lien executed by the client, the lawyer has an obligation to secure the funds claimed by the nonclient. See Ohio Sup.Ct. Bd. of Commissioners on Grievances and Discipline, Op. 2007-7 (Dec. 7, 2007), noted in 24 ABA/BNA MANUAL ON PROF. CONDUCT 15 (Jan. 9, 2008).

[32]The Wyoming Supreme Court has held that a lawyer who fails pay a holder of a valid state lien may be li-

able to that third party. See Winship v. Gem City Bone & Joint, P.C., 2008 WY 68, 185 P.3d 1252 (Wyo. 2008).

[Section 1.15–2]

[1]Matter of Conroy, 56 N.J. 279, 266 A.2d 279 (1970), explained that this procedure protects the interests of all three parties to the transaction, the insured, the successful litigant, and the litigant's lawyer.

See Restatement of the Law Governing Lawyers, Third, § 43 ("Lawyer Liens") (Official Draft 2000).

[2]Sampson v. State Bar, 12 Cal.3d 70, 115 Cal.Rptr. 43, 524 P.2d 139 (1974) (lawyer disciplined by endorsing client's name to settlement check without client authorization and for other matters).

Notification.[3] This Model Rule—which is not part of the ABA Model Rules of Professional Conduct—simply requires the insurer, when paying more than a certain amount (such as more than $5,000) in settlement of any third-party liability claim, to send a written notice to the claimant if the claimant is a natural person, and the payment is delivered to the claimant's lawyer or other representative by draft, check or otherwise.[4]

Many lawyers put in their fee agreement a written requirement that all checks in settlement of the case or in payment of the verdict be made out jointly to the client and lawyer and that the client will endorse the check and allow the lawyer to place it in a trust account. This practice is proper and gives the client notice of the lawyer's receipt of the funds while preserving the lawyer's charging lien on the funds. The lawyer then would comply with Rule 1.15 by promptly delivering the funds once the checks had been endorsed and deposited.

If the lawyer does not put the charging lien in writing, there is the real risk that the court will not enforce an *oral charging lien* because a lawyer's charging lien against the client's recovery could become detrimental to the client, and Rule 1.8(a) requires the client's informed *written* consent to the lawyer's acquisition of an interest adverse to the client.[5]

§ 1.15–3 AUDITS OF TRUST FUND ACCOUNTS

Neither the Model Rules nor the Model Code require any spot or systematic auditing by the bar authorities of client trust funds. However, the ABA, in its Model Rules for Lawyer Disciplinary Enforcement, recommends that bar discipline counsel should have ready access to records of the location and number of client trust fund accounts held by all of the lawyers in the state.[1] The ABA also recommends that Bar Counsel should be able to verify the accuracy of these accounts *if* there is "probable cause" that the funds have not been maintained properly or have been

---

[3]ABA Model Rule for Payee Notification (Aug. 13, 1991) is reprinted in Appendix D of the Lawyer's edition of this book.

[4]ABA Model Rule for Payee Notification, § A.

[5]*Fletcher v. Davis*, 33 Cal.4th 61, 90 P.3d 1216, 14 Cal.Rptr.3d 58 (2004), *on remand*, 2004 WL 2429613 (Cal. App.2004). In this case, a lawyer sued several parties to enforce a charging lien he had obtained from a former cli-

ent. The state Supreme Court held that the lawyer could not enforce the lien because he did not comply with Rules of Professional Conduct requiring the client's informed *written* consent to the attorney's acquisition of an interest adverse to the client.

[Section 1.15–3]

[1]ABA Model Rules for Lawyer Disciplinary Enforcement, Rule 29 (ABA 1996).

mishandled.[2] The ABA justified this limitation on bar counsel on the grounds that it was necessary in order to preserve client confidences. However, clients would be more protected if the Bar Counsel had more power to examine trust fund accounts without having to cross the hurdle of probable cause.

In addition, the ABA has proposed random audits of lawyers' trust fund accounts and approved a Model Rule for Random Audit of Lawyer Trust Accounts.[3] The empirical evidence has shown that random audits are a proven deterrent to the misuse of money and property in the practice of law and that examination of trust accounts by court-designated auditors provide practitioners with expert and practical assistance in maintaining necessary records and supporting books of account. The burden that this proposed rule would impose on law firms is minimal, because all audits would be random and would not be imposed on any law firm more than once every three years.[4] But, one cannot effectuate a complete audit if one cannot verify the accuracy of the trust fund account, and neither the Model Rules nor the Model Code require any spot or systematic auditing by the bar authorities of client trust funds.

Several states require spot checks, and some Canadian provinces require accounting certificates of trust fund accounts. Some commentators have also proposed that all attorneys be bonded, or that at least lawyers who have been suspended or disbarred and are seeking reentry to the profession should be bonded.[5]

§ 1.15–4 TRUST ACCOUNT OVERDRAFT NOTIFICATION

In addition to the establishment of random trust fund audits, the ABA has established another useful procedure to protect clients from the occasional dishonest or overwhelmed lawyer. The ABA has recommended establishing trust account overdraft notification, and has drafted the Model Rules for Trust Account Overdraft Notification.[1]

The ABA solution is both simple and elegant. The evidence shows that if the bank dishonors drafts for insufficient funds drawn from a client trust account, that event is an early warning

---

[2] ABA Model Rules for Lawyer Disciplinary Enforcement, Rule 30 (ABA 1996).

[3] The ABA Model Rule for Random Audit of Lawyer Trust Accounts (Aug. 11, 1993), is reprinted in Appendix C of the Lawyer's edition of this book.

[4] ABA Model Rule for Random Audit of Lawyer Trust Accounts (Aug. 11, 1993), at § I.

[5] Ronald D. Rotunda & Mary M. Devlin, *Permanent Disbarment: A Market Oriented Proposal*, 9 THE PROFESSIONAL LAWYER 2 (A.B.A., No. 9, 1997).

[Section 1.15–4]

[1] ABA Model Rules for Trust Account Overdraft Notification (Feb. 9, 1988), Rules 1 to 6.

that mischief is afoot: the lawyer is engaging in conduct likely to injure clients. An overdraft notification program has the potential to reduce significantly the level of lawyer defalcations across the country. The costs of providing overdraft notification are minimal and can be assessed against the lawyer who caused the overdraft.

The Model Rules for Trust Account Overdraft Notification require financial institutions that maintain lawyer trust accounts to notify the appropriate lawyer disciplinary agency of overdrafts. In order for a financial institution to be eligible to hold lawyer trust accounts, it must agree to provide this overdraft notification. Because the appropriate disciplinary authorities are given sufficient warning, they are able to intervene before major losses occur and many clients are harmed.

The prophylactic nature of this rule also allows the appropriate authorities to advise and admonish deviant lawyers to take corrective action before the misconduct becomes more serious.

§ 1.15–5 CLIENT PROTECTION FUNDS

The ABA has been active in encouraging lawyers to contribute to client security trust funds. In response to the ABA lead on this issue, some states have established client security trust funds or client protection funds, which offer some protection to clients by reimbursing them in whole or in part when their attorneys have misappropriated their money. These funds are typically funded by periodic assessments on the members of the bar. Neither the 1983 Model Rules nor the Code required the establishment of such funds, but both urged individual lawyers to participate in this effort of reimbursement.[1] The drafters of the 2002 Rules added the phrase to the 1983 Comment providing that, if a state has a mandatory protection plan, the lawyer must participate in it. If it is voluntary, the lawyer should participate in it.

[Section 1.15–5]

[1] 1983 Model Rule 1.15, Comment 5; EC 9-7.

Model Rules for Lawyers' Funds for Client Protection. The ABA House of Delegates approved Model Rules For Lawyers' Funds for Client Protection on August 9, 1989. The original Rules were designed to encourage and assist courts, bar associations, and legislative bodies in organizing new and basic programs to reimburse clients for losses caused by dishonest conduct of lawyers. The revised Rules address procedural and organizational deficiencies in the earlier version. They offer standards for the effective financing of client protection programs. The new Rules streamline the procedures for the processing, evaluation, and payment of reimbursements. They also clarify provisions relating to creditor rights.

The Model Rules For Lawyers' Funds for Client Protection are reprinted in Appendix E of the Lawyer's edition of this book.

§ 1.15–6 INTEREST EARNED ON CLIENT TRUST FUNDS

Under common law rules going back many years, any interest earned on client trust accounts does not belong to the lawyer. If funds are invested, the interest earned (whether small or large in amount) on the client's property belongs to the client, not to the lawyer.[1] The ethics rules reflect this common law principle. Thus, the 1908 Canons of Professional Ethics state quite clearly that client funds should not "be commingled with [the lawyer's] own *or be used by* him."[2] Nor may the lawyer use interest earned to defray the expense of handling the agency account.[3] Of course, the attorney may always bill the client separately for disbursements.

Neither the Model Rules nor the Model Code specifically deal with the question of the investment of client trust accounts. Normally a lawyer would be under no duty to invest client funds because she is usually keeping these funds in her capacity as a safe guarder, not as an investor. However, in some cases the large amount of money and length of time involved may require the lawyer to secure instructions from the client regarding investments.[4]

Historically, because client funds are held for such a short time, the lawyer keeps the funds in non-interest-bearing bank accounts. The administrative difficulty of apportioning to each of the clients their share of interest in a multi-client account with other clients' funds encourages non-interest bearing accounts. However, with modern computers, the assumed burden imposed by administrative difficulty should be a thing of the past. Banks now pay interest on funds held in checking accounts, while in the past banks paid no interest on certain accounts, such as checking accounts.

In recent years, the organized bar has responded to the fact that client funds can be placed in interest bearing accounts. The organized bar has attempted to capture the interest generated by pooling small amounts of funds into a much larger trust fund. The bar has created an exception to these basic rules in order to collect the interest from the pool of trust fund accounts and use this otherwise untapped resource to fund law-related public service projects, such as indigent legal services. The nominal interest from many small accounts can add up quickly.[5]

The ABA Ethics Committee ruled that the Model Code did not

[Section 1.15–6]

[1]ABA Formal Opinion 348 (July 23, 1982).

[2]Canons of Professional Ethics, Canon 11 (emphasis added).

[3]ABA Informal Opinion 991 (July 3, 1967).

[4]ABA Formal Opinion 348 (July 23, 1982).

[5]The Law Foundation of British

stand in the way of such programs. Even without prior client consent or notice, the "interest earned on bank accounts in which are deposited client's funds, nominal in amount or to be held for short periods of time, under state-authorized programs providing for the interest to be paid to tax-exempt organizations" is not treated as funds of the client within the meaning of the ethics rules.[6] The Model Rules do not undercut support for these programs, which are typically called IOLTA plans (an acronym that stands for "Interest on Lawyer Trust Account.")

The future of such programs is was placed in doubt for several years after the 1998 U.S. Supreme Court decision in *Phillips v. Washington Legal Foundation*.[7] *Phillips* found constitutional problems when the state takes the interest earned from these pooled income fund accounts. The question before the Court was narrow. The Court assumed that a lawyer was required to put funds into an IOLTA account only if the interest generated on the funds would be insufficient to offset bank service charges and accounting for the interest. The issue was whether the interest was nevertheless "property" of the lawyer or client in such a case so that the Takings Clause could apply. By a five to four vote, the Court, speaking through Chief Justice Rehnquist, held such interest on a client's funds in a lawyer's hands is property of the client even if bank charges would mean the client could never spend it. Because the questions had not been decided below, the Court left for another day whether the IOLTA program constituted an unconstitutional taking of the clients' property and what, if any, compensation might be due.

In 2003, the Supreme Court addressed these issues in *Brown v. Legal Foundation of Washington*,[8] a case examining the constitutionality of the State of Washington's IOLTA program. All nine justices agreed that the IOLTA program was equivalent to a physical, not regulatory, taking of client property.[9] They also agreed that the State of Washington had taken the property for a

---

Columbia receives interest on lawyer's trust fund accounts, and by 1976, interest income totaled over $2 million a year. *See In re Interest on Trust Accounts*, 356 So.2d 799, 804 (Fla. 1978).

[6] ABA Formal Opinion 348 (July 23, 1982). *See also* Rule 6.1, below.

[7] *Phillips v. Washington Legal Foundation*, 524 U.S. 156, 118 S.Ct. 1925, 141 L.Ed.2d 174 (1998).

[8] *Brown v. Legal Foundation of Washington*, 538 U.S. 216, 123 S.Ct. 1406, 155 L.Ed.2d 376 (2003). *See*

Ronald D. Rotunda, *Found Money: IOLTA, Brown v. Legal Foundation of Washington, and the Taking of Property without the Payment of Compensation*, 2002–2003 CATO SUPREME COURT REV. 245 (2003) (analyzing the IOLTA issue in general and criticizing the majority's analysis of just compensation).

[9] 538 U.S. at 235, 123 S.Ct. at 1419 ("As was made clear in *Phillips*, the interest earned in IOLTA accounts 'is the 'private property' of the owner of the principal.' ").

public purpose. The court, however, divided (5 to 4) on the issue of whether Washington owed just compensation to the clients who lost interest in IOLTA programs. The majority held that under the Washington IOLTA program, the clients suffered no net loss, and therefore the state program owed no compensation to the clients under the Takings Clause.

To the extent that states pattern their IOLTA statutes after the Washington State plan, one can presume that such plans will withstand future constitutional attack. These decisions are discussed in more detail in the discussion on pro bono activities of lawyers. At this time, lawyers must comply with IOLTA requirements as they have been held constitutional in the *Brown* decision.[10]

A study of state IOLTA programs finds that 37 jurisdictions have mandatory programs, 13 jurisdictions have programs that allow lawyers to opt out of IOLTA, and 2 jurisdictions (South Dakota and the Virgin Islands) have purely voluntary programs.[11]

---

[10]See further discussion of IOLTA plans in Rule 6.1. *See* Chapter 6.1.

[11]*See* http://www.abanet.org/legal services/iolta/ioltus.html.

CHAPTER 1.16
DECLINING OR TERMINATING REPRESENTATIONS

RULE 1.16: DECLINING OR TERMINATING REPRESENTATION

(a) Except as stated in paragraph (c), a lawyer shall not represent a client or, where representation has commenced, shall withdraw from the representation of a client if:

(1) the representation will result in violation of the rules of professional conduct or other law;

(2) the lawyer's physical or mental condition materially impairs the lawyer's ability to represent the client; or

(3) the lawyer is discharged.

(b) Except as stated in paragraph (c), a lawyer may withdraw from representing a client if:

(1) withdrawal can be accomplished without material adverse effect on the interests of the client;

(2) the client persists in a course of action involving the lawyer's services that the lawyer reasonably believes is criminal or fraudulent;

(3) the client has used the lawyer's services to perpetrate a crime or fraud;

(4) the client insists upon taking action that the lawyer considers repugnant or with which the lawyer has a fundamental disagreement;

(5) the client fails substantially to fulfill an obligation to the lawyer regarding the lawyer's services and has been given reasonable warning that the lawyer will withdraw unless the obligation is fulfilled;

(6) the representation will result in an unreasonable financial burden on the lawyer or has been rendered unreasonably difficult by the client; or

(7) other good cause for withdrawal exists.

(c) A lawyer must comply with applicable law requiring notice to or permission of a tribunal when terminating a representation. When ordered to do so by a tribunal, a lawyer shall continue representation notwithstanding good cause for terminating the representation.

(d) Upon termination of representation, a lawyer shall take steps to the extent reasonably practicable to protect a client's interests, such as giving reasonable notice to the client, allowing time for employment of other counsel, surrendering papers and property to which the client is entitled and refunding any advance payment of fee or expense that has not been earned or incurred. The lawyer may retain papers relating to the client to the extent permitted by other law.

Comment

[1] A lawyer should not accept representation in a matter unless it can be performed competently, promptly, without improper conflict of interest and to completion. Ordinarily, a representation in a matter is completed when the agreed-upon assistance has been concluded. See Rules 1.2(c) and 6.5. See also Rule 1.3, Comment [4].

Mandatory Withdrawal

[2] A lawyer ordinarily must decline or withdraw from representation if the client demands that the lawyer engage in conduct that is illegal or violates the Rules of Professional Conduct or other law. The lawyer is not obliged to decline or withdraw simply because the client suggests such a course of conduct; a client may make such a suggestion in the hope that a lawyer will not be constrained by a professional obligation.

[3] When a lawyer has been appointed to represent a client, withdrawal ordinarily requires approval of the appointing authority. See also Rule 6.2. Similarly, court approval or notice to the court is often required by applicable law before a lawyer withdraws from pending litigation. Difficulty may be encountered if withdrawal is based on the client's demand that the lawyer engage in unprofessional conduct. The court may request an explanation for the withdrawal, while the lawyer may be bound to keep confidential the facts that would constitute such an explanation. The lawyer's statement that professional considerations require termination of the representation ordinarily should be accepted as sufficient. Lawyers should be mindful of their obligations to both clients and the court under Rules 1.6 and 3.3.

Discharge

[4] A client has a right to discharge a lawyer at any time, with or without cause, subject to liability for payment for the lawyer's services. Where future dispute about the withdrawal may be anticipated, it may be advisable to prepare a written statement reciting the circumstances.

[5] Whether a client can discharge appointed counsel may depend on applicable law. A client seeking to do so should be given a full

explanation of the consequences. These consequences may include a decision by the appointing authority that appointment of successor counsel is unjustified, thus requiring self-representation by the client.

[6] If the client has severely diminished capacity, the client may lack the legal capacity to discharge the lawyer, and in any event the discharge may be seriously adverse to the client's interests. The lawyer should make special effort to help the client consider the consequences and may take reasonably necessary protective action as provided in Rule 1.14.

Optional Withdrawal

[7] A lawyer may withdraw from representation in some circumstances. The lawyer has the option to withdraw if it can be accomplished without material adverse effect on the client's interests. Withdrawal is also justified if the client persists in a course of action that the lawyer reasonably believes is criminal or fraudulent, for a lawyer is not required to be associated with such conduct even if the lawyer does not further it. Withdrawal is also permitted if the lawyer's services were misused in the past even if that would materially prejudice the client. The lawyer may also withdraw where the client insists on taking action that the lawyer considers repugnant or with which the lawyer has a fundamental disagreement.

[8] A lawyer may withdraw if the client refuses to abide by the terms of an agreement relating to the representation, such as an agreement concerning fees or court costs or an agreement limiting the objectives of the representation.

Assisting the Client upon Withdrawal

[9] Even if the lawyer has been unfairly discharged by the client, a lawyer must take all reasonable steps to mitigate the consequences to the client. The lawyer may retain papers as security for a fee only to the extent permitted by law. See Rule 1.15.

Authors' 1983 Model Rules Comparison

The drafters of the 2002 Rules amended Rule 1.16(b) by taking a phrase out of 1.16(b) text and putting it into subsection (b)(1). The 1983 version of Rule 1.16(b) contained the language that a lawyer could withdraw if withdrawal could be accomplished without material adverse effect on the client. The drafters thought it would be clearer to make that a basis under (b)(1) rather than in the lead-in text. They did not intend any change in meaning. *See* Reporter's Explanation of Changes to Model Rule 1.16. By adding a new (b)(1), the old (b)(1) through (b)(6) were renumbered to become (b)(2) through (b)(7).

The drafters modified the language of Rule 1.16(b)(4) to clarify and slightly expand its meaning. The 1983 provision used the words, "pursuing an objective" and the drafters replaced this with "taking action" that the lawyer considers to be repugnant. Lawyers should be able to withdraw when a client orders them to take action regardless of whether the action is an objective or some other aspect of the representation. The 1983 provision also used the word, "imprudent" and the drafters replaced this with "with which the lawyer has a fundamental disagreement." The new language is more precise as to why a lawyer may wish to withdraw under Rule 1.16(b)(4).

The drafters amended Rule 1.16(c) to add the first sentence reminding lawyers to comply with the rules of court when seeking to withdraw.

The drafters amended Rule 1.16(d) to refer to expenses that were not yet incurred as including the amounts that would need to be refunded to the client.

In Comment 1, the drafters added the last line and the cross references to the other Rules. This change defines the normal end to a representation and cites to the provisions that discuss the scope of a representation.

Comments 2, 4, 5, and 8 are identical to the 1983 version.

In Comment 3, the drafters added the second and last lines referring to court approval or notice and reminding lawyers of their obligations under Rule 1.6 and Rule 3.3. They also changed the word, "wish" to "request." No change in meaning was intended by these amendments. *See* Reporter's Explanation of Changes to Model Rule 1.16.

In Comment 6, the drafters changed the terminology to that used in current Rule 1.14 and they referred lawyers to that provision for guidance. The words, "is mentally incompetent" were changed to "has severely diminished capacity." Additional word changes were made to the last line in this Comment.

In Comment 7, the drafters changed the language to mirror the changes made in Rule 1.16(b)(4).

In Comment 9, the drafters deleted, on the ground that the sentence was ambiguous, the following line: "Whether or not a lawyer for an organization may under certain unusual circumstances have a legal obligation to the organization after withdrawing or being discharged by the organization's highest authority is beyond the scope of these Rules." A cross reference to Rule 1.15 was added.

Model Code Comparison

[1] With regard to paragraph (a), DR 2-109(A) provided that a lawyer "shall not accept employment . . . if he knows or it is obvious that [the prospective client] wishes to . . . [b]ring a legal action . . . or otherwise have steps taken for him, merely for the purpose of harassing or maliciously injuring any person. . . ." Nor may a lawyer accept employment if the lawyer is aware that the prospective client wishes to "[p]resent a claim or defense . . . that is not warranted under existing law, unless it can be supported by good faith argument for an extension, modification, or reversal of existing law." DR 2-110(B) provided that a lawyer "shall withdraw from employment . . . . if:

"(1) He knows or it is obvious that his client is bringing the legal action . . . or is otherwise having steps taken for him, merely for the purpose of harassing or maliciously injuring any person.

"(2) He knows or it is obvious that his continued employment will result in violation of a Disciplinary Rule.

"(3) His mental or physical condition renders it unreasonably difficult for him to carry out the employment effectively.

"(4) He is discharged by his client."

[2] With regard to paragraph (b), DR 2-110(C) permitted withdrawal regardless of the effect on the client if:

"(1) His client: (a) Insists upon presenting a claim or defense that is not warranted under existing law and cannot be supported by good faith argument for an extension, modification, or reversal of existing law; (b) Personally seeks to pursue an illegal course of conduct; (c) Insists that the lawyer pursue a course of conduct that is illegal or that is prohibited under the Disciplinary Rules; (d) By other conduct renders it unreasonably difficult for the lawyer to carry out his employment effectively; (e) Insists, in a matter not pending before a tribunal, that the lawyer engage in conduct that is contrary to the judgment and advice of the lawyer but not prohibited under the Disciplinary Rules; (f) Deliberately disregards an agreement or obligation to the lawyer as to expenses and fees.

"(2) His continued employment is likely to result in a violation of a Disciplinary Rule.

"(3) His inability to work with co-counsel indicates that the best interest of the client likely will be served by withdrawal.

"(4) His mental or physical condition renders it difficult for him to carry out the employment effectively.

"(5) His client knowingly and freely assents to termination of his employment.

"(6) He believes in good faith, in a proceeding pending before a tribunal, that the tribunal will find the existence of other good cause for withdrawal."

[3] With regard to paragraph (c), DR 2-110(A)(1) provided: "If permission for withdrawal from employment is required by the rules of a tribunal, the lawyer shall not withdraw . . . without its permission."

[4] The provisions of paragraph (d) are substantially identical to DR 2-110(A)(2) and (3).

§ 1.16–1 ACCEPTING A CASE

The English barrister, like a cab driver, is bound to respond to the first hail. In contrast, the American lawyer is not obligated to accept every client who walks through the door. However, if the court appoints a lawyer to a case, it is unethical for the lawyer to reject that appointment for the wrong reason: the lawyer may not reject an appointed case because the client or the cause is unpopular.[1]

Sometimes, the ethics rules do not allow a lawyer to accept a

---

[Section 1.16–1]

[1]EC 2-27 states that a lawyer "should not decline representation because a client or cause is unpopular or community reaction is adverse." *See also* EC 2-28, 2-29, 2-30.

Rule 6.2 states that a lawyer "shall not seek to avoid appointment

case. For example, a lawyer may not accept a case if doing so will violate a disciplinary rule or other law, or if the lawyer cannot perform prompt and competent service.[2]

§ 1.16–2 TERMINATING REPRESENTATION

§ 1.16–2(a) Overriding Principles

The rules regarding withdrawal are more complex than the rules regarding accepting a case. One must first keep in mind several overriding principles.[1]

First, if a matter is before a tribunal, the lawyer must follow that tribunal's rules, which typically require securing the tribunal's permission before withdrawing.[2] If the tribunal does not grant permission, the lawyer must continue in the case even though the lawyer would otherwise have a right, or duty, to withdraw.[3] If the tribunal asks the lawyer why he is seeking withdrawal, the lawyer's duty to keep client confidences may

---

by a tribunal to represent a person except for good cause, such as. . . ."

On the English "Taxicab Rule" for barristers, see W.W. BOULTON, A GUIDE TO CONDUCT AND ETIQUETTE AT THE BAR OF ENGLAND AND WALES 17–33 (4th ed. 1965). This "Taxicab Rule" does not apply to solicitors.

[2]Rule 1.16(a)(1), (2), Rule 1.16, Comment 1; EC 2-30.

Sex Discrimination When a Law Firm Refuses to Represent a Man? The general rule in all U.S. jurisdictions has been that a lawyer is not legally required to represent any client, except perhaps when appointed by a court to do so. However, in *Stropnicky v. Nathanson*, 1999 WL 33453078 (M.C.A.D.1999), *aff'd* 2003 WL 22480688 (Mass.Super.2003), the Massachusetts Commission Against Discrimination found that a law firm that specialized in representing women in divorce cases violated the state's antidiscrimination law by refusing to represent a man in such a case. This case raises many questions. The lawyers refusing to accept the male may claim a first amendment right of association. If the law forced the law firm to accept the man, the male may not really want to be represented because of the fear that the law firm may not perform satisfactorily but not so unsatisfactory that there is

legal malpractice. And, even if one could prove malpractice, the male client may just wish to hire a law firm, not "buy a second law suit." And, the law firm that refuses to accept males may feel so strongly about that issue that the lawyers do not believe that they can perform competent service, which means, under the ethics rules, that they cannot accept the case even if the state's antidiscrimination law says that they should.

See Symposium, A Duty to Represent? Critical Reflections on Stropnicky v. Nathanson, 20 WEST. NEW ENG. L. REV. 5 (1998); Steve Berenson, *Politics and Plurality in a Lawyer's Choice of Clients: the Case of Stropnicky v. Nathanson*, 35 SAN DIEGO L. REV. 1 (1998).

[Section 1.16–2]

[1]*See generally* Restatement of the Law Governing Lawyers §§ 31 to 33 (Ending Client-Lawyer Relationship) (Official Draft 2000).

[2]The drafters to the 2002 Rules made several changes to reflect the fact that some courts only require notice to the court, not permission. The lawyer is obligated to follow the procedures of the applicable court. Rule 1.16(c).

[3]Rule 1.16(c); DR 2-110(A)(1).

E.g., Hasbro, Inc. v. Serafino,

prevent the lawyer from responding.[4] (However, the confidentiality rules do not prevent the attorney from filing a "notice of the fact of withdrawal" and withdrawing or disaffirming any opinion, document, affirmation, or the like.) If the client discharges the lawyer and the tribunal does not permit the lawyer to withdraw, the lawyer must comply with the orders of the tribunal.[5]

If the matter is before a tribunal, that tribunal may simply refuse to allow the lawyer to withdraw. For example, in *Haines v. Liggett Group, Inc.*,[6] plaintiff's lawyer moved to withdraw in tobacco litigation on the grounds that the firm could no longer absorb the cost of financing the litigation. The judge, relying on Rule 1.16(c), denied the request, noting that unprofitability is an inherent risk of contingent fee litigation; the law firm cannot walk away from its contract because the case may not generate the return initially predicted.

Second (assuming that the matter is not before a tribunal or that, if it is, the tribunal agrees), the client always "has a right to discharge a lawyer at any time, with or without cause, subject to liability for payment of the lawyer's services."[7] In such a case, if the client fires the lawyer, the lawyer must withdraw.[8]

Agency law recognizes the concept of a "power coupled with an interest." An example of such a power is the lender's power to sell the house when the mortgagor defaults.[9] A principal, under the Law of Agency, can normally fire his agent at will, but he cannot fire, at will, an agent who has a power coupled with an interest. But lawyers are not agents with a power coupled with an interest. No lawyer can continue to represent a client who does not wish to be represented.[10] The lawyer cannot even use his

---

966 F.Supp. 108, 110 (D. Mass. 1997), holding that the clients' failure to pay attorney fees of approximately $97,000 did not entitle attorneys and law firm to withdraw as counsel because the lawyers' withdrawal would require the clients to either immediately retain substitute counsel or accept default judgments, and court's own interest would be ill served by permitting counsel to withdraw without substitute counsel.

V.H. v. J.P.H., 62 Mass.App.Ct. 910, 815 N.E.2d 1096 (Mass.App.Ct. 2004), holding that the trial judge did not abuse his discretion in declining to allow the lawyer to withdraw as counsel in a tort action due to the client's failure to pay the lawyer's bill. The trial court noted that the case had

been pending for three years and that it would be extremely difficult for another lawyer to prepare for final discovery and for the trial in a relatively short period of time.

[4]Rule 1.16, Comment 3.

[5]*Compare* Rule 1.16(a), *with* Rule 1.16(c).

[6]*Haines v. Liggett Group, Inc.*, 814 F.Supp. 414 (D.N.J.1993).

[7]Rule 1.16, Comment 4.

[8]DR 2-110(B)(4); Rule 1.16(a)(3).

[9]*See, e.g.*, SELL ON AGENCY § 229 (Foundation Press, 1975).

[10]ABA Informal Opinion 1397 (Aug. 31, 1977). *See also* Rule 1.16, Comment 4.

contingent fee arrangement to prevent the client from discharging him.[11]

The client's normal power to discharge an attorney does not apply to situations controlled by other law. For example, a statute may grant a term of office to a government attorney who cannot be fired except for cause.[12]

Third, the lawyer must make reasonable efforts to protect the client's interests, such as giving reasonable notice to the client, and surrendering any papers and property to which the client is entitled.[13] This duty exists not only when the attorney resigns but also when he or she is discharged.[14]

The client who discharges the lawyer is still liable for any fees earned, or for other contractual or quasi-contractual damages.[15] And, the lawyer must return any fee or cost deposit advances not yet earned or incurred.[16]

§ 1.16–2(b) Mandatory and Permissive Withdrawal

Given these general, overriding principles, the Model Rules—like its predecessor, the Model Code—divide withdrawal into two basic types: mandatory and permissive withdrawal. Both permissive withdrawal and mandatory withdrawal are subject to the three transcending principles discussed above.

§ 1.16–2(b)(1) Mandatory Withdrawal

The lawyer *must* withdraw from a case: (1) if continued employment would result in violating the disciplinary rules or other law; (2) if the lawyer's physical or mental condition results in a material adverse impact on the client; or (3) if the client discharges the attorney.[17] The Rules provide that the lawyer may withdraw without any reason if doing so has no material adverse effect on the client.[18] The Code had no such provision, but prior case law has recognized this right of an attorney, like any other agent.[19]

---

[11]ABA Informal Opinion 1397 (Aug. 31, 1977). *Cf.* DR 5-103(A); Rule 1.8(j) (lawyer may not acquire a proprietary interest in client's cause of action). *See Richette v. Solomon*, 410 Pa. 6, 18–19, 187 A.2d 910, 917 (1963) (clause in retainer agreement prohibiting lawyer discharge is void).

[12]*Pillsbury v. Board of Chosen Freeholders of Monmouth County*, 140 N.J.Super. 410, 356 A.2d 424 (1976) (per curiam), *affirming*, 133 N.J.Super. 526, 337 A.2d 632 (1975).

[13]Rule 1.16(d). *Accord* DR 2-110(A)(2).

[14]*See, e.g., Dayton Bar Association v. Weiner*, 40 Ohio St.2d 7, 317 N.E.2d 783 (1974), *cert. denied*, 420 U.S. 976, 95 S.Ct. 1400, 43 L.Ed.2d 656 (1975).

[15]Rule 1.16(a)(3); Rule 1.16, Comment 4; DR 2-110(A)(3). *See, e.g., Carlson v. Nopal Lines*, 460 F.2d 1209 (5th Cir.1972).

[16]Rule 1.16(d). DR 2-110(A)(3).

[17]Rule 1.16(b). DR 2-110(B).

[18]Rule 1.16(b)(1).

[19]*E.g., Sterling v. Jones*, 255 La. 842, 846, 233 So.2d 537, 539 (1970).

§ 1.16–2(b)(2) Permissive Withdrawal

The Model Rules differ from the Model Code, but the differences are more in detail than in focus. Subject to the three overriding principles discussed above, the Model Rules *permit* withdrawal in all cases where the lawyer can accomplish withdrawal without material adverse effect on the client.[20] The lawyer also may withdraw (even if it causes material adverse impact to the client) on the following basis of good cause: (1) the client persists in using the lawyer's services in an action that the lawyer reasonably believes is a crime or fraud; (2) the client has used the lawyer to perpetrate a past crime or fraud; (3) the client insists on conduct the lawyer believes is repugnant or with which the lawyer has a fundamental disagreement (even though it is not illegal);[21] (4) the client fails substantially to fulfill an obligation to the lawyer and the client has been given reasonable warning that the lawyer will seek to withdraw; or (5) the client has made representation unreasonably difficult.[22]

The Rules add a seventh catch-all—when "other good cause" exists. This catch-all is not limited to cases where the *tribunal* finds good cause.[23] The Rules also add an entirely new reason that was not found anywhere in the Model Code: the lawyer may withdraw when "the representation will result in an unreasonable financial burden on the lawyer . . . ."[24]

Although the lawyer now has many circumstances where she may withdraw, there still are limits. If the lawyer withdraws from representation improperly—in violation of the ethics rules—she is subject to discipline.

In addition, the court may impose other remedies. Consider, for example, *Bell & Marra v. Sullivan.*[25] In that case, the client refused to settle on terms the lawyer thought wise and also refused to sign a new fee agreement. The firm, which had a contingency fee agreement, then withdrew from the representation. After new lawyers successfully concluded the

---

The ABA Model Code explicitly provided that the lawyer may withdraw if the lawyer and client freely assent to the termination. DR 2-110(C)(5). The Model Code allowed withdrawal if: the client insisted on presenting a frivolous claim, or the client insisted on pursuing an illegal course of conduct, or the client insisted that the lawyer violate the law or disciplinary rules, or the client made it unreasonably difficult for the lawyer to perform effectively, or the client insisted (in a matter not in litigation) that the lawyer engage in conduct of which the lawyer disapproves, or the client refused to pay the lawyer's fees or disbursements. DR 2-110(C)(1).

[20] Rule 1.16(b)(1).

[21] Rule 1.16(b)(4). *Cf.* DR 2-110(C)(1)(a); DR 7-101(B)(2).

[22] Rule 1.16(b)(2) to (6).

[23] *Compare* DR 2-110(C)(6), *with* Rule 1.16(b)(7).

[24] Rule 1.16(b)(6).

[25] *Bell & Marra v. Sullivan*, 300 Mont. 530, 6 P.3d 965 (2000).

case for the client, the first firm asserted an attorneys' lien. The court found that the law firm did not have good cause to withdraw based on its claim of financial burdens caused by the unanticipated length of the case and appeals. This unjustified withdrawal from the matter forfeited the firm's right to any of the ultimate fee. The court reversed the lower court that had awarded *quantum meruit* fees for the underlying action and fees for prosecuting the lien foreclosure. The firm received *no* fee.

§ 1.16–2(b)(3) Proportionality and Permissive Withdrawal

The Model Rules provide that the lawyer may withdraw for no reason, "if withdrawal can be accomplished without *material adverse* effect on the interests of the client."[26] This provision, not found in the Model Code, certainly appears to authorize the lawyer to decide simply to take a hike, and the client cannot stop that action, unless the lawyer's withdrawal would harm the client and that harm would be material.

The Restatement the Law Governing Lawyers rejects that view, for the uncomplicated reason that it appears to violate the lawyer's fiduciary obligation to her client. The Restatement proposes a proportionality test. In light of the fiduciary nature of the lawyer-client relationship in instances of permissive withdrawal if there is significant disproportion between the effect on the lawyer of the client's offensive actions or other sources of the difficulty and the effect on the client that the lawyer's withdrawal would cause, the lawyer may not withdraw.[27]

The Reporter's Note to this section acknowledges that the states have "widely adopted" the proposition that lawyers can "permissively withdraw on the ground of no material adverse effect on the client."[28] The Restatement candidly concedes that it has found no authority to support its argument for proportionality as a limit on permissive withdrawal.[29] Nonetheless, it argues that the harm to the client should not be disproportionate to the justification for the lawyer's withdrawal based on general fiduciary principles. In light of this reasoning, a lawyer relying on the plain language of Rule 1.16(b) may be unpleasantly surprised

---

[26]Rule 1.16(b) (emphasis added).

[27]Restatement of the Law Governing Lawyers, Third, § 32(4), and Comment *h(i)* (Official Draft 2000).

[28]Restatement of the Law Governing Lawyers, Third, § 30, Reporter's Note to Comment *h(ii)* (Official Draft 2000).

Breach of Contract and Nominal Damages. This Comment notes that a lawyer's withdrawal in the absence of material adverse effects on the client may constitute breach of contract, but the fact that there are no material adverse effects should mean that any damages flowing from this breach would be nominal. *Id.*

[29]Restatement of the Law Governing Lawyers, Third, § 32, Reporter's Note to Comment *h(i)* (Official Draft 2000).

if the court is persuaded by the Restatement's position regarding proportionality.

§ 1.16–2(b)(4) The Client Fires the Lawyer

The client may exercise control over the client-lawyer relationship by simply terminating it. That is, the client can always fire the lawyer, who then must withdraw, even if the client seeks to terminate the lawyer for a less than noble reason.[30] For example, if the client decides to fire the lawyer for an illegal reason (because, *e.g.*, the lawyer has hired a law associate who is a member of a racial minority, or because the lawyer adheres to a different religious faith than the client), the lawyer still has no right to prevent the client from terminating the representation, but that does not mean that the client might not be liable for damages, for wrongful discharge, a topic to which we now turn.[31]

§ 1.16–3 WRONGFUL DISCHARGE

In recent years, attorneys have brought wrongful discharge suits after being fired by their employers (typically lawyers working as in-house counsel) or by their law firm (typically lawyers working as associates)[1] for refusal to engage in unethical activity. These plaintiffs usually are employees at will. The courts have split on whether to allow this cause of action, but the trend favors it.[2] The fact that a client or a law firm has the right to fire an at-

---

[30]Rule 1.16(a)(3); DR 2-110(B)(4).

[31]Civil rights statutes may also impose sanctions on the client for racial or other forbidden discrimination.

[Section 1.16–3]

[1]On the question of discharge rights of inside counsel, see Rachel S. Arnow Richman, *A Cause Worth Quitting For? The Conflict Between Professional Ethics and Individual Rights in Discriminatory Treatment of Corporate Counsel*, 75 IND. L.J. 963 (2000). Professor Arnow Richmond discusses the literature, the case law, the Model Rules, and Title VII of the Civil Rights Act, and argues that present law fails to account for in-house counsel's legitimate need for job protection where she is treated as much as an employee as a lawyer.

[2]See Wieder v. Skala, 80 N.Y.2d 628, 593 N.Y.S.2d 752, 609 N.E.2d 105 (1992) (lawyer who alleges that he was

discharged from law firm because he insisted that his firm comply with its ethical obligation to report a fellow associate to the state bar disciplinary authorities has a cause of action for breach of contract; the duty to comply with the state bar's ethical rules is an implied-in-law condition of the employment contract). *See also Nordling v. Northern States Power Co.*, 478 N.W.2d 498 (Minn.1991); *General Dynamics v. Superior Court*, 7 Cal.4th 1164, 32 Cal.Rptr.2d 1, 876 P.2d 487 (Cal. 1994). *Accord* Oregon State Ethics Committee Opinion 1994-136 (1994) (lawyer, in action for wrongful discharge, may reveal employer's secrets—lawyer claimed he was fired for failure to file a patent for his employer for invention that the employer's customer had really invented—to the extent necessary to establish wrongful discharge).

See generally Kenneth J. Wilbur, *Wrongful Discharge of Attorneys: A Cause of Action to Further Professional*

torney for no reason does not imply a right to fire for the wrong reason.

The Model Rules do not prohibit a lawyer from suing her former client and employer for wrongful discharge, but the lawyer must take care not to disclose client information beyond that information the lawyer reasonably believes is necessary to establish her claim.[3]

The typical defendants in these suits are either law firms (which do not have a client relationship with the lawyers that they employ) or corporations (which hire in-house counsel, so the corporations are both clients and employers). The general rule is that clients have the legal power to fire their counsel at any time, with or without cause.[4] Hence, the remedy for wrongful discharge for those jurisdictions that recognize this tort would not be reinstatement but damages. In other words, the court will not normally order the client/employer to retain the wrongfully discharged lawyer but rather the court will order the client to pay damages for the wrongful discharge of that lawyer. This remedy respects the various interests involved. The client "can" fire, *i.e.*, has the power to fire, the lawyer for no reason. But the lawyer has a cause of action for damages if the discharge has been for the wrong reason.

In addition to lawyers having claims against their employer-clients for wrongful discharge, they also may have claims against their law firms. Although courts often say that clients retain an unreviewable right to discharge their lawyers for no reason—a

---

Responsibility, 92 DICKINSON. L.REV. 777 (1988).

Illinois has been the major jurisdiction unfriendly to a cause of action for wrongful discharge if an employer-client (or a law firm) wrongly discharges a lawyer. *Herbster v. North American Co. for Life & Health Insurance*, 150 Ill.App.3d 21, 103 Ill.Dec. 322, 501 N.E.2d 343 (1986)(no cause of action for chief legal officer of corporation fired because he had refused to destroy or remove documents that were subject to a discovery order in federal court and that tended to show the company's fraud in the sale of annuities); *Balla v. Gambro*, 145 Ill.2d 492, 164 Ill.Dec. 892, 584 N.E.2d 104, 16 A.L.R.5th 1000 (1991) (no cause of action for lawyer who refused to follow the client's order to destroy evidence that kidney dialysis devices were faulty; client was a corporation and

the lawyer was the in-house counsel).

The Illinois decisions have not been persuasive in other states, which have either declined to follow or explicitly rejected them. *See, e.g., General Dynamics Corp. v. Superior Court*, 7 Cal.4th 1164, 32 Cal.Rptr.2d 1, 876 P.2d 487 (1994)(declined to follow *Balla*); *GTE Products Corp. v. Stewart*, 421 Mass. 22, 653 N.E.2d 161 (1995) (declined to follow *Balla*); *Willy v. Coastal States Management Co.*, 939 S.W.2d 193 (Tex.App.-Houston (1 Dist.), 1996), writ granted (Sep 04, 1997), writ denied (Jul 14, 1998) (disagreed with *Balla*); *Kachmar v. SunGard Data Systems, Inc.*, 109 F.3d 173 (3d Cir.1997) (declined to follow *Balla*).

[3]ABA Formal Opinion 01-424 (Sept. 22, 2001).

[4]Rule 1.16, Comment 4.

right that the common law or modern statutes may modify, as discussed above—law firms that employ lawyers as partners or associates do not have the same right. The law firm or similar legal organization does not the rights of a client but only the rights of an employer.[5]

In the cases thus far, all of the defendants are either law firms (which do not have the rights of clients) or corporations (or other entities) that hire lawyers to represent them. We do not have a case yet where a client fires its law firm for an improper reason. For example, assume that a client (an individual, or an entity) hires a law firm and then fires that law firm for an *improper* reason, *e.g.*, the lawyer's law firm hired a minority lawyer, or the law firm complied with its mandatory duties under Rule 3.3 to expose client perjury. There is no case yet ruling on the question of whether this type of client must pay the law firm damages for wrongful discharge.

---

[5]Law firms have certain responsibilities towards their employees and subordinate lawyers, an issue discussed more fully in connection with the analysis of Rule 5.1 ("Responsibilities of a Partner or Supervisory Lawyer"), Rule 5.2 ("Responsibilities of a Subordinate Lawyer"), and Rule 5.6 ("Restrictions on Right to Practice"). These responsibilities impose duties on the law firm to restrain and train these employees.

CHAPTER 1.17

SALE OF A LAW PRACTICE

§ 1.17–1 Selling a Law Practice
§ 1.17–2 The Disposition of Client Files and Property When a
　　　　　Sole Practitioner Dies

RULE 1.17: SALE OF LAW PRACTICE

A lawyer or a law firm may sell or purchase a law practice, or an area of law practice, including good will, if the following conditions are satisfied:

(a) The seller ceases to engage in the private practice of law, or in the area of practice that has been sold, [in the geographic area] [in the jurisdiction] (a jurisdiction may elect either version) in which the practice has been conducted;

(b) The entire practice, or the entire area of practice, is sold to one or more lawyers or law firms;

(c) The seller gives written notice to each of the seller's clients regarding:

(1) the proposed sale;

(2) the client's right to retain other counsel or to take possession of the file; and

(3) the fact that the client's consent to the transfer of the client's files will be presumed if the client does not take any action or does not otherwise object within ninety (90) days of receipt of the notice.

If a client cannot be given notice, the representation of that client may be transferred to the purchaser only upon entry of an order so authorizing by a court having jurisdiction. The seller may disclose to the court in camera information relating to the representation only to the extent necessary to obtain an order authorizing the transfer of a file.

(d) The fees charged clients shall not be increased by reason of the sale.

Comment

[1] The practice of law is a profession, not merely a business. Clients are not commodities that can be purchased and sold at will. Pursuant to this Rule, when a lawyer or an entire firm ceases to practice,

or ceases to practice in an area of law, and other lawyers or firms
take over the representation, the selling lawyer or firm may obtain
compensation for the reasonable value of the practice as may
withdrawing partners of law firms. See Rules 5.4 and 5.6.

Termination of Practice by the Seller
[2] The requirement that all of the private practice, or all of an area
of practice, be sold is satisfied if the seller in good faith makes the
entire practice, or the area of practice, available for sale to the
purchasers. The fact that a number of the seller's clients decide not
to be represented by the purchasers but take their matters
elsewhere, therefore, does not result in a violation. Return to private
practice as a result of an unanticipated change in circumstances
does not necessarily result in a violation. For example, a lawyer
who has sold the practice to accept an appointment to judicial office
does not violate the requirement that the sale be attendant to ces-
sation of practice if the lawyer later resumes private practice upon
being defeated in a contested or a retention election for the office or
resigns from a judiciary position.
[3] The requirement that the seller cease to engage in the private
practice of law does not prohibit employment as a lawyer on the
staff of a public agency or a legal services entity that provides legal
services to the poor, or as in-house counsel to a business.
[4] The Rule permits a sale of an entire practice attendant upon
retirement from the private practice of law within the jurisdiction.
Its provisions, therefore, accommodate the lawyer who sells the
practice on the occasion of moving to another state. Some states are
so large that a move from one locale therein to another is tanta-
mount to leaving the jurisdiction in which the lawyer has engaged
in the practice of law. To also accommodate lawyers so situated,
states may permit the sale of the practice when the lawyer leaves
the geographical area rather than the jurisdiction. The alternative
desired should be indicated by selecting one of the two provided for
in Rule 1.17(a).
[5] This Rule also permits a lawyer or law firm to sell an area of
practice. If an area of practice is sold and the lawyer remains in the
active practice of law, the lawyer must cease accepting any matters
in the area of practice that has been sold, either as counsel or co-
counsel or by assuming joint responsibility for a matter in connection with the division of a fee with another lawyer as would
otherwise be permitted by Rule 1.5(e). For example, a lawyer with a
substantial number of estate planning matters and a substantial
number of probate administration cases may sell the estate planning portion of the practice but remain in the practice of law by
concentrating on probate administration; however, that practitioner
may not thereafter accept any estate planning matters. Although a
lawyer who leaves a jurisdiction or geographical area typically
would sell the entire practice, this Rule permits the lawyer to limit
the sale to one or more areas of the practice, thereby preserving the
lawyer's right to continue practice in the areas of the practice that
were not sold.

Sale of Entire Practice or Entire Area of Practice
[6] The Rule requires that the seller's entire practice, or an entire

area of practice, be sold. The prohibition against sale of less than an entire practice area protects those clients whose matters are less lucrative and who might find it difficult to secure other counsel if a sale could be limited to substantial fee-generating matters. The purchasers are required to undertake all client matters in the practice or practice area, subject to client consent. This requirement is satisfied, however, even if a purchaser is unable to undertake a particular client matter because of a conflict of interest.

Client Confidences, Consent and Notice

[7] Negotiations between seller and prospective purchaser prior to disclosure of information relating to a specific representation of an identifiable client no more violate the confidentiality provisions of Model Rule 1.6 than do preliminary discussions concerning the possible association of another lawyer or mergers between firms, with respect to which client consent is not required. Providing the purchaser access to client-specific information relating to the representation and to the file, however, requires client consent. The Rule provides that before such information can be disclosed by the seller to the purchaser the client must be given actual written notice of the contemplated sale, including the identity of the purchaser, and must be told that the decision to consent or make other arrangements must be made within 90 days. If nothing is heard from the client within that time, consent to the sale is presumed.

[8] A lawyer or law firm ceasing to practice cannot be required to remain in practice because some clients cannot be given actual notice of the proposed purchase. Since these clients cannot themselves consent to the purchase or direct any other disposition of their files, the Rule requires an order from a court having jurisdiction authorizing their transfer or other disposition. The Court can be expected to determine whether reasonable efforts to locate the client have been exhausted, and whether the absent client's legitimate interests will be served by authorizing the transfer of the file so that the purchaser may continue the representation. Preservation of client confidences requires that the petition for a court order be considered in camera. (A procedure by which such an order can be obtained needs to be established in jurisdictions in which it presently does not exist).

[9] All elements of client autonomy, including the client's absolute right to discharge a lawyer and transfer the representation to another, survive the sale of the practice or area of practice.

Fee Arrangements Between Client and Purchaser

[10] The sale may not be financed by increases in fees charged the clients of the practice. Existing arrangements between the seller and the client as to fees and the scope of the work must be honored by the purchaser.

Other Applicable Ethical Standards

[11] Lawyers participating in the sale of a law practice or a practice area are subject to the ethical standards applicable to involving another lawyer in the representation of a client. These include, for example, the seller's obligation to exercise competence in identifying a purchaser qualified to assume the practice and the purchaser's

obligation to undertake the representation competently (see Rule 1.1); the obligation to avoid disqualifying conflicts, and to secure the client's informed consent for those conflicts that can be agreed to (see Rule 1.7 regarding conflicts and Rule 1.0(e) for the definition of informed consent); and the obligation to protect information relating to the representation (see Rules 1.6 and 1.9).

[12] If approval of the substitution of the purchasing lawyer for the selling lawyer is required by the rules of any tribunal in which a matter is pending, such approval must be obtained before the matter can be included in the sale (see Rule 1.16).

Applicability of the Rule

[13] This Rule applies to the sale of a law practice of a deceased, disabled or disappeared lawyer. Thus, the seller may be represented by a non-lawyer representative not subject to these Rules. Since, however, no lawyer may participate in a sale of a law practice which does not conform to the requirements of this Rule, the representatives of the seller as well as the purchasing lawyer can be expected to see to it that they are met.

[14] Admission to or retirement from a law partnership or professional association, retirement plans and similar arrangements, and a sale of tangible assets of a law practice, do not constitute a sale or purchase governed by this Rule.

[15] This Rule does not apply to the transfers of legal representation between lawyers when such transfers are unrelated to the sale of a practice or an area of practice.

Authors' 1983 Model Rules Comparison

The 1983 Rules did not contain a Rule 1.17. In 1990, the ABA adopted Rule 1.17 to regulate the sale of a law practice.

The ABA made several changes in Rule 1.17 in 2002, based upon an evaluation of this practice in the various states. The major change is that a lawyer now may sell an entire area of practice rather than the entire practice.

The text of Rule 1.17 and section (a) were amended to refer to the sale of an area of practice.

Rule 1.17(b) was amended to make clear that an entire area of practice may be sold to one or more lawyers or law firms.

In Rule 1.17(c), the drafters made it clear that the seller must give notice to the clients of the sale. Subsection (c)(2) was deleted; this was a reference to section (d) which addressed the topic whether the fee could be increased to the clients. Subsections (c)(3) and (c)(4) were renumbered as (c)(2) and (c)(3).

In Rule 1.17(d), the ABA deleted the following statement: "The purchaser may, however, refuse to undertake the representation unless the client consents to pay the purchaser fees at a rate not exceeding the fees charged by the purchaser for rendering substantially similar services prior to the initiation of the purchase negotiations." Lawyers had used this statement to demand higher fees or else the client would be dropped and the ABA thought this result was improper.

In Comment 1, the ABA modified the language to permit a lawyer to cease an entire area of practice that is then taken over by one or more lawyers or law firms.

In Comment 2, the ABA amended the language to add the sale of all of an area of practice. It also amended the language relating to a lawyer's return to practice. The words, "does not necessarily" were added to describe whether a change in circumstances that resulted in a lawyer to return to practice would violate this Rule. At the end of the Comment, the ABA added a resignation from a judicial position as a change in circumstances that would permit a lawyer to return to practice.

Comment 3 was not amended.

In Comment 4, the ABA made a minor change adding sale of an entire practice to the first sentence.

Comment 5 is new and describes in detail the manner in which a lawyer may sell an area of practice.

Old Comment 5 was renumbered as Comment 6 and amended to reflect that a practice or area of practice could be sold to more than one purchaser.

Old Comment 6 was renumbered as Comment 7 and amended to remove the following phrase: "and any proposed change in the terms of the future representation." This was removed as Rule 1.17(d) was modified to remove the possibility of increasing the fee.

Old Comment 7 was renumbered as Comment 8 and it was not modified.

Old Comment 8 was renumbered as Comment 9 and a reference to sale of an area of practice was added.

Comment 9 was amended to remove the discussion of the old Rule 1.17(d), which permitted a purchasing lawyer to increase the fee. This practice is no longer permitted.

Old Comment 10 was deleted because it discussed the fact that lawyers should not intentionally fragment a practice so as to sell it under the old Rule.

Old Comment 11 was amended to add an area or practice and to make clear the need of the purchaser lawyer to satisfy Rule 1.7 (conflicts of interest) and informed consent.

Comment 12, 13, and 14 were not amended.

In Comment 15, the ABA added a phrase dealing with the sale of an area of practice.

Model Code Comparison

There was no counterpart to this Rule in the Model Code.

§ 1.17–1 SELLING A LAW PRACTICE

The Model Code prohibited a lawyer from "selling" the law practice[1] because "clients are not merchandise."[2] However, this same Code did not concern itself with division of fees among

---

[Section 1.17–1]

[1] EC 4-6.

[2] ABA Formal Opinion 266 (June 2, 1945).

lawyers within the same firm.[3] Thus, a firm could always add another lawyer as a partner in the firm, and have that new partner purchase equity in the firm. This equity typically included not only the cost of physical assets like law books and desks, but also "good will," that is, the expectation of continued business.

In effect, this arrangement allowed lawyers to sell a law practice when a law partnership accepted new members into the partnership. Thus, under the Model Code there was a disparity of treatment between lawyers practicing in a partnership compared to sole practitioners, who were forbidden from selling "good will,"[4] and law firms who were not. Because of this difference in treatment, efforts were made to change the rules regarding sale of a law practice.

California initially responded to such concerns by adopting a new rule allowing for the sale of a law practice by a living lawyer or the estate of a deceased lawyer.[5] The California State Bar urged the ABA to adopt a similar rule, and it did so in February 1990, when it added Rule 1.17, "Sale of Law Practice." The purpose of this Rule is to allow "solo practitioners to sell their practice in much the same way as withdrawing or retiring partners and shareholders in firms, in effect, do when the firm pays for their interest in the practice with future installment payments or agrees to continue the salary and benefits for a period of time without requiring the withdrawing or retiring attorney to perform any services."[6]

Rule 1.17 begins by reaffirming that: "[c]lients are not commodities that can be purchased and sold at will."[7] The remainder of the Rule explains the proper way to sell the law practice as a going concern. The 1990 version of Rule 1.17 required that a lawyer sell his or her entire practice to one lawyer or law firm.

The reason this Rule prohibits piecemeal sale of a practice was to protect clients "whose matters are less lucrative and who might find it difficult to secure other counsel if the sale could be limited to substantial fee-generating matters."[8] Rule 1.17 was drafted to force the purchaser to subsidize those clients with less lucrative cases, including clients with lawsuits that the purchaser candidly calculated should not have been brought to begin with. The prohibition against the piecemeal purchase of a practice would encourage the purchaser to avoid accepting the clients with the

---

[3]DR 2-107.

[4]*See O'Hara v. Ahlgren, Blumenfeld & Kempster*, 127 Ill.2d 333, 130 Ill.Dec. 401, 537 N.E.2d 730 (1989), holding that a sole practitioner may not sell good will.

[5]Rule 2-300, California Rules of

Professional Conduct.

[6]*Norton Frickey, P.C. v. James B. Turner, P.C.*, 94 P.3d 1266, 1270 (Colo.App.,2004).

[7]Rule 1.17, Comment 1.

[8]1990 Model Rule 1.17, Comment 6.

less lucrative cases by trying to raise their fees. To deal with this problem, Rule 1.17(d) prohibits raising any fees because of the sale. These restrictions were intended to prevent the seller from financing the sale by increasing the new clients' fees.

The 2002 Rules do not allow the purchasing lawyer to buy only a particular case or particular cases, but the revised Rule does permit a lawyer to sell either the entire practice *or* an entire *area of practice* to one or more lawyers or law firms. After much debate, the drafters endorsed a provision that relaxed the entire practice and one buyer requirements. They did so because "the present requirement was unduly restrictive and potentially disserves clients."[9] Many lawyers argued for an ability to sell an area of practice when they wanted to downsize their practice or shift resources into another direction. The drafters eventually accepted the multiple purchaser option so as to allow the areas to go to the firm that best suits the area of practice.

The 2002 Rule 1.17 continues to impose various restrictions on the sale of a law practice.

First, the seller must cease to engage in the practice of law, or in an entire area of practice, in the jurisdiction (or a particular geographic area) [the state court adopting Rule 1.17 is to choose one of these alternatives], unless the seller returns to private practice because of unanticipated circumstances.[10] A seller who becomes in-house counsel, or works for the government, or a legal services entity is not considered to be returning to private practice.[11]

Second, the sale of a law practice raises questions of client confidentiality, for the purchaser is not the lawyer whom the clients hired.[12] Consequently, each of the seller's clients must receive written notice of the proposed sale, the right to retain other counsel, and the right to take possession of his file.[13] These clients are given a reasonable chance to consent or withhold consent *before* the confidences are revealed.

Unfortunately, not all clients may respond to their mail in general and this notice in particular. To take this fact into account,

---

[9]Reporter's Explanation of Changes to Rule 1.17.

[10]Rule 1.17 & Rule 1.17, Comment 2.

[11]Rule 1.17, Comment 3.

[12]*See* Arizona State Bar Opinion 06–01 (Apr. 2006) (permitting Arizona lawyers who wish to sell their law practice to disclose some limited confidential information (*e.g.*, client names

and general description of work performed, but not fees) to the potential buyer before obtaining client consent), *noted in* 22 ABA/BNA MANUAL ON PROFESSIONAL CONDUCT, Current Reports News 188 (Apr. 19, 2006).

[13]Rule 1.17(c)(1),(2), & (3). Even after the sale of the law practice, a client may always transfer the representation to another lawyer. Rule 1.17, Comment 9.

this Rule provides that if a client does not object or does not respond within 90 days, his consent is presumed.[14]

If the client cannot be given notice, the purchaser must secure a court order authorizing the transfer. The court can determine if there have been reasonable efforts to find the clients and whether it serves the legitimate interests of these absent clients to have the purchaser continue the representation of them. To protect the client's confidentiality, the seller may disclose to the court *in camera* information about the proposed representation only to the extent necessary to obtain this order.[15]

Third, Rule 1.17(d) prohibits the purchasing lawyer from increasing the fee charged to the clients who choose to come over to the new firm because of the sale. The Comments state that the purchasing lawyer must honor the prior lawyer's agreements with the client as to scope and fee. The 1990 version of this provision had a line that permitted a purchasing lawyer to decline any representation where the client refused to increase the fee to the level of other clients of the lawyer. The ABA deleted this line and the commentary explaining it because apparently purchasing lawyers used it to threaten to drop clients who would not agree to a fee increase.[16]

Recall that, if a lawyer divides fees with another lawyer in a different law firm, each lawyer must assume joint responsibility for the representation, pursuant to Rule 1.5(e)(1).[17] Rule 1.17 does not refer to that section; in fact, a Comment to Rule 1.17 specifically provides that this Rule does *not* apply to the transfer of legal representation unrelated to the sale of a practice.[18]

One would think, as a logical matter, that the responsibilities assumed under Rule 1.17 should be no less than those assumed pursuant to Rule 1.5(e)(1). Comment 11 to Rule 1.17 does note that the seller has the obligation to exercise competence in identifying a qualified purchaser.[19] While the seller cannot exercise continuing supervision (he has, after all, left the practice), it is not unreasonable to make him share joint malpractice liability (as if they were partners) with the person whom he hand picks to buy his practice. Such a rule would assure that the seller picks carefully, and it is no more onerous than the burden placed by Rule 1.5(e)(1).[20]

---

[14]Rule 1.17(c)(3)

[15]Rule 1.17, Comment 8.

[16]*See* Margaret Colgate Love, *The Revised ABA Model Rules of Professional Conduct: Summary of the Work of Ethics 2000*, 15 GEORGETOWN J. OF LEGAL ETHICS 441, 462 (2002).

[17]Rule 1.5(e)(1).

[18]Rule 1.17, Comment 15.

[19]Rule 1.17, Comment 11.

[20]**Occurrences Made and Claims Made Malpractice Policies.** The lawyer selling the practice has to buy malpractice insurance to cover the

§ 1.17–2 THE DISPOSITION OF CLIENT FILES AND PROPERTY WHEN A SOLE PRACTITIONER DIES

If a law firm has more than one attorney, the death of one of the partners does not end the law practice, because there is a least one other attorney to carry on the work. However, in the case of sole practitioners who do not first sell their practice, there arises the question of what happens to the files of the various clients.

When the Model Rules added Rule 1.17 to allow a lawyer to sell her law practice to another lawyer,[1] the ABA also added Rule 5.4(a)(2). This Rule provides that if a lawyer (e.g., Lawyer *A*) purchases the law practice of "a deceased, disabled, or disappeared lawyer," (e.g., Lawyer *B*), then Lawyer *A* may agree to pay the purchase price to the estate or other representative of Lawyer *B*.

The ABA recommends that the sole practitioner have a plan to provide for the protection of her clients' interests in the event of her death, in order to assure that client matters (*e.g.*, document filings, statute of limitations) are not neglected.[2] The plan should designate another lawyer who would make reasonable efforts to notify the clients of the sole practitioner's death, review the files, and determine which need immediate attention. Because the

---

cases open as of the time of the insurance. There are two basic types of malpractice coverage: "occurrences made," and "claims made."

Under an "occurrences made" policy, the policy covers all claims made for any alleged malpractice that occurred at the time the policy was in force, even if the claim is made years later and the lawyer is no longer insured by that particular insurance company. So, a lawyer retiring from practice would be covered if he or she had that type of insurance in force covering all claims made during that time period. This type of policy is rare now, because insurance companies found it difficult to work out the actuarial costs.

Under a "claims made" policy, the policy covers all claims made while the policy is in force, even if the lawyer did not have that policy in effect at the time the alleged malpractice occurred. If the selling lawyer would be liable for the malpractice of the person to whom he or she sold the practice, the selling lawyer would have to continue to buy a "claims made" policy. However, the expenses related to this policy could be worked out and factored into the sale of the law practice. The selling lawyer, for example, could require—as a condition of sale—that the purchasing lawyer buy malpractice insurance and continue it for a reasonable length of time.

[Section 1.17–2]

[1] Rule 1.17.

[2] ABA Formal Opinion 92-369 (Dec. 7, 1992). Rule 1.1, requiring competence, and Rule 1.3, prohibiting neglect, reinforce this obligation. *See also* DR 6-101(A)(1), (3).

The ABA Model Rule on Financial Recordkeeping § E (Feb. 9, 1993), *reprinted in* **Appendix B** of the Lawyer's edition of this book, reaches the same conclusion. When a law practice is sold, the seller must make appropriate arrangements for the maintenance of the trust fund and financial records.

designated lawyer does not represent these clients, she should only review as much of the files as needed to identify the clients and determine which files need immediate attention. The drafters of the 2002 Rules added this obligation of a sole practitioner to a Comment to Rule 1.3 on diligence.[3]

[3]Rule 1.3, Comment 5.

CHAPTER 1.18
DUTIES TO PROSPECTIVE CLIENTS

RULE 1.18: DUTIES TO PROSPECTIVE CLIENT

(a) A person who discusses with a lawyer the possibility of forming a client-lawyer relationship with respect to a matter is a prospective client.

(b) Even when no client-lawyer relationship ensues, a lawyer who has had discussions with a prospective client shall not use or reveal information learned in the consultation, except as Rule 1.9 would permit with respect to information of a former client.

(c) A lawyer subject to paragraph (b) shall not represent a client with interests materially adverse to those of a prospective client in the same or a substantially related matter if the lawyer received information from the prospective client that could be significantly harmful to that person in the matter, except as provided in paragraph (d). If a lawyer is disqualified from representation under this paragraph, no lawyer in a firm with which that lawyer is associated may knowingly undertake or continue representation in such a matter, except as provided in paragraph (d).

(d) When the lawyer has received disqualifying information as defined in paragraph (c), representation is permissible if:

(1) both the affected client and the prospective client have given informed consent, confirmed in writing, or:

(2) the lawyer who received the information took reasonable measures to avoid exposure to more disqualifying information than was reasonably necessary to determine whether to represent the prospective client; and

(i) the disqualified lawyer is timely screened from any participation in the matter and is apportioned no part of the fee therefrom; and

(ii) written notice is promptly given to the prospective client.

Comment

[1] Prospective clients, like clients, may disclose information to a lawyer, place documents or other property in the lawyer's custody, or rely on the lawyer's advice. A lawyer's discussions with a prospective client usually are limited in time and depth and leave both the prospective client and the lawyer free (and sometimes required) to proceed no further. Hence, prospective clients should receive some but not all of the protection afforded clients.

[2] Not all persons who communicate information to a lawyer are entitled to protection under this Rule. A person who communicates information unilaterally to a lawyer, without any reasonable expectation that the lawyer is willing to discuss the possibility of forming a client-lawyer relationship, is not a "prospective client" within the meaning of paragraph (a).

[3] It is often necessary for a prospective client to reveal information to the lawyer during an initial consultation prior to the decision about formation of a client-lawyer relationship. The lawyer often must learn such information to determine whether there is a conflict of interest with an existing client and whether the matter is one that the lawyer is willing to undertake. Paragraph (b) prohibits the lawyer from using or revealing that information, except as permitted by Rule 1.9, even if the client or lawyer decides not to proceed with the representation. The duty exists regardless of how brief the initial conference may be.

[4] In order to avoid acquiring disqualifying information from a prospective client, a lawyer considering whether or not to undertake a new matter should limit the initial interview to only such information as reasonably appears necessary for that purpose. Where the information indicates that a conflict of interest or other reason for non-representation exists, the lawyer should so inform the prospective client or decline the representation. If the prospective client wishes to retain the lawyer, and if consent is possible under Rule 1.7, then consent from all affected present or former clients must be obtained before accepting the representation.

[5] A lawyer may condition conversations with a prospective client on the person's informed consent that no information disclosed during the consultation will prohibit the lawyer from representing a different client in the matter. See Rule 1.0(e) for the definition of informed consent. If the agreement expressly so provides, the prospective client may also consent to the lawyer's subsequent use of information received from the prospective client.

[6] Even in the absence of an agreement, under paragraph (c), the lawyer is not prohibited from representing a client with interests adverse to those of the prospective client in the same or a substantially related matter unless the lawyer has received from the prospective client information that could be significantly harmful if used in the matter.

[7] Under paragraph (c), the prohibition in this Rule is imputed to other lawyers as provided in Rule 1.10, but, under paragraph (d)(1), imputation may be avoided if the lawyer obtains the informed consent, confirmed in writing, of both the prospective and affected clients. In the alternative, imputation may be avoided if the condi-

tions of paragraph (d)(2) are met and all disqualified lawyers are timely screened and written notice is promptly given to the prospective client. See Rule 1.0(k) (requirements for screening procedures). Paragraph (d)(2)(i) does not prohibit the screened lawyer from receiving a salary or partnership share established by prior independent agreement, but that lawyer may not receive compensation directly related to the matter in which the lawyer is disqualified.

[8] Notice, including a general description of the subject matter about which the lawyer was consulted, and of the screening procedures employed, generally should be given as soon as practicable after the need for screening becomes apparent.

[9] For the duty of competence of a lawyer who gives assistance on the merits of a matter to a prospective client, see Rule 1.1. For a lawyer's duties when a prospective client entrusts valuables or papers to the lawyer's care, see Rule 1.15.

Authors' 1983 Model Rules Comparison

There was no counterpart to this Rule in the 1983 Model Rules. The 1983 Rules did contain a line in the Scope that stated, "But there are some duties, such as that of confidentiality under Rule 1.6 that may attach when the lawyer agrees to consider whether a client-lawyer relationship shall be established." 1983 Model Rules, Scope [3]. The 2002 Rules retain this language and cite to Rule 1.18. See Rule Scope 17.

Authors' Model Code Comparison

EC 5-20 stated that: "A lawyer is often asked to serve as an impartial arbitrator or mediator in matters which involve present or former clients. He may serve in either capacity if he first discloses such present or former relationships. After a lawyer has undertaken to act as an impartial arbitrator or mediator, he should not thereafter represent in the dispute any of the parties involved."

§ 1.18–1 DUTIES OWED TO PROSPECTIVE CLIENTS

§ 1.18–1(a) Introduction

Origins of Rule 1.18. The Model Code and the initial version of the Model Rules did not have a specific provision dealing with *prospective* clients, but this category of persons has always existed. Before the ABA House of Delegates approved Rule 1.18 in 2002, many of the Rules already applied to lawyer contacts with prospective clients.[1] Lawyers owe a duty of competence to prospective clients—when a lawyer tells a prospective client that the lawyer will look into the client's rights, the lawyer undertakes

---

[Section 1.18–1]

[1]The ABA addressed this topic in Formal Opinion 90-358. See American Bar Association, Formal Opinion 90-358 (Sept. 13, 1990). See also Restatement of the Law Governing Lawyers, Third, § 15 (Official Draft 2000) ("Duties to Prospective Clients"). Rule 1.18 is based upon the principles found in Opinion 90-358 and the Restatement.

an obligation to perform this task competently.[2] Lawyers also owe a duty of loyalty to prospective clients because—before they may consider accepting the representation—lawyers must examine their past and present relationships to determine whether a potential or actual conflict of interest exists.[3] If a lawyer obtains a confidence from a prospective client, the lawyer owes an obligation to protect it.[4] These obligations arise from fiduciary principles[5] and the application of other Rules that protect clients. Not all prospective clients become clients, but all current and former clients were once prospective clients.[6]

The drafters of the 2002 Rules examined the duties owed to prospective clients and created Model Rule 1.18. Prospective clients are like clients for several reasons. They often disclose confidential information to a lawyer in an effort to retain him. They also place documents or other property in the lawyer's custody, even if only temporarily. And, they may rely on his advice even if they decide not to retain him, or the lawyer decides not to retain them. For example, they may rely on the lawyer's advice that the statute of limitations has run and that therefore the prospective client has no case.[7]

However, "a lawyer's discussions with a prospective client often are limited in time and depth of exploration, do not reflect full consideration of the prospective client's problems. . . ."[8] Consequently, prospective clients receive some but not all of the protection afforded clients. Rule 1.18 reflects that principle.

Defining "Prospective Client." The first subsection, Rule 1.18 (a), initially defines a "prospective client" very broadly, as any "person who discusses with a lawyer the possibility of form-

---

[2] Rule 1.1.

See, e.g., Togstad v. Vesely, Otto, Miller & Keefe, 291 N.W.2d 686 (Minn. 1980), holding that a lawyer who advises prospective clients that they have no claim is liable for negligent advice.

[3] Rule 1.7.

[4] Rule 1.6.

[5] See, e.g., Westinghouse Elec. Corp. v. Kerr-McGee Corp., 580 F.2d 1311, 1319 (7th Cir.1978):

"The fiduciary relationship existing between lawyer and client extends to preliminary consultation by a prospective client with a view to retention of the lawyer, although actual employment does not result." (footnote omitted).

[6] See Margaret Colgate Love, Duties to Prospective Clients, 87 ABA J. 59 (May 2001).

[7] Miller v. Metzinger, 91 Cal.App.3d 31, 154 Cal.Rptr. 22 (1979), held that a lawyer who advises a prospective client must mention statute-of-limitations problem when the limitations period is about to expire.

[8] Restatement of the Law Governing Lawyers, Third, § 15, Comment b (Official Draft 2000). Rule 1.18, Comment 1 quotes from this portion of the Restatement, although without using quotation marks.

ing a client-lawyer with respect to a matter is a prospective client."[9]

However, one should not read that language too literally. This person must have a "reasonable expectation" of forming a client-lawyer relationship, as the Comments explain. While the text of Rule 1.18 focuses on the actions and motive of the prospective client, the Comments interpret this language to make clear that a person does not become a perspective client merely by talking to the lawyer. It must be "reasonable" for the prospective client to expect that a lawyer-client relationship could come to pass. "A person who communicates information unilaterally to a lawyer without any expectation that the lawyer is willing to discuss the possibility of forming a client-attorney relationship is not a 'prospective client' within the meaning of paragraph (a)."[10] This language focuses on the reasonableness of the client's communication to the lawyer.

For example, one could find that a person who simply sends (out of the blue) confidential information to a lawyer via mail or email for the purposes of exploring a possible attorney-client relationship is not a prospective client because the client had no reason to believe that the lawyer was willing to consider the employment.[11] However, a website *encouraging* prospective clients to contact the law firm may change such expectations, particularly if the website gave no cautionary instructions.[12]

Let us hypothesize a person who calls his lawyer-friend to ask about a possible divorce. The lawyer says, "I am a patent lawyer, and I do not practice divorce law. Moreover, I am a friend of your spouse too, and I do not want to become involved. I can listen to your problems as a friend, but I have to warn you that we cannot establish a lawyer-client relationship and nothing you tell me

---

[9]Rule 1.18(a).

[10]Rule 1.18, Comment 2.

[11]*See* Association of Bar of City of New York, Committee on Professional and Judicial Ethics, Formal Opinion 2001-1 (Mar. 1, 2001) "Duty to Preserve Confidences of a Prospective Client" (Pre-Retention Communication; Conflicts of Interest). The Opinion states that if law firm website does not warn persons not to send confidential information the lawyer must keep any information received confidential, but lawyer is not disqualified from representing adverse party. The Opinion reasons that law firm websites and other advertisements do not constitute

invitations for person to provide specific confidential information about a matter.

[12]Many law firm websites encourage communication from unknown persons but they ask that persons not send confidential information to the law firm and warn that no attorney-client relationship arises until both the person and the lawyer sign an agreement. Is the person who responds to a website soliciting persons injured by a particular pharmaceutical drug a prospective client? Suppose the website provides general information about the law firm and its lawyers and provides an email address?

will be privileged." This person has no "reasonable expectation"[13] that a lawyer-client relationship will be established and he is not a perspective client under Rule 1.18.

On the other hand, assume a lawyer announces, in a website or newspaper advertisement: "I never form a lawyer-client relationship with strangers, but you are free to propose your facts in an email, or mail, or in person, and I will consider your request." This warning may not be detailed enough to avoid the lawyer's obligations under Rule 1.18. The lawyer may be trying to avoid creating "any reasonable expectation" that a lawyer-client relationship might be formed, but a lawyer cannot avoid the obligations of Rule 1.18 simply making a blanket statement that there is no lawyer-client relationship until both the lawyer and the client agree to create one.[14]

When the Rule focuses on a "reasonable expectation," we measure what is reasonable from the perspective of the client, not the lawyer. The client is typically a layperson, and what is "reasonable" to a layperson is different than what is reasonable to a trained lawyer. For example, consider *DeVaux v. American Home Assurance Co.*[15] The purported client, who had been injured in a store, wrote the law firm asking for help regarding a possible tort claim. The secretary answered the call. She told the purported client to write a letter to the firm requesting legal assistance. The secretary also arranged a medical examination for the plaintiff with the store's insurance company. The purported client wrote the letter to the firm, but the lawyer's secretary misfiled it so that no lawyer in the firm ever saw it until after the statute of limitations had run. The prospective client had called the office several times about her case but no one returned the calls. The prospective client sued the law firm for malpractice and the court denied summary judgment for the law firm. It concluded that a jury might reasonably find that the firm had formed a lawyer-client relationship. From the perspective the lawyer, there was no lawyer-client relationship because no lawyer had ever spoken to the prospective client. But, from the perspective of the client,

---

[13]Rule 1.18, Comment 2.

[14]*Bridge Products Inc. v. Quantum Chemical Corp.*, 1990 WL 70857 (N.D. Ill.1990). The court ordered a law firm's disqualification when the prospective client conducted what is called a "beauty contest" among various firms to decide which firm to hire. In the course of a one-hour discussion, the prospective client disclosed its settlement terms and strategic advice of its other lawyers. The lawyer did not seek the potential client's waiver prior to the prospective client's disclosure of confidence.

[15]*DeVaux v. American Home Assurance Co.*, 387 Mass. 814, 444 N.E.2d 355 (1983).

it was reasonable to think that she has created such a relationship.[16]

The purpose of Rule 1.18 is to protect a prospective client's reasonable expectations. Consequently, it does not protect prospective clients who contact lawyers as part of a ruse, for the purpose of disqualifying the lawyer.[17] A person who communicates with a lawyer for the purpose of disqualifying the lawyer from representing another party to the dispute, instead of for the purposes of determining whether the person would like to employ the lawyer, is not a prospective client. For example, if a woman had hired Lawyer A to represent her in a divorce, and the woman subsequently interviewed Lawyer B and Lawyer C for the purposes of disqualifying Lawyer B and Lawyer C, the woman is not a prospective client under Rule 1.18(a). Therefore Lawyer B and Lawyer C have no duties of confidentiality and loyalty to the woman and could represent the woman's husband because there is no conflict of interest. This result makes sense because the woman is intentionally providing confidential information for the purpose of using the Rules advantageously to create a purported conflict. The Rules do not protect such conduct.

Once a person is classified as a prospective client, the lawyer owes such a person obligations with respect to confidential information, documents or other property delivered to the lawyer, and any legal advice the lawyer provides to such a person.[18] The lawyer owes these duties, even though the prospective client does not become a client and even though the "lawyer's discussions with a prospective client are limited in both time and depth."[19] Prospective clients receive some but not all of the protection afforded to clients. As to what is the scope of those protections, that is the issue to which we now turn.

§ 1.18–1(b) Duty of Confidentiality

Prospective clients often must reveal confidential information to a lawyer in order to permit the lawyer to determine whether the lawyer can accept the representation. If the lawyer is willing to accept the representation of the prospective client, the lawyer may need confidential information to determine possible conflicts, the expected cost of representation, and the proposed course of conduct.

---

[16]A Virginia Ethics Opinion examines different hypotheticals that may or may not create an expectation that a law firm will treat unsolicited contacts as confidential. *See* Va. State Bar Comm. on Legal Ethics, Op. 1842 (Sept. 30, 2008), noted in 24 ABA/BNA Law. Man. Prof. Conduct 543 (Oct. 15, 2008). Note that Virginia has not adopted a version of Rule 1.18.

[17]*See* ABA Formal Opinion 90-358 (Sept. 13, 1990), at n.3; North Carolina Ethics Opinion 244 (1997).

[18]Rule 1.18, Comment 1.

[19]Rule 1.18, Comment 1.

If no attorney-client relationship ensues from the prospective client's inquiries, the lawyer who has obtained confidential information from the prospective client may not disclose or use that information except as permitted by the former client provision, Rule 1.9.[20] In other words, Rule 1.18 treats a prospective client as a former client for the purposes of confidential information.[21] The lawyer's obligation to protect these confidences attaches even when the conversation with the prospective client is brief in time.[22]

Rule 1.18, governing "prospective clients" whom the lawyer does not represent, creates a category that could be called "former prospective clients." A lawyer may not use this confidential information to the disadvantage of the former client or former prospective client.[23] The lawyer may use information to the disadvantage of the prospective client (or former client) if the information has become generally known or if another Rule such as Rule 1.6 or 3.3 permits or requires.[24] Otherwise the lawyer may not reveal information about a prospective (or former client) unless one of the other Rules permit or require disclosure.[25]

The conversations that a lawyer has with a prospective client are not confidential if the parties agree that they will not be confidential.[26]

For example, assume that the President of Prospective Client (Corporation A) meets with Lawyer. When the meeting begins, Lawyer informs the President of Corporation A that he must first obtain information about Corporation A and its affiliates and about the general nature of the legal matter to perform a conflicts check pursuant to procedures followed in Lawyer's firm. Lawyer also explains that he will be willing to discuss matters only if Prospective Client agrees that it will not require Lawyer to keep confidential information revealed during these preliminary discussions. President of Prospective Client (Corporation A) agrees, and they engage in preliminary discussions over several aspects of the dispute. Lawyer later declines the representation because of a conflict involving another firm client. Thereafter, Lawyer is approached by Company B to represent it in its contract dispute with Company A. Lawyer may accept the representation. Because of President's agreement, Lawyer is not required to keep confidential from Company B the information he

---

[20] Rule 1.18(b).

[21] *Compare* ABA Formal Opinion 90-358 (Sept. 13, 1990)(adopting current client analysis).

[22] Rule 1.18, Comment 3.

[23] Rule 1.9(c).

[24] Rule 1.9(c)(1).

[25] Rule 1.9(c)(2).

[26] Rule 1.18, Comment 5. Restatement of the Law Governing Lawyers, Third, § 15(2)(b) (Official Draft 2000).

learned during the initial consultation with President of Corporation A.[27]

§ 1.18–1(c) Duty of Loyalty

Confidential Information from a Former Prospective Client. A lawyer who acquires confidential information from a prospective client about a possible representation may owe an obligation of loyalty to the prospective client even though the lawyer does not undertake the representation. If the prospective client does not ever become a client, the lawyer, in general, may not represent a new client "with interests materially adverse to those of a prospective client in the same or substantially related matter if the lawyer received information from the prospective client that could be significantly harmful to that person in the matter."[28]

If a lawyer discusses a potential matter with a prospective client and obtains information from the person and a representation does not occur, Rule 1.18 essentially applies the principles, but not the exact test, that applies to former clients under Rule 1.9. The requirements of Rule 1.18 are not exactly the same as Rule 1.9. Let us consider several examples to clarify the distinction.

Under Rule 1.9, if a lawyer had formerly represented Client #1 in a matter, the lawyer cannot later represent Client #2 in that matter or a matter substantially related to that matter if the interests of Client #1 and Client #2 are "materially adverse" and the lawyer had acquired material information that is confidential.[29]

Assume that Client #1 later asks a lawyer to represent Client #1 in a matter adverse to someone who had been a prospective client in the same or substantially related matter, and the information that the lawyer learned from the "former prospective client" is information that "could be significantly harmful" to the prospective client. In that case, Rule 1.18 disqualifies the lawyer from accepting the new representation,[30] because the information is not merely confidential but "could be significantly harmful" to the prospective client. Rule 1.18, unlike Rule 1.9, requires that the confidential information be not only relevant but also "could be significantly harmful" to the prospective client.

Significantly Harmful Information. If a lawyer has interviewed a prospective client and has decided not to undertake the representation or if the client has decided not to hire the lawyer,

---

[27]Restatement of the Law Governing Lawyers, Third, § 15(2)(b), Comment c, Illustration 4.

[28]Rule 1.18(c).

[29]Rule 1.9(b).

[30]Rule 1.18(c).

the lawyer may represent a party who is adverse to the prospective client in the same or substantially related matter unless the lawyer has acquired information from the prospective client that is likely to be "significantly harmful" to that person.[31] Thus, lawyers do not generally owe prospective clients a broad duty of loyalty. They only owe them a duty not to use confidential information acquired in the interview process that is likely to be "significantly harmful" to the prospective client.[32] The possession of this particular type of confidential information forms the basis for the disqualification.

Hence, in order to avoid disqualification, a lawyer may ask a prospective client not to share any confidential information—or any confidential information that is "significantly harmful" to the prospective client. The lawyer can avoid disqualification if the prospective client agrees that he will not provide confidential information to the lawyer. However, if the client cannot discuss the problem without revealing confidences to his prospective lawyer, then the prospective client's choices are limited. The prospective client will either waive the confidence or move on to a different lawyer. Or the lawyer will accept the opportunity cost and hear the significantly harmful information.

The Rules are not too clear in defining what is likely to be information "that could be significantly harmful." If the former prospective client argues that he gave the lawyer information "that could be significantly harmful," it may not be possible for the judge deciding the disqualification motion to determine if the information is likely to "be significantly harmful" unless she knows what the information is, and once the information is disclosed to the judge on the record it is no longer confidential.

In addition, one may not be able to determine if information is "significantly harmful" unless one knows the theory of the case. The information may be the fact that the former prospective client received a letter on May 15, 2004. The opposing party may learn, only after extensive discovery, that the date was important because it undercut a theory of laches.

To avoid these problems, the courts should interpret very narrowly the language regarding information that "could be

---

[31] Rule 1.18, Comment 6.

See *Sturdivant v. Sturdivant*, 2006 WL 3030681, 367 Ark. 514 (Ark. 2006), *noted in* 22 ABA/BNA MANUAL ON PROFESSIONAL CONDUCT, Current Reports News 528 (Nov. 1, 2006). The court disqualified a lawyer from representing the wife in a child custody proceeding because the father had previously consulted with, but chose

not to retain, another lawyer in the same firm. The court reinforced, "The duty to a prospective client exists regardless of how brief the initial conference may have been and regardless of the fact that no client-attorney relationship ensued."

[32] *See also* Restatement of the Law Governing Lawyers, Third, § 15(2) (Official Draft 2000).

significantly harmful." If the court concludes that the prospective client disclosed confidences that could not be significantly harmful, then Rule 1.18(c) will not treat the prospective client as having all the rights of a former client.

Clark Capital Management Group, Inc. v. Annuity Investors Life Insurance Co.,[33] is a trademark infringement cause of action that illustrates how the courts may implement Rule 1.18(d)(2), although the court decided this case before that Rule existed. The defendant moved to disqualify plaintiff's counsel because of earlier telephone conversations between the defendant's attorney and Lawyer Biemer, a member of plaintiff's law firm. The defendant's lawyer had discussed possibly retaining Biemer's firm as co-counsel, but the lawyers never reached any retention agreement concerning representation, and the defendant later hired another firm. The defendant's lawyer said that he revealed confidential client information to Biemer that he had a reasonable expectation that Biemer would keep confidential. The court found, however, that the plaintiff's expectation of confidentiality was unreasonable: no actual offer had been made to Biemer. Both the defendant's lawyer and Biemer had recognized Biemer's need to perform a conflict check before consenting to represent him. Biemer testified that if the other lawyer has disclosed anything to him, he had no recollection of it. Biemer was not working on the case because the firm had already screened him from any involvement with it, and the likelihood that confidential information would reach the trial attorneys was minimal.

Placing Limits on the Initial Interview. There will be cases where it is reasonable for the prospective client to discuss all the relevant facts with his prospective lawyer without disclosing any confidences. For example, if the dispute about which the prospective client has approached the lawyer has appeared in the local newspaper and all of the relevant facts are public, the lawyer does not need confidential information to evaluate the prospective matter. The prospective client could say to the lawyer, "read the paper and you will learn about the matter in which I need legal representation."

If the lawyer deals with a sophisticated prospective client and explains the matter fully, the courts are likely to take the prospective client at his word when he said that there was no relevant confidential information. But, the court should be more sympathetic to the prospective client if the lawyer who proposed such an agreement did not explain the matter fully, in a way that the

---

[33]*Clark Capital Management Group, Inc. v. Annuity Investors Life* *Insurance Co.,* 149 F. Supp. 2d 193 (E.D. Pa. 2001).

prospective client could understand.[34] If the prospective client unknowingly gave confidential information to his prospective lawyer, the court is likely to interpret Rule 1.18(c) to disqualify the lawyer, if the information was likely to be significantly harmful.

Anytime the lawyer talks to a prospective client may create an opportunity cost to the lawyer. For example, the lawyer interviews the prospective client and the client chooses not to hire the lawyer, or the lawyer chooses not to accept the retention. That is not the end of the matter because the interview could prevent the lawyer from undertaking representation from a client. That lost opportunity is the opportunity cost of the interview.

If the matter can be discussed without disclosure of confidential information, the lawyer and the prospective client can agree that the prospective client will not provide confidential information to the lawyer. That way, the lawyer reduces her opportunity cost. Even if no conflict exists with the prospective client's matter, the lawyer may decline the representation for any of a number of reasons. For example, the lawyer may decline the matter on grounds of profitability, workload, expertise, and future direction of the lawyer's practice. By imposing sufficient limits for the initial interview, the lawyer can keep her options open in the future.

Rule 1.18 tells a lawyer how to limit her opportunity cost that prospective clients would otherwise impose. The lawyer can limit the scope and type of information that she obtains from a prospective client during the initial interview.[35] In order to avoid disqualification, the lawyer should ask for only such information that is needed to determine whether the lawyer should undertake the new matter. In many cases, the lawyer should begin by asking the prospective client to provide objective facts about the prospective client, the potential adversaries, and the general nature of the dispute or transaction. By limiting the information to basic objective information, the lawyer may be able to perform a reasonable conflicts of interest inquiry before acquiring more specific factual information that could lead to the lawyer's disqualification with respect to this matter.

In short, the lawyer can agree with a prospective client at the outset that the prospective client will provide no confidential information during the interview that will later prohibit the lawyer from representing an adverse client in the same or substantially

---

[34]*See* Rule 1.0(e), defining "informed consent."

[35]Rule 1.18, Comment 4.

related matter.[36] The prospective client must give informed consent. The lawyer and client can expressly provide that the lawyer could use the information learned in the prospective client interview in the subsequent representation.

One would assume that a lawyer should use such waivers primarily with sophisticated prospective clients and not lay persons who may not understand the consequences of their consent. For example, when a sophisticated prospective client conducts a "beauty contest" with several law firms,[37] the Rules permit the law firms and the prospective client to agree that the beauty contest will not disqualify the firms that do not represent the company to accept adverse representations in the same matter.[38] However, the Rules do not permit the lawyers to secure broad waivers of disqualification in order to use the adverse information against an unsophisticated prospective client who did not appreciate the potential harm of consent in a situation involving harmful confidential information.

Rule 1.18, in short, rewards lawyers who proceed carefully in interviewing prospective clients because the lawyers can limit their opportunity cost and avoid disqualification by placing limits on the initial interview. Prospective clients are also served because they will have more choices in interviewing law firms and conducting beauty contests if the initial interviews do not impose unnecessary opportunity costs. The lawyer can also represent a party adverse to the former prospective client if the client and the former prospective client waive their rights in writing, after being fully informed about their rights.[39]

---

[36]Rule 1.18, Comment 5. The advance waiver of disqualification seems less rigorous than the advance consent under Rule 1.7. See Rule 1.7, Comment 22.

[37]See, e.g. Bridge Products Inc. v. Quantum Chemical Corp., 1990 WL 70857 (N.D.Ill.1990).

The term, "beauty contest," refers to a competition established by a sophisticated prospective client who seeks to compare the financial terms and legal approach of several law firms in a prospective representation before it decides which firm it will retain to represent it in the matter.

See generally Kenneth D. Agran, The Treacherous Path to Diamond-Studded Tiaras: Ethical Dilemmas in Legal Beauty Contests, 9 GEORGETOWN J. LEGAL ETHICS 1307 (1996).

[38]Compare B.F. Goodrich Co. v. Formosa Plastics Corp., 638 F.Supp. 1050 (S.D.Tex.1986) (prospective client corporation interviewed five lawyers before choosing one firm and court declined to disqualify one of the firms interviewed from representing an adverse party).

[39]Rule 1.18(d)(1) & Rule 1.0(e), defining "informed consent."

§ 1.18–2 IMPUTED DISQUALIFICATION RESULTING FROM PROSPECTIVE CLIENT CONFLICTS

Rule 1.10 generally imputes the conflicts of interests of one lawyer in a law firm to all of the lawyers in the firm.[1] However, Rule 1.18 limits the application of the imputed disqualification principle when the conflict arises from a prospective client contact with one of the lawyers in the firm. If a lawyer is disqualified from representation because she has information from a prospective client that "could be significantly harmful" to the former prospective client if the lawyer were to represent a client adverse to the former prospective client, then "no lawyer in a firm with which the lawyer is associated may knowingly undertake or continue representation in such a matter, *except* as provided in paragraph (d)."[2] Rule 1.18(d) provides important, albeit limited, exceptions to the imputed disqualification.

Waiver. First, the law firm can avoid the imputed disqualification by securing waivers from the new client and the former prospective client. If one lawyer in the firm has received disqualifying information from a prospective client and the lawyer does not represent the client in the matter, the other lawyers in the firm may obtain the informed consent, confirmed in writing, from the prospective client and the affected client.[3] In many situations, prospective clients and adverse parties may consent to permit the law firm to represent the adverse party. The parties may not consider the information to be damaging or they may plan to disclose it in the representation.

While it is important to provide for waiver, this exception may be of limited practicality because parties may be unwilling to waive the strategic benefits of disqualifying their opponents' lawyers, particularly if the confidential information is at all relevant. Hence, the Rule also allows screening.

The Basic Elements of Screening. Rule 1.9, dealing with the former client, does not provide for this screening, but Rule 1.18, dealing with the former prospective client, does allow limited screening. This type of screen is similar to the screen that Rule 1.11 allows for lawyers entering and leaving government.

Rule 1.18(d) comes into effect when it disqualifies the lawyer who personally dealt with the former prospective client. Rule 1.18 allows the law firm to take the adverse representation if it screens the disqualified lawyer. Like Rule 1.11, the firm must institute the opaque screen in a timely manner. The notice to the prospective client should include "a general description of the

---

[Section 1.18–2]
    [1] Rule 1.10.

[2] Rule 1.18(c)(emphasis added).
[3] Rule 1.18(d)(1).

subject matter about which the lawyer was consulted, and of the screening procedures employed . . .."[4]

The law firm must also promptly inform the former prospective client in writing. And, the individually-disqualified lawyer, like the lawyer governed by Rule 1.11 must not be apportioned any part of the fee from this matter.[5]

There are a few differences in comparing the Rule 1.18 screen dealing with prospective clients and the Rule 1.11 screen dealing with lawyers entering or leaving the government. Under Rule 1.18, the law firm can only use screening when the lawyer who interviewed the prospective client "took reasonable measures to avoid exposure to more disqualifying information than was reasonably necessary to determine whether to represent the prospective client . . .."[6] The purpose of this requirement is to encourage lawyers who interview prospective clients to limit their acquisition of confidential information to only such information that they need to decide whether the firm can represent the prospective client. If the firm possesses limited information, the lawyers are more likely to comply with the screening requirements, and the prospective client is more likely to be comfortable with the screening procedure.

Rationale. The ABA's use of screening in the prospective client conflicts area departs from its general position that the Rules should limit screening to the government lawyer context.[7] However, many prospective client relationships last only a short period of time and the imposition of proper procedures by lawyers address the most serious concern of confidentiality.

In some regions of the country and in some areas of law, the disqualifications created through imputing prospective client conflicts impose significant costs on the choice of counsel by other parties. The Model Rules sought to balance these concerns and costs in its Rule 1.18.

---

[4]Rule 1.18, Comment 8.
[5]Rule 1.18(d)(2).

[6]Rule 1.18(d)(2).
[7]Rule 1.11, Rule 1.12.

II. THE LAWYER AS COUNSELOR

CHAPTER 2.1

THE LAWYER AS ADVISOR

§ 2.1–1 Advisor Versus Advocate
§ 2.1–2 Distinction Between Rule 2.1 Advisor and Rule 2.3
Evaluator

RULE 2.1: ADVISOR

In representing a client, a lawyer shall exercise independent professional judgment and render candid advice. In rendering advice, a lawyer may refer not only to law but to other considerations such as moral, economic, social and political factors, that may be relevant to the client's situation.

Comment

Scope of Advice

[1] A client is entitled to straightforward advice expressing the lawyer's honest assessment. Legal advice often involves unpleasant facts and alternatives that a client may be disinclined to confront. In presenting advice, a lawyer endeavors to sustain the client's morale and may put advice in as acceptable a form as honesty permits. However, a lawyer should not be deterred from giving candid advice by the prospect that the advice will be unpalatable to the client.

[2] Advice couched in narrow legal terms may be of little value to a client, especially where practical considerations, such as cost or effects on other people, are predominant. Purely technical legal advice, therefore, can sometimes be inadequate. It is proper for a lawyer to refer to relevant moral and ethical considerations in giving advice. Although a lawyer is not a moral advisor as such, moral and ethical considerations impinge upon most legal questions and may decisively influence how the law will be applied.

[3] A client may expressly or impliedly ask the lawyer for purely technical advice. When such a request is made by a client experienced in legal matters, the lawyer may accept it at face value. When such a request is made by a client inexperienced in legal matters, however, the lawyer's responsibility as advisor may include indicating that more may be involved than strictly legal considerations.

[4] Matters that go beyond strictly legal questions may also be in the domain of another profession. Family matters can involve

problems within the professional competence of psychiatry, clinical psychology or social work; business matters can involve problems within the competence of the accounting profession or of financial specialists. Where consultation with a professional in another field is itself something a competent lawyer would recommend, the lawyer should make such a recommendation. At the same time, a lawyer's advice at its best often consists of recommending a course of action in the face of conflicting recommendations of experts.

Offering Advice

[5] In general, a lawyer is not expected to give advice until asked by the client. However, when a lawyer knows that a client proposes a course of action that is likely to result in substantial adverse legal consequences to the client, the lawyer's duty to the client under Rule 1.4 may require that the lawyer offer advice if the client's course of action is related to the representation. Similarly, when a matter is likely to involve litigation, it may be necessary under Rule 1.4 to inform the client of forms of dispute resolution that might constitute reasonable alternatives to litigation. A lawyer ordinarily has no duty to initiate investigation of a client's affairs or to give advice that the client has indicated is unwanted, but a lawyer may initiate advice to a client when doing so appears to be in the client's interest.

Authors' 1983 Model Rules Comparison

The text of the 2002 version is identical to the Rule adopted by the ABA House of Delegates in 1983.

The drafters of the 2002 Rules added the following sentence to Comment 5: "Similarly, when a matter is likely to involve litigation, it may be necessary under Rule 1.4 to inform the client of forms of dispute resolution that might constitute reasonable alternatives to litigation." They also made a few word changes in Comment 5 for stylistic and clarification purposes.

Model Code Comparison

There was no direct counterpart to this Rule in the Disciplinary Rules of the Model Code. DR 5-107(B) provided that a lawyer "shall not permit a person who recommends, employs, or pays him to render legal services for another to direct or regulate his professional judgment in rendering such legal services." EC 7-8 stated that "[a]dvice of a lawyer to his client need not be confined to purely legal considerations. . . . In assisting his client to reach a proper decision, it is often desirable for a lawyer to point out those factors which may lead to a decision that is morally just as well as legally permissible. . . . In the final analysis, however, . . . the decision whether to forego legally available objectives or methods because of nonlegal factors is ultimately for the client. . . ."

§ 2.1–1 ADVISOR VERSUS ADVOCATE

The lawyer's role in giving advice often depends on whether the lawyer is acting as an advocate or as a consultant.[1] When the client consults the attorney who is acting primarily as advocate, the attorney may urge upon the courts any nonfrivolous interpretation of the law that favors the client. In contrast, when the client consults the attorney in order to seek advice on how to proceed in a matter, the attorney should give the client his or her good faith opinion on how the courts will likely rule, and the full effects of such a decision. The distinction accords with the reality of law practice, because a client typically wants to know how the decisions are likely to come out. It is not enough for the client to know that he can raise an issue that is not frivolous if the lawyer neglects to tell him that this non-frivolous issue is unlikely to win any votes either at trial or on appeal.

Model Rule 2.1 recognizes this role of the lawyer when it provides that the lawyer must render to her client her candid opinion of what the court is likely to do. She also should inform her client of the practical effects of such a ruling.[2] The lawyer's efforts to comfort the client cannot limit her duty to give an honest assessment of unpleasant facts.[3]

The drafters of the 2002 Rules added to Comment 5 a statement reminding lawyers in matters that are likely to involve litigation to inform their clients about "forms of dispute resolution that might constitute reasonable alternatives to litigation."[4] This change recognizes the rise in alternative dispute resolution movement in the last two decades as well as the fact that clients need legal advice on the choice of process to resolve a dispute.[5]

In offering legal advice, the lawyer need not limit her comments to purely technical legal considerations but may refer to economic, political, social and moral considerations. The lawyer may offer her judgment as to what effects are morally just as well as legally permissible.[6] The lawyer who couches her advice too

---

[Section 2.1–1]

[1] Typically, we think of lawyers as advocates in litigation and as consultants in a non-litigative situation. However, a lawyer can be an advocate outside of litigation, *i.e.*, in a negotiation or a presentation or lobbying effort before Congress. And, one can be an advisor to a party who is in litigation.

[2] EC 7-5; Rule 2.1.

[3] Rule 2.1, Comment 1.

[4] Rule 2.1, Comment 5.

[5] *See* Reporter's Explanation of Changes to Model Rule 2.1.

[6] EC 7-8, 7-9; Rule 2.1. *See also* Restatement of the Law Governing Lawyers, Third, § 94(3) (Official Draft 2000).

Fees for Nonlegal Advice. The Restatement has an usual provision that advises: "Whether a lawyer may appropriately charge a fee for advice defined in this Comment ["Advice concerning non-legal consider-

narrowly is a lawyer who ill-serves her client.[7] Of course, the client, not the lawyer, ultimately must make the final decision whether to accept the lawyer's judgment based on nonlegal considerations.[8] But the client cannot make this judgment to ignore the lawyer's nonlegal considerations if the lawyer never tells the client.

The client may instruct the lawyer, either expressly or impliedly, to limit her advice to only technical legal matters. In that case, the lawyer should follow this limitation, unless the client's inexperience indicates that she must say more.[9] Normally the lawyer need not give unsought advice, but she may initiate advice to a client when doing so appears to be in the client's interest.[10]

§ 2.1–2 DISTINCTION BETWEEN RULE 2.1 ADVISOR AND RULE 2.3 EVALUATOR

Sometimes the client asks the lawyer to evaluate a matter for the benefit of a third person, such as when she writes a legal opinion concluding that it is legal to sell certain securities registered for sale under the securities laws.[1] If the opinion is to be made public, the agency may seek to use that opinion to justify

---

ations"] depends on whether the parties contemplated that the lawyer's compensated services would include such advice (see § 38)." Restatement of the Law Governing Lawyers, Third, § 94, Comment *h* (Official Draft 2000), at p. 12. Section 38 merely offers several general statements regarding fee agreements. It does not require that there be a separate section in the bill for time spent on "non-legal considerations."

It is difficult to understand how this Comment is supposed to be applied. If the lawyer decides to spend several days studying Aristotle's *Ethics*, or St. Augustine's *Confessions* before advising a client, then one supposes that the lawyer should not charge for that time unless the client and lawyer contemplated that. However, what is much more likely to happen is that the lawyer, in advising the client whether to pursue a course of action, also advises that the particular course of action may be unwise from the standpoint of publicity, morality, etc. What the law "should be" often influences the direction of the case law. One cannot imagine that the law-

yer—in the course of advising the client that a defamation suit in a specific context may be viewed by others as an attempt to stifle free speech—must separately bill the quarter-hour of the hour conversation that referred to moral issues.

[7] Rule 2.1, Comment 2. *See also* William Simon, The Practice of Justice: A Theory of Lawyers' Ethics (1998); Deborah L. Rhode, *Symposium Introduction: In Pursuit Of Justice*, 51 Stan. L. Rev. 867 (1999); Symposium, *The Lawyer's Duty to Promote the Common Good*, 40 So. Tex. L. Rev. 1-309 (1999). James E. Fleming, *The Lawyer as a Citizen*, 70 Fordham L. Rev. 1699 (2002).

[8] EC 7-8.

[9] Rule 2.1, Comment 3.

[10] Rule 2.1, Comment 5. *See* EC 7-8 ("lawyer ought to initiate this decision-making process").

[Section 2.1–2]

[1] Rule 2.3, Comment 1. *See also* ABA Formal Opinion 335 (1974); *ABA Third-Party Opinion Report*, 47 Business Lawyer 167 (1991).

its action. The lawyer is then an *evaluator*, governed by Rule 2.3, discussed below.[2] However, if the agency asks for *confidential* advice, then the lawyer is an advisor, governed by Rule 2.1.[3]

The lawyer's role as evaluator for the benefit of a third party also should be distinguished from the lawyer's role as *investigator* solely for the benefit of her client. A prospective purchaser may retain a lawyer to do a title search on property that the purchaser is planning to purchase. The lawyer's client is the purchaser, not the seller, and the lawyer's duty of loyalty is only to this client.

Some law firms have found the investigation practice so lucrative that they now have special teams to conduct them. Many courts will tend to dismiss shareholder suits against officials if a law firm finds the officials to be without blame after an investigation and evaluation, and companies often believe that they can avoid more extensive government inquiries by showing that they are willing to clean their own house by hiring a lawyer-evaluator.[4] The companies treat these investigations as secret, though they may loudly trumpet the conclusions. These investigations may turn into "evaluations" for the benefit of third parties, when the companies and the lawyers whom they hire seek to have third parties rely on these evaluations.

For example, assume that the seller of real estate retains a lawyer to conduct a title search and furnish an opinion that the title is good. The seller plans to show this legal opinion to the purchaser. In this case, the seller retains the lawyer to evaluate the property for the benefit of the purchaser, a nonclient.[5] The lawyer's duty of loyalty is to the client,[6] but the lawyer also has assumed legal obligations to the third party whom he knows will rely on his evaluation.[7]

Similarly, a lawyer who drafts a tax shelter opinion knowing

---

[2] *See also* Rule 2.3, Comment 2.

[3] Restatement of the Law Governing Lawyers, Third, § 95 (Official Draft 2000).

[4] Laurie P. Cohen, *Firms Faulted for "Independent" Inquiries*, WALL STREET JOURNAL, June 14, 1989, at col. 4–6.

[5] Rule 2.3, Comment 3.

[6] Rule 2.3, Comment 3. Restatement of the Law Governing Lawyers, Third, § 95 (Official Draft 2000), Comment *b*, at pp. 19 to 20 explains:

"In the course of providing legal services to a client, a lawyer may be asked to investigate or analyze issues of fact or law and report the results to persons who are not clients . . .. In a real estate transaction, a title opinion rendered by the lawyer for the seller may be addressed to the purchaser or a financial institution lending funds to the purchaser to be secured by the property. In such cases, the evident intent of the parties is that an opinion so addressed may be relied on by the addressee. The client's interest is advanced by making it possible for the third person to proceed with the transaction on the basis of the evaluation."

[7] Restatement of Torts, Second § 552; Restatement of the Law Governing Lawyers § 51 ("Duties of Care to Certain Non-Clients") (Official Draft

that it will be shown to and relied on by investors may be liable
to those investors. Thus, the lawyer's assumption of the role as
evaluator carries with it important malpractice risks.[8]

2000).

See also Greycas v. Proud, 826
F.2d 1560 (7th Cir.1987), *cert. denied*,
484 U.S. 1043, 108 S.Ct. 775, 98
L.Ed.2d 862 (1988).

[8]*DuPont v. Brady*, 680 F.Supp.
613, Fed. Sec. L. Rep. ¶ 93,618 (S.D.N.
Y.1988). An investor sued a tax
adviser-lawyer alleging violations of
federal securities laws, state securities
laws, and common-law fraud and attorney malpractice, arising out of
investment in tax shelter. On remand
from the Second Circuit, the trial court
held that this tax adviser-lawyer who
had been sued under Rule 10b-5 for

failing to disclose potential nondeduc-
tability of tax shelter investment failed
to rebut presumption of reliance arising from this material nondisclosure.
This case was on remand from *duPont
v. Brady*, 828 F.2d 75, 56 U.S.L.W.
2158, 56 U.S.L.W. 2218, Fed. Sec. L.
Rep. ¶ 93,376 (2d Cir.1987).

*Norman v. Brown, Todd &
Heyburn*, 693 F.Supp. 1259, 1265 (D.
Mass.1988). The lawyer drafted a tax
opinion letter knowing that it would
be published in the offering material
and relied on by purchasers. The lawyer was liable for negligently drafting
this letter.

CHAPTER 2.2
THE LAWYER AS INTERMEDIARY

DELETED RULE 2.2: INTERMEDIARY

(a) A lawyer may act as intermediary between clients if:

(1) the lawyer consults with each client concerning the implications of the common representation, including the advantages and risks involved, and the effect on the attorney-client privileges, and obtains each client's consent to the common representation;

(2) the lawyer reasonably believes that the matter can be resolved on terms compatible with the clients' best interests, that each client will be able to make adequately informed decisions in the matter and that there is little risk of material prejudice to the interest of any of the clients if the contemplated resolution is unsuccessful; and

(3) the lawyer reasonably believes that the common representation can be undertaken impartially and without improper effect on other responsibilities the lawyer has to any of the clients.

(b) While acting as intermediary, the lawyer shall consult with each client concerning the decisions to be made and the considerations relevant in making them, so that each client can make adequately informed decisions.

(c) A lawyer shall withdraw as intermediary if any of the clients so request, or if any of the conditions stated in paragraph (a) is no longer satisfied. Upon withdrawal, the lawyer shall not continue to represent any of the clients in the matter that was the subject of the intermediation.

Comment

[1] A lawyer acts as intermediary under this Rule when the lawyer represents two or more parties with potentially conflicting interests. A key factor in defining the relationship is whether the parties share responsibility for the lawyer's fee, but the common representation may be inferred from other circumstances. Because confusion can arise as to the lawyer's role where each party is not separately represented, it is important that the lawyer make clear the relationship.

[2] The Rule does not apply to a lawyer acting as arbitrator or mediator between or among parties who are not clients of the lawyer, even where the lawyer has been appointed with the concurrence of the parties. In performing such a role the lawyer may be subject to applicable codes of ethics, such as the Code of Ethics for Arbitration in Commercial Disputes prepared by a joint Committee of the American Bar Association and the American Arbitration Association.

[3] A lawyer acts as intermediary in seeking to establish or adjust a relationship between clients on an amicable and mutually advantageous basis; for example, in helping to organize a business in which two or more clients are entrepreneurs, working out the financial reorganization of an enterprise in which two or more clients have an interest, arranging a property distribution in settlement of an estate or mediating a dispute between clients. The lawyer seeks to resolve potentially conflicting interests by developing the parties' mutual interests. The alternative can be that each party may have to obtain separate representation, with the possibility in some situations of incurring additional cost, complication or even litigation. Given these and other relevant factors, all the clients may prefer that the lawyer act as intermediary.

[4] In considering whether to act as intermediary between clients, a lawyer should be mindful that if the intermediation fails the result can be additional cost, embarrassment and recrimination. In some situations the risk of failure is so great that intermediation is plainly impossible. For example, a lawyer cannot undertake common representation of clients between whom contentious litigation is imminent or who contemplate contentious negotiations. More generally, if the relationship between the parties has already assumed definite antagonism, the possibility that the clients' interests can be adjusted by intermediation ordinarily is not very good.

[5] The appropriateness of intermediation can depend on its form. Forms of intermediation range from informal arbitration, where each client's case is presented by the respective client and the lawyer decides the outcome, to mediation, to common representation where the clients' interests are substantially though not entirely compatible. One form may be appropriate in circumstances where another would not. Other relevant factors are whether the lawyer subsequently will represent both parties on a continuing basis and whether the situation involves creating a relationship between the parties or terminating one.

Confidentiality and Privilege

[6] A particularly important factor in determining the appropriateness of intermediation is the effect on client-lawyer confidentiality and the attorney-client privilege. In a common representation, the lawyer is still required both to keep each client adequately informed and to maintain confidentiality of information relating to the representation. See Rules 1.4 and 1.6. Complying with both requirements while acting as intermediary requires a delicate balance. If the balance cannot be maintained, the common representation is improper. With regard to the attorney-client privilege, the prevailing rule is that as between commonly represented clients the privi-

lege does not attach. Hence, it must be assumed that if litigation eventuates between the clients, the privilege will not protect any such communications, and the clients should be so advised.

[7] Since the lawyer is required to be impartial between commonly represented clients, intermediation is improper when that impartiality cannot be maintained. For example, a lawyer who has represented one of the clients for a long period and in a variety of matters might have difficulty being impartial between that client and one to whom the lawyer has only recently been introduced.

Consultation

[8] In acting as intermediary between clients, the lawyer is required to consult with the clients on the implications of doing so, and proceed only upon consent based on such a consultation. The consultation should make clear that the lawyer's role is not that of partisanship normally expected in other circumstances.

[9] Paragraph (b) is an application of the principle expressed in Rule 1.4. Where the lawyer is intermediary, the clients ordinarily must assume greater responsibility for decisions than when each client is independently represented.

Withdrawal

[10] Common representation does not diminish the rights of each client in the client-lawyer relationship. Each has the right to loyal and diligent representation, the right to discharge the lawyer as stated in Rule 1.16, and the protection of Rule 1.9 concerning obligations to a former client.

Authors' 1983 Model Rules Comparison

The ABA House of Delegate *deleted* Rule 2.2 from the 2002 version of the Rules.

The drafters of the 2002 Rules based their recommendation to completely delete the Rule on the following observations:

The Commission recommends deleting Rule 2.2 and moving any discussion of common representation to the Rule 1.7 Comment. The Commission is convinced that neither the concept of "intermediation" (as distinct from either "representation" or "mediation") nor the relationship between Rules 2.2 and 1.7 has been well understood. Prior to the adoption of the Model Rules, there was more resistance to the idea of lawyers helping multiple clients to resolve their differences through common representation; thus, the original idea behind Rule 2.2 was to permit common representation when the circumstances were such that the potential benefits for the clients outweighed the potential risks. Rule 2.2, however, contains some limitations not present in Rule 1.7; for example, a flat prohibition on a lawyer continuing to represent one client and not the other if intermediation fails, even if neither client objects. As a result, lawyers not wishing to be bound by such limitations may choose to consider the representation as falling under Rule 1.7 rather than Rule 2.2, and there is nothing in the Rules themselves that clearly dictates a contrary result.

Rather than amending Rule 2.2, the Commission believes that the ideas expressed therein are better dealt with in the Comment to Rule 1.7. There is much in Rule 2.2 and its Comment that applies to all examples of common representation and ought to appear in Rule 1.7. Moreover, there is less resistance to common representation today than there was in 1983; thus, there is no longer any particular need to establish the propriety of common representation through a separate Rule.

Reporter's Explanation of Changes to Model Rule 2.2.

Model Code Comparison

There was no direct counterpart to this Rule in the Disciplinary Rules of the Model Code. EC 5-20 stated that a "lawyer is often asked to serve as an impartial arbitrator or mediator in matters which involve present or former clients. He may serve in either capacity if he first discloses such present or former relationships." DR 5-105(B) provided that a lawyer "shall not continue multiple employment if the exercise of his independent judgment in behalf of a client will be or is likely to be adversely affected by his representation of another client, or if it would be likely to involve him in representation of differing interests, except to the extent permitted under DR 5-105(C)." DR 5-105(C) provided that "a lawyer may represent multiple clients if it is obvious that he can adequately represent the interests of each and if each consents to the representation after full disclosure of the possible effect of such representation on the exercise of his independent professional judgment on behalf of each."

§ 2.2–1 INTERMEDIATION AMONG MULTIPLE CLIENTS: BACKGROUND

In 1983, the ABA adopted Rule 2.2 as a provision to govern situations where a lawyer represents two or more clients with potentially conflicting interests.[1] At the time, the drafters believed that the Model Code did not offer sufficient guidance to lawyers who wanted to accept such representations.[2] Thus, they drafted a detailed rule creating a new role, referred to as intermediation, for lawyers who sought to represent multiple clients.[3] "Intermediation" is a term that did not pass into general professional us-

---

[Section 2.2–1]

[1] Deleted Rule 2.2, Comment 1.

[2] The Model Code made few references to the concept of the lawyer as intermediary between clients. DR 5-105(B) recognizes that the lawyer may represent multiple clients with differing interests if, under DR 5-105(C), the clients consent and it is "obvious" that the lawyer can represent each adequately. *See also* EC 5-20, concerning the lawyer as "impartial arbitrator or mediator." But, there was no direct counterpart in the Model Code to Rule 2.2.

[3] The Reporter to the 1983 Model Rules, Professor Geoffrey Hazard, created the concept of a lawyer as intermediary from his study of Louis Brandeis' "counsel for the situation." *See* GEOFFREY C. HAZARD, JR., ETHICS IN THE PRACTICE OF LAW 58–68 (Yale Press 1978). At several times during the legal career of Brandeis, he had represented multiple clients with conflicting interests. In the 1916 Senate hearings involving the confirmation of Brandeis to the Supreme Court, several opponents claimed that he had violated the conflicts of interest rules by representing multiple clients. The

age, and the American Law Institute's Restatement of the Law Governing Lawyers does not employ it.[4]

Generally, Rule 2.2 allowed the lawyer to represent multiple clients in order to intermediate their differences if the clients knowingly consented, the lawyer reasonable believed that the matter could be resolved on terms that were compatible with the clients' best interest, there was little risk of material prejudice to any of the clients if the matter was not resolved successfully, and the lawyer reasonably believed that she could act impartially and that there would be no improper effect on her other clients.[5]

The Model Rules delineated the role of the lawyer as intermediary as a recognition of what had been a common role for lawyers to play. Because clients often sought multiple client representation to save costs and time, it was "common practice" for attorneys to act "for both partners in drawing articles of copartnership or drawing agreements for the dissolution of copartnership, in acting for both the grantor and the grantee in the sale of real property, in acting for both the seller and purchaser in the sale of personal property, in acting for both the lessor and the lessee in the leasing of property, and in acting for both the lender and borrower in handling a loan transaction. . . ."[6]

The 1983 Model Rules sometimes used the term "intermediation" as meaning anything from "informal arbitration" to "mediation."[7] However, it is important to realize that in arbitration or mediation the lawyer-arbitrator or lawyer-mediator represents *none* of the parties. Intermediation is different: in intermediation the lawyer represents *all* of the parties involved in the intermediation. In fact, one of the requirements of intermediation is that the lawyer must reasonably believe that the matter can be resolved "on terms compatible with the *clients'* best interests, that *each client* will be able to make adequately informed decisions in the matter and that there is little risk of material prejudice to the interest of *any of the clients* if the contemplated resolution is unsuccessful. . . ."[8]

---

proponents argued that Brandeis was a "counsel for the situation" serving the common goals of the clients and therefore did not violate any ethical norms.

[4]Restatement of the Law Governing Lawyers, Third, § 130 (Official Draft 2000), Comment *a*.

[5]Deleted Rule 2.2(a).

[6]*Lessing v. Gibbons*, 6 Cal.App.2d 598, 606, 45 P.2d 258, 261 (1935).

[7]Rule 2.2, Comment 5 (intermediation ranges from "informal arbitration" to "mediation" to common representation).

[8]Deleted Rule 2.2(a)(2) (emphasis added).

Although one Comment to Deleted Rule 2.2 treated "interme-diation" as including "mediation,"[9] another made clear that Rule 2.2, governing the intermediary, did "*not* apply to a lawyer acting as arbitrator or *mediator* between or among parties who are not clients of the lawyer, even where the lawyer has been appointed with the concurrence of the parties."[10] When a lawyer was intermediating between his own clients, Rule 2.2 was designed to protect the lawyer's clients. Deleted Rule 2.2 did not cover cases of formal arbitration where the lawyer was selected by parties who were *not* his clients.[11]

§ 2.2–2 REASONS UNDERLYING THE DELETION OF RULE 2.2

Despite its detail, Deleted Rule 2.2 presented many interpre-tive problems for lawyers.[1] First, the rule did not clearly define the term "intermediary" and therefore lawyers did not know whether the Rule governed all multiple client representations or only those that lawyers and clients designated as intermediations. Second, the drafters did not clarify the relationship between Deleted Rule 2.2 and Rule 1.7(b) and therefore lawyers were confused about the inconsistencies between the two provisions. Third, the Deleted Rule 2.2 did not clarify whether the client in an intermediation was each person, the group, or the situation. Finally, it also did not address the lawyer's duty of confidential-ity as it related to the multiple clients in an intermediation.

Apart from these interpretive problems, when clients in a multiple client representation sued their lawyers for malpractice or breach of fiduciary duty, these clients often used the failure of the lawyer to follow the details in Deleted Rule 2.2 as evidence that their lawyers had committed malpractice.[2] In an era of mal-practice suits against lawyers, one could view Deleted Rule 2.2 as providing too much bright line guidance to lawyers.

The drafters of the 2002 Rules chose to combine the notion of intermediation into the multiple client representation language of the general conflicts of interest Rule 1.7.[3] After all, much of the guidance in Deleted Rule 2.2 related to conflicts of interest when

---

[9]Deleted Rule 2.2, Comment 5.

[10]Deleted Rule 2.2, Comment 2 (emphasis added).

[11]*See* Deleted Rule 2.2, Comment 2. *Cf.* Rule 1.12.

[Section 2.2–2]

[1]*See generally* John S. Dzien-kowski, *Lawyers as Intermediaries: The Representation of Multiple Clients*

in the Modern Legal Profession, 1992 U.ILL.L.REV. 741.

[2]*See, e.g., McNair v. Rainsford*, 330 S.C. 332, 499 S.E.2d 488 (App. 1998)(reversing a summary judgment and ordering a trial on the grounds that a lawyer representing multiple clients may have violated Rule 1.7 and 2.2 in South Carolina).

[3]Reporter's Explanation of

a lawyer represented multiple clients.[4] By combining much of the language into the Comments under Rule 1.7, the ABA solved several of the problems relating to inconsistent language. However, only time will tell whether this change will reduce lawyer malpractice liability in the multiple client representation context.

Changes to Model Rule 2.2. Although the drafters moved the notion of intermediation into the Comments to Rule 1.7, they no longer refer to this representation as involving an "intermediary" or "intermediation." Instead, they use the terms, "common representation" of clients in a more general discussion of multiple client representation.

[4] A previous edition of this book presciently noted: "All of the issues under Rule 2.2 could probably be handled just as well under Rule 1.7. Rule 2.2 really appears to be just a specific application of the general principles of Rule 1.7."

CHAPTER 2.3
THE LAWYER AS EVALUATOR

§ 2.3–1 The Lawyer As Evaluator
§ 2.3–2 Client Consent to the Lawyer Acting As Evaluator
§ 2.3–3 Client-Imposed Limitations on the Scope of an
　　　　　Evaluation

RULE 2.3: EVALUATION FOR USE BY THIRD PERSONS

(a) A lawyer may provide an evaluation of a matter affecting a client for the use of someone other than the client if the lawyer reasonably believes that making the evaluation is compatible with other aspects of the lawyer's relationship with the client.

(b) When the lawyer knows or reasonably should know that the evaluation is likely to affect the client's interests materially and adversely, the lawyer shall not provide the evaluation unless the client gives informed consent.

(c) Except as disclosure is authorized in connection with a report of an evaluation, information relating to the evaluation is otherwise protected by Rule 1.6.

Comment

Definition

[1] An evaluation may be performed at the client's direction or when impliedly authorized in order to carry out the representation. See Rule 1.2. Such an evaluation may be for the primary purpose of establishing information for the benefit of third parties; for example, an opinion concerning the title of property rendered at the behest of a vendor for the information of a prospective purchaser, or at the behest of a borrower for the information of a prospective lender. In some situations, the evaluation may be required by a government agency; for example, an opinion concerning the legality of the securities registered for sale under the securities laws. In other instances, the evaluation may be required by a third person, such as a purchaser of a business.

[2] A legal evaluation should be distinguished from an investigation of a person with whom the lawyer does not have a client-lawyer relationship. For example, a lawyer retained by a purchaser to analyze a vendor's title to property does not have a client-lawyer relationship with the vendor. So also, an investigation into a person's affairs by a government lawyer, or by special counsel by a

government lawyer, or by special counsel employed by the government, is not an evaluation as that term is used in this Rule. The question is whether the lawyer is retained by the person whose affairs are being examined. When the lawyer is retained by that person, the general rules concerning loyalty to client and preservation of confidences apply, which is not the case if the lawyer is retained by someone else. For this reason, it is essential to identify the person by whom the lawyer is retained. This should be made clear not only to the person under examination, but also to others to whom the results are to be made available.

Duties Owed to Third Person and Client

[3] When the evaluation is intended for the information or use of a third person, a legal duty to that person may or may not arise. That legal question is beyond the scope of this Rule. However, since such an evaluation involves a departure from the normal client-lawyer relationship, careful analysis of the situation is required. The lawyer must be satisfied as a matter of professional judgment that making the evaluation is compatible with other functions undertaken in behalf of the client. For example, if the lawyer is acting as advocate in defending the client against charges of fraud, it would normally be incompatible with that responsibility for the lawyer to perform an evaluation for others concerning the same or a related transaction. Assuming no such impediment is apparent, however, the lawyer should advise the client of the implications of the evaluation, particularly the lawyer's responsibilities to third persons and the duty to disseminate the findings.

Access to and Disclosure of Information

[4] The quality of an evaluation depends on the freedom and extent of the investigation upon which it is based. Ordinarily a lawyer should have whatever latitude of investigation seems necessary as a matter of professional judgment. Under some circumstances, however, the terms of the evaluation may be limited. For example, certain issues or sources may be categorically excluded, or the scope of search may be limited by time constraints or the noncooperation of persons having relevant information. Any such limitations that are material to the evaluation should be described in the report. If after a lawyer has commenced an evaluation, the client refuses to comply with the terms upon which it was understood the evaluation was to have been made, the lawyer's obligations are determined by law, having reference to the terms of the client's agreement and the surrounding circumstances. In no circumstances is the lawyer permitted to knowingly make a false statement of material fact or law in providing an evaluation under this Rule. See Rule 4.1.

Obtaining Client's Informed Consent

[5] Information relating to an evaluation is protected by Rule 1.6. In many situations, providing an evaluation to a third party poses no significant risk to the client; thus, the lawyer may be impliedly authorized to disclose information to carry out the representation. See Rule 1.6(a). Where, however, it is reasonably likely that providing the evaluation will affect the client's interests materially and adversely, the lawyer must first obtain the client's consent after the

client has been adequately informed concerning the important possible effects on the client's interests. See Rules 1.6(a) and 1.0(e).

Financial Auditors' Requests for Information

[6] When a question concerning the legal situation of a client arises at the instance of the client's financial auditor and the question is referred to the lawyer, the lawyer's response may be made in accordance with procedures recognized in the legal profession. Such a procedure is set forth in the American Bar Association Statement of Policy Regarding Lawyers' Responses to Auditors' Requests for Information, adopted in 1975.

Authors' 1983 Model Rules Comparison

The drafters of the 2002 Rules revised the text and comments of Rule 2.3 to reflect the view that lawyer evaluations of a client may fall into two categories: (1) evaluations that provide benefit (and no significant risk) to the client, and (2) evaluations that are likely to have a material adverse effect on the client. In the first category, lawyers may be impliedly authorized to perform the evaluation. For the second category, the lawyer must obtain the client's informed consent before proceeding with the evaluation representation. To facilitate this change, the drafters inserted new text in a new Rule 2.3(b) and renumbered the former (b) as (c). See Appendix N for a redlined version of the old rule and the Reporter's explanation.

In Comment 1, the drafters added the clause recognizing that some evaluations may be impliedly authorized from a larger representation.

In Comment 2, the drafters deleted the following paragraph relating to evaluations performed by government lawyers:

> [2] Lawyers for the government may be called upon to give a formal opinion on the legality of contemplated government agency action. In making such an evaluation, the government lawyer acts at the behest of the government as the client but for the purpose of establishing the limits of the agency's authorized activity. Such an opinion is to be distinguished from confidential legal advice given agency officials. The critical question is whether the opinion is to be made public.
>
> The remaining paragraphs were renumbered to reflect this deleted language.

The drafters modified the title of new Comment 3 to reflect an obligation to the client.

In new Comment 4, the drafters added the last sentence to reaffirm Rule 4.1's requirement that lawyers not make false statements of law or fact in an evaluation.

Comment 5 on obtaining client consent is completely new and reflects the drafters' belief that lawyers should obtain a client's informed consent when the evaluation involves material risk of harm.

Model Code Comparison

There was no counterpart to this Rule in the Model Code.

§ 2.3–1 THE LAWYER AS EVALUATOR

Clients often hire lawyers to evaluate a matter for the benefit of third parties. In such a situation, the lawyer assumes the role of an evaluator—authoring a document, in some cases referred to as an opinion letter, examining the legal position of a client.[1] Third parties, such as banks, investors, and purchasers, request such evaluations to determine whether to enter into a transaction with a client and to provide information about the value of the potential investment. The lawyer is an evaluator when she issues a legal opinion "concerning the title of property rendered at the behest of a vendor for the information of a prospective purchaser, or . . . an opinion concerning the legality of the securities registered for sale under the securities laws."[2] Lawyers have frequently assumed this special role, particularly in recent times.[3]

In 1983, the ABA House of Delegates adopted Rule 2.3 to govern the situations where lawyers accept the role of an evaluator of a client matter for use by third persons. Rule 2.3 affirms that lawyers may accept this type of representation even though the role of the lawyer as evaluator may create some duties to third persons or may require that the lawyer disclose information adverse to the clients' interests. Given the divided loyalties that may arise in the context of an evaluation, Rule 2.3 establishes the conditions that a lawyer must satisfy before accepting this unique representation.

Evaluation for the benefit of a third party should be distinguished from investigation for the benefit of a client. There is, in short, an important difference between a lawyer's opinion that is expected to be made *public* and shown to third parties, versus a lawyer's opinion that is expected to *remain private* and only shown to the client. If, for example, a client asks for confidential advice about whether it has complied with the law, then the lawyer is acting as an adviser, and is therefore governed by Rule 2.1.

For example, a prospective buyer of an apartment building may hire a lawyer to complete a title search on this property, which the buyer is planning to purchase. The lawyer's client is the buyer, not the seller, and the lawyer's duty of loyalty is only to his client. In contrast, if the seller retains a lawyer to furnish

---

[Section 2.3–1]

[1] The 1983 version of Rule 2.3 contained a Comment 2 describing the role of an evaluator in the context of a government lawyer. *See* Authors' 1983 Model Rules Comparison to Rule 2.3. The drafters of the 2002 Rules deleted this Comment because "neither its meaning nor function was clear." Reporter's Explanation of Changes to Model Rule 2.3. The deletion of this language does not suggest that government lawyers may never be evaluators, it simply reflects the notion that the remaining language can properly address the role of government lawyers who act as evaluators.

[2] Rule 2.3, Comment 1. *See also* ABA Formal Opinion 335 (1974).

[3] Rule 2.3. *See also* Restatement of the Law Governing Lawyers, Third, §95 (Official Draft 2000).

a title opinion that the seller plans to show to the buyer to bolster his claim that the title is a good one, then the lawyer is retained by the client to *evaluate* the property for the benefit of a nonclient.[4] The lawyer's duty of loyalty is to the client,[5] but the lawyer may also have assumed legal obligations to the third parties who rely on the evaluation.[6]

In the practice of law, there are many recurring contexts where clients routinely ask lawyers for evaluations.[7] Lawyers perform evaluations in the areas of: (1) tax—evaluating the tax consequences of an actual or proposed transaction or evaluating whether the transaction constitutes a tax shelter, (2) securities—evaluating a client's compliance with the securities law or exemption from securities registration, (3) environmental—evaluating a client's compliance with environmental laws and regulations, (4) commercial real estate—evaluating the validity or the mortgage loan, and (5) litigation risk—evaluating the risk that the client's ongoing litigation may result in a material loss for purposes of financial reporting in an auditor's statement.

In many of these areas, practice groups and the ABA have sought to develop model standards for issuing opinions.[8] The specific details of these standards are generally beyond the scope of this discussion. Two areas have drawn the attention of the legal profession.

In the litigation risk context, Model Rule 2.3 has a special Comment titled, "Financial Auditors' Requests for Information." The Comment simply states that when the lawyer for a corporation responds to an auditor's request for information, the lawyer should follow ABA recommended policies on this issue.[9] Case law has confirmed that: "An attorney's responsibility with respect to responses to auditor's inquiries is governed by the American Bar

---

[4] Rule 2.3, Comment 2.

[5] Rule 2.3, Comment 2.

[6] Restatement of the Law of Torts, Second, § 552.

[7] *See* ABA/BNA Lawyers' Manual on Professional Conduct ¶ 71:701 (2004) (examining legal opinions and evaluations).

[8] *See, e.g., Circular 230,* 31 C.F.R. pt. 10 (2004) (regulating the issuance of tax shelter opinions); *Report of the Special Committee on Lawyers' role in Securities Transactions,* 33 BUSINESS LAWYER 1343 (1978) (offering guidance

in securities opinions); *Mortgage Loan Opinion Report,* 54 BUSINESS LAWYER 119 (1998) (examining different standards for mortgage loan opinions).

[9] Rule 2.3, Comment 6. The Comment incorporates, by reference, the ABA's *Statement of Policy Regarding Lawyers' Responses to Auditors' Requests for Information,* adopted in 1975, and reprinted in, 31 BUSINESS LAWYER 1709 (1976). For further discussion, see James J. Fuld, *Lawyers' Responses to Auditors—Some Practical Aspects,* 44 BUSINESS LAWYER 159 (1985).

Association 'Statement of Policy Regarding Lawyer's Responses to Auditor's Request For Information.' "[10]

In these circumstances, it is helpful to think of the lawyer as the client's agent in responding to requests from the auditors. If the lawyer is not really the agent, then this rule does not obligate the lawyer to respond. Thus, *Tew v. Arky, Freed, Stearns, Watson, Greer, Weaver & Harris, P.A.*[11] granted summary judgment to defendant-lawyer because he had "no legal duty" to advise a company's auditors of his alleged knowledge of the company's financial problems when he did virtually no work for company, and the company had never retained him regarding its financial problems. There is no malpractice liability for failure to disclose unless there is a duty to disclose.[12]

In the tax shelter context, the Treasury and Internal Revenue Service (IRS) have sought to regulate lawyers who draft tax shelter opinions. In 2003, the Treasury and the IRS issued proposed modifications to Circular 230 that would significantly increase the burden on lawyers who issued opinions in the tax shelter context.[13] In the same year, the government adopted list maintenance regulations that required law firms and accounting firms to keep lists of clients who relied upon tax shelters.[14] During the last year, the IRS has used these rules and its subpoena power to obtain records from lawyers and other firms about client participation in tax shelters. In several highly publicized cases, the IRS and law firms have fought over the confidentiality of client identity and records in the tax shelter opinion context.[15] This federal regulation of tax lawyers demonstrates the exercise of the

---

[10]*Tew v. Arky, Freed, Stearns, Watson, Greer, Weaver & Harris, P.A.*, 655 F.Supp. 1571, 1572 (S.D.Fla.,1987), *affirmed*, 846 F.2d 753 (11th Cir. 1988) (TABLE, NO. 87-5248), certiorari denied, 488 U.S. 854, 109 S.Ct. 142, 102 L.Ed.2d 114 (1988).

[11]*Tew v. Arky, Freed, Stearns, Watson, Greer, Weaver & Harris, P.A.*, 655 F.Supp. 1571, 1572–73 (S.D.Fla. 1987). There was:

"no evidence that ESM [the corporation] ever retained Mr. Stearns to devote substantive attention to its financial problems. In fact, the record in this case establishes without question that Mr. Stearns did virtually no work at all for ESM. Accordingly, even *under the ABA Statement*, it is patently clear as a matter of law that *Mr. Stearns owed no legal duty* to disclose. Having rendered almost no services to

ESM—*and never having been retained by ESM regarding its financial problems*—Mr. Stearns simply cannot be sued for legal malpractice for not disclosing his alleged knowledge of ESM's financial problems. In addition, there is no evidence that ESM ever identified its financial problems in its auditor's inquiry letters or requested comment thereon." (emphasis added).

[12]ROBERT J. HAFT AND MICHELE H. HUDSON, LIABILITY OF ATTORNEYS AND ACCOUNTANTS FOR SECURITIES TRANSACTIONS § 6:20 ("Attorneys—Lawyers 'Responses To Auditors' Requests For Information") (Thomson West 2004).

[13]*See* IR-2003-147 at www.irs.gov

[14]*See* Treas. Reg. § 301.612-1 (2004).

[15]*United States v. Sidley, Austin, Brown & Wood, LLP*, 2004 WL 905930

supremacy clause in preempting the state regulation of the conduct of lawyers.

It is common, at the closing of a business transaction involving, for example, a lender, acquirer, or buyer that the lawyer for the borrower or acquired company or seller to issue a closing opinion that refers to legal proceedings involving the company. This opinion letter often includes a paragraph that refers to legal proceedings that may involve the company. This "paragraph does not express any legal conclusions (and, therefore, is sometimes referred to as a 'confirmation' rather than an opinion). Instead, it simply states a fact, namely that counsel knows of no legal proceedings that have not otherwise been disclosed to the recipient."[16]

If the lawyer gives a negligent opinion—an opinion that does not reflect customary diligence[17]—that results in damage to the recipient of the opinion, the recipient has a cause of action against the lawyer, even though the lawyer was not his client.[18]

A leading decision applying these principles is *Dean Foods Co. v. Pappathanasi*.[19] The opinion letter said that, to the law firm's knowledge, without investigation, "except as disclosed in a sched-

---

(N.D.Ill.2004), enforced an IRS summons requiring the law firm to turn over names of its tax shelter clients. Sidley & Austin allegedly marketed tax shelters at very high fees and also sold opinion letters reassuring the clients that the shelters would work. The IRS believed the schemes are unlawful and ineffective, but without the lists, it cannot know who used them. In this opinion, the court rejected arguments from "John Doe" intervenors alleging that the summonses are indefinite. *See also United States v. Jenkens & Gilchrist, P.C.*, 2004 WL 1091009 (N.D.Ill. 2004) (same result in the case of another firm). As one indication of what is involved in such cases, on May 14, 2004, Judge Scheindlin gave preliminary approval to a settlement with investors in one such shelter called COBRA. The amount of the settlement was reported to be $75 million, making it one of the largest malpractice settlements ever. See *Denney v. Jenkens & Gilchrist, P.C.*, 2004 WL 936843 (S.D.N.Y. 2004), for an earlier opinion developing some of the allegations in the case.

[16]Donald W. Glazer & Arthur Norman Field, *No-Litigation Opinions Can Be Risky Business: Looking at the Facts and Beyond*, 14 ABA BUSINESS LAW TODAY (No. 6, July/August 2005), http://www.abanet. org/buslaw/blt/2005–07–08/field.shtml.

[17]Restatement of the Law Governing Lawyers, Third, § 52, Comment b & § 95(3) (ALI 2000).

[18]*E.g., Greycas, Inc. v. Proud*, 826 F.2d 1560 (7th Cir. 1987); *Nycal Corp. v. KPMG Peat Marwick LLP*, 426 Mass. 491, 493–99, 688 N.E.2d 1368 (1998).

Third-party "Closing" Opinions: A Report of the TriBar Opinion Committee, 53 BUSINESS LAWYER 591–679 (1998).

[19]18 Mass. L. Rptr. 598, 2004 WL 3019442 (Mass. Super. 2004). The case was settled so there is no appellate report. However, it is commonly cited as a thoughtful and leading case. *E.g.* Donald W. Glazer & Arthur Norman Field, *No-Litigation Opinions Can Be Risky Business: Looking at the Facts and Beyond*, 14 ABA BUSINESS LAW TODAY (No. 6, July/August 2005), http://www.abanet.

ule to the acquisition agreement: (a) there was no investigation of any kind pending or threatened against the Company and (b) the Company was not 'subject to any . . . continuing' governmental investigation."[20] However, three months after the closing, the U.S. Attorney sent a target letter to the acquired company, which later pled guilty and paid a fine of over $7 million.[21] The court found, after a bench trial, that the firm had negligently misrepresented and should have disclosed an investigation. The court tied together the various bits of knowledge that the individual members of the law firm had and used that to find negligence.[22] The law firm was liable for more than $9 million.

Negative Assurances. In light of *Dean Foods Co. v. Pappathanasi*,[23] commentators have recommended that lawyers avoid negative assurances in opinion letters:

> Opinion preparers should avoid stating expressly in their opinion letters that they are unaware of (or that nothing has come to their attention that leads them to believe that there are) any inaccuracies in the factual representations or certificates on which they are relying. Such statements can be read as providing negative assurance and, if incorrect, may serve as a basis for a claim even if all the opinions given are correct. Ordinarily, negative assurance should only be given to financial intermediaries (such as placement agents and underwriters) in securities offerings to assist them in establishing defenses from liability under the securities laws.[24]

§ 2.3-2 CLIENT CONSENT TO THE LAWYER ACTING AS EVALUATOR

To protect the clients, and to take into account the needs of third parties, Rule 2.3 places several important restrictions on the evaluations. The lawyer must reasonably believe that conducting an evaluation is compatible with other aspects of the

---

org/buslaw/blt/2005–07–08/field.shtml.

[20]Donald W. Glazer & Arthur Norman Field, *No-Litigation Opinions Can Be Risky Business: Looking at the Facts and Beyond*, 14 ABA BUSINESS LAW TODAY (No. 6, July/August 2005), http://www.abanet. org/buslaw/blt/2005–07–08/field.shtml.

[21]*Dean Foods Co. v. Pappathanasi*, 2004 WL 3019442, *10. This case specifically relied on Third-party "Closing" Opinions: A Report of the TriBar Opinion Committee, 53 BUSINESS LAWYER 591–679 (1998).

[22]In contrast, *Greycas, Inc. v. Proud*, 826 F.2d 1560 (7th Cir. 1987) involved a single lawyer. *Dean Foods* involved knowledge of various members of the same law firm. The court wove the various bits of knowledge to find negligence.

[23]18 Mass. L. Rptr. 598, 2004 WL 3019442 (Mass. Super. 2004).

[24]Donald W. Glazer & Arthur Norman Field, *No-Litigation Opinions Can Be Risky Business: Looking at the Facts and Beyond*, 14 ABA BUSINESS LAW TODAY (No. 6, July/August 2005), http://www.abanet. org/buslaw/blt/2005–07–08/field.shtml, *citing*, Report of ABA Task Force on Securities Law Opinions, Negative Assurance in Securities Offerings: Special Report of the Task Force on Securities Law Opinions, ABA Section of Business Law, 59 BUSINESS LAWYER 1513 (2004).

lawyer's relationship with the client.[1] For example, if the lawyer had been an advocate defending the client on charges of fraud, it would usually not be compatible for the lawyer to conduct an evaluation of the same or related transaction.[2]

The 1983 version of Rule 2.3 required that the client should also knowingly consent to this arrangement.[3] The text of the rule required that the lawyer obtain this knowing consent in every representation where the lawyer planned to perform an evaluation for use by a third person. The thrust of this requirement was that the client should know that the lawyer does not plan to act as a typical partisan advocate because of "the lawyer's responsibilities to third persons and the duty to disseminate the findings."[4]

The drafters of the 2002 Rule 2.3 believed that this consent requirement did not properly reflect the circumstances under which lawyers perform evaluations. In some cases, the nature of the representation provides implied authorization for the lawyer to perform an evaluation of the client for a third party.[5] This situation arises when the main reason for the representation is to provide the evaluation for a third person.[6] Another situation may arise when the evaluation is part of a larger representation of the client, and the evaluation was contemplated by the attorney and the client from the outset of the representation. In such circumstances, if the evaluation is contemplated by the attorney-client representation and no significant risk of injury to the client exists, the lawyer does not need to obtain the client's informed consent.[7]

Rule 2.3(b) provides that the lawyer must obtain the client's informed consent if "the lawyer knows or reasonably should know that the evaluation is likely to affect the client's interests materially and adversely. . . . " The lawyer needs to disclose information to the client about the effect of producing an evaluation for disclosure to a third party.[8]

[Section 2.3–2]

[1] Rule 2.3(a).

[2] Rule 2.3, Comment 4.

[3] Rule 2.3(a)(2).

[4] Rule 2.3, Comment 3.

[5] Rule 2.3(a).

[6] Rule 2.3, Comment 1.

[7] Rule 2.3, Comment 5. The drafters seem to link the impliedly authorized approach to consent with the little risk of material prejudice standard. Although one could often find that a lawyer's judgment that the evaluation poses little risk of prejudice or adverse effect on the client usually arises when a lawyer has implied authorization to perform an evaluation, these two inquiries are separate and distinct. A lawyer should determine whether under the facts of the representation, the lawyer is or is not impliedly authorized to perform an evaluation. If the risk of adverse effect is serious and material, the lawyer may be under an obligation to ensure that the client understands these risks even if implied authorization exists.

[8] See Rule 2.3, Comment 5.

§ 2.3–3 CLIENT-IMPOSED LIMITATIONS ON THE SCOPE OF AN EVALUATION

A client may place limits on the scope of an evaluation, for example, by excluding certain issues, or imposing time constraints.[1] Or, some persons may simply refuse to cooperate; Rule 2.3 does not arm the lawyer with a subpoena power. The lawyer's evaluation should disclose in the evaluation all material limits so that third persons may consider such information in determining whether to rely on the lawyer's evaluation.[2] Of course, lawyers need to be mindful about their obligation under Rule 4.1 not to "knowingly make a false statement of material fact or law."[3]

To the extent that the lawyer with client approval or consent shows an evaluation to a third party, the expectation of client confidentiality is removed with respect to the evaluation. Otherwise, all information relating to the evaluation is confidential because of the client-lawyer relationship.[4] Thus, if communications are not required to be disclosed in the evaluation, these communications, which are not included in the report, continue to be protected by Rule 1.6.[5] Third parties may request that the lawyer disclose such information, however, the lawyer must obtain the client's informed consent before complying with

---

[Section 2.3–3]

[1] Rule 2.3, Comment 4.

[2] Rule 2.3, Comment 4. **Selective Waiver**. *In re Pacific Pictures Corp.*, ___ F.3d ___, ___, 2012 WL 1293534 (9th Cir. 2012). This court, like most circuits, rejected the selective waiver theory of *Diversified Industries, Inc. v. Meredith*. Once a litigant produces documents to the government in compliance with a grand jury subpoena, these documents lose their attorney client privilege. The court said, 2012 WL 1293534, *3:

"Petitioners' primary contention is that because Toberoff disclosed these documents to the government, as opposed to a civil litigant, his actions did not waive the privilege as to the world at large. That is, they urge that we adopt the theory of 'selective waiver' initially accepted by the Eighth Circuit, *Diversified Industries, Inc. v. Meredith*, 572 F.2d 596 (8th Cir.1978) (en banc), but rejected by every other circuit to consider the issue since, *see In re Qwest Commc'ns Int'l*, 450 F.3d 1179, 1197 (10th Cir.2006); *Burden–Meeks v.*

Welch, 319 F.3d 897, 899 (7th Cir.2003); *In re Columbia/HCA Healthcare Corp. Billing Practices Litig*. ., 293 F.3d 289, 295 (6th Cir.2002) [hereinafter " *In re Columbia* "]; *United States v. Mass. Inst. of Tech.*, 129 F.3d 681, 686 (1st Cir.1997); *Genentech, Inc. v. United States Int'l Trade Comm'n*, 122 F.3d 1409, 1416–18 (Fed.Cir.1997); *In re Steinhardt Partners, L.P.*, 9 F.3d 230, 236 (2d Cir.1993); *Westinghouse Elec. Corp. v. Republic of Philippines*, 951 F.2d 1414, 1425 (3d Cir.1991); *In re Martin Marietta Corp.*, 856 F.2d 619, 623–24 (4th Cir.1988); *Permian Corp. v. United States*, 665 F.2d 1214, 1221 (D.C.Cir.1981)."

[3] Rule 2.3, Comment 4.

[4] Rule 2.3(c). A leading case in this area is *Diversified Industries, Inc. v. Meredith*, 572 F.2d 596 (8th Cir. 1977).

[5] Rule 2.3(c). That is the ethical rule. Of course, a court may decide that the information will not be protected under the law of evidence.

a third party request.[6]

---

[6]See Rule 1.6(a).

THE LAWYER AS A THIRD-PARTY NEUTRAL

RULE 2.4: LAWYER SERVING AS THIRD-PARTY NEUTRAL

(a) A lawyer serves as a third-party neutral when the lawyer assists two or more persons who are not clients of the lawyer to reach a resolution of a dispute or other matter that has arisen between them. Service as a third-party neutral may include service as an arbitrator, a mediator or in such other capacity as will enable the lawyer to assist the parties to resolve the matter.

(b) A lawyer serving as a third-party neutral shall inform unrepresented parties that the lawyer is not representing them. When the lawyer knows or reasonably should know that a party does not understand the lawyer's role in the matter, the lawyer shall explain the difference between the lawyer's role as a third-party neutral and a lawyer's role as one who represents a client.

Comment

[1] Alternative dispute resolution has become a substantial part of the civil justice system. Aside from representing clients in dispute-resolution processes, lawyers often serve as third-party neutrals. A third-party neutral is a person, such as a mediator, arbitrator, conciliator or evaluator, who assists the parties, represented or unrepresented, in the resolution of a dispute or in the arrangement of a transaction. Whether a third-party neutral serves primarily as a facilitator, evaluator or decisionmaker depends on the particular process that is either selected by the parties or mandated by a court.

[2] The role of a third-party neutral is not unique to lawyers, although, in some court-connected contexts, only lawyers are allowed to serve in this role or to handle certain types of cases. In performing this role, the lawyer may be subject to court rules or other law that apply either to third-party neutrals generally or to lawyers serving as third-party neutrals. Lawyer-neutrals may also be subject to various codes of ethics, such as the Code of Ethics for

Arbitration in Commercial Disputes prepared by a joint committee of the American Bar Association and the American Arbitration Association or the Model Standards of Conduct for Mediators jointly prepared by the American Bar Association, the American Arbitration Association and the Society of Professionals in Dispute Resolution.

[3] Unlike nonlawyers who serve as third-party neutrals, lawyers serving in this role may experience unique problems as a result of differences between the role of a third-party neutral and a lawyer's service as a client representative. The potential for confusion is significant when the parties are unrepresented in the process. Thus, paragraph (b) requires a lawyer-neutral to inform unrepresented parties that the lawyer is not representing them. For some parties, particularly parties who frequently use dispute-resolution processes, this information will be sufficient. For others, particularly those who are using the process for the first time, more information will be required. Where appropriate, the lawyer should inform unrepresented parties of the important differences between the lawyer's role as third-party neutral and a lawyer's role as a client representative, including the inapplicability of the attorney-client evidentiary privilege. The extent of disclosure required under this paragraph will depend on the particular parties involved and the subject matter of the proceeding, as well as the particular features of the dispute-resolution process selected.

[4] A lawyer who serves as a third-party neutral subsequently may be asked to serve as a lawyer representing a client in the same matter. The conflicts of interest that arise for both the individual lawyer and the lawyer's law firm are addressed in Rule 1.12.

[5] Lawyers who represent clients in alternative dispute-resolution processes are governed by the Rules of Professional Conduct. When the dispute-resolution process takes place before a tribunal, as in binding arbitration (see Rule 1.0(m)), the lawyer's duty of candor is governed by Rule 3.3. Otherwise, the lawyer's duty of candor toward both the third-party neutral and other parties is governed by Rule 4.1.

Authors' 1983 Model Rules Comparison

There was no counterpart to this Rule in the 1983 Model Rules.

Authors' Model Code Comparison

EC 5-20 stated that: "A lawyer is often asked to serve as an impartial arbitrator or mediator in matters which involve present or former clients. He may serve in either capacity if he first discloses such present or former relationships. After a lawyer has undertaken to act as an impartial arbitrator or mediator, he should not thereafter represent in the dispute any of the parties involved."

§ 2.4–1 LAWYERS SERVING AS THIRD-PARTY NEUTRALS

In the last twenty-five years, the alternative dispute resolution movement has occupied a prominent place in American dispute resolution.[1] Legislatures have mandated the use of mediation and negotiation before parties may proceed to litigation. Judges around the country encourage parties to mediate and negotiate disputes to facilitate voluntary settlement. Parties seeking to reduce costs and delay have turned to arbitration, mediation, mini-trials, conciliation and other ADR procedures to resolve their disputes. Many of these ADR procedures use third-party neutrals—independent individuals who are not representing the parties but who are seeking to facilitate the resolution of disputes—to conduct the proceedings. Although many ADR processes do not require that third-party neutrals be licensed lawyers,[2] the legal nature of disputes makes it natural to use lawyers as third-party neutrals in a vast majority of cases.[3]

Rule 2.4 authorizes lawyers to serve as third-party neutrals "in the resolution of a dispute or the arrangement of the transaction."[4] In fact, the provision recognizes the benefits served when lawyers assume the role of a third-party neutral.

The particular role of the lawyer who serves as a third-party neutral is defined by the process "selected by the parties or mandated by the court."[5] And, many ADR processes are subject to a variety of mandated and voluntary rules and guidelines.[6] Rule 2.4 does not attempt to supplant any of these rules and guidelines. Lawyers who serve as third-party neutrals should continue to follow these other sources for their conduct.[7] Instead, Rule 2.4 addresses unique problems that may arise when a

---

[Section 2.4–1]

[1]*See* KIMBERLEE K. KOVACH, MEDIATION: PRINCIPLES AND PRACTICE 1–34 (West Publishing Co., 3rd ed. 2004) (discussing ADR movement in the United States).

[2]Courts often require that only lawyers serve as third-party neutrals in court sponsored ADR procedures. *See* Rule 2.4, Comment 1.

[3]**Unauthorized Practice of Law.** A third-party neutral need not be a lawyer unless the neutral is practicing law. *See* ABA Section on Dispute Resolution, *Resolution on Mediation and the Unauthorized Practice of Law Adopted by the Section on February 2, 2002*, 13 WORLD ARBITRATION & MEDIATION REP. 135 (2002), ("Lawyer-mediators should be aware that, unless they are admitted to the bar in every state, they too are potentially affected by the issue of

UPL and mediation . . .. If mediation is considered the practice of law, lawyer-mediators could be accused of violating UPL statutes when they serve in a jurisdiction in which they are not admitted to the bar").

[4]Rule 2.4, Comment 2.

[5]Rule 2.4, Comment 1.

[6]Many state legislatures have enacted mediation and arbitration statutes. *See* Uniform Arbitration Act (2000); Uniform Mediation Act (2002). Many court rules permit or require judges to encourage ADR processes in litigation. And, several groups have promulgated standards and guidelines in various ADR processes. *See, e.g.,* AAA/ABA Code of Ethics for Arbitrators in Commercial Disputes (1977); AAA/ABA/SPIDR Model Standards for Conduct for Mediators (1994).

[7]Rule 2.4, Comment 2.

lawyer serves as a third-party neutral apart from the rules of these processes.

§ 2.4–2 RESPONSIBILITIES OF A LAWYER SERVING AS THIRD-PARTY NEUTRAL

Rule 2.4(b) provides that a lawyer who acts as a third-party neutral "shall inform unrepresented parties that the lawyer is not representing them."[1] The reason for imposing this requirement on lawyers who serve as third-party neutrals is that the role of a lawyer as a representative of a client and the role of the lawyer as a third-party neutral differ significantly. Comment 3 of Rule 2.4 warns: "The potential for confusion is significant when the parties are unrepresented in the process."[2]

This Comment also explains that when unrepresented clients are familiar with ADR processes, the lawyer's warning will be sufficient to inform them not to rely upon the lawyer for providing legal advice to the unrepresented party. However, in some circumstances, the unrepresented party will not understand the lawyer's role in the proceeding. In such a case, the lawyer third-party neutral "who knows or reasonably should know that a party does not understand the lawyer's role in the matter . . . shall explain the differences between the lawyer's role as a third-party neutral and a lawyer's role as one who represents a client."[3] This obligation is parallel to a lawyer's obligation when representing a client against a party who is not represented by counsel. Under Rule 4.3, a lawyer has a similar obligation to correct a misunderstanding that the unrepresented party may have about the lawyer's role in the matter.

The drafters of Rule 2.4 chose not to extend these obligations to represented parties in ADR proceedings. On one hand, represented parties are less likely to rely on a lawyer third-party neutral for legal advice. On the other hand, a party's lawyer is in a better position to determine that a lay person does not understand the role of a third-party neutral. Thus, it makes sense to place this burden on the party's lawyer and not on the third-party neutral to educate the party about the ADR process.

Rule 2.4 leaves unresolved many other questions about the

[Section 2.4–2]

[1] This Rule is really a reiteration of Rule 4.3, which requires that a lawyer who knows, or reasonably should know, that an unrepresented person misunderstands the lawyer's role, should correct the misunderstanding.

[2] Rule 2.4, Comment 3.

[3] See Rule 2.4, Comment 3. According to the Comment, the facts and circumstances will inform the lawyer whether such disclosure needs to be specific and detailed or general. The lawyer needs to make sure that the unrepresented party does not rely upon the decisions or actions of the third-party neutral to make choices in the ADR process.

lawyer's role as a third-party neutral. It does not address whether a lawyer who is a third-party neutral should participate in drafting agreements in principle or contracts between the parties in an ADR process. The Rule does not address whether a lawyer has an obligation to explain to the parties the legal consequences of proposed courses of action. It does not address possible disclosures that a lawyer who acts as a third-party neutral should make to inform the parties or potential biases. The Rule does not address the third-party neutral's obligations of confidentiality to the parties in an ADR proceeding. And, it does not address the fees that lawyers who are third-party neutrals may charge. The drafters chose not to define these and other specific duties of a third-party neutral because no consensus exists about the proper answers to these questions and duties of a lawyer third-party neutral often depend upon the ADR process implicated in the specific case.[4]

A Comment to Rule 2.4 discusses possible conflicts of interest that arise after a lawyer serves as a third-party neutral. One of the parties may ask the lawyer to represent them in future proceedings related to the matter that was the subject of the ADR process. In such a situation, the lawyer will need to turn to Rule 1.12, which has been expanded to include conflicts of interest issues involving mediators and other third-party neutrals.[5]

§ 2.4–3 RESPONSIBILITIES OF LAWYERS REPRESENTING CLIENTS IN AN ADR PROCEEDING

Although Rule 2.4 is entitled "Lawyer Serving as Third-Party Neutral," Comment 5 deals with the topic of lawyers representing clients in an ADR proceeding. The Comment states that "lawyers who represent clients in alternative dispute-resolution proceedings are governed by the Rules of Professional Conduct."[1] Clients who hire lawyers to represent them in resolving a dispute would assume that the lawyer's conduct would comply with the same standards as in other representations. No reason exists to depart from such a conclusion. One might only add that a lawyer

---

[4]Carrie Menkel-Meadow, *Ethics Issues in Arbitration and Related Dispute Resolution Processes: What's Happening and What's Not*, 56 U. MIAMI. L. REV. 949, 976 n. 117 (2002) (in hearings, author had urged the drafters to add more guidance in Rule 2.4). *See also* Carrie Menkel-Meadow, *Ethics in Alternative Dispute Resolution: New Issues, No Answers From the Adversary Conception of Lawyers' Responsibilities*, 38 S. TEX. L. REV. 407 (1997)

For a detailed discussion of the drafting history of Rule 2.4 and the related ethical issues in ADR proceedings, see Douglas H. Yarn, *Lawyer Ethics in ADR and the Recommendations of Ethics 2000 to Revise the Model Rules of Professional Conduct: Considerations for Adoption and State Application*, 54 ARK. L. REV. 207 (2001).

[5]*See* Chapter 1.12.

[Section 2.4–3]

[1]Rule 2.4, Comment 5.

participating in a formal ADR process would be expected to follow the rules of the process in the same way that a lawyer would be expected to follow the rules of court in litigation.

The Comment goes on to make a distinction between a lawyer's representation of clients in arbitrations and in other ADR processes. When the lawyer represents a client in a binding arbitration procedure, the lawyer is expected to follow the rules relating to tribunals, such as Rule 3.3 on candor to the tribunal.[2] When the lawyer represents a client in other ADR processes, the lawyer is expected to treat the opposing side and the third-party neutral under Rule 4.1's obligation to third persons.[3] This result is consistent with the Rule 1.0(m)'s definition of a tribunal. A tribunal includes binding arbitration proceedings and other proceedings that are designed to adjudicate the rights of the parties.[4] In light of the significant number of legal disputes that are diverted away from litigation to binding arbitration, society should expect that lawyers representing clients in binding arbitration should follow the same ethical rules that apply in a judicial forum.

---

[2] See Chapter 3.3.

[3] See Chapter 4.1.

[4] See Rule 1.0(m) (definition of tribunal).

III. THE LAWYER AS AN ADVOCATE

CHAPTER 3.1
MERITORIOUS CLAIMS AND CONTENTIONS

§ 3.1–1 Meritorious Claims and Frivolous Positions
§ 3.1–2 Related Judicial Management Tools Including Rule 11
      of the Federal Rules of Civil Procedure

RULE 3.1: MERITORIOUS CLAIMS AND CONTENTIONS

A lawyer shall not bring or defend a proceeding, or assert or controvert an issue therein, unless there is a basis in law and fact for doing so that is not frivolous, which includes a good faith argument for an extension, modification or reversal of existing law. A lawyer for the defendant in a criminal proceeding, or the respondent in a proceeding that could result in incarceration, may nevertheless so defend the proceeding as to require that every element of the case be established.

Comment

[1] The advocate has a duty to use legal procedure for the fullest benefit of the client's cause, but also a duty not to abuse legal procedure. The law, both procedural and substantive, establishes the limits within which an advocate may proceed. However, the law is not always clear and never is static. Accordingly, in determining the proper scope of advocacy, account must be taken of the law's ambiguities and potential for change.

[2] The filing of an action or defense or similar action taken for a client is not frivolous merely because the facts have not first been fully substantiated or because the lawyer expects to develop vital evidence only by discovery. What is required of lawyers, however, is that they inform themselves about the facts of their clients' cases and the applicable law and determine that they can make good faith arguments in support of their clients' positions. Such action is not frivolous even though the lawyer believes that the client's position ultimately will not prevail. The action is frivolous, however, if the lawyer is unable either to make a good faith argument on the merits of the action taken or to support the action taken by a good faith argument for an extension, modification or reversal of existing law.

[3] The lawyer's obligations under this Rule are subordinate to federal or state constitutional law that entitles a defendant in a

criminal matter to the assistance of counsel in presenting a claim or contention that otherwise would be prohibited by this Rule.

Authors' 1983 Model Rules Comparison

The drafters of the 2002 Rules added "in law and fact" to the first sentence. The drafters did not intend any change in meaning. They simply wanted to clarify that lawyers need to have a basis in law and fact for positions they take on behalf of clients. Reporter's Explanation of Changes to Model Rule 3.1.

Comment 1 is identical to the 1983 version.

In Comment 2, the drafters of the 2002 Rules added the following sentence: "What is required of lawyers, however, is that they inform themselves about the facts of their clients' cases and the applicable law and determine that they can make good faith arguments in support of their clients' positions." This change was made to make clear that lawyers must make a reasonable inquiry into the facts and the law of their client's case. The 1983 Comment 2 also included a clause stating that an action is frivolous if the client takes the action for the primary "purpose of harassing or maliciously injuring a person." The drafters deleted this clause because they believed that the duty of a lawyer not to bring frivolous cases and arguments does not rest on whether the client has a subjective intent to harass or injure a third person.

Comment 3 is new and explains that in criminal cases the lawyer's obligations are subordinate to any federal or state constitutional rights given to the lawyer's client.

Model Code Comparison

DR 7-102(A)(1) provided that a lawyer may not "[f]ile a suit, assert a position, conduct a defense, delay a trial, or take other action on behalf of his client when he knows or when it is obvious that such action would serve merely to harass or maliciously injure another." Rule 3.1 is to the same general effect as DR 7-102(A)(1), with three qualifications. First, the test of improper conduct is changed from "merely to harass or maliciously injure another" to the requirement that there be a basis for the litigation measure involved that is "not frivolous." This includes the concept stated in DR 7-102(A)(2) that a lawyer may advance a claim or defense unwarranted by existing law if "it can be supported by good faith argument for an extension, modification, or reversal of existing law." Second, the test in Rule 3.1 is an objective test, whereas DR 7-102(A)(1) applied only if the lawyer "knows or when it is obvious" that the litigation is frivolous. Third, Rule 3.1 has an exception that in a criminal case, or a case in which incarceration of the client may result (for example, certain juvenile proceedings), the lawyer may put the prosecution to its proof even if there is no nonfrivolous basis for defense.

§ 3.1–1 MERITORIOUS CLAIMS AND FRIVOLOUS POSITIONS

When the client consults the attorney as adviser, the attorney should give the client his or her good faith, candid opinion on how the courts will likely rule, and the full effects of such a decision. She also should inform her client of the practical effects of such a ruling.[1] The lawyer's efforts to comfort the client cannot limit her duty to give an honest assessment of unpleasant facts.[2]

In contrast, when the client consults the attorney as an advocate, the attorney may urge upon the courts any nonfrivolous interpretation of the law that favors the client. The ethics rules prohibit lawyers from asserting any frivolous positions, claims, defenses, or motions.[3] Nor may lawyers make frivolous discovery requests or fail to make a reasonably diligent effort to comply with discovery requests.[4]

However, the mere fact that a legal position is "creative" or contrary to existing law does not make that position frivolous. Existing law often has ambiguities and, even if it is clear, there is always the potential for change.[5] A permissible, nonfrivolous position includes any good faith argument for extension, modification, or even *reversal* of existing law.[6]

A claim does not become frivolous merely because the lawyer believes that the client will not prevail. And, whether the case is civil or criminal, the lawyer need not first fully substantiate the facts before making a claim. The lawyer may expect to develop vital evidence by discovery.[7] Discovery, after all, normally comes *after* the complaint is filed, not before. "It is obvious that the

---

[Section 3.1–1]

[1]Rule 2.1; EC 7-5.

[2]Rule 2.1, Comment 1.

[3]Rule 3.1. DR 7-102(A); DR 2-109(A). A lawyer also must refuse to accept a case if the client seeks to maintain a frivolous action. Rule 3.1; EC 2-30; DR 2-109(A); DR 7-102(A)(1). *See also* Restatement of the Law Governing Lawyers § 110 (Official Draft 2000).

In re Sarelas, 360 F.Supp. 794 (N.D.Ill.1973) (attorney suspended and fined for filing frivolous immigration appeals); *In re Bithoney*, 486 F.2d 319 (1st Cir.1973) ("baseless defenses").

[4]Rule 3.4(a), (d).

See, e.g., WALL STREET JOURNAL, Feb. 29, 1995, at B8, col. 6, reporting that a law firm for a computer company paid to settle a tort claim against it. The law firm footed the bill for the settlement, because it discovered that, due to an oversight, it had failed to turn over to plaintiff documents subject to discovery, and the trial judge had threatened to declare a mistrial

or impose sanctions. The document omissions came to light when the law firm was about to turn over the same documents to another plaintiff in a different case.

[5]Rule 3.1, Comment 1.

[6]Rule 3.1; DR 2-109(A)(2); DR 7-102(A)(2). *Cf.* Rule 3.4(c) (lawyer should not knowingly disobey tribunal unless there is "open refusal based on an assertion that no valid obligation exists."). *Cf.* DR 7-106(A). EC 7-4; DR 7-102(A)(1), (2); DR 2-109(A).

See Sanford V. Levinson, *Frivolous Cases: Do Lawyers Really Know Anything At All?*, 24 OSGOODE HALL L.J. 353 (1986) (examining the difficulty of categorizing legal arguments as frivolous).

If lawyers could not seek to have settled law overturned, then the "separate but equal" doctrine of *Plessy v. Ferguson*, 163 U.S. 537, 16 S.Ct. 1138, 41 L.Ed. 256 (1896) would not have been overruled in *Brown v. Board of Education*, 347 U.S. 483, 74 S.Ct. 686, 98 L.Ed. 873 (1954).

[7]Rule 3.1, Comment 2. E.g., *Kamen v. American Telephone &*

drafters of the rules acknowledged that when lawyers prepare and file pleadings in civil actions, they routinely make factual allegations in support of their theories of liability and assert defenses thereto, some of which ultimately provide to be unsubstantiated."[8]

It is only when the pleading or oral representation are made "*without any* reasonable basis *and* is designed merely to embarrass or [for] . . . some other ill-conceived or improper motives," that "such a pleading or oral representation would clearly be subject to disciplinary action."[9]

Lawyers should not file "frivolous" lawsuits. Rule 3.1 prohibits that and also responds to a common complaint of the general public, *i.e.*, that lawyers file too many frivolous lawsuits. When people are asked what they dislike most about lawyers, one of the major complaints is that lawyers file "too many unnecessary lawsuits," (27%).[10]

In spite of the adverse perceptions of the general public, one

---

Telegraph Co., 791 F.2d 1006, (2d Cir. 1986). The trial court granted Rule 11 sanctions and the Second Circuit reversed. The lawyer's reliance on his client's assertion that defendant received federal grants in connection with its work for the military was "reasonable" so that lawyer would not be subject to sanctions for failing to make a reasonable inquiry as to the jurisdictional bases of the complaint.

Kraemer v. Grant County, 892 F.2d 686 (7th Cir.1990)(per curiam). The trial court ordered a lawyer in a Rule 11 case to pay $3,000 toward legal fees that the adverse parties incurred in defending a civil rights case brought by lawyer on behalf of a client claiming conspiracy to evict her from land. The Seventh Circuit reversed and held that the trial court had abused its discretion. The lawyer acted reasonably in gathering information and instituted suit only after the hostile attitude of the potential defendants made it necessary to use the discovery process to gather additional information.

[8]*Lawyer Disciplinary Board v. Neely*, 207 W.Va. 21, 528 S.E.2d 468, 473 (1998).

[9]*State v. Anonymous (1974–5)*, 31 Conn.Supp. 179, 326 A.2d 837, 838

(1974)(emphasis added). The requirement in this case that the filing be without any reasonable basis and designed merely to embarrass, relied upon the Model Code's subjective intent requirement.

[10]Randall Samborn, *Anti-Lawyer Attitude Up, But NLJ/West Poll Also Shows More People Are Using Attorneys*, NATIONAL LAW JOURNAL, Aug. 9, 1993, at 1, col. 1. The top complaint is that lawyers are "too interested in money," (31%). The third major complaint is that lawyers "manipulate the legal system without regard for right or wrong," (26%).

A 1986 National Law Journal survey reaches similar conclusions. The top faults of lawyers were, according to the average person on the streets, that lawyers are "too interested in money," (32%); that lawyers "manipulate the legal system without any concern for right or wrong," (22%); and that lawyers "file too many unnecessary lawsuits," (20%). *What America Really Thinks About Lawyers*, NATIONAL LAW JOURNAL, Aug. 18, 1986, at S3, *discussed in* Robert C. Post, *On the Popular Image of the Lawyer: Reflections in a Dark Glass*, 75 CALIF. L. REV. 379, 380 (1987).

See also James Podgers, *Public: "Shyster" OK—If He's on Your Side*,

should not apply or interpret Rule 3.1 too broadly, because lawyers are allowed to bring creative lawsuits and novel legal theories. Consider another set of statistics. What do people like about lawyers? For the general public, the most positive aspect of lawyers is, "Putting clients' interests first," (46%); second, protecting people's rights (25%).[11]

When we put the two sets of statistics together, we discover that people both like lawyers—lawyers fight zealously for their clients, file lawsuits, and "cut through red tape"—and dislike lawyers—they are guns for hire who manipulate the legal system—for the same reasons.[12] Litigants want tough litigators on their side, and nice, easy-going people for adversaries.[13]

Rule 3.1 is supposed to navigate the narrow shoals between Scylla and Charybdis. Although lawyers should not file "frivolous" law suits, they may file "creative" law suits.

§ 3.1–1(a) Objective Test

The drafters of the Model Rules maintain that, unlike the com-

---

67 A.B.A. J., 695–96 (1981) (members of a San Diego Focus Group blame lawyers for being "sue crazy," filing too many law suits). Ronald D. Rotunda, *Epilogue*, in PRIME TIME LAW: FICTIONAL TV LAWYERS AND THEIR IMPACT ON AMERICA—FROM PERRY MASON AND *L.A. LAW* TO *LAW & ORDER* AND *ALLY McBEAL* 265 (Robert M. Jarvis & Paul R. Joseph, eds., Carolina Academic Press, 1998).

[11]Randall Samborn, *Anti-Lawyer Attitude Up, But NLJ/West Poll Also Shows More People Are Using Attorneys*, NATIONAL LAW JOURNAL, Aug. 9, 1993, at 1, col. 1.

The 1986 National Law Journal poll results were similar. The most admired quality was that lawyers' top "priority is to their clients," (38%); and, second, lawyers "know how to cut through bureaucratic red tape," (31%). *What America Really Thinks About Lawyers*, NATIONAL LAW JOURNAL, Aug. 18, 1986, at S3, discussed in, Robert C. Post, *On the Popular Image of the Lawyer: Reflections in a Dark Glass*, 75 CALIF. L. REV. 379, 380 (1987).

[12]*See* James Podgers, *Public: "Shyster" OK—If He's on Your Side*, 67 A.B.A. J. 695 (1981), concluding

that the people who complain that lawyers have bad attributes admit that, when they hire lawyers, they want lawyers with these attributes. *See also* Robert C. Post, *On the Popular Image of the Lawyer: Reflections in a Dark Glass*, 75 CALIF. L. REV. 379, 386 (1987). Professor Post noted that lawyers are "simultaneously praised and blamed for the very same actions." *Id.*

"We expect lawyers to fulfill both desires, and so they are a constant irritating reminder that we are neither a peaceable kingdom of harmony and order, nor a land of undiluted individual autonomy, but somewhere disorientingly in between. Lawyers, in the very exercise of their profession, are the necessary bearers of that bleak winter's tale, and we hate them for it."

[13]William Brewer & John Bickel, *Etiquette of the Advocate?*, TEXAS LAWYER 20, 21 (Mar. 21, 1994). *See also* James Podgers, *Public: "Shyster" OK—If He's on Your Side*, 67 A.B.A. J., 695–96 (1981), pointing out that members of a San Diego Focus Group who blamed lawyers for being "sue crazy," filing too many law suits, were more willing to acknowledge the need for lawyers to protect their interests.

parable provision of the Model Code,[14] the test of Rule 3.1 is "an objective test."[15] This objective test is thought to be a more stringent standard.[16]

Granted, one can infer motive from objective facts, but the test is not limited to objective facts. This "objective" test defines "not frivolous" in terms of a *good faith* argument" for a change or modification in the law.[17] "Good faith" does tend to suggest a subjective test. A Comment in the 1983 Model Rules stated that an action is frivolous if "taken *primarily for the purpose of* harassing or maliciously injuring a person" or if made in bad faith.[18] Such a test was very similar to that found in the Model Code.[19] This test, defined partly in terms of motivation, hardly appeared to be objective.

The drafters of the 2002 Rules removed the subjective test in the Comment. That Comment used to stated that an action was frivolous if the client sought the lawyer's work to harass or maliciously injure a third person. The drafters removed this language because they thought that this standard should be more objective and less dependent on the motives of the client in pursuing the action.

§ 3.1–1(b) Tax Cases

If a lawyer is representing a client before a tribunal and is seeking an *ex parte* order, the lawyer must disclose to the court not only all of the applicable law, even if adverse, but also all material facts that the lawyer reasonably believes are necessary for the tribunal to make an informed decision.[20] The Internal Revenue Service is not treated like a court and the tax return is not treated like a request for an *ex parte* order.

The lawyer, advising a client with respect to a tax return, is acting both as an advisor[21] and as an advocate.[22] The general rule is that the lawyer may advise her client on taking a position on a tax return—

> even where the lawyer believes the position *probably will not prevail*, there is no "substantial authority" in support of the position, and there will be no disclosure of the position in the [tax]

---

[14]DR 7–102(A)(1).

[15]*See* Rule 3.1, Code Comparison 1.

[16]Note, James W. MacFarlane, *Frivolous Conduct Under Model Rules of Professional Conduct 3.1*, 21 J. LEGAL PROFESSION 231, 234–38 (1996–1997).

[17]Rule 3.1.

[18]Rule 3.1, Comment 2 (emphasis

added).

[19]DR 7–102(A) and DR 2–109(A).

[20]Rule 3.3(d) & Comment 15.

[21]Rule 2.1.

[22]Rule 3.1. *See also* Rule 1.2(d) (lawyer may counsel client to make a good faith effort to determine the validity, scope, meaning, or application of the law).

return. However, the position to be asserted must be one which the lawyer in good faith believes is warranted in existing law or can be supported by a good faith argument for an extension, modification *or reversal* of existing law. This requires that there is *some realistic possibility of success* if the matter is litigated.[23]

But, the lawyer also must advise the client of the risks of taking this position on the tax return, including any adverse legal consequences or possible penalties that the Internal Revenue Service might impose, if the client takes the position on the tax return that the lawyer has offered.[24]

§ 3.1–1(c) Criminal Cases

The duty to refrain from asserting frivolous claims includes the duty to refrain from pursuing dilatory tactics, which are not permissible even in criminal cases.[25] However, the duty to avoid frivolous claims does not preclude the attorney from putting the state to its burden of proof in a criminal case.[26] The government, in every criminal case, has the constitutional duty to prove every element of the charge if the defendant pleads not guilty. The government cannot constitutionally shift that burden to the defendant.[27] In any criminal case—or in any case that can result in incarceration—the defense lawyer may force the prosecutor to establish every element of the case.[28] The defense lawyer is acting properly in requiring the state to prove all elements of the crime, even though the defense offers no legal or factual defenses to the charges.

The criminal defendant has the right to decide whether to appeal, although he should exercise this right after "full consultation" with the defense counsel.[29] If there is a criminal appeal, the appellate defense counsel "should not seek to withdraw from a case solely on the basis of his or her determination that the appeal lacks merit."[30]

If the appellate lawyer can find no non-frivolous ground for appeal, the U.S. Supreme Court has ruled that the lawyer must file what is called an *Anders* brief—named after the case of that

---

[23]ABA Formal Opinion 85-352 (July 7, 1985), at 4. This Formal Opinion reconsidered revised part of Formal Opinion 314 (Apr. 27, 1965).

[24]ABA Formal Opinion 85-352 (July 7, 1985), at 3 to 4.

[25]*State v. Darnell*, 14 Wash.App. 432, 542 P.2d 117, 120 (1975). *See also* Rule 3.2; DR 7-102(A)(1).

[26]Rule 3.1.

[27]*Mullaney v. Wilbur*, 421 U.S. 684, 95 S.Ct. 1881, 44 L.Ed.2d 508 (1975).

[28]*Accord* Restatement of the Law Governing Lawyers, Third, § 170(2) (Tent. Draft No. 8, March 21, 1997).

[29]ABA STANDARDS ON THE DEFENSE FUNCTION, STANDARD 4-5.2(a) (v), *Control and Direction of the Case* (ABA, 3rd ed. 1992).

[30]ABA STANDARDS ON THE DEFENSE FUNCTION, STANDARD 4-8.3(a), *Counsel on Appeal* (ABA, 3rd ed. 1992).

name.[31] In that brief, the appellate defense lawyer explains why there are no non-frivolous grounds for the appeal. However, the client has no constitutional right to force the appointed counsel to press all non-frivolous issues that the client wants advanced, if the defense counsel, as a matter of professional judgment, decides not to present all points. Experienced appellate counsel know that they might decide to focus on a few arguments and winnow out weaker ones.[32]

Because the criminal defendant and defense lawyer can force the prosecutor to prove every component of the crime even if there are no factual or legal defenses, it is rare that a criminal defense lawyer will be sanctioned for taking a frivolous position.[33] But it can happen. If the lawyer takes a position that is truly frivolous, there is precedent for sanctioning the lawyer. For

---

[31]*Anders v. California*, 386 U.S. 738, 87 S.Ct. 1396, 18 L.Ed.2d 493 (1967). The procedures outlined in *Anders* are not the only procedures that are constitutional. In *Smith v. Robbins*, 528 U.S. 259, 120 S.Ct. 746, 145 L.Ed.2d 756 (2000), the Court (5 to 4) stated that the procedure delineated in *Anders* "is a prophylactic one; the States are free to adopt different procedures, so long as those procedures adequately safeguard a defendant's right to appellate counsel." 528 U.S. at 264, 120 S.Ct. at 753. The California post-*Anders* procedure is discussed in *People v. Wende*, 25 Cal.3d 436, 441–42, 158 Cal.Rptr. 839, 842–43, 600 P.2d 1071, 1074–75 (1979). Counsel following *Wende* does not explicitly state that his review has led him to conclude "that the appeal would be frivolous (although that is considered implicit) nor requests leave to withdraw. Instead, he is silent on the merits of the case and expresses his availability to brief any issues on which the court might desire briefing." 528 U.S. at 264, 120 S.Ct. at 753. In order for the criminal defendant to succeed in arguing that his counsel was ineffective in not filing a merits brief, the defendant must satisfy both prongs of the test previously articulated in *Strickland v. Washington*, 466 U.S. 668, 104 S.Ct. 2052, 80 L.Ed.2d 674 (1984).

[32]*Jones v. Barnes*, 463 U.S. 745, 103 S.Ct. 3308, 77 L.Ed.2d 987 (1983).

[33]One may ask whether it is frivolous for a criminal defense lawyer to argue jury nullification to the jury. D.C. Bar Ethics Opinion 320 (2003) discusses the extent to which it is acceptable for a criminal defense lawyer to make an argument urging the jury to exercise its power of nullification (the power to refuse to follow the judge's instructions). The Opinion notes that, historically, juries had wide powers of nullification. Only in the 20th century did the courts draw a sharp division drawn between the court's power to declare the law and the jury's power to find the facts. Rule 1.3 states that attorneys have "a duty to 'represent a client zealously and diligently within the bounds of the law.'" Rule 3.1 requires an attorney to defend her client even if convinced of the client's guilt. Rule 3.3(b) imposes an "absolute obligation of candor to the tribunal" on an attorney, but not a limitation on the right of argument. The Opinion reads these rules together, in the context of arguments regarding jury nullification, as stating that "unless the advocate expressly urges nullification . . . or has been prohibited by the presiding officer from making a particular argument, a criminal defense counsel may zealously represent his client and may offer any argument for which he has a good faith evidentiary basis," including "arguments with incidental nullification effects."

example, in one criminal case when the lawyer filed a petition for rehearing claiming that the federal tax laws did not apply to resident U.S. citizens, the Court of Appeals sanctioned the lawyer for this frivolous legal position.[34]

§ 3.1–2 RELATED JUDICIAL MANAGEMENT TOOLS INCLUDING RULE 11 OF THE FEDERAL RULES OF CIVIL PROCEDURE

§ 3.1–2(a) Other Rules and Statutes

Other rules and statutes, as well as a court's inherent powers, give judges various tools to control the proceedings before them. For example, 28 U.S.C. § 1927 prohibits a lawyer from unduly multiplying proceedings, "unreasonably and vexatiously." This section does not require the lawyer to file any writing. Rule 38, Federal Rules of Appellate Procedure, confers on federal appellate courts power similar to that which Rule 11 confers on district courts. The appellate courts can award "just damages and single or double costs" for an appeal judged to be "frivolous." In addition, state and federal courts have the contempt power and the "inherent power" to control the proceedings and lawyers before them.[1]

---

[34]*In re Becraft*, 885 F.2d 547 (9th Cir.1989), relying on Rule 38, Federal Rules of Appellate Procedure, held that in a criminal case the defense counsel's conduct in filing petition for rehearing, based on the argument that federal tax laws did not apply to resident United States citizens, was "frivolous conduct." The court imposed sanctions of $2,500.

This sanction was imposed on the lawyer who made a frivolous argument in a criminal case under the following circumstances:

"Kenneth Nelson was convicted in the District Court for the District of Nevada on three counts of failure to file income tax returns in violation of 26 U.S.C.A. § 7203. Nelson, represented by counsel Lowell H. Becraft, Jr., then appealed to this court claiming, inter alia, that the district court erred in refusing to give his proposed jury instruction that a United States citizen residing in the United States is not subject to the federal income tax laws. By memorandum disposition dated March 22, 1989, this court af-

firmed Nelson's conviction, noting that Becraft's argument regarding the inapplicability of the federal tax laws to resident United States citizens had no basis in law. Becraft thereafter filed a petition for rehearing and/or suggestion for rehearing en banc [hereafter 'petition for rehearing']. In the petition for rehearing, Becraft once again argued that the federal tax laws are inapplicable to resident United States citizens.

"Upon receipt of the petition for rehearing, we, *sua sponte*, issued a show cause order requesting Becraft to explain why damages in the sum of $2500 should not be assessed against him for filing a frivolous petition for rehearing. See Appendix A. We have now reviewed Becraft's several-hundred-page reply to our show cause order [hereinafter 'reply'] and have reached the conclusion that Becraft's conduct warrants sanctions."

885 F.2d at 547.

[Section 3.1–2]

[1]*See, e.g., Chambers v. NASCO Inc.*, 501 U.S. 32, 111 S.Ct. 2123, 115

§ 3.1–2(b) Common Law Torts

In addition, in some circumstances common law torts provide a remedy for those injured by the lawyer's conduct. Common tort remedies include abuse of process,[2] malicious prosecution,[3] defamation,[4] false arrest,[5] and so forth.[6] However, there are strict requirements that must be met for these causes of action to be viable against lawyers, who are often protected by various privileges and immunities.[7]

§ 3.1–2(c) Rule 11

Rule 11 of the Federal Rules of Civil Procedure was amended in 1983 to provide that every pleading, motion, or other paper must be signed by an individual lawyer; this signature certifies that she has read the paper, that to the best of her knowledge,

---

L.Ed.2d 27 (1991); *Phillips v. Brisebois*, 72 Haw. 146, 808 P.2d 370 (Hawaii 1991).

[2]*See, e.g., Board of Education v. Farmingdale Classroom Teachers Association*, 38 N.Y.2d 397, 380 N.Y.S.2d 635, 343 N.E.2d 278 (N.Y.1975) (cause of action against attorney who subpoenaed 87 teachers to appear and testify on the very same day as a means of obliging the Board of Education to hire substitute teachers).

In *Zamos v. Stroud*, 32 Cal.4th 958, 12 Cal.Rptr.3d 54, 87 P.3d 802 (2004), attorney Zamos accused attorney Stroud of malicious prosecution. The underlying case had accused Zamos of fraud in recommending that client Brookes settle an earlier case. When Stroud filed the fraud case, he thought it had merit, but as the case went on, transcripts produced by Zamos showed it had none. Stroud, however, refused to dismiss the case, and in this proceeding, the California Supreme Court considered whether a malicious prosecution claim can be based on "continuing" an invalid case or whether it is limited simply to filing one. The Court acknowledged that giving excessive breadth to the tort of malicious prosecution could discourage lawyers from pursuing risky cases, but relying on § 674 of the Restatement Second of Torts, it unanimously held that improper continuation of a clearly invalid claim could indeed be the basis for such an action.

[3]*See, e.g., Voytko v. Ramada Inn*, 445 F.Supp. 315 (D.N.J.1978) (cause of action against private attorney who threatened a party with criminal prosecution, assisted in filing charges; in addition, his associate acted as the prosecutor pursuant to a law that allowed private attorneys to prosecute criminal actions).

[4]*See, e.g., Green Acres Trust v. London*, 141 Ariz. 609, 688 P.2d 617 (Ariz.1984) (cause of action against attorney for his statements in a press conference, a forum in which the statements were not privileged).

[5]*See, e.g., Havens v. Hardesty*, 43 Colo.App. 162, 600 P.2d 116 (Colo.App. 1979) (cause of action against attorney for false arrest when he, in error, arranged for the arrest of a person having the same name as the person who should have been arrested).

[6]Tortious Interference with Contract. *E.g., Duggin v. Adams*, 234 Va. 221, 360 S.E.2d 832 (Va.1987)(lawyer advised his client to breach a sales contract so that he, the lawyer, could purchase the property himself).

[7]*See, e.g.,* Restatement, Second, of the Law of Torts §§ 37, 45A, 653 674, 675, 682, 766 to 774A. However, these immunities do not protect the lawyer in certain factual circumstances.

"formed after reasonable inquiry," it is well grounded in fact and is warranted by existing law or good faith argument to extend, modify, or reverse existing law, and that it is not filed for any improper purpose.[8] For violation of this rule the court may sanction the party *or the attorney*. The purpose of this amendment was to provide the federal courts with powers to use the Rules of Civil Procedure to counteract what many judges saw as an increase in the use of dilatory practices and the filing of frivolous motions in federal courts.[9] Many states have enacted their own versions of federal Rule 11.

Rule 11 has spawned a great deal of controversy over its scope, meaning, procedures, and application.[10] Opponents claim that it has chilled lawyers' enthusiasm over pursuing novel legal theories; that it is biased against plaintiffs, particularly against plaintiffs in civil rights suits; and that it has not reduced but increased the cost of litigation by imposing expensive and time consuming satellite litigation. Since adoption of Rule 11 in 1983 there have been thousands of decisions dealing with Rule 11 sanctions; in one case alone the lawyers (to vindicate their reputations) spent $100,000 to reverse a $3,000 sanction. In many circuits, a very few judges are responsible for a disproportionate number of Rule 11 sanctions.[11]

The Advisory Committee on the Federal Rules of Civil Procedure responded to these criticisms, and a new Rule 11 went into effect in late 1993. The Advisory Committee Notes to the 1993 amendments explained that the new Rule 11 was drafted to place "greater constraints on the imposition of sanctions" and to "reduce the number of motions for sanctions presented to the court." The amended Rule 11 provides protection against sanctions—and a safe harbor for the subject of the Rule 11 sanction—if the challenged paper, claim, defense, etc. is withdrawn or appropriately

---

[8]Rule 11 is one response to the "litigation explosion," the existence of which is a matter of some dispute. *See, e.g.,* Marc S. Galanter, *Reading the Landscape of Disputes: What We Know and Don't Know (and Think We Know) About Our Allegedly Contentious and Litigious Society,* 31 U.C.L.A. L. REV. 4 (1983) (challenging the empirical and conceptual bases of the "litigation explosion").

[9]Ronald D. Rotunda, *The Litigator's Professional Responsibility,* 77 ILLINOIS BAR JOURNAL 192 (1988), *reprinted in* 25 TRIAL MAGAZINE 98 (Mar. 1989), and *in* 30 LAW OFFICE ECONOMICS AND MANAGEMENT 61

(1989).

[10]*See* Rule 11 *in* TRANSITION: THE REPORT OF THE THIRD CIRCUIT TASK FORCE ON THE FEDERAL RULES OF CIVIL PROCEDURE (Steven Burbank, Reporter, 1989).

[11]*See, e.g.,* 3 ABA/BNA LAWYERS' MANUAL ON PROFESSIONAL CONDUCT 266–67 (Aug. 19, 1987); Ronald D. Rotunda, *Learning the Law of Lawyering,* 136 U.PA.L.REV. 1761, 1773–75 (1988); Victor H. Kramer, *Viewing Rule 11 as a Tool to Improve Professional Responsibility,* 75 MINN. L. REV. 793 (1991).

corrected.[12] Moreover, the judge's sanctions must be limited to "what is sufficient to deter repetition" of the conduct.

Rule 11 now gives the judge a greater range of choices in imposing a remedy for a violation of the Rule.[13] Sanctions may include "directives of a nonmonetary nature" or an order to pay a penalty to the court, or an order to pay the movant "*some* or all of the reasonable attorneys' fees and other expenses incurred as a direct result of the violation."[14] Although Rule 11 is still an important weapon in the judicial arsenal, the changes in Rule 11 have lessened the problems associated with the earlier version.

§ 3.1–2(d) The Basic Elements of the Procedural Rules Against Frivolous Litigation

In general, procedural rules, like Rule 11, that impose sanctions for "frivolous" litigation, usually have four elements. The Restatement of the Law Governing Lawyers divides these elements into four parts. First, the lawyer may not file a pleading or other paper unless he or she first makes "an inquiry about facts and law that is reasonable in the circumstances."[15] Second, the lawyer's conclusions regarding these facts and law "must meet an

---

[12]Fed. R. Civ. P. 11(c)(1)(A).

[13]The following cases illustrate the flexibility courts have in fashioning a remedy under the current version of Rule 11.

In *Jimenez v. Madison Area Technical College*, 321 F.3d 652 (7th Cir.2003), Jimenez sued her employer and former colleagues for race, ethnic origin, and sex discrimination, but she was found to have falsified documents to support the claims. The documents included supposed emails calling her a "money hungry spic" and a "stupid Mexican." Defendants had told her lawyer that they denied authorship of the documents, but the lawyer apparently did nothing to verify their authenticity, saying only that he would wait until the depositions to test the documents' credibility. As a sanction for these acts under Rule 11, Jiminez' case was dismissed with prejudice, and the Seventh Circuit upheld that sanction, finding that "Jimenez' claim was so unmeritorious and her behavior so deceptive that the filing of her baseless claim amounted to veritable attack on our system of justice." 321 F.3d at 657. Moreover, the court also imposed sanctions under Rule 38 of

the Federal Rules of Appellate Procedure for filing a frivolous appeal.

Whitehead v. Food Max of Mississippi, Inc., 332 F.3d 796 (5th Cir.2003), *cert. denied*, 540 U.S. 1047, 124 S.Ct. 807, 157 L.Ed.2d 694 (2003), affirmed a Rule 11 sanction for attorney Minor's behavior in trying to execute a judgment against Kmart. After getting a $3.4 million judgment, Minor invited the media to accompany him to a local Kmart store where he attempted to execute the judgment by seizing currency in the cash registers and vault. News reports about the execution of the writ included "Minor's extremely hyperbolic, intemperate, and misleading comments." 332 F.3d at 800. The Fifth Circuit upheld a finding that Minor acted with an improper purpose in obtaining the writ of execution, in violation of Rule 11(b)(1), so sanctions were warranted. The Court held that Minor's improper purposes in obtaining the writ were "to embarrass Kmart and advance his personal position." *Id.* at 808.

[14]Federal Rule 11(c)(2) (emphasis added).

[15]Restatement of the Law Governing Lawyers, Third, § 110, Comment *c*,

objective, minimal standard of supportability."[16] Third, the Restatement advises, "litigation measures may not be taken for an improper purpose, *even in instances in which they are otherwise minimally supportable.*"[17] And, fourth, remedies for violation may include sanctions such as fee shifting, which in appropriate cases may be imposed directly on an offending lawyer.[18]

The third element in the American Law Institute's analysis raises important First Amendment problems. It is certainly true that some cases appear to argue that a nonfrivolous motion can be treated as harassing and sanctionable when the lawyer is motivated by less than honorable intentions,[19] but that argument should be fatally undercut by the U.S. Supreme Court's decision in *Bill Johnson's Restaurants, Inc. v. NLRB.*[20] This labor law case ruled that, given the "First Amendment right of access to the courts," the "filing and prosecution of a well-founded lawsuit may not be enjoined as an unfair labor practice, even if it would not have been commenced but for the *plaintiff's desire to retaliate* against the defendant for exercising rights protected by the [National Labor Relations] Act."[21]

Plaintiffs do not have to like their adversaries. In fact, many parties in litigation do not have good feelings toward each other. That is why some people consider litigation to be the modern form of dueling. Consequently, the plaintiff's bad feelings towards their opponents (or defendant's bad feelings toward plaintiff) should not convert a meritorious motion into a motion that should be sanctioned.

Initially the American Law Institute opined that "objectively non-frivolous, even meritorious, steps" can be, "nonetheless improper."[22]

In its final draft, the American Law Institute's position softened. It now only argues that "litigation may not be taken for

---

[16] Restatement of the Law Governing Lawyers, Third § 110, Comment c, at 172 (Official Draft 2000).

[17] Restatement of the Law Governing Lawyers, Third § 110, Comment c, at 172 (Official Draft 2000) (emphasis added).

[18] Restatement of the Law Governing Lawyers, Third § 110, Comment c, at 172 (Official Draft 2000).

[19] The Reporter's Note to § 110 states:

"On objectively non-frivolous, even meritorious, steps that are nonetheless improper, see, e.g., *Aetna Life Ins. Co. v. Alla Medical Services, Inc.*,

855 F.2d 1470 (9th Cir.1988) (successive motions for the purpose of delaying need to file answer)."

Restatement of the Law Governing Lawyers, Third, § 110, Reporter's Note to Comment c, at p. 179 (Official Draft 2000).

[20] *Bill Johnson's Restaurants, Inc. v. NLRB*, 461 U.S. 731, 103 S.Ct. 2161, 76 L.Ed.2d 277 (1983).

[21] 461 U.S. at 742–43, 103 S.Ct. at 2169–70 (emphasis added).

[22] Restatement of the Law Governing Lawyers, Third, § 170, Comment c, at p. 361 (Tent. Draft No. 8, Mar. 21, 1997).

an *improper purpose*, even in instances in which they are otherwise minimally supportable."[23] However, the fact still remains that if a lawyer has not, for example, mislead his opponent or the court or violated any court order, and his motion or other legal position is objectively nonfrivolous, there should be no ethical violation. If the motion is without merit, the litigant's bad feelings offer a motive as to why such a motion was filed.

Although frivolous motions and unjustified delays cannot be tolerated, it appears that Rule 11 actually aggravates those problems. Not only does it heighten tension and increase the number of motions and appeals in litigation, but it tends to be enforced arbitrarily, because judges differ on what constitutes a frivolous motion. For example, an empirical study sponsored by the Federal Judicial Center presented adaptations of actual Rule 11 cases to the federal district court judges that it surveyed.[24] In no case did the judges unanimously agree that there was a Rule 11 violation. In only three of the ten cases did more than 75% of the judges agree that there was a violation.[25] Furthermore, Rule 11 has tended to operate against plaintiffs.[26]

A better system might have judges report lawyers who abuse the system to the appropriate disciplinary agency.[27] Judges would have to take this responsibility seriously. Some judges are responding to the problem of delay and backlog in the courts by resorting to fact pleading. Requiring the plaintiff to allege detailed facts does tend to reduce litigation, but it often is to the detriment of plaintiffs even if plaintiffs have a good case, because the elaborate facts have to be alleged before discovery has begun.[28] Judges can more easily reduce delay by simply deciding motions more quickly and refusing to grant continuances unless the mov-

---

[23]Restatement of the Law Governing Lawyers, Third, § 110, Comment *c*, at p. 172 (emphasis added).

[24]SAUL M. KASSIN, AN EMPIRICAL STUDY OF RULE 11 SANCTIONS (1987).

[25]SAUL M. KASSIN, AN EMPIRICAL STUDY OF RULE 11 SANCTIONS (1987), at 12 & at 17 table 3. *See also* Sanford V. Levinson, *Frivolous Cases: Do Lawyers Really Know Anything At All?*, 24 OSGOODE HALL L.J. 353 (1986).

[26]Ronald D. Rotunda, *Lawyers and Professionalism: A Commentary on the Report of the American Bar Association Commission on Professionalism*, 18 LOYOLA U. CHI. L.J. 1149, 1166 (1987).

[27]ABA Model Code of Judicial

Conduct, Canon 3D(2) (1990):

"A judge having knowledge that a lawyer has committed a violation of the Rules of Professional Conduct should take appropriate action. A judge having knowledge that a lawyer has committed a violation of the Rules of Professional Conduct that raises a substantial question as to the lawyer's honesty, trustworthiness or fitness as a lawyer in other respects shall inform the appropriate authority."

[28]Ronald D. Rotunda, *Lawyers and Professionalism: A Commentary on the Report of the American Bar Association Commission on Professionalism*, 18 LOYOLA U. CHI. L.J. 1149, 1169 (1987).

ing party has a good reason to delay.[29]

---

[29]*See* Ronald D. Rotunda, *Law, Lawyers, and Managers, in* CLARENCE WALTON, ed., THE ETHICS OF CORPORATE CONDUCT 127, 144 (Prentice-Hall, Inc., The American Assembly of Columbia University, 1977) (describing how the Southern District of New York substantially reduced delay in criminal cases by converting from a central to an individual calendar system, so that judges could no longer avoid deciding motions by continuing them until another judge assumed the rotating obligation to hear all criminal pretrial motions).

CHAPTER 3.2
EXPEDITING LITIGATION

§ 3.2–1 Making "Reasonable" Efforts to Expedite Litigation
§ 3.2–2 Delay for the Convenience of the Lawyer

RULE 3.2: EXPEDITING LITIGATION

A lawyer shall make reasonable efforts to expedite litigation consistent with the interests of the client.

Comment

[1] Dilatory practices bring the administration of justice into disrepute. Although there will be occasions when a lawyer may properly seek a postponement for personal reasons, it is not proper for a lawyer to routinely fail to expedite litigation solely for the convenience of the advocates. Nor will a failure to expedite be reasonable if done for the purpose of frustrating an opposing party's attempt to obtain rightful redress or repose. It is not a justification that similar conduct is often tolerated by the bench and bar. The question is whether a competent lawyer acting in good faith would regard the course of action as having some substantial purpose other than delay. Realizing financial or other benefit from otherwise improper delay in litigation is not a legitimate interest of the client.

Authors' 1983 Model Rules Comparison

The text of the 2002 version of Rule 3.2 is identical to the Rule adopted by the ABA House of Delegates in 1983.

The 1983 version of Rule 3.2 addressed delay for the convenience of the lawyer in the following way: "Delay should not be indulged merely for the convenience of the advocates. . . ." The drafters deleted this sentence and replaced it with the following: "Although there will be occasions when a lawyer may properly seek a postponement for personal reasons, it is not proper for a lawyer to routinely fail to expedite litigation solely for the convenience of the advocates." The drafters believed that the old language did not permit lawyers to delay a work in litigation purely for their convenience. The new language allows lawyers to make limited and reasonable requests for delay.

Model Code Comparison

DR 7-101(A)(1) stated that a lawyer does not violate the duty to represent a client zealously "by being punctual in fulfilling all professional commitments." DR 7-102(A)(1) provided that a lawyer "shall not . . . file a suit, assert a position, conduct a defense [or] delay a trial . . . when he knows or when it is obvious that such action would serve merely to harass or maliciously injure another."

§ 3.2–1 MAKING "REASONABLE" EFFORTS TO EXPEDITE LITIGATION

The Model Code imposed ethical restraints on dilatory practices in litigation.[1] The Model Rules continue those restrictions but phrase the ethical rule regarding dilatory motions in a more affirmative manner, by requiring the lawyer to make "reasonable efforts to expedite litigation," but those efforts must be "consistent with the interests of the client."[2]

The Model Code forbade a lawyer from delaying when the lawyer "*knows* or when it is *obvious* that such action would serve *merely to harass* or maliciously injure another."[3] This change in language from the Code to the Rules does not represent a substantive change in result but more a change in mood: the language of the Model Rules is more affirmative, but the duties of the lawyer remain the same. The duty to expedite litigation must be balanced against the duty to act "consistent with the interests of the client."

If it is in the client's best interest to expedite litigation, then a lawyer will have no problem in complying with Rule 3.2. But sometimes, expeditious, prompt litigation is not in the client's best interest. Some well-known lawyers have gloated about their ability to delay a case for years. One well-known New York litigator, who later had a chair named for him at Harvard Law School, bragged that he was a born procrastinator who could keep antitrust litigation going for years.[4]

If the motion or other action is not "frivolous," does the lawyer violate Rule 3.2 simply because the client benefits from the delay? May a lawyer file a non-frivolous motion that is likely to fail when the real purpose of the motion is to take advantage of the delay that it causes? The test that Model Rule 3.2 proposes may appear, at first, to say no: "The question is whether a competent lawyer acting in good faith would regard the course of action as having some substantial purpose *other than delay*. Realizing financial or other benefit *from otherwise improper* delay is not a legitimate interest of the client."[5]

The first sentence quoted above may say that, in determining whether to take a position in litigation, or file a motion, and so

---

[Section 3.2–1]

[1] DR 7-101(A)(1) (ethically proper for lawyer, in representing a client zealously to be "punctual in fulfilling all professional commitments"); DR 7-102(A)(1) (lawyer "shall not . . . file a suit, assert a position, conduct a defense [or] delay a trial . . . when he knows or when it is obvious that such action would serve merely to harass or

maliciously injure another.").

[2] Rule 3.2.

[3] DR 7-102(A)(1) & DR 2-109(A)(1) (emphasis added).

[4] Bruce Bromley, *Judicial Control of Antitrust Cases*, 23 F.R.D. 417 (1976).

[5] Rule 3.2, Comment (emphasis added).

forth, the lawyer cannot consider the benefits of delay that flow from the action. On the other hand, the second sentence points in the opposite direction, for it says that when the lawyer considers the legitimate interests of the client, he may not consider the benefits of delay if the delay is "otherwise improper." If the motion, filing, or other action is non-frivolous, then it is not otherwise improper.

If a non-frivolous motion or other action has a very small chance of winning, but the client is quite happy to assume the expenses associated with the motion because of the benefits of delay, then the delay should not be "otherwise improper" because the motion or other action is not frivolous. In one case, for example, the court found that it was proper for a criminal defense lawyer not to raise a speedy trial defense in view of the lawyer's tactic to delay the trial "as long as possible" so that "witnesses' memories might deteriorate, or witnesses might become unavailable."[6]

A non-frivolous motion or lawsuit does not become frivolous merely because the proponent harbors ill will towards his litigation adversary. Plaintiffs and defendants often do not like each other; "ill will is not uncommon in litigation."[7] As Justice Stevens once noted: "We may presume that every litigant intends harm to his adversary."[8]

The reference in the second sentence to *financial benefit* from otherwise improper delay creates an ambiguity in how the Rules should be interpreted. If the motion is frivolous or violates a court rule (such as Rule 11), then the Comment makes sense. If the client is using delay to obtain a nuisance value settlement in a frivolous case, the delay is improper.[9] But does the Comment try to prohibit delay in litigation if the client plans to file for bankruptcy or if the client gains from delaying payment to a defendant because the law includes no prejudgment interest? Because many decisions in litigation are made for many complicated reasons, it may be rare to find a nonfrivolous motion used for delay where the only reason for the tactics is client financial gain. Many clients would take issue with the notion that Rule 3.2

---

[6] *People v. Moody*, 676 P.2d 691, 695 (Colo.1984). The court thus rejected the claim that the trial lawyer had provided ineffective assistance of counsel by not raising the speedy trial motion.

[7] *BE & K Construction Co. v. National Labor Relations Board*, 536 U.S. 516, 534, 122 S.Ct. 2390, 2400–01, 153 L.Ed.2d 499 (2002).

[8] *Professional Real Estate Investors v. Columbia Pictures Indus.*, 508 U.S. 49, 69, 113 S.Ct. 1920, 1933, 123 L.Ed.2d 611 (1993) (Stevens, J., concurring in judgment). He went on to say: "Access to the courts is far too precious a right for us to infer wrongdoing from nothing more than using the judicial process to seek a competitive advantage in a doubtful case." *Id.*

[9] *See* Restatement of the Law Governing Lawyers, Third, § 106, Comment e (Official Draft 2000).

prohibits their lawyers from considering the financial benefit aspects of nonfrivolous delays in litigation.

One commentator on Rule 3.2 concluded that: "[p]lainly, under the Rules delay in litigation can no longer be justified simply by invoking client interest," but he also admitted that actual enforcement of this Rule "will probably require an adjustment to the professional expectations of many lawyers and judges."[10]

In the meantime, judges have not relied on Rule 3.2 to sanction lawyers in cases where the lawyer has filed a non-frivolous motion or taken other non-frivolous action that results in delay. Instead, judges have sanctioned lawyers for misconduct that involved a great deal more than merely filing dilatory but non-frivolous motions or engaging in other foot-dragging but non-frivolous practices.[11]

Judges realize that there is a First Amendment protection (a lawsuits is a "petition" to the Government for a redress of "grievances")[12] to file non-frivolous cases. The fact that a lawsuit or motion is ultimately unsuccessful does not mean that it is baseless. "[T]he text of the First Amendment [does not] speak in terms of successful petitioning—it speaks simply of 'the right of the people . . . to petition the Government for a redress of grievances.' "[13]

BE & K Construction Co. v. National Labor Relations Board,[14] offers a useful example. In that case, unions filed health and safety charges against a non-union contractor who had secured a large contract. The contractor retaliated by filing secondary-boycott and antitrust claims against the unions. After the court either dismissed these claims or the plaintiff voluntarily withdrew them with prejudice, the unions complained to the NLRB, which found (1) the contractor's suits were "unmeritorious" and (2) the employer had a bad motive because it had filed the suits in order to retaliate against union members who were engaged in conduct that the NLRB protects. The NLRB agreed that this employer conduct constituted an unfair labor practice, but the Supreme Court reversed.

Justice O'Connor, speaking for the Court, held that such a

---

[10] CHARLES W. WOLFRAM, MODERN LEGAL ETHICS 600 (West Pub. Co. 1986) (footnote omitted).

[11] *See, e.g., Carter v. Mississippi*, 654 So.2d 505 (Miss.1995) (attorney violates Rule 3.2 when he promises clients that he would represent them in exchange for the money he took from them and then does nothing).

[12] This First Amendment right to petition is one of "the most precious of the liberties safeguarded by the Bill of Rights," *Mine Workers v. Illinois Bar Association*, 389 U.S. 217, 222, 88 S.Ct. 353, 356, 19 L.Ed.2d 426 (1967).

[13] *BE & K Construction Co. v. National Labor Relations Board*, 536 U.S. 516, 532, 122 S.Ct. 2390, 2400, 153 L.Ed.2d 499 (2002).

[14] *BE & K Construction Co. v. National Labor Relations Board*, 536 U.S. 516, 122 S.Ct. 2390, 153 L.Ed.2d 499 (2002).

lawsuit cannot constitute an unfair labor practice because it was not "sham litigation," which she defined as litigation that is (1) *subjectively* brought with a bad motive, *and* (2) "objectively baseless." These lawsuits did not meet that test. The NLRB may not "burden an unsuccessful but reasonably based suit" even if it "was brought with a retaliatory purpose."[15] If the litigant's "purpose is to stop conduct he reasonably believes is illegal, petitioning is genuine both objectively and subjectively."[16] Justice Scalia, concurring, concluded that the implication of this decision is that the Court, to avoid First Amendment problems, will interpret the relevant statutes to allow courts to "prohibit only lawsuits that are both objectively baseless and subjectively intended to abuse process."[17]

§ 3.2–2 DELAY FOR THE CONVENIENCE OF THE LAWYER

Obviously, judges, lawyers, and litigants balance their schedules and matters to accommodate their work load. Inevitably, personal and professional matters come into conflict with a lawyer's representation of a client. The text of Rule 3.2 places a professional obligation of the lawyer to expedite litigation consistent with the legitimate interests of the client. The Comment to the 1983 Rules prohibited a lawyer from delaying litigation "merely for the convenience" of the lawyer.[1] The legal profession has never ascribed a literal meaning to this Comment. But the drafters of the 2002 Rules believed that they should amend the Comment so that it would actually offer guidance to lawyers.

The amended Comment to Rule 3.2 now states: "Although there will be occasions when a lawyer may properly seek a postponement for personal reasons, it is not proper for a lawyer to routinely fail to expedite litigation solely for the convenience of the advocates." Thus, lawyers are permitted to ask for delay to accommodate a personal matter, but they should not routinely delay matters solely on personal grounds. Although this is not stated in the Comments, a lawyer who seeks delay for a purely personal reason must first examine whether the delay will affect the client's interests. If such delay may harm client interests, the lawyer would need to examine Rule 1.1 (Competence), Rule 1.7(a) (Conflicts of Interest), and Rule 1.4 (duty to keep the client

---

[15]536 U.S. at 534, 122 S.Ct. at 2401, 153 L.Ed.2d at 516.

[16]536 U.S. at 534, 122 S.Ct. at 2401, 153 L.Ed.2d at 516. See also, *Bill Johnson's Restaurants, Inc. v. N.L.R. B.*, 461 U.S. 731, 742–43, 103 S.Ct. 2161, 2170, 76 L.Ed.2d 277, 289 (1983) *Professional Real Estate Investors, Inc. v. Columbia Pictures Industries, Inc.*, 508 U.S. 49, 60–61, 113 S.Ct. 1920, 1928, 123 L.Ed.2d 611 (1993).

[17]536 U.S. 516, 537, 122 S.Ct. 2390, 2402 (Scalia, J., joined by Thomas, J., concurring).

[Section 3.2–2]

[1]1983 Rule 3.2, Comment 1.

informed). A lawyer who seeks delay, for more than a few days, based upon a personal reason should consider informing the client about the lawyer's need for a delay.

CHAPTER 3.3
CANDOR TOWARD THE TRIBUNAL

RULE 3.3: CANDOR TOWARD THE TRIBUNAL

(a) A lawyer shall not knowingly:

(1) make a false statement of fact or law to a tribunal or fail to correct a false statement of material fact or law previously made to the tribunal by the lawyer;

(2) fail to disclose to the tribunal legal authority in the controlling jurisdiction known to the lawyer to be directly adverse to the position of the client and not disclosed by opposing counsel; or

(3) offer evidence that the lawyer knows to be false. If a lawyer, the lawyer's client, or a witness called by the lawyer, has offered material evidence and the lawyer comes to know of its falsity, the lawyer shall take reasonable remedial measures, including, if necessary, disclosure to the tribunal. A lawyer may refuse to offer evidence, other than the testimony of a defendant in a criminal matter, that the lawyer reasonably believes is false.

(b) A lawyer who represents a client in an adjudicative proceeding and who knows that a person intends to engage, is engaging or has engaged in criminal or fraudulent conduct related to the proceeding shall take reasonable remedial measures, including, if necessary, disclosure to the tribunal.

(c) The duties stated in paragraphs (a) and (b) continue to the conclusion of the proceeding, and apply even if compliance requires disclosure of information otherwise protected by Rule 1.6.

(d) In an ex parte proceeding, a lawyer shall inform the tribunal of all material facts known to the lawyer that will enable the tribunal to make an informed decision, whether or not the facts are adverse.

Comment

[1] This Rule governs the conduct of a lawyer who is representing a client in the proceedings of a tribunal. See Rule 1.0(m) for the definition of "tribunal." It also applies when the lawyer is representing a client in an ancillary proceeding conducted pursuant to the tribunal's adjudicative authority, such as a deposition. Thus, for example, paragraph (a)(3) requires a lawyer to take reasonable remedial measures if the lawyer comes to know that a client who is testifying in a deposition has offered evidence that is false.

[2] This Rule sets forth the special duties of lawyers as officers of the court to avoid conduct that undermines the integrity of the adjudicative process. A lawyer acting as an advocate in an adjudicative proceeding has an obligation to present the client's case with persuasive force. Performance of that duty while maintaining confidences of the client, however, is qualified by the advocate's duty of candor to the tribunal. Consequently, although a lawyer in an adversary proceeding is not required to present an impartial exposition of the law or to vouch for the evidence submitted in a cause, the lawyer must not allow the tribunal to be misled by false statements of law or fact or evidence that the lawyer knows to be false.

Representations by a Lawyer

[3] An advocate is responsible for pleadings and other documents prepared for litigation, but is usually not required to have personal knowledge of matters asserted therein, for litigation documents ordinarily present assertions by the client, or by someone on the client's behalf, and not assertions by the lawyer. Compare Rule 3.1. However, an assertion purporting to be on the lawyer's own knowledge, as in an affidavit by the lawyer or in a statement in open court, may properly be made only when the lawyer knows the assertion is true or believes it to be true on the basis of a reasonably diligent inquiry. There are circumstances where failure to make a disclosure is the equivalent of an affirmative misrepresentation. The obligation prescribed in Rule 1.2(d) not to counsel a client to commit or assist the client in committing a fraud applies in litigation. Regarding compliance with Rule 1.2(d), see the Comment to that Rule. See also the Comment to Rule 8.4(b).

Legal Argument

[4] Legal argument based on a knowingly false representation of law constitutes dishonesty toward the tribunal. A lawyer is not required to make a disinterested exposition of the law, but must recognize the existence of pertinent legal authorities. Furthermore,

771

as stated in paragraph (a)(2), an advocate has a duty to disclose directly adverse authority in the controlling jurisdiction that has not been disclosed by the opposing party. The underlying concept is that legal argument is a discussion seeking to determine the legal premises properly applicable to the case.

Offering Evidence

[5] Paragraph (a)(3) requires that the lawyer refuse to offer evidence that the lawyer knows to be false, regardless of the client's wishes. This duty is premised on the lawyer's obligation as an officer of the court to prevent the trier of fact from being misled by false evidence. A lawyer does not violate this Rule if the lawyer offers the evidence for the purpose of establishing its falsity.

[6] If a lawyer knows that the client intends to testify falsely or wants the lawyer to introduce false evidence, the lawyer should seek to persuade the client that the evidence should not be offered. If the persuasion is ineffective and the lawyer continues to represent the client, the lawyer must refuse to offer the false evidence. If only a portion of a witness's testimony will be false, the lawyer may call the witness to testify but may not elicit or otherwise permit the witness to present the testimony that the lawyer knows is false.

[7] The duties stated in paragraphs (a) and (b) apply to all lawyers, including defense counsel in criminal cases. In some jurisdictions, however, courts have required counsel to present the accused as a witness or to give a narrative statement if the accused so desires, even if counsel knows that the testimony or statement will be false. The obligation of the advocate under the Rules of Professional Conduct is subordinate to such requirements. See also Comment [9].

[8] The prohibition against offering false evidence only applies if the lawyer knows that the evidence is false. A lawyer's reasonable belief that evidence is false does not preclude its presentation to the trier of fact. A lawyer's knowledge that evidence is false, however, can be inferred from the circumstances. See Rule 1.0(f). Thus, although a lawyer should resolve doubts about the veracity of testimony or other evidence in favor of the client, the lawyer cannot ignore an obvious falsehood.

[9] Although paragraph (a)(3) only prohibits a lawyer from offering evidence the lawyer knows to be false, it permits the lawyer to refuse to offer testimony or other proof that the lawyer reasonably believes is false. Offering such proof may reflect adversely on the lawyer's ability to discriminate in the quality of evidence and thus impair the lawyer's effectiveness as an advocate. Because of the special protections historically provided criminal defendants, however, this Rule does not permit a lawyer to refuse to offer the testimony of such a client where the lawyer reasonably believes but does not know that the testimony will be false. Unless the lawyer knows the testimony will be false, the lawyer must honor the client's decision to testify. See also Comment [7].

Remedial Measures

[10] Having offered material evidence in the belief that it was true, a lawyer may subsequently come to know that the evidence is false.

Or, a lawyer may be surprised when the lawyer's client, or another witness called by the lawyer, offers testimony the lawyer knows to be false, either during the lawyer's direct examination or in response to cross-examination by the opposing lawyer. In such situations or if the lawyer knows of the falsity of testimony elicited from the client during a deposition, the lawyer must take reasonable remedial measures. In such situations, the advocate's proper course is to remonstrate with the client confidentially, advise the client of the lawyer's duty of candor to the tribunal and seek the client's cooperation with respect to the withdrawal or correction of the false statements or evidence. If that fails, the advocate must take further remedial action. If withdrawal from the representation is not permitted or will not undo the effect of the false evidence, the advocate must make such disclosure to the tribunal as is reasonably necessary to remedy the situation, even if doing so requires the lawyer to reveal information that otherwise would be protected by Rule 1.6. It is for the tribunal then to determine what should be done—making a statement about the matter to the trier of fact, ordering a mistrial or perhaps nothing.

[11] The disclosure of a client's false testimony can result in grave consequences to the client, including not only a sense of betrayal but also loss of the case and perhaps a prosecution for perjury. But the alternative is that the lawyer cooperate in deceiving the court, thereby subverting the truth-finding process which the adversary system is designed to implement. See Rule 1.2(d). Furthermore, unless it is clearly understood that the lawyer will act upon the duty to disclose the existence of false evidence, the client can simply reject the lawyer's advice to reveal the false evidence and insist that the lawyer keep silent. Thus the client could in effect coerce the lawyer into being a party to fraud on the court.

Preserving Integrity of Adjudicative Process

[12] Lawyers have a special obligation to protect a tribunal against criminal or fraudulent conduct that undermines the integrity of the adjudicative process, such as bribing, intimidating or otherwise unlawfully communicating with a witness, juror, court official or other participant in the proceeding, unlawfully destroying or concealing documents or other evidence or failing to disclose information to the tribunal when required by law to do so. Thus, paragraph (b) requires a lawyer to take reasonable remedial measures, including disclosure if necessary, whenever the lawyer knows that a person, including the lawyer's client, intends to engage, is engaging or has engaged in criminal or fraudulent conduct related to the proceeding.

Duration of Obligation

[13] A practical time limit on the obligation to rectify false evidence or false statements of law and fact has to be established. The conclusion of the proceeding is a reasonably definite point for the termination of the obligation. A proceeding has concluded within the meaning of this Rule when a final judgment in the proceeding has been affirmed on appeal or the time for review has passed.

Ex Parte Proceedings

[14] Ordinarily, an advocate has the limited responsibility of pre-

senting one side of the matters that a tribunal should consider in reaching a decision; the conflicting position is expected to be presented by the opposing party. However, in any ex parte proceeding, such as an application for a temporary restraining order, there is no balance of presentation by opposing advocates. The object of an ex parte proceeding is nevertheless to yield a substantially just result. The judge has an affirmative responsibility to accord the absent party just consideration. The lawyer for the represented party has the correlative duty to make disclosures of material facts known to the lawyer and that the lawyer reasonably believes are necessary to an informed decision.

Withdrawal

[15] Normally, a lawyer's compliance with the duty of candor imposed by this Rule does not require that the lawyer withdraw from the representation of a client whose interests will be or have been adversely affected by the lawyer's disclosure. The lawyer may, however, be required by Rule 1.16(a) to seek permission of the tribunal to withdraw if the lawyer's compliance with this Rule's duty of candor results in such an extreme deterioration of the client-lawyer relationship that the lawyer can no longer competently represent the client. Also see Rule 1.16(b) for the circumstances in which a lawyer will be permitted to seek a tribunal's permission to withdraw. In connection with a request for permission to withdraw that is premised on a client's misconduct, a lawyer may reveal information relating to the representation only to the extent reasonably necessary to comply with this Rule or as otherwise permitted by Rule 1.6.

Authors' 1983 Model Rules Comparison

The 1983 version of Rule 3.3 set forth a lawyer's duty of candor to the court in four specific subsections to Rule 3.3(a):

(a) A lawyer shall not knowingly:

(1) make a false statement of material fact or law to a tribunal;

(2) fail to disclose a material fact to a tribunal when disclosure is necessary to avoid assisting a criminal or fraudulent act by the client;

(3) fail to disclose to the tribunal legal authority in the controlling jurisdiction known to the lawyer to be directly adverse to the position of the client and not disclosed by opposing counsel; or

(4) offer evidence that the lawyer knows to be false. If a lawyer has offered material evidence and comes to know of its falsity, the lawyer shall take reasonable remedial measures.

The drafters of the 2002 Rules reorganized and clarified a lawyer's duty of candor to the tribunal. *See* Reporter's Explanation of Changes to Model Rule 3.3. The drafters sought to strengthen a lawyer's duties in addressing frauds related to documents or frauds related to the client's perjury. The drafters also broadened the lawyer's general obligation of candor to the tribunal by adding language in the Rule and in the Comments "to ensure the integrity of the adjudicative process." Comment 2.

Rule 3.3(a)(1) now imposes a duty on lawyers to correct prior statements made to the court that the lawyer later discovers were false.

The 2002 revisions deleted a clause in Rule 3.3(a)(2) that had stated a lawyer should not knowingly fail to disclose facts to the tribunal needed to avoid assisting the client's criminal or fraudulent act. The purpose of that deletion was not to take away the lawyer's duty of candor but to reorganize Rule 3.3 and make the disclosure obligation clearer. The drafters renumbered section (a)(3) as (a)(2) without modification, and renumbered section (a)(4) as (a)(3) while making significant revisions. The drafters combined all rules dealing with frauds related to documents into the new Rule 3.3(a)(3). This revision includes language that came from old Rule 3.3(c).

The drafters added a new Rule 3.3(b) that significantly rewrites the old Rule 3.3(a)(2) dealing with client crimes and frauds against the tribunal.

The 1983 version of Rule 3.3(b) is now Rule 3.3(c); Rule 3.3(b) now includes a reference to (a) and (b).

The drafters did not amend Rule 3.3(d).

Comment 1 is new and explains that this Rule applies representations before tribunals, not merely courts. A tribunal includes any legal body acting in an adjudicative capacity. *See* Rule 1.0(m).

Old Comment 1 is now renumbered as Comment 2 and modified to clarify the purpose of Rule 3.3.

Old Comments 2 and 3 are now renumbered as Comments 3 and 4 without modification.

Old Comments 4 and 5 are deleted.

The drafters added new Comments 5, 6, and 7, which explain the lawyer's role of candor in offering evidence to a tribunal. The drafters did not amend Comment 8, which deals with the same topic. The drafters moved and amended old Comment 14 so it is now new Comment 9. It deals with the exception that lawyers must permit criminal defendant clients to testify even when the lawyer knows that they intend to testify falsely.

The drafters deleted old Comments 7, 8, 9, and 10 on the topic of perjury by a criminal defendant.

Old Comment 11 is now revised and renumbered as Comment 10. It discusses the ABA's new approach to remedial measures when the lawyer knows that the client is committing a fraud on the tribunal.

Old Comment 6 is now Comment 11 with one sentence deleted.

Old Comment 12 was deleted. The new Comment 12 addresses client conduct that undermines the integrity of the adjudicative process, such as bribery or destruction of documents.

Old Comment 13 was amended to make clear when the obligations under Rule 3.3 end.

Old Comment 15 is renumbered as new Comment 14 without revision.

The drafters added new Comment 15 to discuss explicitly the interaction between Rule 1.6 and withdrawal.

Model Code Comparison

[1] Paragraph (a)(1) is substantially identical to DR 7-102(A)(5), which provided that a lawyer shall not "knowingly make a false statement of law or fact."

[2] Paragraph (a)(2) is implicit in DR 7-102(A)(3), which provided that "a lawyer shall not . . . knowingly fail to disclose that which he is required by law to reveal."

[3] Paragraph (a)(3) is substantially identical to DR 7-106(B)(1).

[4] With regard to paragraph (a)(4), the first sentence of this subparagraph is similar to DR 7-102(A)(4), which provided that a lawyer shall not "knowingly use" perjured testimony or false evidence. The second sentence of paragraph (a)(4) resolves an ambiguity in the Model Code concerning the action required of a lawyer who discovers that the lawyer has offered perjured testimony or false evidence. DR 7-102(A)(4), quoted above, did not expressly deal with this situation, but the prohibition against "use" of false evidence can be construed to preclude carrying through with a case based on such evidence when that fact has become known during the trial. DR 7-102(B)(1), also noted in connection with Rule 1.6, provided that a lawyer "who receives information clearly establishing that . . . [h]is client has . . . perpetrated a fraud upon . . . a tribunal shall [if the client does not rectify the situation] . . . reveal the fraud to the . . . tribunal. . . ." Since use of perjured testimony or false evidence is usually regarded as "fraud" upon the court, DR 7-102(B)(1) apparently required disclosure by the lawyer in such circumstances. However, some states have amended DR 7-102(B)(1) in conformity with an ABA-recommended amendment to provide that the duty of disclosure does not apply when the "information is protected as a privileged communication." This qualification may be empty, for the rule of attorney-client privilege has been construed to exclude communications that further a crime, including the crime of perjury. On this interpretation of DR 7-102(B)(1), the lawyer has a duty to disclose the perjury.

[5] Paragraph (c) confers discretion on the lawyer to refuse to offer evidence that the lawyer "reasonably believes" is false. This gives the lawyer more latitude than DR 7-102(A)(4), which prohibited the lawyer from offering evidence the lawyer "knows" is false.

[6] There was no counterpart in the Model Code to paragraph (d).

§ 3.3–1 INTRODUCTION: THE DUTY OF CANDOR

Rule 3.3, titled, "Candor Towards the Tribunal," brings together several different rules that focus on this duty of the lawyer as advocate. When a lawyer deals with a tribunal, in some very important respects, he or she must do more than merely tell the truth. Instead, the litigator must be "candid," *i.e.*, frank, without guile, aboveboard, straightforward. Although lawyers have the duty not to lie to their opponents,[1] the title of Rule 3.3 advises that lawyers have a higher duty to judges, the duty to be candid. Let us consider several different topics that all fall under this general rubric.[2]

THE DEFINITION OF "TRIBUNAL." Note that Rule 3.3 applies to a

---

[Section 3.3–1]

[1]*See, e.g.,* Rule 8.4(c).

[2]Rule 3.3(a)(1), in part, forbids lawyers from making certain false

"tribunal." It is not limited to a court.[3] A "tribunal" is any legal body or entity that acts in an adjudicative capacity.

For example, an arbitrator in a private arbitration is a "tribunal" for purposes of Rule 3.3. This interpretation advances the disclosure obligations of Rule 3.3, because arbitrators have the power to issue subpoenas, compel the production of relevant documentary evidence, administer oaths and affirmations, find the law and facts of the case, and, in general, exercise the powers of a court in the management and conduct of the hearing. "The effectiveness of arbitration as an alternative to formal litigation clearly would be undermined if counsel did not deal candidly with arbitrators."[4] In contrast, a grand jury is not a "tribunal" –at least as applied to defend.

Mediation. Rule 3.3 does not apply to a stand-alone mediation, because a mediator does not preside over a "tribunal" as defined in Rule 1.0(m).[5] Typically in mediation, a consensual process, a neutral third party works with the disputants to help them reach agreement as to some or all of the issues in controversy. The mediator does not have any power to impose a resolution so the mediation is not a "tribunal," because the Rules define "tribunal" to include a court or "an arbitrator in a *binding* arbitration." Usually, the mediator meets with the parties simultaneously and attempts to moderate and direct their discussions and negotiations. Because everyone is in the room together, all participants in the mediation know what the others have said. Rule 4.1 governs such mediation.[6]

Caucused Mediation. ABA Formal Opinion 06–439 (2006)

---

statements, but it also imposes some duties of candor, some duties to volunteer information. See Rule 3.3(a)(3) ("if necessary, disclosure to the tribunal"); Rule 3.3(b) ("shall take reasonable remedial measures").

[3]*See* Rule 1.0(m).

[4]*In the Matter of Forrest*, 158 N.J. 428, 435, 730 A.2d 340, 344 (1999) (per curiam) (internal citations omitted).

[5]ABA Formal Opinion 06–439 (Apr. 12, 2006).

[6]Examples of permissible "puffing" versus impermissible falsehoods include the following:

"A party in a negotiation also might exaggerate or emphasize the strengths, and minimize or deemphasize the weaknesses, of its factual or legal position. A buyer of products or services, for example, might overstate its confidence in the availability of alternate sources of supply to reduce the appearance of dependence upon the supplier with which it is negotiating. . . . .. An example of a false statement of material fact would be a lawyer representing an employer in labor negotiations stating to union lawyers that adding a particular employee benefit will cost the company an additional $100 per employee, when the lawyer knows that it actually will cost only $20 per employee. Similarly, it cannot be considered 'posturing' for a lawyer representing a defendant to declare that documentary evidence will be submitted at trial in support of a defense when the lawyer knows that such documents do not exist or will be inadmissible. In the same vein, neither a prosecutor nor a criminal defense lawyer can tell the other party

focused on a type of mediation, called "caucused mediation." In caucused mediation, the mediator meets privately with the parties. Each of these individual caucuses is confidential. The mediator controls the flow of information, subject to the agreement of the parties. Because of the nature of the mediator's involvement—she transmits information from one party to another—the successive transmissions of information tends to distort the information, and this distortion increases with subsequent transmissions. In addition, empirical research shows that mediators tend to embellish information, and sometimes distort it "to meet the momentary needs of their efforts to achieve a settlement."[7]

The question is whether the parties have a higher standard of truthfulness or candor than Rule 4.1 imposes. Rule 3.3 is a higher standard, and the issue is whether Rule 3.3 applies to mediation entered into by the parties to litigation pursuant to a statute or court order, or entered into voluntarily. One would think that the principles of candor to the court apply to such mediations because they are proceedings ancillary to the court proceedings (like depositions are ancillary to a court proceeding).

ABA Formal Opinion 06–439 (2006)[9] looked at this question and disagreed. It announced that Rule 4.1(a) governs "caucused mediation," not Rule 3.3. It did, however, concede that Rule 3.3 would apply to statements made to a tribunal *if* the tribunal itself is participating in settlement negotiations, including court-sponsored mediation in which a judge participates.[8]

If one takes this statement literally, candor to the court would

---

during a plea negotiation that they are aware of an eyewitness to the alleged crime when that is not the case." ABA Formal Opinion 06–439 (Apr. 12, 2006).

See also, Jeffrey Krivis, *The Truth About Using Deception in Mediation*, 20 Alternatives to High Cost Litigation 121, 123 (2002), listing similar examples.

[7]John W. Cooley, *Mediation Magic: Its Use and Abuse*, 29 Loy. U. Chi. L.J. 1, 101 (1997)(footnotes omitted). The author also explains, "one could make a persuasive argument that a heightened standard of truthfulness by advocates in mediation should apply because of the 'deception synergy' syndrome resulting from a third-party neutral's involvement. Practical experience shows that the accuracy of communication deteriorates on succes-sive transmissions between and among individuals. Distortions tend to become magnified on continued transmissions. Also, available behavioral research concerning mediator's strategies and tactics reveals that mediators tend to embellish information, translate it, and sometimes distort it to meet the momentary needs of their efforts to achieve a settlement. To help protect against 'deception synergy' perhaps more truthfulness should be required from mediation advocates and mediators." (footnotes omitted).

[8]ABA Formal Opinion 06–439 (Apr. 12, 2006), at note 2: "Rule 3.3 does apply, however, to statements made to a tribunal when the tribunal itself is participating in settlement negotiations, including court-sponsored mediation in which a judge partici-pates.", citing ABA Formal Opinion 93–370 (1993) (Judicial Participation

not apply to a majority of mediations conducted in conjunction with state and federal litigation. That result would be troubling because a lawyer should not be constrained from the obligations of candor (and disclosure) when a client commits a fraud in a mediation. Obviously, courts and state ethics committees are free to apply Rule 3.3 to all mediations performed as ancillary to judicial proceedings. ABA Formal Opinion 06–439 (2006) did acknowledge that Rule 4.1 applies, forbidding the lawyer from making a false statement of material fact or law to a third party.

In addition, if one considers mediation (whether caucused mediation or otherwise) to be a "nonadjudicative proceeding," then Rule 3.9 applies. That Rule says that Rules 3.3(a) through 3.3(c), 3.4(a) through 3.4(c), and Rule 3.5 all apply to nonadjudicative proceedings. ABA Formal Opinion 06–439 never mentioned Rule 3.9.

It is now quite clear that Rule 3.3 applies not only to proceedings before a tribunal but also any "ancillary proceeding[s] conducted pursuant to the tribunal's adjudicative authority, such as a deposition."[9] Essentially, Rule 3.3 duties begin to apply when a lawyer enters an appearance for a client and files a complaint in a case. For ethical purposes, it is quite irrelevant that a witness testifies in a deposition conducted in the informal atmosphere of a lawyer's office rather than the pomp and circumstance of a court proceeding.

While Rule 3.3 states that it applies to representations before a *tribunal,* its application is really broader than that because Rule 3.9 provides that the principles in Rule 3.3(a) through (c) apply to advocacy in a nonadjudicative proceeding.[10]

§ 3.3–2 CANDOR IN STATEMENTS ABOUT THE LAW AND DISCLOSURE OF ADVERSE LEGAL AUTHORITY

False Statements of the Law. A lawyer is subject to discipline if he knowingly makes a false statement of law to a tribunal.[1] Lawyers may not knowingly offer a false representation about the law. It does not matter if the representation is in a filing or made in open court.[2] The new Rule deletes the word, "material" in Rule 3.3 because the 2002 drafters believed that lawyers should not knowingly make any false statement of law to the tribunal, whether or not they are material. The lawyer may

---

in Pretrial Settlement Negotiations).

[9]Rule 3.3, Comment 1.

[10]**Other Tribunals Outside of the Judicial Branch.** This rule applies whether or not the tribunal is judicial, legislative, or administrative.

See Rule 3.9. *See also* Restatement of the Law Governing Lawyers, Third, § 111(2) (Official Draft 2000).

[Section 3.3–2]

[1]Rule 3.3(a)(1); DR 7-102(A)(5).

[2]Rule 3.3, Comment 4.

not lie, even if the lawyer privately seeks to justify the lie on the grounds that it was an immaterial little white lie.

Material Misstatements. While the lawyer may not make any false statement of law, the duties of the lawyer are different if the lawyer unintentionally makes a false statement of law to the tribunal and later discovers that is was false. *If* the statement is material, then the lawyer must correct the statement about the law made to the court.[3]

This clause clearly strengthens an advocate's duty to inform the tribunal that a prior statement about the law or the facts needs to be corrected if it is at all relevant to the proceedings.

Disclosure of Adverse Authority. The lawyer also has an affirmative duty to volunteer to the tribunal any legal authority in the controlling jurisdiction that he knows is directly adverse to his client's position and that opposing counsel has not already disclosed.[4] This Rule does not require a lawyer to make "a disinterested exposition" of the law.[5] A lawyer, after all, is not the judge or a law professor. An interested party hired his lawyer to promote his interests. The lawyer is engaged in advocacy, not a seminar discussion.

While the advocate must disclose pertinent, adverse legal authority in the controlling jurisdiction, he need not confess error. Of course, after disclosing these legal decisions he may seek to distinguish them, argue that the court should overrule them, challenge their soundness, "or present reasons which he believes would warrant the court in not following them in the pending case."[6]

The policy underlying this Rule is clear. Because the court should have full knowledge of all authority bearing directly upon the issue at hand, the lawyers who appear should arm the judges with the pertinent legal knowledge. Lawyers have an incentive to cite and argue authority that furthers their legal positions. However, absent this Rule, advocates would be tempted to ignore adverse authority with the hope that the opposing party will neglect to cite them. This state of affairs would result in court decisions that would not have the benefit of adverse legal authority. At minimum, it would place the burden on the tribunal to search for such authority. If the lower court does not consider this authority, an appellate decision may discover the case and then reverse the decision to the lower court for reconsideration. That would correct the legal error, but result in time-consuming remands. If the appellate court did not discover the adverse pre-

---

[3] Rule 3.3(a)(1).
[4] Rule 3.3(a)(2); DR 7-106(B)(1).
[5] Rule 3.3, Comment 4.

[6] ABA Formal Opinion 146 (July 17, 1935).

cedent, we would eventually find two lines of authority pointing in opposite directions. While the appellate courts would eventually correct their error, the parties and the law would suffer in the interval. Hence, the Rule requires an advocate who discovers adverse legal authority in the controlling jurisdiction to cite it, in the interests of judicial efficiency.

Note that the rule does *not* speak of "controlling authorities." It is broader and refers to "legal authority in the controlling jurisdiction." This language rejects the narrow view that the lawyer must only cite decisions that are decisive of the pending case. The legal "authority" is also broader than case law. The test is whether the decision, or statute, or regulation, or other law is something that court should clearly consider in deciding the case.[7] The disclosure rule applies to—

> a decision directly adverse to any proposition of law on which the lawyer expressly relies, which would reasonably be considered important by the judge sitting on the case . . .. The test in every case should be: *Is the decision which opposing counsel has overlooked one which the court should clearly consider in deciding the case?* Would a reasonable judge properly feel that a lawyer who advanced, as the law, a proposition adverse to the undisclosed decision was lacking in candor and fairness to him? Might the judge consider himself misled by an implied representation that the lawyer knew of no adverse authority.[8]

Case law has adopted a similar test.[9]

The Rules extend the duty to disclose adverse legal authority

---

[7] *See, e.g., Brundage v. Estate of Carambio*, 195 N.J. 575, 951 A.2d 947 (N.J.2008) (refusing to find a duty of a lawyer to disclose a similar case that the lawyer had unsuccessfully litigated in the same jurisdiction because the decision was contained in an unpublished decision that was not controlling; but the court castigated the lawyer for "sharp" practices).

[8] ABA Formal Opinion 280 (June 18, 1949) (emphasis added).

[9] *See, e.g., Shaeffer v. State Bar of California*, 26 Cal.2d 739, 160 P.2d 825 (1945). A lawyer, who relied on a California Supreme Court case to argue that his opponent's complaint should be dismissed, neglected to mention that the California Court of Appeal had issued a decision expressly rejecting the lawyer's interpretation of the California Supreme Court case. After the court of appeal's decision was discovered, the lawyer said that he omitted telling the trial judge about that decision because he thought that the court of appeal's discussion of the point was dictum, and that there was still no controlling authority contrary to his interpretation of the supreme court case. The California Supreme Court viewed the matter differently. Because of the lawyer's "familiarity with the [court of appeal] case [where, six months earlier he had appeared as counsel for appellant], he should . . . have directed the trial court's attention to the decision and [openly] argued [his] contentions . . . that the case was not controlling." 26 Cal.2d 739, 747–48, 160 P.2d at 829.

In re Greenberg, 15 N.J. 132, 137, 104 A.2d 46, 49 (1954). The duty to disclose applies "to decisions of the courts of this State and, with respect to federal questions, to decisions of the courts of the United States."

A lawyer's "ostrich-like tactic of pretending that potentially dispositive

until the proceedings are concluded "even if compliance requires disclosure of information otherwise protected by Rule 1.6."[10]

§ 3.3–3 CANDOR IN STATEMENTS ABOUT THE FACTS

§ 3.3–3(a) Affirmative Misrepresentations

Rule 3.1 governs the lawyer's ethical duties when she files motions or makes arguments based on evidence.[1] The lawyer does *not* need to have *personal knowledge* of the statements contained in any files she makes on behalf of her client.[2] The lawyer is "responsible" for these litigation documents in the sense that the lawyer, in good faith, has a basis in law and fact for doing so that is not frivolous.

Rule 3.3(a)(1), in contrast, covers situations where the lawyer makes representations of fact or law to a tribunal. The general principle, whether or not the lawyer is representing a party in litigation, is that a lawyer may not make any misrepresentation or engage in any dishonest, fraudulent or deceitful conduct.[3] A specific corollary of this principle is that a lawyer may not make

---

authority against a litigant's contention does not exist is as unprofessional as it is pointless." *Hill v. Norfolk and Western Ry.*, 814 F.2d 1192, 1198 (7th Cir.1987), *citing Bonds v. Coca-Cola Co.*, 806 F.2d 1324, 1328 (7th Cir. 1986).

Mannheim Video, Inc. v. County of Cook, 884 F.2d 1043, 1047 (7th Cir. 1989): "an attorney should not ignore potentially dispositive authorities; the word 'potentially' deliberately included those cases arguably dispositive. Counsel is certainly under obligation to cite adverse cases which are ostensibly controlling and then may argue their merits or inapplicability. But counsel may not hide from virtually controlling cases, only later to argue that the omission was due to a scintilla of difference between the already decided cases and the one being litigated." The court did not impose sanctions under Rule 11 of the Federal Rules of Civil Procedure because it declined to hold that the trial judge had "abused his discretion."

Tyler v. State, 47 P.3d 1095, 1105–1106 (Alaska App.2001). A "court decision can be 'directly adverse' to a lawyer's position even though the lawyer reasonably believes that the decision is factually distinguishable

from the current case or the lawyer reasonably believes that, for some other reason, the court will ultimately conclude that the decision does not control the current case." The court imposed sanctions in the form of a fine of $250. The court cited, RONALD D. ROTUNDA, PROFESSIONAL RESPONSIBILITY 163 (West Publishing 3rd ed.1992).

[10]Rule 3.3(b).

[Section 3.3–3]

[1]Rule 3.1. Other rules—as exemplified by Rule 11 of the Federal Rules of Civil Procedure—cover the obligations of a lawyer when the lawyer places client information and other factual assertions into a filing.

[2]Rule 3.3, Comment 3.

[3]Rule 8.4(c); DR 1-102(A)(4). *Cincinnati Bar Assn. v. Statzer*, 101 Ohio St.3d 14, 800 N.E.2d 1117(2003), reconsideration denied by *Cincinnati Bar Assn. v. Statzer*, 101 Ohio St.3d 1471, 804 N.E.2d 43, 2004-Ohio-819 (2004).— The lawyer taking a deposition (in this disciplinary proceeding!) waved around "suggestively" labeled tapes implying that the tapes contained conversations of the deponent and the lawyer. "By suggestively labeling the tapes and referring to them during questioning, respondent im-

a false statement of fact *to a tribunal*.[4] As in the case of false statements about the law, if a lawyer makes a statement about a fact to the tribunal and he later learns that his statement was both false and material to the proceeding, the lawyer must correct the false statement of fact. The drafters of the 2002 Rules added this obligation to correct prior statements of fact if the lawyer learns of their falsity.

Lawyers normally do not make testify as to statements of fact to a tribunal during an official proceeding.[5] Instead, they present evidence, argue about proper interpretations of the law, and ask the finder of fact to draw reasonable inferences from the evidence. However, in some cases lawyers do make representations to the tribunal. If the lawyer makes an assertion of fact in open court purporting to be based on her own knowledge (e.g., "my client is late for our hearing today because he just called me and said he had a flat tire"), or files an affidavit, the lawyer may make such assertions only when she *knows* the assertion is true or believes it to be true on the basis of a *reasonably* diligent inquiry.[6]

Rule 3.3 not only governs the conduct of a lawyer who is representing a client before a tribunal, but it also covers any

---

plied that she had recorded conversations with the legal assistant that could impeach and personally embarrass the legal assistant. Respondent also intermittently cautioned the legal assistant to answer truthfully or risk perjuring herself."— 101 Ohio St.3d 14, 15, 800 N.E.2d 1117, 1120.— The tapes were blanks. The court found this action was deceptive and therefore a violation of DR 1-102(A)(4) & Rule 8.4(c), and ordered the lawyer suspended for six months (suspension stayed for good behavior). The lawyer defended her conduct by claiming the ruse "worked." The court was unimpressed.

Kim v. Westmoore Partners, Inc., 201 Cal. App. 4th 267, 273, 133 Cal. Rptr. 3d 774 (4th Dist. 2011). The court imposed a $10,000 fine on an appellate lawyer who sought an extension of time to file his brief "under false pretenses," and who also filed a recycled brief full of irrelevant allegations, and then sent another lawyer to appear at his sanction hearing.

[4] Rule 3.3(a)(1). Cf. DR 7-102(A)(5). Rule 3.3(a)(1), showing the changes and deletions that the ABA House of Delegates made in 2002 provides:

"(a) A lawyer shall not knowingly:

"(1) make a false statement of ~~material~~ fact or law to a tribunal <u>or fail to correct a false statement of material fact or law previously made to the tribunal by the lawyer</u>; . . . . "

The Reporter's Explanation of Changes states:

<u>"Paragraph (a)(1): Amplify lawyer's duty not to make false statements to tribunal and add obligation to correct false statements previously made</u>

"The Commission recommends deletion of the term "material" that presently qualifies the lawyer's duty not to knowingly make false statements of fact or law to a tribunal, bringing this duty into conformity with the duty not to offer false evidence set forth in paragraph (a)(3). A new phrase addresses the lawyer's duty to correct a false statement of material fact or law previously made to the tribunal, also paralleling the duty to take remedial measures in paragraph (a)(3)."

[5] Rule 3.3, Comment 3.

[6] Rule 3.3, Comment 3 (emphasis added).

ancillary proceeding, such as a deposition, which is conducted pursuant to the tribunal's adjudicative authority. In general, the lawyer's duty to the tribunal is greater than her duty to the adversary. As we discuss in more detail elsewhere [Rules 4.1 and 8.4(c)], the lawyer may not lie to the adversary, but the lawyer has a broader duty of candor to the judge.

§ 3.3–3(b) Misrepresentation by Omission

It is not always necessary, or even permissible, to volunteer[7] adverse facts when appearing before a tribunal. However, in some circumstances, the "failure to make a disclosure is the equivalent of an affirmative misrepresentation."[8] Because lawyers may not affirmatively misrepresent,[9] they must make the necessary disclosures in such circumstances.[10]

---

[7]Volunteering adverse facts without the client's permission, where there is no duty to volunteer, may well violate Rule 1.1's obligation to represent the client competently.

[8]Rule 3.3, Comment 3.

[9]Rule 8.4(c); DR 1-102(A)(4).

Settling litigation without informing the court or opposing counsel of a prior, material false statement made in the course of that litigation may constitute a violation of the lawyer's duty of candor to the court. *In re Mines*, 523 N.W.2d 424, 426 (S.D. 1994). The court held that a lawyer's failing to remedy inadvertent misrepresentation, upon which the court relied is conduct involving deceit, dishonesty, misrepresentation and fraud and is prejudicial to administration of justice. The court imposed public censure. The court said: "This Court has given Mines the benefit of the doubt that his original misstatement of the fact to Judge Johns was made in good faith: without any knowledge whatsoever that the federal case had not been filed. Even so there remains the disturbing reality of his continued silence after he became aware of the non-filing." 523 N.W.2d at 427.

[10]*Matter of Jeffers*, 3 Cal. State Bar Ct. Rptr. 211, 1994 WL 715918 (Cal. State Bar Ct. 1994). The Review Department of the State Bar Court of California concluded that a lawyer had "intentionally" misled a trial judge as to his client's death. 1994 WL 715918,*4, 3 Cal. State Bar Ct. Rptr. at 218. In this case, the lawyer was not "directly asked if" his client was dead, and "his answers to the judge's questions may have been facially truthful" but that "is not a defense" because it is settled law that "concealment of material facts is just as misleading as explicit false statements, and accordingly, is misconduct calling for discipline." 1994 WL 715918,*6, 3 Cal. State Bar Ct. Rptr. 211, 220. This lawyer failed to inform the court of the client's death and represented to the court, during settlement discussions, that he could not communicate with client because "client's brain was not functioning." Because of this and other misconduct, the disciplinary court placed the respondent on probation for two years and required him to take and pass the professional responsibility examination.

ABA Formal Opinion 98-412 (Sept. 9, 1998), concluded that a lawyer who discovers that his client has violated a court order prohibiting or limiting the transfer of assets *must* reveal that fact to the court if that is necessary to avoid, or to correct, a lawyer's affirmative representation to the court. The lawyer must also disclose the client's conduct or withdraw from continued representation in the litigation if withdrawal is necessary to

§ 3.3–4 THE LAWYER'S DUTIES IN OFFERING EVIDENCE TO A TRIBUNAL

When a lawyer has knowledge that evidence is false, the lawyer must refuse to offer the evidence.[1] For example, if a client informs the lawyer that the client fabricated a document that is relevant and would be admitted into evidence it if were not made-up, the lawyer must refuse to admit the document. If a client finds a witness who is willing to testify falsely, the lawyer must refuse to call the witness. If the witness will testify about some things truthfully and other matters falsely, the lawyer must refrain from asking the witness about matter about which the lawyer knows the witness will lie. If the witness, in response to the adversary's question, gives a false answer, the lawyer, as discussed below, must take reasonable measures to undo this testimony, including revealing it to the judge.[2] Similarly, the lawyer may not falsify evidence or aid in its creation or preservation "if he knows, or it is obvious that the evidence is false."[3]

Rule 3.3(a)(3) does not prevent a lawyer from admitting evidence in order to prove its falsity.[4] For example, if an opposing party made a statement to the authorities shortly after the accident and later contradicted it, the lawyer could admit the false statement for the purpose of proving its falsity.

The purpose of these provisions is clear. Lawyers as officers of the tribunal must not participate in misleading the court or jury even when the client insists that the lawyer do so.

If a lawyer reasonably believes that evidence is false, but does not "know," Rule 3.3(a)(3) provides that the lawyer *may* refuse to offer the evidence.[5] This provision leaves up to the discretion of the lawyer whether to seek admission of questionable evidence. Some lawyers may err on the side of inclusion and risk the need to correct the submission at a later time. Other lawyers may

avoid assisting the client's fraud on the court. If the lawyer continues to represent the client, that may be treated as assisting the client's fraud on the court if the client's conduct destroys the court's ability to grant effective relief to the opposing party. If the lawyer withdraws, the lawyer's obligation is not fulfilled: the lawyer must make a disclosure sufficient to warn the court not to rely on the lawyer's prior representation that the lawyer now knows are false. *Id.*

[Section 3.3–4]

[1] Rule 3.3(a)(3); DR 7-102(A)(4). *See also* Restatement of the Law Governing Lawyers, Third, §§ 111(1), 120(1) (Official Draft 2000).

[2] Rule 3.3(a)(3) & Comments 6 & 10.

[3] Rule 3.4(b); DR 7-102(A)(6).

[4] Rule 3.3, Comment 5.

[5] Rule 3.3(a)(3). *See also* Restatement of the Law Governing Lawyers, Third, §§ 111(1), 120(3) (Official Draft 2000).

prefer to be cautious and demand additional proof of its authenticity. This Rule permits a lawyer's decision to override client choice on whether to admit the evidence.

If the lawyer, the client, or a witness called by the lawyer has offered material evidence to the tribunal and the lawyer later learns that this evidence was false when admitted, the lawyer shall take reasonable remedial measures.[6] In some situations, the lawyer learns of the falsity at a later time and in other cases the lawyer knows of the falsity when the witness utters the answer to the question posed by the lawyer or the opposing counsel. For example, the witness may want to testify falsely about a particular matter. The lawyer will tell the witness not to testify falsely. The witness might respond, "Don't worry; I'll tell the truth. Just put me on the stand." The lawyer puts the witness on the stand and, at the crucial moment, the witness lies and tells the lie. During the recess the witness might say: "I was willing to lie under oath, so you should not be surprised that I lied when I told you that I would tell the truth."

In all these cases, if the lawyer learns of the falsity prior to the conclusion of the proceeding, the lawyer should meet with the client and remonstrate as to the need to correct the false evidence. If the witness or client will not tell the truth and refuses to cooperate with the lawyer's attempt to correct the false evidence, the lawyer must take further remedial action.[7]

First, the lawyer must consider withdrawing from the representation. If withdrawal is not possible *or* if it will not undo the effect of the false evidence, the lawyer must disclose the information to the tribunal and the tribunal will then make a decision on how to handle the situation. The tribunal may inform the trier of fact, may order a mistrial, or do nothing.[8]

Commentators have long debated the degree of disclosure appropriate when the lawyer discovers that he or she has submitted material, false documentary or testimonial evidence. Some commentators have cogently argued that, particularly in criminal cases, the lawyer must keep client confidences: while the client has no right to commit perjury, if the client does testify falsely, the lawyer must not violate the client's trust by revealing the perjury.[9] After a debate that lasted years, the Model Rules

---

[6] Rule 3.3(a)(3).

[7] Rule 3.3, Comment 10.

[8] Rule 3.3, Comment 10.

[9] A major proponent of this view, and its most articulate defender is, Monroe Freedman, Lawyers' Ethics in an Adversary System (1975); Freed-man, Getting Honest About Client Perjury, 21 Geo. J. Legal Ethics 133 (2008); Monroe Freedman, Understanding Lawyers' Ethics 109-41 (1990). The most recent edition of this popular book is, Monroe H. Freedman & Abbe Smith, Understanding Lawyers' Ethics (4th ed.2010); Freed-

purported to reject this alternative.[10] The Rules say that they come down on the side of disclosure.[11]

Oddly enough, Professor Geoffrey Hazard, who promoted the present position of Rule 3.3, later said, "Distinguishing the function of criminal defense counsel from other advocate roles. I have come to the view that requiring a criminal defense lawyer to 'blow the whistle' on client perjury is futile or counterproductive."[12] Yet, he also acknowledges, "Many judges hold that the lawyer must disclose the perjury or fabrication to the court."[13]

The U.S. Supreme Court has not held that the U.S. Constitution requires the defense counsel to present the client's perjured

---

man, The Cooperating Witness Who Lies—A Challenge to Defense Lawyers, Prosecutors, and Judges, 740 Ohio St. J. Crim. L. 739 (2010). For a contrary position, *see, e.g.,* Rotunda, Book Review of Lawyers' Ethics in an Adversary System, 89 Harv. L. Rev. 622 (1976). *See generally* Rule 3.3, Comments 4 to 14.

[10]As Professor Monroe Freedman has pointed out, in Freedman, Getting Honest About Client Perjury, 21 Geo. J. Legal Ethics 133, 162 (2008):

However, the appearance that Model Rule 3.3 brought about a major policy change from the traditional view has been rendered practically meaningless by the requirement that a lawyer have "actual knowledge" before taking any remedial action. The result is that a defense lawyer may refrain from concluding that her client's testimony is perjurious, despite the fact that the client has told the lawyer inconsistent versions of the truth, and despite the fact that the client's testimony is far-fetched or preposterous, unsupported by other evidence, and dramatically contradicted by credible evidence. Through the disingenuous use of the "knowing" requirement, therefore, the courts and the ABA have effectively maintained the result of the traditional view.

Nevertheless, there remains a critical policy issue under Model Rule 3.3 because there are still some occasions when lawyers conclude that their clients are lying and then betray their clients' confidences. Unfortunately,

those lawyers are almost always court-appointed attorneys representing criminal defendants who are poor and members of minority groups. This has produced a race- and class-based double standard, resulting in a de facto denial of equal protection of the laws.

[11]The Model Code was unclear as to what to do. Rotunda, When the Client Lies: Unhelpful Guidelines from the ABA, 1 Corp. L. Rev. 34 (1978). In contrast, the Rules come down on the side of disclosure. *See* Model Rule 3.3. *Compare* ABA Formal Opinion 341 (Sept. 30, 1975) (discussing the position of the ABA Model Code), *with* ABA Formal Opinion 87-353 (Apr. 20, 1987) (discussing the position of the ABA Model Rules).

See also Rotunda, Client Fraud: Blowing the Whistle, Other Options, 24 Trial Mag. 92 (Nov., 1988); Rotunda, The Notice of Withdrawal and the New Model Rules of Professional Conduct: Blowing the Whistle and Waiving the Red Flag, 63 Or. L. Rev. 455 (1984), reprinted in, 1985 Criminal L. Rev. 533, and excerpted in 34 Law Review Digest 14 (Mar./Apr. 1985).

[12]Hazard, Jr., The Client Fraud Problem as a Justinian Quartet: An Extended Analysis, 25 Hofstra L. Rev. 1041, 1060 (1997).

[13]Hazard, Jr., The Client Fraud Problem as a Justinian Quartet: An Extended Analysis, 25 Hofstra L. Rev. 1041, 1049 (1997) (footnote omitted).

testimony. There is no federal constitutional right for the defendant to lie under oath or for the lawyer to assist that perjury.[14]

However, it is possible that some state court might hold that the state constitution gives a party in a civil or criminal case, or the accused in a criminal case, the right to lie under oath or present knowingly false evidence. Or, court rules might provide that if the accused want to give his own perjured testimony, his lawyer must allow him to do so if he gives the testimony in a narrative form. In the narrative format, the lawyer asks her client to tell his story. The lawyer asks no questions and the jury listens and does not argue the perjurious testimony to the jury.[15] Perhaps the prosecutor will not object to the narrative format, even though, under the laws of evidence, the lawyer must ask direct, non-leading questions and not simply ask a witness or party to "tell your side of the story."

If court rules or some other law require the lawyer to use the narrative approach, or to keep silent the perjury, the lawyer must follow that other law.[16] In other words, if a court decides to allow or authorize the lawyer to introduce client perjury or other false evidence, the Model Rules take that into account when it provides that the lawyer should obey that other law.[17] The Model Rules do not allow the lawyer to lie or assist the client to lie, but

---

[14]*Nix v. Whiteside*, 475 U.S. 157, 106 S.Ct. 988, 89 L.Ed.2d 123 (1986).

[15]The narrative format allows "the defendant to take the stand and deliver his statement in narrative form; the defendant's attorney does not elicit the perjurious testimony by questioning nor argue the false testimony during closing argument. The attorney, of course, is not precluded from arguing sound, non-perjurious testimony or attacking the state's case. Under this procedure, a defendant is afforded his right to speak to the jury under oath and the constitutional right to assistance of counsel is preserved, but the defense attorney is protected from participating in the fraud. Under such a formula, the responsibility for committing or not committing fraud on the tribunal lies with the defendant, and not with his attorney, and the jury will decide whether the defendant's testimony is credible." *Sanborn v. State*, 474 So.2d 309, 313 (Fla.App. 3d Dist.1985) (internal citations and footnotes omitted).

[16]Rule 3.3, Comment 7.

[17]*See, e.g., The Florida Bar v. Rubin*, 549 So.2d 1000 (Fla.1989), was a disciplinary proceeding that upheld a contempt and publicly reprimanded a lawyer because he failed to obey court order denying him permission to withdraw in case of expected client perjury. The trial court also ordered the lawyer to follow the narrative approach. The state charged the defendant with first-degree murder charge. For various reasons, the court had granted each of his three prior lawyers permission to withdraw. This lawyer was the fourth lawyer to represent this defendant. The Florida Supreme Court said that Florida did not adopt the narrative approach but the lawyer should have followed the court order rather than disobey it and refuse to proceed to trial, citing Rule 1.16(c).

If the bar later tried to discipline the lawyer for using the narrative approach, the state supreme court said: "However, if Rubin had been cited for violation of the Code for fol-

the Model Rules do provide that if other law controls, the lawyer should follow that other law.

But if the lawyer is practicing in a jurisdiction that follows the Model Rules instead of other law, the lawyer must not use the narrative approach and must not hide the client's or witness' perjury. Instead, the "advocate must disclose the existence of perjury with respect to a material fact, even that of a client. . . ."[18]

The Rule is now clear, but the ABA did not come to this conclusion casually. It was the product of years of debate. It is to that debate we now turn, in the next section.

§ 3.3–5 THE PROBLEM OF PERJURED TESTIMONY—THE ROAD LEADING TO DISCLOSURE

§ 3.3–5(a) The Model Code

The Model Code was not clear regarding the duty to correct fraud on a tribunal. It appeared to draw a distinction between fraud by the client and fraud by others, such as witnesses. DR 7-102(B)(2) provided that, if the lawyer "clearly" learns that someone "other than the client has perpetrated a fraud upon a tribunal," then the lawyer "shall promptly reveal the fraud to the tribunal." However, if the client in the course of representation "perpetrated a fraud upon a person or tribunal," then the lawyer must "promptly call upon his client to rectify" it. If his client refuses or is unable to do so, the lawyer must "reveal the fraud to the affected person or tribunal, *except when the information is protected as a privileged communication.*"[1] The ABA added the italicized language in 1974. Many states refused to adopt this 1974 amendment.

ABA Formal Opinion 341 interpreted "privileged" [used in DR 7-102(B)(1)] to include both "confidences" and "secrets" within the meaning of Canon 4.[2] Because "secret" is a term of art that the former Model Code defined very broadly, if one interpreted "privileged" to include "secret," the prohibition on disclosure became so broad that the casual reader might conclude that DR 7-102(B)(1) became a bar to any disclosure. The authors of Formal Opinion 341 may have embraced that meaning.

---

lowing the court-prescribed procedure, his good faith reliance on the trial court's order and the mandate of the district court would have been a *good, and most likely a complete, defense.*" 549 So.2d 1000, 1003 (emphasis added). The italicized phrase is intriguing. One would think that court should say that obeying the court order has to be a complete defense, given that this court had just held that the lawyer could not disobey the order.

[18] 1983 Model Rule 3.3, Comment 12.

[Section 3.3–5]

[1] DR 7-102(B)(1) (emphasis added).

[2] ABA Formal Opinion 341 (Sept. 30, 1975).

However, by incorporating Canon 4, this Formal Opinion also incorporated all of Canon 4's exceptions, including the exception for disclosure necessary to prevent "crimes" such as fraud. These exceptions were broad enough to engulf the new rule promulgated by this Formal Opinion.[3] Under this interpretation of DR 7-102(B)(1), the lawyer has a duty to disclose the perjury.[4]

The lawyer should not be able to avoid this disclosure requirement by claiming that the perjury had already been committed, because that distinction is mere sophistry. Assume that the lawyer tells the client what the law appears to provide after ABA Formal Opinion 341, which was based on the Model Code: "If you tell me that you will commit perjury, then I cannot put you on the stand. But, if you tell me that you will not commit perjury, then I can put you on the stand. If you 'surprise me' and then commit perjury even though you earlier promised that you would not do so, then I cannot disclose your false testimony because it is a past act."

If the client is a person who is considering committing perjury, the client will have no trouble figuring out how to do so without triggering disclosure by the lawyer. The lawyer is practically inviting the client to lie. The only thing missing is a cynical wink.

The best way to "prevent" the crime of perjury or fraud is to tell the client that if the client testifies falsely, the lawyer will reveal it to the judge. Model Rule 3.3's disclosure requirement avoids the subterfuge and guile suggested by the formalistic distinction between "past" and "future" perjury, and thus prevents the lawyer from aiding and abetting client perjury.

§ 3.3–5(b) A Constitutional Right of Perjury?

The rules of ethics obviously cannot override a state or federal constitutional guarantee. Consequently, some commentators have argued that the accused should have a right to testify, and to testify falsely, without his or her lawyer revealing the client's perjury.[5] The Comments to Rule 3.3 acknowledge this position and deal with it by providing that, if a jurisdiction imposes a dif-

---

[3]Ronald D. Rotunda, *When the Client Lies: Unhelpful Guidelines from the ABA*, 1 CORPORATION L. REV. 34 (1978). Ronald D. Rotunda, *Ethics*, USA TODAY, Feb. 15, 1983, at p. 10A; Ronald D. Rotunda, *The Notice of Withdrawal and the New Model Rules of Professional Conduct: Blowing the Whistle and Waiving the Red Flag*, 63 OREGON LAW REVIEW 455 (1984), *reprinted in* 1985 CRIMINAL LAW REVIEW 533, and excerpted in 34 Law Review Digest 14 (Mar./Apr. 1985); Geoffrey

C. Hazard, Jr., *Rectification of Client Fraud: Death and Revival of a Professional Norm*, 33 EMORY L. J. 271 (1984); W. William Hodes, *Two Cheers for Lying (About Immaterial Matters)*, 5 THE PROFESSIONAL LAWYER 1 (1994).

[4]Rule 3.3, Code Comparison 4.

[5]Professor Monroe Freedman is an articulate thoughtful supporter of this position. Several of his insightful books and articles, have argued that the defendant has a right to testify falsely. However, his contributions to

ferent rule or requires, as a constitutional matter, that the lawyer present the accused as a witness, then if the accused wishes to testify "even if counsel knows the testimony will be false," the lawyer must follow the state constitutional requirement.[6]

§ 3.3–5(c) *Nix v. Whiteside*

This constitutional issue arose in the Supreme Court decision in *Nix v. Whiteside*.[7] In that case, the Supreme Court, with no dissent, held that a lawyer's refusal to cooperate with a criminal defendant in presenting perjured testimony at trial does not violate the Sixth Amendment right to effective assistance of counsel.

In *Nix*, the lawyer told the defendant Whiteside that if he (Whiteside) insisted on committing perjury, then "it would be my duty to advise the Court of what he [Whiteside] was doing and that I felt he was committing perjury; also, that I probably would be allowed to impeach that particular testimony." The lawyer also said that he would seek to withdraw from further representation. Whiteside, to buttress his self-defense claim in a murder charge, wanted to testify that he had seen something "metallic" in the victim's hand. However, until a week before

---

the law of ethics go well beyond this particular issue *See, e.g.,* Freedman, *The Professional Responsibility of the Criminal Defense Lawyer: The Three Hardest Questions,* 64 Mich. L. Rev. 1469 (1966); Monroe H. Freedman, *Judge Frankel's Search for Truth,* 123 U. Pa. L. Rev. 1060 (1975); Monroe Freedman, Lawyers' Ethics in an Adversary System (1975); Freedman, Perjury: The Lawyer's Trilemma, 1 Litig. 26 (1975); Freedman, *The Aftermath of Nix v. Whiteside: Slamming the Lid on Pandora's Box,* 23 Crim. L. Bull. 25 (1987); Freedman, *Client Confidences and Client Perjury: Some Unanswered Questions,* 136 U. Pa. L. Rev. 1939 (1988); Freedman, *Getting Honest About Client Perjury,* 21 Geo. J. Legal Ethics 133 (2008); Monroe Freedman, Understanding Lawyer's Ethics (1990), now in its fourth edition: Monroe H. Freedman & Abbe Smith, Understanding Lawyers' Ethics (4th ed.2010); Freedman, *The Cooperating Witness Who Lies—A Challenge to Defense Lawyers, Prosecutors, and Judges,* 740 Ohio St. J. Crim. L. 739 (2010).

The 1983 ABA Model Rules,

while rejecting Professor Freedman's proposal, acknowledged and expressed respect for it. 1983 Model Rule 3.3, Comment 9:

"One [suggested solution to the issue of the client who wishes to testify perjuriously] is to permit the accused to testify by a narrative without guidance through the lawyer's questioning. This compromises both contending principles; it exempts the lawyer from the duty to disclose false evidence but subjects the client to an implicit disclosure of information imparted to counsel. Another suggested resolution, of relatively recent origin, is that the advocate be entirely excused from the duty to reveal perjury if the perjury is that of the client. *This is a coherent solution* but makes the advocate a knowing instrument of perjury." (emphasis added).

[6]Rule 3.3, Comment 7. *See* Ronald D. Rotunda, *Book Review of Freedman's "Lawyers' Ethics in an Adversary System,"* 89 HARV. L. REV. 62 (1976).

See, e.g., The Florida Bar v. Rubin, 549 So.2d 1000 (Fla. 1989).

[7]*Nix v. Whiteside,* 475 U.S. 157, 106 S.Ct. 988, 89 L.Ed.2d 123 (1986).

trial, Whiteside had consistently stated that he had not actually seen the victim with a gun. When asked about the change in testimony, Whiteside said: "If I don't say I saw a gun I'm dead."

At trial Whiteside testified that he knew that the victim had a gun, but admitted that he had not actually seen a gun in the victim's hand. Whiteside was convicted and claimed ineffective assistance of counsel because his counsel's admonition had prevented his giving false testimony. The Eighth Circuit actually granted habeas relief to Whiteside but the Supreme Court reversed, relying in part on Model Rule 3.3.

§ 3.3–5(d) ABA Formal Opinion 87-353

One year after *Nix*, ABA Formal Opinion 87-353, elaborated on Rule 3.3 and advised that the disclosure obligation of Rule 3.3 is "strictly limited" to the case where "the lawyer *knows* that the client has committed perjury. The lawyer's suspicions are not enough."[8]

"Know" does not mean, "know" in an existential sense. "Know" simply means "actual knowledge of the fact in question. A person's *knowledge may be inferred from circumstances.*"[9] Hence, the lawyer may not engage in willful ignorance or conclude that no one really ever "knows" anything for sure.

This Opinion also advised the lawyer that, if she cannot dissuade her client from testifying perjuriously, and if she cannot withdraw from representation, then she either should not call the client as a witness (when the lawyer knows "that the only testimony the client would offer is false"), or she should call the client and question him only on those matters that would not produce perjury. If the client does testify falsely, the lawyer cannot sit idly. She *must disclose* the false testimony under Rule 3.3(a)(3) and Rule 3.3(b).[10] Rule 3.3 overrides Rule 1.6 and adopts this test.[11] It does not countenance perjury and requires the lawyer to undo that perjury.

§ 3.3–5(e) The Narrative Approach

ABA Formal Opinion 87-353 makes clear that the lawyer cannot avoid the responsibility that Rule 3.3 imposes by having the

---

[8]ABA Formal Opinion 87-353 (Apr. 20, 1987) (emphasis in original). *See also* Restatement of the Law Governing Lawyers, Third, § 120 ("False Testimony or Evidence") (Official Draft 2000).

[9]Model Rule 1.0(f) (emphasis added).

[10]If the lawyer is able to withdraw *before* the client testifies perjuriously, then withdrawal is sufficient to enable

the lawyer to conclude that he is not assisting a criminal or fraudulent act by the client. "If the lawyer no longer represents the client, then the lawyer will not be in a position to engage in any conduct covered by Rule 3.3(a)." ABA Formal Opinion 98-412 (Sept. 2, 1998), at 9.

[11]Rule 3.3(c)("even if compliance requires disclosure of information otherwise protected by Rule 1.6. ").

client testify in a narrative form, without questioning.[12] The 1983 Model Rules decisively rejected the narrative approach outlined in the 1979 version of the ABA Proposed Defense Function Standards.[13] A lawyer "can no longer rely on the narrative approach to insulate him from a charge of assisting a client's perjury."[14] Hence, the present ABA Defense Standards now explicitly reject the narrative approach.[15]

Some jurisdictions have continued to allow or require the defendant to give his perjurious testimony in the form of a narrative, without his lawyer asking questions.[16] This result—apparently intended to allow the client to testify perjuriously without the lawyer obviously assisting the perjury—serves to notify the judge, the jury, and the prosecutor that some mischief is afoot because witnesses are not normally allowed to testify without their counsel asking direct questions.[17] Defense counsel is supposed to ask direct questions so that the prosecutor knows whether to object. For example, through use of the narrative, the defendant would be able to introduce into evidence a lot of hearsay testimony. In fact, it would be unusual for anyone to tell a narrative story without relying on hearsay. That is why the prosecutor will object and the trial court has every right under the law of evidence to sustain that objection.

Clearly, the drafters of the 2002 Rules would prefer that the law prohibit a lawyer from putting on the stand a client who has expressed a clear intention to commit perjury. However, the Comments now state: "In some jurisdictions, . . . courts have required

---

[12]ABA Formal Opinion 87-353 (Apr. 30, 1987).

[13]*See* ABA Proposed Defense Function Standard 4-7.5 (1979).

[14]ABA Formal Opinion 87-353 (Apr. 30, 1987). *Cf.* ABA Formal Opinion 98-412 (Sept. 9, 1998), which concluded that a lawyer who discovers that his client has violated a court order prohibiting or limiting the transfer of assets *must* reveal that fact to the court if that is necessary to avoid, or to correct, a lawyer's affirmative representation to the court. The lawyer must also disclose the client's conduct or withdraw from continued representation in the litigation if withdrawal is necessary to avoid assisting the client's fraud on the court.

Continued representation of the client may be treated as assisting the client's fraud on the court if the client's conduct destroys the court's ability to grant effective relief to the opposing party. If the lawyer withdraws, the lawyer's obligation is not ended: the lawyer must make a disclosure sufficient to warn the court not to rely on the lawyer's prior representation that the lawyer now knows is false. *Id.*

[15]ABA STANDARDS RELATING TO THE ADMINISTRATION OF CRIMINAL JUSTICE, THE DEFENSE FUNCTION, STANDARD 4-7.5, and related Commentary (ABA, 3d ed. 1992).

[16]Washington, D.C. Rules of Professional Conduct, Rule 3.3 (b), and Comments 7, 8 (1998). For a defense of the narrative approach, see Norman Lefstein, *Client Perjury in Criminal Cases: Still in Search of an Answer*, 1 GEORGETOWN J. LEGAL ETHICS 521 (1988).

[17]1983 Model Rule 3.3, Comment 9.

counsel to present the accused as a witness or to give a narrative statement if the accused so desires, even if counsel knows that the testimony or statement will be false."[18] In a system that gives the defendant a right to be put on the stand and testify, the Rules still reject the narrative approach. The defendant will be able to testify, but the lawyer must still disclose the perjury if the defendant testifies falsely.[19]

Granted, defendant has "a sense of betrayal," but the client should clearly understand that the lawyer will fulfill her duty to disclose the existence of false evidence. Under the narrative approach or any other approach that allows or requires the lawyer to introduce this evidence and argue it to the jury as if it were true, the client will "simply reject the lawyer's advice to reveal the false evidence and insist that the lawyer keep silent. Thus the client could in effect coerce the lawyer into being a party to fraud on the court."[20]

§ 3.3–5(f) Duration of the Obligation to the Court

If the lawyer has offered material evidence and later learns of its falsity, the lawyer "must take reasonable remedial measures" to undo the effect of the false testimony.[21] This duty applies "even if compliance requires disclosure of information otherwise protected" by the confidentiality requirements of Rule 1.6.[22]

Similarly, the lawyer's duty continues *"to the conclusion of the proceeding"* even though "compliance requires disclosure of information otherwise protected by Rule 1.6."[23]

In a criminal case, a verdict of acquittal concludes the proceedings, given that the double jeopardy clause prevents the state from retrying the defendant. In a criminal case where the defendant was nonetheless convicted, the defendant may wish to appeal to secure a new trial or an outright reversal; the defendant should not be able to benefit from his earlier perjury. Accordingly, the proceeding is not "concluded" until at least the time for direct appeal (as opposed to collateral attack via a writ of habeas corpus) has passed.[24] Hence, in a criminal case, the proceeding has concluded if the jury has acquitted the defendant, or if the time for appeal has not yet passed or the case has been affirmed.

In a civil case, the proceedings should not be treated as concluded until the time for appeal has passed. If the civil case has just concluded with a jury verdict in defendant's favor, and the defense lawyer then learned that she won the case with her

---

[18]Rule 3.3, Comment 7.

[19]Rule 3.3(c).

[20]Rule 3.3, Comment 11. *Accord* Ronald D. Rotunda, *Book Review of Lawyers' Ethics in an Adversary*

System, 89 HARV.L.REV. 622 (1976).

[21]Rule 3.3(a)(4).

[22]*See* Rule 3.3(b).

[23]Rule 3.3(b) (emphasis added).

[24]Rule 3.3, Comment 13.

client's perjury, the proceedings have not yet concluded, because post trial motions are still in order and the time for appeal has not yet passed.[25] Hence, in a civil case, the proceeding has not concluded until the time for any final appeal has passed or the case has been affirmed and there is no further appeal.

In some cases, the lawyer will have to reveal the fact that his client committed perjury in order to comply with the candor requirements of Rule 3.3. Before making this dramatic disclosure, there are other options the lawyer should pursue. First, of course, the lawyer should seek to persuade the client to correct the falsehood.[26] The lawyer should "remonstrate with the client confidentially"[27] and, if the client is still adamant, the lawyer "should seek to withdraw if that will remedy the situation."[28]

However, in some cases withdrawal will not remedy the situation. Then, it will not be enough for the lawyer, like Pontius Pilate, to wash his hands of the situation. In other cases, withdrawal will not be possible because the court will not allow it. In the middle of a trial or even on the eve of a trial, for example, the court is unlikely to allow the lawyer to simply walk away. In those circumstances, the lawyer must disclose the relevant information to the court.[29] The court then decides what to do next: (1) make a statement to the trier of fact; (2) order a mistrial; or (3) "perhaps nothing."[30]

If the lawyer discloses client perjury to the court, and the client disputes the charge, then the lawyer obviously cannot represent the client in resolution of this factual issue because the lawyer will be a witness and have a view of the facts that is contrary to the client's.[31] Thus, the judge may declare a mistrial.

Prior to the 2002 revision, a Comment to Rule 3.3 acknowledged that an "unscrupulous client might in this way attempt to produce a series of mistrials and thus escape prosecution. However, the Comment argued that a second such encounter could be construed as a deliberate abuse of the right to counsel and, as such, a waiver of the right to further representation."[32] Ethics 2000, the ABA Commission that proposed major changes to the Model Rules, deleted that Comment, and several others, along with a notation that said it had "been deleted as no longer help-

---

[25]Rule 3.3, Comment 13.

[26]Rule 3.3, Comment 5.

[27]Rule 3.3, Comment 10.

[28]Rule 3.3, Comment 10.

[29]Rule 3.3, Comment 10.

[30]Rule 3.3, Comment 10. *See*

Ronald D. Rotunda, *Client Fraud: Blowing the Whistle, Other Options*, 24 TRIAL MAGAZINE 92 (Nov. 1988).

[31]Rule 3.7.

[32]Rule 3.3, Comment 10, now deleted when the ABA House of Delegates adopted major changes in 2002.

ful to the analysis of questions arising under this Rule. *No change in substance is intended.*"[33]

While this Comment is no longer in the Model Rules, the possibility that this scenario will come to pass is quite real. There is constitutional support for the proposition that the client may lose the right to counsel.[34] However, rather than speak of "waiver of the right to further representation," one should more precisely speak of "forfeiture."[35] The client is not "waiving" if we think of a waiver in its ordinary sense: a voluntary relinquishment of a known right. The client is forfeiting a right because of its abuse.

§ 3.3–5(g) Candor in Civil Litigation

Although the lawyer's obligation to the tribunal in the situation of a lying criminal defendant is well known in the criminal defense bar, lawyers litigating civil cases are sometimes not as well versed as to how this candor should apply in the civil context. Of course, if a client informs a lawyer that a document is false, lawyers know that they may not admit it into evidence. And, if a client informs a lawyer that he will lie on the stand during trial, a lawyer must seek to dissuade the client from such action and will often seek to withdraw if this does not occur. The problems in civil cases tend to arise when the client has already committed the crime or fraud and the lawyer now must decide what to do.

If a client has perpetuated a past crime or fraud that is ongoing (e.g., the client lied in a deposition), the lawyer should not go to trial and act as if nothing is amiss. However, some lawyers believe that they can avoid the problem by settling the case. In the view of some people, the lawyer would be careful not to refer to the falsehood during the settlement discussions, but otherwise would take advantage of the false evidence that was uncovered during discovery.

However, Rule 3.3 does not differentiate between civil and criminal cases in the context of a client fraud on the court. If one is to take seriously the lawyer's obligation of candor to the court, Rule 3.3 does not allow a lawyer to settle a case without disclosing a fraud that is material enough to affect the underlying settlement, because Rule 3.3 covers any "ancillary proceeding conducted pursuant to the tribunal's adjudicative authority, such as a deposition."[36] See also the discussion of this issue in the following section.

---

[33]Reporter's Explanation of Changes to Rule 3.3 (emphasis added).

[34]*Cf. Illinois v. Allen*, 397 U.S. 337, 90 S.Ct. 1057, 25 L.Ed.2d 353 (1970) (defendant's courtroom disruption justifies conducting trial without defendant's presence).

[35]*See* Peter Westen, *Away from Waiver: A Rationale for the Forfeiture of Constitutional Rights in Criminal Procedure*, 75 MICH. L. REV. 1214 (1977).

[36]Rule 3.3, Comment 1.

§ 3.3–6 THE LAWYER'S OBLIGATION OF CANDOR IN PRETRIAL DISCOVERY

If a lawyer in a civil case discovers that her client has lied in a deposition, the lawyer must use all reasonable means to remedy the fraud, even though the lawyer may have acted completely innocently. For example, the lawyer should first remonstrate with the client. If that fails, the lawyer must take other measures, including revealing the perjury to the judge.[1]

Consider the situation where the other party's attorney asked

[Section 3.3–6]

[1]An interesting example of a lawyer informing the court of false statements is found in *Jones v. Clinton*, 36 F.Supp.2d 1118 (E.D.Ark.1999). In the course of the judge's opinion, she noted:

"Indeed, even though the President's testimony at his civil deposition was entirely consistent with Ms. Lewinsky's affidavit denying 'sexual relations' between herself and the President, the President's *attorney later notified this Court pursuant to his professional responsibility* that portions of Ms. Lewinsky's affidavit were reported to be 'misleading and not true' and that this Court should not rely on Ms. Lewinsky's affidavit or remarks of counsel characterizing that affidavit. See Letter of September 30, 1998. The President's testimony at his deposition that Ms. Lewinsky's denial in her affidavit of a 'sexual relationship' between them was 'absolutely true' likewise was 'misleading and not true.' " 36 F.Supp.2d 1118, 1130 n. 15 (emphasis added).

This case grew out of *Clinton v. Jones*, 520 U.S. 681, 117 S.Ct. 1636, 137 L.Ed.2d 945 (1997), the decision denying the President any Presidential immunity (permanent or temporary) from the civil suit filed by Ms. Paula Jones. See discussion in Ronald D. Rotunda, *Paula Jones Day in Court*, 17 LEGAL TIMES 24, 27 (May 30, 1994). *See also* Roberto Suro & John Harris, *No Appeal Planned on Contempt Order; Clinton Aides Await Sanctions Decision*, WASHINGTON POST, Apr. 14, 1999, at A1. Subsequently, the President paid $90,686 in civil contempt fines. Linda Satter, *Court Lies Cost Clinton $90,686*, ARKANSAS DEMOCRAT-GAZETTE, July 30, 1999, at p. 1.

On President Clinton's last day in office, January 19, 2001, he accepted a five-year suspension from the Arkansas bar, which ended both the criminal probe and the state disbarment proceedings. Under the terms of the suspension, the President also had to pay a $25,000 fine. In the consent order the President acknowledged that he "knowingly gave evasive and misleading answers" concerning his relationship with Ms. Lewinsky. That order included a finding that the President thereby violated Arkansas Rule 8.4(d).

In a public statement, also released on January 19, 2001, President Clinton said: "I tried to walk a fine line between acting lawfully and testifying falsely, but I now recognize that I did not fully accomplish this goal and that certain of my responses to questions about Ms. Lewinsky were false."

Independent Counsel Robert W. Ray announced that same day that, by agreement with President Clinton upon entry of the consent order and issuance of Clinton's public statement, "President Clinton will be discharged from all criminal liability for matters within the remaining jurisdiction of this Office." The President agreed not to seek any reimbursement of his legal fees. The Arkansas outside counsel to the Supreme Court Committee on Professional Conduct said that the Committee "wanted the suspension to start while Clinton was still in office as an added stigma." *Clinton Accepts Five-Year Suspension to End Disbarment Case, Criminal Probe*, ABA/BNA

a question during deposition, to which her client responded with an answer that the lawyer thought was correct at the time. However, the lawyer later learned that the client lied in the deposition. Even though the lawyer did not rely on that deposition to file a motion for summary judgment, and no misrepresentations took place in open court, Rule 3.3 applies. Both Rules 3.3(a)(1) & (3) apply to pretrial discovery situations and neither Rule requires that the lawyer must have been aware of the false evidence at the time that it was introduced.[2]

Rule 3.3 does not allow a lawyer to settle a case without disclosing a fraud that is material enough to affect the underlying settlement, because Rule 3.3 covers any "ancillary proceeding conducted pursuant to the tribunal's adjudicative authority, such as a deposition."[3] The case law and ethics opinions come to the same conclusion.

In fact, the Rule does not even require the judge to be aware of the false evidence. In the typical discovery situation, the judge will not have read the depositions and therefore will not be aware of the specific testimony. Nonetheless, Rule 3.3 requires the lawyer to take reasonable remedial measures to rectify the false testimony or evidence, including disclosure to the judge, so that the client cannot take advantage of the false evidence.[4]

LAWYER'S MANUAL ON PROFESSIONAL CONDUCT, Current Reports, vol. 17, no. 3, Jan. 31, 2001, at p. 73.

Following the Arkansas suspension, the U.S. Supreme Court ordered that "Bill Clinton, of New York, New York, is suspended from the practice of law in this Court, and a rule will issue, returnable within 40 days, requiring him to show cause why he should not be disbarred from the practice of law in this Court." *In re Discipline of Clinton*, 534 U.S. 806, 122 S.Ct. 36, 151 L.Ed.2d 254 (2001). The former President promptly announced that he would contest the disbarment, but instead, on the fortieth day, he resigned from the Supreme Court bar rather than fighting his disbarment. *President Would Drop High Court Privilege*, WASHINGTON POST, Nov. 10, 2001, at p. A3. A few days later, the Court announced: "Bill Clinton, of New York, New York, having requested to resign as a member of the Bar of this Court, it is ordered that his name be stricken from the roll of

attorneys admitted to the practice of law before this Court. The Rule to Show Cause, issued on October 1, 2001, is discharged." *In the Matter of Bill Clinton*, 534 U.S. 1016, 122 S.Ct. 584, 151 L.Ed.2d 454 (2001).

[2] *Jones v. Clinton*, 36 F.Supp.2d 1118, 1130 n. 15 (E.D.Ark.1999).

[3] Rule 3.3, Comment 1.

[4] *See, e.g., Kath v. Western Media, Inc.*, 684 P.2d 98 (Wyo.1984). The lawyer, during the course of negotiations to settle the suit for attorney fees and costs from a prior action had a duty to disclose a letter was contrary to what a witness said or necessarily implied in his April 6, 1983, deposition.

In re Mack, 519 N.W.2d 900, 901 (Minn.1994). The court disciplined a lawyer for failure to take reasonable measures to disclose falsity of testimony of client in deposition. The lawyer "neither advised his client to disclose her misrepresentation nor disclosed it himself to either the court

§ 3.3–7 THE LAWYER'S DUTY TO PREVENT CRIMINAL AND FRAUDULENT CONDUCT RELATED TO THE PROCEEDING

The Rule 3.3(a)(2) of 1983 Model Rules stated that "A lawyer shall not knowingly . . . fail to disclose a material fact to a tribunal when disclosure is necessary to avoid assisting a criminal or fraudulent act by the client."[1] Rule 3.3(a)(4) of the 1983 Rules also stated that lawyer should not offer evidence known to be false and if such evidence is offered and the lawyer discovers its falsity, the lawyer shall take reasonable remedial measures.[2] These two duties of the Rule 3.3—requiring the lawyer to have candor to the court—caused some confusion: which types of frauds on the court fell under which rule. A criminal or fraudulent act by a client could involve introduction of evidence or it could be outside of the traditional role of the lawyer as one who introduces evidence to a tribunal. This confusion was largely theoretical because the result under Rule 3.3(a)(2) and (a)(4) was similar.

The drafters of the 2002 Rules kept the provision on a lawyer's involvement with evidence in Rule 3.3(a) and elaborated upon it slightly. They also deleted the language in 1983 Rule 3.3(a)(2) and moved its principle to Rule 3.3(b), which now deals with client behavior that constitutes criminal or fraudulent conduct related to the proceeding. Now it is clear that Rule 3.3(a)(3) deals with fraud on the court related to introducing evidence and Rule 3.3(b) deals with other frauds outside of the area of evidentiary frauds, such as bribes, intimidation or unlawful communications with a witness, juror, court official or other participant in the proceeding, unlawful destruction or concealment of documents or other evidence, or failure to disclose information to the tribunal when required by law to do so. The drafters reorganized the Comments to reflect this change, and added a new Comment, entitled "Preserving the Integrity of the Adjudicative Process."[3]

Now, under Rule 3.3(b), when a lawyer representing a client

---

or the adversary."

See also, Virginia State Bar Opinion 1451 (1992), http://www.vacle.org/opinions/1451.TXT. "[I]t would be unjust to allow the false deposition testimony [of defendant] to stand, regardless of whether the case proceeds to trial. [T]he defendant's attorney must reveal the client's knowingly false statement (fraud) to the tribunal if the client is unwilling to do so."

ABA Formal Opinion 93-376 (Aug. 6, 1993): "A lawyer in a civil case

who discovers that her client has lied in responding to discovery requests must take all reasonable steps to rectify the fraud, which may include disclosure to the court. In this context, the normal duty of confidentiality in Rule 1.6 is explicitly superseded by the obligation of candor toward the tribunal in Rule 3.3."

[Section 3.3–7]

[1] 1983 Model Rule 3.3(a)(2).
[2] 1983 Model Rule 3.3(a)(4).
[3] Rule 3.3, Comment 12.

before an adjudicative body learns that the client "intends to engage, is engaging, or has engaged in criminal or fraudulent conduct related to the proceeding," then the lawyer "shall take reasonable remedial measures, including, if necessary, disclosure to the tribunal."[4]

Thus, in a sense, Rule 3.3(b) is broader and a catchall for criminal and fraudulent behavior that does not require the lawyer to admit false evidence into the record.[5] When such conduct is involved, the lawyer's obligation to the client must give way to the broader obligation that lawyers have as officers of the tribunal.

§ 3.3–8 THE LAWYER'S WITHDRAWAL FROM THE CASE AND THE PROTECTION OF A CLIENT'S SECRETS

In many cases, a lawyer's withdrawal from the case, even the lawyer's "noisy withdrawal," will not be entirely effective to undo the fraud's impact on the case. For example, the opposing party might drop the case or settle it, in reliance on the false deposition, in spite of the noisy withdrawal. Consequently, "[d]irect disclosure under Rule 3.3, to the opposing party or, if need be, to the court, may prove to be the only reasonable remedial measure in the client fraud situations most likely to be encountered in pretrial proceedings."[1]

In other cases, however, withdrawal will be effective to fulfill the lawyer's obligations, but the very fact of the lawyer's withdrawal will undermine the client's confidences or secrets. The client may even specifically instruct the lawyer not to broadcast the fact of his withdrawal. The client, in short, would like the lawyer to slink quietly away and not publicly announce his withdrawal.

The Model Rules make clear that they do not respect the client's interest in keeping secret his lawyer's withdrawal in this situation. The Rules advise, generally, that if the lawyer has of-

---

[4]Rule 3.3(b).

"Criminal or fraudulent" means crimes or frauds directed toward a matter pending before the court. ABA Formal Opinion 98-412 (Sept. 9, 1998), at 7 n. 11.

[5]Rule 3.3(b) may reach a lawyer's direct or indirect conduct relating to litigation tactics that including packing the courtroom with sympathetic persons. *See Norris v. Risley*, 918 F.2d 828 (9th Cir.1990) (15 women from local organizations wearing Women Against Rape buttons in courtroom); *State v. Rose*, 112 N.J. 454, 548 A.2d

1058 (1988) (9 or 10 uniformed officers sat in courtroom during trial against person accused of murdering an officer).

[Section 3.3–8]

[1]ABA Formal Opinion 93-376 (Aug. 6, 1993). *See also* ABA Formal Opinion 98-412 (Sept. 9, 1998) at 5, & n. 9, noting that the lawyer has a duty to disclose a client's false statement (the client's correct name) to a probation officer when the client gave the false name in an effort to obtain a lighter sentence.

fered material evidence and later learns of its falsity, the lawyer "must take reasonable remedial measures."[2] This duty applies "even if compliance requires disclosure of information otherwise protected" by the confidentiality requirements of Rule 1.6.[3]

In addition, if the client will use a lawyer's services to further the client's "criminal or fraudulent conduct," then the lawyer must also withdraw.[4] In some circumstances the fact of a lawyer's withdrawal from representation may amount to a disclosure of client confidences or secrets. For example, if a lawyer withdraws in such a manner as to suggest that the client intends to commit fraud, then the lawyer will have disclosed information detrimental to the client. In some instances "the very act of disassociation would have the effect of violating" the lawyer's obligation of protecting the client's secrets and confidences.[5] Under the Model Code and its predecessors, there were those who argued that the lawyer must respect the client's secrets in such a situation.[6] This is no longer true. In those cases where Rule 3.3 does not require the lawyer disclose his client's nefarious activities, the lawyer must withdraw and may even make this withdrawal noisy.[7]

---

[2]Rule 3.3(a)(3).

[3]See Rule 3.3(b).

[4]Rule 1.16(a)(1). The Model Code had similar requirements. DR 2-110(B)(2); DR 7-102(A)(7).

[5]ABA Formal Opinion 314 (Apr. 27, 1965), referring to Canon 37. Canon 37 of the ABA Canons of Professional Ethics (1908, as amended) was the predecessor to DR 4-101 of the Model Code. The confidentiality sections are now found in Rule 1.6 of the Model Rules.

[6]For example, the AMERICAN LAWYER'S CODE OF CONDUCT (The Roscoe Pound—American Trial Lawyers Foundation, Rev. Draft, May 1982), *reprinted in* THOMAS D. MORGAN & RONALD D. ROTUNDA, 1999 SELECTED STANDARDS ON PROFESSIONAL RESPONSIBILITY (Foundation Press, 1999), at 251, et seq. reflects this position. *See id.* at Rule 6.5 [at p. 270]: "In any matter other than criminal litigation, a lawyer may withdraw from representing a client if the lawyer comes to know that the client has knowingly induced the lawyer to take the case or to take action on behalf of the client on the basis of material representations about the case, *and if withdrawal can be accomplished without a direct violation of confidentiality.*" (emphasis added).

See also American Lawyer's Code of Conduct, Illustrative case 6(a), which argues that, in a criminal case, where the client intends to commit perjury, the lawyer would commit a disciplinary violation by asking to withdraw and giving an equivocal explanation if the judge thinks an equivocal explanation is an indication that the client will commit perjury. In Illustrative case 6(c), the proposed American Lawyer's Code of Conduct applies in a civil case or a regulatory proceeding. Thus, if a lawyer, by agency or court rule, must give a reason for withdrawal, and the lawyer asks to withdraw because of the client's insistence on filing documents with material misrepresentations, the lawyer would "commit a disciplinary violation by withdrawing and thereby directly violating the client's confidences in making the required explanation."

[7]*See* Ronald D. Rotunda, *The*

§ 3.3–9 CANDOR IN *EX PARTE* PROCEEDINGS

The law allows a tribunal to hold an *ex parte* proceeding, a hearing with only one side present, when an emergency arises that required immediate attention of the tribunal in light of the imminent harm. The Model Rules require that a lawyer representing a client in an *ex parte* proceeding has a special affirmative duty to disclose all material facts (whether or not thought to be adverse) to the tribunal. The disclosure requirement is necessary so that the tribunal can make an informed decision.[1] In an *ex parte* proceeding, the tribunal cannot rely on the adversary system to uncover the truth; however, the tribunal has a duty to afford the absent party a balanced and fair consideration. Because the lawyer cannot rely on the other side to balance her presentation, she has this broader affirmative duty.[2]

For example, in *Goodsell v. The Mississippi Bar*,[3] the court found that a lawyer violated this rule when he represented to the court that his client had signed a motion for a temporary restraining order, when in fact, the lawyer had signed the document himself. The nature of signature and the fact that the client was not even present when the lawyer signed client's name to the motion were material facts. For this violation and others, the court suspended the lawyer for 180 days.

The lawyer can violate this section even if he does not make a "knowingly" false misrepresentation, *if* he fails to make a "reasonable investigation" before asserting to the court as true, in an *ex parte* proceeding, that which he does not reasonably know to be true.[4]

Notice of Withdrawal and the New Model Rules of Professional Conduct: Blowing the Whistle and Waiving the Red Flag, 63 OREGON L. REV. 455 (1984).

This rule requiring withdrawal has ancient roots. When young Abraham Lincoln was practicing law and learned that his client had lied in court, he left the courtroom and refused to proceed with the trial. " 'My hands are dirty and I've gone to wash them,' the future President told the judge." Andrew Napolitano, *Clinton's Perjury and His Lawyer's Ethics*, WALL STREET JOURNAL, Sept. 24, 1998, at A18. Mr. Napolitano is a former judge.

[Section 3.3–9]

[1] Rule 3.3(d).

[2] Rule 3.3, Comment 14. No similar provision exits in the Model Code, but the principle of Rule 3.3(a) reflects the case law. *Cf. Precision Instrument Mfg. Co. v. Automotive Maintenance Machinery Co.*, 324 U.S. 806, 818, 65 S.Ct. 993, 999, 89 L.Ed. 1381, 1388 (1945) (patent applicant must report to the Patent Office all facts concerning possible fraud or inequities underlying patent application).

[3] *Goodsell v. The Mississippi Bar*, 667 So.2d 7, 10 (1996).

[4] *Matter of Brantley*, 260 Kan. 605, 629, 920 P.2d 433, 447 (1996)(per curiam): "There does not appear to be any evidence in the record that Brantley made knowingly false statements to the court. [But his] failure to make a reasonable investigation regarding

CHAPTER 3.4

FAIRNESS TO OPPOSING PARTY AND OPPOSING COUNSEL

RULE 3.4: FAIRNESS TO OPPOSING PARTY AND COUNSEL

A lawyer shall not:

(a) unlawfully obstruct another party's access to evidence or unlawfully alter, destroy or conceal a document or other material having potential evidentiary value. A lawyer shall not counsel or assist another person to do any such act;

(b) falsify evidence, counsel or assist a witness to testify falsely, or offer an inducement to a witness that is prohibited by law;

(c) knowingly disobey an obligation under the rules of a tribunal, except for an open refusal based on an assertion that no valid obligation exists;

(d) in pretrial procedure, make a frivolous discovery request or fail to make reasonably diligent effort to comply with a legally proper discovery request by an opposing party;

---

the Hendrix fund transfers before accusing Hendrix in court of misappropriating funds may be considered a violation of the rule. Making such accusations in an ex parte setting violates MRPC 3.3(d). The record does not show that Brantley provided the judge complete information about these transfers, such as the dates of the transfers (the last one well over a year before the conservatorship) and the fact that they involved only Hendrix's own account."

803

(e) in trial, allude to any matter that the lawyer does not reasonably believe is relevant or that will not be supported by admissible evidence, assert personal knowledge of facts in issue except when testifying as a witness, or state a personal opinion as to the justness of a cause, the credibility of a witness, the culpability of a civil litigant or the guilt or innocence of an accused; or

(f) request a person other than a client to refrain from voluntarily giving relevant information to another party unless:

(1) the person is a relative or an employee or other agent of a client; and

(2) the lawyer reasonably believes that the person's interests will not be adversely affected by refraining from giving such information.

Comment

[1] The procedure of the adversary system contemplates that the evidence in a case is to be marshalled competitively by the contending parties. Fair competition in the adversary system is secured by prohibitions against destruction or concealment of evidence, improperly influencing witnesses, obstructive tactics in discovery procedure, and the like.

[2] Documents and other items of evidence are often essential to establish a claim or defense. Subject to evidentiary privileges, the right of an opposing party, including the government, to obtain evidence through discovery or subpoena is an important procedural right. The exercise of that right can be frustrated if relevant material is altered, concealed or destroyed. Applicable law in many jurisdictions makes it an offense to destroy material for purpose of impairing its availability in a pending proceeding or one whose commencement can be foreseen. Falsifying evidence is also generally a criminal offense. Paragraph (a) applies to evidentiary material generally, including computerized information. Applicable law may permit a lawyer to take temporary possession of physical evidence of client crimes for the purpose of conducting a limited examination that will not alter or destroy material characteristics of the evidence. In such a case, applicable law may require the lawyer to turn the evidence over to the police or other prosecuting authority, depending on the circumstances.

[3] With regard to paragraph (b), it is not improper to pay a witness's expenses or to compensate an expert witness on terms permitted by law. The common law rule in most jurisdictions is that it is improper to pay an occurrence witness any fee for testifying and that it is improper to pay an expert witness a contingent fee.

[4] Paragraph (f) permits a lawyer to advise employees of a client to refrain from giving information to another party, for the employees may identify their interests with those of the client. See also Rule 4.2.

Authors' 1983 Model Rules Comparison

The text of the 2002 version of Rule 3.4 is identical to the Rule adopted by the ABA House of Delegates in 1983.

In Comment 2, the drafters of the 2002 Rules added the following language: "Applicable law may permit a lawyer to take temporary possession of physical evidence of client crimes for the purpose of conducting a limited examination that will not alter or destroy material characteristics of the evidence. In such a case, applicable law may require the lawyer to turn the evidence over to the police or other prosecuting authority, depending on the circumstances." The drafters believed that lawyers needed more guidance regarding the law of possession of evidence of the crime. *See* Reporter's Explanation of Changes to Model Rule 3.4.

Model Code Comparison

[1] With regard to paragraph (a), DR 7-109(A) provided that a lawyer "shall not suppress any evidence that he or his client has a legal obligation to reveal." DR 7-109(B) provided that a lawyer "shall not advise or cause a person to secrete himself . . . for the purpose of making him unavailable as a witness. . . ." DR 7-106(C)(7) provided that a lawyer shall not "[i]ntentionally or habitually violate any established rule of procedure or of evidence."

[2] With regard to paragraph (b), DR 7-102(A)(6) provided that a lawyer shall not participate "in the creation or preservation of evidence when he knows or it is obvious that the evidence is false." DR 7-109(C) provided that a lawyer "shall not pay, offer to pay, or acquiesce in the payment of compensation to a witness contingent upon the content of his testimony or the outcome of the case. But a lawyer may advance, guarantee or acquiesce in the payment of: (1) Expenses reasonably incurred by a witness in attending or testifying; (2) Reasonable compensation to a witness for his loss of time in attending or testifying; [or] (3) A reasonable fee for the professional services of an expert witness." EC 7-28 stated that witnesses "should always testify truthfully and should be free from any financial inducements that might tempt them to do otherwise."

[3] Paragraph (c) is substantially similar to DR 7-106(A), which provided that "A lawyer shall not disregard . . . . a standing rule of a tribunal or a ruling of a tribunal made in the course of a proceeding, but he may take appropriate steps in good faith to test the validity of such rule or ruling."

[4] Paragraph (d) has no counterpart in the Model Code.

[5] Paragraph (e) substantially incorporates DR 7-106(C)(1), (2), (3) and (4). DR 7-106(C)(2) proscribed asking a question "intended to degrade a witness or other person," a matter dealt with in Rule 4.4. DR 7-106(C)(5), providing that a lawyer shall not "fail to comply with known local customs of courtesy or practice," was too vague to be a rule of conduct enforceable as law.

[6] With regard to paragraph (f), DR 7-104(A)(2) provided that a lawyer shall not "give advice to a person who is not represented . . . other than the advice to secure counsel, if the interests of such person are or have a reasonable possibility of being in conflict with the interests of his client."

§ 3.4–1 THE DISTINCTION BETWEEN THE LAWYER'S DUTY OF CANDOR TO THE COURT AND THE LAWYER'S DUTY OF FAIRNESS TO OPPOSING COUNSEL

The ethics rules impose on lawyers certain affirmative obligations of *candor* to a tribunal, for example, to disclose material adverse legal authority.[1] However, with respect to opposing parties or third parties, the lawyer's duty is, in general, more limited. Subject to various exceptions,[2] the fundamental principle of ethics is that lawyers may not knowingly misrepresent either a material fact or law to opposing parties or other persons.[3] This principle applies whether the lawyer is involved in litigation or negotiation.

It is interesting how often the Rules repeat the proposition that a lawyer may neither make *any misrepresentation* nor engage in any dishonest, fraudulent or deceitful conduct.[4] For example, Rule 4.1(a) states that, in the course of representing a client, the lawyer "shall not knowingly make a false statement of material fact or law to a third person."[5] Rule 8.4(c) provides that a lawyer engages in "professional misconduct" when he or she engages in conduct "involving dishonesty, fraud, *deceit* or misrepresentation."[6] And then there is Rule 3.4, which is the subject of this section. Its title captures the basic principle for which it stands: Fairness to Opposing Party and Counsel.

Consider, for example this situation. The plaintiff's lawyer ("*L*") plans to file a claim against defendant. Both *P* and plaintiff know that the statute of limitations has run, but they hope that defendant and her counsel ("*D*") will not plead the statute. During the course of negotiations, P discovers that both defendant and her counsel, *D*, are unaware of the limitations defense. *L* is careful not to make any affirmative misrepresentation about the facts showing that the claim is time-barred. *L* is acting properly. "Indeed, the lawyer may not, consistent with her responsibilities to her client, refuse to negotiate or break off negotiations merely

---

[Section 3.4–1]

[1] Rule 3.3, Candor to a Tribunal.

[2] There are circumstances where a lawyer has the duty to come forward to correct a problem. For example, Rule 4.1(b) requires the lawyer not to "fail to disclose a material fact to a third person when disclosure is necessary to avoid assisting a criminal or fraudulent act by a client unless disclosure is prohibited by Rule 1.6."

[3] Rule 4.1(a); Rule 8.4(c). The Model Code has similar provisions. DR 7-102(A)(5); DR 7-102(A)(4).

[4] Rule 8.4(c). The Model Code has a similar provision. DR 1-102(A)(4).

[5] Rule 4.1(a). Notice that this section uses the term "material." Although the Code (unlike the Rules) does not specifically use the term "material," it should be considered an implicit requirement.

[6] Rule 8.4(c) (emphasis added).

because the claim is or becomes time-barred."[7] The lawyer for one party does not normally have the duty to volunteer the existence of adverse facts or adverse law to the other party.

On the other hand, even though the lawyer does not have to volunteer to her opponent a statutory defense, the lawyer cannot keep the judge in the dark. The Rules impose an affirmative duty, requiring that the lawyer shall not "fail to disclose to the tribunal legal authority in the controlling jurisdiction known to the lawyer to be directly adverse to the position of the client and not disclosed by opposing counsel."[8] The lawyer may neither explicitly misrepresent the state of the law nor implicitly do so, by, for example, making an apparently complete recital of relevant authorities but omitting the relevant statute that provides for the limitations defense.[9]

Let us assume that a new state law tolls the statute of limitations. Let us further assume that the defendant pleads the statute of limitations, but does not disclose the new tolling statute to the court.Rule 3.3 requires the lawyer to make this disclosure of the adverse statute to the court, but not to opposing counsel. However, the defendant's lawyer may not speak *ex parte* to the judge about this matter. Consequently, the lawyer will disclose the adverse law to the judge in the presence of the opposing counsel. That means that lawyer is not obligated to make this disclosure in the course of negotiations with the opposing lawyer. But the lawyer still must not mislead opposing counsel about the existence of the new statute.

ABA Formal Opinion 94-387, while ruling that the lawyer, in negotiations, cannot tell the opposing party about the statute of limitations defense, also admits that the lawyer "must be careful not to make any affirmative misrepresentations about the facts showing that the claim is time-barred, or suggest that she plans to do something to enforce the claim (*e.g.,* file suit) that she has no intention of doing."[10] But, then it also asserts that the lawyer *need not* volunteer this information about the existence of the statute of limitations to the tribunal (if a case is filed). This Formal Opinion argues that there is no "failure of candor toward the tribunal in violation of Rule 3.3"—because the lawyer is making "no misrepresentations in pleadings or orally to the court or

---

[7]ABA Formal Opinion 94-387 (Sept. 26, 1994).

[8]Rule 3.3(a)(3). *See also* Restatement of the Law Governing Lawyers, Third, § 111 (Official Draft 2000).

[9]Restatement of the Law Governing Lawyers, Third, § 111 (Official Draft 2000), Comment *b*, at p. 183. The particular reference is to "omitting a recent adverse decision," but omitting a reference to a statute directly on point falls in the same category.

[10]ABA Formal Opinion 94-387 (Sept. 26, 1994), at 3.

opposing counsel, she has breached no ethical duty towards either."[11]

That argument is, to say the least, conclusory. If the lawyer does not volunteer a *fact* to the judge (and this fact would establish a statute of limitations defense), that is appropriate under Rule 3.3 because the lawyer does not normally have to volunteer "facts."[12] But the polling statute is a law, not a fact. If the lawyer fails to disclose that a newly-enacted statute has tolled the statute of limitations from five years to three, and this limitation is a complete defense under the facts as pleaded by plaintiff, Rule 3.3(a)(2) directly applies. The lawyer has to volunteer ("shall not knowingly . . . fail to disclose") to the judge that there is legal authority in the controlling jurisdiction "directly adverse to the position of the client and not disclosed by opposing counsel."[13] A statute, no less than a Supreme Court precedent, is "legal authority."

The conclusion of Formal Opinion 94-387, that the lawyer should *not* inform the court of the existence of the statute, drew a strong dissent from a member of the Ethics Committee, who remarked:

> I look upon this opinion as Julia Child would regard a fly in her soup. It is unneeded, unwarranted, and too much to swallow. In short, a practice note for the lawyer interested in developing a "sharp" practice.[14]

This dissent's view of a lawyer's ethical obligation finds support in the American Law Institute's Restatement of the Law Governing Lawyers. As the relevant Comment explains:

> Tribunals must be able to rely upon advocates for reasonably accurate statements of the law. No worthwhile purpose is served by permitting *misstatements of the law* . . . .. The rule also prohibits *implicit misrepresentations*, such as making an apparently complete recital of relevant authorities but omitting an adverse decision that should be considered by the tribunal for a fair determination of the point.[15]

If the lawyer must offer the judge a "reasonably accurate statement of the law," then this new tolling statute is something that must not be swept under the rug. Consider what would happen if the defendant prevails in the trial court because the defense lawyer did not disclose the adverse law (the tolling statute) to the

---

[11]ABA Formal Opinion 94-387 (Sept. 26, 1994), at 4.

[12]Except for the special case of *ex parte* proceedings under Rule 3.3(d).

[13]Rule 3.3(a)(2). Restatement of the Law Governing Lawyers, Third, § 111 (Official Draft 2000).

[14]ABA Formal Opinion 94-387 (Sept. 26, 1994), at 8 (Richard C. McFarlain, dissenting).

[15]*See* Restatement of the Law Governing Lawyers, Third, § 111 (Official Draft 2000), Comment *b*, at 183.

trial judge and no one else discovered the existence and applicability of the statute. The plaintiff now appeals on various grounds, but still fails to discover the tolling defense. During oral argument a member of the Court of Appeals (having discovered the existence of the statute on her own) asks defense counsel, "What about this statute? Is that not a complete defense?" What does defense counsel say now?—"Yes. You're right. It's a shame that you discovered it."

§ 3.4–2 OBSTRUCTING ACCESS TO EVIDENCE

A corollary to the general principle that a lawyer may not engage in deceitful behavior or misrepresent the facts or the law,[1] is the Rule 3.4 requirement that a lawyer may not unlawfully obstruct access to, alter, or conceal evidence, or witnesses, or encourage a witness to testify falsely.[2] In addition, the Rules give the lawyer discretion to refuse to offer evidence he or she "reasonably believes is false."[3] Similarly the lawyer may not falsify evidence or aid in its creation or preservation "if he knows, or it is obvious that the evidence is false."[4]

§ 3.4–2(a) Physical Evidence of a Crime by the Client

One leading decision, *In re Ryder*,[5] involved a criminal defense lawyer who accepted from his client stolen money and a sawed-off shotgun used in an armed bank robbery and deposited it in a safe deposit box. The lawyer knew that his client had given him the fruits and the instrumentality of a crime. The lawyer intended to keep possession of this evidence that linked his client to robbery until his client's trial unless the government discovered it

---

[Section 3.4–2]

[1]Rule 8.4(c).

[2]Rule 3.4(a),(b); DR 7-109(A),(B) ,(C); DR 7-106(C)(7). Restatement of the Law Governing Lawyers, Third, § 116(2) (Official Draft 2000).

See also Jerista v. Murray,185 N.J. 175, 883 A.2d 350 (2005). This case held that the plaintiffs were entitled to a spoliation instruction against the defendant, a lawyer who did not destroy evidence but concealed his negligent dismissal of the underlying case for 9 years. The lawyer had represented an injured customer and her husband in a negligence lawsuit against a supermarket for an injury that an automatic door had caused. The lawyer concealed the dismissal of the underlying tort claim, and thus his own negligence, for nine years. By the time his concealment ended, evidence regarding the fault of the underlying tort defendant was either lost or destroyed. Plaintiffs claimed they could have prevailed in the underlying case under the *res ipsa loquitur* doctrine, and defendant argued to the contrary. Among other things, the court held that if, in fact, plaintiffs could make a threshold showing that the defendant's concealment of the dismissal led to the loss or destruction of relevant evidence, the jury would be entitled to infer that the missing evidence would have assisted plaintiffs' case.

[3]Rule 3.3(a)(3).

[4]DR 7-102(A)(6). *See also* Rule 3.4(b).

[5]*In re Ryder*, 263 F.Supp. 360 (E.D.Va.1967), *aff'd*, 381 F.2d 713 (4th Cir.1967) (per curiam).

before then. The court explained that the defense lawyer intended, by his possession, to destroy the chain of evidence linking his client to the contraband and thereby prevent it from being used at trial against his client. The court suspended the lawyer for 18 months, and explained that the sanction would have been greater but for the fact that the lawyer intended to return the bank's money after the trial. This lawyer also had consulted with reputable lawyers to determine what course he should take, another fact that mitigated the sanction imposed against him.[6]

Notice that we are discussing possession of the fruits and materials of a crime. Possession of this type of physical evidence is different than other items, such as photographs that the lawyer took of the crime scene,[7] or trial exhibits that the lawyer prepared. These materials are not pre-existing physical evidence

---

[6]*See also, e.g., In re January 1976 Grand Jury*, 534 F.2d 719 (7th Cir.1976). The attorney refused to comply with a grand jury's subpoena duces tecum to turn over moneys received by him from clients suspected of bank robbery. The trial court held the lawyer in contempt and the Seventh Circuit affirmed.

Shortly after robbing a savings and loan association, the robbers delivered the stolen money to appellant-lawyer. The money was delivered either for safekeeping, with or without the lawyer's knowledge that it was stolen, or it was delivered as an attorney's fee. Thus, the court reasoned, if the money was a fee, then the robbers voluntarily relinquished the money and with it any arguable claim that might have arisen from their possession or constructive possession. The payment of an attorney's fee is not a privileged communication. The money itself is non-testimonial and thus there is no plausible argument left for resisting the subpoena.

If the money was not given as a fee but for safekeeping, then the delivery of the money was an act in furtherance of the crime, whether or not the lawyer knew it was stolen. The delivery of the money was not assertive conduct and therefore was not a privi-

leged communication. And, as noted above, the money itself is non-testimonial. The lawyer simply witnessed a criminal act. The fact that he also participated in the act (presumably without knowledge of its criminal nature) is irrelevant because he was not asserting his own privilege against self incrimination.

Thus, Judge Tone, joined by Judge Bauer, concluded, there is no reason, based on any constitutional provision or the attorney-client privilege, to shield from judicial inquiry either the fruits of the robbery or the fact of the later criminal act of turning over the money to the lawyer. It is therefore irrelevant that the lawyer, in response to the subpoena, will be making an assertion about who turned over the money and when. The only issue left is a constitutional one. When the robbers chose to make their lawyer a witness to their crime, may they now invoke the Sixth Amendment right to effective assistance of counsel to bar his eyewitness testimony at trial? Judge Tone remarked, that, for him, "to ask that question is almost to answer it."

[7]*See People v. Belge*, 83 Misc.2d 186, 372 N.Y.S.2d 798 (1975)(lawyer took photographs of crime scene and deceased victims).

of the client's crime; the lawyer creates them and they are normally protected by the work product privilege.[8]

When one considers the cases where the lawyer is asked to take possession of physical evidence of a crime, the general principle that one may draw from them is that a lawyer, when necessary, may take possession of the physical evidence and retain it for a reasonable amount of time in order to examine it, but this examination must not alter or destroy the evidence.[9] After that time, the lawyer must either return the evidence to the site from where it was obtained (if that can be done without destroying the evidentiary value of the material)[10] or notify the prosecuting authorities that the lawyer has possession of the evidence.[11]

---

[8]Restatement of the Law Governing Lawyers, Third, § 119 (Official Draft 2000), at Comment a.

[9]The drafters of the 2002 Rules added the last line to Comment 2 of Rule 3.4 to clarify a lawyer's handling of evidence of the crime.

[10]In light of advances in forensic science, it is hard to imagine how a lawyer could return physical evidence to the scene of the crime without leaving the lawyer's DNA on the evidence or without feeling the need to remove fingerprints and other indicia of the lawyer's possession of the evidence. Such conduct would constitute tampering or altering the evidence.

[11]Restatement of the Law Governing Lawyers, Third, § 119 (Official Draft 2000).

Morrell v. State, 575 P.2d 1200 (Alaska 1978), which upheld the decision of the trial court to admit incriminating evidence of a kidnapping plan allegedly written by the defendant. A friend of the defendant turned the plan over to defense counsel, who then aided the friend in turning the evidence over to the police. Defense counsel then withdrew from the case. The Alaska Supreme Court held that:

"[A] criminal defense attorney must turn over to the prosecution real evidence that the attorney obtains from his client. Further, if the evidence is obtained from a non-client third party who is not acting for the client, then the privilege to refuse to testify concerning the manner in which the evidence was obtained is inapplicable. [Defense counsel] would have been obligated to see that the evidence reached the prosecutor in this case even if he had obtained the evidence from Morrell. His obligation was even clearer because he acquired the evidence from [a third party], who made the decision to turn the evidence over to [defense counsel] without consulting Morrell and therefore was not acting as Morrell's agent.

"[Defense counsel] could have properly turned the evidence over to the police himself and would have been obliged to do so if [the third party] had refused to accept the return of the evidence.

"[Finally, while] statutes which address the concealing of evidence are generally construed to require an affirmative act of concealment in addition to the failure to disclose information to the authorities, taking possession of evidence from a nonclient third party and holding the evidence in a place not accessible to investigating authorities would seem to fall within the statute's ambit. Thus, [the defense lawyer] breached no ethical obligation to his client which may have rendered his legal services to Morrell ineffective." 575 P.2d at 1210–12.

In *People v. Meredith*, 29 Cal.3d 682, 175 Cal.Rptr. 612, 631 P.2d 46

§ 3.4–2(b) Discovery Abuses in Civil Cases

The problem of lawyers and clients destroying or withholding evidence that is subpoenaed is not limited to solo practitioners representing criminal defendants. Unfortunately, there have been cases where judges have discovered that law firms and large corporations have violated these principles. In some instances, lawyers have been integrally involved in a scheme of deception.[12]

(1981), the defendant had told his lawyer the location of the robbery-murder victim's wallet. The lawyer then had his investigator remove it. The client's disclosure to the lawyer was privileged, and that privilege was not destroyed when the lawyer told the investigator where the wallet was. On the other hand, removing the wallet did destroy the privilege, because when defense counsel removes or alters evidence, he necessarily deprives the prosecution of the opportunity to observe that evidence in its original condition or location. The lawyer's decision to remove evidence is therefore tactical; if he leaves the evidence where he discovered it, his observations derived from privileged communications are insulated from revelation. If he removes the evidence to examine or test it, the original location and condition of that evidence loses the protection of the privilege. *Accord People v. Nash*, 418 Mich. 196, 341 N.W.2d 439, 446–51 (1983).

In *Clutchette v. Rushen*, 770 F.2d 1469 (9th Cir.1985), *cert. denied,* 475 U.S. 1088, 106 S.Ct. 1474, 89 L.Ed.2d 729 (1986) the defendant was accused of shooting a man in his car. The defendant's wife voluntarily turned over some receipts to the police. She had been acting as an investigator for her husband's defense lawyer, and the lawyer had sent her to Los Angeles to retrieve (and possibly to destroy) the receipts that showed that her husband had arranged for the car to be reupholstered shortly after the murder. The police used these receipts to find the former seat covers and matched the blood type to the victim's. The court held that the wife's surrender of the receipts was not a

violation of the defendant's attorney-client privilege. If the attorney had not done anything to retrieve the receipts, he would not have had to tell the police about them. Having taken the receipts into his possession, however, through the wife-investigator, the receipts were fair game for police discovery. There was no deprivation of Sixth Amendment rights, particularly because the police engaged in no overt act to get the receipts.

People v. Superior Court, 192 Cal.App.3d 32, 237 Cal.Rptr. 158 (1987) held that if a lawyer takes possession of stolen property, the lawyer must inform the court of the action. "The court, exercising care to shield privileged communications and defense strategies from prosecution view, must then take appropriate action to ensure that the prosecution has timely access to physical evidence possessed by the defense and timely information about alteration of any evidence."

[12]*Feld's Case,* 149 N.H. 19, 815 A.2d 383 (2002), *cert. denied,* 540 U.S. 815, 124 S.Ct. 67, 157 L.Ed.2d 31 (2003), suspended attorney Feld for one year as result of violations of Rules 3.4 and 8.4 during discovery. The underlying matter involved an eviction claim against Bussiere by Feld's clients, recent purchasers of a piece of property. Prior to the purchase, Bussiere notified the clients that he had a leasehold interest and enclosed supporting documentation. When questioned during discovery, however, Field's clients denied knowledge of Bussiere's documentation. The Professional Discipline Committee found, after a hearing, "that Feld 'orchestrated, assisted, counseled and tolerated the formulation of inaccurate and incom-

In *Compaq Computer Corp. v. Ergonome Inc.*[13] the court, relying on Federal Rules of Civil Procedure, Rule 37(b)(2)(A), upheld the trial court's imposition of nearly $2.8 million in attorney's fees for the defendant because of discovery abuse. The court also upheld the trial court's finding that the book's author was the alter ego of the publisher as a sanction for repeated discovery violations: "Compaq struggled for well over two years to obtain sufficient alter ego discovery from Brown and Ergonome. Brown and Ergonome engaged in abusive practices for the sole purpose of frustrating Compaq's ability to extract the discovery. . . . The entire egregious course of overlitigation and discovery abuse is among the worst we have seen."[14]

Sometimes, the court will order sanctions, but there is no record in the official reporter systems because the judge neither issues a written opinion nor publishes an opinion.[15]

In one situation, for example, judges in three states have taken

---

plete sworn responses that he knew were inaccurate' in violation of New Hampshire Rules of Professional Conduct 3.4 and 8.4." The Court also found that: "The response, reviewed by Feld, claimed that the letter 'was never received by Carolyn M. Roberge.' Feld, however, knew that this answer was false when he signed it, as Ms. Roberge had already shown Feld the July 28 letter along with the unrecorded documents." 815 A.2d at 387. In addition, Feld was present during [his client's] deposition in which she gave numerous evasive answers to such questions. "Given the importance placed by Bussiere upon this line of inquiry, and Feld's repeated involvement with false answers, the record does not support Feld's claim that his assistance with the response to the request for admission was inadvertent." *Id.* In a second incident, the client was questioned on the nature of his involvement with the financing of the property, which he answered evasively. "A pattern of evasive or non-responsive conduct, such as that demonstrated in the responses to the interrogatory," the Court held, "demonstrates a lawyer's failure 'to make reasonably diligent effort to comply with a legally proper discovery request made by an opposing party.' " *Id.* at 388. Further, when Feld invoked the

attorney-client privilege in a deposition after such evasive answers were made, it was "a bad faith effort to impede Bussiere's discovery," *Id.* at 390. The Court imposed a one year suspension, which was based on similar sanctions imposed for intentional deceit during trial.

[13]*Compaq Computer Corp. v. Ergonome Inc.*, 387 F.3d 403 (5th Cir. 2004).

[14]*Compaq Computer Corp. v. Ergonome Inc.*, 387 F.3d 403 (5th Cir. 2004). See also, *Rottlund Co., Inc. v. Pinnacle Corp.*, 222 F.R.D. 362 (D. Minn. 2004) (court holds that the defendant's record of abuse of the judicial process, its discovery incompetence, and its defiance of court orders warranted a discovery sanction award of $50,000.00 in reasonable attorney fees and costs for the plaintiff's prosecution of its motion for sanctions).

[15]*See generally* MARGARET M. KOESEL, DAVID A. BELL AND TRACEY L. TURNBULL, DANIEL F. GOURASH, EDITOR, SPOLIATION OF EVIDENCE: SANCTIONS AND REMEDIES FOR DESTRUCTION OF EVIDENCE IN CIVIL LITIGATION (ABA 2000).

See, e.g., John J. Fialka, *Lawyer Says He Was Told to Destroy Documents,* WALL STREET JOURNAL, Mar. 26, 1999, at B8, col. 4–6. A lawyer

DuPont Corporation, the chemical giant, to task for withholding evidence, destroying evidence and other litigation misconduct involving various law suits concerning Benlate DF, a fungicide blamed for causing massive crop damage in 40 states.[16] In a Georgia case, a federal judge threatened criminal contempt. Then, DuPont struck "an unusual deal" with the federal judge who had ordered the U.S. Attorney to investigate and prosecute allegations of obstruction of justice. "The court agreed to drop the criminal investigation if DuPont paid $11 million."[17] The judge did not order the money to go to the plaintiffs, but to "four Georgia law schools and a state commission that trains lawyers." The Atlanta law firm that represented DuPont during the Benlate litigation also agreed to pay $250,000 to the state commission. And, as part of this deal, neither DuPont nor its law firm admitted any wrongdoing. The case is troubling because the sanction did not help make the victim whole, and it appears to pave the way for

in the Interior Department told Federal Judge Royce C. Lambert that the agency's deputy solicitor "directed" him to have "purged from the files" certain documents involving allegations that Indian trust funds had been mishandled. Judge Lambert ordered the Interior Department not to take any retaliatory action against the lawyer. Earlier, this judge cited for contempt Interior Secretary Bruce Babbitt and Treasury Secretary Richard Rubin for their failure to produce trust fund records.

Paul M. Barrett, *Libel Verdict Against Dow Jones To Be Thrown Out, Says Judge*, WALL STREET JOURNAL, Apr. 9, 1999, at B19, col. 1–2. The trial judge announced that he will throw out a $22.7 million libel verdict against Dow Jones & Co., publisher of the Wall Street Journal. Plaintiff sued over a 1993 Wall Street Journal article about a now defunct investment firm, MMAR Group, Inc. The judge said: "From clear and convincing evidence, the Court finds that MMAR obtained its favorable verdict through its own misconceptions and misrepresentations." The judge's opinion explained that MMAR should have, during discovery, surrendered secret tape recordings that would have helped Dow Jones prove the truth of three of the five statements that the jury found

false and defamatory. A former MMAR employee told Dow Jones lawyers that a MMAR official pressured him to erase certain tapes. Note that the judge planned to dismiss the entire case for failure to comply with discovery, although the secret tape recordings only affected three of the five defamatory statements. A lesser sanction would have really placed no real penalty on MMAR for discovery abuse.

Elizabeth Amon, *Working on the RRS: Simple Property Case Sparks 25 Class Actions Against RRS, Telecoms*, 21 NATIONAL L. JOURNAL A1, A12 (Aug. 16, 1999), noting that the trial judge found conduct by two defendants to be a "conscious and pervasive course of misrepresentation and misconduct," and thus sanctioned the two defendants $600,000 plus any prejudgment interest on any damages that the plaintiffs might later recover, in the case of *Firestone v. Penn Central Corp. & U.S. Railroad Vest, Inc.*, No. 29 D03-9210-CP-500.

[16] The case was *Bush Ranch v. DuPont* [unreported]. *See* Jan Hollingsworth, *Benlate Focus Shifts to Miami*, THE TAMPA TRIBUNE, Jan. 9, 1999, reprinted in:

http://tampatrib.com/news/envir o0x.htm.

[17] *Id.*

richer lawyers and clients to buy themselves out of trouble while poorer lawyers and clients must suffer the consequences of criminal contempt.

§ 3.4–3 MONEY PAYMENTS TO WITNESSES

§ 3.4–3(a) Introduction

The Model Code specifically prohibited a lawyer from paying a witness any money contingent on the outcome of the case.[1] The lawyer may advance, guarantee, or acquiesce in the payment of (1) a witness' expenses in attending or testifying; (2) compensation for the witness' loss of time because of attending or testifying; and (3) a reasonable fee for an expert witness' professional services.[2]

Oddly enough, the Rules have no explicit provision against paying contingent fees to fact witnesses or to expert witnesses. However, a Comment maintains that the "common law rule in most jurisdictions is that it is improper to pay an occurrence witness any fee for testifying and that it is improper to pay an expert witness a contingent fee."[3] The purpose of this Comment is apparently to incorporate by reference a state's prohibition against contingent fees into the black letter rule that provides it is improper for a lawyer to "offer an inducement to a witness that is prohibited by law."[4]

Indeed, most jurisdictions forbid paying contingent fees to witnesses,[5] whether they are expert witnesses or fact witnesses.[6]

[Section 3.4–3]

[1]DR 7-109(C).

[2]DR 7-109(C).

[3]Rule 3.4, Comment 3. *See also* Restatement of the Law Governing Lawyers, Third, § 117 ("Compensating Witnesses") (Official Draft 2000).

[4]Rule 3.3(b).

[5]This prohibition is long-standing. *See, e.g., In re Schapiro*, 144 App.Div. 1, 128 N.Y.S. 852 (N.Y.App. Div.1911), disbarring a lawyer who paid a contingent fee to a witness. *See also In re O'Keefe*, 49 Mont. 369, 142 P. 638 (1914). The very first Restatement of the law of Contracts repeats this prohibition. ALI, Restatement of the Law of Contract, § 552(2) (1932). Modern cases follow this rule. *Belfonte v. Miller*, 212 Pa.Super. 508, 243 A.2d 150 (1968).

Attacks on Constitutionality of Rule Against Paying Contingent Fees to Expert Witnesses. Although plaintiffs have attacked DR 7-109(C), which directly prohibited lawyers from paying contingent fees to expert witnesses—unlike Rule 3.4, Comment 3, which incorporates state law by reference—no appellate court has found this argument valid. *See Person v. Association of the Bar of the City of New York*, 554 F.2d 534 (2d Cir.1977) (reversing the trial court, which had found the rule unconstitutional), *cert. denied*, 434 U.S. 924, 98 S.Ct. 403, 54 L.Ed.2d 282 (1977).

[6]Washington, D.C. is an exception to the general rule. It does have an unusual and explicit provision that allows a fee to an expert witness to be contingent on the outcome of the proceeding but not contingent on the amount actually recovered.

The Model Rules do not make this particular disqualification explicit, but the Restatement of the Law Governing Lawyers does.[7]

§ 3.4–3(b) Lawyer-Witnesses and Contingent Fees

Just as a lawyer cannot pay a witness a contingent fee, a lawyer/witness may not collect a contingent fee. Thus, if a lawyer is both a witness in the case and is representing the plaintiff with the lawyer's payment being a contingent fee, courts have disqualified the lawyer because the lawyer will, in effect, be collecting a contingent fee for his testimony.[8] Further, a lawyer who attempts to sell his or her testimony to another party may violate the criminal laws.[9]

§ 3.4–3(c) Comparing Expert Witnesses to Fact Witnesses

The general rule is that lawyers can pay *expert* witnesses for their time, but not for their testimony. In other words, the lawyer can pay an expert witness an hourly fee, which represents a fee for the expert's advice and expert opinion. But the lawyer may not make this fee contingent on the outcome of the expert

---

Washington, D.C. Rules of Professional Conduct, Rule 3.4, Comment 8, reprinted in, THOMAS D. MORGAN & RONALD D. ROTUNDA, 2002 SELECTED STANDARDS ON PROFESSIONAL RESPONSIBILITY (Foundation Press, 2002):

"A fee for the services of a witness who will be proffered as an expert may be made contingent on the outcome of the litigation, provided, however, that the fee, while conditioned on recovery, shall not be a percentage of the recovery."

The Restatement rejects whatever reasoning that may be behind this D.C. Rule. Restatement of the Law Governing Lawyers, Third, § 117(2) (Official Draft 2000) (the lawyer may not pay a witness based "on the content of the witness's testimony or the outcome of the litigation").

[7]Restatement, of the Law Governing Lawyers, Third, § 117(2) (Official Draft 2000), Comment *d*, at p. 214.

[8]*Cresswell v. Sullivan & Cromwell*, 922 F.2d 60, 72–73 (2d Cir.1990), *cert. denied*, 505 U.S. 1222, 112 S.Ct. 3036, 120 L.Ed.2d 905 (1992). The court based its ruling on two grounds. The contingency fee arrangement (the lawyer who represented the plaintiffs in litigation was to perform legal work in connection with subsequent related securities litigation and to appear as witness for the plaintiffs in that litigation) violated two basic ethical rules. First, a lawyer shall not accept employment in contemplated or pending litigation if he knows or it is obvious that he ought to be called as witness. Second, a lawyer shall not acquiesce in payment of compensation to a witness contingent upon the content of his testimony or the outcome of a case. The court upheld an order barring the lawyer from representing plaintiffs and from receiving a contingent fee. The court cited both DR 5-101(B) and DR 7-109(C) of the ABA Model Code.

[9]*United States v. Blaszak*, 349 F.3d 881 (6th Cir.2003) involved Blaszak, a lawyer convicted, under 18 U.S.C. § 201(c)(3), of offering to sell his testimony to the defendants in an antitrust case. His contention on appeal was that making it a crime to seek such payments for truthful testimony denied his First Amendment right to freedom of speech. (We kid you not.) The Sixth Circuit rejected that view. The lawyer is free to speak freely; the law only prevents getting paid for it in these circumstances.

witness's testimony or the outcome of the litigation.[10] If one pays a witness for the content of the testimony, there is a real risk that the money will corrupt the witness and interfere with the truth-finding process of the trial.

When lawyers deal with fact witnesses, the lawyers may only pay these witnesses for the "reasonable expenses of the witness incurred in providing evidence except an expert witness may be offered and paid a non-contingent fee."[11] Lawyers cannot pay fact witnesses money for their testimony even if the lawyer and witness agree that the purpose of the payment is to make sure that the client testifies "truthfully."[12] In one case, a court disqualified a lawyer for promising to give a witness a percentage of the potential recovery in the case, purportedly in order to induce a witness to "tell the truth."[13]

Although lawyers may not pay witnesses for their testimony, they can pay certain expenses associated with testifying. The Model Code explicitly allowed the lawyer to "advance, guarantee, or acquiesce in the payment" of: (1) the expenses that the witness (whether fact or opinion witness) occurred in "attending or testify-

---

[10]Restatement of the Law Governing Lawyers, Third, § 117(1), (2) (Official Draft 2000).

Hiring a Medical-Legal Consulting Firm on a Contingent Fee Basis. ABA Formal Opinion 87-354 (Nov. 7, 1987) advised that ethical questions are raised when a lawyer recommends that a client hire a medical-legal consulting firm on a contingent basis. The arrangement, depending on the facts, may violate Rule 3.4(b): "If the contingent fee arrangement constitutes an improper inducement to an expert witness under applicable state law, the lawyer's recommendation of the Consultant and cooperation with the Consultant would violate Rule 8.4(a), which prohibits violation of the Rules 'through the acts of another.' *Id.* at 3. This Formal Opinion explicitly superseded Informal Opinion 1375 (1976).

[11]Restatement of the Law Governing Lawyers, Third, § 117(1) (Official Draft 2000).

[12]*In re Howard*, 69 Ill.2d 343, 14 Ill.Dec. 360, 372 N.E.2d 371 (Ill.1977). *See also Florida Bar v. Wohl*,

842 So.2d 811 (Fla.2003). *Wohl* is an interesting case on paying a witness. Attorney Wohl represented Bruce Winston, son of jeweler Harry Winston, in a dispute with his brother over his mother's estate. Wohl solicited the help of Kerr, a former employee of the Winston jewelry business, and offered compensation of $25,000 for her first 50 hours of service, and up to a one million dollars "bonus" depending on the "usefulness" of the information. The Florida Supreme Court agreed with a referee that this agreement violated Rule 3.4(b), prohibiting an unlawful inducement to a witness. Kerr was a fact witness, not an expert. The Court imposed a 90-day suspension on attorney Wohl, one year probation, and his successful completion of a Practice and Professional Enhancement Program.

[13]*Wagner v. Lehman Bros. Kuhn Loeb Inc.*, 646 F.Supp. 643 (N.D.Ill. 1986). *See also* Restatement of the Law Governing Lawyers, Third, § 117(2) ("Compensating Witnesses") (Official Draft 2000).

ing," and (2) "reasonable compensation to the witness for his loss of time in attending or testifying."[14]

The Model Rules has no such explicit provision. However, in a unanimous ethics opinion, the ABA Ethics Committee has opined that the lawyer may pay a non-expert witness reasonable compensation for his or her loss of time in attending the trial and testifying.[15] In fact, the lawyer may also properly compensate the witness for the time spent in attending and preparing for his or her deposition by reviewing and researching records germane to his or her testimony.[16] This ABA Formal Opinion even allows the lawyer to pay the witnesses for their time when they have not sustained any direct loss of income, such as when the witness is retired or unemployed. In that case, the Formal Opinion offers a test that is none too clear: the lawyer "must determine the reasonable value of the witness's time based on all relevant circumstances."[17]

This Opinion creates risks. It may invite less scrupulous lawyers to, in effect, pay witnesses for the content of their testimony. Unprincipled lawyers will have no incentive to pay witnesses for their time if the content of the testimony is not helpful. Even if the lawyers are principled, the witnesses may not be: cunning and dishonest witnesses will soon figure out that the money does not flow unless the testimony is helpful.

§ 3.4–3(d) Prosecutors and Inducements to Witnesses

A prosecutor cannot pay a witness for the content of testimony, but it is ethically proper for her to reimburse the reasonable expenses of attendance at court or in depositions or for pretrial interviews.[18]

Prosecutors also offer witnesses other inducements to testify. Sometimes these witnesses are informants who receive money from law enforcement authorities; sometimes they are criminal defendants who testify in exchange for immunity from prosecution or for the possibility of securing a lighter sentence. Courts have permitted these inducements, because their purpose is not to change the content of the testimony but simply to get informa-

---

[14]DR 7-109(C)(1), (2).

[15]ABA Formal Opinion 96-402 (Aug. 2, 1996).

[16]ABA Formal Opinion 96-402 (Aug. 2, 1996), at 2. On the other hand, at least one state opinion has questioned whether lawyers can pay witnesses for the time spent preparing for their testimony. Pennsylvania Bar Association, Committee on Legal Ethics and Professional Responsibil-

ity, Opinion 95-126 (1995).

[17]ABA Formal Opinion 96-402 (Aug. 2, 1996), at 3.

[18]ABA Standards Relating to the Administration of Justice, The Prosecution Function, Standard 3-3.2(b) (ABA 3rd ed. 1992). This Standard explicitly states that there must be "no attempt to conceal the fact of reimbursement." This requirement is implicit in the Model Rules.

tion that, realistically, would not otherwise normally be given.[19] Indeed, courts are often involved in the decision to grant a favor (immunity, or a reduced sentence) in exchange for the witness' cooperation.

On the federal level, for example, a variety of federal statutes "allow the government, upon proper disclosure and/or court approval, to trade certain items of value for testimony."[20] Sections 3553(e) and 994(n), of title 18, United States Code,[21] allow the federal courts, acting pursuant to the Sentencing Guidelines and upon motion of the government, to reduce sentences for individuals who provide "substantial assistance in the investigation or prosecution of another." The federal immunity statutes[22] require courts, upon the request of the government, to confer immunity upon witnesses for their testimony in aid of the prosecution. The Witness Relocation and Protection Act,[23] allows the government to bestow various benefits for the protection of cooperating witnesses.

There is a federal statute, the anti-gratuity statute,[24] that makes it a crime to "promise anything of value to any person, for or because of the testimony under oath . . . ." A panel of the Tenth Circuit, in 1998, concluded that this section prevents Assistant U.S. Attorneys from offering leniency to an accomplice in exchange for truthful testimony.[25] The panel reasoned that, when the Government offers a witness statutory immunity—the court

---

[19]*See United States v. Gray*, 626 F.2d 494 (5th Cir.1980), *cert. denied*, 449 U.S. 1091, 101 S.Ct. 887, 66 L.Ed.2d 820 (1981) (the fact that one informant was paid about $37,000 for his services and that other informant received $25,000 did not establish misconduct, in absence of proof that a contingent fee was promised to the informants). The court said: "Although high informant fees are and must be suspect, an informant's testimony will not be rejected unless there is evidence that he was promised payment contingent upon conviction of a particular person." 626 F.2d at 499.

[20]Lucero, J., joined by Henry, J., concurring, in *United States v. Singleton*, 165 F.3d 1297, 1303 (10th Cir.1999).

[21]These sections were passed as part of the Sentencing Reform Act of 1984.

[22]8 U.S.C.A. §§ 6001 to 6005. These sections were passed as part of the Organized Crime Control Act of 1970.

[23]8 U.S.C.A. §§ 3521 to 3528, which were passed as part of the Comprehensive Crime Control Act of 1974.

[24]18 U.S.C.A. § 201(c)(2) provides:
"(c) Whoever—

. . . .

"(2) directly or indirectly, gives, offers, or promises anything of value to any person, for or because of the testimony under oath or affirmation given or to be given by such person as a witness upon a trial . . . before any court . . . shall be fined under this title or imprisoned for not more than two years, or both."

[25]*United States v. Singleton*, 144 F.3d 1343 (10th Cir.1998), *rev'd*, 165 F.3d 1297 (10th Cir.1999).

technically grants it[26]—the court promises that his immunized testimony cannot be used to prosecute him. It must grant immunity or the defendant would have a Fifth Amendment right not to incriminate himself.[27] Thus, the witness is given something of value (immunization) and the Government also receives something of value, the immunized testimony.

The *en banc* court quickly reversed this panel decision.[28] The majority ruled that the reference in the statute to "whomever" does not include the United States acting in its sovereign capacity, and thus does not include Assistant U.S. Attorneys who act as alter egos of the Federal Government.[29] The Government, in short, did not intend, by one statute, to criminalize that which other federal statutes specifically authorize.

The U.S. Supreme Court has periodically acknowledged the importance of using immunity and other techniques to secure testimony in criminal cases. Immunity statutes "reflect[ ] the importance of testimony, and the fact that many offenses are of such a character that the only persons capable of giving useful testimony are those implicated in the crime."[30] Immunity is "essential to the effective enforcement of various criminal statutes,"[31] and "so familiar that immunity statutes have become part of our 'constitutional fabric.' "[32] The purpose of these inducements is not to change testimony; prosecutors routinely seek corroboration of the witness' testimony to be assured that the witness is not simply making up a story, and they often grant immunity in order to secure documents and similar evidence that they could not

---

[26]*Pillsbury Co. v. Conboy*, 459 U.S. 248, 254 n. 11, 103 S.Ct. 608, 612, 74 L.Ed.2d 430 (1983) (" 'The court's role in granting the [immunity] order is merely to find the facts on which the order is predicated.' ").

[27]*Kastigar v. United States*, 406 U.S. 441, 446, 92 S.Ct. 1653, 1657, 32 L.Ed.2d 212 (1972).

[28]*United States v. Singleton*, 165 F.3d 1297 (10th Cir.1999), *reversing*, 144 F.3d 1343 (10th Cir.1998). In this case, the defendant, Sonya Singleton, was convicted of money laundering and conspiring to distribute cocaine. The conspiracy forming the basis of Ms. Singleton's conviction required her to send and receive drug proceeds by Western Union wires. Her co-conspirator, Napoleon Douglas, entered into a plea agreement in which he agreed to testify truthfully in return for the government's promise not to prosecute him for related offenses,

to advise the sentencing court of his cooperation, and to advise a state parole board of the "nature and extent" of his cooperation.

[29]The court ruled that the word "whoever" in the statute connotes a being; but the United States is an inanimate entity, and applying the statute to the government would deprive the sovereign of a recognized or established prerogative. 165 F.3d at 1299.

[30]*Kastigar v. United States*, 406 U.S. 441, 446, 92 S.Ct. 1653, 1657, 32 L.Ed.2d 212 (1972).

[31]*Kastigar v. United States, 406 U.S. at 447, 92 S.Ct. at 1658.*

[32]*United States v. Mandujano*, 425 U.S. 564, 575–76, 96 S.Ct. 1768, 1775–76, 48 L.Ed.2d 212 (1976) (plurality opinion), *quoting Lefkowitz v. Turley*, 414 U.S. 70, 81–82, 94 S.Ct. 316, 324–325, 38 L.Ed.2d 274 (1973).

otherwise obtain.[33] Rather, the purpose is to get documents, other real evidence, and cooperation that the government would not otherwise get.[34]

§ 3.4–3(e) Coaching Witnesses, Preparing Witnesses, and Counseling a Witness to Testify Falsely

Lawyers may interview witnesses and prepare them for trial, but lawyers may not "suggest" that a client or witness testify falsely.[35] If the suggestion is baldly made, the lawyer is suborning perjury. However, lawyers cannot avoid their ethical responsibilities by a wink of their eye or a knowing smile. Thus, in *Harlan v. Lewis*,[36] the Eight Circuit ruled that a defense lawyer, in a medical malpractice case, violated Rule 3.4 "by suggesting" to another treating physician that, although he also could be sued by plaintiff, that suit would be unsuccessful if he did not testify.[37]

---

[33]For example, in the perjury investigation of Monica Lewinsky, the Independent Counsel immunized Ms. Lewinsky primarily for the purpose of securing a blue dress. She offered little new testimonial information (other investigations had already uncovered the salient facts). But the immunity agreement meant that Ms. Lewinsky had to turn over a blue dress. This blue dress had physical evidence (the President's DNA) that implicated the President in perjury, conspiracy, and obstruction. The blue dress corroborated and authenticated Ms. Lewinsky's story. *See* REFERRAL TO THE UNITED STATES HOUSE OF REPRESENTATIVES, pursuant to Title 28, United States Code, § 595(c), SUBMITTED BY THE OFFICE OF THE INDEPENDENT COUNSEL SEPT. 9, 1998. The House of Representatives subsequently impeached the President and the Senate refused to convict him.

[34]*United States v. Juncal*, 1998 WL 525800, at *1 (S.D.N.Y.1998): "The concept of affording cooperating accomplices with leniency dates back to the common law in England and has been recognized and approved by the United States Congress, the United States Courts and the United States Sentencing Commission."

[35]Restatement of the Law Governing Lawyers, Third, § 116(1) (Official Draft 2000).

[36]*Harlan v. Lewis*, 982 F.2d 1255, 1257 (8th Cir.1993), *cert. denied*, 510 U.S. 828, 114 S.Ct. 94, 126 L.Ed.2d 61 (1993).

[37]**Undercover Operations.** Sometimes prosecutors use undercover agents to ferret out crime. When these undercover operatives lie to the court—in order to keep their cover—courts have often been displeased, even though the judges suggest no better alternative under the circumstances. One must realize that the lies are not intended to secure any improper advantage from the court: the lie does not continue because the prosecutor reveals the truth as soon as the circumstances permit. *See* § 32-1.2.

In *People v. Reichman*, 819 P.2d 1035 (Colo.1991), a prosecutor created a drug task force that used undercover investigators. One of these investigators identified a lawyer as a possible drug user. This investigator also expressed concern that his cover might have been compromised. In response, the prosecutor had the investigator arrested for a fictitious crime. This investigator then hired the suspected lawyer to defend him. Charges were filed,

In court trials, attorneys often prepare witnesses by trying to refresh their recollection.[38] For example, witnesses are shown documents that they may have seen (or even written themselves) years earlier. But when lawyers cross the line and put their own words into witnesses' mouths, there is a danger that lawyers are not preserving evidence but simply making it up.

Careful trial lawyers must find out if the witness is giving his own testimony or merely repeating what a lawyer told him to say. If a witness' testimony appears to have been memorized or rehearsed or if it appears that the witness is testifying using the lawyer's words rather than his own, or has been improperly coached, such matters should be explored on cross-examination.

---

the investigator was arraigned, and the trial judge knew nothing of the deception. The purpose of this charade was to convince the lawyer that the investigator was really not a police undercover agent. When the Court found out the truth it was incensed. The prosecutor was publicly censured for engaging in fraud, deceit, and prejudicing the administration of justice.

In re Friedman, 76 Ill.2d 392, 30 Ill.Dec. 288, 392 N.E.2d 1333 (1979), was another case where the prosecutor allowed false testimony to be introduced in court. The respondent, an attorney in the criminal division of the Cook County State's Attorney office, learned that the defense lawyer solicited a police officer to commit perjury. The respondent instructed the officer to agree to commit the perjury so that the state could then apprehend the briber. After the officer testified falsely under oath that a witness was unavailable, the defense lawyer gave the officer $50. The state indicted the defense lawyer for bribery.

Although the assistant State's Attorney allowed the false testimony to be introduced solely for the purpose of developing evidence to be used in a subsequent prosecution, a disciplinary action was brought against him. Two justices found a violation of DR 7–102(A)(4), (6), & DR 7–109(B); they argued: "The integrity of the courtroom is so vital to the health of our legal system that no violation of that integrity, no matter what its motivation, can be condoned or ignored." These Justices refused to impose any sanctions, however, because respondent had acted without the guidance of settled opinion, and because of the belief of many lawyers that respondent's conduct in the circumstances of this case was proper. Two justices went further and found the respondent guilty of prejudicing the administration of justice. Two justices found that the respondent did not violate any ethical proscriptions at all.

[38] Preparing a witness is different than creating testimony. Good faith "preparation" and "creation" are each on different sides of a great divide. As the court noted in State v. McCormick, 298 N.C. 788, 259 S.E.2d 880 (1979):

"It is not improper for an attorney to prepare his witness for trial, to explain the applicable law in any given situation and to go over before trial the attorney's questions and the witness' answers so that the witness will be ready for his appearance in court, will be more at ease because he knows what to expect, and will give his testimony in the most effective manner that he can. Such preparation is the mark of a good trial lawyer, See, e. g., A. Morrill, Trial Diplomacy, Ch. 3, Part 8 (1973), and is to be commended because it promotes a more efficient administration of justice and saves court time."

State v. McCormick, 298 N.C. 788, 791, 259 S.E.2d 880, 882 (1979).

The jury then decides what weight to be given to the witness' testimony.[39] As one commentator has noted:

> A potential example of an attorney overreaching ethical lines would occur if the attorney said, "You will be asked if you ever saw any WARNING labels on containers of asbestos. It is important to maintain that you NEVER saw any labels on asbestos products that said WARNING or DANGER." On its face, this statement suborns perjury, unless the attorney already knows that the witness never actually saw any warning labels and is just reminding him of that fact.[40]

Courses in legal ethics often refer to Judge John D. Voelker's famous novel, *Anatomy of a Murder*.[41] There, the defense lawyer, in developing a successful homicide defense of temporarily impaired mental capacity, coached the defendant and planted the right words in his mouth. The defendant supplied the requisite "facts" after having been told in advance by counsel what types of facts would constitute the defense. The lawyer in effect told his client: "Given the facts that you told me, you have no legal defense and are likely to be electrocuted. However, if you acted in a blind rage, that would be a defense, and I could save your life. Think it over tonight, and tomorrow, when we talk see if you can remember just how crazy you were." This is an example of what lawyers are not supposed to do.

There is no scientific study that measures accurately how often attorneys cross the line from jogging the witness' memory to planting false memories, but there is some empirical evidence that the problem is real.[42]

Lawyers should not improperly coach witnesses, inducing them to "remember" events or words that did not occur.[43] This risk is exacerbated by the fact that it is in the witnesses' own economic self-interest to remember what is prompted by these "memory

---

[39]*State v. McCormick*, 298 N.C. 788, 259 S.E.2d 880 (1979), relying on ABA Code of Professional Responsibility, DR 7-102.

[40]Renee Salmi, *Don't Walk the Line: Ethical Considerations in Preparing Witnesses for Deposition and Trial*, 18 REVIEW OF LITIGATION 135, 143 (Winter, 1999) (footnote omitted).

[41]It was published in 1958, written under the pseudonym of R. Traver.

[42]Approximately sixteen to seventeen years ago, workers testified that 70 to 80 percent of the asbestos products in certain workplaces were manufactured by Johns-Mansville. Mansville filed for bankruptcy in 1982

Practically overnight, after that date, workers began to testify that Mansville's product share was only 10 to 20 percent. Mansville was no longer a solvent defendant. As other companies being sued went bankrupt, testimony again changed. *See* Lester Brickman & Ronald D. Rotunda, *When Witnesses Are Told What to Say*, WASHINGTON POST, January 13, 1998, at A15, col. 2–4.

[43]*State v. Earp*, 319 Md. 156, 571 A.2d 1227, 1235 (Md.1990), warning that "The attorney should exercise great care to avoid suggesting to the witness what his or her testimony should be."

joggers."[44] Lawyers, in preparing their witnesses, may refresh their recollections, but they may not coach witnesses to testify falsely.[45]

§ 3.4–4 DISCOVERY REQUESTS

Just as Rule 3.1 prohibits frivolous claims and contentions, and Rule 3.2 urges lawyers to make "reasonable efforts to expedite litigation," Rule 3.4 emphasizes these general principles by its more specific command that prohibits lawyers from making frivolous discovery requests. This Rule also covers the failure to make a reasonably diligent effort to comply with discovery requests.[1] The mere fact that a legal position is "creative" or contrary to existing law does not make that position frivolous. The existing law often has ambiguities and always has potential for change.[2] Therefore a lawyer, in seeking to subpoena a document that appears to be protected as privileged, may still make a "good faith argument for an extension, modification or reversal of existing law."[3]

---

[44]In one case that was much discussed in the legal press, a law firm involved with asbestos litigation gave this memorandum to their clients before their deposition:

"The only documents you should ever refer to in your deposition are your Social Security Print Out, your Work History Sheets and photographs of [asbestos-containing] products you were shown, but ONLY IF YOU ARE ASKED ABOUT THEM AND ONLY IF YOUR BARON & BUDD ATTORNEY INSTRUCTS YOU TO ANSWER! Any other notes, such as [this 20 page memorandum on *Preparing for Your Deposition* that] you are reading right now, are 'privileged' and should never be mentioned."

Bob Van Voris, *Client Memo Embarrasses Dallas Firm: Baron & Budd Coaching of Witnesses Called Improper*, National Law Journal, Oct. 13, 1997, at A30.

[45]Renee Salmi, *Don't Walk the Line: Ethical Considerations in Preparing Witnesses for Deposition and Trial*, 18 Review of Litigation 135 (Winter, 1999); ABA/BNA Lawyers Manual on Professional Conduct, Current Reports, vol. 14, No. 2 (Feb. 18, 1998); Richard C. Wydick, *The Ethics of*

Witness Coaching, 17 Cardozo L. Rev. 1, 4–5 (1995); Joseph D. Piorkowski, *Professional Conduct and the Preparation of Witnesses for Trial: Defining the Acceptable Limitations of "Coaching,"* 1 Georgetown J. Legal Ethics 389 (1987); Fred C. Zacharias & Shaun Martin, *Litigating Zealously Within the Bounds of the Law*, 87 Kentucky L.J. 1001 (1998–99).

[Section 3.4–4]

[1]Rule 3.4(a), (d). *See also* Restatement of the Law Governing Lawyers, Third, § 118(1),(2) (Official Draft 2000).

See, e.g., Wall Street Journal, Feb. 29, 1995, at B8, col. 6, reporting that a law firm for Apple Computer paid to settle a tort claim against Apple. The law firm footed the bill for the settlement, because it discovered that, due to an oversight, it had failed to turn over to plaintiff documents subject to discovery, and the trial judge had threatened to declare a mistrial or impose sanctions. The document omissions came to light when the law firm was about to turn over the same documents to another plaintiff in a different case.

[2]Rule 3.1, Comment 1.

[3]Rule 3.1; DR 2-109(A)(2); DR

§ 3.4–5 DISOBEYING A TRIBUNAL EXCEPT FOR OPEN REFUSALS

In general, the ethics rules mandate the lawyer's obedience to a judge's orders.[1] The lawyer and client, of course, have the right to claim an evidentiary privilege, but should do so openly,[2] so that the judge can rule on the validity of the claim.

§ 3.4–5(a) Citing Unpublished Opinions

If a tribunal has a clear rule forbidding lawyers from citing certain cases (typically, unpublished opinions that can be found through the use of computerized research, such as Westlaw), the lawyer has an ethical obligation to obey that rule, because Rule 3.4(c) incorporates, by reference, a tribunal's local rules.[3] Yet, even in the jurisdictions that clearly forbid counsel from citing to a court its own previously written but unpublished opinions, the lawyer may ethically *"ask permission of the court* to cite an unpublished opinion, pointing out that there now appears to be a trend in other jurisdictions to relax the prohibition against such citations."[4]

In April 2006, the U.S. Supreme Court approved an appellate rule that requires federal appeals courts to permit lawyers to cite to unpublished opinions in court submissions.[5] The rule will become effective in December 2006 if Congress does not block its implementation. Federal Rule of Appellate Procedure 32.1 requires the circuit courts to permit parties to cite unpublished authorities issued after January 1, 2007. Prior to the adoption of this rule, the circuits were split among three positions: litigants may not cite unpublished decisions, litigants are discouraged from citing unpublished decisions unless there is no published authority, and litigants may cite unpublished decisions.[6]

§ 3.4–5(b) Misleading the Court as to the Identity of the Individual Sitting at Counsel's Table

Eye witness identification is one of the most persuasive types

---

7-102(A)(2). *See also* Rule 3.4(c) (lawyer should not knowingly disobey tribunal unless there is "open refusal based on an assertion that no valid obligation exists."). *Cf.* DR 7-106(A).

[Section 3.4–5]

[1] Restatement of the Law Governing Lawyers, Third, § 105 (Official Draft 2000).

[2] Rule 3.4(c)(requiring lawyer to obey tribunal's rules except for "open refusal"). *Cf.* Rule 8.1, Comment 2 (one who claims privilege "should do so openly and not use the right of nondisclosure as a justification for failure to comply. . . . ").

[3] ABA Formal Opinion 94-386 (Aug. 6, 1994).

[4] ABA Formal Opinion 94-386 (Aug. 6, 1994), at 2 (emphasis in original).

[5] 22 ABA/BNA MANUAL ON PROFESSIONAL CONDUCT, Current Reports News 194 (Apr. 19, 2006) (discussing the adoption of Federal Rule of Appellate Procedure 32.1).

[6] 22 ABA/BNA MANUAL ON PROFESSIONAL CONDUCT, Current Reports News 194 (Apr. 19, 2006).

of evidence, but it is often wrong, as shown by a blitz of overturned jury verdicts based on eye witness testimony and later contradicted by modern DNA testing.[7] Consequently, some lawyers have sought to conduct their own in-court lineups, by having someone who is not their client sit at counsel table and pretend to be the accused.

Courts have held lawyers in contempt for that tactic, on the grounds that it violates court custom or rules of the tribunal governing who may sit at counsel table and misleads the court.[8] Other courts do not appear to be concerned with this tactic.[9] In

---

[7] John Gibeaut, *"Yes, I'm Sure That's Him: Eyewitness Reliability Under Question By Experts, Courts,"* 85 ABA J., Oct. 1999, at 26–27.

[8] *E.g., United States v. Thoreen,* 653 F.2d 1332 (9th Cir.1981), *cert. denied,* 455 U.S. 938, 102 S.Ct. 1428, 71 L.Ed.2d 648 (1982). This court relied on, *inter alia,* DR 7-106(C)(5), which corresponds to Rule 3.4(b); DR 7-102(A)(6), which corresponds to Rule 3.3(a)(4); and DR 1-102(A)(4), which corresponds to Rule 8.4(c).

Attorney Grievance Commission of Maryland v. Rohrback, 323 Md. 79, 591 A.2d 488 (App.1991), where a divided court held that: (1) an attorney who is informed by client that he has been arrested and that he already had provided authorities with a false name is not required to inform the authorities and correct his client's prior misstatement; (2) this attorney also is not required to inform the court commissioner when the client (but not the attorney) obtained a bond using a false name where there is no evidence that the attorney was even present in the room at the time; but (3) the attorney may not misrepresent the identity of the client to the agent conducting a pre-sentence investigation. This misrepresentation was by the attorney and it warranted a 45 day suspension.

People v. Simac, 161 Ill.2d 297, 204 Ill.Dec. 192, 641 N.E.2d 416 (1994), held (4 to 3) (1) that the evidence supported the finding that the defense counsel, by substituting a similar-looking individual for defen-

dant at counsel's table without notifying court (resulting in misidentification by prosecution witness) intended to embarrass, hinder, and obstruct the court and the proceedings, thereby supporting his conviction of direct criminal contempt; and that (2) requiring the defense counsel to notify the court before substituting an individual for defendant at counsel's table would not violate any principles of professional responsibility.

[9] *E.g., Duke v. State,* 260 Ind. 638, 298 N.E.2d 453 (1973). The Indiana Supreme Court quoted from the trial record as follows:

"JUDGE: If this is not the man here—I'm not sure he has cleared the case against Duke.

"MR. DIETZEN [the lawyer]: Can the court say positively that this man wearing pink trousers is the same man who was wearing pink trousers this morning?

"JUDGE: You know I warned about tricks."

260 Ind. 638, 640, 298 N.E.2d 453, 454.

The man identified was not the defendant. "The following day it was discovered that the fingerprints of Wilson, who was taken to jail, did not match the fingerprints of the man, Albert Norris Duke, who had originally been charged with the crime." 260 Ind. 638, 640, 298 N.E.2d 453, 454. The appellate court therefore reversed the conviction. The court did not question the ethics of the trial counsel.

light of this divergence of authority, the careful lawyer who wishes to engage in such conduct, should tell the judge first.[10]

§ 3.4–6 TRIAL TACTICS, INADMISSIBLE EVIDENCE, AND CLOSING ARGUMENTS

The ABA Rules provide that, during the trial the lawyer may not "allude" to any matter not reasonably believed to be relevant, or admissible.[1]

Assume for example, that the local evidence rule prohibits introducing evidence that the plaintiff has remarried. A lawyer who asks the witness, "You have remarried, haven't you?," should be violating Rule 3.4(e). The other lawyer's objection will not undo the harm because the lawyer could not reasonably believe that the evidence is relevant or admissible—the local rule having clearly prohibited the question.[2]

Hearsay would not normally be in that category of Rule 3.4(e). It may not be clear that the question calls for hearsay that is inadmissible because often there is an exception to the hearsay rule. Many times a lawyer will decide, for tactical reasons, not to object to a particular question. Sometimes the question is simply in poor form, and can be rephrased to avoid the hearsay objection. Particular in bench trials many judges will allow evidence that is hearsay, but the judge will discount its value. We have found no case ever disciplining a lawyer merely for asking a question that a judge ruled called for hearsay.

During the trial, the lawyer may not, in closing argument or otherwise, assert his personal opinion or knowledge regarding facts at issue, unless he is actually testifying as a witness.[3] However, the lawyer may argue for any position or conclusion based on his analysis of the evidence.[4]

Consider two examples that illustrate this principle. First, as-

---

[10]The *Thoreen* court suggested that counsel could first seek the court's permission to (1) have more than one person seated at counsel table, without identifying which one is the witness, or (2) have no one seated at counsel's table except counsel, or (3) have an in-court line-up. 653 F.2d at 1342 n. 7.

[Section 3.4–6]

[1]Rule 3.4(e). *See also* Restatement of the Law Governing Lawyers, Third, § 107(1) (Official Draft 2000).

[2]*See, e.g., Falkowski v. Johnson,* 148 F.R.D. 132 (D.Del.1993) (reference of plaintiff's lawyer to insurance in an automobile case required a mistrial); *People v. Blackington,* 167 Cal.App.3d 1216, 213 Cal.Rptr. 800 (4th Dist. Ct.App.1985) (prosecutor's repeated references to codefendant's inadmissible and inculpatory statements during cross-examination of defendant, for purpose of establishing premeditation and countering self-defense claim, entitled defendant to mistrial, particularly where he was denied his right to cross-examine codefendant as to those statements when codefendant invoked privilege not to testify).

[3]Rule 3.4(e); DR 7-106(C)(1), (3), (4). Restatement of the Law Governing Lawyers, Third, § 107(1) (Official Draft 2000).

[4]DR 7-106(C)(4).

sume that in closing argument the lawyer states: "How can you believe Witness? I've seen many people testify over the years, and in my experience, Witness is lying. I don't believe him, can you?" The lawyer's action is improper, even if Lawyer really believes that Witness is lying because the lawyer may not assert his personal opinions regarding the facts at issue.[5]

Now, assume that in closing argument the lawyer states: "How can you believe Witness? His testimony contradicts the sworn testimony of three other people who, unlike Witness, have no financial interest in this case." The lawyer's action is proper, because he is just arguing from the evidence that is in the record.

Is this distinction meaningful? Why does the law permit one form of argument and not the other? We must realize that whenever the law offers a bright line rule, it may appear arbitrary that one will violate the law by being one inch outside the line and follow the law by being one inch inside the law. That is the price we pay for precision. In this case, the bright line is not difficult to justify. The law does not want lawyers purporting to be witnesses, vouching for their client's veracity. Yet, lawyers can argue from the evidence, and that argument can be colorful, use metaphor and simile.

§ 3.4–7 ASKING POTENTIAL WITNESSES NOT TO VOLUNTEER INFORMATION

A lawyer may not obstruct her opponents' ability to collect evidence.[1] However, she may advise her client that he should not volunteer any information to the opponent. Then, the only way for the other side to secure information would be via subpoena or deposition of the lawyer's client. In those circumstances the lawyer will be able to protect the client's interest by reviewing documents before they are turned over to make sure that no privileges are waived. And, during the deposition, the lawyer's participation will similarly serve to protect the client's interest.

There are certain types of nonclients whom lawyers can request not to volunteer information. The general rule is that, on behalf of his client, the lawyer may always request an *unrepresented nonclient* witness to refrain from voluntarily giving relevant information to another party *if* the witness is the client's relative,

---

[5]Rule 3.4(e); Restatement of the Law Governing Lawyers, Third, § 107(1) (Official Draft 2000).

§§ 116(2), 118(1),(2) (Official Draft 2000).

[Section 3.4–7]

[1]Rule 3.4(a). Restatement of the Law Governing Lawyers, Third,

employee, or agent whose interests will not be adversely affected if this request is honored.[2]

The lawyer, however, cannot forbid such witnesses from being interviewed. Whether they are in fact interviewed is up to them. They can always insist on being subpoenaed and then deposed. The lawyer is merely informing them that they need not volunteer and can require the other lawyer to subpoena them.

However, lawyers have no right to request other nonclients— *i.e.*, witnesses with no connection to the client—to refrain from volunteering information to the opposing lawyer. For example, in *North Carolina State Bar v. Graves*,[3] the court upheld the discipline of an attorney who attempted to influence a witness (who was not his client) to refuse to testify or, in the alternative, to plead the Fifth Amendment. Although the witness had a constitutional right to plead the Fifth Amendment, it is still a *criminal act* for someone "with corrupt motive to induce a witness to exercise that privilege."[4]

People v. Kenelly,[5] offers another interesting example. In that case the court suspended an attorney because he drew a contract under which his client settled a civil case against *X,* and, in exchange, agreed to evade a subpoena in *X*'s upcoming criminal trial.[6]

---

[2] Rule 3.4(f). Restatement of the Law Governing Lawyers, Third, § 116(4) (Official Draft 2000). *See* Robert C. Hacker & Ronald D. Rotunda, *Ethical Restraints on Communications with Adverse Expert Witnesses*, 5 CORPORATION L. REV. 348 (1982).

[3] *North Carolina State Bar v. Graves*, 50 N.C.App. 450, 274 S.E.2d 396 (1981).

Catherine D. Perry, J., citing treatise in, *Synergetics, Inc. v. Hurst*, 2007 WL 2422871, *10 at n. 11 (E.D. Mo. 2007).

[4] *North Carolina State Bar v. Graves*, 50 N.C.App. 450, 274 S.E.2d 396 (1981). *See also United States v. Baker*, 611 F.2d 964, 968 (4th Cir. 1979).

See also Restatement of the Law Governing Lawyers, Third, §§ 116(3) ,(4) (Official Draft 2000).

[5] *People v. Kenelly*, 648 P.2d 1065 (Colo.1982).

[6] *Accord In the Matter of Lutz*, 101 Idaho 24, 607 P.2d 1078 (1980).

See also Snyder v. State Bar, 18 Cal.3d 286, 291, 133 Cal.Rptr. 864, 867, 555 P.2d 1104, 1107 (1976) (attorney disbarred, inter alia, for advising clients not to be available for depositions); *Florida Bar v. Machin*, 635 So.2d 938 (Fla.1994) (lawyer suspended for offering to establish a trust fund for the child of a murder victim if the victim's family agreed not to testify at the client's sentencing hearing). *Cf. Taylor v. Commonwealth*, 192 Ky. 410, 233 S.W. 895 (1921) (attorney disbarred when he was party to an arrangement under which a witness was paid to leave the jurisdiction and not return).

§ 3.4–8 MARY CARTER AGREEMENTS

The term "Mary Carter Agreement," is derived from *Booth v. Mary Carter Paint Co.*[1] In Arizona, these agreements are often called, "Gallagher Agreements," named after *City of Tucson v. Gallagher.*[2] Essentially, in these agreements, the plaintiff sues several defendants and then secretly settles with one or more of the defendants, but the settling defendants retain a financial stake in the plaintiff's recovery. Those defendants who have settled do not withdraw from the trial but continue as defendants as if they had not been dismissed. The secretly-settled defendants agree with the plaintiff that the defendants' maximum liability is fixed by the settlement, and the payment that they must make to the plaintiff will be diminished proportionately by the liability of the non-settling defendants.[3]

Consider *Elbaor v. Smith.*[4] In this case, after plaintiff sued several defendants for medical malpractice, she signed Mary Carter Agreements with two doctors and a hospital but not the third doctor, Dr. Elbaor. The Mary Carter Agreements required the settling defendants to pay a total of $425,010 to plaintiff. In addition, the Mary Carter defendants were to participate in the trial as defendants, although they had settled the case. The Mary Carter Agreement included a payback clause, so that the Mary Carter defendants would be reimbursed all or part of the settlement money paid to the plaintiff out of the recovery from Dr. Elbaor. Thus, several defendants shared a mutual financial interest with the plaintiff: the Mary Carter defendants had a financial stake in any recovery that plaintiff received from the remaining defendant because the Mary Carter defendants would be financially rewarded to the extent that they could persuade the jury to shift the blame to the remaining defendant.

During the trial, the lawyers for the defendants (hereinafter, the Mary Carter defendants) who had settled the case with the plaintiff sat at the table with the lawyer for Dr. Elbaor. The Mary Carter defendants were not like ordinary defendants, for they vigorously assisted the plaintiff in pointing the finger of culpability at Dr. Elbaor. This scenario, in the view of the Texas Supreme Court, "created some odd conflicts of interest and some

---

[Section 3.4–8]

[1]*Booth v. Mary Carter Paint Co.*, 202 So.2d 8 (Fla.App.1967). The Florida Supreme Court first used this term in a later case, where it concluded that Mary Carter Agreements tend to skew the trial process. The court then established supervisory guidelines to limit

their effects. *See Ward v. Ochoa*, 284 So.2d 385 (Fla.1973).

[2]*City of Tucson v. Gallagher*, 108 Ariz. 140, 493 P.2d 1197 (1972).

[3]*See, e.g., Ward v. Ochoa*, 284 So.2d 385, 387 (Fla.1973).

[4]*Elbaor v. Smith*, 845 S.W.2d 240, 22 A.L.R.5th 879 (Tex. 1992).

questionable representations of fact."[5] For example, although the plaintiff's experts testified that Dr. Syrquin (one of the Mary Carter defendants) committed malpractice, the plaintiff's lawyer stated during voir dire and in her opening statement that Dr. Syrquin's conduct was "heroic" and that it was Dr. Elbaor's negligence that caused the plaintiff's damages. And during her closing argument, plaintiff's lawyer urged the jury to find that Dr. Syrquin had *not* caused plaintiff's damages, an unusual statement from a plaintiff's lawyer regarding a named defendant.

The Mary Carter defendants remained defendants of record, but the Mary Carter defense lawyers asserted during voir dire that plaintiff's damages were "devastating," "astoundingly high," and "astronomical." Furthermore, on their purported cross examination they elicited testimony from plaintiff that was favorable to her and they requested recovery for pain and mental anguish. The Mary Carter defendants' attorneys also abandoned their pleadings on plaintiff's contributory negligence, argued that plaintiff should be awarded all of her alleged damages, and urged that Dr. Elbaor was 100 percent liable.

In these types of cases, if one or more defendants settle the case and they are removed as parties, there is no Mary Carter Agreement. However, if these defendants, who are no longer parties to the case, testified, they would be testifying as a non-party witness, not as purported "defendants." It would be unethical for the plaintiff's lawyer to pay these witnesses for the content of their testimony or make payment contingent on the content of their testimony.[6] If these defendants stay in the case and are not removed as parties, then they will receive money, a financial reward, in the form of a reduced settlement obligation, based on the content of their testimony. Mary Carter defendants receive financial reward to the extent that they can shift the blame to the remaining non-Mary Carter defendant. Some courts have found that this situation violates the rules of ethics, in particular, Rule 3.4(b), by offering a witness an inducement to testify falsely.[7]

---

[5] 845 S.W.2d at 246.

[6] *See* Rule 3.4(b)(offer inducement to witness "that is prohibited by law"), which is what the court relied on in *Elbaor v. Smith*, 845 S.W.2d 240, 247 n.14 (Tex.1992).

[7] *Elbaor v. Smith*, 845 S.W.2d 240, 247 n. 14 (Tex.1992):

"However, Rule 3.04(b) [corresponding to Model Rule 3.4(b)] of the Texas Disciplinary Rules of Professional Conduct prohibits a lawyer from paying or offering to pay a witness contingent upon the content of the testimony of the witness or the outcome of the case. Certainly Rule 3.04(b) mandates that an attorney has an ethical duty to refrain from making a settlement contingent, in any way, on the testimony of a witness who was also a settling party."

Many commentators[8] and courts[9] have attacked Mary Carter Agreements as unethical, because they give one or more of the defendants a stake in the plaintiff's recovery, mislead the jury (because a nominal defendant really has the financial incentives of a plaintiff and participates in the trial on behalf of the plaintiff),[10] tend to promote unethical collusion between the plaintiff and the Mary Carter defendant, and corrupt the testimony of the Mary Carter defendants, because their maximum liability is fixed and will be diminished proportionately by increasing the liability of the non-Mary Carter defendants.[11]

In addition, courts complain that they require too much judicial supervision. Court rules may require that Mary Carter Agreements are discoverable. If a trial court learns of a Mary Carter Agreement, it may try to deal with it by reapportioning peremptory challenges of jurors, ruling on who may examine a witness as an adverse witness, disclosing the agreement to jury at the

---

[8]See, e.g., David Jonathan Grant, Comment, The Mary Carter Agreement—Solving the Problems of Collusive Settlements and Joint Tort Actions, 47 So. Calif. L.Rev. 1393, 1409 (1974); David R. Miller, Comment, Mary Carter Agreements: Unfair and Unnecessary, 32 Sw. L. J. 779 (1978); June F. Entman, Mary Carter Agreements: An Assessment of Attempted Solutions, 38 U. Fla. L. Rev. 521 (1986); Robin Renee Green, Comment, Mary Carter Agreements: The Unsolved Evidentiary Problems in Texas, 40 Baylor L. Rev. 449 (1988); John E. Benedict, Note, It's A Mistake to Tolerate the Mary Carter Agreement, 87 Colum. L. Rev. 368 (1987); Richard Casner, Note, Admission into Evidence of a Mary Carter Agreement from a Prior Trial is Harmful Error, 18 Tex. Tech L. Rev 997 (1987).

[9]See, e.g., Vermont Union School v. H.P. Cummings Const., 143 Vt. 416, 469 A.2d 742, 749 (1983); Elbaor v. Smith, 845 S.W.2d 240, 247–250 (Tex.1992) (Mary Carter agreements held to be against public policy and void).

Daniel v. Penrod Drilling Co., 393 F.Supp. 1056 (E.D.La.1975), held that the Mary Carter Agreement, between the plaintiff and one defendant, not revealed to the jury or the other defendant, to dismiss one defendant at the end of the trial in exchange for the defendant's agreement to offer no resistance to the plaintiff's case, required a new trial. The vice of such an agreement is not eliminated by the last minute offer to disclose it to the jury because the remaining defendant would not have sufficient opportunity to adapt its trial strategy. Even if this agreement had been made known to the jury, it "might in itself prejudice the defendant's case since the jurors might infer that all parties to the agreement believed that the nonagreeing defendant was the party really at fault. . . ." 393 F. Supp. at 1060.

[10]See, e.g., Daniel v. Penrod Drilling Co., 393 F.Supp. 1056, 1060 (E.D. La.1975): "Courts are not merely arenas where games of counsel's skill are played. Even in football we do not tolerate point shaving." Slayton v. Ford Motor Co., 140 Vt. 27, 435 A.2d 946, 947 (1981), concluding that a jury may wrongly infer that the non-settling defendant must be the most culpable defendant because plaintiff had not settled with that defendant.

[11]Elbaor v. Smith, 845 S.W.2d 240, 247 n. 14 (Tex.1992).

very beginning of the trial, so that it is no longer secret, and giving cautionary jury instructions.[12]

Although proponents of Mary Carter Agreements claim that they promote settlement, opponents point out that they only allow a partial settlement and virtually assure a trial against the non-settling defendants,[13] because the Agreement gives the Mary Carter defendant a veto power over the plaintiff's settlement with the remaining defendants.[14]

Some courts do not invalidate Mary Carter Agreements on ethical and other policy grounds but allow them and then strictly police them.[15] Other courts have decided that the best remedy is prophylactic, and thus declare that these agreements are void and unethical.[16]

---

[12]*See, e.g., Elbaor v. Smith*, 845 S.W.2d 240, 246 & n. 12 (Tex.1992), describing what the trial judge did to mitigate the effects of the Mary Carter Agreement. However, in this case, the trial judge did *not* enter the Agreement into evidence. The Texas Supreme Court held that all Mary Carter Agreements are void as against public policy.

[13]As, *Stein v. American Residential Management*, 781 S.W.2d 385, 389 (Tex.App.-Houston [14th Dist.] 1989), *writ denied per curiam*, 793 S.W.2d 1 (Tex.1990) concluded: "Only a mechanical jurisprudence could characterize Mary Carter arrangements as promoting compromise and discouraging litigation—they plainly do just the opposite."

See, e.g., Lum v. Stinnett, 87 Nev. 402, 488 P.2d 347, 348 (1971); *Bedford School Dist. v. Caron Construction Co.*, 116 N.H. 800, 367 A.2d 1051, 1054 (1976) (Mary Carter Agreement obliged plaintiff to prosecute claim against the remaining defendant, and plaintiff could not settle the claim for under $20,000 without the consent of the Mary Carter defendant).

[14]*See, e.g., Bass v. Phoenix Seadrill/78 Ltd.*, 749 F.2d 1154, 1156 (5th Cir.1985) (Mary Carter agreement gave settling defendant veto power).

[15]*See, e.g., Sequoia Manufacturing Co. v. Halec Construction Co.*, 117 Ariz. 11, 570 P.2d 782, 793–95 (1977); *Vermont Union School v. H.P. Cummings Construction Co.*, 143 Vt. 416, 469 A.2d 742, 749–50 (1983); *Shelton v. Firestone Tire and Rubber Co.*, 281 Ark. 100, 662 S.W.2d 473 (1983); *Abbott Ford, Inc. v. Superior Court*, 43 Cal.3d 858, 239 Cal.Rptr. 626, 633, 741 P.2d 124, 131 (1987); *Carter v. Tom's Truck Repair, Inc.*, 857 S.W.2d 172 (Mo.1993).

[16]*See, e.g., Trampe v. Wisconsin Tel. Co.*, 214 Wis. 210, 252 N.W. 675 (1934), holding Mary Carter Agreements to be void; *Lum v. Stinnett*, 87 Nev. 402, 488 P.2d 347 (1971) (same); *Elbaor v. Smith*, 845 S.W.2d 240, 246 & n. 12 (Tex.1992) (same).

The Supreme Court of Oklahoma offered a more elaborate procedure, which, in effect, voids Mary Carter Agreements. *Cox v. Kelsey-Hayes Co.*, 594 P.2d 354, 359 (Okl.1978), held that a trial court must—

"*either hold that portion of the agreement granting agreeing defendant an interest in a large plaintiff's verdict unenforceable as against public policy, or dismiss the agreeing defendant from the suit.* In no circumstances should a defendant who will profit from a large plaintiff's verdict be allowed to remain in the suit as an ostensible defendant. If agreeing defendant is dismissed, cross-examination affecting his interest and credibility should protect the interest of non-agreeing defendant. If agreeing

---

RULE 3.5: IMPARTIALITY AND DECORUM OF THE TRIBUNAL

A lawyer shall not:

(a) seek to influence a judge, juror, prospective juror or other official by means prohibited by law;

(b) communicate ex parte with such a person during the proceeding unless authorized to do so by law or court order;

(c) communicate with a juror or prospective juror after discharge of the jury if:

(1) the communication is prohibited by law or court order;

(2) the juror has made known to the lawyer a desire not to communicate; or

(3) the communication involves misrepresentation, coercion, duress or harassment; or

(d) engage in conduct intended to disrupt a tribunal.

Comment

[1] Many forms of improper influence upon a tribunal are proscribed by criminal law. Others are specified in the ABA Model Code of Judicial Conduct, with which an advocate should be familiar. A

---

defendant remains in the suit and the agreement has been declared void as against public policy, then the adversary nature of the proceedings has been preserved and the agreement is no longer relevant. In most cases full disclosure to the jury of the exact terms of the agreement is probably inadvisable. Full disclosure could in some cases be detrimental to the non-agreeing defendant who would be torn between need to inform the jury of the agreement and the potentially self-serving statements of plaintiff and agreeing defendant contained therein." 594 P.2d 354, 359–60 (emphasis in original)(footnote omitted)

lawyer is required to avoid contributing to a violation of such provisions.

[2] During a proceeding a lawyer may not communicate ex parte with persons serving in an official capacity in the proceeding, such as judges, masters or jurors, unless authorized to do so by law or court order.

[3] A lawyer may on occasion want to communicate with a juror or prospective juror after the jury has been discharged. The lawyer may do so unless the communication is prohibited by law or a court order but must respect the desire of the juror not to talk with the lawyer. The lawyer may not engage in improper conduct during the communication.

[4] The advocate's function is to present evidence and argument so that the cause may be decided according to law. Refraining from abusive or obstreperous conduct is a corollary of the advocate's right to speak on behalf of litigants. A lawyer may stand firm against abuse by a judge but should avoid reciprocation; the judge's default is no justification for similar dereliction by an advocate. An advocate can present the cause, protect the record for subsequent review and preserve professional integrity by patient firmness no less effectively than by belligerence or theatrics.

[5] The duty to refrain from disruptive conduct applies to any proceeding of a tribunal, including a deposition. See Rule 1.0(m).

Authors' 1983 Model Rules Comparison

The drafters of the 2002 Rules modified the text of Rule 3.5 to take into account the practice of lawyers interviewing jurors after the trial is over.

The drafters of the 2002 Rules modified Rule 3.5(b) to narrow the prohibition against ex parte conduct to lawyer conduct "during the proceeding." This change recognizes that lawyers may contact jurors and possibly others after the proceeding is completed. Rule 3.5(b) also now recognizes that ex parte contact may be authorized by court order in some cases.

Rule 3.5(c) is new and reflects the case law that the ban on contact with jurors after a verdict may violate the First Amendment. *See* Reporter's Explanation of Changes to Model Rule 3.5. The drafters of the 2002 Rules imposed three possible situations where a lawyer may not speak with a juror after the completion of the proceedings.

The 1983 version of Rule 3.5(c) was renumbered as Rule 3.5(d) without any changes.

The current Comment 1 is identical to the 1983 version.

Comments 2 and 3 are new and reflect the changes made to the text of the Rule.

The drafters renumbered the 1983 Comment 2 as Comment 4, but no changes were made to the language.

Comment 5 is new and explains that the obligation of lawyers not to disrupt the tribunal applies to all proceedings associated with the tribunal, including depositions.

Model Code Comparison

[1] With regard to paragraphs (a) and (b), DR 7-108(A) provided

that "[b]efore the trial of a case a lawyer . . . shall not communicate with . . . anyone he knows to be a member of the venire. . . ." DR 7-108(B) provided that during the trial of a case a lawyer "shall not communicate with . . . any member of the jury." DR 7-110(B) provided that a lawyer shall not "communicate . . . as to the merits of the cause with a judge or an official before whom the proceeding is pending, except . . . upon adequate notice to opposing counsel," or as "otherwise authorized by law."

[2] With regard to paragraph (c), DR 7-106(C)(6) provided that a lawyer shall not engage in "undignified or discourteous conduct which is degrading to a tribunal."

§ 3.5–1 SEEKING TO INFLUENCE CORRUPTLY

Rule 3.5 makes a lawyer subject to discipline for engaging in conduct that already is illegal. The purpose of this rule is to make clear that the lawyer who engages in such conduct must fear not only the sanctions that other law imposes but also the sanction of losing his or her license to practice law. Thus, the lawyer may not attempt to influence a judge, juror, prospective juror, or other official by means that are prohibited by law.[1] These ethics rules incorporate by reference other law and then impose the threat of legal discipline.[2]

§ 3.5–2 DISRUPTING THE TRIBUNAL

The lawyer may disobey a tribunal's order if there is an *"open refusal based on an assertion that no valid obligation exists. . . ."*[1] That is the lawful way to disagree with the judge. The ethics rules forbid unlawful ways to disobey a court order, and thus they explicitly forbid disrupting the tribunal.[2]

Thus, the court in the decision of *In the Matter of McAlevy*[3] severely reprimanded an attorney who, at a side bar conference, threatened (in vulgar terms) physical violence to the Deputy Attorney General; this lawyer also later attacked the Deputy Attorney General during a conference in the judge's chambers.

[Section 3.5–1]

[1] Rule 3.5(a). DR 7-108(A), (B).

[2] Rule 8.4(a).

[Section 3.5–2]

[1] Rule 3.4(d) (emphasis added). *See also* DR 7-102(A).

[2] Rule 3.5(d). DR 7-106(C)(6).

[3] *In the Matter of McAlevy*, 69 N.J. 349, 354 A.2d 289 (1976). Contrast *Attorney Grievance Commission of Maryland v. Link*, 380 Md. 405, 844 A.2d 1197 (2004). The lawyer's conduct in *Link* (criticizing and engaging in confrontation with the agent of the custodian of records that the lawyer was attempting to obtain) were unlike the facts in *McAlevy*, which occurred during the actual litigation process. *Link* explained that the confrontation and resulting conduct and remarks were the result of the lawyer's perception that requirements for accessing information imposed by agent were improper and even illegal, offending conduct was not during the course of litigation or court proceedings; the lawyer's conduct was rude and insensitive, but not criminal. Part of the issue involved the question whether the word "Sparky" is racially offensive.

When the judge and his law clerk tried to separate the two men now locked in combat, they were drawn into the fight and at one point all four men were rolling on the floor.[4]

Just as the lawyer-official may not accept anything of value offered to influence her own actions as a public official, neither may a lawyer seek to influence a public official (or juror) improperly.[5]

A lawyer may not use his public position in order to gain a corrupt advantage for himself or his client.[6] The basic question is whether the effort to influence the tribunal was corrupt. Consider, for example, a lawyer-legislator who appears before the state commerce commission to urge a rate increase on behalf of a private client. This lawyer-legislator is also on the state house committee that oversees the state commerce commission and sets the administrators' salaries. Such circumstantial facts alone do not show anything improper. The lawyer-legislator must also have actually engaged in an overt attempt to exert improper influence over the state commerce commission.[7]

§ 3.5–3 *EX PARTE* COMMUNICATIONS DURING THE PROCEEDING

The Model Rules and the Model Code forbid improper *ex parte* communications with jurors or prospective jurors.[1] Similarly, both the Rules and the Code forbid improper efforts to influence judges, jurors, prospective jurors, or other officials.[2] The main difference in this instance between the two sets of rules—and a typical difference that exists throughout the two codes—is that the Rules simply incorporate the requirements of other law.[3] The Code, on the other hand, is much more specific in describing the forbidden conduct.

As part of the ground rules of litigation, lawyers are prohibited from contacting "persons serving in an official capacity in the proceeding, such as judges, masters or jurors," unless permitted by law or court order. Canon 3B(7) of the Code of Judicial Conduct regulates ex parte communications in judicial proceedings. This provision and other court rules delineate what judges and court personnel may do with respect to ex parte conduct. As one can

---

[4]The judge suffered minor injuries. *See* Ronald D. Rotunda, *The Litigator's Professional Responsibility*, 25 Trial Magazine 98 (Mar. 1989).

[5]Rule 3.5(a); *Cf.* EC 7-35; DR 9-101(C). Restatement of the Law Governing Lawyers, Third, § 113(2) (Official Draft 2000).

[6]DR 8-101(A)(2); Rule 3.5(a).

[7]ABA Informal Opinion 1182 (Dec. 5, 1971). *See also State ex rel.* *Nebraska State Bar Association v. Holscher*, 193 Neb. 729, 738, 230 N.W.2d 75, 80 (1975).

[Section 3.5–3]

[1]Rule 3.5(b); DR 7-108. Restatement of the Law Governing Lawyers, Third, §§ 113(1), 115 (Official Draft 2000).

[2]DR 7-108(A); DR 7-110(A); Rule 3.5(a).

[3]Rule 3.5(a), (b).

imagine, courts and parties need to communicate about scheduling and other administrative matters. However, ex parte communications that address the merits of a matter undermine the public confidence in the judiciary. When all parties are not present to hear a communication with the court, the litigants cannot voice their positions or preserve their rights on appeal. Of course, there may be exceptional circumstances where ex parte conduct is permitted by law or court order.[4]

§ 3.5–4 COMMUNICATING WITH JURORS AFTER DISCHARGE OF THE JURY

Disciplinary Rule 7-108(D) of the former Model Code of Professional Responsibility allowed communications after the discharge of the jury, as long as they were not "calculated merely to harass or embarrass the juror or to influence his action in future jury service." Under this rule, it was not unethical for a lawyer to question jurors after they were discharged, as long as the lawyer did not harass, induce, or embarrass the juror.[1]

Rule 3.5(b), however, *before* the 2002 revisions, stated that a lawyer may not "communicate ex parte" with a jury "during the proceeding unless authorized to do so by law or court order." The 1983 version of Rule 3.5 was sometimes interpreted to prohibit lawyers from communicating with jurors after they were discharged. One study of the state of the law concluded that, as of 1994, in the majority of federal district courts, a lawyer "seeking a postverdict interview with jurors, at minimum, must petition the court for permission and, more often than not, must show some external evidence of the suspected impropriety in order to gain such authorization."[2] In most trial courts, a lawyer needed judicial permission to interview the jurors and the judge granted such permission only upon a showing of good cause.[3] A strong rule on no impeachment of jury verdicts led courts to grant very few motions to contact jurors after the verdict.[4]

In 1996, a federal district court held that the Hawaiian version of Rule 3.5 was unconstitutional as applied to *post-verdict* contact

---

[4]Rule 3.5(b).

[Section 3.5–4]

[1]ABA Committee on Ethics and Professional Responsibility, Formal Opinion 319 (1967).

[2]Benjamin M. Lawsky, *Note, Limitations on Attorney Postverdict Contact with Jurors: Protecting the Criminal Jury and Its Verdict at the Expense of the Defendant*, 94 COLUM. L. REV. 1950, 1958 (1994).

[3]*See* Benjamin M. Lawsky, *Note, Limitations on Attorney Postverdict Contact with Jurors: Protecting the Criminal Jury and Its Verdict at the Expense of the Defendant*, 94 COLUM. L. REV. 1950 (1994).

[4]*See* Federal Rule of Evidence 606(b) (no impeachment rule).

with jurors.[5] The case involved a pro se plaintiff who was also a lawyer and therefore covered by the Rules. He asked the defendant and the court if they could stay behind after the verdict so that he could ask the jurors some questions:

> He claims that he desires to talk with the jurors for various purposes, including: (1) to thank them for their service, attention, and their verdict, (2) to discuss with the jurors their thinking, reasoning, and reaction to the case and to Rapp's performance, (3) to explore the possibility of "extrinsic fraud," jury misconduct, error, or other grounds upon which the verdict might be called into question by the Schmidts, (4) to answer any questions the jurors may have, (5) for other "proper and legitimate" reasons not calculated to harass or embarrass jurors or to influence their actions . . . .[6]

The district court found that Rule 3.5(b) was unconstitutionally vague and overbroad and that Hawaii, in practice, allowed *joint* counsel interviewing of jurors. The Hawaii court system, in practice, did not prohibit all post-verdict communications; it simply gave a veto to one of the lawyers. Thus, the court concluded that a complete prohibition against lawyer contact with jurors post-verdict was contrary to the First Amendment.[7]

The drafters of the 2002 Rules believed that in response to the Hawaii federal district court decision, they should redraft the Rule 3.5 prohibition on lawyer contact with jurors after their discharge from the case. The new Rule 3.5(c) states that a lawyer should not "communicate with a juror or prospective juror after discharge of the jury" if: a court order or law prohibits such contact, or the person has informed the lawyer that he or she desires that no communication takes place, or the lawyer's communication involves "misrepresentation, coercion, duress or harassment."[8] Otherwise, Rule 3.5 permits lawyer contact with jurors *after* the jury is discharged.

The new Rule 3.5 will raise other issues for the litigation process. Will this Rule create a duty that all lawyers stay and interview jurors to determine if a basis for appeal exists? Will such new information cause the standard or review on the no impeachment rule to be changed? Can juror statements potentially hurt a client's case on appeal?[9] Should judges give jurors the right to leave the courtroom through a side door without any contact, or should a judge encourage jurors to help educate the

---

[5]*See Rapp v. Disciplinary Board of the Hawaii Supreme Court*, 916 F.Supp. 1525 (D.Hawaii, 1996).

[6]916 F.Supp. at 1529.

[7]*See also Benton v. Commission of Discipline*, 933 S.W.2d 784 (Tex. App.—Corpus Christi 1996).

[8]Rule 3.5(c), & Comment 3.

[9]For example, if a lawyer believes that the judge improperly admitted some evidence and the lawyer asks the jury whether they considered it and they say no, does that waive the lawyer's argument on appeal?

lawyers as to how the case was decided?[10] Some jurors, particularly after trials involving celebrities, like face time with the press. Should the judge ban such post-verdict communications on the grounds that the possibility of this face time may affect how the jurors vote, or that these post-verdict discussions will affect the jury deliberations by compromising their secrecy? Must the judge instruct the jurors that they have a right not to talk to the lawyers?

---

[10]In some cases, the judge encourages and asks the jurors to stay behind. In one case (unreported) the judge told the jurors that lawyer interviews of juries "are very helpful to educate the lawyers as to how to conduct similar litigation in the future. It will show them errors and strengths. I urge you to stay 15 minutes so that all of us can ask you some questions." In another instance (also unreported), the judge instructed the lawyers not to talk to the lawyers afterwards.

CHAPTER 3.6
TRIAL PUBLICITY

RULE 3.6: TRIAL PUBLICITY

(a) A lawyer who is participating or has participated in the investigation or litigation of a matter shall not make an extrajudicial statement that the lawyer knows or reasonably should know will be disseminated by means of public communication and will have a substantial likelihood of materially prejudicing an adjudicative proceeding in the matter.

(b) Notwithstanding paragraph (a), a lawyer may state:

(1) the claim, offense or defense involved and, except when prohibited by law, the identity of the persons involved;

(2) information contained in a public record;

(3) that an investigation of a matter is in progress;

(4) the scheduling or result of any step in litigation;

(5) a request for assistance in obtaining evidence and information necessary thereto;

(6) a warning of danger concerning the behavior of a person involved, when there is reason to believe that there exists the likelihood of substantial harm to an individual or to the public interest; and

(7) in a criminal case, in addition to subparagraphs (1) through (6):

(i) the identity, residence, occupation and family status of the accused;

(ii) if the accused has not been apprehended, information necessary to aid in apprehension of that person;

(iii) the fact, time and place of arrest; and

(iv) the identity of investigating and arresting officers or agencies and the length of the investigation.

(c) Notwithstanding paragraph (a), a lawyer may make a

841

statement that a reasonable lawyer would believe is required to protect a client from the substantial undue prejudicial effect of recent publicity not initiated by the lawyer or the lawyer's client. A statement made pursuant to this paragraph shall be limited to such information as is necessary to mitigate the recent adverse publicity.

(d) No lawyer associated in a firm or government agency with a lawyer subject to paragraph (a) shall make a statement prohibited by paragraph (a).

Comment

[1] It is difficult to strike a balance between protecting the right to a fair trial and safeguarding the right of free expression. Preserving the right to a fair trial necessarily entails some curtailment of the information that may be disseminated about a party prior to trial, particularly where trial by jury is involved. If there were no such limits, the result would be the practical nullification of the protective effect of the rules of forensic decorum and the exclusionary rules of evidence. On the other hand, there are vital social interests served by the free dissemination of information about events having legal consequences and about legal proceedings themselves. The public has a right to know about threats to its safety and measures aimed at assuring its security. It also has a legitimate interest in the conduct of judicial proceedings, particularly in matters of general public concern. Furthermore, the subject matter of legal proceedings is often of direct significance in debate and deliberation over questions of public policy.

[2] Special rules of confidentiality may validly govern proceedings in juvenile, domestic relations and mental disability proceedings, and perhaps other types of litigation. Rule 3.4(c) requires compliance with such rules.

[3] The Rule sets forth a basic general prohibition against a lawyer's making statements that the lawyer knows or should know will have a substantial likelihood of materially prejudicing an adjudicative proceeding. Recognizing that the public value of informed commentary is great and the likelihood of prejudice to a proceeding by the commentary of a lawyer who is not involved in the proceeding is small, the rule applies only to lawyers who are, or who have been involved in the investigation or litigation of a case, and their associates.

[4] Paragraph (b) identifies specific matters about which a lawyer's statements would not ordinarily be considered to present a substantial likelihood of material prejudice, and should not in any event be considered prohibited by the general prohibition of paragraph (a). Paragraph (b) is not intended to be an exhaustive listing of the subjects upon which a lawyer may make a statement, but statements on other matters may be subject to paragraph (a).

[5] There are, on the other hand, certain subjects that are more likely than not to have a material prejudicial effect on a proceeding, particularly when they refer to a civil matter triable to a jury, a criminal matter, or any other proceeding that could result in incarceration. These subjects relate to:

(1) the character, credibility, reputation or criminal record of a party, suspect in a criminal investigation or witness, or the identity of a witness, or the expected testimony of a party or witness;

(2) in a criminal case or proceeding that could result in incarceration, the possibility of a plea of guilty to the offense or the existence or contents of any confession, admission, or statement given by a defendant or suspect or that person's refusal or failure to make a statement;

(3) the performance or results of any examination or test or the refusal or failure of a person to submit to an examination or test, or the identity or nature of physical evidence expected to be presented;

(4) any opinion as to the guilt or innocence of a defendant or suspect in a criminal case or proceeding that could result in incarceration;

(5) information that the lawyer knows or reasonably should know is likely to be inadmissible as evidence in a trial and that would, if disclosed, create a substantial risk of prejudicing an impartial trial; or

(6) the fact that a defendant has been charged with a crime, unless there is included therein a statement explaining that the charge is merely an accusation and that the defendant is presumed innocent until and unless proven guilty.

[6] Another relevant factor in determining prejudice is the nature of the proceeding involved. Criminal jury trials will be most sensitive to extrajudicial speech. Civil trials may be less sensitive. Nonjury hearings and arbitration proceedings may be even less affected. The Rule will still place limitations on prejudicial comments in these cases, but the likelihood of prejudice may be different depending on the type of proceeding.

[7] Finally, extrajudicial statements that might otherwise raise a question under this Rule may be permissible when they are made in response to statements made publicly by another party, another party's lawyer, or third persons, where a reasonable lawyer would believe a public response is required in order to avoid prejudice to the lawyer's client. When prejudicial statements have been publicly made by others, responsive statements may have the salutary effect of lessening any resulting adverse impact on the adjudicative proceeding. Such responsive statements should be limited to contain only such information as is necessary to mitigate undue prejudice created by the statements made by others.

[8] See Rule 3.8(f) for additional duties of prosecutors in connection with extrajudicial statements about criminal proceedings.

Authors' 1983 Model Rules Comparison

In 1991, the Supreme Court in *Gentile v. State Bar of Nevada*, 501 U.S. 1030, 111 S.Ct. 2720, 115 L.Ed.2d 888 (1991), called into question the constitutionality of parts of the 1983 Model Rule 3.6. The opinion and the 1983 version of Rule 3.6 are discussed below. From 1991 to 1994, the ABA worked to draft an amendment that would conform to the *Gentile* decision. In August 1994, the ABA House of Delegates adopted a new Rule 3.6 with many new Comments and a new Model Code Comparison.

The drafters of the 2002 Model Rules made very few changes from the 1994 version of Rule 3.6. In Rule 3.6(a), the drafters clarified the standard regarding the state of mind of the lawyer who disseminates the public statement. They changed the standard from that of a "reasonable person" to a "reasonable lawyer." And, they changed the language on the state of mind of the lawyer from "would expect" to "knows or reasonably should know." *See* Reporter's Explanation of Changes to Model Rule 3.6.

Comments 1 to 7 are identical to the 1994 Rule 3.6.

Comment 8 is new and references Rule 3.8(f) as the standard applicable for prosecutors.

Model Code Comparison

Rule 3.6 is similar to DR 7-107, except as follows: First, Rule 3.6 adopts the general criteria of "substantial likelihood of materially prejudicing an adjudicative proceeding" to describe impermissible conduct. Second, Rule 3.6 transforms the particulars in DR 7-107 into an illustrative compilation that gives fair notice of conduct ordinarily posing unacceptable dangers to the fair administration of justice. Finally, Rule 3.6 omits DR 7-107(C)(7), which provided that a lawyer may reveal "[a]t the time of seizure, a description of the physical evidence seized, other than a confession, admission or statement." Such revelations may be substantially prejudicial and are frequently the subject of pretrial suppression motions, which, if successful, may be circumvented by prior disclosure to the press.

§ 3.6–1 TRIAL PUBLICITY, PRETRIAL PUBLICITY, AND THE LAWYER'S RIGHT TO COMMENT

The compatibility of a commitment to an "uninhibited, robust, and wide-open" discussion of public issues in a free press[1] with a commitment to a criminal process in which the "conclusions to be reached in a case will be induced only by evidence and argument in open court"[2] has been a subject of long standing debate.[3] The problem becomes more acute with the growth of national news coverage and the electronic media. The prominent issue within this area is the extent to which the disciplinary rules may insulate a courtroom from the intrusion of outside prejudice caused by publicity surrounding the case. The rights of the press often conflict with the rights of the accused.

The primary ethics rule is Rule 3.6. Like its predecessor, DR 7-107, Rule 3.6 attempts to balance the right of free speech with the right to a fair trial. Rule 3.6, after it was amended in response to *Gentile v. State Bar of Nevada*,[4] discussed immediately below, is more sympathetic to the First Amendment concerns.

[Section 3.6–1]

[1] *New York Times Co. v. Sullivan*, 376 U.S. 254, 84 S.Ct. 710, 11 L.Ed.2d 686 (1964).

See generally HARRY KALVEN, JR., ED. BY JAMIE KALVEN, A WORTHY TRADITION: FREEDOM OF SPEECH IN AMERICA 24–32 (Harper & Row, 1988).

[2] *Patterson v. Colorado*, 205 U.S. 454, 27 S.Ct. 556, 51 L.Ed. 879 (1907).

[3] See Chief Justice Burger's discussion of the history of this conflict in *Nebraska Press Association v. Stuart*, 427 U.S. 539, 547–51, 96 S.Ct. 2791, 2797–99, 49 L.Ed.2d 683 (1976).

[4] *Gentile v. State Bar of Nevada*, 501 U.S. 1030, 111 S.Ct. 2720, 115 L.Ed.2d 888 (1991).

See Ronald D. Rotunda, *Reporting Sensational Trials: Free Press, a Responsible Press, and Cameras in the Courts*, 3 COMMUNICATIONS LAW AND POLICY 295 (1998); 5 RONALD D. ROTUNDA & JOHN E. NOWAK, TREATISE ON CONSTITUTIONAL LAW: SUBSTANCE AND PROCEDURE § § 20.23 to 20.25 (Thomson- West, 4th ed. 2008) (6 vol-

§ 3.6–2 THE *GENTILE* DECISION

Any limits on a lawyer's right to comment raise serious questions regarding possible unconstitutional restrictions on the lawyer's First Amendment rights. Several courts have found various First Amendment problems with DR 7-107,[1] the predecessor to Rule 3.6.

A leading decision is *Gentile v. State Bar of Nevada*,[2] where a very fragmented Supreme Court held that a Nevada Supreme Court Rule governing a lawyer's pretrial statements about a case incorporated a standard that was consistent with the First Amendment, but was void for vagueness as interpreted.[3]

Attorney Gentile had held a press conference a few hours after Nevada had indicted his client. Gentile made a brief statement, mentioned generally his client's defense, and that he thought

---

umes).

[Section 3.6–2]

[1] *See Chicago Council of Lawyers v. Bauer*, 522 F.2d 242 (7th Cir.1975), *cert. denied sub nom.*, *Cunningham v. Chicago Council of Lawyers*, 427 U.S. 912, 96 S.Ct. 3201, 49 L.Ed.2d 1204 (1976); *Markfield v. Association of the Bar of City of New York*, 49 A.D.2d 516, 370 N.Y.S.2d 82 (1975), *appeal dismissed*, 37 N.Y.2d 794, 375 N.Y.S.2d 106, 337 N.E.2d 612 (1975); *Hirschkop v. Snead*, 594 F.2d 356 (4th Cir.1979) (per curiam).

[2] *Gentile v. State Bar of Nevada*, 501 U.S. 1030, 111 S.Ct. 2720, 115 L.Ed.2d 888 (1991).

[3] The Nevada Rule was almost identical to the original version of ABA Model Rule 3.6. The ABA amended Rule 3.6 on August 10, 1994 to respond to *Gentile v. Nevada State Bar*, 501 U.S. 1030, 111 S.Ct. 2720, 115 L.Ed.2d 888 (1991). In *Gentile*, the Nevada Supreme Court had ruled that certain conduct violated Rule 177(1), even though Rule 177(3) purported to provide a safe harbor from Rule 177(1). Nevada Supreme Court Rule 177 was based on ABA Model Rule 3.6. The U.S. Supreme Court held that the Nevada rule was unconstitutionally vague as interpreted.

The black letter rule of the *original version* of Model Rule 3.6 had read as follows:

RULE 3.6 Trial Publicity

(a) A lawyer shall not make an extrajudicial statement that a reasonable person would expect to be disseminated by means of public communication if the lawyer knows or reasonably should know that it will have a substantial likelihood of materially prejudicing an adjudicative proceeding.

(b) A statement referred to in paragraph (a) ordinarily is likely to have such an effect when it refers to a civil matter triable to a jury, a criminal matter, or any other proceeding that could result in incarceration, and the statement relates to:

(1) the character, credibility, reputation or criminal record of a party, suspect in a criminal investigation or witness, or the identity of a witness, or the expected testimony of a party or witness;

(2) in a criminal case or proceeding that could result in incarceration, the possibility of a plea of guilty to the offense or the existence or contents of any confession, admission, or statement given by a defendant or suspect or that person's refusal or failure to make a statement;

(3) the performance or results of any examination or test or the refusal or failure of a person to submit to an examination or test, or the identity or nature of physical evidence expected to be presented;

(4) any opinion as to the guilt or innocence of a defendant or suspect in a criminal case or proceeding that could result in incarceration;

that the police were upset. But he declined to answer reporters' questions seeking more detailed comments. Six months later, a jury acquitted Gentile's client of all counts. Then the State Bar of Nevada filed a complaint against Gentile for allegedly violating Nevada's Supreme Court Rule 177, governing pretrial publicity. That ethics rule was almost identical to the then current version of ABA Model Rule 3.6.[4] The Nevada Disciplinary Board recommended a private reprimand for Gentile and the State Supreme Court agreed. The U.S. Supreme Court reversed.[5]

---

(5) information the lawyer knows or reasonably should know is likely to be inadmissible as evidence in a trial and would if disclosed create a substantial risk of prejudicing an impartial trial; or

(6) the fact that a defendant has been charged with a crime, unless there is included therein a statement explaining that the charge is merely an accusation and that the defendant is presumed innocent until and unless proven guilty.

(c) Notwithstanding paragraph (a) and (b)(1–5), a lawyer involved in the investigation or litigation of a matter may state without elaboration:

(1) the general nature of the claim or defense;

(2) the information contained in a public record;

(3) that an investigation of the matter is in progress, including the general scope of the investigation, the offense or claim or defense involved and, except when prohibited by law, the identity of the persons involved;

(4) the scheduling or result of any step in litigation;

(5) a request for assistance in obtaining evidence and information necessary thereto;

(6) a warning of danger concerning the behavior of a person involved, when there is reason to believe that there exists the likelihood of substantial harm to an individual or to the public interest; and

(7) in a criminal case:

(i) the identity, residence, occupation and family status of the accused;

(ii) if the accused has not been apprehended, information necessary to aid in apprehension of that person;

(iii) the fact, time and place of arrest; and

(iv) the identity of investigating and arresting officers or agencies and the length of the investigation.

Comments [2] and [3] of the original Model Rule read as follows:

[2] No body of rules can simultaneously satisfy all interests of fair trial and all those of free expression. The formula in this Rule is based upon the ABA Model Code of Professional Responsibility and the ABA Standards Relating to Fair Trial and Free Press, as amended in 1978.

[3] Special rules of confidentiality may validly govern proceedings in juvenile, domestic relations and mental disability proceedings, and perhaps other types of litigation. Rule 3.4(c) requires compliance with such Rules.

[4]Reprinted in, THOMAS D. MORGAN & RONALD D. ROTUNDA, 1991 SELECTED STANDARDS ON PROFESSIONAL RESPONSIBILITY 71–72 (Foundation Press, 1991).

[5]Kennedy, J., announced the judgment of the Court, and delivered the opinion of the Court with respect to Parts III and VI. Marshall, Blackmun, Stevens, & O'Connor, JJ., joined that opinion. Kennedy, J. (joined by Marshall, Blackmun, & Stevens, JJ.) also delivered a separate opinion as to Parts I, II, IV, & V.

Rehnquist, C.J. delivered the opinion of the Court with respect to Parts I & II. White, O'Connor, Scalia, and Souter, JJ., joined that opinion. Rehnquist, C.J., also delivered a dissenting opinion with respect to Part

Different majorities of the Court supported each holding. Justice Kennedy, for the Court, concluded that the "notwithstanding" language [now found in Model Rule 3.6(b)] purported to create a safe harbor, listing statements that can be made (*e.g.*, the general nature of the claim or defense, information contained in a public record) without fear of discipline. Nevada's decision to discipline Gentile in spite of this purported safe harbor provision raised concerns of vagueness and selective enforcement. The Rule misled Gentile to believe that he could make statements on those issues at a press conference, even if he knew or reasonably should know that these statements would have a substantial likelihood of prejudicing an adjudicative proceeding.[6] The present version of Rule 3.6(b) does create a safe harbor and should avoid the problem that existed in *Gentile*.[7]

Part I of Justice Kennedy's separate opinion[8] emphasized that it was important to realize what this case was about:

> [O]ne central point must dominate the analysis: this case involves classic political speech. The State Bar of Nevada reprimanded petitioner for his assertion, supported by a brief sketch of his client's defense, that the State sought the indictment and conviction of an innocent man as a "scapegoat," and had not "been honest enough to indict the people who did it; the police department, crooked cops." At issue here is the constitutionality of a ban on political speech critical of the government and its officials.[9]

This central fact placed Gentile's speech squarely within the protections of the First Amendment.

§ 3.6-3 THE POST-*GENTILE* RULE 3.6

Rule 3.6—like its predecessor, DR 7-107—distinguishes between criminal and civil cases by providing a bit more restriction of speech in criminal cases.[1] Rule 3.6(a) adopts a general test restricting speech if the extrajudicial statement "will have a substantial likelihood of materially prejudicing an adjudicative

---

III; White, O'Connor, & Souter, JJ. joined that dissenting opinion. Finally, O'Connor, J., also filed a concurring opinion.

[6]*See* Ronald D. Rotunda, *Can You Say That?*, 30 TRIAL MAGAZINE 18 (Dec. 1994).

[7]Rule 3.6, Comment 4. *See also* Restatement of the Law Governing Lawyers, Third, § 109(1) (Official Draft 2000).

[8]Only Marshall, Blackmun, & Stevens, JJ., joined this part.

[9]501 U.S. at 1030, 111 S.Ct. at 2720 (Opinion of Kennedy, J., joined by Marshall, Blackmun, & Stevens, JJ.).

[Section 3.6-3]

[1]DR 7-107(F) also applies the restrictions of criminal cases to professional discipline proceedings and juvenile proceedings. However, the Model Code provided that none of the restrictions on trial publicity—whether in a civil or criminal case—apply if the lawyer is (1) replying to charges of misconduct publicly made against the lawyer or (2) participating in any proceeding of any legislative, administrative, or other investigative body. DR 7-107(I).

proceeding in the matter."[2] The Code had no such general test, though it at times used a test less protective of the free speech interests: "reasonably likely to interfere with a fair trial" or similar proceeding.[3]

There are several important differences between the Model Code and the Model Rule. In part, these differences reflect the change in First Amendment law, which has recognized the important free speech interests in commentary involving the criminal justice system. In other situations, the Model Rule reflects a belief that there is a lessened public interest justifying certain publicity.

For example, the Model Code specifically allowed the attorney to describe, at the time of seizure, physical evidence seized except for a confession, admission, or statement.[4] In contrast, Rule 3.6 does not allow such announcements, viewing them as "substantially prejudicial. . . ."[5] DR 7-107 stated specifically what attorneys may or may not publicly disclose.[6] Rule 3.6, in contrast, treats these specifics as illustrations of conduct that will usually meet the "substantial likelihood" test of Rule 3.6(a).

The drafters of the 2002 Rules changed the language and clarified the standard in Rule 3.6. First, the 2002 Rule now makes clear that one should judge the substantial likelihood of materially prejudicing the proceeding from the perspective of a reasonable lawyer not from the perspective a reasonable person, so that the perspective of the test changes from that of the recipient to that of the lawyer professional making the statement.[7] In addition, in order to past First Amendment scrutiny, the Rule must

---

[2]*See also* Restatement of the Law Governing Lawyers, Third, § 109(1) (Official Draft 2000).

[3]*See* DR 7-107(D), (F), (G)(5), & (H)(5).

[4]DR 7-107(C)(7).

[5]Rule 3.6, Code Comparison 1.

[6]DR 7-107(A) stated:

"DR. 7-107 Trial Publicity.

"(A) A lawyer participating in or associated with the investigation of a criminal matter shall not make or participate in making an extrajudicial statement that a reasonable person would expect to be disseminated by means of public communication and

that does more than state without elaboration:

"(1) Information contained in a public record.

"(2) That the investigation is in progress.

"(3) The general scope of the investigation including a description of the offense and, if permitted by law, the identity of the victim.

"(4) A request for assistance in apprehending a suspect or assistance in other matters and the information necessary thereto.

"(5) A warning to the public of any dangers."

[7]*See* Reporter's Explanation of Changes to Model Rule 3.6.

be interpreted to require that the statement in question "must be one reasonably likely to affect the outcome" of the proceeding.[8]

Second, the drafters of the 2002 Rule changed the scienter requirement from would "expect" to "knows or reasonably should know." This change is not intended to make a substantive difference; the drafters thought that the new language was more consistent with standards existing elsewhere in the Model Rules.[9]

Whether the case is civil or criminal, with or without a jury, it is important to remember that certain extrajudicial statements are allowed, including, for example, information contained in a public record, a request for assistance in obtaining evidence, a warning of the danger concerning an individual if there is reason to believe that there exists the likelihood of substantial harm, the scheduling or results of any steps in litigation, the general nature of the claim, the general scope of an investigation, the identity of the accused, and the identity of the arresting and investigating officers.[10]

Rule 3.6(c) adds a new right not found in the Model Code: a lawyer may make an extrajudicial statement that would otherwise be improper, if it is in response to statements by others, when a reasonable lawyer believes that the response is necessary to avoid prejudicing his client. These self-defense-type statements should be limited to information that is necessary to mitigate any undue prejudice created by the statements that others have made. In a sense, the lawyer can fight fire with fire, by using his free speech rights to counteract negative publicity about his client.

Rule 3.8(f) added in 1994 along with the revision of Rule 3.6 specifically warns prosecutors to refrain from making any

---

[8]*Iowa Supreme Court Board of Professional Ethics and Conduct v. Visser*, 629 N.W.2d 376, 381 (2001). The Grievance Commission found that the lawyer's statement to a newspaper reporter violated an Iowa disciplinary rule that prohibited a lawyer who was involved in civil litigation from making extrajudicial statements; it recommended a public reprimand. The Iowa Supreme Court held, in light of First Amendment rights, that it must interpret the disciplinary rule had to require that the statement as issue must be reasonably likely to affect the fairness of the proceeding. Then the court found no violation of this rule as interpreted. However, it did admonish the lawyer for violating another rule prohibiting misleading statements.

[9]*See* Reporter's Explanation of Changes to Model Rule 3.6.

[10]Rule 3.6(b); DR 7-107(B), (G). *See also* Restatement of the Law Governing Lawyers, Third, § 169(1) (Tent. Draft No. 8, Mar. 21, 1997); Restatement of the Law Governing Lawyers, Third, § 190(1) (Official Draft 2000).

See Ronald D. Rotunda, *Dealing with the Media: Ethical, Constitutional, and Practical Parameters*, 84 ILL. STATE BAR JOURNAL 614 (Dec. 1996), discussing these issues in more detail; Ronald D. Rotunda, *Reporting Sensational Trials: Free Press, a Responsible Press, and Cameras in the Courts*, 3 COMMUNICATIONS LAW AND POLICY 295 (No. 2, Spring, 1998).

extrajudicial comments that serve no legitimate law enforcement purpose and have a substantial likelihood of heightening public opprobrium of the accused.[11] Prosecutors are "clearly in a different position than that of defense counsel in this regard. We must not prejudice the defendant by seeking improper publicity in a case and in fact, we must prevent others from doing so as well, even though the audience of the media is our 'client.' "[12]

---

[11]On the constitutional issues, see 5 RONALD D. ROTUNDA & JOHN E. NOWAK, TREATISE ON CONSTITUTIONAL LAW: SUBSTANCE AND PROCEDURE § 20.25 (Thomson- West, 4th ed. 2008) (6 volumes). *See also* Ronald D.Rotunda, *Independent Counsel and the Charges of Leaking: A Brief Case Study*, 68 FORDHAM LAW REVIEW 869 (1999).

[12]Maria Collins Warren, *Ethical Prosecution: A Philosophical Field Guide*, 41 WASHBURN L.J. 269, 273 (2002)(footnote omitted, citing Model Rule 3.6). *See also* Restatement of the Law Governing Lawyers, Third, § 109(2), *An Advocate's Public Comment on Pending Litigation* (Official Draft 2000).

CHAPTER 3.7
LAWYER AS WITNESS

RULE 3.7: LAWYER AS WITNESS

(a) A lawyer shall not act as advocate at a trial in which the lawyer is likely to be a necessary witness unless:

(1) the testimony relates to an uncontested issue;

(2) the testimony relates to the nature and value of legal services rendered in the case; or

(3) disqualification of the lawyer would work substantial hardship on the client.

(b) A lawyer may act as advocate in a trial in which another lawyer in the lawyer's firm is likely to be called as a witness unless precluded from doing so by Rule 1.7 or Rule 1.9.

Comment

[1] Combining the roles of advocate and witness can prejudice the tribunal and the opposing party and can also involve a conflict of interest between the lawyer and client.

Advocate-Witness Rule

[2] The tribunal has proper objection when the trier of fact may be confused or misled by a lawyer serving as both advocate and witness. The opposing party has proper objection where the combination of roles may prejudice that party's rights in the litigation. A witness is required to testify on the basis of personal knowledge, while an advocate is expected to explain and comment on evidence given by others. It may not be clear whether a statement by an advocate-witness should be taken as proof or as an analysis of the proof.

[3] To protect the tribunal, paragraph (a) prohibits a lawyer from simultaneously serving as advocate and necessary witness except in those circumstances specified in paragraphs (a)(1) through (a)(3). Paragraph (a)(1) recognizes that if the testimony will be uncontested, the ambiguities in the dual role are purely theoretical. Paragraph (a)(2) recognizes that where the testimony concerns the extent and value of legal services rendered in the action in which

851

the testimony is offered, permitting the lawyers to testify avoids the need for a second trial with new counsel to resolve that issue. Moreover, in such a situation the judge has firsthand knowledge of the matter in issue; hence, there is less dependence on the adversary process to test the credibility of the testimony.

[4] Apart from these two exceptions, paragraph (a)(3) recognizes that a balancing is required between the interests of the client and those of the tribunal and the opposing party. Whether the tribunal is likely to be misled or the opposing party is likely to suffer prejudice depends on the nature of the case, the importance and probable tenor of the lawyer's testimony, and the probability that the lawyer's testimony will conflict with that of other witnesses. Even if there is risk of such prejudice, in determining whether the lawyer should be disqualified, due regard must be given to the effect of disqualification on the lawyer's client. It is relevant that one or both parties could reasonably foresee that the lawyer would probably be a witness. The conflict of interest principles stated in Rules 1.7, 1.9 and 1.10 have no application to this aspect of the problem.

[5] Because the tribunal is not likely to be misled when a lawyer acts as advocate in a trial in which another lawyer in the lawyer's firm will testify as a necessary witness, paragraph (b) permits the lawyer to do so except in situations involving a conflict of interest.

Conflict of Interest

[6] In determining if it is permissible to act as advocate in a trial in which the lawyer will be a necessary witness, the lawyer must also consider that the dual role may give rise to a conflict of interest that will require compliance with Rules 1.7 or 1.9. For example, if there is likely to be substantial conflict between the testimony of the client and that of the lawyer the representation involves a conflict of interest that requires compliance with Rule 1.7. This would be true even though the lawyer might not be prohibited by paragraph (a) from simultaneously serving as advocate and witness because the lawyer's disqualification would work a substantial hardship on the client. Similarly, a lawyer who might be permitted to simultaneously serve as an advocate and a witness by paragraph (a)(3) might be precluded from doing so by Rule 1.9. The problem can arise whether the lawyer is called as a witness on behalf of the client or is called by the opposing party. Determining whether or not such a conflict exists is primarily the responsibility of the lawyer involved. If there is a conflict of interest, the lawyer must secure the client's informed consent, confirmed in writing. In some cases, the lawyer will be precluded from seeking the client's consent. See Rule 1.7. See Rule 1.0(b) for the definition of "confirmed in writing" and Rule 1.0(e) for the definition of "informed consent."

[7] Paragraph (b) provides that a lawyer is not disqualified from serving as an advocate because a lawyer with whom the lawyer is associated in a firm is precluded from doing so by paragraph (a). If, however, the testifying lawyer would also be disqualified by Rule 1.7 or Rule 1.9 from representing the client in the matter, other lawyers in the firm will be precluded from representing the client by Rule 1.10 unless the client gives informed consent under the conditions stated in Rule 1.7.

Authors' 1983 Model Rules Comparison

The drafters the 2002 Rules made one stylistic change to the text of the 1983 version of Rule 3.7. They substituted the word, "unless" for the words, "except where" as the introductory language to the exceptions to the Rule.

In Comment 1, the drafters added a reference to tribunals as another effect of the prejudice of the confusion of advocate and witness.

Comments 2, 3, and 4 have been amended to include references to the tribunal. The first lines of Comments 2 and 3 are new and refer to the tribunal's interest in enforcing the Rule. In Comment 4, the first two sentences were amended to include references to the tribunal's interests. The last line in Comment 4 has been modified to clarify the relationship between the general conflicts of interest provisions and the basic advocate witness problem.

Comment 5 is new and provides another justification why normally the firm is not disqualified from representing the client when one of its lawyers is a likely witness.

The drafters renumbered old Comment 5 as new Comment 6 and substantially modified the language to clarify the situations where the testimony of the witness may create a conflict with the representation of the client. *See* Reporter's Explanation of Changes to Model Rule 3.7.

Comment 7 is new and it examines the scope of imputed disqualification in application of this Rule.

Model Code Comparison

[1] DR 5-102(A) prohibited a lawyer, or the lawyer's firm, from serving as advocate if the lawyer "learns or it is obvious that he or a lawyer in his firm ought to be called as a witness on behalf of his client." DR 5-102(B) provided that a lawyer, and the lawyer's firm, may continue representation if the "lawyer learns or it is obvious that he or a lawyer in his firm may be called as a witness other than on behalf of his client . . . until it is apparent that his testimony is or may be prejudicial to his client." DR 5-101(B) permitted a lawyer to testify while representing a client: "(1) If the testimony will relate solely to an uncontested matter; (2) If the testimony will relate solely to a matter of formality and there is no reason to believe that substantial evidence will be offered in opposition to the testimony; (3) If the testimony will relate solely to the nature and value of legal services rendered in the case by the lawyer or his firm to the client; (4) As to any matter if refusal would work a substantial hardship on the client because of the distinctive value of the lawyer or his firm as counsel in the particular case."

[2] The exception stated in paragraph (a)(1) consolidates provisions of DR 5-101(B)(1) and (2). Testimony relating to a formality, referred to in DR 5-101(B)(2), in effect defines the phrase "uncontested issue," and is redundant.

§ 3.7–1 THE ADVOCATE AS WITNESS

§ 3.7–1(a) Policies Underlying the Rule

Both the Model Code and the Model Rules regulate when an advocate may simultaneously act as a witness. The Model Rules, like the Model Code, treat the case where the advocate is asked to be a witness as an instance of conflict of interests.[1]

The primary rationale supporting Rule 3.7 is that the fact-finder may be confused if the person actually acting as an advocate before the fact-finder also offers testimony with his or her argument: "It may not be clear whether a statement by an advocate-witness should be taken as proof or as an analysis of the proof."[2] The jury may be confused if the advocate gets up from counsel's chair, sits in the witness box, and later addresses the jury in closing argument. This reason implicates the quality of the judicial proceeding and therefore involves potential direct harm to the tribunal.[3]

The real rationale for the advocate-witness rule is that there is a danger of confusing the fact-finder. That rationale does not apply in a bench trial. In other words, if the fact-finder is a judge and not a jury, there is less change of confusion by the fact-finder. In bench trials, judges have broader leeway in allowing hearsay evidence because we expect the judge to be able to discount the evidence. That same rationale applies to the situation where the lawyer offers testimony in a bench trial. The lawyer's dual role as advocate and witness should not confuse the judge, who may allow the testimony.[4]

This point is valid, but that is what happens when someone represents himself *pro se*. The advocate-witness rule would not prevent a *pro se* litigant (even a lawyer who represents himself

---

[Section 3.7–1]

[1]The Code places the relevant rules in Canon 5, the conflicts Canon—DR 5-101(B). Both DR 5-102 and the Rules specifically refer to the problem as a "conflict of interest." Rule 3.7, Comment 1.

See also Restatement of the Law Governing Lawyers, Third, § 108 (Official Draft 2000).

[2]Rule 3.7, Comment 2.

[3]The drafters of the 2002 Rules modified the Comments to this Rule to emphasize the strength of the tribunal's interests in enforcing the Rule. One could also argue that the tribunal has an incentive to prevent a fact witness from being exposed to the types of zealous advocacy that litigators engage in to prepare themselves for trial. In other words, a lawyer witness may subconsciously alter his or her recollection of events if they are responsible for preparing the case at trial.

[4]Courts, without discussion, do not focus on this distinction, or, they allow the judge to exclude the testimony in his discretion. *Spivey v. United States*, 912 F.2d 80, 84 (4th Cir.1990) (lawyer's "in limine" affidavit submitted after bench trial was improper for various reasons, including the advocate-witness rule). Mt. Rushmore Broadcasting, Inc. v. Statewide Collections 42 P.3d 478, 479 (Wyo. 2002): "Jan Charles Gray (Gray), the sole shareholder, director and officer of Mt. Rushmore, is an active member of the Wyoming State Bar and represented Mt. Rushmore during the bench trial at the district court. Mt. Rushmore challenges the district court's refusal to allow Gray to testify based on Rule 3.7 of the Wyoming Rules of Professional Conduct. We find no abuse of discretion and affirm the district court's decision."

pro se) from testifying and representing himself. Rule 3.7 does not try to accomplish the impossible. It simply seeks to eliminate unnecessary confusion imposed on the fact-finder by requiring that the trial advocate and the witness not be the same person if that is reasonably possible. Indeed, one of the specific subsections of Rule 3.7 provides an important exception of the advocate-witness rule—when disqualification of the lawyer "would work substantial hardship on the client."[5]

A second policy reason underlying Rule 3.7 involves the right of the opposing counsel not to deal with a witness that is also an advocate. Litigators deal with opposing witnesses in a variety of ways. They may choose to minimize their testimony or may choose to impeach their testimony at deposition or trial. When an opposing witness is also an advocate, the cross examining lawyer may feel constrained from impeaching the witness if the lawyer doing the questioning believes that the jury has developed warm feelings towards an advocate. Some people believe that, in such a case, the opposing counsel may be injured by attacking the testifying lawyer or by foregoing an aggressive style of cross examination. Hence, some lawyers argue that just the fact that opposing counsel may face a witness that the jury has seen as an advocate is a source of potential prejudice to the lawyer's client.

Others argue that the lawyer-witness who has developed a friendly rapport with the jury is no different than any other witness who has developed a friendly empathy with the trier of fact. The lawyer who is cross-examining that kind of charismatic witness may also feel that he or she must forego an aggressive style of cross examination. If a witness, whether or not a party, has developed a good rapport with the jury, there is nothing special about the fact that the witness is also an advocate.

While Litigant #1 may wish to use the advocate-witness rule to prevent the lawyer for Litigant #2 from appearing as an advocate, the law of ethics does not always grant Litigant #2's request, because another principle tells us that, unless there is a good reason to the contrary, the client (Litigant #2) should be free to choose counsel of his or her choice.

The advocate-witness rule does not create immunity from testifying; it is a limitation on who can be an advocate. It is not a rule of evidence but a rule of ethics grounded in the notion that there is sometimes a systemic interest—an interest in the system of justice focussed on confusion of the trier of fact—that requires the lawyer not to be both the advocate in court and the witness at the same time. If the advocate-witness rule applies, the lawyer still provides the testimony, but that lawyer must withdraw from being an advocate.

---

[5]Rule 3.7(a)(3).

The Rule basically provides that the advocate should withdraw if she is "likely to be called as a necessary witness" unless the testimony relates to an uncontested issue, or it relates to the nature and value of legal services in that case, or disqualification would work a "substantial hardship on the client."[6] The lawyer should not accept employment if she "ought to be called as witness" unless one of these exceptions is applicable.[7]

§ 3.7–1(b) Exceptions to the Rule

Rule 3.7 provides three exceptions to the advocate witness rule. In other words, a lawyer may serve as an advocate and a witness in three limited circumstances.

First, a lawyer may represent a client in litigation when the lawyer's testimony relates to an uncontested issue. When the testimony relates to an uncontested issue, none of the policies against allowing a lawyer to occupy a dual role underlying Rule 3.7 are present. Comment 3 more aptly states that, when the testimony is uncontested, "the ambiguities in the dual role are theoretical."[8] Further, in many cases in court, counsel stipulate to the admission of evidence that is uncontested and therefore the lawyer will never need to take the witness stand as a sworn witness.

Second, a lawyer may be an advocate and a witness when the lawyer's testimony relates "to the nature and value of the legal services rendered in the case . . . ."[9] In many litigation matters, the prevailing party is entitled to legal fees from the opposing side under authority of statute or contract. When the merits of the case are over, if the result triggers the recovery of legal fees and after a motion is filed, the judge schedules a briefing and hearing schedule for the court's determination of appropriate fees. One could argue that the lawyers who tried the case on the merits should step aside and allow other lawyers to represent the client in the attorneys' fees phase of the litigation. Such a rule, however, would necessitate a second trial in many cases[10] and significant delay. There is also a question whether on the issue of fees, other lawyers in the advocate's firm could represent the client because such lawyers inevitably share fees in the law firm

---

[6]Rule 3.7(a)(1), (2), (3); DR 5-102(A). *See generally* Douglas R. Richmond, *Lawyers as Witnesses*, 36 NEW MEXICO L. REV. 47 (2006) (analyzing the operation of Model Rule 3.7).

[7]DR 5-101(B).

The Code also has a special, additional rule, which provides that if a lawyer, after accepting the case, is called as a witness "other than on behalf of the client," then the lawyer need not withdraw "until it is apparent" that the testimony may be "prejudicial" to the client. DR 5-102(B).

[8]Rule 3.7, Comment 3.

[9]Rule 3.7(a)(2).

[10]Rule 3.7, Comment 3 (stating that this exception avoids the need for a second trial).

partnership. Therefore, for the sake of efficiency and the fact that the concerns of the advocate witness rule are not usually present in a dispute over fees, Rule 3.7 does not require disqualification of the lawyers who will testify about the fees earned in the case on the merits.[11]

Rule 3.7 provides an exception for situations where disqualification of the advocate witness would present a substantial hardship on the client. An exception based upon hardship to the client is based upon equitable principles for relief to a strict rule of disqualification. It requires a balancing of interests between the policies underlying the Rule, including the effect on the tribunal with the hardship placed upon the client when the lawyer is disqualified.[12]

Clearly, the substantial hardship exception needs to be interpreted very narrowly or else it would eliminate the general rule. It does not apply when a client foresees that a lawyer will be a necessary witness but simply wishes to consent to have the lawyer as an advocate and a witness. One source of hardship focuses on the value or need of this particular lawyer to be the advocate in this case.[13] For example, if a lawyer had represented a defense contractor client in contracts with the government, and such contracts involved security clearances, one could possibly see an argument to allow this lawyer occupy both roles. A second source of hardship would focus on the timing of the opposing party's desire to depose the client's lawyer as a witness.[14]

§ 3.7–2 IMPUTATION TO OTHER LAWYERS IN THE FIRM

The Model Code, without discussing the imputation question, explicitly imputed the advocate-witness disqualification to all lawyers in the firm.[1] However, given the rationale of the rule, the

---

[11]Many, but not all, hearings regarding attorneys' fees are heard by a judge not a jury. In this case, the exception makes more sense. When the attorneys' fees issue is heard by a jury, the jury has already decided the merits and in most cases turns to a decision on the reasonableness of fees to be awarded.

[12]See *D.J. Investment Group LLC v. DAE/Westbrook LLC*, 147 P.3d 414 (Utah 2006), *noted in* 22 ABA/BNA MANUAL ON PROFESSIONAL CONDUCT, Current Reports News 578 (Nov. 29, 2006) (holding that the substantial hardship determination requires a

balancing between the interests of the lawyer's client with those of the opposing party and the tribunal).

Sternberg, J., in *People v. Pasillas-Sanchez*, 214 P.3d 520, 2009 WL 706883, *5 (Colo. App. 2009), citing Treatise.

[13]DR 5-101 focused its hardship exception on distinctive value to the client.

[14]*Murray v. Metropolitan Life Ins. Co.*, 583 F. 3d 173, 178–79 (2d Cir. 2009).

[Section 3.7–2]

[1]DR 5-101(B); DR 5-102(A), (B).

Model Rules do not impute the advocate-witness prohibition.[2] The reason for this change is apparent once one looks at the reason for the initial disqualification. The Code, in seeking to justify the disqualification of the lawyer-witness, offered various inconsistent rationales. Lawyers were told that the restrictions on the testifying advocate should exist because, *e.g.*, such an advocate may be "more easily impeachable for interest." At the same time that they were told that the lawyer-witness should be disqualified because "the opposing counsel may be handicapped in challenging the credibility of the lawyer . . . ."[3] These rationales, although presented simultaneously, cannot both be true for they are inconsistent with each other. Thus, where the witness is a partner of another lawyer who is the advocate, there is no automatic imputation because there is no realistic danger of confusing the fact-finder. The same person will not be testifying and then arguing the significance of that testimony to the jury.[4] One additional reason for allowing the firm to represent the client when a lawyer in the firm is likely to be a necessary witness is the preservation of client choice in hiring a law firm. Although the specific lawyer is disqualified, the client can use the resources of the firm and more easily involve the disqualified lawyer in the preparation of the matter.

Rule 3.7(b) states that a lawyer may represent the client when "another lawyer in the lawyer's firm is likely to be called as a witness unless precluded from doing so by Rule 1.7 or Rule 1.9." Lawyers have obligations to present clients under Rule 1.7 and former clients under 1.9. Before the lawyer may accept the matter, the lawyer must determine whether such conflicts rules are implicated in the representation and override Rule 3.7(b). One possible source of conflict would involve the substance of the testifying lawyer's statement. If the lawyer will testify against interests of the client, the litigator, another lawyer in the firm, has a present client conflict of interest. If the law firm may have been negligent in handling the matter for the client, a conflict also exists. It is the obligation of the lawyer to determine whether such conflicts exist and to comply with the applicable rules.[5]

Courts are very reluctant to disqualify a law firm because a particular lawyer is personally disqualified by the advocate-witness rule. The court will not disqualify a law firm by imputation unless the moving party "proves by clear and convincing evidence that [A] the witness will provide testimony prejudicial to

---

[2]Rule 3.7(b).   F.Supp. 350, 363 (N.D.Ill.1984).
[3]EC 5-9.   [5]Rule 3.7, Comment 6.
[4]*See Jones v. City of Chicago*, 610

the client, and [B] the integrity of the judicial system will suffer as a result."[6]

§ 3.7–3 WAIVER BY CLIENT OR OPPOSING COUNSEL

Given this rationale of confusion of the fact-finder—an interest of the judicial system rather than an interest of the client—nothing in either the Code or the Rules provides for client or opposing counsel waiver of the advocate-witness rule.[1] In other words, if it is confusing to the trier of fact if the advocate also testifies, it the does not solve this problem if the client "waives" the conflict. If the only purpose of this rule is to protect the client, then the client can waive its protection. But if the purpose of the rule is to protect the fact-finder or the system of justice, waiver makes no sense. The client cannot waive the rights of the fact-finder.

The party represented by the advocate-witness may seek to "waive" the disqualification because the client wants jury confusion. Or, the client may seek to waive or consent to the advocate witness because of bad advice from the lawyer who desires to remain in the case as a litigator. Or the attorney for the other side may avoid pressing for disqualification out of a desire to avoid clashing with opposing counsel or to obtain tactical advantages. None of these reasons implicate the rationale of the Rule and thus none justify waiver. Accordingly, in cases where neither party moves for disqualification, the court should act *sua sponte*.[2]

---

[6]*Murray v. Metropolitan Life Ins. Co.*, 583 F.3d 173, 178-79 (2d Cir. 2009). The court reversed the trial judge. In this class action, the plaintiffs were policyholders of Metropolitan Life Insurance Company when it was a mutual insurance company. Plaintiffs alleged that they were misled and shortchanged in the transaction that demutualized the company in 2000. "Nine years after the action was commenced and five weeks before trial was scheduled to begin, plaintiffs moved to disqualify the lead counsel for Metropolitan Life Insurance Company and MetLife, Inc. ('MetLife'), Debevoise & Plimpton LLP ('Debevoise'). The grounds alleged related to that firm's representation of MetLife in the underlying demutualization." 583 F.3d 173, 174.

"In this case, four Debevoise lawyers are likely to be called to testify at trial. Three of them are transac-

tional lawyers who are not and will not be trial advocates; the fourth, a litigator, is a member of the trial team, but will not act as an advocate before the jury. None of these witnesses, then, is properly considered trial counsel for purposes of Rule 3.7(a)." 583 F.3d 173, 178-79.

[Section 3.7–3]

[1]*See, e.g., Supreme Beef Processors, Inc. v. American Consumer Industries, Inc.*, 441 F.Supp. 1064, 1068 (N.D.Tex.1977); *Draganescu v. First National Bank of Hollywood*, 502 F.2d 550, 552 (5th Cir.1974). The California Rules of Professional Conduct, surprisingly, do provide for client waiver, though it does not explain why a waiver would be appropriate. California Rule 5-210(C).

[2]*MacArthur v. Bank of New York*, 524 F.Supp. 1205, 1209 (S.D.N.Y. 1981).

§ 3.7–4 SCOPE OF THE DISQUALIFICATION OF THE ADVOCATE WITNESS

If the advocate-witness rule requires a lawyer to be disqualified, then the disqualified lawyer may consult with the party's substitute counsel and assist in preparing for trial.[1] None of the reasons offered for the advocate-witness rule (confusion of fact-finder, difficulty of challenging credibility of advocate-witness, etc.) justify prohibiting the disqualified advocate-witness from consulting with the new lawyer (or with other lawyers in his firm, if the other lawyers become the trial counsel). For example, the disqualified lawyer will not divulge any forbidden confidences or other improper information to the new lawyer, because the lawyer-witness was not disqualified for that reason; nor will the lawyer-witness, who is no longer a lawyer-advocate, be able to confuse the fact-finder.

Even though the disqualified lawyer may participate in the litigation counsel's preparation of the case, the litigator—i.e., the advocate who is actually conducting the trial—should be careful not to undermine the credibility of the testimony of his client's lawyer (the one who is disqualified from being an advocate.). This caveat applies to all the witnesses that the lawyer calls.

§ 3.7–5 JUDICIAL ENFORCEMENT OF THE ADVOCATE WITNESS RULE

Many ethical restrictions are enforced primarily in the course of legal discipline. Not so with the advocate-witness rule. Courts routinely enforce the advocate-witness rule in the course of litigation by disallowing the witness to also act as the trial lawyer.[1] This enforcement is proper, because a violation of the advocate-witness rule infects the truth-finding process by confusing the fact-finder, whether judge or jury.[2] Because judges have an obligation to preside over a fair proceeding, one of the main policies underlying the Rule is to limit the confusion that results when a lawyer occupies a dual role.

Some courts have been concerned about the use of this Rule for

---

[Section 3.7–4]

[1]*MacArthur v. Bank of New York*, 524 F.Supp. 1205, 1211 n. 3 (S.D.N.Y. 1981); *Jones v. Chicago*, 610 F.Supp. 350, 363 (N.D.Ill.1984).

[Section 3.7–5]

[1]*See, e.g., Weil v. Weil*, 283 App.Div. 33, 35, 125 N.Y.S.2d 368, 370 (1953) (new trial granted because of violation of advocate-witness rule);

Supreme Beef Processors, Inc. v. American Consumer Industries, Inc., 441 F.Supp. 1064, 1069 (N.D.Tex.1977) (judgment vacated because of violation of advocate-witness rule); *MacArthur v. Bank of New York*, 524 F.Supp. 1205 (S.D.N.Y.1981) (mistrial because of violation of advocate-witness rule).

[2]Ronald D. Rotunda, *Learning the Law of Lawyering*, 136 U. PENN. L. REV. 1761, 1766–67 (1988).

tactical advantage.[3] An opposing party may call the client's lawyer as a witness at the eleventh hour before trial. In some cases, such late efforts to call a witness require court permission and the court may inquire into the need to call the lawyer as a witness. In the cases, when the court perceives that an opposing party seeks to use Rule 3.8 to impose a burden on the client of the lawyer witness, the court may require that the party moving to disqualify counsel show actual prejudice.[4] In many cases, it will be obvious that a lawyer involved in the proceeding will be a necessary witness and thus apply Rule 3.8 early in the litigation. However, in some cases, courts will need to weigh the application Rule 3.7 in the facts and circumstances presented.

To prevent litigants from imposing unnecessary costs of the opposing party, the courts will requiring the moving party to establish that the lawyer's testimony will cause substantial prejudice and harm the integrity of the judicial system.[5] "Prejudice" means testimony that is "sufficiently adverse to the factual assertions or account of events offered on behalf of the client, such that the bar or the client might have an interest in the lawyer's independence in discrediting that testimony."[6]

---

[3]See ABA CENTER FOR PROFESSIONAL RESPONSIBILITY, ANNOTATED MODEL RULES OF PROFESSIONAL CONDUCT 386–87 (ABA, 5th ed. 2003).

[4]See, e.g., Zurich Insurance Co. v. Knotts, 52 S.W.3d 555 (Ky.2001). Some states, such as Texas, have modified the language and comments of Rule 3.8 to remove the strategic edge to the remedy of disqualification. See Texas Disciplinary Rule 3.08.

[5]Lamborn v. Dittmer, 873 F.2d 522, 531 (2d Cir. 1989).

[6]Lamborn v. Dittmer, 873 F.2d 522, 531 (2d Cir. 1989); Murray v. Metropolitan Life Ins. Co., 583 F.3d 173, 178 (2d Cir. 2009).

CHAPTER 3.8
SPECIAL RESPONSIBILITIES OF A PROSECUTOR

RULE 3.8: SPECIAL RESPONSIBILITIES OF A PROSECUTOR

The prosecutor in a criminal case shall:

(a) refrain from prosecuting a charge that the prosecutor knows is not supported by probable cause;

(b) make reasonable efforts to assure that the accused has been advised of the right to, and the procedure for obtaining, counsel and has been given reasonable opportunity to obtain counsel;

(c) not seek to obtain from an unrepresented accused a waiver of important pretrial rights, such as the right to a preliminary hearing;

(d) make timely disclosure to the defense of all evidence or information known to the prosecutor that tends to negate the guilt of the accused or mitigates the offense, and, in connection with sentencing, disclose to the defense and to the tribunal all unprivileged mitigating information known to the prosecutor, except when the prosecutor is relieved of this responsibility by a protective order of the tribunal;

(e) not subpoena a lawyer in a grand jury or other criminal proceeding to present evidence about a past or present client unless the prosecutor reasonably believes:

(1) the information sought is not protected from disclosure by any applicable privilege;

(2) the evidence sought is essential to the successful completion of an ongoing investigation or prosecution; and

(3) there is no other feasible alternative to obtain the information;

(f) except for statements that are necessary to inform the public of the nature and extent of the prosecutor's action and that serve a legitimate law enforcement purpose, refrain from making extrajudicial comments that have a substantial likelihood of heightening public condemnation of the accused and exercise reasonable care to prevent investigators, law enforcement personnel, employees or other persons assisting or associated with the prosecutor in a criminal case from making an extrajudicial statement that the prosecutor would be prohibited from making under Rule 3.6 or this Rule.

(g) When a prosecutor knows of new, credible and material evidence creating a reasonable likelihood that a convicted defendant did not commit an offense of which the defendant was convicted, the prosecutor shall:

(1) promptly disclose that evidence to an appropriate court or authority, and

(2) if the conviction was obtained in the prosecutor's jurisdiction,

(i) promptly disclose that evidence to the defendant unless a court authorizes delay, and

(ii) undertake further investigation, or make reasonable efforts to cause an investigation, to determine whether the defendant was convicted of an offense that the defendant did not commit.

(h) When a prosecutor knows of clear and convincing evidence establishing that a defendant in the prosecutor's jurisdiction was convicted of an offense that the defendant did not commit, the prosecutor shall seek to remedy the conviction.

Comment

[1] A prosecutor has the responsibility of a minister of justice and not simply that of an advocate. This responsibility carries with it specific obligations to see that the defendant is accorded procedural justice, that guilt is decided upon the basis of sufficient evidence, and that special precautions are taken to prevent and to rectify the conviction of innocent persons. The extent of mandated remedial action is a matter of debate and varies in different jurisdictions. Many jurisdictions have adopted the ABA Standards of Criminal Justice Relating to the Prosecution Function, which are the product of prolonged and careful deliberation by lawyers experienced in both criminal prosecution and defense. Competent representation of the sovereignty may require a prosecutor to undertake some procedural and remedial measures as a matter of obligation. Applicable law may require other measures by the prosecutor and knowing disregard of those obligations or a systematic abuse of prosecutorial discretion could constitute a violation of Rule 8.4.

[2] In some jurisdictions, a defendant may waive a preliminary

hearing and thereby lose a valuable opportunity to challenge probable cause. Accordingly, prosecutors should not seek to obtain waivers of preliminary hearings or other important pretrial rights from
unrepresented accused persons. Paragraph (c) does not apply,
however, to an accused appearing *pro se* with the approval of the
tribunal. Nor does it forbid the lawful questioning of an uncharged
suspect who has knowingly waived the rights to counsel and silence.

[3] The exception in paragraph (d) recognizes that a prosecutor may
seek an appropriate protective order from the tribunal if disclosure
of information to the defense could result in substantial harm to an
individual or to the public interest.

[4] Paragraph (e) is intended to limit the issuance of lawyer
subpoenas in grand jury and other criminal proceedings to those
situations in which there is a genuine need to intrude into the
client-lawyer relationship.

[5] Paragraph (f) supplements Rule 3.6, which prohibits extrajudicial statements that have a substantial likelihood of prejudicing an
adjudicatory proceeding. In the context of a criminal prosecution, a
prosecutor's extrajudicial statement can create the additional
problem of increasing public condemnation of the accused. Although
the announcement of an indictment, for example, will necessarily
have severe consequences for the accused, a prosecutor can, and
should, avoid comments which have no legitimate law enforcement
purpose and have a substantial likelihood of increasing public opprobrium of the accused. Nothing in this Comment is intended to
restrict the statements which a prosecutor may make which comply
with Rule 3.6(b) or 3.6(c).

[6] Like other lawyers, prosecutors are subject to Rules 5.1 and 5.3,
which relate to responsibilities regarding lawyers and nonlawyers
who work for or are associated with the lawyer's office. Paragraph
(f) reminds the prosecutor of the importance of these obligations in
connection with the unique dangers of improper extrajudicial statements in a criminal case. In addition, paragraph (f) requires a
prosecutor to exercise reasonable care to prevent persons assisting
or associated with the prosecutor from making improper extrajudicial statements, even when such persons are not under the direct
supervision of the prosecutor. Ordinarily, the reasonable care standard will be satisfied if the prosecutor issues the appropriate cautions to law-enforcement personnel and other relevant individuals.

[7] When a prosecutor knows of new, credible and material evidence creating a reasonable likelihood that a person outside the
prosecutor's jurisdiction was convicted of a crime that the person
did not commit, paragraph (g) requires prompt disclosure to the
court or other appropriate authority, such as the chief prosecutor of
the jurisdiction where the conviction occurred. If the conviction was
obtained in the prosecutor's jurisdiction, paragraph (g) requires the
prosecutor to examine the evidence and undertake further investigation to determine whether the defendant is in fact innocent or
make reasonable efforts to cause another appropriate authority to
undertake the necessary investigation, and to promptly disclose the
evidence to court and, absent court-authorized delay, to the
defendant. Consistent with the objectives of Rules 4.2 and 4.3,
disclosure to a represented defendant must be made through the

defendant's counsel, and in the case of an unrepresented defendant, would ordinarily be accompanied by a request to a court for the appointment of counsel to assist the defendant in taking such legal measures as may be appropriate.

[8] Under paragraph (h), once the prosecutor knows of clear and convincing evidence that the defendant was convicted of an offense that the defendant did not commit, the prosecutor must seek to remedy the conviction. Necessary steps may include disclosure of the evidence to the defendant, requesting that the court appoint counsel for an unrepresented indigent defendant and, where appropriate, notifying the court that the prosecutor has knowledge that the defendant did not commit the offense of which the defendant was convicted.

[9] A prosecutor's independent judgment, made in good faith, that the new evidence is not of such nature as to trigger the obligations of sections (g) and (h), though subsequently determined to have been erroneous, does not constitute a violation of the Rule.

Authors' 1983 Model Rules Comparison

The 1983 version of Rule 3.8 contained sections (a) through (e). It did not contain a provision dealing with prosecutor subpoenas of defense counsel. Also, only Rule 3.8(e) addressed trial publicity:

[The prosecutor in a criminal case shall] exercise reasonable care to prevent investigators, law enforcement personnel, employees or other persons assisting or associated with the prosecutor in a criminal case from making an extrajudicial statement that the prosecutor would be prohibited from making under rule 3.6.

In 1990, the ABA added the text in subparagraph (f) to original Model Rule 3.8 and added a new Comment 4. This amendment sought to address the profession's concerns over the increased use of subpoenas that are directed towards attorneys for information about their clients. The adopted rule seeks to limit the use of such subpoenas because of their potential to disrupt the attorney-client relationship.

In 1994, the ABA added new section (g) permitting prosecutors to make public statements for legitimate law enforcement purposes. In 1995, the ABA amended Rule 3.8(f) to remove the requirement that prosecutors obtain prior judicial approval after a hearing before serving a subpoena on a defense attorney. This requirement was deleted because the ABA believed that such requirements are better left to procedural rules rather than ethical standards.

The drafters of the 2002 Rules did not modify the language of the Rule 3.8 as amended over the years. Instead, they combined sections (e) and (g) into a new (f) and moved the old (f) to (e). By doing so, this brought all of the language dealing with trial publicity into one provision.

In Comment 1, the drafters of the 2002 Rules deleted the following sentence because of the view that grand jury proceedings are not ex parte proceedings: "See also Rule 3.3(d), governing *ex parte* proceedings, among which grand jury proceedings are included." *See* Reporter's Explanation of Changes to Model Rule 3.8.

Comment 2 was significantly expanded to explain the policy

underlying the obligation of prosecutors not to seek waiver of pretrial rights from unrepresented persons. The amendment also explains the difference between pro se representation and unrepresented persons and states that Rule 3.8 should not prevent prosecutors from questioning uncharged suspects.

Comments 3, 4, and 5, were not amended except to update the references to the changed subsection numbers in the Rule.

Comment 6 is new and explains Rule 3.8(f), including the language about controlling personnel outside of the prosecutor's office. No change in meaning is intended with this language. *See* Reporter's Explanation of Changes to Model Rule 3.8.

Post February 2008 Amendment:

At the February 2008 ABA Meeting, the House of Delegates added section (g) and (h) and Comments [7] to [9] to Model Rule 3.8 as well as a modification to Comment [1]. These amendments are based in part upon proposed amendments to the New York Code of Professional Responsibility. In 2006, the New York State Bar Association proposed changes to their rule on the ethical responsibilities of prosecutors. These changes addressed the responsibilities of prosecutors to criminal defendants and their lawyers who seek to demonstrate their clients' innocence in a post conviction proceeding. The view that prosecutors needed some guidance on how to address such post conviction efforts was supported by the case law and made in light of the many high profile cases demonstrating innocence despite a criminal conviction.

Model Code Comparison

DR 7-103(A) provided that a "public prosecutor . . . shall not institute . . . criminal charges when he knows or it is obvious that the charges are not supported by probable cause." DR 7-103(B) provided that "[a] public prosecutor . . . shall make timely disclosure . . . of the existence of evidence, known to the prosecutor . . . that tends to negate the guilt of the accused, mitigate the degree of the offense, or reduce the punishment."

§ 3.8–1 INTRODUCTION

It is often said that the duty of the public prosecutor "is to seek justice, not merely to convict."[1] From this principle, certain limitations have been developed that modify the duty of zealous behavior of government attorneys when they are acting as prosecutors in criminal cases. Sometimes, courts state that

---

[Section 3.8–1]

[1]EC 7-13; Rule 3.8, Comment 1. Accord, *Foute v. State*, 4 Tenn. (3 Hayw.) 98, 99, 1816 WL 355 (1816); *Berger v. United States*, 295 U.S. 78, 55 S.Ct. 629, 79 L.Ed. 1314 (1935).

See Bruce A. Green & Fred C. Zacharias, *Prosecutorial Neutrality*, 2004 Wisconsin L. Rev. 837, 840 (2004) (arguing that prosecutors should make decisions "based on articulable principles or subprinciples that command broad societal acceptance"); Fred C. Zacharias, *Structuring the Ethics of Prosecutorial Trial Practice: Can Prosecutors Do Justice?*, 44 VAND. L. REV. 45, 48 (1991); Kevin C. McMunigal, *Are Prosecutorial Ethics Standards Different?*, 68 FORDHAM L. REV. 1453 (2000).

government lawyers, *even in civil cases*, are under a higher standard than their civil counterparts.[2] However, if one actually looks at the case results, as opposed to the dictum, one finds that, outside of the area of criminal prosecution, government lawyers in civil cases are under the same ethics standard as private lawyers in civil cases. They have the same duty to represent their clients loyally while complying with all of the ethics rules.[3]

Because criminal and civil prosecutors work primarily before courts, violations of Rule 3.8 and other constraints on their conduct are often scrutinized in the litigation process. Defense lawyers routinely seek to bring violations of these norms into the proceeding as prosecutorial misconduct that should affect the government's case on the merits. The proper forum and sanction for violation of Rule 3.8 is the subject of a vigorous debate.[4]

The obligations of government lawyers in criminal cases and civil cases are discussed in separate sections below.

§ 3.8–2 SPECIAL RESPONSIBILITIES OF PROSECUTORS IN CRIMINAL CASES

§ 3.8–2(a) The Requirement of Probable Cause

Ordinarily a lawyer may bring any nonfrivolous action.[1] The criminal prosecutor's obligations are stricter: a prosecutor may not institute charges—even if they are not frivolous—if he knows that they are not supported by probable cause.[2] Comment 1 reaffirms the notion that prosecutors are not simply zealous advocates; they are "ministers of justice."

Prosecutors have been given wide discretion to conduct their activities and their conduct is largely protected by broad governmental immunity. Thus, the ABA has decided to impose upon prosecutors an obligation that they "refrain from prosecuting a charge that the prosecutor knows is not supported by prob-

---

[2]*See, e.g., Freeport-McMoRan Oil & Gas Co. v. Federal Energy Regulatory Commission*, 962 F.2d 45 (D.C. Cir.1992).

[3]*See, e.g.*, Geoffrey Miller, Government Lawyers' Ethics in a System of Checks and Balances, 54 U. CHICAGO L. REV. 1293, 1294, 1295 (1987) ("Despite its surface plausibility, the notion that government attorneys represent some transcendental 'public interest' is, I believe, incoherent."); Catherine J. Lanctot, *The Duty of Zealous Advocacy and the Ethics of*

the Federal Government Lawyer: The Three Hardest Questions, 64 So. CAL. L. REV. 951 (1991).

[4]*See* ABA CENTER FOR PROFESSIONAL RESPONSIBILITY, ANNOTATED MODEL RULES OF PROFESSIONAL CONDUCT 397–399 (ABA, 5th ed. 2003) (examining the remedies for violations of the ethics rules).

[Section 3.8–2]

[1]*See* Rule 3.1. DR 2–109(A); 7–102(A)(1).

[2]Rule 3.8(a). DR 7–103(A).

able cause . . . ."[3] Rule 3.8(a)'s requirement that a prosecutor have knowledge about the lack of probable cause make it unlikely that this provision will serve as a basis for discipline in the vast majority of cases.[4]

---

[3] Rule 3.8(a).

[4] For a rare case where the court did impose discipline based on this section, see *Iowa Supreme Court Attorney Disciplinary Board v. Howe*, 706 N.W.2d 360 (Iowa 2005). The court disciplined a part-time state prosecutor whom the disciplinary board charged with violating the Iowa Code of Professional Responsibility for Lawyers by filing charges in more than 170 misdemeanor cases that were not supported by probable cause. Technically, the court based discipline on DR 7–103(A), which states that a prosecutor "shall not institute or cause to be instituted criminal charges when the lawyer knows or it is obvious that the charges are not supported by probable cause"). This section is analogous to Rule 3.8(a).

The Board alleged that on numerous occasions the respondent amended traffic citations to charge violations of the cowl-lamp statute found in Iowa Code section 321.406, later incorporated into the city ordinances. Defendants would subsequently enter guilty pleas to the amended charges, although the fact there was no factual basis for the pleas. The Board alleged Howe, the part-time prosecutor and respondent-knew there was no factual basis for the charges and that the charges were not supported by probable cause. The cowl-lamp statute, a remnant from a long-ago era, states that a motor vehicle "may be equipped with not more than two side cowl or fender lamps which shall emit an amber or white light without glare." Iowa Code § 321.406. As Howe acknowledged, vehicles have not been equipped with cowl or fender lamps "for a considerable number of years." The respondent admitted he knew there was no probable cause to believe this offense had

been committed by the 174 persons charged with violating this law, but he did not think he was doing anything illegal or wrong by allowing defendants to plead guilty to these fictitious charges. He thought that as long as the charging police officer agreed to the deal and the reduction benefited the defendant, the plea bargains were consistent with his obligation as a prosecutor to see that justice was done. His actions were always above board. Magistrate Whittenburg testified she understood at the time she accepted the guilty pleas that there was no factual basis for them. She believed none was required for simple misdemeanors.

The court concluded: "We think the respondent's conduct clearly violated the Iowa Code of Professional Responsibility. DR 7–103(A) states that a prosecutor "shall not institute or cause to be instituted criminal charges when the lawyer knows or it is obvious that the charges are not supported by probable cause." There is no dispute in the present case that the *cowl-lamp charges* were not supported by probable cause and that the respondent knew it." 706 N.W.2d 360, 368 (footnote omitted)." The court added: "The fact that the *original* traffic citations may have been supported by probable cause is beside the point because Howe is not being disciplined for instituting the *original* charges. His ethical violation arises from the *amended* charges alleging cowl-lamp violations, which clearly lacked probable-cause support." 706 N.W.2d 360, 368 (emphasis in original).

The court said simply announced that "the fact that plea bargains to lesser or related charges are authorized by our rules of criminal procedure is also irrelevant," because "Howe is not being disciplined for allowing the defendant to plead guilty

§ 3.8–2(b) Dealing with Unrepresented Defendants

Two provisions of Rule 3.8 address prosecutorial conduct towards unrepresented persons.

The Sixth Amendment of the Constitution gives persons accused of a crime the right "to have Assistance of Counsel for his defence."[5] Rule 3.8(b) states that a prosecutor must provide the accused a reasonable opportunity to obtain counsel. This obligation requires that the prosecutor determine whether the accused has been informed of his or her right to obtain counsel and if that has not been done, to fulfill this duty to inform the accused. It also requires that the prosecutor discuss the procedure by which the accused may obtain legal representation. And, the accused should be given a reasonable opportunity to obtain counsel.

State and federal criminal justice systems have put in place procedural safeguards to protect the state and federal constitutional rights of accused persons. Such safeguards may include hearings for probable cause, bail, and disclosure of charges. Under Rule 3.8(c), a prosecutor should not urge an unrepresented accused to waive important pretrial rights, such as the right to a preliminary hearing.[6] This standard focuses on the prosecutor's conduct and words directed towards an accused that ask the person to waive important rights. If the accused voluntarily waives such rights without prompting from the prosecutor, this Rule is not implicated.

In the course of a criminal investigation or proceeding, two situations may arise that would not implicate Rules 3.8(b) and

---

to a reduced charge." *Id.* Finally, the court was unmoved by the fact that "there is no Iowa case or rule requiring that there be a factual basis for guilty pleas to simple misdemeanors." The court simply responded: "whether or not the *guilty plea* must be supported by a factual basis is a different question from whether or not the *charge* must be supported by probable cause." 706 N.W.2d at 368. The court concluded that "[f]iling charges that are blatantly bogus—even when defendants are willing to plead guilty to them—does not promote confidence in the integrity of the judicial process." 706 N.W.2d at 371. For this violation and others, the court suspended the respondent indefinitely with no possibility of reinstatement for a period of four months from the date of the filing of this opinion. Justice Carter concurred specially and did not believe that discipline should be imposed on

the basis of Howe's acceptance of misdemeanor guilty pleas to equipment violations that had not occurred where the alleged offenders agreed to that disposition. Justice Larson dissented.

One should not read too much into this case. The court added that it "conclusion that the respondent's conduct was improper should not be applied too broadly. Certainly prosecutors have the authority to negotiate plea bargains, and may ethically reduce a charge in exchange for a defendant's guilty plea to the reduced charge. The only restriction placed on this process by DR 7–103(A) is the requirement that any charge—original or reduced—be supported by probable cause." 706 N.W.2d at 371.

[5] U.S. Const. Amend. VI (1791).

[6] Rule 3.8(b), (c). *Cf.* DR 7–104(A) (2).

(c). First, if the accused has decided to appear *pro se* with the consent of the tribunal, the government attorney must negotiate directly with the accused.[7] Essentially, in a pro se representation, the accused has been informed of his or her right to counsel and has chosen pro se representation. In that situation, prosecutors may engage in typical negotiations with the accused about series of choices they wish to make.

Second, prosecutors and law enforcement personnel should have the right to question persons who have not been charged with a crime.[8] For those who are not yet charged with a crime, the right to counsel (or the right to seek certain pretrial safeguards) do not come into play until the government detains them and charges them with a crime.

§ 3.8–2(c) Volunteering Exculpatory Evidence[9]

Civil litigants have, in general, no ethical duty to volunteer adverse information to their opponents in litigation.[10] In contrast, criminal prosecutors (but usually not criminal defense lawyers) have the ethical duty to volunteer adverse information. The prosecutor must inform the accused of the existence of evidence that tends to negate the guilt of the accused or mitigate the punishment.[11] Moreover, the prosecutor should not intentionally fail to follow certain leads because he believes the information secured might damage his case.[12] Prosecutors must turn over not only evidence that is considered exculpatory but also evidence that can be used for impeachment of the government witnesses.[13]

The obligation of a prosecutor under Rule 3.8(d) to "make timely disclosure to the defense of all evidence of information known to the prosecutor that tends to negate the guilt of the ac-

---

[7] Rule 3.8, Comment 2. *Cf.* EC 3-7.

[8] Rule 3.8, Comment 2.

[9] Salmon, J., citing Treatise, in *Clark v. State*, 140 Md.App. 540, 781 A.2d 913 (2001).

[10] Rule 3.4.

[11] Rule 3.8(d). DR 7-103(B).

[12] EC 7-13.

DNA and Scientific Evidence of Post-Conviction Innocence. *See, e.g.,* Judith A. Goldberg & David M. Siegel, *The Ethical Obligations of Prosecutors in Cases Involving Postconviction Claims of Innocence*, 38 Calif. W. L. Rev. 389 (2002). This article argues for new ethical rules in light of new scientific methods, such as DNA testing, that are now available. Pros-

ecutors are often in control of this evidence. Therefore, the article argues that, as an ethical duty, "when faced with an innocence-based postconviction claim requesting the application of 'new' science to 'old' evidence, prosecutors should promptly seek the fullest accounting of the truth, effect the fullest possible disclosure, and use the most accurate science." 38 Cal. W. L. Rev. 389, at 389.

[13] *See, e.g., United States v. Boyd*, 55 F.3d 239 (7th Cir.1995), *affirming*, 833 F.Supp. 1277 (N.D.Ill.1993).

See also, e.g., Bruce Green, Why Should Prosecutors 'Seek Justice'?, 26 Fordham Urb.L.J. 607 (1999); Bennett L. Gershman, *The Prosecutor's Duty to Truth*, 14 Georgetown J. Legal Ethics 309 (2001).

cused or mitigates the offense" is sometimes confused with federal and state constitutional and criminal law requirements imposed upon prosecutors.[14] This confusion has led to some to look to the federal and state authorities for guidance as to how to interpret the Rule 3.8 obligations of a prosecutor. Formal Opinion 09-454 seeks to clarify this confusion by reaffirming that the ethical duty imposed upon prosecutors is separate and distinct from the other legal duties that prosecutors must follow.[15] First, the Opinion makes clear that the duty to disclose under Rule 3.8 is "more extensive" than the federal constitutional obligation. Rule 3.8 does not contain a materiality requirement nor does it require only disclosure of information that is "likely to lead to an acquittal."[16] "Rule 3.8(d) is more demanding than the constitutional case law, in that it requires the disclosure of evidence or information favorable to the defense without regard to the anticipated impact of the evidence or information on a trial's outcome."[17] The Opinion goes as far as saying that prosecutors under their ethical duties should err on the side of disclosure because of their role as ministers of justice. Of course, this duty only applies to information known by the prosecutor and does not require that the prosecutor undertake an investigation to discover additional information. But prosecutors who supervise others must take reasonable steps to ensure that others in the office are complying with the rules of ethics and law. And, such a duty would apply to different lawyers working on the same case together or as a case is passed on from prosecutor to prosecutor.[18]

Second, Formal Opinion 09-454 requires that prosecutors disclose favorable information to the defense in a timely manner. Timely is interpreted as at a time when the information can be used "effectively." Thus, prosecutors must disclose such information "as soon as reasonably practical."[19] Finally, the Opinion examines whether prosecutors may be relieved of the obligation of disclosing favorable information to the defense if the defendant

---

[14]For example, some believe that Rule 3.8 codifies the constitutional requirements of *Brady v. Maryland*, 373 U.S. 83, 83 S. Ct. 1194, 10 L. Ed. 2d 215 (1963).

[15]ABA Formal Opinion 09-454 (July 9, 2009). *See* Peter A. Joy & Kevin C. McMunigal, *ABA Explains Prosecutor's Ethical Disclosure Duty*, 24 CRIMINAL JUSTICE 41 (2010). *But see Disciplinary Counsel v. Kellogg-Martin*, 124 Ohio St. 3d 415, 2010-Ohio-282, 923 N.E.2d 125 (2010) (limiting prosecutor's ethical duties to the requirements of the law).

[16]ABA Formal Opinion 09-454, at 3 (July 9, 2009).

[17]ABA Formal Opinion 09-454, at 3 (July 9, 2009).

[18]ABA Formal Opinion 09-454, at 6 (July 9, 2009).

[19]ABA Formal Opinion 09-454, at 4 (July 9, 2009).

waives a right of access to such information.[20] Prosecutors have often proposed plea bargains or promises of leniency if a criminal defendant consents to a prosecutor's noncompliance with Rule 3.8(d). The ABA Opinion states that a defendant's consent does not relieve the prosecutor of the duty to disclose favorable information. The ethical obligations of prosecutors are designed to promote the fair administration of a criminal justice system. Thus, in the absence of a "legitimate and overriding purpose," a defendant cannot waive the prosecutor's duties under Rule 3.8(d).

The prosecutor must also inform the sentencing tribunal of all mitigating information not covered by a protective order or otherwise privileged.[21] Whenever the prosecutor is proceeding *ex parte,* as in a grand jury hearing, the ethics rules provide that he should offer the tribunal "all material facts" whether or not adverse.[22] On the other hand, as a matter of constitutional law, a court may not dismiss an otherwise valid indictment on the ground that the prosecutor failed to disclose to the grand jury "substantial exculpatory evidence" in his or her possession.[23]

The 1983 version of Comment 1 to Rule 3.8 contained a sentence that said: "See also Rule 3.3(d), governing ex parte proceedings, among which grand jury proceedings are included." The House of Delegates, in 2002, accepted the advice of the Ethics 2000 Commission and deleted this sentence, because "grand-jury proceedings are not ex parte *adjudicatory* proceedings."[24]

§ 3.8–2(d) Subpoenaing Lawyers

The 1983 Model Rules did not contain any provision dealing with prosecutor subpoenas of lawyers. In 1990, the ABA House of Delegates amended Rule 3.8 to place ethical limits on a prosecutor who seeks to subpoena an attorney.[25] In recent years, the Government has appeared to increase its subpoenas of criminal defense lawyers to testify before the grand jury. In the District of Massachusetts, for example, the Federal Government, during most of the 1980's, subpoenaed attorneys in approximately 10%

---

[20]ABA Formal Opinion 09–454, at 5 (July 9, 2009).

[21]Rule 3.8(d). Comment 3 notes that prosecutors may seek court orders to restrict disclosure of exculpatory evidence when this is needed to protect the public or an individual from harm.

[22]Rule 3.3(d). *See* Rule 3.8, Comment 1.

[23]*See, e.g., United States v. Williams,* 504 U.S. 36, 112 S.Ct. 1735, 118 L.Ed.2d 352 (1992).

[24]Reporter's Explanation of Changes to Rule 3.8 (emphasis added).

[25]In the 1990 amendment of the 1983 Rules, the House of Delegates added section (f). The drafters of the 2002 Model Rules renumbered the sections, so now the limitation is contained in Rule 3.8(e). For a discussion of the 1990 amendment, see Ronald D. Rotunda, *Abuse of Ethics Rule Hinders Prosecutors,* CHICAGO SUN-TIMES, Aug. 14, 1991, at p. 12, col. 1–2.

to 32% of the criminal cases.[26] The Government often seeks information on the amount of the fee paid to the attorney, whether it was paid in cash, and whether the client or a third party paid it. The answers to these questions are relevant in light of various federal laws such as the Racketeer Influenced and Corrupt Organizations Act[27] and the Continuing Criminal Enterprise Statute.[28] The fee information may be useful in determining whether any fee is subject to forfeiture because it was acquired through certain criminal activity, or is evidence of a criminal enterprise. A client cannot prevent evidence from being subpoenaed by the simple expedient of turning it over to her lawyer.[29]

An attorney, just like any other witness who is called to testify

---

[26]*United States v. Klubock,* 832 F.2d 649, 658 (1st Cir.1987) (amended panel opinion), *aff'd by equally divided en banc court,* 832 F.2d 664 (1st Cir. 1987).

[27]18 U.S.C.A. §§ 1961 to 1968.

[28]21 U.S.C.A. §§ 848 to 853.

[29]Attorneys who are witnesses to criminal acts have no privilege to refuse to testify about those acts, even if the perpetrator is their client. An interesting case on this issue is: *In re January 1976 Grand Jury,* 534 F.2d 719 (7th Cir.1976). The attorney refused to comply with a grand jury's subpoena duces tecum to turn over moneys received by him from clients suspected of bank robbery. The Court of Appeals affirmed the contempt order, and Judge Tone, joined by Judge Bauer, offered a perceptive analysis of this question:

"We must assume for purposes of this appeal that shortly after robbing a savings and loan association, the robbers delivered money stolen in the robbery to appellant. If that occurred, the money was delivered either for safekeeping, with or without appellant's knowledge that it was stolen, or as an attorney's fee.

"If it was the latter, the robbers voluntarily relinquished the money and with it any arguable claim that might have arisen from their possession or constructive possession. As Judge Pell points out, the payment of a fee is not a privileged communication. The money itself is non-

testimonial and no plausible argument is left for resisting the subpoena.

"If the money was not given as a fee but for safekeeping, the delivery of the money was an act in furtherance of the crime, regardless of whether appellant knew it was stolen. The delivery of the money was not assertive conduct and therefore was not a privileged communication, and, as we just observed, the money itself is non-testimonial. The attorney is simply a witness to a criminal act. The fact that he is also a participant in the act, presumably without knowledge of its criminal quality, is irrelevant since he is not asserting his own privilege against self incrimination. There is no authority or reason, based on any constitutional provision or the attorney-client privilege, for shielding from judicial inquiry either the fruits of the robbery or the fact of the later criminal act of turning over the money to appellant. Accordingly, it is immaterial that in responding to the subpoena appellant will be making an assertion about who turned over the money and when.

"Finally, the proceedings have not yet reached the point at which we must decide whether, when the robbers have chosen to make appellant a witness to their crime, they may invoke the Sixth Amendment [right to effective assistance of counsel] to bar his eyewitness testimony at trial, although, for me, to ask that question is almost to answer it."

before the grand jury, can always raise any applicable privilege, such as the attorney-client evidentiary privilege. In fact, in the context of government subpoenas, the lawyer has a special ethical obligation "to seek to limit the subpoena or court order [such as a search warrant] on any legitimate available grounds so as to protect documents that are deemed to be confidential under Rule 1.6."[30] However, if the client consents to the lawyer producing privileged documents, then the lawyer is no longer obligated to avoid producing those documents.[31]

Notwithstanding this fact, attorneys have typically argued that they should not even be subpoenaed unless there is first an adversary hearing before a judge, who is to determine that the information is not privileged, that the evidence is "essential," and that there is "no other feasible alternative" to secure this evidence. After most courts rejected this position,[32] the ABA (in February, 1990) added new Rule 3.8(f) and Comment 4, which imposes such a requirement on the prosecutor as a matter of legal ethics.

Some commentators have questioned what the ABA has done in this matter, on the grounds that the ABA has sought, via the ethical rules, to create a rule of substantive law or a rule of procedure or evidence. The ABA has, in effect, sought to impose a special, additional requirement on federal and state prosecutors if they wish to subpoena a lawyer in a criminal proceeding. This rule does not apply to lawyers subpoenaing other lawyers in civil proceedings, nor does it impose any requirement on prosecutors who subpoena other individuals who may have a confidential relationship with the accused, such as a spouse, priest, accountant, medical doctors, and so forth. And, this new restriction applies even though the substantive law gives witnesses other perfectly reasonable remedies if they believe they should not be subpoenaed.[33]

If the ABA had merely proposed a statute, or a rule of evidence or criminal procedure, it would not go into effect until a court or legislature adopted the proposal. Moreover, if a state court adopted such a rule of procedure or evidence, it would not bind federal prosecutors in federal court. But if a state court adopts a provision from the ABA Model Rules—and the great majority of jurisdictions largely follow the Model Rules—this state rule of ethics will bind all lawyers who are members of the bar of that state. Federal prosecutors, because they are members of at least one state bar, will normally not only be subject to federal law but also to the ethics rules of the state where they are practicing.

---

[30] ABA Formal Opinion 94-385 (July 5, 1994).

[31] ABA Formal Opinion 94-385 (July 5, 1994).

[32] See, e.g., United States v. Perry, 857 F.2d 1346 (9th Cir.1988).

[33] For example, they can move the court to quash the subpoena.

In 1995, the ABA House of Delegates removed the requirement that prosecutors obtain "prior judicial approval after an opportunity for an adversarial hearing."[34] The Committee Report supporting the deletion of this requirement noted that a hearing requirement is more properly set forth in a rule of procedure, not a rule of ethics, and the new Rule should receive more widespread acceptance without the hearing requirement.[35]

The full effect of new Rule 3.8(f) remains to be seen. In the legislative history surrounding Rule 3.8(f), some lawyers argued that it should have a very broad scope.[36] Proponents of Rule 3.8(f) argued that the attorney-client evidentiary privilege does not offer enough protection because it does not cover client "secrets," as defined in DR 4-101(A) and 1.6(a) and Comment 5. On the other hand, the Model Rules themselves advise that the "lawyer must comply with the final orders of a court or other tribunal of competent jurisdiction requiring the lawyer to give information about the client."[37] Courts will uphold the evidentiary privilege, but not the protection of client "secrets" because that is not an evidentiary privilege.

Similarly, in the legislative history of Rule 3.8(f), some commentators complained that "an attorney in possession of documents received from a client in the course of a case may be compelled by subpoena to produce those documents assuming that the client personally could be compelled to produce the documents were they in the client's hands." True enough, but a client has no legal right to avoid a subpoena merely by turning over the requested documents to her attorney.[38]

---

[34]1994 Model Rule 3.8(f)(2).

[35]In 1995, the ABA House of Delegates deleted this requirement, conceding that "it sets out a type of implementing requirement that is properly established by rules of criminal procedure rather than established as an ethical norm." The action responded to cases that had ruled that the original Rule 3.8(f) was inconsistent with the Federal Rules of Criminal Procedure and exceeded the rule-making power of the lower federal courts. *Baylson v. Disciplinary Board of Supreme Court of Pennsylvania*, 975 F.2d 102 (3d Cir.1992), *cert. denied*, 507 U.S. 984, 113 S.Ct. 1578, 123 L.Ed.2d 147 (1993), relying on Rule 17 of the Federal Rules of Criminal Procedure. *See also*

Stephen Gillers & Roy D. Simon, REGULATION OF LAWYERS: STATUTES AND STANDARDS 2001, at 247–48 (Aspen Law Pub. 2001)(quoting the Report Explaining 1995 Amendment).

[36]*See* Report Accompanying Proposed Rule 3.8(f), by the ABA Standing Committee on Ethics and Professional Responsibility (1990).

[37]Rule 1.6, Comment 19.

[38]*See* Report Accompanying Proposed Rule 3.8(f), by the ABA Standing Committee on Ethics and Professional Responsibility (1990). When Rule 3.8(f) was first added to the Model Rules, it required the prosecutor to secure judicial approval prior to issuing the subpoena to the lawyer

In *United States v. Klubock*,[39] an equally divided federal appellate court approved a federal rule similar to Rule 3.8(f). However, other federal courts have invalidated, on supremacy clause grounds, similar state rules to the extent that the state seeks to apply this disciplinary rule to federal prosecutors.[40] Critics of this rule are concerned that it distorts evidentiary privileges, imposes the organized bar's view of positive law on criminal prosecutors, disrupts existing subpoena practice, and compromises the authority and investigative function of the modern grand jury.[41] Proponents believe that the rule does not hamstring prosecutors and protects the client-lawyer relationship.

The current Rule 3.8(f) seeks to limit prosecutorial subpoenas against lawyers to only those cases where "a genuine need [exists] to intrude into the client-lawyer relationship."[42] The Rule continues to limit prosecutorial subpoenas to situations where the information is not privileged, very important to the criminal investigation or prosecution, and otherwise not accessible.

§ 3.8–2(e) Trial Publicity by Prosecutors and Their Agents

The drafters of the 1983 Model Rules addressed the topic of trial publicity in litigation in Rule 3.6. However, they still felt the need to elaborate upon the general limitations in the specific context of prosecutor's ethics. In the 1983 version of Rule 3.8(e), criminal prosecutors were to "exercise reasonable care to prevent investigators, law enforcement personnel, employees or other persons assisting or associated with the prosecutor in a criminal case from making an extrajudicial statement that the prosecutor would be prohibited from making under rule 3.6."[43]

In 1994, the ABA added a new section, Rule 3.8(g) to specifi-

---

[39] *United States v. Klubock*, 832 F.2d 649 (1st Cir.1987) (en banc).

[40] *See, e.g., Baylson v. Disciplinary Board of Supreme Court of Pennsylvania*, 764 F.Supp. 328 (E.D.Pa.1991), *aff'd*, 975 F.2d 102 (3d Cir.1992), cert. denied, 507 U.S. 984, 113 S.Ct. 1578, 123 L.Ed.2d 147 (1993), holding that a state rule patterned after Rule 3.8(f) cannot be enforced against federal prosecutors. *See also Almond v. U.S. District Court for the District of Rhode Island*, 852 F.Supp. 78 (D.N.H.1994) (invalidating this Rule 3.8(f) as applied to federal prosecutors), *modified in, Whitehouse v. U.S. District Court for the District of Rhode Island*, 53 F.3d 1349 (1st Cir.1995) (upholding federal court lo-

cal rule as applied to federal prosecutors).

[41] *See, e.g.,* Fred Zacharias, *A Critical Look at Rules Governing Grand Jury Subpoenas of Attorneys*, 76 MINN. L. REV. 917 (1992); Roger Cramton & Lisa Udell, *State Ethics Rules and Federal Prosecutors: The Controversies over the Anti-Contact and Subpoena Rules*, 53 U. PITT. L. REV. 291 (1992); Bruce A. Green & Fred C. Zacharias, *Regulating Federal Prosecutors' Ethics*, 55 VANDERBILT L. REV. 381 (2002); Bennett L. Gershman, PROSECUTORIAL MISCONDUCT § 3:24 (2d ed.)(Updated August 2004).

[42] *See* Rule 3.8, Comment 5.

[43] 1983 Model Rule 3.8(e). The Model Code did not have a special pro-

cally address what a prosecutor could and could not say. Prosecutors could make "statements that are necessary to inform the public of the nature and extent of the prosecutor's action and that serve a legitimate law enforcement purpose, [but should] refrain from making extrajudicial comments that have a substantial likelihood of heightening public condemnation of the accused."[44] This Rule recognized that the public expects prosecutors to make announcements about criminal activity. Yet, excessive publicity about a crime and the accused can influence the public and the citizens who may constitute the jury pool.[45] Thus, prosecutors should refrain from making any extrajudicial comments that serve no legitimate law enforcement purpose and have a substantial likelihood of heightening public opprobrium of the accused.[46]

The drafters of the 2002 Rules combined old Rule 3.8(e) and (g) into one new Rule 3.8(f). Comment 5 states that Rules 3.6 (b) and (c) are still important sources for prosecutorial statements and Rule 3.8 does not attempt to cut back on them. The drafters of the 2002 Rules also added new Comment 6, which deals with statements made by other affiliated with the prosecutor's office. Rules 5.1 and 5.3 require that the prosecutor supervise those in the office so that they do not violate Rule 3.6 and Rule 3.8(f). However, law enforcement personnel are often not under the direct supervision of the prosecutor's office. Thus, Comment 6 requires that prosecutors "exercise reasonable care to prevent persons assisting or associated with the prosecutor from making

---

vision dealing with prosecutor's public statements.

[44] 1994 Model Rule 3.8(g).

[45] In a world of ubiquitous publicity about trials, *Maryland Attorney Grievance Commission v. Gansler*, 377 Md. 656, 835 A.2d 548 (2003), represents a relatively rare reprimand for it. Respondent, the State's Attorney for one of Maryland's largest counties, had held press conferences about highly publicized cases and reporting evidentiary details, prior criminal records, and alleged confessions and offered plea deals. The Maryland Supreme Court agreed with Gansler that "information contained in a public record" includes all information made public from any source, including the media. Thus, publicly revealing a defendant's criminal record is permissible, even if prejudicial to the defendant, if the speaker can show that a private citizen could discover the record from public documents. Confessions, however, could not be so discovered, nor could information about plea discussions, so Gansler's reference to them was improper. Further, the fact Gansler was a public official was important, the Court said. "Prosecutors are held to even higher standards of conduct than other attorneys due to their unique role as both advocate and minister of justice. * * * [Moreover,] a prosecutor's opinion of guilt is much more likely to create prejudice, given that his or her words carry the authority of government and are especially persuasive in the public eye." 835 A.2d at 572. The Court concluded that a formal reprimand, issued publicly, would adequately deter future violations of professional standards.

[46] Rule 3.8(g).

improper extrajudicial statements, even when such persons are not under the direct supervision of the prosecutor."[47] The Comment goes on to say that a prosecutor will satisfy this reasonable care standard by issuing "appropriate cautions" to the individuals outside of the supervision of the lawyer. The drafters sought to impose some burden on prosecutors to attempt to control law enforcement personnel even though those individuals are not under the control and supervision of the prosecutor's office.

§ 3.8-3 DUTIES OF A PROSECUTOR IN POST CONVICTION PROCEEDINGS

In the last twenty years, over three hundred criminal defendants have been exonerated through post conviction proceedings.[1] Seventy-four of these defendants had received death sentences. Advances in science have facilitated the ability of these defendants to prove that they were wrongfully convicted.[2]

In light of the number of these exonerations, legislatures in over thirty states have enacted laws to permit convicted persons to submit to a DNA test that would be matched with the DNA possessed by law enforcement authorities.[3] Although convicted defendants often must proclaim innocence and must provide evidences to substantiate their claim that they were wrongfully convicted, the statutes provide that once the defendant meets this burden the authorities must cooperate with the request for retesting of the DNA.[4] The requirement of cooperation is consistent with judicial opinions considering the responsibilities of prosecutors in post conviction matters. In 1976, the Supreme Court in *Imbler v. Pachtman* held that prosecutors must inform the appropriate authority when they learn of information that calls into question the "correctness of a conviction."[5] These developments support a more general obligation for prosecutors to cooperate with the search for justice when the system has produced a wrongful conviction.[6]

In 2006, the Association of the Bar of the City of New York proposed a set of rules for prosecutors and these rules included

---

[47]Rule 3.8, Comment 6.

[Section 3.8-3]

[1]*See* Samuel R. Gross, Kristen Jacoby, Daniel J. Matheson, Nicholas, Montgomery, & Sujata Patil, *Exonerations in the United States 1989 Through 2003*, 95 J. Crim. L. & Criminology 523 (2005).

[2]*See* Jane Campbell Moriarty, *"Misconvictions," Science, and the Ministers of Justice*, 86 Neb. L.Rev. 1 (2007).

[3]*See* Kathy Swedlow, *Don't Believe Everything You Read: A Review of the "Post-Conviction" DNA Testing Statutes*, 38 Cal.W.L.Rev. 355 (2002)

[4]Id. at 376–82.

[5]*Imbler v. Pachtman*, 424 U.S. 409, 96 S. Ct. 984, 47 L. Ed. 2d 128 (1976).

[6]*See* Fred C. Zacharias, *The Role of Prosecutors in Serving Justice After Convictions*, 58 Vand. L.Rev. 171 (2005)

an obligation for prosecutors to consider credible assertions of innocence in the post-conviction context.[7] The proposals were considered at the New York State level during a review of the ethics rules. And, the ABA Section of Criminal Justice examined these proposals in its report, "Achieving Justice: Freeing the Innocent, Convicting the Guilty."[8] This consideration led to the proposed amendment to Model Rule 3.8. In February 2008, the ABA House of Delegates adopted new sections (g) and (h) along with some new commentary. These changes are discussed below.

§ 3.8-3(a) Knowledge of New, Credible, and Material Evidence Demonstrating Reasonable Likelihood of a Wrongful Conviction

Under Rule 3.8(g), the prosecutor has two new obligations in a post conviction context. First, when a prosecutor has knowledge of "new, credible and material evidence creating a reasonable likelihood" that the convicted defendant did not commit the crime for which he or she was convicted, the prosecutor has an obligation to promptly disclose it to the court or appropriate authority.[9] The appropriate authority, according to the Comments, may be the prosecutor in the jurisdiction.[10] The obligation to disclose such information is designed to place the issue of innocence and a wrongful conviction clearly before the court or prosecutor responsible for the original conviction. Mere disclosure when the prosecutor with the knowledge is outside of their jurisdiction is all that Rule 3.8(g)(1) requires.

Second, when a prosecutor has knowledge of such evidence on a conviction within the prosecutor's jurisdiction, Rule 3.8(g) requires that the prosecutor promptly inform the defendant and undertake an investigation to determine whether the convicted defendant may be innocent of committing the crime.[11] The prosecutor may delay in informing the defendant with the court's permission.[12] This provision imposes a duty upon a prosecutor to examine new, credible, and material evidence creating a reasonable likelihood that the convicted individual did not commit the crime. The prosecutor may do this directly or may make reasonable efforts to cause another authority to investigate the question of the convicted defendant's innocence.[13]

In the states with a statute authorizing convicted defendants to request a DNA match upon the completion of certain prerequi-

---

[7]Proposed Prosecution Ethics Rules, The Committee on Professional Responsibility, 61 The Record of the Association of the Bar of the City of New York 69 (2006).

[8]*See* ABA Criminal Justice Section, Report to the House of Delegates 105B (2008).

[9]See Rule 3.8(g)(1).

[10]Comment 7 to Rule 3.8.

[11]Rule 3.8(g)(2)(i).

[12]Rule 3.8(g)(2)(i).

[13]Rule 3.8(g)(2)(ii).

sites, one would think that such statutes the standard for triggering an investigation under Rule 3.8(g)(2). But the Rule does not address whether lesser proof and evidence will trigger an investigation. A broad meaning of this provision may require prosecutors to follow many leads based upon new, credible and material evidence to determine whether the convicted defendant is innocent.[14] For example, would a signed confession by another inmate currently imprisoned in another state or country provided to the prosecutor trigger this duty?

§ 3.8-3(b) Knowledge of Clear and Convincing Evidence Establishing a Wrongful Conviction

Under Rule 3.8(h), a prosecutor who has knowledge of "clear and convincing evidence" that a convicted defendant in the prosecutor's jurisdiction did not commit the crime for which he or she was convicted "shall seek to remedy the conviction." The Comments offer the following possible actions that a prosecutor should consider taking: disclosing the facts to the defendant, seeking the appointment of counsel for the defendant, informing the tribunal of the facts, and other action consistent with remedying a wrongful conviction.[15] When the jurisdiction does not have a judicial remedy for a wrongful conviction, the prosecutor may seek an executive pardon or clemency from a parole board.[16] The duty to seek a remedy for a wrongful conviction of an innocent human arises from the general obligation of the prosecutor to seek justice.

§ 3.8-3(c) A Good Faith Safe Harbor for Prosecutors

Comment 9 to Rule 3.8 states that the duties imposed by Rules 3.8(g) and (h) are subject to a good faith safe harbor. In other words, if a prosecutor interprets the rules and facts in good faith

---

[14]The following question was raised by Department of Justice lawyers and addressed by Stephen Saltzburg, in 23 SPR Criminal Justice 1 (2008):

"Q: How can a prosecutor who did not prosecute a case know that evidence is "new, credible, and material"?

"A: At times, a prosecutor will know that evidence the prosecutor has received exculpates someone who was convicted in another jurisdiction. This may occur, for example, when an arrested individual confesses to a crime for which the prosecutor knows that someone in another jurisdiction was convicted. But unless a prosecutor actually does *know* of the conviction in another jurisdiction, *knows* the evidence is relevant to that conviction, and *knows* that the evidence is "new, credible, and material," the rule imposes no obligation. Even so, as a matter of prudence, a prosecutor who receives evidence that appears to support a claim of innocence in another jurisdiction ought to refer that evidence to the prosecutor in the other jurisdiction for evaluation. The burden of action would be minimal and would place in appropriate hands the determination of whether the evidence satisfies the standard."

[15]Comment 8 to Rule 3.8.

[16]*See* Stephen Saltzburg, 23 SPR Criminal Justice 1 (2008).

and determines that they do not apply, and such action turns out to be incorrect, the prosecutor will not be considered to have violated the duties to remedy wrongful convictions. The purpose of a safe harbor is to encourage states to adopt this amendment to Rule 3.8 and for prosecutors to work to seek justice by correcting erroneous convictions. The Comment forgives prosecutors for decisions that are incorrect but made in good faith.

§ 3.8–4 SPECIAL RESPONSIBILITIES OF GOVERNMENT LAWYERS IN CIVIL CASES

The Model Code said that the government lawyer's special duty to seek justice extends to civil or administrative proceedings. The lawyer should not use her position or the government's economic power to "harass parties," or to cause "unjust settlements or results."[1] If the government lawyer believes that litigation is unfair, she should use her discretionary power not to proceed, or offer such a recommendation to her superiors.[2] The Model Rules do not repeat this language, and scholarly commentary suggests that when government lawyers are representing the government in civil cases, the rules of ethics place on them no higher (or lower) duty than they place on lawyers who represent private parties.[3]

ABA Formal Opinion 94-387[4] concluded that the Model Rules do not require a lawyer to inform the opposing party in negotiations that the statute of limitations has run on her client's claims (though the lawyer must not make affirmative misrepresentations).[5] The Formal Opinion concluded that there is no basis in the Model Rules to hold a lawyer representing the government in a *civil* case to any different ethical standard: "the government lawyer operating within the adversarial system has no greater or lesser right or duty than the private lawyer to sit in presumptive judgment of the client's cause."[6]

To the extent that the government lawyer does not misstate or distort facts, or refuses to volunteer adverse information to the opposing counsel that would indicate that the statute of limitations has expired on the government's claim, the ABA Formal

---

[Section 3.8–4]

[1]EC 7-14.

[2]EC 7-14.

[3]Catherine J. Lanctot, *The Duty of Zealous Advocacy and the Ethics of the Federal Government Lawyer: The Three Hardest Questions*, 64 So. CALIF. L. REV. 951 (1991).

[4]ABA Formal Opinion 94-387 (Sept. 26, 1994).

[5]Indeed, the Formal Opinion argued that it would violate Rules 1.3 and 1.6 to reveal this information without client consent. The lawyer, according to this Opinion, also may file a suit to enforce a claim that she knows is time-barred (unless the rules of the jurisdiction prohibit that).

[6]ABA Formal Opinion 94-387 (Sept. 26, 1994) (footnote omitted).

Opinion appears to be correct.[7] The government lawyer, just like a private lawyer, may not obstruct the other party's access to evidence but usually need not volunteer adverse facts.[8] However, this ethics opinion appears to go further than that; it appears to argue that the government lawyer need not volunteer knowledge of the adverse law to the court.[9]

That conclusion of the majority in Formal Opinion 94-387 appears incorrect: in order to enforce the claim, the government will be prosecuting the case in court. Rule 3.3(a)(2) places an affirmative duty on the lawyer (whether a government lawyer or a private lawyer) to volunteer to the court adverse legal authority in the controlling jurisdiction.[10] Hence the lawyer must disclose to the court the existence of the adverse statute of limitations, because it is a law.

This ABA Opinion also appears incorrect when it states that the government lawyer may ethically file a suit to enforce a claim that she knows is time-barred by statute. If she files such a suit, she is involved in a proceeding within the meaning of Rule

---

[7] Formal Opinion 94-387 drew a dissent that rejected all of its conclusions. The dissent also argued, citing EC 7-14, that the "worst part of this opinion is its theory that government lawyers do not owe a greater duty to the public than other lawyers, particularly the pettifogger described in this opinion."

Cf. Freeport-McMoRan Oil & Gas Co. v. Federal Energy Regulatory Commission, 962 F.2d 45 (D.C.Cir. 1992). In this case, the counsel for an agency, FERC, did not bother to disclose in its brief that FERC had no objection to vacating a challenged order. The court vacated the orders and, at oral argument, FERC counsel rejected the idea that counsel for a public agency has any special obligations. Judge Mikva, for the court, cited EC 7-14 and responded: "We find it astonishing that an attorney for a federal administrative agency could so unblushingly deny that a government lawyer has obligations that might sometimes trump the desire to pound an opponent into submission." 962 F.2d at 48.

[8] *See, e.g.,* Rule 3.4. There are exceptions, for example, in an *ex parte* proceeding, the lawyer must volunteer adverse facts to the tribunal. Rule

3.3(d). If the lawyer submits evidence that he *later* learns is false, he must undo the harm caused by taking "reasonable remedial measures," including making disclosure of otherwise confidential information. Rule 3.3(b).

[9] Granted, the statute of limitations is an affirmative defense, which the defendant is free to waive. However, under the facts of this opinion, the defendant does not waive because the defendant is unaware of the law, the statute. And the trial court is similarly unaware. The statute is "legal authority in the controlling jurisdiction known to be directly adverse to the position of the client and not disclosed by opposing counsel." Rule 3.3(a)(2). Once the court knows of the statute, the defendant can still waive it.

There may be a situation where the statute is known to all parties, but defendant did not bother to subpoena a letter that would have demonstrated that facts existed to make this statute applicable. The plaintiff cannot engage in fraud but he does not have to volunteer this letter. The letter is a fact; the statute is law, a distinction that is crucial under Rule 3.3.

[10] Rule 3.3(a)(2).

3.3(a)(2), and so she must disclose the adverse legal authority that demonstrates that her case is time-barred. This duty extends until the "conclusion of the proceeding."[11] So even if she won the case on the trial level, and the time for appeal has not yet passed, she must inform the court that there is a statute of limitations that is directly applicable to this case.[12]

---

[11]Rule 3.3(b).

[12]The lawyer would not have to volunteer to the court the existence of facts that would make a claim time-barred because Rule 3.3(a)(3) applies to the law, not to facts.

CHAPTER 3.9
ADVOCATE IN NONADJUDICATIVE PROCEEDINGS

§ 3.9–1 Disclosure of Representative Authority
§ 3.9–2 The Distinction Between Adjudicative Proceedings and Other Proceedings
§ 3.9–3 Duties Applicable to Lawyers Representing Clients in Nonadjudicative Proceedings

---

RULE 3.9: ADVOCATE IN NONADJUDICATIVE PROCEEDINGS

A lawyer representing a client before a legislative body or administrative agency in a nonadjudicative proceeding shall disclose that the appearance is in a representative capacity and shall conform to the provisions of Rules 3.3(a) through (c), 3.4(a) through (c), and 3.5.

Comment

[1] In representation before bodies such as legislatures, municipal councils, and executive and administrative agencies acting in a rule-making or policy-making capacity, lawyers present facts, formulate issues and advance argument in the matters under consideration. The decision-making body, like a court, should be able to rely on the integrity of the submissions made to it. A lawyer appearing before such a body must deal with it honestly and in conformity with applicable rules of procedure. See Rules 3.3(a) through (c), 3.4(a) through (c) and 3.5.

[2] Lawyers have no exclusive right to appear before nonadjudicative bodies, as they do before a court. The requirements of this Rule therefore may subject lawyers to regulations inapplicable to advocates who are not lawyers. However, legislatures and administrative agencies have a right to expect lawyers to deal with them as they deal with courts.

[3] This Rule only applies when a lawyer represents a client in connection with an official hearing or meeting of a governmental agency or a legislative body to which the lawyer or the lawyer's client is presenting evidence or argument. It does not apply to representation of a client in a negotiation or other bilateral transaction with a governmental agency or in connection with an application for a license or other privilege or the client's compliance with generally applicable reporting requirements, such as the filing of income-tax returns. Nor does it apply to the representation of a client in connection with an investigation or examination of the client's affairs conducted by government investigators or examiners. Representation in such matters is governed by Rules 4.1 through 4.4.

Authors' 1983 Model Rules Comparison

The drafters of the 2002 Rules made one change to the text of the 1983 version of Rule 3.9. They substituted the words, "legislative body or administrative agency" for the words, "legislative or administrative tribunal." This change clarifies that legislatures are not typically referred to as tribunals, especially in a Rule that deals with nonadjudicative proceedings. No change in substance was intended. *See* Reporter's Explanation of Changes to Model Rule 3.9.

In Comment 1, the drafters strengthened the lawyer's duty to act honestly and to comply with procedural rules. The words, "should comply" were changed to "must comply" with reference to the lawyer's duty. The drafters also added a citation to Rules 3.3(a) through (c), 3.4(a) through (c) and 3.5.

No changes were made to Comment 2.

In Comment 3, the drafters of the 2002 Rules significantly modified this Comment to clarify the application of this Rule. Some ambiguity existed whether the Rule applied to government investigations or negotiations. The drafters added the clause that the Rule "only applies when a lawyer represents a client in connection with an official hearing or meeting of a governmental agency or a legislative body to which the lawyer or the lawyer's client is presenting evidence or argument." They also added one additional clause and a new sentence. This Rule is not intended to apply to a lawyer's representation of a client "in connection with an application for a license or other privilege or the client's compliance with generally applicable reporting requirements, such as the filing of income-tax returns." The drafters also stated, "[N]or does it apply to the representation of a client in connection with an investigation or examination of the client's affairs conducted by government investigators or examiners." Such representations are governed by Rules 4.1 through 4.4.

Model Code Comparison

EC 7-15 stated that a lawyer "appearing before an administrative agency, regardless of the nature of the proceeding it is conducting, has the continuing duty to advance the cause of his client within the bounds of the law." EC 7-16 stated that "[w]hen a lawyer appears in connection with proposed legislation, he . . . should comply with applicable laws and legislative rules." EC 8-5 stated that "[f]raudulent, deceptive, or otherwise illegal conduct by a participant in a proceeding before a . . . legislative body . . . should never be participated in . . . by lawyers." DR 7-106(B)(1) provided that "[i]n presenting a matter to a tribunal, a lawyer shall disclose . . . [u]nless privileged or irrelevant, the identity of the clients he represents and of the persons who employed him."

§ 3.9–1 DISCLOSURE OF REPRESENTATIVE AUTHORITY

A lawyer appearing before a tribunal may not mislead the tribunal regarding the fact that the lawyer appears in a representative capacity. This point is understood in any normal court proceeding, because lawyers have to file as counsel of record. Many nonadjudicative proceedings are a different matter, because there often is no formal procedure requiring the lawyer to "enter an appearance" as counsel of record. For example, lawyers will appear and give testimony before a legislative hearing or appear before an administrator and may never be asked if the attorney is there on behalf of a client or on her own behalf.[1] Rule 3.9 corrects that anomaly by requiring the lawyer to disclose if she is representing another party or representing her own interests.[2]

The identity of the lawyer's client is rarely privileged.[3] Even when it is, the lawyer may not mislead a judicial tribunal, an administrative agency, or a legislative body regarding the fact that the lawyer appears in a representative capacity. It is not misleading for a lawyer to disclose that she appears on behalf of another, whose name is privileged; it is misleading for the lawyer to pretend that she appears pro se when in fact she does not.[4] In judicial as well as nonadjudicative proceedings (such as those involving lobbying), the government has a legitimate need to know "who is being hired, and who is putting up the money, and how much."[5]

§ 3.9–2 THE DISTINCTION BETWEEN ADJUDICATIVE PROCEEDINGS AND OTHER PROCEEDINGS

Rule 3.9 does not apply to cases where one represents a client in negotiations or other bilateral transactions with an agency. Sometimes it may be unclear if the administrative proceeding should be treated as "bilateral," and therefore not governed by Rule 3.9, or "nonadjudicative," and therefore governed by Rule 3.9. There is very little case law in this area, but what there is suggests that term "nonadjudicative" is interpreted broadly, even though the organized bar may have a more narrow interpretation.[1]

The drafters of the 2002 Rules added additional language to

[Section 3.9–1]

[1]Of course, a legislative body or agency may have its own disclosure rules that require lawyers to provide this information as a condition of appearing before the forum.

[2]See also Restatement of the Law Governing Lawyers, Third, § 104(1) (Official Draft 2000).

[3]See, e.g., Colton v. United States, 306 F.2d 633, 637 (2d Cir.1962).

[4]Rule 8.4(c). Cf. Rule 3.9; DR 7-106(B)(2); DR 1-102(A)(4).

[5]United States v. Harriss, 347 U.S. 612, 625, 74 S.Ct. 808, 816, 98 L.Ed. 989, 1000 (1954) (upholding

disclosure provisions of Federal Lobbying Act, 2 U.S.C.A. §§ 261 et seq.).

This principle goes back many years. DR 7-106(B)(2); ABA Canons of Professional Ethics (1908, as amended), Canon 26: "[I]t is unprofessional for a lawyer [appearing before legislative or other bodies] to conceal his attorneyship. . . . "

[Section 3.9–2]

[1]In re LaCava, 615 N.E.2d 93 (Ind.1993) (per curiam) ruled that a medical malpractice review panel is a rule-making or policy-making tribunal for purposes of Rule 3.9. In that case, the court reprimanded and admonished the respondent.

Comment 3 to attempt to clarify this ambiguity. Rule 3.9 is not intended to apply to a lawyer's representation of a client "in connection with an application for a license or other privilege or the client's compliance with generally applicable reporting requirements, such as the filing of income-tax returns."[2] Also it does not govern situations when a lawyer represents a client in government investigation or examination of the client's conduct. In those cases, the lawyer is governed by the rules that govern transactions where the lawyer is dealing with nonclients on behalf of clients.[3]

§ 3.9–3 DUTIES APPLICABLE TO LAWYERS REPRESENTING CLIENTS IN NONADJUDICATIVE PROCEEDINGS

In general, if the lawyer represents a client in an adjudicative proceeding before any legislative or administrative agency, or involving the agency as a participant, then the lawyer has the legal rights and responsibilities of any lawyer acting as an advocate in a proceeding before a judicial tribunal. In other types of proceedings and matters involving the lawyer's representation of a client before the government agency, the lawyer has the same rights and duties in dealing with the agency as would a lawyer dealing with a private person.[1]

Even in the situation where the lawyer represents the client

But see ABA Formal Opinion 93-375 (Aug. 6, 1993), arguing that when a lawyer represents a client in a bank examination, the banking regulatory agency is not a "tribunal" for purposes of Rule 3.3, and the banking examination is not a "adjudicative proceeding" for purposes of Rule 3.3. Furthermore, this ABA Formal Opinion stated that the banking examination is also not a "nonadjudicative proceeding" for purposes of Rule 3.9. The ABA Formal Opinion stated that the lawyer's relationship with the banking agency should be treated as a bilateral proceeding for purposes of Rule 3.9. However, even in these circumstances, the Formal Opinion advised that the lawyer may not lie or mislead agency officials and be careful to avoid assisting her client's course of action if she (the lawyer) reasonably believes that course of action to be fraudulent.

For further discussion of this issue in the context of administrative actions brought by the federal Office of Thrift Supervision, see Harris Weinstein, *Attorney Liability in the Savings and Loan Crisis*, 1993 U. ILL. L. REV. 53; Symposium, *In the Matter of Kaye, Scholer, Fierman, Hays & Handler—Government Regulations, Lawyers' Ethics, and the Rule of Law*, 66 So. CALIF. L. REV. 977 (1993).

[2] Rule 3.9, Comment 3. The drafters of the 2002 Rules sought to bolster the ABA's position in ABA Formal Opinion 93-375 that the government investigation in a banking proceeding is not governed by Rule 3.9.

[3] Rule 3.9, Comment 3. This Comment refers to Rule 4.1 through 4.4. For example, Rule 4.2 regulates the lawyer's dealings with persons represented by counsel.

[Section 3.9–3]

[1] Restatement of the Law Governing Lawyers, Third, § 104(3)(b) (Official Draft 2000).

See, e.g., Attorney General of the

before an agency, Rule 3.9 does not impose on a lawyer all of the ethical requirements that are thrust on lawyers who represent clients in litigation in court. Rule 3.9 provides that the lawyer must conform to Rule 3.3(a) through 3.3(c),[2] as well as Rule 3.4(a) through 3.4(c).[3]

However, Rule 3.9 does not incorporate Rule 3.3(d), which governs *ex parte* proceedings, because those proceedings involve applications for a type of relief—a temporary restraining order, a default judgment—that are simply inapplicable to the nonadjudicative proceedings governed by Rule 3.9. Similarly, Rule 3.9 does not incorporate the portions of Rule 3.4 governing, for example, a lawyer's obligations regarding discovery, or the limitations on a lawyer asserting personal knowledge, because they are often inapplicable before municipal councils, legislatures, and agencies acting in a rule-making capacity. Of course, a lawyer who appears before an agency must follow the particular rules of procedure adopted by the agency.[4]

Rule 3.9 incorporates Rule 3.5, requiring a lawyer to deal with the tribunal with impartiality and not to seek to influence it corruptly or engage in *ex parte* communications unless other law permits those communications.[5] But Rule 3.9 does not incorporate the restriction in Rule 3.1 that prohibits making frivolous arguments because, in politics, it is standard operating procedure to design arguments that appeal to emotion and may not necessarily follow the rules of logic. So the cross-references in Rule 3.9 likewise deliberately omit any citation to Rule 3.1.[6]

United States v. Covington & Burling, 411 F.Supp. 371 (D.D.C.1976), where the court held that a lawyer who represents a foreign principal and who has registered as an agent under the Foreign Agents Registration Act of 1938 may validly claim the attorney-client privilege to withhold from disclosure to the Attorney General documents that are required to be kept under the Act

[2]This Rule requires candor to a court, prohibits misleading legal argument and presentation.

[3]This Rule governs matters such as destruction of evidence and disobedience to a tribunal's rules.

[4]Rule 3.9, Comment 1. Restatement of the Law Governing Lawyers, Third, § 104(2) (Official Draft 2000).

[5]*In re LaCava,* 615 N.E.2d 93 (Ind.1993) (per curiam).

[6]2 Geoffrey C. Hazard, Jr. & W. William Hodes, The Law of Lawyering: A Handbook on the Model Rules of Professional Misconduct (Aspen Law Pub., Inc. 3d ed. 2000 Supplement) § 35-1, at p. 512.

IV. TRANSACTIONS WITH PERSONS OTHER THAN CLIENTS

CHAPTER 4.1
TRUTHFULNESS IN STATEMENTS TO OTHERS

§ 4.1–1 Introduction
§ 4.1–2 Prohibitions Against False Statements of Material Facts or Law to Third Persons
§ 4.1–3 Disclosures Necessary to Avoid Assisting Client Crimes and Frauds Against Third Persons

---

RULE 4.1: TRUTHFULNESS IN STATEMENTS TO OTHERS

In the course of representing a client a lawyer shall not knowingly:

(a) make a false statement of material fact or law to a third person; or

(b) fail to disclose a material fact when disclosure is necessary to avoid assisting a criminal or fraudulent act by a client, unless disclosure is prohibited by Rule 1.6.

Comment

Misrepresentation

[1] A lawyer is required to be truthful when dealing with others on a client's behalf, but generally has no affirmative duty to inform an opposing party of relevant facts. A misrepresentation can occur if the lawyer incorporates or affirms a statement of another person that the lawyer knows is false. Misrepresentations can also occur by partially true but misleading statements or omissions that are the equivalent of affirmative false statements. For dishonest conduct that does not amount to a false statement or for misrepresentations by a lawyer other than in the course of representing a client, see Rule 8.4.

Statements of Fact

[2] This Rule refers to statements of fact. Whether a particular statement should be regarded as one of fact can depend on the circumstances. Under generally accepted conventions in negotiation, certain types of statements ordinarily are not taken as statements of material fact. Estimates of price or value placed on the subject of a transaction and a party's intentions as to an acceptable settlement of a claim are ordinarily in this category, and so is the existence of an undisclosed principal except where nondisclosure of

the principal would constitute fraud. Lawyers should be mindful of their obligations under applicable law to avoid criminal and tortious misrepresentation.

Crime or Fraud by Client

[3] Under Rule 1.2(d), a lawyer is prohibited from counseling or assisting a client in conduct that the lawyer knows is criminal or fraudulent. Paragraph (b) states a specific application of the principle set forth in Rule 1.2(d) and addresses the situation where a client's crime or fraud takes the form of a lie or misrepresentation. Ordinarily, a lawyer can avoid assisting a client's crime or fraud by withdrawing from the representation. Sometimes it may be necessary for the lawyer to give notice of the fact of withdrawal and to disaffirm an opinion, document, affirmation or the like. In extreme cases, substantive law may require a lawyer to disclose information relating to the representation to avoid being deemed to have assisted the client's crime or fraud. If the lawyer can avoid assisting a client's crime or fraud only by disclosing this information, then under paragraph (b) the lawyer is required to do so, unless the disclosure is prohibited by Rule 1.6.

Authors' 1983 Model Rules Comparison

The drafters of the 2002 Rules did not modify the text of the 1983 version of Rule 4.1. They did, however, modify several Comments in response to perceived problems with the prior language.

In Comment 1, the drafters of the 2002 Rules deleted a phrase that suggested that a misrepresentation "may occur by a failure to act." They added the notion that a misrepresentation may occur when a lawyer makes a "partially true, but misleading" statement. The drafters also added a cross reference to Rule 8.4 for false statements or misrepresentations outside of the context of an attorney-client representation.

In Comment 2, the drafters added the qualification "ordinarily" to make clear that sometimes an estimate of price or value or intentions as to a settlement or the existence of an undisclosed principal does constitute a false statement of fact. Whether there is permissible "puffing" or misrepresentation depends on the circumstances. This change recognizes that in certain conditions a lawyer may mislead a party in the context of such discussions. The drafters also added a new sentence to the end of Comment 2 to remind lawyers to "avoid criminal and tortious" misrepresentations.

In Comment 3, the drafters refocused the language from a short discussion of fraud to a broader comment about crimes and a reference to lawyer participation in client crimes and frauds. Much of this Comment contains new language and references to Rule 1.2(d) and Rule 1.6.

Model Code Comparison

[1] Paragraph (a) is substantially similar to DR 7-102(A)(5), which stated that "[i]n his representation of a client, a lawyer shall not . . . [k]nowingly make a false statement of law or fact."

[2] With regard to paragraph (b), DR 7-102(A)(3) provided that a lawyer shall not "[c]onceal or knowingly fail to disclose that which he is required by law to reveal."

§ 4.1–1 INTRODUCTION

Rule 4.1 governs the lawyer's obligations to persons other than the lawyer's own client.[1] It is important to understand that if the failure to disclose a material fact involves a *tribunal*, Rule 4.1 is not applicable. Instead, Rule 3.3 is the basic Rule governing the lawyer's duty of candor to a tribunal.[2] A lawyer's obligations under Rule 3.3 are greater than a lawyer's obligations under Rule 4.1.[3]

At first, the disclosure obligations that Rule 4.1 imposes may appear to be broad. Rule 4.1(a) appears to forbid making any false statements of law or fact to anyone, and Rule 4.1(b) appears to create affirmative duties when it provides that lawyers may not "fail to disclose a material fact" to a third person.[4] Neither of these obligations is as significant as they first appear. Sometimes what the right hand gives, the left hand takes away. In this case, the Comments to Rule 4.1 appear to take away some of the black letter in Rule 4.1. This was the result under the 1983 Model Rules and it was continued under the 2002 Model Rules. The amendments adopted by the ABA House of Delegates in 2002, however, seem to change the narrow obligation of lawyers to disclose information under Rule 4.1.

§ 4.1–2 PROHIBITIONS AGAINST FALSE STATEMENTS OF MATERIAL FACTS OR LAW TO THIRD PERSONS

Rule 4.1(a) states that a lawyer, while representing her client, "shall not knowingly . . . make a false statement of material law or fact to a third person." This obligation covers statements made to all third persons such as opposing parties or their counsel in the course of a representation.[1] This Rule applies to litigation

---

[Section 4.1–1]

[1]*See also* Restatement of the Law Governing Lawyers § 98 ("Statements to Non-Client") (Official Draft 2000).

[2]The specific subsection is Rule 3.3(b), which governs that situation and prohibits the misrepresentation.

[3]The lawyer's duty in the event of a falsehood under Rule 3.3 may even require disclosure of the perjury to the tribunal because of the lawyer's duty of candor owed to tribunals. Rule 3.3(c).

Adjudicative Proceedings. Concerning the lawyer's duty in litigation, *see also* Rule 3.4. For example, during the trial the lawyer may not "allude" to any matter not reasonably believed to be relevant, or admissible. Nor may he, in closing argument or otherwise, assert his personal opinion or knowledge regarding facts at issue, unless he is actually testifying as a witness. Rule 3.4(e). DR 7-106(C)(1), (3), (4).

Nonadjudicative proceedings. For more information about truthfulness in nonadjudicative proceedings, see Rule 3.9.

[4]Rule 4.1(b).

[Section 4.1–2]

[1]If a lawyer makes a misrepresentation outside of a client representation, that conduct would be governed

and nonlitigation representations and in litigation applies in addition to the obligations to the tribunal under Rule 3.3.

The Comments reaffirm the need for lawyers to be truthful, even when dealing with adversaries.[2] However, they also make it clear that lawyers usually have no duty to inform to opposing parties relevant facts if they are not asked. Of course, when other law or the procedures of a court (such as the discovery rules) require disclosure, that other law overrides this general view that lawyering takes place within the context of an adversary system.

If a lawyer makes an affirmative statement, that statement should be truthful and not misleading. The drafters of the 2002 Rules elaborated on how Rule 4.1(a) prohibits misleading statements. A misleading statement encompasses statements that are partially true but misleading or statements that omit a material fact needed for the statement to be accurate.[3] Half-truths are whole lies.[4]

Lawyers violate Rule 4.1 if they refer to, incorporate, or affirm the statement of another person, such as the client, that the lawyer knows is false.[5] The lawyer cannot avoid responsibility by truthfully stating that another person has made a statement when the lawyer knows that other statement is false. A lawyer makes a false statement if he simply repeats the false statements of another when he knows that those other statements are false.

For example, assume that Client has contracted to sell interests in Client's business to Buyer. To assist Client, Lawyer for Client prepares an offering statement to present to Buyer. Lawyer knows that information in the statement, provided by Client, is materially misleading because it shows that Client's business as profitable and growing, but Lawyer knows that its assets are heavily encumbered, business is declining and unprofitable, and

---

by Rule 8.4. *See* Rule 4.1, Comment 1.

[2]Rule 4.1, Comment 1: "A lawyer is required to be truthful when dealing with others on a client's behalf."

[3]Rule 4.1, Comment 1 (prohibiting "partially true but misleading statements or omissions" that are the equivalent of affirmative false statements).

[4]*See, e.g.,* Restatement of Torts, Second, § 529: "A representation stating the truth so far as it goes but which the maker knows or believes to be materially misleading because of

his failure to state additional or qualifying matter is a fraudulent misrepresentation." Restatement of Contracts, Second, § 159, Comment b, stating that a half-truth may be as misleading as an entirely false statement.

In the Matter of Silverman, 113 N.J. 193, 549 A.2d 1225 (1988): A lawyer's omissions and affirmative misrepresentations in prospectus and loan applications intended to induce favorable decisions by lenders amounted to false statements.

[5]Rule 4.1, Comment 1.

the company has substantial debts. Lawyer's knowing actions assisted Client's fraud.[6]

Rule 4.1(a) prohibits lawyers from *knowingly* making false or misleading statements.[7] Knowledge comes from statements made by clients, documents in the lawyer's possession and other information that the lawyer learns in the course of a representation.

Lawyers should also be careful not to make affirmative representations when they in fact do not know if those statements are accurate or not. Although a statement made in reckless disregard of the truth or negligently by a lawyer may not violate Rule 4.1, such statements may expose a lawyer to civil liability to a third person.

In addition, there is the risk that a court will later conclude that the lawyer did "know" because she made a statement implying that she knew although she had no basis in fact for so implying. Consider *Slotkin v. Citizens Casualty of New York*.[8] A lawyer represented a defendant in a personal injury case that a brain-damaged child and his mother brought. The lawyer stated during settlement negotiations that "to the best of his knowledge" there was only $200,000.00 in potential insurance coverage. Documents in his possession, however, showed the existence of an additional $1 million excess policy. Based on the misrepresentation of coverage, the plaintiff settled the case and later learned of the truth. Instead of moving to set aside the settlement, the plaintiff sued the defense lawyer alleging, among other claims, that that lawyer was liable for fraud. The jury found for the plaintiff, but the trial judge granted the lawyer judgment as a matter of law. The Second Circuit reversed, concluding that the plaintiff had established sufficient *scienter*, which the court explained included " 'a reckless indifference to error,' 'a pretense of exact knowledge,' or '(an) assertion of a false material fact "susceptible of accurate knowledge" but stated to be true on the

---

[6]Restatement of the Law Governing Lawyers, Third, § 98, Illustration 1 (2000). This illustration is based on, *Molecular Technology Corp. v. Valentine*, 925 F.2d 910 (6th Cir.1991).

[7]Rule 1.0(f) (defining knowing to include "actual knowledge of the fact in question" and stating that "knowledge may be inferred from the circumstances").

See, e.g., Alvin B. Rubin, *A Causerie on Lawyers' Ethics in Negotiation*, 35 LA. L. REV. 577, 589, 591 (1975); Gerald Wetlaufer, *The Ethics Of Lying In Negotiations*, 75 IOWA L.

REV. 1219 (1990); Charles B. Craver, *Negotiation Ethics: How To Be Deceptive Without Being Dishonest / How To Be Assertive Without Being Offensive*, 38 S. Tex. L. Rev. 713 (1997); Brian C. Haussmann, *The ABA Ethical Guidelines For Settlement Negotiations: Exceeding The Limits Of The Adversarial Ethic*, 89 CORNELL L. REV. 1218 (2004).

[8]*Slotkin v. Citizens Casualty of New York*, 614 F.2d 301 (2d Cir.1979), *cert. denied*, 449 U.S. 981, 101 S.Ct. 395, 66 L.Ed.2d 243 (1980).

personal knowledge of the representer.' "[9] Later, a court disciplined the lawyer who made the false statement.[10]

Rule 4.1(a) prohibits a lawyer from making false statements of *material* fact or law. It applies to statements of fact and not opinions. "Whether a particular statement should be regarded as one of fact can depend on the circumstances."[11] Some of those circumstances can depend upon whether the statement is made in response to a specific question, whether it contains qualifications, or whether it is made in a disputed negotiation between represented parties.[12]

The Comments to Rule 4.1 elaborate by announcing that, "Under generally accepted conventions in negotiation, certain types of statements ordinarily are not taken as statements of material fact. Estimates of price or value placed on the subject of a transaction and a party's intentions as to an acceptable settlement of a claim are in this category, and so is the existence of an undisclosed principal except where nondisclosure of the principal would constitute fraud."[13] Hence, lawyers may engage in puffing about facts and values.[14]

One cannot "lie," but a lawyer can make statements regarding the party's intention as to an acceptable settlement, such as: "My client will never accept a penny less than $285,000," even when the lawyer knows that statement is simply not true. This "false"

---

[9]614 F.2d 301, 314 (2d Cir.1979).

[10]*In re McGrath*, 96 A.D.2d 267, 468 N.Y.S.2d 349 (N.Y.App.Div., 1st Dept.1983). The court held that held that the lawyer's negligent misrepresentation of his medical malpractice client's insurance coverage, his failure to appear at scheduled pretrial conferences, and his failure to cooperate in disciplinary committee investigations, after having received private admonishments and public censure in connection with other matters, warranted six-month suspension.

[11]Rule 4.1, Comment 2.

[12]*See Office of Disciplinary Counsel v. DiAngelus*, 589 Pa. 1, 907 A.2d 452 (Pa. 2006), *noted in* 22 ABA/BNA MANUAL ON PROFESSIONAL CONDUCT, Current Reports News 537 (Nov. 1, 2006). In *DiAngelus*, the court suspended the defense lawyer for five years for falsely telling a prosecutor that the charging officer in a traffic violation case had agreed to a plea bargain. The court held that the false

statement, which induced the prosecutor not to contest exonerating evidence presented by defense at hearing, was a "material" misrepresentation.

[13]Rule 4.1, Comment 2. *See also* ABA Informal Opinion 1283 (Nov. 20, 1973)(unethical in settlement negotiations to represent that class action will be brought if this intention is false). Although the Model Code would probably exclude "puffing" or immaterial misstatements, nothing in the Model Code specifically approves of the exceptions found in Rule 4.1, Comment 2.

[14]*Ausherman v. Bank of America Corp.*, 212 F.Supp.2d 435, 446 (D.Md. 2002): "Patently, certain aspects of the process unavoidably involve statements that are less than completely accurate, such as posturing or puffery, intentional vagueness regarding a negotiating party's 'bottom line,' estimates of price or value, and the party's ultimate intentions regarding what an acceptable settlement would be—all of which are thought to encompass representations that are not 'material.' "

statement is not a "lie" because, the official Comment announces: "a party's intentions as to an acceptable settlement of a claim" are not considered a material fact.[15] I suppose it depends on how one defines the word "lie." When a lawyer deals with another lawyer in negotiation, the ethics rules allow both lawyers to assume that they are not bargaining with the devil. The opposing counsel is not like the adversary selling allegedly genuine Persian carpets in an oriental bazaar.

For example, the lawyer cannot lie about insurance coverage.[16] Nor may the lawyer falsely assert that he is not tape-recording a conversation when, in fact, he is tape-recording a conversation.[17] The problem is not the taping, which violated no ethics rule or other law in this instance, but the lie about the taping.

For tort liability, it is typically necessary for the plaintiff to show reliance and injury. But for disciplinary purposes, there is no requirement for the disciplinary authorities to show that another person relied on the lawyer's false statement and was suffered injury.[18]

An ABA Formal Opinion[19] explains that Rule 4.1 really only allows a "certain amount of posturing or puffery in settlement negotiations" as an "acceptable convention *between opposing counsel*." But, the Opinion warns, a party's actual "bottom line" is a material fact. And, a "deliberate misrepresentation or lie *to a judge* in pretrial negotiations would be improper under Rule 4.1."[20] So, it appears that one could not falsely tell the judge, in a settlement conference, that "My client will never accept a penny less than $285,000," even though one may be able to make that same false statement to the opposing party when the judge is not there.

A more recent ABA Formal Opinion reaffirmed the view that lawyers may engage in "puffing" or "posturing" when making

---

[15]Rule 4.1, Comment 2.

[16]*See, e.g., Shafer v. Berger, Kahn, Shafton, Moss, Figler, Simon & Gladstone*, 107 Cal.App.4th 54, 67, 72, 69, 74, 79, 81, 85, 131 Cal.Rptr.2d 777, 788, 789, 791, 793, 797, 798, 801 (Cal.App.2d Dist.2003). The court held that the adversary lawyer owed plaintiffs a duty not to make fraudulent statements about insurance coverage. The litigation privilege did not protect the lawyer's fraudulent statements. The plaintiffs justifiably relied on the opposing lawyer's misrepresentation. The court relied on the Restatement of the Law Governing Lawyers, Third, § 98, which corresponds to Rule 4.1.

[17]*Mississippi Bar v. Attorney ST*, 621 So.2d 229 (Miss.1993), reversed the complaint tribunal and held that a lawyer's denial of surreptitiously taping telephone conversations that were, in fact, being taped warrants a private reprimand. "Attorney ST's actions, therefore violate the very precepts of Rule 4.1." 621 So.2d 229, 230 (Miss. 1993).

[18]Restatement of the Law Governing Lawyers, Third, § 98, Comment c (2000).

[19]ABA Formal Opinion 93-370 (Feb. 5, 1993).

[20]ABA Formal Opinion 93-370 (Feb. 5, 1993)(emphasis added).

remarks about willingness to make concessions or when making a demand in negotiations.[21] "A party in negotiation also might exaggerate or emphasize the strengths, and minimize or deemphasize the weaknesses, of its factual or legal position."[22]

The Opinion also considered whether the same rules should apply in a "caucused mediation," and it similarly adopted a view that a lawyer may engage in puffing with respect to negotiating goals or willingness to compromise.[23] It rejected the argument that when a third-party neutral becomes involved in a mediation, the parties should impose a higher standard to govern their mediation conduct.

In some circumstances, Rule 4.1(a) has real bite. In order for Rule 4.1(a) to apply, the statement made by the lawyer needs to be a *false* statement *fact* of that is *material*.

Virzi v. Grand Trunk Warehouse & Cold Storage Co.[24] is a leading case offering an example of an affirmative obligation to volunteer a special type of material fact to opposing counsel. The court held that when the lawyer's client dies in the midst of a settlement of a pending lawsuit, the lawyer has the duty to so inform the opposing counsel and the court. The lawyer not only has a

---

[21]*See* ABA Formal Opinion 06–439 (Apr. 12, 2006).

The ABA Opinion offers the following example:

"We emphasize that . . . care must be taken by the lawyer to ensure that communications regarding the client's position, which otherwise would not be considered statements "of fact," are not conveyed in language that converts them, even inadvertently, into false factual representations. For example, even though a client's Board of Directors has authorized a higher settlement figure, a lawyer may state in a negotiation that the client does not wish to settle for more than $50. However, it would not be permissible for the lawyer to state that the Board of Directors had formally disapproved any settlement in excess of $50, when authority had in fact been granted to settle for a higher sum.

"We emphasize that, whether in a direct negotiation or in a caucused mediation, care must be taken by the lawyer to ensure that communications regarding the client's position, which otherwise would not be considered statements "of fact," are not conveyed in language that converts them, even inadvertently, into false factual representations. For example, even

though a client's Board of Directors has authorized a higher settlement figure, a lawyer may state in a negotiation that the client does not wish to settle for more than $50. However, it would not be permissible for the lawyer to state that the Board of Directors had formally disapproved any settlement in excess of $50, when authority had in fact been granted to settle for a higher sum."

Id.

[22]ABA Formal Opinion 06–439 (Apr. 12, 2006), at 1. This Opinion expressly rejects the commentators' calls for fairness in negotiation. *Id.* at 2.

[23]"[T]he mediator in a caucused mediation meets privately with the parties either individually or in aligned groups. These caucuses are confidential, and the flow of information among the parties and their counsel is controlled by the mediator subject to the agreement of the respective parties." ABA Formal Opinion 06–439 (Apr.12, 2006).

[24]*Virzi v. Grand Trunk Warehouse & Cold Storage Co.*, 571 F.Supp. 507 (E.D.Mich.1983).

duty of candor to the *court*,[25] but, on this particular issue, she has a duty *"to opposing counsel."*[26] In *Virzi* the court set aside the settlement because of the lawyer's failure to volunteer this fact. The lawyer in such a case may also be subject to discipline.[27]

Virzi does not mean that counsel has a general ethical duty to volunteer adverse facts to her opponent. The death of a client is an unusual fact; it means that the lawyer no longer represents that client and—if she continues in the case—will be appearing on behalf of another client, *i.e.*, the estate. The lawyer is no longer the agent of a principal because the principal is now dead. Once the client dies, "any subsequent communication to opposing counsel with respect to the matter would be the equivalent of a knowing, affirmative misrepresentation should the lawyer fail to disclose the fact that she no longer represents the previously identified client."[28] The duty to disclose the death of the client is an exception to the rule that, in general, the lawyer has no ethical duty to volunteer adverse facts to her opponent. There is a duty, in short, to volunteer to the court and the opposing counsel that you no longer have a client to represent but that you now represent the estate of the client.

---

[25] Rule 3.3(a)(1), (2), (4).

[26] 571 F.Supp. at 512 (emphasis in original).

[27] *See Toledo Bar Association v. Fell*, 51 Ohio St.2d 33, 364 N.E.2d 872, 873 (1977), imposing an indefinite suspension from practice of law on a Workers' Compensation attorney who "understood that it had been the long established practice . . . to deny any claim for permanent-total disability benefits upon notice of the death of the claimant, [and] deliberately withheld information concerning his client's death prior to the hearing on the motion concerning the claim."

See also Di Sabatino v. State Bar, 27 Cal.3d 159, 162, 162 Cal.Rptr. 458, 459, 606 P.2d 765, 766 (1980). A lawyer misled the bail commissioner by failing to disclose all facts surrounding previous efforts to obtain reduction of bail for clients; that action constitutes misconduct warranting public reproval, i.e., reprimand.

Franklin v. State Bar, 41 Cal.3d 700, 709, 224 Cal.Rptr. 738, 743, 715 P.2d 699, 703 (1986) (misrepresentation regarding the dismissal of a court case); *Bach v. State Bar*, 43 Cal.3d 848, 855–856, 239 Cal.Rptr. 302, 306–307, 740 P.2d 414, 417–418 (1987) (misrepresentation regarding the existence of a court order); *Kentucky Bar Association v. Geisler*, 938 S.W.2d 578 (Ky.1997) (lawyer's failure to disclose her client's death to opposing counsel amounted to affirmative misrepresentation and warranted public reprimand).

With *Geisler*, contrast, *Gailor v. Alsabi*, 990 S.W.2d 597 (Ky.1999). The court explained: "the sole basis for our decision in *Geisler* was that she had violated the Code of Professional Conduct, specifically SCR 3.130-4.1, and ABA Formal Opinion 95-397. Whatever duties the Code of Professional Conduct may impose upon licensed attorneys, it has no relevance to the conduct of laypersons." 990 S.W.2d at 605.

[28] ABA Formal Opinion 95-397 (Sept. 18, 1995) (footnote omitted).

§ 4.1–3 DISCLOSURES NECESSARY TO AVOID ASSISTING CLIENT CRIMES AND FRAUDS AGAINST THIRD PERSONS

§ 4.1–3(a) Introduction

The introductory phrase of Rule 4.1(b)—a lawyer shall not "fail to disclose a material fact" to a third person—appears, at first blush, to impose a broad affirmative disclosure obligation on lawyers. But this obligation is followed by an important, restrictive "unless" clause. Rule 4.1(b) provides that a lawyer shall not knowingly "fail to disclose a material fact [to a third person] when disclosure is necessary to avoid assisting a criminal or fraudulent act by a client, *unless* disclosure is prohibited by Rule 1.6."[1] The "unless" clause places meaningful limitations on the disclosure obligation found in the first part of that Rule, because the "unless" clause incorporates, by reference, Rule 1.6—the broad rule governing client confidences.[2] Thus, the obligation to mandatory disclosure completely depends upon the language in Rule 1.6.

Nonetheless, although Rule 4.1's affirmative disclosure obligation is more modest than it first appears, the Rule still is relevant. Rule 4.1(b) does not require a lawyer to assist a client in a crime or fraud even if failure to assist would amount to a disclosure prohibited by Rule 1.6. So, in the situation where the lawyer has an affirmative obligation to do something, but cannot disclose because of Rule 1.6, the only alternative must be that he or she must withdraw. The lawyer may also file a notice of withdrawal, if required.[3]

Rule 4.1(b) cannot mean that a lawyer may assist the client in a criminal or fraudulent act if failure to so assist would amount to a disclosure prohibited by Rule 1.6. If Rule 4.1(b) means that, it conflicts with Rule 1.2.[4] In such a situation, the lawyer, in order to avoid violating either Rule 1.2 or 4.1(b), would have to

---

[Section 4.1–3]

[1] Rule 4.1(b) (emphasis added).

[2] Note that some jurisdictions (*e.g.,* Hawaii, Texas) have not accepted the "unless" clause.

[3] This topic is considered in the discussion of Rule 1.6. *See also* Ronald D. Rotunda, *The Notice of Withdrawal and the New Model Rules of Professional Conduct: Blowing the Whistle and Waving the Red Flag,* 63 ORE. L. REV. 455 (1984), reprinted in, 1985 CRIMINAL LAW REVIEW 533, and excerpted in 34 LAW REVIEW DIGEST 14 (Mar./Apr. 1985).

[4] Rule 1.2 (d) provides:

"A lawyer shall not counsel a client to engage, or assist a client, in conduct that the lawyer knows is criminal or fraudulent. . . . "

The lawyer may counsel or assist his client "to make a good faith effort to determine the validity, scope, meaning or application of the law." Rule 1.2(d). *See also* DR 2-109(A)(2); DR 7-102(A)(2); EC 7-4; DR 7-106(A).

General Counsel to a Criminal Syndicate. Consider the situation where the lawyer is hired to be, in effect, the general counsel for a criminal syndicate, or criminal organization.

withdraw under Rule 1.16(a)(1).[5] When withdrawing, even though the lawyer may not be able to blow the whistle, he *may waive a red flag* by filing a "notice of withdrawal."[6] He should also inform the client of the lawyer's obligations under the Model Rules.[7]

This analysis is confirmed by language added by the drafters of the 2002 Rules. The drafters explicitly cite to Rule 1.2 and state that Rule 4.1(b) is an "application of the principle set forth in Rule 1.2(d) and addresses the situation where a client's crime or fraud takes the form of a lie or misrepresentation."[8] The Comment notes that in most cases withdrawal and compliance with Rule 1.2 and Rule 1.16 will sufficiently discharge the lawyer's responsibilities. In some cases, "it may be necessary for the lawyer to give notice of withdrawal and to disaffirm an opinion, document, affirmation or the like."[9]

When a lawyer discovers that a client is committing a crime or fraud against a third person, the lawyer must under Rule 1.2(d) inform the client that the lawyer cannot participate in the crime or fraud. If the crime or fraud is ongoing and if the lawyer has provided legal services intertwined with the crime or fraud and if the client refuses to change course, the lawyer will need to withdraw under Rule 1.16(a). The lawyer may be required to inform the opposing party that the lawyer no longer represents the client. If documents, which contain falsehoods, have been given to the opposing party, the lawyer will probably need to disaffirm them even though this signals implicitly that a problem exists with those documents. Whether a lawyer may go further

---

Perhaps the lawyer has a retainer from a drug cartel, where the lawyer agrees to represent (and secure bail for) any runners who are caught by the police. Prior to the Model Rules, legal authority concluded that it was improper for a lawyer to be, in effect, the general counsel of an organized criminal organization. ABA Formal Opinion 281 (Mar. 11, 1952); ABA Defense Function Standards, Standard 4-3.7(c); *In re Abrams*, 56 N.J. 271, 266 A.2d 275 (1970).

The Model Rules have no provision that explicitly comes to that conclusion. However, a Comment to Rule 1.2 provides that a lawyer may agree to undertake "a criminal defense incident to a general retainer for legal services to a lawful enterprise." Rule 1.2, Comment 12. So, the Rules prohibit a lawyer from being general counsel to a criminal mob by negative implication.

In other words, a lawyer may have a general retainer to a large corporation that is a lawful enterprise, even though the lawyer fully expects that she may represent the corporation from time to time on criminal antitrust or criminal environmental defense matters. But, by negative implication, she may not ethically agree to be the general counsel for a criminal enterprise (*e.g.*, the Mafia, a criminal prostitution ring, or an illegal drug cartel), because those enterprises are not lawful.

[5] Rule 1.6, Comment 14.

[6] Rule 1.6, Comment 15. *See* Ronald D. Rotunda, *Client Fraud: Blowing the Whistle, Other Options*, 24 TRIAL MAGAZINE 92 (Nov., 1988).

[7] Rule 1.2(e).

[8] Rule 4.1, Comment 3.

[9] Rule 4.1, Comment 3.

and disclose information about the crime or fraud, depends upon the state's version of Rule 1.6.

§ 4.1–3(b) Analysis under the 2002 Rule 1.6

Under Rule 4.1(b), "a lawyer shall not knowingly . . . fail to disclose a material fact when disclosure is necessary to avoid assisting a criminal or fraudulent act by a client, unless disclosure is prohibited by Rule 1.6."

As was discussed in Chapter 1.6, the drafters of the 2002 Model Rules sought to expand permissive disclosure under Rule 1.6. However, the ABA House of Delegates, in 2002, rejected the effort to allow a lawyer to disclose to prevent a financial crime or fraud. The ABA House of Delegates adopted a version of Rule 1.6 that limited disclosure to situations (1) to prevent "reasonably certain death or substantial bodily harm," (2) "to secure legal advice about the lawyer's compliance with these Rules," (3) to allow a lawyer to defend against civil or criminal charges or to pursue a claim, and (4) to comply with the order of a court.[10]

This 2002 version of Rule 1.6 had a short life span, as discussed below. But it is still important to appreciate what it prohibited and outlawed, because that is the best way to understand what led to the 2003 revisions. When Rule 4.1(b) was combined with the 2002 version of Rule 1.6, it was unlikely that the mandatory disclosure would come into play in the vast majority of cases where the client used the lawyer's legal services to commit a crime or fraud against a third person because situations involving reasonably certain death or substantial bodily harm in connection with financial frauds are unlikely. The disclosure obligation of Rule 4.1(b) provision could apply if a client used the services of a lawyer to sell real property to a developer and the lawyer discovers that the client buried toxic waste in the soil that was reasonably certain to cause death or substantial bodily harm to the homeowners who would eventually live on the property. If the client refused to back out of the transaction, Rule 4.1(b) would require a lawyer whose services were being used to commit this crime or fraud to disclose this information to the third person.

However, if the client was involved in a financial crime or fraud against a third person that was not reasonably certain to cause death or substantial bodily harm, the 2002 version of Rule 1.6 would have prohibited a lawyer from disclosing the information and therefore Rule 4.1(b) would similarly prohibit the lawyer from making any disclosures to the third person. That was because the disclosure obligation of Rule 4.1(b) does not apply to information that Rule 1.16 protects. As noted above, the lawyer in many cases must withdraw from the representation under

---

[10]2002 Model Rule 1.6.

Rule 1.16(a), but disclosure is not an option open to the lawyer under Rule 4.1.

§ 4.1–3(c) Analysis After the 2003 Amendment to Rule 1.6

As discussed in Chapter 1.6, the ABA House of Delegates adopted two amendments to Rule 1.6 in 2003 in response to the Report of the Task Force on Corporate Responsibility. The changes increased the lawyer's ability to disclose information that otherwise would have been within the protection of Rule 1.6. The ABA followed the lead of many states, which had already increased the lawyer's ability to disclose in order to prevent or rectify financial frauds.[11]

The 2003 version of Rule 1.6 provides two new bases for disclosure. Rule 1.6(b)(2) allows a lawyer to disclose confidential client information to prevent crimes or frauds likely to result in substantial financial injury when the client has used the lawyer's services to further the crime or fraud.[12] Rule 1.6(b)(3) allows a lawyer to disclose confidential client information to prevent, mitigate, or rectify a past crime or fraud likely to result in substantial financial injury when the client used the lawyer's services to further client's nefarious purposes.[13] In both cases, the Rule obviously assumes that the lawyer was unwittingly helping the client. These provisions are likely to be involved in a significant percentage of crimes or frauds where the client uses a lawyer's services to injury a third person.

Rule 4.1(b) states that "a lawyer shall not knowingly . . . fail to disclose a material fact when disclosure is necessary to avoid assisting a criminal or fraudulent act by a client, unless disclosure is prohibited by Rule 1.6." When this provision is read in combination with Rule 1.6(b)(2) or Rule 1.6(b)(3), many situations will arise where a lawyer *must disclose* confidential client information to a third person to avoid assisting the client's criminal or fraudulent act. When Rule 4.1(b) is mandatory unless limited by Rule 1.6, the expansion of permissive disclosure in Rule 1.6 will lead to mandatory disclosure under Rule 4.1 to third persons in the context of financial crimes likely to cause substantial injury.

For example, assume that Seller (whom Lawyer S represents) is selling a large commercial mall to Buyer (whom Lawyer B represents). Buyer has asked Seller to sign a long list of representations and Lawyer S provides the representations to the Lawyer B. Lawyer S has helped Seller answer the representations and both attend the closing of the transaction. During the

---

[11] *See, e.g.,* Morgan Cloud, *Privileges Lost? Privileges Retained?*, 69 TENN. L. REV. 65, 90 (2001).

[12] Rule 1.6(b)(2).

[13] Rule 1.6(b)(3).

closing, Seller informs Lawyer S that a major tenant has given notice of an intent to vacate and that he has not disclosed this material information in the representations that he and Lawyer S had provided to Buyer and Lawyer B. The loss of this tenant significantly impairs the value of the property involved in the transaction, and Seller's failure to make this disclosure is fraud.

Rule 1.2(d) and Rule 4.1(b) now *require* Lawyer S disclose to Buyer this material fact; if Lawyer S remains silent, he would be participating in the fraud against Buyer.[14] Rather than rush to blow the whistle on his client, Lawyer S should first inform Seller about the requirements under 4.1(b). When Lawyer S examines Rule 1.6(b)(2), which *permits* a lawyer to disclose information to prevent this future fraud, and Rule 4.1(b), which *requires* the lawyer to disclose information to avoid assisting this fraud, Lawyer S must inform B if Seller will not do so.

However, Seller will, in practice, inform Buyer because Seller really has no choice, once Seller knows that the ethics rules do not permit Lawyer S to solve his ethical obligations simply by withdrawing from the representation. Lawyer S must act because Rule 4.1(b) provides that the lawyer "*shall not* knowingly *fail to disclose* a material fact to a third person" in these circumstances. Unlike Pontius Pilate, Lawyer S cannot wash his hands of the problem by simply withdrawing from further involvement.

One must presume that the ABA House of Delegates knew about the interaction between Rule 4.1 and Rule 1.6 when they adopted the amendments to Rule 1.6 in 2003. It is curious that the ABA, under Rule 4.1(b), imposes a mandatory disclosure while Rule 1.6(b) only provides for permissive disclosure. The result is that Rule 1.6 only imposes permissive disclosure for reasonably certain *death* or substantial bodily harm and but Rule 4.1(b) makes disclosure mandatory for *financial crimes* and frauds involving substantial harm.

---

[14]*See, e.g., In re Rausch*, 272 Kan. 308, 318, 32 P.3d 1181, 1189 (2001) (per curiam), holding that a lawyer violated Rule 4.1(b) because, among other things, he failed to disclose to investors that "the investment program was a sham." The lawyer argued that his actions were not in "the course of representing a client," but the court responded: "he *did* act as an attorney for Deerfield." He also acted: "(2) as incorporator of Deerfield, (3) as regis- tered agent for Deerfield, (4) as Secretary of the Board of Directors of Deerfield, (5) as Secretary/Treasurer of Deerfield, (6) as a shareholder of Deerfield, and (7) as trustee of the trust which initially held the monies to be invested by Deerfield in [sic] behalf of the investors." 272 Kan. 308, 329, 32 P.3d 1181, 1196 (emphasis in original). The court suspended the lawyer for two years.

CHAPTER 4.2

COMMUNICATIONS WITH A PERSON REPRESENTED BY COUNSEL

RULE 4.2: COMMUNICATION WITH PERSON REPRESENTED BY COUNSEL

In representing a client, a lawyer shall not communicate about the subject of the representation with a person the lawyer knows to be represented by another lawyer in the matter, unless the lawyer has the consent of the other lawyer or is authorized to do so by law or a court order.

Comment

[1] This Rule contributes to the proper functioning of the legal system by protecting a person who has chosen to be represented by a lawyer in a matter against possible overreaching by other lawyers who are participating in the matter, interference by those lawyers with the client-lawyer relationship and the uncounselled disclosure of information relating to the representation.

[2] This Rule applies to communications with any person who is represented by counsel concerning the matter to which the communication relates.

[3] The Rule applies even though the represented person initiates or consents to the communication. A lawyer must immediately terminate communication with a person if, after commencing communication, the lawyer learns that the person is one with whom communication is not permitted by this Rule.

[4] This Rule does not prohibit communication with a represented person, or an employee or agent of such a person, concerning matters outside the representation. For example, the existence of a controversy between a government agency and a private party, or between two organizations, does not prohibit a lawyer for either from communicating with nonlawyer representatives of the other regarding a separate matter. Nor does this Rule preclude com-

munication with a represented person who is seeking advice from a lawyer who is not otherwise representing a client in the matter. A lawyer may not make a communication prohibited by this Rule through the acts of another. See Rule 8.4(a). Parties to a matter may communicate directly with each other, and a lawyer is not prohibited from advising a client concerning a communication that the client is legally entitled to make. Also, a lawyer having independent justification or legal authorization for communicating with a represented person is permitted to do so.

[5] Communications authorized by law may include communications by a lawyer on behalf of a client who is exercising a constitutional or other legal right to communicate with the government. Communications authorized by law may also include investigative activities of lawyers representing governmental entities, directly or through investigative agents, prior to the commencement of criminal or civil enforcement proceedings. When communicating with the accused in a criminal matter, a government lawyer must comply with this Rule in addition to honoring the constitutional rights of the accused. The fact that a communication does not violate a state or federal constitutional right is insufficient to establish that the communication is permissible under this Rule.

[6] A lawyer who is uncertain whether a communication with a represented person is permissible may seek a court order. A lawyer may also seek a court order in exceptional circumstances to authorize a communication that would otherwise be prohibited by this Rule, for example, where communication with a person represented by counsel is necessary to avoid reasonably certain injury.

[7] In the case of a represented organization, this Rule prohibits communications with a constituent of the organization who supervises, directs or regularly consults with the organization's lawyer concerning the matter or has authority to obligate the organization with respect to the matter or whose act or omission in connection with the matter may be imputed to the organization for purposes of civil or criminal liability. Consent of the organization's lawyer is not required for communication with a former constituent. If a constituent of the organization is represented in the matter by his or her own counsel, the consent by that counsel to a communication will be sufficient for purposes of this Rule. Compare Rule 3.4(f). In communicating with a current or former constituent of an organization, a lawyer must not use methods of obtaining evidence that violate the legal rights of the organization. See Rule 4.4.

[8] The prohibition on communications with a represented person only applies in circumstances where the lawyer knows that the person is in fact represented in the matter to be discussed. This means that the lawyer has actual knowledge of the fact of the representation; but such actual knowledge may be inferred from the circumstances. See Rule 1.0(f). Thus, the lawyer cannot evade the requirement of obtaining the consent of counsel by closing eyes to the obvious.

[9] In the event the person with whom the lawyer communicates is not known to be represented by counsel in the matter, the lawyer's communications are subject to Rule 4.3.

Authors' 1983 Model Rules Comparison

Since the adoption of the 1983 version of Rule 4.2, the ABA House of Delegates has considered many proposed amendments to the Rule. In 1995, the ABA amended the Rule by changing the word "party" to the word "person." The amendment added to the Comments three new paragraphs (2, 5 & 6) and revised the remaining paragraphs.

The drafters of the 2002 Rules considered many proposals on this Rule, but they ultimately resisted any provisions that addressed the special problems of federal prosecutors. The drafters of the 2002 Rules amended the 1983 version of Rule 4.2 to permit communication with a represented party if the contact is authorized by court order. *See* Reporter's Explanation of Changes to Model Rule 4.2. Despite this minor change in text, the drafters significantly modified the Comments.

Comment 1 is new and addresses the reasons underlying this Rule.

Old Comment 1 is moved to Comment 4 and modified to state that this Rule does not prohibit clients from seeking second opinions from lawyers not representing persons in this matter.

Old Comment 2 is moved to Comment 5 and modified to explain more precisely the right of citizens to communicate with their government. The drafters also added two sentences for government communications with an accused criminal defendant. Such contacts implicate this Rule as well as constitutional rights of the accused.

Old Comment 3 is moved to Comment 2 and modified. The Comment now explains the expansive scope of Rule 4.2.

Comment 3 is new and states that the Rule applies even when the client initiates the communication. The lawyer must discontinue the communication and comply with Rule 4.2.

Comment 6 is new and discusses the possibility that a party may seek a court order to permit contact with a represented party.

Old Comment 4 is moved to Comment 7 and modified to narrow the definition of persons in an organization who are covered by this Rule.

Old Comment 5 is moved to Comment 8 and modified.

Old Comment 6 is moved to Comment 9 with no changes.

MODEL CODE COMPARISON

This Rule is substantially identical to DR 7–104(A)(1) except for the substitution of the term "person" for "party."

§ 4.2–1 THE GENERAL PRINCIPLE

§ 4.2–1(a) Introduction

Rule 4.2 is often called the anti-contact rule. It places important restrictions on lawyers who seek to contact other persons whom the lawyer knows are represented in the matter. If a lawyer for a client (Lawyer #1) knows that another party is represented by his own attorney (Lawyer #2), then Lawyer #1 may not communicate with the party represented by Lawyer #2 in that matter unless Lawyer #2 consents.[1]

The obvious reason for this requirement is to prevent lawyers from overreaching the person contacted.[2] In addition, Rule 4.2 helps to protect the attorney-client privilege.[3] During the ABA debates on Rule 4.2, the Reporter for the Model Rules said that "the purpose of Rule 4.2 was to protect the lawyer-client relationship against breach by a lawyer representing another."[4]

This Rule has a long lineage. The original ABA Canons of Professional Ethics included a no contact rule.[5] The ABA Model Code[6] adopted this requirement, as did the Restatement of the Law Governing Lawyers.[7]

The same no-contact rule applies to non-parties who happen to be represented by counsel for that particular matter.[8] This extension of the requirement to all "persons" (whether or not parties to a lawsuit), is quite consistent with the rationale of preventing overreaching by counsel for another person.

Although nonparties (*e.g.,* witnesses) usually do not retain counsel to represent them, sometimes they do. A witness, such as the complaining witness in a criminal rape case, may be represented by her counsel. The prosecutor represents the govern-

---

[Section 4.2–1]

[1]Rule 4.2; DR 7-104(A)(1); ABA Canons of Professional Ethics, Canon 9 (1990). See the extended discussion in, ABA Formal Opinion 95-396 (July 28, 1995).

[2]Rule 4.2 and Comment 1; DR 7-104(A)(1). John Leubsdorf, *Communicating with Another Lawyer's Client: the Lawyer's Veto and the Client's Interests,* 127 U. PA. L. REV. 683 (1979).

Douglas R. Richmond, *Let's Talk: Critical Aspects Of The Anti-Contact Rule For Lawyers,* 76 DEFENSE COUNSEL J. 40 (2008).

[3]*Cf.* Restatement of the Law Governing Lawyers § 102 (Official Draft 2000), which provides that when a lawyer speaks to a nonclient who is not represented by counsel, the lawyer should not seek to obtain information that the lawyer should reasonably know that the nonclient may not reveal without violating a duty of confidentiality imposed by law.

[4]*See* The Legislative History of the Model Rules of Professional Conduct 148 (ABA, 1987).

[5]ABA Canons of Professional Ethics, Canon 9 (1908): "A lawyer should not in any way communicate upon the subject of controversy with a party represented by counsel; much less should he undertake to negotiate or compromise the matter with him, but should deal only with his counsel. It is incumbent upon the lawyer most particularly to avoid everything that may tend to mislead a party not represented by counsel, and he should not undertake to advise him as to the law."

[6]DR 7-104(A)(1).

[7]Restatement of the Law Governing Lawyers, Third, §§ 99 to 102 (Official Draft 2000).

[8]The Model Code, in DR 7-104(A)(1) used the word "party." Initially, the title to Rule 4.2 used the word "person," although the Rule itself used the narrower term, "party." In 1995, Rule 4.2 was amended to make clear that it applies to any represented "person," whether or not a party to the litigation or other matter.

ment, not the complaining witness. The no-contact rule applies to these nonparties.

Rule 4.2 and Contacts with Corporate In–House Counsel. Rule 4.2 generally does not prohibit a lawyer who represents an organization in a matter from communicating with the organization's inside counsel about the subject of the representation, even though outside counsel represents the organization in the matter. There is no ethical rule that requires the lawyer to obtain first the prior consent of the organization's outside counsel. The rationale is easy to understand. When "the constituent of an organization is a lawyer employee of that organization who is acting as a lawyer for that organization," then the protections that Rule 4.2 provides are not needed.[9]

There are a few exceptions to this general principle. If an inside counsel has her own independent counsel in the matter (and is not using the organization's counsel), then Rule 4.2 would apply. If the inside counsel is in fact a party in the matter (whether she uses or own counsel or uses the organization's counsel), then Rule 4.2 applies. The inside lawyer may be a part of a constituent group of the organization, "for example, when the lawyer participated in giving business advice or in making decisions which gave rise to the issues which are in dispute."[10] If the outside counsel asks the adverse lawyer not to communicate with inside counsel, that would be "a rare case," and in that instance, "contact by the adverse counsel might violate Rule 4.4."[11] If the inside counsel asks the opposing lawyer to contact only the corporation is outside counsel, the opposing lawyer should respect that.

§ 4.2–1(b) Undercover Operations

Literally, Rule 4.2 would prevent lawyers—either in civil or criminal cases—from participating in undercover operations. First, the undercover investigators would be misrepresenting whom they represent and their real purpose.[12] Second, these investigators would be contacting persons who are represented by lawyers, in apparent violation of the anti-contact rule.

Criminal Undercover Operations. A few courts have not looked with favor on undercover operations controlled by lawyers, on the grounds that lawyers should not be engaged in any decep-

---

[9]ABA Formal Opinion 06–443 (Aug. 5, 2006).

[10]ABA Formal Opinion 06–443 (Aug. 5, 2006) (citing Model Rule 4.2 Comment 7).

[11]ABA Formal Opinion 06–443

(Aug. 5, 2006) (emphasis added).

[12]Rule 8.4(c) forbids the lawyer from engaging in misrepresentation. Rule 8.4(a) forbids the lawyer from violating this rule "through acts of another," *i.e.*, the investigator.

tions, even when they are a part of legitimate law enforcement.[13] However, the alternative, in such cases, would be that police would still continue clandestine undercover operations but that lawyers would have no control over them and no ability to restrain them, because the lawyer would be forbidden to participate in an activity that is unlawful.[14]

---

[13]In *People v. Reichman*, 819 P.2d 1035 (Colo.1991), a prosecutor created a drug task force that used undercover investigators. One of these investigators identified a lawyer as a possible drug user. This investigator also expressed concern that his cover might have been compromised. In response, the prosecutor had the investigator arrested for a fictitious crime. This investigator then hired the suspected lawyer to defend him. Charges were filed, the investigator was arraigned, and the trial judge knew nothing of the deception. The purpose of this charade was to convince the lawyer that the investigator was really not a police undercover agent. When the Court found out the truth it was incensed. The prosecutor was publicly censured for engaging in fraud, deceit, and prejudicing the administration of justice.

In re Friedman, 76 Ill.2d 392, 30 Ill.Dec. 288, 392 N.E.2d 1333 (1979), was another case where the prosecutor allowed false testimony to be introduced in court. The respondent, an attorney in the criminal division of the Cook County State's Attorney's office, learned that the defense lawyer solicited a police officer to commit perjury. The respondent instructed the officer to agree to commit the perjury so that the state could then apprehend the person who offered the bribe. After the officer testified falsely under oath that a witness was unavailable, the defense lawyer gave the officer $50. The state indicted the defense lawyer for bribery.

Although the assistant State's Attorney allowed the false testimony to be introduced solely for the purpose of developing evidence to be used in a subsequent prosecution, a disciplinary

action was brought against him. Two justices found a violation of DR 7-102(A)(4), (6), & DR 7-109(B); they argued: "The integrity of the courtroom is so vital to the health of our legal system that no violation of that integrity, no matter what its motivation, can be condoned or ignored." These Justices refused to impose any sanctions, however, because respondent had acted without the guidance of settled opinion, and because of the belief of many lawyers that respondent's conduct in the circumstances of this case was proper. Two justices went further and found the respondent guilty of prejudicing the administration of justice. Two justices found that the respondent *did not violate* any ethical proscriptions at all.

[14]The Department of Justice has encouraged "federal prosecutors to play a larger role in preindictment, prearrest investigations." 59 Fed. Reg. 39,910, 39,911 (1994), because "greater participation of lawyers at the preindictment stage of law enforcement has been regarded as helpful in assuring that police investigations comply with legal and ethical standards." 59 Fed Reg. at 39,911. These undercover operations, by hypotheses, are lawful.

For example, the U.S. Supreme Court has specifically approved the use of testers in civil rights cases. These testers give out false information concerning the availability of a particular dwelling. The Court said that they, nonetheless, have standing to sue under the Fair Housing Act of 1968. *Havens Realty Corp. v. Coleman*, 455 U.S. 363, 102 S.Ct. 1114, 71 L.Ed.2d 214 (1982). In that case, the Court reasoned that the enforceable right to truthful information concerning housing is statutorily conferred on

On the other hand, the purpose of the prohibition against lawyers engaging in deceit or asking others (investigators) to engage in deceit on their behalf is to make sure that the lawyer does not overreach when dealing with a third party or abuse a fiduciary relationship. The purpose of the general prohibition against misrepresentation is not to prohibit investigatory techniques that are lawful and sometimes essential in the effort to uncover crime. Thus, other courts have ruled that, assuming the lawyer's conduct does not violate any other provision of law or a Disciplinary Rule, then, notwithstanding Rule 8.4(c), a lawyer, personally or through an employee or agent, may misstate or fail to state his or her identity and/or purpose in contacting someone who is the subject of an investigation for the purpose of gathering facts before filing suit or investigating possible criminal activity.[15]

In criminal investigations, courts recognize that it is often difficult to uncover criminal activity without undercover operations, and undercover operations involve deception. In some cases, the people who engage in such deceptions may be lawyers (some

---

all persons by 42 U.S.C. § 3604, and may be enforced without regard to an individual's actual interest in a house or apartment. 455 U.S. at 373, 102 S.Ct. at 1121.

The Rules of Professional Conduct, by definition, only apply to lawyers. If the only restriction prohibiting communication with a person is one of these ethics rules, then this restriction only applies to lawyers and results in forbidding lawyers from doing that which anyone else may do lawfully. Hence, a rule forbidding a lawyer's involvement while continuing to allow undercover operations operates to prevent lawyers from serving as a brake or restraint on over-zealous undercover operations by lay-investigators.

[15]*See, e.g.,* Christopher J. Shine, Note, *Deception and Lawyers: Away From a Dogmatic Principle and Toward a Moral Understanding of Deception*, 64 NOTRE DAME L. REV. 722 (1989); David V. Isbell & Lucantinoi N. Salvi, *Investigators and Discrimination Testers: An Analysis of the Provisions Prohibiting Misrepresentation Under the Model Rules of Professional Conduct*, 8 GEORGETOWN J. LEGAL ETHICS 791, 801–04 (1995).

United States v. Lemonakis, 485 F.2d 941, 955–56, 158 U.S.App.D.C. 162, 177–77 (D.C.Cir.1973), holding that, in a non-custodial situation, the Government's instructions to its informant, although provided by a U. S. Attorney as well as the investigating officers, were not such as to constitute the informant as the "alter ego" of the U. S. Attorney's office. "This was not a case where a defendant was in danger of being tricked by a lawyer's artfully contrived questions into giving his case away." 485 F.2d at 956, 158 U.S.App.D.C. at 177. "Finally, we cannot say that at this stage of the Government's investigation of a criminal matter, the public interest does not—as opposed to the different interests involved in civil matters—permit advantage to be legally and ethically taken of a wrongdoer's misplaced belief that a person to whom he voluntarily confides his wrongdoing will not reveal it. We find there was *no ethical breach by the U.S. Attorneys* prosecuting the case; accordingly, we need not reach what legal consequences might flow had we concluded otherwise." (internal citations omitted). 485 F.2d at 956, 158 U.S.App.D.C. at 177 (emphasis added).

909

F.B.I. agents are lawyers) and in other cases the people who supervise the undercover operatives are lawyers.

As Chief Justice Warren noted many years ago:

At this late date in the annals of law enforcement, it seems to me that we cannot say either that every use of informers and undercover agents is proper or, on the other hand, that no uses are. There are some situations where the law could not adequately be enforced without the employment of some guile or misrepresentation of identity. A law enforcement officer performing his official duties cannot be required always to be in uniform or to wear his badge of authority on the lapel of his civilian clothing. Nor need he be required in all situations to proclaim himself an arm of the law. It blinks the realities of sophisticated, modern-day criminal activity and legitimate law enforcement practices to argue the contrary.[16]

In pursuing crime the Government does not limit itself to behavior expected in your grandmother's drawing room. It uses sting operations, bait to trap a criminal, decoys, stoolies, and undercover operatives. Thus, there are many courts that have found no problem with criminal undercover operations.[17] Courts recognize that, in crimes leaving no complaining witnesses, active participation by law enforcement agents may be necessary to establish an effective case. "The agents' acts merely *appear* criminal; they are not, because they are performed without the state of mind necessary to support a conviction."[18]

In *United States v. Murphy*,[19] the court upheld the mail fraud conviction of a corrupt state judge. Some of the counts on which he was convicted grew out of contrived cases staged by the FBI and federal prosecutors as part of what was called "Operation Greylord," an investigation of the Cook County courts. Federal Bureau of Investigation and federal prosecutors established and ran this operation in which agents pretended to be defendants, prosecutors and defense attorneys. They tried phantom cases,

---

[16]*Hoffa v. United States*, 385 U.S. 293, 315, 87 S.Ct. 408, 420, 17 L.Ed.2d 374 (1966) (Warren, C.J., dissenting). In this case, the majority held that the use of testimony of government informer concerning conversations between defendant and informer or in his presence did not violate Fourth, Fifth and Sixth Amendment rights.

[17]Courts often explicitly recognize that the use of deception in compelling circumstances is not repugnant to justice, and is not sanctioned. *See, e.g., People v. Archer*, 68 A.D.2d 441, 449, 417 N.Y.S.2d 507, 513 (1979), *affirmed*, 49 N.Y.2d 978, 428 N.Y.S.2d 949, 406 N.E.2d 804 (1980), *cert. denied*, 449

U.S. 839, 101 S.Ct. 117, 66 L.Ed.2d 46 (1980).

[18]*United States v. Murphy*, 768 F.2d 1518, 1529, 18 Fed. R. Evid. Serv. 981 (7th Cir.1985) (emphasis in original).

[19]*United States v. Murphy*, 768 F.2d 1518, 18 Fed. R. Evid. Serv. 981 (7th Cir.1985). *Cf. United States v. Blackwood*, 768 F.2d 131 (7th Cir. 1985). (a lawyer and agent of the FBI describes two other concocted cases in which he represented "defendants" and paid a bribe through yet another police officer to obtain the corrupt disposition).

and offered bribes to judges (while they obviously concealed their undercover operations) in order to separate honest judges from dishonest ones. Agents of the FBI took the stand in the Circuit Court of Cook County and lied about their made-up cases in order to gather evidence about a corrupt state judge. The Government presented most of the evidence about the judge fixing cases through witnesses who had concocted the cases for the purpose of the Greylord investigation. An FBI agent, posing as a corrupt lawyer, would represent the defendants in phantom cases. Agents filed fabricated complaints and testified about made-up events. The corrupt judge would accept a bribe and acquit the "defendant."

The convicted state judge argued that the agents (including the lawyers involved) committed "frauds" on the court because the "cases" in which the judge accepted bribes were not cases at all. The Seventh Circuit rejected that argument. The law forbids extortion and a scheme to defraud, not merely a completed fraud. And the court explicitly rejected challenges to the ethics of the lawyers involved:

> The FBI and the prosecutors behaved honorably in establishing and running Operation Greylord. . . . The Greylord cases did not interfere with the smooth operation of the local courts or diminish the rights of any third party. They were, in this respect, less offensive than "sting" operations in which the police go into business as a "fence" for stolen goods. The existence of a well-paying fence may induce people to steal goods to sell to the fence. Here no stranger was at risk. Operation Greylord harmed only the corrupt.[20]

Undercover operations are a fact of life—for both criminal[21] and civil investigations—and they continue in spite of what some may regard as the literal restrictions of Rule 4.2. The majority of courts have held that the no-contact rule does not prevent non-custodial pre-indictment communications by undercover agents with represented parties that occur in the course of legitimate criminal investigations.[22] Such contacts are "authorized by law," and thus not prohibited by Rule 4.2.[23]

---

[20]768 F.2d 1518, 1529.

[21]Federal regulations allow such undercover operations. 28 C.F.R. § 77.6 lists various exceptions to the no-contact rule, one of which is when there is an investigation of "additional different or ongoing crimes or civil violations," including "undercover or covert" operations. See § 32-2.2, below.

[22]*United States v. Ryans*, 903 F.2d 731, 739 (10th Cir.1990): "We

agree with the majority of courts which have considered the question that [the no-contact rule] was not intended to preclude undercover investigations of unindicted suspects merely because they have retained counsel." *See also United States v. Dobbs*, 711 F.2d 84, 86 (8th Cir.1983): "Assuming that [the no-contact rule applies] it does not require government investigatory agencies to refrain from any contact with a criminal suspect because he or

Civil Undercover Operations. On the civil side, a typical undercover operation involves civil rights "testers," *e.g.*, people who seek to rent an apartment in order to discover if the landlord really is enforcing a racial quota or refusing to rent to blacks. The testers (an inter-racial couple) are not really intending to lease the apartment and so they misrepresent their true purpose when discussing the situation with the landlord. Commentators and courts have pointed out that, in these circumstances, applying the misrepresentation rules does not further their purposes.[24] Public policy supports an exception that, at the least, would allows investigators and discrimination testers to misrepresent their identity and purpose when they are investigating persons who are suspected of engaging in unlawful conduct.[25]

If the testers said that they were undercover investigators, it would undercut the whole point of the investigation. When a restaurant critic reviews restaurants, she does not announce, when she sits down, that she is there to review the restaurant for the next edition of the Michelin Travel Guide and that she "wants to be treated like anyone else." Instead, she acts like everyone else and does not impugn the integrity of her investigation by announcing her visit, anymore than a grade school teacher announces that "tomorrow there will be a surprise quiz."

Distinguishing Between Civil and Criminal Undercover Operations. Some courts have drawn a distinction between civil and criminal undercover operations, and only seek to sanction

---

she has retained counsel. [The Government's] noncustodial interview of Dobbs prior to the initiation of judicial proceedings against the appellant did not constitute an ethical breach."

[23]*United States v. Grass*, 239 F.Supp.2d 535, 541 (M.D.Pa.2003) (McDade Amendment, 28 U.S.C.A. § 530B, does not prevent preindictment undercover contacts because they are authorized by law).

[24]*See, e.g., Apple Corps Ltd. v. International Collectors Soc.*, 15 F. Supp.2d 456, 475 (D.N.J.1998) (lawyers in private practice may use "an undercover investigator to detect ongoing violations of the law . . ., especially where it would be difficult to discover the violations by other means").

See also David V. Isbell & Lucantinoi N. Salvi, *Investigators and Discrimination Testers: An Analysis of the Provisions Prohibiting Misrepresentation Under the Model Rules of Professional Conduct*, 8 GEORGETOWN J. LEGAL ETHICS 791, 801–04 (1995).

[25]*Apple Corps Ltd. v. International Collectors Soc.*, 15 F. Supp. 2d 456, 476 (D.N.J. 1998) held that an investigator's and tester's misrepresentation of identity is not a misrepresentation of "such gravity as to raise questions as to a person's fitness to be a lawyer," quoting David B. Isbell & Lucantonia N. Salvi, *Ethical Responsibility of Lawyers for Deception by Undercover Investigators and Discrimination Testers; An Analysis of the Provisions Prohibiting Misrepresentation Under the Model Rules of Professional Conduct*, 8 GEORGETOWN J. LEGAL ETHICS 791, 816 (1995).

lawyers who engage in deceptive undercover *civil* operations.[26] They would not sanction lawyers who engage in or supervise *bona fide* criminal undercover operations.

Banning All Undercover Operations. Some people would go further and completely ban all undercover operations involving lawyers. Undercover operations could still exist, but lawyers (including members of the bar who are FBI agents or other law enforcement personnel) could not be involved in them, and lawyers who would participate in, or supervise, or order them, would be subject to discipline.

The Oregon Supreme Court accepted this broad ban in 2000, when it reprimanded a lawyer who engaged in a civil undercover operation.[27] The court broadly held that any lawyer violates DR 7-102(A)(5) [or its counterpart in the Model Rules] by misrepresenting the lawyer's identity while engaged in the practice of law. The court said that the "prohibitions against dishonesty, fraud, deceit, and misrepresentation in DR 1-102(A)(3) are not limited to litigation or even to the representation of clients."[28] Moreover, this court added, lawyers—whether in either the private practice of law or government lawyers investigating a civil *or* a criminal

---

[26]*Sequa Corp. v. Lititech Inc.*, 807 F.Supp. 653, 663 (D.Colo.1992), stating: "Law enforcement authorities are afforded license to engage in unlawful or deceptive acts to detect and prove criminal violations. Private attorneys are not."

David V. Isbell & Lucantinoi N. Salvi, *Investigators and Discrimination Testers: An Analysis of the Provisions Prohibiting Misrepresentation Under the Model Rules of Professional Conduct*, 8 GEORGETOWN J. LEGAL ETHICS 791, 805 (1995), argue for a broader exemption, that there is no valid distinction to be drawn between civil and criminal investigations for purposes of the ethics rules governing undercover operations. *Cf. Hamilton v. Miller*, 477 F.2d 908, 909 n. 1 (10th Cir.1973), explaining that "it would be difficult indeed to prove discrimination in housing without [the testers'] means of gathering evidence."

[27]*In re Conduct of Gatti*, 330 Or. 517, 8 P.3d 966 (2000)(per curiam). This court acknowledged that "this court is aware that there are circumstances in which misrepresentations, often in the form of false statements of fact by those who investigate violations of the law, are useful means for uncovering unlawful and unfair practices, and that lawyers in both the public and private sectors have relied on such tactics." 330 Or. 517, 532, 8 P.3d 966, 976.

See also In re Chambers, 292 Or. 670, 680–81, 642 P.2d 286, 292–93 (1982), holding that a lawyer's knowing misrepresentation of himself as independent insurance agent violates DR 7-102(A)(5).

[28]330 Or. at 527–28, 8 P.3d at 973. In 2002, the Oregon Supreme Court amended its disciplinary rule to allow lawyers to advise and supervise otherwise lawful undercover investigations ('an effort to obtain information on unlawful activity through the use of misrepresentations or other subterfuge'). Art Garwin, *Covert Work OK: New Rule Lets Lawyers Supervise Undercover Probes*, 1 NO. 6 A.B.A. J. E-Report 9 (Feb. 15, 2002) (on Westlaw).

matter—may not misrepresent their identity or purpose in investigating a matter.[29]

A leading case that approved of undercover operations when they are conducted in ways that do not violate the basic purposes behind the anti-contact rule is *Gidatex, S.r.L., Plaintiff v. Campaniello Imports, Ltd.*[30] A furniture manufacturer sued to terminate a distributor for alleged trademark infringement. The defendant moved to exclude evidence on the ground that the plaintiff had used private investigators to secretly tape conversations with defendant's salespeople.

The court held that this conduct did not violate New York disciplinary rules against attorney misrepresentations and contact with represented parties because the investigators did not intrude on the distributor's lawyer-client privilege and did not attempt to use superior legal knowledge to take advantage of the salespeople. The lawyer had private investigators secretly tape conversations with terminated distributor's salespeople, in an effort to gain evidence in trademark infringement suit. The court announced: "hiring investigators to pose as consumers is an

---

[29]330 Or. at 539–40, 8 P.3d at 979–80. The U.S. Attorney said that one of his greatest challenges is coping with this state Supreme Court ruling because it virtually stops undercover investigations in Oregon. *See Ethics Rules 'Nearly Halt' Large-Scale Federal Criminal Probes*, AP, Fox News, Nov. 14, 2001, *http://www.foxn ews.com/story/0,2933,38803,00.html*, reporting that an "Oregon Supreme Court ruling on legal ethics has essentially shut down federal probes statewide into crimes such as drug trafficking, child pornography and extortion, officials say in court documents."

[30]*Gidatex, S.r.L., Plaintiff v. Campaniello Imports, Ltd.*, 53 U.S.P. Q.2d 1008, 82 F.Supp.2d 119 (S.D.N. Y.1999).

See also United States v. Parker, 165 F.Supp.2d 431 (W.D.N.Y. 2001), upholding the use of a "sting" type of undercover investigation in enforcing the federal criminal statute in question. The conduct did not, in the view of the court, violate any ethical rules and was not prohibited by DR 1-102(A) (4), because the sting operation required deceit.

Restatement of the Law Governing Lawyers, Third, § 99, illustration 2 (Official Draft 2000) approves of the contact in illustration 2 because the communication is on an "unrelated matter." The illustration states: "Plaintiff, represented by Lawyer B, has filed a personal-injury action against Defendant. Lawyer A, who is representing Defendant, directs Investigator to make an appointment at Plaintiff's place of business, a beauty parlor. While Plaintiff shampoos, cuts, and sets Investigator's hair, Plaintiff and Investigator engage in small talk unrelated to Plaintiff's lawsuit or physical condition. Investigator reports to Lawyer A, including several observations indicating that Plaintiff is not physically impaired as alleged. Lawyer A has not violated the rule of this Section because Investigator did not engage Plaintiff in conversation relevant to the matter on which Plaintiff is represented and only engaged Plaintiff in activities that Plaintiff engages in regularly in dealing with the public." This illustration was based on, *Mondelli v. Checker Taxi Co.*, 197 Ill.App.3d 258, 143 Ill.Dec. 331, 554 N.E.2d 266 (1990).

accepted investigative technique, not a misrepresentation." The court went on to say that the "policy interests behind forbidding misrepresentations by attorneys are to protect parties from being tricked into making statements in the absence of their counsel and to protect clients from misrepresentations by their own attorneys." In this case, the "presence of investigators posing as interior decorators did not cause the sales clerks to make any statements they otherwise would not have made. There is no evidence to indicate that the sales clerks were tricked or duped by the investigators' simple questions . . . ."[31]

Opinion 737 of the New York County Lawyers' Association Committee on Professional Ethics addresses the topic of undercover operations and dissemblance in a very meticulous way.[32] The opinion finds that some level of dissemblance serves societal goals in uncovering illegal practices. Thus, the general rule is that obtaining evidence under false pretenses is unethical for lawyers to do unless you fall within a narrow set of exceptions. The exceptions must involve: (1) seeking evidence of illegal activity that the lawyer believes in good faith is taking place or is imminent or evidence of illegal activity in the areas of civil rights or

---

[31]82   F.Supp.2d   119 (S.D.N.Y.1999) (footnote omitted).

Exclusion of Evidence as Inappropriate Remedy. The court went on to say that, even if there had been a violation of the New York ethics rule, the court would not, in these circumstances, enforce it by excluding evidence. 82 F.Supp.2d 119 (S.D.N.Y.1999). *See also United States v. Hammad*, 858 F.2d 834, 837 (2d Cir.1988) (discouraging suppression of evidence to punish unethical conduct of prosecutor); *Stagg v. New York City Health & Hosp. Corp.*, 162 A.D.2d 595, 556 N.Y.S.2d 779 (2d Dep't 1990) (court admitted testimony allegedly obtained in violation of New York's DR 7-104(A)(1)).

See also United States v. Parker, 165 F.Supp.2d 431 (W.D.N.Y.2001), holding that, even if the prosecuting attorney had violated ethical rules, suppression of evidence is not the proper remedy. The defendants based their suppression motion on three propositions: (1) there was no judicial approval of the use of a "sting" type of undercover investigation in enforcing the federal criminal statute in question; (2) the undercover operations did not meet the requirements of DR 1-102(A)(4) of the Code of Professional Responsibility, which prohibits attorneys from engaging in "conduct involving dishonesty, fraud, deceit, or misrepresentation"; and (3) the undercover investigation involved the Government's attorneys in unprofessional conduct as prohibited by DR 1-102(A) (4) because the sting operation required deceit.

One can find the rare occasion where a court will exclude evidence, but without citing precedent or discussing the issue. *Mundt v. U.S. Postal Service*, 2001 WL 1313780, *4 (N.D.Ill. 2001): "Mundt is barred from relying on the affidavits of both Michael Taylor and Stephen Brown," which were taken in violation of Rule 4.2. However, this comment is dictum because the court went on to say that it would reach the same result even if it admitted the affidavits, because "they do not generate a genuine issue of material fact that would preclude summary judgment." *Id.*

[32]*See* N.Y. County Lawyers' Ass'n Comm. On Prof. Ethics, Formal Op. 737 (May 23, 2007).

intellectual property, (2) the evidence is not readily available through other lawful means, (3) the conduct does not violate specific provisions of the ethics code, and (4) the conduct does not violate the law or ethics rules protecting third persons. In particular, investigators must not violate the anti-contact rule or misrepresenting the purpose of the investigation to unrepresented parties, or making false and misleading statements.

§ 4.2–2 SECURING CONSENT FROM THE PERSON'S LAWYER

If a person, let us say "Alpha," is represented by counsel, then the lawyer [Lawyer #1] who wants to talk to Alpha, a represented person, has to go through Alpha's lawyer [Lawyer #2]. Lawyer #1 asks to speak to Alpha. Lawyer #2 may allow Lawyer #1 to speak to Alpha alone, or Lawyer #2 may insist on being there in person, or Lawyer #2 may refuse to give Lawyer #1 permission to talk to Alpha, in which case Lawyer #2 may only talk to Alpha pursuant to subpoena and deposition.[1] This requirement of securing the lawyer's consent clearly "covers any person, whether or not a party to a formal proceeding, who is represented by counsel concerning the matter in question."[2]

§ 4.2–2(a) Knowing that the Person is Represented

Lawyer #1 will not know that she must ask Lawyer #2 for consent to contact a person unless Lawyer #1 first "knows" that Lawyer #2 represents this person in the matter. In typical litigation, counsel for plaintiffs and defendants will normally know that the other party is represented. All counsel file their appearances in court. However, in some cases—particularly in cases where a witness is separately represented, or where litigation has not yet begun—the lawyer may not "know" that the particular person is already represented by a lawyer for the matter in question.

[Section 4.2–2]

[1]Recall that, on behalf of her client, the lawyer may always *request* an unrepresented nonclient witness to refrain from voluntarily giving relevant information to another party *if* the witness is the client's relative, employee, or agent whose interests will not be adversely affected if this request is honored. Rule 3.4(f). The lawyer, however, cannot forbid such witnesses from being interviewed. Whether they are in fact interviewed is up to them. They can always insist on being subpoenaed and then deposed. At the deposition, opposing counsel will be present.

[2]Rule 4.2, Comment 2. *See also* EC 7-18 (using the word "person"). ABA Formal Opinion 95-396 (July 28, 1995), at 7 (interpreting the word, "party," in the original version of Rule 4.2, to mean "person").

"Know" means "really know;" that is, "actual knowledge of the fact in question."[3] It does not mean, merely "suspect," or "may have known" or "should have known." The lawyer must have "actual knowledge of the fact of the representation; but such knowledge may be inferred from the circumstances."[4] However, the lawyer cannot evade her obligations merely by closing her eyes to the obvious.[5] In other words, "know" means "know pragmatically," not "know existentially."

If the opposing party tells the lawyer that he is not represented by counsel, the lawyer is no longer bound by Rule 4.3. In one case, a lawyer met with an opposing party in a civil case at the request of the opposing party. Prior to this meeting, the opposing party stated that he was no longer represented by counsel in this matter, but his former lawyer had not moved to withdraw. The Texas Supreme Court held that the lawyer should not be disqualified in such circumstances because there had been no violation of Rule 4.2.[6] A lawyer cannot represent one whom he is not authorized to represent, even if the lawyer had filed a notice of appearance.

If the lawyer does not know that the person is represented, then Rule 4.3 applies.[7]

§ 4.2–2(b) Other Law[8]

Other law may preempt the no-contact Rule of 4.2.[9] This "other law" can include a statute or a regulation authorized by statute, a constitutional provision, or a judicial precedent.[10] If another

---

[3] Rules 1.0(f).

[4] Rule 4.2, Comment 8. *Accord* ABA Formal Opinion 95-396 (July 28, 1995), at 13:

" 'Know' does not mean 'reasonably should know'. . . . *Rule 4.2 does not,* like Rule 4.3, *imply a duty to inquire.*" (emphasis added).

[5] Once can infer that the lawyers "knows" if there is "substantial reason to believe that the person with whom communication is sought is represented in the matter to be discussed." Rule 4.2, Comment 8.

[6] *In re Users System Services, Inc.,* 22 S.W.3d 331 (Tex.1999). This court specifically disagreed with the dictum in ABA Formal Opinion 95-396 (1995), which said that the lawyer may not communicate with the adverse party "until the lawyer has withdrawn her appearance." The court said that the

party may not want his co-defendants to know about his decision to meet with opposing counsel. The court concluded: "We disagree, for reasons already stated, that communication concerning litigation is not allowed if a party's former lawyer has not withdrawn his appearance. The ABA opinion cites authority for other statements but none for this one." 22 S.W.3d 331.

[7] Rule 4.2, Comment 9.

[8] Castillo, J., citing Treatise, in *Parker v. Pepsi-Cola General Bottlers, Inc.,* 249 F. Supp.2d 1006, 1010 (N.D. Ill.2003).

[9] Rule 4.2, Comment 4. The last clause of the black letter Rule makes the same point.

[10] Rule 4.2, Comment 4. *See New York State Association for Retarded Children v. Carey,* 706 F.2d 956, 960–61

(2d Cir.1983), *cert. denied*, 464 U.S. 915, 104 S.Ct. 277, 78 L.Ed.2d 257 (1983), holding that it was proper for the trial judge to permit counsel for plaintiffs, as well as plaintiffs' experts, to interview government staff in order to determine if the government had complied with court rulings.

Undercover Criminal Investigations.

Rule 4.2, Comment 5 acknowledges that a communication "authorized by law" includes "investigative activities of lawyers representing governmental entities, directly or through investigative agents, prior to the commencement of criminal or civil enforcement proceedings, when there is applicable judicial precedent that has either found the activity permissible under this Rule or has found this Rule inapplicable." Sometimes the prosecutors and investigators under their supervision engage in surreptitious operations to catch criminals.

ABA Formal 94-396 (July 28, 1995), at 12, has similarly acknowledged this exception for undercover operations:

"[T]here is a body of decisional law that, in effect, concludes that the public interest in investigating crime may outweigh the interests served by the Rule in the criminal context, at least where the contacts are made with represented persons who have been neither arrested nor formally charged, and the contacts are made by undercover agents or informants and not by the government lawyers themselves (or by agents acting so closely under the lawyers' direction as to be their 'alter egos'). Accordingly, the Committee believes that so long as this body of precedent remains good law, it is appropriate to treat contacts that are recognized as proper by such decisional authority as being 'authorized by law' within the meaning of that exception stated in the Rule." (footnote omitted).

In *People v. Reichman*, 819 P.2d 1035 (Colo.1991), a prosecutor created a drug task force that used undercover investigators. One of these investigators identified a lawyer as a possible drug user. This investigator also expressed concern that his cover might have been compromised. In response, the prosecutor had the investigator arrested for a fictitious crime. This investigator then hired the suspected lawyer to defend him. Charges were filed, the investigator was arraigned, and the trial judge knew nothing of the deception. The purpose of this charade was to convince the lawyer that the investigator was really not a police undercover agent. When the Court discovered the truth it was incensed, and publicly censured the prosecutor for engaging in fraud, deceit, and for prejudicing the administration of justice.

Cf. In re Friedman, 76 Ill.2d 392, 30 Ill.Dec. 288, 392 N.E.2d 1333 (Ill.1979). The respondent was an Assistant State's Attorney working in the criminal division of the Cook County State's Attorney office. When respondent learned that the defense lawyer solicited a police officer to commit perjury he instructed the officer to agree to accept the bribe in order to apprehend the briber. After the officer testified falsely under oath that a witness was unavailable, the defense lawyer gave the officer $50, and the state indicted the defense lawyer for bribery. The state disciplinary authorities brought a disciplinary action against the prosecutor even though he had allowed the false testimony to be introduced into evidence solely for the purpose of developing evidence to be used in a subsequent prosecution against the briber.

Two justices on the Illinois Supreme Court found a violation of DR 7-102(A)(4), (6), & DR 7-109(B): "The integrity of the courtroom is so vital to the health of our legal system that no violation of that integrity, no matter what its motivation, can be condoned or ignored." 30 Ill.Dec. at 289, 392 N.E.2d at 1335. However, they refused to impose any sanctions because re-

law authorizes the contact, then Lawyer #1 may communicate directly with a person about the subject of the representation.

For example, in a class action, defense attorneys may secure a court order allowing communication with members of the plaintiff class in appropriate circumstances.

A statute, a court rule, or a constitutional provision may authorize a party or lawyer in a controversy with a government agency to speak directly to government officials about the matter.[11]

The First Amendment right to "petition the Government for a redress of grievances,"[12] is a constitutional right that Rule 4.2 obviously does not override.[13] For instance, let us assume that an Indian tribe is suing the U.S. Government complaining as to the Federal Government's interpretation of a treaty. The Indian Chief should have the same right as any other individual to complain to the Government (the House of Representatives, the Senate, the Attorney General, the President) that the Executive Branch should change its interpretation of the treaty. The trial lawyer handling the case may not like it that the lawyers for the tribe are going over his head, but the President of the United States

---

spondent had acted without the guidance of settled opinion, and because of the belief of many lawyers that respondent's conduct in the circumstances of this case was proper. Two justices went further and found the respondent guilty of prejudicing the administration of justice. Two justices found that the respondent did not violate any ethical proscriptions at all.

[11]Rule 4.2, Comment 4.

[12]**The Right of Petition.** The Court has held that the right is not limited solely to religious or political causes, but is applicable to any field of human endeavor including business or other economic activity. *Thomas v. Collins*, 323 U.S. 516, 65 S.Ct. 315, 89 L.Ed. 430 (1945), *rehearing denied*, 323 U.S. 819, 65 S.Ct. 557, 89 L.Ed. 650 (1945). Thus, a state statute cannot require labor union organizers to register with a state official before urging workers to join a union, for such a statute imposes a prior restraint on free speech and free assembly. 323 U.S. at 532, 65 S.Ct. at 323–24.

On the right of petition, see Gregory A. Mark, *The Vestigial Constitution: The History and Significance of the Right to Petition*, 66 FORDHAM L.

REV. 2153 (1998); Carol Rice Andrews, *A Right of Access to Court Under the Petition Clause of the First Amendment: Defining the Right*, 60 OHIO ST. L. J. 557 (1999); 5 RONALD D. ROTUNDA & JOHN E. NOWAK, TREATISE ON CONSTITUTIONAL LAW: SUBSTANCE AND PROCEDURE §§ 20.53 to 20.55 (Thomson- West, 4th ed. 2008) (6 volumes).

[13]*See* John Leubsdorf, *Communicating with Another Lawyer's Client: the Lawyer's Veto and the Client's Interests*, 127 U. Pa. L. Rev. 683 (1979).

CHARLES W. WOLFRAM, MODERN LEGAL ETHICS 614 to 615 (West Pub. Co. Practitioner's Ed. 1986) states:

"Requiring the consent of an adversary lawyer seems particularly inappropriate when the adversary is a government agency. Constitutional guarantees of access to government and statutory policies encouraging government in the sunshine seem hostile to a rule that prohibits a citizen from access to an adversary governmental party without prior clearance from the government party's lawyer." (footnote omitted).

does not need the permission of the government trial lawyer before he directly speaks with these lawyers.[14]

One can think of other illustrations. The U.S. Government may be suing a Fortune 500 company claiming that a violation of federal export controls. The CEO of that company has the same right as any other individual to complain to the Government (the House of Representatives, the Senate, the Attorney General, the President) that the suit is not justified, improperly interprets federal law, or is simply bad policy. The lawyers for the company have similar rights under the petition clause of the First Amendment.[15] The trial lawyer handling the case may not like it that the lawyers for the company are going over his head, but the President of the United States does not need the permission of the Department of Justice trial lawyer before he directly speaks with these lawyers.[16]

The purpose of this contact must be "to petition" the government. Petitions may be oral or in writing. The purpose of the petition may include settling a lawsuit or other controversy. Its purpose should not include the objective of trying to gain useful admissions against interest or confessions from a low-level government employee who is in no position to resolve any controversies.[17]

If a government official is separately represented in a particular matter—often the case if a litigant is suing both the govern-

---

[14]If the lawyer for the Indian tribe may not talk to the President unless the lawyer in charge of the case first gives his consent to the Indian lawyer pursuant to Rule 4.2, then the President will never be able to make the decision to overrule the government lawyer because the President will never learn of the interest of the Indian tribe's lawyer unless the government's trial lawyer first gives permission to this direct communication.

[15]The principle-called the *Noerr-Pennington Doctrine* after the leading cases, which construed the antitrust laws in light of the First Amendment Right of Petition-is that business interests may combine and lobby to influence the legislative, executive, or judicial branches of government or the administrative agencies. The antitrust laws cannot prohibit these concerted lobbying efforts because of the Right of Petition. *Eastern R.R. Presidents Conference v. Noerr Motor Freight, Inc.*,

365 U.S. 127, 81 S.Ct. 523, 5 L.Ed.2d 464 (1961), *rehearing denied*, 365 U.S. 875, 81 S.Ct. 899, 5 L.Ed.2d 864 (1961); *United Mine Workers v. Pennington*, 381 U.S. 657, 85 S.Ct. 1585, 14 L.Ed.2d 626 (1965), *on remand*, 257 F.Supp. 815 (E.D.Tenn. 1966), *aff'd in part, rev'd in part*, 400 F.2d 806 (6th Cir.1968), *cert. denied*, 393 U.S. 983, 89 S.Ct. 450, 21 L.Ed.2d 444 (1968), *rehearing denied*, 393 U.S. 1045, 89 S.Ct. 616, 21 L.Ed.2d 599 (1969); *California Motor Transport Co. v. Trucking Unlimited*, 404 U.S. 508, 92 S.Ct. 609, 30 L.Ed.2d 642 (1972). Rule 4.2 also cannot prohibit these lobbying efforts.

[16]Of course, this example assumes that the contact is not otherwise corrupt. In other words, the lawyers or individuals would be complaining about the policy, not trading campaign contributions for political favors.

[17]ABA Formal Opinion 97-408 (Aug. 2, 1997) at 10 n.15.

ment official in her personal capacity and the government—then the petition clause does not create an exception to Rule 4.2 as to this separately-represented official. The lawyer may not talk to the represented official, although the right to petition still applies to the government.[18]

ABA Formal Opinion 97-408[19] acknowledges that the First Amendment right to petition the government for redress of grievances modifies Rule 4.2, and admits that the legal commentators conclude that the no-contact requirement of Rule 4.2 "has limited, if any, application to contacts with represented government entities, in light of First Amendment considerations."[20] Nonetheless, this Opinion advises that the private lawyer "*must give* government counsel reasonable advance notice of his intent to communicate with such officials, to afford an opportunity for consultation between government counsel and the officials on the advisability of their entertaining the communication."[21]

One looks in vain at the language of Rule 4.2 for any evidence that the private lawyer, when exercising the First Amendment right to petition the government for redress of grievances, "*must* give government counsel reasonable *advance notice* of his intent to communicate. . . ." (Several members of the ABA Ethics Committee, which drafted this Formal Opinion, concluded that the advance notice should be permissive, not mandatory.[22]) The ABA House of Delegates could certainly amend this Model Rule and add such language, but it has not done so. The only language that specially relates to the constitutional issue appears to broadly exempt such government contacts from the no-contact requirements of Rule 4.2.[23]

Some jurisdictions have special rules to take into account the First Amendment rights at issue. California simply exempts all contacts with a represented government official.[24] The Washington, D.C. Rules expressly state that Rule 4.2 "does not prohibit communication by a lawyer with government officials who have the authority to redress the grievances of the lawyer's client

---

[18]ABA Formal Opinion 97-408 (Aug. 2, 1997), at 3 n.2.

[19]ABA Formal Opinion 97-408 (Aug. 2, 1997).

[20]ABA Formal Opinion 97-408 (Aug. 2, 1997), at 5 to 6, note 9, omitted, citing various authorities.

[21]ABA Formal Opinion 97-408 (Aug. 2, 1997), at 1 (emphasis added).

[22]ABA Formal Opinion 97-408 (Aug. 2, 1997), at 8, n.12.

[23]*See* Rule 4.2, Comment 5, exempts communications "authorized by

law." Professor Wolfram examined this Comment and concluded that Rule 4.2, Comment 5 made clear that Rule 4.2 does not apply at all to these types of contacts with governmental officials. CHARLES W. WOLFRAM, MODERN LEGAL ETHICS 614 to 615 (West Pub. Co. Practitioner's Ed. 1986)

[24]California Rules of Professional Conduct, Rule 7-103: "This rule shall not apply to communications with a public officer, board, committee or body."

. . . ."[25] Of course, the private lawyer contacting the government employee should not misrepresent his role. The private lawyer should also advise the government employee that there is pending litigation and that the government is represented by its lawyer.[26]

The Restatement of the Law Governing Lawyers recommends, in general, that the no-contact rule simply should not apply to communications with a government agency or government officer. If there is litigation involving a specific claim, contact is still permitted "so long as it does not create an opportunity for substantially unfair advantage against the governmental party."[27] The proposal satisfies both the interests in free speech and the interest of the government in protecting its valid concerns.

§ 4.2–2(c) Sanctions

A lawyer who violates Rule 4.2 is obviously subject to discipline. In addition, courts have sometimes imposed other sanctions. If the lawyer has approached the opposing parties directly, and negotiated an agreement with them, even though he knew that they were represented by counsel, the court may void the agreement.[28]

If the no contact violation occurs in the course of civil litigation, the courts have used a variety of sanctions. It is possible for courts to exclude from use at trial the evidence and information obtained during an improper ex parte communication until the excluded evidence is later obtained through properly conducted discovery.[29] This sanction does *not* exclude evidence, but requires counsel to cure the problem.[30] Courts have required the party who engaged in the improper ex parte communications to pro-

---

[25]Rule 4.2(d), Washington D.C. Rules of Professional Conduct. *See also* Rule 4.2, Comment 6, of the Washington D.C. Rules. This Comment expressly states that the lawyer may communicate "without the prior consent of the lawyer representing the government in such cases."

[26]Utah State Bar, Opinion 115 (1993).

[27]Restatement of the Law Governing Lawyers, Third, § 101 (Official Draft 2000). The Reporters for this Restatement would go even further than the American Law Institute and simply adopt the California approach, exempting *all* communications with a represented government client. *See id.*, Reporter's Note, Comment b, at 104.

[28]*Mintwood Corp. v. Fonseca*, 47 U.S.L.W. 2019 (D.C. Super. Ct. 1978).

[29]*Cagguila v. Wyeth Laboratories, Inc.*, 127 F.R.D. 653 (E.D.Pa.1989); *University Patents Inc. v. Kligman*, 737 F.Supp. 325, 328 (E.D.Pa.1990).

The court in *Cagguila* made clear that if the excluded evidence were later obtained through discovery that was properly conducted, then the information could be used at trial. 127 F.R.D. at 655 n. 3.

[30]Suppression of Evidence is not the remedy for a violation of the no-contact rule. *See, e.g., United States v. Grass*, 239 F.Supp.2d 535, 546 (M.D.Pa. 2003): "Assuming that AUSA Daniel violated the no-contact rule, suppression of the Noonan tapes is an

duce for the opposing party the information obtained during the communications.[31] Still other courts have elected to disqualify the party's counsel who improperly engaged in ex parte communications with the represented party.[32]

§ 4.2–3 CRIMINAL PROSECUTIONS

Rule 4.2 is intended to govern not only civil but also criminal cases.[1] The applicability of the Rule in that situation has spawned a great deal of controversy.[2]

First, it has long been quite clear that Rule 4.2 is inapplicable to grand jury proceedings. Prosecutors routinely question witnesses in grand jury proceedings, without their counsel's presence.[3] The grand jury rules do not even allow the witness to

inappropriate remedy."

[31]*University Patents Inc. v. Kligman*, 737 F.Supp. 325, 328 (E.D. Pa.1990).

Work Product Exception. The lawyer may object to turning over the evidence on the grounds of the attorney work product privilege, but the court is unlikely to be sympathetic to that plea. *Haffer v. Temple University*, 115 F.R.D. 506, 513 n. 3 (E.D.Pa. 1987).

[32]*Cronin v. Eighth Judicial District Court*, 105 Nev. 635, 781 P.2d 1150 (1989). The court noted that it was "undisputed" that the lawyer "had repeated and pervasive ex parte communications with management level employees of the Imperial Palace to discuss the Scanlon case." 105 Nev. 846, at 641, 781 P.2d 1150, at 1153.

[Section 4.2–3]

[1]Rule 4.2, Comment 5. This Comment also makes clear that "The fact that a communication does not violate a state or federal constitutional right is insufficient to establish that such a communication is permissible under this Rule."

But cf. State v. Richmond, 114 Ariz. 186, 560 P.2d 41 (1976), *cert. denied*, 433 U.S. 915, 97 S.Ct. 2988, 53 L.Ed.2d 1101 (1977), which said that DR 7-104 and EC 7-8 [the predecessors to Rule 4.2] "are generally assumed to be for the purpose of affording civil litigants some of the

protection which the Constitution guarantees to criminal defendants . . . .. *As long as law enforcement officers comply with the requirement of the Constitution in pursuit of their investigation,* an incriminating statement which is freely and voluntarily given is admissible." (emphasis added).

[2]The applicability of the no-contact rule goes back many years, before the existence of the Model Rules. *United States v. Ryans*, 903 F.2d 731 (10th Cir.1990) *cert. denied*, 498 U.S. 855, 111 S.Ct. 152, 112 L.Ed.2d 118 (1990), involved the secret recording of a conversation between the target of an investigation, known to be represented by his regular lawyer, and a cooperating witness prior to indictment. The court did not suppress the evidence obtained but reported that "it is now well settled that DR 7-104(A)(1) applies to criminal as well as civil litigation," and that it applies to agents of public prosecutors "when they act as the alter ego of the prosecuting attorneys." 903 F.2d 731 at 735.

[3]*Cf. Nai Cheng Chen v. INS*, 537 F.2d 566, 568–69 (1st Cir.1976), where the court refused to exclude evidence obtained from an interview for which there had been a failure to provide notice to counsel. The court noted that the immigration proceeding was not criminal, and that Immigration Service investigators are "authorized by law" to interrogate aliens or suspected

be attended by her lawyer. The witness may plead the Fifth Amendment, or leave the grand jury room between questions to consult with her lawyer, but the lawyer has no right to be present during her client's examination.

Prosecutors have tools of criminal investigation that go beyond the grand jury, and the exercise of these other tools has provoked controversy with the defense bar.[4] Often, the prosecutor may wish to secure evidence from a suspect covertly (by wiring an undercover agent or informant) without seeking permission from the suspect's counsel. Defense attorneys in some criminal cases have argued that such investigative techniques violate the ethics rules,[5] and that courts should enforce these rules by suppressing any evidence acquired by their violation.[6] The U.S. Attorney General disagreed and argued that prosecutors are authorized "by law" to make such contacts directly or through agents. In addition, the Attorney General, by promulgating a rule, has attempted to preempt and override any state or federal court ethics rule to the contrary.[7] State supreme courts and state disciplinary authorities do not take kindly to claims that the U.S. Attorney General has the power to exempt federal prosecutors from state rules of ethics.[8]

---

aliens, thus coming within the exception to the ethics rule. 537 F.2d at 569 & n. 7. However, the court said, it would be "better practice" to give such notice.

[4]*See* William Stuntz, *Lawyers, Deception, and Evidence Gathering*, 79 VA. L. REV. 1903 (1993).

[5]*See* Rule 4.2 and DR 7-104(A) (1).

[6]*See, e.g.,* Jerry Norton, *Ethics and the Attorney General*, 74 Judicature 203 (Dec.–Jan.1991).

[7]Richard Thornburgh, *Ethics and the Attorney General: The Attorney General Responds*, 74 JUDICATURE 290 (April–May 1991). *See also* Ronald D. Rotunda, *Abuse of Ethics Rule Hinders Prosecutors*, CHICAGO SUN-TIMES, Aug. 14, 1991, at p. 12, col. 1–2.

The Reno Memorandum and Rules. Attorney General Janet Reno issued formal regulations supporting the position of her predecessor, Attorney General Richard Thornburgh.

Her rules are complex (they occupy seven pages of the Code of Federal Regulations and another eight pages of the U.S. Attorney's Manual) and allow various exceptions, such as for "exceptional circumstances".

See Communications with Represented Persons, 28 Code of Federal Regulations, Part 77 (1994). In the comments accompanying this rule, Attorney General Reno emphasized that the Department of Justice "has long maintained, and continues to maintain, that it has authority to exempt its attorneys from the application of DR 7-104 and Model Rule 4.2 and their state counterparts." 59 Fed. Register 39910, 39911 (Aug. 4, 1994).

See also 59 Fed. Reg. 39910, 39927.

See 28 C.F.R. Part 77.

[8]Roger C. Cramton & Lisa K. Udell, *State Ethics Rules and Federal Prosecutors: The Controversies Over the Anti-Contact and Subpoena Rules*, 53 U. Pitt. L. Rev. 291 (1992).

The Attorney General's effort to override the ethics rules has, thus far, not succeeded.[9] The leading case is the New Mexico State Supreme Court decision, *In re Howes*.[10] When a murder suspect (represented by counsel) *initiated* a conversation with an Assistant U.S. Attorney ("AUSA"), and the AUSA responded by talking with the suspect without the suspect's lawyer being present or consenting to the contact, the New Mexico Supreme Court assumed disciplinary jurisdiction over the AUSA.[11] The AUSA was practicing in Washington, D.C. at the time but admitted in New Mexico. Both the DOJ and the AUSA filed unsuccessful federal suits challenging New Mexico's state court jurisdiction.[12]

The New Mexico Supreme Court admitted that there was "no evidence" that the AUSA's contact with the suspect "resulted in actual injury to either the defendant or the legal process in general," but the potential for injury "is obvious."[13] In addition, it was also troubled that the AUSA had not shown, in the court's view, sufficient remorse. The court reached this conclusion because the AUSA said:[14]

> I would never put myself in a position again to be a guinea pig, a test case, whether or not [the chief of the felony section] gave me the right directions, whether or not the Attorney General or the Thornburgh Memorandum, whether or not the District of Columbia Court of Appeals two years later said what happened was—if it was constitutional, it was proper. [W]hen you asked me if I would ever

---

[9]*E.g., United States v. Lopez*, 4 F.3d 1455 (9th Cir.1993), *appeal after remand*, 106 F.3d 309 (9th Cir.1997). Lopez was charged with a drug offense and feared his children were being abused while he was in prison. He wanted to discuss cooperation with the government. However, his lawyer had a reputation for refusing to negotiate. Thus, Lopez tried to deal with the government directly.

The District Court in *Lopez* held that—even where the defendant initiated the contact—it was so improper for the U.S. Attorney's office to talk to him in the absence of his lawyer that the court dismissed the indictment. The Ninth Circuit opinion was disdainful of the Thornburgh memorandum (on which the Department of Justice relied) and critical of the U.S. Attorney, but it concluded that dismissing the indictment went too far.

It has been argued that Rule 4.2 should not apply in criminal cases because prosecutors do not have "cli-

ents" in the sense that private lawyers do. F. Dennis Saylor, IV & J. Douglas Wilson, *Putting a Square Peg in a Round Hole: The Application of Model Rule 4.2 to Federal Prosecutors*, 53 U. Pitt. L. Rev. 459 (1992). However, the American Bar Association and state supreme courts have not accepted that argument. ABA Formal Opinion 95-396 (July 28, 1995), at 5 to 6.

[10]*In re Howes*, 123 N.M. 311, 940 P.2d 159 (1997) (per curiam).

[11]*In re Howes*, 123 N.M. 311, 940 P.2d 159 (1997) (per curiam).

[12]*In re Doe*, 801 F.Supp. 478 (D. C.N.M.1992); *United States v. Ferrara*, 847 F.Supp. 964 (D.D.C.1993), *aff'd*, 54 F.3d 825 (D.C.Cir.1995). Both of these lawsuits were resolved in favor of New Mexico's jurisdiction.

[13]123 N.M. 311, 321, 940 P.2d 159, 169.

[14]123 N.M. 311, 322, 940 P.2d 159, 170.

do this again, my answer was not to say that what I did then was wrong. I believe I was ethical and proper under those circumstances. And I would, given the same circumstances today, without any other changes, if this happened again, I would do the same thing. I wouldn't change.

The New Mexico Supreme Court also rejected the AUSA's contention that he should be excused under Rule 5.2[15] because he was acting at the direction of a superior. The court said that there was "no 'arguable question of professional duty' needing resolution."[16] The AUSA could rely neither on DOJ memoranda nor the direction of his superiors because the court thought that the no-contact principle of Rule 4.2 is quite clear. Consequently, the state court censured the AUSA.[17]

In the wake of that case, Department of Justice officials have expressed concern that the states' enforcement of their versions of Rule 4.2 has prevented U.S. Attorneys from investigating effectively. One Department of Justice official has claimed that the fear of being caught up in state ethics charges "has a severe chilling effect, which, I can testify to, happens every day at the Department of Justice."[18]

---

[15]Rule 5.2 (b) and Comment 2.

[16]123 N.M. 311, 316, 940 P.2d 159, 164.

[17]*In re Howes*, 123 N.M. 311, 322, 940 P.2d 159, 170 (1997) (per curiam).

After the New Mexico court censured the AUSA, Eric Holder, who was the Deputy Attorney General of the Department of Justice under Janet Reno, wrote a letter for the lawyer that said:

"It is the view of the Department of Justice that the sanction against you was inappropriate and should not have been imposed."

Quoted in, David S. Cloud *Did Starr Go Too Far in Questioning Lewinsky? The Rules are Unclear: Justice Department Allows More Leeway Than States in Grilling Some Suspects*, WALL STREET JOURNAL, March 5, 1999, at A1, A8, col. 1.

[18]*See* David S. Cloud, *Did Starr Go Too Far in Questioning Lewinsky? The Rules are Unclear: Justice Department Allows More Leeway Than States in Grilling Some Suspects*, WALL STREET JOURNAL, Mar. 5, 1999, at A1,

col. 1, quoting David Ogden, a top official in the Justice Department then headed by Attorney General Janet Reno.

Application of Rule 4.2 in Proceedings Involving Detainees Held by the Military. In response to the terrorist attacks of September 11, 2001, the United States invaded Afghanistan and Iraq, and captured alleged terrorists. The Supreme Court ruled that detainees held at the Naval Base at Guantánamo, Cuba, had jurisdiction to file petitions for habeas relief, but the Court did not indicate the nature of their substantive right. *Rasul v. Bush*, 542 U.S. 466, 124 S.Ct. 2686, 159 L.Ed.2d 548 (2004), *on remand*, 103 Fed.Appx. 676 (C.A.D.C. 2004). In another case involving a U.S. citizen captured in Afghanistan, the Court ruled that the Government must hold a hearing so that the alleged terrorist (who had been captured with an assault rifle but did not wear a uniform) would have "a chance to prove military error," that is, that he had been captured by mistake, for he may have been an "errant tourist, embedded journalist, or local aid worker."

§ 4.2–3(a) Congressional Statutory Response

In 1998, Congress enacted a new law that provides that U.S. government lawyers are subject to state laws, state rules, and federal court rules governing lawyers in each state "to the same extent and in the same manner as other attorneys in that State." The statute also requires the Attorney General to make and amend Department of Justice rules to "assure compliance with this section."[19]

The McDade Amendment "made the entire Rule 4.2, *including the authorized by law exception*, applicable to the conduct of Government attorneys."[20]

§ 4.2–4 COMMUNICATIONS WITH REPRESENTED PERSONS ABOUT MATTERS OUTSIDE OF THE REPRESENTATION

The requirements of Rule 4.2 are inapplicable if the communication does not concern the subject of representation but rather another, separate matter. For example, if a person files for personal bankruptcy and hires a lawyer to represent him in that matter, that does not mean that this person is "represented" by counsel in a hit and run accident. Similarly, in a controversy between two corporations involving one matter (a boundary line

---

Hamdi v. Rumsfeld, 542 U.S. 507, 535, 124 S.Ct. 2633, 2649, 159 L.Ed.2d 578 (2004), *on remand*, 378 F.3d 426 (4th Cir.2004) (O'Connor plurality). The Government offered hearings to all of the detainees held at the Naval Base. Many of the lawyers or purported lawyers, relying on Rule 4.2, filed motions before the habeas courts to preclude any questioning of these detainees unless they were present, for Temporary Restraining Orders, and for other relief. The Government argued that Rule 4.2 was inapplicable. Different trial judges, in unpublished oral orders and without written opinions, denied these various motions of the lawyers for the detainees. E.g., *Lakhdar Boumediene v. Bush*, CV04-1166 (D.D.C. Aug. 3, 2004) (trial transcript); *Salim Gherebi v. Bush*, 2004 WL 1729443 (D.D.C.2004) (trial transcript); (D.D.C. Aug. 3, 2004); *Jamil El-Banna v. Bush*, CV04-1144 (Aug. 6, 2004) (trial transcript).

[19] 28 U.S.C.A. § 530B, "Ethical Standards for Attorneys for the Government." This law went into effect 180 days after its enactment date of October 21, 1998. For a thorough article analyzing this statute, see Fred C. Zacharias & Bruce A.Green, *The Uniqueness of Federal Prosecutors*, 88 Georgetown L.J. 210 (2000). The authors are very critical and argue that the Citizens Protection Act, 28 U.S.C.A. § 530B, is "casual and flawed legislation." 88 Georgetown L.J. at 259.

McDade Amendment. This law, 28 U.S.C.A. § 530B, is often called the "McDade Amendment," after its sponsor. Congressman Joseph McDade. In 1992, a federal grand jury indicted Congressman McDade on five counts of offenses related to bribery. McDade claimed that there was prosecutorial misconduct and that Department of Justice officials violated various ethics standards. The trial court did not agree, and the jury eventually acquitted McDade, who introduced what eventually became the McDade Amendment.

[20] *United States v. Grass*, 239 F.Supp.2d 535, 545 (M.D.Pa. 2003) (emphasis added).

dispute), a lawyer for either of the corporations can communicate with nonlawyer representatives of the other on a different matter (a contract dispute).[1] However, if the two matters are related, such as co-employees each suing their employer for employment discrimination, the Rule applies.[2]

If the government has indicted a defendant on crime A, that does not prevent the government prosecutor from communicating with the defendant, either directly or through investigators, on crime B.[3]

§ 4.2–5 CLIENTS SPEAKING TO EACH OTHER DIRECTLY WITHOUT THEIR LAWYERS BEING PRESENT

This Rule does not prohibit lawyers from advising principals to speak directly with their counterparts. The Rule governs lawyers, not their clients, so "parties to a matter may communicate directly with each other . . . ."[1] However, when a lawyer represents himself pro se, Rule 4.2 can be interpreted to prohibit the lawyer-party from communicating directly with an opposing represented party.[2]

Rule 4.2, when read in connection with Rule 8.4(a)—a lawyer may not violate a Rule "through the acts of another"—suggests that a lawyer is precluded from "using an intermediary to carry a

---

[Section 4.2–4]

[1] Rule 4.2, Comment 1.

[2] *Parker v. Pepsi-Cola*, 249 F.Supp.2d 1006 (N.D.Ill.2003), involved Robert Gena (represented by his counsel) who had sued Pepsi for employment discrimination. Pepsi subpoenaed Gena for a deposition on the "Lopez Litigation," a related discrimination case. Pepsi's counsel served Gena personally with the subpoena and did not send a copy to Gena's lawyer. When Gena arrived at the deposition and informed Pepsi counsel that he had not notified his attorneys about it, the lawyer nevertheless proceeded and asked Gena questions pertaining to Gena's suit against Pepsi. Gena moved for a default judgment against Pepsi and its lawyers. The Court found that Pepsi and its attorneys violated Illinois' version of Model Rule 4.2. But because the court believed that any prejudice could be mitigated through discovery limita-

tions and other sanctions, it denied plaintiffs request for a default judgment. Instead, the Court barred Pepsi from using Gena's deposition testimony or any evidence obtained from it, required Pepsi to destroy all copies, summaries, and analyses of the testimony, and granted Plaintiff attorney's fees for the motion.

[3] ABA Formal Opinion 95-396 (July 28, 1995), at 14 & n. 42.

[Section 4.2–5]

[1] Rule 4.2, Comment 1.

[2] See *In re Jeffrey T. Haley, Attorney at Law*, 156 Wash. 2d 324, 126 P.3d 1262 (2006). The state supreme court held that Rule 4.2 applies to a lawyer proceeding *pro se*. However, given the ambiguity in application of the rule prior to this case, and the vague language of the rule, the court held that it would apply this interpretation prospectively only.

message from the lawyer to the opposing party . . . ."[3] On other hand, Model Rule 4.2, unlike its predecessor, specifically does not include in its command, the phrase—"or cause another to communicate."[4] In fact, the ABA House of Delegates specifically rejected a proposal to add that phrase to Rule 4.2.[5] Furthermore, the lawyer's client is not a mere "intermediary." Should not the client be able to talk to the other client directly if they wish?

Given these concerns, the general principle is that the lawyer cannot use a paralegal or other aide or "intermediary" to contact the adverse party directly. However, the lawyer "has a duty" to discuss with his client "not only the limits on the lawyer's ability to communicate" with the adverse party directly, "but also the freedom of the" client to "communicate with the opposing" party directly.[6]

Consider the situation where a lawyer representing a party believes that the opposing lawyer is not communicating a reasonable settlement offer to the opposing party. If Lawyer A (on behalf of Client A) makes a settlement offer to the opposing party's lawyer (Lawyer B), but Lawyer A believes that Lawyer B will not communicate that offer to Client B, even then Lawyer A may not communicate directly with Client B to determine whether the offer has been communicated. But Lawyer A may advise Client A that Client A may communicate directly with Client B about the offer.[7]

The lawyer may advise her client that she may (and perhaps should) talk directly to the opposing party. Sometimes, such direct encounters may lead to a fruitful settlement. And, in some cases, such direct encounters may be quite natural: if General Motors sues General Electric, the two CEOs may find it quite natural to meet face to face and talk.

---

[3]*See* ABA, THE LEGISLATIVE HISTORY: THE DEVELOPMENT OF THE MODEL RULES OF PROFESSIONAL CONDUCT 1982–2005 536 (ABA Center for Professional Responsibility, 2006).

[4]*Compare* Rule 4.2 *with* DR 7-104(A)(1), which uses the phrase, "or cause another to communicate." Note that the official "Model Code Comparison" asserts that Rule 4.2 is "substantially identical to DR 7-104(A)(1) except for the substitution of the term 'person' for 'party.' "

[5]ABA, THE LEGISLATIVE HISTORY: THE DEVELOPMENT OF THE MODEL RULES OF PROFESSIONAL CONDUCT 1982–2005 532 (ABA Center for Professional Responsibility, 2006).

[6]ABA Formal Opinion 92-362 (July 6, 1992), at 5.

[7]ABA Formal Opinion 92-362 (July 6, 1992) (a lawyer who has made an offer to opposing counsel may not call the opposing party to see if the offer has been communicated; but the lawyer may advise her client that she may talk to the opposing party directly to see if that party received the offer).

Some commentators advise that the lawyer, as a matter of ethics should not write "scripts" for their clients to follow.[8] This advice gives a competitive advantage to clients who are already articulate as compared to clients who need their lawyers as ghost writers. Thus, the ABA recognizes that parties to a legal matter have the right to communicate directly with each other. Hence, a lawyer may (1) advise a client of that right, and (2) may assist the client regarding the substance of any proposed communication. It is not necessary for the client to initiate the request for the lawyer's help in ghost writing any proposed communication. Of course, the lawyer may not use his client as a mean to overreach the other party.[9]

§ 4.2–6 EMPLOYEES AND AGENTS OF ORGANIZATIONS AND OTHER PARTIES

§ 4.2–6(a) Alter Egos

A corporation or other entity only speaks through flesh and blood agents. Consequently, the restrictions of Rule 4.2 apply to these flesh and blood agents when they are, in effect, alter egos of the entity. The general rule is that if a corporation or other entity is represented by counsel, then alter egos of that organization are also treated as persons represented by that counsel for purposes of the rule restricting communications to persons represented by counsel.[1]

In determining who is an "alter ego," an ABA Informal Opinion interpreting the Model Code concluded that if the officers and employees that the lawyer proposes to interview "*could commit the corporation* because of their authority as corporate officers or employees or for some other reason the law cloaks them with authority, then they, as the alter egos of the corporation, are parties for purposes of [the ethics rules]."[2]

The 1995 ABA Model Rules adopted the alter ego test, elaborated on it, and appeared to expand it as well:

> In the case of an organization, this Rule [4.2] prohibits communications by a lawyer for another person or entity concerning the matter in representation with persons [1] having a managerial responsibility on behalf of the organization, and [2] with any other person whose act or omission in connection with that matter may

---

[8]State Bar of California, Formal Opinion 1993-131 (1993). *Cf.* ABA Formal Opinion 95-396 (July 28, 1995), at 21: "Whether in a civil or criminal matter, if the investigator acts as the lawyer's 'alter ego,' the lawyer is ethically responsible for the investigator's conduct."

[9]ABA Formal Op. 11-461 (Aug.

4, 2011).

[Section 4.2–6]

[1]ABA Informal Opinion 1410 (Feb. 14, 1978).

[2]ABA Informal Opinion 1410 (Feb. 14, 1978) (emphasis added), citing DR 7-104(A)(1), the predecessor to the Model Rules.

be imputed to the organization for purposes of civil or criminal liability *or* [3] whose statement may constitute an admission on the part of the organization. If an agent or employee of the organization is represented in the matter by his or her own counsel, the consent by that counsel to a communication will be sufficient for purposes of this Rule. Compare Rule 3.4(f).[3]

If clause [2] was an independent test, it appeared to cover every employee-witness in certain cases. This interpretation was supported by the cross reference at the end of this Comment: "Compare Rule 3.4(f)." Rule 3.4(f) authorizes a lawyer to request someone not her client to refrain from volunteering relevant information if the person is "an employee or other agent of a client" and the lawyer reasonably believes that the interests of this employee or other agent would not be adversely affected by refusing to volunteer this information. The term, "employee or other agent of a client" was quite broad, covering all employees and even those independent contractors who are agents of the client. On the other hand, the Code Comparison to Rule 4.2 suggests a much less ambitious interpretation of Rule 4.2. It advises: "This Rule is substantially identical to DR 7-104(A)(1)."[4]

Under an overly broad interpretation, a lawyer could not interview any corporate employee for whom the organization may have vicarious liability on the matter in question (no matter how low they were in the corporate hierarchy) unless corporate counsel agreed. Indeed, if all employees were automatically included within the protective wings of Rule 4.2, every employee at the lowest end of the pecking order would be covered. Such a broad anti-contact rule would make the fact gathering of litigation more expensive and protect the entity in circumstances where there is no real need to protect it.[5]

Consequently, commentators have often argued for a narrower interpretation, stating that the purpose of the anti-contact rule

---

[3]1995 Rule 4.2, Comment 4 (emphasis added).

[4]1995 Rule 4.2, Code Comparison 1:

[5]*See, e.g., Niesig v. Team I*, 76 N.Y.2d 363, 559 N.Y.S.2d 493, 558 N.E.2d 1030 (1990), involved a plaintiff's personal injury lawyer who wished to interview a corporate defendant's employees who had witnessed an accident. This employee was merely an eyewitness, not someone who would subject the corporation to vicarious liability. The court rejected this overly-broad interpretation of the anti-contact rule.

The *Niesig* court noted that, when a corporation is a party to a lawsuit, the incorporeal entity is, technically, the only "party." However, because a corporation only acts through natural persons, and unless one or more of these employees is also sued, the corporation would have no protection under DR 7-104(A)(1) or Rule 4.2. Thus, "parties" for purposes of the no-contact rule should include: (1) only corporate employees whose acts or omissions in the matter under inquiry are binding on the corporation (that is, who are the corporation's alter egos); (2) employees whose acts or omissions are imputed to the corpora-

is to prevent improvident settlements and similarly major capitulations of legal position on the part of a momentarily uncounseled, but represented, party and to enable the corporation's lawyer to maintain an effective lawyer-client relationship with members of management. Thus, in the case of corporate and similar entities, the anti-contact rule should prohibit contact with those officials, *but only those,* who have the legal power to bind the corporation in the matter or who are responsible for implementing the advice of the corporation's lawyer, or any member of the organization whose own interests are directly at stake in a representation.[6] The trend in the case law favors this view.[7]

Thus, if an employee's only relation to a case is as a holder of factual information, the employee-witness should be freely accessible to either lawyer.[8] For such witnesses the interviewing lawyer need not secure any permission from the party's lawyer. If

---

tion for purposes of its liability; or (3) employees implementing the advice of counsel. All other employees may be interviewed informally.

The court noted that there should be a public policy of reducing litigation costs by allowing plaintiffs to use informal, off the record, private interviews rather than costly depositions or interviews attended by the adversary counsel. Allowing the plaintiff's lawyer to conduct these interviews does not prevent the corporation from interviewing its own employees, gathering facts, and counseling employees so that they do not make improvident disclosures.

[6]CHARLES W. WOLFRAM, MODERN LEGAL ETHICS 613 (West Pub. Co., 1986) (emphasis added), citing Rule 4.2 and DR 7-104(A)(1).

[7]*Niesig v. Team I*, 76 N.Y.2d 363, 559 N.Y.S.2d 493, 558 N.E.2d 1030 (1990). *See also State ex rel. Charleston Area Medical Center v. Zakaib*, 190 W.Va. 186, 437 S.E.2d 759 (W.Va. 1993), reviewed an order allowing plaintiff's counsel to interview all present and former employees of a medical center in a malpractice action. The court barred interviews with present employees "who are responsible for implementing the advice of the corporation's lawyer." The court also adopted the majority view, discussed below, that Rule 4.2 does not bar

interviews with former employees of an opponent.

[8]CHARLES W. WOLFRAM, MODERN LEGAL ETHICS 613 (West Pub. Co., 1986). *See also* ABA Formal Opinion 117 (1934).

ABA Formal Opinion 95-396 (July 28, 1995), "Communications with Represented Persons." This Formal Opinion makes clear that Rule 4.2 only applies to a person (whether or not a formal party to the proceeding) who is represented by counsel. Fact witnesses normally are not represented, so Rule 4.2 would not apply in that case. If the fact witness is represented by counsel (*e.g.,* the complaining witness in a criminal rape prosecution) the lawyer seeking to question the witness must secure permission from the witness' personal lawyer. Formal Opinion 95-396 states that Rule 4.2 applies to "any person who has retained counsel in a matter and whose interests are potentially distinct from those of the client on whose behalf the communicating lawyer is acting." The qualifying phrase—"and whose interests are potentially distinct"—should not be read literally; it does not narrow the reach of Rule 4.2. In other words, if the witness has retained counsel, the other lawyer must secure the permission of that counsel, even if (in the view of the communicating lawyer) the interests are not "potentially distinct." It is up

this nonparty occurrence witness (or fact witness) has independent legal representation, the lawyer seeking the interview should secure the permission of the witness' personal lawyer for this matter but should not have to secure any permission from the opposing party's lawyer.

The lawyer for the client-employer could instruct the client's employees that they should not volunteer information to the other side and should only speak through deposition, but the lawyer for the client-employer could not prohibit the other party's lawyer from speaking with these witnesses[9] if the witnesses wanted to speak to the other party's lawyer. If the witness is an employee of a corporation or other organization, the 1995 version of Rule 4.2 only prohibited a lawyer from communicating with a person "having managerial responsibility" or any person whose "act or omission in connection with that matter may be imputed to the organization" for civil or criminal liability, or "whose statement may constitute an admission on the part of the organization."[10] The restrictions of 1995 version of Rule 4.2 should not be read too broadly, so that it "remains a rule of ethics rather than of corporate immunity."[11]

The drafters of the 2002 Rules responded to the criticism that this interpretation was overly broad and they redrafted the language into what is now Comment 7. This Comment states:

> In the case of a represented organization, this Rule prohibits communications with a constituent of the organization who supervises, directs or regularly consults with the organization's lawyer concerning the matter or has authority to obligate the organization with respect to the matter or whose act or omission in connection with the matter may be imputed to the organization for purposes of civil or criminal liability. Consent of the organization's lawyer is not required for communication with a former constituent. If a constituent of the organization is represented in the matter by his or her own counsel, the consent by that counsel to a communication will be sufficient for purposes of this Rule. Compare Rule 3.4(f). In communicating with a current or former constituent of an organization, a lawyer must not use methods of obtaining evidence that violate the legal rights of the organization. See Rule 4.4.

The drafters sought to provide clearer guidance for those who deal with entities.[12]

§ 4.2–6(b) Expert Witnesses

Normally, expert witnesses have no separate legal

---

to the witness's counsel to make that determination.

[9] Rule 3.4(f).

[10] Rule 4.2, Comment 4. *Accord* ABA Formal Opinion 95-396 (July 28, 1995).

[11] *Johnson v. Cadillac Plastic Group*, 930 F.Supp. 1437, 1442 (D. Colo.1996).

[12] *See* Reporter's Explanation of Changes to Model Rule 4.2.

representation. If a lawyer knows that an expert witness has separate legal representation in a particular matter, then she must first contact that lawyer for permission to speak to the expert witness.

If the expert witness has no separate legal representation, the lawyer who hired the expert witness can advise her that she should not volunteer information to the other side and should only speak through deposition.[13] But the lawyer for the client-employer cannot prohibit the other party's lawyer from speaking with this witness if the witness wants to speak to the other party's lawyer.[14]

There may be jurisdictions where local court rules prohibit the lawyer from contacting the expert witness.[15] Obviously, then the lawyer must follow those rules; failure to follow those rules would constitute an ethical violation.[16]

§ 4.2–6(c) Former Employees, in General

Neither Rule 4.2 nor its Comments require a lawyer representing a client in a matter adverse to a corporation to seek permission of that corporation's attorney before interviewing *former employees* of the corporate party about the subject of the representation.[17] State and federal courts and state ethics opinions have split on this issue[18] but most support the view

---

[13]Rule 3.4(f).

[14]*See* Robert C. Hacker & Ronald D. Rotunda, *Ethical Restraints on Communications with Adverse Expert Witnesses*, 5 CORP.L.REV. 348 (1982). *See also In re Investigation of FMC Corporation*, 430 F.Supp. 1108 (S.D. W.Va.1977).

[15]*See, e.g.,* Fed. Rules Civ. Procedure, Rule 26(b)(4)(A).

[16]The lawyer who did not follow a local rule of procedure would be violating Rule 3.4(c), which prohibits a lawyer from disobeying a tribunal's rules unless he is testing the rule ("except for an open refusal based on an assertion that no valid obligation exists"). *See* ABA Formal Opinion 93-378 (Nov. 8, 1993).

[17]Rule 4.2, Comment 7 ("Consent of the organization's lawyer is not required for communication with a former constituent.").

[18]*State ex rel. Charleston Area Medical Center v. Zakaib*, 190 W.Va.

186, 437 S.E.2d 759 (W.Va.1993). The lower court had authorized plaintiff's counsel to interview all present and former employees of a medical center in a malpractice action. The court, on appeal, adopted the majority view that Rule 4.2 does not bar interviews with former employees of an opponent. With respect to present employees, the court order only barred interviews with present employees "who are responsible for implementing the advice of the corporation's lawyer."

Other cases supporting the view that Rule 4.2 does not cover former employees include: *Wright v. Group Health Hospital*, 103 Wash.2d 192, 691 P.2d 564, 569 (Wash.1984); *United States v. Western Electric Co.*, 1990 WL 39129 (D.D.C.1990); *Aiken v. Business and Industry Health Group, Inc.*, 885 F.Supp. 1474, 1478–79 (D. Kan.1995); *H.B.A. Management Inc. v. Estate of Schwartz*, 693 So.2d 541, 543–46 (Fla.1997); *Spencer v. Steinman*, 179 F.R.D. 484, 491 (E.D.Pa. 1998); Washington, D.C. Legal Ethics

expressed in an ABA Formal Opinion,[19] which has made clear that neither the text nor the Comments cover former employees.

Any other reading of Rule 4.2 is unnatural and stained. It is not the purpose of Rule 4.2 to prevent the disclosure of prejudicial testimony but to protect the client-lawyer relationship.[20] The attorney for the employer does not have a client-lawyer relationship with a former employee. Moreover, to so interpret the Rule would make it more expensive for the lawyer to obtain information about her case, because she would have to proceed by way of deposition rather than interview if the opposing lawyer refused consent. Furthermore, Rule 4.2 protects a person from being damaged by a binding disclosure made without that person's lawyer being present. But former employees are not represented by the employer's lawyer.

§ 4.2–6(d) Former Employees Who Have Privileged Information

A more difficult question arises when the former employee knows information that is privileged from disclosure. For example, the former employee may be a chemist who is privy to trade secrets that his former employer has a legal right to prevent him from revealing. Or, the former employee may be a lawyer

---

Committee, Opinion 287 (Jan. 19, 1999).

The court in *In re Opinion 668 of Advisory Committee on Professional Ethics*, 134 N.J. 294, 633 A.2d 959 (N. J.1993)(per curiam), sent the issues back for further study but, as an interim matter, concluded that Rule 4.2 barred interviews with both present and former employees in the company control group. Notice to the corporation, but not permission, was also required to talk to present or former "employees whose conduct, in and of itself, establishes the organization's liability."

[19] ABA Formal Opinion 91-359 (Mar. 22, 1991).

[20] In *Clark v. Beverly Health & Rehabilitation Services, Inc.*, 440 Mass. 270, 797 N.E.2d 905 (2003), plaintiff's estate sued for wrongful death resulting from a morphine overdose of plaintiff. During the course of discovery, plaintiff's counsel made an ex parte contact with a nurse whom defendant had formerly employed, and who was involved with the subject matter of the litigation. The nurse was not represented by counsel and agreed to speak with plaintiff's counsel, who later deposed her. Defendants' counsel filed a motion seeking to bar plaintiff's counsel from making any future ex parte contacts with former employees. The State Supreme Court found that the scope of Rule 4.2 and Comment 4 were limited only to certain categories of current employees and did not extend to former employees. Thus the Court found that the plain language of the Rule did not prevent ex parte contacts with all former employees. The Court found that the policies underlying Rule 4.2 were two-fold: (1) to protect the attorney-client relationship and (2) to prevent an employee from making an ill-advised comment that could later impute liability to the company. The Court found that neither of these policy considerations were served by prohibiting all ex parte communications with former employees. Thus, the court remanded for a fuller evaluation of the contact actually made in this case.

who was in the Office of General Counsel of the employer and who has information about the former employer that is protected by the attorney-client privilege.

There are two major alternatives for dealing with this issue. Under one view, the lawyer interviewing the former employee does not worry whether the former employee should or should not answer a particular question. The duty would be placed on the employer to instruct its former employees that they have a legal obligation to refuse to reveal certain information and, if they are not clear what that information is, they should inform the employer and require the lawyer to proceed by way of deposition, where the rights of the employer can be protected.

Under this view of the law, the primary burden would fall on the employer and former employee. It is the former employee— and not the lawyer adverse to the interests of the former employer—who has the obligation to keep some information confidential. The adverse lawyer should not deal corruptly with this former employee—for example, by bribing him to reveal information, or by not disclosing that he is a lawyer representing a party with interests adverse to the employer.[21] But otherwise, it is up to the employer to protect its rights.

Alternatively, the initial burden may be placed on the adverse lawyer (that is, the lawyer who is seeking to question the witness and who is representing the party with interests adverse to the employer). Then, if the former employee "has been *extensively* exposed to confidential information,"[22] the adverse lawyer should not solicit this information if the lawyer knows or should reasonably know that this information is privileged. If the adverse lawyer violates this rule, she may find that the court will disqualify her and strike the testimony of the witness who should not have spoken on such matters.[23]

This, in fact, is the rule that courts are adopting. If a lawyer in

---

[21]*See* Rule 4.3, providing that, if the lawyer is dealing with an unrepresented person, she should not "state or imply" that she is disinterested. If the lawyer knows, or reasonably should know, that the unrepresented person does not understand the lawyer's role, she must take reasonable steps to correct the misunderstanding. *See also* Restatement of the Law Governing Lawyers § 103 (Official Draft 2000).

[22]*Camden v. State of Maryland,* 910 F.Supp. 1115, 1122 (D.Md.1996) (emphasis in original).

In re Domestic Air Transportation Antitrust Litigation, 141 F.R.D. 556, 561 (N.D.Ga.1992) (adverse lawyer permitted to interview former employees but may not ask about information covered by the attorney-client privilege).

Note that ABA Formal Opinion 91-359 (Mar. 22, 1991) concludes that the prohibition of Rule 4.2 regarding a lawyer's contacts with the employees of an opposing party does not extend to the *former* employees of that party.

[23]*Zachair, Ltd. v. Driggs,* 965 F.Supp. 741 (D.Md.1997), *aff'd,* 141 F.3d 1162 (4th Cir.1998)(lawyer is disqualified for various reasons, including engaging in ex parte contact with the former general counsel of a defen-

a matter is questioning a non-client and the anti-contact provisions of Rule 4.2 are not applicable, then the lawyer should "not seek to obtain information that the lawyer reasonably should know the non-client may not reveal without violating a duty of confidentiality to another imposed by law."[24] Just as a lawyer may not reveal his client's secrets, he has "the duty not to seek to cause another to do so."[25]

This burden imposed on the adverse lawyer only relates to confidences that are based on fundamental and general law, such as the work product doctrine, or the attorney-client privilege, or the physician-patient privilege. It does not cover "confidentiality duties based only on contract . . . ."[26]

---

dant, when the lawyer knew or reasonably should have known that the former general counsel possessed substantial privileged information).

[24]Restatement of the Law Governing Lawyers, Third, § 102 (Official Draft 2000).

[25]*American Protection Insurance*

Co. v. MGM Grand Hotel-Las Vegas, 748 F.2d 1293, 1301 (9th Cir.1984), *opinion withdrawn and appeal dismissed on other grounds*, 765 F.2d 925 (9th Cir.1985).

[26]Restatement of the Law Governing Lawyers, Third, § 102, Comment *b* (Official Draft 2000), at 106.

CHAPTER 4.3
DEALING WITH UNREPRESENTED PERSONS

RULE 4.3: DEALING WITH UNREPRESENTED PERSON

In dealing on behalf of a client with a person who is not represented by counsel, a lawyer shall not state or imply that the lawyer is disinterested. When the lawyer knows or reasonably should know that the unrepresented person misunderstands the lawyer's role in the matter, the lawyer shall make reasonable efforts to correct the misunderstanding. The lawyer shall not give legal advice to an unrepresented person, other than the advice to secure counsel, if the lawyer knows or reasonably should know that the interests of such a person are or have a reasonable possibility of being in conflict with the interests of the client.

Comment

[1] An unrepresented person, particularly one not experienced in dealing with legal matters, might assume that a lawyer is disinterested in loyalties or is a disinterested authority on the law even when the lawyer represents a client. In order to avoid a misunderstanding, a lawyer will typically need to identify the lawyer's client and, where necessary, explain that the client has interests opposed to those of the unrepresented person. For misunderstandings that sometimes arise when a lawyer for an organization deals with an unrepresented constituent, see Rule 1.13(d).

[2] The Rule distinguishes between situations involving unrepresented persons whose interests may be adverse to those of the lawyer's client and those in which the person's interests are not in conflict with the client's. In the former situation, the possibility that the lawyer will compromise the unrepresented person's interests is so great that the Rule prohibits the giving of any advice, apart from the advice to obtain counsel. Whether a lawyer is giving impermissible advice may depend on the experience and sophistication of the unrepresented person, as well as the setting in which the behavior and comments occur. This Rule does not prohibit a lawyer from negotiating the terms of a transaction or settling a dispute with an unrepresented person. So long as the lawyer has explained that the lawyer represents an adverse party and is not

representing the person, the lawyer may inform the person of the terms on which the lawyer's client will enter into an agreement or settle a matter, prepare documents that require the person's signature and explain the lawyer's own view of the meaning of the document or the lawyer's view of the underlying legal obligations.

Authors' 1983 Model Rules Comparison

The drafters of the 2002 Rules amended the 1983 version of Rule 4.3 to bring into the text from the Comments the discussion about whether a lawyer may give legal advice to an unrepresented party. *See* Reporter's Explanation of Changes to Model Rule 4.4. The last line of the 2002 version of Rule 4.3 is new.

In Comment 1, the drafters deleted the sentence about giving advice to an unrepresented person. And, they added to the Comment the last two sentences dealing with identifying the client to the unrepresented person.

Comment 2 is new and explains the new language about giving legal advice to an unrepresented person.

Model Code Comparison

There was no direct counterpart to this Rule in the Model Code. DR 7-104(A)(2) provided that a lawyer shall not "[g]ive advice to a person who is not represented by a lawyer, other than the advice to secure counsel. . . ."

§ 4.3–1 DEALING WITH INDIVIDUALS WHO ARE NOT REPRESENTED BY COUNSEL

Rule 4.3 restricts the lawyer's communications with unrepresented persons. This provision is derived, in part, from DR 7-104(A)(2).[1] If a person is not represented by counsel, the lawyer for the represented person may neither state nor imply that the lawyer is disinterested. If the unrepresented person does not understand the lawyer's role, the lawyer should try to correct the misunderstanding.[2] In the absence of a misunderstanding, the Rule, however, does not affirmatively require that a lawyer identify that she is representing a client. And, the Rule does not require that lawyers disclose the identity of the client to the unrepresented persons, although many lawyers do so as a matter of normal practice.

For example, assume that the attorney ("Attorney") for an employer prepares settlement papers in a worker's compensation case for the employee ("Employee") to sign. Employee, who signs

---

[Section 4.3–1]

[1]Although Rule 4.3 is phrased differently than DR 7-104(A)(2), Rule 4.3 generally reflects the prior case law interpretation of DR 7-104(A)(2).

[2]*See* Restatement of the Law Governing Lawyers § 103 (Official Draft 2000) (requiring that lawyer clarify any misunderstanding if a failure to do so would materially prejudice the unrepresented person). *See also* ABA Section of Litigation, Ethical Guidelines for Settlement Negotiations 4.3.4 (2002) (examining the obligations of negotiating with an unrepresented person).

these papers, is not represented by any lawyer. Attorney must not advise or mislead Employee as to the law or Attorney's role in this matter. Attorney should also advise the court, which must approve the settlement, that Employee is appearing *pro se*. In this situation, Attorney's actions are proper.[3]

A leading case in this area is *W.T. Grant Co. v. Haines*.[4] This case involved a corporation's antitrust action against one of its former employees and others. The employee moved to disqualify the corporation's law firm, alleging that it had violated DR 7-104(A) when corporate attorneys had earlier interviewed the employee. When this interview took place, the corporation's lawyer correctly identified the character and nature of their representation, but he failed to disclose various facts that the employee would have found quite interesting, such as that earlier that morning the corporation had filed a lawsuit naming that employee as a defendant. The lawyer for the corporation told the employee that candid answers might clear his name. This lawyer also secured the employee's authorization to examine his taxes, credit cards, etc.

The court found no violation of DR 7-104(A)(1) because the employee was not yet represented by counsel and corporate counsel had accurately said whom they represented. The employee was said to be sophisticated, "neither a callow youth nor a befuddled widow." As for the principle reflected in DR 7-104(A)(2)—not giving advice to unrepresented persons with interests opposed to the client's—the court said that the question was "close," but that, even assuming a violation, the court would not disqualify the

---

[3]ABA Formal Opinion 102 (Dec. 15, 1933).

[4]*W.T. Grant Co. v. Haines*, 531 F.2d 671 (2d Cir.1976).

"Imminent public harm" Exception? With *Haines*, compare, *In re Pautler*, 47 P.3d 1175 (Colo2002). A deputy district attorney deceived a murder suspect by pretending to be a defense attorney in order to encourage the suspect's surrender. The court found a violation of Rule 4.3. It court said that "Pautler went further than implying he was disinterested; he purported to represent Neal. Without doubt, Pautler's conduct violated the letter of Colo. RPC 4.3." 47 P.3d at 1182. As a sanction, the court suspended the lawyer for three months, which was stayed during twelve

months of probation during which he had to take ethics courses and retake the professional responsibility examination.

The court said specifically that it would not "address whether, under some unique circumstances, an 'imminent public harm' exception could ever apply to the Colorado Rules of Professional Conduct. We hold only that this is not such case." *In re Pautler*, 47 P.3d 1175, 1181 n. 6 (Colo. 2002). *See* Livingston Keithley, *Should A Lawyer Ever Be Allowed To Lie? People v. Pautler and a Proposed Duress Exception*, 75 U. Colo. L. Rev. 301 (2004); Douglas R. Richmond, *Deceptive Lawyering*, 74 U. Cinn. L. Rev. 577 (2005)

lawyer because the defense counsel failed to establish that the corporate lawyer's behavior tainted the trial.[5]

The failure to clarify the lawyer's role in the matter can lead to finding that the lawyer represented the employee. In *Perez v. Kirk & Carrigan*,[6] the court reversed a summary judgment and sent a case back for trial over the issue of whether a lawyer who interviewed an employee in a hospital room had developed an attorney-client relationship with the employee. Mr. Perez, a truck driver for the Valley Coca Cola Bottling Company, was involved in an accident with a school bus that killed 22 children. The Company's outside lawyer took a statement from Mr. Perez, who alleged that that the lawyer had told him that, even though the lawyer was representing the Company, he was also there to protect Mr. Perez's interests and would keep any information confidential. However, this lawyer turned this statement over to the local prosecutor, who then filed criminal charges against the employee. After the meeting with Mr. Perez, the company lawyer arranged for an outside criminal defense lawyer to represent Mr. Perez, and the company lawyer had no further contact with him. The liability insurer paid for all counsel for the company and Mr. Perez. Mr. Perez sued the lawyer for breach of trust and fiduciary duty claiming that the lawyer told him that, even though the lawyer was representing the Company, he was also there to protect Mr. Perez's interests and would keep any information confidential.

In applying Rule 4.3 to this case, if the lawyer is really representing the Company, he must take reasonable efforts to ensure that the employee understands that salient fact.[7] A long line of cases holds that the fact-finder may imply an attorney-client relationship from the conduct of the parties. It is not necessary that the alleged client or prospective client pay a fee, for lawyers can work for free.[8] In addition—although the court did not mention these facts—the employee's physical and mental state, as well as possible language difficulties, should increase the lawyer's burden to ensure that the employee knows that anything he says can be used for the benefit of the Company.

Of course, such warnings (like the *Miranda* warning that po-

---

[5]The court stated that the appropriate forum was the Grievance Committee of the bar association.

[6]*Perez v. Kirk & Carrigan*, 822 S.W.2d 261 (Tex.App.—Corpus Christi 1991 writ denied).

[7]Rule 1.13(f) & Comments 10 & 11.

[8]*See, e.g., E.F. Hutton & Co. v.* *Brown*, 305 F.Supp. 371, 388 (S.D.Tex. 1969); *United States v. Evans*, 113 F.3d 1457, 1465 (7th Cir. 1997) (clients needs reasonable subjective belief that attorney-client relationship has been formed); *State ex rel. Oklahoma Bar Association v. Green*, 936 P.2d 947, 952 (Okl. 1997)(attorney-client relationship may be implied from the conduct of the parties).

lice give to suspects in custody) may scare the employee into not cooperating with the investigation.

Application of Rule 4.3 to Contact by Counsel with Putative Members of a Class Before Class Certification. When plaintiffs and defense counsel seek to contact putative members of a class before it has been certified, several potential ethics issues arise.[9] In 2007, the ABA addressed the various ethics issues when making such communications.[10] One threshold issue hinged on whether the plaintiffs' lawyers represent the entire potential class before it has been certified. If so, defense lawyers could not contact potential class members because such communications would violate Rule 4.2. ABA Formal Opinion 07-445 holds that "putative class members are not represented parties for purposes of the Model Rules prior to certification of the class and expiration of the opt-out period."[11] Therefore, Rule 4.2 only applies when communicating with persons who have retained counsel by choosing to participate in the class.

Although trial judges have the power to regulate lawyer contact with putative clients, such discretion is not unlimited because such communications have the benefit of informing potential class members of the existence and merits of the litigation.[12] When plaintiffs and defense counsel communicate with putative clients who are not represented by counsel, Rule 4.3 applies. Such communications may inquire about facts, but these communications may not contain legal advice other than the advice to retain counsel. If such communications are intended to attract potential clients, then Rule 7.3 on contacts with prospective clients will apply.

§ 4.3–2 PROVIDING LEGAL ADVICE TO UNREPRESENTED PERSONS

The 1983 version of Rule 4.3 did not contain any statement in the text of the Rule as to whether a lawyer may provide legal advice to an unrepresented party. The Comments stated that "During the course of a lawyer's representation of a client, the lawyer should not give advice to an unrepresented person other than the advice to obtain counsel."[1] Although this standard provided a bright line for lawyers, it is rather unworkable in practice if read literally. Unrepresented persons ask lawyers

---

[9]*See generally* Debra Lyn Bassett, *Pre-Certification Communication Ethics in Class Actions*, 36 GA. L.REV. 353 (2002); Vincent R. Johnson, *The Ethics of Communicating with Putative Class Members*, 17 REV. LIT. 497 (1998).

[10]ABA Formal Opinion 07-445

(Apr. 11, 2007).

[11]Id.

[12]*Gulf Oil Co. v. Bernard*, 452 U.S. 89, 101 S. Ct. 2193, 68 L. Ed. 2d 693 (1981).

[Section 4.3–2]

[1]1983 Rule 4.3, Comment 1.

questions and in many cases the answers do not involve issues on which the lawyer's client and the unrepresented person disagree. In other words, the interests of the parties may be aligned and therefore a lawyer should be able to answer the questions of the unrepresented third person. The other party may ask, "Where do I sign on the document?" or "Do I need to get my signature notarized?"

The drafters of the 2002 Rules removed this language from the Comment and added in the black letter rule a provision that addresses this issue. Under Rule 4.3, a lawyer ordinarily should not provide legal advice to an unrepresented person if the lawyer knows or reasonably should know that the interests of the client and the unrepresented person have a "reasonable possibility of being in conflict."[2] Of course, a lawyer may also inform the unrepresented person to obtain counsel to help in this matter. But, as long as the lawyer does not mislead the unrepresented party into thinking he or she does not need separate counsel, the lawyer has no obligation to advise the unrepresented party to secure separate counsel.[3] Clearly, the Rule is designed to give lawyers leeway to give some basic advice in situations where the interests of the client and the unrepresented person are aligned.

The Comment to Rule 4.3 elaborates on this issue.[4] It explains that the Rule is designed to prevent a lawyer from compromising the legal position of unrepresented persons whose interests are adverse to those of the client. The Comment advises: "Whether a lawyer is giving impermissible advice may depend on the experience and sophistication of the unrepresented person, as well as the setting in which the behavior and comments occur."[5] One should not interpret this language to authorize the lawyer to provide advice on issues where the interests of the client and unrepresented person are in conflict as long as the unrepresented person is experienced and sophisticated. Such a view conflicts

---

[2] Rule 4.3. The 1983 Comment used the word advice, but the text of the 2002 Rule 4.3 uses the words legal advice. Is this a conscious change, or should the provision focus on the lawyer's attempt to influence the decision of the unrepresented person?

[3] **Comparing Rule 4.3 to** *Miranda* **Warnings.** Rule 4.3 does not impose *Miranda* obligations on private lawyers. Rule 4.3 "does not impose an affirmative duty on a lawyer to advise an unrepresented person to consult an attorney; it merely states, 'During the course of a lawyer's representation of a client, the lawyer should not give advice to an unrepresented person other than the advice to obtain counsel.' " *Suck v. Sullivan*, 1999 WL 33437564, *2, n.4 (Mich.App. 1999) (per curiam). In other words, the lawyer may, but need not, advice the unrepresented person to secure counsel. Rule 4.3 "does not impose a duty on an attorney to recommend that a person who is not represented by counsel confer with an attorney under any circumstances." 1999 WL 33437564, *2.

[4] Rule 4.3, Comment 2.

[5] Rule 4.3, Comment 2.

with the language of the black letter Rule and the purpose behind it.

The Comment also makes clear that the prohibition on giving advice does not limit the lawyer's ability to talk to the unrepresented person, draft documents for that person's signature and explain factual positions in the matter. One must not view this Comment as giving the lawyer general permission to provide legal advice or interpretations of language dependent upon external cases or statutes. The lawyer in such a case must make clear that she represents the client, and not the unrepresented person, in such negotiations.[6]

For example, assume that a minor and the minor's parents are unrepresented by counsel during negotiation and settlement of the minor's injury claim. The tortfeasor's insurer, however, has retained a lawyer to represent its interests. This lawyer may prepare the application for guardianship appointment and the application for approval of settlement of the minor's claim, and she may appear before the court to secure final approval of the settlement, provided that she informs the minor and the minor's parents that she is retained by the insurer and does not represent the minor; she must also inform the minor and the minor's parents that she (the attorney) prepared the documents and that they may secure counsel to review the documents; she should also make these disclosures to the court to create a record. But, she must not give legal advice to the unrepresented minor and the minor's parents.[7] In this circumstance, the fact that the lawyer prepared "documents for the court to appoint a guardian and to approve the guardian's settlement of a minor's claim does not constitute the giving of legal advice to an unrepresented party."[8]

Parker v. Carnahan exemplifies the problems that can result from too much interaction between the lawyer and the unrepre-

---

[6]*X-It Products, LLC v. Walter Kidde Portable Equipment, Inc.*, 227 F.Supp.2d 494, 548 (E.D.Va. 2002), which relied on Rule 4.3 to conclude that when the lawyer knows or reasonably should know that the unrepresented person misunderstands the lawyer's role in the matter, the lawyer shall make reasonable efforts to correct the misunderstanding: "As Ive made clear in his testimony, and as his letter to Oslakovic makes equally plain, Ive, who was not represented by counsel, believed that Oslakovic was acting not as Kidde's counsel but as a third party neutral who would keep the claims in X-It's patent application confidential and merely come to a professional opinion regarding the strength of the application in order to facilitate negotiations between the parties."

[7]Ohio Advisory Opinion 96-2, 1996 WL 92873 (the Supreme Court of Ohio Board of Commissioners on Grievances and Discipline (February 2, 1996)).

[8]Ohio Advisory Opinion 96-2, 1996 WL 92873, *3.

sented person.[9] In this decision, Mrs. Parker's husband failed to file federal income tax returns although he had informed her that he was filing the returns on time. Mrs. Parker decided to divorce her husband and the IRS had brought proceedings against both of them. The husband had hired a lawyer and an accountant to prepare back tax returns and they called Mrs. Parker to come in and sign the returns. The lawyer and the accountant did not inform Mrs. Parker that by signing back joint tax returns, instead of separate returns, she was waiving the innocent spouse defense before the IRS. In other words, if Mrs. Parker signed the joint tax returns, the IRS could collect penalties and interest from her and if she prepared her own separate returns she could argue an innocent spouse defense. Mrs. Parker came to the lawyer's office and after asking several questions, she signed the returns and the IRS collected a larger portion of the penalties and interest from her. Mrs. Parker sued the attorney and the accountant. The court sent the case back for trial on the issue of whether the lawyer was negligent for failing to inform Mrs. Parker that he was not representing her interests in getting a non-client to sign the tax returns.[10] The court sent the case back for trial, because, given the allegations, the fact-finder could determine "that the attorneys were aware or should have been aware that their conduct would have led a reasonable person to believe that she was being represented by the attorneys."[11]

Parker demonstrates that, even when no attorney-client relationship exists, a lawyer who answers questions of an unrepresented person risks a lawsuit where the unrepresented party later claims that the lawyer failed to inform that person about the risk involved in signing documents prepared by the lawyer. As the court warned: "The general rule is that in absence of evidence that the attorney knew that the parties had assumed that he was representing them in a matter, the attorney had no affirmative duty to inform the person that he was not their attorney. On the other hand, an attorney can be held negligent where he fails to advise a party that he is not representing them on a case *where the circumstances lead the party to believe that the attorney*

---

[9]*Parker v. Carnahan*, 772 S.W.2d 151 (Tex.App.—Texarkana 1989, writ denied). The IRS threatened the husband with criminal liability if the taxes were not paid, and thus the lawyer sought to have the wife sign the returns and pay the husband's share of the taxes, penalties, and interest.

[10]772 S.W.2d at 159. The court found that no attorney client relation-

ship existed between the lawyer and Mrs. Parker because she at all times knew that the husband had hired the lawyer for his IRS problems. The court also sent the case against the accountant back for trial on the theory that accountants who prepare joint returns may have an obligation to explain the consequences of signing the returns.

[11]*Parker v. Carnahan*, 772 S.W.2d 151, 157.

is representing him."[12]

---

[12]*Parker v. Carnahan*, 772 S.W.2d 151, 157 (emphasis added; internal citations omitted).

CHAPTER 4.4
RESPECT FOR THE RIGHTS OF THIRD PERSONS

RULE 4.4: RESPECT FOR RIGHTS OF THIRD PERSONS

(a) In representing a client, a lawyer shall not use means that have no substantial purpose other than to embarrass, delay, or burden a third person, or use methods of obtaining evidence that violate the legal rights of such a person.

(b) A lawyer who receives a document relating to the representation of the lawyer's client and knows or reasonably should know that the document was inadvertently sent shall promptly notify the sender.

Comment

[1] Responsibility to a client requires a lawyer to subordinate the interests of others to those of the client, but that responsibility does not imply that a lawyer may disregard the rights of third persons. It is impractical to catalogue all such rights, but they include legal restrictions on methods of obtaining evidence from third persons and unwarranted intrusions into privileged relationships, such as the client-lawyer relationship.

[2] Paragraph (b) recognizes that lawyers sometimes receive documents that were mistakenly sent or produced by opposing parties or their lawyers. If a lawyer knows or reasonably should know that such a document was sent inadvertently, then this Rule requires the lawyer to promptly notify the sender in order to permit that person to take protective measures. Whether the lawyer is required to take additional steps, such as returning the original document, is a matter of law beyond the scope of these Rules, as is the question of whether the privileged status of a document has been waived. Similarly, this Rule does not address the legal duties of a lawyer who receives a document that the lawyer knows or reasonably should know may have been wrongfully obtained by the sending person. For purposes of this Rule, "document" includes e-mail or other electronic modes of transmission subject to being read or put into readable form.

[3] Some lawyers may choose to return a document unread, for example, when the lawyer learns before receiving the document that it was inadvertently sent to the wrong address. Where a lawyer is not required by applicable law to do so, the decision to voluntarily return such a document is a matter of professional judgment ordinarily reserved to the lawyer. See Rules 1.2 and 1.4.

Authors' 1983 Model Rules Comparison

The drafters of the 2002 Rules amended the 1983 version of Rule 4.4 to add a section relating to a lawyer's receipt of inadvertently sent documents. *See* Reporter's Explanation of Changes to Model Rule 4.4.

The original text of 1983 Rule 4.4 was placed into section (a).

The drafters added Rule 4.4(b).

In Comment 1, the drafters added a clause to the last sentence of Comment 1 that attempts to limit unwarranted intrusions into the attorney-client relationship.

Comments 2 and 3 are new and explain the new section (b) of the Rule.

Model Code Comparison

DR 7-106(C)(2) provided that a lawyer shall not "[a]sk any question that he has no reasonable basis to believe is relevant to the case and that is intended to degrade a witness or other person." DR 7-102(A)(1) provided that a lawyer shall not "take . . . action on behalf of his client when he knows or when it is obvious that such action would serve merely to harass or maliciously injure another." DR 7-108(D) provided that "[a]fter discharge of the jury . . . the lawyer shall not ask questions or make comments to a member of that jury that are calculated merely to harass or embarrass the juror. . . ." DR 7-108(E) provided that a lawyer "shall not conduct . . . . a vexatious or harassing investigation of either a venireman or a juror."

§ 4.4–1 USING MEANS THAT EMBARRASS, DELAY, OR BURDEN A THIRD PERSON

§ 4.4–1(a) Harassment

A lawyer's duty to represent a client competently and effectively does not allow a lawyer to harass another person. The Model Code had several specific provisions addressing this issue. It prohibited a lawyer from asking questions that the lawyer had "no reasonable basis to believe [were] . . . relevant to the case and that [were] . . . intended to degrade a witness or other person."[1] Also, a lawyer shall not "take . . . action on behalf of his client when he knows or when it is obvious that such action would serve merely to harass or maliciously injure another."[2] The drafters of the Model Rules used a more general prohibition. Lawyers shall not use means that serve no substantial purpose

---

[Section 4.4–1]   [2]Model Code DR 7-102(A)(1).
[1]Model Code DR 7-106(C)(2).

but to "embarrass, delay, or burden a third person . . . ."[3] Of course, if the lawyer's conduct disrupts a tribunal, it is prohibited by Rule 3.5(d).

§ 4.4–1(b) Threatening Criminal or Disciplinary Charges

The ABA Model Code included a specific provision that forbade a lawyer from threatening to present or presenting "criminal charges solely to obtain an advantage in a civil matter."[4] The Model Rules have no such provision.

However, that omission in the Model Rules does not mean that a lawyer is free to engage in such conduct. If the lawyer's threats amount to criminal extortion under state law, then Model Rule 8.4(b) would apply, for that provision prohibits a lawyer from committing a criminal act that reflects adversely on honesty, trustworthiness or fitness as a lawyer in other respects.[5] Crimes like extortion, that involve "serious interference with the administration of justice," fall in this category.[6]

Assuming that there is no violation of other law (such as the state law of extortion), the Rules do not prohibit a lawyer, in a civil case, from using the possibility of presenting criminal charges against the opposing party to gain relief for her client, provided that the criminal matter is related to the civil claim, the lawyer reasonably believes that the civil claim and the possible criminal charge are warranted, and the lawyer does not attempt to exert "improper influence" over the criminal process. Thus, an ABA Formal Opinion in 1992 concluded that a lawyer may also agree (and have her client agree) to refrain from pursuing criminal charges in return for satisfaction of the civil claim, assuming that other law does not prevent this agreement.[7]

Two years later, the ABA Ethics Committee issued a very different opinion, Formal Opinion 92-363, that deals with the case where a lawyer threatens to file a disciplinary complaint against an opposing lawyer in order to gain advantage in a civil case (or

---

[3]Rule 4.4(a). *See also* DR 7-108(D), (E); Restatement of the Law Governing Lawyers § 106 (Official Draft 2000).

Douglas R. Richmond, *Lawyer's Professional Responsibilities and Liabilities in Negotiations*, 22 GEORGETOWN J. LEGAL ETHICS 249 (2009).

[4]DR 7-105 (A). *See also* EC 7-21. The Rules have no such provision.

[5]*See* American Law Institute, Model Penal Code § 223.4 (1962) (a person commits a crime of theft by extortion if he accuses anyone of a criminal offense in order to obtain property that is not honestly claimed as indemnification for harm caused by conduct relating to the accusation). This issue, a lawyer's threats and the crime of extortion, is discussed in, Ronald D. Rotunda, *The Lawyer's Duty To Report Another Lawyer's Unethical Violations in the Wake of Himmel*, 1988 UNIVERSITY OF ILLINOIS LAW REVIEW 977 (1988).

[6]Rule 8.4, Comment 1.

[7]ABA Formal Opinion 92-363 (July 6, 1992).

the lawyer agrees not to report the lawyer if a satisfactory settlement is made).[8] The Opinion acknowledged that the Model Rules have no express prohibition governing this fact situation but nonetheless concluded that it presents a disciplinary violation. When ABA Model Rule 8.3 requires the lawyer to report another lawyer's violation of the Rules of Professional Conduct,[9] then the lawyer must report. It is improper for the lawyer to threaten to report the opposing lawyer but then agree not to report if the other side agrees to a satisfactory settlement. Even if Rule 8.3 is inapplicable, the Formal Opinion concludes that such action will "frequently" violate "one of the more general restraints on advocacy imposed by the Model Rules." It referred to Rule 4.4, prohibiting a lawyer from using means that have no substantial purpose other than to embarrass or burden a third party. It even claimed that "such a threat may prejudice the administration of justice," in violation of Rule 8.4(d).

If counsel does file a disciplinary complaint against the opposing lawyer, that fact alone normally neither requires nor permits the lawyer to withdraw from representing the client in the matter.[10] However, the filing of a complaint may create or expose circumstances that do justify withdrawal. For example, if the lawyer seeks to defend the accusation by exposing client confidences,[11] his interests may diverge from his client's thereby creating a disqualifying conflict of interest.

§ 4.4–1(c) Conduct for the Purpose of Burdening the Opponent

Rule 4.4(a) prohibits a lawyer from engaging in conduct that has no substantial purpose other than to delay or burden a third person. In a Texas Ethics Opinion, the committee addressed the question whether a lawyer may advise a client to hire all of the lawyers in a small community so as to conflict out the available local attorneys from representing the opposing party.[12] The opinion acknowledged that the analysis would depend upon the facts and circumstances and the reasons for the lawyer's advice; but if a lawyer's sole purpose for advising a client to hire all

---

[8]ABA Formal Opinion 94-383 (July 5, 1994).

[9]Rule 8.3(a) required the lawyer to report another lawyer's violation of the ethics rules when that violation raises "a substantial question as to that lawyer's honesty, trustworthiness or fitness as a lawyer in other respects. . . ."

[10]Formal Opinion 94-384 (July 5, 1994).

[11]Rule 1.6(b)(5).

[12]See State Bar of Texas Prof. Ethics Comm., Op. 585 (Sept 2008).

available attorneys in a small community was to burden the opposing side, the lawyer would violate Rule 4.4.[13]

Normally, the lawyer suing a corporation may deal directly with the in-house legal counsel and not be concerned about the no-contact provisions of Rule 4.2.[14] The Restatement agrees that "Inside legal counsel for a corporation is not generally within" the no contact prohibition, and therefore "contact with such counsel is not generally limited" by the no-contact rule.[15]

However, if the corporation asks the adverse lawyer not to contact its in-house counsel, the ABA advises, "contact by the adverse counsel might violate Rule 4.4."[16] There may also be a problem under Rule 4.4 if the in-house lawyer is himself a party to the litigation, or if the in-house counsel participated in giving business advice or making decisions that gave rise to the issues now in dispute.[17]

One commentator raises the valid point that the effort to bring violations of Rule 4.2 within the parameters of Rule 4.4 "seems to be a stretch."[18] If there is a violation of Rule 4.2, there is no need to bring in Rule 4.4. If there is a violation of Rule 4.4 ("embarrass" a third party), there is no need to bring in Rule 4.2.

§ 4.4-2 USING METHODS TO OBTAIN EVIDENCE THAT VIOLATE THE LEGAL RIGHTS OF A THIRD PERSON

§ 4.4-2(a) Gathering Evidence

Clients often use lawyers to obtain information and gather evidence. Such methods may be in the context of filed litigation or expected litigation. Or clients may hire lawyers to conduct an internal corporate investigation. Or they may retain lawyers to represent them in a transaction and to find out information about

---

[13]*See* Va. Standing Comm. on Legal Ethics, Op. 1794 (June 30, 2004) (a lawyer violates Rule 4.4 by asking client to interview all available lawyers in a community with intent to prevent them from representing the opposing party with no intent of hiring them).

[14]ABA Formal Op. 06-443 (Aug. 5, 2006).

[15]Restatement Third, The Law Governing Lawyers § 100, comment c.

[16]ABA Formal Op. 06-443 (Aug. 5, 2006).

[17]Rule 1.4, Comment 7. *See* North Carolina State Bar Ethics Opinion 128 (Apr. 16, 1993), 1993 WL 833052, "Communication with Adverse Corporation's House Counsel." This opinion concluded that (unless the corporation's independent counsel consented) the opposing lawyer may not communicate with the adverse party's in-house counsel if that in-house counsel participated at the trial as a person having managerial responsibility, without consent of corporation's independent counsel.

[18]These issues are carefully discussed in, Richmond, Let's Talk: Critical Aspects of the Anti-Contract Rule for Lawyers, 76 Def. Couns. J. 40, 47–48 (2009). The ABA position "seems to be a stretch." 76 Def. Couns. J. 40, 48.

opposing parties. Rule 4.4(a) prohibits a lawyer from using "methods of obtaining evidence that violate the legal rights of such a person." Thus, under the Model Rules, a lawyer who obtains evidence or information for a client may not violate the law. In such representations, lawyers must properly supervise those who work for them, under Rule 5.1 and Rule 5.3 as well as their agents under Rule 8.4(a), to ensure that those related individuals do not violate the law and Rule 4.4(a).

§ 4.4–2(b) Surreptitious Tape Recordings

In 1974, shortly after the Senate Watergate Committee discovered that President Nixon (who was also a lawyer) had created an elaborate taping system and had been secretly taping many of his Oval Office conversations, the ABA Ethics Committee issued ABA Formal Opinion 337[1] concluding that it was unethical for a lawyer to engage in secret tape recordings, even if the recordings were not a violation of criminal law. The Opinion concluded that "no lawyer should record any conversation whether by tapes or other electronic device, without the consent or prior knowledge of *all* parties to the conversation."[2]

This Formal Opinion also turned its attention to lawyers who are law enforcement personnel engaged in secret tape recordings that are both constitutional and authorized by statute. The Opinion said that such tape recordings, under "extraordinary circumstances," may be ethical, but this Opinion specifically "does not address" such cases, which should be examined "on a case by case basis." Ominously, the Opinion issued a caveat: "It should be *stressed*, however, that the mere fact that secret recordation in a particular instance is not illegal will not necessarily render the conduct of a public law enforcement officer in making such a recording ethical."[3]

ABA Formal Opinion 337 relied on general language found in the Model Code. There was no provision in the Model Code that

---

[Section 4.4–2]

[1]ABA Formal Opinion 337 (Aug. 10, 1974).

[2]Emphasis added. In ABA Formal Opinion 01-422 (June 24, 2001), the ABA formally withdrew Formal Opinion 337 discussed below.

[3]Emphasis added. Note that this ABA promulgation does not bind the courts, because ethics opinions are not law, although they may be persuasive.

In this instance, the courts were not persuaded. *See, e.g., United Sates v. Jamil*, 707 F.2d 638, 646 (2d Cir. 1983):

"We reject appellee's contention that the introduction of the tapes in evidence by the prosecutor would constitute a violation of DR 7-104(A)(1). Such a holding would bar prosecutors from utilizing the fruits of government investigations which are found to be lawfully conducted."

addresses this question precisely, though some states have followed this Formal Opinion.[4]

The Model Rules also have no specific provision prohibiting a lawyer from engaging in surreptitious tape recordings of their conversations with witnesses, opposing parties, or clients if these recordings are otherwise legal. Secret tape recordings where one party consents to the taping (but the other party remains unaware) are not illegal under federal law and the laws of many states.[5] Most state ethics opinions appear to allow such secret tape recordings.[6] Consequently, the Restatement of the Law Governing Lawyers does not follow ABA Formal Opinion 337. Instead, the Restatement allows lawyers to make secret recording's of conversations with another person, without that person's

---

[4]*See, e.g., In re Warner*, 286 S.C. 459, 335 S.E.2d 90 (1985) (per curiam), holding that a lawyer's participation with his client in scheme to first entrap, then secretly record a conference with the family court judge in the judge's chambers warranted a public reprimand.

Committee on Professional Ethics v. Mollman, 488 N.W.2d 168 (Iowa 1992). The Court held that the lawyer engaged in misconduct by wearing a concealed microphone to record a conversation with a friend and former client in order to lure the friend into a trap set by federal law enforcement officials. The lawyer engaged in this conduct to secure leniency in his own prosecution for drug possession. This misconduct warranted a 30-day suspension.

Cf. Kimmel v. Goland, 51 Cal.3d 202, 271 Cal.Rptr. 191, 793 P.2d 524 (1990), cross-defendants had secretly taped a conversation involving cross-complainants in violation of Penal Code section 632, which made it unlawful to record a telephone conversation without consent of all the parties. The court held that the plaintiffs had alleged a cause of action against a lawyer [Mr. Farnell] for unlawfully tape recording a telephone conversation with the opposing party. "As alleged in the cross-complaint, between January and April of 1983, plaintiffs taped confidential telephone conversa-

tions without park management's consent or knowledge. During this period, plaintiffs delivered the tapes to Farnell on five separate occasions. Although Farnell was not present during the actual recording of the conversations, he transcribed the tapes and 'furthered the unlawful agreement [to record the confidential conversations] by aiding, abetting, counseling, advising and encouraging' plaintiffs in their recording of the calls." 51 Cal.3d 202, 207–08, 271 Cal.Rptr., 191, 193–94, 793 P.2d 524, 526–27 (footnote omitted).

[5]*See, e.g., United States v. White*, 401 U.S. 745, 91 S.Ct. 1122, 28 L.Ed.2d 453 (1971), holding that the Omnibus Crime Control and Safe Streets Act of 1968, 18 U.S.C.A. §§ 2510 to 2520, allow a participant to a conversation to record it secretly. There is an FCC rule that regulates secret recordings of telephone conversations (there must be a tone warning device and so forth), but failure to follow these instructions is not criminal, and evidence obtained in violation of these FCC rules are still admissible. *Battaglia v. United States*, 349 F.2d 556 (9th Cir.1965), *cert. denied*, 382 U.S. 955, 86 S.Ct. 430, 15 L.Ed.2d 360 (1965).

[6]Restatement of the Law Governing Lawyers § 106 (Official Draft 2000), Reporter's Note at 142.

consent to being recorded, *if* that recording does not violate the law of the relevant jurisdiction.[7]

Subsequently, in 2001, the ABA formally withdrew Formal Opinion 337. In ABA Formal Opinion 01–422[8] the ABA Ethics Committee concluded that it is not inherently "misleading" for a lawyer to tape record a conversation. In short, the new ABA position is that a lawyer who electronically records a conversation without the knowledge of the other party or parties to the conversation does not necessarily violate the Model Rules. A lawyer may not, however, record conversations in violation of the law in a jurisdiction that forbids such conduct without the consent of all parties. Nor may a lawyer falsely represent that she is not recording a conversation when she, in fact, is doing so. The Committee could not agree whether a lawyer may secretly record a client-lawyer conversation without the knowledge of the client, but the members agreed that it is inadvisable for a lawyer to do so.

Although many people find surreptitious tape recording to be offensive as a general matter, there are specific circumstances where the practice seems reasonable. For example, lawyers might tape record (or advise the client to tape record) obscene phone calls or threats in order to document the calls or threats. Law enforcement personnel and civil rights testers may need to record in order to document claims of violations of illegal discrimination. Lawyers may feel the need to record a conversation with a potential witness when there is a realistic risk that the witness may decide later to commit perjury.[9]

Remedy. If the lawyer engages in surreptitious tape recording in violation of the ethics rules, the lawyer is, of course, subject to

---

[7]Restatement of the Law Governing Lawyers § 106 (Official Draft 2000), at Comment *b*: "When secret recording is not prohibited by law, doing so is permissible for lawyers conducting investigations on behalf of their clients, but should be done only when compelling need exists to obtain evidence otherwise unavailable in as reliable a form."

[8]Formal Opinion 01-422 (June 24, 2001), titled, *Electronic Recordings by Lawyers Without the Knowledge of All Participants*.

[9]*Storment v. Gossage*, 791 F.Supp. 215 (C.D.Ill.1992), where the court, *sua sponte* sanctioned a lawyer $5,000 for filing meritless suit against the defendant (a second lawyer) who had reported the contents of a tape-recorded conversation that proved that the first lawyer had urged his client to commit perjury. The court also held that this second lawyer had not violated any provisions of the Federal Communications Privacy Act. The court found that the first lawyer had instituted the entire suit to harass the reporting attorney and delay the inevitable result of a state disciplinary proceeding.

discipline. In addition, the aggrieved party may sue the lawyer in tort if there is a violation of other law.[10]

However, a court is most unlikely to exclude the evidence, a remedy that is typical in Fourth Amendment violations but not typical at all for violations of ethical rules.[11]

§ 4.4–3 RECEIPT OF PRIVILEGED DOCUMENTS THROUGH INADVERTENT DISCLOSURE

§ 4.4–3(a) The Misdirected Fax, Email, or Mailed Package

The situation where a fax, containing confidential material, is sent to the wrong party involves a case of inadvertent disclosure. Initially two important ABA Formal Opinions dealt with the issues presented when a law firm receives a misdirected fax. The

---

[10]*Kimmel v. Goland*, 51 Cal.3d 202, 271 Cal.Rptr. 191, 793 P.2d 524 (1990), holding that an injured party can sue a lawyer for invasion of privacy because of the lawyer's *"illegal recording of confidential telephone conversations."* 51 Cal.3d 202, 205, 793 P.2d 524, 525, 271 Cal.Rptr. 191, 192 (emphasis added).

[11]*See, e.g., Universal Athletic Sales Co. v. American Gym, Recreational & Athletic Sales Equipment Corp.*, 546 F.2d 530, 539 (3d Cir.1976), held that ethics rules regulate lawyer conduct but do "not delineate rules of evidence but only sets forth strictures on attorney conduct.".

In *United States v. Jamil*, 707 F.2d 638, 646 (2d Cir.1983), Chief Judge Jack B. Weinstein suppressed and excluded from evidence the tape recording of a conversation in which defendant participated. The Second Circuit reversed, holding that it will not bar prosecutors from "utilizing the fruits of government investigations" that were "lawfully conducted."

In *United States v. Starusko*, 729 F.2d 256 (3d Cir.1984) the trial court precluded key Government witness from testifying at the trial in criminal case as sanction for the Government's failure to turn over to the defendant certain exculpatory evidence prior to trial. The Government appealed pursuant to 18 U.S.C.A. § 3731, and the Third Circuit reversed and held that the trial court had

abused its discretion. Even if the prosecutor is subject to disciplinary sanction for failing to turn over constitutionally required exculpatory evidence before trial, the court will not exclude the prosecution witness's testimony.

Contra, Midwest Motor Sports, Inc. v. Arctic Cat Sales, Inc., 144 F.Supp.2d 1147 (D.S.D.2001), *aff'd*, 347 F.3d 693 (8th Cir.2003), held that when the defense attorneys directed an investigator to tape record conversations with plaintiffs' employees without plaintiffs' consent, that violated professional conduct rules, and these violations warranted exclusion of this evidence as sanction. The court said: "It is not illegal in South Dakota for one party to a conversation to record the conversation without the other party's knowledge or consent. It is, however, unethical for an attorney or his investigator or other agent to record a conversation without the other party's knowledge or consent because such conduct involves deceit or misrepresentation." Id. at 1158–59 (internal citations and quotations omitted). Note that this case relied on ABA Formal Opinion 337 (1974). Id. at 1159. However, this decision did not even cite Formal Opinion 01-422 (June 24, 2001) (*Electronic Recordings by Lawyers without the Knowledge of All Participants*), which explicitly withdrew (overruled) ABA Formal Opinion 337!

first opinion[1] addressed the situation where a law firm *inadvertently* receives information from the opposing party that, on its face, appears to be covered by the attorney-client privilege or is otherwise confidential.

In the typical case, a clerk in a law firm mistakenly faxes a document to opposing counsel instead of faxing it to co-counsel. The ABA Opinion, while conceding that is there no satisfactory answer in the black letter provisions of the 1983 Model Rules, concluded that the lawyer should refrain from reviewing the materials, notify the sending lawyer, and abide by that lawyer's instructions.[2] However, in a second Formal Opinion, the ABA Ethics Committee concluded that if an unauthorized source, *e.g.*, a whistle-blower, *intentionally* sends the information to counsel, then the receiving lawyer should either inform the adversary's lawyer and follow her instructions, or refrain from using the unsolicited material until a court makes a definitive resolution of the proper disposition of the materials.[3]

These ABA Formal Opinions distinguished on the question of whether the fax was sent inadvertently or deliberately by a disgruntled employee. In some cases the receiving lawyer will not know if the sender is a whistle-blower or an inattentive employee. Not all whistle-blowers announce their intention in the cover memorandum attached to the fax. But much turns on this unknown fact.

Consider the effect of these ABA Opinions if the misdirected fax is sent in a jurisdiction that would regard the evidentiary privilege as lost in those circumstances. If the misdirected fax from lawyer #1 causes his client to lose the evidentiary privilege, why should the ethics rules prohibit lawyer #2 (the recipient of the misdirected fax) from using the faxed information? If lawyer #1 lost the attorney-client evidentiary privilege in any other situation,[4] then lawyer #2 would take advantage of this difficulty, in the same way that he would take advantage of the circumstance where lawyer #1 mistakenly filed a complaint the day after, instead of the day before, the statute of limitations has run.

[Section 4.4–3]

[1] ABA Formal Opinion 92-368 (Nov. 10, 1992).

   See generally Andrew M. Perlman, *Untangling Ethics Theory from Attorney Conduct Rules: The Case of Inadvertent Discosures*, 13 GEO. MASON L. REV. 767 (2005)

[2] ABA Formal Opinion 92-368 (Nov. 10, 1992).

[3] ABA Formal Opinion 94-382 (July 5, 1994).

[4] For example, if a question is asked during a trial and lawyer #1 did not object on the grounds that the answer was protected by the attorney-client privilege, then the objection would be lost and treated as "waived."

   See, e.g., Granada Corp. v. Honorable First Court of Appeals, 844 S.W.2d 223 (Tex.1992) (even inadvertent disclosure of documents waives privilege).

Because of these difficulties, some state bar opinions and court cases have rejected the ABA solution.[5] Granted, it is the general principle that a lawyer may not cajole, coax or induce another lawyer to violate that other lawyer's duty of confidentiality. However, it "is not, a violation to accept the advantage of inadvertent, and even negligent, disclosure of confidential information by the other lawyer, if the effect of the other lawyer's action is to waive the right of that lawyer's client to assert confidentiality."[6]

In 2002, the ABA added a comment to Rule 4.4 that was inconsistent with the ABA position stated in the formal opinions on the inadvertent disclosure of a document:

> Whether the lawyer is required to take additional steps, such as returning the original document, is a matter of law beyond the scope of these Rules, as is the question of whether the privileged status of a document has been waived. . . .
>
> Some lawyers may choose to return a document unread, for example, when the lawyer learns before receiving the document that it was inadvertently sent to the wrong address. Where a lawyer is not required by applicable law to do so, the decision to voluntarily return such a document is a matter of professional judgment ordinarily reserved to the lawyer. See Rules 1.2 and 1.4.[7]

In light of this inconsistent language, the ABA withdrew the formal opinion and reaffirmed the position in the comments to Rule 4.4: "Rule 4.4(b) thus only obligates the receiving lawyer to notify the sender of the inadvertent transmission promptly."[8]

For these reasons, the simplest solution is for the lawyer to avoid the problem by taking reasonable care to ensure that no faxes are misdirected.[9] The general trend in the law is to hold that the attorney-client privilege is not waived by inadvertent disclosure if the lawyer and client take *reasonable* precautions to guard against inadvertent disclosure.[10] What is "reasonable"

---

[5]*See, e.g., Aerojet-General Corp. v. Transport Indemnity Insurance*, 18 Cal.App.4th 996, 22 Cal.Rptr.2d 862 (1993), reversing the lower court and holding that even if the documents were sent inadvertently, the lawyer who received them through no wrongdoing on his part may keep them and need not inform opposing counsel.

[6]Restatement of the Law Governing Lawyers, Third, § 102, Comment *e* (Official Draft 2000), at 109.

[7]Rule 4.4, comments 3 & 4.

[8]ABA Formal Opinion 05–368 (Oct 1, 2005).

[9]If the fax is misdirected, then both the receiving lawyer and the sending lawyer have to look to their local jurisdiction to determine what happens next.

[10]*See, e.g., Transamerica Computer Co. v. IBM Corp.*, 573 F.2d 646, 652 (9th Cir.1978) (review of 17 million pages of documents with "demanding timetable" and "logistical difficulties;" held, no waiver by inadver-

depends on the circumstances, including the sensitivity of the information.[11]

If a lawyer receives the misdirected fax in a jurisdiction where these issues are not decided by the relevant decisional law, then

---

tent disclosure).

See also, SCM Corp. v. Xerox Corp., 70 F.R.D. 508, 519 (D.Conn. 1976). The Restatement of the Law Governing Lawyers, Third, § 79, Comment h, Illustration 6 (Official Draft 2000), is based on the SCM case, where the lawyer failed to edit matters turned over in course of en bloc copying because of production pressures. "Xerox's affidavits imply that after documents were screened for production to the FTC they were thereafter simply copied en masse and not examined again for privileged information. If that was the case, the somewhat troublesome claim of inadvertence will be accepted and the claim to privilege sustained."

But remember, not all cases follow this principle. Wichita Land & Cattle v. American Federal Bank, 148 F.R.D. 456, 457–58 (D.D.C.1992), holding that the law firm's inadvertent disclosure of two privileged documents that were among 40 boxes that were released meant a waiver of the attorney-client privilege. The law firm claimed that it "took all reasonable steps to shield privileged documents from the discovering party," and the disclosure was "inadvertent." 148 F.R.D. at 458.

Some courts are even less sympathetic and harken back to Dean Wigmore, who believed any disclosure (even to an eavesdropper) mandated a loss of the privilege because the privilege was in derogation of the search for truth. 8 JOHN HENRY WIGMORE, EVIDENCE §§ 2325–2326 (McNaugton rev. 1961). See Suburban Sew 'N Sweep, Inc. v. Swiss-Bernina, Inc., 91 F.R.D. 254 (N.D.Ill.1981) (opposing party discovers handwritten draft of client's letter to lawyer after two years of digging around the trash dumpster examining the waste basket scraps of the client; held, privilege waived).

[11]Restatement of the Law Governing Lawyer, Third, § 79, Comment h (Official Draft 2000), at p. 600.

See, e.g., In re Reorganization of Electric Mutual Liability Insurance Co. (Bermuda), 425 Mass. 419, 681 N.E.2d 838 (1997). An anonymous source disclosed a document. The issue before the court was whether this disclosure mandated a conclusion that the privilege had been waived. The court ruled that, if the client shows that adequate protective steps were taken to preserve the confidentiality of the information, then the disclosure will be presumed not to have been voluntary. See also Abamar Housing & Development Inc. v. Lisa Daly Lady Decor Inc., 698 So.2d 276 (Fla.App. 1997), to the same effect.

United States v. Gangi, 1 F.Supp.2d 256 (S.D.N.Y.1998) involved an unusual fact situation where it appears that proper precautions were not taken. A lawyer handed to a Magistrate Judge in open court in Arizona a sensitive government strategy memorandum in a securities and bank fraud case in the mistaken belief that it was a copy of the indictment. However, this memorandum also contained highly confidential wiretap material and information about witnesses. It bore the legend "This Document Contains Grand Jury Material" but it was not marked confidential or privileged. The judge turned the document over to defense counsel, it got into the hands of other corporate officers, and for three weeks it was in the public court file. Only when the case was moved to New York did the government realize the mistake and ask for all copies of the document back.

The Gangi court held that the document still constitutes government work product. The court ruled that the defendants who had not seen the document have an interest in not being

the safest policy is for the lawyer receiving these documents to submit the document to the court, advise the court that the privilege may be waived due to its disclosure (whether due to inadvertence, negligence, or whistle-blowing) and ask the court if the lawyer must return the documents, or whether the evidentiary privilege is waived in these circumstances.[12] Then, the lawyer will know what to do and not risk being sanctioned for violating ethical rules.[13]

Accessing Emails Legally

Sometimes one litigant has the capacity to read the emails or other information (typically electronic information) of the other litigant *without* engaging in illegal hacking or violating any promise, expressed or implied. The typical situation occurs when an employer has access to the employee's work computer. The mere fact that the employer has access does not mean that the employer has legal access. The one court noted, "Property rights are no less offended when an employer examines documents stored on a computer as when an employer rifles through a folder containing an employee's private papers or reaches in and examines the contents of an employee's pockets."[14]

When a lawyer is representing the employee, then "as soon as practical" after there is a client-lawyer relationship, a lawyer "typically should instruct the employee-client to avoid using a workplace device or system for sensitive or substantive com-

---

worse off than defendants who had seen it. Thus, the court held that the privilege was waived but it permitted redacting of a limited amount of sensitive information after approval of the court before sharing it with the other defendants.

[12]*See* Heidi L. McNeil & Christopher J. Littlefield, *The Inadvertent Disclosure of Privileged Documents, State Bar of Arizona*, 30 ARIZONA ATTORNEY 10 (Nov. 1993). *See also State Compensation Insurance Fund v. WPS, Inc.*, 70 Cal.App.4th 644, 82 Cal.Rptr.2d 799 (Cal.App. 1999) (arguing that the inadvertent fax did not waive the privilege and advising counsel to return a misdirected fax).

[13]However, there is case law that, in effect, rewards the lawyer receiving the inadvertently disclosed documents *if* that lawyer examines these documents. *In re United Mine Workers of America Employee Benefit Plans Litiga-*

tion, 156 F.R.D. 507, 513 (D.D.C.1994). In this case, the court ruled that the plaintiffs' inadvertent disclosure waived the privilege, but remanded to the magistrate judge to determine if the "defendants had succeeded in establishing that they learned the 'gist' of the privileged documents at issue." (footnote omitted). Defendants' knowledge of these documents reflects the degree of disclosure that took place. "A certain degree of disclosure is necessary to constitute a waiver. A privileged document is deemed 'disclosed' when a party has learned the 'gist' of the document's contents." 156 F.R.D. at 513 n. 9. Thus, if defendants did not obtain sufficient knowledge of the contents of plaintiffs' documents (if they did not learn the gist of them), a waiver would not occur.

[14]*Stengart v. Loving Care Agency, Inc.*, 408 N.J. Super. 54, 69–70, 973 A.2d 390, 399 (App. Div. 2009).

munications, and perhaps for any attorney-client communications, because even seemingly ministerial communications involving matters such as scheduling can have substantive ramifications."[15]

For the lawyer representing the employer in these circumstances, the employer may have access to these emails (assuming, again, that there is no hacking and that the employer has not violated any express or implied promise of confidentiality). If there is a court rule, or statute, labor agreement, or something else that creates a reasonable expectation of privacy that requires the employer (or the employer's lawyer) to notify the employee (the opposing litigant or prospective opposing litigant), then the lawyer should follow those rules. If the law governing potential disclosure is "unclear," then Rule 1.6(b)(6) allows the employer's lawyer to disclose to the opposing litigant that the employer has retrieved the employee's attorney-client e-mail communications "to the extent the lawyer reasonably believes it is necessary to do so to comply with the relevant law." If the law governing "potential disclosure is unclear, the lawyer need not risk violating a legal or ethical obligation"[16]

Assuming that it is clear that no rule or promise forbids the employer's access to the employee's email, then the lawyer's duty is different. Then, let us assume that the employer's lawyer receives copies of an employee's private communications with his or her lawyer. Moreover, assume that the reason the employer has access to these emails is that the information is located in the employee's business e-mail file or on the employee's workplace computer or other device. Under those circumstances, "neither Rule 4.4(b) nor any other Rule requires the employer's lawyer to notify opposing counsel of the receipt of the communications."[17]

§ 4.4–3(b) Remedies for Inadvertent Disclosure

Many courts have been unsympathetic of the lawyer or client who inadvertently discloses attorney-client material to the adverse party, even if the disclosure was not negligent.[18] Yet, in other cases, courts have ordered that when lawyers receive

---

[15]ABA Formal Op. 11-459 (Aug. 4, 2011), "Duty to Protect the Confidentiality of E-mail Communications with One's Client."

[16]ABA Formal Op. 11-460 (Aug. 4, 2011), "Duty when Lawyer Receives Copies of a Third Party's E-mail Communications with Counsel."

[17]ABA Formal Op. 11-460 (Aug. 4, 2011), "Duty when Lawyer Receives

Copies of a Third Party's E-mail Communications with Counsel."

[18]*United Mine Workers v. Arch Mineral Corp.*, 145 F.R.D. 3, 6 (D.D.C. 1992). The court rejected the application of the attorney-client privilege to documents that had allegedly been misappropriated and leaked to opposing counsel. The opposing counsel, who received the documents, said that he had gained access to them only be-

inadvertently-disclosed attorney-client material, they must return the documents and destroy all copies in their hands.[19]

This remedy—return of the documents to the original party and destruction of any remaining copies—is not difficult to implement. Moreover, this judicial relief will prevent the document in question from being introduced into evidence or used in a deposition.[20] However, it is no panacea. It may not be possible for the lawyer to forget what he or she has read. Thus, litigants have also sought an additional, more onerous remedy: they want the court to disqualify the lawyer who has received the material.

This remedy of disqualifying the lawyer is much more difficult to understand than a court order forcing the party to return the inadvertently disclosed document. First, court-ordered disqualification will not affect the situation where the client has also seen the document in question. The court cannot disqualify the defendant, the adverse party who received the misdirected fax.[21]

The remedy of disqualification would, in effect, punish lawyer #2 (and the client of lawyer #2) because lawyer #1 (or the client of lawyer #1) turned over material that they should not have disclosed. Whether their disclosure was negligent or simply a reasonable error, the fact remains that it was the other side (lawyer #1 or the client of lawyer #1) that did it and now the other side wants to disqualify opposing counsel because of what they (and not opposing counsel) did.

Second, even if the unintentional disclosure was not negligent,[22] the fact is that the remedy of disqualification serves to disadvantage one party because an adverse party made a mistake and the receiving party read a document that may be labeled "confidential," but was sent to him anyway. We are not speaking of a situation where a lawyer has stolen the documents or bribed some-

---

cause an anonymous source sent multiple copies. Although the documents were marked, "Confidential-Attorney and Client Communication/Do not copy or further distribute," the court ruled that the privilege was lost because the other side had not taken "all possible precautions to maintain their confidentiality." 145 F.R.D. at 8–10.

[19] *Resolution Trust Corp. v. First of America Bank*, 868 F.Supp. 217 (W.D.Mich.1994).

[20] *Resolution Trust Corporation v. First of America Bank*, 868 F.Supp. 217 (W.D.Mich.1994) (although plaintiff's counsel knew what the documents said, they could not be used in evidence).

[21] *Kusch v. Ballard*, 645 So.2d 1035 (Fla.Dist.App.1994), involved a privileged document mistakenly faxed to the opposing party. The court held that the inadvertent faxing did not constitute waiver of the lawyer-client privilege but disqualification of the innocent recipient was neither necessary nor appropriate.

[22] We do not, after all, require the lawyer to personally type the addresses of each envelope. The fact that a document is mailed to the wrong party does not necessarily mean that there was negligence. Reasonable people are allowed to make reasonable mistakes.

one to steal them.[23] The court may not wish to punish the sending lawyer because of his error (particularly if the error was not negligent), but neither should the court reward him by allowing his mistake to result in the disqualification of the receiving lawyer. Consequently, some courts have refused to disqualify the receiving lawyer in this situation.[24]

---

[23]**Dismissal of Complaint As Sanction When Documents Are Stolen.** *Lipin v. Bender*, 193 A.D.2d 424, 597 N.Y.S.2d 340 (1993). The plaintiff stole privileged documents from defense counsel who had brought them to a hearing. Plaintiff's lawyer then copied the documents and used them against the defendant. The court dismissed the complaint as a sanction against the plaintiff.

Matter of Wisehart, 281 A.D.2d 23, 721 N.Y.S.2d 356 (2001), *appeal dismissed*, 96 N.Y.2d 935, 733 N.Y.S.2d 370, 759 N.E.2d 369 (2001) (per curiam), is the next chapter in *Lipin v. Bender*, 193 A.D.2d 424, 597 N.Y.S.2d 340 (1993), *affirmed*, 84 N.Y.2d 562, 620 N.Y.S.2d 744, 644 N.E.2d 1300 (1994), the case, where the client had stolen opposing counsel's documents. Later in the underlying case, the lawyer sought a rehearing alleging in part that the trial judge was suffering from breast cancer that caused her to behave irrationally and that the Chief Judge of the Court of Appeals had been covering up for her. The court held that the lawyer's condoning the use of his opponent's documents that had been copied by his client/employee, his failure to advise the court and his opponent immediately of the theft of those documents, his use of those documents to try to extract a settlement from adversary, his reckless accusations against judges, and his disregard of a court directive to make no use of documents in litigation and to secure all copies was conduct that warranted a two-year suspension from practice of law. The court said that the lawyer had an unblemished record in practice of almost 50 years, but that his conduct in this case was so bizarre

that a two year suspension was appropriate.

[24]*Resolution Trust Corp. v. First America Bank*, 868 F.Supp. 217 (W.D. Mich.1994), holding that disqualification of plaintiff's counsel was not warranted. "First of all, the cat is out of the bag." 868 F.Supp. at 220. The lawyer did read material, which was "clearly labeled on its face 'PRIVILEGED AND CONFIDENTIAL,'" was directed to a Senior Vice President of defendant and contained the caption of the case." 868 F.Supp. at 218. The document in question was a seven page letter from the defendant's counsel to the defendant laying out the facts of the case to date and the defense strategy. *Id.*

Contrast In re Bank of America, N.A., 45 S.W.3d 238 (Tex.App.2001), involved a situation where the trial judge had made an in camera inspection of 158 pages of defendant's documents and ruled they were neither privileged nor work product. Over defense objection and before it could seek review of the determination, the trial judge simply handed the papers to the plaintiff's counsel who took and immediately read them. On review, the state appellate court upheld the documents' privileged character, and the bank moved to disqualify plaintiff's counsel. This court found that while the plaintiff's counsel had not done anything ethically wrong, neither had the defendant, and in this case the best way to protect the defendant was to make the plaintiff retain new counsel who had not seen the confidential material, even though the plaintiff will "undoubtedly suffer extraordinary prejudice if its attorneys were disqualified after more than four years of liti-

§ 4.4–3(c) Model Rule 4.4(b)

The drafters of the 2002 Rules studied the ethics opinions and judicial decisions involving the receipt of privileged documents through inadvertent disclosure and they decided to include a provision in Rule 4.4 to address this topic. Rule 4.4(b) states that if a lawyer receives a document relating to a representation and that lawyer knows or reasonably should know that the document was delivered inadvertently, the lawyer should inform the sender in a prompt manner.[25] Apart from this obligation to inform the sender, the text of the Rule imposes no further obligation.

Comment 2 advises that the Rule takes no position on the questions of privilege, whether further action is required, or whether the lawyer may read the documents.[26] Once the lawyer notifies the sender, either the sender or the receiver can file appropriate motions in court and let the court decide what to do next. The court will look at the law of evidence to determine if the inadvertent disclosure constitutes a waiver of the privilege. The court will also decide if the receiving-lawyer must return the documents to the sender and whether the receiving-lawyer may retain copies of the documents.

There is also the problem of what to do when someone sends documents to a lawyer that sender may have obtained unlawfully.[27] The drafters of 2002 Rules concluded that a provision must address this topic, but the rule that was finally adopted does not impose any additional duties on the lawyer other than notifying the sender, who then can go to court to seek what protective order he or she wants. As to what the court should do, that issue then becomes one of other law (such as the law of evidence), not of legal ethics.

The lawyer, in short, should inform the court, which will issue a ruling as to what should be done. Consider, for example, Daniel Ellsberg, who sent to the public media copies of the Pentagon Papers,[28] which were classified and were not supposed to be revealed. Other laws, not the ethics rules, will tell us what the lawyer should do in that situation.

---

gation" 45 S.W.3d at 245.

One should also note that it is becoming increasingly common for lawyers to include on the cover sheet of all faxes sent to anyone a standard boilerplate statement proclaiming that the fax is "privileged and confidential," even when the fax is intended to be sent to opposing counsel and the information (*e.g.*, a proposed deposition schedule) is not "privileged and confidential." It should not be surprising that this boilerplate is not quite the warning to the recipient that a lawyer may later contend it is.

[25] Rule 4.4(b).

[26] Rule 4.4, Comment 2.

[27] Rule 4.4, Comment 2.

[28] *New York Times v. United States*, 403 U.S. 713, 91 S.Ct. 2140, 29 L.Ed.2d 822 (1971). See also *Daniel Ellsberg, Secrets: A Memoir of Vietnam and the Pentagon Papers* (Viking Penguin, 2002).

The drafters took one stand in the Comments relating to whether the lawyer or the client has the authority to make a decision regarding whether to read an inadvertently sent document. However, this stand is much less significant than it first appears. In the actual language, the first clause of this Comment takes away the discretion that the remainder of the Comment appears to give: "Where a lawyer is not required by applicable law to do so, the decision to voluntarily return such a document is a matter of professional judgment ordinarily reserved to the lawyer."[29]

Hence, to avoid a malpractice suit, the lawyer should file motion in court to find out what she should do in such circumstances, unless the law is already quite clear. If the court rules that there is no privilege, the lawyer may, indeed, *must* read and use the document to the disadvantage of the other side. If the court rules that the document must not be used, the lawyer cannot use it even if the client says otherwise. The matter, in practice, is not one of professional judgment; it is an issue of the law of evidence. As the Restatement advised:

> It is not a violation to accept the advantage of inadvertent, and even negligent, disclosure of confidential information by the other lawyer, if the effect of the other lawyer's action is to waive the right of that lawyer's client to assert confidentiality.[30]

The Reporter's Notes to the Restatement explicitly acknowledge that its position is contrary to the view of ABA Formal Opinion 92-368 (1992).[31]

Indeed, consistent with this treatise, the Restatement advises: "If the disclosure operates to end legal protection for the information, the lawyer may use it for the benefit of the lawyer's own client *and may be required to do so* if that would advance the client's lawful objectives."[32]

Rule 4.4(b) does not apply to the lawyer's receipt of intention-

---

[29]Rule 4.4, Comment 3 (citing Rule 1.2 and Rule 1.4).

[30]Restatement of the Law Governing Lawyer, Third, § 102, Comment e (Official Draft 2000).

[31]Restatement of the Law Governing Lawyer, Third, § 102, Reporter's Notes to Comment e (Official Draft 2000).

[32]Restatement of the Law Governing Lawyer, Third, § 60, Comment m (Official Draft 2000).

See also, e.g., In re Polypropylene Carpet Antitrust Litigation, 181 F.R.D. 680, 698 (N.D. Ga. 1998):

"The Court therefore concludes that, although Opinion 92-368 represents one view regarding an attorney's obligation to return inadvertently produced documents, it is debatable whether Opinion 92-368 establishes an ethical rule that governs the conduct of attorneys in this circuit. A court should be hesitant to 'deprive an attorney of the opportunity to practice his profession on the basis of a determination after the fact that conduct is unethical if responsible attorneys would differ in appraising the propriety of that conduct.' *Schlumberger Technologies, Inc. v. Wiley*, 113 F.3d 1553, 1560–61 (11th Cir.1997) (internal quotations omitted)."

ally or advertently sent documents.[33] Thus, a lawyer who receives documents from a whistleblower does not have an obligation under Rule 4.4(b) to disclose such fact to the opposing side.[34] However, the lawyer must be mindful of other law when dealing with such information. If the information is accompanied by a personal contact from the sending person, the lawyer needs to be mindful of Model Rule 4.2 (the anti-contact rule), Model Rule 3.4(a) and (b)(dealing with evidence and witnesses), and Model Rule 3.7 (the lawyer himself or herself may become a witness to the parties disclosure). When a tribunal is involved and when the whistleblowing involves candor to the court, the lawyer should consider bringing the documents to the attention of the court and to allow the court to complete the investigation.

In re Polypropylene Carpet Antitrust Litigation, 181 F.R.D. 680, 698 (N.D.Ga.1998). The court explicitly relied on the Restatement view.

[33]ABA Formal Opinion 06–442, at n. 7 (Aug. 5, 2006).

[34]*But see Burt Hill, Inc. v. Hassan*, 2010 WL 419433 (W.D. Pa. 2010) (package left outside defendant's office by an anonymous source required that attorney comply with Pa. Rule 4.4(b)).

V. LAW FIRMS AND ASSOCIATIONS

CHAPTER 5.1

RESPONSIBILITIES OF A PARTNER OR SUPERVISORY LAWYER

RULE 5.1: RESPONSIBILITIES OF PARTNERS, MANAGERS, AND SUPERVISORY LAWYERS

(a) A partner in a law firm, and a lawyer who individually or together with other lawyers possesses comparable managerial authority in a law firm, shall make reasonable efforts to ensure that the firm has in effect measures giving reasonable assurance that all lawyers in the firm conform to the Rules of Professional Conduct.

(b) A lawyer having direct supervisory authority over another lawyer shall make reasonable efforts to ensure that the other lawyer conforms to the Rules of Professional Conduct.

(c) A lawyer shall be responsible for another lawyer's violation of the Rules of Professional Conduct if:

(1) the lawyer orders or, with knowledge of the specific conduct, ratifies the conduct involved; or

(2) the lawyer is a partner or has comparable managerial authority in the law firm in which the other lawyer practices, or has direct supervisory authority over the other lawyer, and knows of the conduct at a time when its consequences can be avoided or mitigated but fails to take reasonable remedial action.

Comment

[1] Paragraph (a) applies to lawyers who have managerial authority over the professional work of a firm. See Rule 1.0(c). This includes members of a partnership, the shareholders in a law firm organized as a professional corporation, and members of other associations authorized to practice law; lawyers having comparable managerial authority in a legal services organization or a law department of an

enterprise or government agency; and lawyers who have intermediate managerial responsibilities in a firm. Paragraph (b) applies to lawyers who have supervisory authority over the work of other lawyers in a firm.

[2] Paragraph (a) requires lawyers with managerial authority within a firm to make reasonable efforts to establish internal policies and procedures designed to provide reasonable assurance that all lawyers in the firm will conform to the Rules of Professional Conduct. Such policies and procedures include those designed to detect and resolve conflicts of interest, identify dates by which actions must be taken in pending matters, account for client funds and property and ensure that inexperienced lawyers are properly supervised.

[3] Other measures that may be required to fulfill the responsibility prescribed in paragraph (a) can depend on the firm's structure and the nature of its practice. In a small firm of experienced lawyers, informal supervision and periodic review of compliance with the required systems ordinarily will suffice. In a large firm, or in practice situations in which difficult ethical problems frequently arise, more elaborate measures may be necessary. Some firms, for example, have a procedure whereby junior lawyers can make confidential referral of ethical problems directly to a designated senior partner or special committee. See Rule 5.2. Firms, whether large or small, may also rely on continuing legal education in professional ethics. In any event, the ethical atmosphere of a firm can influence the conduct of all its members, and the partners may not assume that all lawyers associated with the firm will inevitably conform to the Rules.

[4] Paragraph (c) expresses a general principle of personal responsibility for acts of another. See also Rule 8.4(a).

[5] Paragraph (c)(2) defines the duty of a partner or other lawyer having comparable managerial authority in a law firm, as well as a lawyer who has direct supervisory authority over performance of specific legal work by another lawyer. Whether a lawyer has supervisory authority in particular circumstances is a question of fact. Partners and lawyers with comparable authority have at least indirect responsibility for all work being done by the firm, while a partner or manager in charge of a particular matter ordinarily also has supervisory responsibility for the work of other firm lawyers engaged in the matter. Appropriate remedial action by a partner or managing lawyer would depend on the immediacy of that lawyer's involvement and the seriousness of the misconduct. A supervisor is required to intervene to prevent avoidable consequences of misconduct if the supervisor knows that the misconduct occurred. Thus, if a supervising lawyer knows that a subordinate misrepresented a matter to an opposing party in negotiation, the supervisor as well as the subordinate has a duty to correct the resulting misapprehension.

[6] Professional misconduct by a lawyer under supervision could reveal a violation of paragraph (b) on the part of the supervisory lawyer even though it does not entail a violation of paragraph (c) because there was no direction, ratification or knowledge of the violation.

[7] Apart from this Rule and Rule 8.4(a), a lawyer does not have disciplinary liability for the conduct of a partner, associate or subordinate. Whether a lawyer may be liable civilly or criminally for another lawyer's conduct is a question of law beyond the scope of these Rules.

[8] The duties imposed by this Rule on managing and supervising lawyers do not alter the personal duty of each lawyer in a firm to abide by the Rules of Professional Conduct. See Rule 5.2(a).

Authors' 1983 Model Rules Comparison

The drafters of the 2002 Rules changed the caption of Rule 5.1 to add "Managers" and made the words "Partner" and "Lawyer" plural.

In Rule 5.1(a), the drafters added to the responsibility placed on partners, a similar responsibility on "a lawyer who individually or together with other lawyers possesses comparable managerial authority in a law firm." The drafters sought to impose explicitly in text Rule 5.1(a) duties on "managing lawyers in corporate and government legal departments and legal services organizations." Reporter's Explanation of Changes to Rule 5.1. This change would also impose Rule 5.1(a) duties upon lawyers who are managers of law firms, but who may not be a partner.

In Rule 5.1(c)(2), the drafters added the words, "or has comparable managerial authority" to similarly bring into this provision those lawyers who are managers of legal departments.

Comment 1 is reorganized just to address Rule 5.1(a) first and to explain the addition of the language about manager and lawyers having comparable managerial authority. The last line in the Comment notes the application of paragraph (b) to supervisory lawyers.

Comment 2 is new and explains the duties and responsibilities of those lawyers with managerial authority.

Comment 3 is the old Comment 2 and the drafters slightly amended the language to make clear that the policies needed to comply with Rule 5.1(a) will depend upon the firm's size, structure, and nature of the practice.

Comment 4 is old Comment 3 with a slight modification to focus it on 5.1(c) generally and to add the word "personal" to modify responsibility.

Comment 5 is old Comment 4, with an amendment to reflect the addition of managers to the Rule. It explains the operation of Rule 5.2(c)(2) with the addition of managers in firms and other organizations.

Comments 6 and 7 are old Comments 5 and 6, but they were not modified.

Comment 8 is new and reflects the drafter's view that all lawyers must comply with the Model Rules for their own conduct and those who have partner, managerial, or supervisory authority have additional responsibilities. The responsibilities in Rule 5.1 do not affect a lawyer's duty to follow the Rules generally if they are involved in the situation.

Model Code Comparison

There was no direct counterpart to this Rule in the Model Code. DR

1-103(A) provided that a lawyer "possessing unprivileged knowledge of a violation of DR 1-102 shall report such knowledge to . . . authority empowered to investigate or act upon such violation."

§ 5.1–1 INTRODUCTION: THE LAWYER'S OBLIGATIONS AS A MEMBER OF A FIRM

Part 5 of the Model Rules has a specific section dealing with "Law Firms and Associations." Many of these provisions have no explicit counterpart in the Model Code. For the most part, however, Part 5 does not change the law. Rather, it codifies and amplifies provisions already found in scattered sections of the Model Code and adds or elaborates on topics already implicit in the laws of agency and of tort.[1] To the extent that Part 5 adds provisions already existing in the law of agency,[2] it serves to subject a lawyer to discipline for conduct that, previously, may have subjected the lawyer only to the risk of civil liability.

General Counsel of Law Firms. Because of the realistic possibility of tort suits against law firms based on alleged violations of the ethics rules, including the firm's lack of reasonable supervision, a growing number of law firms are designating one partner as the "general counsel of the law firm."[3]

This arrangement heightens ethical awareness by fixing responsibility in one lawyer to whom other lawyers, whether partners or associates, may turn for a more objective evaluation of legal ethics issues. Second, creating a post of general counsel to the firm means that this general counsel must stay up-to-date

---

[Section 5.1–1]

[1] **Vicarious Liability Involving Civil Liability and Discipline.** Part 5 of the Model Rules does not purport to impose any liability on a *law firm*. However, other law, such as tort, agency, or contract, may impose vicarious liability on the law firm. Restatement of the Law Governing Lawyers § 58 (Official Draft 2000).

[2] Restatement of the Law of Agency, Second §§ 503, 507, 510 (1958).

[3] *See, e.g.*, Epstein, The In-House Ethics Advisor: Practical Benefits for the Modern Law Firm, 7 Geo. J. Legal Ethics 1011 (1994); Gillers, Preserving the Attorney Client Privilege for the Advice of a Law Firm's In-House Counsel, 2000 A.B.A. Prof. Law. 107 (2000); Chambliss and Wilkins, The Emerging Role of Ethics Advisors, General Counsel, and Other Compliance Specialists in Large Law Firms, 44 Ariz. L. Rev. 559 (2002); Richmond, Law Firm Internal Investigations: Principles And Perils, 54 Syracuse L. Rev. 69 (2004); Richmond, Essential Principles for Law Firm General Counsel, 53 U. Kan. L. Rev. 805 (2005); Chambliss, The Scope of In-Firm Privilege, 80 Notre Dame L. Rev. 1721 (2005); Fortney, Law Firm General Counsel as Sherpa: Challenges Facing the In-Firm Lawyer's Lawyer, 53 U. Kan. L. Rev 835 (2005); Chambliss, The Professionalization of Law Firm In-House Counsel, 84 N.C. L. Rev. 1515 (2006); Rotunda, Lawyers: Why We Are Different and Why We Are the Same: Creating Structural Incentives in Large Law Firms to Promote Ethical Behavior—In-House Ethics Counsel, Bill Padding, and In-House Ethics Training, 44 Akron Law Rev. 679 (2011) (Miller-Becker Professional Responsibility Distinguished Lecture Series).

on the development of the case law and regulations that govern the practice of law. Lawyers who practice in creditors' rights, or antitrust, government contact law, etc. have an economic incentive to keep up with the latest law. Unless a lawyer is practicing in the area of legal ethics, he or she does not have the same incentive to keep up with the ever-increasing complications area of law. In addition, the law firm is more likely to protect, under the attorney-client evidentiary privilege, conversations and communications between its law firm lawyers and the law firm's general counsel, who is also a member of the firm.[4]

It is increasingly common for ethics specialists to advise law firms to create an "ethics partner" or in-house lawyer to advice on matters of legal ethics.[5]

Several ethics issues regarding clients arise if a law firm creates a separate department or lawyer to handle all ethics issues within a firm.[6]

First, may a lawyer in a law firm share confidential client information with an in-house ethics counsel in order to discuss an ethics issue? The answer is yes. Rule 1.6(b)(4) permits a lawyer to consult with someone outside of the firm to ascertain the lawyer's compliance with the ethics rules. ABA Formal Opinion 08-453 reminds us that the language in Comment 5 of Rule 1.6 provides that, unless instructed otherwise by a client, lawyers may share client information with others in the firm. Thus, unless a client has specifically restricted the sharing of information with the firm, lawyers may discuss client matters with ethics counsel.[7]

Second, does the lawyer have an obligation to inform the client of the consultation or the advice received at any point in time? Of course, a lawyer is free to disclose the fact that he or she consulted with in-house ethics counsel to the client. And, if the lawyer had planned on billing the client for the work of ethics counsel, the lawyer should disclose the impending consultation and obtain the client's consent. But, ABA Formal Opinion 08-453 takes the position that the Model Rules only require disclosures of the facts, circumstances, and legal standard of the rule in

---

[4]*In re Sunrise*, 130 F.R.D. 560, 595 (E.D.Pa.1989); *Lama Holding Co. v. Shearman & Sterling*, No. 89 Civ. 3639 (KTD), 1991 WL 115052, at *1 (S.D.N.Y.1991); *United States v. Rowe*, 96 F.3d 1294 (9th Cir.1996).

[5]Professor Roy Simon, for example, recommends: "Many law firms already have an 'ethics committee' or 'ethics partner' to serve as the firm's internal resource for deciding ethics questions, and firms of more than a dozen lawyers that do not yet have an ethics committee ought to form one." Roy D. Simon, Simon's New York Code of Professional Responsibility Annotated 68 (2005).

[6]*See* ABA Formal Ethics Op. 08-453 (Oct. 17, 2008).

[7]Id.

question; the lawyer need not disclose the fact that the lawyer sought the advice of ethics counsel to reach this conclusion. Therefore, lawyers are not required to disclose that their advice comes from an in-house ethics counsel.[8]

A third question about a consultation with ethics counsel is whether the referral of the ethics issue creates a conflict of interest between the law firm and the client. According to ABA Formal Opinion 08-453, the answer depends upon "the nature of the consultation and the respective interests of the firm and its client at the time." Usually, the lawyer consults with ethics counsel so as to help him or her properly represent the client. Thus the consultation does not create a conflict. In such cases, the interests of the client and the lawyer are aligned.

However, a situation may arise when the interests become divergent. For example, if the lawyer has committed malpractice and the consultation with ethics counsel is to "protect the interests of the consulting lawyer or the firm" against the interests of the client, a conflict has arisen. Normally, one would think that the conflict arises from the malpractice and not the consultation, but the ABA Opinion seems to suggest that conflicts arise from both. The Opinion states, "there is a significant risk that the representation of that client will be materially limited by the interests of the consulting lawyer and every lawyer in the firm." Thus, the Opinion suggests that Rule 1.10 disqualifies all lawyers in the firm unless the client waives disqualification. The lawyer must address the Rule 1.10 issue and the 1.7 conflict issue in such a case in order to continue the representation.

This analysis inevitably must rely on a formalistic view of the consultation with the in-house ethics counsel. In other words, when a lawyer consults with an ethics counsel, the law firm develops an attorney-client relationship with that ethics counsel and one must compare this relationship to the role of the law firm in representing the client. There may be disputes where a law firm does form an attorney-client relationship with ethics counsel, but this characterization does not seem necessary in all cases. Why use this characterization when a lawyer simply calls an ethics counsel as a sounding board? The normal rule is that the client hires the "law firm," and every lawyer in the firm owes a duty to the client. The law firm's ethics counsel, in that sense, is not different than any other lawyer in the firm. So why should

---

[8]The New York State Bar Association proposed a similar result was proposed in 2005. See N.Y. State Bar Association Committee On Prof. Ethics, Consultation with a Law Firm's In-House Counsel on Matters of Professional Ethics Involving One or More Clients of the Law Firm, Op. 789 (Oct. 26, 1005) (law firm "has no duty to advise the client that the law firm has consulted with its own in-house counsel in reaching those conclusions").

the Model Rules (or the ABA Formal Opinion) create role differentiation for an ethics counsel? The problem of a firm that has committed an act of malpractice is adequately addressed through Rule 1.7. That possible conflict arises whether or not the firm has an individual formally designated as "an ethics counsel."

If there is a dispute between the client and the law firm, many cases do not allow the law firm to assert an adverse attorney-client privilege against an existing client. In other words, the attorney client privilege does not protect a law firm's communication with its own in-house counsel if the communication implicates or creates a conflict between the law firm's fiduciary duties to itself and its duties to the client seeking to discover the communication.[9]

Some courts have recognized that the law should encourage law firms to use a general counsel, in order for the firm lawyers to have a person to whom they can submit their legal ethics questions. These courts, to encourage development in this area, generally treat as privileged the conversations that the firm lawyers have with the firm's inside general counsel.

> The court recognizes that law firms should and do seek advice about their legal and ethical obligations in connection with representing a client and that firms normally seek this advice from their own lawyers. Indeed, many firms have in-house ethics advisers for this purpose. A rule requiring disclosure of all communications relating to a client would dissuade attorney's from referring ethical problems to other lawyers, thereby undermining conformity with ethical obligations. Such a rule would also make conformity costly by forcing the firm either to retain outside counsel or terminate an existing attorney-client relationship to ensure confidentiality of all communications relating to that client. This

---

[9]*In re Sunrise Securities Litigation*, 130 F.R.D. 560, 597 (E.D. Pa. 1989). See also, e.g., *Koen Book Distributors, Inc. v. Powell, Trachtman, Logan, Carrle, Bowman & Lombardo, P.C.*, 212 F.R.D. 283, 286 (E.D.Pa.2002): "The [Work Product] doctrine does not apply where a client, as opposed to some other party, seeks discovery of the lawyer's mental impressions. *Spivey v. Zant*, 683 F.2d 881, 885 (5th Cir.1982). It cannot shield a lawyer's papers from discovery in a conflict of interest context anymore than can the attorney-client privilege." *Bank Russells Lambert v. Credit Lyonnais (Suisse) S. A.*, 220 F. Supp. 2d 283, 287 (S.D.N.Y.2002), holding that the law firm "was under an ethical duty to disclose to [its client] the results of its internal conflict check, and in no position to claim a privilege against their client. While the privilege will be applicable as against all the world, it cannot be maintained against [its client]." *Versuslaw, Inc. v. Stoel Rives, LLP*, 127 Wash. App. 309, 334, 111 P.3d 866, 879 (Div. 1, 2005): "When a law firm seeks advice from its in-house lawyer concerning potential malpractice in its representation of a client, the law firm's position can be adverse to or limit the law firm's representation of its client and create a conflict of interest."

court declines to follow such a strict rule, preferring one that is consistent with a law firm in-house ethical infrastructure.[10]

Hence, a court has held (in the course of multidistrict litigation concerning a bankrupt securities broker) that a law firm's internal e-mail was privileged as work product because the client's presumptive access to its file does not apply to documents intended solely for internal law office.[11] In these e-mails, the law partners shared their preliminary thoughts concerning the law firm's representation of SPhinX and PlusFunds in various matters, including the Refco bankruptcy proceedings. Plaintiffs claimed that the law firm engaged in malpractice and in a conflict of interests.

Similarly, if lawyers within a firm have communications among themselves regarding the firm's potential malpractice in an existing client, the attorney-client privilege protects those communications from later discovery by the client:

> recognition of the privilege promotes the affected attorney's ability promptly to seek advice and to obtain it based on a complete disclosure of the circumstances which led them to believe that some loss prevention communication was warranted.[12]

The view that the ethics counsel is the law firm's lawyer is confirmed by ABA Formal Opinion's discussion of "identifying Ethics Counsel's Client." Although this discussion primarily focuses on conflicts between the law firm and the consulting lawyer, it is clear that the ABA has adopted this formal characterization of the role of ethics counsel. As the firm's lawyer, the ethics counsel has a duty to the entity (*i.e.*, the law firm) and to its compliance with the rules of professional responsibility. Rules 1.13, 5.1, and 8.3 all provide guidance for the ethics counsel

---

[10]*Thelen Reid & Priest LLP v. Marland*, 2007 WL 578989, *7 (N.D. Cal. 2007). See also *Versuslaw, Inc. v. Stoel Rives, LLP*, 127 Wash App. 309, 332, 111 P.3d 866, 878 (Wash. App. Div. 1, 2005), *review denied*, 132 P.3d 147 (Wash. 2006): "Lawyers in a law firm seeking legal advice from another lawyer in the same firm can assert the attorney-client privilege," *citing United States v. Rowe*, 96 F.3d 1294 (9th Cir. 1996); *Hertzog, Calamari & Gleason v. Prudential Ins. Co.*, 850 F. Supp. 255 (S.D.N.Y.1994).

[11]*In re Refco Securities Litigation*, __ F.Supp.2d __, 2011 WL 497441 (S.D.N.Y. 2011). Compare, *Sage Realty Corp. v. Proskauer Rose Goetz & Mendelsohn, LLP*, 91 N.Y.2d 30, 37, 666 N.Y.S.2d 985, 689 N.E.2d 879 (1997), holding that a client has "presumptive access to the attorney's entire file on the represented matter, subject to narrow exceptions," and one of those exceptions is "documents intended for internal law office review and use." This court said that there was a "need for lawyers to be able to set down their thoughts privately in order to assure effective and appropriate representation warrants keeping such documents secret from the client involved." *Thelen Reid & Priest LLP v. Marland*, 2007 WL 578989, *7 (N.D. Cal. 2007).

[12]*TattleTale Alarm Systems, Inc. v. Calfee, Halter & Griswold, LLP*, 2011 WL 382627, *10 (S.D. Ohio 2011).

in the discharge of his or her responsibilities. Thus, the ethics counsel has an obligation to report information to the lawyers in charge of the law firm as well as to the bar if a lawyer is engaged in conduct not protected by client confidentiality that raises substantial questions as to that lawyer's honesty, trustworthiness, and fitness as a lawyer.

The law should encourage law firms to create in-house general counsel, and then treat those general counsels the way it treats general counsel of any other entity, such as a corporation, union, or partnership; the courts, in short, should respect the attorney-client privilege of a law firm's general counsel as a way of encouraging behavior that is more ethical.

If a law firm appoints one of its partners as its own in-house general counsel, then this in-house counsel can offer candid and confidential advice to the younger lawyers. The creation of this office will signal that the law firm wants to create the right culture, and foster the right habits.[13] The in-house counsel is likely to be more objective than the lawyers initially involved with the matter. For one thing, the in-house counsel will not be personally involved with the particular matter. If the client is the problem, she should be viewing the client as a client of "the firm" rather than a client of the particular billing partner.

The in-house counsel will make the decision more objectively than either the partner in charge or the senior associate. That is because the client's billings may represent 20% or more of the billings of the partner or associate, but only a minute percentage of the billings of the entire law firm. If necessary, the in-house counsel can decide whether the issue is such that she should kick it upstairs to the relevant law firm committee (such as the committee that decides if there is a disqualification issue or a conflict of interests).

When the firm creates an in-house ethics counsel to whom partners and associates can easily confide about ethics issues, they promote the development of a culture of ethics. The existence of an in-house ethics counsel sends an important signal to all the lawyers in the firm. The associate can simply talk to another lawyer (the in-house counsel) confidentially. There is no need to go over anyone's head. The law firm does not have to decide if the issue is worth the expense of hiring outside counsel.

If there is no in-house counsel to whom the junior associate can turn, the junior associate is less likely to turn to anyone. If the junior associate sees that the senior associate and the billing partner have decided not to turn over the document, it is harder

---

[13]Davis, Legal Ethics and Risk Management: Complementary Visions of Lawyer Regulation, 21 Geo. J. Legal Ethics 95, 108–10 (2008).

for the junior associate to go over their heads and make waves. However, it is easy to walk down the hall for a confidential conversation with the in-house counsel.

It is often difficult to make the initial decision to get involved. But if the firm makes that decision easier, more people are likely to make the first step. If young lawyers know that they can easily and confidentially seek the solace of the in-house general counsel, they should be less likely to follow the herd. Just as it is easy to ask *inside* counsel, it is a lot bigger step to seek the solace of the law firm's *outside* counsel; it is a particularly big step for junior associates. The existence of an in-house general counsel should encourage junior partners or associates (particularly junior associates) to report suspicions in a way that does not disadvantage those who do report.

Thus, it is becoming more common for law firms to appoint one of the partnership's lawyers as "general counsel" to the law firm.[14] A survey of the largest 197 law firms in 2005 reported that nearly 70% now have a designated general counsel. That is up from 63% in the prior year. Each is an inside counsel rather than an outside general counsel (*i.e.*, a lawyer in another law firm), and, 92% of these general counsel are partners in their firm.[15]

It should take little effort for the young associate to turn to this general counsel, who may be the lawyer down the hall or on the next floor, in order to seek candid advice. When a lawyer sees a problem—or thinks she sees a problem but she is not sure and her colleagues are doing nothing—she can inform the general counsel about what she sees and know that she is speaking confidentially. The general counsel, by definition, will not be one of the passive bystanders who chose to walk around the fallen body crying for help. That is because it is the business of the general counsel to become involved. That is part of her job description. If the lawyer can confidentially seek advice or report to a general counsel, then that lawyer is less likely to do nothing.

---

[14]Epstein, The In-House Ethics Advisor: Practical Benefits for the Modern Law Firm, 7 Geo. J. Legal Ethics 1011 (1994); Chambliss and Wilkins, The Emerging Role of Ethics Advisors, General Counsel, and Other Compliance Specialists in Large Law Firms, 44 Ariz. L. Rev. 559 (2002); Richmond, Essential Principles for Law Firm General Counsel, 53 U. Kan. L. Rev. 805 (2005); Chambliss, The Scope of In-Firm Privilege, 80 Notre Dame L. Rev. 1721 (2005) [hereinafter Chambliss, The Scope of In-Firm Privilege]; Fortney, Law Firm General Counsel as Sherpa: Challenges Facing the In-Firm Lawyer's Lawyer, 53 U. Kan. L. Rev 835 (2005); Chambliss, The Professionalization of Law Firm In-House Counsel, 84 N.C. L. Rev. 1515 (2006) [hereinafter Chambliss, Professionalization of Law Firm In-House Counsel]; Davis, *supra* note 1.

[15]Results of Confidential "Flash" Survey on Law Firm General Counsel, (Mar. 2005), http://www.altmanweil.com/dir__docs/resource/d0f1e347-e90b-40ae-9b92-808a7eff6ffd__document.pdf.

If the general counsel concludes there is no problem, the junior lawyer will have ethical reasons to defer to that decision.[16] If there is a problem, the inside counsel can take appropriate action to correct it.

The empirical evidence demonstrates that: one study showed that, over a five-year period, law firms that employ a general counsel (or similar position, such as ethics advisor or loss prevention counsel) spend $1 million less on defense costs and indemnity payments in connection with malpractice claims.[17] Because these firms are more ethical, they have fewer malpractice claims.

The law should encourage law firms to create an in-house legal counsel.[18] The ethics rules authorize lawyers to seek confidential advice from other lawyers about their ethical duties.[19] Although the ABA Model Rules do not use the title "in-house counsel," they do specifically contemplate that law firms, particularly larger firms, may designate a senior lawyer as a designated ethics lawyer.[20] The ABA advises that a lawyer who consults the law firm's general counsel in an effort to conform her conduct to the

---

[16]Rule 5.2(b) (subordinate lawyer does not violate the ethics rules by acting in accordance with a supervisory lawyer's reasonable resolution of an arguable ethical issue).

[17]Davis, The Emergence of Law Firm General Counsel and the Challenges Ahead, 20 Prof. Lawyer, no. 14, at 1.

[18]*Thelen Reid & Priest LLP v. Marland*, 2007 WL 578989, *7 (N.D. Cal. 2007), "The court recognizes that law firms should and do seek advice about their legal and ethical obligations in connection with representing a client and that firms normally seek this advice from their own lawyers. Indeed, many firms have in-house ethics advisers for this purpose. A rule requiring disclosure of all communications relating to a client would dissuade attorneys from referring ethical problems to other lawyers, thereby undermining conformity with ethical obligations. Such a rule would also make conformity costly by forcing the firm to either retain outside counsel or terminate an existing attorney-client relationship to ensure confidentiality

of all communications relating to that client. This court declines to follow such a strict rule, preferring one that is consistent with a law firm in-house ethical infrastructure. Accordingly, Thelen is to produce some but not all communications in which a Thelen lawyer seeks or gives advice on the firm's ethical obligations to Marland." *Versuslaw, Inc. v. Stoel Rives, LLP*, 127 Wash. App. 309, 111 P.3d 866, 878 (Div. 1 2005) ("Lawyers in a law firm seeking legal advice from another lawyer in the same firm can assert the attorney-client privilege."), citing *U.S. v. Rowe*, 96 F.3d 1294 (9th Cir. 1996); *Hertzog, Calamari & Gleason v. Prudential Ins. Co. of America*, 850 F. Supp. 255 (S.D. N.Y. 1994); *In re Sunrise Securities Litigation*, 130 F.R.D. 560 (E.D. Pa. 1989).

[19]Rule 1.6(b)(4) (lawyer may seek advice of other lawyer about ethical duties without losing confidentially) and R. 5.1(a) (law firm should have measures in effect to assure that law firm complies with its ethical obligations).

[20]Rule 5.1, Comment 3.

ethics rules is not engaging in a conflict of interest with the client. Instead, she is engaging in an "inherent" part of her work.[21]

Lawyers are less likely to violate the ethics rules when they seek objective advice from other lawyers about their ethical duties—e.g., is there a conflict of interest with another client,[22] or is there a conflict with the lawyer's personal interest;[23] or is a client's prospective waiver of a conflict of interest still valid in light of changing factual circumstances; or, must the law firm withdraw from a particular case because of the client's misstatements during discovery.[24]

Instead of encouraging law firms to appoint a general counsel, some courts,[25] but not others,[26] have shown hostility by denying the attorney-client privilege to lawyers who consult their law

---

[21]In-House Consulting on Ethical Issues, ABA Formal Ethics Op. 08-453 (Oct. 17, 2008), quoting N.Y. State Bar Association Committee on Professional Ethics, Consultation with a Law Firm's In-House Counsel on Matters of Professional Ethics Involving One or More Clients of the Law Firm, Op. 789 (Oct. 26, 2005), 2005 WL 3046319, at *3 ("A lawyer's interest in carrying out the ethical obligations imposed by the Code is not an interest extraneous to the representation of the client. It is inherent in that representation and a required part of the work in carrying out the representation.").

[22]Rule 1.7.

[23]Rule 1.8(j).

[24]Rule 3.3(a)(3).

[25]In re Sunrise Securities Litigation, 130 F.R.D. 560, 597 (E.D. Pa. 1989) ("[A] law firm's communication with in-house counsel is not protected by the attorney client privilege if the communication implicates or creates a conflict between the law firm's fiduciary duties to itself and its duties to the client seeking to discover the communication."); Koen Book Distributors, Inc. v. Powell, Trachtman, Logan, Carrle, Bowman & Lombardo, P.C., 212 F.R.D. 283, 285 (E.D. Pa. 2002) ("[T]o the extent that the seeking or obtaining of legal advice by one lawyer from another lawyer inside the firm 'implicates or creates a conflict of interest,' the attorney-client privilege between the lawyers in the firm is viti-

ated.") (footnote omitted); Bank Brussells Lambert v. Credit Lyonnais (Suisse), 220 F. Supp. 2d 283, 288 (S.D. N.Y. 2002) ("law firm cannot invoke the attorney-client privilege against a current client when performing a conflict check in furtherance of representing that client"); Asset Funding Group, LLC v. Adams & Reese, LLP, No. 07-2965, 2008 U.S. Dist. 2008 WL 4948835, at *4 (E.D. La. Nov. 17, 2008); In re SonicBlue Inc., 2008 WL 170562, *9 (Bankr. N.D. Cal. 2008) (no privilege for the law firm because there was conflict of interest when the firm sought advice from another lawyer within the same firm).

[26]E.g., Board of Overseers of Bar v. Warren, 2011 ME 124, 34 A.3d 1103 (Me. 2011), which held that the crime-fraud exception to the attorney-client privilege that existed between a law firm and its former general counsel did not apply to defeat the privilege. The law firm asserted protected from disclosure to Bar Counsel of firm documents that Bar Counsel sought concerning the former general counsel's investigation of the law firm's former partner for misconduct. The law firm was not planning or engaged in any fraudulent activity at the time it enlisted its former general counsel's help in the investigation, and the law firm did not intend to facilitate or conceal any fraudulent or criminal conduct in the communications with former general counsel.

firm's in-house general counsel. The lawyer seeks legal advice from the general counsel on what to do in order to comply with the ethics rules. These cases argue that there should be no attorney-client privilege because the lawyer who consults with the law firm's in-house counsel is in a conflict of interest with the law firm's fiduciary duties to its client. That, says the courts, should cause the lawyer to lose the privilege. As one court argued:

> Permeating the documents is consideration of how best to position the firm in light of a possible malpractice action. They clearly establish that the law firm was in a conflict of interest relationship with its clients.[27]

Yet, in identical circumstances, these courts appear to be quite willing to protect the law firm's communications with its *outside* counsel.[28] That distinction makes little sense. If a lawyer really cannot confidentially consult with a lawyer in the same law firm about his or her ethical duties, then consulting with a lawyer in a different law firm is not any different.[29] It is just more expensive. If the lawyer seeks legal advice on what to do in order to comply with the ethics rules (including the ethical obligation of competence)[30] it should make no difference to treat one consultation as a breach of fiduciary duties and the other as proper. Instead of encouraging lawyers to seek ethics advice, these cases serve to discourage that alternative by prescribing a procedure that is more costly.

The principle that motivates these courts—the argument that there is an inherent conflict of interest when the lawyer seeks advice of the in-house general counsel—is false. Assume for example, that the in-house general counsel advises a lawyer in the firm that this lawyer has committed malpractice. The ethics rules envisage that the law firm should advise the firm's client of the possible malpractice.[31] It does not matter whether inside counsel or outside counsel has advised that there is malpractice.

---

[27]*Koen Book Distrib.*, 212 F.R.D. at 286. *In re Sunrise Securities*, 130 F.R.D.at 595. *See also Burns ex rel. Office of Public Guardian v. Hale and Dorr LLP*, 242 F.R.D. 170, 173 (D. Mass. 2007) ("The 'client' invoking the privilege is H & D itself, which is being represented by another lawyer of the firm. Because the firm owed a fiduciary duty to Alexis Burns as the trust beneficiary, there is no policy reason why the court should allow H & D should be allowed to withhold disclosure of information relevant to her claim. Because the privilege is inapplicable to this circumstance, the plaintiff's motion to compel will be allowed.").

[28]*In re Sunrise Securities*, 130 F.R.D. at 597 n.12. *See also Liberty Mut. Ins. Co. v. Tedford*, 2009 WL 2425841, *6 (N.D. Miss. 2009).

[29]Barker, Law Firm In-House Attorney-Client Privilege Vis-à-Vis Current Clients, 70 Def. Couns. J. 467, 471 (2003).

[30]Rule 1.1. It is no accident that competence is the first rule. The drafters believed that the first rule of ethics, the prime directive, is competence.

[31]Rule 1.4 & Comment 3 (duty to

The case law agrees that if the law firm discovers that it has committed malpractice, the lawyer should inform the law firm's client,[32] as part of its duty to keep the client well informed. The law firm's obligation does not depend on whether inside or outside counsel has delivered the bad news.[33]

Lawyers are always supposed to do what they can to protect themselves from a malpractice lawsuit; we call that acting competently. It is not a conflict of interests for the lawyer to seek advice from another lawyer about what she should do to act competently and ethically.[34] The law firm benefits both the client and itself when it creates procedures to assure that it acts competently and without conflicts. The ethics rules require that.[35] Because the factual landscape is always changing and lawyers must apply the law to these changing situations, lawyers must constantly determine if they have violated any ethical rules.

The ethical rules also place limits on how the lawyer can protect herself from malpractice: the lawyer may not ethically ask the client to sign a retainer agreement waving his right to

---

inform client of "significant developments affecting" the representation), and Comment 7 ("lawyer may not withhold information to serve the lawyer's own interest"). Rule 1.6(b)(4) & Comment 9. *See also* In-House Consulting on Ethical Issues, ABA Formal Ethics Op. 08-453 (Oct. 17, 2008) ("Duty to Inform the Client of an Ethics Consultation").

[32]For example of inside counsel delivering the bad news, *see Versuslaw, Inc. v. Stoel Rives, LLP*, 127 Wash. App. 309, 111 P.3d 866, 878 (Div. 1 2005). Lawyer Elvins was the Stoel Rives lawyer who represented VersusLaw in its arbitration with Matthew Bender. Lawyer Dean was Stoel Rives' in-house counsel (its loss prevention lawyer). Dean provided legal advice to Stoel Rives attorneys on ethical and legal issues. Dean advised Elvins about Stoel Rives' representation of VersusLaw in the arbitration and the two-year limitation for filing VersusLaw's claim for royalties under the License Agreement. When Elvins learned about a possible malpractice claim that its client could have against Elvins and the Stoel Rives law firm, Elvins informed Acton, the President and CEO of VersusLaw. *See also, In re SRC Holding Corp.*, 364

B.R. 1, 37-42 (D. Minn. 2007), rev'd, 553 F.3d 609 (8th Cir. 2009) (law firm has duty to inform its client about malpractice claim that client may have against it) (no general counsel).

[33]Restatement Third, The Law Governing Lawyers § 20, Comment c ("If the lawyer's conduct of the matter gives the client a substantial malpractice claim against the lawyer, the lawyer must disclose that to the client. For example, a lawyer who fails to file suit for a client within the limitations period must so inform the client, pointing out the possibility of a malpractice suit and the resulting conflict of interest that may require the lawyer to withdraw.").

[34]N.Y. State Bar Association Committee on Professional Ethics, Consultation with a Law Firm's In-House Counsel on Matters of Professional Ethics Involving One or More Clients of the Law Firm, Op. 789 (Oct. 26, 2005), 2005 WL 3046319, at *3.

[35]Rule 5.1(a), requiring the firm "shall make reasonable efforts to ensure that the firm has in effect measures giving reasonable assurance that all lawyers in the firm conform to the Rules of Professional Conduct."

sue for malpractice.[36] But that limitation is a far cry from a rule that denies the attorney-client privilege to lawyers merely because they seek legal advice on how best to comply with their ethical duties. The ethics rules and good law firm practices "create an obligation to establish protocols, appropriate for the size and practice of the firm, to enable the firm to enforce these standards internally. To envision such a system without access to confidential advice on legal and ethical issues affecting the firm's obligations is difficult."[37]

Thus, the ABA Model Rules specifically authorize the lawyer to seek confidential legal advice in order for the lawyer and law firm to comply with the ethics rules.[38] The ethics rules encourage lawyers to seek confidential advice from other lawyers in order to comply with their ethical duties of competence as well as their other ethical duties.[39] The Rules make no distinction between consulting a lawyer outside the law firm versus consulting a lawyer inside the law firm.[40]

If lawyers must hire outside counsel in order enjoy the protections of the attorney client privilege, it will be more expensive to seek advice, and that means fewer lawyers will seek the advice. In particular, younger lawyers, the junior associates, are a lot less likely to tell the partner that they need to seek outside legal advice to second-guess what another partner is doing. It is a lot easier for the junior associate simply to walk down the hall or take the elevator to another floor and talk in confidence to the in-house counsel, whose job is to be the independent legal ear and independent conscience. Instead of encouraging this consultation, many courts are discouraging it. They are creating a regime where the junior associate has to tell the partner, "I am not sure that what you are doing is right; I want the law firm to pay to hire an outside counsel to second-guess you."

The law should encourage lawyers to consult other lawyers on legal ethics issues for the same reason that the law encourages corporations to consult with their in-house counsel.[41] The attorney-client privilege encourages the client (in this case, the

---

[36]Rule 1.8(h)(1).

[37]N.Y. State Bar Association Committee on Professional Ethics, Consultation with a Law Firm's In-House Counsel on Matters of Professional Ethics Involving One or More Clients of the Law Firm, Op. 789 (Oct. 26, 2005), 2005 WL 3046319, at *2.

[38]Rule 1.6(b)(4) & Comment 9. *See also* In-House Consulting on Ethical Issues, ABA Formal Ethics Op. 08-453 (Oct. 17, 2008) ("The Model Rules con-

template the existence of some structure or process within a firm for resolution of questions about professional conduct . . . .").

[39]In fact, lawyers can make disclosures that would otherwise violate their duty of confidentiality in order to protect themselves from a charge of wrongful conduct. Rule 1.6(b)(5).

[40]Rule 1.6, Comment 9.

[41]Chambliss, The Scope of In-Firm Privilege, *supra* note 14. *See also,*

associate or partner with the ethics question) to speak candidly. It also encourages the general counsel of the firm to respond candidly. The privilege should encourage the in-house general counsel to conduct an internal investigation if that is appropriate, just as in-house corporate counsel conduct internal investigations when appropriate to keep the client out of trouble. The lawyer who becomes in-house counsel develops expertise on such issues as conflicts of interest, applicability of attorney-client privilege, and so on. Of course the law firm has a fiduciary duty to its client, but, as Professor Elizabeth Chambliss has pointed out, the law firm's in-house counsel has a duty to the law firm, and courts should encourage this development.[42]

The law firm's general counsel is more likely to be objective regarding a particularly lucrative client than the lawyer whose billings disproportionately depend on that particular client. A lawyer whose status and rank within the law firm depends on a major client is more likely to rationalize that what the client is doing is permissible. For example, the lawyer will strive mightily not to confront that client with a charge that the lawyer thinks the client has concealed a document that should be turned over in discovery. If the law firm confronts the client and loses the client, the law firm suffers a slight loss in business; if the billing partner confronts the client and loses the client, that partner may lose 20% or more of her entire billings.[43]

§ 5.1–2 LAWYERS' DUTY TO SUPERVISE OTHER LAWYERS

§ 5.1–2(a) Responsibility of Partners to Ensure that Lawyers in the Firm Comply with Ethics Rules.

The partners in a law firm have the duty to make reasonable efforts to assure that all of the lawyers in the firm comply with

---

e.g., *U.S. v. Buitrago-Dugand*, 712 F. Supp. 1045, 1048 (D.P.R. 1989) ("The attorney-client privilege exists to encourage people to seek legal advice freely and to speak candidly to the attorney without fear that the communication will be disclosed."); *U.S. v. Saccoccia*, 898 F. Supp. 53, 57 (D.R.I. 1995) ("The purpose of the attorney-client privilege is to encourage the client to make full disclosure of all pertinent facts to the attorney so that the attorney may render informed legal advice with respect to the matters about which the attorney is consulted.").

[42]Chambliss, The Scope of In-Firm Privilege, *supra* note 14, at 1723–24.

[43]Lawyers want to move up the law firm structure, from associates to partners, and from low-level partners to high-level partners. *See* Galanter & Palay, *supra* note 14. *See* Wilkins and Gulati, Reconceiving the Tournament of Lawyers: Tracking, Seeding, and Information Control in the Internal Labor Markets of Elite Law Firms, 84 Va. L. Rev. 1581 (1998). Ethics rules place some restrictions on lawyer mobility while market forces may encourage it. Sahl, Thinking about Leaving? The Ethics of Departing One Firm for Another, 18 Prof. Lawyer, no. 1, 2008, at 2.

the ethics rules.[1] This duty similarly applies to other lawyers with general supervisory powers, such as the head of a corporate law department, the head of a government agency, or the shareholders of a professional legal corporation.[2] The drafters of the 2002 Rules imposed the same obligation on "a lawyer who individually or together with other lawyers possesses comparable managerial authority in a law firm."[3] When this language is combined with the definition of a firm in Rule 1.0(c), this Rule now applies more clearly to managers in in-house corporate departments, government law offices, and legal services organizations.

The Rules do not provide a definition of "appropriate procedural safeguards." Rather, the Rules provide that the question whether the lawyers have instituted reasonable measures depends on all the facts and the measures may vary depending on the size of the firm.[4] On issues such as conflicts of interest, all law firms must have a conflicts checking system to properly comply with this Rule. Once a firm reaches a certain size, the firm will need to centralize intake of prospective clients. And, Rule 5.1(a) requires that large firms have ethics or conflicts committees and procedures in place to address the reporting and compliance with the Rules. The drafters of the 2002 Rules added new Comment 2 to emphasize the need for procedures to detect and resolve ethics issues.[5] The failure to have such measures in place constitutes a violation of this Rule.

[Section 5.1–2]

[1] Rule 5.1(a). *Cf.* DR 4-101(D); EC 4-5. Restatement of the Law Governing Lawyers, Third, § 11 (Official Draft 2000).

Douglas R. Richmond, *Law Firm Partners As Their Brothers' Keepers*, 96 KENTUCKY L.J. 231 (2008).

[2] Rule 5.1, Comment 1.

[3] Rule 5.1(a).

[4] Rule 5.1, Comment 2.

See, e.g., Dresser Industries, Inc. v. Digges, 1989 WL 139234 (D.Md. 1989), holding that even though a partner committed an intentional tort (fraudulently billing a client), a jury may hold his partners liable vicariously because there was no monitoring system in place to prevent this type of fraud.

See, e.g., In re Cohen, 847 A.2d 1162, 1166 (D.C.2004), holding that a partner's failure, in 12 person firm, to exercise proper supervisory responsibility over a dishonest associate under this supervision violated Rule 5.1 and justified his suspension for 30 days: "Respondent conceded before the Hearing Committee and the Board that there was no system in place to impart rudimentary ethics training to lawyers in the firm, particularly the less experienced ones. Equally troubling was the lack of a review mechanism which allowed an associate's work to be reviewed and guided by a supervisory attorney."

[5] Rule 5.1, Comment 2. The Comment identifies conflicts, statutes of limitations, filing deadlines, client trust fund compliance, and supervision of inexperienced lawyers as key aspects of focus to comply with Rule 5.1(a).

§ 5.1–2(b) Responsibility of Supervisory Lawyers to Ensure that Supervised Lawyers Comply with Ethics Rules.

Even if a lawyer is not a partner or other general manager, he or she may have direct supervisory authority over another lawyer.[6] For example, a senior associate may have some authority over a junior associate. Such a supervisor has the same responsibility as a partner or manager to assure compliance with the ethical rules by those lawyers under her direct supervisory authority.[7] Although the partner's or general manager's responsibilities relate to *all* lawyers in the firm, the supervisory lawyer's responsibilities relate only to those lawyers under her direct supervisory authority.[8]

The very nature of a lawyer designated as a supervisory lawyer involves the supervision and ultimate responsibility for the performance and quality of the work of the supervised lawyers. It makes sense to impose an obligation on these individuals to ensure that the other lawyers follow the Rules. Supervisory lawyers must be available to answer questions from other lawyers and if they notice that a supervised lawyer's conduct or work raises a question as to whether an ethical problem exists, the supervisory lawyer must address the situation promptly.[9]

The firm may be able to accommodate the impaired lawyer. For example, if a mental impairment prevents the lawyer from working in areas with deadline pressures, the lawyer may shift to legal areas that are less pressured.

The Impaired Lawyer. Sometimes a lawyer is impaired and cannot function as she should. The problem may be mental, or physical. There may be a drug or alcohol addiction. "When a supervising lawyer knows that a supervised lawyer is impaired, close scrutiny is warranted because of the risk that the impairment will result in violations."[10] The supervisory lawyer must engage in action to reasonably assure that the impairment will not cause a violation of the ethics rules. If the impaired lawyer causes a violation of the Rules, the supervisory lawyer may have an obligation to report the lawyer pursuant to Rule 8.3. "If the

---

[6] Rule 5.1(b).

[7] Rule 5.1(b).

[8] Rule 5.1(b).

[9] A Maryland court suspended two name partners (not licensed to practice in Maryland) who had opened a law office in Maryland and hired an associate to operate most facets of the office. The name partners were disciplined for failing to properly supervise, train, and offer support to the associate who had full responsibility to handle all of the cases in the Maryland office. See *Attorney Grievance Com'n of Maryland v. Kimmel*, 405 Md. 647, 955 A.2d 269 (2008).

[10] ABA Ethics Opinion 03-429, Obligations With Respect To Mentally Impaired Lawyer In The Firm (June 11, 2003).

firm removes the impaired lawyer in a matter, it may have an obligation to discuss with the client the circumstances surrounding the change of responsibility." If the impaired lawyer leaves the firm, the ABA has advised that the firm "may have disclosure obligations to clients who are considering whether to continue to use the firm or shift their relationship to the departed lawyer, but [it] must be careful to limit any statements made to ones for which there is a factual foundation. The obligation to report a violation of the Model Rules by an impaired lawyer is not eliminated by departure of the impaired lawyer."[11]

On the other hand, a Philadelphia ethics opinion does not advise informing the clients of the departing lawyer. The ethics committee considered the situation of a two-person firm that was dissolving. One lawyer ("W") had a permanent reading disability and some memory impairment as a result of several strokes. That lawyer intended to solicit the present clients of the firm and not disclose to these clients his disability. "In view of the Committee, there does not, however, appear to be an obligation under the Rules to inform the clients to be solicited of W's disability and his consequent inability to personally handle their matters." The Committee was concerned that the impaired lawyer could sue another lawyer if that lawyer disclosed W's impairment to the clients. The Committee recognized that, under Rule 5.1(c)(2), the lawyer "may have some responsibility for violation by W of the Rules," but the lawyer could fulfill that responsibility "urging that W desist from misrepresenting his ability to serve the firm's clients, and informing the Disciplinary Board if W fails to comply with inquirer's request."[12]

The ABA advises that, if the impaired lawyer's partners or supervising lawyers take steps to assure that the impaired lawyer is not representing clients while materially impaired, "there is no obligation to report the affected lawyer's *past failure* to withdraw from representing clients." However, if the "affected lawyer's firm is not responsive to the concerns brought to their attention, the lawyer must make a report under Rule 8.3." The reporting lawyer has "no affirmative obligation to speak with either the affected lawyer or her firm about her conduct or condition before reporting to the appropriate authority."[13] In 2008, the ABA House of Delegates approved a controversial rule on conditional admission to practice law that is designed to be used when an individual

---

[11]ABA Ethics Opinion 03-429, Obligations With Respect To Mentally Impaired Lawyer In The Firm (June 11, 2003). *See* George Edward Bailly, *Impairment, The Profession and Your Law Partner*, 11 PROFESSIONAL LAWYER 2 (No. 1, 1999).

[12]Philadelphia Bar Association Professional Guidance Committee Ethics Opinion 2000-12 (Dec. 2000), 2000 WL 33173008, *1.

[13]ABA Ethics Opinion 03-431, Lawyer's Duty To Report Rule Violations By Another Lawyer Who May

has a history of substance abuse, mental illness, or emotional problems.[14]

Partners and supervising lawyers have a responsibility to ensure that lawyers in their own firms comply with the rules of professional conduct, but "no lawyer is obligated under the Model Rules to take any action to ensure compliance with the rules by lawyers in other firms."[15]

§ 5.1–2(c) Responsibility of Lawyers Who Order or Ratify Another Lawyer's Conduct.

As a general principle, a lawyer may not knowingly assist another to violate the ethics rules or to violate those rules through the acts of another.[16] Consequently, a lawyer is responsible for another lawyer's ethics violation if the first lawyer orders the second to engage in misconduct, or knowingly ratifies the second lawyer's misconduct.[17]

A lawyer who orders another lawyer to engage in conduct that violates a provision of the Model Rules or other law necessarily has committed a violation of that Rule. The notion of ratification is slightly more difficult. Rule 5.1(c)(1) states that a lawyer is responsible for the violation if the lawyer "with knowledge of the specific conduct, ratifies the conduct." The knowledge requirement would arise when the second lawyer informs the first lawyer about the conduct he or she intends to take and the conduct is a clear violation of the Rules and the first lawyer does nothing to modify the conduct of the second lawyer. The first lawyer could also ratify the conduct by informing the second lawyer, "Do as

---

Suffer From Disability Or Impairment (Aug. 8, 2003). This Opinion, in general, dealt with reporting obligation of a the obligation of a lawyer who acquires knowledge that another lawyer, *not in his firm*, suffers from a mental condition that materially impairs that lawyer's ability to represent a client. However, it also elaborated on the responsibilities of lawyers who supervise other lawyers in the same firm.

[14]*See* ABA Model Rule on Conditional Admission to Practice Law (Feb. 11, 2008).

[15]ABA Ethics Opinion 03-431, Lawyer's Duty To Report Rule Violations By Another Lawyer Who May Suffer From Disability Or Impairment (Aug. 8, 2003), at n. 14.

[16]Rule 8.4(a); DR 1-102(A)(2).

[17]Rule 5.1(c)(1). Easterbrook, J.,

citing this Treatise, in *Decatur Ventures, LLC v. Daniels*, 485 F.3d 387, 392 (7th Cir. 2007).

Lawyers do not have *vicarious* liability for the ethical violations of other lawyers. They do have liability for their ethical failure to supervise or their failure to mitigate the subordinate's ethical violations. *E.g., In re Anonymous Member of South Carolina Bar*, 346 S.C. 177, 184, 552 S.E.2d 10, 13 (2001) (per curiam): Rule 5.1(c) "imposes ethical duties on subordinate and supervisory lawyers. Rule 5.1(c)'s liability is not vicarious liability because the obligation does not arise merely from the relationship between the attorneys. The supervising attorney's ethical violation will be based on his participation in the underlying misconduct or his failure to mitigate it."

you wish" or "Go ahead with the course you have proposed." These responses stop short of ordering the second lawyer on how to act but clearly bring the first lawyer into the definition of ratification of the second lawyer's conduct. The notion of ratification seems to imply that the first lawyer had knowledge of the second lawyer's proposed course of conduct (which is a violation of the Rules) and did nothing to stop it from taking place.

§ 5.1–2(d) Responsibility of Partners and Supervisory Lawyers Who Fail to Take Reasonable Remedial Action to Avoid or Mitigate the Consequences of a Violation.

Partners, supervisory lawyers, and managers are also responsible for the other lawyer's ethical misconduct if the partner or supervisory lawyer fails to take reasonable remedial action to avoid or mitigate the misconduct.[18] For example, "if a supervisory lawyer knows that a subordinate misrepresented a matter to an opposing party in negotiation, the supervisor as well as the subordinate has a duty to correct the resulting misapprehension."[19] The obligation of lawyers to take corrective action to remedy another lawyer's violation of the rules is based the duties that partners, supervisory lawyers, and firm managers owe to their clients and the legal profession. If those lawyers can avoid or mitigate the consequences of a past rule violation, Rule 5.1(c)(2) imposes on them the obligation to act.

In some cases, the obligation to act is clear. For example, the lawyer discovers the violation of Rule 3.3 (candor to the court) or discovery rules in a case that is still pending before the court. In other cases, the possibility of avoiding or mitigating the consequences of the Rule violation appears to be present even if the attorney-client relationship has ended. For example, if a managing partner discovers that a business lawyer in the firm had overbilled clients routinely, the managing partner should conduct an audit of the billing records of the business lawyer. If the audit produces conclusive evidence of overbilling of a former client, this Rule would apply. After all, returning the overbilled monies would avoid or mitigate the Rule 1.5(a) violation. As more partners in the firm learn of the business lawyer's Rule violation, each of the partners then becomes responsible for taking reasonable remedial action or else they violate Rule 5.1(c)(2) for failing to act.

§ 5.1–3 LAW FIRM DISCIPLINE

The ethics codes have always directed their mandates and guidelines towards persons and not entities. States license individual lawyers and not law firms as possessing the right to

---

[18]Rule 5.1(c)(2). *Cf.* DR 1–103(A).   [19]Rule 5.1, Comment 5.

practice law, thus rules and discipline systems are directed to regulating the license holder. Also, the ethics codes were developed when a significant number of lawyers practiced in solo or small firm arrangements. Thus, the Model Code and the Model Rules have not made a "law firm," as an entity, subject to legal discipline.

In 1991, Professor Ted Schneyer called for the expansion of discipline to cover law firms.[1] He argued that,

> First, even when a firm has clearly committed wrongdoing, courts may have difficulty, as an evidentiary matter, in assigning blame to particular lawyers, each of who has an incentive to shift responsibility for an ethical breach onto others in the firm. . . . Second, even when courts and disciplinary agencies can link professional misconduct to one or more lawyers in a firm as an evidentiary matter, they may be reluctant to sanction those lawyers for fear of making them scapegoats for others in the firm who would have taken the same actions in order to further the firm's interests . . . . Third and most important, a law firm's organization, policies, and operating procedures constitute an "ethical infrastructure" that cuts across particular lawyers and tasks. Large law firms are typically complex organizations. Consequently, their infrastructures may have at least as much to do with causing and avoiding unjustified harm as do the individual values and practice skills of their lawyers.[2]

His reasoning makes a strong case that the implementation of firm discipline could have some positive incentive effects as well as providing disciplinary authorities with needed power to assess penalties against the proper actors.

The drafters of the 2002 Model Rules considered extending the obligation to comply with the Rules to law firms and also to permit disciplinary actions against law firms as well as individual lawyers. The opponents argued that the benefits of this proposal were relatively small and the costs could be very high because firm responsibility may de-emphasize individual responsibility of licensed professionals.[3] Therefore, the drafters of the 2002 Rules rejected any amendments along these lines.

New York[4] and New Jersey[5] became the first jurisdictions to make a "law firm" subject to discipline. When a law firm does not

---

[Section 5.1–3]

[1] *See* Ted Schneyer, *Professional Discipline for Law Firms?*, 77 CORNELL L. REV. 1 (1991). Contrast, Julie Rose O'Sullivan, *Professional Discipline For Law Firms? A Response To Professor Schneyer's Proposal*, 16 GEORGETOWN J. OF LEGAL ETHICS 1 (2002).

[2] 77 Cornell at 8–10 (footnotes omitted).

[3] Margaret Colgate Love, *The Revised ABA Model Rules of Professional Conduct: Summary of the Work of Ethics 2000*, 15 GEORGETOWN J. OF LEGAL ETHICS 441, 470–71 (2002).

[4] **New York.** New York DR 1-104(a), (c), 22 N.Y. Code, Rules & Regulations, Part 1200.5(a), (c):

"(a) A law firm shall make reasonable efforts to ensure that all law-

implement a reasonable system for checking out potential conflicts, or when the firm does not offer adequate training of its paralegals, or when the firm does not supervise its associates, it will be easier for the disciplinary authorities to seek to have "the law firm" sanctioned than to spend the resources to find out which particular lawyers should be the ones who should be charged with a careless conflicts check, or which lawyers did not supervise which associates. Consequently, given the policy considerations that favor law firm discipline, one should not be surprised if the actions of New York and New Jersey portend a trend in the law.

Law firms are also subject to the regulation of several federal bodies such as the Securities and Exchange Commission and the Treasury Department. The SEC may suspend a firm from practicing before the SEC or may require that the firm notify all of its securities clients about a violation of SEC Rules.[6] The Office of Thrift Supervision used its power to freeze the assets of a law firm.[7] Many of the federal statutes provide for criminal as well as civil liability for law firms as well as individual lawyers for violations. Thus, law firms as entities do have some exposure to direct sanctions.

Whether or not the ethics rules recognize the law firm as responsible for the actions of its lawyers, the law of tort and agency independently may impose *respondeat superior* civil liability.

---

yers in the firm conform to the disciplinary rules. . . . (c) A law firm shall adequately supervise, as appropriate, the work of partners, associates and nonlawyers who work at the firm. . . ."

[5]**New Jersey.** After New York's actions, New Jersey changed its Rules to allow for a law firm to be subject to discipline. New Jersey Rule of Professional Conduct 5.1(a) states:

"(a) *Every law firm* and organization authorized by the Court Rules to practice law in this jurisdiction shall make reasonable efforts to ensure that member lawyers or lawyers otherwise participating in the organization's work undertake measures giving reasonable assurance that all lawyers conform to the Rules of Professional Conduct." (emphasis added).

In 1998 [effective Sept. 1, 1998]

the New Jersey Supreme Court amended the rule on disciplinary jurisdiction to include every "business entity authorized to practice law" to "be subject to the disciplinary jurisdiction of the Supreme Court. . . ."West's New Jersey Rules of Court, Part I, Rules of General Application Chapter II, Conduct of Lawyers, Judges and Court Personnel Rule 1:20, Discipline of Members of the Bar.

[6]*See Securities and Exchange Commission v. National Student Marketing Corp.*, 457 F.Supp. 682 (D. D.C.1978)(SEC enforcement against corporation and two of its law firms as entities).

[7]*See* James O. Johnstone, Jr. & Daniel Scott Schecter, *Introduction: Kaye Scholer and the OTS—Did Anyone Go Too Far?*, 66 S.CAL.L.REV. 977 (1993).

§ 5.1–4 COMPARING TORT AND ETHICS LIABILITY

One should keep in mind the distinction between Rule 5.1 and tort liability, as well as the distinction, within Rule 5.1, between the failure to supervise and the ordering or ratifying of unethical conduct.

For example, assume that Lawyer A is the supervisor of Lawyer B. Neither the firm nor Lawyer A exercises any care to assure that Lawyer B will protect client confidences. Even though there is no supervision, it turns out that Lawyer B in fact does not violate any confidences. Nonetheless, Lawyer A still has violated Rule 5.1(b) [because of Lawyer A's failure to supervise], but not Rule 5.1(c) [which governs a supervising lawyer's liability for ratifying or failure to take reasonable remedial action]. A client would not have a cause of action in tort against Lawyer A for failure to supervise because there are no damages.

Now, let us change the facts. Assume, in the above example, that Lawyer A does exercise reasonable supervisory care over Lawyer B, but Lawyer B nonetheless violates a client's confidences, causing the client monetary damage. Lawyer A has not violated Rule 5.1(b) [there has been adequate supervision] nor 5.1(c) [the supervising lawyer does not ratify the action and does not know about it in time to avoid or mitigate it]. But the supervisory lawyer is still liable in tort under a theory of vicarious liability.

Now, assume, in the prior example, that Lawyer A discovers Lawyer B's breach of confidence in time to prevent it, but Lawyer A acts unreasonably and fails to take any remedial action. Lawyer A has not violated Rule 5.1(b) but has violated Rule 5.1(c)(2), and is also liable in tort, under a theory of vicarious liability.

CHAPTER 5.2
RESPONSIBILITIES OF A SUBORDINATE LAWYER

RULE 5.2: RESPONSIBILITIES OF A SUBORDINATE LAWYER

(a) A lawyer is bound by the Rules of Professional Conduct notwithstanding that the lawyer acted at the direction of another person.

(b) A subordinate lawyer does not violate the Rules of Professional Conduct if that lawyer acts in accordance with a supervisory lawyer's reasonable resolution of an arguable question of professional duty.

Comment

[1] Although a lawyer is not relieved of responsibility for a violation by the fact that the lawyer acted at the direction of a supervisor, that fact may be relevant in determining whether a lawyer had the knowledge required to render conduct a violation of the Rules. For example, if a subordinate filed a frivolous pleading at the direction of a supervisor, the subordinate would not be guilty of a professional violation unless the subordinate knew of the document's frivolous character.

[2] When lawyers in a supervisor-subordinate relationship encounter a matter involving professional judgment as to ethical duty, the supervisor may assume responsibility for making the judgment. Otherwise a consistent course of action or position could not be taken. If the question can reasonably be answered only one way, the duty of both lawyers is clear and they are equally responsible for fulfilling it. However, if the question is reasonably arguable, someone has to decide upon the course of action. That authority ordinarily reposes in the supervisor, and a subordinate may be guided accordingly. For example, if a question arises whether the interests of two clients conflict under Rule 1.7, the supervisor's reasonable resolution of the question should protect the subordinate professionally if the resolution is subsequently challenged.

Authors' 1983 Model Rules Comparison
The 2002 version is identical to the Rule adopted by the House of Delegates in 1983.

Model Code Comparison

There was no counterpart to this Rule in the Model Code.

§ 5.2–1 THE RESPONSIBILITY OF A LAWYER WHO IS SUBJECT TO SUPERVISION BY ANOTHER LAWYER

All lawyers, whether they are supervisory lawyers or subordinates, are obligated to follow the Model Rules of professional responsibility. However, subordinate lawyers may claim that because all of their work is subject to the direction and supervision of a supervisory lawyer or partner, they should somehow have less responsibility. And, associates have the additional claim that they are at will employees without an ownership stake in the firm and thus they have limited control.[1] Both the Model Rules and Restatement address this argument.

A lawyer cannot escape responsibility for ethical misconduct merely by claiming that she followed orders.[2] There is no "good

---

[Section 5.2–1]

[1] *See generally* Douglas R. Richmond, *Professional Responsibilities of Law Firm Associates*, 45 BRANDEIS L.J. 199 (2007)(providing a comprehensive examination of ethical issues faced by law firm associates, including Model Rule 5.2).

[2] Rule 5.2(a). *See also* Restatement of the Law Governing Lawyers, Third, § 12(1), (2) (Official Draft 2000); *In re Knight*, 129 Vt. 428, 430, 281 A.2d 46, 48 (1971) (per curiam).

Leonard Gross, *Ethical Problems of Law Firm Associates*, 26 WM. & MARY L. REV. 259 (1985), criticizing Rule 5.1(b) on several grounds:

"First, the Rule makes it much easier for an associate to follow the questionable instructions of a partner. Failure to follow the instructions would violate the associate's duty of obedience to the partner. Therefore, absent some defense to the violation of the duty of obedience, the partner would be justified if he dismissed the associate. Unless the rules of professional responsibility impose disciplinary sanctions for failure to report the questionable conduct of the partner, in some states the associate's ability to report such conduct and still maintain a civil action for abusive or wrongful discharge is reduced. Model Rule 5.2(b) leaves the conscientious associate in a real quandary. Furthermore, because an associate might be less likely to report questionable ethical practices, Model Rule 5.2(b) might have the effect of further lowering the public's unfavorable opinion of the legal profession. The Rule might also have a detrimental impact on attorneys' self-perception. Finally, Model Rule 5.2(b) fails to account for those particular situations in which an associate is as well equipped as a partner to make ethical decisions. In such cases, deference by the associate to the questionable ethical decisions of a partner is unwarranted." *Id.* at 299–300 (footnotes omitted).

Carol Rice, *The Superior Orders Defense in Legal Ethics: Sending the Wrong Message To Young Lawyers*, 32 WAKE FOREST L. REV. 887 (1997), criticizing Rule 5.2(b): "Because the senior lawyer takes the responsibility for any misjudgment, the junior lawyer has little incentive to even consider tough ethical issues, let alone raise them." *Id.* at 889.

soldier" defense in the law governing lawyers if there is no arguable question of professional responsibility needing resolution.[3]

On the other hand, if the ethical violation is not clear, the subordinate lawyer may defer to the judgment of the supervisory attorney. The subordinate does not violate her ethical duties if she follows the supervisor's "reasonable resolution of an arguable question of professional duty."[4] One cannot escape one's ethical duties by merely claiming that one is only following orders, but one can escape by following reasonable orders.[5]

The terms, "arguable question of professional responsibility" and "reasonable resolution" are subject to debate and interpretation. Clearly, an associate could not escape responsibility for participating in the litigation team's destruction of litigation documents subject to discovery.[6] Also, an associate who follows the orders of a partner to perform work that violates an explicit provision of the Rules is responsible for the violation.[7] The purpose underlying the Rule is to encourage associates to bring to the attention of the supervisory lawyers and partners questions of professional responsibility. After all, those individuals are responsible for ensuring that the firm complies with ethics rules and they ultimately profit from the legal work the firm performs.

In general, Rule 5.2(b) may provide false comfort to a junior lawyer. In practice, many of the cases may give lip service to this rule but do not embrace it with enthusiasm, and instead conclude

---

[3]*In re Ockrassa*, 165 Ariz. 576, 799 P.2d 1350 (Ariz.1990), holding that it is no defense for a prosecutor if his superiors allowed him to prosecute the same person whom he has earlier defended in a substantially related matter because the ethics rule prohibiting this conflict is quite clear. *In the Matter of Howes*, 123 N.M. 311, 316, 940 P.2d 159, 164 (1997) (per curiam), holding that a prosecutor cannot avoid discipline by relying on the view of his superior because there was no reasonable grounds to believe that the anti-contact principle of Rule 4.2 was inapplicable.

[4]Rule 5.2(b).

[5]*Cf.* ABA Formal Opinion 347 (Dec. 1, 1981), and ABA Formal Opinion 96-399 (Jan. 18, 1996), exten-sively discussing the ethical obligations of lawyers working for the Legal Service Corporation when funding is reduced and the remaining funding subjects the lawyer's representation to restrictive conditions. Carol Rice, *The Superior Orders Defense in Legal Ethics: Sending the Wrong Message to Young Lawyers*, 32 WAKE FOREST L. REV. 887 (1997) argued that there should be no defense of superior orders.

[6]Lawrence J. Fox, *Save Us From Ourselves*, 50 RUTGERS L. REV. 2189, 2192 (1998).

[7]*See, e.g.,* Rule 1.8(c) (preparing an instrument for a client that gives a lawyer in the firm a substantial gift when the lawyer is not related to the client).

that it was not reasonable for the junior lawyer to follow orders because the junior lawyer should look up the law.[8]

Inquiring Into the Decision-Making Process of the Supervisory or Subordinate Lawyer.

Rule 5.2 does not address the issue whether a supervised lawyer has an obligation to inquire into the decisionmaking process that the partners use to resolve the ethics dilemma and whether the partner has an obligation to provide such information to the supervised lawyer. In other words, if the supervised lawyer informs a partner about an ethics problem and the partner says, we will take care of it, should the associate demand more information from the firm to comply with Rule 5.2? Does the firm have any obligation to provide such information to the associate?

In Texas Ethics Opinion 523, an associate discovered that the law firm had committed negligence against a client in the past. The associate informed the shareholders in the firm and resigned, but demanded that the partners inform the client and take rea-

---

[8]*See, e.g., In re Knight*, 129 Vt. 428, 430, 281 A.2d 46, 48 (1971) (per curiam), acknowledged that the respondent, an "inexperienced attorney," was afraid of losing his job and was under the "domination" of an experienced practitioner who was later convicted of extortion and disbarred. The court said: "It is true in the instant case that the respondent was a relatively inexperienced attorney and was under the domination of an older and experienced practitioner, possessed of a forceful personality which brooked no interference with his wishes." 129 Vt. 428, 430, 281 A.2d 46, 48. Nonetheless, the inexperienced lawyer could not "assign to another his duty to his oath." The court suspended the inexperienced lawyer for three months.

In the Matter of Rivers, 285 S.C. 492, 331 S.E.2d 332 (1984), holding that inexperienced attorneys are held to same standards as their more experienced colleagues because it is the duty of attorneys to discover and comply with the rules of practice and professional responsibility governing the profession. In this case, the court ruled that when a lawyer causes a private investigator to communicate, before the trial of a case, with persons known to be members of jury venire and their relatives, and the lawyer failed to reveal such conduct to the court or the Board of Commissioners on Grievances and Discipline, that conduct warranted public reprimand (in light of mitigating factors).

Kelley's Case, 137 N.H. 314, 627 A.2d 597 (1993), concluding that the ethics rule that states that a subordinate lawyer does not violate the Rules of Professional Conduct if the subordinate lawyer acts in accordance with supervisory lawyer's reasonable resolution of arguable question of professional duty, does not constitute a defense to the charge of violating the conflict of interest rule where the conflict would be so clearly fundamental to a disinterested attorney that undertaking joint representation of clients is per se unreasonable. In this case, the court held that public censure was the appropriate sanction for lawyers who represented two clients with substantially different interests in the estate, even though these lawyers maintained that they reasonably believed no actual conflict of interest would develop, that both clients were aware of the potential conflict, and that both clients signed written waivers of conflict.

sonable remedial action. More specifically, the associate demanded that the shareholders provide proof of remedial action to him and, if they did not, he said he would be obligated to report this information to the disciplinary authorities. The shareholders told the associate that remedial action had been taken, but that they would not provide specific information to the associate because it would violate the duty of confidentiality. They also forbade the former associate from communicating with the client. The former associate asked for an advisory opinion from the state ethics opinion committee. The Committee answered:

> [I]t was also *prudent and proper* for the former associate to insist that the shareholders in the law firm assure him in writing that the affected client was told about the negligent legal services so that the remedial action could be taken. Otherwise the former associate attorney would not have an adequate basis for concluding that he had complied with his obligations under the disciplinary rules. If the shareholders refuse, within a reasonable time, to provide to the former associate written assurances that the client in fact has been told of the negligence, then the associate *would be obligated* to inform the client about the specific negligent legal services.[9]

Many law partners might not welcome the advice provided in this ethics opinion. While the Rules clearly impose ethical obligations on all lawyers, including associates, the partners do not envision themselves as reporting to the associates, or former associates. This Opinion may assume a factual situation where it was reasonable for the lawyer to ask for a written assurance (even though lawyers are supposed to regard their word as their bond) because the lawyer had independent reasons not to trust his former supervisors.

Even then, it is difficult to *require* the subordinate, as an ethical obligation, to become what he may see as an officious intermeddler and seek out the client of the firm, particularly in the context of this Opinion, which tells us that the negligent act occurred "prior to the associate's employment." That means that the former associate must find this client, who was never the associate's client, introduce himself, and disclose his version of events.

Notice that the first part of this Opinion merely says that the lawyer may ask for written assurances. Then, the lawyer can protect himself if someone later claims that he never informed the powers-that-be about the problem that needs corrective action. The second part of this Opinion, however, jumps from an ethical aspiration to a command: unless the partners or share-

---

[9]Texas Professional Ethics Committee, Opinion 523 (Oct. 1997) (emphasis added).

holders provide "written assurances," the associate (or former associate) *must* inform the client of the law firm. What if the lawyers did inform the client and thought that the associate was too overbearing so that it would not provide written assurances? The Opinion notes, "The shareholders told the associate that remedial action had been taken, but that they would not provide specific information to the associate because it would violate the duty of confidentiality." What if that information had been a writing, or an email (a digital form of writing), or a voice mail? Would that be enough to satisfy the former associate? The Opinion does not say, but it does conclude that the former associate is *not obligated* to report the partners' alleged negligent conduct to the disciplinary authorities because the negligence did not rise to the level of a Rule 8.3(a) violation.

Partners do not normally think that they have to justify their conduct to the associates, whom Rule 5.2 calls the "subordinate" lawyers because they are the underlings.

Compare this opinion with *McCurdy v. Kansas Dept. of Transportation*.[10] A civil service lawyer working for the state Department of Transportation objected to a five-day suspension that she received for declining a work assignment from her supervisor. The court overturned the suspension. She argued that she could not accept a case from her public-agency employer because of a conflict of interest. She discovered that the lawyer representing the landowner in the matter was a lawyer in the same firm she had consulted previously about a personal legal matter. She told her supervisor that she could not investigate the landowner's claim because she had an attorney-client relationship, which preceded the assignment, with the same law firm that was representing the landowner. She refused to supply her supervisor with more information about her legal problem.

The court said that she (the subordinate lawyer) did not have to respond to the supervisory lawyer's request for information. She concluded: "McCurdy did not have to reveal the exact nature of her conflict to properly decline the work assignment, nor did she have to transfer to [her supervisor] the responsibility for determining if she had a conflict of interest."[11]

§ 5.2–2 WRONGFUL DISCHARGE

In recent years, when attorneys have been fired by their clients or their law firms, allegedly for their refusal to engage in unethical activity, they have brought wrongful discharge suits. These lawyers sue even though they are employees at will. Typically,

---

[10]*McCurdy v. Kansas Dept. of Transportation*, 21 Kan.App.2d 262, 898 P.2d 650 (Kan.App. 1995).

[11]21 Kan.App.2d 262, 265, 898 P.2d 650, 653 (Kan.App.1995).

the plaintiff-lawyer asserts that he or she was discharged for not following the direction of a supervisory lawyer when that direction violated the ethics rules.[1] Consequently, the discharged lawyers complain that the termination was wrongful.

The courts have split on this issue, but the trend favors this cause of action.[2] The fact that a client or a law firm has the right to fire an attorney for no reason does not imply a right to fire for

---

[Section 5.2–2]

[1] Rule 5.2(a).

[2] **New York.** A leading case is *Wieder v. Skala*, 80 N.Y.2d 628, 593 N.Y.S.2d 752, 609 N.E.2d 105 (1992) (lawyer who alleged that he was discharged from law firm because he insisted that his firm comply with its ethical obligation to report a fellow associate to the state bar disciplinary authorities has a cause of action for breach of contract; the duty to comply with the state bar's ethical rules is an implied-in-law condition of the employment contract).

In *Wieder* the law firm fired the lawyer, and the lawyer sued the firm for wrongful discharge. In other cases, the client sued the lawyer, and the courts have upheld a cause of action when the lawyer sued the client for wrongful discharge. *See, e.g., General Dynamics v. Superior Court*, 7 Cal.4th 1164, 32 Cal.Rptr.2d 1, 876 P.2d 487 (Cal.1994), upholding the cause of action for wrongful discharge by in-house counsel who claimed that mandatory ethical norms in the California Rules of Professional Conduct conflicted with illegitimate demands of the employer.

California. *General Dynamics Corp. v. Superior Court of San Bernardino County*, 7 Cal.4th 1164, 32 Cal.Rptr.2d 1, 876 P.2d 487 (1994) held that an in-house attorney is not precluded from pursuing an action in tort for retaliatory termination. More than with outside counsel, corporate in-house counsel may be faced with a moral dilemma between ethical norms and the client's interest, because in-house counsel is dependent on one employer to provide his or her livelihood and career success. Therefore, an in-house attorney faced with a choice between the demands of an employer and the requirements of an ethical code "has an even greater claim to judicial protection than a nonattorney employee."

If the conduct in which the attorney has engaged is merely ethically permissible, but not required by statute or ethical code, then *General Dynamics* said that court must answer yes to two questions in order to allow the cause of action: first, is the employer's conduct of the kind that would give rise to a retaliatory discharge action by a non attorney employee; second, does some statute or ethical rule, such as the statutory exceptions to the attorney-client privilege, specifically permits the attorney to depart from the usual requirement of confidentiality with respect to the client-employer and engage in the "nonfiduciary" conduct for which he was terminated.

On the other hand, if the in-house counsel is asked to commit a crime, or to engage in an act that would subject him to disbarment and is discharged for refusing to engage in such an act, and counsel would have been discharged for adhering to a mandatory ethical obligation then, said *General Dynamics*, "under most circumstances," this lawyer will have a retaliatory discharge cause of action against the employer because the governing professional rules or statutes "expressly remove" the requirement of attorney confidentiality.

Oregon. Oregon State Bar Ethics Committee Opinion 1994-136 (1994) concluded that a lawyer who was allegedly terminated for failure to file a patent claim for his employer on an invention made by the employer's customer may reveal his employer's

the wrong reason. Of course, because clients can always fire their counsel at any time, with or without cause,[3] it may be that, absent special circumstances, one should expect that the typical remedy for wrongful discharge would not be reinstatement of the lawyer but damages paid to the lawyer.[4]

---

secrets insofar as necessary to establish his wrongful discharge claim.

Illinois. A rare case rejecting the *Wieder* approach is, *Balla v. Gambro, Inc.*, 145 Ill.2d 492, 164 Ill.Dec. 892, 584 N.E.2d 104 (1991). A corporation's in-house counsel alleged that he had been fired because he had reported the client to the FDA regarding faulty kidney dialysis machines, as he was legally obligated to do. The Illinois Supreme Court agreed that the lawyer was ethically required to report the employer's wrongdoing, but, it argued, to say the employer cannot fire him for doing so would impose the cost of ethical compliance on the client instead of the lawyer. Further, once the lawyer did report on the client, as the law required him to do, the client would no longer trust the lawyer. Therefore the court concluded that there should be no tort of retaliatory discharge for lawyers.

Illinois has refused to allow lawyers to sue for retaliatory discharge. *See, e.g., Jacobson v. Knepper & Moga P.C.*, 185 Ill.2d 372, 235 Ill.Dec. 936, 706 N.E.2d 491, 78 Fair Employment Practice Cases (BNA) 1160, 137 Lab. Cases ¶ 58,562 (1998) (plaintiff, an associate in the law firm, alleged that he was fired after he had complained several times to his supervising partner that the firm was continuously filing debt-collection suits in the Cook County court system even though the defendants did not live in that jurisdiction). The Illinois Supreme Court overturned two lower courts to reach this result. *See* Darryl Van Duch, *OK to Fire Whistleblower Lawyer*, National Law Journal, Jan. 18, 1999, at A6.

See, e.g., Leonard Gross, *Ethical Problems of Law Firm Associates*, 26 William & Mary L.Rev. 259 (1985);

Stephen Gillers, *Protecting Lawyers Who Just Say No*, 5 Georgia St. U. L. Rev. 1 (1988); Michael Franck, *MRPC 5.1: Responsibilities of Partners and Other Supervisory Lawyers*, 67 Michigan Bar J. 1086 (1988).

Kentucky. *Gadlage v. Winters & Yonker, Attorneys at Law, P.S.C.*, 2011 WL 6888538 (W.D. Ky. 2011). An at-will law associate sued his former law firm for wrongful discharge and retaliation: the termination allegedly was for the lawyer' refusal to violate ethics rules that the state supreme court promulgated. This federal court concluded that Kentucky would offer a remedy for wrongful discharge of an at-will employee if the termination violated constitutional or statutory provision, but violating the ethics rules is not violating a constitutional or statutory provision. Hence, the law firm associate has no viable wrongful discharge claim against the law firm that terminated him because of his refusal to take part in what he believed was a suspect referral arrangement with medical providers. The court added: "This is not a pretty business that Mr. Gadlage has seen and fought against in his own way. Unfortunately, Kentucky does not afford him a legal remedy in these circumstances." *Gadlage v. Winters & Yonker, Attorneys at Law, P.S.C.*, 2011 WL 6888538, *2 (W.D. Ky. 2011).

[3] Rule 1.16, Comment 4.

[4] *Parker v. M & T Chemicals, Inc.*, 236 N.J.Super. 451, 566 A.2d 215 (1989). In this case, a former-in-house attorney sued an employer and supervisors under the state Conscientious Employee Protection Act. The employer moved to dismiss for failure to state claim. The court held that the Conscientious Employee Protection Act is not inconsistent with the Code of

§ 5.2–3 LAWYER SUING PRESENT CLIENT FOR EMPLOYMENT DISCRIMINATION

Wrongful termination cases should be distinguished from cases where the lawyer sued the client (or the law firm) for discrimination or other allegedly wrongful action. These cases are typically based on state or federal statutes. In the wrongful termination suit, the client-lawyer relationship has necessarily ended, but in the discrimination lawsuit, the lawyer may wish to pursue the claim while remaining employed by the corporation or other employer, and federal or state statutory anti-retaliation provisions may operate to protect the lawyer's job status while he or she is suing the client (or the law firm).[1]

We then have a situation where the client (or the law firm)

Professional Ethics adopted by the New Jersey Supreme Court to extent that a discharged attorney seeks monetary damages, as opposed to reinstatement, and thus the retaliating employer may be compelled to pay damages to employee attorney who was wrongfully discharged or mistreated for refusing to join a scheme to cheat a competitor or for any reason violative of law, fraudulent, criminal, or incompatible with a clear mandate of public policy.

[Section 5.2–3]

[1]**Retaliatory Firing.** *Jones v. Flagship International*, 793 F.2d 714 (5th Cir.1986), *cert. denied*, 479 U.S. 1065, 107 S.Ct. 952, 93 L.Ed.2d 1001 (1987), holding, on the facts before the court, that the employer did not impermissibly retaliate against the employee, a licensed attorney, because she filed an EEOC complaint; instead the employer suspended this employee (in view of the sensitive role that she played as the equal opportunity manager for the employer), because she had solicited others to file EEOC complaints and was seeking to be the vanguard of a class action.

Santa Clara County Counsel Attorneys Association v. Woodside, 7 Cal.4th 525, 28 Cal.Rptr.2d 617, 869 P.2d 1142 (1994). The court held that a state statute authorized this suit by the county attorneys' employee association, and the county was barred from discharging attorneys for exercis-

ing their right to sue under this statute.

Verney v. Pennsylvania Turnpike Commission, 903 F.Supp. 826 (M.D. Pa.1995). The court held that the terminated employee proved a causal link between filing of her EEOC complaint and her termination nearly two years later for purposes of establishing prima facie case of retaliation under Title VII. The employer admitted that one of the factors that led to the employee's discharge was her suit against the employer for sex discrimination. However, the employer articulated legitimate, nondiscriminatory reasons for its termination of employee due to erosion of trust and confidence in her ability as an attorney as evidenced by her surreptitious documentation of conversations with employees, as well as staff meetings, inability to deal with outside counsel, withdrawal from other members of the legal department, and actions that reflected poor judgment.

Douglas v. DynMcDermott Petroleum Operations Co., 144 F.3d 364 (5th Cir.1998) Following her termination as in-house counsel, a black female attorney brought suit against her employer alleging, inter alia, retaliation in violation of Title VII. The trial court found for the employee on her Title VII retaliation claim and awarded her back pay, and compensatory and punitive damages. The employer appealed and the Fifth Circuit held that the employee's conduct of

may likely believe that it no longer can trust this lawyer, that it does not believe that the lawyer is loyal, and that it is concerned that the lawyer may reveal confidential information in the course of the lawsuit. The lawyer, after all, is suing a present client or is suing the law firm for whom the lawyer continues working. On the other hand, the civil rights statutes and similar laws are intended to protect all employees, even those who are lawyers.[2]

In *Hull v. Celanese Corp.*,[3] an employee of Celanese Corp. sued her employer alleging sex-based discrimination. Hull's lawyers later moved to allow five other women to intervene as plaintiffs. One of these women was Attorney X, who was also on the corporate legal staff of Celanese. Celanese then sought to deny intervention and to disqualify Hull's lawyers based on the risk that confidential Celanese information received by X might be used by Hull's lawyers against Celanese to work on the prosecution of the joint Hull-X lawsuit. In fact, Celanese had earlier assigned Attorney X to work on the defense of the Hull lawsuit.

Hull's (and Attorney X's) lawyers argued that the lawyers never had any direct access to confidences of Celanese and, because they had carefully cautioned Attorney X not to reveal any confidential information, there was no danger of even an indirect transfer of confidential information. Nonetheless, the court disqualified Hull's (and Attorney X's) lawyers but said, without further explanation, that the factual situation was "novel" and that this "decision should not be read to imply that either Hull or [Attorney X] cannot pursue her claim of employment discrimination based on sex."[4]

The general rule is that inside counsel may sue her employer,

---

disclosing informally to third parties information relating to interoffice complaints of discrimination constituted breach of her duties of confidentiality and loyalty to employer, and was not protected activity under Title VII.

[2]*Plessinger v. Castleman & Haskell*, 838 F.Supp. 448 (N.D.Cal. 1993). A fired associate sued his firm for age discrimination and also sued the firm's client (Allstate Insurance) for tortious interference with business relations. The complaint alleged that Allstate had ordered the firm to fire him because it wanted younger lawyers working on its cases. Allstate asserted that it had an absolute right to counsel of its choice and that therefore the claim must be dismissed. The judge disagreed, saying if that were the rule, clients could demand that no

women or racial minorities work on its cases. The court denied Allstate's motion to dismiss.

[3]*Hull v. Celanese Corp.*, 513 F.2d 568 (2d Cir.1975). *See also Alexander v. Tandem Staffing Solutions, Inc.*, 881 So.2d 607 (Fla.App.4th Dist.2004) (Former general counsel filed whistle-blower lawsuit against former employer. Corporation sought to disqualify the client's lawyer because she had disclosed privileged corporate information to him. The trial court permitted the disqualification, but the appellate court reversed. It stated that the exception to the confidentiality rule dealing with breaches of duty by the lawyer authorized these disclosures.).

[4]513 F.2d at 572. *See* ABA Formal Opinion 01-424 (Sept. 22, 2001), con-

the corporation, for causes of action such as employment discrimination or retaliatory discharge, *but* that they may do so only insofar as they protect their client's (or former client's) secrets and confidences.[5] Hence, it is unlikely that the court would allow the inside counsel to maintain a class action because an individual action will protect the plaintiff in pursuing the lawsuit without unnecessarily disclosing client confidences and secrets.

For example, in *Doe v. A. Corp.*,[6] in-house counsel provided legal advice concerning employee benefits to the corporation and to the administrators of its benefit plan. Then, this lawyer (who now was a former inside counsel) sued the corporation and administrators of its benefit plan seeking benefits allegedly due to him under the corporation's pension and life insurance plans. He also sought to represent a class of other employees allegedly entitled to those benefits. The district court in *Doe* held that plaintiff's ethical obligations as a lawyer barred him from prosecuting such litigation. He appealed. The Court of Appeals, speaking through Judge Alvin B. Rubin, held that the plaintiff's ethical obligations barred him from prosecuting the action as class representative of other employees, but he could prosecute an action in his own behalf. In other words, if the lawyer were the lawyer for the class, or were a class representative, the lawyer would be disclosing confidential information to the class member. But the lawyer may not do that. The lawyer may, however, assert her own claims in an individual suit, but she must take precautions to reveal only to persons with a need to know. Class members do not fall in that category. She also should make other arrangements to safeguard the client's confidential information.

The Fifth Circuit cited, with apparent approval, the action of the trial court, in issuing various orders to protect the corporation's privileged information:

> To prevent identification of the company and the possible disclosure of confidential information concerning its affairs, the district court granted the defendant corporation's motion to seal the record; require the suit to be prosecuted without revealing the name of either the lawyer or the corporation; and enjoin Doe and his co-counsel from pursuing any actions arising out of the facts on which

---

cluding that a former in-house lawyer may pursue a wrongful discharge claim against her former employer and client as long as the lawyer does not disclose client information beyond that which the lawyer reasonably believes is necessary to establish her claim.

[5]*Heckman v. Zurich Holding Co. of America*, 2007 WL 1347753, 242 F.R.D. 606 (D. Kan. 2007) (citations omitted): "The overwhelming majority of courts" that have considered the issue, "have permitted in-house attorneys to bring retaliatory discharge claims against their former employers/clients *so long as they do not run afoul of their duty of confidentiality*." (emphasis added).

[6]*Doe v. A Corp.*, 709 F.2d 1043 (5th Cir. 1983).

his suits were based, communicating with other persons to induce them to bring a similar action, and disclosing or using any information Doe gained during his employment by the corporation.[7]

---

[7]*Doe v. A Corp.*, 709 F.2d 1043, 1044 n.1 (5th Cir. 1983). ABA Formal Opinion 01–424 also cites with approval this footnote. ABA Formal Opinion 01–424, text at notes 10–11.

Accord, Wise v. Consolidated Edison Co. of New York, Inc., 282 A.D.2d 335, 723 N.Y.S.2d 462 (1st Dep't 2001) N.Y.A.D. (1st Dept. 2001). A former in-house counsel sued his employer for wrongful termination. The Supreme Court denied the employer's motion to dismiss and permanently seal record, and the Appellate Division reversed. The Appellate Division, held that: (1) it would bar this suit if permitting it to go forward would entail the former in-house counsel's improper disclosure of client confidences, and (2) the employer was entitled to have the record sealed. "[P]ermitting the action to go forward would entail the improper disclosure by plaintiff, an attorney who was in-house counsel to defendant prior to his termination, of client confidences, including specific corporate tax strategies." *Wise v. Consolidated Edison Co. of New York, Inc.*, 282 A.D.2d 335, 723 N.Y.S.2d 462, 463 (1st Dep't 2001).

Kachmar v. SunGard Data Systems, Inc., 109 F.3d 173 (3d Cir. 1997). A former in-house lawyer brought claims against her former employer including claims of sex discrimination and retaliatory discharge under Title VII. The court allowed the suit but warned:

"In balancing the needed protection of sensitive information with the in-house counsel's right to maintain the suit, the district court may use a number of equitable measures at its disposal 'designed to permit the attorney plaintiff to attempt to make the necessary proof while protecting from disclosure client confidences subject to the privilege.' *General Dynamics*, 32 Cal.Rptr.2d at 18, 876 P.2d at 504. Among those referred to in General Dynamics were '[t]he use of sealing and protective

orders, limited admissibility of evidence, orders restricting the use of testimony in successive proceedings, and, where appropriate, in camera proceedings.' *Id.* Admittedly, this may entail more attention by a judicial officer than in most other Title VII actions, but . . . that permits vindicating Kachmar's rights while preserving the core values underlying the attorney-client relationship." 109 F.3d at 182.

Kachmar also cited with approval the *Doe* case.

Douglas v. DynMcDermott Petroleum Operations Co., 144 F.3d 364 (5th Cir.1998) Following her termination as in-house counsel, a black female attorney brought suit against her employer alleging, inter alia, retaliation in violation of Title VII. The trial court found for the employee on her Title VII retaliation claim and awarded her back pay and compensatory and punitive damages. The employer appealed and the Fifth Circuit held that the employee's conduct of disclosing informally to third parties information relating to interoffice complaints of discrimination constituted breach of her duties of confidentiality and loyalty to employer, and was not protected activity under Title VII.

Alexander v. Tandem Staffing Solutions, Inc., 881 So. 2d 607 (Fla. Dist. Ct. App. 4th Dist. 2004). The corporation's former general counsel filed a lawsuit against her former employer pursuant to a state law (the Florida Whistleblower Act). The corporation sought to disqualify the client's lawyer because she had disclosed privileged corporate information to him. The trial court permitted the disqualification, but the appellate court reversed. Disclosures *to her own lawyer* reasonably pertaining to her whistleblower claim were permissible and did not require disqualification of attorney. However, the court added, 881 So.2d at 610:

"the former in-house attorney has a

CHAPTER 5.3

THE LAWYER'S RESPONSIBILITIES
REGARDING NONLAWYER ASSISTANTS

§ 5.3–1 Supervising Nonlawyer Employees
§ 5.3–2 Sharing Client Information with Outside Contractors

'duty to minimize disclosures" and that the trial court has numerous tools it must employ to prevent unwarranted disclosure of the confidential information, including 'the use of sealing and protective orders, limited admissibility of evidence, orders restricting the use of testimony in successive proceedings, and, where appropriate, in camera proceedings.'" (quoting *Spratley v. State Farm Mut. Auto. Ins. Co.*, 2003 UT 39, 78 P.3d 603 (Utah 2003).

Ackerman v. National Property Analysts, Inc., 887 F. Supp. 510 (S.D. N.Y. 1993). The former inside counsel of a corporation (Leonard Hirschhorn, Esq.) filed a fraud action against his former employer. Hirschhorn was involved, either as counsel for claimants or a litigant in own right. Defendants claimed that plaintiffs' counsel obtained confidential information from Hirschhorn in drafting the complaints against defendants. The court disqualified plaintiffs' counsel for violating ethics rules. The court also dismissed both actions with prejudice. *See also* 887 F.Supp. at 516: "Hirschhorn was assisting in the representation of the plaintiffs while also acting as a party. Accordingly, it is presumed that the NPA and United Growth Defendants disclosed confidences and secrets to Hirschhorn which bear directly on the subject matter of this action." (citations omitted).

Crews v. Buckman Laboratories Intern., Inc., 78 S.W.3d 852, 862–63 (Tenn. 2002), held that an in-house associate general counsel may sue his client alleging wrongful discharge, and then citing cases that concluded that the suit is permissible "only if the lawyer could do so without breaching the duty of confidentiality."

Breckinridge v. Bristol–Myers Co., 624 F. Supp. 79 (S.D. Ind. 1985). Breckinridge, a lawyer, retired at age 65. He sued claiming that the company forced him to retire in violation of the Age Discrimination in Employment Act. The court advised that the lawyer may disclose what is necessary for his lawsuit, but no more: "He should not, however, disclose more than is necessary for his own protection." 624 F.Supp. at 84.

Siedle v. Putnam Investments, Inc., 147 F.3d 7 (1st Cir.1998). The former in-house counsel sued, claiming breach of contract, interference with advantageous business relationships and conversion. The company claimed that the plaintiff's filings contained information that was subject to attorney-client privilege. The trial court issued an order to seal the paper, but later rescinded it. The company appealed, and the First Circuit held that it was an abuse of discretion for the trial court to rescind the seal order unsealing all the filings.

See also, RESTATEMENT OF THE LAW GOVERNING LAWYERS, THIRD, § 64 & Comment *e* (A.L.I. 2000).

RULE 5.3: RESPONSIBILITIES REGARDING NONLAWYER ASSISTANTS

With respect to a nonlawyer employed or retained by or associated with a lawyer:

(a) a partner, and a lawyer who individually or together with other lawyers possesses comparable managerial authority in a law firm shall make reasonable efforts to ensure that the firm has in effect measures giving reasonable assurance that the person's conduct is compatible with the professional obligations of the lawyer;

(b) a lawyer having direct supervisory authority over the nonlawyer shall make reasonable efforts to ensure that the person's conduct is compatible with the professional obligations of the lawyer; and

(c) a lawyer shall be responsible for conduct of such a person that would be a violation of the Rules of Professional Conduct if engaged in by a lawyer if:

(1) the lawyer orders or, with the knowledge of the specific conduct, ratifies the conduct involved; or

(2) the lawyer is a partner or has comparable managerial authority in the law firm in which the person is employed, or has direct supervisory authority over the person, and knows of the conduct at a time when its consequences can be avoided or mitigated but fails to take reasonable remedial action.

Comment

[1] Lawyers generally employ assistants in their practice, including secretaries, investigators, law student interns, and paraprofessionals. Such assistants, whether employees or independent contractors, act for the lawyer in rendition of the lawyer's professional services. A lawyer must give such assistants appropriate instruction and supervision concerning the ethical aspects of their employment, particularly regarding the obligation not to disclose information relating to representation of the client, and should be responsible for their work product. The measures employed in supervising nonlawyers should take account of the fact that they do not have legal training and are not subject to professional discipline.

[2] Paragraph (a) requires lawyers with managerial authority within a law firm to make reasonable efforts to establish internal policies and procedures designed to provide reasonable assurance that nonlawyers in the firm will act in a way compatible with the Rules of Professional Conduct. See Comment [1] to Rule 5.1. Paragraph (b) applies to lawyers who have supervisory authority over the work of a nonlawyer. Paragraph (c) specifies the circumstances in which a lawyer is responsible for conduct of a nonlawyer that would be a violation of the Rules of Professional Conduct if engaged in by a lawyer.

Authors' 1983 Model Rules Comparison

The drafters of the 2002 version amended Rule 5.3(a) and 5.3(c)(2) to reflect the changes made in Rule 5.1 to include lawyers who have managerial authority over others.

Rule 5.1(a) contains the following clause, "and a lawyer who individually or together with other lawyers possesses comparable managerial authority."

Rule 5.3(c)(2) similarly contains the following language, "has comparable managerial authority."

Comment 2 was added to explain the changes in text relating to lawyers with managerial authority.

Model Code Comparison

There was no direct counterpart to this Rule in the Model Code. DR 4-101(D) provided that a lawyer "shall exercise reasonable care to prevent his employees, associates, and others whose services are utilized by him from disclosing or using confidences or secrets of a client . . . ." DR 7-107(J) provided that "[a] lawyer shall exercise reasonable care to prevent his employees and associates from making an extrajudicial statement that he would be prohibited from making under DR 7-107." .

§ 5.3–1 SUPERVISING NONLAWYER EMPLOYEES

A lawyer's responsibility over nonlawyer employees parallels that over subordinate lawyers.[1] The Comment to Model Rule 5.3 emphasizes a lawyer's duty to instruct nonlawyer employees about the ethical aspects of their employment.[2] It is reasonable for lawyers to disclose client confidences to nonlawyer employees, such as secretaries, and the rules of ethics have no jurisdiction over these nonlawyer employees.[3] However, the ethics rules do require that the lawyer exercise "reasonable care to prevent his employees or associates" from violating the obligation regarding client confidences or secrets.[4]

A lawyer who fails in her duty of supervision violates Rule 5.3 even though no secrets are in fact disclosed, because the disciplinable violation is the failure to supervise. Conversely, a lawyer

---

[Section 5.3–1]

[1] See Rule 5.3. Cf. DR 4-101(D); EC 4-5; DR 7-107(J). Restatement of the Law Governing Lawyers, Third, § 11(4) (Official Draft 2000). This basic restriction is derived from the rules of agency. See Restatement of the Law of Agency, Second §§ 503, 507, 510 (1958).

[2] See Rule 5.3, Comment 1. A useful tool to help the lawyer in fulfilling this responsibility is THE LEGAL ASSISTANT'S PRACTICAL GUIDE TO PROFESSIONAL RESPONSIBILITY (ABA, 2d ed. 2004).

[3] See Rule 5.3, Comment 1.

[4] Rule 5.3; DR 4-101(D); EC 4-5.

See, e.g., In re Bonanno, 208 A.D.2d 1117, 617 N.Y.S.2d 584 (N.Y. App.Div.1994)(per curiam). A lawyer hired a nonlawyer assistant. Because of the assistant's "exemplary" work, the lawyer decreased his supervision. "Without respondent's knowledge or authorization, the assistant began holding himself out as an attorney, representing clients, and embezzling client funds. When respondent became aware of the assistant's misconduct, he fired the assistant." 208 A.D.2d 1117, at 1117, 617 N.Y.S.2d 584, at 584. The court censured the lawyer for failure to supervise this employee.

who adequately supervises her employees has fulfilled her obligation, even though the employee nonetheless violates his instructions and improperly discloses a client secret or confidence.

The policies underlying this Rule are obvious. Clients hire lawyers and law firms to represent their interests and although they may understand that parts of the work may be performed by nonlawyers, clients expect lawyers to adequately supervise the delivery of legal services by the firm. Also, a lawyer may not circumvent the Rules by permitting employees and independent contractors to violate them.

Rule 5.3 applies to partners, lawyers who individually or collectively have managerial authority, and lawyers who supervise nonlawyer employees or independent contractors. The reference to lawyers with managerial authority was added in 2002 to clarify that Rules 5.1 and 5.3 applied "to managing lawyers in corporate and government legal departments and legal services organizations."[5] This amendment is not intended to change the prior law under Rule 5.3.

Rule 5.3 applies to law firm employment of law clerks for the purpose of evaluating the clerk's work for the prospect of future employment. Law clerks, who are not licensed to practice law, are not directly responsible for following the Rules. However, when law firms employ them, the lawyers in the firm are responsible for properly supervising their work and for informing the law clerks about their need to follow the Rules.[6]

If a clerk intends to work for two firms in the same location and in the same substantive legal sections of the firms, the law firms should take special precautions not to put the clerk in a position to violate confidentiality or loyalty to the clients of the firm. If a law clerk intends to spend the first half of a summer with Firm A and the second half with Firm B, the law firms should take care not to give the law clerk legal work where the other firm is representing a client adverse to the firm's client. For example, if Firm A represents the plaintiff and Firm B represents the defendant in the same litigation, both firms should ask the law clerk about the current employment plans for the summer. Once they know that the law clerk will be at Firm A and Firm B, both firms should avoid asking the clerk to work on the matter where the firms are on opposite sides. If Firm A asks the clerk to write a memorandum on a possible takeover target for an aggressor client, and later in the summer, Firm B begins to represent

---

[5] Reporter's Explanation of Changes to Rule 5.3.

[6] *In re Kellogg*, 269 Kan. 143, 154, 4 P.3d 594, 602 (2000)(per curiam): Rule 5.3 "requires a lawyer to make reasonable efforts to ensure that a nonlawyer assistant's conduct and training is compatible with the lawyer's obligation and may be violated by a lack of training."

the target of this takeover, Firm B should not give the law clerk work on this matter and should not ask the clerk about confidential information gained while working in Firm A.

The supervising lawyer must exercise reasonable care. For example, the prudent lawyer will require the nonlawyer assistants to read the current Rules, and then focus on and explain the reasons behind those rules with "special significance for nonlawyer employees." The "short list would include the rules governing diligence, communication, confidentiality, conflicts of interest, trust accounts, candor and honesty, communications with persons represented by counsel, and the unauthorized practice of law." The lawyer can emphasize the requirement of confidentiality "by having employees sign a confidentiality agreement," and then retain a copy of that agreement in the employee's files. "Use internal memoranda to remind people of their responsibilities, and put copies in the personnel files as appropriate."[7]

§ 5.3-2 SHARING CLIENT INFORMATION WITH OUTSIDE CONTRACTORS

The lawyer may employ outside contractors for accounting, photocopying, storage, data processing, or other legitimate purposes but the lawyer must exercise due care in selecting the contractor, because these outside agencies employ nonlawyers who may have some access to client files.[1]

Lawyers must make reasonable efforts to satisfy themselves that the outside service provider does not make unauthorized disclosures of client confidences or secrets.[2] For example, the lawyer who contracts with a recycling firm to dispose of trash should take care to instruct the recycling firm on the importance of protecting client confidences and secrets.[3] Similarly, the law firm that hires a computer maintenance company that will have

---

[7]Kate A. Toomey, *Practice Pointer: Training And Supervising Non-Lawyer Assistants*, 17 UTAH BAR JOURNAL 16 (April, 2004).

[Section 5.3-2]

[1]Rule 5.3, Comment 1 (referring to "independent contractors"); EC 4-3.

Cf. ABA Formal Opinion 95-393 (Apr. 24, 1995), concluding that a government lawyer may disclose to nonlawyer supervisor information relating to representation if this disclosure helps carry out the client's representation. If it is not used for that purpose, the lawyer can disclose it only if the client expressly consents, after consultation with his lawyer. If

there is no consent, the lawyer may disclose data (*e.g.*, demographic information) from the client's files only in a way that does not identify the client or compromise the confidentiality of any particular client's data or permit the data to be traced back to that client.

[2]*See* Virginia Standing Committee on Legal Ethics, Opinion 1787 (Dec. 22, 2003) (imposing the obligation to inform nonlawyer expert witness about the importance of confidentiality of documents provided to the expert by the lawyer).

[3]Oregon State Bar, Formal Opinion No. 1995-141 (1995).

access to client files must take reasonable efforts to make sure that this outside contractor will establish reasonable procedures to protect client confidences and secrets. If a significant breach of confidentiality has occurred, the lawyer may be obligated to inform the affected clients.[4]

Outsourcing Legal Services to Lawyers and Nonlawyers Outside of the United States. In recent years, American companies have sought to reduce their costs of operation by outsourcing services to companies located outside of the United States. Some American law firms and corporations have also begun to outsource legal work to lawyers and nonlawyers located around the world.[5]

The outsourcing of legal services raises many ethics issues for the lawyers who are sending the work to other lawyers and nonlawyers.[6] A New York City Bar Opinion examines the ethics issues and concludes that New York lawyers may outsource legal work if they comply with the special ethics issues that outsourcing creates.[7] These issues include the obligation to: "(a) supervise the non-lawyer and ensure that the non-lawyer's work contributes to the lawyer's competent representation of the client; (b) preserve the client's confidences and secrets when outsourcing; (c) avoid conflicts of interest when outsourcing; (d) bill for outsourcing appropriately; and (e) obtain advance client consent for outsourcing."[8]

The failure to supervise the work of the out-of-jurisdiction legal service provider could lead to the lawyer assisting another in the unauthorized practice law as well as a violation of Model Rule 5.3. The inability of the New York lawyer to supervise personally

---

[4]ABA Formal Opinion 95–398 (Oct. 27, 1995), concluding that sometimes the lawyer's disclosure to the client of a breach of security "would be required under Rule 1.4(b)."

[5]*See* Tom Ramstack, *Law Firms Send Case Work Overseas to Boost Efficiency,* THE WASHINGTON TIMES, at C14, Sept. 26, 2005 available at http://www.washingtontimes.com/business/20050925–102112–4588r.htm. *See also* Mimi Samuel & Laurel Currie Oates, *From Oppression to Outsourcing: New Opportunities for Uganda's Growing Number of Attorneys in Today's Flattening World,* 4 SEATTLE J. FOR SOCIAL JUSTICE 835 (2006).

[6]Note that outsourcing refers to sending work to another location to someone who can more efficiently ac-

complish the work, but the work has no factual or legal relationship to the jurisdiction where the work is sent.

[7]Association of the Bar of the City of New York, Committee on Professional and Judicial Ethics, Ethics Opinion 2006–3 (Aug. 2006). *See also* Fl. Bar Prof. Ethics Comm., Op. 07-2 (July 25, 2008) (generally approving outsourcing if US lawyers appropriately safeguard client information and properly supervise the lawyers or paralegals performing the work), *noted in* 24 ABA/BNA Law. Man. Prof. Conduct 437 (Aug. 20, 2008).

[8]Association of the Bar of the City of New York, Committee on Professional and Judicial Ethics, Ethics Opinion 2006–3 (Aug. 2006) (footnote omitted).

the work of the out-of-country legal services provider poses many challenges. Hence, lawyers should consider the following checklist when determining how to supervise outsourced legal work:

(a) obtain background information about any intermediary employing or engaging the non-lawyer, and obtain the professional résumé of the non-lawyer; (b) conduct reference checks; (c) interview the non-lawyer in advance, for example, by telephone or by voice-over-internet protocol or by web cast, to ascertain the particular non-lawyer's suitability for the particular assignment; and (d) communicate with the non-lawyer during the assignment to ensure that the non-lawyer understands the assignment and that the non-lawyer is discharging the assignment according to the lawyer's expectations.[9]

In addition to supervision, the lawyer may need to disclose and obtain the client's consent to outsourcing legal services. If the outsourcing requires the disclosure of confidential information, the lawyer would need to obtain the client's consent.[10]

Perhaps, one could draw a distinction between outsourcing to lawyers and outsourcing to nonlawyers.[11] One does not, for example, need client consent to outsource a messenger or package delivery service (e.g., Federal Express). However, the City Bar of New York Opinion notes that there are some situations where outsourcing to nonlawyers would also require the lawyer to secure client consent to the outsourcing:

if (a) non-lawyers will play a significant role in the matter, e.g., several non-lawyers are being hired to do an important document review; (b) client confidences and secrets must be shared with the non-lawyer, in which case informed advance consent should be secured from the client; (c) the client expects that only personnel employed by the law firm will handle the matter; or (d) non-lawyers are to be billed to the client on a basis other than cost, in which case the client's informed advance consent is needed.[12]

The ABA addressed the issues raised by outsourcing of legal and nonlegal support services in Formal Opinion 08-451.[13] In light of the varying types of work that are outsourced in the practice of law, the ABA takes a facts and circumstances approach to the ethical issues that may be involved in a particular situation. Some forms of outsourcing require direct supervision under Rules 5.1 and 5.2 and, when confidential information is disclosed to outside parties, client consent may be required under Rule 1.6. The opinion raises several special issues that may arise

---

[9]Association of the Bar of the City of New York, Committee on Professional and Judicial Ethics, Ethics Opinion 2006–3 (Aug. 2006).

[10]Model Rule 1.6.

[11]Model Rule 1.5(e).

[12]Association of the Bar of the City of New York, Committee on Professional and Judicial Ethics, Ethics Opinion 2006–3 (Aug. 2006).

[13]ABA Formal Op. 08-452 (Aug. 5, 2008).

when a law firm outsources work to foreign lawyers, including the increased need for specific supervision and the need to examine the skills and risks that arise when work is sent to another jurisdiction.[14] Ultimately, the opinion rests on the duty of the lawyer to competently deliver legal services to the client with appropriate disclosure required by the rules of professional responsibility.[15] The ABA Opinion approves the concept of outsourcing and raises some potential concerns but it does not provide the detailed guidance that is contained in some state opinions.

The ABA Opinion approves the concept of outsourcing and raises some potential concerns but it does not provide the detailed guidance that is contained in some state opinions.[16]

---

[14]The Opinion states: "When engaging lawyers trained in a foreign country, the outsourcing lawyer first should assess whether the system of legal education under which the lawyers were trained is comparable to that in the United States . . . . The lack of rigorous training or effective lawyer discipline does not mean that individuals from that nation cannot be engaged to work on a particular project. What it does mean is that, in such circumstances, it will be more important than ever for the outsourcing lawyer to scrutinize the work done by the foreign lawyers—perhaps viewing them as nonlawyers—before relying upon their work in rendering legal services to the client . . . . Consideration also should be given to the legal landscape of the nation to which the services are being outsourced, particularly the extent that personal property, including documents, may be susceptible to seizure in judicial or administrative proceedings notwithstanding claims of client confidentiality. ABA Formal Op. 08-452 (Aug. 5, 2008).

[15]A lawyer may be required to disclose outsourcing to the client: (1) when it involves disclosure of confidential information, (2) when it involves using an outside lawyer who is sharing legal fees, (3) when it involves largely unsupervised delegation of independent work to another lawyer (ABA Formal Op. 88-356 (Dec. 16,

1988), and (4) when the firm marks up the costs paid to outside sources in a manner that exceeds the imposition of allocable overhead of the law firm.

[16]**Cloud Computing and On-Line Data Storage**. E.g., New York State Bar Association, Committee on Professional Ethics, Eth. Op. 842, 2010 WL 3961389 (Sept. 10, 2010), which advises that lawyers may use an online data storage system to store and back up client confidential information, *if* the lawyer takes reasonable care to ensure that confidentiality will be maintained in a manner consistent with the lawyer's obligations under Rule 1.6. The lawyer should also "stay abreast of technological advances to ensure that the storage system remains sufficiently advanced to protect the client's information, and should monitor the changing law of privilege to ensure that storing the information online will not cause loss or waiver of any privilege."

See also, Iowa State Bar Association, Committee on Ethics and Practice Guidelines, Op. 11-01 (Sept. 9, 2011) ("Software as a Service - Cloud Computing") advises that lawyers who take advantage of "cloud computing" must "perform due diligence to assess the degree of protection that will be needed and to act accordingly." The Committee concluded that the lawyer may discharge her duties to protect client information "by relying on the due

CHAPTER 5.4

PROFESSIONAL INDEPENDENCE OF A LAWYER

RULE 5.4: PROFESSIONAL INDEPENDENCE OF A LAWYER

(a) A lawyer or law firm shall not share legal fees with a nonlawyer, except that:

(1) an agreement by a lawyer with the lawyer's firm, partner, or associate may provide for the payment of money, over a reasonable period of time after the lawyer's death, to the lawyer's estate or to one or more specified persons;

(2) a lawyer who purchases the practice of a deceased, disabled, or disappeared lawyer may, pursuant to the provisions of Rule 1.17, pay to the estate or other representative of that lawyer the agreed-upon purchase price;

(3) a lawyer or law firm may include nonlawyer employees in a compensation or retirement plan, even though the plan is based in whole or in part on a profit-sharing arrangement; and

(4) a lawyer may share court-awarded legal fees with a nonprofit organization that employed, retained or recommended employment of the lawyer in the matter.

(b) A lawyer shall not form a partnership with a nonlawyer if any of the activities of the partnership consist of the practice of law.

(c) A lawyer shall not permit a person who recommends, employs, or pays the lawyer to render legal services for another to direct or regulate the lawyer's professional judgment in rendering such legal services.

---

diligence services of independent companies, bar associations or other similar organizations or through its own qualified employees."

(d) A lawyer shall not practice with or in the form of a professional corporation or association authorized to practice law for a profit, if:

(1) a nonlawyer owns any interest therein, except that a fiduciary representative of the estate of a lawyer may hold the stock or interest of the lawyer for a reasonable time during administration;

(2) a nonlawyer is a corporate director or officer thereof or occupies the position of similar responsibility in any form of association other than a corporation; or

(3) a nonlawyer has the right to direct or control the professional judgment of a lawyer.

Comment

[1] The provisions of this Rule express traditional limitations on sharing fees. These limitations are to protect the lawyer's professional independence of judgment. Where someone other than the client pays the lawyer's fee or salary, or recommends employment of the lawyer, that arrangement does not modify the lawyer's obligation to the client. As stated in paragraph (c), such arrangements should not interfere with the lawyer's professional judgment.

[2] This Rule also expresses traditional limitations on permitting a third party to direct or regulate the lawyer's professional judgment in rendering legal services to another. See also Rule 1.8(f) (lawyer may accept compensation from a third party as long as there is no interference with the lawyer's independent professional judgment and the client gives informed consent).

Authors' 1983 Model Rules Comparison

In 1990, the House of Delegates added a new subsection (Rule 5.4(a)(2)) to reflect the newly adopted Rule 1.17 on sale of a law practice. The original text of Rule 5.4(a)(2) read as follows:

"(a) A lawyer or law firm shall not share legal fees with a nonlawyer, except that:

"(2) a lawyer who undertakes to complete unfinished legal business of a deceased lawyer may pay to the estate of the deceased lawyer that proportion of the total compensation which fairly represents the services rendered by the deceased lawyer; and.
. . . "

The drafters of the 2002 Model Rules added a new subsection (a)(4) to Rule 5.4 to clarify whether a lawyer may share court-awarded legal fees with a non-profit organization. They also amended 5.4(d)(2) to add the following language—"or occupies the position of similar responsibility in any form of association other than a corporation"—to cover situations where lawyers practice in the form of limited liability companies or other organizations.

Comment 2 was added in 2002 to reaffirm the legal profession's prohibition on third party interference with the attorney-client relationship and to provide a cross reference to Rule 1.8(f). The drafters did not intend to change prior law in this Comment.

Model Code Comparison

[1] Paragraph (a) is substantially identical to DR 3-102(A).

[2] Paragraph (b) is substantially identical to DR 3-103(A).

[3] Paragraph (c) is substantially identical to DR 5-107(B).

[4] Paragraph (d) is substantially identical to DR 5-107(C).

§ 5.4–1 SHARING FEES WITH LAY PERSONS

§ 5.4–1(a) General Prohibition

In general, a lawyer or law firm may not share legal fees with a nonlawyer.[1] The ABA has embraced a prohibition on the sharing of legal fees with nonlawyers because it seeks to limit nonlawyer involvement in the control and delivery of legal services. The ban on sharing legal fees with nonlawyers not only limits nonlawyer control over the services, but it also supports the bar's enforcement of the Model Rules. Because the Rules do not apply to nonlawyers and the bar does not have jurisdiction over nonlawyers who work outside of a law firm, the bar would have a difficult time regulating the legal profession if nonlawyers working outside of law firms had an incentive to profit from the practice of law.

The prohibition against fee sharing limits the types of arrangements that a law firm may have with nonlawyers. If a law firm hires a nonlawyer to perform services as part of litigation, such as accounting or financial planning, the law firm must pay the nonlawyer on an hourly or fixed basis. It cannot pay the nonlawyer on a contingent basis because this would constitute the sharing of legal fee, the spoils of the litigation, with the nonlawyer. Similarly, a lawyer may not pay a nonlawyer for referring a case to the lawyer. That conduct would violate Rule 7.2(b) and Rule 5.4(a) because the source of payment of the referral is legal fees.

Rule 5.4(a) contains several major exceptions to the prohibition on sharing legal fees with nonlawyers. These exceptions are discussed below.

§ 5.4–1(a)(1) Paying Fees to a Placement Agency Based on a Percentage of the Lawyer's Compensation

Sometimes a law firm has a short term need to hire lawyers for a specific project or staffing problem or to offer special expertise on a particular issue. In such cases, the law firm typically hires a "temporary lawyer," "lawyer-temp," or "law-temp." This type of hiring has increased appreciably in recent times.[2] The firm may hire the lawyer-temp either directly or use the services of a placement agency.

[Section 5.4–1]

[1] Rule 5.4(a); DR 3-102(A). Restatement of the Law Governing Lawyers, Third, § 10(3) (Official Draft 2000).

[2] See generally Vincent R. Johnson & Virginia Coyle, On the Transformation of the Legal Profession: The Advent of Temporary Lawyering, 66 NOTRE DAME L. REV. 359 (1990).

If the law firm uses a placement agency, the agency that charges the law firm for its services (locating, recruiting, screening, and supplying temporary lawyer with particular credentials) may base its fee on a percentage of the temporary lawyer's compensation. This fee arrangement raises the question of whether it constitutes an improper sharing of legal fees with nonlawyers. Some have argued that this type of payment is an unethical sharing of a "legal fee,"[3] but they do not explain why this type of fee sharing compromises the lawyer's independence. The ABA Ethics Committee has opined that this payment is ethical, for the simple reason that paying it does not compromise at all the rationale behind Rule 5.4(a), which is to maintain the lawyer's professional independence.[4]

§ 5.4–1(b) Sharing Legal Fees with the Estate of a Deceased Lawyer

Under Rule 5.4(a)(1), a law firm may agree to pay money to the estate of a deceased lawyer (or to other specified persons) for a reasonable period of time after the lawyer's death.[5] The estate (or the beneficiaries of the estate) need not be lawyers.

The purpose of this exception is clear. After the death of a lawyer, the lawyer's beneficiaries have a right to receive the lawyer's assets through the operation of wills and estates law. A portion of the assets may include paying out the deceased lawyer's share of the law firm's capital account and another portion may include paying the legal fees that the deceased lawyer earned in the practice of law. This exception does not threaten the professional independence of the law firm paying out the monies owed to the estate or beneficiaries of the deceased lawyer.

The only requirement under the provision is that the payments may only last a reasonable time. The Rule and Comments do not define what may constitute a reasonable time. Of course, it would make sense to determine this time by reference to the estate in question. The purpose for this limitation is to prohibit a firm

---

[3] Committee on Professional and Judicial Ethics of the Association of the Bar of the City of New York, Opinion No. 1988-3 (Apr. 6, 1988), amended in Opinion No. 1988-3-A (May 23, 1988) concluded that a lawyer unethically shared fees with a nonlawyer if it paid the agency, which then paid the temporary lawyer, or if it paid the temporary lawyer directly and paid the agency a placement fee related to the compensation paid to the lawyer. This Opinion is, frankly, conclusory.

[4] ABA Formal Opinion 88-356 (Dec. 16, 1988), at 12. *Accord* Connecticut Bar Association, Committee on Professional Ethics, Informal Opinion 88-15 (Aug. 1, 1988).

Cf. ABA Formal Opinion 87-355 (Dec. 5, 1987), concluding that the sponsor of a for-profit legal service plan may keep a portion of the monthly fee paid by the members of the legal service plan in order to give the plan sponsor money to cover expenses and also for profit.

[5] Rule 5.4(a)(1); DR 3-102(A)(2).

from making a nonlawyer beneficiary a *de facto* partner in the law firm entity. In other words, a law firm could not pay out the monies owed over a ten year period as the nonlawyer beneficiary continue to draw from the ongoing practice of law.

§ 5.4–1(c) Sharing Legal Fees with a Lawyer's Beneficiaries after the Sale of a Law Practice

Since 1990, the Model Rules permit a lawyer to sell her law practice to another lawyer.[6] The ABA added Rule 5.4(a)(2) in order to make Rule 5.4 consistent with Rule 1.17, which is the Rule that authorizes a lawyer to sell her practice. Rule 5.4(a)(2) provides that if a lawyer (*e.g.*, Lawyer A) purchases the law practice of "a deceased, disabled, or disappeared lawyer," (*e.g.*, Lawyer B), then Lawyer A may agree to pay the purchase price to the estate or other representative of Lawyer B. The lawyer is, in effect, sharing legal fees with a nonlawyer (the estate or other representative of Lawyer B).

This provision is more controversial than the payment of a lawyer's estate to nonlawyer beneficiaries in Rule 5.4(a)(1). Under Rule 1.17, a lawyer's practice may be sold after a lawyer's death or disappearance by the nonlawyer beneficiaries.[7] The Comment to Rule 1.17 contemplates this problem: "This Rule applies to the sale of a law practice of a deceased, disabled or disappeared lawyer. Thus, the seller may be represented by a non-lawyer representative not subject to these Rules. Since, however, no lawyer may participate in a sale of a law practice which does not conform to the requirements of this Rule, the representatives of the seller as well as the purchasing lawyer can be expected to see to it that they are met."[8]

When Rule 1.17 is combined with Rule 5.4(a)(2), a nonlawyer beneficiary or spouse could sell a law practice and receive the agreed-upon price. The text and Comments of Rule 5.4 do not seem to place any restrictions on the time or the manner of payment to the nonlawyer. The problems that can arise are illustrated by the facts of *O'Hara v. Ahlgren, Blumenfeld & Kempster*.[9] In O'Hara, a widow sold a law practice of her deceased husband lawyer based upon a percentage of future fees that would be generated from the deceased lawyer's clients and for goodwill. The Illinois Supreme Court invalidated the contract as against public policy and on the grounds that it involved sharing of legal fees with nonlawyers. *O'Hara* involved the Illinois Rules based upon the Model Code. But would a nonlawyer be able to

---

[6]See discussion of Rule 1.17, in Chapter 1.17.

[7]The Rules seem to use the term, "disabled," in the sense of a lawyer who is too disabled to continue to practice law.

[8]Rule 1.17, Comment 13.

[9]*O'Hara v. Ahlgren, Blumenfeld & Kempster*, 537 N.E.2d 730 (Ill.1989).

sell a practice and structure it to involve future payments for many years under Rule 5.4(a)(2)? The answer is uncertain.

The lawyer who is disabled or deceased or who has simply disappeared cannot exercise any continuing oversight or be available for consultation regarding legal matters because the lawyer is not there. In contrast, a retired lawyer can exercise continuing oversight or be available for consultation. Hence, Rule 5.4 does not deal with the situation where a lawyer is sharing fees with other *lawyers* who are not in the same firm. Other rules deal with that issue.[10]

§ 5.4–1(d) Employee Profit-Sharing Plans Based Upon Profits of the Law Firm

Under Rule 5.4(a)(3), a lawyer may include nonlawyer employees in a compensation or retirement plan "even though the plan is based in whole or in part on a profit-sharing arrangement."[11] For example, at the end of the year a law firm may give each of its secretaries a bonus because the firm has just settled a significant case on very favorable terms. The firm's actions do not constitute a prohibited sharing of fees. However, as discussed in the next section, the law firm may not give these people any managerial control.

Rule 5.4 and its Comments are relatively straightforward on the profit sharing exception; they do not present a definition of a profit sharing plan or nuances that may be prohibited. Such distinctions have appeared in the state interpretations of Rule 5.4. Some authorities have states that the profits sharing plan must be calculated on net profits and never on the law firm's receipt of a specific legal fee in a specific case.[12] ABA Informal Opinion 1440 approved a compensation plan to a nonlawyer administrator based upon net profits.[13] But one would hope that if the ABA had sought this result, the drafters would have put language in the Rule or Comments to this effect. Many law firms give lawyers and nonlawyers bonuses based upon a large verdict in a particular case and law firms also tend to compensate lawyers and nonlawyers that worked on the case with a greater share of the profits. Also, economists would argue that the gross profit, net profit distinction is meaningless as both can be manipulated to reach the same result. Of course, a firm should not be able to compensate nonlawyers based upon cases that they

---

[10] Rule 1.5(e) (division of fees with lawyers not in the same firm); Rule 1.17 (sale of entire law practice); Rule 5.6(a) (restrictions on right to practice in connection with retirement). *Accord* DR 2-107(B); DR 2-108(A).

[11] Rule 5.4(a)(3). DR 3-102(A)(3).

[12] *See* ABA/BNA Lawyer's Manual on Professional Conduct: Practice Guide 41:809 (2004).

[13] ABA Informal Opinion 1440 (Aug. 12, 1979) (approving a net profits compensation plan to a law office administrator who is a nonlawyer).

have brought into the law firm because this would violate Rule 7.2(b).

§ 5.4–1(e) Sharing Court-Awarded Attorney's Fees with a Bona Fide Pro Bono Organization

Before the adoption of the 2002 Rules, the strict language in Rule 5.4(a) certainly appeared to prohibit a lawyer from sharing court-awarded legal fees (or any other legal fees) with a nonlawyer entity (such as the ACLU, the NAACP, etc.) that recommended that lawyer's employment. A separate provision in Rule 7.2 emphasized that prohibition.[14] On the other hand, lawyers could, in effect, "share fees" with placement agencies that the law firm uses to find temporary lawyers.[15] The purpose of Rule 5.4(a) was to make sure that the fee sharing arrangement does not compromise the lawyer's independence. The reason for this prohibition is simply inapplicable in this circumstance. If a lawyer may "share fees" with a placement agency, may the lawyer ethically "share fees" with a non-profit legal services organization, if that turn-over of fees does not compromise the lawyer's independence?

American Civil Liberties Union / Eastern Missouri Fund v. Miller[16] answered no to that question. The state supreme court held that Missouri's Rule 5.4(a)—which corresponded to its ABA counterpart—prohibited a former ACLU staff attorney from complying with his employment contract, which required him to turn over court-awarded fees to the ACLU. After that decision, the ACLU won a court order permanently enjoining Missouri from enforcing its ethical rules so as to invalidate the fee turn-over provision in the ACLU employment contract.[17] In response to that result, the ABA Ethics Committee reached a different

---

[14]Rule 7.2(c) prohibits payment of a referral fee, again with a few limited exceptions not applicable to this issue.

[15]ABA Formal Opinion 88-356 (Dec. 16, 1988): "The use of a lawyer placement agency to obtain temporary lawyer services *where the agency's fee is a proportion of the lawyer's compensation* does not violate the Model Rules or predecessor Model Code as long as the professional independence of the lawyer is maintained without interference by the agency, the total fee paid by each client to the law firm is reasonable, and the arrangement otherwise is in accord with the guidelines in this opinion." (emphasis added).

[16]*American Civil Liberties Union / Eastern Missouri Fund v. Miller*, 803 S.W.2d 592 (Mo.), *cert. denied*, 500 U.S. 943, 111 S.Ct. 2239, 114 L.Ed.2d 481 (1991).

[17]*Susman v. Missouri, No. 91-4429-CV-C-5* (W.D. Mo., June 1, 1992).

Other courts, without discussing the issue, have simply awarded attorneys' fees to nonprofit legal service organizations because of work that staff lawyers have performed. *See, e.g., Oldham v. Ehrlich*, 617 F.2d 163, 165 n. 3, 168–69 (8th Cir.1980); *New York State Association for Retarded Children, Inc. v. Carey*, 711 F.2d 1136,

result in Formal Opinion 93-374.[18] It considered the same situation discussed in *ACLU/Eastern Missouri Fund*: a non-profit pro bono organization asks an attorney to undertake pro bono litigation. The Opinion concluded that the lawyer (whether an employee of the organization or a member of a law firm) may agree in advance or later to turn over some or all of the court-awarded fees to the non-profit organization. Although two provisions in the Model Rules[19] appear to apply "literally" to prohibit the turnover of fees, they should not be interpreted that way, because application of these Rules would not further the purposes behind them. However, the Formal Opinion advised that lawyers who enter into such agreements should disclose the arrangement to their clients, because of the possibility of improper lay interference.[20]

The drafters of the ABA Rules, in an effort to clarify the ambiguity caused by the case law, drafted a new Rule 5.4(a)(4) that codifies Formal Opinion 93-374. This provision expressly permits a lawyer to pay to a nonprofit organization part of the court-awarded attorneys fees relating to a case referred to the lawyer by the organization. The drafters agreed with the ABA Opinion and its conclusion that the threat to the independence of the lawyer's judgment is less here than in cases involving for-profit organizations.[21]

1139, 1154 (2d Cir.1983); *McLean v. Arkansas Board of Education*, 723 F.2d 45, 47 (8th Cir.1983)(per curiam).

Cf. Atkins v. Tinning, 865 S.W.2d 533 (Tex.App.1993), concluding that even if a fee sharing agreement with a non-lawyer is unethical, that does not mean the agreement itself is unenforceable. The contract question and the ethical issue are distinct, the court said. However, that would mean that the court is enforcing a contract that its own rules conclude is against public policy. A better rationale for this decision is simply that this type of fee sharing does not compromise the lawyer's independence. The purpose of the fee sharing prohibition is to protect the lawyer's independent judgment, and the reason for this prohibition is simply inapplicable in this circumstance.

[18]ABA Formal Opinion 93-374 (June 7, 1993).

[19]Rules 5.4(a) and 7.2(c).

[20]ABA Formal Opinion 93-374 (June 7, 1993) attracted a strong dissent, arguing that the majority's interpretation of the Rules was contrary to their plain meaning. The dissenters argued that drafting errors should be corrected by redrafting, not by ignoring the language and amending the rule in the guise of creative interpretation.

[21]*See* Reporter's Explanation of Changes to Model Rule 5.4 (*See* Appendix N of the Lawyer's edition of this book).

§ 5.4–1(e)(1) In-House Corporate Counsel Representing Third Parties

ABA Formal Opinion 93-374[22] explains that the rule it adopted only applies to bona fide pro bono organizations, so that lawyers cannot share legal fees with a corporation that hires it out to third parties. In other words, corporations cannot share legal fees with their in-house lawyers; they cannot make a profit from their in-house lawyers by allowing their in-house lawyers to provide legal services to third parties—by "renting" these in-house lawyers to third parties—and then collecting profits on this rent. Assume, for example, a corporation has in-house counsel but the amount of work these salaried lawyers perform is not enough to keep them busy. The corporation may allow these lawyers to work for third parties. These *lawyers can receive* fees directly from the third parties, and these fees can be in excess of the corporation's costs, but *the corporation cannot* ethically receive a fee for the legal services that is higher than the cost to the corporation employing them.[23] There is unethical fee-sharing in violation of Rule 5.4(a) because the lawyer is sharing legal fees with a nonlawyer (the corporate employer).

On the other hand, the same rationale for allowing fee sharing with pro bono organizations[24] or with for-profit placement agencies[25] should apply to for-profit corporations if there is also no realistic risk of compromising the lawyer's independent judgment. Remember, the ABA Opinion does not object to corporate in-house lawyers providing legal services to third parties, as long as the corporation does not profit from the lawyers' representation; the lawyers may profit, but their employer may not *if* the employer is a for-profit institution.

§ 5.4–1(e)(2) In-House Counsel Sharing Attorney's Fees with the Corporation

Consider another factual variant involving fee sharing. Assume that an in-house lawyer who wins a case on behalf of the corporation is entitled to attorney's fees under a fee-shifting statute. The ABA Ethics Committee has concluded that it would be a violation of Rule 5.4(c) for the lawyer to "share with her corporate employer a 'reasonable attorney's fee' based on an hourly rate that exceeds the cost the corporation incurred in employing" that lawyer.[26]

Normally, in these fee-shifting cases, the client (not the lawyer)

---

[22]ABA Formal Opinion 93-374 (June 7, 1993).

[23]ABA Formal Opinion 95-392 (Apr. 24, 1995).

[24]ABA Formal Opinion 93-374 (June 7, 1993).

[25]ABA Formal Opinion 88-356 (Dec. 16, 1988).

[26]ABA Formal Opinion 95-392 (Apr. 24, 1995), at 1 to 2.

ABA Formal Opinion 95-392 reflects the case law. *See, e.g., National*

collects the fee award and then pays his or her lawyer the agreed-upon fee. That arrangement is assumed to violate no ethics rule. Given that this arrangement is proper, why not the other way around, where the lawyer passes on the fee award to the client? Note that when the court gives the fee award to the client, the lawyer can always waive any fee that the client offers. Lawyers are not ethically required to charge for their services. If lawyers can pass on the entire fee award (by declining to charge for their services) should they not be able to pass on part of the fee award?

When an in-house corporate lawyer is entitled to attorney's fees under a fee-shifting law, there is no danger that this particular fee arrangement will compromise the lawyers' independent professional judgment. The lawyers are representing their corporate client whether or not the lawyers also share legal fees with that client. Yet, the ABA Ethics Committee disapproves of this arrangement although it would allow the lawyers to share legal fees with a for-profit law placement agency.[27]

§ 5.4–2 THE PROHIBITION ON SHARING MANAGERIAL RESPONSIBILITY WITH NONLAWYERS

Although lawyers may include lay employees in a profit-sharing arrangement, lawyers may not give these people any managerial control. Thus, lay people cannot be partners in law firms.[1] However, they can be profit-sharing employees. A major difference is that "partners" own the firm; they are the managers in control. In contrast, "employees" work for the firm; they have no managerial control even if they enjoy profit-sharing.

Because the ethics rules allow lawyers to give nonlawyer-employees a share of the profits but not a share in the management, the Rules do not allow a law firm to sell shares to an investing public. This ethics rule tends to limit the size of law firms

---

Treasury Employees Union v. U.S. Department of the Treasury, 656 F.2d 848 (D.C.Cir.1981) (union may not ethically receive attorney's fees in excess of its financial outlay for these lawyers).

Contrast ABA Formal Opinion 93-374 (June 7, 1993), which concluded that the lawyer (whether an employee of the organization or a member of a law firm) may agree in advance or later to turn over some or all of the court-awarded fees to the *non-profit* organization (in this case, the ACLU), "because the expectation of receiving a fee is unlikely in these circumstances to be the source of lay interference with the lawyer's professional judgment."

[27]ABA Formal Opinion 88-356 (Dec. 16, 1988).

[Section 5.4–2]

[1]*See, e.g.,* Rule 5.4(b): "A lawyer shall not form a partnership with a nonlawyer if any of the activities of the partnership consist of the practice of law." *Accord* DR 3-103(A). Restatement of the Law Governing Lawyers, Third, § 10(2) (Official Draft 2000).

because it limits their sources of capital.[2] Unlike brokerage firms, law firms cannot sell shares to raise capital to expand.

The rule prohibiting nonlawyers from sharing managerial responsibility with lawyers applies whether or not the lawyers are practicing in the form of a partnership. If the lawyer is practicing law in the form of a professional legal corporation, no lay person may be a director or officer, or control the lawyer's legal judgment, or own any financial interest (except that a deceased lawyer's fiduciary representative may hold the lawyer's interest for a reasonable period of time during the administration of the estate).[3]

§ 5.4–3 THE PROHIBITION ON SHARING OWNERSHIP OF A LAW FIRM WITH NONLAWYERS

§ 5.4–3(a) General Prohibition Against Co-ownership of Law Firms with Nonlawyers

The Model Code prohibited lawyers from entering into a partnership with a nonlawyer.[1] During the debate over the drafting of the Model Rules, an early draft of the proposed Rules recommended that nonlawyers be permitted to form partnerships with lawyers if there would be no interference with the lawyers' independent professional judgment or with the client-lawyer relationship, client confidentiality would be maintained, and any advising and fee arrangements did not otherwise violate the Rules governing lawyers. During the ABA floor debates an ABA delegate asked: "Does this rule mean Sears & Roebuck will be able to open a law office?" Professor Geoffrey C. Hazard, Jr., the Reporter for the Model Rules, answered "Yes." The proposal was promptly defeated.[2]

Perhaps some day the ABA will change the Model Rules, and

---

[2] Larry E. Ribstein, *Ethical Rules, Agency Costs, and Law Firm Structure*, 84 VA. L. REV. 1707 (1998), noting that the rule against non-lawyer ownership of law firms "ensures that lawyers control the firm that provides legal services. This tends to constrain the size of law firms. . . ." *Id.* at 1707.

[3] Rule 5.4(d); DR 5-107(C).

[Section 5.4–3]

[1] *See* Model Code, DR 3-103(A).

[2] *See* Rita H. Jensen, *Ethics Row Looms on [Law Firm] Affiliates*, NATIONAL LAW. JOURNAL, Feb. 20, 1989, at 1, 28. *Compare, e.g.*, Faye A. Silas, *Diversification*, 72 A.B.A.J., May 1986, at 17, *with* A.B.A. COMMISSION ON PROFESSIONALISM, "IN THE SPIRIT OF PUBLIC SERVICE:" A BLUEPRINT FOR THE REKINDLING OF LAWYER PROFESSIONALISM 30–31 (ABA, Aug.1986). For an analysis of the Report of this ABA Commission, see Ronald D. Rotunda, *Lawyers and Professionalism: A Commentary on the Report of the American Bar Association Commission on Professionalism*, 18 LOYOLA U. OF CHICAGO L. J. 1149 (1987) (the Baker-McKenzie Foundation Lecture).

Rule 5.4 thus reemphasizes the provision found in Rule 1.8(f)(2), which provides that if someone other than the client pays for the client's legal services, the lawyer's obligations are still to the client. The lawyer may not allow the third party (who pays for the

Sears will be allowed to own a law firm.[3] In the meantime, it is interesting to note that on January 1, 1991, the District of Columbia became the first jurisdiction to amend its Rule 5.4(b) in order to allow nonlawyers to become partners in law firms, subject to various conditions.[4] However, even the Washington, D.C. Rules do not allow Sears, Roebuck & Co. to hold or control a law firm as a subsidiary.[5]

---

services or who recommends the lawyer) to interfere with the lawyer's professional judgment. Rule 5.4(c); DR 5-107(B). *Cf.* Rule 1.8(f).

[3]*The End of the Legal Profession?*, TAX NOTES, Feb. 15, 1999, at 948, 950, which refers to the Sears Roebuck comment and notes that some accounting and law professionals believe "maybe that is where the market is telling us all they should be delivered," and, "We need an immediate reexamination of our rules."

[4]District of Columbia Court of Appeals Rule 5.4 provides, as of 1998, the following:

"(b) A lawyer may practice law in a partnership or other form of organization in which a financial interest is held *or managerial authority* is exercised by an individual nonlawyer who performs professional services which assist the organization in providing legal services to clients, but only if:

"(1) The partnership or organization has as its sole purpose providing legal services to clients;

"(2) All persons having such managerial authority or holding a financial interest undertake to abide by these rules of professional conduct;

"(3) The lawyers who have a financial interest or managerial authority in the partnership or organization undertake to be responsible for the nonlawyer participants to the same extent as if nonlawyer participants were lawyers under Rule 5.1;

"(4) The foregoing conditions are set forth in writing."

Comment 5 to this Rule explains that nonlawyer participants "ought not to be confused with nonlawyer assistants under Rule 5.3. *Non-lawyer participants are persons having managerial authority* or financial interests in organizations which provide legal services." (emphasis added).

As of 1999, very few law firms in Washington, D.C. have chosen to have nonlawyer partners. First, D.C. Rule 5.4(b)(1) requires that the law firm have, as its "sole purpose" the provision of legal services to its clients. Second, ABA Formal Opinion 91-360 (July 11, 1991) states that if a law firm has offices in more than one jurisdiction, it cannot have a non-lawyer partner in its Washington, D.C. office.

[5]Washington, D.C. Rules on Professional Conduct, Rule 5.4, Comment 8 adds that the Rule "does not permit an individual or entity to acquire all or any part of the ownership of a law practice organization for investment or other purposes" because "such an investor would not be an individual performing professional services within the law firm or other organization. . . . ". So, even in Washington, D.C., a corporation, like Sears, cannot own a law firm.

In the two examples discussed earlier in this section, a corporation tried to "rent out" its in-house counsel and make a profit from the lawyers' legal work. The ethics opinions concluded that it was unethical for the lawyers to share fees with the corporation even though the lawyers did not share managerial responsibility with laypeople. ABA Formal Opinion 95-392 (Apr. 24, 1995). *Contrast* ABA Formal Opinion 93-374 (June 7, 1993). It appears that one effect of the fee-sharing rule is to prevent lay entities from profiting from law firms even when there is no interference with the law-

A law firm may ethically own a department store as a subsidiary, because no ethical rules prohibit law firms and lawyers from investing in such businesses.[6] But Sears cannot own a law firm.

§ 5.4–3(b) Partnerships with Lawyers Admitted in Other American Jurisdictions and Foreign Jurisdictions

The Model Rules do not allow a lawyer to be in partnership with a nonlawyer if any of the business of the partnership is the practice of law.[7] However, the Model Rules draw a distinction between people who are not lawyers (no partnership permitted) versus people who are lawyers but who are not admitted in every jurisdiction in which the partnership has an office (partnership permitted). If the partnership has offices in several states, but not all the lawyers in the partnership are admitted in all jurisdictions, then the listings of the law firm (*e.g.*, the letterhead, bar listing, professional card) should list the pertinent jurisdictional limitations on the lawyer's entitlement to practice.[8]

There are somewhat different concerns if the person is not admitted to the practice of law in the United States at all, but is considered a lawyer in a foreign country. The ABA has advised that the ethics rules do not prohibit U.S. lawyers from forming partnerships or other entities to practice law in which foreign lawyers are partners or owners, "as long as the foreign lawyers are members of a recognized legal profession in a foreign jurisdiction and the arrangement is in compliance with the law of jurisdictions where the firm practices." However, if the foreign person is a member of a profession that is not recognized as a legal profession by the foreign jurisdiction, that person would be deemed a "nonlawyer," so that admitting them to the American

---

yer's independent professional judgment.

The nature of law firm practice is changing more quickly abroad, in Great Britain and Australia, which share our common law heritage. The Legal Services Act of 2007 allows British lawyers to operate in firms with nonlawyers and the attorney-client privilege extends to communication with the nonlawyers. Australia now permits its lawyers to practice in corporate entities that sell stock to the general public. The European Union is considering similar changes in lawyer regulation. THOMAS D. MORGAN, THE VANISHING AMERICAN LAWYER 89–91 (Oxford U. Press 2010).

[6] Model Rule 5.7 places certain limitations on law-related services. The department store (no surprise here) is not law-related.

[7] Model Rule 5.4(b). *See also* Rule 5.4(d). *But see* Va. State Bar Standing Comm. Ethics, Op. 1843 (2008), *noted in* 24 Law. Man. Prof. Conduct 216 (2008). In Virginia, lawyers may form a partnership or professional corporation with nonlawyer patent agents if the sole purpose of the entity is to practice patent law. The result is supported by the federal preemption arguments of *Sperry v. State of Fla. ex rel. Florida Bar*, 373 U.S. 379, 83 S. Ct. 1322, 10 L. Ed. 2d 428 (1963).

[8] Model Rule 7.5(b); Model Code DR 2-102(D). *See also*, ABA Formal Opinion 90-357 (May 10, 1990).

partnership would violate Rule 5.4, governing the professional independence of a lawyer.

The responsible lawyers in a U.S. law firm, before accepting a foreign lawyer as a partner, must take reasonable steps to ensure that the foreign lawyer qualifies under this standard and that the arrangement is also in compliance with the other law in the jurisdictions where the firm practices. The ABA Ethics Committee has advised that the responsible lawyers in the U.S. law firm must take reasonable steps to assure that matters in their U.S. offices involving representation in a foreign jurisdiction are managed in accordance with relevant ethical rules, and that all the lawyers in the firm comply with other pertinent ethical rules.[9]

---

[9]*See* Laurel S. Terry, *GATS' Applicability to Transnational Lawyering and its Potential Impact on U.S. State Regulation of Lawyers*, 34 VANDERBILT J. TRANSNATIONAL L. 989 (2001) for a thorough discussion of the potential impact of GATS, the General Agreement on Trade in Services on legal services and legal ethics rules in the United States. This article was revised in, Laurel S. Terry, *Corrections To Laurel S. Terry, GATS' Applicability To Transnational Lawyering And Its Potential Impact On U.S. State Regulation Of Lawyers*, 34 Vand. J. Transnat'l L. 989 (2001), 35 VANDERBILT J. TRANSNATIONAL L. 1387 (2001). *See also* Howard A. Levine, *The Regulation Of Foreign-Educated Lawyers In New York: The Past, Present, And Future Of New York's Role In The Regulation Of The International Practice Of Law*, 47 N.Y.L. SCHOOL L. REV. 631 (2003).

CHAPTER 5.5

UNAUTHORIZED PRACTICE OF LAW; MULTIJURISDICTIONAL PRACTICE OF LAW

§ 5.5–1 Introduction
§ 5.5–2 Multijurisdictional Practice of Law
§ 5.5–3 Unauthorized Practice of Law: Defining the "Practice of Law"?
§ 5.5–4 Rationale for Rules Against Unauthorized Practice
§ 5.5–5 Remedies for Unauthorized Practice
§ 5.5–6 Aiding in the Unauthorized Practice of Law
§ 5.5–7 Practice of Law by Corporations, Associations, and Partnerships

---

RULE 5.5: UNAUTHORIZED PRACTICE OF LAW; MULTIJURISDICTIONAL PRACTICE OF LAW

(a) A lawyer shall not practice law in a jurisdiction in violation of the regulation of the legal profession in that jurisdiction, or assist another in doing so.

(b) A lawyer who is not admitted to practice in this jurisdiction shall not:

(1) except as authorized by these Rules or other law, establish an office or other systematic and continuous presence in this jurisdiction for the practice of law; or

(2) hold out to the public or otherwise represent that the lawyer is admitted to practice law in this jurisdiction.

(c) A lawyer admitted in another United States jurisdiction, and not disbarred or suspended from practice in any jurisdiction, may provide legal services on a temporary basis in this jurisdiction that:

(1) are undertaken in association with a lawyer who is admitted to practice in this jurisdiction and who actively participates in the matter;

(2) are in or reasonably related to a pending or potential proceeding before a tribunal in this or another jurisdiction, if the lawyer, or a person the lawyer is assisting, is authorized by law or order to appear in such proceeding or reasonably expects to be so authorized;

(3) are in or reasonably related to a pending or poten-

tial arbitration, mediation, or other alternative dispute resolution proceeding in this or another jurisdiction, if the services arise out of or are reasonably related to the lawyer's practice in a jurisdiction in which the lawyer is admitted to practice and are not services for which the forum requires pro hac vice admission; or

(4) are not within paragraphs (c)(2) or (c)(3) and arise out of or are reasonably related to the lawyer's practice in a jurisdiction in which the lawyer is admitted to practice.

(d) A lawyer admitted in another United States jurisdiction, and not disbarred or suspended from practice in any jurisdiction, may provide legal services in this jurisdiction that:

(1) are provided to the lawyer's employer or its organizational affiliates and are not services for which the forum requires pro hac vice admission; or

(2) are services that the lawyer is authorized by federal or other law to provide in this jurisdiction.

Comment

[1] A lawyer may practice law only in a jurisdiction in which the lawyer is authorized to practice. A lawyer may be admitted to practice law in a jurisdiction on a regular basis or may be authorized by court rule or order or by law to practice for a limited purpose or on a restricted basis. Paragraph (a) applies to unauthorized practice of law by a lawyer, whether through the lawyer's direct action or by the lawyer assisting another person.

[2] The definition of the practice of law is established by law and varies from one jurisdiction to another. Whatever the definition, limiting the practice of law to members of the bar protects the public against rendition of legal services by unqualified persons. This Rule does not prohibit a lawyer from employing the services of paraprofessionals and delegating functions to them, so long as the lawyer supervises the delegated work and retains responsibility for their work. See Rule 5.3.

[3] A lawyer may provide professional advice and instruction to nonlawyers whose employment requires knowledge of the law; for example, claims adjusters, employees of financial or commercial institutions, social workers, accountants and persons employed in government agencies. Lawyers also may assist independent nonlawyers, such as paraprofessionals, who are authorized by the law of a jurisdiction to provide particular law-related services. In addition, a lawyer may counsel nonlawyers who wish to proceed pro se.

[4] Other than as authorized by law or this Rule, a lawyer who is not admitted to practice generally in this jurisdiction violates paragraph (b) if the lawyer establishes an office or other systematic and continuous presence in this jurisdiction for the practice of law. Presence may be systematic and continuous even if the lawyer is

not physically present here. Such a lawyer must not hold out to the public or otherwise represent that the lawyer is admitted to practice law in this jurisdiction. See also Rules 7.1(a) and 7.5(b).

[5] There are occasions in which a lawyer admitted to practice in another United States jurisdiction, and not disbarred or suspended from practice in any jurisdiction, may provide legal services on a temporary basis in this jurisdiction under circumstances that do not create an unreasonable risk to the interests of their clients, the public or the courts. Paragraph (c) identifies four such circumstances. The fact that conduct is not so identified does not imply that the conduct is or is not authorized. With the exception of paragraphs (d)(1) and (d)(2), this Rule does not authorize a lawyer to establish an office or other systematic and continuous presence in this jurisdiction without being admitted to practice generally here.

[6] There is no single test to determine whether a lawyer's services are provided on a "temporary basis" in this jurisdiction, and may therefore be permissible under paragraph (c). Services may be "temporary" even though the lawyer provides services in this jurisdiction on a recurring basis, or for an extended period of time, as when the lawyer is representing a client in a single lengthy negotiation or litigation.

[7] Paragraphs (c) and (d) apply to lawyers who are admitted to practice law in any United States jurisdiction, which includes the District of Columbia and any state, territory or commonwealth of the United States. The word "admitted" in paragraph (c) contemplates that the lawyer is authorized to practice in the jurisdiction in which the lawyer is admitted and excludes a lawyer who while technically admitted is not authorized to practice, because, for example, the lawyer is on inactive status.

[8] Paragraph (c)(1) recognizes that the interests of clients and the public are protected if a lawyer admitted only in another jurisdiction associates with a lawyer licensed to practice in this jurisdiction. For this paragraph to apply, however, the lawyer admitted to practice in this jurisdiction must actively participate in and share responsibility for the representation of the client.

[9] Lawyers not admitted to practice generally in a jurisdiction may be authorized by law or order of a tribunal or an administrative agency to appear before the tribunal or agency. This authority may be granted pursuant to formal rules governing admission pro hac vice or pursuant to informal practice of the tribunal or agency. Under paragraph (c)(2), a lawyer does not violate this Rule when the lawyer appears before a tribunal or agency pursuant to such authority. To the extent that a court rule or other law of this jurisdiction requires a lawyer who is not admitted to practice in this jurisdiction to obtain admission pro hac vice before appearing before a tribunal or administrative agency, this Rule requires the lawyer to obtain that authority.

[10] Paragraph (c)(2) also provides that a lawyer rendering services in this jurisdiction on a temporary basis does not violate this Rule when the lawyer engages in conduct in anticipation of a proceeding or hearing in a jurisdiction in which the lawyer is authorized to practice law or in which the lawyer reasonably expects to be admit-

ted pro hac vice. Examples of such conduct include meetings with the client, interviews of potential witnesses, and the review of documents. Similarly, a lawyer admitted only in another jurisdiction may engage in conduct temporarily in this jurisdiction in connection with pending litigation in another jurisdiction in which the lawyer is or reasonably expects to be authorized to appear, including taking depositions in this jurisdiction.

[11] When a lawyer has been or reasonably expects to be admitted to appear before a court or administrative agency, paragraph (c)(2) also permits conduct by lawyers who are associated with that lawyer in the matter, but who do not expect to appear before the court or administrative agency. For example, subordinate lawyers may conduct research, review documents, and attend meetings with witnesses in support of the lawyer responsible for the litigation.

[12] Paragraph (c)(3) permits a lawyer admitted to practice law in another jurisdiction to perform services on a temporary basis in this jurisdiction if those services are in or reasonably related to a pending or potential arbitration, mediation, or other alternative dispute resolution proceeding in this or another jurisdiction, if the services arise out of or are reasonably related to the lawyer's practice in a jurisdiction in which the lawyer is admitted to practice. The lawyer, however, must obtain admission pro hac vice in the case of a court-annexed arbitration or mediation or otherwise if court rules or law so require.

[13] Paragraph (c)(4) permits a lawyer admitted in another jurisdiction to provide certain legal services on a temporary basis in this jurisdiction that arise out of or are reasonably related to the lawyer's practice in a jurisdiction in which the lawyer is admitted but are not within paragraphs (c)(2) or (c)(3). These services include both legal services and services that nonlawyers may perform but that are considered the practice of law when performed by lawyers.

[14] Paragraphs (c)(3) and (c)(4) require that the services arise out of or be reasonably related to the lawyer's practice in a jurisdiction in which the lawyer is admitted. A variety of factors evidence such a relationship. The lawyer's client may have been previously represented by the lawyer, or may be resident in or have substantial contacts with the jurisdiction in which the lawyer is admitted. The matter, although involving other jurisdictions, may have a significant connection with that jurisdiction. In other cases, significant aspects of the lawyer's work might be conducted in that jurisdiction or a significant aspect of the matter may involve the law of that jurisdiction. The necessary relationship might arise when the client's activities or the legal issues involve multiple jurisdictions, such as when the officers of a multinational corporation survey potential business sites and seek the services of their lawyer in assessing the relative merits of each. In addition, the services may draw on the lawyer's recognized expertise developed through the regular practice of law on behalf of clients in matters involving a particular body of federal, nationally-uniform, foreign, or international law. Lawyers desiring to provide *pro bono* legal services on a temporary basis in a jurisdiction that has been affected by a major disaster, but in which they are not otherwise authorized to practice law, as well as lawyers from the affected jurisdiction who seek to

practice law temporarily in another jurisdiction, but in which they are not otherwise authorized to practice law, should consult the [*Model Court Rule on Provision of Legal Services Following Determination of Major Disaster*].

[15] Paragraph (d) identifies two circumstances in which a lawyer who is admitted to practice in another United States jurisdiction, and is not disbarred or suspended from practice in any jurisdiction, may establish an office or other systematic and continuous presence in this jurisdiction for the practice of law as well as provide legal services on a temporary basis. Except as provided in paragraphs (d)(1) and (d)(2), a lawyer who is admitted to practice law in another jurisdiction and who establishes an office or other systematic or continuous presence in this jurisdiction must become admitted to practice law generally in this jurisdiction.

[16] Paragraph (d)(1) applies to a lawyer who is employed by a client to provide legal services to the client or its organizational affiliates, i.e., entities that control, are controlled by, or are under common control with the employer. This paragraph does not authorize the provision of personal legal services to the employer's officers or employees. The paragraph applies to in-house corporate lawyers, government lawyers and others who are employed to render legal services to the employer. The lawyer's ability to represent the employer outside the jurisdiction in which the lawyer is licensed generally serves the interests of the employer and does not create an unreasonable risk to the client and others because the employer is well situated to assess the lawyer's qualifications and the quality of the lawyer's work.

[17] If an employed lawyer establishes an office or other systematic presence in this jurisdiction for the purpose of rendering legal services to the employer, the lawyer may be subject to registration or other requirements, including assessments for client protection funds and mandatory continuing legal education.

[18] Paragraph (d)(2) recognizes that a lawyer may provide legal services in a jurisdiction in which the lawyer is not licensed when authorized to do so by federal or other law, which includes statute, court rule, executive regulation or judicial precedent.

[19] A lawyer who practices law in this jurisdiction pursuant to paragraphs (c) or (d) or otherwise is subject to the disciplinary authority of this jurisdiction. See Rule 8.5(a).

[20] In some circumstances, a lawyer who practices law in this jurisdiction pursuant to paragraphs (c) or (d) may have to inform the client that the lawyer is not licensed to practice law in this jurisdiction. For example, that may be required when the representation occurs primarily in this jurisdiction and requires knowledge of the law of this jurisdiction. See Rule 1.4(b).

[21] Paragraphs (c) and (d) do not authorize communications advertising legal services to prospective clients in this jurisdiction by lawyers who are admitted to practice in other jurisdictions. Whether and how lawyers may communicate the availability of their services to prospective clients in this jurisdiction is governed by Rules 7.1 to 7.5.

Authors' 1983 Model Rules Comparison

The 1983 Model Rules had a very straightforward rule entitled Unauthorized Practice. This Rule read as follows:

A lawyer shall not:

(a) practice law in a jurisdiction where doing so violates the regulation of the legal profession in that jurisdiction; or

(b) assist a person who is not a member of the bar in the performance of activity that constitutes the unauthorized practice of law.

The drafters of the 2002 Model Rules debated possible changes to Rule 5.5, and they made specific proposals, but the consideration of such proposals was deferred for the final report of the Commission on Multijurisdictional Practice.

Post February 2002 Amendment:

The Commission on Multijurisdictional Practice made its final recommendations to the ABA in August 2002. Based upon this Report, the ABA House of Delegates adopted significant amendments to Rule 5.5 at the August meeting.

In Rule 5.5, the ABA combined sections (a) and (b) into Rule 5.5(a). The ABA adopted new sections (b) through (d) that address the topic of multijurisdictional practice of law.

Comment 1 and 4 to 21 are new and explain the new provisions in Rule 5.5.

Comment 2 is old Comment 1 with slight modifications.

Comment 3 is old Comment 2 with slight modifications.

Post February 2007 Amendment:

At the February 2007 meeting, the ABA Standing Committee on Client Protection proposed that the ABA House of Delegates adopt a modification to Model Rule 5.5 Comment 14 and a Model Rule on Provision of Legal Services Following Determination of Major Disaster. The impetus underlying the proposal was the practical problems that lawyers faced after the Katrina hurricane. Louisiana lawyers sought refuge in neighboring states, despite the fact that they were not licensed to practice law in those states. And, lawyers from all over the country sought to offer legal services in Louisiana to help address the legal issues caused by this natural disaster. The ABA adopted the amendment to Comment 14 by adding the last line to this Comment and adopted the proposed ABA Model Rule noted above. The Model Rule on Provision of Legal Services Following Determination of Major Disaster is reprinted in Appendix M of the Lawyer's edition of this book.

Model Code Comparison

[1] With regard to paragraph (a), DR 3-101(B) of the Model Code provided that "[a] lawyer shall not practice law in a jurisdiction where to do so would be in violation of regulations of the profession in that jurisdiction."

[2] With regard to paragraph (b), DR 3-101(A) of the Model Code provided that "[a] lawyer shall not aid a non-lawyer in the unauthorized practice of law."

§ 5.5–1 INTRODUCTION

The Model Code and the 1983 Model Rules generally prohibited lawyers from engaging in unauthorized practice of law and from assisting others to violate unauthorized practice of law restrictions. In 2000, the ABA formed a Commission on Multijurisdictional Practice (MJP Commission) to study issues on the problems of lawyers who practice across state lines and to formulate a rational regulatory model for controlling multijurisdictional practice.

The drafters of the 2002 Model Rules deferred their consideration of any amendments to Rule 5.5 to the MJP Commission. In August 2002, the MJP Commission's recommendations to the ABA were presented and were adopted.

This chapter first examines Rule 5.5's regulation of multijurisdictional practice of law issues. It then turns to traditional unauthorized practice of law issues developed primarily in the case law.

§ 5.5–2 MULTIJURISDICTIONAL PRACTICE OF LAW

§ 5.5–2(a) Background

The fact that a person is a graduate of a law school does not make him authorized to practice law unless he is first admitted to the bar of the relevant jurisdiction. "Authority to engage in the practice of law conferred in any jurisdiction is not *per se* a grant of the right to practice elsewhere, and it is improper for a lawyer to engage in practice where he is not permitted by law or by court order to do so."[1] These interstate limitations are often confusing, leading to much litigation and frequent criticism.[2]

The Model Code encouraged members of the bar, as well as the organized bar itself, to remove unnecessary restrictions on interstate practice.[3] The Rules, interestingly, do not have any corresponding exhortation in favor of removing needless barriers to entry.

There are many jurisdictional questions involving the practice of law, as our society has become more mobile, with high speed highways and airplanes causing people to measure distance in hours instead of miles. Technology has also changed our method of communication, with conference calls, video-conferencing, wire-

---

[Section 5.5–2]

[1] EC 3-9. See DR 3-101(B); Rule 5.5(a).

[2] *See, e.g.,* Fred Zacharias, *Federalizing Legal Ethics,* 73 TEXAS L. REV. 335 (1994); Edward A. Carr & Allan Van Fleet, *Professional Responsibility Law in Multijurisdictional Litigation: Across the Country and Across the Street,* 36 So. TEX. L. REV. 859 (1995); Teresa Stanton Collett, *Foreword, Ethics and the Multijurisdictional Practice of Law,* 36 So. TEX. L. REV. 657 (1995); Mary C. Daly, *Resolving Ethical Conflicts in Multijurisdictional Practice—Is Model Rule 8.5 the Answer, an Answer, or No Answer at All,* 36 So. TEX. L. REV. 715 (1995); John Sutton, *Unauthorized Practice by Transactional Lawyers: A Post-Seminar Reflection on "Ethics and Multijurisdictional Practice of Law,"* 36 So. TEX. L. REV. 1027 (1995); Charles Wolfram, *Sneaking Around in the Legal Profession: Interjurisdictional Unauthorized Practice of Law by Transactional Lawyers,* 36 So. TEX. L. REV. 665 (1995).

[3] *See* EC 3-9; EC 8-3.

less communications, and the Internet. Lawyers routinely communicate in one jurisdiction to a client in a different jurisdiction about advice involving the effects or application of federal or state law in yet another jurisdiction.[4]

In one significant New York case, *El Gemayel v. Seaman,*[5] the court allowed a foreign attorney to collect his fees because, the court said, he did not "practice" in New York when he *telephoned* his client there and discussed with the client the progress of legal proceedings in Lebanon.[6] The lawyer in *El Gemayel* was not physically present in New York and did not have an office there

---

[4]*See generally* John Sutton, *Unauthorized Practice by Transactional Lawyers: A Post-Seminar Reflection on "Ethics and Multijurisdictional Practice of Law,"* 36 So. Tex. L. Rev. 1027 (1995); Charles Wolfram, *Sneaking Around in the Legal Profession: Interjurisdictional Unauthorized Practice of Law by Transactional Lawyers,* 36 So. Tex. L. Rev. 665 (1995).

[5]*El Gemayel v. Seaman,* 72 N.Y.2d 701, 536 N.Y.S.2d 406, 533 N.E.2d 245 (1988).

Global Practice of Law. The coming years will witness the transformation of American law practice because of the global practice of law. *See discussion,* in, *e.g.*, Davis, Regulation of the Legal Profession in the United States and the Future of Global Law Practice, 19 Prof. Law. 1 (2009); Morgan, Should the Public Be Able to Buy Stock in Law Firms?, 11 Engage: The Journal of the Federalist Society's Practice Groups 111 (#2, Sept. 2010).

[6]In response to foreign pressure, and the pressure of American lawyers who want to open access to legal markets abroad, the Court of Appeals of the State of New York has amended its rules for licensing foreign legal consultants. The new rules allow foreign lawyers to form partnerships with New York lawyers. *In the Matter of the Amendments of the Rules of the Court of Appeals for the Licensing of Legal Consultants,* 197 A.D.2d 392, 603 N.Y.S.2d 20-117 (Nov. 17, 1993, effective Dec. 8, 1993), amending 22 N.Y.C. R.R. Part 421.

New York is moving towards what is already quite common in Europe. The Treaty of Rome, which created what is now the European Union, seeks to remove obstacles to the free movement of capital, persons, and services among the member states. Under the Treaty, a qualified EC lawyer may provide legal services in another member state either by visiting on an occasional basis or by setting up a permanent office. He or she may provide this legal service using the qualifications of his or her original home ("home title"), or by obtaining additional qualifications, as an "integrated lawyer" from the place where he or she is setting up the permanent office. If the lawyer is using only home qualifications and is not an integrated lawyer, then the lawyer cannot undertake activities "specifically reserved to full members of the local legal profession."

In the United Kingdom, activities specifically reserved to the local legal profession or an integrated lawyer are confined "to appearing in court on his own and to undertaking probate and conveyancing work." A lawyer from one country in the European Community relying on his or her home title while practicing in another country in the EC may give legal advice, "including advice in local law." Toulmin, *Legal Practice in Europe,* INTERNATIONAL FINANCIAL LAW REVIEW, Aug., 1989.

See also Detlev F. Vagts, *Professional Responsibility in Transborder Practice: Conflict and Resolution,* 13 Georgetown J. Legal Ethics 677 (2000);

purporting to practice in New York. If he had a permanent presence in the state, i.e., an office in the state, but was not admitted to that jurisdiction, the typical rule would regard him as engaging in the unauthorized practice of law even though he only gave advice on Lebanese law.

For example, a lawyer admitted in the District of Columbia but not in Maryland could not operate from a Maryland office and represent clients, even if the lawyer (on behalf of his clients) was filing suit in the District of Columbia, where he was admitted, or in the federal district court in Maryland.[7]

Owen Bonheimer & Paul Supple, *Unauthorized Practice Of Law By U.S. Lawyers In U.S.-Mexico Practice*, 15 GEORGETOWN J. LEGAL ETHICS 697 (2002); George C. Nnona, *Multidisciplinary Practice In The International Context: Realigning The Perspective On The European Union's Regulatory Regime*, 37 CORNELL INTERNATIONAL L.J. 115 (2004–2005).

[7]*Kennedy v. Bar Association of Montgomery County, Inc.*, 316 Md. 646, 561 A.2d 200 (1989), holding that "unauthorized practice of law" was not limited to a law practice utilizing the common law and statutes of Maryland and would also include advice to clients and preparation of legal documents on basis of federal or foreign law by a lawyer who was not admitted to practice in Maryland, was admitted to practice in federal district court in Maryland, *and* had his principal office in Maryland. A lawyer who is not admitted to practice law in Maryland, but who is admitted to practice in federal district court in Maryland is *not* permitted to sort through the clients in his principal office in that state and represent only those whose legal matters would require suit or defense in federal court in Maryland or a court in which the attorney had been admitted.

Kennedy v. Bar Association also concluded that no tension exists between its prohibition against unauthorized practice of law and the lawyer's admission to the bar of a federal court in Maryland if the attorney (who is not admitted in Maryland) maintains his principal office for practice of law in Maryland:

"Kennedy may not utilize his admission to the bar of the federal court in Maryland, or his admission in Washington, D.C., as a shield against injunctive relief by asserting that he will operate a triage. He is not permitted to sort through clients who may present themselves at his Maryland office and represent only those whose legal matters would require suit or defense in a Washington, D.C. court or in the federal court in Maryland because the very acts of interview, analysis and explanation of legal rights constitute practicing law in Maryland. For an unadmitted person to do so on a regular basis from a Maryland principal office is the unauthorized practice of law in Maryland." 316 Md. at 666, 561 A.2d at 210.

Federal Practice in a State where the Lawyer is not Admitted. For a different view, arguing that the lawyer should be able to set up a permanent presence and office and law practice in a state without being admitted to that state if he limits his practice to federal issues, see William T. Barker, *Extrajurisdictional Practice By Lawyers*, 56 Bus. Law. 1501 (2001). The author reads federal supremacy law and *Sperry v. Florida ex rel. Florida Bar*, 373 U.S. 379, 83 S.Ct. 1322, 10 L.Ed.2d 428 (1963), very broadly. He argues that "federal law authorizes some forms of practice. As one would expect, federal supremacy precludes state restriction of such practice, leaving only the question of defining the scope of the practice authorized." 56

Bus. Law. 1501, 1536–37 (footnote omitted). He candidly admits that his argument is based on analogy:

> *Though there is scant authority* on the point, *I would think* the authority to practice before an agency includes planning advice: advising a client, based on the federal law administered by the agency admitting the practitioner, on what steps a client might take, under state law, to pursue agency proceedings with maximum benefit or prospect of success." 56 Bus. Law. 1501, 1540 (emphasis added).

The lawyer who is not admitted to practice in a state and who opens an office there and establishes a permanent presence is engaged in unauthorized practice, even if he limits his practice to federal issues *unless* he comes within the *Sperry* exemption, which is discussed later in this chapter.

The Restatement of the Law Governing Lawyers does not embrace Mr. Barker's argument. See Restatement of the Law Governing Lawyers § 3(2) *Jurisdictional Scope Of The Practice Of Law By A Lawyer* (2000), which provides that a lawyer admitted in one jurisdiction may practice "before a tribunal or administrative agency of another jurisdiction or the federal government in compliance with requirements for temporary or regular admission to practice before that tribunal or agency." This provision does not allow a lawyer who is not admitted in State #1 to open up an office in State #1 and put up a shingle that says, e.g., "Legal Practice admitted to Federal Income Tax Advice."

See also Ginsburg v. Kovrak, 392 Pa. 143, 139 A.2d 889 (1958). The court held that an injunction enjoining defendant, who was admitted to practice law in United States Supreme Court, the Court of Appeals of District of Columbia, and the United States District Courts of District of Columbia and Eastern District of Pennsylvania, but who was not admitted to practice in State court from practicing law in Philadelphia County or from advertis-ing that he practiced law or was authorized to practice law did not infringe upon any Federal rights guaranteed to defendant by either the statutes or Constitution of the United States.

Bluestein v. State Bar, 13 Cal.3d 162, 118 Cal.Rptr. 175, 529 P.2d 599 (1974) held that if a lawyer introduced an unlicensed person to his clients at a law office, informing these clients that the unlicensed person is an attorney in another state and has practiced law in Europe, and subsequently allowed the unlicensed person to consult with these clients without any supervision by a licensed lawyer, that action would constitute aiding and abetting the unlicensed person to practice law whether or not the unlicensed person in fact does advise a client in California regarding foreign law and notwithstanding the contention that the unlicensed person would be doing nothing but assisting the clients to obtain counsel in a foreign country

Ranta v. McCarney, 391 N.W.2d 161 (N.D.1986) held that out-of-state attorney not licensed to practice law in state could not recover compensation for services rendered in state. The court remanded that case to determine whether any fees related to practice of law conducted outside of the state.

Cleveland Bar Association v. Misch, 82 Ohio St.3d 256, 695 N.E.2d 244 (1998). The court issued an injunction against Ohio practice by an Ohio resident, who was admitted only in Illinois and in the federal court in Ohio. Pursuant to a "consulting agreement" with an Ohio firm, the performed extensive services in Ohio for various clients. This lawyer became a resident of Ohio in 1988, but took no steps to seek admission to the bar of Ohio by examination or on motion. Nor did he register under an Ohio Bar Rule. This lawyer did not maintain an office for the practice of law in Illinois. To the extent that the activities of this lawyer constituted the rendering of legal services in Ohio, he was engaged in the unauthorized practice of law.

El Gemayel, in fact, specifically distinguished another New York decision, *Spivak v. Sachs*,[8] which had held that a California attorney engaged in the unlawful practice of law by assisting an acquaintance in New York with her divorce. In so doing, the California attorney became substantially involved in the client's New York affairs, spending 14 days physically in New York attending meetings, reviewing drafts of a separation agreement, discussing the client's financial and custody problems, recommending a change in New York counsel and, based on his knowledge of New York and California law, rendering his opinion as to the proper jurisdiction for the divorce action and related marital and custody issues. The court concluded that these activities plainly constituted the "practice of law."

A controversial decision that adopts a view of unauthorized practice of law that makes life difficult for multistate law firms is *Birbrower, Montalbano, Condon & Frank, P.C. v. Superior Court (ESQ Business Services, Inc.)*.[9] That case found unauthorized practice in a fact pattern that has caused dread and tremors in all multi-jurisdictional law firms.[10]

Office Of Disciplinary Counsel v. Marcone, 855 A.2d 654 (Pa. 2004), held that a suspended attorney who maintained a law office within Commonwealth was engaged in the practice of law, and that conduct violated a prior Supreme Court order suspending attorney from the practice of law. No federal statute or local rule preempted Pennsylvania's regulation of a suspended attorney's ability to maintain a law office within Pennsylvania.

If a valid federal law authorizes the lawyer to practice in the state, then, under the supremacy clause, the state cannot bar the lawyer from practice. *Silverman v. Texas*, 405 F.2d 410 (5th Cir.1968), holding that an opinion of the Texas Bar committee interpreting its ethics rules to preclude a patent attorney enrolled by United States Commissioner of Patents, who was also a licensed practitioner in Texas, from listing himself both under 'attorneys' and 'patent attorney' in classified section of local telephone directory was invalid as in conflict with regulation of Patent Commissioner, pursuant to statute, permitting patent attorneys to list themselves in a classified telephone or city directory.

[8]*Spivak v. Sachs*, 16 N.Y.2d 163, 167, 263 N.Y.S.2d 953, 955, 211 N.E.2d 329, 331 (1965).

[9]*Birbrower, Montalbano, Condon & Frank, P.C. v. Superior Court (ESQ Business Services, Inc.)*, 17 Cal.4th 119, 70 Cal.Rptr.2d 304, 949 P.2d 1 (Cal.1998).

[10]In *Florida Bar v. Rapoport*, 845 So.2d 874 (Fla.2003), *cert. denied*, 540 U.S. 967, 124 S.Ct. 441, 157 L.Ed.2d 313 (2003), the Florida Supreme Court enjoined Rapoport, a D.C. lawyer, from representing parties in Florida securities arbitration proceedings and advertising his services in a Florida newspaper. The court found that Rapoport was a "nonlawyer" [as defined by Rule Regulating the Florida Bar 10-2.1(c)] who was performing the traditional tasks of a lawyer. He received no hearing, but the court held that he had adequate notice and opportunity to be heard, because he failed to raise any factual dispute. The two dissenting judges argued that the court denied Rapoport his constitutional right to due process. Rapoport had undergone three-vessel coronary artery bypass surgery and was in recovery at the time of the motion for summary judg-

A New York firm represented ESQ, a California corporation, in claims it had against Tandem Computers, Inc., relating to a software and marketing contract. California law governed the contract, and New York firm partners traveled to California for a few briefs trips on several occasions. The dispute ultimately was settled, and the firm asked for the million dollar fee due under its agreement with ESQ. The client refused to pay, the lower court upheld the refusal, and the California Supreme Court affirmed over a vigorous dissent because it said that the New York law firm was engaged in the unauthorized practice of law in California. Commentators have vigorously attacked the decision.[11]

The court acknowledged that enforcement of its unauthorized practice rule in this case was not necessary to protect a naive client from an incompetent lawyer. But, said the court, each state has power to decide who can practice there, and that is the end of the inquiry. The New York lawyers lost their fee because they were physically present in California when they advised the California company about an impending arbitration proceeding governed by California law. However, the court warned that even non-physical presence in California—such as the New York lawyers' communications with the California client by fax from New York, by email from New York, and by telephone from New York—could constitute unauthorized practice of law. The court also cautioned that even if the New York counsel had associated with California counsel, that association would not have cured the violation of the unauthorized practice laws. The court did

---

ment. He was representing himself, had asserted there were material issues of fact to be tried, and had asked for a continuance, which the Court had denied. "The right to be heard is fundamental," the dissenters argued, "and Rapoport has been denied this right."

In *Ford Motor Credit Co. v. Sperry*, 344 Ill.App.3d 1068, 280 Ill.Dec. 9, 801 N.E.2d 954 (2003), Sperry alleged that Ford had engaged in consumer fraud, a charge the court rejected. Ford then sought its attorneys' fees from Sperry for defending against the charge. The court denied the request because the law firm representing Ford had not registered as a professional corporation under Illinois Supreme Court Rule 721(c). Hence, although all the firm's lawyers were properly licensed in Illinois, the firm itself was ineligible to practice in Illinois and hence could not receive a fee award.

In *Preston v. University of Arkansas for Medical Sciences*, 354 Ark. 666, 128 S.W.3d 430 (2003), plaintiffs had filed a malpractice complaint against several doctors associated with a medical school. The plaintiffs' lawyers were from Oklahoma and had not applied for pro hac vice admission. The Arkansas Supreme Court held that the complaint was thus a nullity—a very strict remedy that enforces unauthorized practice in a way that directly hurts the innocent client. The Court did not even toll the statute of limitations, which had now run. It sounds like the medical malpractice case will now be for lawyer malpractice, so the client has to begin anew with different lawyers.

[11]*See, e.g.,* Stephen Gillers, *Protecting Their Own,* THE AMERICAN LAWYER, Nov. 1998, at 118.

concede that payment for the New York lawyers' services might be due for services rendered to ESQ in New York, but only if those could be severed from the rest of the agreement.[12]

Other cases such as *Fought & Co. v. Steel Engineering and Erection, Inc.*,[13] reject this parochial California rule. The case involved an Oregon firm acting as general counsel to an international client that built an airport on Maui. The client won a judgment against the state of Hawaii in a case handled by lawyers licensed there, but the Oregon firm sought a portion of the statutory attorney's fees for work it did in aiding that firm in preparing for the litigation. The court understood that making it impossible for mainland firms to collect fees for work relating to Hawaii would make it more difficult for Hawaiian clients to get high quality legal services at competitive rates. Even applying the standards set forth in *Birbrower*, the Court said the Oregon firm had retained local counsel for work done in Hawaii. It could be seen as assisting Hawaiian counsel and thus not barred from collecting a fee.

The Restatement of the Law Governing Lawyers also rejects *Birbrower* as "unduly restrictive."[14] The test that the Restatement proposes makes more sense and satisfactorily protects the interests of the client in competent representation. First, if the lawyer is admitted in State #1, she may practice law anywhere

---

[12]Subsequently, the California legislature reversed part of *Birbrower*, but it did so only on the narrow facts of the case and only for a short time. The New York lawyers represented the California corporation in an arbitration proceeding, and the new statute allows a party to an arbitration proceeding to be represented by an out-of-state lawyer. Cal. Code Civ. Proc., § 1282.4 (1999). This statute was automatically repealed on January 1, 2001. See § 1282.4(j). The Financial Industry Regulatory Authority has amended its arbitration and mediation code to allow representation by attorneys licensed anywhere in the United States and by non-attorneys, subject to state regulations on the unauthorized practice of law. *See* FINRA, Regulatory Notice 07-57: Representation of Parties in Arbitration and Mediation (Nov. 2007).

[13]*Fought & Co. v. Steel Engineering and Erection, Inc.*, 87 Hawai'i 37, 951 P.2d 487 (Hawaii 1998). *See also, e.g., Colmar, Ltd. v. Fremantlemedia*

North America, Inc., 344 Ill.App.3d 977, 983, 801 N.E.2d 1017, 1022, 280 Ill.Dec. 72, 77 (Ill.App. 1 Dist., 2003), which rejected *Birbrower*. It held that the fact that the lawyer who represented a movie distributor in an arbitration with a movie producer was not admitted to practice in the state where arbitration was conducted was irrelevant to the validity of the arbitration award and did not constitute unauthorized practice of law. The court reasoned that the arbitration was reasonably related to the lawyer's regular representation of the distributor in the lawyer's home state; arbitration did not involve issues specific to the law of the state where the arbitration was conducted; the arbitration rules permitted party to be represented by a nonlawyer; and there was no arbitration procedure that corresponded to *pro hac vice* admission.

[14]Restatement of the Law Governing Lawyers, Third, § 3 (Official Draft 2000), Reporter's Note, Comment *e*.

within State #1. Second, she may practice before any tribunal or administrative agency of any other state or the federal government if she complies with the temporary or regular admission rules of that tribunal or agency. For example, she may be admitted *pro hac vice*.[15] Third, she may practice "within a jurisdiction

---

[15]**Pro Hac Vice Admission for Litigation.** Lawyers who are litigating in court but who are not admitted in a particular state typically ask the tribunal for admission for the purposes of the particular case. Lawyers who give advice, and aid in putting together various transactions have no procedure to become admitted for purposes of a particular transaction.

In *Paciulan v. George*, 229 F.3d 1226 (9th Cir.2000), the court upheld the constitutionality of a California rule permitting non-resident lawyers to appear *pro hac vice*, but not permitting lawyers without California licenses who resided in California to appear *pro hac vice*. The Ninth Circuit explained that a state has a significant interest in not letting its residents secure a license elsewhere and then regularly practice in California. Granting non-residents occasional *pro hac vice* status is not inconsistent with that interest. The court rejected plaintiff's argument that the rule violated the Privileges and Immunities Clause, the Fourteenth Amendment's Privileges or Immunities Clause, the First Amendment; and the residents' property rights.

Admission in Federal Court. A lawyer litigating in federal court has to be admitted to the bar of that court, either permanently or pro hac vice. *See, e.g., Office of Disciplinary Counsel v. Scuro*, 36 Ohio St.3d 205, 522 N.E.2d 572 (Ohio 1988)(per curiam), where a lawyer was admitted in Ohio, but not in the federal court for the Western District of Texas. He practiced law for years in the W. D. Tex., in violation of the laws of that district and of Ohio and of Texas. The court suspended him for six months.

If a lawyer is admitted in State #1 (but not State #2) and she is also admitted in the federal court that sits in State #2, she can practice law before the federal court in state #2 as long as her practice is limited to cases filed in the federal court for State #2.

Some federal courts, before admitting a lawyer to practice before the federal court, require her to be admitted to the state where the federal court sits. The Restatement criticizes this practice as creating an unnecessary barrier to entry. "Local rules in some few federal districts additionally require admission to the bar of the sitting state as a condition of admission to the federal court. The requirement is inconsistent with the federal nature of the court's business." Restatement of the Law Governing Lawyers, Third, § 3 (Official Draft 2000), Comment *f*.

Admission Before Federal Agencies. The rules of some federal agencies allow nonlawyers to appear before them (*e.g.,* the Patent Office). The Supreme Court, relying on the Supremacy Clause, has overturned state rules to the contrary. *Sperry v. Florida ex rel. Florida Bar*, 373 U.S. 379, 83 S.Ct. 1322, 10 L.Ed.2d 428 (1963).

Of course, there must be a federal rule or statute that authorizes the practice. If there is no such rule, the state can enforce its unauthorized practice rules. The general rule is that a lawyer cannot establish a permanent presence in a state without being admitted to that state, even if he puts up a shingle that says, "practice limited to advice on federal law." *Office Of Disciplinary Counsel v. Marcone*, 855 A.2d 654 (Pa. 2004), holding that a suspended attorney who maintained a law office within Commonwealth was engaged in the practice of law, and that conduct violated a prior Supreme Court order suspending attorney from the practice of law. No federal statute

in which the lawyer is not admitted to the extent that the lawyer's activities in the matter arise out or are otherwise reasonably related to the lawyer's practice" under parts (1) or (2), above.[16]

For example, assume that Lawyer is admitted in State A and has an office there. Some of her clients are residents of State B, where Lawyer is not admitted. She may represent these residents of State B and research the law of State B, but she may not open a law office in State B for the general practice of law in that state unless she is first admitted there.[17]

Given these same facts, let us assume that Lawyer also represents a regulated utility ("Utility") in State A near the border with State B. Sometimes, to service her client, Lawyer must research the law of State B as well as the law of State A and federal law. Lawyer may do that as well as "travel to State B to deal with governmental officials with respect to environmental issues arising out of Utility's activities."[18] In fact, according to the Restatement, she may represent Utility in rate applications in other states, even though that will involve her in "extensive presence and activities in each of the other states until the necessary rates have been established." She may retain local counsel or conduct "those activities in the other states on behalf of Utility."[19]

In the above example, let us assume that Lawyer represents a different utility, located in the southeastern United States. This utility, Utility #1, is planning a hostile takeover of Utility #2, located in the Northeast. Lawyer is admitted in California. Lawyer will have to be physically present in a number of different states in which she is not admitted. She will also represent Utility #1

---

or local rule preempted Pennsylvania's regulation of a suspended attorney's ability to maintain a law office within Pennsylvania.

If federal rules allow the practice, they are supreme over state law. *In re Desilets*, 291 F.3d 925 (6th Cir 2002), holding that a lawyer licensed to practice law in Texas could practice bankruptcy law before bankruptcy court in Western District of Michigan, without being admitted to Michigan state court, where lawyer was eligible for admission to bar of Western District of Michigan and was properly admitted pursuant to local rule.

Casey v. F.D.I.C., 583 F.3d 586 (8th Cir. 2009), cert. denied, 2010 WL 265883 (U.S. 2010). Homeowners sued their mortgage lenders, claiming that fees charged for preparing loan-related documents violated Missouri's statu-tory prohibition on the unauthorized practice of law. The Court held that a federal regulation, governing federal savings association lenders, preempted Missouri's state unauthorized practice of law statute.

[16]Restatement of the Law Governing Lawyers, Third, § 3 (Official Draft 2000).

[17]Restatement of the Law Governing Lawyers, Third (Official Draft 2000), at § 3, Comment *e*, Illustration 1.

[18]Restatement of the Law Governing Lawyers, Third (Official Draft 2000), at § 3, Comment *e*, Illustration 2.

[19]Restatement of the Law Governing Lawyers, Third (Official Draft 2000), at § 3, Comment *e*, Illustration 3.

before at least one federal agency in Washington, DC. "Given the multistate and federal nature of the legal work, Lawyer and other members of Lawyer's firm may represent Utility as requested."[20]

Another practical example illustrates the Restatement's rejection of unauthorized practice rules that simply do not reflect the way law is practiced today. Assume that Lawyer is admitted in Illinois and drafts a will and estate plan for Client A, in Illinois. Later, Client A moves to Florida, and requests Lawyer to draft a codicil to A's will. Lawyer does so and visits Client A in Florida to obtain the necessary signatures. Then Client A introduces Lawyer to Client B, also in Florida. Client B also asks Lawyer to draft an estate plan for him, and she does so, conducting legal research in Illinois and conferring with Client B by telephone and letter. Lawyer then travels to Florida so that Client B and the necessary witnesses can sign the documents. The Restatement concludes: "Lawyer's activities in Florida on behalf of both A and B were permissible."[21]

In *Spivak*, the court, while finding unauthorized practice, offered a little comfort to the modern lawyer whose practice frequently crosses state lines. The court acknowledged that, given "the numerous multi-state transactions and relationships of modern times, we cannot penalize every instance in which an attorney from another State comes into our State for conferences or negotiations relating to a New York client and a transaction somehow tied to New York."[22] The Restatement of the Law Governing Lawyers should be influential in persuading courts not to interpret vague criminal statutes drafted in an earlier era to create complex entry barriers to multistate legal practice that are not necessary to protect clients from incompetent legal representation. Moreover, restrictive interpretation of unauthorized practice statutes may, at first, appear to protect in-state lawyers from out of state competition, but it does so at a substantial cost: the Balkanization of the legal profession. These in-state lawyers who are protected from out-of-state competition will find themselves precluded from practicing in other states, as these other states respond to compensatory trade barriers.

In 2002, the MJP Commission presented its recommendations to the House of Delegates and the ABA in August amended Rule 5.5 to address multijurisdictional practice of law issues. The following sections examine the new language of this Rule.

---

[20] Restatement of the Law Governing Lawyers, Third (Official Draft 2000), at § 3, Comment *e*, Illustration 4.

[21] Restatement of the Law Governing Lawyers, Third (Official Draft 2000), at § 3, Comment *e*, Illustration 5.

[22] *Spivak v. Sachs*, 16 N.Y.2d 163, 168, 263 N.Y.S.2d 953, 956, 211 N.E.2d 329, 331 (1965) (citations omitted).

§ 5.5–2(b) Establishing a Systematic and Continuous Presence in Another State.

Rule 5.5(a) states that a "lawyer shall not practice law in a jurisdiction in violation of the regulation of the legal profession in that jurisdiction . . . .." This provision acknowledges that states may adopt and apply their own unauthorized practice of law rules and lawyers are expected to follow those rules.

Rule 5.5(b) prohibits a lawyer from establishing "an office or other systematic or continuous presence" in another jurisdiction for the purposes of delivering legal services. The notion of unauthorized practice involves prohibiting those that are not licensed to practice law in a jurisdiction from delivering legal services to the citizen of that jurisdiction. In all fifty states, an out-of-state lawyer may not open a permanent law office and establish a continuous presence of practicing law in that jurisdiction. A lawyer who seeks to establish a permanent presence in another state must either become licensed in that state or open an office with a lawyer who is licensed to practice law in that state.

Rule 5.5(b) also prohibits a lawyer from holding himself out as licensed in a jurisdiction, or making a misrepresentation about the state of licensure, when that in fact is not the case. Such conduct would also implicate a violation of Rule 7.1 (false and misleading statements regarding a lawyer's services) and Rule 8.4(c) (engaging in conduct that involves dishonesty and misrepresentation). Rule 5.5 makes it clear that lawyers need to be completely accurate about their jurisdiction of licensure.

§ 5.5–2(c) Providing Legal Services on a Temporary Basis in Another State.

Of all of the provisions in Rule 5.5, the most important one for the vast majority of lawyers is the provision that authorizes lawyers to offer temporary legal services in another jurisdiction.[23] Under Rule 5.5(c), a lawyer in good standing may offer legal services in another state on a temporary basis in four situations.

First, the lawyer may associate with local counsel and require that the local lawyer actively participate in the representation.[24] Prior to the adoption of new Rule 5.5, many lawyers associated with local counsel because they felt that it would be difficult for the client or the local bar authorities to complain if the out-of-state lawyer used a local lawyer. The policy underlying this exception is clear: when the out-of-state lawyer hires a local lawyer,

---

[23]Rule 5.5 does not define temporary legal services. "Services may be 'temporary' even though the lawyer provides services in this jurisdiction on a recurring basis, or for an extended period of time, as when the lawyer is representing a client in a single lengthy negotiation or litigation." Rule 5.5, Comment 6.

[24]Rule 5.5(c)(1).

the client and the public are protected.[25] Of course, before a lawyer can associate with local counsel, the lawyer would need to meet the requirements of Rule 1.5(e) (division of fees between lawyers not in the same firm), which include a responsibility to inform the client of the arrangement between the local counsel and the out-of-state lawyer.

Second, the lawyer may practice law on a temporary basis in another jurisdiction if the representation is "related to a pending or potential proceeding before a tribunal" in which the lawyer is authorized or expects to be authorized to represent the client.[26] This exception is based upon the longstanding practice of *pro hac vice* admission of lawyers for one time only. When a lawyer seeks to represent a client in a litigation matter and the lawyer is not licensed to practice law in the state, the lawyer may apply to the court for *pro hac vice* admission. Past practice permitted a lawyer who sought and received such admission to generally perform all matters necessary to the litigation in the state where the tribunal was located even though the lawyer was not licensed to practice law in that jurisdiction. However, Rule 5.5(b) is more permissive; it allows a lawyer to perform work in the other state just on the anticipation that the lawyer will be admitted *pro hac vice*.[27] Additionally, it protects subordinate lawyers who work on the case but do not expect to appear before the tribunal.[28] The policy underlying this exception involves the existence of a tribunal that can monitor the lawyer's representation of a client. Modern litigation depends upon limited admission, thus the Rule removes any possible ambiguity with respect to litigation practice.

Third, the lawyer may participate in a pending or potential arbitration, mediation, or other ADR proceeding in the state where the lawyer is licensed or another state if the proceeding is reasonably related to or arises out of a representation in a jurisdiction where the lawyer is licensed to practice law.[29] This exception could be named the anti-*Birbrower* rule and is designed to permit lawyers to follow clients to other jurisdictions to perform legal work on arbitrations, mediations, and other ADR proceedings. Often, lawyers draft agreements that implement arbitration or mediation in neutral jurisdictions. Because these

---

[25] Rule 5.5, Comment 8.

[26] Rule 5.5(c)(2).

[27] The Comments provide several examples of the type of work that may fall under preadmission conduct: "meetings with the client, interviews of potential witnesses, and review of document." Rule 5.5, Comment 10.

[28] Rule 5.5, Comment 11 (authoriz-ing subordinate lawyers to perform "research, review documents, and attend meetings").

[29] Rule 5.5(c)(3). For a definition of reasonably related, see Rule 5.5, Comment 14. Accord, *Colmar, Ltd. v. Fremantlemadia North America, Inc.*, 344 Ill.App.3d 977, 983, 801 N.E.2d 1017, 1022, 280 Ill.Dec. 72, 77 (Ill.App. 1 Dist., 2003).

ADR proceedings often do not require the involvement of lawyers, it would be a strange result to find the participation of the lawyers to be the unauthorized practice of law. However, if the mediation is court-annexed or sponsored, the lawyer will need to seek *pro hac vice* admission to perform work for the client in the ADR proceeding.[30]

Fourth, lawyers may represent a client in a matter in another state, not covered under *pro hac vice* admission or not part of an ADR proceeding, when that matter is closely and reasonably related to a representation in a state in which they are licensed to practice law.[31] This provision is a broad catch-all, but it also embodies some of the principles that the Restatement promoted.[32] Too many facets of today's practice of law depend upon parties, funding, or property that is located in multiple states.

These four exceptions provide a safe harbor for temporary practice out of state. Although these exceptions represent a bold step towards new latitude in multijurisdictional practice of law,[33] they recognize that such activity is taking place whether or not bar authorities sanction it. Thus, the ABA sought to regulate this behavior and limit it to instances of temporary law practice, rather than allow it to go unregulated.

Despite the breadth of the four exceptions for temporary practice under Model Rule 5.5, the exceptions proved to be too narrow to address the out-of-state practice problems created by Hurricane Katrina, which made landfall in August, 2005. After this natural disaster, the ABA formed a Task Force on Hurricane Katrina.[34] The Task Force recommended that the unauthorized practice of law rules be suspended to allow lawyers to help the many organizations that were trying to assist the affected public and to rebuild the damaged areas. Initially, the Task Force proposed a new Model Rule 5.8, but it later refocused its efforts on drafting a Model Court rule that could be implemented by the courts of the affected jurisdiction.

In February 2007, the ABA House of Delegates adopted a one

---

[30]Rule 5.5, Comment 12.

[31]Rule 5.5(c)(4).

[32]Restatement of the Law Governing Lawyers, Third (Official Draft 2000), at § 3.

[33]A few states may take a narrower stance on multijurisdictional practice than the ABA Model Rules. *See* Wyoming Rule of Prof. Conduct, Rule 5.5, *noted in* 22 ABA/BNA MANUAL ON PROFESSIONAL CONDUCT, Current Reports News 241 (May 17, 2006). There are only three instances when an out-of-state lawyer may practice in Wyoming: practicing as in-house counsel, providing legal services authorized by federal law, or representing a client in a case with the active participation of local counsel (provided that the appearance is authorized by law or a court order).

[34]*See* ABA Standing Committee on Client Protection, Report 104 to the ABA House of Delegates, Revised (Jan. 29, 2007), available at *http://www.abanet.org/cpr/jclr/katrina_report.pdf*.

sentence addition to Comment 14 of Model Rule 5.5 and a Model Court Rule on the Provision of Legal Services Following a Determination of Major Disaster.[35] The language in Comment 14 makes clear that lawyers from other areas who wish to provide pro bono services on a temporary basis in a state affected by a major disaster as well as lawyers from the affected state who wish to practice on a temporary basis in other states should look to the Model Court Rule on provision of legal services following a major disaster. The Model Court Rule on the Provision of Legal Services Following the Determination of Major Disaster provides that courts in a state suffering a major disaster and courts in other jurisdictions may make a finding that a determination of a major disaster must be made to ensure provision of legal services to the affected area and for lawyers affected by the disaster.[36]

One aspect of this rule is to allow lawyers who are in good standing, licensed to practice outside of the affected area to provide legal services to those residents who have moved out of the affected jurisdiction. Such legal services must be pro bono and supervised "an established not-for-profit bar association, *pro bono* program or legal services program or through such organization(s) specifically designated by this Court."[37] Another aspect of the rule is to allow lawyers from the affected jurisdiction to offer legal services from a jurisdiction outside of their licensure.[38] When the representation involves a court matter, the lawyer must follow the pro hac vice rules, but the costs shall be waived. The rule provides that courts shall have the power to end such practice 60 days after announcing that the effects of the major disaster are no longer present. And, the rule requires that lawyers register with the local bar within 30 days of providing legal services under the rule.

Hurricane Katrina had a significant impact on the legal system and legal rights of the residents of Alabama, Louisiana, and Mississippi. The jurisdictional limitations on lawyers from within and outside of the affected states potentially limited the legal work that could occur. The changes that the ABA adopted in 2007 address the need to loosen jurisdictional limitations so that lawyers can participate in the recovery and rebuilding efforts of the country. The difficulties of addressing such jurisdictional rules in the context of a disaster, whether caused by acts of

---

[35] The model court rule is reprinted in Appendix M of the Lawyer's edition of this book.

[36] Provision (a) of the Model Court Rule on the Provision of Legal Services Following the Determining of Major Disaster.

[37] Provision (b) of the Model Court Rule on the Provision of Legal Services Following the Determining of Major Disaster.

[38] Provision (c) of the Model Court Rule on the Provision of Legal Services Following the Determining of Major Disaster.

nature, acts of war, or acts of terror, require a well thought out rule considered in advance.

§ 5.5–2(d) Representing Entities in Another State.

Rule 5.5(d) covers two specific situations where lawyers may offer either continuous or temporary legal services in a state in which they are not licensed apart from Rules 5.5(b) and (c).

First, a lawyer in good standing, who is an employee, may represent his or her organizational employer throughout the country. In other words, in-house corporate lawyers may practice law on behalf of the corporation in jurisdictions in which they are not licensed to practice law.[39] The reason underlying this rule is that corporations and their affiliates and other entities such as government entities hire lawyer employees for the sole purpose of having the lawyer represent the entity. The Comment states:

> The lawyer's ability to represent the employer outside the jurisdiction in which the lawyer is licensed generally serves the interests of the employer and does not create an unreasonable risk to the client and others because the employer is well situated to assess the lawyer's qualifications and the quality of the lawyer's work.[40]

The lawyer as employee exception is limited to representing the employer, not other employees of the entity.[41] And, the lawyer cannot represent the entity in litigation unless the out-of-state lawyer seeks pro hac vice admission under the rules of the court where the litigation is pending.[42] Based upon these two principles, one could take the position that an out-of-state in-house lawyer should not file an evaluation for use by a third person because that third person should not be asked to rely upon the legal advice of a lawyer who is not licensed in the jurisdiction in question.

The ABA's passage of Rule 5.5(d) authorizing corporate lawyers from representing the entity throughout the country appears to parallel the developments in a national practice of law. However, the states have responded by enacting several requirements for out-of-state corporate attorneys who represent the corporate entity.[43] These licensing regulations may include: (1) registration with the state bar, (2) payment of an initial licensing fee, (3) payment of annual renewal fees, (4) compliance with a character and fitness inquiry, and (5) compliance with annual continuing legal education in the state. The failure to comply with these regula-

---

[39]Delaware's version of Rule 5.5 permits in-house lawyers who are licensed in a foreign country to perform nonlitigation work for the corporation. *See* Del. Rule of Prof. Conduct, Rule 5.5(d) (Jan. 7, 2008), *noted in* 24 ABA/BNA MANUAL OF PROF. CONDUCT, CURRENT REPORTS 66 (Feb. 6, 2008).

[40]Rule 5.5, Comment 16.

[41]Rule 5.5, Comment 16.

[42]Rule 5.5(d)(1).

[43]*See* http://www.abanet.org/cpr/mjp/in-house_rules.pdf (chart listing states with licensure requirements).

tions will subject the corporate lawyer to a claim of unauthorized practice of law and subject the lawyer to discipline.[44]

On one hand, one could view these developments as a natural extension of state bars to control those out-of-state lawyers who are practicing in their jurisdiction. On the other hand, it is difficult to see how they protect the public as the multinational corporation is the client and they have full knowledge of the licensure of their employees. Additionally, a high percentage of corporations doing business in a state either have employees who are licensed or have hired outside law firms to represent their interests. So, do these rules really protect the corporate entity?

Thus, these regulations look anticompetitive and enacted primarily for the collection of the annual dues. And, in many of these states, the lawyers still do not have full local bar membership and therefore they cannot represent the corporation in court or prepare opinions for use by third parties.

In 2008, the ABA followed the states that had implemented in-house out-of-state counsel licensure with the promulgation of the ABA Model Rule for the Registration of In-House Counsel.[45] Perhaps the in-house lawyers were better off before the passage of Rule 5.5(d).

Second, a lawyer in good standing may provide legal services in a jurisdiction where the lawyer is not licensed to practice law if authorized by federal or other law.[46] This covers such situations as areas of practice where the federal government may control or regulate the practice and therefore there is a federal preemption claim. It may also include internal rules that permit government lawyers to practice law on behalf of the government as long as they are licensed in one state.

§ 5.5–3 UNAUTHORIZED PRACTICE OF LAW: DEFINING THE "PRACTICE OF LAW"?

§ 5.5–3(a) Introduction

In the United States, it is commonly understood that one needs to be licensed by a state to practice law within that state.

---

[44]*See Corporate Counsel Must Be Mindful of Proliferating State Licensing Regulations*, 25 ABA/BNA Law. Man. Prof. Conduct 93 (Feb. 18, 2009) (noting that in five years the number of states requiring licensing of in-house lawyers has increased from 14 to 32). Of course, these corporate lawyers must keep their bar licenses valid in their home state or else face discipline. *See, e.g., In re DeBacher*, 184 P.3d 506 (Okla. 2008); *Hipwell v. Kentucky Bar Ass'n*, 267 S.W.3d 682 (Ky. 2008) (corporate in-house counsel suspended for one year).

[45]*See* ABA Model Rule for the Registration of In-House Counsel (2008) (requiring registration within 180 days after employment begins in state).

[46]The defintition of "other law" includes "statute, court rule, executive regulatoin or judicial precedent." Rule 5.5, Comment 18.

However, in Europe and most places around the world, the concept of "unauthorized practice of law" is alien. In the United States, one does not need an M.B.A. (Master of Business Administration) to "practice business." The M.B.A. may be useful, and some employers may prefer to hire those who have it, but one can engage in business without the degree. Many foreign countries treat much of the practice of law the way the United States treats the practice of business.[1]

But in this country, only licensed professionals can legally practice law. What constitutes the unauthorized practice of law is a matter of state law. The Model Rules, like the Model Code, merely incorporate by reference these local rules, case law, and statutes.[2] The Rules leave it at that. The Model Code asserted that it was "neither necessary nor desirable to attempt the formulation of a single, specific definition of what constitutes the practice of law."[3]

§ 5.5–3(b) A Hodgepodge of Case Law

State law definitions of unauthorized practice are a hodgepodge, varied and often confusing.[4] A 1994 ABA survey indicated that 13

[Section 5.5–3]

[1] In France, for example, anyone, without any restrictions of citizenship, residency, or even training, can legally offer legal advice. Unregulated advisors include law departments of banks that offer below cost legal service in order to attract business, the law departments of accounting firms, telephone services that offer legal advice, and so forth. These people are not subject to any regulations, except that they may not hold themselves out to be a member of one of the regulated professions, such as a *conseil juridique* (legal advisor). Members of one of the regulated professions of law can render any form of legal advice and appear before some lower courts. Only an *avocat* is allowed to appear before higher courts. *See generally* MISSION D'ETUDE SUR L'EUROPE ET LES PROFESSIONS DU DROIT: RAPPORT (Juin 1989).

The "Consultation Paper on the Review of the Regulatory Framework for Legal Services in England and Wales" (March 2004) suggests substantial changes in this area of the law. Among other things, this report would allow banks to offer legal services to their customers. *See* http://www.legal-services-review.org.uk.

[2] Rule 5.5(a), Rule 5.5, Comment 2. *See also* DR 3-101(A); EC 3-5. Restatement of the Law Governing Lawyers, Third, § 4 (Official Draft 2000).

The anticompetitive aspects of the unauthorized practice rules are thoughtfully discussed in several important articles, which include, Thomas D. Morgan, *The Evolving Concept of Professional Responsibility*, 90 HARV. L. REV. 702, 707–12 (1977); Barlow Christensen, *The Unauthorized Practice of Law: Do Good Fences Really Make Good Neighbors or Even Good Sense?*, 1980 AM. BAR FOUNDATION RESEARCH J. 159; Deborah Rhode, *Policing the Professional Monopoly: A Constitutional and Empirical Analysis of Unauthorized Practice Prohibitions*, 34 STAN. L. REV. 1 (1981); Jonathan Rose, *Unauthorized Practice of Law in Arizona: A Legal and Political Problem that Won't Go Away*, 34 ARIZ. ST. L.J. 585 (2002).

[3] EC 3-5.

[4] *See* Deborah Rhode, *Policing the Professional Monopoly: A*

jurisdictions have adopted *no* definition of the "practice of law," and three others did not respond to the survey. Of the 35 jurisdictions that reported that they had a definition, one could find that definition only in the case law in 28 of the 35 jurisdictions. Eight jurisdictions reported that their enforcement mechanism was either inactive or non-existent.[5]

If a person appears in court on behalf of another person, that appearance has historically been treated as constituting the practice of law. But the practice of law is not limited to litigation. Indeed, many lawyers rarely step inside a court room, unless they are defending their own traffic ticket. When lawyers give transactional advice and engage in similar non-court representation of clients, the cases hold that they are practicing law.[6] Beyond such general statements, one finds that the devil is in the details, and it is difficult to find universal agreement in the case law.

Even the case law within a single jurisdiction has sometimes appeared to throw its hands into the air and given up trying to define what constitutes the "practice of law" and what Rule 5.5 therefore actually prohibits. The Connecticut Supreme Court, for example, defined the "practice of law" by using, in the definition, the term to be defined. It said that the "practice of law" is the "performance of any acts by persons not admitted as attorneys, in or out of court, commonly understood to be the practice of law."[7] The Arizona Supreme Court once said that "it is impossible to lay down an exhaustive definition of 'the practice of law' by attempting to enumerate every conceivable act performed by lawyers in the normal course of their work."[8] Courts in Texas have admitted that "a comprehensive definition of just what qualifies as the

---

Constitutional and Empirical Analysis of Unauthorized Practice Prohibitions, 34 STAN.L.REV. 1 (1981).

[5] ABA Standing Committee on Lawyer's Responsibility for Client Protection, 1994 Survey and Related Materials on the Unauthorized Practice of Law/Nonlawyer Practice 5 to 6 (ABA 1996). *See also*, ABA Commission on Nonlawyer Practice, Nonlawyer Activity in Law-Related Situations: A Report with Recommendations (ABA Aug. 1995).

[6] Restatement of the Law Governing Lawyers, Third (Official Draft 2000), at § 3, Comment *e*.

[7] *Grievance Committee v. Payne*, 128 Conn. 325, 330, 22 A.2d 623, 626 (1941).

[8] *State Bar of Arizona v. Arizona Land Title & Trust Co.*, 90 Ariz. 76, 87, 366 P.2d 1, 8–9 (1961), *modified*, 91 Ariz. 293, 371 P.2d 1020 (1962).

The Arizona situation is particularly interesting because, in 1985, the state legislature repealed the statute prohibiting the unauthorized practice of law. Nonetheless, the state supreme court continues to enforce the prohibition by use of its contempt powers against disbarred lawyers. *In re Creasy*, 198 Ariz. 539, 12 P.3d 214 (2000). In *Creasy* the court found the previously disbarred lawyer guilty of contempt for violating his order of disbarment. This disbarred lawyer had acted in a private arbitration unconnected to any judicial proceeding. It is unclear if the state court would enjoin nonlawyers

practice of law is 'impossible,' and 'each case must be decided upon its own particular facts.' "[9] And, sometimes the courts disagree with the local bar authorities as to what constitutes the practice of law.[10]

In general it may be said that a person practices law when he or she *applies the law to the facts of a particular case.* "Functionally, the practice of law relates to the rendition of service for others that calls for the professional judgment of a lawyer. The essence of the professional judgment of the lawyer is his educated ability to relate the general body of and philosophy of law to a specified legal problem of a client . . . ."[11]

Delegating Duties to Paralegals. The lawyer may delegate various tasks to secretaries, law clerks, or paralegals, and, so long as the lawyer supervises the work and is ultimately responsible for it, there is no unauthorized practice.[12] Lawyers nowadays routinely delegate repetitive legal tasks, such as keeping track of calendar calls, to paralegals in order to keep costs down. The lawyer must supervise, but the lawyer does not commit per se neglect if the paralegal makes a mistake, as long as the lawyer exercised reasonable supervision.[13]

---

who had not earlier been disbarred and subject to the jurisdiction of the court. Jonathan Rose, *Unauthorized Practice of Law in Arizona: A Legal and Political Problem That Won't Go Away*, 34 ARIZ. ST. L. J. 585, 585 n.2 (2002), analyzes *Creasy.* The court explicitly did not reach the question of the "extent of our power to regulate 'practitioners' who are not and have never been lawyers." *In re Creasy*, 198 Ariz. 539, 541, 12 P.3d 214, 216.

[9]*Unauthorized Practice of Law Committee v. Parsons Technology, Inc.*, 1999 WL 47235, *4 (N.D.Tex.1999), *vacated and remanded*, 179 F.3d 956 (5th Cir.1999), quoting *Palmer v. Unauthorized Practice Committee*, 438 S.W.2d 374, 376 (Tex.Civ.App.-Houston 1969)(no writ).

[10]*Countrywide Home Loans Inc. v. Kentucky Bar Association*, 113 S.W.3d 105 (Ky. 2003), rejected a Kentucky Bar Association advisory opinion arguing that performance of a real estate closing by a lay closing agent is the unauthorized practice of law. The Court understood the "closing" to be the "final event" where all parties

"gather around a table to complete their transaction by signing and exchanging documents and transferring funds." The record showed that 95% of the documents are identical in all closings; largely for regulatory reasons, none are subject to negotiation or change. Other aspects of real estate work are different, e.g., preparation of a title commitment letter and the preparation of deeds and mortgages. The Court held, a closing is largely ministerial and involves little or no legal judgment. A layperson may conduct it without violating the prohibition against the unauthorized practice of law.

[11]EC 3-5. *See, e.g., State v. Winder*, 42 A.D.2d 1039, 348 N.Y.S.2d 270 (1973) (no unauthorized practice in distribution of do-it-yourself divorce kits with forms and instructions because the kit did not contain personalized advice applied to a particular person).

[12]Rule 5.5, Comment 2; EC 3-6.

[13]*Pincay v. Andrews*, 389 F.3d 853 (9th Cir.2004) (en banc).

"[T] the delegation of such tasks to spe-

Thus, *Pincay v. Andrews*,[14] the court held that a lawyer's reliance on a paralegal calendaring clerk to determine the deadline to file a notice of appeal may be excusable neglect from which a court can grant relief if the subordinate miscalculates the time period.[15] In this case, a sophisticated law firm had what it thought was a sophisticated system to determine and calendar filing deadlines. Nonetheless, it missed a critical 30-day time period in which to file a notice of appeal. The court stated that delegation of the task of ascertaining the deadline was not per se inexcusable neglect.[16]

Paralegals and Others Following the Lawyer's Directions. If a police officer tells you that the speed limit is 55 m.p.h., or the court clerk instructs you that reply briefs should be printed on blue-backed paper, these people use the law, but they are not practicing law.[17] If a lawyer instructs these people (or similar people, such as a claims adjuster) about the law, the lawyer is not normally assisting in the unauthorized practice of law because these people, the recipients of the lawyers' aid, do not practice law. They simply follow the lawyer's instructions.

While the lay investigator asks questions, or the paralegal conducts legal research, or the secretary prepares letters for the lawyer to sign, the lawyer is the person who applies the law to the facts; *viz.*, the lawyer decides when the cause of action lies more in tort than in contract, or whether research is useful, or whether to send a letter and what that letter should contain.[18]

In 2002, the ABA established a Task Force on the Model Defi-

---

cialized, well-educated non-lawyers may well ensure greater accuracy in meeting deadlines than a practice of having each lawyer in a large firm calculate each filing deadline anew. The task of keeping track of necessary deadlines will involve some delegation. The responsibility for the error falls on the attorney regardless of whether the error was made by an attorney or a paralegal. We hold that delegation of the task of ascertaining the deadline was not per se inexcusable neglect." (citation omitted, citing Rule 5.5, Comment 2).

[14]*Pincay v. Andrews*, 389 F.3d 853 (9th Cir.2004)(en banc).

[15]The court relied on Rule 4(a)(5), Federal Rules of Civil Procedure and Model Rule 5.5, Comment 2.

[16]The notice of appeal was due in 30 days, but a paralegal charged with calendaring the filing deadlines mis-

read the rule and incorrectly advised the lawyer that the notice was not due for 60 days, which was the time allowed when the government is a party to the case.

[17]EC 3-5.

[18]*See, e.g., In re Opinion 24*, 128 N.J. 114, 607 A.2d 962 (1992), held that paralegals who are supervised by—but not employed by—lawyers do not engage in the practice of law. Lawyers may delegate legal tasks to a paralegal, regardless of whether the paralegal is employed by a lawyer or a law firm or is an independent retained by a lawyer or a firm, if the lawyers maintain direct relationships with their clients, supervise the paralegal's work, and remain responsible for the work product.

Doe v. Condon, 341 S.C. 22, 532 S.E.2d 879 (per curiam), holding that "a non-lawyer employee conducting

nition of the Practice of Law. The Commission issued a Report and Recommendation to the ABA in August 2003.[19] The Recommendation states that every jurisdiction should adopt its own definition of the practice of law.[20] The Task Force recommended that any definition should be based upon applying legal principles and judgment to an individualized fact pattern. Such a definition should focus on protecting the public and weighing benefits of nonlawyers performing services for the public. The Task Force's Report provides more specific advice for how states should go about defining the practice of law. In August 2003, the ABA House of Delegates adopted the Task Force Report concluding that it was not possible to craft a one-size-fits-all definition of the practice of law.[21]

§ 5.5–3(c) Accountants, the Practice of Law, and the Emergence of Multidisciplinary Practice ("MDP")

Accountants obviously can engage in accounting without practicing law. Yet, when they prepare complex income tax returns and give tax advice regarding complex transactions, there can come a time when the accountant may be said to be applying the law to the specific facts and, in effect, practicing law.[22] If the accountant is found to be practicing law, it does not matter that he performs legal services as well as, or even better than, a lawyer in the particular matter,[23] because it has never been a defense to a charge of unauthorized practice of law that the advice rendered is completely competent.

If the accountant is also a lawyer admitted to the bar, the

---

unsupervised legal presentations for the public and answering legal questions for the public or for clients of the attorney/employer engages in the unauthorized practice of law." 341 S.C. 22, 23, 532 S.E.2d 879, 880 (2000). *See, e.g.,* Candy M. Kern-Fuller, *Doe v. Condon: Lawyers Beware—This Unauthorized-Practice-of-Law Case May Affect You!,* 53 SOUTH CAROLINA L. REV. 661 (2002).

[19]http://www.abanet.org/cpr/model_def_home.html. This site also lists information regarding what some states have done to create their own definitions as suggested by the Task Force.

[20]*See* http://www.abanet.org/cpr/model-def/taskforce_rpt_803.pdf.

[21]Many lawyer groups, such as the Association of Professional Responsibility Lawyers, argued against the

adoption of a uniform definition of the practice of law. *See* Letter from the Association of Professional Responsibility Lawyers to the American Bar Association (Dec. 17, 2002)("In our view, it is neither possible nor desirable to adopt a single definition of the practice of law that will work even reasonably well in the many and varied contexts in which some definition might be useful.").

[22]*See Lowell Bar Association v. Loeb,* 315 Mass. 176, 52 N.E.2d 27 (1943); *Matter of Bercu,* 273 App.Div. 524, 78 N.Y.S.2d 209 (1st Dept.1948).

[23]Donald Weckstein, *Limitations on the Right to Counsel: The Unauthorized Practice of Law,* 1978 UTAH L. REV. 649, 650 (tax accountants may know more of tax law than lawyers who are not tax lawyers).

lawyer-accountant still may not practice law today *if* he is employed by an accounting firm, because accounting firms (just like corporations) may not practice law. On the other hand, if a law firm hired an accountant, there would be no problem with the accountant practicing accountancy because the law forbids the unauthorized practice of law, not of accountancy.

The laws that American jurisdictions have regarding the practicing of law by accountants are not reflected abroad. Accounting firms in Europe, for example, are able to offer their clients both accounting advice and legal advice with respect to drafting documents, negotiating transactions, and so forth. So far, this multidisciplinary practice by accounting firms has not been permitted in this country, though the issue is the subject of intense debate.[24]

Large accounting firms are expanding in this country and abroad, and they are hiring a great many lawyers who understand both accounting and law. PricewaterhouseCoopers is a major accounting firm that operates both in the United States and abroad. In early 1999, this firm had more than 1,500 lawyers working around the world.[25] And the accounting firms are expanding. In 1999, several big name tax lawyers who are rainmakers left law firms to join the Big Five accounting firms.[26] In some cases, these lawyers are offered to clients as "legal consultants," offering advice, but not engaged in the practice of law.[27] Traditional law

---

[24]*See, e.g.,* Gianluca Morello, *Big Six Accounting Firms Shop World Wide for Law Firms: Why Multi-Disciplinary Practices Should Be Permitted in the United States*, 21 FORDHAM INTERNATIONAL L. J. 190 (1997).

American Law Firm Expansion Abroad. American law firms are expanding abroad and joining forces with foreign firms. *See, e.g.,* Paul Barrett, *Rogers & Wells and U.K. Firm Plan to Merge*, WALL STREET JOURNAL, May 24, 1999, at A3, col. 4 & A8, col. 3 (Midwest ed.). The two firms mentioned in this article are Rogers & Wells based in New York and Clifford Chance, based in London. The combined firm will have 2,400 lawyers in Europe, Asia, and the United States. These mergers raise various issues given that foreign law does not embrace American distinctions regarding unauthorized practice.

See generally ABA Commission on Multidisciplinary Practice, *Background Paper on Multidisciplinary Practice: Issues and Developments*, 10 THE PROFESSIONAL LAWYER 1 (ABA, No. 1, Fall, 1998); John Gibeaut, *Share the Wealth: ABA Panel Proposes Fee-Splitting with Other Professionals*, 14 ABA JOURNAL 14 (July 1999).

[25]Paul M. Barrett, *Drive to Go Global Spurs Law-Firm Merger Talk*, WALL STREET JOURNAL, Mar. 18, 1999, at B1, col. 5.

[26]Tom Herman, *Tax Report*, WALL STREET JOURNAL, March 24, 1999, at p. A1, col. 5.

[27]*See The Tanina Rostain, Emergence of Law Consultants*, 75 FORDHAM L. REV. 1397 (2006) (examining the legal and ethical issues involving law consultants).

firms are finding themselves in a competitive disadvantage,[28] and some lawyers are rethinking the rules regarding multidisciplinary practice.[29]

§ 5.5–3(d) Legal Kits and Computer Programs

Publishers market law books to lawyers and to lay people. Legal casebooks, for example, are marketed to lay people, who are usually called law students. Sometimes, Unauthorized Practice Committees and others raise eyebrows when legal "how to" books are marketed to lay audiences who are not law students but simply the average persons on the street.

Occasionally the sale of the law kit or how-to book is joined with the author or another person giving specific, personalized advice to the lay purchaser of the book. In those cases, the courts are more likely to find the unauthorized practice of law.[30]

In other cases, some courts just seem to be antagonistic to people selling these books on how to avoid probate, how to do your own divorce, how to draft your own lease, how to avoid hiring a lawyer, and so forth. In *People v. Macy*,[31] for example, the lawyer reviewed a package of living trust forms for a nonlawyer, knowing that this nonlawyer planned to sell them to other lay people. The Colorado Supreme Court held that the attorney should be suspended for two years because this activity aided a nonlawyer in the unauthorized practice of law. The court said, in very broad language: "The creation and sale of trust documents by nonlawyers constitutes the unauthorized practice of law. This

---

[28] John Gibeaut, *Squeeze: As Accountants Edge into the Legal Market, Lawyers May Find Themselves Blindsided by the Assault But Also Limited by Professional Rules*, A.B.A. J., Feb. 1998, at 42.

[29] *See, e.g., The Bar Must Change Model Rules, MDP [Multidisciplinary Panel] Panel Told*, TAX NOTES, Feb. 15, 1999, at 951:

"The bar must abolish or amend the ethical rules that prevent lawyers from engaging in some form of multidisciplinary practice, according to an overwhelming majority of witnesses appearing before an American Bar Association commission in Los Angeles February 4–6."

See also National Conference of Lawyers and CPAs Endorse MDPs, TAX NOTES, Mar. 15, 1999, at 1543. John S.

Dzienkowski & Robert J. Peroni, *Multidisciplinary Practice and the American Legal Profession: A Market Approach to Regulating the Delivery of Legal Services in the Twenty-First Century*, 69 FORDHAM L. REV. 83 (2000).

[30] Cases involving unauthorized practice where the lay advisor has gone beyond writing books and has started giving specific, personalized legal advice, include, *e.g., People v. Divorce Associated & Publishing Limited*, 95 Misc.2d 340, 407 N.Y.S.2d 142 (1978); *Matter of Estate of Margow*, 77 N.J. 316, 390 A.2d 591 (1978); *Florida Bar v. Brower*, 402 So.2d 1171 (Fla.1981).

[31] *People v. Macy*, 789 P.2d 188 (Colo.1990).

court has suspended an attorney in the past for aiding a nonlawyer in marketing trusts to the public."[32]

A similar decision antagonistic to the notion that lay publishers should be able to compete with practicing lawyers is *Unauthorized Practice of Law Committee v. Parsons Technology, Inc.*[33] Parsons Technology sold computer software, including a computer program called *Quicken Family Lawyer*. This computer program contained various forms and asked users various questions.[34] The initial screen displayed by the computer program stated:

> This program provides forms and information about the law. We cannot and do not provide specific information for your exact situation. For example, we can provide a form for a lease, along with information on state law and issues frequently addressed in leases. But we cannot decide that our program's lease is appropriate for you. [Y]ou must use your own judgment and, to the extent you believe appropriate, the assistance of a lawyer.[35]

The computer program also explained that the product was developed and reviewed by expert attorneys.

Nonetheless, the trial court in *Parsons Technology* actually *enjoined* selling this computer program, because it found that the selling of a will manual or a will program constitutes the unauthorized practice of law even though there is no personal contact or other relationship between the publisher and the alleged

---

[32]789 P.2d 188, 189, internal citations omitted, citing *People v. Schmitt*, 126 Colo. 546, 251 P.2d 915 (1952) and *People v. Boyls*, 197 Colo. 242, 591 P.2d 1315 (1979).

[33]*Unauthorized Practice of Law Committee v. Parsons Technology, Inc.*, 1999 WL 47235 (N.D.Tex.1999) (Senior Judge Barefoot Sanders), *vacated and remanded*, 179 F.3d 956 (5th Cir.1999) (per curiam); *In re Reynoso*, 477 F.3d 1117, Bankr. L. Rep. P 80,864 (9th Cir. 2007), upheld the bankruptcy court's finding that bankruptcy petition preparers (BPPs) who sold web-based software that prepared bankruptcy petitions, engaged in the unauthorized practice of law under California law. In this case, the individual who owned and operated the company was not an attorney, the BPPs held themselves out as offering legal expertise, offering customers extensive advice on how to take advantage of so-called loopholes in the Bankruptcy Code, promising services comparable to those of a "top-notch bankruptcy lawyer," and describing their software as "an expert system" that would do more than function as a "customized word processor." This software went beyond providing clerical services, because it provided personalized guidance by determining in which schedules to place information provided by BPPs' customers, selecting exemptions for the customers, and supplying relevant legal citations.

[34]The software package contained over 100 legal forms that are said to be "valid in 49 states." It asked questions about the user and suggested forms to deal with the user's problem in the user's jurisdiction, although it expressly disclaimed providing "specific information for your exact situation."

[35]1999 WL 47235, at *2.

client.[36] The trial court—after simply announcing that there was no First Amendment, free speech problem[37]—broadly declared that Parsons should have been on notice that "in Texas, the selling of forms, without more, may be considered the unauthorized practice of law."[38]

After the decision, the Texas legislature enacted a law providing that "the 'practice of law' does not include the design, creation, publication, distribution, display, or sale . . . [of] computer software, or similar products if the products clearly and conspicuously state that the products are not a substitute for the advice of an attorney." That law was effective immediately. The Fifth Circuit then vacated the injunction and judgment and remanded in light of the new statute.[39]

In spite of cases such as *Macy* and the trial court ruling in *Parsons Technology*, the general rule is that "selling forms or kits is not unauthorized practice so long as they are not accompanied by advice, either in writing or in person, that is personalized in the sense of being directed to the specific problem of a designated

---

[36]1999 WL 47235, at *6, *11.

[37]"The Statute at issue is aimed at eradicating the unauthorized practice of law. The Statute's purpose has nothing to do with suppressing speech." 1999 WL 47235, at *8.

[38]1999 WL 47235, at *11.

This sweeping claim—that a publication of a book of forms, or a computer program that collects forms with an easy way to access them—is troubling. First, it is not unauthorized practice of law for a layperson to represent himself or herself. Given that rule, is it unauthorized practice for a lawyer to help a layperson represent himself or herself? The Model Rules say no. Rule 5.4, Comment 1 says explicitly: "a lawyer may counsel non-lawyers who wish to proceed *pro se*." So, a lawyer can write a book on how to write your own will. And a law library can stock that book.

Assume that a lay person wishes to write her or his own will. If the lay person asks the law librarian where the self-help books on writing wills are located, the law librarian, without violating the rules against unauthorized practice, can direct a layperson to the books on wills. "Go to aisle 14, and there are the books on

wills." The law-librarian is not aiding the "unauthorized" practice of law because the lay person is authorized to represent herself or himself.

If a law book publisher can publish a book that tells one how to write a will, one would think that Quicken could do that too. If lawyers have the right to write a book or develop computer software to help laypeople to represent themselves, then Quicken should have the right to market it. Granted, a lay person may be foolish to rely on a form book, but the law already gives lay people the right to represent themselves, even if doing so is foolish.

[39]*Unauthorized Practice of Law Committee v. Parsons Technology, Inc.*, 179 F.3d 956 (5th Cir.1999) (per curiam) (vacating and remanding to the trial court in light of the new statute). *See* Richard Zorza, *Re-conceptualizing the Relationship Between Legal Ethics And Technological Innovation in Legal Practice: from Threat to Opportunity*, 67 FORDHAM L. REV. 2659, 2686 (1999); Bruce Green, *Foreword: Rationing Lawyers: Ethics and Professional Issues in the Delivery of Legal Services to Low-Income Clients*, 67 FORDHAM L. REV. 1713, 1729 (1999).

or readily identifiable person."[40] A leading case illustrating this principle is *Matter of New York Co. Lawyers' Association v. Dacey.*[41]

Dacey published a widely popular book entitled, *How to Avoid Probate,* which consisted of 55 pages of text and 310 pages of forms. In the dissenting opinion in the lower court, which the New York Court of Appeals adopted, Justice Stevens analyzed the pertinent legal principle:

> It cannot be claimed that the publication of a legal text which purports to say what the law is amounts to legal practice. And the mere fact that the principles or rules stated in the text may be accepted by a particular reader as a solution to his problem does not affect this . . . .. Apparently it is urged that the conjoining of these two, that is, the text and the forms, with advice as to how the forms should be filled out, constitutes the unlawful practice of law. But that is the situation with many approved and accepted texts. Dacey's book is sold to the public at large. There is no personal contact or relationship with a particular individual. Nor does there exist that relation of confidence and trust so necessary to the status of attorney and client. This is the essential of legal practice—the representation and the advising of a particular person in a particular situation . . . .. At most the book assumes to offer general advice on common problems, and does not purport to give personal advice on a specific problem peculiar to a designated or readily identified person.[42]

Even the distinction found in most cases—between selling a book of forms or a kit and accompanying that sale with personal advice—should be reconsidered. Many of these cases were decided before the Supreme Court imposed some constitutional limitations on the power of the state to regulate lawyer solicitation. Now, many forms of personal advice, such as direct mail legal

---

[40]CHARLES W. WOLFRAM, MODERN LEGAL ETHICS § 15.1.3, at 840 (West Pub. Co., 1986) (footnote omitted).

Accord State v. Winder, 42 A.D.2d 1039, 348 N.Y.S.2d 270 (1973), holding that there was no unauthorized practice when a lay person merely distributes "do-it-yourself divorce kits" with forms and instructions, because these kits did not contain personalized advice applied to a particular person; however the lay author of these "divorce yourself kits" who gave legal advice in the course of personal contacts concerning particular problems that might arise in the preparation and presentation of the purchasers' asserted matrimonial

cause of action or pursuit of other legal remedies and who provided assistance and preparation of necessary documents was guilty of unauthorized practice of law.

[41]*Matter of New York Co. Lawyers' Association v. Dacey,* 28 A.D.2d 161, 283 N.Y.S.2d 984 (1967), *rev'd on the dissenting opinion in the Appellate Division,* 21 N.Y.2d 694, 287 N.Y.S.2d 422, 234 N.E.2d 459 (1967).

[42]28 A.D.2d 161, 173, 283 N.Y.S.2d 984, 997. Justice Stevens was the only dissent in the lower court (the appellate division). Justice Scileppi was the only dissent in New York Court of Appeals.

advertising, merit some important constitutional protections.[43] So, to the extent that lawyers admitted to practice in the jurisdiction are selling these kits, these cases have to be rethought and what was forbidden in the past may now be permissible.

§ 5.5–4 RATIONALE FOR RULES AGAINST UNAUTHORIZED PRACTICE

Proponents often defend unauthorized practice rules as designed to protect lay people from being injured by incompetents or by those who lack the integrity to practice law compared to those who have been licensed to practice law.[1] But scholars have often criticized these justifications as a pretext, arguing that historically lawyers have often used the unauthorized practice rules to suppress competition by lay persons seeking to perform services at less cost than those charged by members of the Bar, and to make it more difficult for out-of-state lawyers to compete with those licensed within the state.[2]

Unauthorized practice rules can represent guild rules, efforts

---

[43]See the discussion of Rule 7.1, et seq. *See also Shapero v. Kentucky Bar Association*, 486 U.S. 466, 108 S.Ct. 1916, 100 L.Ed.2d 475 (1988) (targeted direct mail constitutionally protected).

In *Florida Bar v. Went for It, Inc.*, 515 U.S. 618, 115 S.Ct. 2371, 132 L.Ed.2d 541 (1995), on remand 66 F.3d 270 (11th Cir.1995), the Court did not disturb *Shapero*, but held (5 to 4) that, even though targeted mailing is constitutionally protected, Florida may ban targeted mailing by plaintiffs' attorneys for 30 days after the cause of action has occurred. Justice O'Connor, who dissented in *Shapero*, wrote the majority opinion in *Went for It*. O'Connor's dissent in *Shapero* was joined by Rehnquist, C.J. and Scalia, J. Both of these Justices, along with Thomas & Breyer, JJ., joined the five person majority. The majority in *Shapero* included Kennedy, J. (who joined all of the Brennan plurality) & Stevens, J. (who joined Parts I and II of the Brennan plurality). In *Went For It*, Kennedy, J. filed a dissenting opinion joined by Stevens, Souter, & Ginsburg, JJ.

See also Ronald D. Rotunda, *Professionalism, Legal Advertising, and Free Speech In the Wake of Florida Bar v. Went For It, Inc.*, 49 Ark. L. Rev. 703 (1997); 5 Ronald D. Rotunda & John E. Nowak, Treatise on Constitutional Law: Substance and Procedure § 20.31 (Thomson- West, 4th ed. 2008) (6 volumes).

[Section 5.5–4]

[1]EC 3-1. *See also, e.g., Spivak v. Sachs*, 16 N.Y.2d 163, 168, 263 N.Y.S.2d 953, 956, 211 N.E.2d 329, 331 (1965), stating that the purpose of the prohibition against "unauthorized practice of law" is to protect the public in this State from "the dangers of legal representation and advice given by persons not trained, examined and licensed for such work, whether they be laymen or lawyers from other jurisdictions."

[2]*See, e.g.,* Thomas D. Morgan, *The Evolving Concept of Professional Responsibility*, 90 Harv. L. Rev. 702, 707–08 (1977). *See also* Barlow F. Christensen, *The Unauthorized Practice of Law: Do Good Fences Really Make Good Neighbors—or Even Good Sense*, 1980 Am. Bar Foundation Research J. 159; Deborah Rhode, *Policing the Professional Monopoly: A Constitutional and Empirical Analysis of Unauthorized Practice Prohibitions*, 34 Stan. L. Rev. 1 (1981).

to protect a cartel and prevent reform that might lead to competition from nonlawyers. The late Professor Arthur Sutherland once remarked that one "can scarcely imagine a speaker at a meeting of a county medical society discussing the possible elimination of some disease by public health measures, and then qualifying his observations by the statement that many practitioners make a living out of treating the disease in question; and that unless the physicians are vigilant to prevent the adoption of such measures, this source of business will be taken from them. Yet speakers at bar association meetings are frequently heard to make similar observations about the effects of proposed reforms."[3]

Much of the litigation involving unauthorized practice deals with subjects where nonlawyers often provide services that many lay people find are competently performed with less expense: debt collection, divorce kits or divorce forms, kits to avoid or deal with probate, real estate contracts, tax preparation and planning, and appearances before specialized administrative agencies.[4]

---

[3]Quoted in, MARTIN MAYER, THE LAWYERS 28 (1967).

[4]Thomas D. Morgan, *The Evolving Concept of Professional Responsibility*, 90 HARV. L. REV. 702, 707–08 & nn. 16–21 (1977).

Supremacy Clause. In this category of specialized agencies, federal rules allow nonlawyers to appear before certain agencies (*e.g.*, the Patent Office). The Supreme Court, relying on the Supremacy Clause, has overturned state rules to the contrary. *Sperry v. Florida ex rel. Florida Bar*, 373 U.S. 379, 83 S.Ct. 1322, 10 L.Ed.2d 428 (1963).

Casey v. F.D.I.C., 583 F.3d 586 (8th Cir. 2009), cert. denied, 2010 WL 265883 (U.S. 2010). Plaintiffs sued mortgage lenders claiming that mortgage lenders had engaged in the unauthorized practice of law by charging a fee for preparation of loan documents by nonlawyers. The Court held that a federal regulation preempted Missouri's state unauthorized practice of law statute.

Other Constitutional Challenges. General, broad-based challenges to the constitutionality of unauthorized practice rules have failed. *See, e.g., Lawline v. American Bar Association*, 956 F.2d 1378 (7th Cir.1992), *cert. denied*, 510 U.S. 992, 114 S.Ct. 551, 126 L.Ed.2d 452 (1993), a suit by an association of lawyers, paralegals, and lay people who had organized a service that proposed to answer legal questions from the public over the phone. It also planned to make referrals to legal aid and to lawyers who would charge reduced fees. The suit, in general, challenged the constitutionality of DR 3-101 and DR 3-103 and Model Rules 5.4(b) and 5.5(b) on their face. The Court dismissed the action. The cited rules were all rationally related to the goal of "safeguard[ing] the public, maintain[ing] the integrity of the profession, and protect[ing] the administration of justice from reproach."

On the other hand, more limited challenges have succeeded. *See, e.g., National Revenue Corp. v. Violet*, 807 F.2d 285 (1st Cir.1986), invalidating, under the dormant commerce clause, a Rhode Island law that prevented anyone not a member of the Rhode Island bar from engaging in all aspects of debt collection, even preliminary, non-litigation work.

The Supreme Court has held that there is a First Amendment right of access to the courts, which can place

§ 5.5–5 REMEDIES FOR UNAUTHORIZED PRACTICE

Fees. Typically state laws or state common law provides that it is a defense to a lawsuit for the payment of fees that the party seeking fees engaged in the unauthorized practice of law. The client can thus avoid paying a fee even though he has no complaint as to the quality of work that the nonlawyer performed.[1] Courts routinely state that a contract to provide services in violation of the prohibition against unauthorized practice of law is unenforceable as against public policy.[2]

Disgorging Fees. Courts can order the person or entity who engaged in unauthorized practice to *disgorge fees*, even when no client has complained. Consider *State ex rel. Indiana State Bar Association v. United Financial Systems Corporation.*[3] The Indiana State Bar Association sued an insurance marketing agency for engaging in unauthorized practice of law, and sought injunctive relief disgorgement of the fees it had charged its client, who were not complaining.

United Financial Systems Corporation targeted potential clients with mailings that included information on how to avoid probate. The company's sales representatives, who were not attorney's, met with those who responded to the mailings. During the meetings, the sales representatives obtained the clients' financial information and sold them estate planning services, including wills and trusts. The sales representatives then forwarded this financial information to the company's in-house counsel, who sent the information to list of attorneys who contracted with the company. Lawyers on this list or panel would then would call the client to discuss briefly the services they had purchased, and then prepare the documentation. These panel lawyers typically limited their contact with the client to this one phone call. After the lawyers prepared the documents, the nonlawyer sales representatives within the company took the documents to the clients, explained the nature of the documents

---

some limits on a state's overly restrictive laws. *United Transp. Union v. State Bar of Michigan*, 401 U.S. 576, 91 S.Ct. 1076, 28 L.Ed.2d 339 (1971); *United Mine Workers v. Illinois State Bar Association*, 389 U.S. 217, 88 S.Ct. 353, 19 L.Ed.2d 426 (1967); *Brotherhood of R.R. Trainmen v. Virginia*, 377 U.S. 1, 84 S.Ct. 1113, 12 L.Ed.2d 89 (1964); *NAACP v. Button*, 371 U.S. 415, 83 S.Ct. 328, 9 L.Ed.2d 405 (1963). *See also Ohralik v. State Bar*, 436 U.S. 447, 98 S.Ct. 1912, 56 L.Ed.2d 444 (1978); *In re Primus*, 436 U.S. 412,

98 S.Ct. 1893, 56 L.Ed.2d 417 (1978).

[Section 5.5–5]

[1] *See, e.g., State v. Midland Equities of New York, Inc.*, 117 Misc.2d 203, 458 N.Y.S.2d 126 (1982).

[2] *See, e.g., El Gemayel v. Seaman*, 72 N.Y.2d 701, 705, 536 N.Y.S.2d 406, 409, 533 N.E.2d 245, 248 (1988).

[3] *State ex rel. Indiana State Bar Association v. United Financial Systems Corporation*, 926 N.E.2d 8 (Ind. 2010).

and assisted the clients with their execution. They would also attempt to sell the clients insurance products and annuities.

The court found that the company's use of attorney's did not avoid the problem of unauthorized practice. The company's business model "marginalized the attorney's role to such a degree as to cross the line of permissible practices." The corporation's business model runs "afoul of the prohibition against the unauthorized practice of law."[4]

It also noted that the disparity between commissions paid to sales representatives for the sale of the estate planning services ($750 to $900 per sale), and fees paid to the panel lawyers ($225 per client) "indicative of an emphasis on sales and revenue rather than the provision of objective, disinterested legal advice."[5] The court enjoined the company from continuing its style of practice.

In addition, the court ordered the corporation to disgorge its fees because it had engaged in the unauthorized practice of law by selling estate planning products and services to its clients. To make this disgorgement remedy truly effective, the court ordered the corporation to give notice of its unauthorized conduct to all readily identifiable persons to whom it had sold such products since the corporation's inception, and to provide separate individual notice to all who purchased such services after the corporation had notice of its illegality, informing them that they were entitled to refund, upon request, of what they had paid.[6]

Criminal Prosecution. The unauthorized practice of law is often a criminal violation as well.[7] Those who hold themselves out as lawyers in a jurisdiction where they are not properly admitted have been jailed and fined.[8]

---

[4] 926 N.E.2d 8, 15.

[5] 926 N.E.2d 8, 13.

[6] 926 N.E.2d 8, 17-20.

[7] For example, in June, 1991, a paralegal in Green Bay, Wisconsin, was sentenced to nine months in jail for helping people file petitions in federal bankruptcy court in Madison. He was released on probation after 30 days. WALL ST. JOURNAL, Aug. 28, 1991, at B4, col. 6 (Midwest ed.). *See* Deborah Rhode, *Policing the Professional Monopoly: A Constitutional and Empirical Analysis of Unauthorized Practice Prohibitions*, 34 STAN. L. REV. 1, 11 n.39 (1981).

[8] *See, e.g., Satterwhite v. Texas*, 979 S.W.2d 626 (Tex.Crim.App.1998).

The defendant did not pay his bar dues. He made efforts to pay the dues but did not pay the proper amounts, so he was suspended from practice for nonpayment of dues. Still, he held himself out as a lawyer in good standing with the state bar. He was sentenced to four and one-half years in prison and a fine of $7,500.

Falsely Holding Oneself Out To Be a Lawyer. *In the Matter of Contempt of the Supreme Court of Indiana*, 693 N.E.2d 555 (Ind.1998). The respondent resigned from the state bar when faced with a pending disciplinary action. However, he then became "vice president and general counsel" of an estate planning company. His business card printed these two titles and added the word, "Es-

Injunctive and Declaratory Relief. Courts may also grant declaratory or injunctive relief.[9]

Contempt. A court may enforce unauthorized practice rules by use of its contempt power against previously disbarred lawyers who continue to practice law in violation of their disbarment order.[10] In these cases, it is not unusual for a local bar association to lead the charge and become a prime enforcement authority.[11] In contrast, in 1999, an American Bar Association Commission proposed removing or limiting unauthorized practice rules when they pose barriers to entry.[12] The ABA House of Delegates decided, instead, to adopt a recommendation advising that "[e]ach

---

quire," after his name. On his office wall he displayed his original bar admission. The court found that he was falsely holding himself out to be a lawyer. He was fined $500 and warned that if he continued such activities, he might face imprisonment.

[9] *See, e.g., Dauphin County Bar Association v. Mazzacaro*, 465 Pa. 545, 351 A.2d 229 (1976); *In re Banks*, 561 A.2d 158 (D.C.1987). In *Matter of Murgatroyd*, 741 N.E.2d 719 (Ind. 2001), an out-of-state lawyer sent letters proposing to represent victims of a plane crash in Indiana. Even though he presumably could have been admitted *pro hac vice* if he had represented any clients, the court found the letters affirmatively misleading because they did not say the lawyer was not licensed in Indiana. For its remedy, the court enjoined the lawyer from ever taking an Indiana case in the future without associating an Indiana lawyer.

[10] *In re Creasy*, 198 Ariz. 539, 12 P.3d 214 (2000). *See* Gerard E. Wimberly, Jr., *The Unauthorized Practice of Law by Licensed Attorneys: a Perilous Paradox*, 37 Arizona Attorney 29 (June 2001); Jonathan Rose, *Unauthorized Practice of Law in Arizona: A Legal and Political Problem That Won't Go Away*, 34 ARIZ. ST. L. J. 585, 585 n.2 (2002).

[11] Notice the name of the plaintiff in many of the cases: *Dauphin County Bar Association v. Mazzacaro*, 465 Pa. 545, 351 A.2d 229 (1976); *The Florida Bar v. Neckman*, 616 So.2d 31 (Fla. 1993); *Toledo Bar Association v. Doyle*,

68 Ohio St.3d 24, 623 N.E.2d 37 (Ohio 1993).

[12] ABA Commission on Multidisciplinary Practice: Report to the House of Delegates (ABA, June 8, 1999), recommending:

"A lawyer should be permitted to share legal fees with a nonlawyer, subject to certain safeguards that prevent erosion of the core values of the legal profession." [Resolution No. 2.]

"A lawyer should be permitted to deliver legal services through a multidisciplinary practice (MDP), defined as a partnership, professional corporation, or other association or entity that includes lawyers and nonlawyers and has as one, but not all, of its purposes the delivery of legal services to a client(s) other than the MDP itself or that holds itself out to the public as providing nonlegal, as well as legal, services. It includes an arrangement by which a law firm joins with one or more other professional firms to provide services, including legal services, and there is a direct or indirect sharing of profits as part of the arrangement." [Resolution No. 3.]

In 1986, the ABA Commission on Professionalism recommended that, in order to reduce legal costs to the client, paralegals should be licensed to perform relatively simple tasks now being performed by lawyers admitted to the bar. ABA Commission on Professionalism, " . . . In the Spirit of Public Service:" A Blueprint for Rekindling Lawyer Professionalism 43 (ABA 1986). *See* Ronald D. Rotunda, *Lawyers*

jurisdiction should reevaluate and refine to the extent necessary the definition of the 'practice of law,' " and that "[j]urisdictions should retain and enforce laws that generally bar the practice of law by entities other than law firms."[13]

Loss of the Attorney-Client Privilege Is Not a Remedy for Unauthorized Practice. The basic restatement of the attorney client privilege is that it applies when a person engages in a communication for the purpose of obtaining or providing legal assistance and the non-client party to that communication is a lawyer or someone whom the client or prospective client reasonably thinks is a lawyer. Under the law of evidence, the communication is privileged if the client or prospective client consults with a lawyer or someone "who the client or prospective client reasonably believes is a lawyer."[14]

Hence, the Restatement restates the general rule that a client does not lose the attorney client privilege simply because the person with whom the client deals has falsely represented that he is a lawyer. A client or prospective client secured the protection of the attorney-client privilege even if he or she communicates with someone who is a fraud or charlatan, one who falsely claims to be a lawyer, so long as the confiding client "reasonably believes that the imposter is a lawyer."[15] Obviously, the client or prospective client does not lose the protection merely because the lawyer failed to pay his bar dues, or is practicing outside the jurisdiction in which he is admitted.[16] The purported purpose of the privilege is to safeguard the client or prospective

---

and Professionalism: A Commentary on the Report of the American Bar Association Commission on Professionalism, 18 LOYOLA UNIVERSITY CHICAGO L.J. 1149 (1987) (the Baker-McKenzie Foundation Lecture).

[13]See Recommendation 10F, July 2000 ABA Annual Meeting, available at: http://www.abanet.org/cpr/mdprecom10f.html.

[14]Proposed Federal Rules of Evidence, Rule 503(a)(2)(1973); Hickman v. Taylor, 329 U.S. 495, 508, 67 S.Ct. 385, 392, 91 L.Ed. 451 (1947). Restatement of the Law Governing Lawyers, § 72(1) (Official Draft 2000).

[15]Restatement of the Law Governing Lawyers, § 72(1), comment e (Official Draft 2000).

[16]See, e.g., Georgia-Pacific Plywood Co. v. United States Plywood Corp., 18 F.R.D. 463 (S.D.N.Y.1956).

The issue before the court was "whether one who is resident and practicing law by acting as house counsel for a corporation in a state in which he has not been admitted to the bar, may nevertheless qualify as an attorney for purposes of the privilege if he has been licensed elsewhere." 18 F.R.D. at 465. The court supported the privilege.

Cf. Mitts & Merrill, Inc. v. Shred Pax Corp., 112 F.R.D. 349, 352 (N.D. Ill.1986), accepting the privilege when the lawyer was admitted in Europe. The court held that the better rule, "where, as in the present case, 'substantive' information regarding foreign law is communicated to the United States lawyer, is that the communication is privileged either because the foreign patent agent is acting as the agent of the United States lawyer or the foreign patent agent is engaged in substantive lawyering which would be

client. That purpose is hardly furthered when the client or prospective client acts reasonably in dealing with a pretender or a member of the bar who has not yet received *pro hac vice* admission and the court punishes the reasonable client or prospective client by denying the protection of the privilege. When a client hires a lawyer, he does not usually ask the lawyer to supply a receipt for his most recent bar dues.

§ 5.5–6 AIDING IN THE UNAUTHORIZED PRACTICE OF LAW

§ 5.5–6(a) The General Rule

A lawyer may engage in the unauthorized practice of law either: (1) by practicing in a jurisdiction in which she is not admitted,[1] or (2) by assisting a lay person in the unauthorized practice of law.[2]

That fact of life leads to another important way to enforce the

---

held privileged by the foreign country. There has been no attempt to determine German law on the issue, but the communication itself shows that the patent agent was at least acting as Mr. Santisi's agent on this case." (internal citation omitted).

Corporate Counsel, Unauthorized Practice, and the Application of the Attorney Client Privilege. An aberrational case is *Financial Technologies Intern., Inc. v. Smith*, 2000 WL 1855131, 49 Fed Rules Service 3d 961 (S.D.N.Y.2000). Defendant's counsel argued that the plaintiff should not be able to assert the attorney client privilege because its counsel, although he graduated from Hofstra Law School in 1978 and had passed the New York State Bar Examination later that year, was not a member of any bar because he failed to submit the paperwork necessary for admission.

The court emphasized: "the facts demonstrate that Peter Smith was not an attorney admitted to the bar of any state at the time the communications were made, and thus an essential element necessary for invocation of the privilege is absent." 2000 WL 1855131 *3. The court accepted the general rule that: "an individual who reasonably believed that the person consulted was a duly admitted attorney should be af-

forded a measure of protection." 2000 WL 1855131 *6. But the court tried to carve out an exception for the corporate client:

"Here, FTI employed Smith as their general counsel. This is strong evidence that they believed him to be an attorney. There is, however, no indication that FTI checked Smith's background to ascertain whether or not he was a duly licensed attorney or even asked Smith for credentials proving admission to the bar . . .. While an investigation of this magnitude, though not time consuming, could prove onerous for an individual seeking legal advice, it is not unduly burdensome for a corporation . . . to require a corporation to determine whether their general counsel, or other individuals in their employ, are licensed to perform the functions for which they have been hired." 2000 WL 1855131 *6.

[Section 5.5–6]

[1] Rule 5.5(a); DR 3-101(B). *See also* Restatement of the Law Governing Lawyers, Third, § 3 ("Jurisdictional Scope of Practice of Law by Lawyer") (Official Draft 2000).

[2] Rule 5.5(a); DR 3-101(A). *See also* Restatement of the Law Governing Lawyers, Third, § 4 ("Unauthorized Practice of Law by Non-Lawyer")

rules against unauthorized practice—by disciplining lawyers who either engage in the unauthorized practice of law or aid those who do.[3]

§ 5.5–6(b) *Pro Se* Litigants

The rule against unauthorized practice only applies to a person seeking to represent another. A lay person may represent himself, even if doing so requires that the lay person appear in court and otherwise practice law.[4] In fact, in criminal cases defendants have a constitutional right to defend themselves.[5]

However, while a lay person can represent himself, the general rule is that he cannot represent another lay person.[6] In the same lawsuit, a party can represent himself but not another codefendant or coplaintiff.[7]

If a lay person wishes to proceed *pro se,* a lawyer may assist him. This assistance does not violate the rule against aiding a lay person in the unauthorized practice of law because the lay person, while practicing law, is not engaged in the *unauthorized* practice of law. A lawyer who helps a nonlawyer appearing *pro se* is not

---

(Official Draft 2000).

[3]Rule 5.5, Rule 5.5, Comment 2. DR 3-101(A); EC 3-5. *See also* Restatement of the Law Governing Lawyers, Third, § 4 (Official Draft 2000).

[4]For example, a federal statute gives litigants the right to proceed pro se in both civil and criminal cases. 28 U.S.C.A. § 1654. *See also,* EC 3-7.

[5]*Faretta v. California,* 422 U.S. 806, 95 S.Ct. 2525, 45 L.Ed.2d 562 (1975).

[6]*See, e.g., Brown v. Ortho Diagnostic Systems, Inc.,* 868 F.Supp. 168 (E.D.Va.1994).

Special Rules of a Tribunal Allowing Non-Lawyers to Practice Law. Many jurisdictions allow nonlawyers to aid other nonlawyers in small claims court, landlord-tenant courts, and some administrative agencies. In addition, many jurisdictions allow law students, under the direction of lawyers, to represent indigents as part of a clinical legal education. Restatement of the Law Governing Lawyers, Third (Official Draft 2000),

§ 4 at Comment *c.*

In addition, federal rules allow nonlawyers to appear in before certain agencies, like the Patent Court. If there is such a rule authorizing appearance, then the Supremacy Clause overrides state rules to the contrary. *Sperry v. Florida ex rel. Florida Bar,* 373 U.S. 379, 83 S.Ct. 1322, 10 L.Ed.2d 428 (1963).

On the other hand, if the federal rule does not authorize law practice, the state can impose its unauthorized practice rules. *E.g., Office Of Disciplinary Counsel v. Marcone,* 855 A.2d 654 (Pa. 2004), holding that a suspended attorney who maintained a law office within Commonwealth was engaged in the practice of law, and that conduct violated a prior Supreme Court order suspending attorney from the practice of law. The court went on to hold that no federal statute or local rule preempted Pennsylvania's regulation of a suspended attorney's ability to maintain a law office within Pennsylvania.

[7]*Lutz v. Lavelle,* 809 F.Supp. 323 (M.D.Pa.1991).

aiding the unauthorized practice of law because the pro se litigant is "authorized" to represent himself.[8]

For similar reasons, a law librarian may answer a layperson's questions about where to go in the library to find books about litigation, or drafting a will. The lay person may be foolish to represent himself—it is often said that the lawyer who represents himself has a fool for a client—and a nonlawyer who represents himself is likely to be just as foolish. But, the law allows both a lawyer and a layperson to engage in such foolishness.

§ 5.5–6(c) Aiding Disbarred or Suspended Lawyers in the Practice of Law[9]

On the other hand, a lawyer may not assist a disbarred lawyer or a suspended lawyer in the practice of law.[10] The disbarred or suspended lawyer is not authorized to practice law, and a licensed lawyer should not aid him or her in representing third parties. Some courts allow suspended or disbarred lawyers to work as paralegals, if a lawyer admitted to practice engages in adequate supervision.[11] However, many other jurisdictions do not allow a suspended or disbarred lawyer to engage in such work related to the practice of law, even though a paralegal (who also is not licensed to practice law) may lawfully engage in the same tasks.[12] State bar authorities tend to scrutinize disbarred and suspended lawyers more carefully as they may have the temptation to continue to practice law under the guise of a nonlegal activity.[13]

Lawyers can use paralegals, law clerks, and other employees to

---

[8] Rule 5.5, Comment 2.

[9] Droney, J. citing Treatise, *Haye v. Ashcroft*, ___ F.Supp.2d ___, 2004 WL 1936204 (D.Conn.2004).

[10] *See, e.g., In re Anderson*, 409 N.W.2d 220 (Minn.1987) (per curiam). The respondent hired a suspended attorney, as a "paralegal" to assist him in legal work and did not supervise him. The court, based on these facts and other circumstances, indefinitely suspended the lawyer.

[11] *In re Mitchell*, 901 F.2d 1179 (3d Cir.1990).

[12] A 1994 survey listed 12 states that do not allow suspended or disbarred lawyers from engaging in any law-related activity, even work as a paralegal or law clerk, although one does not have to be licensed to hold these positions. ABA Standing Committee on Lawyer's Responsibility for Client Protection, 1994 Survey and Related Materials on the Unauthorized Practice of Law/Nonlawyer Practice 43 to 47 (AA 1996).

Restatement of the Law Governing Lawyers, Third (Official Draft 2000), § 3, Comment *d*: "Either by rule, decisional law, or specific order, a jurisdiction may, for example, prohibit a disbarred or suspended lawyer from functioning as a paralegal in a law firm, *even beyond the prohibition against practicing as a lawyer* or holding oneself out as such." (emphasis added)(internal cross reference omitted).

[13] *See, e.g., United States v. Johnson*, 327 F.3d 554 (7th Cir.2003), *cert. denied*, 540 U.S. 1111, 124 S.Ct. 1087, 157 L.Ed.2d 900 (2004), held that the National Legal Professional Associates (NLPA), headed by a disbarred attorney, was engaged in the unauthorized practice of law. NLPA was a paralegal service that sought to

engage in various tasks, as long as the lawyers adequately supervise their employees.[14] Even then, these lay people cannot do certain things, like appear in court on behalf of a client, unless a special court rule allows it.[15]

§ 5.5–7 PRACTICE OF LAW BY CORPORATIONS, ASSOCIATIONS, AND PARTNERSHIPS

§ 5.5–7(a) *Pro Se* Corporate Litigants

Although an individual may represent himself, the typical rule is that corporations, partnerships, other associations, and so forth, may not appear *pro se*. Because a corporation is a separate legal entity, this incorporeal entity can only appear through

---

deliver pretrial, sentencing, and post-conviction counseling services directly to criminal defendants. The district court found that NLPA interfered with the attorney-client relationship, and "insofar as they created a practical reversal of the traditional roles of supervising attorney and subordinate paralegal, [the NLPA's] activities exceeded the scope of their permitted paralegal function and reached the level of practicing law." 327 F.3d at 558–559. On review, the Seventh Circuit found that the district court had the inherent power to regulate and sanction conduct that abuses the judicial process, and it agreed that the NLPA was engaged in the unauthorized practice of law. The Court found that the practice of law in Illinois includes "providing *any* advice or other service 'requiring the use of any legal skill or knowledge, . . . the legal effect of which, under the facts and conditions involved, must be carefully determined.' " *Id.* at 562. Because NLPA conducted legal services without attorney supervision, it was engaged in the unauthorized practice of law. However, because it did not do so in bad faith, the Court ruled that the district court's imposition of punitive sanctions was an abuse of discretion.

[14]*In re Sledge*, 859 So.2d 671 (La. 2003), involved Sledge, a high volume solo practitioner who nominally ran his office but in fact largely left the cases in the hands of law clerks and other non-lawyers who used a rubber stamp to put the lawyer's name on pleadings, discovery responses, and correspondence. In most cases, Sledge only went to court and attended depositions. Sometimes, he was not present in the office for months at a time while he attended Scientology retreats and wrote a novel. Meanwhile, his staff signed-up clients, wrote letters and pleadings, and negotiated settlements. There were obviously several grounds on which the Louisiana Supreme Court could discipline Sledge, including utter neglect of cases, but it focused on his facilitation of the unauthorized practice of law by his staff. The sanction for complete delegation of "professional judgment to a non-lawyer" was disbarment.

See also In re Valinoti, 2002 WL 31907316 (Cal.Bar.Ct. 2002), involving a lawyer who ran a similar office of non-lawyer immigration counselors whom he only rarely supervised. He met few of his 1700 clients, leaving non-lawyers to fill out all applications and other documents. That lawyer received a three year suspension.

[15]*See People v. Perez*, 24 Cal.3d 133, 155 Cal.Rptr. 176, 594 P.2d 1 (1979), *reversing* 82 Cal.App.3d 89, 147 Cal.Rptr. 34 (1978) (the intermediate court of appeals held student representation to be unauthorized practice; the California Supreme Court reversed, later approved State Bar Rules Relating to Practical Training of Law Students).

PRACTICE OF LAW BY ENTITIES   § 5.5–7

lawyers because the corporation cannot practice law.¹ Courts, on their own motion, have ruled that partnerships and other organizations must be represented by counsel and no non-lawyer member of the organization can appear on the organization's behalf.²

Sometimes, courts have created exceptions to this general principle (by relying on their inherent powers or similar authority), but the exceptions are few and far between.³

§ 5.5–7(b) Insurance Companies' Use of In-House Counsel to Represent the Insured

Typically, an insurance policy provides that, if the policyholder is sued, the insurance company will supply coverage (*i.e.*, pay the judgment up to a certain amount) and also supply a lawyer to represent the defendant. Often, insurance companies hire outside law firms to represent the insured/defendant in court. However, other insurance companies prefer to use their own in-house lawyers to represent the defendant because it is easier to keep costs under control. These lawyers are often paid a flat, yearly salary, while the insurance company may have to pay outside lawyers an hourly fee. The decision whether to use the in-house lawyers or the outside lawyers is one that raises important questions regarding the law of unauthorized practice.⁴

Some states conclude that the insurance company may not use its in-house salaried lawyers to represent the insured because that would mean that the insurance company would be practic-

[Section 5.5–7]

¹*See, e.g., Simbraw, Inc. v. United States*, 367 F.2d 373 (3d Cir.1966) (per curiam); *MOVE Organization v. United States Department of Justice*, 555 F.Supp. 684, 692–94 (E.D.Pa.1983).

Merco Construction Engineers, Inc. v. Municipal Court, 21 Cal.3d 724, 147 Cal.Rptr. 631, 581 P.2d 636 (1978) (statute designed to reverse the rule preventing corporations from appearing *pro se* held unconstitutional).

²*First Amendment Foundation v. Village of Brookfield*, 575 F.Supp. 1207 (N.D.Ill.1983) (court, on its own motion, holds that a statute barring corporations from appearing pro se applies to partnerships and other organizations.)

³*See, e.g., United States v. Reeves*, 431 F.2d 1187 (9th Cir.1970) (per

curiam) (when state law gives each partner a specific right to property, and the government sues to foreclose partnership property, the individual partner may appear *pro se* because he is pleading his own case); *In re Victor Publishers, Inc. (Appeal of Pace)*, 545 F.2d 285, 286 n. 8 (1st Cir.1976) (corporate officer demonstrated extraordinary legal ability).

In re Holliday's Tax Services, Inc., 417 F.Supp. 182, 183–85 (E.D.N.Y.1976) (court has inherent power to allow bankruptcy debtor to be represented by sole shareholder), *aff'd mem.*, 614 F.2d 1287 (2d Cir.1979).

⁴*See, e.g.*, Debra Baker, *A Grab for the Ball: Insurers Are Setting Up Their Own Lawyers to Handle Claims, Leaving Defense Firms with Nothing to Show*, 85 A.B.A.J 42 (April, 1999).

ing law.[5] However, other states allow the practice because they do not view the arrangement as a corporation practicing law.[6] This issue is subject to varying treatment in the courts and so one must look to one's local jurisdiction to determine the applicable rule.

The ABA has examined the issues at stake when an insurance company's in-house counsel represents individual policyholders in ABA Formal Opinion 03-430.[7]

First, the Opinion said that staff attorneys could represent both the insurance company and the insured. In the majority of cases, the insurance company and the insured have a common interest, and thus there is no inherent conflict of interest. The Opinion also says, however, that in cases where a conflict exists, the attorney will be required either to secure the permission of the insured to continue the representation or terminate his representation of the insured. Model Rule 5.4(c) requires the attorney to exercise independent judgment in representation, thus safeguarding the interests of the insured. Model Rule 1.8(f) also requires the insurance company staff to disclose his relationship with the insurance company to the insured at the earliest possible opportunity. With these safeguards in place, however, the

---

[5]*Gardner v. North Carolina State Bar*, 316 N.C. 285, 341 S.E.2d 517 (1986), stating that: "Since a corporation cannot practice law directly, it cannot do so indirectly by employing lawyers to practice for it."

[6]*In re Allstate Insurance Co.*, 722 S.W.2d 947 (Mo.1987) (*en banc*) specifically refused to follow *Gardner* and concluded that the insurance company may either hire independent lawyers or use its own employee-lawyers instead. The court reasoned that if the insurer can hire an independent contractor it can act through its employee. Any danger of conflict of interest is minimized because the insurance company uses its employee-lawyers "only when there is no question of coverage, and when the claim is within policy limits."

See also, e.g., Cincinnati Ins. Co. v. Wills, 717 N.E.2d 151 (Ind. 1999), holding, first, a liability insurer does not necessarily engage in the unauthorized practice of law by using an in-house lawyer to represent an insured; and, second, such an arrangement also does not create an inherent conflict of

interest. However, the insurer's captive law firm used a deceptive name. The court held that the lawyers practicing under the name Berlon & Timmel must take immediate action to discontinue use of Berlon & Timmel or any other name suggesting a legal entity other than Cincinnati Insurance Co. to describe their practice as employees of Cincinnati Insurance Co. 717 N.E.2d at 165.

See also Petition of Youngblood, 895 S.W.2d 322 (Tenn. 1995), holding that the Tennessee Board of Professional Responsibility was in error in erred in finding a per se conflict of interest implicit in employer-employee relationship between insurer and lawyers representing insureds. The Board also erred in concluding that the arrangement constituted an improper lay corporation practicing law. However, the Board properly held that holding out in-house lawyer-employee as part of separate and independent law firm constitutes unethical and deceptive practice.

[7]ABA Formal Opinion 03-430 (July 9, 2003).

possibility of undue influence should be low and dual representation permissible.

Second, the Opinion addressed the issue of under what trade name the attorneys would be permitted to practice. It determined that the staff attorneys were often physically and organizationally different from the rest of the insurance company, had their own staff, and did act as a "firm." Thus, the Opinion staff attorneys could refer to themselves as a "firm" and could name the "firm" after one or more of the staff attorneys. The Opinion, however, reiterated the need of the "firm" to be in compliance with Model Rule 7.1 and refrain from giving any misleading information regarding the nature of the firm or the services that were offered. Finally, the Opinion found that the firm must disclose their affiliation with the insurance company to any insured-clients, but need not add other public disclaimers, nor inform any non-clients of their affiliation.

The Florida Supreme Court has adopted amendments to its conflicts of interest rules that track many of the ideas in the ABA Opinion.[8] One of the provisions in the conflicts of interest rules states that "a lawyer has a duty to ascertain whether the lawyer will be representing both the insurer and the insured as clients, or only the insured, and to inform both the insured and the insurer regarding the scope of the representation."[9] The comments to the rule add that this unique tripartite relationship creates ambiguity as to whom the lawyer represents: the desire of this rule is to minimize confusion and inconsistent expectations that may arise. Another section of the rules adds special rules for Insurance Staff Attorneys.[10] The Staff Attorneys may practice under a name that does not constitute a material misrepresentation, but 1) the firm name must include the name of the lawyer with supervisory responsibilities; 2) signs, letterhead, etc. must disclose that the lawyers in the unit are employees of the insurer; 3) the name of insurer and the lawyer's relationship with the insurer must be disclosed to all insured and prospective clients, and must be disclosed in the lawyer's first appearance in the tribunal; 4) offices/personnel/records must be functionally/physically separate; and 5) additional disclosure should occur when lawyer reasonably knows the relationship is misunderstood. The comments to the Florida Rule add that use of a name to identify the attorneys is permissible if there is such physical and functional separation to constitute a separate law firm; otherwise,

---

[8] *See Amendment to Rules Regulating the Florida Bar re: Rules of Professional Conduct,,* 838 So.2d 1140 (Fla.2003).

[9] Florida Rules of Professional Conduct, Rule 4-1.7(e)(Conflict of Interest).

[10] Florida Rule of Professional Conduct, Rule 4-7.10.

it would be a material misrepresentation. The lawyers do not have to make such disclosures in their pleadings and papers filed in court proceedings because that would negate the policy of not telling juries about the fact of insurance coverage.

§ 5.5–7(c) Nonprofit Corporate Legal Aid Clinics

States often permit legal aid societies to practice in a nonprofit corporate form in order to help provide access to justice for the poor and the economically disadvantaged. Courts generally conclude that the nonprofit nature of the enterprise reduces or eliminates the risk that the corporate entity will compromise the loyalty of lawyer-employees to clients or otherwise threaten clients' interests.[11] Nonprofit public-interest groups provide a "unique and indispensable vehicle through which citizens can systematically sponsor and assist litigation advancing broad public interests."[12] A significant source for these groups is statutory attorney fees awarded to prevailing plaintiffs.[13]

In *Frye v. Tenderloin Housing Clinic, Inc.*,[14] a nonprofit housing clinic sued a landlord on behalf of a tenant. Following this successful suit against the landlord, the tenant (now the former

---

[11]Grace M. Giesel, *Corporations Practicing Law Through Lawyers: Why the Unauthorized Practice of Law Doctrine Should Not Apply*, 65 Mo. L. Rev. 151, 194–97 (2000). *E.g., Azzarello v. Legal Aid Society of Cleveland*, 117 Ohio.App 471, 478, 185 N.E.2d 566, 570 (1962); *Dixon v. Georgia Indigent Legal Services, Inc.*, 388 F.Supp. 1156 (S.D. Ga. 1974), aff'd without opinion, 532 F.2d 1373 (5th Cir.1974) (applying Georgia law); *In Re Education Law Center, Inc.*, 86 N.J. 124, 429 A.2d 1051 (1981).

See also, Judge (later Justice) Souter, in, *In re New Hampshire Disabilities Rights Center, Inc.*, 130 N.H. 328, 336, 541 A.2d 208, 213 (1988):

"Organizations, their members and their staff lawyers may assert a protected first amendment right of associating for non-commercial purposes to advocate the enforcement of legal and constitutional rights of those members, or of others within a definite class whom the organization exists to serve. When such advocacy may reasonably include the provision of legal advice or take the form of litigation, the organization may itself provide legal representation to its members or beneficiaries despite State regulations restricting legal practice and the solicitation of clients, provided that the organization and its lawyers do not engage in the specific evils that the general State regulations are intended to prevent."

[12]Roy D. Simon, Jr., *Fee Sharing Between Lawyers and Public Interest Groups*, 98 YALE L.J. 1070, 1114 (1989).

Compare NAACP v. Button, 371 U.S. 415, 428–431, 83 S.Ct. 328, 9 L.Ed.2d 405 (1963). The Court invalidated statutes that would have prohibited NAACP attorneys and lay members or NAACP supporters from urging others to join them in undertaking litigation challenging discriminatory practices. The state could not show that its rules, which infringed upon the fundamental First Amendment rights of the NAACP lawyers, members, and supporters, served a compelling state interest in its rules.

[13]Roy D. Simon, Jr., *Fee Sharing Between Lawyers and Public Interest Groups*, 98 YALE L.J. 1070, 1070 (1989) (footnote omitted).

[14]38 Cal.4th 23, 40 Cal.Rptr.3d 221, 129 P.3d408 (2006).

client of the nonprofit corporate housing clinic) sued that clinic, alleging that the clinic was not entitled to statutory attorney fees that the court had awarded against the landlord. The state supreme court, reversing the court of appeals, disagreed. First, a state statute permitting incorporation of nonprofit legal corporations and related statutes that required such corporations to register with State Bar did not occupy the entire field of law governing practice of law by nonprofit corporations. Second, even assuming that the clinic was not exempt from the statutory registration requirement, the nonprofit legal corporation's failure to register did not injure the client, and, thus, he was not entitled to the remedy of disgorgement of fees.[15]

---

[15]The court distinguished *Birbrower, Montalbano, Condon & Frank v. Superior Court*, 17 Cal.4th 119, 70 Cal.Rptr.2d 304, 949 P.2d 1 (1998):

"In *Birbrower*, we concluded that an out-of-state law firm was not entitled to a judgment enforcing its client's obligations under a fee agreement for legal services rendered in California, because neither the firm nor its lawyers were authorized to practice law in California. *Birbrower* is inapposite. It concerned a law firm's action to recover contractual fees owed by its client. The question in the present case is whether Frye, the plaintiff tenant for whom THC won a favorable judgment, is entitled to statutory attorney fees that the court ordered the defendant landlords in the underlying action to pay—despite the contract assigning such fees to THC and despite the circumstance that the defendant landlords paid the fees without objecting that THC was not authorized to practice law."

Frye v. Tenderloin Housing Clinic, Inc., 38 Cal.4th 23, 48, 40 Cal.Rptr.3d 221, 239, 129 P.3d 408, 426 (2006).

CHAPTER 5.6
RESTRICTIONS ON THE RIGHT TO PRACTICE LAW

§ 5.6–1 Employment Contracts That Restrict the Right of a
Lawyer to Practice Law
§ 5.6–2 Restrictive Covenants and Settlements of a Law Suit

RULE 5.6: RESTRICTIONS ON RIGHT TO PRACTICE

A lawyer shall not participate in offering or making:

(a) a partnership, shareholders, operating, employment, or other similar type of agreement that restricts the right of a lawyer to practice after termination of the relationship, except an agreement concerning benefits upon retirement; or

(b) an agreement in which a restriction on the lawyer's right to practice is part of the settlement of a client controversy.

Comment

[1] An agreement restricting the right of lawyers to practice after leaving a firm not only limits their professional autonomy but also limits the freedom of clients to choose a lawyer. Paragraph (a) prohibits such agreements except for restrictions incident to provisions concerning retirement benefits for service with the firm.

[2] Paragraph (b) prohibits a lawyer from agreeing not to represent other persons in connection with settling a claim on behalf of a client.

[3] This Rule does not apply to prohibit restrictions that may be included in the terms of the sale of a law practice pursuant to Rule 1.17.

Authors' 1983 Model Rules Comparison

The text of Rule 5.6(a) was modified in 2002 to cover "shareholders, operating . . . or other similar type of agreement."

In Rule 5.6(b), the drafters changed "controversy between private parties" to "client controversy."

Comment 1 changed the words, "partners or associates" to the word, "lawyers" to reflect that lawyers often practice in forms of organizations other than a partnership.

Model Code Comparison

This Rule is substantially similar to DR 2-108.

§ 5.6–1 EMPLOYMENT CONTRACTS THAT RESTRICT THE RIGHT OF A LAWYER TO PRACTICE LAW

§ 5.6–1(a) Introduction

The ABA Model Rules and the ABA Model Code both prohibit a lawyer from either requiring or agreeing to accept an employment contract or other agreement restricting his or her right to practice law after termination of the relationship created by the agreement. This prohibition applies to "a partnership, shareholders, operating, employment, or other similar type of agreement. . . . "[1] Such restrictive covenants violate the discipline rules even if they are limited to a stated period and geographic area.[2]

For example, a lawyer may not accept or propose a restriction in an employment agreement prohibiting counsel for a corporation from representing anyone in any future action against the corporation. Although the former lawyer for the corporation could not ethically engage in subsequent adverse representation that is *substantially related* to the prior representation,[3] a prohibition of *all* future adverse representation, including matters that are *unrelated,* violates Rule 5.6(a).[4]

Rule 5.6 is part of a long, unbroken tradition. It is virtually identical to DR 2-108, which in turn reflects pre-Code authority.[5] Oddly enough, some lawyers have vigorously attacked Rule 5.6 without appreciating its extended pedigree and traditional origins.[6] Other commentators argue that the legal profession's prohibition of non-compete agreements is economically inefficient,

---

[Section 5.6–1]

[1] Rule 5.6(a). The 1983 Rule 5.6(a) referred to partnership and employment agreements. The drafters of the 2002 Rules expanded the language to include other forms of law firm practice as well as other agreements. They also amended Comment 1 to apply the prohibition more broadly against lawyers instead of partners or associates. This modification does not change prior law; it simply clarifies the broad application of the rule to different types of agreements that may govern law firm organization.

[2] ABA Formal Opinion 300 (Aug. 7, 1961). *See also* Restatement of the Law Governing Lawyers, Third, § 13 ("Restrictions on Right to Practice Law") (Official Draft 2000).

[3] Rule 1.9.

[4] ABA Formal Opinion 94-381 (May 9, 1994).

[5] ABA Formal Opinion 300 (Aug. 7, 1961), citing ABA Canons of Professional Ethics, Canon 7 (1908), which stated, in part, that: "Efforts, direct or indirect, in any way to encroach upon the professional employment of another lawyer, are unworthy of those who should be brethren at the Bar. . . ." For a short and excellent history of the law leading to DR 2-108, see, ROBERT W. HILLMAN, HILLMAN ON LAWYER MOBILITY: THE LAW AND ETHICS OF PARTNER WITHDRAWALS AND LAW FIRM BREAKUPS § 2.3.3 (Little Brown & Co. 1994).

[6] *See* Louis Jackson & Anthony H. Atlas, *The Ethics of Stealing Clients,* 69 A.B.A.J. 706, 707 (1983) ("Firms are being bled and even destroyed [but Rule 5.6 does] nothing to protect the attorney who has built a law practice.").

because it makes it harder for law firms to "develop reputational capital and to motivate their lawyers to police lawyer-client agency costs."[7] Thus, regardless of the reasons for the covenant to compete, courts should not enforce them in the United States.[8]

§ 5.6–1(b) Court Enforcement

Most courts will not enforce a restrictive agreement that violates this rule.[9] Because lawyers should not sign or require other lawyers to sign such agreements, the courts will typically refuse to enforce them even when the lawyer who signed the agreement (the departing lawyer) brings an action to strike the

---

[7]Larry E. Ribstein, *Ethical Rules, Agency Costs, and Law Firm Structure*, 84 VA. L. REV. 1707, 1708 (1998). Steven Gillers & Richard W. Painter, *Free the Lawyers: A Proposal to Permit No-Sue Promises in Settlement Agreements*, 18 GEORGETOWN J. LEGAL ETHICS 291, 323 (2005), arguing that "the ethics rules should recognize that the defendant has a legitimate interest in buying total peace from the plaintiff's lawyer on matters factually related to the action it is settling and that the plaintiff's lawyer (with approval of her client) has a legitimate interest in being free to sell that peace."

[8]A New York court refused to enforce an agreement by two law firms in discussions for a potential merger to not hire away each other's lawyers for a two year period of time if the merger was unsuccessful. *See* 24 ABA/BNA Law. Man. Prof. Conduct 588 (Nov. 12, 2008) (citing unpublished opinion in Nixon Peabody LLP v. de Senihes, Valsarndidis, Arnsallem, Jonath, Flaicher Associes No. 2008/10374 (Sept. 16, 2008)).

[9]*See, e.g., Cohen v. Lord, Day & Lord*, 75 N.Y.2d 95, 551 N.Y.S.2d 157, 550 N.E.2d 410 (1989)(law firm partnership agreement that conditions payment of earned but uncollected partnership revenues upon a withdrawing partner's obligation to refrain from practicing law in competition with the former law firm restricts the practice of law in violation of New York's DR 2-108(A) "and is unenforce-

able in these circumstances as against public policy."). *Peroff v. Liddy, Sullivan, Galway, Begler & Peroff, P.C.*, 852 F.Supp. 239 (S.D.N.Y.1994)(same) (provision in partnership agreement entitling withdrawing partner to less compensation if he took clients with him violated public policy and was unenforceable); *Whiteside v. Griffis & Griffis, P.C.*, 902 S.W.2d 739, 1995-2 Trade Cases ¶ 71,223 (Tex.App.1995) (provision in law firm agreement, requiring that good will be taken into consideration in determining compensation for shares if withdrawing shareholder did not compete with corporation within designated area and time period, violated Code of Professional Responsibility prohibition against agreements restricting right of attorney to practice law).

California is an exception to this rule. *Howard v. Babcock*, 6 Cal.4th 409, 25 Cal.Rptr.2d 80, 863 P.2d 150 (1993), *appeal after remand*, 40 Cal.App.4th 569, 46 Cal.Rptr.2d 907 (1995), arguing that law firms should be treated no differently from other business partnerships, such as accountants' and doctors' practices, which California permits to enter into agreements restricting competition: "A revolution in the practice of law has occurred requiring economic interests of the law firm to be protected as they are in other business enterprises." Justice Kennard wrote a vigorous and thoughtful dissent in *Babcock*.

provision in the agreement restricting her right to practice in competition with her former firm.[10]

This principle is quite logical. If the court imposes a rule on lawyers, one would think that the court should not aid and abet its violation by enforcing contracts that violate the rule that the court has promulgated.[11] If a court now decides that law firms should be protected by restrictive covenants just like other business enterprises, then the logical thing for the court to do is to repeal its rule banning such contracts. That makes more sense than imposing the ethics rule while simultaneously refusing to enforce it. If the lawyer's signature on the invalid agreement serves to waive her rights, then the court, in effect, will be enforcing the agreement that is, by the court's own rules, against public policy.

Rule 5.6(a) prohibits agreements that serve to restrict the rights of a lawyer to practice after he or she leaves the law firm. Thus, a law firm cannot create a financial penalty that goes into effect if the lawyer leaves the law firm and then competes with it because that penalty is a form of restriction.[12] Consider, for example, *Stevens v. Rooks Pitts and Poust.*[13]

In the *Rooks Pitts case,* a lawyer departing his law firm brought suit challenging, as contrary to public policy, language in the partnership agreement limiting the compensation payable to any withdrawing partner if the partner competed with the firm in a certain geographic area. Although the lower court granted the law firm's motion for summary judgment, the appellate court reversed, relying on Rule 5.6. First, the financial disincentive clause in the partnership agreement between lawyers, which required the departing lawyer to give up certain compensation due to him if he competed with the firm in a certain geographic area within

---

[10]The lawyer does not waive her right to challenge the financial disincentive provision, simply because she earlier signed the agreement and had earlier benefitted from this provision when other lawyers withdrew from the law firm before she did. *Stevens v. Rooks Pitts and Poust,* 289 Ill.App.3d 991, 225 Ill.Dec. 48, 682 N.E.2d 1125 (Ill.App. 1 Dist.1997).

[11]*Gray v. Martin,* 63 Or.App. 173, 182, 663 P.2d 1285, 1290 (Or.App. 1983), *review denied, Gray v. Martin,* 295 Or. 541, 668 P.2d 384 (1983) (because contract violates this disciplinary rule it is unenforceable).

[12]Financial disincentives may involve either forfeiting compensation that is due to the departing lawyer or requiring that the departing lawyer remit to the firm a part of profits earned from representing former clients of the firm. *See* ABA/BNA Lawyer's Manual on Professional Conduct 51:1205 (2004) (examining financial disincentives involved in Rule 5.6). *See also Law Offices of Ronald J. Palagi, P.C. v. Howard,* 275 Neb. 334, 747 N.W.2d 1 (2008) (holding that a contract requiring a departing lawyer to remit all attorneys' fees from law firm clients who choose to follow the lawyer as unenforceable).

[13]*Stevens v. Rooks Pitts and Poust,* 289 Ill.App.3d 991, 225 Ill.Dec. 48, 682 N.E.2d 1125 (Ill.App. 1 Dist.1997).

one year after his departure, was unenforceable as against public policy; second, the financial penalty provision would be severed from the remainder of the partnership agreement, which the departing lawyer could then enforce as written; and third, the lawyer did not waive his right to challenge the financial disincentive provision simply because he had signed the agreement and had benefited from this provision when several attorneys withdrew before him.

Another example is *Anderson v. Aspelmeier, Fisch, Power, Warner Engberg*.[14] In this case, the law firm suspended its contractual obligation to pay its former partner, because the partner committed an "act detrimental to the partnership" by accepting business from clients who left the old firm. The court did not allow the law firm to reduce its payout to the departing partner because doing so would violate the ethical rule prohibiting lawyers from using covenants not to compete. The clients have every right to follow a former partner who withdrew from the law firm, and the law firm cannot financially penalize the departing partner for accepting these clients.[15]

In some cases, courts have drawn fine lines and exacting distinctions. Thus, *Hackett v. Milbank, Tweed, Hadley & McCloy*[16] ruled that if the financial penalty for leaving is not directed solely against lawyers who practice in competition against their former firm, then it is not really anticompetitive and therefore is not invalid under Rule 5.6(a). In that case, the law firm agree-

---

[14] *Anderson v. Aspelmeier, Fisch, Power, Warner Engberg*, 461 N.W.2d 598 (Iowa 1990).

[15] *See also Denburg v. Parker Chapin Flattau & Klimpl*, 82 N.Y.2d 375, 604 N.Y.S.2d 900, 624 N.E.2d 995 (1993), which considered the validity of a provision in the Parker Chapin partnership agreement that required withdrawing partners to make certain payments to the firm upon demand: if the withdrawing partner practiced law in the private sector prior to July 1988, he or she was to pay the firm either (1) 12.5% of the firm's profits allocated to that partner over the two previous years or (2) 12.5% of any billings to former Parker Chapin clients by the partner's new firm during the ensuing two years, whichever amount was greater. An exception was provided for withdrawing partners whose previous year's profit share was less than $85,000, providing that the part-

ner's new firm did no work for Parker Chapin clients during the two-year period following the withdrawal.

The court concluded, in light of *Cohen v. Lord, Day & Lord*, that the provision violated, and intended to violate, the public policy against anticompetition clauses. The provision, by its terms, applied only to withdrawing partners who went into private practice and hence into potential competition with Parker Chapin. It required the payment of the higher of two possible amounts, one of which was "directly proportional to the success of a departing partner's competitive efforts." And the exemption for a low-paid partner applied only if no Parker Chapin clients were served 82 N.Y.2d at 381, 604 N.Y.S.2d 900, 624 N.E.2d 995.

[16] *Hackett v. Milbank, Tweed, Hadley & McCloy*, 86 N.Y.2d 146, 630 N.Y.S.2d 274, 654 N.E.2d 95 (1995).

ment provided for reducing supplemental payments to a withdrawing partner based on the withdrawing partner's new income in other pursuits. The provision was not "inevitably anticompetitive on its face," because the clause did not discriminate between partners departing for private practice in competition with the former law firm and those departing the law firm for other pursuits, such as to enter academia or to accept a government position, neither of which compete with the former law firm.[17] The court upheld an arbitration award enforcing this agreement.

A court will enforce a partnership agreement that requires departing lawyers to share, with the former firm, 50% of contingent fees eventually received on cases the departing lawyers took with them when they left. Such an agreement does not violate Rule 5.6 because it does not prevent, "as a matter of fact or economic reality," the departing lawyer's ability to continue his practice or to handle cases that clients wanted him to take from plaintiff firm.[18] This partnership clause recognizes the value of the firm's willingness to risk the time and money to develop the claim, knowing that any of its lawyers could leave at any time, and that the client may decide to keep his case with the person who was most heavily involved with the litigation.[19]

§ 5.6–1(c) Restrictive Covenants and Retirement Agreements

The drafters of the Rules implemented an important exception to the general rule against covenants not to compete. A restrictive covenant may be imposed as a condition of collecting retirement benefit.[20]

The restrictions imposed in connection with retirement benefits

---

[17]86 N.Y.2d 146, 149, 630 N.Y.S.2d 274, 654 N.E.2d 95, 97 (1995). The law firm claimed that the petitioner was not entitled to any withdrawal payments because the amount of his annual income at his new firm foreclosed payments under the Milbank, Tweed scheme (which reduced the amount of the supplemental payments in proportion to a withdrawing partner's new earned income) and that the provisions of the partnership's agreement were not unlawfully anticompetitive.

[18]*Groen, Laveson, Goldberg & Rubenstone v. Kancher*, 362 N.J.Super. 350, 361, 827 A.2d 1163, 1169 (N.J.Super.A.D. 2003).

[19]For an opinion with an analysis of different contractual provisions for sharing fees with a departing lawyer who is taking a client, see N.C. State Bar Ethics Comm., Formal Op. 2008-8 (Oct. 24, 2008), *noted in* 24 ABA/BNA Law. Man. Prof. Conduct 640 (Dec. 10, 2008). The Opinion states: "The procedure or formula for dividing a fee must be reasonably calculated to protect the economic interests of the law firm while not restricting the right to practice law. It should fairly reflect the firm's investment of resources in the client's representation as of the time of the lawyer's departure and the investment of resources that will be required of the departing lawyer to complete the representation."

[20]Rule 5.6(a). DR 2-108(A). Restatement of the Law Governing Lawyers, Third, § 13(1) (Official Draft 2000).

must affect benefits that are available only to a lawyer who is in fact retiring from the practice of law. The restrictions may not impose a forfeiture of income that the lawyer had already earned, for that would fun afoul of Rule 5.6(a).

For example, the law firm may impose restrictions on the right to practice that delay or forfeit retirement benefits if the lawyer continues to practice law. It also may limit the restriction temporally, geographically, or to certain types of practice. The law firm, consistent with Rule 5.6(a), may permit the departing lawyer to engage in non-competitive employment, "such as service as a judge, a law professor, an elected or appointed government official, a public defender, a legal services lawyer, or an in-house counsel for a charitable or other non-profit organization, activities that a law firm may not wish to discourage."[21] The law firm has an interest in preventing the retiring partner from competing with her former law firm because it may fund the retirement out of its present income. But, a lawyer's employment as a judge, law professor, and so forth is not employment that competes with the former law firm.

Because Rule 5.6(a) expresses "a strong disapproval of restrictive covenants in lawyer agreements," we must construe them "strictly and narrowly." In order to be—

> an agreement concerning retirement benefits under Rule 5.6(a), the provision in question must affect benefits that are available only to a lawyer who is in fact retiring from the practice of law, and cannot work a forfeiture of Income already earned by the lawyer. Beyond that, however, law firms and employers have significant latitude in shaping the nature and scope of the restriction on practice and the penalties for noncompliance.[22]

Two reasons are often advanced to justify this exception to the normal rule against restrictions on the departing lawyer's right to practice. First, the law firm may use its current income to fund the retirement payout benefits that it must pay to the lawyers leaving the firm and retiring. Thus, some people argue that, if these lawyers were then to compete against the law firm, they would be undercutting the firm's source of income to meet the retirement payout. On the other hand, this is true of any firm payments.

The second justification is more persuasive. The exception in Rule 5.6(a) applies, by its own terms, to lawyers who are "retiring." If the lawyer is actually retiring from the practice of law, placing a restriction on her right to practice would not interfere with the right of her former clients to choose her as their lawyer because she is no longer available to serve former

---

[21] ABA Formal Opinion 06–444 (Sept. 13, 2006) (footnote omitted).

[22] ABA Formal Opinion 06–444 (Sept. 13, 2006).

clients. Thus, if there really is not an authentic and genuine retirement, the restrictive covenant is invalid.[23]

Given that a law firm could restrict a lawyer's right to practice in order for the lawyer to receive retirement benefits, the Rule is potentially open to abuse. Law firms could structure employment agreements and partnership or professional corporation provisions so as to include in retirement all payments to departing lawyers. Unfortunately, the Comments do not define retirement benefits and they do not provide much elaboration on the operation of this exception.

Courts should not permit law firms to use this exception to withhold payments conditioned on an agreement not to compete other than payments that related to those benefits on retirement as the term is normally understood.[24] The lack of specificity in defining retirement benefits have led the New Jersey courts to issue three opinions on this topic. One decision invalidated a law firm agreement that paid lawyers who left on non-competitive terms but denied any compensation for those who left on competitive terms.[25] In that decision, the agreement did not focus on lawyer retirement, just whether the lawyer continued to practice law in competition with the firm.

A second decision invalidated a law firm agreement that paid greater retirement benefits to a lawyer who left the practice of law, paid slightly smaller benefits to lawyers who left the state to practice law, and substantially penalized lawyers who stayed in state and practiced law.[26] The court found that the law firm did not have a bona fide retirement agreement.

In the third decision, the New Jersey Supreme Court held that in order for an agreement to fit within the exception in Rule 5.6,

---

[23]*Gray v. Martin*, 63 Or.App. 173, 181–82, 663 P.2d 1285, 1290 (Or.App. 1983), *review denied*, *Gray v. Martin*, 295 Or. 541, 668 P.2d 384 (1983):

"Paragraph 25 [of the partnership agreement] fits squarely within the prohibition contained in DR2-108(A). It affects defendant's right to practice law in Jefferson, Crook or Deschutes counties by requiring that if he does so he loses the benefits that would otherwise be his. This is certainly a restriction on his right to practice. The agreement is not a condition to payment of retirement benefits as plaintiffs claim. If retirement has the same meaning as withdrawal in DR2-108(A), then the disciplinary rule has no meaning. Every termination of

a relationship between law partners would be a retirement, and agreements restricting the right to practice would always be allowed. We conclude that Paragraph 25 of the partnership agreement violates DR2-108(A)."

[24]*See* CENTER FOR PROFESSIONAL RESPONSIBILITY, ANNOTATED MODEL RULES OF PROFESSIONAL CONDUCT 494–495 (ABA, 5th ed. 2003).

[25]*Jacob v. Norris, McLaughlin & Marcus*, 128 N.J. 10, 607 A.2d 142 (1992)

[26]*Apfel v. Budd, Larner, Gross, Rosenbaum, Greenberg & Sade*, 324 N.J.Super. 133, 734 A.2d 808 (App.Div. 1999), *certification denied*, 162 N.J. 485, 744 A.2d 1208 (Table) (1999).

it must contain sufficient indicia of a bona fide agreement.[27] The fact that an agreement includes: (1) minimum age requirements, (2) benefit calculation formulas, (3) a defined term for benefit payouts, and (4) benefits that increase as years of service to the firm increase are evidence of a bona fide retirement plan. The New Jersey Supreme Court directed its Professional Responsibility Rules Committee to review its version of Rule 5.6 and the question whether benefits upon retirement should be defined in the Rule so as to give more guidance to law firms in that state.[28]

ABA Formal Opinion 06–444 provides guidance on bona fide retirement plan restrictions on the right to practice law.[29] ABA Formal Opinion requires that the benefits be "available only to lawyers who are in fact retiring and thereby terminating or winding down their legal careers."[30] The availability of the benefits should be tied to a lawyer's age and years of service; thus providing support for a lawyer upon retirement from practice of law. If the benefits are available "during the prime of a lawyer's career and after only a relatively modest period of service with the firm," any restriction on practice in order to receive such benefits would seem to prevent a lawyer from competing against the law firm and not for retirement purposes.[31] Several factors that one should consider when deciding whether the benefits are are bona fide retirement benefits that can be conditioned upon a restriction of practice are:

> (i) the presence of benefit calculation formulas, (ii) benefits that increase as the years of service to a firm increase, and (iii) benefits that are payable over the lifetime of a retired partner. Similarly, if there is an interrelationship between the benefits and payments from other retirement funds, such as Social Security and defined contribution retirement plans (that is, the payments from the firm decrease as other sources of retirement income phase in), the benefits are more likely to be considered "retirement benefits" under Rule 5.6(a).[32]

Essentially, the court or disciplinary committee needs to examine the benefits and restrictions as a whole to determine whether the law firm has improperly used the retirement label to implement a covenant not to compete with its productive lawyers.

---

[27]*Borteck v. Riker, Danzig, Scherer, Hyland & Perretti*, 179 N.J. 246, 255, 844 A.2d 521, 527 (2004) (basing this list of indicia on the testimony of an expert witness).

[28]179 N.J at 260, 844 A.2d at 530.

[29]ABA Formal Opinion 06–444 (Sept. 13, 2006) ("It would not be proper under Rule 5.6(a), for example, for a law firm to place a "retirement benefit" label on a partner's capital account or on income already earned by the partner, and thereby seek to divest lawyers of such sums if they compete with the firm.")

[30]ABA Formal Opinion 06–444 (Sept. 13, 2006).

[31]ABA Formal Opinion 06–444 (Sept. 13, 2006).

[32]ABA Formal Opinion 06–444 (Sept. 13, 2006) (footnote omitted).

Rule 5.6 also makes clear that it does not apply to restrictions that may be included in the terms of the sale of an entire law practice.[33] Complete sales of a law practice are governed by Model Rule 1.17.

§ 5.6–1(d) Departing Lawyers Seeking to Take Clients With Them

The partnership, shareholder, or other type of agreement may also provide how the law firm should handle the situation where many lawyers leave the firm and the firm breaks up, or one or more lawyers leave the firm to join another firm or start their own firm. Any such agreement must comply with the ethical restrictions of Rule 5.6(a). Thus, when lawyers leave their firm, they retain the right to practice law in competition with the firm from which they departed. But, to what extent may the departing lawyers seek to take with them the clients of that firm (or, in the view of the departing lawyers, "their clients")? The question is, to what extent may departing lawyers solicit clients from their previous law firm? These issues are considered in the analysis of Rule 7.3.

§ 5.6-1(e) Confidentiality Agreements Imposed on Departing Lawyers

Rule 1.9(c) requires, in general, that a lawyer must neither use nor reveal confidential information that the lawyer learned from a former client, unless the information has become "generally known." Hence, clients sometimes may wish to use Rule 1.9(c) to expand the restrictions on the lawyer's right to practice after the client becomes a former client.

The fact pattern is similar to the situation where parties seek to impose limits on a lawyer's right to practice.[34] However, this situation involves the employer (about to become the former employer) imposing (as a condition of employment) restrictions on the lawyer when he or she leaves employment. The principles, however, are similar. Both involve the relationship between Rule 1.9 and Rule 5.6(b).

A typical situation involves a corporation that employs various

---

[33]Rule 5.6, Comment 3.

[34]ABA Formal Op. 00-417 (Apr. 7, 2000) explains that a lawyer may participate in a settlement agreement that prohibits him from revealing information relating to the representation of his client, because Rule 1.6 protects that information as to the present client and Rule 1.9 protects it as to the former client. However, the lawyer may not participate or comply with a settlement agreement that prevents him from using information gained during that representation in later representations against the opposing party, or a related party, except in very limited circumstances. An agreement not to use any information learned during the representation effectively would restrict the lawyer's right to practice and hence would violate Rule 5.6(b).

lawyers. The ethics rules govern lawyers so they will determine whether the general counsel may ethically require the assistant general counsels or staff lawyers to sign confidentiality agreements that "arguably" extend the lawyers' confidentiality obligations, after their employment ends, to information that goes beyond confidential client information. The New York New York State Bars Association's Committee on Professional Ethics concluded that such agreements are proper *if* the agreement makes clear that it does not restrict the lawyer's right to practice law after he or she leaves employment and does not expand the lawyer's duty to protect client information under the ethics rules.[35]

In the particular agreement that the Ethics Committee considered, a savings clause specifically provided that, as applied to lawyers, the agreement is "not meant to restrict the employee's post-termination right to practice law in violation of the applicable rules of professional conduct or in violation of the ethics rules of the jurisdictions in which the attorney is licensed." Thus, even if the general corporate agreement goes beyond Rules 1.6 and 1.9, "the savings clause keeps the agreement within the confines of the Rules and renders further analysis under Rule 5.6 unnecessary."[36]

§ 5.6–2 RESTRICTIVE COVENANTS AND SETTLEMENTS OF A LAW SUIT

§ 5.6–2(a) Introduction

Model Rule 5.6(b) makes clear that lawyers may not restrict their right to practice as part of the settlement of a client's controversy.[1] Clients always have a right to discharge their lawyers at any time and hire new counsel. And a lawyer can turn down a prospective client. But, if lawyers were forced to (or were allowed to force others to) agree to restrictive covenants, then these covenants would impose restraints, not only on the lawyer's professional autonomy, but also on the new client's freedom to choose a lawyer. Thus, the Model Rules justify Rule 5.6(b) based on two rationales: lawyer freedom and client freedom.[2]

This type of constraint is different from a lawyer's unencumbered decision to reject proffered employment because of the manner in which this restraint comes about. It is not the product of the lawyer's voluntary forbearance; third parties impose this restriction at the time of settlement. A lawyer would be in an inher-

---

[35]N.Y. State Bar Association, Committee on Professional Ethics, Op. 858 (Mar. 17, 2011).

[36]N.Y. State Bar Association, Committee on Professional Ethics, Op. 858 (Mar. 17, 2011), 2011 WL 1351745,

*4. *See also*, Connecticut Informal Opinion 02-05 (2002), 2002 WL 570602.

[Section 5.6–2]

[1]DR 2-108(B); Rule 5.6(b).
[2]Rule 5.6, Comment 1.

ent and inevitable conflict of interests situation whenever, for example, his client (the plaintiff) wants to settle and agree to the opposing party's condition that the lawyer not represent any future plaintiffs against this defendant, or not represent any future plaintiffs in this type of law suit. The restriction on the plaintiff-lawyer's right to practice costs the plaintiff nothing. It is, as the saying goes, no skin off of the plaintiff's nose if the plaintiff's lawyer must forego future restrictions on that lawyer's right to practice law. But it does limit the lawyer's ability to practice law and the ability of future clients to hire that lawyer, so it is against public policy.

Therefore, Rule 5.6 limits Rule 1.2(a), which provides, in general, that the lawyer must abide by the client's decisions concerning settlement.[3] A lawyer may not accept or be part of a settlement agreement that would limit the ability of the lawyer to accept representation of future clients.[4]

Similarly, a lawyer may not settle a case on the condition that she not use any information learned against the defendant in the future.[5] A settlement term that prohibited a lawyer from, *e.g.*, using the same expert witness or subpoenaing certain records on behalf of the new client that the lawyer had previously subpoenaed on behalf of the former client would, in practice, effectively bar the lawyer from future representations, because the lawyer's inability to use that information might materially limit her representation of a future client. The ABA Ethics Opinion on this issue reminds us that "the subsequent use of information relating to the representation of a former client is treated quite liberally as compared to restrictions regarding disclosure of client information."[6] Rule 1.9(c) restrains only use that is *disadvantageous* to the former client and does not even apply when the information has become generally known or when other exceptions apply. "As long as the lawyer does not disclose information relating to the representation of the former client to a third party, the

---

[3]ABA Formal Opinion 93-371 (Aug. 16, 1993).

[4]*See, e.g.*, Oregon State Bar Legal Ethics Committee, Opinion 258 (1974); D.C. Bar Legal Ethics Committee, Opinion 35 (1977); ABA Formal Opinion 93-371 (Aug. 16, 1993).

[5]ABA Formal Opinion 00-417 (Apr. 7, 2000) reaches this conclusion after examining, in particular, Rules 1.9 and 5.6. Although a lawyer may participate in a settlement agreement that prohibits him from revealing information relating to the representation of his client, the lawyer may not

participate or comply with a settlement agreement that would prevent him from using information gained during the representation in later representations against the opposing party, or a related party, except in very limited circumstances. An agreement not to use information learned during the representation effectively would restrict the lawyer's right to practice and hence would violate Rule 5.6(b).

[6]ABA Formal Opinion 00-417 (Apr. 7, 2000).

lawyer may use that information in subsequent representations, subject to the limited restrictions of Rule 1.9(c)(1)."[7]

The introductory clause to Rule 5.6 makes clear that both Rule 5.6(a) and Rule 5.6(b) prohibit lawyers from "participat[ing] in offering or making" the prohibited agreement. Thus a lawyer may not ethically agree to the restriction and the opposing lawyer may not propose or require the restriction.

Moreover, a lawyer is not subject to estoppel if she later objects to the agreement that she had earlier signed.[8] The other party to the agreement, seeking its enforcement, may argue that the lawyer should not be able to deceive the other party by signing it and then seeking to avoid its enforcement. However, if estoppel did apply, the courts would be enforcing agreements that their own rules forbid, because the most likely candidate to object to an agreement against public policy is, in this circumstance, one who has signed it.[9]

Hiring the Former Adversary. There are powerful market incentives for defendants to prevent plaintiffs' lawyers from suing them in the future. Some defendants, typically large corporations, have responded by putting the adverse counsel on retainer, after the case is settled. Then, the former adversaries cannot ethically sue them in the future because of the conflict created by this arrangement: the lawyer (now a consultant to the corporation) cannot sue a present client.[10] Professor Geoffrey Hazard, the Reporter for the ABA Model Rules, acknowledges that this ar-

---

[7]ABA Formal Opinion 00-417 (Apr. 7, 2000).

[8]See Cardillo v. Bloomfield 206 Corp., 411 N.J. Super. 574, 988 A.2d 136 (2010).

[9]Cf. Stevens v. Rooks Pitts and Poust, 289 Ill.App.3d 991, 225 Ill.Dec. 48, 682 N.E.2d 1125 (Ill.App. 1 Dist. 1997).

[10]See, e.g., Jackson v. Bellsouth Telecommunications, Inc., 181 F.Supp.2d 1345 (S.D.Fla.2001). The court explained, that, when entering into the global settlement agreement with Bellsouth, the defendants also entered into two separate agreements that the plaintiffs in this case alleged to be unethical and unlawful. First, the Ruden McClosky defendants [the law firm that represented the plaintiffs in the underlying case] "agreed not to sue Bellsouth for any claims of employment discrimination for a period of one year. Plaintiffs here claim that 'the effect of this side agreement was to impede the ability of [those plaintiffs who signed the general release] to enforce the terms' of the settlement and that this provision of the settlement was never disclosed to them.. Second, the Bellsouth and Ruden McClosky defendants entered into a four-year 'consulting agreement,' under the terms of which Bellsouth paid $120,000 taken from the settlement proceeds directly to the Ruden McClosky defendants and without the plaintiffs' knowledge. Plaintiffs allege that the defendants took this action in order to create a conflict of interest that would disqualify the Ruden McClosky defendants from representing any plaintiff in future actions against BellSouth, which in effect 'bought' the loyalty of Plaintiffs' attorneys from the Plaintiffs, to whom their duty was owed." 181 F.Supp.2d at 1354.

rangement is a mere "contrivance," but "it's significantly within the rules," if the lawyers fully disclose this side arrangement to their clients.[11]

The lawyers, settling with the defendant on behalf of their clients, must disclose this arrangement so that the clients can decide if the lawyers are involved in a conflict of interest—there is always the risk that the lawyer might sell the client short and advise acceptance of a poor offer so that the lawyer can accept the lucrative settlement agreement.[12]

§ 5.6–2(b) Imposing Restrictions on the Lawyer's Practice When the Lawyer Is the Respondent

A disciplinary authority, or another government agency, as part of a settlement of its controversy with a lawyer, may impose restrictions on that lawyer's right to practice. In this case, the

---

See also 181 F.Supp.2d at 1360: "Further, the plaintiffs allege that the purpose of the four-year 'consulting agreement' entered into by the Bellsouth and Ruden McClosky defendants was to 'create a conflict of interest for Plaintiffs' attorneys [the Ruden McClosky defendants] and to prevent future representation of any plaintiffs in legal action against Bellsouth.' "

The court ended up dismissing these counts with prejudice. However, in an earlier part of this litigation, the judge was less sympathetic. BellSouth Corp. negotiated a consulting deal with a group of Miami lawyers to settle a workplace-discrimination lawsuit they filed on behalf of 56 employees and former employees.

The "company left it to the plaintiffs' lawyers to determine their own consulting fees and told them to take the amount out of a $1.6 million settlement fund created for their clients. The clients knew nothing about the deal until one of them complained about the lawyers for other reasons to the federal judge in Miami overseeing the case, which led to an investigation of the settlement. 'Simply put, this situation thrust plaintiffs' counsel into a direct conflict of interest with their clients,' Judge Donald Middlebrooks wrote last January, after the investigation. 'It enabled them to take a direct cut of the settlement money—a paradigmatic payoff to a plaintiffs' lawyer if there ever was one.' Judge Middlebrooks ordered two BellSouth in-house law-

yers who negotiated the deal to take a five-hour ethics course and referred the conduct of a paralegal for the lead plaintiffs lawyer in the case, Norman Gantz, to federal prosecutors for possible criminal charges. [That lawyer] who wasn't sanctioned by the judge but has stopped practicing law in Florida, couldn't be reached for comment. Bell-South says it acted in good faith. 'The BellSouth lawyers were told in no uncertain terms by plaintiffs' lawyers that [the consulting agreement] was in fact going to be disclosed,' says Lawrence Robbins, a Washington, D.C., attorney for BellSouth who wasn't involved in the case."

Milo Geyelin, *Some Companies Pay Lawyers Not to Sue Again: Ethics Codes Say Agreements Must Be Disclosed to Clients But Not All Lawyers Do So,* WALL STREET JOURNAL, May 16, 2001, at B1, B6.

[11]Milo Geyelin, *Some Companies Pay Lawyers Not to Sue Again: Ethics Codes Say Agreements Must Be Disclosed to Clients But Not All Lawyers Do So,* WALL STREET JOURNAL, May 16, 2001, at p. B1.

[12]*See* Model Rule 1.4(b) (lawyer must explain matter to client to extent reasonable necessary to permit client to make informed decisions); Model Rule 1.8(g) & Comment 4 (lawyer representing two or more clients and making aggregate settlement must disclose the participation of each person in the settlement).

lawyer is the party (the defendant or respondent). The lawyer is not settling a claim on behalf of a client; he is settling a disciplinary proceeding or other claim against him.[13] The ABA Ethics Committee, in reaching this conclusion, did not discuss how its conclusion is consistent with the Comment to Rule 5.6 that purports to justify Rule 5.6 on the basis of the new client's freedom to hire counsel unencumbered by restrictions that third parties have imposed on the lawyer's ability to accept a client retainer.[14] That suggests that the client freedom rationale is more of a make-weight and that the lawyer freedom rationale is the primary justification for this Rule.

§ 5.6–2(c) Restrictive Covenants with Government Lawyers

The language of Rule 5.6(b) and its prohibition against lawyers agreeing to a restriction of their right to practice as part of a settlement of a controversy uses the phrase "between private parties." However, that language does not exempt government agencies from this rule.[15] Lawyers in a state or federal government agency may not ethically seek to impose such settlement restrictions on the opposing counsel as part of the government's settlement with a client represented by that lawyer, and private lawyers may not enter into such agreements with government agencies.[16]

---

[13]ABA Formal Opinion 95-394 (July 24, 1995).

[14]Rule 5.6, Comment 1.

[15]This Rule does not apply to prohibit government agencies from having conflicts rules for lawyers who leave employment to joint private practice. For example, an agency could have a one year prohibition against representing clients before the agency after leaving government employment.

[16]ABA Formal Opinion 95-394 (July 24, 1995).

CHAPTER 5.7
RESPONSIBILITIES REGARDING LAW-RELATED SERVICES

§ 5.7–1 Defining Law-Related Services
§ 5.7–2 Special Ethics Issues Related to Law-Related Services

---

RULE 5.7: RESPONSIBILITIES REGARDING LAW-RELATED SERVICES

(a) A lawyer shall be subject to the Rules of Professional Conduct with respect to the provision of law-related services, as defined in paragraph (b), if the law-related services are provided:

(1) by the lawyer in circumstances that are not distinct from the lawyer's provision of legal services to clients; or

(2) in other circumstances by an entity controlled by the lawyer individually or with others if the lawyer fails to take reasonable measures to assure that a person obtaining the law-related services knows that the services are not legal services and that the protections of the client-lawyer relationship do not exist.

(b) The term "law-related services" denotes services that might reasonably be performed in conjunction with and in substance are related to the provision of legal services, and that are not prohibited as unauthorized practice of law when provided by a nonlawyer.

Comment

[1] When a lawyer performs law-related services or controls an organization that does so, there exists the potential for ethical problems. Principal among these is the possibility that the person for whom the law-related services are performed fails to understand that the services may not carry with them the protections normally afforded as part of the client-lawyer relationship. The recipient of the law-related services may expect, for example, that the protection of client confidences, prohibitions against representation of persons with conflicting interests, and obligations of a lawyer to maintain professional independence apply to the provision of law-related services when that may not be the case.

[2] Rule 5.7 applies to the provision of law-related services by a lawyer even when the lawyer does not provide any legal services to the person for whom the law-related services are performed and whether the law-related services are performed through a law firm

or a separate entity. The Rule identifies the circumstances in which all of the Rules of Professional Conduct apply to the provision of law-related services. Even when those circumstances do not exist, however, the conduct of a lawyer involved in the provision of law-related services is subject to those Rules that apply generally to lawyer conduct, regardless of whether the conduct involves the provision of legal services. See, e.g., Rule 8.4.

[3] When law-related services are provided by a lawyer under circumstances that are not distinct from the lawyer's provision of legal services to clients, the lawyer in providing the law-related services must adhere to the requirements of the Rules of Professional Conduct as provided in paragraph (a)(1). Even when the law-related and legal services are provided in circumstances that are distinct from each other, for example through separate entities or different support staff within the law firm, the Rules of Professional Conduct apply to the lawyer as provided in paragraph (a)(2) unless the lawyer takes reasonable measures to assure that the recipient of the law-related services knows that the services are not legal services and that the protections of the client-lawyer relationship do not apply.

[4] Law-related services also may be provided through an entity that is distinct from that through which the lawyer provides legal services. If the lawyer individually or with others has control of such an entity's operations, the Rule requires the lawyer to take reasonable measures to assure that each person using the services of the entity knows that the services provided by the entity are not legal services and that the Rules of Professional Conduct that relate to the client-lawyer relationship do not apply. A lawyer's control of an entity extends to the ability to direct its operation. Whether a lawyer has such control will depend upon the circumstances of the particular case.

[5] When a client-lawyer relationship exists with a person who is referred by a lawyer to a separate law-related service entity controlled by the lawyer, individually or with others, the lawyer must comply with Rule 1.8(a).

[6] In taking the reasonable measures referred to in paragraph (a)(2) to assure that a person using law-related services understands the practical effect or significance of the inapplicability of the Rules of Professional Conduct, the lawyer should communicate to the person receiving the law-related services, in a manner sufficient to assure that the person understands the significance of the fact, that the relationship of the person to the business entity will not be a client-lawyer relationship. The communication should be made before entering into an agreement for provision of or providing law-related services, and preferably should be in writing.

[7] The burden is upon the lawyer to show that the lawyer has taken reasonable measures under the circumstances to communicate the desired understanding. For instance, a sophisticated user of law-related services, such as a publicly held corporation, may require a lesser explanation than someone unaccustomed to making distinctions between legal services and law-related services, such as an individual seeking tax advice from a lawyer-accountant or investigative services in connection with a lawsuit.

[8] Regardless of the sophistication of potential recipients of law-related services, a lawyer should take special care to keep separate the provision of law-related and legal services in order to minimize the risk that the recipient will assume that the law-related services are legal services. The risk of such confusion is especially acute when the lawyer renders both types of services with respect to the same matter. Under some circumstances the legal and law-related services may be so closely entwined that they cannot be distinguished from each other, and the requirement of disclosure and consultation imposed by paragraph (a)(2) of the Rule cannot be met. In such a case a lawyer will be responsible for assuring that both the lawyer's conduct and, to the extent required by Rule 5.3, that of nonlawyer employees in the distinct entity that the lawyer controls complies in all respects with the Rules of Professional Conduct.

[9] A broad range of economic and other interests of clients may be served by lawyers' engaging in the delivery of law-related services. Examples of law-related services include providing title insurance, financial planning, accounting, trust services, real estate counseling, legislative lobbying, economic analysis, social work, psychological counseling, tax preparation, and patent, medical or environmental consulting.

[10] When a lawyer is obliged to accord the recipients of such services the protections of those Rules that apply to the client-lawyer relationship, the lawyer must take special care to heed the proscriptions of the Rules addressing conflict of interest (Rules 1.7 through 1.11, especially Rules 1.7(a)(2) and 1.8(a), (b) and (f)), and to scrupulously adhere to the requirements of Rule 1.6 relating to disclosure of confidential information. The promotion of the law-related services must also in all respects comply with Rules 7.1 through 7.3, dealing with advertising and solicitation. In that regard, lawyers should take special care to identify the obligations that may be imposed as a result of a jurisdiction's decisional law.

[11] When the full protections of all of the Rules of Professional Conduct do not apply to the provision of law-related services, principles of law external to the Rules, for example, the law of principal and agent, govern the legal duties owed to those receiving the services. Those other legal principles may establish a different degree of protection for the recipient with respect to confidentiality of information, conflicts of interest and permissible business relationships with clients. See also Rule 8.4 (Misconduct).

Authors' 1983 Model Rules Comparison

Rule 5.7 was not part of the 1983 Model Rules. In 1991, the ABA adopted a version of Rule 5.7 in response to pressures for a rule governing the delivery of law-related services by law firms. The original Rule 5.7 was completely repealed in 1992 and a new Rule 5.7 was adopted in 1994. The text of this 1994 rule forms the basis for the text of the current rule.

The drafters of the 2002 Rules only made one slight change to the text of Rule 5.7. In Rule 5.7(a)(2), they deleted the word, "separate," and added the clause "in other circumstances." This change was designed to broaden the way in which lawyers may offer law-related services.

Comments 1, 4, 5, 6, 7, 8, 9, and 11 were not modified.

In Comment 2, the drafters added a clause at the end of the first sentence stating that the Rule applies "whether the law-related services are performed through a law firm or a separate entity."

In Comment 3, the drafters added several sentences to the end of the Comment to make clear that providing law-related services through a separate entity is not sufficient to remove the services from the protection of the Rule. The lawyer must comply with the other aspects of the Rule.

In Comment 10, the drafters amended a reference to the conflicts of interest (Rule 1.7) to reflect changes made to that rule in 2002.

Model Code Comparison

There was no counterpart to this Rule in the Model Code.

§ 5.7–1 DEFINING LAW-RELATED SERVICES

Someday, Sears may be able to own a law firm. In the meantime, may a law firm (or partners of a law firm) invest in, or own and operate a department store? Absolutely. The department store is not ancillary to the business of a law firm, so the Model Rules do not concern themselves with this issue.

May a law firm also own a business that is ancillary to the practice of law, such as a patent consulting firm? Patent work is related to legal services. In August of 1991, the ABA House of Delegates narrowly approved a new rule to deal with this question, Model Rule 5.7, "Provision of Ancillary Services."[1] At its August, 1992 annual meeting, the ABA repealed this Rule. It was the first time that the ABA House of Delegates simply repealed, outright, a Rule.[2] Less than two years after this repeal, the ABA approved a new Rule 5.7, at its February, 1994 midyear meeting. The new Rule 5.7 is titled "Responsibilities Regarding Law-Related Services."[3]

"Law-related services" are services that are reasonably performed in conjunction with, and are related to, legal services,

---

[Section 5.7–1]

[1] *See* Dennis J. Block, Irwin H. Warren, & George F. Meierhofer, Jr., *Model Rule of Professional Conduct 5.7: Its Origin and Interpretation*, 5 GEORGETOWN J. OF LEGAL ETHICS 739 (1992).

[2] For a complete review of the history of Model Rule 5.7, see A Legislative History: The Development of the ABA Model Rules of Professional Conduct, 1982–2005 (ABA 2006) at 245.

[3] Rule 5.7 has a complicated history. The Kutak Commission proposed a "quite permission" rule, but the ABA decided to adopt no regulation when it approved the 1983 ABA Model Rules. Then, by a narrow vote, it embraced a "highly prohibitory Rule 5.7" in 1991, only to repeal it a year later, by another narrow vote. In 1994, it adopted a "much more permissive" by a significant majority. Restatement of the Law Governing Lawyers, Third, § 10 ("Limitations On Nonlawyer Involvement In A Law Firm") (Official Draft 2000), Reporter's Notes to Comment g.. The 2003 revisions made slight changes to the 1994 version of Rule 5.7.

but these services would not constitute the unauthorized practice of law if they were performed by a nonlawyer.[4] Examples include "title insurance, financial planning, accounting, trust services, real estate counseling, legislative lobbying, economic analysis, social work, psychological counseling, tax return preparation, and patent, medical or environmental consulting."[5] Customers of these ancillary businesses may include clients and nonclients.

---

[4]Rule 5.7(b). *See* Restatement of the Law Governing Lawyers, Third, § 11 ("Limitations on Non-Lawyer Involvement in Law Firm") (Official Draft 2000), at Comment *g*, "Lawyer involvement in ancillary business activities."

[5]Rule 5.7, Comment 9.

Lawyers as Expert Witnesses. If a lawyer testifies as an expert witness on behalf of a party who is the client of another law firm, the lawyer does not thereby assume an attorney-client relationship with that party or provide a "law-related" service under Rule 5.7. ABA Formal Opinion 97-407 (May 13, 1997). The situation would be different if the law firm hired the other lawyer as a non-testifying expert consultant, rather than as a testifying expert witness. The nontestifying expert consultant is an advocate. In contrast, the testifying expert witness, like any non-lawyer expert witness, is hired to present expert testimony to aid the trier of fact. "A duty to advance a client's objectives diligently through all lawful measures, which is inherent in a client-lawyer relationship, is inconsistent with the duty of a testifying expert." ABA Formal Opinion 97-407 (May 13, 1997) at 4.

This conclusion—that a lawyer testifying as an expert witness is not engaging in a "law-related" service—is not obvious. An expert witness (even one testifying on the standards of the legal profession) does not have to be admitted to the bar to testify, just as a law professor does not have to be admitted to the bar to teach law. Similarly, a lawyer could engage in the business of practicing law and also be an expert witness in legal malpractice cases. A law firm could practice law, supply economic analysis (a "law-related service" under Rule 5.7), and supply an expert witness in legal malpractice cases. The same law firm would not supply the expert witness in the situation where it was also representing the plaintiff (or defendant), but it still would appear to be engaging in a "law-related service."

See also E.E.O.C. v. Exxon Corporation, 202 F.3d 755 (5th Cir. 2000). The EEOC alleged that Exxon's failure to permit a recovering alcoholic to hold a safety-sensitive position such as an oil tanker pilot violates the Americans with Disabilities Act. Exxon defended its actions, in part, on the grounds that its policy grew out of a requirement that the Federal Government had placed on it in connection with Exxon's settling criminal charges arising out of the Exxon Valdez oil spill. In support of this defense, Exxon hired two former Justice Department lawyers (now in private practice) as expert witnesses to testify about the events leading up to the earlier settlement. The Justice Department argued that their testimony would violate the Ethics in Government Act, but the District Judge permitted the testimony insofar as it was limited to publicly-known information. The Fifth Circuit affirmed, because being an expert witness (or a fact witness) is not the same as representing a party, so it is not forbidden by either the Federal statute, the ABA Model Rules, or the Texas or DC Bar Rules. "The ABA Model Rules and the corresponding state rules all permit a lawyer to use information that has become publicly known. See ABA Model R. 1.9(c)(1); Tex. Bar R. 1.05(b)(3); D.C. Bar R. 1.6 Comment 8. These rules

Law firms create these non-law subsidiaries for economic reasons. First, one-stop shopping makes the law firm more convenient for the client when the client has a problem that requires the services of several professionals. In addition, in these non-law subsidiaries, the law firm can ethically give the nonlawyer professionals—the former ambassador, a former economist for the federal reserve, or a former chief trade negotiator—the status and titles that they believe they deserve. Having the affiliates may help the firm retain existing clients and bring in new clients, thus offering new sources of revenue. Accordingly, various law firms, particularly in the Washington, D.C. area (a location with a disproportionate number of former ambassadors, former agency head, and so forth), have created subsidiaries to perform law-related services.

§ 5.7–2 SPECIAL ETHICS ISSUES RELATED TO LAW-RELATED SERVICES

§ 5.7–2(a) Relevance of Rule 1.8

Whether or not a jurisdiction adopts Rule 5.7, the lawyer is still governed by Rule 1.8(a), which already regulates business transactions with a client. In fact, one can think of Rule 5.7 as an elaboration of the general principles found in Rule 1.8(a).[1]

The existence of these subsidiaries raises various ethical issues mainly relating to conflicts of interest and attorney-client privilege. Rule 5.7 outlines the basic rules the law firm must follow to deal with these ethical issues.

§ 5.7–2(b) Applying Rule 5.7

Rule 5.7(a) is drafted in a very indirect way. Essentially, it states that the provisions of the Model Rules will apply to regulate the conduct of lawyers who deliver law-related services to clients if one of two conditions is met. Implicit in this Rule is the fact that law firms may offer law-related services, and they may do so with partnerships with non-lawyers. The Rule also does not require the lawyer to disclose the lawyer's ownership interests in the law-related service. And, it is reasonable to presume that most, but not all, lawyers wish to exclude the application of the Rules to the law-related service.[2]

The 1994 version of Rule 5.7(a) provided that a lawyer was

---

suggest that the sharing of public information in itself does not present an ethical bar." *EEOC v. Exxon Corp.*, 202 F.3d 755, 759 (5th Cir.2000).

[Section 5.7–2]

[1] *See, e.g., Florida Bar v. Slater*, 512 So.2d 191 (Fla.1987), where the court suspended a lawyer for 2 years and 4 months for referring law clients who sustained personal injuries to a physical therapy clinic: "Respondent concealed his involvement in the organization and operation of the clinic from his law firm, the claimants, and the insurance companies." *Id.* at 191.

[2] For example, a litigation law firm may own a separate copying and

subject to *all* of the Model Rules when providing these services *if*: (1) she provided them in circumstances that are indistinct from her provision of legal services to clients, *or* (2) the lawyer (individually or with others) controlled a separate, distinct entity that provided these law-related services *but* she did not take reasonable measures to make sure that the recipient of the law-related services knew that these services were not legal services and that therefore the typical protections of the lawyer-client relationship (*e.g.*, attorney-client privilege, conflict of interest rules) did not apply.[3]

The purpose of the 1994 version of the Rule was clear. The ABA sought to channel the provision of law-related services into separate and distinct entities and to require that lawyers inform clients that these services were not the practice of law in order to suspend the application of the Rules.

The drafters of the 2002 Rules removed the language about offering the law-related services through a separate entity. The new language states that "if the law-related services are provided . . . in other circumstances by an entity controlled by the lawyer individually or with others . . . ."[4] Thus, in order to escape application of the Rules, the lawyer should offer the services in a manner that is distinct from the legal services and inform the client that these services are not the practice of law and therefore the protections of the Rules do not apply.[5]

Rule 5.7(a) significantly motivates the lawyer to make sure

---

brief printing company. It may expressly inform clients that they are free to use any copying services they wish, however, the law firm owned copying service gives our clients accurate, prompt, and confidential copying services for a reasonable cost. If the client chooses another service, they do so at their own risk on quality and confidentiality. In this example, the firm is perfectly willing to provide the protections of the Model Rules to the operation of the separate copying firm.

[3]*See, e.g., In re Pappas*, 159 Ariz. 516, 768 P.2d 1161 (Ariz.1988). The lawyer performed legal services for clients and also investment advisory services for these same clients without making clear the distinction between the two. Because the clients reasonably believed that the lawyer was acting as their lawyer for both the legal and investment services, the court ruled that all of the ethics rules regarding conflicts of interest applied. The court disciplined the lawyer.

[4]Rule 5.7(a). The removal of the word separate entity pushes the focus on providing the law-related services in a manner that is distinct from the legal services. This can be accomplished through a separate entity, but it also can be done directly in the law firm.

[5]Comment 3 is instructive:

Even when the law-related and legal services are provided in circumstances that are distinct from each other, for example through separate entities or different support staff within the law firm, the Rules of Professional Conduct apply to the lawyer as provided in paragraph (a)(2) unless the lawyer takes reasonable measures to assure that the recipient of the law-related services knows that the services are not legal services and that the protections of the client-lawyer relationship do not apply.

these law-related services are distinct from her legal business in order to avoid the more demanding and stringent requirements of several of the sections in the Model Rules. If the lawyer provides law-related services that are distinct from her provision of legal services to clients, and she makes clear that the protections of the lawyer-client relationship do not apply, then, with respect to those law-related services, she is not subject to those provisions of the Model Rules that apply to lawyers only when acting as lawyers (*e.g.*, advertising, conflicts of interest, disclosure of confidential information). She still would be subject to those other portions of the Model Rules that apply to lawyers whether or not they are acting in their capacity as lawyers (*e.g.*, prohibition of deceit).[6]

This Rule applies to all law-related services provided by a law firm, even if the firm is not providing legal services to the client of the law-related service.[7] The lawyer must explain the meaning of a warning that the protections of the Model Rules do not apply to this service.[8] And, the lawyer must comply with this Rule before entering into a contract for the law-related services.[9] The Comments place the burden of proof on the lawyer to ensure compliance with the Rule and they note that sophisticated clients may need far less disclosure than unsophisticated clients.[10]

In some cases, the law firm may have a difficult or impossible time separating the delivery of legal services and law-related services to the client. The two types of services may relate to the same facts or the delivery of the services may be so entwined that they cannot be separated.[11] In such situations, the lawyer must ensure that the Rules are properly complied with especially Rule 5.3's requirement that the lawyer supervise the nonlawyers in the delivery of their law-related services.

If the ancillary business (the real estate firm, or the consulting firm) bills the customer separately and does not engage in the practice of law, then the fact that both the law firm and the ancillary business are involved in the same matter does not constitute illegal fee-splitting with non-lawyers, "even if nonlawyers have ownership interests or exercise management powers in the ancillary enterprise."[12]

Still, a lawyer involved with ancillary businesses must take

Rule 5.7, Comment 3.

[6]*See, e.g.,* Rule 8.4(c) (lawyer may not engage in conduct "involving dishonesty, fraud. . . . "). Rule 5.7, Comments 1, 3, 8.

[7]Rule 5.7, Comment 2.

[8]Rule 5.7, Comment 6 (client should understand the practical effect

of a statement that the services do not receive the protections of the Rules).

[9]Rule 5.7, Comment 6.

[10]Rule 5.7, Comment 7.

[11]Rule 5.7, Comment 8.

[12]Restatement of the Law Governing Lawyers, Third, § 10 (Official Draft 2000), at Comment *g*, p. 101.

care to avoid typical pitfalls. First, a lawyer who advises a client in dealing with the business entity that is really the lawyer's affiliate may not have the independent judgment needed to give sound advice, such as the advice to fire the affiliate. The lawyer must be sure that her self-interest in promoting the ancillary business does not distort her judgment in recommending the lawyer's own ancillary services to the client.[13] These affiliates inevitably involve the lawyer in business transactions with the client, which also raise separate problems under other ethics rules.[14]

In addition, law firms with these ancillary subsidiaries should be concerned about the risk of liability for the acts of their affiliates, ranging from simple negligence to dishonesty. While all the conflict of interest rules may not apply to these ancillary businesses, there remains the ethical risk that the affiliate will expand the number of situations disqualifying the law firm. For example, the affiliate may work on behalf of its customer, who has an interest conflicting with a different client of the law firm. In addition, a dissatisfied customer may turn to other ethical rules to create a cause of action. For example, a customer of the affiliate may claim that Rule 1.5(a) should apply to affiliates and that a fee was "unreasonable," in light of that Rule.

Only time will tell if law firms increase the creation of these law firm subsidiaries. To the extent that law firms become one-stop shopping centers, state legislators may step in, because lawyers may have less of a claim that only lawyers and judges can regulate them. Lawyers could lose their power of self-regulation, and the state supreme courts, which usually claim an inherent power to regulate the practice of law, may lose that claim of authority as well.[15]

---

[13]Restatement of the Law Governing Lawyers, Third, § 10 (Official Draft 2000), at Comment g, p. 101.

[14]See, e.g., Rule 1.8(a) and its predecessor, DR 5-104(A).

[15]See discussion in, THOMAS D. MORGAN & RONALD D. ROTUNDA, PROBLEMS AND MATERIALS ON PROFESSIONAL RESPONSIBILITY 539–40 (Foundation Press, 6th ed. 1995).

Moreover, if a law firm is allowed to set up a non-lawyer affiliate, a non-lawyer entity might be allowed to set up a law firm subsidiary. This issue is related to the emergence of MDP's or Multi-Disciplinary Practice, discussed in Rule 5.5, which deals with the unauthorized practice of law.

VI. PUBLIC SERVICE

CHAPTER 6.1
VOLUNTARY PRO BONO PUBLICO SERVICE

RULE 6.1: VOLUNTARY PRO BONO PUBLICO SERVICE

Every lawyer has a professional responsibility to provide legal services to those unable to pay. A lawyer should aspire to render at least (50) hours of pro bono publico legal services per year. In fulfilling this responsibility, the lawyer should:

(a) provide a substantial majority of the (50) hours of legal services without fee or expectation of fee to:

(1) persons of limited means or

(2) charitable, religious, civic, community, governmental and educational organizations in matters that are designed primarily to address the needs of persons of limited means; and

(b) provide any additional services through:

(1) delivery of legal services at no fee or substantially reduced fee to individuals, groups or organizations seeking to secure or protect civil rights, civil liberties or public rights, or charitable, religious, civic, community, governmental and educational organizations in matters in furtherance of their organizational purposes, where the payment of standard legal fees would significantly deplete the organization's economic resources or would be otherwise inappropriate;

(2) delivery of legal services at a substantially reduced fee to persons of limited means; or

(3) participation in activities for improving the law, the legal system or the legal profession.

In addition, a lawyer should voluntarily contribute

financial support to organizations that provide legal services to persons of limited means.

Comment

[1] Every lawyer, regardless of professional prominence or professional work load, has a responsibility to provide legal services to those unable to pay, and personal involvement in the problems of the disadvantaged can be one of the most rewarding experiences in the life of a lawyer. The American Bar Association urges all lawyers to provide a minimum of 50 hours of pro bono services annually. States, however, may decide to choose a higher or lower number of hours of annual service (which may be expressed as a percentage of a lawyer's professional time) depending upon local needs and local conditions. It is recognized that in some years a lawyer may render greater or fewer hours than the annual standard specified, but during the course of his or her legal career, each lawyer should render on average per year, the number of hours set forth in this Rule. Services can be performed in civil matters or in criminal or quasicriminal matters for which there is no government obligation to provide funds for legal representation, such as postconviction death penalty appeal cases.

[2] Paragraphs (a)(1) and (2) recognize the critical need for legal services that exists among persons of limited means by providing that a substantial majority of the legal services rendered annually to the disadvantaged be furnished without fee or expectation of fee. Legal services under these paragraphs consist of a full range of activities, including individual and class representation, the provision of legal advice, legislative lobbying, administrative rule making and the provision of free training or mentoring to those who represent persons of limited means. The variety of these activities should facilitate participation by government lawyers, even when restrictions exist on their engaging in the outside practice of law.

[3] Persons eligible for legal services under paragraphs (a)(1) and (2) are those who qualify for participation in programs funded by the Legal Services Corporation and those whose incomes and financial resources are slightly above the guidelines utilized by such programs but nevertheless, cannot afford counsel. Legal services can be rendered to individuals or to organizations such as homeless shelters, battered women's centers and food pantries that serve those of limited means. The term "governmental organizations" includes, but is not limited to, public protection programs and sections of governmental or public sector agencies.

[4] Because service must be provided without fee or expectation of fee, the intent of the lawyer to render free legal services is essential for the work performed to fall within the meaning of paragraphs (a)(1) and (2). Accordingly, services rendered cannot be considered pro bono if an anticipated fee is uncollected, but the award of statutory attorneys' fees in a case originally accepted as pro bono would not disqualify such services from inclusion under this section. Lawyers who do receive fees in such cases are encouraged to contribute an appropriate portion of such fees to organizations or projects that benefit persons of limited means.

[5] While it is possible for a lawyer to fulfill the annual responsibil-

ity to perform pro bono services exclusively through activities described in paragraphs (a)(1) and (2), to the extent that any hours of service remained unfulfilled, the remaining commitment can be met in a variety of ways as set forth in paragraph (b). Constitutional, statutory or regulatory restrictions may prohibit or impede government and public sector lawyers and judges from performing the pro bono services outlined in paragraphs (a)(1) and (2). Accordingly, where those restrictions apply, government and public sector lawyers and judges may fulfill their pro bono responsibility by performing services outlined in paragraph (b).

[6] Paragraph (b)(1) includes the provision of certain types of legal services to those whose incomes and financial resources place them above limited means. It also permits the pro bono lawyer to accept a substantially reduced fee for services. Examples of the types of issues that may be addressed under this paragraph include First Amendment claims, Title VII claims and environmental protection claims. Additionally, a wide range of organizations may be represented, including social service, medical research, cultural and religious groups.

[7] Paragraph (b)(2) covers instances in which lawyers agree to and receive a modest fee for furnishing legal services to persons of limited means. Participation in judicare programs and acceptance of court appointments in which the fee is substantially below a lawyer's usual rate are encouraged under this section.

[8] Paragraph (b)(3) recognizes the value of lawyers engaging in activities that improve the law, the legal system or the legal profession. Serving on bar association committees, serving on boards of pro bono or legal services programs, taking part in Law Day activities, acting as a continuing legal education instructor, a mediator or an arbitrator and engaging in legislative lobbying to improve the law, the legal system or the profession are a few examples of the many activities that fall within this paragraph.

[9] Because the provision of pro bono services is a professional responsibility, it is the individual ethical commitment of each lawyer. Nevertheless, there may be times when it is not feasible for a lawyer to engage in pro bono services. At such times a lawyer may discharge the pro bono responsibility by providing financial support to organizations providing free legal services to persons of limited means. Such financial support should be reasonably equivalent to the value of the hours of service that would have otherwise been provided. In addition, at times it may be more feasible to satisfy the pro bono responsibility collectively, as by a firm's aggregate pro bono activities.

[10] Because the efforts of individual lawyers are not enough to meet the need for free legal services that exists among persons of limited means, the government and the profession have instituted additional programs to provide those services. Every lawyer should financially support such programs, in addition to either providing direct pro bono services or making financial contributions when pro bono service is not feasible.

[11] Law firms should act reasonably to enable and encourage all lawyers in the firm to provide the pro bono legal services called for by this Rule.

[12] The responsibility set forth in this Rule is not intended to be enforced through disciplinary process.

Authors' 1983 Model Rules Comparison

The 1983 version of Rule 6.1 called for all lawyers to "render public interest legal service." In 1993, the ABA amended the pro bono rule with an aspirational plea for lawyers to render 50 hours a year directed towards economically disadvantaged clients.

The text of the 2002 version of Rule 6.1 is only slightly different from the language adopted in 1993. In order to reaffirm the obligation of pro bono services to the poor, the drafters added the following line as the first sentence in the new Rule: "Every lawyer has a professional responsibility to provide legal services to those unable to pay."

The drafters of the 2002 Rules also added Comment 11 and renumbered old Comment 11 to Comment 12. The added language, "Law firms should act reasonably to enable and encourage all lawyers in the firm to provide the pro bono legal services called for by this Rule" recognizes that law firms play an important role in encouraging pro bono services for their lawyers.

Model Code Comparison

There was no counterpart of this Rule in the Disciplinary Rules of the Model Code. EC 2-25 stated that the "basic responsibility for providing legal services for those unable to pay ultimately rests upon the individual lawyer . . . . Every lawyer, regardless of professional prominence or professional work load, should find time to participate in serving the disadvantaged." EC 8-9 stated that "[t]he advancement of our legal system is of vital importance in maintaining the rule of law . . . [and] lawyers should encourage, and should aid in making, needed changes and improvements." EC 8-3 stated that "[t]hose persons unable to pay for legal services should be provided needed services."

§ 6.1–1 REPRESENTING CLIENTS AND CAUSES IN PRO BONO REPRESENTATION

Pro Bono Publico means, "for the public good," or for the welfare of the whole. As applied to the work of lawyers, it usually refers to work that lawyers do without fee, or with no expectation of a fee, or for a reduced fee for clients of limited means. Lawyers may also represent charitable organizations, such as the Y.M.C.A., the Boy Scouts, the A.C.L.U., and the N.A.A.C.P. on a no fee or reduced fee basis.[1] The Model Rules, like the Model Code, encourage, but do not require, lawyers to engage in pro bono activities.[2]

If a lawyer represents a client on a pro bono basis, it does not

---

[Section 6.1–1]

[1] ABA Rule 6.1, Comment 6 (e.g., "social service, medial research, cultural and religious groups" may qualify as pro bono).

[2] In February 1993, the ABA House of Delegates replaced the original version of Model Rule 6.1 with an aspirational plea for 50 hours a year from each lawyer. This more specific

imply that the client is necessarily right, or that the public interest is served only if the client's claim is vindicated. Rather, it means that the public interest is served because that client's views are represented. The client then has his or her day in court.

Law reform activities (when a lawyer, without fee, represents a cause rather than a client) are also considered part of pro bono work.[3] Such activities may include: (1) testifying before legislative or administrative hearings urging law reform; (2) lobbying for law reform in the selection and retention of judges; or (3) participating in bar association activities.

The fact that the lawyer engages in any given law reform activities does not imply that the lawyer's view of law reform is correct. Rather, the public is served because lawyers offer their services, judgment, and experience, to promote causes that they, in good faith, believe promote law reform. The lawyer advocates a viewpoint that might otherwise not be heard, and this airing of the viewpoint adds another voice to the marketplace of ideas.

§ 6.1–2 MANDATORY PRO BONO SERVICE

§ 6.1–2(a) An Aspirational Rule

The Model Code did not require a lawyer to engage in pro bono activities. In fact, no disciplinary rule in the Model Code even dealt with this issue. Only in the ethical considerations did we find the concern expressed that persons who are unable to pay "all or a portion of a reasonable fee" still should be able to obtain "necessary legal services," and that, consequently, "lawyers should support and participate in ethical activities designed to achieve that objective."[1] Although the Ethical Considerations of the Model Code stated that it was an "obligation" of each lawyer to render "free legal services to those unable to pay reasonable fees,"[2] the failure to meet this "obligation" was not disciplinable.

The drafters of the 1983 Model Rules thought that pro bono activities were too important to find no mention in the black letter rules. So, unlike the Model Code, an entire section of the Model Rules is labeled "Public Service," and a specific Rule—Rule 6.1 and the accompanying Comments—address the topic of performing pro bono services.[3] Rule 6.1 is the only Black Letter Rule that never uses the word "shall" and only uses the word

---

Rule also seeks to direct lawyers to provide pro bono services to the economically disadvantaged, rather than charitable and nonprofit organizations. For a complete review of the history of Model Rule 6.1, see A LEGISLATIVE HISTORY: THE DEVELOPMENT OF THE ABA MODEL RULES OF PROFESSIONAL CONDUCT, 1982–1998 (ABA 1999) AT 270.

[3] Rule 6.1, Comments 2, 8.

[Section 6.1–2]

[1] EC 2-16.

[2] EC 2-25.

[3] Rule 6.1.

"should."[4] However, the fact that Rule 6.1 is not enforced through the disciplinary process,[5] does not take away from its importance or the controversy it has provoked.[6]

When the ABA initially adopted the Model Rules in 1983, Rule 6.1 was a vague call urging lawyers to engage in pro bono work for people of limited means or for public service or charitable groups. In February 1993, the ABA House of Delegates approved a much more specific Rule, although it is still aspirational and not intended to be enforced by discipline.

The revised Rule 6.1 offers more than a vague exhortation. It urges lawyers to aspire "to render at least (50) hours of pro bono publico legal services per year," a statement that is followed by a detailed explanation as to whom the lawyers should render these services.[7] The hours are in parenthesis because the ABA recognized that states might well choose a different figure.[8] States may choose a higher or lower number, or express the number as a percentage of a lawyer's professional time. Work may include legal representation in court, legal advice, lobbying, free training or mentoring to persons of limited means.[9]

If any of these 50 hours are unfulfilled, then lawyers can fulfill the "remaining [aspirational] commitment" by engaging in pro bono work for individuals or groups seeking to protect civil rights or public rights (*e.g.*, environmental rights), by pro bono work for charitable, religious, civil, etc. organizations (*e.g.*, bar association activities, Law Day activities, or legislative lobbying).[10]

§ 6.1–2(b) Proposals for Compulsory Pro Bono

The ABA Commission that drafted the 1983 Model Rules wrestled with the question of whether the Model Rules should require lawyers to engage in pro bono work for clients of limited

---

[4] Rule 1.5(b) does use the word "preferably," but the other provisions in that Rule are mandatory.

[5] Rule 6.1, Comment 11.

[6] An incomplete list of articles and books on this issue would include, F. Raymond Marks, et al., The Lawyer, the Public and Professional Responsibility 288–92 (1972). David L. Shapiro, *The Enigma of the Lawyer's Duty to Serve*, 55 N.Y.U. L. Rev. 735, 738–39 (1980); Esther F. Lardent, *Mandatory Pro Bono in Civil Cases: The Wrong Answer to the Right Question*, 49 Md.L. Rev.8 (1990); Suzanne Bretz, Note, *Why Mandatory Pro Bono Is a Bad Idea*, 3 Georgetown J. Legal Ethics 623 (1990);

Symposium, Mandatory Pro Bono, 19 Hofstra L.Rev. 739 (1991); Donald Patrick Harris, *Let's Make Lawyers Happy: Advocating Mandatory Pro Bono*, 19 N.Ill.U.L.Rev. 287 (1999); Christina M. Rosas, *Mandatory Pro Bono Publico for Law Students: The Right Place to Start*, 30 Hofstra L. Rev. 1069 (2002); Judith L. Maute, *Changing Conceptions of Lawyers' Pro Bono Responsibilities: From Chance Noblesse Oblige to Stated Expectations*, 77 Tulane L. Rev. 91 (2002).

[7] Rule 6.1(a) (1), (2).

[8] Rule 6.1, Comment 1.

[9] Rule 6.1, Comment 2.

[10] Rule 6.1(b) & Comments 5 to 8.

means. Although Rule 6.1 makes clear that it is not intended to be enforced through the disciplinary process,[11] that idea has been periodically proposed and justified or criticized under various theories.

In 1976 in California, for example, the state legislature considered, and defeated, a bill requiring active members of the bar to engage in a minimum of 40 hours per year of mandatory pro bono work for no fee or a "substantially reduced" fee.[12]

That defeat did not end discussion of the issue. Several years later, in 1979, Thomas Ehrlich, the first President of the Legal Services Corporation and a member of the ABA Commission that drafted the Model Rules, argued "with enthusiasm" that the Model Rules should mandate (not merely encourage) pro bono activities by private attorneys to help the poor.[13] Consequently, an early draft of the 1983 Model Rules initially proposed: "A lawyer *shall* render unpaid public interest legal service . . . [and] shall make an annual report concerning such service to the appropriate regulatory authority."[14] Many ABA members opposed this rule, and the Commission withdrew its proposal.

The Ethics 2000 Commission similarly debated the issue of mandatory pro bono. It invited commentary on this issue and debated the prospect of using an ethics rule to enforce a minimum contribution-of-hours pro bono rule. Ultimately, the Commission came to the same conclusion as had been done in 1983 and in 1993: amending Rule 6.1 is not the appropriate answer to the problem.[15] Instead, it added a sentence to the beginning of Rule 6.1 which reaffirms a lawyer's "responsibility to provide legal services to those unable to pay."

---

[11]Rule 6.1, Comment 12.

[12]Assembly Bill No. 4050 (1976).

[13]Thomas Ehrlich, *Rationing Justice*, 34 THE RECORD OF THE ASSOCIATION OF THE BAR OF THE CITY OF NEW YORK 729, 743 (Dec. 1979).

[14]Proposed Rule 8.1, Discussion Draft (Jan. 30, 1980), reprinted in THOMAS D. MORGAN & RONALD D. ROTUNDA, 1980 SELECTED NATIONAL STANDARDS SUPPLEMENT 142 (Foundation Press, 1980).

[15]The Reporter's Explanations to the 2002 Model Rules contains the following comment:

the Commission remains committed to the proposition that providing pro bono legal service to persons of limited means is an important obligation of every lawyer. The Commission also believes that the current system for mobilizing lawyers to provide pro bono legal service is not adequate to the task at hand. After considerable reflection, however, the Commission has concluded that amending Rule 6.1 to require all lawyers to provide pro bono legal service is not an appropriate response to the problem. Rather, the Commission encourages the ABA to heighten its efforts to find more appropriate and effective means to increase the voluntary participation of lawyers in the provision of legal services to persons of limited means.

Reporter's Explanation of Changes to Model Rule 6.1.

In *Schwarz v. Kogan*,[16] plaintiff challenged the constitutionality of a Florida rule that required far less than mandatory pro bono; it only required Florida lawyers to report the number of pro bono hours they worked each year. The rule also encouraged them to pay $350 to a legal aid organization if they did not want to do the pro bono work themselves. The court held that the Florida program was a rational way to keep the need for pro bono service before Florida lawyers, and a lawyer may be professionally disciplined for a failure to report. The Eleventh Circuit said Florida "undoubtedly has a legitimate interest" in encouraging pro bono service and "the free provision of legal services to the poor has long been recognized as an essential component of the practice of law."[17] Indeed, the court said, "one of the traditions of the legal profession is that a lawyer, as an officer of the Court, is 'obligated to represent indigents for little or no compensation upon court order'."[18]

§ 6.1–2(c) Rationales for Mandatory Pro Bono

It is settled that, in individual cases, the courts have the power to compel attorneys to accept appointment to cases before the court. "Attorneys are officers of the court, and are bound to render service when required by such an appointment."[19] Less certain is the extent to which counsel are required to assume this burden with little or no compensation.

A related question is the extent to which a state bar association or the state disciplinary machinery can or should require mandatory pro bono representation in civil, rather than criminal cases, and mandatory pro bono counseling and advice in non-litigative situations.

These issues are occasionally litigated in the courts. Although courts have held that there is no constitutional right to compensation for compelled jury service,[20] the difference between compelled jury service and compelled legal representation is not only in the amount of time and effort typically required, but also in the nature of the limited and discrete class burdened. The burden of uncompensated criminal defense representation is borne only by trial lawyers while the burden of jury service does not single out

---

[16]*Schwarz v. Kogan*, 132 F.3d 1387 (11th Cir.1998), *cert. denied*, 524 U.S. 954, 118 S.Ct. 2372, 141 L.Ed.2d 740 (1998).

Reporting Pro Bono. In addition to Florida, there are a few jurisdictions that now require lawyers to report how much time or money they devote to pro bono activities each year. These state include Illinois, Maryland, Mississippi, and Nevada. 22 Lawyers Manual on Professional Conduct 321 (June 28, 2006).

[17]*132 F.2d at 1391.*

[18]*Id.*

[19]*Powell v. Alabama*, 287 U.S. 45, 73, 53 S.Ct. 55, 65, 77 L.Ed. 158, 172 (1932).

[20]*Maricopa County v. Corp.*, 44 Ariz. 506, 39 P.2d 351 (1934) (per curiam).

any discrete class of individuals. A purpose of the Just Compensation Clause is to prevent the majority from requiring discrete classes of people to bear special burdens without just compensation. Thus, the Alaska Supreme Court held that, under the state Constitution, the court could not compel a private attorney to represent an indigent criminal defendant unless the state paid just compensation, defined as, "the compensation received by the average competent attorney operating in the open market."[21]

Proponents of mandatory pro bono offer various rationales to justify the right of society to mandate that lawyers work for free or for substantially lessened compensation. Some commentators have argued that lawyers, but not medical doctors, are obliged to offer free service because

> lawyers are an essential part of the public justice system, with monopolistic access to the workings of the system. With that monopoly comes a public obligation to help ensure the sound workings of the system—otherwise the rationing of justice becomes warped in ways that are dangerous not only to poor people, who are denied an opportunity to use the system, but also to the public generally, which is denied a legal system that works fairly.[22]

Others reply that although lawyers have a legal monopoly over the practice of law, medical doctors have a legal monopoly over the practice of medicine. Thus, the President of the California State Bar once proposed that medical doctors, lawyers, and dentists all should be obligated to contribute one-half day per month of free services.[23] In 1987, the *ABA Journal* and the *Journal of the American Medical Association* each published an editorial advocating that "all doctors and all lawyers, as a matter of ethics and good faith, should contribute a significant percentage of their total professional efforts without expectation of financial remuneration."[24] They contended that 50 hours a year was "an appropriate minimum amount."[25]

In reply, some have argued that the fact that there is a legal monopoly proves little: if the monopoly is bad, it should be eliminated; if the monopoly is good and needed for independent reasons, then its existence adds little to the pro bono debate. Some states monopolize the sale of liquor, but do not provide free alcohol to those who cannot afford it. When the ABA Commission that drafted the Model Rules initially proposed a *mandatory* pro

---

[21] *DeLisio v. Alaska Superior Court*, 740 P.2d 437, 443 (Alaska 1987) (overruling prior cases).

[22] Thomas Ehrlich, *Rationing Justice*, 34 RECORD OF THE ASSOCIATION OF THE BAR OF THE CITY OF NEW YORK 729, 743 (Dec. 1979).

[23] SAN JOSE MERCURY, Nov. 29, 1976, at 26, col. 1.

[24] 73 A.B.A.J. 55 (Dec. 1, 1987).

[25] *Id.*

bono requirement, it did not rely on any theory of legal monopoly. Instead, the ABA Commission relied on "the lawyer's commitment to the law's idea of equal justice."[26]

Others argue that to say that free legal services to the poor and less advantaged will promote justice does not lead to the conclusion that it is an individual lawyer's duty to provide such services for free. These people argue that it is society's duty to fund services and pay the lawyers who perform them.[27] Society benefits when there is more justice, and society benefits when people are more educated. Society does not require teachers to work for free; the public school system pays the teachers for their service. Similarly, it is argued, society should pay in those cases where it wants lawyers for the poor, rather than impose the financial burden on a few lawyers.

§ 6.1–2(d) Mandatory Pro Bono and Alternative Service

Some proposals for mandatory pro bono provide forms of alternative service for those who do not perform pro bono work directly. For example, if a partner in a large firm is appointed by the court to represent an indigent, can he fulfill this responsibility by assigning the case to one of the young associates?

Lawyers in solo practice or in small firms often believe that this opt out in effect places a proportionately heavier burden on them, because it is easier for the larger firms to assign the case to a less expensive associate in their office. Moreover, when firms are large enough, with a supply of young associates who do not yet have any client base, the marginal cost to the larger firm of assigning an extra associate to a pro bono activity is not significant. The associates are paid by the year, and if some associates must work a little harder on a pro bono case on which

---

[26]Proposed Model Rule 8.1, Comment 1 (Discussion Draft, Jan. 30, 1980), reprinted in THOMAS D. MORGAN & RONALD D. ROTUNDA, 1980 SELECTED NATIONAL STANDARDS SUPPLEMENT 142 (Foundation Press 1980).

[27]See, e.g., State v. Green, 470 S.W.2d 571, 573 (Mo.1971), where the court said that it "will not *compel* the attorneys . . . to discharge alone a 'duty which constitutionally is the burden of the State' "(emphasis in original); State ex rel. Scott v. Roper, 688 S.W.2d 757 (Mo.1985) (en banc)(extensive historical discussion and holding that court does not have power to appoint counsel in civil cases

without compensation).

See David L. Shapiro, The Enigma of the Lawyer's Duty to Serve, 55 N.Y.U. L. REV. 735, 738–39 (1980):

"Although frequently urged as rooted in the firmest of traditions, the 'duty to serve' in fact has a history shrouded in obscurity, ambiguity, and qualification, and this murkiness is reflected in recent struggles of courts and commentators to deal rationally with the issues. Imposition of a duty by the state. . . . raises substantial constitutional issues and is perhaps even more vulnerable on economic and other policy grounds."

they also gain useful experience, the cost to the large firm is lessened.[28]

Alternatively, should a lawyer be permitted to fulfill his pro bono responsibility by paying another lawyer in a different firm to do the work? Should a lawyer simply be allowed to buy out of this obligation? Such a buy out would be equally available to solo practitioners as well as members of the larger firms. The burden, however, would be relatively greater for the poorer lawyer.

If Alpha could simply buy out his obligation, that buy-out provision emphasizes that mandatory pro bono is really a tax, and, as such, some argue that it is better for the state legislature to tax each lawyer directly and use that money to hire attorneys to staff legal aid offices.[29]

The Model Rules recognize that it may not be feasible for some lawyers to engage in pro bono service; for example, a state might impose legal restrictions on government lawyers or judges that will limit their ability to perform personally pro bono activities for people of limited means or for charitable and similar organizations that address the needs of persons of limited means.[30] In that case, lawyers "may discharge the pro bono responsibility" by making financial contributions to support pro bono services.[31] One might consider this provision to be a form of buy-out.

Some proponents of mandatory pro bono would oppose any type of opt out provision. They argue that what is needed is not just the lawyer's money but the lawyer's time. "The responsibility for pro bono service should be borne *by each lawyer individually*."[32] Lawyers, it is thought, should personally engage

---

[28]ARTHUR L. LIMAN, WITH PETER ISRAEL, LAWYER: A LIFE OF COUNSEL AND CONTROVERSY 173 (Public Affairs, N.Y. 1998) (emphasis added), explaining when Arthur Liman's law firm accepted a docket of cases involving prisoners' rights, "The lion's share of the work in those cases was done by Paul, Weiss *associates*, under partner supervision, and they took them on with zeal, *honing their skills* and achieving some spectacular victories, including the case of the Black Muslim minister."

[29]Obviously, this tax could be made progressive if that is what the legislature wants.

[30]Rule 6.1, Comment 5 & Rule 6.1(a).

[31]Rule 6.1, Comment 9:

"[T]here may be times when it is not feasible for a lawyer to engage in pro bono services. At such times a lawyer may discharge the pro bono responsibility by providing financial support to organizations providing free legal services to persons of limited means."

[32]Proposed Model Rule 8.1, Comment 1 (Discussion Draft, Jan. 30, 1980) (emphasis added), reprinted in THOMAS D. MORGAN & RONALD D. ROTUNDA, 1980 SELECTED NATIONAL STANDARDS SUPPLEMENT 142 (Foundation Press 1980).

Note that Rule 6.1, Comment 9, states: "[A]t times it may be more feasible to satisfy the pro bono responsibility *collectively*, as by a *firm's aggregate pro bono activities*." (emphasis added.)

in this work not only to help clients but to understand, first hand, the legal problems of the poor.[33]

If lawyers, personally, must engage in pro bono representation, that would mean that even in a very large firm, the senior partner in charge of securities law could not assign to the junior partner or associate in the family law section of the law firm the duty of handling a no fault divorce for a poor person, even though the younger lawyer might be more efficient in performing this type of work. Granted, "many legal aid programs have found that, with relatively modest amounts of training, even bond indenture lawyers can re-emerge from their specialist shells."[34] Yet, opponents of this view argue that, if the real purpose of pro bono work is to help the poor, the poor would be more efficiently helped by a legal service lawyer specializing in their problems rather than a municipal bond lawyer who was forced to learn about the law of evictions.

§ 6.1–3 FINANCIAL SUPPORT FOR PRO BONO AND IOLTA PROGRAMS

§ 6.1–3(a) Charitable Contributions

Because pro bono activities are voluntary, it is a fact of life that some lawyers are more forthcoming than others in offering free (or reduced fee) legal services to those unable to pay the normal fee. The legal needs of the poor are not entirely met by the lawyers who donate their time by engaging in personal pro bono activities. It is also the case that state and federal governments and some foundations also fund various legal service organizations that hire lawyers to represent the poor.

These programs are part of an effort to provide more representation for those unable to hire private lawyers. These organizations take the form of legal aid offices, state public defender offices (for the defense of criminal cases), and bar-sponsored lawyer referral services. Lawyers "should support all proper efforts" of these programs.[1] Programs such as these are a response to the fact that there is more demand for free legal services from the poor than there is a supply of lawyers able to donate sufficient time and resources to the problem. Lawyers should "voluntarily

---

[33]*See* EC 2-25: "[P]*ersonal involvement* in the problems of the disadvantaged can be one of the most rewarding experiences in the life of a lawyer" (emphasis added). *Accord.* Rule 6.1, Comment 1.

[34]Thomas Ehrlich, *Rationing Justice*, 34 RECORD OF THE ASSOCIATION

OF THE BAR OF THE CITY OF NEW YORK 729, 744 (Dec. 1979).

[Section 6.1–3]

[1]Rule 6.1, Comment 3. *Accord* EC 2-25; EC 2-16; EC 2-33.

In the United States, legal aid is often traced back to 1876 and the

contribute financial support to organizations that provide legal services to persons of limited means."[2]

§ 6.1–3(b) IOLTA Programs

"IOLTA" stands for Interest on Lawyer Trust Accounts. These accounts grew out of a series of trust law and tax law provisions. First, some background.[3]

Lawyers must not commingle their funds with client funds.[4] However, it is not necessary that each client have a separately established trust fund account, as long as the funds from clients are deposited in a trust fund account, with proper records.[5] Although the funds of each client are typically commingled together with the funds of other clients, they may not be commingled with the lawyer's personal funds. Usually, these funds are held for a short time, and, although any amount deposited for any particular client may not be large, the total amount for all the clients' funds may be substantial.

When lawyers establish trust funds for their clients, they typically place those funds in non-interest bearing accounts. First, the law of ethics regarding this issue requires safekeeping, not commingling, and accounting, not investing. In some circumstances, the trust law might require that funds be invested, but this rule does not apply when the trustee is not under a duty to invest trust money but merely to safeguard it.[6] Many lawyer trust fund accounts fall in that category. In addition, before the advent of computers, it was administratively difficult to calculate how much interest should be assigned to a particular client when the funds were held for a short time and combined with the funds of other clients.

The Model Rules and the Model Code allow—but do not require—lawyers to invest their short term client trust funds in interest-bearing accounts. If trust funds are placed in interest-bearing accounts, then, under standard trust rules, any interest

---

formation of a legal aid society for German immigrants living in New York. By 1916, there were legal aid societies in 37 American cities. For a discussion of the early history, see REGINALD HEBER SMITH, JUSTICE AND THE POOR (1919); EMERY A. BROWNELL, LEGAL AID IN THE UNITED STATES (1951).

[2] Rule 6.1 (last ¶). See also, Comments 9, 10.

[3] For further elaboration on IOLTA plans, see the earlier discussion under Rule 1.15.

[4] See discussion of Rule 1.15 ("Safekeeping property"), above.

[5] Rule 1.15, Comment 1, advising that monies of clients or third persons should be kept "in one or more trust accounts. Separate trust accounts may be warranted when administering estate monies or acting in similar fiduciary capacities."

[6] 2A AUSTIN WAKEMAN SCOTT & WILLIAM FRANKLIN FRATCHER, THE LAW OF TRUSTS, §§ 180.3, 181 (4th ed. 1987).

would have to be credited to each client.[7] If the funds draw interest, that interest, under normal trust rules, becomes the property of the client, not the lawyer, because the client owns the principal from which the interest accrues. The general rule is that interest follows the principal. Consequently, the legal ethics rules provided that the lawyer could not use the interest earned on client funds to defray the lawyer's own operating expenses (such as bank handling fees, accounting costs, record keeping and notification expenses) unless she had "the specific and informed consent of the client."[8]

Because the money in these trust funds accounts often has to be available on short notice, lawyers keep these funds in demand deposits. That fact led to another reason why these short time funds were kept in non-interest bearing accounts: prior to 1980, federal law did not allow interest paid on a federally-insured checking account. Consequently, the depository institutions benefitted by free use of the money.

In 1980, when Congress allowed interest to be paid on demand deposits (called "Negotiable Order of Withdrawal" or "NOW" accounts), it still prohibited for-profit corporations and partnerships from earning interest on demand deposits.[9] However, the Federal Reserve Board later ruled that such funds could be held in NOW accounts *if* the funds were held in trust pursuant to which charitable organizations had the "exclusive right to the interest."[10] And the Internal Revenue Service ruled that it would not attribute the interest earned from such accounts to the income of the individual clients if they had no control over the decision to place the funds in the IOLTA account and did not designate who would receive the interest generated by the account.[11] A leading ABA Formal Opinion also approved IOLTA programs as permissible under the rules of ethics.[12]

Armed with this change in the law, bar associations and courts then sought to recapture this interest—which would otherwise inure to the benefit of the banks and other depository institu-

---

[7]ABA Formal Opinion 348 (July 23, 1982).

[8]ABA Formal Opinion 348 (July 23, 1982). As this ethics opinion noted, the principle it articulated was not new. ABA Informal Opinion 545 (1962) (lawyer may not keep interest earned on trust account even though it was "quite difficult to allocate" interest to particular clients, unless clients specifically authorize this action); ABA Informal Opinion 991 (1967)(law firm may not use interest earned on savings account to defray expenses of handling agency account unless clients specifically consent).

[9]12 U.S.C.A. § 1832.

[10]*See* Donald Middlebrooks, *The Interest on Trust Accounts Program: Mechanics of Its Operations*, 56 Fla. Bar J. 115, 117 (Feb. 1982).

[11]*See* Revenue Ruling 81-209, 1981-2 C.B. 16; Revenue Ruling 87-2, 1987-1 C.B. 18.

[12]ABA Formal Opinion 348 (July 23, 1982).

tions—and use it to fund various public service projects, such as funding of legal services projects and similar pro bono activities. These programs are called, Interest on Lawyer Trust Accounts, or IOLTA.

Phillips v. Washington Legal Foundation,[13] was the first Supreme Court case to begin to ask whether state IOLTA plans constitute an unconstitutional taking of client funds. Under the Texas IOLTA program, an attorney who received client funds must place them in a separate, interest-bearing, federally authorized account if he or she determined that the funds "could not reasonably be expected to earn interest for the client" or the interest that might be earned "is not likely to be sufficient to offset the cost of establishing and maintaining the account, service charges, accounting costs and tax reporting costs which would be incurred in attempting to obtain the interest."[14]

The respondents alleged that the Texas IOLTA program violated their rights under the Fifth Amendment, which provides that "private property" shall not "be taken for public use, without just compensation." The question before the Court was narrow. The Court assumed that a lawyer was required to put funds into an IOLTA account only if the interest generated on the funds would be insufficient to offset bank service charges and accounting for the interest. The issue was whether the interest was nevertheless "property" of the lawyer or client in such a case so that the Takings Clause could apply. The Court held that the interest on client funds held in IOLTA accounts is property of the client for purposes of the takings clause of the Fifth Amendment.

Chief Justice Rehnquist, for the Court (5 to 4), held that the interest on a client's funds in a lawyer's hands is "property" of the client even if bank charges would mean the client could never spend it. For example, the Court said, rental income would be the property of the owner of a building even if collecting the rent cost more than the tenant had paid. The general rule is that "interest follows principal."[15] There is no traditional property law principle that allows the owners of funds temporarily deposited in an attorney trust account to be deprived of the interest the funds generates.[16]

Although the decision in *Phillips* is narrow, it has raised sig-

---

[13]*Phillips v. Washington Legal Foundation*, 524 U.S. 156, 118 S.Ct. 1925, 141 L.Ed.2d 174 (1998).

[14]Phillips, 524 U.S. at 162, 118 S.Ct. at 1929, 141 L.Ed.2d at 182.

[15]This common law rule dates back law hundreds of years. *Beckford v. Tobin, 1 Ves.Sen. 308, 310, 27* Eng.Rep. 1049, 1051 (Ch. 1749): "[I]nterest shall follow the principal, as the shadow the body."

[16]Because the questions had not been decided below, the Court left for another day whether the IOLTA program constituted an unconstitutional taking of the clients' property and

nificant constitutional doubt about the ultimate viability of IOLTA plans.[17] This doubt was increased because of an earlier decision, *Webb's Fabulous Pharmacies, Inc. v. Beckwith*,[18] where the Court broadly held that the interest on deposited funds is "property," and that the state may not constitutionally take this property without paying just compensation.[19] This uncertainty prevailed for five years as the cases made their way through the lower courts.

In 2003, the Supreme Court addressed these issues in *Brown v. Legal Foundation of Washington*,[20] a case examining the constitutionality of the State of Washington's IOLTA program. All nine

---

what, if any, compensation might be due. 524 U.S. at 172, 118 S.Ct. at 1934. On remand, *Washington Legal Foundation v. Texas Equal Access to Justice Foundation*, 270 F.3d 180 (5th Cir.2001), held that the IOLTA program of Texas was a *per se* "taking" under Takings Clause; that declaratory and injunctive relief were available remedies; and that the Texas Supreme Court justices were not legislatively immune from declaratory and injunctive relief claim. The court then reversed and remanded for further proceedings. In contrast, *Washington Legal Foundation v. Legal Foundation of Washington*, 271 F.3d 835 (9th Cir.2001) (en banc), held that the IOLTA requirement of Washington State was not a Fifth Amendment taking of the clients' property; and, even if it were a taking, the value of any just compensation was nil. The court remanded for consideration of First Amendment issues.

[17]Souter, J. (joined by Breyer, Stevens, & Ginsburg, JJ.) and Breyer, J. (joined by Stevens, Souter, & Ginsburg, JJ.) filed dissenting opinions. They argued that the Court had reached out unnecessarily to decide an abstract issue, and that it could only properly decide the property issue in light of the issues that were not before the Court. They also believed, however, that it was meaningless to talk of "taking" or calling "property" an asset that had no practical value to the client. Under pre-existing federal law, the client's principal could not generate interest (because federal law pro-

hibits for-profit corporations and partnerships from earning interest on demand deposits unless the interest is earned in an IOLTA account).

[18]*Webb's Fabulous Pharmacies, Inc. v. Beckwith*, 449 U.S. 155, 159, 101 S.Ct. 446, 450, 66 L.Ed.2d 358 (1980), *on remand*, 394 So.2d 1009 (Fla.1981). The Supreme Court held that a Florida county's taking of the interest earned on an interpleader fund while the fund was temporarily held by the county court, in addition to a fee for the county's services for holding such fund, constituted a taking of property violating the Fifth and Fourteenth Amendments.

[19]The general rule is that, when the government takes physical possession of money or property that otherwise would accrue to the benefit of a private person, the private person's claim for just compensation is established unless the government can demonstrate that its action in fact constituted only a regulation of the property use, or payment of an amount lawfully owed to the government. Because a state statute authorized a separate clerk's fee for services rendered, the taking of the interest could not be justified as payment of an obligation to the government.

[20]*Brown v. Legal Foundation of Washington*, 538 U.S. 216, 123 S.Ct. 1406, 155 L.Ed.2d 376 (2003). *See* Ronald D. Rotunda, *Found Money: IOLTA, Brown v. Legal Foundation of Washington, and the Taking of Property without the Payment of Compensation*, 2002–2003 Cato Supreme Court Rev.

justices agreed that the IOLTA program was equivalent to a physical, not regulatory, taking of client property.[21] They also agreed that the State of Washington had taken the property for a public purpose. The court, however, divided (5 to 4) on the issue of whether Washington owed just compensation to the clients who lost interest in IOLTA programs. The majority held that under the Washington IOLTA program, the clients suffered no net loss, and therefore the state program owed no compensation to the clients under the Takings Clause.

Justice Stevens writing for the majority held that just compensation should be measured by the property owner's "net losses rather than the value of the public's gain."[22] The opinion then focused on the Washington Supreme Court's IOLTA rule that required lawyers to place client funds in a non-IOLTA account when such funds could generate net earnings for clients. Given that requirement, the majority of client deposits into the IOLTA accounts could not have earned net earnings for the clients. Thus, according to the majority, these clients have suffered no loss. For the clients whose principal was mistakenly placed in an IOLTA account, their lawyers violated the terms of the IOLTA rule itself. Improper private decisions of lawyers and not state action caused some client funds that would earn net interest to end up in IOLTA accounts; therefore, these clients have no entitlement to compensation.[23]

The majority sums up its analysis as follows:

> It is neither unethical nor illegal for lawyers to deposit their clients' funds in a single bank account. A state law that requires client funds that could not otherwise generate net earnings for the client to be deposited in an IOLTA account is not a "regulatory taking." A law that requires that the interest on those funds be transferred to a different owner for legitimate public use, however, could be a *per se* taking requiring the payment of "just compensation" to the client. Because that compensation is measured by the owner's pecuniary loss—which is zero whenever the Washington law is obeyed—there has been no violation of the Just Compensation Clause of the Fifth Amendment in this case.[24]

---

245 (2003) (analyzing the IOLTA issue in general and criticizing the majority's analysis of just compensation).

[21] 538 U.S. at 235, 123 S.Ct. at 1418 ("As was made clear in *Phillips*, the interest earned in IOLTA accounts 'is the 'private property' of the owner of the principal.' ").

[22] 538 U.S. at 237, 123 S.Ct. at 1420. Although the majority opinion states that this view of compensation is supported by precedent, the more traditional view of just compensation is the market value on the date the property is taken.

[23] 538 U.S. at 239–40, 123 S.Ct. at 1420.

[24] 538 U.S. at 240, 123 S.Ct. at 1421 (citations omitted).

The primary dissent written by Justice Scalia vigorously disagreed with Justice Steven's narrow reading of the IOLTA statute and his "net loss" theory of just compensation.

Some in the legal profession view the *Brown* decision as a broad endorsement that IOLTA plans generally can withstand a Takings Clause challenge as well as other general challenges. However, the majority opinion is written on very narrow grounds. Justice Stevens relies heavily on the Washington IOLTA statute's requirement that lawyers place client funds in a non-IOLTA account when the clients could earn net interest. Thus, an IOLTA statute without such a requirement may present constitutional problems.

If the lawyer makes a mistake about whether the principal could earn net interest, the majority opinion states that a lawyer could be directly liable to the clients for failing to exclude the deposit from the IOLTA account.

Finally, advances in computer technology will make it feasible for law firms to credit net interest to client with little or no additional cost to the client or to the lawyer. The majority understood its opinion would take into account these advances in technology and automatically adjust what the lawyer must return to the client.[25]

One additional basis exists for future IOLTA litigation. Justice Kennedy in a separate dissent explained the First Amendment issues implicated in IOLTA:

> Had the State, with the help of Congress, not acted in violation of its constitutional responsibilities by taking for itself property which all concede to be that of the client, the free market might have created various and diverse funds for pooling small interest amounts. These funds would have allowed the true owners of the property the option to express views and policies of their own choosing. Instead, as these programs stand, the true owner cannot even opt out of the State's monopoly.
>
> The First Amendment consequences of the State's action have not been addressed in his case, but the potential for a serious violation is there. One constitutional violation (the taking of property) likely will lead to another (compelled speech). These matters may have to come before the Court in due course.[26]

Therefore, given the issues left open in *Brown*, clients and

---

[25]The majority quoted a lower court's view of advances in technology and the impact on IOLTA:

" 'Thus, as cost effective subaccounting services become available, making it possible to earn net interest for clients on increasingly smaller amounts held for increasingly shorter periods of time, more tried money will have to be in-vested for the clients' benefit under the new rule. The rule is therefore self-adjusting and is adequately designed to accommodate changes in banking technology without running afoul of the state or federal constitutions.' "

538 U.S. at 227, 123 S.Ct. at 1414

[26]538 U.S. at 253, 123 S.Ct. at

lawyers may identify a successful challenge to state IOLTA programs in the future.[27]

§ 6.1–4 FEES, REDUCED FEES, AND PRO BONO REPRESENTATION

§ 6.1–4(a) Indigents, the Middle Class, and Price Differential

Sometimes the lawyer may charge one of her clients a fee for certain work, although the same lawyer will charge a different client no fee for the same work, because this other client cannot afford to pay anything.[1] However, in order for a lawyer to be engaged in pro bono work, it is not necessary that the lawyer refuse to charge any fee. Often a person of moderate means can afford some fee, but not the lawyer's customary fee. Then the lawyer should charge a reduced fee.[2]

The Model Rules do not set a minimum fee—to do so would raise a problem of price-fixing under the antitrust laws,[3] but the tradition of the ethics rules recognizes that "adequate compensation is necessary in order to enable the lawyer to serve his client effectively and to preserve the integrity and independence of the profession."[4]

A lawyer, therefore, may charge a "reasonable fee" of clients able to afford it. Those clients who only can afford less, should be charged a lesser fee. It "is proper to define the extent of services in light of the client's ability to pay."[5] In effect, the Rules and the Code permit a lawyer to charge one client less (or more) than another client is charged, based on the clients' ability to pay. If one charges a client *less* because the client is less wealthy, the other side of the coin must be that one is charging another client *more* because that client is more wealthy.[6] Some people might be surprised to learn that lawyers may ethically charge them more because they can afford a higher fee, but that is an inevitable

---

1428 (citations omitted).

[27]*See* Ronald D. Rotunda, *Found Money: IOLTA, Brown v. Legal Foundation of Washington, and the Taking of Property without the Payment of Compensation*, 2002–2003 CATO SUPREME COURT REV. 245, 268–69 (2003).

[Section 6.1–4]

[1]Rule 6.1, Comment 1. EC 2-24, 2-25.

[2]EC 2-16, 2-24. Rule 6.1, Comment 1.

[3]*Goldfarb v. Virginia State Bar*, 421 U.S. 773, 95 S.Ct. 2004, 44 L.Ed.2d

572 (1975) (minimum fee schedule published by Fairfax County Bar Association, enforced through the prospect of professional discipline from the state bar, constitutes price fixing in violation of § 1 of the Sherman Antitrust Act).

[4]EC 2-17.

[5]Rule 1.5, Comment 3.

[6]*Cf.* EC 2-18, which explicitly approves of price discrimination in a special circumstance (it provides that it is appropriate to charge less to a fellow lawyer or members of a fellow lawyer's immediate family).

result of any rule that allows lawyers to charge some people less or nothing because of their inability to afford the standard rate.

Consider this example: Attorney Alpha represents Client A, another lawyer, in the purchase of a home. Attorney Alpha charges $50 per hour for her services. Attorney Alpha also represents Client B, a wealthy manufacturer, in the purchase of his home. Attorney Alpha charges Client B $100 per hour for her services. Client C, an indigent, asks Attorney Alpha to represent him in reviewing his rental contract with Landlord in a low income housing project. Attorney Alpha charges nothing. Finally, Client D, a person of moderate means, asks Attorney Alpha to represent him in the purchase of his moderate cottage. Attorney Alpha charges Client D only $40 per hour for her services, which is all that D can afford. Assuming that none of these charges is unreasonably high, Attorney has done nothing improper under the ethics rules. Client B (or any other client) may be upset that Attorney Alpha has charged him more per hour than she has charged other clients; it is a free country and Client B can be upset, but he has no claim that Attorney Alpha has done anything that is ethically improper.

§ 6.1–4(b) Sharing Court-Awarded Fees with Pro Bono Organizations

A lawyer may begin a pro bono project with no expectation of a fee, but it may later develop that the lawyer may collect a fee, such as a statutory award of attorneys' fees.[7] This possibility of being awarded fees raises an ethics issue when the lawyer is acting on behalf of a private organization, such as the American Civil Liberties Union. The question is whether the lawyer may properly share his legal fees with a nonlawyer. The answer to this question was uncertain under the 1983 Model Rules. However, the drafters of the 2002 Model Rules explicitly addressed this question in Rule 5.4(a)(4).

This problem encompasses several rules that are not found in Part 6 of the Model Rules. The 1983 version of Rule 5.4(a) prohibited a lawyer from sharing fees with a nonlawyer, subject to a few limited exceptions. Rule 7.2(c) prohibited payment of a referral fee, again with a few limited exceptions not relevant here. An ABA Formal Opinion[8] concluded that where a non-profit pro bono organization asks an attorney to undertake pro bono litigation, the lawyer (whether an employee of the organization or a member of a law firm) may agree in advance or later to turn over

---

[7] Rule 6.1, Comment 4.

[8] ABA Formal Opinion 93-374 (June 7, 1993).

For a thorough and careful dis-

cussion of these issues, see Roy D. Simon, Jr., *Fee Sharing Between Lawyers and Public Interest Groups*, 98 Yale L. J. 1969 (1989).

some or all of the court-awarded fees to the non-profit pro bono organization. Although Rules 5.4(a) and 7.2(c) literally appeared to prohibit the turnover of fees, ABA Formal Opinion 93-374 argued that they should not be interpreted that way, because application of these rules would not further the purposes behind them. However, lawyers who entered into such agreements should disclose the arrangement to their clients, because of the possibility of improper lay interference.[9]

This ABA Formal Opinion attracted a strong dissent, arguing that the majority's interpretation of the Rules was contrary to their plain meaning.[10] This Opinion is also contrary to *American Civil Liberties Union/Eastern Missouri Fund v. Miller*,[11] which held that Missouri's Rule 5.4(a) prohibited a former ACLU staff attorney from complying with his employment contract, which required him to turn over court-awarded fees.[12]

Most courts followed the view expressed by the majority in Formal Opinion 93-374. Although the courts did not always discuss the issue in any detail, they allowed the attorneys' fee awards to be turned over to the nonprofit organization for work performed by their lawyers.[13]

The drafters of the 2002 Model Rules thought that it was important to resolve this dispute through a change in the provision that examines sharing of legal fees with nonlawyers. Rule 5.4(a) prohibits the sharing of legal fees with a nonlawyer, but the rule includes an explicit exception for sharing "court-awarded legal fees with a nonprofit organization that employed, retained

---

[9]ABA Formal Opinion 93-374 (June 7, 1993).

Contrast Formal Opinion 95-392 (April 24, 1995), which concluded that it would be illegal fee-sharing if in-house corporate lawyers shared with their employers any fee-shifting award (*i.e.*, a "reasonable attorney's fee" based on an hourly rate that is in excess of the actual cost the corporation incurred in employing the lawyer). The Ethics Committee distinguished its earlier Opinion 93-374 as limited to non-profit organizations, "because the expectation of receiving a fee is unlikely in these circumstances to be the source of lay interference with the lawyer's professional judgment." Formal Opinion 95-392 (April 24, 1995), at 8.

[10]ABA Formal Opinion 93-374 (June 7, 1993) (dissent).

[11]*American Civil Liberties Union/Eastern Missouri Fund v. Miller*, 803 S.W.2d 592, 43 ALR 5th 901 (Mo.1991), *cert. denied*, 500 U.S. 943, 111 S.Ct. 2239, 114 L.Ed.2d 481 (1991).

[12]The ACLU later won a court order permanently enjoining Missouri from enforcing its ethical rules to prevent the fee turn-over provision in the ACLU employment contract. *Susman v. Missouri, No. 91-4429-CV-C-5 (W.D. Mo., June 1, 1992)*.

[13]*E.g.*, *Oldham v. Ehrlich*, 617 F.2d 163, 165 n. 3, 168–69 (8th Cir. 1980); *New York State Association for Retarded Children, Inc. v. Carey*, 711 F.2d 1136, 1139, 1154 (2d Cir.1983); *McLean v. Arkansas Board of Education*, 723 F.2d 45, 47 (8th Cir.1983).

or recommended employment of the lawyer in the matter."[14] The
drafters of the 2002 Rules sought to reaffirm the position taken
by the ABA Formal Opinion 93-374 because the threat to the
professional independence of a lawyer is significantly reduced
when dealing with a nonprofit organization.[15]

---

[14]Rule 5.4(a)(4).

[15]*See* Reporter's Explanation of

Changes to Model Rule 5.4 (*See*
Appendix A).

CHAPTER 6.2
ACCEPTING APPOINTMENTS

RULE 6.2: ACCEPTING APPOINTMENTS

A lawyer shall not seek to avoid appointment by a tribunal to represent a person except for good cause, such as:

(a) representing the client is likely to result in violation of the Rules of Professional Conduct or other law;

(b) representing the client is likely to result in an unreasonable financial burden on the lawyer; or

(c) the client or the cause is so repugnant to the lawyer as to be likely to impair the client-lawyer relationship or the lawyer's ability to represent the client.

Comment

[1] A lawyer ordinarily is not obliged to accept a client whose character or cause the lawyer regards as repugnant. The lawyer's freedom to select clients is, however, qualified. All lawyers have a responsibility to assist in providing pro bono publico service. See Rule 6.1. An individual lawyer fulfills this responsibility by accepting a fair share of unpopular matters or indigent or unpopular clients. A lawyer may also be subject to appointment by a court to serve unpopular clients or persons unable to afford legal services.

Appointed Counsel

[2] For good cause a lawyer may seek to decline an appointment to represent a person who cannot afford to retain counsel or whose cause is unpopular. Good cause exists if the lawyer could not handle the matter competently, see Rule 1.1, or if undertaking the representation would result in an improper conflict of interest, for example, when the client or the cause is so repugnant to the lawyer as to be likely to impair the client-lawyer relationship or the lawyer's ability to represent the client. A lawyer may also seek to decline an appointment if acceptance would be unreasonably burdensome, for example, when it would impose a financial sacrifice so great as to be unjust.

[3] An appointed lawyer has the same obligations to the client as retained counsel, including the obligations of loyalty and confidentiality, and is subject to the same limitations on the client-lawyer relationship, such as the obligation to refrain from assisting the client in violation of the Rules.

Authors' 1983 Model Rules Comparison

The 2002 version is identical to the Rule adopted by the ABA House of Delegates in 1983.

Model Code Comparison

There was no counterpart to this Rule in the Disciplinary Rules of the Model Code. EC 2-29 stated that when a lawyer is "appointed by a court or requested by a bar association to undertake representation of a person unable to obtain counsel, whether for financial or other reasons, he should not seek to be excused from undertaking the representation except for compelling reasons. Compelling reasons do not include such factors as the repugnance of the subject matter of the proceeding, the identity or position of a person involved in the case, the belief of the lawyer that the defendant in a criminal proceeding is guilty, or the belief of the lawyer regarding the merits of the civil case." EC 2-30 stated that "a lawyer should decline employment if the intensity of his personal feelings, as distinguished from a community attitude, may impair his effective representation of a prospective client."

§ 6.2–1 ACCEPTING PRO BONO CASES

A lawyer is not like the cab driver waiting at a taxi stand. The lawyer need not accept every client who walks through the door. However, it is improper for a lawyer to refuse an appointed case for the wrong reason. To achieve the goal of making legal services fully available, a lawyer "should not lightly decline proffered employment;" a lawyer should accept "his share of tendered employment which may be unattractive both to him and to the bar generally."[1]

For example, a lawyer must refuse a case because he is too busy to give it his competent attention.[2] A lawyer also must refuse a case if the client seeks to maintain a frivolous action or one brought only to harass another.[3] And a lawyer must refuse a case if accepting it would result in violation of "other law."[4]

On the other hand, a lawyer should not decline representation

---

[Section 6.2–1]

[1] EC 2-26.

[2] Rule 1.1; Rule 6.2, Comment 2. EC 2-30; DR 6-101(A)(1).

See, e.g., *Zarabia v. Bradshaw,* 185 Ariz. 1, 912 P.2d 5 (1996), which held that the superior court's system of appointing private attorneys for indigent defendants offended requirement that indigent defendants receive effective assistance of counsel. The lower court was appointing lawyers on a random, rotational basis, which did not take into account the skill required in handling particu-

lar case. A lawyer with no trial or criminal experience was not likely to become reasonably competent to represent defendant charged with a serious crime simply by having a mentor to consult. The plaintiffs objecting to this system were an estate-planning lawyer who had never tried a jury case or practiced criminal law, and a second lawyer who had "minimal experience in criminal representation," and concentrated "on civil transactional work."

[3] Rule 3.1. EC 2-30; DR 2-109(A); DR 7-102(A)(1).

[4] Rule 6.2(a). *See* ABA Formal Opinion 347 (Dec. 1, 1981), and ABA

merely because the client, or the client's cause, is unpopular[5] or because influential members of the community oppose the lawyer's involvement.[6] In addition, a lawyer need not refuse a case merely because he or she does not believe in the merits of a client's case, or believes, in a criminal case, that the client is guilty.[7] However, if the lawyer's personal feelings are so intense that his effective representation is impaired, then he must not take the case.[8]

§ 6.2–2 REJECTING APPOINTED CASES

In contrast to Rule 6.1's aspirational goal of pro bono legal services to persons of limited means, Rule 6.2 recognizes that courts generally have the power to appoint lawyers to represent indigent clients. Depending upon the jurisdiction and the court, the power of a judge to appoint a lawyer to represent a client may be derived from constitutional sources, statutory provisions, inherent powers of the court, or social policy justifications.[1] The open question is whether such appointments may be made with little or no compensation.[2]

In light of the mandatory nature of court appointments, Rule 6.2 provides that a lawyer should not refuse a court appointment to handle a pro bono case except for "compelling reasons" or "good cause."[3] The rule provides three general categories of good cause to serve as a basis for rejecting a court appointment.

First, a lawyer must decline an appointment when the representation "is likely to result in a violation of the Rules . . . or

---

Formal Opinion 96-399 (Jan. 18, 1996), extensively discussing the ethical obligations of lawyers working for the Legal Service Corporation when funding is reduced and the remaining funding limits the lawyer's representation or subjects it to restrictive conditions.

[5]Rule 6.2, Comment 1. EC 2-27.

[6]EC 2-28.

[7]EC 2-29.

[8]Model Rule 6.2(c) & Comment 2; EC 2-30.

[Section 6.2–2]

[1]*Powell v. Alabama*, 287 U.S. 45, 73, 53 S.Ct. 55, 65, 77 L.Ed. 158, 172 (1932). *See generally* ABA/BNA Lawyers' Manual on Professional Conduct ¶ 91:6202-07 (2004).

[2]*See, e.g., DeLisio v. Alaska Superior Court*, 740 P.2d 437 (Alaska 1987) (court could not compel an attorney to represent an indigent client without offering just compensation).

See, e.g., State v. Citizen, 898 So.2d 325 (La. 2005), holding that two statutes did not authorize the use of local funds to pay for appointed defense counsel for indigent criminal defendants and that these statutes did not violate the due process, equal protection, or right to counsel rights of the defendants. However, a trial court may halt a prosecution until adequate funding for appointed counsel for the indigent criminal defendant is likely to become available.

[3]EC 2-29; Rule 6.2(a).

other law."[4] It is obvious that a lawyer should not be required to accept an appointment when the Model Rules or other law permit or require a lawyer to avoid certain conduct in a representation. There are many examples of such cases, including representations that involve a conflict of interest with another client or those that would involve the lawyer in a crime or fraud.

Second, Rule 6.2 permits a lawyer to refuse an appointed case if taking it would result in "an unreasonable financial burden."[5] This rule restates the provision in Rule 1.16 that a lawyer may withdraw from a representation when "the representation will result in an unreasonable financial burden on the lawyer . . . ."[6] Thus, one could view this rule as reaffirming the idea that a lawyer may withdraw when the burden of the representation rises to the level of a serious and unreasonable financial burden. In the context of a court appointment, however, this provision could be viewed more broadly as encompassing the compensation structure in place for court appointed lawyers and the individual lawyer's recent participation in other court appointed or pro bono matters.

Finally, Rule 6.2 states that a lawyer may decline an appointed

---

[4]Rule 6.2(a).

[5]Rule 6.2(b).

The Model Code had no such specific provision, but earlier case law has allowed this excuse when the burden is truly unreasonable. *Compare People ex rel. Conn v. Randolph*, 35 Ill.2d 24, 219 N.E.2d 337 (1966) (State paid fee in excess of statutory maximum allowed in appointed case in order to prevent an unconstitutional taking of property when the financial burden was staggering), *with People v. Sanders*, 58 Ill.2d 196, 317 N.E.2d 552 (1974)(only $250 statutory maximum awarded in capital punishment case because financial burden in this instance is not unreasonable).

Brown v. Board of County Commissioners of Washoe County, 85 Nev. 149, 451 P.2d 708 (1969) held that a "minor" loss of income should be borne by attorney. However, in that case, many people would think the loss was not that minor. The court has appointed the lawyer to represent an indigent defendant in noncapital criminal case that was both complex and long. The length of the indigent's trial forced the lawyer to associate with other counsel in other matters; he also was not able to see other clients for over two months; he lost several regular clients; and he was compelled to return retainers in excess of $1,000. Nonetheless, the court held that the lawyer was not entitled to recover more than the statutory limit of $300 as compensation. After this case, the legislature amended the relevant statute to provide for fee payments in excess of the established limits in "unusual circumstances." See *Wood v. State*, 113 Nev. 1455, 1457, 951 P.2d 601, 602 (1997).

Contrast, New York County Lawyers' Association v. State, 192 Misc.2d 424, 433, 745 N.Y.S.2d 376, 385 (N.Y.Sup. 2002). The court held that the New York County lawyer's association satisfied its burden of showing that it was likely that indigent litigants in New York City family and criminal courts were being denied effective assistance of counsel, resulting from lawyers' compensation rates that were too low. The court granted a preliminary injunction directing payment of interim rate of $90 an hour for in- and out-of-court work.

[6]Rule 1.16(b)(6).

representation if the "the cause is so repugnant to the lawyer" so as to impair the lawyer-client relationship or the quality of the representation.[7] It is improper for a lawyer to refuse an appointed case because the client is unpopular.[8] However, the lawyer should not take a case if his or her own personal feelings against the client or cause are so strong that the lawyer could not do a competent job.[9] Indeed, it would be unethical for the lawyer to accept such a case, because the first rule of legal ethics is competence.[10]

The appointing courts, rather than state bar disciplinary systems, enforce the standard of "good cause" for rejecting a court appointment. A court appointed lawyer must inform the court that he or she wishes to decline the representation. Thus, lawyers are less likely to test the margins of what constitutes "good cause" because of the social and professional pressure to comply with requests of judges before whom they regularly litigate cases.

---

[7] Rule 6.2(c).

[8] EC 2-27.

[9] EC 2-30; Rule 6.2(c). The Code said that "[c]ompelling reasons [not to take a case] do not include such factors as the repugnance of the subject matter . . . " EC 2-29. In contrast, Rule 6.2(c) states that a proper reason to refuse to accept an appointed case is that "the client or the cause is so repugnant . . . " to the lawyer. *See also* Rule 6.2, Comment 1 ("A lawyer ordinarily is not obliged to accept a client whose character or cause the lawyer regards as repugnant.").

These two sections are not re-ally in conflict. EC 2-30 explains that a lawyer should decline representation if "the intensity of his personal feelings" may "impair his effective representation . . .," and Comment 1 to Rule 6.2 qualifies the reference to repugnancy by explaining that it is modified by the lawyer's responsibility to provide pro bono service: "An individual lawyer fulfills this responsibility [to assist in providing pro bono publico service] by accepting a fair share of unpopular matters or indigent or unpopular clients."

[10] Rule 1.1.

CHAPTER 6.3

MEMBERSHIP IN LEGAL SERVICES ORGANIZATIONS

§ 6.3–1 Lawyers As Officers or Directors of a Legal Services Organization

§ 6.3–2 Constitutional Limitations on the Power of the Federal Government to Use Its Spending Power to Regulate Legal Services

---

RULE 6.3: MEMBERSHIP IN LEGAL SERVICES ORGANIZATION

A lawyer may serve as a director, officer or member of a legal services organization, apart from the law firm in which the lawyer practices, notwithstanding that the organization serves persons having interests adverse to a client of the lawyer. The lawyer shall not knowingly participate in a decision or action of the organization:

(a) if participating in the decision or action would be incompatible with the lawyer's obligations to a client under Rule 1.7; or

(b) where the decision or action could have a material adverse effect on the representation of a client of the organization whose interests are adverse to a client of the lawyer.

Comment

[1] Lawyers should be encouraged to support and participate in legal service organizations. A lawyer who is an officer or a member of such an organization does not thereby have a client-lawyer relationship with persons served by the organization. However, there is potential conflict between the interests of such persons and the interests of the lawyer's clients. If the possibility of such conflict disqualified a lawyer from serving on the board of a legal services organization, the profession's involvement in such organizations would be severely curtailed.

[2] It may be necessary in appropriate cases to reassure a client of the organization that the representation will not be affected by conflicting loyalties of a member of the board. Established, written policies in this respect can enhance the credibility of such assurances.

Authors' 1983 Model Rules Comparison

The 2002 version is identical to the Rule adopted by the ABA House of Delegates in 1983.

Model Code Comparison

There was no counterpart to this Rule in the Model Code.

§6.3–1 LAWYERS AS OFFICERS OR DIRECTORS OF A LEGAL SERVICES ORGANIZATION

An attorney in a private law firm may also be a member, officer, or director of a legal services organization engaged in pro bono activities.[1] In fact, after Congress established the federal Legal Services Corporation in 1974,[2] in order to offer noncriminal legal services to indigents, the relevant regulations required that at least 60% of the local governing bodies should be attorneys admitted in that state and supportive of the delivery of quality legal services to the poor.[3] The pro bono activities of the legal services organization may include lawsuits against private parties represented by the attorney's private firm. Such a situation may raise a conflict of interest question. Rule 6.3 is drafted to deal with this ethical issue.

If an attorney in private practice is a member of a legal services board, in a matter of time it may come to pass that the staff members of the legal services organization, on behalf of an indigent client, will file suit against one of the private attorney's private clients, or defend the indigent against suit brought by the private client. This situation may raise a practical problem: the client may not approve of the fact that its private lawyer is serving on the legal services board. However, there is no ethical conflict of interest because the private attorney who is a member of the Board does not have an attorney-client relationship with the Legal Service Organization's clients.[4] The individual legal service clients do not confer with the Board members; nor do they place any confidences or secrets with these Board members.[5] The Board's role is restricted solely to establishing broad policy for

---

[Section 6.3–1]

[1] May a lawyer serve on an advisory committee of a public interest organization? Utah State Bar Ethics Advisory Comm. Op. 06–05 (Dec. 29, 2006), *noted in* 23 ABA/BNA MANUAL ON PROFESSIONAL CONDUCT, Current Reports News 37 (Jan. 24, 2007), stated that lawyers who serve on an ad hoc litigation advisory board for a public interest group are not automatically barred from participation by conflicts of interest between their clients and the group's clients. The committee felt that the exemption afforded to directors, officers, or members should also apply to advisors. However, the opinion cautioned that lawyers serving as advisors still may have to recuse themselves from certain matters of the organization, and the organization should have implement clear policies requiring lawyer recusal.

[2] *See* 42 U.S.C.A. § 2996b.

[3] 45 C.F.R. § 1607.3(b)(1982).

[4] ABA Formal Opinion 345 (July 12, 1979); Rule 6.3, Comment 1.

[5] ABA Formal Opinion 334 (Aug. 10, 1974).

the Program, not managing or directly participating in the Program's client representation.[6]

Nonetheless, ABA Formal Opinion 345,[7] based on the Model Code, concluded that there remains a problem when a Board member represents a client adverse to the client of a legal services program. Perhaps, said the Opinion, one of the counsel might feel self-restrained in exercising zeal. Or, a client (particularly an indigent one) may acquiesce only because he believes that he has no choice in the matter.

Consequently, Formal Opinion 345 concluded that the clients on both sides must be made aware of the Board member's role. The lawyers and clients on either side should "feel comfortable," and "if, in the course of the representation, it becomes apparent that independent representation is not being afforded on both sides or one or the other of the clients perceives that it is not afforded, *no matter what the reality,* then the lawyers should assist in change of counsel for one or both clients."[8] If the Board member's law firm is large enough, the Opinion continued, a lawyer other than the Board member should represent the firm's clients in disputes with the legal services program, so that the Board member is not directly involved. This ABA Formal Opinion urged the Board member's law firm to provide "screening procedures."[9] Finally, because of the "extreme value" of having active lawyers serve as Board members, the legal services staff lawyer "should not seek unfairly to gain advantage for their clients by disqualification of the Board member or his firm."[10]

The approach of the Model Rules is a little different. The Rules try to solve the problem of any perceived conflicts by selectively screening the private lawyer from the decision-making process of the legal services organization. If the private lawyer is also a member, director, or officer of the legal services organization, then the private lawyer should not "knowingly" participate in any decision or action of the legal services organization if such participation would be inconsistent with the lawyer's obligation, under the general conflicts of interest rule (Rule 1.7), to his or

---

[6]ABA Formal Opinion 345 (July 12, 1979). *See also* 45 C.F.R. § 1607.4(b) (1982). *Cf.* DR 5-107(B) (lawyer should not permit person who employs him to render services for another to direct his professional judgment); Rule 5.4(c) (same); ABA Formal Opinion 334 (Aug. 10, 1974) (same). Finally, public policy favors having active practitioners involved in the ac-

tivities of legal service organizations. ABA Formal Opinion 345 (July 12, 1979); Rule 6.3, Comment 1.

[7]ABA Formal Opinion 345 (July 12, 1979).

[8]*Id.* (emphasis added).

[9]*Cf.* Rule 1.11.

[10]ABA Formal Opinion 345 (July 12, 1979).

her private clients.[11] Similarly, the private lawyer should not knowingly participate in a decision on behalf of the legal services organization if the decision could have a "material adverse effect" on a legal services' client whose interests are adverse to the lawyer's private client. The private lawyer, then, is not disqualified from serving on the Board; that lawyer is disqualified from participating in certain Board decisions.[12] The legal services organization also should establish written policies regarding the role of the legal services decision-making process in order to enhance the credibility of the assurances that it gives to its indigent.

§ 6.3–2 CONSTITUTIONAL LIMITATIONS ON THE POWER OF THE FEDERAL GOVERNMENT TO USE ITS SPENDING POWER TO REGULATE LEGAL SERVICES

When the Federal Government spends money, it has a great deal of power to attach conditions to the use of that money. The general rule is that he who pays the piper calls the tune.[1] Consider, for example, *Rust v. Sullivan*,[2] where the Government hired private speakers (doctors and other medical personnel) to act on behalf of the Government and transmit information about Government programs relating to family planning. The Court held that the Federal Government could engage in viewpoint discrimination (limiting the medical personnel's speech that proposed abortion) in order to make sure that the Government's own message (about pre-conception family planning) is being delivered. In this situation, the Court gave the Government wide power to place limits on the type of speech that it wishes to subsidize, because the Government is the speaker and it is hiring people to represent *its* interests.

The situation is different when the Government hires lawyers to represent other people's interests, not its own interests. When the Government spends money to facilitate *private* speech, is does not have the same latitude to engage in viewpoint discrimi-

---

[11]Rule 6.3 requires that a lawyer place the interests of private clients above the lawyer's interests to the legal services organization. See John S. Dzienkowski, *Positional Conflicts of Interest*, 71 Tex. L. Rev. 457, 531–36 (1993) (examining public interest positional conflicts of interest).

[12]*Accord* Restatement of the Law Governing Lawyers, Third, § 135 (Official Draft 2000), Comment *e*, "Lawyer as director of legal services organiza-

tion."

[Section 6.3–2]

[1]1 RONALD D. ROTUNDA & JOHN E. NOWAK, TREATISE ON CONSTITUTIONAL LAW: SUBSTANCE AND PROCEDURE § § 5.1, 5.7 (Thomson-West, 4th ed. 2007) (6 volumes).

[2]*Rust v. Sullivan*, 500 U.S. 173, 111 S.Ct. 1759, 114 L.Ed.2d 233 (1991).

nation because it is not promoting *Government* speech.[3] Public defenders, for example, represent their clients, not the Government, which is represented by its own prosecutors. The purpose of the public defender program is not to transmit information about Government programs, and the public defender does not speak on behalf of the Government even though the Government pays the salary of the public defender.

There is a constitutional difference, for First Amendment purposes, when the Government hires lawyers (such as legal services lawyers in civil cases or public defenders in criminal cases) to represent other people. When the Government funds legal services, it is not subsidizing Government speech because these lawyers—unlike prosecutors or other lawyers who represent the Government—represent their clients. The Government may not engage in viewpoint discrimination when it hires lawyers to represent the interests of others.

The Court relied on this distinction in *Legal Services Corporation v. Velazquez.*[4] Congress established the Legal Services Corporation (LSC) to provide legal representation for the poor. LSC distributes federal funds to provide financial support for legal assistance in noncriminal matters to persons financially unable to afford legal assistance. From its inception in 1974, Congress has placed various restrictions on the LSC's use of funds. The statute prohibits LSC funds from going to any political party, or to any political campaign, or for use in advocating or opposing any ballot measures. The Act further prohibits use of funds in most criminal proceedings and in litigation involving nontherapeutic abortions, secondary school desegregation, military desertion, or violations of the Selective Service. The law also bars fund recipients from bringing class action suits unless they first obtain express approval from LSC.

One section of the law, enacted in 1996 as part of a compromise set of restrictions, prohibits funding any organization that—

initiates legal representation or participates in any other way, in

---

[3]*Rust v. Sullivan*, 500 U.S. 173, 111 S.Ct. 1759, 114 L.Ed.2d 233 (1991) (Government uses private speakers to transmit information concerning its own program); *Compare Board of Regents of University of Wisconsin System v. Southworth*, 529 U.S. 217, 229, 235, 120 S.Ct. 1346, 1353, 1357, 146 L.Ed.2d 193 (2000) (the Government is the speaker), *with Rosenberger v. Rector and Visitors*, 515 U.S. 819, 833, 115 S.Ct. 2510, 2518, 132 L.Ed.2d 700 (Government subsidizes private speech). Ronald D. Rotunda,

Subsidized Speech for the Rich, CHICAGO TRIBUNE, Dec. 12, 1999, at § 1, p. 23.

[4]*Legal Services Corporation v. Velazquez*, 531 U.S. 533, 121 S.Ct. 1043, 149 L.Ed.2d 63 (2001). Justice Kennedy, wrote the opinion for the Court, joined by Justices Stevens, Souter, Ginsburg, & Breyer. Justice Scalia dissented, in an opinion joined by Chief Justice Rehnquist and Justices O'Connor and Thomas.

litigation, lobbying, or rulemaking, involving an effort to reform a Federal or State welfare system, except that this paragraph shall not be construed to preclude a recipient from representing an individual eligible client who is seeking specific relief from a welfare agency if such relief does not *involve an effort to amend or otherwise challenge existing law in effect on the date of the initiation of the representation.*[5]

The italicized phrase was the focus of the Court in *Legal Services Corporation v. Velazquez.*

The Second Circuit held that the restrictions placed on litigation, lobbying, or rulemaking, involving welfare reform were constitutional because they were not based on viewpoint discrimination. The LSC grantee could not participate in these endeavors regardless of the side of the issue. However, the Second Circuit concluded that the italicized phrase (the qualification that representation could "not involve an effort to amend or otherwise challenge existing law") was impermissible viewpoint discrimination because it "clearly seeks to discourage challenges to the status quo." The Second Circuit severed this portion of the statute—which allowed LSC attorneys to represent individual clients seeking welfare benefits so long as these lawsuits did not involve an attempt to amend or challenge existing law. The Second Circuit then invalidated it.

The Supreme Court accepted certiorari only on this issue, reviewed this clause, and, in a five to four opinion, concurred that it violated the First Amendment. The Court declined to address the severability issue because it was not contested before the Court. To reach its result, the Court used several justifications that are not usually combined—freedom of speech, the duties of lawyers to their clients, the role of courts in the adversary process, and separation of powers—so that this holding is somewhat unique and may not spawn an extensive line of cases in its wake.

Justice Kennedy, for the Court, agreed that Congress need not fund an LSC lawyer to represent indigents, and when it did so, it need not fund the whole range of legal representations or relationships. But, what Congress may not do is define the scope of the litigation it funds to exclude certain constitutional theories.

The attempted restriction is designed to insulate the Government's interpretation of the Constitution from judicial challenge. The Constitution does not permit the Government to confine litigants and their attorneys in this manner. We must be vigilant when Congress imposes rules and conditions which in effect insulate its own laws from legitimate judicial challenge. Where private speech is involved,

---

[5]Section 504(b)(16) (emphasis added). The restrictions were part of a compromise set of restrictions enacted in the Omnibus Consolidated Rescissions and Appropriations Act of 1996 (1996 Act), §§ 504, 110 Stat. 1321 to 1353, and continued in each subsequent annual appropriations Act.

even Congress' antecedent funding decision cannot be aimed at the suppression of ideas thought inimical to the Government's own interest.[6]

The LSC program was designed to facilitate private speech, not to promote a governmental message. The LSC lawyer is not the government's speaker, unlike the *Rust* decision.[7]

In addition, the LSC restriction interferes with the lawyer's duty to his or her client.[8] The restriction seeks to "truncate" the lawyer's argument to the courts and prohibit speech "upon which courts must depend for the proper exercise of the judicial power. . . . A scheme so inconsistent with accepted separation-of-powers principles is an insufficient basis to sustain or uphold the restriction on speech."[9]

Justice Scalia, in his dissent, contended that the restrictions were viewpoint-neutral and the litigation ban is symmetrical, because the LSC can sponsor neither challenges to, nor defenses of, existing welfare reform law: "litigants challenging the covered statutes or regulations do not receive LSC funding, and neither do litigants defending those laws against challenge."[10] If the issue arises at trial, the LSC provides that "the lawyer should discontinue the representation, 'consistent with the applicable rules of professional responsibility.' " The LSC lawyers "may, however, and indeed *must* explain to the client why they cannot represent him. They are also free to express their views of the legality of the welfare law to the client, and they may refer the client to another attorney who can accept the representation."[11]

---

[6]531 U.S. 533, 547, 121 S.Ct. 1043, 1052, 149 L.Ed.2d 63. Compare, Ronald D. Rotunda, *Media Account-ability In Light of the First Amend-ment*, 21 SOCIAL PHILOSOPHY & POLICY 269 (Cambridge University Press, No. 2, 2004), *reprinted in*, ELLEN FRANKEL PAUL, FRED D. MILLER JR., & JEFFREY PAUL, eds., FREEDOM OF SPEECH (Cambridge U. Press 2004).

[7]531 U.S. 533, 541, 121 S.Ct. 1043, 1049, 149 L.Ed.2d 63.

[8]531 U.S. at 545, 121 S.Ct. at 1051, arguing that the restriction "is inconsistent with the proposition that attorneys should present all the rea-sonable and well-grounded arguments necessary for proper resolution of the case."

[9]531 U.S. 533, 545, 121 S.Ct. 1043, 1051, 149 L.Ed.2d 63.

[10]531 U.S. 533, 549–51, 121 S.Ct. 1043, 1053–54, 149 L.Ed.2d 63 (Scalia, J., dissenting).

[11]531 U.S. 533, 551, 121 S.Ct. 1043, 1054, 149 L.Ed.2d 63 (Scalia, J., dissenting) (emphasis in original). The dissent also argued that the Second Circuit's decision to sever this funding clause from the statute created a piece of legislation that Congress would not have approved.

CHAPTER 6.4
LAW REFORM ACTIVITIES AFFECTING CLIENT INTERESTS

§ 6.4–1 Law Reform Activities Adverse to a Private Client's Interest

§ 6.4–2 Law Reform Activities That Coincide with a Private Client's Interests

§ 6.4–3 When the Client's Identity Is Secret

RULE 6.4: LAW REFORM ACTIVITIES AFFECTING CLIENT INTERESTS

A lawyer may serve as a director, officer or member of an organization involved in reform of the law or its administration notwithstanding that the reform may affect the interests of a client of the lawyer. When the lawyer knows that the interests of a client may be materially benefitted by a decision in which the lawyer participates, the lawyer shall disclose that fact but need not identify the client.

Comment

[1] Lawyers involved in organizations seeking law reform generally do not have a client-lawyer relationship with the organization. Otherwise, it might follow that a lawyer could not be involved in a bar association law reform program that might indirectly affect a client. See also Rule 1.2(b). For example, a lawyer specializing in antitrust litigation might be regarded as disqualified from participating in drafting revisions of rules governing that subject. In determining the nature and scope of participation in such activities, a lawyer should be mindful of obligations to clients under other Rules, particularly Rule 1.7. A lawyer is professionally obligated to protect the integrity of the program by making an appropriate disclosure within the organization when the lawyer knows a private client might be materially benefitted.

Authors' 1983 Model Rules Comparison
The 2002 version is identical to the Rule adopted by the ABA House of Delegates in 1983.

Model Code Comparison
There was no counterpart to this Rule in the Model Code.

§ 6.4–1 LAW REFORM ACTIVITIES ADVERSE TO A PRIVATE CLIENT'S INTEREST

It is not generally considered a conflict of interest for a lawyer to engage in law reform activities even though such activities are adverse to the financial interests of the lawyer's private clients. A lawyer only represents a client in the lawyer's professional capacity. It is not necessary that the lawyer agree with, adopt, or support his or her client's views.[1] "The obligation of loyalty to his client applies only to a lawyer in the discharge of his professional duties and implies no obligation to adopt a personal viewpoint favorable to the interests or desires of his client."[2] Lawyers who abhor cigarettes may represent tobacco companies but write letters to their Senators advocating bans on smoking. Their clients may object, but those objections find no support in the ABA Model Rules.

In fact, the ABA Model Code expressly provided that a lawyer "may take positions on public issues and espouse legal reforms he favors without regard to the individual views of any client."[3] The Rules are not quite as specific on this issue, though their general tenor supports the principle expressed in the Code.

For example, the first sentence of Model Rule 6.4 states that a lawyer may be a director, officer, or member of a group involved in law reform activities "notwithstanding that the reform may affect the interests of a client of the lawyer." If no breach of loyalty arises when the lawyer is a member of an organization advocating law reform contrary to a client's interest, there should be little legal argument that there is a breach of loyalty when the lawyer speaks out on his own behalf.[4] In both cases the Model Rules and the Model Code conclude that any alleged benefits to clients of treating the situation as a conflict of interests are outweighed by the social costs of prohibiting lawyers from engaging in law reform efforts, either individually or through bar associations, legal service organizations, the NAACP, the Washington Legal Foundation, or similar groups.

The client may not like the fact that the lawyer is publicly advocating law reform views contrary to the client's private

---

[Section 6.4–1]

[1]Some law firms may use an overly broad definition of positional conflicts to avoid taking some pro bono cases, but it is not the ethics rules that compel that interpretation. Esther F. Lardent, *Positional Conflicts in the Pro Bono Context: Ethical Considerations and Market Forces*, 67 Fordham L. Rev. 2279, 2289–90 (1999) (arguing that some firms apply an overly broad definition of positional conflicts to avoid upsetting paying clients).

[2]EC 7-17. Accord Rule 1.2(b). On positional conflicts, see, John Dzien-

kowski, *Positional Conflicts of Interest*, 71 Tex.L.Rev. 457 (1993); Esther F. Lardent, *Positional Conflicts in the Pro Bono Context: Ethical Considerations and Market Forces*, 67 Fordham L.Rev. 2279 (1999); and Norman W. Spaulding, *The Prophet and the Bureaucrat: Positional Conflicts in Service Pro Bono Publico*, 50 Stan.L.Rev. 1395 (1998); Comment, *Effects of Legal Ethics in the Business World*, 17 St. John's J. Legal Comment 247, 262 (2003).

[3]EC 7-17.

[4]*Cf.* EC 8-4.

interests. Indeed, if the client is upset enough, he or she may always fire the lawyer.[5] But the client could not validly charge that the lawyer acted unethically in taking the contrary position, unless the lawyer is violating client secrets.[6] In practice, of course, the client—even if she is very upset—might not discharge the lawyer because lawyers are not fungible.

The American Law Institute's Restatement of the Law Governing Lawyers agrees that a lawyer acts properly if he or she openly takes a public position on a controversial issue that is contrary to the views of some or all of that lawyer's clients. The Restatement broadly concludes that there is no conflict and that it is unnecessary to secure the clients' consent.[7] Lawyers are supposed to bring "professional detachment" to their clients, who should understand that the lawyers do not necessarily adopt the clients' views as the lawyers' personal views.[8] Moreover, a contrary rule leads to a bad policy result. For example, if "tax lawyers advocating positions about tax reform were obliged to advocate only positions that would serve the positions of their present clients, the public would lose the objective contributions to policy making of some persons most able to help."[9]

It may be bad for the lawyer's business if a lawyer advocates tax reform that is inconsistent with a paying client's interests, but it is not unethical. It is one thing for a client to charge that the lawyer is making a mistake; it is quite another for the client to be able to charge that the lawyer is acting unethically.

---

[5]Rule 1.16(a)(3); DR 2-110(B)(4). In spite of the ethics rules, some clients do affect the willingness of a law firm to undertake unpopular representation. Norman W. Spaulding, *The Prophet and the Bureaucrat: Positional Conflicts in Service Pro Bono Publico*, 50 STAN. L. REV. 1395, 1420 (1998).

[6]If the lawyer uses or reveals secret information (*e.g.* confidential test results that the client knows but that are otherwise secret and not generally known) then the lawyer has violated Rule 1.6.

[7]RESTATEMENT (THIRD) OF THE LAW GOVERNING LAWYERS § 125 Comment *e* (2000).

[8]*Id.*

[9]*Id.* See also John S. Dzienkowski, *Positional Conflicts of Interest*, 71 TEXAS L. REV. 457 (1993); Norman W. Spaulding, *The Prophet and the Bureaucrat: Positional Conflicts in Service Pro Bono Publico*, 50 STAN. L. REV. 1395 (1998); Ester F. Lardent, *Positional Conflicts in the Pro Bono Context: Ethical Considerations and Market Forces*, 67 FORDHAM L. REV. 2279 (1999).

Scott L. Cummings, *The Politics of Pro Bono*, 52 U.C.L.A. L. REV. 1, 117–18 (2004) (footnotes omitted): "Particularly as corporate clients become more aggressive about ensuring that law firms do not switch sides on important business matters, law firms are reluctant to accept pro bono cases that even appear to adopt antagonistic positions. Moreover, when a positional conflict does emerge, law firms are generally unwilling to sacrifice fee-generating cases for those undertaken for free. Firms therefore tend to take an expansive view of positional conflicts in the pro bono context, making cautious case selection decisions that screen out potentially troublesome pro bono work."

Government Lawyers and Pro Bono Activities. Although Rule 6.4 does not specifically include attorneys in public office, the policy reasons supporting Rule 6.4 applies to such lawyers, Thus, an Illinois advisory ethics opinion saw "no reason to restrict permitted associational activities to attorneys in the private sector."[10]

This Illinois ethics opinion concluded that even though a state's attorney has the statutory duty to represent the county clerk in the county clerk's official capacity, an assistant state's attorney (who is president of a non-profit organization) from urging the legislature adopt an amendment to a state law even though the county clerk is opposed to the amendment. In the particular case, an assistant state's attorney was also president of a genealogical society. He wanted to advocate an amendment to the Vital Records Act to allow broader and easier access to birth records sought by individuals for bona fide genealogical research. The local county clerk, whose office the state's attorney represents by statute, is opposed to the amendment.

§ 6.4–2 LAW REFORM ACTIVITIES THAT COINCIDE WITH A PRIVATE CLIENT'S INTERESTS

The client's interest and the personal law reform interests of the lawyer may coincide. If the lawyer is representing a private client while, for example, appearing before a legislative committee and asking for law reform, the lawyer may not mislead the committee as to the true identity of the client.[1]

If the lawyer personally believes in an item of law reform and his own belief coincides with the interest of his client, it was unclear under the Model Code whether the lawyer must nonetheless disclose that fact even if such disclosure does not identify the client.[2] Rule 6.4 is much more specific, at least in the situation where the lawyer serves an organization involved in law reform: "When the lawyer knows that the interests of a client may be materially *benefitted* by a decision in which the lawyer participates, the lawyer shall disclose that fact but need not identify the client."[3] The disclosure of the fact of representation helps to

---

[10]Illinois State Bar Association, *Law Reform Activities Affecting Client Interests*, ISBA Advisory Opinion on Professional Conduct Opinion No. 91–27 (April 3, 1992), 1992 WL 754625.

[Section 6.4–2]

[1]Rules 3.9 & 4.1(a); DR 7-106(B).

[2]*See* EC 8-4, which only states that if the lawyer purports to act on behalf of the public, then the lawyer should conscientiously believe in the position advocated.

[3]Rule 6.4 (emphasis added). Comment 1 adds:

"A lawyer is professionally obli-

preclude the suspicion that the lawyer exercised improper influence on behalf of a client.[4]

The Restatement of the Law Governing Lawyers agrees with the ABA. The Restatement makes clear that the lawyer need not secure client consent to participate in a decision that *hurts* a client, but she should disclose to the legal reform group that the decision will *help* a present client (although she need not identify the name of the private client). Similarly, the fact that a lawyer represents a client, whether pro bono or fee-based, implies nothing about what the lawyer's personal beliefs are.[5]

Let us assume that the lawyer represents Alpha Corporation in negotiations with the Internal Revenue Service. The lawyer wants the IRS to permit Alpha Corporation to employ accelerated depreciation methods for machinery purchased in a prior tax year. While the lawyer is negotiating, she personally believes that the accelerated depreciation laws for manufacturing equipment are unwise public policy. Because of her beliefs, she is also working with a bar association committee to develop a policy statement against the accelerated depreciation allowance. Indeed, let us further assume that the committee chair has requested this lawyer to testify before Congress in support of the report and its proposal to repeal all depreciation allowances. This new legislation, (like typical tax enactments) would apply only for current and future tax years, thus not directly affecting Alpha Corporation's case before the IRS. However, the proposed legislation is against Alpha's economic interests. Nonetheless, the ALI advises that the lawyer, without Alpha's consent, may continue to represent Alpha while simultaneously working to repeal the accelerated depreciation allowance.[6]

The same principles apply to a government lawyer. Assume a lawyer works for a government agency, and her boss tells her that she may not attend a public hearing because her views on a policy are contrary to the views of the agency and he is afraid that one of the legislators at the hearing will see her in the audience and call her to testify. In this circumstance, *Johnston v.*

---

gated to protect the integrity of the program [*e.g.*, pro bono, bar association, or other program] by making an appropriate disclosure within the organization when the lawyer knows a private client might be materially benefitted."

[4]Law reform organizations may have more stringent disclosure or participation requirements than those embodied in Rule 6.4. *See, e.g.*, ABA Section of Taxation, Guide to Committee Operations ch. 3.2 (2004) (statement of conflicts of interest policy).

[5]Restatement of the Law Governing Lawyers, Third, § 125 (2000).

[6]Restatement of the Law Governing Lawyers, Third, § 125 & Illustration 6 (2000).

Koppes[7] held that the supervisor may not sanction the government lawyer-employee for private policy positions that she advocates. "Loyalty to a client requires subordination of a lawyer's personal interests *when acting in a professional capacity*. But loyalty to a client does not require extinguishment of a lawyer's deepest convictions" when *acting in a private capacity*.[8] In this example, the lawyer attended the hearing in her private capacity, making her attendance appropriate.

A contrary rule would change the practice of law and the public activities of lawyers dramatically. Practicing lawyers are typically members of the committees that draft new rules of civil or criminal procedure. A broad conflicts rule would disqualify all of these lawyers because whatever rules they propose will affect their present clients, some adversely.

There is no conflict in this fact situation; otherwise, no lawyer who was ever planning to work in the private sector could serve as counsel to, or a witness for, a House or Senate tax committee, or testify before the Internal Revenue Service about new laws or regulations affecting taxes. Not only would new tax laws or regulations affect that lawyer's future private clients, the new laws or regulations would also directly affect the taxes that the lawyer himself will have to pay.

§ 6.4–3 WHEN THE CLIENT'S IDENTITY IS SECRET

If the identity of the client is privileged or secret, the lawyer should at least alert the legislative committee or similar entity that she is representing a private client whose identity cannot be revealed.[1]

---

[7] 850 F.2d 594 (9th Cir. 1988).

[8] 850 F.2d 594, 596 (9th Cir. 1988) (emphasis added).

[Section 6.4–3]

[1] Rules 3.9 & 4.1(a). *Cf.* Rule 6.4.

CHAPTER 6.5

NONPROFIT AND COURT-ANNEXED LIMITED LEGAL SERVICES PROGRAMS

RULE 6.5: NONPROFIT AND COURT-ANNEXED LIMITED LEGAL SERVICES PROGRAMS

(a) A lawyer who, under the auspices of a program sponsored by a nonprofit organization or court, provides short-term limited legal services to a client without expectation by either the lawyer or the client that the lawyer will provide continuing representation in the matter:

(1) is subject to Rules 1.7 and 1.9(a) only if the lawyer knows that the representation of the client involves a conflict of interest; and

(2) is subject to Rule 1.10 only if the lawyer knows that another lawyer associated with the lawyer in a law firm is disqualified by Rule 1.7 or 1.9(a) with respect to the matter.

(b) Except as provided in paragraph (a)(2), Rule 1.10 is inapplicable to a representation governed by this Rule.

Comment

[1] Legal services organizations, courts and various nonprofit organizations have established programs through which lawyers provide short-term limited legal services—such as advice or the completion of legal forms—that will assist persons to address their legal problems without further representation by a lawyer. In these programs, such as legal-advice hotlines, advice-only clinics or pro se counseling programs, a client-lawyer relationship is established, but there is no expectation that the lawyer's representation of the client will continue beyond the limited consultation. Such programs are normally operated under circumstances in which it is not feasible for a lawyer to systematically screen for conflicts of interest as is generally required before undertaking a representation. See, e.g., Rules 1.7, 1.9 and 1.10.

[2] A lawyer who provides short-term limited legal services pursuant to this Rule must secure the client's informed consent to the limited scope of the representation. See Rule 1.2(c). If a short-term limited representation would not be reasonable under the circumstances, the lawyer may offer advice to the client but must also advise the client of the need for further assistance of counsel. Except as provided in this Rule, the Rules of Professional Conduct, including Rules 1.6 and 1.9(c), are applicable to the limited representation.

[3] Because a lawyer who is representing a client in the circumstances addressed by this Rule ordinarily is not able to check systematically for conflicts of interest, paragraph (a) requires compliance with Rules 1.7 or 1.9(a) only if the lawyer knows that the representation presents a conflict of interest for the lawyer, and with Rule 1.10 only if the lawyer knows that another lawyer in the lawyer's firm is disqualified by Rules 1.7 or 1.9(a) in the matter.

[4] Because the limited nature of the services significantly reduces the risk of conflicts of interest with other matters being handled by the lawyer's firm, paragraph (b) provides that Rule 1.10 is inapplicable to a representation governed by this Rule except as provided by paragraph (a)(2). Paragraph (a)(2) requires the participating lawyer to comply with Rule 1.10 when the lawyer knows that the lawyer's firm is disqualified by Rules 1.7 or 1.9(a). By virtue of paragraph (b), however, a lawyer's participation in a short-term limited legal services program will not preclude the lawyer's firm from undertaking or continuing the representation of a client with interests adverse to a client being represented under the program's auspices. Nor will the personal disqualification of a lawyer participating in the program be imputed to other lawyers participating in the program.

[5] If, after commencing a short-term limited representation in accordance with this Rule, a lawyer undertakes to represent the client in the matter on an ongoing basis, Rules 1.7, 1.9(a) and 1.10 become applicable.

Authors' 1983 Model Rules Comparison

There was no counterpart to this Rule in the 1983 Model Rules.

Model Code Comparison

There was no counterpart to this Rule in the Model Code.

§ 6.5–1 LAWYER PARTICIPATION IN NONPROFIT AND COURT-ANNEXED LIMITED LEGAL SERVICE PROGRAMS

Nonprofit organizations, such as bar associations, law schools, and public interest organizations, often organize limited legal services programs for the general public. Law days, taxpayer assistance programs, telephone hotlines are sponsored as a way of reaching out to the public to offer limited legal services. Similarly, courts often sponsor court-annexed limited legal services programs for the public. These programs deliver pro bono legal services of a limited nature to persons of limited means who would otherwise not seek legal representation. In many instances, an attorney-client relationship is formed between the lawyer and a lay person participating in such a program. However, all of the concerned parties presume that the representation will consist of one meeting and will not continue beyond this first contact.

The Ethics 2000 Commission was concerned that "a strict application of the conflict-of-interest rules may be deterring lawyers from serving as volunteers in programs in which clients are provided short-term limited legal services under the auspices of a nonprofit organization or a court-annexed program."[1] In light of the profession's commitment to pro bono programs for persons of limited means, the House of Delegates adopted a new Rule 6.5 to encourage the organized delivery of short term limited legal services to the public.

Rule 6.5 applies only to limited short term legal services programs sponsored by a nonprofit organization or a court.[2] The drafters chose not to relax the conflicts of interest rules for all limited short term legal representations generally, only those offered under the auspices of a nonprofit organization or court. The drafters included this restriction for several reasons.[3] They wanted to encourage lawyers to participate in organized pro bono programs without fear of violating the ethics rules. And, they believed that limiting the rule to lawyer participation in nonprofit organizations would minimize the risk to clients. Such organizations and courts usually have specific guidelines for lawyers participating in these programs.

§ 6.5–2 LIMITING THE APPLICATION OF THE CONFLICTS OF INTEREST RULES

In the typical course of events, when a prospective client seeks to establish an attorney-client relationship with a lawyer, the lawyer must conduct a relatively elaborate inquiry as to whether the lawyer may accept the representation under the ethics rules.[1] A major aspect of this inquiry involves the conflict of interest rules. The lawyer must examine the current and former conflicts of interest rules as they apply to the representation of the prospective client. Usually, the lawyer must spend significant time and money to properly conduct the evaluation of actual and

---

[Section 6.5–1]

[1]Reporter's Explanation of Changes to Model Rule 6.5.

[2]Rule 6.5 does not apply to a program sponsored by a nonprofit organization or court that results in a traditional legal representation between a participating lawyer and client. For example, a lawyer who works through a nonprofit organization to es-tablish a normal attorney-client relationship with a client on a pro bono basis needs to comply with all of the conflicts of interest rules. See Rule 6.5 Comment 5.

[3]Reporter's Explanation of Changes to Model Rule 6.5.

[Section 6.5–2]

[1]Rules 1.1, 1.2, 1.7, 1.9, 1.10, 1.18.

potential conflicts of interest that may result from the new representation.

In the situation of a limited short term representation performed under the auspices of a nonprofit or court-annexed program, it is not practical to conduct such a conflicts of interest inquiry. The lawyer in such a program donates time to discuss a legal problem with a client on a one time basis. No further legal representation is contemplated. In order for the lawyer to conduct a full conflicts of interest inquiry, the lawyer would need to have access to the law firm's conflicts databases. Thus, such an inquiry would cause delay in answering the client's questions. Given the limited nature of the relationship and the fact that this is done in a pro bono context to provide general legal advice to clients of limited means, it does not make sense to require a full conflicts of interest inquiry.[2]

Rule 6.5(a)(1) provides that a lawyer who provides short term limited legal services under a nonprofit or court-annexed program does not need to meet the requirements of Rule 1.7 (current client conflicts) or Rule 1.9(a) (former client conflicts) unless the lawyer has actual knowledge of the existence of a conflict of interest.[3] Therefore, when a lawyer meets an individual in such a program and the person describes the facts of her problem, the lawyer is obligated to conduct a present or former client conflicts check only if the lawyer knows that this specific person or the facts described raise a conflict of interest with the lawyer's practice. If the lawyer knows that this person's interests are in conflict with the lawyer's practice, the lawyer cannot go forward with the representation of this person in the limited short term relationship without complying with the conflicts of interest rules. If the lawyer does not know of an actual or potential conflict, the lawyer may form the limited attorney-client relationship and provide the short term legal advice.

Rule 6.5(a)(2) further provides that Rule 1.10, the imputed disqualification rule, would apply also only if the lawyer knows that a current or former conflict exists with respect to other lawyers in the firm.[4] Therefore, the lawyer who participates in a qualifying pro bono program does not need to conduct a conflicts check with respect to conflicts of interest between the prospective client and the lawyer's law firm, unless the lawyer knows of a conflict as a result of the imputation.

Once a lawyer accepts a limited short term representation, another conflicts problem may arise. The representation of a client in one of these programs could be imputed back to the other

---

[2] Rule 6.5 Comment 1.
[3] Rule 6.5 Comment 3.

[4] Rule 6.5 Comment 4.

lawyers in the firm to disqualify them from current or future representations of persons adverse to the client served in this pro bono limited representation program. Rule 6.5(b) specifically removes the application of Rule 1.10 from all short term representations conducted under the auspices of a nonprofit or court-annexed program. The Comments to Rule 6.5 state that given the limited nature of the representation, it does not make sense to impute the representation to the other lawyers in the firm.[5]

Of course, if the lawyer expands the scope of the representation from a limited short term one to a normal attorney-client relationship, the lawyer must abide by all of the traditional conflicts of interest rules. Thus, the suspension of the present and former client rules and the imputed disqualification rule is only limited to a very small category of limited short term representations.

§ 6.5–3 LIMITING THE SCOPE OF THE ATTORNEY-CLIENT RELATIONSHIP

By their very nature, limited legal services programs imply the creation of a limited attorney-client relationship.[1] The lawyer participates in a program that is presumed to have a short-term duration. In other words, the lawyer will meet with the client for one short visit or participate in one telephone call and will analyze the client's problems or situation and offer limited legal advice.

When a lawyer participates in such a program, an attorney-client relationship is formed between the attorney and the client. And, the lawyer owes to the client many of the traditional duties given the circumstances of the representation. A lawyer owes a duty of competence and diligence to such clients. The lawyer owes a duty of confidentiality to such clients. And, to the extent discussed in the previous section, the lawyer owes the client a limited duty of loyalty.

Lawyers who participate in such programs must inform the prospective client about the limited nature of the representation and must obtain the prospective client's consent.[2] This obligation simply involves the application of Rule 1.2(c)'s reasonable limitation of the scope of the attorney-client relationship with the prospective client's informed consent to the situation of the limited legal service.

Individuals who seek legal services through a telephone bank

---

[5]Rule 6.5 Comment 1 adds: "Such programs are normally operated under circumstances in which it is not feasible for a lawyer to systematically screen for conflicts of interest as is generally required before undertaking a representation."

[Section 6.5–3]

[1]Reporter's Explanation of Changes to Model Rule 6.5.

[2]Rule 6.5 Comment 1.

or limited clinic should objectively realize that the representation is limited in duration and less involved than when an individual seeks advice from a lawyer in a law firm on an ongoing basis. When the lay person explains her problem to the lawyer, the lawyer must determine whether it is reasonable to address this problem in a limited legal service.[3] If it is a problem suited for a limited legal service, the lawyer should explain the fact that the legal services are provided in a one time meeting and that the client should have no expectation that the relationship will last beyond this meeting. If a limited representation is not reasonable given the individual's problems, the lawyer should inform the person of this fact and urge the person to seek further assistance of another lawyer. After such a disclosure, the lawyer may offer advice to the client in light of the understanding that further legal services are needed.

It is important to note that the view that a lawyer may offer advice to a client after the lawyer has decided that a limited short term representation is not reasonable in the situation differs from the result that is obtained in the context of a general limitation on the scope of an attorney client representation. Under Rule 1.2(c), if a lawyer determines that it is not reasonable to limit the scope of the representation, the lawyer should not seek to do so with the client.[4] Rule 6.5 deals with organized pro bono programs delivering limited short term legal services to the public. The drafters must have thought that given the short term nature of the legal services and the required disclosure, clients are better off receiving some advice about the problem and being told to seek additional legal services rather than receiving no advice whatsoever. This view also authorizes the lawyer in such a situation to be more descriptive about the advice that a client needs. Otherwise, a lawyer could only state, this problem is not capable of resolution by a limited short term legal service and I cannot answer any more of your questions. Such descriptive information can lead the client to seek additional legal services from another lawyer.

§ 6.5–4 UNBUNDLED LEGAL SERVICES DIRECTED AT PRO SE CLIENTS AND PERSONS OF LIMITED MEANS

Rule 6.5 provides a very narrow exception for limited legal services offered by nonprofit or court annexed programs. This provision however represents one aspect of a much larger movement, referred to as "unbundled legal services," that is gaining some momentum in the ABA and the states. The phrase, unbundled

---

[3] Rule 6.5 Comment 2.

[4] Rule 1.2(c) Comment 7 (the limitation must be reasonable under the circumstances).

legal services, has been used to describe a situation in which the lawyer is asked to offer very limited legal services to a client.[1] In most of these cases, the client cannot afford to hire the lawyer for a complete representation and therefore the client intends to represent herself pro se after receiving the limited legal services.

The broader question whether lawyers may ethically offer unbundled legal services implicates many ethics rules. Can a lawyer deliver competent representation under Rule 1.1 when legal services are unbundled? May a lawyer limit the scope of the representation under Rule 1.2 or will that rule need to be modified? Will such services be limited to persons of limited means or may all clients receive limited legal services? Will a court permit a lawyer to assist a pro se client without requiring that the lawyer enter an appearance? How are questions of confidentiality and candor to the court handled in an unbundled representation? May a lawyer draft a document that will be entered into a court record without disclosing that it had been prepared by the lawyer? Does a lawyer who intends to perform limited services to a pro se client need to conduct a conflicts of interest check before accepting the limited representation? What type of agreements should the lawyer draft when accepting a limited representation? How does one define a reasonable fee in an unbundled representation? How do Rules 4.2 and 4.3 apply when a lawyer is performing a limited representation? Are there circumstances when a lawyer will need to withdraw from a limited representation under Rule 1.16? What is the proper standard of conduct for malpractice when a lawyer offers limited legal services?

The ABA is involved in encouraging a debate and analysis of the concept of unbundled legal services. The Standing Committee on the Delivery of Legal Services has developed a website, The Pro Se/Unbundling Resource Center, to encourage a debate and study of "the issues involved in self-representation and unbundled legal services."[2] The ABA Section of Litigation commissioned a task force to author a "Handbook on Limited Scope Legal Assistance."[3] An underlying feature of this debate involves the relaxation or modification of the existing norms and rules for

---

[Section 6.5–4]

[1]See Mary Helen McNeal, *Redefining Attorney-Client Roles: Unbundling and Moderate-Income Elderly Clients*, 32 Wake Forest L.Rev. 295 (1997); Fred C. Zacharias, *Limited Performance Agreements: Should Clients Get What They Pay For?*, 11 Georgetown Journal of Legal Ethics 915 (1998); James M. McCauley, *Current Ethical and Unauthorized Practice Issues Relating to Endeavors to Assist Pro Se Litigants*, Virginia Lawyer 43 (Dec. 2002).

[2]See http://www.abanet.org/legalservices/delivery/delunbund.html (visited Aug. 1, 2004).

[3]See ABA Section of Litigation, A Report of the Modest Means Task Force: Handbook on Limited Scope Legal Assistance (2003).

legal representation of clients to allow lawyers to offer limited scope legal assistance to persons of limited means.

Several states have adopted ethics and court rules directed to lawyer delivery of unbundled legal services. For example, the Florida Supreme Court has amended the Comments to their version of Rule 1.2 to permit a lawyer to draft a document for a *pro se* litigant without the lawyer signing it.[4] It also amended Florida's version of Rules 4.2 and 4.3 to address the issue whether a person who received limited legal services is considered represented or unrepresented for the purposes of these two rules. Washington similarly amended its ethics rules and civil rules of court to authorize limited legal representations.[5] There are several other examples in California, Colorado, Maine, Nevada, and Wyoming.[6]

The trend in the cases is in favor of allowing ghost written legal papers. As one commentator has noted:

> Almost all of the federal cases and state ethics opinions opposing ghostwriting were issued before the May 2007 ABA opinion. Because most states look to the ABA Model Rules when adopting and amending their own rules of professional conduct, the coming years may see a number of courts and states take a more relaxed stance on ghostwriting.[7]

Thus, the Second Circuit, following the recommendation of an ABA Formal Opinion, refused to discipline a lawyer for ghost writing a pro se brief because there was no clear rule prohibiting the practice.[8]

---

[4] *Amendment to the Rules Regulating the Florida Bar and the Florida Family Law Rules of Procedure (Unbundled Legal Services)*, 860 So.2d 394 (2003)(the document must indicate that it was prepared with the assistance of a lawyer).

Ghost Writing. *See* John C. Rothermich, *Ethical and Procedural Implications of "Ghostwriting" for Pro Se Litigants: Toward Increased Access to Civil Justice*, 67 Fordham L.Rev. 2687 (1999). The 10th Circuit has held:

> We hold that the participation by an attorney in drafting an appellate brief is per se substantial, and must be acknowledged by signature. In fact, we agree with the New York City Bar's ethics opinion that "an attorney must refuse to provide ghostwriting assistance unless the client specifically commits herself to disclosing the attorney's assistance to the court upon filing."

Duran v. Carris, 238 F.3d 1268, 1273 (10th Cir. 2001)(footnote omitted). *But see* ABA Formal Op. 07-446 (May 5, 2007) ("Undisclosed Legal Assistance to Pro Se Litigants"). This Opinion permits a lawyer to assist a pro se litigant without disclosing the lawyer's participation with or the extent of work given to the litigant.

[5] *See* Washington Rules of Prof. Conduct, Rules 1.2, 4.2, 4.3; Washington Civil Rules, Rules 4.2, 11, 70.1.

[6] The ABA has collected the various state rules authorizing unbundled legal services on its website. *See* http://www.abanet.org/legalservices/delivery/delunbundrules.html visited Aug. 1, 2004.

[7] Robbins, Ghostwriting: Filling in the Gaps of Pro Se Prisoners' Access to the Courts, 23 Geo. J. Legal Ethics 271, 290 (2010) (footnote omitted).

VII. INFORMATION ABOUT LEGAL SERVICES

CHAPTER 7.0

HISTORICAL AND CONSTITUTIONAL BACKGROUND

---

§ 7.0–1 THE ORIGINS OF THE RESTRICTIONS ON LEGAL ADVERTISING

The 1908 Canons of Ethics originally allowed lawyers to advertise, and advertise they did. Publication of business cards in newspapers and directories as well as advertisements of a lawyer's specialty were quite common, but some of them were considered unseemly, unprofessional, or misleading. For example, one 1911 lawyer's advertisement in the *Los Angeles Daily Times* included the following (in all capital letters): "WE GET THE COIN."[1]

By 1937, a complete redraft of Canon 27 severely restricted lawyer advertising.[2] The organized bar maintained this virtual prohibition until the 1970s when consumer groups, some attorneys, and others began actively opposing the bar's position, leading to court decisions that forced the bar to change the rules.

Consequently, before considering Rule 7.1 and the other Rules in Part 7—all dealing with regulations governing the way that lawyers communicate to the lay public information about legal

---

[8]*See also, In re Fengling Liu*, 664 F.3d 367 (2d Cir. 2011)(per curiam), which cited, with approval, ABA Formal Opinion 07-446 (2007) (Undisclosed Legal Assistance to *Pro Se* Litigants (2007). Because there was no specific rule on ghost writing, the Second Circuit recommended that the court consider an amendment to the Second Circuit rules to resolve the issue and make a clear rule. *In re Fengling Liu*, 664 F.3d 367, 373 n.7

(2d Cir. 2011).

[Section 7.0–1]

[1]*See* Myrna Oliver, *Lawyer Advertising*, Calif. Lawyer, July, 1987, at 29. *See also* Ronald D. Rotunda, *Lawyer Advertising and the Philosophical Origins of the Commercial Speech Doctrine*, 36 U. Richmond L. Rev. 91 (2002).

[2]*See* ABA Formal Opinion 276 (Sept. 20, 1947).

services—we shall first consider and analyze the major U.S. Supreme Court cases that focus on the special issue of the commercial speech of lawyers.[3]

§ 7.0–2 THE *BATES* CASE AND ITS PROGENY

All commercial speech constitutional law cases dealing with lawyer advertising are the progeny of *Bates v. State Bar*.[1] In 1977, *Bates* struck down Arizona's limitations on attorney advertising and held that the right of free speech protects truthful newspaper advertising of availability and fees for routine legal services. However, the Court allowed the states to subject legal advertising to reasonable restrictions on time, place and manner, and to prohibit false or misleading advertising.

The Court in *Bates* was tentative in expanding the right of free speech as applied to advertising by lawyers. The majority noted that the case did not involve person-to-person solicitation or advertising as to the quality of legal services, but only the question of whether lawyers may constitutionally advertise truthful information about the prices of routine services, such as uncontested divorces, uncontested adoptions, simple personal bankruptcies, and changes of name.[2] This advertising, the Court ruled, is constitutionally protected under the First Amendment.

At this point in the development of the case law, the *Bates* Court also left open the extent to which certain types of advertising may be misleading, though it found appellants' particular advertisement not misleading. The Court also raised the questions of whether: (1) advertising claims as to the *quality* of ser-

---

[3]On the commercial speech doctrine, *See* Ronald D. Rotunda, *The Commercial Speech Doctrine in the Supreme Court*, 1976 U. OF ILL. LAW FORUM 1080 (1976); Ronald D. Rotunda, *The First Amendment Now Protects Commercial Speech*, 10 THE CENTER MAGAZINE: A Publication of the Center For the Study of Democratic Institutions 32 (May/June 1977); Ronald D. Rotunda, *The Constitutional Future of the Bill of Rights: A Closer Look at Commercial Speech and State Aid to Religiously Affiliated Schools*, 65 NORTH CAROLINA L. REV. 917 (1987); Ronald D. Rotunda, *Commercial Speech and the Platonic Ideal: Libre expression et libre enterprise*, in, DAVID SCHNEIDERMAN, ed., FREEDOM OF EXPRESSION AND THE CHARTER 319 (Centre for Constitutional Studies/Centre d'études constitutionnelles, Carswell, Canada 1991); 5

RONALD D. ROTUNDA & JOHN E. NOWAK, TREATISE ON CONSTITUTIONAL LAW: SUBSTANCE AND PROCEDURE § § 20.26 to 20.31 (Thomson- West, 4th ed. 2008) (6 volumes).

[Section 7.0–2]

[1]*Bates v. State Bar*, 433 U.S. 350, 97 S.Ct. 2691, 53 L.Ed.2d 810 (1977), *reh'g denied* 434 U.S. 881, 98 S.Ct. 242, 54 L.Ed.2d 164 (1977).

See, e.g., Lori Andrews, *Lawyer Advertising and the First Amendment*, 1981 A.B. FOUNDATION RESEARCH J. 967 (1981); Ronald D. Rotunda, *Professionalism, Legal Advertising, and Free Speech In the Wake of Florida Bar v. Went For It, Inc.*, 49 ARK. L. REV. 703 (1997); Rodney A. Smolla, *The Puffery of Lawyers*, 36 U. RICHMOND L REV. 1 (2002).

[2]433 U.S. at 366, 97 S.Ct. at 2700.

vices "may be so likely to be misleading as to warrant restriction," and (2), whether "the special problems of advertising on the electronic broadcast media will warrant special consideration."[3]

§ 7.0–2(a) The Four-Part Test of *Central Hudson*

Following *Bates*, the Supreme Court developed a four-part test for all commercial speech cases, in *Central Hudson Gas & Electric Corporation v. Public Service Commission*.[4] In this case, the Court invalidated a regulation of the state Public Service Commission that completely banned all public utility advertising promoting the use of electricity. The Commission argued that all such promotional advertising was contrary to the national policy of conserving energy. The Court outlined a four-part analysis:

> At the outset we must determine whether the expression is protected by the First Amendment. For commercial speech to come within that provision, it at least [1] must concern lawful activity and not be misleading. [2] Next we ask whether the asserted governmental interest is substantial. If both inquiries yield positive answers, we must determine [3] whether the regulation directly advances the governmental interest asserted, and [4] whether it is not more extensive than is necessary to serve that interest.[5]

---

[3]433 U.S. at 383–84, 97 S.Ct. at 2709.

After *Bates* the American Bar Association did not wait to test the restrictions in the ABA Model Code of Professional Responsibility dealing with television and radio. Instead, the ABA, with reasonable promptness, amended the Model Code to allow radio and television advertising subject to certain restrictions. *See, e.g.,* D.R. 2-101(D): "If the advertisement is communicated to the public over television or radio, it shall be prerecorded, approved for broadcast by the lawyer, and a recording of the actual transmission shall be retained by the lawyer."

States have not always followed the ABA lead on advertising, particularly with respect to electronic advertising, imposing more strict rules on electronic advertising, leading to a world where the jurisdictional regulatory differences are greater than ever. See William E. Hornsby, Jr., *Ad Rules Infinitum: The Need for Alternatives to State-Based Ethics Governing Legal Services Marketing*, 36 U. RICHMOND L. REV. 49 (2002). Kandi L. Birdsell &

Joshua D. Janow, *Legal Advertising: Finding Timely Direction in the World of Direct Solicitation, Waiting Periods and Electronic Communication*, 15 GEORGETOWN J. LEGAL ETHICS 671 (2002).

[4]*Central Hudson Gas & Electric Corporation v. Public Service Commission*, 447 U.S. 557, 100 S.Ct. 2343, 65 L.Ed.2d 341 (1980).

[5]447 U.S. at 566, 100 S.Ct. at 2351. Blackmun, J., joined by Brennan, J., concurred in the judgment. They objected to the four-part test, and expressed doubt "whether suppression of information concerning the availability and price of a legally offered product is ever a permissible way for the State to 'dampen' demand for or use of the product." Such a regulatory measure "strikes at the heart of the First Amendment" because the state covertly is attempting to "manipulate the choices of its citizen, not by persuasion or direct regulation, but by depriving the public of the information needed to make a free choice." 447 U.S. at 575, 100 S.Ct. at 2356, citing, Ronald D. Rotunda, *The Commercial Speech Doctrine in the*

Applying this test, the *Central Hudson* Court invalidated the New York regulation. The Court first found that promotional advertising is lawful commercial speech and that the advertisement was not misleading;[6] second, the state interests in conservation are substantial; third, the ban on promotional advertising advances this ban.

But the regulation in *Central Hudson* failed the fourth prong of this test: the state's complete suppression of speech was more extensive than necessary to further energy conservation.[7] For example, some promotional advertising would cause no net increase in energy use. Also more limited restrictions might promote conservation sufficiently. The state could "require that the advertisements include information about the relative efficiency and expense of the offered service, both under current conditions and for the foreseeable future."[8] The state could tax energy inefficient appliances, and thus discourage their use without attempting to manipulate customers by keeping them from hearing truthful messages about lawful activity.

Supreme Court, 1976 U. OF ILL. L. FORUM 1080, 1080–83 (1976).

[6]*Accord Consolidated Edison Co. of New York, Inc. v. Public Service Commission*, 447 U.S. 530, 100 S.Ct. 2326, 65 L.Ed.2d 319 (1980).

In *Bolger v. Youngs Drug Products Corp.*, 463 U.S. 60, 103 S.Ct. 2875, 77 L.Ed.2d 469 (1983), a unanimous court invalidated a federal statute prohibiting the unsolicited mailing of contraceptive advertisements. The majority opinion by Marshall, J., found that the interest in shielding mail recipients from offensive materials was not sufficiently substantial to burden speech, and that the regulation did not directly and narrowly promote a substantial interest in aiding parents' efforts to discuss birth control methods with their children.

Rehnquist and O'Connor, JJ., 463 U.S. at 75, 103 S.Ct. at 2885, 77 L.Ed.2d at 483 (concurring), and Stevens, J., 463 U.S. at 80, 103 S.Ct. at 2888, 77 L.Ed.2d at 486 (concurring), would have considered a government interest in protecting persons from receiving material they find offensive in their homes to be substantial. However these justices believed that the law did not sufficiently promote that interest.

Promotion of illegal activity, or an advertisement that offers to engage in a crime, is not protected advertising. *See Pittsburgh Press Co. v. Pittsburgh Commission on Human Relations*, 413 U.S. 376, 93 S.Ct. 2553, 37 L.Ed.2d 669 (1973), *reh'g denied* 414 U.S. 881, 94 S.Ct. 30, 38 L.Ed.2d 128 (1973); *National Society of Professional Engineers v. United States*, 435 U.S. 679, 697–98 nn. 26, 27, 98 S.Ct. 1355, 1368–69 nn. 26, 27, 55 L.Ed.2d 637, 654 nn. 26, 27 (1978).

[7]*Cf. N.L.R.B. v. Retail Store Employees Union, Local 1001*, 447 U.S. 607, 618, 100 S.Ct. 2372, 2379, 65 L.Ed.2d 377 (1980) (Powell, J., joined by Burger, C.J., Stewart, and Rehnquist, JJ.) (Congress, consistent with First Amendment, may prohibit secondary picketing calculated "to persuade the customers of the secondary employer to cease trading with him in order to force him to cease dealing with, or put pressure upon, the primary employer;" such picketing spreads labor discord by coercing neutral party to join the dispute and furthers an unlawful objective).

[8]447 U.S. at 571, 100 S.Ct. at 2354.

Now, keeping the *Central Hudson* four-part test in mind, let us consider some specific fact scenarios involving lawyer advertising.

§ 7.0–3 ALLEGEDLY MISLEADING ADVERTISING

§ 7.0–3(a) State Restrictions on the Language Used in Lawyer Advertisements

Some states responded to *Bates* by, in effect, declaring that certain types of legal advertising were inherently misleading. Missouri had reprimanded a lawyer because he had deviated from the precise listing of areas of practice included in the state's Rule governing lawyer advertising; his advertisement listed "real estate" instead of "property," and he listed "contracts," although Rule 4 did not list that latter term at all. In a significant opinion, which identified the lawyer only by initials, *In re R.M.J.*,[1] a unanimous Supreme Court rejected this argument. In an opinion by Justice Powell, the Court invalidated various restrictions on types of lawyer advertising that the state claimed were misleading. Missouri had failed to show that R.M.J.'s listing was deceptive and because the state could show no substantial interest that its restriction on advertising promoted, the Court invalidated it.

The Court also invalidated a part of Missouri Rule 4 prohibiting a lawyer from identifying the jurisdictions in which he is licensed to practice law.[2] R.M.J. also emphasized in large boldface type that he was a member of the U.S. Supreme Court bar, a "relatively uninformative fact" but the record did not show that it was misleading. Missouri Rule 4 did not specifically identify this information as misleading, nor place a limitation on the type size, nor require any explanation of the significance of admission to the U.S. Supreme Court bar.[3]

The *R.M.J.* Court also invalidated a prohibition against the lawyer mailing announcement cards to persons other than lawyers, former clients, personal friends, and relatives. These cards announced the opening of his law office to a wide range of people. The state produced no evidence justifying such a restrictive prohibition.

[Section 7.0–3]

[1]*In re R.M.J.*, 455 U.S. 191, 102 S.Ct. 929, 71 L.Ed.2d 64 (1982).

See Charles B. Blackmar, *The Missouri Supreme Court and Lawyer Advertising: RMJ and its Aftermath*, 47 Mo.L.Rev. 621 (1982). Empirically, the evidence is that lawyer advertising rules are under-enforced, but some states are more vigorous than others. *See* Fred C. Zacharias, *What Lawyers Do When Nobody's Watching: Legal Advertising as a Case Study of the Impact of Underenforced Professional Rules*, 87 Iowa L. Rev. 971 (2002).

[2]455 U.S. at 205, 102 S.Ct. at 938.

[3]455 U.S. at 205–06, 102 S.Ct. at 938–39

§ 7.0–3(b) Advertising That a Lawyer Is a "Specialist" or "Certified"

Before 1989, the ABA and many states prohibited lawyers from advertising that they were specialists unless they practiced in admiralty or patent law or unless they met the requirements of a state bar operated specialization program. A Comment to Rule 7.4 stated:

> If a lawyer practices only in certain fields, or will not accept matters except in such fields, the lawyer is permitted so to indicate. However, stating that the lawyer is a "specialist" or that the lawyer's practice "is limited to" or "concentrated in" particular fields is not permitted. These terms have acquired a secondary meaning implying formal recognition as a specialist. Hence, use of these terms may be misleading unless the lawyer is certified or recognized in accordance with procedures in the state where the lawyer is licensed to practice law.[4]

The Supreme Court addressed the specialization issue in *Peel v. Attorney Registration and Disciplinary Commission of Illinois.*[5] The facts of this case were unusual. The ethical rules governing lawyers, which the Illinois Supreme Court promulgated, did not permit an attorney to hold himself out as "certified" or a "specialist" except for patent, trademark, and admiralty lawyers. The Illinois Supreme Court publicly censured Peel because his letterhead *truthfully* stated that he is a civil trial specialist certified by the National Board of Trial Advocacy (NBTA), a bona fide private group that developed a set of objective and demanding standards and procedures for periodic certification of lawyers with experience and competence in trial work. In *Peel*, a splintered U.S. Supreme Court (five to four, with no majority opinion) reversed the Illinois Supreme Court and found that Peel's claims were truthful and constitutionally protected.

The facts on Peel's letterhead were both verifiable and true. The issue before the Court was whether a lawyer has a constitutional right, under the standards applicable to commercial speech, to advertise his or her certification as a trial specialist by NBTA. Though Peel's claim was facially accurate, Illinois argued that Peel's letterhead implied a higher quality or ability, than noncertified lawyers. Justice Stevens' plurality opinion explained that Illinois had confused "the distinction between statements of

---

[4]*See* THOMAS D. MORGAN & RONALD D. ROTUNDA, SELECTED STANDARDS ON PROFESSIONAL RESPONSIBILITY 170 (Foundation Press Inc., 1989).

[5]*Peel v. Attorney Registration and Disciplinary Commission of Illinois,* 496 U.S. 91, 110 S.Ct. 2281, 110 L.Ed.2d 83 (1990).

opinion or quality and statements of objective facts that may support an inference of quality."[6]

Peel's statement of certification by a private group, the NBTA, has no more potential to mislead than an attorney advertising that he is admitted to practice before the U.S. Supreme Court, a statement the Supreme Court had approved in an earlier opinion, *In re R.M.J.*[7] Thus, Peel's letterhead was neither actually nor inherently nor potentially misleading. If the state believes that statements of private certification might be potentially misleading, the state might be able to require a disclaimer about the certifying organization or the standards of a specialty.[8] The U.S. Supreme Court is a little more likely to uphold a state regulation of speech when the state responds by requiring more speech rather than less.[9] In any event, the regulations at issue in *In re R.M.J.* simply banned speech.

The Illinois Supreme Court claimed that Peel's statement that he was certified was misleading because, that court said, everyone knows that "certified" means that he was certified by the state, because a certificate is—and here the Illinois Supreme Court quoted from *Webster's Dictionary*:

[A] document issued by . . . a state agency, . . . certifying that one has satisfactorily . . . attained professional standing in a given field and may officially practice or hold a position in that field. Webster's Third New International Dictionary 367 (1986 ed.)[10]

---

[6]496 U.S. at 101, 110 S.Ct. at 2288. (Stevens, J., joined by Brennan, Blackmun, & Kennedy, JJ.).

Marshall, J., joined by Brennan, J., concurred in the judgment, arguing that the letterhead was potentially misleading and that Illinois could enact regulations other than a total ban in order to protect the public. White, J., dissented and agreed that the letterhead was potentially misleading. O'Connor, J., joined by Rehnquist, C.J. & Scalia, J., also dissented and objected that the Court's "[f]ailure to accord States considerable latitude in this area embroils this Court in the micromanagement of the State's inherent authority to police the ethical standards of the profession within its borders." 496 U.S. at 119, 110 S.Ct. at 2297.

[7]*In re R.M.J.*, 455 U.S. at 205–06, 102 S.Ct. at 938–39.

[8]496 U.S. at 110 n. 17, 110 S.Ct. at 2292 n. 17.

[9]A lawyer's "constitutionally protected interest in *not* providing any particular factual information in his advertising is minimal." *Zauderer v. Office of Disciplinary Counsel*, 471 U.S. 626, 628 and 651, 105 S.Ct. 2265, 2270 and 2282, 85 L.Ed.2d 652 (1985).

[10]*In re Peel*, 126 Ill.2d 397, 405, 128 Ill.Dec. 535, 539, 534 N.E.2d 980, 984 (1989), *rev'd*, 496 U.S. 91, 110 S.Ct. 2281, 110 L.Ed.2d 83 (1990). After this case, the Illinois Supreme Court promptly modified its rules and required lawyers who used the words "certified," "specialist," "expert," or "any other, similar terms", to state, *inter alia*, that "the Supreme Court of Illinois does not recognize certifications of specialists in the practice of law and that the certificate, award or recognition is not a requirement to

1151

The full quotation, to which the Illinois court referred, is quite different if one removes the ellipses that the Illinois Supreme Court had inserted:

> [A] document issued by *a school,* a state agency, *or a professional organization* certifying that one has satisfactorily *completed a course of studies, has passed a qualifying examination, or has* attained professional standing in a given field and may officially practice or hold a position in that field. Webster's Third New International Dictionary 367 (1986 ed.).[11]

The language that the Illinois Supreme Court deleted is in italics. If a lawyer were to manipulate a quotation this way in the course of filing a brief, there is no doubt that the court would be upset at being misled. In this case, the court manipulated the quotation, but the U.S. Supreme Court saw behind the trickery.

As Justice Stevens' plurality opinion noted, the consuming public already knows that states routinely issue licenses for a host of activities—such as licenses to sell liquor, or drive a car—all the time. Similarly, private groups issue certificates to commemorate a solo flight or a hole in one. It is hardly uncommon for people to claim that they are foreign car "specialists" or air conditioning "specialists" without the public automatically believing that the state has formally recognized these claims. Justice Stevens rejected the paternalistic assumption that the reader of Peel's stationery was no more discriminating or sophisticated than those who watch children's television. The state's rule was overbroad: one does not burn down the house to roast the pig.[12]

§ 7.0–3(c) Lawyer's Designation as a Certified Public Accountant and a Certified Financial Planner

In *Ibanez v. Florida Department of Business and Professional Regulation, Board of Accountancy,*[13] Justice Ginsburg, for the Court, held that the Florida Board of Accountancy violated free speech when it reprimanded Silvia Ibanez, an attorney, because she had truthfully stated in her advertising that she was a Certified Public Accountant (CPA) and a Certified Financial Planner (CFP). The state Board of Accountancy licensed her as a CPA,

---

practice law in Illinois." *See* Illinois Amended Rule 7.4 (July 16, 1990), reprinted in, THOMAS D. MORGAN & RONALD D. ROTUNDA, PROBLEMS AND MATERIALS ON PROFESSIONAL RESPONSIBILITY 446 (Foundation Press, 5th ed. 1991).

[11]Although the Illinois Supreme Court criticized Peel for being misleading, one might level the same charge at the Illinois Supreme Court, given the way it edited the dictionary quota-

tion.

[12]496 U.S. at 105–06, 110 S.Ct. at 2290. *Cf. Bolger v. Youngs Drug Products Corp.,* 463 U.S. 60, 74, 103 S.Ct. 2875, 2884, 77 L.Ed.2d 469 (1983).

[13]*Ibanez v. Florida Department of Business and Professional Regulation, Board of Accountancy,* 512 U.S. 136, 114 S.Ct. 2084, 129 L.Ed.2d 118 (1994).

and a bona fide private organization, not the state, licensed her as a CFP. Attorney Ibanez argued her own case.

Justice Ginsburg, for a unanimous Court, upheld Ibanez's right to use the CPA designation. "[W]e cannot imagine how consumers could be misled by her truthful representation" that she is a CPA.[14]

§ 7.0–3(d) Limitations on the State's Power to Mandate "Unduly Burdensome" Disclosure Requirements in Lawyer Advertising

The *Ibanez* Court, seven to two, also rejected sanctions based on the fact that Ms. Ibanez had truthfully stated that she was a CFP. In so doing, the Court placed limits on Florida's right to mandate detailed disclosures. The Board relied on a Florida rule that prohibits the use of "specialist" unless accompanied by a disclaimer "in the immediate proximity of the statement that implies formal recognition as a specialist." It must also state that "the recognizing agency is not affiliated with or sanctioned by the state or federal government," and must set out the requirements for recognition, "including, but not limited to, education, experience[,] and testing."[15]

Justice Ginsburg, for the Court, remarked on the "failure of the Board to point to any harm that is potentially real, not purely hypothetical," and criticized the detail required on the disclaimer, which would effectively rule out use of the designation on a business card, letterhead, or yellow pages listing. She then concluded, "We have never sustained restrictions on constitutionally protected speech based on a record so bare as the one on which the Board relies here."[16]

Zauderer v. Office of Disciplinary Counsel[17] is another important decision significantly limiting the power of the state to mandate detailed disclosures. In *Zauderer*, Justice White for the Court held that Ohio may not discipline an attorney who solicits business by running newspaper advertisements containing nondeceptive illustrations and legal advice. The attorney in question placed an advertisement offering to represent women who had suffered injury from the Dalkon Shield Intrauterine Device. This advertisement included a drawing of the Shield and offered legal advice, such as the advice that claims may not yet be time barred.

---

[14]512 U.S. at 143, 114 S.Ct. at 2089.

[15]*Ibanez*, 512 U.S. at 146, 114 S.Ct. at 2090.

[16]512 U.S. at 143–47, 114 S.Ct. at 2089–91.

O'Connor, J., joined by Rehnquist, C.J., dissented on this point, arguing that the CFP designation is both *inherently* and potentially misleading because a private organization, not the state, confers the designation of Certified Financial Planner.

[17]*Zauderer v. Office of Disciplinary Counsel*, 471 U.S. 626, 105 S.Ct. 2265, 85 L.Ed.2d 652 (1985).

Though the legal advice regarded a specific legal problem, it was neither false nor deceptive, and did not involve face-to-face solicitation.

However, the Court held that the state could discipline an attorney for failure to include in his advertisements some information reasonably necessary to make his advertisement not misleading. The lawyer advertised that he was available to represent clients on a contingent fee basis and that "if there is no recovery, no legal fees are owed by our clients."[18] The advertisement failed to disclose that the clients might be liable for significant litigation costs even though their lawsuits were unsuccessful.

§ 7.0–3(d)(1) Rules Requiring Disclaimers versus Rules that Prohibit Speech

The U.S. Supreme Court is a little more likely to uphold a state regulation of speech when the state responds by requiring more speech rather than less. A disclosure requirement does not prohibit speech, and the lawyer's "constitutionally protected interest in *not* providing any particular factual information in his advertising is minimal."[19] Consequently, it is easier for a state to justify a regulation that requires more disclosure rather than one that totally prohibits all speech.

Accordingly, the *Zauderer* Court first carefully distinguished between disclosure requirements and outright prohibitions of speech. As long as the disclosure requirements (1) are reasonably related to the state's interest in preventing deception of consumers, (2) there is no problem of vagueness,[20] and, (3) they are not "unjustified or unduly burdensome,"[21] there is no First Amendment violation.

This "unduly burdensome" caveat is an important one. The Supreme Court did not give regulatory authorities a blank check to make every advertisement look like a securities prospectus. *Zauderer* made clear that disclosure requirements do implicate free speech, and "unjustified or unduly burdensome disclosure requirements might offend the First Amendment by chilling protected commercial speech."[22] There must be limits to the state's power to mandate detailed disclosures, because a disclosure rule making every brief advertisement look as complex as the Treaty

---

[18]*Zauderer*, 471 U.S. at 631, 105 S.Ct. at 2271.

[19]471 U.S. at 628, 651, 105 S.Ct. at 2270, 2282 (emphasis in original).

[20]471 U.S. at 653 n. 15, 105 S.Ct.

at 2283 n. 15.

[21]471 U.S. at 651, 105 S.Ct. at 2282.

[22]471 U.S. at 651, 105 S.Ct. at 2282.

of Westphalia can be the functional equivalent of prohibiting the advertisement.[23]

If the disclosure requirements meet this three-part test, it is not necessary for the state to demonstrate that they are the least restrictive means to serve the state's purposes. Nor is a disclosure requirement invalid if it is underinclusive, *i.e.*, if it does not get at all facets of the problem it is designed to ameliorate.

Applying these principles *Zauderer* concluded:

> Appellant's advertisement informed the public that "if there is no recovery, no legal fees are owed by our clients." The advertisement makes no mention of the distinction between "legal fees" and "costs," and to a layman not aware of the meaning of these terms of art, the advertisement would suggest that employing appellant would be a no-lose proposition in that his representation in a losing cause would come entirely free of charge. The assumption that substantial numbers of potential clients would be so misled is hardly a speculative one: it is a commonplace that members of the public are often unaware of the technical meanings of such terms as "fees" and "costs"—terms that, in ordinary usage, might well be virtually interchangeable. When the possibility of deception is as self-evident as it is in this case, we need not require the State to "conduct a survey of the . . . public before it [may] determine that the [advertisement] had a tendency to mislead."[24]

§ 7.0–4 SOLICITATION OF LEGAL BUSINESS

§ 7.0–4(a) Face to Face Solicitation

In the year following the *Bates* decision, the Court began to define the limits of state regulation of attorney solicitation of clients. The two leading cases were decided the same day, *Ohralik v. Ohio State Bar*[1] and *In re Primus*.[2] In these cases, the majority, speaking through Justice Powell, appeared to resurrect some

---

[23]*Ibanez v. Florida Department of Business and Professional Regulation, Board of Accountancy*, 512 U.S. 136, 143–47, 114 S.Ct. 2084, 2089–91, 129 L.Ed.2d 118 (1994), and *Zauderer v. Office of Disciplinary Counsel*, 471 U.S. 626, 105 S.Ct. 2265, 85 L.Ed.2d 652 (1985), both discussed below.

[24]471 U.S. at 652, 105 S.Ct. at 2282. Powell, J., took no part in the consideration or decision of this case. Brennan, J., joined by Marshall, J., concurred in part and dissented in part. They did not dispute the Court's basic disclosure principles, but did not believe, inter alia, that Ohio's "vaguely expressed disclosure requirements" were permissible. O'Connor, J., joined by Rehnquist, J., also concurred in

part and dissented in part. They would have upheld Ohio's rule prohibiting the use of unsolicited legal advice in printed advertisements in order to attract clients.

[Section 7.0–4]

[1]*Ohralik v. Ohio State Bar*, 436 U.S. 447, 98 S.Ct. 1912, 56 L.Ed.2d 444 (1978).

[2]*In re Primus*, 436 U.S. 412, 98 S.Ct. 1893, 56 L.Ed.2d 417 (1978).

Doctors' Advertising. Closely related to the issue of advertising and solicitation by lawyers is the question of similar activities by physicians. *See generally* William C. Canby & Ernest Gellhorn, *Physician Advertising: The First Amendment and the Sherman Act*, 1978 DUKE L.J. 543.

elements of the "commercial" speech distinction that had been discredited by the earlier cases. Justice Powell said in *Ohralik* that the distinction between other types of speech and commercial speech is a "commonsense" one, though later he stated in *Primus* that the line between commercial and noncommercial speech "will not always be easy to draw."[3]

It is difficult to derive any specific principle of law from *Ohralik* and *Primus* because language in each case suggests both broad and narrow holdings.[4] The decisions in the two cases, taken together, indicate that the state may regulate lawyer solicitation in order to protect the public from false or deceptive commercial practices, so long as the regulations are reasonable and are not

---

[3] 436 U.S. at 455–56, 438 n.32, 98 S.Ct. at 1918, 1908 n. 32. Justice Powell said that the line is "based in part on the motive of the speaker and the character of the expressive activity. . . ." Id. Justice Rehnquist, dissenting, noted that to the extent this " 'commonsense' distinction focuses on the content of the speech, it is at least suspect under many of the Court's First Amendment cases . . . and to the extent it focuses upon the motive of the speaker, it is subject to manipulation by clever practitioners." 436 U.S. at 441–42, 98 S.Ct. at 1910.

Moreover, Justice Powell's tortured discussion of attorney's fees—in which he sought to demonstrate that there are differences in counsel fees awarded by the court and counsel fees awarded in a "traditional" manner—demonstrates that distinguishing between commercial and noncommercial speech is a fruitless endeavor. Justice Powell said, inter alia, that:

"Counsel fees [here] are awarded in the discretion of the court; awards are not drawn from the plaintiff's recovery, and are usually premised on a successful outcome; and the amounts awarded may not correspond to fees generally obtainable in private litigation." 436 U.S. at 430, 98 S.Ct. at 1903–04.

All of these characteristics, even the last one supposedly unique to the ACLU litigation, apply to many private securities lawsuits where the attorneys secure a benefit for shareholders but create no res. Similar types of fees may be generated by truth in lending cases. *See, e.g., Mills v. Electric Auto-Lite Co.*, 396 U.S. 375, 389–97, 90 S.Ct. 616, 624–28, 24 L.Ed.2d 593 (1970), *appeal after remand*, 552 F.2d 1239 (7th Cir.1977), *cert. denied*, 434 U.S. 922, 98 S.Ct. 398, 54 L.Ed.2d 279 (1977), *reh'g denied*, 434 U.S. 1002, 98 S.Ct. 649, 54 L.Ed.2d 499 (1977); *Mirabal v. General Motors Acceptance Corp.*, 576 F.2d 729 (7th Cir.1978), *cert. denied*, 439 U.S. 1039, 99 S.Ct. 642, 58 L.Ed.2d 699 (1978).

[4] For example, in *Ohralik*, Justice Powell for the majority summarized *Primus* as follows:

"We hold today in *Primus* that a lawyer who engaged in solicitation as a form of protected political association may not be disciplined without proof of actual wrongdoing that the State constitutionally may proscribe." 436 U.S. at 462–63 n. 20, 98 S.Ct. at 1922 n. 20.

Yet in *Primus* itself, Justice Powell for the majority spoke more hesitantly, stating, for example, that "[w]e express no opinion whether an analysis of this case [*Primus*] would be different [if the ACLU had shared court awarded fees between the state chapter and the private attorney cooperating with the ACLU]." 436 U.S. at 430 n. 24, 98 S.Ct. at 1904 n. 24.

§ 7.0–4(b) Comparison of Lawyer Solicitation Cases With Accountant Solicitation Cases

The Court's deference to state regulation that limits the power of lawyers to engage in face-to-face, in-person solicitation of clients should be contrasted with the strict limits the Court has placed on the state powers to limit face-to-face, in person solicitation by accountants. In *Edenfield v. Fane*,[24] the Court invalidated a Florida ban on in-person, uninvited, direct *face-to-face* or telephone contact by Certified Public Accountants soliciting business in the business context. The Court held that, as applied, the Florida ban on CPA solicitation in the business context violated free speech. The CPA who is soliciting business intends to communicate truthful, nondeceptive information proposing a lawful commercial transaction.

This Florida CPA rule, the Court concluded, need only be reasonably tailored to serve a substantial state interest. Yet even under this intermediate standard of review, the Court found that the law is unconstitutional as applied. The Court agreed that Florida has a substantial interest in protecting consumers from fraud and from overreaching, in protecting the privacy of consumers, and in maintaining the fact and appearance of CPA impartiality. However, Florida did not meet its burden to show that its rule is reasonably tailored to meet these interests. Nor could Florida demonstrate that its rule serves these interests in a direct and material manner. For example, the state offered no studies or even anecdotal evidence that personal solicitation by CPAs creates dangers of fraud, overreaching, or compromised independence.

Ohralik does not support the CPA restriction. Its "narrow" holding—said the Court in *Edenfield*—depended on "unique" features of in-person solicitation by lawyers. The CPA, unlike a lawyer, is not trained in the art of persuasion. The CPA, in contrast to the lawyer, is trained in "independence and objectivity, not advocacy." In addition, the CPA's prospective clients, unlike the young accident victim in *Ohralik*, are sophisticated

---

Powell's dictum—at least in its broad form—is not even supported by the American Bar Association. See A.B.A. Formal Opinion 334 (Aug. 10, 1974) (dealing with restrictions on lawyers' activities by legal services offices as they affect independence of professional judgment).

Justice Marshall specifically disassociated himself from Justice Powell's dictum and observed that this dictum "is by no means self-evident,

has never been the actual holding of this Court and is not put in issue by the facts presently before us." 436 U.S. at 471, 98 S.Ct. at 1927. See also 436 U.S. at 439, 98 S.Ct. at 1908 (Blackmun, J., concurring).

[24]*Edenfield v. Fane*, 507 U.S. 761, 113 S.Ct. 1792, 123 L.Ed.2d 543 (1993). Kennedy, J., delivered the opinion of the Court, which voted 8 to 1 to invalidate the state restrictions. Only O'Connor, J., dissented.

experienced business executives. The people whom the CPA wishes to solicit meet the CPA in their own offices, and there is no pressure to retain the CPA on the spot. *Ohralik*, in short, does not relieve the state of the obligation to prove that the preventative measures that it proposes will contribute "in a material way" to relieving a "serious" problem.

§ 7.0–4(c) Targeted Direct Mail Advertising

Shapero v. Kentucky Bar Association[25] invalidated, as a violation of free speech, state prohibitions against attorneys sending truthful, non-deceptive letters to potential clients known to face particular legal problems (*i.e.*, targeted, direct-mail advertising). The state rule was based on what was then the ABA's version of Model Rule 7.3, which prohibited targeted direct mail as a form of in-person solicitation. The Court relied primarily on *Zauderer v. Office of Disciplinary Counsel* and noted that the Supreme Court's lawyer advertising cases have never distinguished among various modes of written advertising to the general public. For example, *In re R.M.J.* treated mailed announcement cards the same as newspaper and telephone directory advertisements.[26]

One would think that the Court, given its previous holdings involving advertising, would have little trouble with this case. As

---

[25]*Shapero v. Kentucky Bar Association*, 486 U.S. 466, 108 S.Ct. 1916, 100 L.Ed.2d 475 (1988), *on remand* 763 S.W.2d 126 (Ky.1989).

See Lori Andrews, *Lawyer Advertising and the First Amendment*, 1981 AM.BAR FOUNDATION RESEARCH J. 967; Note, *Direct-Mail Solicitation by Attorneys: Bates to R.M.J.*, 33 SYRACUSE L.REV. 1041 (1982); Judith Maute, *Scrutinizing Lawyer Advertising and Solicitation Rules Under Commercial Speech and Antitrust Doctrine*, 13 HASTINGS CONST. L.Q. 487 (1986); Louise L. Hill, *Solicitation by Lawyers: Piercing the First Amendment Veil*, 42 MAINE L.REV. 369 (1990).

[26]Brennan, J., in a plurality opinion went on to conclude that petitioner's particular letter was not misleading merely because it engaged in the liberal use of underscored, upper case letters—e.g., "Call NOW, don't wait"; "it is FREE, there is NO charge for calling." Nor was the letter misleading because it contained assertions that stated no objective fact ("It may surprise you what I may be able to do for you"). The plurality said that a "truth-ful and nondeceptive letter, no matter how big its type and how much it speculates can never 'shou[t]' at the recipient' or 'gras[p] him by the lapels,' as can a lawyer engaging in face-to-face solicitation. The letter simply presents no comparable risk of overreaching."

White and Stevens, JJ., dissented from this plurality opinion because they believed that the issue of whether the petitioner's particular letter was misleading should be decided by the state courts in the first instance.

O'Connor, J., joined by Rehnquist, C.J. and Scalia, J., filed a dissenting opinion. They agreed that the reasoning of *Zauderer* supported the majority's conclusion, but they wanted to reexamine the entire line of cases. "The roots of the error in our attorney advertising cases are a defective analogy between professional services and standardized consumer products and a correspondingly inappropriate skepticism about the State's justification for their regulations." 486 U.S. at 487, 108 S.Ct. at 1929.

a logical matter, mass mailing is simply a form of advertising and therefore should also be constitutionally protected. Given that attorneys may engage in mass mailing, it makes little sense for the state to prohibit targeted mailing, which is only a more efficient form of distributing handbills. It is a form of advertising that uses fewer envelopes than mass mailing. It is quite reasonable for an attorney to mail a letter only to those who are more likely to find it of interest.

On the other hand, the fact that the justices were fragmented indicates that they apparently had more trouble with the case. Justice Brennan announced the decision of the Court and delivered an Opinion of the Court only for parts I and II, and an opinion as to Part III in which Justices Marshall, Blackmun, and Kennedy joined. Justice White, joined by Justice Stevens, concurred in part and dissented in part. Justice O'Connor, joined by Chief Justice Rehnquist and Justice Scalia, dissented.[27]

§ 7.0–4(d) Targeted Direct Mail Within 30 Days Of An Accident

The Supreme Court back-tracked from *Shapero* when it considered targeted mail sent to prospective clients soon after an accident. A Florida ethics rule prohibited personal injury lawyers from sending targeted direct mail soliciting employment to victims and their relatives until 30 days following an accident or disaster. This rule prevented the personal injury *plaintiff's* attorney from contacting the accident victim or a relative, but it imposed no restrictions on the *defense* attorney from contacting either the victim or the relative. In *Florida Bar v. Went for It, Inc.*,[28] the Court did not disturb *Shapero*, but held (5 to 4) that, even though targeted mailing is constitutionally protected, Florida may ban targeted mailing by plaintiffs' attorneys for 30 days after the cause of action has occurred. Justice O'Connor, who had dissented in *Shapero*, wrote the majority opinion in *Went for It*.[29]

---

[27]486 U.S. 466, 480, 108 S.Ct. 1916, 1925, 100 L.Ed.2d 475 (1988).

[28]*Florida Bar v. Went for It, Inc.*, 515 U.S. 618, 115 S.Ct. 2371, 132 L.Ed.2d 541 (1995), *on remand* 66 F.3d 270 (11th Cir.1995). *See* Ronald D. Rotunda, *Professionalism, Legal Advertising, and Free Speech In the Wake of Florida Bar v. Went For It, Inc.*, 49 ARKANSAS L. REV. 703 (1997).

[29]O'Connor's dissent in *Shapero* was joined by Rehnquist, C.J. and Scalia, J. Both of these Justices, along with Thomas & Breyer, JJ., joined the five person majority. The majority in *Shapero* included Kennedy, J. (who joined all of the Brennan plurality) & Stevens, J. (who joined Parts I and II of the Brennan plurality). In *Went For It*, Kennedy, J. filed a dissenting opinion joined by Stevens, Souter, & Ginsburg, JJ.

Justice O'Connor, speaking for the Court, applied the basic test advanced in *Central Hudson*,[30] and claimed that the state bar had substantial interests to protect and that its restrictions were narrowly tailored to advance (directly and substantially) those interests. She contended that the Florida rule was necessary to protect the privacy of the victims and to prevent invasive or unwelcome conduct by lawyers. However, an airline crash or similar misfortune is not a private act. It is widely reported in the newspapers, television, and radio. The recipient of the letter does not have to respond; he or she can just throw it away. The Florida rule did nothing to prevent invasive conduct or unwelcome contact by defense counsel or insurance adjusters.

Justice O'Connor also maintained that the Florida rule was necessary in order to prevent "the erosion of confidence in the profession that such repeated invasions have engendered."[31] She emphasized that the situation in *Went For It* was unlike the situation in *Shapero*, because *Shapero* only dealt "with a broad ban on *all* direct-mail solicitations, whatever the time frame and whoever the recipient," and, unlike *Shapero*, the Florida State Bar had collected evidence that it was important to have this 30 day ban on plaintiff-lawyers in order to protect the public perception of lawyers.

The state bar's evidence was both statistical and anecdotal. O'Connor, for example, regarded as particularly "[s]ignificant" a poll showing that "27% of direct-mail recipients reported that their regard for the legal profession and for the judicial process as a whole was 'lower' as a result of receiving the direct mail."[32] However, if 27% did not like the mailing, then for the remaining 73%, the direct mail did not lower their respect for the profession. But O'Connor asserted that the state can keep everyone in the dark because 27% of the people might think better of us if they did not know what was going on.

In a significant passage, the Court announced an important limitation on any broad reading of this case:

> Florida permits lawyers to advertise on prime-time television and radio as well as in newspapers and other media. They may rent space on billboards. They may send *untargeted letters* to the general population, *or to discrete segments thereof*.[33]

So, it appears that lawyers can still send letters, as long as they also send them to people who are less interested in receiving them. This is a strange rule, particularly when it is purportedly grounded on a distinction of Constitutional dimension.

---

[30] *Central Hudson Gas & Electric Corp. v. Public Service Commission*, 447 U.S. 557, 100 S.Ct. 2343, 65 L.Ed.2d 341 (1980).

[31] 518 U.S. at 634, 115 S.Ct. at 2381.

[32] 515 U.S. at 626, 115 S.Ct. at 2377.

[33] 515 U.S. at 632, 115 S.Ct. at 2380 (emphasis added).

As for the recipients, one wonders how they will know if the letters are targeted or not. With modern computers, one can receive magazines that print the recipient's name on the magazine instead of pasting on a label. Similarly, a mass mailing can begin the letter with the phrase, "Dear Mr. Smith," rather than, "Dear Occupant." Unless the letter refers to a very specific fact (e.g., a particular accident rather than the problem of accidents generally) the recipient will not know from the letter whether it was sent only to him or to others, such as his neighbor.

If people really do not like to receive targeted mailing, then this problem should be self-policing. That is, people who do not like to hire lawyers who send letters seeking employment will not hire such lawyers. If most people do not like these letters, lawyers who send them will learn the hard way not to waste money on them. In fact, these letters must have been useful for the majority of recipients because otherwise the lawyers (who were not sending out the letters for their own health or amusement) would not have sent them.

However, now that the Florida Bar rule is in effect, a client may find out that he or she has hired the type of lawyer who (but for the Florida rule) would have sent a targeted letter. Therefore, by keeping people ignorant of the facts, the Florida rule takes away from clients the right to refuse to hire a lawyer who would send this type of targeted mailing. Meanwhile, under the Florida rule, clients are kept in the dark for 30 days while being fair game for defense lawyers, who can contact them.

The majority justified the Florida prohibition as a means to protect the public perception of lawyers. People might think better of lawyers if only they did not know the type of people that many of the lawyers are. Justice Kennedy ominously complained in his dissent that, "for the first time since *Bates v. State Bar of Arizona*,[34] the Court now orders a major retreat from the constitutional guarantees for commercial speech in order to shield its own profession from public criticism."[35]

The constitutionality of any law restricting truthful lawyer advertising is not completely certain after *Bates* and its offspring. Consequently, some of the ethics rules' specific restrictions, either on their face or as applied, may, in the future, fall to constitutional challenges.

---

[34] *Bates v. State Bar of Arizona,* 433 U.S. 350, 97 S.Ct. 2691, 53 L.Ed.2d 810 (1977), *reh'g denied,* 434 U.S. 881, 98 S.Ct. 242, 54 L.Ed.2d 164 (1977).

[35] 515 U.S. at 644, 115 S.Ct. at 2386 (Kennedy, J., dissenting).

§ 7.0–5 THE BAR'S RESPONSE TO *BATES* AND ITS PROGENY

Many of the rules governing attorney advertising have been in response to Supreme Court cases invalidating the earlier rules as a violation of free speech. To some extent, the organized bar has been forced to modify its rules in light of the developing First Amendment law.

The American Bar Association promptly responded to *Bates* by amending DR 2-101 to loosen its restrictions. However, while the knot was loosened, it was still tied. Although the post-*Bates* version of DR 2-110 included an extensive list of the information that an attorney could include in an advertisement, the Model Code still prohibited anything that it did not expressly permit.

The ABA abandoned this approach when it drafted the Model Rules. These Rules were written in an era when it was clear that the First Amendment applies to advertising of legal services. Although the First Amendment does not apply to the advertising of legal services in exactly the same way it applies to other professions such as accounting services,[1] the First Amendment still does apply. Thus, Rule 7.1 and the other provisions of Part 7, *Information About Legal Services*, contrast sharply to DR 2-110. Rules 7.1 through 7.5 allow any advertising that is not expressly prohibited.

[Section 7.0–5]

[1]*Compare Edenfield v. Fane*, 507 U.S. 761, 113 S.Ct. 1792, 123 L.Ed.2d 543 (1993) (Court invalidated, 8 to 1, a Florida ban on in-person, uninvited, direct face-to-face or telephone contact by Certified Public Accountants soliciting business in the business context), *with Florida Bar v. Went For It, Inc.*, 515 U.S. 618, 115 S.Ct. 2371, 132 L.Ed.2d 541 (1995) (Court, 5 to 4, upholds a Florida ban on plaintiff, personal injury lawyers from sending targeted, direct-mail solicitations to victims and their relatives for 30 days following an accident or disaster).

The *Edenfield* majority stated that the holding in *Ohralik v. Ohio State Bar Association*, 436 U.S. 447, 98 S.Ct. 1912, 56 L.Ed.2d 444 (1978), which allowed restrictions on lawyer's was a holding that depended on "certain 'unique' features of in-person solicitation by lawyers." *Edenfield* then noted that CPAs, unlike lawyers, are not trained in the art of persuasion; the prospective clients are "sophisticated business executives," not like the young accident victim in *Ohralik*, and there is little pressure for the business person to retain the CPA on the spot.

CHAPTER 7.1
COMMUNICATIONS CONCERNING A LAWYER'S SERVICES

RULE 7.1: COMMUNICATIONS CONCERNING A LAWYER'S SERVICES

A lawyer shall not make a false or misleading communication about the lawyer or the lawyer's services. A communication is false or misleading if it contains a material misrepresentation of fact or law, or omits a fact necessary to make the statement considered as a whole not materially misleading.

Comment

[1] This Rule governs all communications about a lawyer's services, including advertising permitted by Rule 7.2. Whatever means are used to make known a lawyer's services, statements about them must be truthful.

[2] Truthful statements that are misleading are also prohibited by this Rule. A truthful statement is misleading if it omits a fact necessary to make the lawyer's communication considered as a whole not materially misleading. A truthful statement is also misleading if there is a substantial likelihood that it will lead a reasonable person to formulate a specific conclusion about the lawyer or the lawyer's services for which there is no reasonable factual foundation.

[3] An advertisement that truthfully reports a lawyer's achievements on behalf of clients or former clients may be misleading if presented so as to lead a reasonable person to form an unjustified expectation that the same results could be obtained for other clients in similar matters without reference to the specific factual and legal circumstances of each client's case. Similarly, an unsubstantiated comparison of the lawyer's services or fees with the services or fees of other lawyers may be misleading if presented with such specificity as would lead a reasonable person to conclude that the comparison can be substantiated. The inclusion of an appropriate disclaimer or qualifying language may preclude a finding that a statement is likely to create unjustified expectations or otherwise mislead a prospective client.

[4] See also Rule 8.4(e) for the prohibition against stating or implying an ability to influence improperly a government agency or official or to achieve results by means that violate the Rules of Professional Conduct or other law.

Authors' 1983 Model Rules Comparison

The 1983 version of Rule 7.1 prohibited false and misleading
advertising and then provided three separate definitions of "false
and misleading" in the text of the Rule. Under the old language, a
communication was false or misleading if it:

(a) contains a material misrepresentation of fact or law, or omits a fact necessary to make the statement considered as a whole not materially misleading;

(b) is likely to create an unjustified expectation about results the lawyer can
achieve, or states or implies that the lawyer can achieve results by means that
violate the Rules of Professional Conduct or other law; or

(c) compares the lawyer's services with other lawyers' services, unless the
comparison can be factually substantiated.

The drafters of the 2002 Rules thought that the definitions relating
to unjustified expectations and comparisons in paragraphs (b) and
(c) were too broad to use as enforceable standards. *See* Reporter's
Explanation of Changes to Rule 7.1. Thus, they moved this language
into the comments as a possible example of what may constitute a
false and misleading communication. With respect to the reference
in (b) to lawyers who state or imply that they can achieve results
by means that violate the Rules or other law, the drafters believed
that this prohibition should be included in Rule 8.4(e). This prohibition should extend to all statements made by lawyers, not just to
advertisements.

In Comment 1, the drafters removed the word "should" and replaced
it with must when discussing the obligation that statements made
by lawyers must be truthful. They also deleted several lines about
the unjustified expectation language of Former Rule 7.1(b).

In new Comment 2, the drafters included a new standard for
evaluating whether a statement is false or misleading.

In new Comment 3, the drafters discuss how an advertisement may
be misleading if it creates an unjustified expectation or unsubstantiated comparison.

In new Comment 4, the drafters added language and a reference to
Rule 8.4(e).

Model Code Comparison

DR 2-101 provided that "[a] lawyer shall not . . . use . . . any form
of public communication containing a false, fraudulent, misleading,
deceptive, self-laudatory or unfair statement or claim." DR 2-101(B)
provided that a lawyer "may publish or broadcast . . . the following
information . . . in the geographic area or areas in which the lawyer
resides or maintains offices or in which a significant part of the
lawyer's clientele resides, provided that the information . . .
complies with DR 2-101(A), and is presented in a dignified manner
. . .." DR 2-101(B) then specified twenty-five categories of information that may be disseminated. DR 2-101(C) provided that "[a]ny
person desiring to expand the information authorized for disclosure
in DR 2-101(B), or to provide for its dissemination through other
forums may apply to [the agency having jurisdiction under state

law] . . .. The relief granted in response to any such application shall be promulgated as an amendment to DR 2-101(B), universally applicable to all lawyers."

§ 7.1–1 THE PROHIBITION AGAINST FALSE OR MISLEADING ADVERTISING

§ 7.1–1(a) Background

Rule 7.1 broadly prohibits "false or misleading statements." Subject to the requirements of this Rule, Rule 7.2 permits a lawyer to advertise through a broad spectrum of media. In contrast, the Model Code provided many detailed regulations regarding what a lawyer could or could not do.[1] For example,

---

[Section 7.1–1]

[1] The last version of the Model Code (before it was replaced by the Model Rules) contained extensive regulations dealing with advertising. The Code began with a general prohibition of "false, fraudulent, misleading, deceptive, self-laudatory or unfair" statements or claims. DR 2-101(A). The Code then listed 25 categories of information that may be advertised, subject to the requirement of DR 2-101(B) that any communication be presented "in a dignified manner." DR 2-101(B)(1) to (B)(25).

The Code permitted advertising through both print and broadcast media. DR 2-101(B). *Bates* had reserved the question as to the extent of constitutional protection in light of the possible "special problems of advertising on the electronic broadcast media." The Code also provided that the advertising may cover only the geographic area where the lawyer resides, or where the lawyer maintains offices, or where a "significant part" of the lawyer's clients reside. DR 2-101(B).

The Model Code allowed a lawyer to present biographical information such as her name, DR 2-101(B)(1), schools attended, DR 2-101(B)(5), and foreign language ability. DR 2-101(B)(14). Advertisements could also include office information such as hours, DR 2-101(B)(19), and fee information. DR 2-101(B)(20) to (B)(25). If contingent fees were advertised, the Code explicitly required that any pub-licity about them must include a statement that the percentage is computed before or after deduction of costs. DR 2-101(B)(22).

As a general rule, the Model Code prohibited lawyers from identifying themselves in their advertisements as specialists in a particular field of law. DR2-102(A); DR 2-105; EC 2-14. This rule was subject to several exceptions. First, the Code recognized the traditional exception for patent lawyers. DR2-105(A)(1). In addition, EC 2-14 also included the fields of admiralty and trademark. This EC, by the way, is contrary to DR 2-105(A)(1). The ABA House of Delegates amended DR 2-105(A)(1) in 1977 (eliminating admiralty and trademark) but did not amend the corresponding EC.

Second, the Model Code permitted lawyers to advertise their specialty *if* certified by the appropriate state agency. DR2-105(A)(3). Furthermore, lawyers could indicate that their practice is limited to certain areas *only* by using state-designated terms. DR2-105(A)(2). These restrictions regarding advertising of truthful information are unconstitutional in light of the case law. If a lawyer only handles real estate matters, should he not be able to so advertise, whether he uses state designated terms or not? *In re R.M.J.*, 455 U.S. 191, 102 S.Ct. 929, 71 L.Ed.2d 64 (1982) so held. The Code provided that any person wishing to advertise information not on the "approved list" might apply to the appropriate state agency for an expansion of the Code.

under the Model Code, it was considered improper for a law firm to communicate on its letterhead that it was affiliated or associated with another firm.[2] Now there is no prohibition if the statement is true.[3]

The 1983 Model Rules version of Rule 7.1 contained one general definition of a false or misleading statement and three specific examples of advertising conduct that similarly fell within the false and misleading language. The general definition included as false or misleading affirmative statements that misrepresent the law or facts or omissions of fact that make a statement as a whole materially misleading. The 2002 revision of the Rules retained this definition as the primary interpretation of false or misleading conduct. The first specific definition in the 1983 Model Rules was based upon communications "likely to create an unjustified expectation about the results the lawyer can achieve . . . ."[4] The drafters of the 2002 Rules believed that this statement was too general and likely to lead to prohibitions on advertising that were "not substantially likely to lead a reasonable person to form a specific and unwarranted conclusion about the lawyer or the lawyer's services."[5] Thus, the drafters moved the unjustified expectations language into the Comments and made this one possible source of a false and misleading advertisement, but not a per se basis.[6]

The 1983 Model Rules also prohibited lawyers from stating or implying that they could achieve a result by means that were prohibited by law or the Model Rules. The drafters of the 2002 Rules moved this language into Rule 8.4(e) to broaden its application to all statements made by lawyers. Finally, the 1983 Model Rules contained a prohibition against comparisons made by one law firm against other law firms unless the comparison could be factually substantiated.[7] The drafters of the 2002 Rules removed this from the text of Rule 7.1 and moved it into the Comments because the misleading nature of comparisons must

---

DR 2-101(D).

The Code also included detailed regulations of other aspects of lawyer advertising besides mode, range, and content. For example, if a lawyer used the broadcast media, the lawyer must pre-record the advertisement and retain a copy. DR2-101(D). If a lawyer advertised a specific service for a set fee, the lawyer had to render the service for that fee for a reasonable time after the advertisement appeared. DR 2-101(E), (F), & (G).

[2]ABA Informal Opinion 1173 (1971), and ABA Formal Opinion 330

(1972), both withdrawn in ABA Formal Opinion 84-351 (Oct. 20, 1984).

[3]See discussion, below, of Rule 7.5, ABA Formal Opinion 84-351 (Oct. 20, 1984) and Formal Opinion 94-388 (Dec. 5, 1994).

[4]1983 Model Rule 7.1(b).

[5]Reporter's Explanation of Changes to Model Rule 7.1.

[6]See Rule 7.1, Comment 3.

[7]See 1983 Model Rule 7.1(c).

be evaluated on a case-by-case basis and not by a provision that may be overbroad.[8]

These changes narrow the definition of false and misleading and are likely to result in fewer cases brought on the grounds of unjustified expectations and comparisons among other lawyers. At least the ABA contemplates a more case-by-case basis for examining claims of violations of Rule 7.1. The drafters of the 2002 Rules feared that the old standard might be subject to constitutional challenge.

§ 7.1-1(b) Prohibitory Requirements versus Disclosure Requirements

The states have a broader power to impose disclosure requirements than they have to ban speech, because a disclosure requirement compels more speech, not less.[9] A reasonable disclosure requirement prohibits no speech and the lawyer's "constitutionally protected interest in *not* providing any particular factual information in his advertising is minimal."[10]

On the other hand, the states do not have *carte blanche* to impose excessive, overly burdensome disclosure requirements. The state does not have the power to mandate disclosures that are so detailed that they become "unduly burdensome."[11]

Thus, disclosure requirements do not violate the First Amendment if they are: (1) reasonably related to the state's interest in preventing deception of consumers, (2) not vague,[12] and (3) not "unjustified or unduly burdensome."[13] The state's disclosure requirements regarding lawyer advertising do not have to be the least restrictive means to serve the state's purposes. A disclosure requirement may also be underinclusive, *i.e.*, it need not solve all facets of the problem it is designed to ameliorate. As a general matter, governments are entitled to attack problems piecemeal,

---

[8]*See* Reporter's Explanation of Changes to Model Rule 7.1.

[9]A lawyer's constitutionally protected interest in *not* providing any particular factual information in his advertising is minimal. *Zauderer v. Office of Disciplinary Counsel*, 471 U.S. 626, 628, 105 S.Ct. 2265, 2270, 85 L.Ed.2d 652 (1985). See also discussion in, Ronald D. Rotunda, *Media Accountability in Light of the First Amendment*, 21 SOCIAL PHILOSOPHY & POLICY 269 (2004).

[10]471 U.S. at 628, 651, 105 S.Ct. at 2270, 2282 (emphasis in original).

[11]*Ibanez v. Florida Department of Business and Professional Regulation*,

Board of Accountancy, 512 U.S. 136, 143–47, 114 S.Ct. 2084, 2089–91, 129 L.Ed.2d 118 (1994), and *Zauderer v. Office of Disciplinary Counsel*, 471 U.S. 626, 105 S.Ct. 2265, 85 L.Ed.2d 652 (1985). *Zauderer* made clear that disclosure requirements do implicate free speech, and "unjustified or unduly burdensome disclosure requirements might offend the First Amendment by chilling protected commercial speech." 471 U.S. at 651, 105 S.Ct. at 2282.

[12]471 U.S. at 653 n. 15, 105 S.Ct. at 2283 n. 15.

[13]471 U.S. at 651, 105 S.Ct. at 2282.

unless their policies implicate rights that are so fundamental that strict scrutiny must be applied.

§ 7.1–2 MATERIAL MISSTATEMENTS OR OMISSIONS

The black letter of Rule 7.1 states that a communication regarding a lawyer's services is false or misleading if it contains material misrepresentations of law or fact, or has *omissions* that are necessary to make the statement considered as a whole not materially misleading.[1] The first focus of the Rule is to ensure that any affirmative statements made by lawyers are truthful. To the extent that statements made by a lawyer are false and material to the target of the statement, the lawyer violates Rule 7.1. The second focus of the provision is to require that when a lawyer makes a communication that communication must not omit facts or information needed to make the statements accurate when considered as a whole. The example of such a situation occurred in *Zauderer v. Office of Disciplinary Counsel*,[2] where a lawyer made the statement in a printed advertisement that if there was no recovery, no legal fees were due. Although the statement was accurate about legal fees, it did not mention litigation or court costs that a client would need to pay regardless whether the client had won the case. The Supreme Court upheld the state bar decision that this omission was a misrepresentation under the state ethics law. Therefore, truthful statements may violate this Rule if they are not accurate when considered as a whole.

Comment 2 to Rule 7.1 mentions one other possible category of truthful statements that may violate Rule 7.1:

> A truthful statement is also misleading if there is a substantial likelihood that it will lead a reasonable person to formulate a specific conclusion about the lawyer or the lawyer's services for which there is no reasonable factual foundation.

This language sets forth a new standard for determining whether a truthful statement may be materially misleading. The drafters borrowed the substantial likelihood inquiry from Rule 3.6 on trial publicity because they thought this standard properly balances the lawyers' first amendment rights and the bar's right to protect the public.[3] Although this standard does embrace a reasonable person test, it seems difficult to apply to specific situations, aside from the contexts discussed below in the next section. In other words, one could apply this test to the communication that raises an unjustified expectation about possible

---

[Section 7.1–2]

[1]Rule 7.1(a).

Cf. Securities & Exchange Commission Rule 10b-5.

[2]*Zauderer v. Office of Disciplin-* *ary Counsel*, 471 U.S. 626, 105 S.Ct. 2265, 85 L.Ed.2d 652 (1985).

[3]*See* Reporter's Explanation of Changes to Model Rule 7.1.

results or the comparison that is difficult to substantiate. However, to apply this test to more general situations involving truthful situations would open the Rule to a challenge that it is overbroad.[4]

§ 7.1–3 POTENTIALLY MISLEADING STATEMENTS

In light of the fact that the drafters of the 2002 Rules removed the specific contexts of false and misleading information in the text of the Rule and placed the language in the comments, there are now many bases for potentially misleading statements. This discussion identifies the most common contexts of communications that may lead to a claim of a false or misleading statement.[1]

§ 7.1–3(a) Unjustified Expectations

Comment 3 to Rule 7.1 provides that a lawyer who advertises his or her legal achievements in current or past cases may violate the prohibition against misleading statements. The proper inquiry is whether the advertisement leads "a reasonable person to form an unjustified expectation that the same results could be obtained for other clients in similar matters, without reference to the specific factual and legal circumstances of each client's case."[2]

One could easily apply this test to a television dramatization of an accident, followed by the lawyer's closing argument to the jury, and followed by a jury foreperson reading a multimillion dollar verdict. Such an advertisement is unlikely to contain sufficient detail as to the factual and legal circumstances of the case and also is likely to create an unjustified expectation that this lawyer can produce similar results in all accident cases. Instead of highlighting a specific case, a dramatization may attempt to show that opposing lawyers and insurance companies are fearful of the lawyer and quickly urge settlement. Such a dramatization may falsely mislead the public to believe that the lawyer in most

---

[4]**Pit Bull Logo.** Some courts have a broad view of what is impermissible. The Florida Supreme Court reprimanded two lawyers because of a television advertisement that used the logo of a pit bull with a spiked collar and used the words "pit bull" in the firm's telephone number. *The Florida Bar v. Pape*, 918 So. 2d 240 (Fla. 2005). The court said that the "logo does not assist the public in ensuring that an informed decision is made prior to the selection of the attorney." 918 So.2d 240, 242.

[Section 7.1–3]

[1]For a comprehensive discussion of advertising and examples of false and misleading states as regulated by the Virginia State Bar, see Va. State Bar Standing Comm. on Law. Adv. And Solicitation, Op. 1750 (Dec. 18, 2008), noted in 25 ABA/BNA Law. Man. Prof. Conduct 13 (Jan. 7, 2009).

[2]Comment 3 to Rule 7.1.

cases received favorable results.[3] Similarly, a statement in a print advertisement that the lawyer has won the largest jury verdict in the state in a personal injury case may similarly give potential clients an unjustified hope in a large financial recovery if they retain this attorney.

Lawyers who wish to describe past victories or particular accomplishments may reduce or eliminate any potential unjustified expectations by including a disclaimer or appropriate qualifying language.[4] Thus, lawyers frequently make statements that each case is different and the results obtained in an individual case depend upon the facts and the law or we cannot guarantee results in a particular case because of differences in the law and facts of each matter. The effectiveness of disclaimers often depends upon its placement in print advertisement or how it is displayed in television media. Therefore, the decision on whether an advertisement created unjustified expectations and whether a disclaimer effectively reduces the unjustified expectation is a facts and circumstances analysis made on a case-by-case basis.

The 1983 version of Rule 7.1 indicated in Comments that advertisements containing client endorsements similarly may create unjustified expectations.[5] This statement was deleted; therefore, one can speculate how dramatically the drafters intended a change in meaning. Perhaps, the use of client endorsements should focus on the accuracy of the statements made and proper disclosure through qualifying and disclaimer language.[6] Clients already make endorsements orally if someone asks. If the lawyer puts these statements in writing with the clients' permission, the 2002 revisions to the Model Rules allow those endorse-

---

[3]*Matter of Keller*, 792 N.E.2d 865 (Ind. 2003), involved a lawyer who had purchased television advertising from a national marketing firm that showed insurance adjusters planning to delay payments to an accident victim. One of them asks who is representing the defendant, and when he is told it is Keller & Keller, he says, "Let's settle this one." Actor Robert Vaughn then appears and says, "The insurance companies know the name Keller & Keller."

The Indiana Supreme Court found that this and other ads that the firm used falsely implied that Keller & Keller usually obtained a favorable outcome for their clients. The court imposed a public reprimand, and relied on Indiana Professional Conduct Rule 7.1(d)(4), which prohibited lawyer advertising that: "contains a state-

ment or opinion as to the quality of the services or contains a representation or implication regarding the quality of legal services." The Model Rules do not have that provision.

[4]Comment 3 to Rule 7.1.

[5]1983 Model Rule 7.1, Comment 1.

[6]*See* Iowa State Bar Ass'n Comm. On Ethics and Practice Guidelines, Op. 07-09 (Oct. 30, 2007), *noted in* 24 ABA/BNA MANUAL ON PROF. CONDUCT, CURRENT REPORTS 35 (Jan. 23, 2008). Opinion 07-09 permits lawyers to advertise themselves as "Super Lawyers" and "Best Lawyers in America" because these publications used a peer review system to decide which lawyers were included and how these lawyer should be rated.

ments, *unless* an endorsement violates the general prohibition against a false or misleading communication. That determination is a case-by-case decision. The new Rules favor that approach instead of blanket prohibitions.

The next section examines whether a former judge may continue to use the title of the judicial office while in private practice.

§ 7.1–3(a)(1) Former Judge's Use of the Judicial Title

When judges leave the bench, it is common for lawyers and others to continue to refer to them as "judge," or "your honor." Similarly, when other government officials—Presidents, Ambassadors, etc.—leave their service, it is also common practice to continue to address them by their title, but without the use of the modifier, "former." President Clinton, for example, is never addressed as "former President Clinton."

ABA Formal Opinion 95-391[7] concluded that, if the judge no longer practices law, there is nothing misleading in referring to the former judge by the honorific title of, "judge," or "your honor." However, if the judge continues to practice law, use of the title in legal communications, court pleadings, and even a letterhead or office nameplate is "misleading" in the view of the ABA Ethics Committee because it "creates an unjustified expectation" and implies that the former judge has special influence. In fact, the former judge who now practices law should not refer to himself as judge and should not encourage others to do so,[8] although they may still use the title out of respect.

Most state ethics opinions agree with the ABA, but others reach a contrary conclusion.[9]

§ 7.1–3(b) Comparing Lawyers' Services

Comment 3 to Rule 7.1 provides that "an unsubstantiated comparison of the lawyer's services or fees with the services or fees of other lawyers may be misleading if presented with such specificity as would lead a reasonable person to conclude that the comparison can be substantiated."[10] As in the context of unjustified expectations, the drafters removed the per se violation and created a case-by-case inquiry whether a comparison is unsub-

---

[7]ABA Formal Opinion 95-391 (Apr. 24, 1995).

[8]ABA Formal Opinion 95-391 (Apr. 24, 1995), at 2.

[9]*See, e.g.*, Florida State Bar Association Committee on Professional Ethics, Opinion 87-9, 1987 WestLaw 125124, State Bar of Michigan Standing Committee on Professional and Judicial Ethics, Opinion RI-108, 1991 WL 519879.

Contra Arizona State Bar Committee on Rules of Professional Conduct, Opinion 87-1, (1987) (letterhead includes, after a lawyer's name, the phrase, "judge of the superior court, retired").

[10]Comment 3 to Rule 7.1.

stantiated and is written with such specificity so as to mislead the prospective client into believing that the comparison is substantiated.

The advertisement that the Supreme Court approved in the *Bates* decision[11]—the original case that gave constitutional protection to lawyer advertising—offered "legal services at very reasonable rates."[12] That statement is a form of comparison. One normally determines if rates are "reasonable" by comparing them with other rates in the locality. The Court noted the *Bates* firm advertised the cost of an uncontested divorce as $175 plus $20 court filing fee. Where John Bates and his partner, Van O'Steen, practiced, the rate for this type of service "runs from $150 to $300 in the area."[13] The Court ruled that the $175 fee and $20 court filing charge "seems 'very reasonable' in light of the customary charge."[14] Then the majority said: "*Of course*, advertising will permit the comparison of rates among competitors, thus revealing if the rates are reasonable."[15] In light of this approach, it is likely that the Supreme Court, on First Amendment grounds, will not allow the states simply to announce or assume that comparisons are not factually substantiated. The states will have to demonstrate that conclusion.

An Ohio Ethics Opinion concluded that an intellectual property firm may not tell potential business clients the number of intellectual property cases the firm had won, lost, and settled.[16] The Opinion announced that such statistics are misleading, self-laudatory, and created unjustified expectations.[17]

In *Mezrano v. Alabama State Bar*,[18] the state court affirmed a State Bar Disciplinary Board order that a lawyer be suspended for a period of 120 days. The court ruled that disciplinary rules

---

[11]*Bates v. State Bar of Arizona*, 433 U.S. 350, 97 S.Ct. 2691, 53 L.Ed.2d 810 (1977).

[12]433 U.S. at 385, 97 S.Ct. at 2710 (Appendix to the Opinion of the Court).

[13]433 U.S. at 382, 97 S.Ct. at 2708.

[14]433 U.S. at 382, 97 S.Ct. at 2708.

[15]433 U.S. at 382, 97 S.Ct. at 2708 (emphasis added).

[16]Supreme Court of Ohio Board of Commissioners on Grievances and Discipline, Opinion Number 2003-2, 2003 WL 1848000. One interesting query is whether, particularly when dealing with intellectual property matters and fairly sophisticated clients, such limits on lawyer advertising serve much public purpose. See Model Rule 7.1, Comment 3, which specifically rejects a per se prohibition of comparisons and only says they "may be misleading."

[17]In addition, the Board concluded that it is improper to offer clients a money-back guarantee for intellectual property work. Such an offer, the Board said, created a conflict of interest between attorney and client, created an unjustified expectation about the results the lawyer can achieve, and implied "that the lawyer has improper influence or control over the legal system."

[18]*Mezrano v. Alabama State Bar*, 434 So.2d 732 (Ala.1983).

requiring that commercial advertisements by lawyers contain a disclaimer as to the quality of services or expertise of the lawyer performing such services and requiring that copies of all lawyer advertisements be sent to the State Bar within three days of first publication did not unconstitutionally infringe upon a lawyer's commercial free speech rights. The court simply announced:

> *We opine* that Mezrano should have included the disclaimer in his advertisement as required by disciplinary rule 2-102(A)(7)(f). The Alabama Bar Association has no rating system. Applicants for bar admission in this state do not receive their scores on the bar examination if they pass. The Alabama Bar does not identify attorneys as specialists. Therefore, *we feel* that attorneys' representations about the quality of their legal services could very well mislead the public. Upon passing the bar examination, all attorneys *are presumed* to be on an equal footing. Thus, the Alabama State Bar could reasonably conclude that attorneys should not hold themselves out as being superior to other attorneys when there is no rating system in this state.[19]

One wonders if this analysis follows the analytical approach of *Bates*. In this case, Mezrano did not comply with the disciplinary rule because he did not include the required disclaimer in his advertisement: "no advertisement shall be published unless it contains, in legible print, the following language: 'No representation is made about the quality of the legal services to be performed or the expertise of the lawyer performing such services.' "[20] Thus, the court upheld the discipline. But the court did not justify or explain its conclusion; instead, it relied on its opinion (*"We opine"*), what it believed (*"we feel"*), and what it presumed ("all attorneys *are presumed*").[21] The *Mezrano* court based its conclusion in part on the fact that "The Alabama Bar does not identify attorneys as specialists."[22] But we now know that states cannot simply ban lawyers from using that term.[23]

---

[19]434 So.2d at 735 (emphasis added).

[20]434 So.2d at 734.

[21]This court was unfriendly to legal advertising, as illustrated by its statement that another reason to discipline the lawyer was because the name of his law office was misleading. Mr. Mezrano had engaged in business under the name "University Legal Center" for about two months. The court noted, "that Mezrano's office is located on University Boulevard in very close proximity to the University of Alabama in Birmingham and that he is not affiliated with the University. We feel that the general public may associate Mezrano with the University due to the name of the 'legal center' and its location, thus being misled as to his identity. This use of the name is in violation of DR 2-102(B)." 434 So.2d at 736.

[22]434 So.2d at 735 (emphasis added).

[23]*Peel v. Attorney Registration and Disciplinary Commission of Illinois*, 496 U.S. 91, 110 S.Ct. 2281, 110 L.Ed.2d 83 (1990), discussed above.

§ 7.1–3(c) The "Of Counsel" Relationship

Sometimes a lawyer not in a law firm will work on a brief with that law firm and then be designated "of counsel" on that particular brief. When this term, "of counsel," is used in a circumstance like this one, it only signifies that there is a short term relationship for a particular case. The designation does not imply that there is any continuing relationship.[24]

In other circumstances, a law firm will use the "of counsel" designation—or similar ones, such as "special counsel," "tax counsel," "senior counsel," etc.—in its general announcements, letterheads, office signs, and so forth. The person so designated is neither a "partner" (with the shared liability and managerial responsibility that is implied by the term "partner" or "principal"), nor is the person an "associate" (a junior non-partner). The "of counsel" may be a lawyer who is retired from the firm but still works on occasion on a particular project, or a retired judge who has associated with the firm and may work part time, or a probationary partner-to-be.

In legal circles, the use of the "of counsel" appellation in such circumstances is thought to imply to the world at large that there is some sort of close, on-going general relationship.[25] Thus, the term would be misleading if used on a letterhead, general announcements, and similar communications when there is, in fact, no such on-going relationship.[26] If such a relationship does exist, then the designation is not misleading and the law firm can use it in its advertisements, letterhead, and so forth. If one lawyer is, in fact, "of counsel" to two or more firms, all these firms can tout the "of counsel" relationship.[27]

For example, if a lawyer works on only one case with another law firm, it is certainly permissible to designate him as "of counsel" on the relevant filings, but it would not be ethically permissible to designate him as "of counsel" on the firm letterhead because there is no on-going relationship.[28] Similarly, the ABA Ethics Committee has opined that it is misleading to use the "of

---

[24]ABA Formal Opinion 90-357 (May 10, 1990).

[25]DR 2-102(A)(4) stated: "A lawyer may be designated 'Of Counsel' on a letterhead if he has a continuing relationship with a lawyer or law firm, other than as a partner or associate." The Model Rules do not use the term "Of Counsel."

[26]ABA Formal Opinion 90-357 (May 10, 1990), at 2.

[27]ABA Formal Opinion 90-357 (May 10, 1990), at 5, which specifically

rejected a contrary conclusion in an earlier opinion, ABA Formal Opinion 330 (1972). If one lawyer can have a close, on-going relationship with more than one client, one lawyer can be of-counsel to more than one firm. Of course, if no such an on-going relationship exists, it would be misleading to advertise that such a relationship is in place.

[28]ABA Formal Opinion 90-357 (May 10, 1990), at 4 & n.7, citing ABA Formal Opinion 330 (1972). Note that ABA Formal Opinion 90-357 withdrew

counsel" designation in general communications such as letterheads, announcement cards, or law signs if there is no ongoing collaborative relationship but only a relationship as an
outside consultant or a forwarder or receiver of legal business.[29]

§ 7.1–3(d) Affiliated and Associated Law Firms

Law firms use a variety of terms to describe their relationship
with other firms. One law firm may be listed as "of counsel" to a
different law firm, or several firms may describe themselves as
part of a "strategic alliance," or "associated with" or "affiliated
with" each other. Sometimes a firm may say that it is part of a
"network" or has a "correspondent" firm elsewhere. The English
language is like a living organism that constantly grows. The law
firms' creation of new terms to describe the new relationships
that they have with each other is part of the growth of any living
tongue.

The Model Rules do not regulate the terms that law firms use
to describe their relationship, *except* for the basic requirement
that applies to all legal advertising: communication regarding
the affiliation of law firms must not be false or misleading. In one
Formal Opinion, the ABA Ethics Committee opined that, when
law firms are "affiliated" or "associated," the potential clients "are
led to believe that the firms will not simultaneously represent
persons whose interests conflict with the client's interests, just as
would be true of lawyers who occupy an 'Of Counsel' relationship
with the firm."[30] Consequently, this ABA Formal Opinion advised
that the law firms must adhere to the applicable rules governing
disclosure of confidential information and conflicts of interest.

A decade later the Ethics Committee reexamined the relationship that law firms have with each other, and how they should
communicate their relationships to clients and prospective
clients. This second Formal Opinion declared that some terms
were, in effect, inherently misleading.[31]

Formal Opinion 94-388 begins its discussion by reaffirming the
basic precept that it is "critical, no matter what words are used

---

and rejected other parts of ABA Formal
Opinion 330 (1972).

[29]ABA Formal Opinion 90-357
(May 10, 1990), at 4.

Because conflicts of interest of
one lawyer are often are imputed to
lawyers in the same law firm, it is not
advisable to designate carelessly a
lawyer as of counsel to the law firm.
In fact, if one lawyer is a member of
two different law firms, they need to
merge their client lists for conflict
purposes. *Cinema 5, Limited v.*

Cinerama, Inc., 528 F.2d 1384 (2d
Cir.1976) (conflict of a lawyer in one
firm is imputed to all lawyers in a dif-
ferent law firm because of one lawyer
who is partner in two law firms). *See*
Robert C. Hacker & Ronald D. Rotunda,
Attorney Conflicts of Interest, 2
CORPORATION L. REV. 345 (1979).

[30]ABA Formal Opinion 84-351
(Oct. 20, 1984), at 5.

[31]ABA Formal Opinion 94-388
(Dec. 5, 1994).

to describe the relationship between firms, for clients to receive information that will tell them the exact nature of the relationship and the extent to which resources of another firm will be available in connection with the client's retention of the firm that is claiming the relationship."[32] Then, the Formal Opinion simply announces: "The Committee concludes that the use of one or two word shorthand expressions [correspondent firm, associated firm, etc.] is *not sufficient* to fulfill that requirement."[33] The law firm's obligation under rule 7.1—

> not to mislead or deceive can only be met if a full description of any relationships the firm may have used in marketing its services is provided to all prospective clients as to whom the lawyer reasonably believes the relationship may be relevant, and to all present clients to whom the lawyer reasonably believes the relationship may be relevant if at any time any of those relationships changes.[34]

The mere fact that ABA Formal Opinion 94-388 announced that a particular term is inherently misleading does not mean that it is misleading. Saying that something is so does not make it so. In the past, the Supreme Court, on First Amendment grounds, has not been persuaded that something is "inherently misleading" simply because a state supreme court or a bar group has made that pronouncement.[35] Consequently, we should expect that the regulatory authorities will have the burden to prove why, in a particular context, the use of certain terms is misleading.

Nonetheless, even if the law does not require a law firm to respect the views expressed in ABA Formal Opinion 94-388, a law firm can still choose to follow it and therefore to perhaps avoid a later question as to whether a term should not have been used, or a qualifying phrase should have been added.

Furthermore, the ABA Formal Opinion is instructive in warning law firms that proclaimed relationships between law firms should not mislead the client as to the resources available to a firm (or network of firms).[36] If a law firm does not have the right to draw on the resources of a larger firm or a firm in a distant city, it should not state or imply that it can do so. Some firms

---

[32]ABA Formal Opinion 94-388 (Dec. 5, 1994), at 3.

[33]ABA Formal Opinion 94-388 (Dec. 5, 1994), at 3 (emphasis added).

[34]ABA Formal Opinion 94-388 (Dec. 5, 1994), at 3 to 4.

[35]*See Bates v. State Bar of Arizona*, 433 U.S. 350, 372–73, 97 S.Ct. 2691, 2703–04, 53 L.Ed.2d 810 (1977); *In re R.M.J.*, 455 U.S. 191, 102 S.Ct. 929, 71 L.Ed.2d 64 (1982); *Peel v. Attorney*

Registration and Disciplinary Commission of Illinois, 496 U.S. 91, 110 S.Ct. 2281, 110 L.Ed.2d 83 (1990). *See also* Thomas D. Morgan, *The Evolving Concept of Professional Responsibility*, 90 HARV. L. REV. 702, 741 (1977).

[36]A useful article on these issues is, Thomas D. Morgan, *Conflicts of Interest and the New Forms of Professional Associations*, 39 S. TEX. L. REV. 215 (1998).

now appear to license their names to other firms. If several law firms, by using the same name, hold themselves out to the public as one law firm, but they are not the same firm, that certainly does appear to be misleading under Rule 7.1, as well as Rule 7.5(d).[37]

Finally, it is useful to recognize that there are risks when law firms affiliate with each other. That does not mean that firms should not affiliate, but it does mean that they should act with their eyes wide open. When law firms tout their special relationships[38] with other law firms, those relationships may serve, in some fact scenarios, to impute conflicts of interest[39] from one firm to another. As Professor Morgan has advised:

> As the number and variety of non-traditional organizations expands, the challenge for the courts will be to keep their focus on the issues of loyalty and confidentiality, rather than trying to decide when lawyers have formed a "firm," however that might generally be defined. If court decisions and ethics committee opinions find imputed conflicts only in concrete applications of forms of organization that materially implicate loyalty and confidentiality in actual cases, ethical principles will tend to reinforce, rather than condemn, the profession's flexible growth and development.[40]

§ 7.1-3(e) Law Firm Web sites

ABA Formal Opinion 10-457[41] (focused its attention on law firm Web sites. A law firm's Web site may include biographical information about firm lawyers, and may describe the firm's areas of practice. The Web site may also provide legal information that is general in nature if it warns site visitors not to rely on it as legal advice).

---

[37]Rule 7.5(d) provides that lawyers "may state or imply that they practice law in a partnership or other organization only when that is the fact."

In *Gosselin v. Webb*, 242 F.3d 412 (1st Cir.2001), a group of lawyers shared office space but were not partners. The District Court granted summary judgment for the lawyers, holding that they could not be vicariously liable for each other's conduct. However, the First Circuit reversed. The lawyers practiced under a common trade name and the negligent lawyer represented that he was "with" a firm. Those kinds of holding out as a partnership could be sufficient to make the lawyers vicariously liable for each other's acts. The factual issues as to whether the client's attorney was held out as a partner in the purported "law firm" precluded summary judgment for other lawyers practicing under the same trade name.

[38]**Division of Fees.** These relationships may include financial relationships. Different law firms should be aware of the requirement in Rule 1.5(e) regarding the division of fees among lawyers in different law firms.

[39]**Conflicts of Interest.** Rule 1.10, imputing conflicts, applies to lawyers "associated in a firm. . . ."

[40]Thomas D. Morgan, *Conflicts of Interest and the New Forms of Professional Associations*, 39 S. TEX. L. REV. 215, 243 (1998).

[41]ABA Formal Opinion 10-457 (Aug. 5, 2010).

The ABA advised that issues can arise under ABA Model Rule 1.18 when visitors respond to a Web site's invitation to contact the firm about legal advice or representation.[42] Rule 1.18, Comment 2, recognizes that a "unilateral" communication to a lawyer "without any reasonable expectation that the lawyer is willing to discuss the possibility of forming a client-lawyer relationship" does not make someone a prospective client. However, if a Web site *invites* a visitor to submit confidential information about a proposed representation, the submission is likely be entitled to all Rule 1.18 protections, including the requirement of timely screening all lawyers who received the confidential information. To avoid such consequences, a firm must use warnings or disclaimers on the site that are "reasonably understandable" and "conspicuously placed to assure that the reader is likely to see [the disclaimers] before proceeding."[43]

---

[42]*See Schiller v. City of New York*, 245 F.R.D. 112, 116-17 (S.D.N.Y. 2007). The N.Y. Civil Liberties Union sent questionnaires to protestors arrested during a national political convention seeking information about alleged police misconduct. The NYCLU transmitted a questionnaire through an e-mail list that it maintains, and it also made the form available on its Web site and at its offices. The court held that the attorney-client privilege did not protect these responses from discovery, absent evidence that persons who completed questionnaires believed at that time that they seeking legal representation by the organization. In addition, any such belief would have been unreasonable because the form said nothing about such representation.

[43]*E.g.*, California Bar Committee on Professional Responsibility, Opinion 2005-168, 2005 WL 3068090 *4 (2005), advising that a disclaimer stating that "confidential relationship" would not be formed is not enough to waive confidentiality, because it confused not forming client-lawyer relationship with agreeing to keep communications confidential. A lawyer can owe a duty of confidentiality to a *prospective* client who consults the lawyer in confidence for the purpose of retaining the lawyer. Thus, even though a lawyer-client relationship did not arise from a prospective client's consultation with Law Firm that does not prevent Law Firm from taking on a duty of confidentiality to the prospective client. However, if "Law Firm written its agreement with Wife with a plain-language reference that her submission would lack confidentiality, then that would have defeated a reasonable expectation of confidentiality." 2005 WL 3068090 *4.

Barton v. U.S. Dist. Court for Central Dist. of Cal., 410 F.3d 1104, 1110 (9th Cir. 2005), holding that a disclaimer at the bottom of the law firm's online questionnaire regarding antidepressant drug (it stated that the questionnaire did not constitute a request for legal advice and did not form an attorney-client relationship) did not act as a waiver of confidentiality. Hence, individuals who completed questionnaire were entitled to writ of mandamus preventing disclosure of questionnaire. Communications by *prospective* clients are covered by the attorney-client privilege whether or not the prospective client retained the lawyer. "The text in the checked box to which the court referred is potentially confusing to clients (as their ambiguous responses suggest) and the law firm should have spoken clearly to the laymen to whom its Web site was addressed about what commitments it

§ 7.1–4 STATING OR IMPLYING AN ABILITY TO ACHIEVE RESULTS BY MEANS THAT VIOLATE THE LAW

The 1983 version of Rule 7.1 contained a statement in text that it is false or misleading for a lawyer to state or imply "that the lawyer can achieve results by means that violate the Rules of Professional Conduct or other law. . . . "[1] That statement is no longer there, but its absence does not mean that the ABA Model Rules now approve such conduct. If a lawyer truthfully stated that he or she had such an intention, that would violate the norms of Rule 8.4 or other law. Thus, the drafters of the 1983 Rules sought to prohibit any statements that expressly or through suggestion implied that the lawyer would act contrary to the law on behalf of the client.

The drafters of the 2002 Rules believed that this prohibition should be part of the general provision on misconduct, Rule 8.4, and not just in the advertising rules. Therefore, they moved this language to Rule 8.4(e) in a provision where the Model Rules already prohibited a lawyer from stating or implying "an ability to influence improperly a government agency or official." Given the related nature of these two types of improper conduct, it makes sense to prohibit all such statements and inferences regardless of whether they arise in the context of a lawyer communication in furtherance of obtaining a client or generally in the context of an ongoing representation.

---

did and did not make."

[Section 7.1–4]

[1]1983 Model Rule 7.1(b).

CHAPTER 7.2
ADVERTISING

RULE 7.2: ADVERTISING

(a) Subject to the requirements of Rules 7.1 and 7.3, a lawyer may advertise services through written, recorded or electronic communication, including public media.

(b) A lawyer shall not give anything of value to a person for recommending the lawyer's services except that a lawyer may

(1) pay the reasonable costs of advertisements or communications permitted by this Rule;

(2) pay the usual charges of a legal service plan or a not-for-profit or qualified lawyer referral service. A qualified lawyer referral service is a lawyer referral service that has been approved by an appropriate regulatory authority;

(3) pay for a law practice in accordance with Rule 1.17; and

(4) refer clients to another lawyer or a nonlawyer professional pursuant to an agreement not otherwise prohibited under these Rules that provides for the other person to refer clients or customers to the lawyer, if

(i) the reciprocal referral agreement is not exclusive, and

(ii) the client is informed of the existence and nature of the agreement.

(c) Any communication made pursuant to this rule shall include the name and office address of at least one lawyer or law firm responsible for its content.

Comment

[1] To assist the public in obtaining legal services, lawyers should be allowed to make known their services not only through reputation but also through organized information campaigns in the form of advertising. Advertising involves an active quest for clients, con-

trary to the tradition that a lawyer should not seek clientele. However, the public's need to know about legal services can be fulfilled in part through advertising. This need is particularly acute in the case of persons of moderate means who have not made extensive use of legal services. The interest in expanding public information about legal services ought to prevail over considerations of tradition. Nevertheless, advertising by lawyers entails the risk of practices that are misleading or overreaching.

[2] This Rule permits public dissemination of information concerning a lawyer's name or firm name, address and telephone number; the kinds of services the lawyer will undertake; the basis on which the lawyer's fees are determined, including prices for specific services and payment and credit arrangements; a lawyer's foreign language ability; names of references and, with their consent, names of clients regularly represented; and other information that might invite the attention of those seeking legal assistance.

[3] Questions of effectiveness and taste in advertising are matters of speculation and subjective judgment. Some jurisdictions have had extensive prohibitions against television advertising, against advertising going beyond specified facts about a lawyer, or against "undignified" advertising. Television is now one of the most powerful media for getting information to the public, particularly persons of low and moderate income; prohibiting television advertising, therefore, would impede the flow of information about legal services to many sectors of the public. Limiting the information that may be advertised has a similar effect and assumes that the bar can accurately forecast the kind of information that the public would regard as relevant. Similarly, electronic media, such as the Internet, can be an important source of information about legal services, and lawful communication by electronic mail is permitted by this Rule. But see Rule 7.3(a) for the prohibition against the solicitation of a prospective client through a real-time electronic exchange that is not initiated by the prospective client.

[4] Neither this Rule nor Rule 7.3 prohibits communications authorized by law, such as notice to members of a class in class action litigation.

Paying Others to Recommend a Lawyer

[5] Lawyers are not permitted to pay others for channeling professional work. Paragraph (b)(1), however, allows a lawyer to pay for advertising and communications permitted by this Rule, including the costs of print directory listings, on-line directory listings, newspaper ads, television and radio airtime, domain-name registrations, sponsorship fees, banner ads, and group advertising. A lawyer may compensate employees, agents and vendors who are engaged to provide marketing or client-development services, such as publicists, public-relations personnel, business-development staff and website designers. See Rule 5.3 for the duties of lawyers and law firms with respect to the conduct of nonlawyers who prepare marketing materials for them.

[6] A lawyer may pay the usual charges of a legal service plan or a not-for-profit or qualified lawyer referral service. A legal service plan is a prepaid or group legal service plan or a similar delivery

system that assists prospective clients to secure legal representation. A lawyer referral service, on the other hand, is any organization that holds itself out to the public as a lawyer referral service. Such referral services are understood by laypersons to be consumer-oriented organizations that provide unbiased referrals to lawyers with appropriate experience in the subject matter of the representation and afford other client protections, such as complaint procedures or malpractice insurance requirements. Consequently, this Rule only permits a lawyer to pay the usual charges of a not-for-profit or qualified lawyer referral service. A qualified lawyer referral service is one that is approved by an appropriate regulatory authority as affording adequate protections for prospective clients. See, e.g., the American Bar Association's Model Supreme Court Rules Governing Lawyer Referral Services and Model Lawyer Referral and Information Service Quality Assurance Act (requiring that organizations that are identified as lawyer referral services (i) permit the participation of all lawyers who are licensed and eligible to practice in the jurisdiction and who meet reasonable objective eligibility requirements as may be established by the referral service for the protection of prospective clients; (ii) require each participating lawyer to carry reasonably adequate malpractice insurance; (iii) act reasonably to assess client satisfaction and address client complaints; and (iv) do not refer prospective clients to lawyers who own, operate or are employed by the referral service.)

[7] A lawyer who accepts assignments or referrals from a legal service plan or referrals from a lawyer referral service must act reasonably to assure that the activities of the plan or service are compatible with the lawyer's professional obligations. See Rule 5.3. Legal service plans and lawyer referral services may communicate with prospective clients, but such communication must be in conformity with these Rules. Thus, advertising must not be false or misleading, as would be the case if the communications of a group advertising program or a group legal services plan would mislead prospective clients to think that it was a lawyer referral service sponsored by a state agency or bar association. Nor could the lawyer allow in-person, telephonic, or real-time contacts that would violate Rule 7.3.

[8] A lawyer also may agree to refer clients to another lawyer or a nonlawyer professional, in return for the undertaking of that person to refer clients or customers to the lawyer. Such reciprocal referral arrangements must not interfere with the lawyer's professional judgment as to making referrals or as to providing substantive legal services. See Rules 2.1 and 5.4(c). Except as provided in Rule 1.5(e), a lawyer who receives referrals from a lawyer or nonlawyer professional must not pay anything solely for the referral, but the lawyer does not violate paragraph (b) of this Rule by agreeing to refer clients to the other lawyer or nonlawyer professional, so long as the reciprocal referral agreement is not exclusive and the client is informed of the referral agreement. Conflicts of interest created by such arrangements are governed by Rule 1.7. Reciprocal referral agreements should not be of indefinite duration and should be reviewed periodically to determine whether they comply with these

Rules. This Rule does not restrict referrals or divisions of revenues or net income among lawyers within firms comprised of multiple entities.

Authors' 1983 Model Rules Comparison

The ABA House of Delegates has modified Rule 7.2 several times since its original adoption in 1983. The ABA amended this Rule in 1989 to conform to the holding in *Shapero v. Kentucky Bar Association*, 486 U.S. 466, 108 S.Ct. 1916, 100 L.Ed.2d 475 (1988) and in 1990 to reflect the addition of Model Rule 1.17 on the sale of a law practice.[1] The drafters of the 2002 Model Rules also made several significant changes to Rule 7.2.

The 1983 version of Rule 7.2(a) authorized advertising through public media and then listed several types of public media: "a telephone directory, legal directory, newspaper, or other periodical, outdoor advertising, radio or television, or through written or recorded communication. . . ." The drafters of the 2002 Rules believed that the list of public media was better suited for a Comment and not the text given that new forms of public media may force future amendments of the text.

The 1983 Rule 7.2 contained a section (b), which required that lawyers keep a copy of all advertisements and communications "for two years after its last dissemination along with a record of when and where it was used. . . ." The drafters of the 2002 Rules believed that this recordkeeping requirement was too burdensome and such records were rarely used in disciplinary proceedings and therefore they recommended that the House of Delegates delete this provision. The 2002 Rule 7.2 contains no such requirement.

The 1983 Rule 7.2(c) was renumbered as 7.2(b) in 2002. The drafters of the 2002 Model Rules modified 7.2(b)(2) by changing a reference to a not-for-profit lawyer referral service to a qualified lawyer referral service and then defining it. They also removed a reference to a legal services organization and changed it to legal services plan. The purpose of these changes was to reflect changes in the manner in which the ABA and states regulate such referral service and plans.

The drafters of the 2002 Rules also renumbered Rule 7.2(d) as 7.2(c), and they added a requirement that communications contain the office address of the advertising lawyer or law firm. They also added to the disclosure requirement that the communication may include the name of a lawyer or the law firm. Most state bar authorities had interpreted the old rule as allowing law firms to include their firm name in lieu of one lawyer's name. However, this change in language makes this state bar interpretive practice within the specific language of the Rule.

The drafters of the 2002 Rules did not modify Comments 1, 2, and 4. Comment 5 from the 1983 Rules dealing with the two year record

---

[Rule 7.2]

[1]For a complete review of these changes to Model Rule 7.2, see A Legislative History: The Development of the ABA Model Rules of Professional Conduct, 1982–1998 (ABA 1999) at 289.

keeping requirement was deleted in 2002 and Comment 6 was renumbered as Comment 5.

In Comment 3, the drafters added the last two lines to address the issue of electronic media and the possibility that real time contact may constitute prohibited solicitation under Rule 7.3.

In Comment 5, the drafters deleted most of the 1983 language and rewrote the manner in which lawyers may pay others to recommend clients to the lawyer. Comment 5 deals mostly with payments to third parties for arranging public media advertising.

In new Comment 6, the drafters define legal service plans and qualified lawyer referral services and discuss how lawyers may interact with such organizations.

In new Comment 7, the drafters of the 2002 Rules examine how the advertising rules apply to regulate the conduct of legal service plans and qualified lawyer referral service plans.

Post February 2002 Amendment:

In August 2002, the ABA House of Delegates added new subsection (b)(4) and new Comment 8 to Rule 7.2. These changes implemented a detailed provision authorizing lawyers to enter into nonexclusive reciprocal referral agreements with another lawyer or another nonlawyer professional. The ABA made this change to legitimate informal referral arrangements that have existed in the past between lawyers and others. This change was patterned on the approach adopted by New York to allow lawyers and nonlawyers to cooperate in the delivery of legal services without sharing legal fees or threatening the independence of the lawyers.

Model Code Comparison

[1] With regard to paragraph (a), DR 2-101(B) provided that a lawyer "may publish or broadcast, subject to DR 2-103, . . . in print media . . . or television or radio. . . ."

[2] With regard to paragraph (b), DR 2-101(D) provided that if the advertisement is "communicated to the public over television or radio, . . . a recording of the actual transmission shall be retained by the lawyer."

[3] With regard to paragraph (c), DR 2-103(B) provided that a lawyer "shall not compensate or give anything of value to a person or organization to recommend or secure his employment . . . except that he may pay the usual and reasonable fees or dues charged by any of the organizations listed in DR 2-103(D)." (DR 2-103(D) referred to legal aid and other legal services organizations.) DR 2-101(I) provided that a lawyer "shall not compensate or give anything of value to representatives of the press, radio, television, or other communication medium in anticipation of or in return for professional publicity in a news item."

[4] There was no counterpart to paragraph (d) in the Model Code.

Model Rules.[12] If the referrals came from an independent contractor who is a lawyer, any sharing of legal fees would need to meet the requirements of Rule 1.5(e).

§ 7.2–3(c) Legal Services Organizations and Plans

In order to appreciate the relative simplicity of the Model Rules' approach to legal service organizations, one should consider the position that the Model Code had embraced. The Code, in precise and elaborate detail, defined the types of legal service organizations from which a lawyer may accept a recommendation or client referral. The Code allowed a lawyer to cooperate with, and accept referrals from, certain groups[13]—public defender, military legal assistance, and bar association referral services—if the organization that was recommending or referring exerted no influence and did not interfere with the lawyer's exercise of independent professional judgment on behalf of a client.[14]

The Model Code also extensively regulated other legal services organizations such as employee or union legal benefits plans.[15] This set of complicated rules drew various distinctions involving for-profit and not-for-profit plans; open and closed plans; plans where the organization "bears ultimate liability of its member" (*i.e.*, a typical insurance plan where the insurer bears liability and chooses the attorney to defend the insured); and plans that a lawyer has initiated.[16]

The Rules, in contrast to the old regime, do not have such a Byzantine set of commands. The Model Rules simply require a lawyer to guarantee his or her professional independence.[17] In addition, there are a few general restrictions regarding solicitation.[18]

Even these specific restrictions are hardly onerous. A lawyer may participate in a for-profit prepaid legal service plan if the plan allows the lawyer to exercise independent judgment on behalf of the clients, to keep client confidences, and to practice competently. The participating lawyer must ensure that the plan involves neither improper advertising, nor improper solicitation, nor improper fee sharing, and must be in compliance with other applicable law.[19]

The drafters of the 2002 Rules changed a reference from legal services organization to legal services plan. This change was made because the term organization was not completely

---

[12]Rule 7.2, Comment 5 (reminding lawyers to follow Rule 5.3 when nonlawyers prepare marketing materials for lawyers).

[13]DR 2-103(D).

[14]DR 2-103(D).

[15]DR 2-103(D)(4)(a to g).

[16]DR 2-103(D)(4).

[17]Rule 5.4.

[18]Rule 7.3(d).

[19]ABA Formal Opinion 87-355 (Dec. 14, 1987).

accurate.[20] A legal services organization in the new definition section of Rule 1.0 is a legal services provider. Rule 7.2 refers to a plan which funnels cases to outside lawyers. The Comments define a legal services plan as "a prepaid or group legal services plan or a similar delivery system that assists prospective clients to secure legal representation."[21] The drafters also added more guidance to the Comments regarding the obligation of lawyers to make sure that legal services plans do not violate the advertising rules.[22]

With this background in the Rules, ABA Formal Opinion 87-355[23] concludes that the Model Rules should not be read to prevent a lawyer from participating in a for-profit prepaid legal services plan if certain requirements are met, none of which are peculiar to for-profit (as opposed to not-for-profit) plans. The lawyer must preserve her professional independence, protect client confidences, avoid conflicts of interest, and be competent. Then, the Formal Opinion turned to the issue of fee sharing:

> Although the Rules do not expressly address the question of whether a lawyer may participate in a prepaid legal services plan where the plan sponsor retains a portion of the subscriber's payment in excess of the administrative costs of the plan to provide a profit for the plan sponsor, the legislative history of the Rules and the rationale for the provisions of Rule 5.4 support the conclusion that a lawyer may participate in a for-profit prepaid legal service plan. Significantly, the flat prohibition against a lawyer participating in for-profit plans in DR 2-103(D)(4)(a) of the Model Code was not carried into the Model Rules.[24]

This Formal Opinion concluded that there was no improper fee-sharing under Rule 5.4 simply because the plan sponsor keeps as a profit a portion of the monthly payments from the plan. "Nor does it constitute giving anything of value to a person for recommending the lawyer's services in violation of Rule 7.2(c)."[25]

The ABA approved a less subtle form of fee-sharing in ABA

---

[20]Reporter's Explanation of Changes to Model Rule 7.2.

[21]Rule 7.2, Comment 6.

[22]Rule 7.2, Comment 7.

[23]ABA Formal Opinion 87-355 (Dec. 14, 1987).

[24]ABA Formal Opinion 87-355 (Dec. 14, 1987), at p. 6.

Cf. ABA Formal Opinion 88-356 (Dec. 16, 1988), at 12, concluding that there was no improper sharing of legal fees with a lay person if law firm uses a placement agency to find temporary lawyers, and when that agency charges the law firm for its services

(locating, recruiting, screening, and supplying temporary lawyer with particular credentials), it bases its fee on a percentage of the temporary lawyer's compensation.

[25]ABA Formal Opinion 87-355 (Dec. 14, 1987), at 7. *See also Richards v. SSM Health Care, Inc.*, 311 Ill.App.3d 560, 244 Ill.Dec. 87, 724 N.E.2d 975 (2000). In this case, after the settlement of a medical malpractice suit, the plaintiff's lawyer filed a petition to adjudicate the lawyer's lien, claiming that a fee agreement with a nonprofit lawyer referral service was void and unenforceable. Judge Warren Wolfson, for the appellate court, held

Formal Opinion 93-374,[26] which considered the situation where a non-profit pro bono organization, which refers a case to a lawyer, also wants the lawyer to turn over to it all or some of the court-awarded legal fees. The Opinion concluded that the lawyer (whether an employee of the organization or a member of a law firm) may agree in advance or later to share some or all of the court-awarded fees with the non-profit organization. Although the Opinion acknowledged that Rules 5.4(a) and 7.2(c) appear to apply "literally" to prohibit the turnover of fees, the Opinion said that they should not be interpreted that way, because application of these Rules would not further the purposes behind them. However, lawyers who enter into such agreements should disclose the arrangement to their clients, because of the possibility of improper lay interference.[27]

There is case law that rejects this conclusion and forbids fee-sharing with nonprofit legal aid groups.[28] But most courts, usually without discussing the matter, have simply awarded attorneys' fees to nonprofit legal service organizations for the work that staff lawyers have performed.[29]

§ 7.2–3(d) Qualified Lawyer Referral Services

The 1983 version of Rule 7.2 allowed the lawyer to pay "the usual charges of a not-for-profit lawyer referral service or legal services organization."[30] Obviously, if the organization paid advertising costs and sought reimbursement from the lawyer, the

---

that: first, the referral by a nonprofit lawyer referral service is not a lawyer-to-lawyer referral governed by the Illinois Rule of Professional Conduct requiring the referring counsel to assume legal responsibility for the referred counsel's performance of services, nor are these fee arrangements between such services and the referred attorney a prohibited sharing of fees with a nonlawyer. Second, the court went on to hold that public policy considerations did not bar the referral service from charging the lawyer 25% of the lawyer's contingency fee.

[26] ABA Formal Opinion 93-374 (June 7, 1993).

[27] The dissent to ABA Formal Opinion 93-374 (June 7, 1993) pointed out that the majority's interpretation of the Rules was contrary to their plain meaning.

[28] *American Civil Liberties Union / Eastern Missouri Fund v. Miller*, 803 S.W.2d 592 (Mo.1991), *cert. denied*, 500 U.S. 943, 111 S.Ct. 2239, 114 L.Ed.2d 481 (1991), which held that Missouri's Rule 5.4(a) prohibited a former ACLU staff attorney from complying with his employment contract, which required him to turn over court-awarded fees. After that decision, the ACLU won a court order permanently enjoining Missouri from enforcing its ethical rules so as to invalidate the fee turn-over provision in the ACLU employment contract. *Susman v. Missouri, No. 91-4429-CC-C-5 (W.D. Mo., June 1, 1992).*

[29] *See, e.g., Oldham v. Ehrlich*, 617 F.2d 163, 165 n. 3, 168–69 (8th Cir.1980); *New York State Association for Retarded Children, Inc. v. Carey*, 711 F.2d 1136, 1139, 1154 (2d Cir. 1983); *McLean v. Arkansas Board of Education*, 723 F.2d 45, 47 (8th Cir. 1983).

[30] 1983 Model Rule 7.2(c)(2). *See also* 1983 Model Rule 7.2, Comment 6:

lawyer could pay that reimbursement.[31] That did not appear to be different than the lawyer paying the costs of her own advertising. However, there would be no need to make that statement in Rule 7.2(c)(2) because it is already covered in Rule 7.2(c)(1), allowing the lawyer to pay the reasonable costs of advertising. Moreover, Rule 7.2(c)(2) does not refer to advertising but to "charges."

The negative implication of this 1983 subsection (2) suggested that the lawyer may not pay "the usual charges" of a *for-profit* lawyer referral program, but she may pay the "not-for-profit" lawyer referral service some money for sending cases to her. If that is what the Rule meant, one wonders what policy the distinction is supposed to further.

Moreover, if the lawyer paid a not-for-profit lawyer referral service a fee in order to receive business, that sounds like paying a referral fee ("sharing fees") with a lay person or lay organization, which is generally forbidden under Rule 5.4, whether or not the organization is for-profit or not-for-profit.[32] Although Rule 5.4, regarding fee sharing with nonlawyers has various exceptions, none of them treat for-profit legal referral or prepaid legal service plans any differently than not-for-profit referral plans.[33] In fact, Rule 5.4, in general, allows a lawyer to practice law in the form of a for-profit organization as long as nonlawyers have no right to control the professional judgment of the lawyer.[34]

This confusion that existed in the 1983 Model Rules has been clarified by the ABA in two respects. First, the ABA has completed a project relating to referral programs and this has produced to model documents. The Model Supreme Court Rules Governing Lawyer Referral and Informational Services and the Model Lawyer Referral and Information Quality Assurance Act provide guidance regarding the not-for-profit and for-profit legal referral services.[35] Second, the drafters of the 2002 Rules modified the language in the text of Rule 7.2 to add "qualified lawyer referral plans." Therefore, the text and Comment to Rule 7.2 now

---

"a lawyer may participate in not-for-profit legal services referral programs and pay the usual fees charged by such programs."

[31]ABA Formal Opinion 87-355 (Dec. 14, 1987), at 5 n. 4: "The Committee notes that it is permissible for a plan sponsor to pay to advertise legal services provided under its auspices as long as the advertisement is truthful. Rule 7.2(c)."

[32]Rule 5.4(a): "A lawyer or law firm shall not share fees with a nonlawyer, except that. . . ."

[33]Rule 5.4(d) states that the lawyer may not "practice law in the form of a professional corporation or association authorized to practice law for profit" if various conditions exist, such as the fact that the nonlawyer does not direct or control the professional judgment of the lawyer. This subsection is inapplicable because lawyer referral services or prepaid legal service plans do not "practice law."

[34]*See* Rule 5.4(d)(1), (2), & (3), which lists the various exceptions.

[35]*See* American Bar Association,

explicitly covers both not-for-profit and qualified lawyer referral plans.

The Comments explain the ABA's position on lawyer affiliations and payments to referral services plans:

A lawyer referral service . . . is any organization that holds itself out to the public as a lawyer referral service. Such referral services are understood by laypersons to be consumer-oriented organizations that provide unbiased referrals to lawyers with appropriate experience in the subject matter of the representation and afford other client protections, such as complaint procedures or malpractice insurance requirements. Consequently, this Rule only permits a lawyer to pay the usual charges of a not-for-profit or qualified lawyer referral service. A qualified lawyer referral service is one that is approved by an appropriate regulatory authority as affording adequate protections for prospective clients.[36]

The current position taken by the Model Rules is that unless the referral program is not-for-profit or a qualified plan approved by the appropriate body, a lawyer may not become involved in paying for such an entity to refer cases to the lawyer.[37]

§ 7.2–3(e) Sale of a Law Practice

In 1990, the ABA House of Delegates adopted Rule 1.17 on the sale of a law practice. Once the ABA authorized lawyers to buy a law practice from another lawyer or legal representative, this opened the door for someone to claim that the purchase of a law practice funneled funds to someone who was referring clients to the lawyer who invested in the practice. And, such an exchange of funds could possibly violate Rule 5.4 as well as 7.2. Thus, Rule 7.2(b)(3) authorizes lawyers to pay for a law practice under the requirements set forth in Rule 1.17.

§ 7.2–3(f) Reciprocal Referral Agreements

The prohibition against giving anything of value to a person or organization in exchange for referring clients to the lawyer is applied broadly to prevent a lawyer from paying lawyers and nonlawyers who refers clients to the lawyer. Several other Model Rules may also apply to this situation. If the payment to another lawyer is construed as a legal fee, then the firm must meet the requirements of Rule 1.5(e), dealing with the sharing of legal fees with a lawyer not in the same firm. If the payment is viewed as directed to a nonlawyer, this rule reaffirms Rule 5.4(a)'s prohibition against sharing legal fees with a nonlawyer.

Model Supreme Court Rules Governing Lawyer Referral and Informational Services (1993); Model Lawyer Referral and Information Quality Assurance Act (1993).

[36]*See* Rule 7.2, Comment 6.

[37]Note, even if the plan is not-for-profit or one qualified under the rules of the appropriate agency, the lawyer needs to make sure that the referral program is not violating one of the Model Rules. *See* Rule 7.2, Comment 7.

In August 2002, the ABA House of Delegate considered and adopted a new subsection to Rule 7.2(b) in order to permit on a limited basis reciprocal referral arrangements. This provision is based upon modifications that were adopted in New York at the time the MDP issue was under debate. New York commissioned a Report on multidisciplinary practice: the final document embraced cooperative side-by-side arrangements between lawyers and nonlawyers, but it expressly rejected nonlawyer involvement in the practice of law.[38] One feature of such cooperation is to permit professionals to recommend and refer their clients to other professionals. Rule 7.2(b) provides such an exception to the prohibition on referral arrangements.

Under Rule 7.2(b)(4), a lawyer may enter into a formal reciprocal referral agreement with another lawyer or a nonlawyer professional.[39] Lawyers who enter into such agreements must meet three requirements. The agreement may not be exclusive, the clients need to be "informed of the existence and nature of the agreement," and such agreements should not be of indefinite duration.[40] Of course, such agreements may only involve exchange of clients and/or customers. Lawyers must not include any exchange of fees or payments for referrals, unless the referral agreement is with a lawyer and that arrangement meets Rule 1.5(e).[41]

Rule 7.2(b)(4) does not explain how a lawyer should interpret the nonexclusive requirement for these reciprocal referral agreements. One could interpret this to mean that lawyers must have two of such agreements in place before they can begin to refer clients to another entity. Or one could view this requirement as just prohibiting lawyers from sending all clients to one external party in exchange for that party sending all business to the lawyer. The underlying policy for nonexclusivity is that lawyers should exercise independent judgment before offering a client advice on whether to see another party, whether that party is a lawyer or a nonlawyer. If a better choice exists for the client, the lawyer should be bound by Rule 2.1 to offer candid advice and by Rule 1.7 to limit conflicts of interest that could taint the

---

[38]*See* Sonia E. Miller, Rules *for MDPs, Ancillary Business Often Murky*, NEW YORK L.J. (Oct. 28, 2002) at S9 (discussing the McCrate Report, PRESERVING THE CORE VALUES OF THE AMERICAN LEGAL PROFESSION: THE PLACE OF MULTIDISCIPLINARY PRACTICE IN THE LAW GOVERNING LAWYERS (May 2000)).

[39]The text and commentary to this Rule do not define "nonlawyer professional."

[40]Rule 7.2(b)(4)(i), (ii), Comment 8. The limit on the duration is included only in Comment 8.

[41]Of course, the Rule does not apply to lawyers practicing in different divisions of the same firm. *See* Rule 7.2, Comment 8.

lawyer's judgment. An exclusive agreement could be viewed to violate this requirement of independent judgment.[42]

The adoption of Rule 7.2(b)(4) makes sense for several reasons. Lawyers are often in a unique position to examine a client's entire situation and either voluntarily or by client request are asked to recommend other lawyers or nonlawyer professionals. Such referrals have often led to informal situations where the two parties often send clients to each other. This Rule now provides specific guidance as to how lawyers should structure such arrangements. It also permits a lawyer to develop a network of third party professionals who will deliver integrated services to clients. Ultimately, this Rule does facilitate the development of side-by-side MDP arrangements.

Payments from Nonlawyer Professionals to Lawyers as Compensation for Client Referrals. Rule 5.4(a) prohibits a lawyer from paying a nonlawyer for a client referral. But may a lawyer receive compensation from a nonlawyer professional for sending a law client to the nonlawyer? Since the late 1970's, lawyers in at least 32 states and in several county and city bar associations have asked for ethics opinions asking whether lawyers may ethically receive referral fees for sending clients to nonlawyer professionals for services or products.[43]

Some of these referrals involve investments advisers, others involve insurance agents, and still others involve physicians, banks, loan brokers, real estate agents, and accountants.[44] The state ethics opinions have closely divided as to whether to permit or prohibit such practices. In fact, one state, New Hampshire, deadlocked on the issue and unable to give a definite answer to the question.[45] However, even many of those bar authorities who have approved these arrangements express serious concern about them and, in some cases, impose a heavy burden on the recipient attorney to justify the arrangement.[46]

Thus far, the ABA has refused to decide whether such arrangements are permissible under the Rules; instead, they have left it up to the states.[47] Although one could imagine a detailed disclosure and consent process with the client whose referral

---

[42]See Rule 7.2, Comment 8 (citing to Rule 2.1 and 5.4(c)).

[43]See John S. Dzienkowski & Robert J. Peroni, *Conflicts of Interest in Lawyer Referral Arrangements with Nonlawyer Professionals*, 21 GEORGETOWN J. LEGAL ETHICS 197 (2008) (citing all of the opinions).

[44]See *Louisiana State Bar Ass'n v. Drury*, 455 So. 2d 1387 (La. 1984), cert. denied, 470 U.S. 1004, 105 S. Ct.

1358, 84 L. Ed. 2d 379 (1985) (lawyer suspended for receiving a referral fee from a physician in a personal injury case); KENTUCKY BAR ASS'N ETHICS OPINION No. KBA E-390 (July 1996).

[45]21 GEORGETOWN J. LEGAL ETHICS, at 208–09.

[46]21 GEORGETOWN J. LEGAL ETHICS, at 209–212.

[47]See Can a Lawyer Accept Referral Fees or Commissions from a Non-

generates the fee from the nonlawyer professional, the benefit to the client seems relatively small and the conflict of interest are potentially troubling. Thus, careful lawyers should not participate in such arrangements because such payments will tend to complicate any other ethics or malpractice issues that arise in representing the client.[48]

§ 7.2–4 RULE 7.2(d)—ENFORCEMENT CONCERNS

§ 7.2–4(a) Identification of Lawyers or Law Firms Responsible for the Communication

The 1983 Model Rule 7.3(c) stated that all communications made by a lawyer needed to include the name of one lawyer responsible for its content in the communication. Two possible reasons existed for such a requirement. First, bar authorities wanted one person in a firm to take responsibility for complying with the advertising rules. Firms may delegate such work to nonlawyers or to outside advertising agencies and later try to deflect the blame of noncompliance to such third party entities. By requiring the name of one lawyer who is responsible for its content, the Rule forces one lawyer to more carefully monitor the communication or advertisement. Second, the requirement gives prospective clients information about the advertisement. Prospective clients see that the communication is coming from a lawyer or law firm and they can proceed to contact one specific lawyer at a firm.

The drafters of the 2002 Rules modified this provision in two ways. They added the notion that the advertisement or communication may have the name of the law firm instead of one lawyer responsible for its context. Obviously, law firms act through lawyers; but the drafters believed that it was sufficient for the bar authorities to see that the communication came from one law firm.[1] These authorities can use their power to demand that lawyers answer questions relating to discipline to gain access to the lawyers responsible for its content.[2] The drafters also added a requirement that the advertisement or communication include the address of the law firm. The drafters believed that

---

lawyer?, Your ABA: Eye on Ethics (June 2007) (*available at* http://www.abanet.org/media/youraba/200706/article11.html) (online newsletter) ("In view of the disparity of opinions on this topic, lawyers should carefully check their local rules of professional conduct and ethics opinions before agreeing to accept a referral fee or a commission from a non-lawyer.").

[48] The authors of the Georgetown Journal article ask a series of ques-

tions about referral fees in order to characterize the true nature of the transaction and its implications on the lawyer's competence, confidentiality, and loyalty. *See* 21 GEORGETOWN J. LEGAL ETHICS, at 1

[Section 7.2–4]

[1] Reporter's Explanation of Changes to Model Rule 7.2.

[2] *See* Rule 8.1(b).

prospective clients should know where a law firm is located in this era of multijurisdictional advertising, media that cross geographic boundaries, and lawyers who practice in locations where they do not maintain an office.[3]

§ 7.2–4(b) Record Keeping

The Model Code and the 1983 Model Rules required that lawyers retain a copy of all advertisements and communication.[4] The 1983 Rules required that the copy or recording be kept for two years after its last dissemination.[5] The Code had no time limit.[6] The obvious purpose of this provision was to aid in the enforcement of the prohibition against misleading speech.[7] The evidentiary record permits the disciplinary authorities to investigate more easily if someone later makes a claim that the advertisement was misleading or otherwise violated a Rule. This record-keeping burden protected the lawyer and third parties in case a subsequent claim alleged that a televised commercial or radio announcement or other advertisement was misleading. The 1983 Model Rules requirement that lawyers also keep a record or when and where an advertisement or communication was used allowed the authorities to determine which specific cases and clients resulted from the advertisement in question.

Comment 5 to the 1983 Model Rules provided that lawyers did not need to obtain prior approval from the disciplinary authorities before using an advertisement. That would be invalid under the First Amendment as prior restraint, but the lawyer had to keep a copy.[8]

The drafters of the 2002 Model Rules eliminated the record keeping requirement of Rule 7.2(b) and Comment 5 because they felt that the benefit of keeping the advertisements was small and the burden to the law firm was too significant.[9] This view was consistent with a position taken by the ABA Commission on Responsibility in Client Development. The drafters noted that such records rarely were involved in helping the bar authorities

---

[3]*See* Reporter's Explanation of Changes to Model Rule 7.2.

[4]1983 Model Rule 7.2(b). DR 2-101(D).

[5]1983 Model Rule 7.2(b).

[6]DR 2-101(D) (". . . shall be retained. . . .").

[7]1983 Model Rule 7.2, Comment 5.

[8]At least one state, Texas, has a requirement that lawyers provide the bar authorities with a copy of all advertisements simultaneously when they are distributed to the public for the first time. *See* Texas Disciplinary Rule 7.07 ("Filing Requirements for Public Advertisements and Written Solicitations"). This Rule also contains a procedure for lawyers to obtain an advisory opinion in advance of the distribution of the advertisement.

[9]Reporter's Explanation of Changes to Model Rule 7.2.

to pursue disciplinary charges against a lawyer.[10] Of course, one would expect that the states may vary significantly on this record keeping requirement.

---

[10] Reporter's Explanation of Changes to Model Rule 7.2.

CHAPTER 7.3

DIRECT CONTACT WITH PROSPECTIVE CLIENTS

RULE 7.3: DIRECT CONTACT WITH PROSPECTIVE CLIENTS

(a) A lawyer shall not by in-person, live telephone or real-time electronic contact solicit professional employment from a prospective client when a significant motive for the lawyer's doing so is the lawyer's pecuniary gain, unless the person contacted:

(1) is a lawyer; or

(2) has a family, close personal, or prior professional relationship with the lawyer.

(b) A lawyer shall not solicit professional employment from a prospective client by written, recorded or electronic communication or by in-person, telephone or real-time electronic contact even when not otherwise prohibited by paragraph (a), if:

(1) the prospective client has made known to the lawyer a desire not to be solicited by the lawyer; or

(2) the solicitation involves coercion, duress or harassment.

(c) Every written, recorded or electronic communication from a lawyer soliciting professional employment from a prospective client known to be in need of legal services in a particular matter shall include the words "Advertising Material" on the outside envelope, if any, and at the beginning and ending of any recorded or electronic communication, unless the recipient of the communication is a person specified in paragraphs (a)(1) or (a)(2).

(d) Notwithstanding the prohibitions in paragraph (a), a lawyer may participate with a prepaid or group legal service plan operated by an organization not owned or

directed by the lawyer that uses in-person or telephone contact to solicit memberships or subscriptions for the plan from persons who are not known to need legal services in a particular matter covered by the plan.

Comment

[1] There is a potential for abuse inherent in direct in-person, live telephone or real-time electronic contact by a lawyer with a prospective client known to need legal services. These forms of contact between a lawyer and a prospective client subject the layperson to the private importuning of the trained advocate in a direct interpersonal encounter. The prospective client, who may already feel overwhelmed by the circumstances giving rise to the need for legal services, may find it difficult fully to evaluate all available alternatives with reasoned judgment and appropriate self-interest in the face of the lawyer's presence and insistence upon being retained immediately. The situation is fraught with the possibility of undue influence, intimidation, and overreaching.

[2] This potential for abuse inherent in direct in-person, live telephone or real-time electronic solicitation of prospective clients justifies its prohibition, particularly since lawyer advertising and written and recorded communication permitted under Rule 7.2 offer alternative means of conveying necessary information to those who may be in need of legal services. Advertising and written and recorded communications which may be mailed or autodialed make it possible for a prospective client to be informed about the need for legal services, and about the qualifications of available lawyers and law firms, without subjecting the prospective client to direct inperson, telephone or real-time electronic persuasion that may overwhelm the client's judgment.

[3] The use of general advertising and written, recorded or electronic communications to transmit information from lawyer to prospective client, rather than direct in-person, live telephone or real-time electronic contact, will help to assure that the information flows cleanly as well as freely. The contents of advertisements and communications permitted under Rule 7.2 can be permanently recorded so that they cannot be disputed and may be shared with others who know the lawyer. This potential for informal review is itself likely to help guard against statements and claims that might constitute false and misleading communications, in violation of Rule 7.1. The contents of direct in-person, live telephone or real-time electronic conversations between a lawyer and a prospective client can be disputed and may not be subject to third-party scrutiny. Consequently, they are much more likely to approach (and occasionally cross) the dividing line between accurate representations and those that are false and misleading.

[4] There is far less likelihood that a lawyer would engage in abusive practices against an individual who is a former client, or with whom the lawyer has a close personal or family relationship, or in situations in which the lawyer is motivated by considerations other than the lawyer's pecuniary gain. Nor is there a serious potential for abuse when the person contacted is a lawyer. Consequently, the general prohibition in Rule 7.3(a) and the

requirements of Rule 7.3(c) are not applicable in those situations. Also, paragraph (a) is not intended to prohibit a lawyer from participating in constitutionally protected activities of public or charitable legal-service organizations or bona fide political, social, civic, fraternal, employee or trade organizations whose purposes include providing or recommending legal services to its members or beneficiaries.

[5] But even permitted forms of solicitation can be abused. Thus, any solicitation which contains information which is false or misleading within the meaning of Rule 7.1, which involves coercion, duress or harassment within the meaning of Rule 7.3(b)(2), or which involves contact with a prospective client who has made known to the lawyer a desire not to be solicited by the lawyer within the meaning of Rule 7.3(b)(1) is prohibited. Moreover, if after sending a letter or other communication to a client as permitted by Rule 7.2 the lawyer receives no response, any further effort to communicate with the prospective client may violate the provisions of Rule 7.3(b).

[6] This Rule is not intended to prohibit a lawyer from contacting representatives of organizations or groups that may be interested in establishing a group or prepaid legal plan for their members, insureds, beneficiaries or other third parties for the purpose of informing such entities of the availability of and details concerning the plan or arrangement which the lawyer or lawyer's firm is willing to offer. This form of communication is not directed to a prospective client. Rather, it is usually addressed to an individual acting in a fiduciary capacity seeking a supplier of legal services for others who may, if they choose, become prospective clients of the lawyer. Under these circumstances, the activity which the lawyer undertakes in communicating with such representatives and the type of information transmitted to the individual are functionally similar to and serve the same purpose as advertising permitted under Rule 7.2.

[7] The requirement in Rule 7.3(c) that certain communications be marked "Advertising Material" does not apply to communications sent in response to requests of potential clients or their spokespersons or sponsors. General announcements by lawyers, including changes in personnel or office location, do not constitute communications soliciting professional employment from a client known to be in need of legal services within the meaning of this Rule.

[8] Paragraph (d) of this Rule permits a lawyer to participate with an organization which uses personal contact to solicit members for its group or prepaid legal service plan, provided that the personal contact is not undertaken by any lawyer who would be a provider of legal services through the plan. The organization must not be owned by or directed (whether as manager or otherwise) by any lawyer or law firm that participates in the plan. For example, paragraph (d) would not permit a lawyer to create an organization controlled directly or indirectly by the lawyer and use the organization for the in-person or telephone solicitation of legal employment of the lawyer through memberships in the plan or otherwise. The communication permitted by these organizations also must not be directed to a person known to need legal services in a particular matter, but is to be designed to inform potential plan members generally of another

means of affordable legal services. Lawyers who participate in a legal service plan must reasonably assure that the plan sponsors are in compliance with Rules 7.1, 7.2 and 7.3(b). See 8.4(a).

Authors' 1983 Model Rules Comparison

The ABA amended the 1983 version of Model Rule 7.3 in 1989 because, in 1988, the Supreme Court had declared a blanket restriction on targeted mailings unconstitutional under the First Amendment. *See Shapero v. Kentucky Bar Association*, 486 U.S. 466, 108 S.Ct. 1916, 100 L.Ed.2d 475 (1988) (discussed in greater detail in Chapter 7.0).[1] The Kentucky rule, which was the subject of this Supreme Court decision, was identical to the original Model Rule 7.3. That provision read as follows:

> A lawyer may not solicit professional employment from a prospective client with whom the lawyer has no family or prior professional relationship, by mail, in-person or otherwise, when a significant motive for the lawyer's doing so is the lawyer's pecuniary gain. The term "solicit" includes contact in person, by telephone or telegraph, by letter or other writing or by other communication directed to a specific recipient, but does not include letters addressed or advertising circulars distributed generally to persons not known to need legal services of the kind provided by the lawyer in a particular matter, but who are so situated that they might in general find such services useful.

The ABA House of Delegates also modified the Comments to this Rule in 1989 to reflect the Supreme Court's ruling on targeted mailings.[2]

The drafters of the 2002 Model Rules made several changes to the

---

[Rule 7.3]

[1] For a complete review of these changes to Model Rule 7.3, see A LEGISLATIVE HISTORY: THE DEVELOPMENT OF THE ABA MODEL RULES OF PROFESSIONAL CONDUCT, 1982–2005 (ABA 2006) at 289.

[2] The ABA amended the comments to Model Rule 7.3 in 1989 to reflect changes made in the text of the Rule brought about by the *Shapero* decision. The text of the original comment reads as follows:

COMMENT:

[1] There is a potential for abuse inherent in direct solicitation by a lawyer of prospective clients known to need legal services. It subjects the lay person to the private importuning of a trained advocate, in a direct interpersonal encounter. A prospective client often feels overwhelmed by the situation giving rise to the need for legal services, and may have an impaired capacity for reason, judgment and protective self-

interest. Furthermore, the lawyer seeking the retainer is faced with a conflict stemming from the lawyer's own interest, which may color the advice and representation offered the vulnerable prospect.

[2] The situation is therefore fraught with the possibility of undue influence, intimidation, and over-reaching. This potential for abuse inherent in direct solicitation of prospective clients justifies its prohibition, particularly since lawyer advertising permitted under Rule 7.2 offers an alternative means of communicating necessary information to those who may be in need of legal services.

[3] Advertising makes it possible for a prospective client to be informed about the need for legal services, and about the qualifications of available lawyers and law firms, without subjecting the prospective client to direct personal persuasion that may overwhelm the client's judgment.

[4] The use of general advertising to transmit information from lawyer to prospective client, rather than direct

1989 version of Rule 7.3 to reflect changes in thought about solicitation and to address the new technologies.

In Rule 7.3(a), the drafters of the 2002 Rules added "real-time electronic" contact as a prohibited type of solicitation. They also broke out from the body of (a) into (a)(1) and (a)(2) the exceptions for solicitation. In doing so, the drafters added lawyers and individuals with whom the lawyer has had a close personal relationship as those excluded from the solicitation ban.

In Rule 7.3(b) and (c), the drafters modified the language to address electronic communications by lawyers. The drafters in Rule 7.3(c)

---

private contact, will help to assure that the information flows cleanly as well as freely. Advertising is out in public view, thus subject to scrutiny by those who know the lawyer. This informal review is itself likely to help guard against statements and claims that might constitute false or misleading communications, in violation of Rule 7.1. Direct, private communications from a lawyer to a prospective client are not subject to such third-scrutiny and consequently are much more likely to approach (and occasionally cross) the dividing line between accurate representations and those that are false and misleading.

[5] These dangers attend direct solicitation whether in-person or by mail. Direct mail solicitation cannot be effectively regulated by means less drastic than outright prohibition. One proposed safeguard is to require that the designation "Advertising" be stamped on any envelope containing a solicitation letter. This would do nothing to assure the accuracy and reliability of the contents. Another suggestion is that solicitation letters be filed with a state regulatory agency. This would be ineffective as a practical matter. State lawyer discipline agencies struggle for resources to investigate specific complaints, much less for those necessary to screen lawyers' mail solicitation material. Even if they could examine such materials, agency staff members are unlikely to know anything about the lawyer or about the prospective client's underlying problem. Without such knowledge they cannot determine whether the lawyer's representations are misleading. In any event, such review would be after the fact, potentially too late to avert the undesirable consequences of disseminating false and misleading material.

[6] General mailings not speaking to a specific matter do not pose the same danger of abuse as targeted mailings, and therefore are not prohibited by this Rule. The representations made in such mailings are necessarily general rather than tailored, less importuning than informative. They are addressed to recipients unlikely to be specially vulnerable at the time, hence who are likely to be more skeptical about unsubstantiated claims. General mailings not addressed to recipients involved in a specific legal matter or incident, therefore, more closely resemble permissible advertising rather than prohibited solicitation.

[7] Similarly, this Rule would not prohibit a lawyer from contacting representatives of organizations or groups that may be interested in establishing a group or prepaid legal plan for its members, insureds, beneficiaries or other third parties for the purpose of informing such entities of the availability of and details concerning the plan or arrangement which he or his firm is willing to offer. This form of communication is not directed to a specific prospective client known to need legal services related to a particular matter. Rather, it is usually addressed to an individual acting in a fiduciary capacity seeking a supplier of legal services for others who may, if they choose, become prospective clients of the lawyer. Under these circumstances, the activity which the lawyer undertakes in communicating with such representatives and the type of information transmitted to the individual are functionally similar to and serve the same purpose as advertising permitted under Rule 7.2.

also made some word changes to reflect the breakout of permissible contacts in Rule 7.3(a)(1) and (a)(2).

Rule 7.3(d) was not modified.

In Comment 1, 2, and 3, the drafters added references to "real time electronic" contact. In Comment 3, the drafters made several minor changes in language to reflect changes in the text.

In Comment 4, the drafters expanded on the reasons underlying the exceptions to in person solicitation. They also added the last line: "Also, paragraph (a) is not intended to prohibit a lawyer from participating in constitutionally protected activities of public or charitable legal-service organizations or bona fide political, social, civic, fraternal, employee or trade organizations whose purposes include providing or recommending legal services to its members or beneficiaries."

The drafters of the 2002 Rules did not modify Comments 5, 6, and 7.

In Comment 8, the drafters made a few changes in language that do not alter the meaning of the language.

Model Code Comparison

DR 2-104(A) provided with certain exceptions that "[a] lawyer who has given in-person unsolicited advice to a layperson that he should obtain counsel or take legal action shall not accept employment resulting from that advice. . . ." The exceptions include DR 2-104(A)(1), which provided that a lawyer "may accept employment by a close friend, relative, former client (if the advice is germane to the former employment), or one whom the lawyer reasonably believes to be a client." DR 2-104(A)(2) through DR 2-104(A)(5) provided other exceptions relating, respectively, to employment resulting from public educational programs, recommendation by a legal assistance organization, public speaking or writing and representing members of a class in class action litigation.

§ 7.3–1 SOLICITATION: BACKGROUND AND THE HISTORICAL PERSPECTIVE

§ 7.3–1(a) The Model Code and the Constitutionality of the Ban on Solicitation

Solicitation may be considered a form of advertising, but on a retail, rather than a wholesale, level. The Model Code made a distinction between general media advertising and improper "in-person" solicitation, which involved contact with specific prospective clients motivated by pecuniary gain.[1] The Code never used the term "face-to-face," and it intended "solicitation" to include "in-person" contact that was *not* face-to-face, such as direct mail advertising.

The Model Code had very extensive regulations governing a lawyer's contact with prospective clients. It provided that lawyers

---

[Section 7.3–1]

[1]EC 2-2, 2-3 & 2-4.

could not ethically recommend their services or those of their partners to a prospective client unless the prospective client initiated the consultation.[2] Similarly, lawyers who rendered unsolicited advice to prospective clients could not usually accept employment arising from that advice.[3] But a lawyer could accept employment resulting from unsolicited advice to a "close friend" or relative.[4]

If the lawyer gave unsolicited advice to a former client in order to secure business she could not accept any resulting employment unless the advice was germane to a matter that the lawyer had formerly handled for that client.[5] Similarly, a lawyer could not normally accept employment resulting from participation in educational activities unless those activities were sponsored by a qualified legal services organization.[6] The Code did permit a lawyer to accept employment resulting from her spoken or written legal scholarship, so long as she did not tout her own professional qualifications.[7]

Under the Code a lawyer could not accept employment from a client who sought that lawyer's services as a result of prohibited solicitation.[8] Consequently, a lawyer could not accept employment if the lawyer knew the client had been solicited by the lawyer's employee, partner, or other lawyer affiliated with such lawyer.[9]

The first major U.S. Supreme Court decisions dealing with solicitation were two companion cases, *Ohralik* and *Primus*. In *Ohralik v. Ohio State Bar Association*,[10] the Court responded to a question left open in *Bates* regarding the greater potential for overreaching when an attorney solicits business face-to-face rather than through the media. The Court held that a state may constitutionally discipline a lawyer who solicits clients in-person under circumstances likely to create undue pressure on the client. In *Ohralik*, the state disciplined a lawyer who sought to be hired on a contingency fee basis in a personal injury matter. The prospective client, who was then recovering from her injuries, was confined to a hospital bed. The lawyer confronted her in a face-to-face meeting and solicited employment.

In *Ohralik* the Court emphasized that the state has an interest in protecting the "unsophisticated, injured, or distressed lay person" from "those aspects of solicitation that involve fraud, undue influence, intimidation, overreaching, and other forms of

---

[2] DR 2-103(A).

[3] DR 2-104(A).

[4] DR 2-104(A)(2).

[5] DR 2-104(A)(1).

[6] DR 2-104(A)(2).

[7] DR 2-104(A)(4).

[8] DR 2-103(E).

[9] *Cf.* DR 1-102(A)(2).

[10] *Ohralik v. Ohio State Bar Association*, 436 U.S. 447, 98 S.Ct. 1912, 56 L.Ed.2d 444 (1978).

'vexatious conduct.' "[11] Justice Powell, for the Court, began the opinion by summarizing in detail the appellant's outrageous in-person solicitation, and noted that the lawyer "refused to withdraw" when Mrs. Holbert, the client, "requested him to do so," and that he "continued to represent himself to the insurance company as Wanda Holbert's lawyer."[12]

Justice Marshall's thoughtful concurring opinion specifically would allow "benign" commercial solicitation, that is "solicitation by advice and information that is truthful and that is presented in a noncoercive, non-deceitful and dignified manner to a potential client who is emotionally and physically capable of making a rational decision either to accept or reject the representation with respect to a legal claim or matter that is not frivolous."[13] Nothing in the majority opinion rejects Justice Marshall's conclusions.

In a companion case, *In re Primus*,[14] the Court recognized that certain types of solicitation are entitled to special constitutional protection. *Primus* involved an American Civil Liberties Union (ACLU) lawyer who, through a letter, offered free legal services to a woman allegedly deprived of her civil rights. The Court extended the First Amendment's protection for free speech and association to the lawyer's activities and struck the state's efforts to reprimand the ACLU lawyer for solicitation.

When someone sees or reads general advertising, that person may simply walk away, or turn the page if he is uninterested. But face-to-face solicitation may exert pressure and seek an immediate response from the prospective client, who then has less opportunity for reflection. The Bar and supervisory authorities have less opportunity to engage in counter education in such circumstances. And there is less opportunity for public scrutiny because the face-to-face solicitation often takes place in private, with no witness other than the lawyer and the prospective client.[15] On the other hand, as *Primus* illustrated, some types of solicitation help clients and do not involve overreaching.

§ 7.3–1(b) The 1983 Model Rules and Ban on Targeted Mailings

In 1983, the ABA adopted Rule 7.3 that governed solicitation. This provision sought to work within the contours of the Supreme Court decisions that permitted a ban on in person contact for

---

[11] 436 U.S. at 462, 98 S.Ct. at 1921 (footnote omitted). *See* Robert B. Reich, *Preventing Deception in Commercial Speech*, 54 N.Y.U.L.Rev. 775 (1979).

[12] 436 U.S. at 467, 98 S.Ct. at 1924.

[13] 436 U.S. at 472 n. 3, 98 S.Ct. at 1927 n. 3 (Marshall, J., concurring).

[14] *In re Primus*, 436 U.S. 412, 98 S.Ct. 1893, 56 L.Ed.2d 417 (1978).

[15] 436 U.S. at 466, 98 S.Ct. at 1923–24.

pecuniary gain, but prohibited such a ban for not-for-profit in person contact.

> A lawyer may not solicit professional employment from a prospective client with whom the lawyer has no family or prior professional relationship, by mail, in-person or otherwise, when a significant motive for the lawyer's doing so is the lawyer's pecuniary gain. The term "solicit" includes contact in person, by telephone or telegraph, by letter or other writing or by other communication directed to a specific recipient, but does not include letters addressed or advertising circulars distributed generally to persons not known to need legal services of the kind provided by the lawyer in a particular matter, but who are so situated that they might in general find such services useful.[16]

The 1983 Rules distinguished between mass mailings (which were allowed as advertising) from targeted mail (which was not allowed), claiming "[d]irect mail solicitation cannot be effectively regulated by means less drastic than outright prohibition."[17] However, targeted mailing did not involve face-to-face contact, and the recipient could simply throw the mail away. Moreover, because a mailing is a written form of communication there is a written record of what was said, which furnishes the client protection against lawyer overreaching. In contrast, in an oral solicitation there is no written record and thus it is more difficult for the disciplinary system to police overreaching.

Targeted mailing is really only a more efficient form of advertising than a mass mailing. Indeed, in *Bates v. State Bar of Arizona*,[18] Justice Powell's separate opinion admitted that there was no "principled basis" to distinguish advertisements in newspapers from "handbills, and mail circulations."[19] There is no constitutional difference between a newsboy giving a handbill to someone, or a postal worker delivering a letter to that person with a copy of that same handbill.

In February of 1987, two ABA entities initially proposed that the 1983 Rule 7.3 be amended to allow targeted mailing, but they withdrew this proposal after the ABA Board of Governors opposed it. Then the Supreme Court gave the bar no choice but to allow targeted mail. In *Shapero v. Kentucky Bar Association*,[20] the Court ruled that, under the First Amendment, states may not categorically prohibit lawyers from seeking business by send-

---

[16]1983 Model Rule 7.3.

[17]See former Comment 5 to Rule 7.3 (1988 version).

[18]*Bates v. State Bar of Arizona*, 433 U.S. 350, 97 S.Ct. 2691, 53 L.Ed.2d 810 (1977).

[19]433 U.S. at 402 n.5, 97 S.Ct. at 2718 n.12 (Powell, J., concurring in

part and dissenting in part, joined by Stewart, J.).

[20]*Shapero v. Kentucky Bar Association*, 486 U.S. 466, 108 S.Ct. 1916, 100 L.Ed.2d 475 (1988). *Shapero* is discussed in more detail in the introductory section that precedes Rule 7.1.

ing truthful, nondeceptive letters to potential clients known to face particular legal problems.

In February 1989, the ABA responded to *Shapero* by amending Rule 7.3, to permit direct mail or prerecorded telephone contact unless the recipient has indicated that he or she does not wish to be solicited by the lawyer, or the solicitation involves coercion, duress, or harassment. Any written solicitation must include the words "Advertising Material" on the outside envelope and at the beginning and ending of any recorded message.

The touchstone of the 1989 Rule was to protect the prospective client from direct, personal encounters or live telephone persuasion from a lawyer because those situations may be fraught with the possibility of "undue influence, intimidation, and over-reaching."[21] In addition, in light of the fact that the lawyer can engage in direct mail advertising or employ prerecorded telephone advertising, there is less need for such personal encounters because the recipient of the direct mailing or prerecorded phone call can always invite the prospective client to call the lawyer's office if the recipient wishes more information.[22]

The Court backtracked a bit from *Shapero* when it held in *Florida Bar v. Went for It, Inc.*,[23] (5 to 4) that it was constitutional for the state to prohibit plaintiff-attorneys (but not defense-attorneys) from sending direct mail solicitations to victims and their relatives for 30 days following an accident or disaster.

In this case, which is discussed in detail in the introduction preceding Rule 7.1, *supra*, the state argued that the 30-day ban protected the privacy of victims and their loved ones against invasive, unsolicited contact by lawyers and prevented the erosion of confidence in the legal profession that such invasions engendered. The narrow majority thought it important that, even with the ban—

> Florida permits lawyers to advertise on prime-time television and radio as well as in newspapers and other media. They may rent

---

[21]Rule 7.3, Comment 1.

[22]Ronald D. Rotunda, LAWYER ADVERTISING AND THE PHILOSOPHICAL ORIGINS OF THE COMMERCIAL SPEECH DOCTRINE, 36 U. Richmond L. Rev. 91 (2002) (Allen Chair Symposium of 2001).

[23]*Florida Bar v. Went for It, Inc.*, 515 U.S. 618, 115 S.Ct. 2371, 132 L.Ed.2d 541 (1995). *See* Ronald D. Rotunda, *Professionalism, Legal Advertising, and Free Speech In the*

Wake of Florida Bar v. Went For It, Inc., 49 ARKANSAS L. REV. 703 (1997) (Symposium), *reprinted in*, 12 LAWYER' LIABILITY REV. 1 (No. 10, Oct. 1998) (part I), 12 LAWYER' LIABILITY REV.1 (No. 11, Nov. 1998)(part II), & 12 LAWYER' LIABILITY REV. 1 (No. 12, Dec. 1998)(part III); Steven M. Field, *Thirty-Day Restrictions On Attorney Direct-Mail Solicitation: The United States Supreme Court Went For It*, 21 CARDOZO L. REV. 1999 (2000).

space on billboards. They may send untargeted letters to the general population, or to discrete segments thereof.[24]

Given this caveat by the Supreme Court, one should not read too much into this case. In addition, the ABA has not followed Florida's example and the Model Rules do not contain the restrictions that a divided Court allowed in *Went for It*.

§ 7.3–2 REGULATION OF DIRECT CONTACT WITH PROSPECTIVE CLIENTS

§ 7.3–2(a) Defining Solicitation Under the Model Rules

Rule 7.3 states that lawyer shall not "solicit professional employment from a prospective client when a significant motive for doing so is the lawyer's pecuniary gain . . . ."[1] Solicitation is defined as "in-person, live telephone or real-time electronic contact" with an individual.[2]

Real–Time Electronic Contact. The drafters of the 2002 Rules added the reference to real-time electronic contact because they believed that it was similar to live in-person or telephone contact. Real-time electronic contact is not defined in the Rules; however, it must necessarily only refer to lawyer participation in chat rooms and instant messaging. It cannot refer to lawyer postings on list serves or blogs or email because such activities are not in real time.

The assumption that "real-time electronic contact" is like "live telephone" contact may be an heroic one. When someone calls you on the telephone, and you pick it up, it is considered impolite to hang up in the middle of a conversation. But that is not true of instant messaging or email. I can email a letter to you, and you may receive it in seconds. Instant messaging is even more instant. But in neither case is there any requirement that you respond. People who use email with any frequency know that the recipient may never respond. Ditto for instant messaging. Indeed, you may not be able to respond instantly because of the all-too-common occurrence that the "server is busy," or your computer ran into problems and shut down automatically, or you lost electricity briefly, shutting down your computer entirely unless you have battery backup, and the sender has no idea whether you have battery backup.

Email or instant messaging requires typing, just like sending a fax. In fact, if you send a fax from your computer to another computer—inexpensive software allows that—it is difficult to

---

[24]518 U.S. at 632, 115 S.Ct. at 2380 (emphasis added).

[Section 7.3–2]

[1]Rule 7.3(a).

[2]Rule 7.3(a).

distinguish the "real-time electronic contact" from the fax, but this Rule does not prohibit the fax while it prohibits the instant messaging. Software also allows you to send a fax from your computer to another person's email account. It also is in "real-time" if the recipient bothers to read it. The recipient can just delete it, as recipients do with many messages. Electronic contact is similar to targeted mailings, only faster, like a telegram is faster than the U.S. Post Office. Nonetheless, the Rule makes the distinction and treats typing an email differently than typing a letter sent by fax.

Although the Rule text and Comments do not explicitly discuss a more full definition of solicitation, solicitation does not encompass all in-person contact between a lawyer and a prospective client. It only encompasses such contact that is initiated by the lawyer for the purpose of seeking an attorney-client relationship for pecuniary gain. The facts of *Ohralik* presented a very easy case—lawyer visiting a prospective client in a hospital room seeking legal employment.[3]

But many in-person contacts are more ambiguous. For example, if a lawyer is waiting in a doctor's office for an appointment, and a person sits down next to the lawyer and the two begin to talk, the situation may or may not constitute solicitation. If the lawyer regularly visits doctor's waiting areas for potential contact with prospective clients, that conduct could constitute solicitation because the lawyer's motive is clear. If the lawyer walks up to every person in the room and asks, do you need a lawyer, that conduct constitutes solicitation.

Assume that a prospective client happens to sit next to a lawyer at a banquet, and then describes a set of facts that call for the attention of a lawyer. The lawyer says, "have you seen a lawyer?" If the person responds, "no, but are you perchance a lawyer?," that fact pattern would not constitute solicitation.

The key in these examples is who initiates the contact, for what purpose, and whether the prospective client is seeking information from a rather passive lawyer.[4]

Telephone Contact Offering Legal Seminars. The Los Angeles Bar has opined that if a lawyer makes a cold telephone call offering to conduct an in-house educational seminar to a strange—someone with whom he has had no prior relationship—

---

[3] 436 U.S. 447, 98 S.Ct. 1912, 56 L.Ed.2d 444 (1978).

[4] There is the story of the doctor who sat next to a lawyer at a banquet, learned that the other person was a lawyer, and then said, "I am upset with patients who telephone me at my office and ask for free medical advice. How do I stop that." The lawyer responded, "That's easy. Just send them a bill." The next Monday, the doctor opened his mail and discovered a bill from the lawyer. This lawyer did not engage in improper "face-to-face" solicitation.

that is not solicitation under California law *if* the lawyer does not communicate a message, or offer, concerning his availability for legal representation.[5] This ethics opinion also found no improper solicitation if the lawyer mails bulletins or briefs discussing legal decisions to a prospective consumer of legal services. Even though "a significant motivation for the communication is to obtain legal services," this opinion concluded that the speech is constitutionally protected commercial speech.[6] Of course, these communications must be truthful and not deceptive.

Agents and Friends. Some personal injury lawyers have used employees or independent contractors to find prospective clients for them. A lay person hired by a lawyer to walk around an airport wearing a sandwich board (bearing an ad) is not engaged in solicitation as long as the person does not talk to prospective clients. If the person walks up to people and says, come to this office for a free legal consultation, that communication would constitute solicitation. If the wearer of the board does not talk until the prospective client asks a question, that conversation would not constitute solicitation. Lawyers must carefully supervise nonlawyer agents to ensure that they are not violating the solicitation rules.[7]

Nonlawyer friends of a lawyer may refer clients to the lawyer. If the lawyer formalizes a relationship with a friend to refer prospective clients to the lawyer, that formal relationship is likely to violate the ban on solicitation. A formal relationship would involve, for example, the lawyer paying the nonlawyer to refer business, or a contract or a quid pro quo exchange of benefits to the nonlawyer for referring and talking to prospective clients.

When a lawyer engages in first amendment protected activities such as speeches or radio programs, the lawyer may invite people to call or attend. If the prospective clients ask questions, they are initiating the contact with the lawyer. And, in most instances, this conduct would not involve solicitation.

Witnesses. Also, if a lawyer represents a client in a matter such as a lawsuit against a builder for defective construction, the lawyer (or an agent) can go door to door and initiate live in-person conversations if the lawyer is in fact seeking facts and witnesses to help in the representation of the client. If the layperson asks the lawyer, "can you represent me," that would not constitute solicitation because the lawyer is initiating the live in-person contact to seek evidence for a case.

---

[5]Los Angeles County Bar Association, *Communications and Solicitations: Cold Calling for Legal Seminar and Mailing of Newsletter*, Formal Opinion No. 494 (Oct. 19, 1998).

[6]Los Angeles County Bar Association, supra, Formal Opinion No. 494 (Oct. 19, 1998), at p. 3.

[7]Rule 8.4(a).

§ 7.3–2(b) Recognized Exceptions to the Ban on Solicitation

Rule 7.3 contains four exceptions to the prohibition against solicitation.

First, a lawyer may always contact another lawyer by telephone or in person contact to solicit the lawyer for business.[8] It makes sense to permit a lawyer to call a general counsel of a corporation and ask to represent the company in its legal matters. The general counsel is sophisticated and has relatively equal knowledge and bargaining power. Any policy reasons for supporting a ban on solicitation do not arise when the target is a lawyer licensed to practice law.

Second, a lawyer may contact family members who are in need of legal services.[9] It would be incredulous for the Rules to prohibit lawyers from offering their services to family members who are in legal trouble. Also, the family members can decide whether they wish to hire a family member lawyer and they certainly have opinions about the lawyer's competence and judgment.

Third, a lawyer may contact a person with whom the lawyer has had a close personal relationship.[10] The reason for this exception is the fact that personal friends are likely to know the lawyer and have an opinion whether they wish to be represented by the lawyer. Also, it is less likely that a lawyer will take advantage of a friend with whom the lawyer has a close personal relationship.

Finally, a lawyer may always contact a former client with whom the lawyer has had a prior professional relationship.[11] This exception for lawyers and former clients makes sense because a former client knows whether he or she was satisfied with the lawyer's work and can make an informed judgment to hire the lawyer again or to find another lawyer. Lawyer should not be prohibited from contacting former clients about changes in the law and this Rule permits such contact. Note that the exception does not require that the new matter relate to the former matter, just that the lawyer had a former client relationship with the person. The Rule also appears to apply to former professional relationships that the lawyer had when the lawyer was in another career prior to becoming a lawyer. For example, if a lawyer was an accountant before going to law school and now the lawyer developed a practice in tax litigation, the lawyer could contact former accounting clients and inform them of his new career.

Note, that even if a lawyer's contact with a person falls within one of these exceptions, Rule 7.3(b) prohibits the permitted solicitation if the person has made it known to the lawyer that the

---

[8] Rule 7.3(a)(1).
[9] Rule 7.3(a)(2).

[10] Rule 7.3(a)(2).
[11] Rule 7.3(a)(2).

contact is not welcomed or if the solicitation involves coercion, duress, or harassment. Therefore, it the lawyer contacts a lawyer or a former client and seeks to make a pitch for legal employment, all the lawyer or former client need to do to stop the communication is to say that they would prefer the lawyer not to call them.

§ 7.3–2(c) The Regulation of Targeted Advertising

Rule 7.3 continues to govern targeted advertising, although the Rule has been amended to take into account the latest Supreme Court authority. The Rule prohibits sending letters or emails to prospective clients who have indicated a desire not to be solicited. And, the written communication may not involve coercion, duress, and harassment. The Rule also applies to plaintiffs lawyers who are seeking to find potential clients after a class action has been filed, but before it has been certified.[12]

Rule 7.3(c) requires that lawyers who send targeted letters must use an envelope that states "advertising material" on the outside. It also requires that if a lawyer uses a recorded or electronic communication, the recording or email must indicate advertising material at the beginning and ending of the communication. The purpose of these warnings is to permit a targeted person to first know that the communication is from a lawyer seeking to offer them legal services and second to permit them to throw the envelope away, hang up the telephone, or delete the email without reading or listening to the entire communication.

Targeted communications have always posed problems for the ABA and the state bars because such communications present the most anxiety on the part of the recipient. When the prospective client receives a letter that states, "We are so sorry to see that your spouse has filed for divorce against you," or "We understand that creditors are beginning foreclosure proceedings on your home," the recipient does not know how the lawyer obtained this information. In large cities, prospective clients often receive dozens of letters after an accident, a divorce filing, or a lien filing.

One approach to regulating such behavior is the 30-day ban upheld in Florida's *Went for It* case. Arkansas, Colorado, Georgia, Hawaii, Idaho, Kentucky, Louisiana, New Jersey, Tennessee, and

---

[12]See ABA Formal Opinion 07-445 (Apr. 11, 2007) ("Contact by Counsel with Putative Members of Class Prior to Class Certification").

Wyoming have some form of 30 day ban on targeted communications and Nevada has a 45-day ban.[13]

Another approach, attempted by Texas and found partially unconstitutional, was an amendment of the criminal barratry law and the highway records statute to prohibit communications for 180 days after an incident. The Texas legislature sought to make public records confidential for 180 days after an accident and to criminalize improper solicitation and targeted communications, but this effort was largely invalidated in the courts.[14]

The Rules already forbid targeted communications (and any other type of advertising or solicitation) if the lawyers are misleading or coercive. But it is likely that states will continue to experiment with the regulation of targeted communications even if they are truthful and not coercive. Proponents argue that further regulation is needed because the general public is most dissatisfied by targeted advertising. On the other hand, if that is true, the problem should be self-correcting: people who do not like to receive targeted advertising will not respond by hiring the lawyers who contact them; lawyers will learn that this type of advertising is unsuccessful and they will be mailing fewer letters, particularly those mailed within 30 days of an accident. If targeted advertising and other forms of solicitation are effective, then lawyers will continue to use that type of advertising—because enough of the public finds the information useful.

§ 7.3–2(d) Sanctions

If the solicitations are not misleading or coercive, the solicitation is like a victim-less crime in that the client is not complaining. Instead, the typical complaining party is the bar or a competing lawyer.

The question them becomes what is the sanction for improper solicitation. The most typical sanction is discipline. The court will not disqualify the lawyer for improper solicitation if the only complainant is the opposing lawyer because the solicitation does not taint the proceeding.[15]

If the lawyer is from out of state, the question of discipline is more complex. The court where the lawyer is admitted may, of course, discipline the lawyer even though the improper conduct occurred in another jurisdiction.[16]

In addition, the court where the conduct occurred may sanction

---

[13]ABA/BNA Lawyers' Manual on Professional Conduct: Practice Guide 81:2003 (2004) (summarizing the state rules on targeted communications).

[14]See Moore v. Morales, 63 F.3d 358 (5th Cir.1995).

[15]Fisher Studio, Inc. v. Loew's Inc., 232 F.2d 199, 204 (2d Cir.1956), cert. denied, 352 U.S. 836, 77 S.Ct. 56, 1 L.Ed.2d 55 (1956).

[16]Rule 8.5(a).

the out-of-state lawyer by barring her from practice in that state,[17] assuming that the court rules allow its disciplinary jurisdiction to extend to lawyers who are in the state only for a particular case.[18]

§ 7.3–3 SOLICITATION AND LEGAL SERVICE PLANS

The Model Rules make clear that an attorney may participate in a prepaid legal service plan even though the plan uses personal contact to solicit potential members generally. However, the lawyer may not own or direct this legal services plan himself. In addition, the legal services plan, when it solicits members, may not target particular persons who are known to need legal services in a particular matter.[1]

The Rules thus distinguish between the plan, which can solicit members, and the lawyer, who cannot do so. However, the lawyer can solicit the plan: in other words, the lawyer can contact the representatives of a group, such as a union, insureds, companies, etc., and urge these representatives to set up a prepaid legal services plan for its members. These third parties can then contact (*i.e.*, solicit) their members.

This distinction is purportedly justified by the fact that the

---

[17]*In re Coale*, 775 N.E.2d 1079 (Ind.2002) (per curiam), barring lawyers "licensed in states other than Indiana, solicited potential clients in this state without complying with our rules governing client solicitation, we find today that they should be barred from engaging in acts constituting the practice of law in this state until further order of this Court." 775 N.E.2d at 1080. Thus, the court would not grant these lawyers *pro hac vice* admission.

See Andrea Lynn Evensen, *Disciplining Out-Of-State Conduct And Lawyers Licensed In Other States*, 15 PROFESSIONAL LAWYER 12 (2004).

[18]*Lawyer Disciplinary Board v. Allen, Coale & Van Susteren*, 479 S.E.2d 317, 198 W.Va. 18 (1996). The lawyers violated the state's solicitation rule by contacting potential personal injury clients through agents, but the disciplinary rule required that the lawyers had to "regularly practice" in West Virginia in order to be disciplined there:

"[W]e simply cannot conclude that the conduct reflected by the record rises to a level sufficient to constitute the regu-

lar practice of law in this State. Consequently, because this Court, at the time of the complained of conduct, had made subject to professional discipline only those persons who 'regularly engaged in the practice of law' in West Virginia, we decline to impose any professional discipline on Mr. Coale, Mr. Allen, or Ms. Van Susteren for their conduct. [But under the new] Rule 1 of the Rules of Lawyer Disciplinary Procedure, as amended by this Court on December 6, 1994, a lawyer is subject to discipline in this State for violating the West Virginia Rules of Professional Conduct if he or she engages in the practice of law in this State, whether or not he or she is formally admitted to practice by this Court. Thus, *under the current jurisdiction* of the Lawyer Disciplinary Board, the conduct in which respondents engaged is clearly subject to our disciplinary procedures."

198 W.Va. 18, 37, 479 S.E.2d 317, 336 (1996) (footnote omitted). This case involved Greta Van Susteren, who later became a legal analysis for the Fox News Channel.

[Section 7.3–3]

[1]Rule 7.3, Comment 8.

lawyer, when he is soliciting the representatives of a proposed plan is not engaging in solicitation but in advertising because this "form of communication is not directed to a prospective client," but to the representatives of the plan who are "acting in a fiduciary capacity seeking a supplier of legal services for others who may, if they choose, become prospective clients of the lawyer."[2]

These distinctions do present somewhat of a legal fiction. If the lawyer may solicit—or, in the words of the Model Rules, "contact[] *representatives* of organizations or groups that may be interested in establishing a group or prepaid legal plan for their members"[3]— why cannot the lawyer contact the members directly? The Comments explain that the distinction is that the representatives have a fiduciary responsibility to their members, but the lawyer is a fiduciary too. Nonetheless, the Rules are very clear that the lawyer himself or herself cannot engage in "personal contact" (solicitation) with the members.[4]

As mentioned above, the legal services plan, when it solicits members, may not target particular persons who are known to need legal services in a particular matter.[5] In-person, face-to-face solicitation, or telephone solicitation, comes under this rule. After *Shapero v. Kentucky Bar Association*,[6] which gave constitutional protection to targeted, direct mail advertising, any complete prohibition of targeted mail raises severe constitutional problems.

Rule 7.3(d) does not address the issue whether a lawyer may contact through solicitation a person who has already signed up for a legal services plan and is paying the monthly fee, but who has not sought the lawyer's services. One could view individuals who had signed up for a prepaid legal services plan as having made a step towards receiving protection of a lawyer and therefore a lawyer could make direct in person contact to determine whether they had any legal matters for the lawyer to examine.[7] However, many such plans cover only basic services; therefore, it is likely that the lawyer would be asking the individuals to present legal problems not covered within the monthly payment. An attempt to prohibit such contact could

---

[2] Rule 7.3, Comment 6.

[3] Rule 7.3, Comment 6 (emphasis added).

[4] Rule 7.3, Comment 8.

[5] Rule 7.3, Comment 8.

[6] *Shapero v. Kentucky Bar Association*, 486 U.S. 466, 108 S.Ct. 1916, 100 L.Ed.2d 475 (1988).

[7] Of course, the lawyer could always use direct mailing to such individuals.

implicate associational freedoms raised in several Supreme Court decisions.[8]

A lawyer who participates in a prepaid legal services plan must take reasonable care to make sure than the plan complies with Rules 7.1, 7.2, and 7.3.

§ 7.3–4 DEPARTING LAWYERS SOLICITING CLIENTS OF THE FORMER LAW FIRM

One does not normally think of soliciting *present* clients. These clients have already hired the law firm, and when the firm sends them unsolicited information about their possible legal needs, it is only being pro-active, taking the initiative. However, situations arise where lawyers within a firm have a falling out, and some lawyers depart without buying the entire law practice from the other lawyers.[1] The partnership agreement may provide how the law firm should handle these break-ups, but any agreement must comply with the ethical rule that provides that a partnership or employment agreement may not restrict the right of a lawyer to practice after leaving the firm except an agreement concerning benefits upon retirement.[2] Thus, when lawyers leave the firm, they retain the right to practice law in competition with the firm from which they departed. But, to what extent may the departing lawyers seek to take with them the clients of that firm (or, in the view of the departing lawyers, "their clients")?

Many years ago, joining a law firm was a little like marriage: it was expected to be a lifetime commitment. Now, joining a law firm is a lot like modern marriage: it often is not a lifetime commitment. The fact that some lawyers prosper from grabbing business from the law firm and then leaving—

is likely evidence of market forces at work. A significant factor underlying the growth of grabbing and leaving is the inability of many firms to develop a method of compensation acceptable to their more mobile partners. Because there is now a market for lawyers who can carry a substantial "portfolio" of clients to another firm, these lawyers have something to auction. Viewed from this perspective, the solution to the problem of grabbing [clients and then leaving the law firm] may lie more in the modification of business prac-

---

[8]*See United Transportation Union v. State Bar of Michigan*, 401 U.S. 576, 91 S.Ct. 1076, 28 L.Ed.2d 339 (1971); *United Mine Workers v. Illinois State Bar Association*, 389 U.S. 217, 88 S.Ct. 353, 19 L.Ed.2d 426 (1967); *Brotherhood of Railroad Trainmen v. Virginia Bar*, 377 U.S. 1, 84 S.Ct. 1113, 12 L.Ed.2d 89 (1964).

[Section 7.3–4]

[1]*See* Rule 1.17, "Sale of a Law Practice."

[2]Rule 5.6(a). *See also* Restatement of the Law Governing Lawyers, Third, § 13(1) (Official Draft 2000).

tices, particularly those pertaining to compensation, than in law reform.[3]

In the meantime, lawyers leave for greener pastures.

When lawyers leave their old law firm to start a new one, there is a tension regarding the status of the clients they had with the first law firm. In a sense, the clients are the clients of the first "law firm," but in another sense the clients only deal with individual flesh and blood human beings, and some of those human beings will be the ones who are leaving to start the new firm. The clients may wish to follow the individual lawyers with whom they have dealt in the past. Clients are not merchandise; they have the right to follow the lawyer when she changes law firms.[4]

These cases also implicate free speech interests. A lawyer should be able to tell the truth, for example, that she is leaving one firm and starting a new firm or joining a different firm and the clients are free to follow her. However, the right of free speech does not equate to the right to lie. The departing lawyer may not lie or mislead others as to why she is leaving.[5]

The general principle that one can derive from the cases is that, when a lawyer leaves a law firm, she may solicit clients on whose matters she had previously worked actively and substantially, *but* she should engage in this solicitation only *after* she has left the firm or after she adequately and timely informed the firm of her intent to contact clients for that purpose.[6]

The Restatement of the Law Governing Lawyers fairly summarizes existing law when it advises that lawyers departing or planning to depart from a law firm to go into business in competition with their former law firm may make "pre-departure arrangements as leasing space, printing new letterhead, and obtaining financing. It is also not a breach of duty to a former firm for a

---

[3]ROBERT W. HILLMAN, LAW FIRM BREAKUPS: THE LAW AND ETHICS OF GRABBING AND LEAVING 143 (Little, Brown & Co. June 21, 1945, 1990). *See also id.* at 143–45. The successor treatise is, ROBERT W. HILLMAN, HILLMAN ON LAWYER MOBILITY: THE LAW AND ETHICS OF PARTNER WITHDRAWALS AND LAW FIRM BREAKUPS (Aspen, 1998).

[4]ABA Formal Opinion 266 (June 21, 1945) maintains: "Clients are not merchandise. Lawyers are not tradesmen. They have nothing to sell but personal service. An attempt, therefore, to barter in clients, would appear to be inconsistent with the best concepts of our professional status."
See, e.g., Bray v. Squires, 702 S.W.2d 266 (Tex.App.1985) (holding that former associates of a law firm, after they have left that law firm, may solicit a financial client because they had actively worked on that client's matter while with the first law firm).

[5]*In re Smith*, 315 Or. 260, 843 P.2d 449 (1992). The lawyer had each new law firm client sign letters retaining him individually. When he opened his new firm, he then sent these clients letters that implied that nothing material had changed. The court imposed a four month suspension on this lawyer for his misrepresentations.

[6]Restatement of the Law Governing Lawyers, Third, § 9(3) (Official Draft 2000).

lawyer who has departed the firm to continue to represent clients whom the lawyer actively represented while with the firm."[7]

When a lawyer decides to leave a law firm, she might not leave alone. She ethically may consult with other partners and associates and employees who decide to leave together. The lawyers leaving Firm One should not use the resources of Firm One to solicit clients for Firm Two.[8] The lawyers may agree to departing as a group, or serial departures, so long as, first, "the lawyers and personnel do nothing prohibited to either of them (including impermissible soliciting clients)," second, "they do not misuse firm resources (*such as without permission copying files or client lists or unlawfully removing firm property from its premises*)," or third, they do not "take other action detrimental to the interests

---

[7]Restatement of the Law Governing Lawyers, Third, § 9 (Official Draft 2000), at Comment *i* ("Departure of lawyer to compete.").

[8]*See Meehan v. Shaughnessy*, 404 Mass. 419, 535 N.E.2d 1255 (1989). In this case, two partners left to open a new law office and sued for fees due from their old partners, who countersued them for violation of fiduciary obligations and tortious interference with relations with clients. In July, the two partners had decided to leave the firm at the end of December and had recruited four others to join them. During the summer and fall, while they worked on obtaining office space and financing for their new firm, they kept up their caseload at the firm rather than letting people who would stay at the firm become familiar with the cases. In addition, they expressly denied to the firm's partners any plans to leave. Then they gave the old firm 30 days notice, immediately called clients, and were able to have 142 out of 350 active cases shifted to the new firm. The court said that law partners owe fiduciary obligations to each other. The departing partners "used speed and preemptive" tactics and abused "their position of trust and confidence" in the firm. The court then remanded so that the old firm could show its economic harm from the loss of clients.

The court also imposed on the departing lawyers the burden to prove that the clients would have come anyway had the lawyers acted properly.

See also Fred Siegel Co., L.P.A. v. Arter & Hadden, 85 Ohio St.3d 171, 707 N.E.2d 853 (1999). Karen Bauernschmidt, an expert in real estate property assessments, had worked for Fred Siegel Co. for ten years and then resigned to join Arter & Hadden, another law firm. She told Arter & Hadden that she thought several Siegel clients would follow her. When she left, she took the cards she had in her Rolodex. While at the new firm, she wrote letters to Siegel clients notifying them of her new association and stated: "When you need assistance or have questions, please contact me." The Siegel firm responded by writing the same clients and stating that it was still fully capable of meeting their needs. The Siegel firm also sued Arter & Hadden, claiming tortious interference with business relationships, and sued Bauernschmidt claiming breach of fiduciary duty. The court rejected the tortious interference theory because of the right of fair competition, particularly when a contract is terminable at will. The court then remanded to determine whether Bauernschmidt's use of the names in the Rolodex was an improper use of a trade secret.

of the firm or of clients, aside from whatever detriment may befall the firm due to their departure."[9]

If the clients of law firm #1 decide to retain the lawyers of law firm #2 (made up of lawyers who departed from law firm #1), then law firm #1 must turn its files over to the law firm designated by the clients.[10]

An ABA Informal Opinion[11] approved a departing lawyer sending the following letter:

Dear [Client]:

Effective [date], I became the resident partner in this city of the XYZ law firm, having withdrawn from the ABC law firm. My decision should not be construed as adversely reflecting in any way on my former firm. It is simply one of those things that sometimes happens in business and professional life.

I want to be sure that there is no disadvantage to you, as the client, from my move. The decision as to how the matters I have worked on for you are handled and who handles them in the future will be completely yours, and whatever you decide will be determinative.

The ABA Committee made clear that—

This opinion is limited to the facts presented: (a) the notice is mailed; (b) the notice is sent only to persons with whom the lawyer had an active lawyer-client relationship immediately before the change in the lawyer's professional association; (c) the notice is clearly related to open and pending matters for which the lawyer had direct professional responsibility to the client immediately before the change; (d) the notice is sent promptly after the change; (e) the notice does not urge the client to sever relationship with the lawyer's former firm and does not recommend the lawyer's employment (although it indicates the lawyer's willingness to continue his responsibility for the matters); (f) the notice makes clear that the client has the right to decide who will complete or continue the matters; and (g) the notice is brief, dignified, and not disparaging of the lawyer's former firm.[12]

Note also requirement (g), that the notice be "not disparaging of the lawyer's former firm."[13] Courts, in general, do not favor departing lawyers making statements disparaging of their former

---

[9] Restatement of the Law Governing Lawyers, Third, § 9 (Official Draft 2000), at Comment *i* (emphasis added).

[10] Rule 1.16, Comment 9.

[11] ABA Informal Opinion No. 1457 (Apr. 29, 1980). *Accord* ABA Formal Opinion 99-414 (Sept. 8, 1999). *Cf.*

Restatement of the Law of Agency, Second, § 396(b) (1958).

[12] ABA Informal Opinion No. 1457 (Apr. 29, 1980).

[13] ABA Informal Opinion No. 1457 (April 29, 1980). ABA Formal Opinion 99-414 (Sept. 8, 1999), at 5 & n. 11, repeats that admonition.

law firm.[14] However, one should distinguish disparaging remarks that are factually verifiable and true from other types of disparaging remarks. Lawyers should have the right to tell the truth. For example, if a lawyer left the firm because it had discriminated against him on account of race, the free speech interests dictate that he should be able to tell that to his clients at Law Firm One.

Note also requirement (b)—"the notice is sent only to persons with whom the lawyer had an active lawyer-client relationship immediately before the change in the lawyer's professional association." ABA Formal 99-414[15] elaborated the meaning of that phrase. A lawyer leaving a law firm "does not have a prior professional relationship with a client sufficient to permit in-person or live telephone solicitation solely by having worked on a matter for the client along with other lawyers in a way that afforded little or no direct contact with the client."[16] The lawyer may contact these firm clients by letter or recorded communication *after* she has departed the law firm.

As for the other clients, her "current clients"—those clients for whose active matters the departing lawyer is currently responsible or plays a *principal role* in the current delivery of legal services—the lawyer may contact these current clients *before* she departs from the firm:

> A lawyer who is departing one law firm for another has an ethical obligation, along with responsible members of the law firm who remain, to assure that those clients are informed that she is leaving the firm. This can be accomplished by the lawyer herself, the responsible members of the firm, or the lawyers and those members jointly. Because a client has the ultimate right to select counsel of his choice, information that the lawyer is leaving and where she will be practicing will assist the client in determining whether his legal work should remain with the law firm, be transferred with the lawyer to her new firm, or be transferred elsewhere. Accordingly,

---

[14]*See, e.g., Adler, Barish, Daniels, Levin & Creskoff v. Epstein*, 482 Pa. 416, 393 A.2d 1175 (1978); *Joseph D. Shein v. Myers*, 394 Pa.Super. 549, 576 A.2d 985 (1990), *appeal denied*, 533 Pa. 600, 617 A.2d 1274 (1991). *Paul L. Pratt, P.C. v. Blunt*, 140 Ill.App.3d 512, 94 Ill.Dec. 815, 488 N.E.2d 1062 (Ill.App.1986), holding that a law firm was not precluded from seeking to enjoin former associates from improperly soliciting his clients based on fact that former associates may also have been subject to disciplinary action; (2) former associates' conduct could be enjoined without violating their consti-

tutional rights of free speech; (3) granting preliminary injunction was not abuse of discretion; but (4) order was overbroad.

Feldman & Pinto, P.C. v. Seithel, 2011 WL 6747464 (E.D. Pa. 2011). The federal district court granted a law firm's motion for a preliminary injunction against a lawyer who tried to recruit many of the law firm's clients after she left the law firm.

[15]ABA Formal 99-414 (Sept. 8, 1999).

[16]ABA Formal Opinion 99-414 (Sept. 8, 1999), at 4 & n. 6.

informing the client of the lawyer's departure in a timely manner is critical to allowing the client to decide who will represent him.[17] Hence, Rule 7.3 does not prohibit a departing lawyer from notifying her current clients that she is leaving one firm and joining another. Such conduct is permitted because the departing lawyer has a present professional relationship with these clients. She may similarly inform clients with whom she has a familial or close personal relationship.[18]

---

[17]ABA Formal Opinion 99-414 (Sept. 8, 1999), at 3 (footnotes omitted).

[18]ABA Formal Opinion 99-414 (Sept. 8, 1999), at 4 to 5 & n. 5.

ing with advertisings of fields of practice and advertisings of lawyer specialization. They first added the topic "Specialization" to the title of Rule 7.4. In the text of Rule 7.4, the drafters removed the reference to specialization and moved it to new Rule 7.4(d). They identified this remaining general text as section (a). The drafters then renumbered section (a) as (b) and (b) as (c) without changing the text of old (a) and (b).

The drafters deleted the alternative (c) provisions that were adopted by the ABA in 1992. Those sections basically permitted a lawyer to advertise a specialization awarded to the lawyer by an external organization as long as the advertisement was truthful. The first alternative (c) provision specified appropriate disclosure if the jurisdiction had an regulatory body to approve certifying organizations and the second alternative (c) specified suggested language if the state did not have such a regulatory body to approve certifying organizations.

The drafters of the 2002 Rules decided that the 1992 Amendments were too permissive of lawyer advertisements of specializations. Thus, they adopted a new Rule 7.4(d) permitting lawyers to

---

nificance of the lawyer's status as a certified specialist. The Rule therefore requires that a lawyer who chooses to communicate recognition by such an organization also clearly state the absence or denial of the organization's authority to grant such certification. Since lawyer advertising through public media and written or recorded communications invites the greatest danger of misleading consumers, the absence or denial of the organization's authority to grant certification must be clearly stated in such advertising in the same sentence that communicates the certification.

[5] In jurisdictions where no appropriate regulatory authority has a procedure for approving organizations granting certification, the Rule requires that a lawyer clearly state such lack of procedure. If, however, the named organization has been accredited by the American Bar Association to certify lawyers as specialists in a particular field of law, the communication need not contain such a statement.

(c) [for jurisdictions where there is a regulatory authority granting certification or approving organizations that grant certification] a lawyer may communicate the fact that the lawyer has been certified as a specialist in a field of law by a named organization or authority but only if:

(1) such certification is granted by the appropriate regulatory authority or by an organization which has been approved by the appropriate regulatory authority to grant such certification; or

(2) such certification is granted by an organization that has not yet been approved by, or has been denied the approval available from, the appropriate regulatory authority, and the absence or denial of approval is clearly stated in the communication, and in any advertising subject to Rule 7.2, such statement appears in the same sentence that communicates the certification.

(c) [for jurisdictions where there is no procedure either for certification of specialties or for approval of organizations granting certification] a lawyer may communicate the fact that the lawyer has been certified as a specialist in a field of law by a named organization, provided that the communication clearly states that there is no procedure in this jurisdiction for approving certifying organizations. If, however, the named organization has been accredited by the American Bar Association to certify lawyers as specialists in a particular field of law, the communication need not contain such a statement.

For a complete review of the history of Model Rule 7.4, see A Legislative History: The Development of the ABA Model Rules of Professional Conduct, 1982–1998 (ABA 1999).

advertise certifications or specializations only if they have been awarded by state or ABA approved organizations. They also deleted Comments 4 and 5 which described the 1992 Rule amendments. See Reporter's Explanation of Changes to Model Rule 7.4.

Model Code Comparison

[1] DR 2-105(A) provided that a lawyer "shall not hold himself out publicly as a specialist, as practicing in certain areas of law or as limiting his practice . . . except as follows:

"(1) A lawyer admitted to practice before the United States Patent and Trademark Office may use the designation 'Patents,' 'Patent Attorney,' 'Patent Lawyer,' or 'Registered Patent Attorney' or any combination of those terms, on his letterhead and office sign.

"(2) A lawyer who publicly discloses fields of law in which the lawyer . . . practices or states that his practice is limited to one or more fields of law shall do so by using designations and definitions authorized and approved by [the agency having jurisdiction of the subject under state law].

"(3) A lawyer who is certified as a specialist in a particular field of law or law practice by [the authority having jurisdiction under state law over the subject of specialization by lawyers] may hold himself out as such, but only in accordance with the rules prescribed by that authority."

[2] EC 2-14 stated that "In the absence of state controls to insure the existence of special competence, a lawyer should not be permitted to hold himself out as a specialist, . . . other than in the fields of admiralty, trademark, and patent law where a holding out as a specialist historically has been permitted."

§ 7.4–1 BACKGROUND AND HISTORY

Since the Supreme Court's decision in *Bates v. State Bar*,[1] the ABA has been concerned about lawyer advertising of fields of practice. This concern has been based on the assumption that when a lawyer claims to practice in a particular field, that lawyer is communicating to the general public that the lawyer specializes in that field. In other words, if a lawyer claims to practice tax law, the ABA has been concerned that the general public will assume that this lawyer is a specialist in tax law. This view causes a serious problem for lawyers who wish to advertise. Lawyers who advertise need to communicate their areas of practice to attract prospective clients. In fact, the most effective advertisements target a segment of the public that is in need to legal services in a particular field of law.

The Model Code required that lawyers use certain designations to advertise a particular area of practice. Under DR 2-105(A)(2), the ABA urged state bars to develop approved designations for advertising fields of practice. And, once the state bar adopted

---

[Section 7.4–1]   97 S.Ct. 2691, 53 L.Ed.2d 810 (1977).

[1]*Bates v. State Bar*, 433 U.S. 350,

such approved language, lawyers needed to use the precise language or else they would be subject to discipline.

This regulatory structure was the subject of the leading case, *In re R.M.J.*[2] The Missouri bar authorities had followed the ABA model and had promulgated a set of rules for advertising fields of practice:

> if the [Missouri] lawyer chooses to list areas of practice in his advertisement, he must do so in one of the two prescribed ways. He may list one of the three general descriptive terms specified in the Rule—"General Civil Practice," "General Criminal Practice," or "General Civil and Criminal Practice." Alternatively, he may use one or more of a list of 23 areas of practice, including for example, "Tort Law," "Family Law," "Probate and Trust Law." He may not list a general term and specific subheadings, nor may he deviate from the precise wording stated in the Rule. He may not indicate that his practice is "limited" to the listed areas and he must include a particular disclaimer of certification of expertise following any listing of specific areas of practice.[3]

Missouri reprimanded R.M.J. because he had deviated from the precise listing of certain areas of practice included in the state's Rule 4. For example, R.M.J.'s advertisement listed "real estate" but Rule 4 used the term "property;" R.M.J. listed "contracts" but Rule 4 did not list that term at all. Because the state could neither demonstrate that R.M.J.'s listing was deceptive nor show that its restrictions promoted any substantial interests, a unanimous U.S. Supreme Court found the state limitations unconstitutional. The Court also invalidated a part of Rule 4 that prohibited a lawyer from identifying the jurisdictions in which he was licensed to practice.

R.M.J. had also emphasized in large, boldface type that he was a member of the U.S. Supreme Court bar. Justice Powell, for the Court, acknowledged that this fact was "relatively uninformative," but held that R.M.J. could not constitutionally be disciplined for advertising it; the record did not show that it was misleading, and Rule 4 did not specifically identify it as misleading, nor place a limitation on its type size, nor require any explanatory disclaimer explaining the significance (or lack thereof) of U.S. Supreme Court bar admission.[4]

One year after *In re R.M.J*, the ABA adopted the 1983 Model Rules which stated that a lawyer may communicate through advertising that the lawyer's practice does or does not include

[2] *In re R.M.J.*, 455 U.S. 191, 102 S.Ct. 929, 71 L.Ed.2d 64 (1982). This case is discussed in greater detail in Chapter 7.0.

[3] 455 U.S. at 194–95, 102 S.Ct. at 933, 71 L.Ed.2d 64.

[4] 455 U.S. at 205–06, 102 S.Ct. at 938–39.

particular fields of law.[5] A Comment to 1983 Rule 7.4, however, had provided that the lawyer may not state that his practice "is limited to" or is "concentrated in" a particular area. The ABA believed that such language would lead the public to presume that the lawyer specialized in those areas. In 1988, the Supreme Court's decision in *Shapero v. Kentucky Bar Association*[6] led the ABA to revisit its language in Rule 7.4. In 1989, the ABA House of Delegates removed the language that lawyers could not stated that their practice is limited to or concentrated in an area of law. It is doubtful that the state could meet the difficult burden of demonstrating that the use of language such as "is limited to" is misleading (while "is not limited to" is not misleading).

After the 1989 amendment to Rule 7.4, the ABA still retained the notion that lawyers could not advertise themselves as specialists unless they fell within three specified exceptions: (1) admiralty practice, (2) patent practice, and (3) specialization plans organized by state bar organizations. The third exception recognized that many states offered certification programs for lawyers in various fields of law.

Since the early 1970s, state bar organizations have experimented with plans of specialization to improve the quality of legal services offered to the public. Specialization permits lawyers to focus their practice on an area of law and after satisfying certain requirements to advertise themselves as specialists in a narrow area of law. When lawyers choose the route of specialization, they have an incentive to become knowledgeable in an area of law and clients can locate those lawyers who have made a decision to practice in this area of law. Some have argued that generalist lawyers will be more likely to refer cases to specialists because the specialist lawyers are less likely to compete with the generalist on additional legal representation for the referred client.

In 1969, an ABA committee on specialization encouraged states to experiment with plans of specialization.[7] Four states adopted plans between 1971 and 1975.[8] California and Texas adopted "bar certified" plans, which required that lawyers satisfy a minimum period of time for practice, a special written examination, peer recommendations, and substantial involvement and concen-

---

[5] Rule 7.4.

[6] *Shapero v. Kentucky Bar Association*, 486 U.S. 466, 108 S.Ct. 1916, 100 L.Ed.2d 475 (1988).

[7] At that time, the ABA chose not to adopt a national plan of specialization. Instead, they encouraged states to experiment with different ap-

proaches. *See* John M. Brumbaugh & Tori Jo Wible, *Certification from a National Perspective*, 77 FLORIDA BAR JOURNAL 30 (Apr. 2003).

[8] *See* American Bar Association Standing Committee on Specialization, Report to the House of Delegates, Information Bulletin Number 4 (1978).

tration in the field of specialization. New Mexico adopted a less formalized plans of "self designated" specialization, which has fewer formal requirements than the bar certified plans. Florida adopted a intermediate approach between the New Mexico approach and that of Texas and California. Bar certified plans were designed to improve the competence of the lawyers who sought the certification designation, while self designation plans were viewed as permitting lawyers to focus their practice by themselves to an area of law and then to advertise the self designated certification. In 1990, the ABA published Model Standards for Specialty Areas for states to examine in creating standards for specialization.[9] These standards covered specific guidance for 24 areas of law. The reference in the 1983 Model Rules version of Rule 7.4(c) to state programs of certification was intended to cover the various state plans for certifying lawyers.

The ABA's ban on advertising specializations and certifications unless they fell within the recognized exceptions was challenged in *Peel v. Attorney Registration and Disciplinary Commission of Illinois*.[10] In *Peel*, a divided Court ruled that free speech guarantees prohibited Illinois from disciplining a lawyer who had stated on his letterhead that the National Board of Trial Advocacy had certified him as a "Certified Civil Trial Specialist." The plurality concluded that Peel's statement was neither potentially nor actually misleading (the National Board of Trial Advocacy was a bona fide organization that had made a reasonable inquiry into Peel's fitness), and the state did not have a sufficient interest to justify a categorical ban on the use of such statements. The plurality noted that terms like "air conditioning specialist" or "foreign car specialist" are common, and the public does not think that they imply a claim of formal recognition by the state.

In 1992, the ABA amended Rule 7.4 once again, this time in response to *Peel v. Attorney Registration and Disciplinary Commission*.[11] The post-*Peel* Rule 7.4 generally allowed a lawyer to call herself a "specialist," if the communication is not misleading.[12] When states have tried to limit lawyers from making truthful, non-misleading speech, the states have lost. It is not enough for the state merely to declare that some speech is "inherently misleading." For example, *Ibanez v. Florida Department of*

---

[9]*See* American Bar Association Model Standards for Specialty Areas (1990).

[10]*Peel v. Attorney Registration and Disciplinary Commission of Illinois*, 496 U.S. 91, 110 S.Ct. 2281, 110 L.Ed.2d 83 (1990).

[11]*Peel v. Attorney Registration and Disciplinary Commission*, 496 U.S. 91, 110 S.Ct. 2281, 110 L.Ed.2d 83 (1990). This case is discussed in greater detail in Chapter 7.0.

[12]Rule 7.4, Comment 1.

Business and Professional Regulation[13] held that the Florida Board of Accountancy violated free speech when it reprimanded Silvia Ibanez, an attorney (who argued her own case), because she had truthfully advertised that she was a Certified Public Accountant (CPA) and a Certified Financial Planner (CFP). The state Board of Accountancy had licensed her as a CPA and a bona fide private organization had certified her as a CFP.

Peel plainly recognized that third party organizations could offer their members certification of specialties apart from the specialization plans offered by the state bar organizations. After *Peel*, the ABA and the states bar organizations needed to address how they should constitutionally regulate such third party organizations that desire to enter the certification role for their members. The 1992 Amendments to Rule 7.4 adopted the following system for regulating third party certification of lawyers. If a state has a system to grant certification, the lawyer may communicate her certification if it is from the state or a state-approved group. Even if the state has not yet approved an organization granting certification, or the state has denied approval, the lawyer may still communicate the certification *if* "the absence or denial of approval is clearly stated in the communication." If Rule 7.2 (regulating advertising) applies, then the statement (of the absence or denial of approval) must appear in the same sentence that advertises the certification.[14] If the state has no procedure to certify specialists or to approve private organizations that certify specialists, the lawyer can still communicate that the private organization has certified her, as long as her communication includes a warning that clearly explains that the state has no procedure to approve certifying organizations. However, the ABA Model Rules provide that if the ABA has accredited the organization to certify specialists in a particular area of law,[15] then the communication does not have to contain this warning.[16]

As discussed below, the ABA amended this regulatory and disclosure structure in the 2002 version of Rule 7.4(c).

---

[13]*Ibanez v. Florida Department of Business and Professional Regulation,* 512 U.S. 136, 114 S.Ct. 2084, 129 L.Ed.2d 118 (1994).

[14]Rule 7.4(c).

[15]During the February 1993, midyear meeting, the ABA House of Delegates approved *Standards for Accreditation of Specialty Certification Programs for Lawyers,* which are Standards that seek to ensure that the lawyer has a special proficiency in the specialty and devotes a substantial amount of time to this type of work. These Standards also require that the certifying organization be composed primarily by members who are lawyers.

[16]Rule 7.4(d).

§ 7.4–2 COMMUNICATION OF FIELDS OF PRACTICE

Rule 7.4(a) states that "A lawyer may communicate the fact that the lawyer does or does not practice in particular fields of law." Of course, any such statements must be truthful and not false and misleading.[1] And, the Rules (unlike the Code) require that any advertising contain the name of at least one lawyer or the law firm responsible for its content.[2]

Comment 1 to Rule 7.4 states that a lawyer may state that he or she is a specialist, specializes in, or practices a specialty. But any such statement would need to satisfy Rule 7.1's prohibition against false or misleading advertisements. Presumably, a lawyer could not use such terms lightly. Instead, the lawyer would need to have some objective basis for using the terms "specializes in" or is a specialist in a particular field.

§ 7.4–3 REGULATION OF COMMUNICATION ABOUT SPECIALIZATION

The drafters of the 2002 Rules separated the discussion of specialization from the general provision on advertising fields of practice. Thus, specialization is addressed in sections (b), (c), and (d) of Rule 7.4.

Rule 7.4 continues to accept the specialties of admiralty and patent law, which historically have been allowed, long before *Peel*.[1] The Comment acknowledges that each of these areas has a long established history of recognizing their members as specialists.[2]

When the drafters of the 2002 Rules separated the topic of specialization from communication about fields of practice, they also decided not to place these two designations under the specialization part of the rule. The drafters decided that these areas present unique practice areas that justify an affirmative rule

---

[1] Rule 7.1.

[2] Rule 7.2(d).

[Section 7.4–3]

[1] Rule 7.4(b), (c).

Even the Model Code allowed these specialties: DR 2-105(A)(1) allowed a lawyer admitted to practice before the United States Patent and Trademark Office to use a designation such as "Patent Attorney." EC 2-14 also allowed a lawyer to "hold himself out as a specialist" in "admiralty, trademark, and patent law" because in those areas "holding out as a specialist historically has been permitted."

Note the drafting error: EC 2-14, the ethical aspiration (the supposedly higher goal), was drafted more broadly than DR 2-105(A)(1) (the supposedly bare minimum ethical requirement). Thus, as a disciplinable minimum, the lawyer can only hold himself out as a patent attorney, but as an aspiration, he may also hold himself out as an admiralty or trademark lawyer too.

Even the ABA Canons of Professional Ethics (1908) allowed a lawyer to hold himself out as a proctor in admiralty or as a patent attorney or trademark attorney. Canon 27.

[2] *See* Rule 7.4, Comment 2.

permitting lawyers practicing in these areas to use special designations.[3] Patent law involves a separate admissions system and thus justifies a rule allowing lawyers who practice in this area to use a specialist designation. Proctors in admiralty law are viewed as doing more than simply practicing in an area of law.

The drafters of the 2002 Rules made a significant change in its treatment of advertising of certification of specialties. Rule 7.4(d) prohibits a lawyer from stating or implying that the lawyer has been certified as a specialist in a particular area of law unless the organization that granted to certification has been approved by the state or granted certification by the ABA; the name of the organization must also be clearly disclosed in the communication. This Rule changes the prior law that permitted a lawyer to advertise that he or she had been certified as a specialist by an organization that had not been approved by the state authority or by the ABA. Under the prior Rule, the lawyer could have communicated such information provided that absence of such approval or certification was included in the same sentence as the certification.[4] The drafters were concerned that this forced disclaimer was not sufficient to solve the problem that the certification by an unapproved organization may be false and misleading.

An absolute ban on lawyer communication of certification of specialization when the certifying organization is not authorized by the state or ABA to grant such certifications may conflict with the Supreme Court decision in *Peel*.[5] If the lawyer's statement about a certification is accurate, and the organization is *bona fide* (the facts of *Peel*) how can the state bar constitutionally restrict its use in a communication?

Nonetheless, the drafters believed that, in light of the harm that may result, communications about certifications of specialties should be restricted to ABA and state approved organizations. In order to show that it is possibly misleading for a lawyer to *truthfully* state that she is certified as a specialist by a *bona fide* organization that is not approved by the ABA or the state, the state (using the analogy of the *Went for It* decision[6]) may decide to commission a study to determine whether consumers are mis-

---

[3]Reporter's Explanation of Changes to Model Rule 7.4. The drafters did not intend a substantive change with this reorganization.

[4]*See* 1992 Model Rule 7.4(c) and alternative (c). *See also* Reporter's Explanation of Changes to Model Rule 7.4.

[5]*Peel v. Attorney Registration and Disciplinary Commission*, 496 U.S. 91, 110 S.Ct. 2281, 110 L.Ed.2d 83 (1990).

[6]*Florida Bar v. Went For It, Inc.*, 515 U.S. 618, 115 S.Ct. 2371, 132 L.Ed.2d 541 (1995). In this case, a lawyer and a lawyer referral service

led by lawyer communications that indicate the lawyer is certified as a specialist by a group that has not been approved by the state or the ABA.

Such a study may show that lay persons place great weight on such certifications of specialties and that such importance may not be justified given the lack of controls on the certifying agency. For example, potential clients may believe that certified lawyers are more competent than non-certified lawyers. Or, that certified lawyers have passed a rigorous set of standards when that may not be the case. It would help if there were evidence that some programs grant certifications without established standards to increase competence, but in that case the organization's certification would not really be *bona fide*, and the state's general prohibition of misleading advertising would come into play.[7] The state may also argue that since *Peel*, the ABA has expanded its program to certify third party organizations as qualified to grant specializations status to lawyers. At the time of the *Peel* decision, this regulatory structure was not in place, and these regulations do not pose an insurmountable barrier for third-party certification organizations and lawyers.

Obviously, the drafters of the 2002 Rules believed that a disclaimer was insufficient to protect the public from misleading certifications.[8] But the Court has generally focused on disclaimers so it remains to be seen if this provision of Rule 7.4 will survive a constitutional challenge. It may be that it will be hard to find a case that is ripe if all *bona fide* organizations secure ABA approval.

There is another concern as well regarding a state bar's empiri-

---

brought action challenging constitutional validity of Florida Bar rules that prohibited lawyers from using targeted direct-mail to solicit personal injury or wrongful death clients within 30 days of accident. The Court (5 to 4) upheld this rule in light of empirical support that the Florida Bar had developed; Florida argued that the restriction on targeted mailing by plaintiff-attorneys is necessary to protect the public image of lawyers. *See* Ronald D. Rotunda, *Professionalism, Legal Advertising, and Free Speech In the Wake of Florida Bar v. Went For It, Inc.*, 49 ARKANSAS L. REV. 703 (1997) (Symposium), *reprinted in*, 12 LAWYERS' LIABILITY REV. 1 (No. 10, Oct. 1998)(part I), 12 LAWYERS' LIABILITY REV. 1 (No. 11, Nov. 1998) (part II), & 12 LAWYERS' LIABILITY REV.

1 (No. 12, Dec. 1998)(part III); Steven M. Field, *Thirty-Day Restrictions On Attorney Direct-Mail Solicitation: The United States Supreme Court Went For It*, 21 CARDOZO L. REV. 1999 (2000); William E. Hornsby, Jr., *Ad Rules Infinitum: The Need For Alternatives To State-Based Ethics Governing Legal Services Marketing*, 36 U. RICH. L. REV. 49 (2002).

[7] If the state had adopted its own program of specialization that was based on a self designation model, that fact may hurt a state's case that ABA or state approval somehow protects the public more than its own self-designation plan.

[8] Reporter's Explanation of Changes to Model Rule 7.4.

cal studies that attempt to show that consumers of legal services are misled by truthful claims that one is certified by a *bona fide* private organization. The American Bar Association's extensive study of advertising has demonstrated one remarkably steady correlation: If a state bar association, in preparation for a judicial challenge, sponsors a study linking the public's perception of lawyers with advertising or targeted mail, only then does the study find some sort of relationship.[9]

Rule 7.4(d)(2) requires that a lawyer who refers to a certification of a specialization must clearly identify the certifying organization in the communication. This disclosure of the certifying organization provides prospective clients with information about the identity of the certifying organization and, therefore, gives them a basis to make further inquiry about the value that should be placed on the certification of a specialization.

---

[9]ABA Commission on Advertising, Lawyer Advertising at the Crossroads: Professional Policy Considerations 72 (1995).

lawyer identification because they do not need to do so. This less restrictive regulatory scheme does not prohibit truthful identification of a lawyer as a lawyer whether or not the publicity is "germane."

§ 7.5–3 TRADE NAMES

The Model Code prohibited lawyers in private practice from practicing under a trade name whether or not it was misleading.[1] In other words, a law firm could not call itself, "The 47th Street Law Office," even though it really was located on 47th Street. However, the Model Code did allow a law firm to use the name of one or more deceased partners or retired members of the firm.[2]

The position of the Code was hardly logical. Why should a law firm be allowed to call itself "Isham, Lincoln, & Beale" (where the "Lincoln" referred to Robert Todd Lincoln, the son of Abraham Lincoln) even though Mr. Lincoln was long deceased, but it could not call itself the "47th Street Law Office" when it really was on 47th Street?[3] If the first name is not misleading, why should the state prohibit the second name, which also is not misleading? A firm name that uses the name of a deceased partner is really a form of trade name.[4] A well known firm name develops value and good will over the years. It is understandable that a law firm wishes to retain the name. But 47th Street Law Office may also develop name recognition and good will.

The U.S. Supreme Court has held that, under the First Amendment, a state may constitutionally impose blanket prohibition of trade names of optometrists.[5] However, there may be constitutional problems when the state bans one type of professional trade name ("the 44th Street Clinic") but not another ("Jones & Smith"—a law firm where Jones is no longer associated with the firm because he is dead). In that case, the asserted state justification is undercut by the state's own actions.

The Model Rules are more logical and avoid these constitutional

---

yer as a lawyer and the author of a book, it was also proper to identify the author as a lawyer in dignified advertisements for the book. DR 2-101(H) (5).

[Section 7.5–3]

[1] DR 2-102(B).

[2] DR 2-102(B), stating that a law firm name may include "the name or names of deceased or retired members of the firm or of a predecessor firm in a continuing line of succession." (footnote omitted).

[3] This is especially true now that a lawyer who was never associated with the firm can buy the law practice. Rule 1.17, Sale of a Law Practice, provides: "A lawyer or a law firm may sell or purchase a law practice, *including good will*, if the following conditions are satisfied. . . . " (emphasis added).

[4] The Code pretended that such names were not trade names and consequently did not bother to distinguish them from other trade names.

[5] *Friedman v. Rogers*, 440 U.S. 1, 99 S.Ct. 887, 59 L.Ed.2d 100 (1979).

issues by prohibiting the use of a trade name in private practice only if the name is misleading or implies a connection with a government agency or charity or public legal services organization that does not exist.[6] For example, the "State of Alabama Legal Clinic" may be misleading if it is not connected with the state and is not a public legal aid agency. In that case, an express disclaimer may be necessary.[7] Otherwise, the "47th Street Law Office" or the "ABC Legal Clinic" is a perfectly valid name for a law office.[8]

The Model Rules (like the Model Code) also allow the use of the name of a deceased or retired member in a continuing line of succession.[9] In other words, a law firm cannot call itself "Law Offices of William O. Douglas & Hugo Black" if Douglas and Black were never members of that firm.

Leaving aside the question of deceased or retired partners, only a member of a law firm actively and regularly practicing with that firm may be named in a firm name. Consequently the names of lawyers acting in a public office, in either a judicial, executive, or administrative capacity may not appear in firm names or on professional notices during the period in which the lawyer is serving in that capacity, unless that lawyer is still actively and regularly practicing law with the firm.[10]

The drafters of the 2002 Rules added to Comment 1 language that would prohibit a law firm from using the name of a nonlawyer in the name of the law firm. When a law firm chooses to use the name of a person, the assumption is that this individual is or was at one time licensed to practice law and in fact did practice with the firm. This issue arose when the Washington, D.C. firm of McKee, Nelson Ernst & Young sought to open an office in New York under the same name. The District of Columbia Bar did not object to the addition of Ernest & Young to the name, as the local ethics rules permit non lawyer ownership in law firms. However, the ethics rules of the New York Bar prohibited the firm from using the trade name of a national accounting firm (Ernst & Young) in the name of the law firm.[11]

The rules that apply to firm names have been extended in Rule

---

[6]Rule 7.5(a).

[7]Rule 7.5, Comment 1: "If a private firm uses a trade name that includes a geographical name such as 'Springfield Legal Clinic,' an express disclaimer that it is a public legal aid agency *may* be required to avoid a misleading implication."

[8]Rule 7.5, Comment 1.

[9]Rule 7.5(a) and Comment 1.

[10]DR 2-102(B); Rule 7.5(c) (prohibiting the use of the name of a lawyer serving in public office during any substantial period in which the lawyer is not regularly practicing with the firm).

[11]*See* Otis Bilodeau, *Growing Fast, Firm Gives Up Ernest Young Name*, LEGAL TIMES, May 1, 2001, at 1. The New York Code of Ethics prohibits lawyers from practicing "under a trade

7.5(b) to "other professional designations." The Comment explains this phrase to include "a distinctive website address or comparable professional designation." Law firms have established web sites, list serves, and email addresses that use trade names.[12] It makes sense to apply the same principles to advertising names and other designations in electronic media that have been developed in law firm trade names.

As long as the designation, such as a website address, email address, or other electronic designation is not false and misleading, the lawyer or law firm may use it to identify itself in electronic media. The use of the terms, other professional designation is broad enough to include new designations that may arise in the future.

§ 7.5–4 IMPLIED PARTNERSHIPS AND OTHER LAW FIRM ORGANIZATIONS

A lawyer may state or imply that she is a member of a partnership or other organization only when that in fact is the case.[1] In some cases, lawyers are not practicing as law partners but are only sharing offices. If so, it would be misleading if any of the lawyers falsely stated or implied that they are partners.

If a lawyer falsely states or implies that she is in partnership with another lawyer, she may also find that she has assumed vicarious liability under the law of agency and partnership.[2]

One state ethics opinion has held that a law firm may own a subsidiary law firm that engages in the practice of law, as long as

name, a name that is misleading as to the identity of the lawyer or lawyers practicing under such name, or a firm name containing names other than those of one or more of the lawyers in the firm. . . ." 22 NYCRR 1200.7 (DR 2-102(b)). One would suspect that the Ernst & Young designation would be prohibited under Rule 7.5(a).

[12]Vanessa S. Browne-Barbour, *Lawyer and Law Firm Web Pages as Advertising: Proposed Guidelines*, 28 RUTGERS COMPUTER & TECH. L.J. 275 (2002), discusses the increasing use of law firms of web pages as advertising and argues that there should be a national rule to prevent inadvertent and unavoidable violations of state rules that conflict with each other.

[Section 7.5–4]

[1]Rule 7.5(d); DR 2-102(D). Comment 2 to Rule 7.5 removed the references to partnerships and broad-

ened the discussion to apply to all forms of organizations that lawyers practice in today. This would include partnerships, professional corporations, limited liability partnerships, and limited liability corporations as well as other organizations that exist or may arise in the future.

[2]ALAN R. BROMBERG, CRANE & BROMBERG ON PARTNERSHIP (West Pub. Co., 1968), at § 36, p. 196:

"Partnership by estoppel is not a form of business association. Rather, it is a technique for fixing liability on one who has let it appear that he is in a business association. It is not a voluntary arrangement, except in the sense that the alleged partner acted voluntarily when he did whatever it was that precipitates the liability."

This principle has long been accepted in the law. *See, e.g., Speer v. Bishop*, 24 Ohio St. 598 (1874).

the subsidiary includes below the firm name the phrase, "a subsidiary of X law firm."[3]

---

[3] 3 N.J. Opinion 704 (May 1, 2006); N.J. Advertising Opinion 37 (May 1, 2006), *noted in* 22 ABA/BNA MANUAL ON PROFESSIONAL CONDUCT, Current Reports News 257 (May 31, 2006).

CHAPTER 7.6
POLITICAL CONTRIBUTIONS TO OBTAIN GOVERNMENT LEGAL ENGAGEMENTS OR APPOINTMENTS BY JUDGES

RULE 7.6: POLITICAL CONTRIBUTIONS TO OBTAIN GOVERNMENT LEGAL ENGAGEMENTS OR APPOINTMENTS BY JUDGES

A lawyer or law firm shall not accept a government legal engagement or an appointment by a judge if the lawyer or law firm makes a political contribution or solicits political contributions for the purpose of obtaining or being considered for that type of legal engagement or appointment.

Comment

[1] Lawyers have a right to participate fully in the political process, which includes making and soliciting political contributions to candidates for judicial and other public office. Nevertheless, when lawyers make or solicit political contributions in order to obtain an engagement for legal work awarded by a government agency, or to obtain appointment by a judge, the public may legitimately question whether the lawyers engaged to perform the work are selected on the basis of competence and merit. In such a circumstance, the integrity of the profession is undermined.

[2] The term "political contribution" denotes any gift, subscription, loan, advance or deposit of anything of value made directly or indirectly to a candidate, incumbent, political party or campaign committee to influence or provide financial support for election to or retention in judicial or other government office. Political contributions in initiative and referendum elections are not included. For purposes of this Rule, the term "political contribution" does not include uncompensated services.

[3] Subject to the exceptions below, (i) the term "government legal engagement" denotes any engagement to provide legal services that a public official has the direct or indirect power to award; and (ii) the term "appointment by a judge" denotes an appointment to a position such as referee, commissioner, special master, receiver, guardian or other similar position that is made by a judge. Those terms do not, however, include (a) substantially uncompensated

services; (b) engagements or appointments made on the basis of experience, expertise, professional qualifications and cost following a request for proposal or other process that is free from influence based upon political contributions; and (c) engagements or appointments made on a rotational basis from a list compiled without regard to political contributions.

[4] The term "lawyer or law firm" includes a political action committee or other entity owned or controlled by a lawyer or law firm.

[5] Political contributions are for the purpose of obtaining or being considered for a government legal engagement or appointment by a judge if, but for the desire to be considered for the legal engagement or appointment, the lawyer or law firm would not have made or solicited the contributions. The purpose may be determined by an examination of the circumstances in which the contributions occur. For example, one or more contributions that in the aggregate are substantial in relation to other contributions by lawyers or law firms, made for the benefit of an official in a position to influence award of a government legal engagement, and followed by an award of the legal engagement to the contributing or soliciting lawyer or the lawyer's firm would support an inference that the purpose of the contributions was to obtain the engagement, absent other factors that weigh against existence of the proscribed purpose. Those factors may include among others that the contribution or solicitation was made to further a political, social, or economic interest or because of an existing personal, family, or professional relationship with a candidate.

[6] If a lawyer makes or solicits a political contribution under circumstances that constitute bribery or another crime, Rule 8.4(b) is implicated.

Authors' 1983 Model Rules Comparison
The 1983 Model Rules did not include a Rule 7.6 on the topic of political contributions by lawyers to obtain government or judicial employment. The ABA House of Delegates adopted Rule 7.6 in February 2000.

The 2002 version is identical to the Rule adopted by the ABA House of Delegates in 2000.

Authors' Model Code Comparison
The Model Code did not contain language dealing with this topic.

§ 7.6–1 INTRODUCTION TO RULE 7.6
In the arcane $1.3 trillion municipal bond market, "pay-to-play" has emerged from obscurity. This alliterative title refers to the situation where lawyers give campaign contributions to state and local officials who direct lucrative municipal and state bond business their way.

State and federal laws already forbid bribery—where one can demonstrate proof of a *quid pro quo*—and the ABA Model Rules already provide that such bribery is disciplinable.[1] In addition, Rule 7.2 forbids a lawyer from paying someone in return for that person recommending the lawyer's legal services.[2] However, except for Rule 7.6, there is no restriction in the Model Rules that limits a lawyer's campaign contributions.

Because state and federal statutes do not prohibit pay-to-play if there is no *quid pro quo*, in the late 1990's, Arthur Levitt, then chairman of the Securities and Exchange Commission, along with others, urged the American Bar Association to use the ethics rules to ban pay-to-play. Those proposing this ban did not argue that the lawyers provide incompetent services but, rather, that the practice is fundamentally unfair. Opponents responded that a ban is bad policy because lawyers should be involved in campaigns as part of their civic responsibility. Punishing campaign contributions also raises First Amendment concerns because campaign contributions are a form of free speech.[3]

Moreover, opponents argue that the Rule is difficult to enforce for two reasons. First, it makes crucial a very subjective element—"for the purpose of obtaining." Second, it does not apply to those who receive contributions. Federal disclosure laws can work because they apply to the candidates receiving campaign funds. In contrast, Rule 7.6 is drafted to cover only those who "make" a contribution.[4] It does not embrace the public official who receives the contribution, even if that official is a lawyer.[5]

[Section 7.6–1]

[1] Rule 8.4(b).

[2] Rule 7.2(b). This prohibition is subject to exceptions not relevant to the issue of pay-to-play. Rule 7.2(b)(1) to (4). Rule 7.2(b) may literally cover pay-to-play but it was drafted in order to prevent lawyers from hiring "runners" to secure work for them. E.g., the lawyer pays a hospital orderly to drop the lawyer's business card with an accident victim and recommend that the victim hire the lawyer.

[3] *Blount v. S.E.C.*, 61 F.3d 938 (D.C. Cir.1995) upheld SEC regulation of "pay to play" as applied to municipal securities professionals. In that case, the president of a state political party brought suit against the Securities and Exchange Commission claiming that regulation promulgated by municipal securities rule-making board approved by SEC, violated his First and Tenth Amendment rights.

The D.C. Circuit held that: (1) the regulation restricting ability of municipal securities professionals to contribute to and solicit contributions for political campaigns of state officials from whom they solicit or obtain business, satisfied the test of "strict scrutiny" for restrictions on freedom of speech, and (2) the restrictions also did not violate Tenth Amendment.

[4] The Report accompanying Rule 7.6 acknowledged that lawyers are not the most important actors in the pay-to-play state of affairs. Rather, the public officials receiving the campaign contributions are the primary actors. In addition, the Report recommends the use of competition in public procurement. Report of the ABA Section of Business Law, Section of Business Law Section of State and Local Government Law Standing Committee on Ethics and Professional Responsibility Association of the Bar of the City of New York, *Report with Recommenda-*

In 1998, the ABA House of Delegates rejected a pay-to-play proposal but continued to study the issue. In 2000, the House approved this new Rule, which bans more than that which Mr. Levitt originally proposed.[6] The House placed this new rule in Part 7 of the ABA Model Rules. Part 7 is titled, "Information About Legal Services." This Rule is not really on that topic. However, it relates, in part, to giving money in the hopes of obtaining business, and that may be why the ABA placed the new Rule in Part 7.[7]

There are several important points to remember in considering Rule 7.6. First, it is not limited to the municipal bond industry. It bans the lawyer or law firm from accepting any "legal engagement or an appointment by a judge if the lawyer or law firm makes a political contribution or solicits political contributions

---

tions to the House of Delegates, Nov. 23, 1999, at 5. See discussion in, Ronald D. Rotunda, *Competitive Bidding Would End "Pay-to-Play,"* 20 NATIONAL LAW JOURNAL A23 (June 29, 1998).

[5]In 1999, the ABA added Canon 3C(5) to the Code of Judicial Conduct:

> A judge shall not appoint a lawyer to a position if the judge either knows that the lawyer has contributed more than [$___] within the prior [___] years to the judge's election campaign, or learns of such a contribution by means of a timely motion by a party or other person properly interested in the matter, unless
>
> (a) the position is substantially uncompensated;
>
> (b) the lawyer has been selected in rotation from a list of qualified and available lawyers compiled without regard to their having made political contributions; or
>
> (c) the judge or another presiding or administrative judge affirmatively finds that no other lawyer is willing, competent and able to accept the position.

This judicial rule, like Model Rule 7.6, reflects the concern that some people have about the appearance of impropriety if lawyers make a political contribution to the judge, and the judge then rewards (or appears to reward) those lawyers by appointing them as special masters, guardians, receivers, or similar positions. Canon 3C(5) provides, in general, that a judge should not appoint a lawyer to a particular position if the judge learns or knows that the

appointee has contributed more than a certain amount (the local jurisdiction sets the amount that triggers this prohibition) within a certain period of years (the local jurisdiction also sets the relevant time period). To some extent it reaffirms a more general provision, Canon 3C(4), which instructs judges to exercise their power of appointment on the basis of merit and not on the basis of nepotism. *See* Ronald D. Rotunda, *Judicial Elections, Campaign Financing, and Free Speech,* 2 ELECTION LAW JOURNAL 79, 87–88 (2003).

[6]ABA/BNA LAWYERS' MANUAL ON PROFESSIONAL CONDUCT, Current Reports, vol. 16, at 64–65 (Mar. 1, 2000).

[7]Rule 7.2(b) also deals with paying money in an effort to secure legal employment.

This topic has inspired several articles. *See* Jon B. Jordan, *The Regulation of "Pay-to-Play" and the Influence of Political Contributions in the Municipal Securities Industry,* 1999 COLUMBIA BUSINESS L. REV. 489 (1999); Brian C. Buescher, *ABA Model Rule 7.6: The ABA Pleases The SEC, But Does Not Solve Pay To Play,* 14 GEORGETOWN J. LEGAL ETHICS 139 (2000); John C. Coffee, Jr., *"When Smoke Gets In Your Eyes": Myth And Reality About The Synthesis Of Private Counsel And Public Client,* 51 DEPAUL L. REV. 241 (2001).

for the purpose of obtaining or being considered for that type of legal engagement or appointment."

Second, the rule extends its prohibition to a "lawyer *or law firm*." This marks the first time that ABA House of Delegates has approved a rule that seeks to discipline a law firm and not merely an individual lawyer within a firm.

Third, Rule 7.6 provides a new definition of "lawyer" or "law firm." These terms include any "political action committee or other entity owned or *controlled by* a lawyer or law firm."[8] This proviso would cover the situation where a lawyer sought to launder the contribution. If, in a 300-person firm, an associate's spouse gives $275 to a state politician, should the law firm be affected? The answer would be yes *if* the lawyer controlled the contribution. Otherwise, we would expect regular laundering of campaign funds. The law firm or lawyer would not be subject to discipline if they did not know of the contribution, because then they could not control it. In many circumstances, no law firm can even be expected to know of the relative's contributions. The firm has no power over a lawyer's spouse. The lawyer, as well, would not normally be expected to have any power over the lawyer's spouse.

Fourth, Rule 7.6 only covers the case where the lawyer engages in the prohibited action *and* receives the appointment. The language of Rule 7.6 prohibits "accept[ing] the government legal engagement or an appointment. . . . ."[9] Moreover, the Report accompanying Rule 7.6 makes it clear that the Rule is not "implicated" until the lawyer accepts the appointment.[10]

Presumably, this Rule should *not* be read in conjunction with Rule 8.4(a), which states that a lawyer may be disciplined if he or she "attempt[s] to violate any of the Rules of Professional Conduct," because Rule 7.6 does not prohibit attempts. However, if a lawyer corruptly attempts to secure an appointment but fails, while Rule 7.6 is inapplicable, other Rules, such as Rule 8.4(b), or Rule 7.2(b) are still applicable and cover corrupt conduct or attempted corrupt conduct.

In addition, this Rule is limited to campaign contributions in the form of money, loans, or "anything of value made directly or

---

[8]Rule 7.6, Comment 4 (emphasis added).

[9]Rule 7.6 (emphasis added).

[10]Report of the ABA Section of Business Law, Section of Business Law Section of State and Local Government Law Standing Committee on Ethics and Professional Responsibility Association of the Bar of the City of New York, *Report with Recommendations to the House of Delegates*, Nov. 23, 1999, at 12: "Although the purpose for making or soliciting contributions is an element under the proposed Rule, it is *not* implicated until a government legal engagement or appointment by a judge *is accepted*." (emphasis added).

indirectly" to a candidate, incumbent, political party, etc. The Rule does not cover campaign contributions in the form of uncompensated services, even if the lawyer contributes the services "for the purpose of obtaining" legal work. In other words, if a lawyer endorses a judge for reelection, "for the purpose of obtaining" from a judge a lucrative court appointment, the lawyer has *not* violated Rule 7.6. However, if that same lawyer contributes $1 to the judge's political campaign for the very same purpose, the lawyer has violated Rule 7.6.

The requirement that the services be rendered "for the purpose of obtaining" the appointment is a specific intent requirement that also narrows the application of the rule. "Legal minds will have little difficulty finding this rule inapplicable to the facts of their case, based on the attorney's assertion that his or her motivation was not political."[11]

The Rule does not cover political contributions made in the expectation that the donee (the Governor, the President) will appoint the lawyer to fill a particular position, for example, judge or other appointed government position. The Rule is limited to the donee who gives the lawyer a "government legal engagement" (municipal bond work); when the Rule does cover appointments, it is limited to appointment *by* a judge, not *to* a judgeship. The Rule simply does not concern itself with appointment by an executive or legislative branch official.

§ 7.6–2 ENFORCEMENT OF THE PROHIBITION OF PAY-TO-PLAY CONTRIBUTIONS

Opponents of Rule 7.6 argued that this provision would be difficult to enforce. In fact, the National Organization of Bar Counsel, representing the lawyers who prosecute discipline cases, warned the ABA of enforcement problems. The members of the NOBC unanimously voted that "we cannot enforce Rule 7.6 unless the conduct in question reaches the standard of bribery."[1] In response, supporters of this Rule argued that the Rule should be

---

[11]Rule 7.6, Comment 2. As Professor Coffee notes:

"Even if the ABA rule were adopted by state bars, its language does not prohibit political contributions or bar the attorney from accepting the engagement—except and unless the contribution was made for the 'purpose of obtaining' such engagement. Legal minds will have little difficulty finding this rule inapplicable to the facts of their case, based on the attorney's assertion

that his or her motivation was not political."

John C. Coffee, Jr., *"When Smoke Gets In Your Eyes": Myth And Reality About The Synthesis Of Private Counsel And Public Client*, 51 DePaul L. Rev. 241, 245–46 (2001).

[Section 7.6–2]

[1]ABA/BNA Lawyers' Manual on Professional Conduct, Current Reports, vol. 16, at 64 (Mar. 1, 2000).

"largely self-enforcing."[2] Also, it is not intended to be enforced, "except in extreme circumstances."[3]

However, it is not necessary that the disciplinary authority prove an explicit *quid pro quo*, because typically "pay-to-play" operates without "formal promises or understandings."[4] Unlike proof of a bribe,[5] a criminal act, proof of a violation of Rule 7.6 does not require proof beyond a reasonable doubt. It is only necessary to prove a violation by "clear and convincing evidence."[6]

The drafters of Rule 7.6 intended that "only clear cases will be subject to disciplinary action," those cases that are the most "egregious."[7] The disciplinary authorities must prove that "no reasonable purpose could have existed *except* the consideration of the lawyer or law firm for legal work (e.g., the contribution by a lawyer in one state to the state treasurer of another state, where there is no personal relationship or political issue connection)."[8]

---

[2] Report of the ABA Section of Business Law, Section of Business Law Section of State and Local Government Law Standing Committee on Ethics and Professional Responsibility Association of the Bar of the City of New York, *Report with Recommendations to the House of Delegates*, Nov. 23, 1999, at 10.

[3] House of Delegates Debate of Feb. 14, 2000, quoted in, ABA/BNA LAWYERS' MANUAL ON PROFESSIONAL CONDUCT, Current Reports, vol. 16, at 64 (Mar. 1, 2000) (remarks of Barbara Medel Mayden, representing the Business Law Section).

[4] Report of the ABA Section of Business Law, Section of Business Law Section of State and Local Government Law Standing Committee on Ethics and Professional Responsibility Association of the Bar of the City of New York, *Report with Recommendations to the House of Delegates*, Nov. 23, 1999, at 9.

[5] When the Government prosecutes under the bribery statutes, there is no need to refer to Rule 7.6, which is not part of the criminal law. In 2005, the federal government indicted a dozen people, including two bankers, a lawyer, and a former city treasurer. Mark Whitehouse, *Closing the Deal: As Banks Bid for City Bond Work, 'Pay to Play' Tradition Endures: How 2 Men from J.P. Morgan Rewarded a Fund-Raiser For Philadelphia's Mayor; Invoice for a Job Not Done*, WALL STREET JOURNAL, Mar. 25, 2005, at p. A1.

[6] Report of the ABA Section of Business Law, Section of Business Law Section of State and Local Government Law Standing Committee on Ethics and Professional Responsibility Association of the Bar of the City of New York, *Report with Recommendations to the House of Delegates*, Nov. 23, 1999, at 11.

[7] Report of the ABA Section of Business Law, Section of Business Law Section of State and Local Government Law Standing Committee on Ethics and Professional Responsibility Association of the Bar of the City of New York, *Report with Recommendations to the House of Delegates*, Nov. 23, 1999, at 11.

[8] Report of the ABA Section of Business Law, Section of Business Law Section of State and Local Government Law Standing Committee on Ethics and Professional Responsibility Association of the Bar of the City of New York, *Report with Recommendations to the House of Delegates*, Nov. 23, 1999, at 11 (emphasis added).

Under this test, there may well be no disciplinary enforcement of Rule 7.6, because a lawyer may contribute to the state treasurer of another state based on a "political issue connection"— e.g., the lawyer seeks to support a candidate because the lawyer believes in the issues advocated by the candidate, or the lawyer shares the same party affiliation.

In addition to disciplinary enforcement, a court might enforce the ethical restriction on "pay-to-play" when selecting class action counsel, if the proof of "pay-to-play" is sufficiently strong. *In re Cendant Corp. Litigation,*[9] the court advised, that in a class action lawsuit under the Private Securities Litigation Reform Act (PSLRA), when a court determines that a publicly managed fund is the presumptively most adequate lead plaintiff, the court can require that the fund disclose any campaign contributions by the fund's choice of counsel to any elected officials possessing direct oversight and authority over the fund in order to avoid a pay-to-play situation. If any such contributions have been made, the court could also require that the fund submit a sworn declaration describing the process by which it selected counsel and attesting to the degree to which the selection process was or was not influenced by any elected officials.[10]

---

[9]*In re Cendant Corp. Litigation,* 264 F.3d 201, 269–70 & n. 49, Fed. Sec. L. Rep. ¶ 91,521 (3d Cir.1001), *on remand,* 243 F.Supp.2d 166 (D.N.J. 2003).

[10]**Pay to Play and the Private Securities Litigation Reform Act.** A particular risk in the pay-to-play context is "unique to publicly-managed pension funds." That risk is that "an informal *quid pro quo* could develop" with class action law firms contributing to the campaigns of elected officials who oversee those funds in the hope that those government officials would select those firms to serve as lead counsel in cases where the funds are lead plaintiffs. If that happens, there is the risk that—

"the lead plaintiff would be complacent and unwilling to object to an excessive fee request, thus defeating the [PSLRA's] goal of lead plaintiff-controlled, rather than lead counsel-controlled, litigation. [Then,] the elected official's conduct—besides representing a breach of fiduciary duty to the pensioners—would threaten the best interests of the class members. Though we stress that there is no evidence of such impropriety in this case, Congress does not appear to have considered this risk when it enacted the Reform Act and may wish to revise the PSLRA to account for it."

In re Cendant Corp. Litigation, 264 F.3d 201, 270 n. 49, *on remand,* 243 F.Supp.2d 166 (D.N.J.2003).

VIII. MAINTAINING THE INTEGRITY OF THE PROFESSION

CHAPTER 8.1
BAR ADMISSION AND DISCIPLINARY MATTERS

§ 8.1–1 Scope of Application of Rule 8.1
§ 8.1–2 Prohibiting False Statements of Material Fact and Imposing an Obligation to Correct Misapprehensions
§ 8.1–3 Requiring Compliance and Cooperation with Lawful Requests for Information
§ 8.1–4 Furthering the Application of Candidates for the Bar

RULE 8.1: BAR ADMISSION AND DISCIPLINARY MATTERS

An applicant for admission to the bar, or a lawyer in connection with a bar admission application or in connection with a disciplinary matter, shall not:

(a) knowingly make a false statement of material fact; or

(b) fail to disclose a fact necessary to correct a misapprehension known by the person to have arisen in the matter, or knowingly fail to respond to a lawful demand for information from an admissions or disciplinary authority, except that this rule does not require disclosure of information otherwise protected by Rule 1.6.

Comment

[1] The duty imposed by this Rule extends to persons seeking admission to the bar as well as to lawyers. Hence, if a person makes a material false statement in connection with an application for admission, it may be the basis for subsequent disciplinary action if the person is admitted, and in any event may be relevant in a subsequent admission application. The duty imposed by this Rule applies to a lawyer's own admission or discipline as well as that of others. Thus, it is a separate professional offense for a lawyer to knowingly make a misrepresentation or omission in connection with a disciplinary investigation of the lawyer's own conduct. Paragraph (b) of this Rule also requires correction of any prior misstatement in the matter that the applicant or lawyer may have made and affirmative clarification of any misunderstanding on the part of the admissions or disciplinary authority of which the person involved becomes aware.

[2] This Rule is subject to the provisions of the fifth amendment of the United States Constitution and corresponding provisions of state constitutions. A person relying on such a provision in response to a question, however, should do so openly and not use the right of nondisclosure as a justification for failure to comply with this Rule.

[3] A lawyer representing an applicant for admission to the bar, or representing a lawyer who is the subject of a disciplinary inquiry or proceeding, is governed by the rules applicable to the client lawyer relationship, including Rule 1.6 and, in some cases, Rule 3.3.

Authors' 1983 Model Rules Comparison

The text of the 2002 version is identical to the Rule adopted by the ABA House of Delegates in 1983.

In Comment 1, the drafters of the 2002 Rules added the following clause: "correction of any prior misstatement in the matter that the applicant or lawyer may have made and." This change was made to make clear that Rule 8.1(b) requires a person to correct prior misstatements made as well as to correct misunderstandings. The drafters believed this duty was included in the 1983 version, but thought that they should expressly state it in the Comment. *See* Reporter's Explanation of Changes to Rule 8.1.

In Comment 3, the drafters added the reference to Rule 1.6 and Rule 3.3. The drafters added this language to "remind[] lawyers that bar admission and professional discipline are judicial proceedings subject to the requirements of Rules 1.6 and 3.3."

Comment 2 is identical to the 1983 version.

Model Code Comparison

DR 1-101(A) provided that a lawyer is "subject to discipline if he has made a materially false statement in, or if he has deliberately failed to disclose a material fact requested in connection with, his application for admission to the bar." DR 1-101(B) provided that a lawyer "shall not further the application for admission to the bar of another person known by him to be unqualified in respect to character, education, or other relevant attribute." With respect to paragraph (b), DR 1-102(A)(5) provided that a lawyer shall not engage in "conduct that is prejudicial to the administration of justice."

§ 8.1–1 SCOPE OF APPLICATION OF RULE 8.1

§ 8.1–1(a) Applicability of the Rules to Nonlawyers Applying for Admission to the Bar

The Model Rules, in general, do not govern nonlawyers. However, an important exception concerns the situation of a nonlawyer who intentionally makes a materially false statement in her bar application. That misstatement constitutes "dishonesty" or a "fraud," and thus is disciplinable,[1] even if the person was not a lawyer at the time because the duty of Rule 8.1 "extends to persons seeking admission to the bar as well as to lawyers."[2]

The Rules are quite specific on this point. The applicant may not make a false statement in connection with the bar application.[3] Though the applicant is not, at the time of the application, governed by the Rules of that jurisdiction, a violation of Rule 8.1(a) may form the basis of discipline if the applicant is already a member of the bar in one jurisdiction and is seeking admission elsewhere. In addition, even if the applicant has not yet been admitted to any bar, she would become subject to discipline if she is subsequently admitted.[4]

The Model Rules do not explicitly set forth the standard to determine if an applicant for admission has the requisite character to become a lawyer. However, Rule 8.4 defines professional misconduct for a lawyer, and bar admission authorities, in effect, borrow from this provision, in the sense that they will not admit anyone who commits a criminal act that reflects adversely on the applicant's honesty, trustworthiness or fitness as a lawyer in other respects, or one who engages in conduct involving dishonesty, fraud, deceit or misrepresentation, or engaged in other conduct that is prejudicial to the administration of justice.[5]

Occasionally, applicants raise constitutional challenges to their

---

[Section 8.1–1]

[1]Rule 8.1(a). The former Model Code included a similar provision. DR 1-102(A)(4).

[2]Rule 8.1, Comment 1. *See also* Restatement of the Law Governing Lawyers, Third, § 2 ("Admission to Practice Law") (Official Draft 2000).

[3]Rule 8.1(a). *See* Melissa Rourke & Meredith Schoenfeld, *The Honesty Standard and the Need For a More Stringent Standard: An Update on Model Rule 8.1*, 15 GEORGETOWN J. LEGAL ETHICS 895 (2002).

[4]Rule 8.1, Comment 1.

[5]*See* ABA Model Rule 8.4 (b), (c), (d). Model Rule 8.4 (a) provides that it is professional misconduct for a lawyer to "violate or attempt to violate the Rules of Professional Conduct, knowingly assist another to do so, or do so through the acts of another." This provision is not really applicable to nonlawyers (who are, obviously, not acting as lawyers). For example, it would violate the ethics rules for a lawyer to solicit legal business, Rule 7.3, but it would not be improper for a nonlawyer (such as a nonlawyer) accountant to solicit accounting business. Indeed, nonlawyers would be exercising constitutional rights to engage in such solicitation. *Edenfield v. Fane*, 507 U.S. 761, 113 S.Ct. 1792, 123 L.Ed.2d 543 (1993) invalidated a Florida ban on in-person, uninvited, direct *face-to-face* or telephone contact by Certified Public Accountants soliciting business in the business context.

In Radtke v. Board of Bar Examiners, 230 Wis.2d 254, 601 N.W.2d 642 (1999), the applicant said that he had left an earlier position as a history lecturer because of "low pay" and denied that he had been warned of professional discipline. However, he had been charged with plagiarism of a history article and he left his department as part of a negotiated settlement. The court found that evidence

denial of admission, and these challenges sometimes succeed.[6] As a constitutional matter, and because it is the right thing to do, the admission authorities should not deny an applicant admission in violation an applicant's beliefs, race, and other constitutionally protected categories.[7] In addition, the bar authorities should not deny an applicant admission without due process.[8]

showed that the applicant had been discharged from his position as university lecturer for unprofessional conduct consisting of plagiarism in a professional article, and his statement on his bar admission application of the reasons he left employment as a university lecturer was misleading. The court also ruled that the applicant could reapply for admission after a one-year period from the date of the Board of Bar Examiners' adverse decision.

See also In re Stamps, 874 So.2d 113 (La. 2004), cert. denied, 543 U.S. 1002, 125 S.Ct. 620, 160 L.Ed.2d 462 (2004) (Louisiana Supreme Court disbarred husband and wife who engaged in unauthorized practice of law in an employment arrangement in another state with disclosing the fact of employment on the application for admission to the bar).

[6]Schware v. Board of Bar Examiners, 353 U.S. 232, 77 S.Ct. 752, 1 L.Ed.2d 796 (1957), held that, under the circumstances of that case, the applicant's past membership in the Communist Party and his prior arrest record and use of aliases 15 years earlier could not raise substantial doubts about his present good moral character; hence, the New Mexico court's refusal to grant him the right to qualify for practice of law constituted a denial of due process.

[7]Schware v. Board of Bar Examiners, 353 U.S. 232, 239, 77 S.Ct. 752, 756, 1 L.Ed.2d 796 (1957): "Obviously an applicant could not be excluded merely because he was a Republican or a Negro or a member of a particular church. Even in applying permissible standards, officers of a State cannot exclude an applicant when there is no basis for their finding that he fails to meet these standards, or when their action is invidiously discriminatory." See also Konigsberg v. State Bar of California, 353 U.S. 252, 269, 77 S.Ct. 722, 731, 1 L.Ed.2d 810, 823 (1957): "Government censorship can no more be reconciled with our national constitutional standard of freedom of speech and press when done in the guise of determining 'moral character,' than if it should be attempted directly." Baird v. State Bar of Arizona, 401 U.S. 1, 91 S.Ct. 702, 27 L.Ed.2d 639 (1971); In re Stolar, 401 U.S. 23, 91 S.Ct. 713, 27 L.Ed.2d 657 (1971).

Compare Converse v. Nebraska State Bar Commission, 258 Neb. 159, 602 N.W.2d 500 (Neb. 1999), which involved an applicant who had engaged in bizarre but non-criminal behavior while in law school. The student wrote to the state Supreme Court and prominent federal judges critical of his appellate advocacy teacher. When he got in trouble for displaying a photograph of a "nude female's backside" on his law school carrel, he raised a First Amendment charge. Later, he sold T-shirts with a "nude caricature of [his law school Dean] shown sitting astride . . . a very large hot dog" with a caption "Astride the Peter Principle." The Court denied him admission to the bar. The "threshold question we must answer is whether conduct arguably protected by the First Amendment can be considered by the Commission during an investigation into an applicant's moral character and fitness to practice law. We answer this question in the affirmative." 602 N.W.2d at 505. The Court declared: "abusive, disruptive, hostile, intemperate, intimidating, irresponsible, threatening, or turbulent behavior is a proper basis for the denial of admission to the bar." 602

N.W.2d at 508.

In re Hale, 243 Ill.Dec. 174, 723 N.E.2d 206 (1999), *cert. denied sub nom. Hale v. Committee on Character and Fitness of the Illinois Bar*, 530 U.S. 1261, 1261, 120 S.Ct. 2716, 2716–17, 147 L.Ed.2d 982 (2000), was decided in an unreported character and fitness opinion, so we only see the case as described in an Illinois dissenting opinion and contemporaneous news articles. Matthew Hale, an outspoken white supremacist, founded a "church" to espouse his beliefs. The Illinois admissions panel held that, in lawyer regulation, " 'fundamental truths' of equality and nondiscrimination 'must be preferred over the values found in the First Amendment.' " Thus, the panel asserted, if Hale were admitted to the Bar, he would be "on a collision course with the Rules of Professional Conduct." The Illinois Supreme Court refused to review the character and fitness panel's opinion, and the U.S. Supreme Court denied certiorari. Justice Heiple, dissenting in the Illinois Supreme Court opinion, questioned whether a lawyer who preached racial hatred *after* bar admission would be subject to disbarment. *Cf.* Rule 8.4, Comment 2. Some commentators have attacked this decision on First Amendment grounds. *See, e.g.,* W. William Hodes, *Accepting And Rejecting Clients-The Moral Autonomy Of The Second-To-The-Last Lawyer In Town*, 48 U. Kan. L. Rev. 977 (2000):

> "[T]he Illinois bar admission case of racist Matthew Hale turns in part on the difference between private disapproval and governmental disapproval of how he might go about choosing clients. Although I would personally be disappointed in any lawyer who refused to serve black clients or Jews, I do not wield state power. The Illinois Supreme Court Committee on Character and Fitness does wield state power, however, and its denial of admission to Hale in part on its prediction that he would treat such clients badly, or simply refuse to serve them, is a shock-

ing violation of First Amendment principles."

48 U. Kan. L. Rev. 977, 990 n.18 (citations omitted). *Contra* Richard L. Sloane, *Barbarian At The Gates: Revisiting The Case Of Matthew F. Hale to Reaffirm That Character And Fitness Evaluations Appropriately Preclude Racists From the Practice of Law*, 15 GEORGETOWN J. LEGAL ETHICS 397, 401 (2004): "this Note argues that the melting pot of the American legal system simply is not big enough to accept racists among its ranks."

In re Roots, 762 A.2d 1161 (R.I. 2000), denied admission to an applicant with a long criminal record ranging from shoplifting to resisting arrest to violating probation. The applicant had a cache of weapons and had published articles manifesting "explicit racial and ethnic bias as well as contempt and disdain for the federal government." The court expressly refused to ground its decision on the applicant's political views alone, but after considering his explicit criminal offenses and lack of candor with the character and fitness committee, it found the applicant had not demonstrated that he deserved bar admission: "we have no intention or desire to censor or to punish Roots for his past or present political views or for exercising his rights of free speech. Nevertheless, when as here, a candidate for admission to the bar of a state has published writings that communicate his or her explicit refusal to accept our federal government as the legitimate government of this country, such a candidate raises legitimate questions about whether he or she in good faith can take and abide by the attorney's oath to support the laws and the constitution of the United States while in the exercise of the office of attorney and counselor." 762 A.2d at 1169.

[8]*Douglas v. Noble*, 261 U.S. 165, 43 S.Ct. 303, 67 L.Ed. 590 (1923), holding that a State can require high

If an applicant for admission to the bar has engaged in conduct involving fraud, the admission authorities, in determining if the *past* act should bar *present* admission, will look at several factors: (1) the amount of time that has passed since the applicant's offense in question; (2) the nature of the applicant's offenses;[9] (3) the applicant's current mental state; (4) the applicant's community service and achievements and the opinions of others regarding the applicant's present character; (5) the applicant's candor before the court; and, (6) the age of the applicant at the time of the offenses.[10]

§ 8.1–1(b) Applicability of Rule 8.1 to Lawyers in Connection with a Disciplinary Matter

Rule 8.1 applies to lawyers who are themselves subject of a disciplinary hearing and lawyers who are representing a client who is subject to a disciplinary hearing or seeking admission to a bar.[11] The policy underlying this Rule is clear. Bar authorities expect that applicants and lawyers subject to the jurisdiction of the Bar will cooperate with applications and investigations.

If the lawyer is the subject of a disciplinary investigation, Rule 8.1 expects the lawyer to be truthful, to correct misapprehensions, and to cooperate with bar authorities. The lawyers' obligation not to knowingly make a false statement of material fact is

---

standards of qualification, such as good moral character or proficiency in its law, before it admits an applicant to the bar, but the Constitution requires that any qualification must have a rational connection with the applicant's fitness or capacity to practice law.

[9]**Mental Health and the Americans With Disabilities Act.** *See* John Bauer, *The Character of the Question and the Fitness of the Process: Mental Health, Bar Admissions and the Americans with Disabilities Act*, 49 U.C.L.A. L. REV. 93 (2001); Fred C. Zacharias, *The Humanization Of Lawyers*, 2002 Professional Lawyer 9 (ABA 2002); Adam J. Shapiro, *Defining The Rights Of Law Students With Mental Disabilities*, 58 U. MIAMI L. REV. 923 (2004). *See* ABA Model Rule on Conditional Admission to Practice Law (Feb. 11, 2008) (may be used when applicant has issues relating to substance abuse or mental health).

[10]*Schware v. Board of Bar Examiners*, 353 U.S. 232, 239, 77 S.Ct. 752, 756, 1 L.Ed.2d 796 (1957). *Com-*

pare In re Krule, 194 Ill.2d 109, 251 Ill.Dec. 665, 741 N.E.2d 259 (2000). *Krule* denied admission to a man who had pled guilty to felony theft (insurance fraud) in 1988, years *before* attending law school. The applicant, at a time when he was "a mature adult and a licensed [insurance] professional," had organized a group that arranged for excessive or not-performed treatment of accident victims and then submitted their claims to insurance companies. The court said the applicant had not been candid about his criminal history when he applied to law school (he also did not tell the law school about three previous misdemeanor charges resulting in two guilty pleas), and he was still less than forthcoming about it. He had been generous with his volunteer time in recent years, but the court (over the dissent of one justice) found that work insufficient to support a finding that he had the requisite character to be a lawyer.

[11]Rule 8.1(a) & Comment 1.

covered by Rule 4.1 and 3.3, but Rule 8.1 makes it a separate violation. The obligation to cooperate is limited by the lawyer's constitutional right against self incrimination if the behavior may implicate possible criminal charges.[12] However, the targeted lawyer still must respond to requests by the bar authorities.[13]

If the lawyer represents another lawyer who is the subject of disciplinary proceedings, the legal representative must ensure that the lawyer client complies with Rule 8.1. The failure to do so would subject the client lawyer to an additional violation of the Rules and another possible sanction. Of course, Rule 8.1(b) does refer to client confidentiality as a valid basis for refusal to disclose certain information. Of course, many bar authorities ask the target client to waive confidentiality.

§ 8.1–2 PROHIBITING FALSE STATEMENTS OF MATERIAL FACT AND IMPOSING AN OBLIGATION TO CORRECT MISAPPREHENSIONS

The lawyer (or applicant) may not knowingly make a *material* misstatement.[1] A statement is material if it has "the effect of inhibiting efforts of the bar to determine an applicant's fitness to practice law."[2] Moreover, the misstatement must be *knowingly* false when made.

This Rule has a scienter requirement. There is no violation if the misrepresentation was not deliberate.[3] Because of this scienter requirement, there arises the question of what the lawyer or applicant should do if she *un*knowingly makes a material false statement, but later comes to know of its falsity. Can she now take advantage of the misinformation because she did not act with scienter; should her earlier ignorance be rewarded, or must she now correct the record? The ABA Model Code did not specifically compel the lawyer or applicant to correct a misapprehension that may have arisen on the part of the bar authorities. However, it might be considered, in some circumstances, to be a "fraud"[4] not to correct misunderstandings of the bar authorities.

In contrast, the Model Rules are clear on this point. The lawyer or applicant may *not "fail to disclose* a fact necessary to correct a misapprehension known by the person to have arisen in the

---

[12]*Spevack v. Klein*, 385 U.S. 511, 87 S.Ct. 625, 17 L.Ed.2d 574 (1967).

[13]*See* ABA CENTER FOR PROFESSIONAL RESPONSIBILITY, ANNOTATED MODEL RULES OF PROFESSIONAL CONDUCT 579 (ABA, 5th ed. 2003).

[Section 8.1–2]

[1]Rule 8.1(a); DR 1-101(A).

[2]*Grievance Commission v. Howe*, 257 N.W.2d 420 (N.D.1977).

[3]*Siegel v. Committee of Bar Examiners, State Bar of California*, 10 Cal.3d 156, 110 Cal.Rptr. 15, 514 P.2d 967 (1973).

[4]DR 1-102(A)(4).

matter. . . ."[5] Consequently, she must disclose her earlier false statement even though she did not know it was false when she originally made it.[6] The Rules impose on the applicant an affirmative duty to clarify "any misunderstandings on the part of the admissions or disciplinary authority of which the person involved becomes aware."[7]

This duty exists even if the misapprehension was not caused by something the lawyer or applicant said. The Comment supports a broad interpretation of the duty to correct misunderstandings. It provides that the Rule "also requires *affirmative* clarification of *any misunderstanding* on the part of the admissions or disciplinary authority of which the person involved becomes aware."[8] Hence, an applicant must correct a misapprehension even if she did not cause it.

§ 8.1–3 REQUIRING COMPLIANCE AND COOPERATION WITH LAWFUL REQUESTS FOR INFORMATION

In the case of either an application for admission or a bar disciplinary matter, the bar authorities may request information. The Rules specifically require a lawyer to comply with any "lawful demand for information" in any admissions or disciplinary investigation, including an investigation into the lawyer's own conduct.[1]

The Rules, obviously, only mandate the lawyer's obedience to a "*proper* request" or a "*lawful* demand" for information in either an admissions of disciplinary proceeding.[2] The lawyer or applicant, of course, has the right to claim any evidentiary or constitutional privilege, but "should do so openly and not use the right of nondisclosure as a justification for failure to comply. . . ."[3]

For example, if the bar application asks if the applicant has ever been arrested, even if that arrest has been expunged from the record, the applicant should either answer the question truthfully (*e.g.*, she was arrested 15 years earlier, but that juvenile ar-

---

[5]Rule 8.1(b) (emphasis added).

[6]The drafters of the 2002 Rules added language to Comment 1 that makes this point clear.

[7]Rule 8.1, Comment 1.

[8]Rule 8.1, Comment 1 (emphasis added).

[Section 8.1–3]

[1]Rule 8.1(b).

In comparison, consider the Model Code. DR 1-103(B) specifically required that the lawyer must reveal any "unprivileged knowledge" regard-

ing another lawyer "upon proper request." This rule did not expressly apply to either the bar admission process or to a disciplinary investigation involving the lawyer's *own* conduct (although refusal to obey a lawful subpoena might be held to violate DR 1-102(A)(5)—conduct "prejudicial to the administration of justice").

[2]Rule 8.1(b).

[3]Rule 8.1, Comment 2. *See also* Rule 3.4(c) (requiring lawyer to obey rules of a tribunal "except for an open refusal").

rest was expunged from her record), or challenge the legal authority of the bar authorities to ask about expunged records.[4]

Sometimes, commentators and the courts have spoken of a duty to "cooperate." Although the Model Code encouraged (if not mandated) a lawyer to cooperate with discipline authorities,[5] the Model Rules impose a much more modest burden. The lawyer who is subject to discipline is the respondent in an adversary proceeding, so the limited requirement is that the lawyer merely comply with the investigatory authority's "proper request" for information.[6]

The Rules offer one example of encouraging cooperation, but it does not involve an instance of where the lawyer cooperating is the respondent in a disciplinary investigation. If lawyer #1's client tells lawyer #1 that lawyer #2 has violated a disciplinary rule, that information may be privileged under Rule 1.6. The Model Rules state that if lawyer #1's knowledge of lawyer #2's disciplinable violation is privileged client information, then lawyer #1 "should encourage" his client to waive the privilege if doing so will not "substantially prejudice the client's interests."[7]

Courts have used the respondent's failure to cooperate as relevant in determining the sanctions that they will impose when the respondent's failure is part of plan to obstruct and improperly delay the disciplinary or admissions proceedings.[8]

---

[4]It is not uncommon for the bar authorities to ask about expunged records, but it may not be legal to do so. The purpose of state laws providing for expungement in certain cases (often in juvenile cases) is, after all, to expunge, to absolve. When the bar authorities ask for this information, they are acting against the public policy represented in the expungement rules.

[5]Thus EC 1-4 says that, if requested, lawyers should serve and assist disciplinary committees. DR 1-103(A) mandated whistle-blowing, and DR 1-103 (B) mandated that the lawyer "shall reveal" any unprivileged knowledge relevant to another lawyer or judge if the disciplinary authorities requested it ("upon proper request").

The case law was not of one mind. *Compare State v. Weber*, 55 Wis.2d 548, 550, 200 N.W.2d 577, 580 (1972) (lawyer's deliberate refusal to cooperate is a grounds for sanction),

with Committee on Legal Ethics of West Virginia State Bar v. Mullins, 159 W.Va. 647, 226 S.E.2d 427, 431 (1976) (no separate violation because of refusal to cooperate).

[6]Rule 8.1(b) (a lawyer may not "fail to respond to a lawful demand for information from an admissions or disciplinary authority. . . ."). *Accord* DR 1-103(B).

[7]Rule 8.3, Comment 2.

[8]*In re Samuels*, 126 Ill.2d 509, 129 Ill.Dec. 43, 535 N.E.2d 808 (1989).

"Finally, respondent's lack of cooperation in the disciplinary proceedings indicates substantial discipline is warranted. Prior to the hearing, respondent repeatedly filed frivolous requests and meritless motions which appear solely calculated to delay the proceedings. At the hearing, respondent insisted on arguing irrelevant issues and questioning his clients' veracity and sanity while failing to support his accusations with any cred-

§ 8.1–3(a) Constitutional Concerns

Constitutional limits constrain the ability of the bar authorities to investigate applicants and deny them admission. For example, the bar may lawfully discipline a lawyer or refuse to admit an applicant because the person unlawfully obstructs the investigation.[9] But the bar authorities, because of free speech concerns, may not punish persons simply because they are or

ible evidence. Respondent, to this day, continues to belittle his clients and their cases, and to blame those who worked for him for the neglect." 126 Ill.2d at 531, 129 Ill.Dec. at 52, 535 N.E.2d at 817.

In re Smith, 168 Ill.2d 269, 296, 213 Ill.Dec. 550, 562, 659 N.E.2d 896, 908 (1995):

"In this case, the record reflects that respondent's efforts to cooperate in these proceedings have not been satisfactory. In five response letters to the Administrator, respondent made the unsubstantiated claim that there was something 'seriously wrong' in her handling of the case. In his answer to the disciplinary charges, respondent accused the Administrator of the 'highly unethical' practice of requiring him to educate the Administrator's employees about the proper workings of the court system. Moreover, the record indicates that '[p]rior to the hearing, respondent repeatedly filed frivolous requests and meritless motions which appear solely calculated to delay the proceedings.' " 168 Ill.2d at 296, 213 Ill.Dec. at 562, 659 N.E.2d at 908.

In one case the court cited several factors as relevant to its decision to disbar the respondent, ranging from apparently frivolous delay to the respondent's *pro se* questioning of a judge during the disciplinary proceeding that was "disrespectful and insulting." The court said:

"An attorney's lack of cooperation with the disciplinary process is also relevant to the determination of an appropriate sanction. In the present case, respondent's conduct on several occasions exceeded the bounds of zealous advocacy and instead seemed designed to obstruct, delay, and hinder the proceedings. Shortly after the [disciplinary] complaint was filed in the second matter, respondent sought to disqualify the Springfield members of the Administrator's office, contending that they were prejudiced against him, and to have the matter transferred to the Chicago office. Later, respondent appeared at the second hearing in the company of a camera operator for a cable access channel; respondent stated that he had no objection to videotaping the proceedings for later broadcast. After the panel sustained the Administrator's objection to the videotaping, respondent demanded a jury trial. When that request was denied, respondent sought to engage in a voir dire examination of the three members of the hearing panel. Respondent later submitted a list of more than 60 questions that he wished to ask the panel; these ranged from inquiries about their religious affiliations and income levels to who had ordered and paid for their lunches. In addition, we note that respondent's *pro se* cross-examination of Judge Collier in the second proceeding before the hearing panel was disrespectful and insulting."

In re Ingersoll, 186 Ill.2d 163, 237 Ill.Dec. 760, 710 N.E.2d 390 (1999) (internal citations omitted). This case was a discipline case, not a bar admissions case. However, the same principle should apply: if a lawyer can be disbarred for such activities, an applicant for admission to the bar should not be treated better.

[9] *Konigsberg v. State Bar of California*, 366 U.S. 36, 81 S.Ct. 997, 6 L.Ed.2d 105 (1961) (*Konigsberg II*).

have been members of the Communist Party.[10] Nor may the bar violate a person's associational and privacy rights by charging perjury if one incorrectly answers *vague* inquiries about past associations.[11]

However, a person may be refused admission if, with scienter, she was a *knowing* member in an organization advocating the unlawful overthrow of the Government, and she had the *specific intent* to further these unlawful goals of the organization.[12]

Similarly, the Model Rules make clear that Rule 8.1 is subject to federal constitutional guarantees, such as the Fifth Amendment, and state constitutional guarantees.[13]

§ 8.1–4 FURTHERING THE APPLICATION OF CANDIDATES FOR THE BAR

Lawyers are often asked to supply character references for bar applicants. If the lawyer is asked, the lawyer obviously must reply truthfully, unless the lawyer claims a privilege such as a constitutional privilege. If the lawyer is representing the applicant, then she must claim the attorney-client privilege. No provisions of the Rules require (or even urge) a lawyer to *volunteer* unfavorable information about an applicant.

For example, assume that a lawyer ("Lawyer") hired a summer Law Clerk in her law office. From that experience Lawyer, based on several incidents, believes that Law Clerk is mentally unstable. Law Clerk is now applying for admission to the bar, but does not ask Lawyer for a reference. Lawyer, after learning of Law Clerk's application, does nothing. However, if the bar asks Lawyer for a reference and inquires if Lawyer has any information that may indicate that Law Clerk should not be admitted,

---

[10]*Schware v. Board of Bar Examiners of State of N.M.*, 353 U.S. 232, 77 S.Ct. 752, 1 L.Ed.2d 796 (1957).

[11]*Baird v. State Bar of Arizona*, 401 U.S. 1, 91 S.Ct. 702, 27 L.Ed.2d 639 (1971) (bar threatened to punish applicant for perjury if she answered incorrectly—without a requirement of scienter—whether any of her past memberships, already disclosed, were in organizations that advocated the unlawful overthrow of the government).

[12]*Law Students Civil Rights Research Council, Inc. v. Wadmond*,

401 U.S. 154, 164–66, 91 S.Ct. 720, 727–28, 27 L.Ed.2d 749, 759–60 (1971). *See generally* 5 RONALD D. ROTUNDA & JOHN E. NOWAK, TREATISE ON CONSTITUTIONAL LAW: SUBSTANCE AND PROCEDURE § 20.44 (Thomson-West, 4th ed. 2008) (6 volumes).

[13]Rule 8.1, Comment 2. Although this Comment only refers to the Fifth Amendment and "corresponding provisions of state constitutions," it should not be read too narrowly. If a court, by rule, adopts the ABA Model Rules, a court rule simply cannot override provisions of the state or federal constitution.

she intends to reply truthfully. Lawyer has violated no provision of the Model Rules in either instance.[1]

In contrast to this example, some lawyers read language in the Model Code to impose a whistle-blowing role on lawyers who had heard unfavorable information about an applicant. The Model Code did include a section that stated that lawyers "shall not further," the admission of candidates to the bar whom the lawyer knows lack the required "character," "education," or "other relevant attribute."[2]

One would think that the most natural reading—but not the only interpretation—of this section is that the lawyer should not file such references as to persons "known by him to be unqualified."[3] This meaning was also supported by another section that instructed the lawyer, before recommending an applicant, to "satisfy himself that the applicant is of good moral character."[4] In other words, the lawyer need not become "a self-appointed investigator,"[5] but he should not recommend an applicant if he has no basis for a recommendation (i.e., "should satisfy himself"), and definitely should not "further" the application of one known to be lacking the requisite characteristics.[6]

But this interpretation of the rule is not the only possible one, and some commentators have argued that the rule is phrased too broadly: "An attorney could 'further' the application of a person for admission to the bar by acting as his counsel in a bar admission proceeding."[7] Consequently, the Rules do not contain any

---

[Section 8.1–4]

[1]Some argue that Lawyer has failed to meet the aspirational level of EC 1-3. Lawyer has violated no DR.

[2]DR 1-101(B).

[3]DR 1-101(B).

[4]EC 1-3.

[5]EC 1-3.

[6]In addition, the last sentence of EC 1-6 affirmatively encouraged lawyers to "assist" unqualified applicants to be licensed when the disqualification (e.g., mental or emotional stability) has terminated. Similarly, lawyers should assist suspended or disbarred lawyers to restore their right to practice law when their disqualifications have terminated.

[7]Donald Weckstein, *Maintaining the Integrity and Competence of the Legal Profession*, 48 TEXAS L. REV. 267, 271 (1970).

In addition, a portion of EC 1-3 might be interpreted to encourage whistle-blowing. EC 1-3 provides:

"Before recommending an applicant for admission, a lawyer should satisfy himself that the applicant is of good moral character. Although a lawyer should not become a self-appointed investigator or judge of applicants for admission, *he should report to proper officials all unfavorable information he possesses* relating to the character or other qualifications of an applicant" (emphasis added).

Some commentators rely on the portion of EC 1-3 italicized above to support, as an ethical aspiration, a lawyer's duty to volunteer unfavorable information to the bar authorities about an applicant.

requirement similar to the Model Code.[8] A lawyer representing an applicant for admission is governed not by Rule 8.1 ("Bar Admission and Disciplinary Matters") but by the rules normally governing the attorney-client relationship.[9]

If an applicant asks a lawyer to submit a character reference to the bar admission authorities, the lawyer must respond truthfully. She should not recommend an applicant if she has no basis for the recommendation (*e.g.*, she does not know him at all but knows his father). Like the Code, the Model Rules impose no requirement that the lawyer become a self-appointed investigator.

In context, however, EC 1-3 should not be so interpreted. DR 1-103(A) does contain a whistle-blowing provision that applies to lawyers already admitted to the bar. That provision is quite clear. One would think that if the drafters of the Code wanted to create a whistle-blowing obligation applying to applicants, they would have known how to write one, because they did so in DR 1-103(A).

A more natural reading of EC 1-3 is to regard the second sentence as modifying the first. In other words, if an applicant asks a lawyer for a recommendation, before the lawyer files the affidavit, he or she should be satisfied that the applicant is of good moral character. It is not necessary for the lawyer, in order to be satisfied, to become a self-appointed investigator, but if the lawyer (who has been asked to recommend an applicant) happens to know or come across unfavorable information, then the lawyer should report it to the bar authorities. If the lawyer believes that the applicant is of good moral character notwithstanding the unfavorable information, the lawyer still must report the unfavorable information, and may argue that it should not be disqualifying, but should let the bar authorities evaluate it.

[8]*See, e.g.*, DR 1-101(B).

[9]Rule 8.1, Comment 3.

CHAPTER 8.2

CHARGES AGAINST JUDICIAL AND LEGAL OFFICIALS

§ 8.2–1 Prohibition Against False Accusations
§ 8.2–2 First Amendment Implications in Rule 8.2
§ 8.2–3 Defending Judges from Criticism
§ 8.2–4 Lawyers As Candidates for Judicial Office

RULE 8.2: JUDICIAL AND LEGAL OFFICIALS

(a) A lawyer shall not make a statement that the lawyer knows to be false or with reckless disregard as to its truth or falsity concerning the qualifications or integrity of a judge, adjudicatory officer or public legal officer, or of a candidate for election or appointment to judicial or legal office.

(b) A lawyer who is a candidate for judicial office shall comply with the applicable provisions of the Code of Judicial Conduct.

Comment

[1] Assessments by lawyers are relied on in evaluating the professional or personal fitness of persons being considered for election or appointment to judicial office and to public legal offices, such as attorney general, prosecuting attorney and public defender. Expressing honest and candid opinions on such matters contributes to improving the administration of justice. Conversely, false statements by a lawyer can unfairly undermine public confidence in the administration of justice.

[2] When a lawyer seeks judicial office, the lawyer should be bound by applicable limitations on political activity.

[3] To maintain the fair and independent administration of justice, lawyers are encouraged to continue traditional efforts to defend judges and courts unjustly criticized.

1983 Model Rules Comparison

The 2002 version is identical to the Rule adopted by the House of Delegates in 1983.

Model Code Comparison

[1] With regard to paragraph (a), DR 8-102(A) provided that a lawyer "shall not knowingly make false statements of fact concerning the qualifications of a candidate for election or appointment to a judicial office." DR 8-102(B) provided that a lawyer "shall not knowingly make false accusations against a judge or other adjudicatory officer."

[2] Paragraph (b) is substantially identical to DR 8-103.

§ 8.2-1 PROHIBITION AGAINST FALSE ACCUSATIONS

Rule 8.2 makes a lawyer subject to discipline if he or she knowingly makes any false charges against a judge, judicial candidate, or public legal officer. The lawyer also must not knowingly speak with "reckless disregard" as to the truth or falsity of his or her statements.[1] Oddly enough, the District of Columbia, which has the highest per capital number of judges, other adjudicatory officers (such as administrative law judges), or other public legal officers (such as prosecuting attorneys),[2] did not adopt this portion or any portion of ABA Model Rule 8.2.[3]

The Rules prohibit a lawyer from making any knowingly false "statements" (or false statements made with reckless disregard as to their truth), when the statements relate to the judge's, or judicial candidate's, or public legal officer's qualifications or integrity.[4] However, this Rule also makes clear that it is

---

[Section 8.2-1]

[1] Rule 8.2(a); DR 8-102. Restatement of the Law Governing Lawyers, Third, § 110(2), Comment *f* (Official Draft 2000), at 174.

[2] Rule 8.2, Comment 1, makes clear that this Rule covers all public legal officers "such as, attorney general, prosecuting attorney and public defender."

[3] Washington, D.C. Rules of Professional Conduct, *reprinted in*, THOMAS D. MORGAN & RONALD D. ROTUNDA, 1999 SELECTED STANDARDS ON PROFESSIONAL RESPONSIBILITY 463 (Foundation Press, 1999 ed.), at 463.

[4] Rule 8.2(a). The Model Rules reject the old terminology of the Model Code. The ABA Model Code prohibited knowingly making "false statements of fact," DR 8-102(A) or "false accusations." DR 8-102(B). *See also* Restatement of the Law Governing Lawyers, Third, § 174 (Tent. Draft No. 8, Mar. 21, 1997). Restatement of the Law Governing Lawyers, Third, § 114 (Official Draft 2000), & Reporters Notes to Comment *b*.

Attacking The Judge In Briefs, Letters, Or Other Papers Filed With The Court. There are limits to the judge's power to discipline a lawyer who files what the judge finds is a rude or disrespectful filing. *In re Snyder*, 472 U.S. 634, 647, 105 S.Ct. 2874, 2882, 86 L.Ed.2d 504 (1985), held that, if a letter written that the lawyer had written to the secretary of a district court judge exhibited an "unlawyer-like rudeness," this single incident of rudeness or lack of professional courtesy cannot support a finding of contemptuous or contumacious conduct, or a finding that lawyer was not fit to practice law in federal courts. It also did not amount to a level of conduct unbecoming a member of the bar. The Court reversed the Eight Circuit's order that suspended the lawyer from practice before the Eight Circuit for six months.

However, judges are as human as the rest of us, and it is not wise to awaken the ire of the judge. *See, e.g. In re Wilkins*, 782 N.E.2d 985 (Ind. 2003). This decision disciplined attorney Wilkins because of a footnote in a brief that said: "Indeed, the [Court of Appeals] Opinion is so factually and legally inaccurate that one is left to wonder whether the Court of Appeals was determined to find for Appellee Sports, Inc., and then said whatever was necessary to reach that conclusion (regardless of whether the facts or the law supported its decision)." The Court

important for lawyers to be able to improve the administration of justice by being able to express "honest and candid opinions."[5]

Thus, Rule 8.2 would approve of such cases as *State Bar v. Semaan*,[6] which found no disciplinable offense when an attorney expressed his opinion attacking a judge; because the criticism involved opinion, there was no statement of fact that could be tested as true or false. In contrast, the Rules would *not* approve

---

agreed that important interests require the courts to allow latitude in lawyer argument, but went on to hold that Rule 8.2(a) creates a boundary beyond that a lawyer may not transgress. However, rather than impose the suspension recommended, the Court confined itself to a public reprimand after Wilkins issued a written apology to all involved.

See also Office of Disciplinary Counsel v. Gardner, 99 Ohio St.3d 416, 793 N.E.2d 45 (2003). *Gardner* imposed a six months suspension for filing a motion accusing the appellate court of lacking basic decency, ignoring prior case law, and having a strong prosecutorial bias. The Court found that there was no factual basis for the statements and therefore they violated Model Rule 8.2.

[5]Rule 8.2, Comment 1.

See, e.g., In re Disbarment of Moore, 529 U.S. 1127, 120 S.Ct. 2028, 146 L.Ed.2d 979 (2000). The Court (5 to 4) disbarred Moore, without opinion. Justices Stevens, Kennedy, Souter & Breyer dissented, also without opinion. A contemporary news account explained that the lawyer's "offense was filing two petitions for writs of certiorari filled with invective against the U.S. Court of Appeals for the 2nd Circuit and its 'chief injustice,' Ralph Winter". The lawyer, Teddy I. Moore, was sought review of Second Circuit rulings that had dismissed employment cases brought by two of his clients against New York City government agencies. Moore also "asked the Court to answer some broader questions—namely, whether the 2nd Circuit could be declared a corrupt enterprise under RICO, and whether Winter could be brought to trial for racketeering." Tony Mauro, *Free Speech at the Bar: Disbarment Showcases Court's Hard Line on Nasty Lawyer Talk*, LEGAL TIMES, June 26, 2000, at p. 10.

See also In re Schafer, 149 Wash.2d 148, 66 P.3d 1036 (2003). This decision involved lawyer Schafer and his client, Hamilton, who had told Schafer that Judge Anderson was involved in certain improprieties involving estate property, that he intended to rid himself of the tainted property before becoming a judge, and for that reason, Hamilton could quickly purchase the property. In an unrelated case involving another client, Judge Anderson had ruled against Schafer. Schafer revealed Hamilton's statements about Anderson's improprieties to government agencies, the media, and the FBI. Hamilton objected, claimed that Schafer really just wanted to retaliate because of Judge Anderson's adverse ruling, and filed a grievance. The Washington Supreme Court suspended Schafer for revealing client confidences in the exposé of Judge Anderson. Although he may "have been justified in reporting Anderson's alleged misconduct regarding the estate, he need not have reported his own client's confidences and secrets to accomplish this goal." In addition, although the rule permits disclosures to a judicial disciplinary tribunal, Schafer made disclosures to newspapers and a "sundry assortment of public officials." However, because "Schafer's unethical conduct resulted in the removal of a corrupt judge," the Court reduced his recommended one year suspension to six months.

[6]*State Bar v. Semaan*, 508 S.W.2d 429, 432 (Tex.Civ.App.1974).

of *In re Raggio*,[7] which reprimanded an attorney for charging that a judicial opinion was "shocking."

Board of Professional Responsibility v. Davidson,[8] involved a lawyer who failed to investigate an accusation against a judge before including it in a pleading. The lawyer's client in a domestic relations case directed her lawyer to "do what you have to do" to get the case assigned to someone other than Judge Arnold. The lawyer filed a motion accusing Judge Arnold of engaging in prohibited *ex parte* contact with opposing counsel and of being "rumored" to favor opposing counsel's firm. The lawyer had not investigated her charges, which proved to be false. The court held that the Rule 8.2 standard requires more of lawyers than simply not violating the standard of *N.Y. Times v. Sullivan*. Its sanction was harsh: it suspended lawyer Davidson for two months.

In re Evergreen Security, Ltd.,[9] was also unsympathetic to the free speech interests of lawyers. It upheld a large sanction when lawyer filed a recusal motion charging, among other things, that the bankruptcy judge, Arthur B. Briskman, had engaged in *ex parte* contact with other side. The appellate court ruled that "the bankruptcy court was not clearly erroneous in finding no factual support" for the lawyer's charges.[10]

§ 8.2–2 FIRST AMENDMENT IMPLICATIONS IN RULE 8.2

The free speech implications of this rule should not be ignored.[1] Lawyers may criticize judges. This criticism may be in bad taste,

---

[7]*In re Raggio*, 87 Nev. 369, 487 P.2d 499 (1971) (per curiam).

[8]*Board of Professional Responsibility v. Davidson*, 205 P.3d 1008 (Wyo. 2009).

[9]*In re Evergreen Security, Ltd.*, 570 F.3d 1257 (11th Cir. 2009). This case was full of sanctions and orders. The bankruptcy judge sanctioned two attorney's and their firm, 384 B.R. 882; assessed sanctions in amount of $371,517.69 against third attorney and barred him from practicing before it for five years, 2008 WL 410091; denied request to refer sanctions motion to different judge, 2008 WL 410087, and denied motion for certain disclosures on the record, 2008 WL 410099. In connection with the nondisclosure, the Eleventh Circuit ruled that bankruptcy judge Arthur B. Briskman had no obligation to disclose to parties before it the existence of a judicial ethics complaint against him in unrelated case because the complaint was confidential, it was not disclosed to the public, and filing the complaint was not something, the court said, that would cause any reasonable person to question bankruptcy judge's impartiality. 570 F.3d 1257, 1277-78.

[10]570 F.3d 1257, 1265.

[Section 8.2–2]

[1]*See New York Times Co. v. Sullivan*, 376 U.S. 254, 279–80, 84 S.Ct. 710, 725–26, 11 L.Ed.2d 686, 706–07 (1964)(public officials or figures may not, under the First Amendment, sue for defamation unless they can prove that the defendant published a knowing falsehood, or what is sometimes called, *New York Times Scienter*). On the First Amendment issues, *see* 5 RONALD D. ROTUNDA & JOHN E. NOWAK, TREATISE ON CONSTITUTIONAL

but it is still protected by the First Amendment. Moreover, because judges are ultimately enforcing the rules that discipline lawyers for insulting judges, these judges should be especially careful that they are acting objectively. As the highest court in New York concluded: "Without more, isolated instances of disrespect for the law, Judges and courts expressed by vulgar and insulting words or other incivility, uttered, written, or committed outside the precincts of a court are not subject to professional discipline."[2]

Any ban on lawyers criticizing judges must be very narrowly drafted in order to take into account free speech concerns. Hence, the Restatement of the Law Governing Lawyers prohibits a lawyer from making a defamatory statement only if it (1) is made "knowingly or recklessly," and (2) it is made "publicly" and (3) it is a "false statement of fact concerning the qualifications or integrity" of a judge or a candidate for election to a judicial office.[3] This rule reflects the fact that courts have held that, as a general principle, harsh, rude, even disrespectful comments about judges are free speech and constitutionally protected.[4]

Sometimes courts and commentators raise the question whether the lawyer subject to discipline must have made the comments with "malice." This reference to "malice" finds its origins in the common law of defamation and also in *New York Times v. Sullivan*,[5] but the same word has two very different meanings. Under the common law, "malice" simply meant "hatefulness" or "ill-will."[6] The Supreme Court, in *Sullivan*, cre-

---

LAW: SUBSTANCE AND PROCEDURE §§ 20.32–20.35 (Thomson-West, 4th ed. 2008) (6 volumes).

[2]*Justices of Appellate Division v. Erdmann*, 33 N.Y.2d 559, 347 N.Y.S.2d 441, 301 N.E.2d 426 (1973) (per curiam).

See also Standing Committee v. Yagman, 55 F.3d 1430 (9th Cir.1995) (Kozinski, J., rejecting discipline imposed on lawyer for comments about a federal trial judge). For further factual background regarding this case, *see* Susan Seager, *Judge Sanctions Yagman, Refers Case to State Bar*, L.A. DAILY J., June 6, 1991, at 1.

[3]Restatement of the Law Governing Lawyers, Third, § 114 (Official Draft 2000).

[4]*See, e.g., Ramsey v. Board of Professional Responsibility*, 771 S.W.2d

116, 121–122 (Tenn.1989), *cert. denied*, 493 U.S. 917, 110 S.Ct. 278, 107 L.Ed.2d 258 (1989).

[5]*New York Times v. Sullivan*, 376 U.S. 254, 84 S.Ct. 710, 11 L.Ed.2d 686 (1964), *motion denied*, 376 U.S. 967, 84 S.Ct. 1130, 12 L.Ed.2d 83 (1964).

[6]W. PAGE KEETON, DAN B. DOBBS, ROBERT E. KEETON & DAVID G. OWEN, PROSSER AND KEETON ON THE LAW OF TORTS 833–834 (West Pub. Co. 5th ed. 1984); *Cantrell v. Forest City Publishing Co.*, 419 U.S. 245, 251–52, 95 S.Ct. 465, 469–70, 42 L.Ed.2d 419 (1974). In *Herbert v. Lando*, 441 U.S. 153, 199, 99 S.Ct. 1635, 1660–61, 60 L.Ed.2d 115 (1979), Justice, Stewart, dissenting, noted: "Although I joined the Court's opinion in *New York Times*, I have come greatly to regret the use in that opinion of the phrase 'actual

ated a new rule to offer greater protection of speech that is critical of public officials.

> The constitutional guarantees require, we think, a federal rule that prohibits a public official from recovering damages for a defamatory falsehood relating to his official conduct unless he proves that the statement was made with "*actual malice*" . . ."[7]

Sullivan then went on to define "malice" to mean something quite different than "vindictiveness" or "spitefulness." The Court said that "actual malice" is "knowledge that [the defamation that was published] was false or with reckless disregard of whether it was false or not."[8] In other words, when the Court used the word "malice," it is not referring to "hatefulness;" rather, the Court meant "*scienter.*"[9]

Hence, it would be unconstitutional to punish a lawyer if he or she told the truth about a judge or judicial candidate, even if the lawyer spoke out of spite. The lawyer would similarly be protected if the lawyer spoke a falsehood, but the lawyer did not *know* that it was false, unless the lawyer spoke with reckless disregard of whether it was false or not. Finally, under the provisions of the Restatement, the lawyer is protected unless this statement (which must be made "knowingly or recklessly,") is also made "publicly" and is a "false statement of fact concerning the qualifications or integrity" of a judge or judicial candidate.

Thus, *In re Green*[10] refused to discipline a lawyer who acted without "malice." In this attorney disciplinary proceeding, a state disciplinary hearing board had found that lawyer Green had authored various letters and motions to a trial judge containing "relentless criticism and contempt for the judge." The hearing board concluded that these actions constituted "a serious breach of acceptable behavior for an attorney toward a member of the judiciary."[11] There was no doubt of the lawyer's intentions; at various times he explicitly accused the judge of being racist. For example, "I affirm my right not to have my attorney fees determined by a racist judge."[12]

Nonetheless, the state supreme court rejected the conclusions of its hearing board and held that the First Amendment precludes

---

malice.' . . . In common understanding, malice means ill will or hostility. [But *New York Times* malice] has nothing to do with hostility or ill will. . . ."

[7]376 U.S. at 279–80, 84 S.Ct. at 726 (emphasis added).

[8]376 U.S. at 280, 84 S.Ct. at 726.

[9]5 RONALD D. ROTUNDA & JOHN E. NOWAK, TREATISE ON CONSTITUTIONAL LAW: SUBSTANCE AND

PROCEDURE §§ 20.33(a), 20.33(b) (Thomson-West, 4th ed. 2008) (6 volumes).

[10]*In re Green*, 11 P.3d 1078 (Colo. 2000) (per curiam). *See* Richard A. McGuire, *How Far Can A Lawyer Go In Criticizing A Judge?*, 27 JOURNAL OF THE LEGAL PROF. 227 (2002–2003).

[11]11 P.3d at 1080.

[12]11 P.3d at 1082.

professional discipline for an attorney's criticism of a judge, unless the criticism involves both falsehood and "actual malice." In this case, the attorney's statements that the trial judge was a "racist and bigot" with a "bent of mind" were opinions based upon fully disclosed and uncontested facts, and thus, the court refused to discipline the lawyer for these statements.

§ 8.2–3 DEFENDING JUDGES FROM CRITICISM

The original draft of the Model Rules was much less protective of judges than either the final draft or the Model Code.[1] The Model Rules initially contained no express language that corresponded to that found in EC 8-6 regarding the lawyer's duty to defend judges.[2]

It is not unusual for judges to believe that lawyers should defend judges from unjust criticism.[3] Hence, the final version, as approved by the House of Delegates, added a paragraph to the Comment that encourages lawyers "to continue traditional efforts to defend judges and courts unjustly criticized."[4] However, there is no language (like the language found in EC 8-6) urging lawyers to be "certain" of the merits of their criticism. Rather, the Rules simply urge lawyers to express "honest and candid opinions."[5]

§ 8.2–4 LAWYERS AS CANDIDATES FOR JUDICIAL OFFICE

Judges running for retention or reelection are governed in their campaign activities by the ABA Model Code of Judicial Conduct (1990), as enacted by the individual states. The Rules, in order to prevent lawyers campaigning for judicial office from having an unfair competitive advantage, similarly require that the lawyer-candidate comply with the applicable provisions of the Code of

---

[Section 8.2–3]

[1] The Model Code urged lawyers to defend judges and other adjudicatory officials against "unjust criticism" because these officials are not "wholly free to defend themselves." EC 8-6. Lawyers also should "be certain" of their criticisms of judges, "use appropriate language" and avoid "petty" and "unrestrained" criticism. EC 8-6.

On the other hand, the same EC 8-6 urged lawyers to "protest earnestly against the appointment or election of those who are unsuited for the bench." And elsewhere, the Model Code advised that lawyers "should avoid undue solicitude for the comfort or con-

venience of judge[s]." EC7-36. The Code thus appeared to point in two directions regarding the lawyer's duty to defend judges.

[2] See Rule 8.2 (Proposed Final Draft, May 30, 1981).

[3] Rinaldi v. Holt, Rinehart & Winston, Inc., 42 N.Y.2d 369, 397 N.Y.S.2d 943, 366 N.E.2d 1299 (1977) (concurring opinion of Fuchsberg, J.), cert. denied, 434 U.S. 969, 98 S.Ct. 514, 54 L.Ed.2d 456 (1977) (arguing that lawyers have an affirmative duty to defend judges).

[4] Rule 8.2, Comment 3.

[5] Rule 8.2, Comment 1.

Judicial Conduct.[1]

_____

[Section 8.2–4]

[1]Rule 8.2(b). This provision is derived from DR 8-102(B).

See ABA Model Code of Judicial Conduct, Canon 5, discussed below.

The title of this Canon provides that "a judge *or judicial candidate* shall refrain from inappropriate political activity." (emphasis added).

RULE 8.3: REPORTING PROFESSIONAL MISCONDUCT

(a) A lawyer who knows that another lawyer has committed a violation of the Rules of Professional Conduct that raises a substantial question as to that lawyer's honesty, trustworthiness or fitness as a lawyer in other respects, shall inform the appropriate professional authority.

(b) A lawyer who knows that a judge has committed a violation of applicable rules of judicial conduct that raises a substantial question as to the judge's fitness for office shall inform the appropriate authority.

(c) This Rule does not require disclosure of information otherwise protected by Rule 1.6 or information gained by a lawyer or judge while participating in an approved lawyers assistance program.

Comment

[1] Self-regulation of the legal profession requires that members of the profession initiate disciplinary investigation when they know of a violation of the Rules of Professional Conduct. Lawyers have a similar obligation with respect to judicial misconduct. An apparently isolated violation may indicate a pattern of misconduct that only a disciplinary investigation can uncover. Reporting a violation is especially important where the victim is unlikely to discover the offense.

[2] A report about misconduct is not required where it would involve violation of Rule 1.6. However, a lawyer should encourage a client to consent to disclosure where prosecution would not substantially prejudice the client's interests.

[3] If a lawyer were obliged to report every violation of the Rules, the failure to report any violation would itself be a professional offense. Such a requirement existed in many jurisdictions but proved to be unenforceable. This Rule limits the reporting obligation to those offenses that a self-regulating profession must vigorously endeavor to prevent. A measure of judgment is, therefore,

required in complying with the provisions of this Rule. The term "substantial" refers to the seriousness of the possible offense and not the quantum of evidence of which the lawyer is aware. A report should be made to the bar disciplinary agency unless some other agency, such as a peer review agency, is more appropriate in the circumstances. Similar considerations apply to the reporting of judicial misconduct.

[4] The duty to report professional misconduct does not apply to a lawyer retained to represent a lawyer whose professional conduct is in question. Such a situation is governed by the Rules applicable to the client-lawyer relationship.

[5] Information about a lawyer's or judge's misconduct or fitness may be received by a lawyer in the course of that lawyer's participation in an approved lawyers or judges assistance program. In that circumstance, providing for an exception to the reporting requirements of paragraphs (a) and (b) of this Rule encourages lawyers and judges to seek treatment through such a program. Conversely, without such an exception, lawyers and judges may hesitate to seek assistance from these programs, which may then result in additional harm to their professional careers and additional injury to the welfare of clients and the public. These Rules do not otherwise address the confidentiality of information received by a lawyer or judge participating in an approved lawyers assistance program; such an obligation, however, may be imposed by the rules of the program or other law.

Authors' 1983 Model Rules Comparison

The 1983 version of Rule 8.3 did not contain a reference to lawyer assistance programs. In 1991, the ABA amended Rule 8.3(c) and added Comment 5 to protect information obtained by a lawyer working in an approved lawyer assistance program.

The drafters of the 2002 Model Rules made several minor changes to Rule 8.3.

In the text of Rule 8.3(a) and (b), the 1983 version used the term, "having knowledge" and the drafters changed this term to "who knows" because the word, "know" is defined in Rule 1.0 and better reflects the modern language involving state of mind. *See* Reporter's Explanation of Changes to Rule 8.3.

In Rule 8.3(c), the drafters changed the words, "serving as a member of" to "participating in" because a lawyer does not need to be a formal member of a lawyer's assistance committee; instead, any participation in the work of such committees is protected by confidentiality. The drafters also simplified the language in Rule 8.3(c) by deleting the last clause: "to the extent that such information would be confidential if it were communicated subject to the attorney-client privilege." This language was confusing and was not needed to describe the need for lawyer assistance committees to work outside of Rule 8.3.

Comments 1, 2, 3, and 4 are identical to the 1983 version.

In Comment 5, the drafters sought to remove any reference to the attorney-client privilege and to place the focus back on Rule 1.6 and confidentiality. They also sought to simplify the test for confidentiality within lawyer assistance programs. The drafters deleted two lines that stated:

The Rule therefore exempts the lawyer from the reporting requirements of Paragraphs (a) and (b) with respect to information that would be privileged if the relationship between the impaired lawyer or judge and the recipient of the information were that of a client and a lawyer. On the other hand, a lawyer who receives such information would nevertheless be required to comply with the Rule 8.3 reporting provisions to report misconduct if the impaired lawyer or judge indicates an intent to engage in illegal activity, for example, the conversion of client funds to his or her use.

1991 Model Rule 8.3, Comment 5. Instead, the drafters simplified the notion of confidentiality in a lawyer assistance program by stating that Rule 8.3 does not apply when a lawyer or judge works in such a program. Each state program can make its own guidelines for confidentiality or disclosure when dealing with lawyers who are struggling with an impairment.

Model Code Comparison

DR 1-103(A) provided that "[a] lawyer possessing unprivileged knowledge of a violation of [a Disciplinary Rule] shall report such knowledge to . . . authority empowered to investigate or act upon such violation."

§ 8.3–1 THE LAWYER'S ROLE REGARDING REPORTING DISCIPLINABLE VIOLATIONS OF LAWYERS

In general, lawyers have an obligation to volunteer information of another lawyer's serious disciplinable violations unless the information is privileged.

§ 8.3–1(a) The Historical Background of the Reporting Obligation in the Model Code

It is easier to appreciate the changes that the Model Rules have made regarding a lawyer's duty to whistle-blow about another lawyer's alleged misconduct if we compare the Rules to the Code. First, the ABA Model Code required, under threat of discipline, that lawyers voluntarily report *any* disciplinable violation by a lawyer to the appropriate authority.[1] This affirmative duty of whistle-blowing applied not only against a lawyer in another firm but also against a partner or associate in the reporting lawyer's own firm.[2] The relevant rule did not use the phrase "another lawyer," so that it appeared to require the lawyer to voluntarily report himself.[3]

Courts have held that this DR conferred standing on a lawyer

[Section 8.3–1]

[1]DR 1-103(A); EC 1-4.

[2]ABA Informal Opinion 1203 (Feb. 9, 1972).

[3]DR 1-103(B) used the phrase "other lawyer," but that was only in connection with responding to a sub-poena or other request for information from the tribunal investigating that other lawyer. DR 1-103(A), the whistle-blowing section, said:

"A lawyer possessing unprivileged knowledge of a violation of DR 1-102 shall report such knowledge to a tribu-

The Illinois Supreme Court in *Himmel* interpreted "unprivileged knowledge" in its version of DR 1-103(A) to mean only "confidence," the evidentiary privilege, and not "secret," which is the broader ethical obligation that is included within DR 4-101(A). In contrast to *Himmel*, the ABA—when it uses the word "privileged" in the Model Code—defines that term to mean both "confidence" and "secret."[12] The Model Rules also protect more than the narrow evidentiary privilege. Model Rule 8.3 "does not require disclosure of information otherwise protected by Rule 1.6. . . ."[13] And Rule 1.6 protects all "client information," a term that is broad enough to cover both evidentiary "confidences" and ethical "secrets."[14]

Thus far, other states have not followed Illinois' lead and have not disciplined lawyers for failure to report when the lawyer's information is included in that broad term, "client information," under Model Rule 1.6.

§ 8.3-1(c) Reporting Obligation of a Lawyer Who Represents Another Lawyer Accused of Conversion, Fraud, or Other Conduct Involving a Substantial Question as to That Lawyer's Fitness as a Lawyer

Himmel's knowledge clearly was a "secret" as defined by the Illinois ethics rule.[15] In February, 1985, after Himmel filed the civil complaint against Mr. Casey (the lawyer whom he failed to report), the question is much less clear, but it is possible that even then the information contained in that complaint may not have lost its "secret" status. Once Ms. Forsberg's case is filed in a court, her complaint against her former lawyer, Mr. Casey was "public" in the sense that someone could uncover it and read about it. Yet, after the complaint was filed, information about it might still be "secret" in the sense that the information had not become "generally known."

In a busy court system where many cases are filed, Ms. Forsberg's judicial action against Casey was not front page news (in fact, it was not even news buried on page twenty-four). Her case was simply one of many cases thrown into an anonymous judicial system. Whether it is a federal or state case, even if it reaches verdict, it may (like most cases) never reach an appeal and never be immortalized in a published decision. Even though the information is "public" in the sense that it is not covered by

---

[12]ABA Formal Opinion 341 (Sept. 30, 1975).

[13]Rule 8.3(c). Cf. EC 4-4.

[14]Rule 1.6, Comment 5: "The confidentiality rule applies not merely to matters communicated in confidence by the client but also to all information relating to the representation, whatever its source."

[15]Illinois Rule 4-101(a), which corresponds to DR 4-101(A) and Model Rule 1.6(a).

the attorney-client evidentiary privilege, it may be unknown or "secret" in the sense that knowledge of it is not widely available. The case may remain obscure and uncelebrated, not "generally known": that is how the American Bar Association uses the word "secret." It states that the "ethical precept, unlike the evidentiary privilege, exists without regard to the nature or source of information or the fact that others share the knowledge."[16]

The *Himmel* decision is significant not only because it disciplines a lawyer solely for the failure to report—there were no other disciplinary charges filed against Mr. Himmel—but primarily because it interprets the word "privileged"[17] very narrowly and differently than the way the ABA uses the very same term.[18] Illinois interprets "privileged" in its ethics code to exclude the ethical privilege, so a lawyer who has knowledge of another lawyer's disciplinary violations must report those violations unless that knowledge is protected by the more narrow attorney-client evidentiary privilege.

Given this result, what about the lawyer representing Mr. Casey? Should not this lawyer have the same obligation to report Mr. Casey as the lawyer for Ms. Forsberg? Casey's lawyer is bound by the evidentiary privilege to the extent that he received confidential information from his client, Mr. Casey. However, Mr. Himmel eventually had to file suit against Casey. The information that Himmel alleged in her complaint is not privileged under the law of evidence as to Casey. Nor is anything in the defendant's answer privileged under the law of evidence. Similarly, whatever Mr. Himmel told Casey's lawyer in negotiations is also not protected in any way by the attorney-client evidentiary privilege. One could think that Casey's lawyer should also have the same reporting obligation as Mr. Himmel. Both have evidence not protected by the evidentiary privilege. Granted, Mr. Casey's lawyer may not believe the evidence against his client, but neither DR 1-103 nor Rule 8.3(a) require the lawyer to "believe" the allegations. If the lawyer has "knowledge," that is enough.[19] *Himmel* appears to hold that when the lawyer representing another lawyer in a malpractice case or other matter acquires "knowledge" of a possible disciplinary violation that relates to the lawyer's fitness as a lawyer, and this knowledge is not privileged under the law of evidence, that lawyer has an ethical obligation to report it.

And then, of course, there is the judge who presided at the trial of Forsberg versus Casey. Because this case was brought before a

---

[16]EC 4-4. *See also* Model Rule 1.6, Comment 5.

[17]This term is used in Illinois Rule 1-103(a).

[18]*See* ABA Formal Opinion 341 (Sept. 30, 1975).

[19]Rule 8.3, Comment 3.

court, a judge had to hear the allegations regarding Mr. Casey. The judge is also a member of the bar and therefore should be subject to same Illinois reporting requirement. In such a case, the judge should also report Mr. Casey. Whether it is a bench trial and whether the jury issues a verdict in favor of the plaintiff, the judge is made aware that he or she does have "knowledge" of claims against a lawyer. These claims are serious indeed, for they involved questions of Casey's honesty and his willingness to convert funds. The *Himmel* court did not discuss these issues regarding a judge's duty to report just as they did not discuss any reporting duty that might be imposed on Casey's lawyer. But, in the wake if *Himmel*, these reporting issues remain, even though the court did not delve into them.

§ 8.3–1(d) The Different Reporting Obligation of the Model Rules

§ 8.3–1(d)(1) Serious Violations Only

The Rules impose a duty to report, but it is more limited than the reporting obligation under the Model Code. The whistle-blowing duty only covers conduct that raises a "substantial question" regarding the other lawyer's "honesty, trustworthiness or fitness as a lawyer."[20] The drafters of the Rules hoped that, by limiting the obligation to report only the more serious violations, the duty would be more realistic and therefore might be more enforceable.[21]

The Rules define "substantial" to mean "a material matter of clear and weighty importance."[22] Thus, "substantial" refers not to the amount of evidence of which the lawyer is aware, but to the "seriousness of the possible offense."[23] Although the ABA Model Code required the lawyer to exercise judgment with respect to the quantum of evidence of violation, the ABA Model Rules, in contrast, require the lawyer to exercise judgment with regard to the seriousness of the violation.[24]

---

[20]Rule 8.3(a). *See also* Restatement of the Law Governing Lawyers, Third, § 5(3) (Official Draft 2000). This obligation to report extends to reporting lawyers who engage in misconduct outside of the practice of law as long as such conduct calls into question the lawyer's honesty, trustworthiness and fitness to practice law and is not protected by Rule 1.6. *See* ABA Formal Opinion 04-433 (Aug. 25, 2004) ("Obligation of a Lawyer to Report Professional Misconduct by a Lawyer Not Engaged in the Practice of Law").

[21]Rule 8.3, Comment 3.

[22]Rule 1.0(l).

[23]Rule 8.3, Comment 3.

Absolute certainty is not necessary to trigger the obligation to report another lawyer. *Board of Overseers of Bar v. Warren*, 2011 ME 124, 34 A.3d 1103, 1115 (Me. 2011), quoting, Rotunda, The Lawyer's Duty to Report Another Lawyer's Unethical Violations in the Wake of Himmel, 1988 U. Ill. L. Rev. 977, 985 (1988).

[24]*In re Riehlmann*, 891 So.2d 1239

§ 8.3–1(d)(2) Obligation to Report Another Lawyer Suffering from Alcoholism, Drug Addiction, or Other Mental Impairment

ABA Formal Opinion 03-431 examines the difficult question of a lawyer's duty to report another lawyer suspected of suffering from alcoholism, drug addiction or other mental impairment.[25] Model Rule 1.16(a)(2) prohibits a lawyer's representation of a client when the lawyer's physical or mental condition "materially impairs the lawyer's ability to represent the client," and Model Rule 8.3(a) requires other lawyers to report such a problem to regulatory authorities. The ABA Committee notes that a lack of fitness to practice can evidence itself through either a pattern of conduct or a single act. The key is whether the substance abuse or mental condition causes a material impairment of the lawyer's ability to practice law.

If a lawyer recognizes symptoms of mental impairment that materially impair the affected lawyer's representation of clients,[26] she has discretion to (1) consult with a mental health care professional about the significance of the observed conduct; (2) speak with the affected lawyer herself; (3) contact "an established lawyer assistance program"; or (4) speak with the supervising lawyers or partners of the affected lawyer's firm who may take steps to ensure that the affected lawyer is not representing clients while materially impaired. Unless the affected lawyer's firm takes appropriate action, the lawyer observing impairment has a duty to report her observations to the appropriate authority. Of course, if the reported information would disclose matters relating to the

---

(La. 2005), presents a very compelling story for disclosure of another lawyer's misconduct in light of the consequences of the lawyer's violation. A lawyer met for drinks with one of his lawyer friends and the friend confessed that he was terminally ill with cancer. The friend further confessed that he had as a prosecutor once suppressed exculpatory blood evidence in a case and the defendant was convicted in the matter. The lawyer asked his friend, the prosecutor, to disclose this information to the court, but the friend refused. The friend later died and five years after the initial disclosure the lawyer discovered that the defendant in the criminal case with the exculpatory information was on death row and about to die through lethal injection. The lawyer disclosed his friend's violation to the state disciplinary authorities and in turn the disci-

plinary authorities disciplined the lawyer for failing to report the misconduct in a more timely fashion. The Louisiana Supreme Court issued a public reprimand to the lawyer for failing to discharge his obligation to report misconduct to the proper authorities.

[25] ABA Formal Opinion 03-431 (Aug. 8, 2003).

[26] The ABA Opinion acknowledges that most lawyers are not trained to discern medical problems suffered by other lawyers. But, "a lawyer may not shut his eyes to conduct reflecting generally recognized symptoms of impairment, (e.g., patterns of memory lapse or inexplicable behavior not typical of the subject lawyer, such as repeated missed deadlines)." ABA Formal Opinion 03-431 (Aug. 8, 2003).

representation of the reporting lawyer's client, the lawyer must get the client's informed consent.[27]

If the impaired lawyer is a member of the law firm, the firm's partners and supervisory lawyers have obligations that are described in ABA Formal Opinion 03-429.[28] Clearly, partners and supervisory lawyers have obligations under Rule 5.1 to ensure that an impaired lawyer's work is supervised so as not to injure clients. Depending on the impairment, in some cases, the partners and supervisory lawyers may have a duty to prevent the impaired lawyer from performing certain types of legal work. If the impaired lawyer cannot competently represent clients in the long run, the other lawyers continue to have an obligation under Rule 8.3 to report the lawyer to the appropriate authority.[29] And, this obligation exists even if the impaired lawyer leaves the firm.

§ 8.3–1(d)(3) No Obligation to Self-Report

Under the Model Code, a lawyer was required to report knowledge of unprivileged information of disciplinable conduct. Given the way in which it is drafted, this rule could be interpreted to require a lawyer to report his or her own misconduct.[30] Failure to report would then be a separate disciplinable violation. Of course, this interpretation would not require a lawyer to waive the Fifth Amendment privilege against self-incrimination because DR 1-103(A) only refers to "unprivileged knowledge or information."

This interpretation is supported by the contrasting language in DR 1-103(B), which specifically refers to "another lawyer." In addition, the ABA interpreted DR 1-103(A) to require a lawyer to report himself if the information was "unprivileged."[31] And, case law has also ruled that a lawyer must promptly notify a client of possible malpractice claims that a client may have against him.[32]

In contrast, some commentators have argued that the "report-

---

[27]Rule 8.3(c).

[28]ABA Formal Opinion 03-429 (June 11, 2003).

[29]This Opinion discusses short term impairments which would not trigger disclosure under Rule 8.3 as long as the firm monitored the lawyer's work versus long term impairments which call into question this person's ability to represent clients competently. ABA Formal Opinion 03-429 (June 11, 2003).

[30]DR 1-103(A). Note, in contrast, that DR 1-103(B) used the term, "another lawyer."

[31]Thus, ABA Informal Opinion 1279 (Aug. 29, 1973) concluded:

"Does [DR 1-103(A)] require a lawyer to 'report' his knowledge that he has, himself, violated DR 1-102, in the situation where his unethical conduct is not privileged because, for example, he clearly cannot be exposed to criminal sanctions for having engaged in such unethical conduct? We construe DR 1-103(A) as requiring the lawyer *to report himself* in that situation."

[32]*Tallon v. Committee on Professional Standards, Third Judicial Dept.*, 86 A.D.2d 897, 447 N.Y.S.2d 50, 51 (3d Dept.1982) (respondent suspended for six months for this and other violations).

ing provision of . . . DR 1-103(A) should not apply to the lawyer's own conduct."[33]

The Rules avoid all of these problems and do not raise this question of interpretation at all, because the relevant provision explicitly refers to knowledge regarding "another lawyer."[34]

§ 8.3–1(d)(4) Consequences of a Violation of Rule 8.3

In the *Himmel* decision examined above, the lawyer received a one year suspension for a failure to report the other lawyer's misconduct. Rule 8.3 is designed to provide bar authorities with information about lawyers who violate laws and rules and place their clients and the public at risk. The failure to report misconduct of another lawyer may have consequences other than bar discipline. If the incompetent or dishonest lawyer is a member of the lawyer's firm who discovers the misconduct, the obligations under Rule 5.1 or Rule 5.2 may be implicated. A partner or supervisory lawyer would have an obligation to take reasonable remedial action and an associate would need to bring these issues to the attention of the partners. When the misconduct occurs within the firm, the violations of Rules 8.3 and 5.1 or 5.2 may also violate a lawyer's standard of care to the client in a malpractice action.[35]

§ 8.3–2 APPLICABILITY OF CONFIDENTIALITY

§ 8.3–2(a) Client Confidences

The Rules, avoiding the interpretation problems found in the Model Code,[1] explicitly provide that the relevant Rules mandating whistle-blowing do not apply to information protected by Rule

---

[33]2 RONALD MALLEN & JEFFREY SMITH, LEGAL MALPRACTICE § 19.6 at 162, note 20 (West Pub. Co., 3rd ed. 1989).

[34]Rule 8.3(a).

[35]*Compare Estate of Spencer v. Galvin*, 946 A.2d 1051 (N.J.Super. 2008). In *Spencer*, two lawyers not in the same firm represented a client. One of the attorneys was engaged in active theft of the client's funds and the other lawyer worked closely on the client's matter and may have witnessed the misconduct. In denying summary judgment, the court stated that if the lawyer had actual knowledge of the theft, by failing to report the misconduct under Rule 8.3, the lawyer may be responsible to the cli-

ent under a malpractice cause of action.

[Section 8.3–2]

[1]The Model Rules did not change the law on this issue. The Model Code reached this same conclusion, but only through a more circuitous route. DR 1-103 referred to "unprivileged knowledge" but did not explain if "privilege" included only the attorney-client evidentiary privilege, or the much broader privilege protected by Canon 4. DR 7-102(B)(1), governing a different issue, also referred to "a privileged communication." ABA Formal Opinion 341 (Sept. 30, 1975) interpreted "privileged communication" in DR 7-102(B)(1) as referring to "those confidences and secrets that are required to be

1.6.[2] Rule 1.6, of course, protects all client information, a category that is much broader than the attorney-client evidentiary privilege.

A lawyer would receive such information protected by Rule 1.6 in one of two situations. First, the lawyer represents a client who informs the lawyer that another lawyer has committed serious professional misconduct such as in the *Himmel* decision. Second, the lawyer represents a lawyer who has committed a serious act of professional misconduct. In the first situation, the lawyer could always obtain the client's consent to disclose to the appropriate professional authority. But if the client declined and if the information was confidential under Rule 1.6 with no exceptions, the lawyer could not report the misconduct. In the second situation, when a lawyer represents another lawyer in the matter that is the subject of the misconduct, the Rules permit the formation and existence of the attorney-client relationship to override the duty to disclose misconduct to the proper authority.

§ 8.3–2(b) Lawyer Assistance Programs

A Lawyer Assistance Program (often called by the acronym LAP) is designed to help lawyers and judges who suffer from alcoholism or drug abuse.[3] Lawyers and judges help other lawyers and judges who are afflicted with these problems. LAPs promise confidentiality to their participants in order to encourage their involvement in the program.[4]

If the lawyers who are active in a LAP were required to reveal the confidential information that they learn from their colleagues who suffer from alcohol or substance abuse, the LAP would be severely undercut. Consequently, Rule 8.3 makes it clear that the reporting requirements that it imposes do not apply in this

---

preserved by DR 4-101." This Formal Opinion found it undesirable to interpret "privileged" to mean only information protected as an evidentiary privilege because the lawyer's ethical duty would then vary from jurisdiction to jurisdiction, depending on the local rules of evidence. Also, the Formal Opinion argued, in some cases it might be difficult to determine which jurisdiction's evidence law should govern.

Because this interpretation of "privileged" under DR 7-102(B)(1) is equally applicable to DR 1-103, the same definition should also apply; that is, "unprivileged knowledge" or "evidence" under DR 1-103 means any information not protected by Canon 4.

[2] See Rule 8.1(b), 8.3(c).

[3] See Fred C. Zacharias, *A Word of Caution for Lawyer Assistance Programming*, 18 GEORGETOWN J. LEGAL ETHICS 237 (2005) (arguing that a real tension exists in LAPs between the goal of rehabilitating a lawyers and the other goals of the disciplinary system).

[4] See, e.g., 2001 North Carolina Formal Ethics Opinion 5, 2001 WL 1949445 (N.C.St.Bar. July 27, 2001), advising that disclosures made during a LAP support group meeting are confidential and not reportable to the State Bar under Rule 8.3.

situation.[5] The Rule treats the relationship between the volunteer lawyers and judges in a LAP and the impaired lawyers or judges as if it were a client-lawyer relationship for purposes of this Rule. Thus, the information received from the impaired lawyer or judge is treated as protected by Rule 1.6.[6]

Prior to the 2002 revisions, a Comment to Rule 8.3 advised that, "if the impaired lawyer or judge indicates an intent to engage in illegal activity, for example, the conversion of client funds to his or her own use," then the lawyer who receives this information "would nevertheless be required to comply with the Rule 8.3 reporting provisions to report misconduct. . . ."[7]

In 2002, the ABA House of Delegates deleted that provision. Now, the Comment simply advises that the Model Rules, other than providing for the confidentiality of information received pursuant to a LAP program, "do not otherwise address the confidentiality of information received by a lawyer or judge participating in an approved lawyers assistance program," but the rules of the LAP program "or other law" may impose such a disclosure obligation.[8]

§ 8.3–2(c) Self-Incrimination and Other Constitutional Privileges

Rule 8.3(c) makes clear that its reporting obligation does not apply to information "otherwise protected by Rule 1.6. . . ."[9] If a lawyer represents a lawyer-respondent in a disciplinary proceeding, the lawyer has no obligation to report the privileged information that she has obtained from her client in confidence.

The drafters of Rule 8.3 make sure that the reporting obligation did not override the client's right to keep client information confidential under Rule 1.6.[10] But, would any other privileges produce a similar result? The drafters may appear to have given protection to one privilege (the attorney-client privilege) but not to others, such as the Fifth Amendment right against self-incrimination. Moreover, the drafters of Rule 8.3 specifically refer to the self-incrimination privilege in Rule 8.1,[11] further suggesting that Rule 8.3 does not incorporate that privilege or any privilege other than the attorney-client privilege.

However, it would be incorrect to read this reference to the

---

[5] Rule 8.3(c); Rule 8.3, Comment 5.

[6] Rule 8.3, Comment 5.

[7] Rule 8.3, Comment 5 (deleted in the 2002 revisions to the Model Rules).

[8] Rule 8.3, Comment 5 (as revised in 2002).

[9] Rule 8.3(c). DR 1-103 restricted its application to "unprivileged knowledge" but did not define the term.

[10] Rule 1.6, in turn, does not refer to self-incrimination. *See* Rule 8.1(b), 8.3(c).

[11] Rule 8.1, Comment 2: "This Rule [8.1] is subject to the provisions of the Fifth Amendment of the United States Constitution and corresponding provisions of state constitutions."

attorney-client privilege as a negative pregnant, excluding all other privileges not specifically mentioned. Clearly the rule cannot apply to knowledge protected by a constitutional privilege, such as the privilege against self-incrimination; otherwise the rule would be unconstitutional.[12] To preserve the constitutionality of these Rules, the self-incrimination protection must be read into them.

As a constitutional matter, bar authorities cannot discipline or otherwise sanction a lawyer simply because he or she has asserted the privilege against self-incrimination.[13] However, the attorney may be disciplined for refusing to testify if that testimony would not expose him to criminal prosecution.[14]

Consequently, the state can grant a lawyer "use immunity"—*i.e.*, a guarantee that the compelled testimony will not be used against the person in a criminal prosecution—and then use this testimony to disbar or otherwise discipline the lawyer. The justification for allowing the use of this compelled testimony for bar discipline is that bar discipline is not a criminal matter.[15] The bar prosecutors can use the compelled testimony (given pursuant to use immunity) in the disciplinary proceeding but the criminal prosecutors cannot use that immunized testimony in the lawyer's criminal prosecution.

§ 8.3–2(d) Court Orders

Skolnick v. Altheimer & Gray[16] held that the lawyer's duty to report another lawyer prevails over the duty to obey a protective order sealing the relevant documents. In this case, a law firm associate and the firm itself had accused a partner of creating and filing a false document in a case. The Illinois Attorney Registration and Disciplinary Commission (ARDC) filed a charge but later dismissed it for lack of evidence. Later, the accused lawyer sued the firm and its associate for defamation and for damaging his practice. The court allowed discovery under a protective order. The associate then allegedly turned up information proving the lawyer's fraud. She wanted to use it in a counterclaim *and* to send it to the ARDC, but the lower court did not allow that. The Illinois Supreme Court reversed.

---

[12] *See* ABA Informal Opinion 1279 (Aug. 29, 1973) (DR 1-103 does not require lawyer to engage in self-incrimination).

[13] *Spevack v. Klein*, 385 U.S. 511, 87 S.Ct. 625, 17 L.Ed.2d 574 (1967).

[14] *Zuckerman v. Greason*, 20 N.Y.2d 430, 285 N.Y.S.2d 1, 231 N.E.2d 718 (1967).

[15] *See, e.g., Matter of Ungar*, 27 A.D.2d 925, 282 N.Y.S.2d 158 (1967);

Anonymous Attorneys v. Bar Association of Erie County, 41 N.Y.2d 506, 393 N.Y.S.2d 961, 362 N.E.2d 592 (1977); *In re Schwarz*, 51 Ill.2d 334, 282 N.E.2d 689 (1972); *In re Daley*, 549 F.2d 469 (7th Cir.1977), *cert. denied*, 434 U.S. 829, 98 S.Ct. 110, 54 L.Ed.2d 89 (1977).

[16] *Skolnick v. Altheimer & Gray*, 191 Ill.2d 214, 246 Ill.Dec. 324, 730 N.E.2d 4 (2000).

The state supreme court held that the duty to report to the ARDC is absolute and transcends protective orders. Indeed, it held that the protective order itself was unjustified even as to the requirement that the counterclaim be sealed. The associate had adequate knowledge to trigger her duty to report. The former partner also failed to rebut the presumption that the counterclaim was a matter of public record subject to disclosure under the First Amendment and under the common law. In short, the state supreme court ruled that the trial court abused its discretion by refusing to modify the protective order to allow the associate to fulfill her ethical duty to report suspected misconduct by the former partner.

§ 8.3–3 REPORTING MISCONDUCT OF JUDGES

In contrast to the Model Code,[1] the Rules clearly *require* a lawyer to volunteer to the appropriate authorities any nonconfidential information showing that a judge (whether or not a lawyer)[2] violated the judicial rules if the conduct raises "a substantial question as to the judge's fitness for office. . . ."[3]

[Section 8.3–3]

[1]Although DR 1-103(A) mandates a whistle-blowing role for lawyers, there is no analogous disciplinary rule mandating the lawyer to make an unsolicited report of misconduct by a judge. However, DR 1-103(A) would apply to judges who are also lawyers in the relevant jurisdiction. Not all judges fall in that category. If a lawyer reported a judge's misconduct to the judicial discipline authority, which many states have created, that authority could impose sanctions on the judge.

As an ethical aspiration (rather than a mandatory obligation) a lawyer should report to "appropriate authorities" (presumably including a judicial discipline commission) any fraudulent, deceptive, or otherwise illegal conduct of any "participant in a proceeding before a tribunal" if the information is not protected as a client confidence. EC 8-5. This language would apply to judges as well as lawyers and laypeople. The Code does explicitly provide that, "upon proper request," the lawyer must reveal unprivileged knowledge or evidence regarding a judge. DR 1-103(B).

[2]Yes, some judges in the United States are not lawyers. In 1983, one source reported that in 44 states approximately 14,000 judges were not licensed to practice law. TIME MAGAZINE, Sept. 26, 1983, at 62, col. 1.

[3]Rule 8.3(b).

MISCONDUCT

RULE 8.4: MISCONDUCT

It is professional misconduct for a lawyer to:

(a) violate or attempt to violate the Rules of Professional Conduct, knowingly assist or induce another to do so, or do so through the acts of another;

(b) commit a criminal act that reflects adversely on the lawyer's honesty, trustworthiness or fitness as a lawyer in other respects;

(c) engage in conduct involving dishonesty, fraud, deceit or misrepresentation;

(d) engage in conduct that is prejudicial to the administration of justice;

(e) state or imply an ability to influence improperly a government agency or official or to achieve results by means that violate the Rules of Professional Conduct or other law; or

(f) knowingly assist a judge or judicial officer in conduct that is a violation of applicable rules of judicial conduct or other law.

Comment

[1] Lawyers are subject to discipline when they violate or attempt to violate the Rules of Professional Conduct, knowingly assist or induce another to do so or do so through the acts of another, as when they request or instruct an agent to do so on the lawyer's behalf. Paragraph (a), however, does not prohibit a lawyer from advising a client concerning action the client is legally entitled to take.

[2] Many kinds of illegal conduct reflect adversely on fitness to practice law, such as offenses involving fraud and the offense of willful failure to file an income tax return. However, some kinds of offenses carry no such implication. Traditionally, the distinction was drawn in terms of offenses involving "moral turpitude." That concept can be construed to include offenses concerning some matters of personal morality, such as adultery and comparable offenses, that have no specific connection to fitness for the practice of law. Al-

though a lawyer is personally answerable to the entire criminal law, a lawyer should be professionally answerable only for offenses that indicate lack of those characteristics relevant to law practice. Offenses involving violence, dishonesty, breach of trust, or serious interference with the administration of justice are in that category. A pattern of repeated offenses, even ones of minor significance when considered separately, can indicate indifference to legal obligation.

[3] A lawyer who, in the course of representing a client, knowingly manifests by words or conduct, bias or prejudice based upon race, sex, religion, national origin, disability, age, sexual orientation or socioeconomic status, violates paragraph (d) when such actions are prejudicial to the administration of justice. Legitimate advocacy respecting the foregoing factors does not violate paragraph (d). A trial judge's finding that peremptory challenges were exercised on a discriminatory basis does not alone establish a violation of this rule.

[4] A lawyer may refuse to comply with an obligation imposed by law upon a good faith belief that no valid obligation exists. The provisions of Rule 1.2(d) concerning a good faith challenge to the validity, scope, meaning or application of the law apply to challenges of legal regulation of the practice of law.

[5] Lawyers holding public office assume legal responsibilities going beyond those of other citizens. A lawyer's abuse of public office can suggest an inability to fulfill the professional role of lawyers. The same is true of abuse of positions of private trust such as trustee, executor, administrator, guardian, agent and officer, director or manager of a corporation or other organization.

Authors' 1983 Model Rules Comparison

The drafters of the 2002 Model Rules made one change to the text of Rule 8.4. In Rule 8.4(e), the drafters added the last clause to this provision. This clause refers to the prohibition against a lawyer stating or implying that he or she can achieve results by means that violate the Rules or other law. This language was contained in Rule 7.1(b) of the 1983 Model Rules and it was moved to Rule 8.4 because this language applies to all of a lawyer's statements whether or not they are made in the context of an advertisement. *See* Reporter's Explanation of Changes to Rule 8.4 (*See* Appendix M of the Lawyer's edition of this book).

Comment 1 is new and explains the prohibition in Rule 8.4(a) against using an agent to do what the lawyer cannot do directly. The Comment states that a lawyer does not violate this Rule when advising a client to take a position that the client is legally entitled to take.

Old Comments 1, 2, 3, and 4 are identical to the 1983 version and are renumbered as Comments 2 through 5.

Model Code Comparison

[1] With regard to paragraphs (a) through (d) DR 1-102(A) provided that a lawyer shall not:

"(1) Violate a Disciplinary Rule.

"(2) Circumvent a Disciplinary Rule through actions of another.

"(3) Engage in illegal conduct involving moral turpitude.

"(4) Engage in conduct involving dishonesty, fraud, deceit, or misrepresentation.

"(5) Engage in conduct that is prejudicial to the administration of justice.

"(6) Engage in any other conduct that adversely reflects on his fitness to practice law."

[2] Paragraph (e) is substantially similar to DR 9-101(C).

[3] There was no direct counterpart to paragraph (f) in the Disciplinary Rules of the Model Code. EC 7-34 stated in part that "[a] lawyer . . . is never justified in making a gift or a loan to a [judicial officer] except as permitted by . . . the Code of Judicial Conduct." EC 9-1 stated that a lawyer "should promote public confidence in our [legal] system and in the legal profession."

§ 8.4–1 DEFINING DISCIPLINABLE CONDUCT

Rule 8.4 defines what constitutes misconduct for a lawyer. In general it provides that a lawyer may be disciplined for violating a mandatory requirement of the Rules, or for engaging in conduct forbidden by other laws *if* such conduct demonstrates that the lawyer should not be entrusted with the confidence that clients normally place in a lawyer.[1]

§ 8.4–1(a) Acts Not Done In a Legal Capacity

State bar authorities may discipline a lawyer for wrongful conduct even though she was not acting in her capacity as a lawyer while she was engaging in the wrong, *if* the conduct functionally relates to her capacity to practice law because any "illegal conduct" or any conduct "involving dishonesty, fraud, deceit, or misrepresentation" adversely affects the lawyer's capacity to practice law.[2]

For example, if a news reporter interviews several people near the court house about judicial candidates, and if one of those interviewed is a lawyer who knowingly makes a false statement of fact about a judicial candidate[3] he has evidenced lack of trustworthiness and is subject to discipline. If the lawyer, not acting in his capacity as a lawyer, misappropriates money from a bank, or defrauds a homeowner, or perjures himself in defending

---

[Section 8.4–1]

[1] *See also* Restatement of the Law Governing Lawyers, Third, § 5 ("Professional Discipline") (Official Draft 2000). *Cf. id.* at § 1, which explains that a lawyer admitted to the bar thereby becomes subject to all law governing such matters as professional discipline, procedure, evidence, civil remedies, and criminal sanctions.

[2] ABA Formal Opinion 336 (June 3, 1974). *See* Rule 8.4(b), (c); DR 1-102(A)(3), (4). See *Neal v. Clinton,* 2001 WL 34355768 (Ark.Cir.Ct.2001) (Not Reported in S.W.3d), involving a negotiated sanction of five-year suspension and $25,000 fine for President Clinton, who admitted that he "evasive and misleading answers" in order "to conceal from plaintiff Jones' lawyers the true facts about his improper relationship with" Monica Lewinsky.

[3] Rule 8.2(A); DR 8-102(A).

a lawsuit,[4] the lawyer is subject to discipline because those crimes have a functional relationship to the qualities required to practice

---

[4]*See Jones v. Clinton*, 36 F.Supp.2d 1118 (E.D.Ark.1999). Paula Corbin Jones sued President Clinton alleging that he had sexually harassed her while she was an Arkansas state employee and he was Governor. During his deposition, the President denied having a sexual relationship with Monica Lewinsky (who had been a federal employee in the White House during part of the Clinton Presidency). The trial court later held President Clinton in civil contempt and ordered him to pay plaintiff's reasonable attorney's fees and the trial court's expenses in traveling to Washington, D.C. "to preside over this tainted deposition." 36 F.Supp.2d at 1132. The President did not contest the findings and paid $90,686 because of the finding of civil contempt. *See* Linda Satter, *Court Lies Cost Clinton $90,686*, ARKANSAS DEMOCRAT-GAZETTE, July 30, 1999, at p. 1. This case marked the first time that a court had held a President in contempt of court. *See Franklin v. Massachusetts*, 505 U.S. 788, 827, 112 S.Ct. 2767, 2789, 120 L.Ed.2d 636 (1992) (Scalia, J., concurring).

The disciplinary authorities could use this conduct as the basis for imposing discipline on the deponent, a member of the bar, even though, in the deposition, he acted in his capacity as a witness and not as a lawyer. Judge Wright referred the matter to state disciplinary authorities. Later, the Arkansas Supreme Court granted a private lawyer's mandamus action against the state disciplinary authority and ordered it to look into the complaint against "Arkansas licensed attorney William Jefferson Clinton, Arkansas Bar No. 73019." *Hogue v. Neal*, 340 Ark. 250, 12 S.W.3d 186 (2000) (per curiam). The concurring opinion agreed that the Committee should follow its procedures and emphasized that the court's order and opinion did not judge the merits of the allegations against the President.

On January 19, 2001, his last day in office, President Clinton accepted a five-year suspension from the Arkansas bar, and paid a $25,000 fine, thus ending both his criminal probe and the disbarment proceedings. The date was not fortuitous: the Arkansas outside counsel to the Supreme Court Committee on Professional Conduct said that the Committee "wanted the suspension to start while Clinton was still in office as an added stigma." In his consent order, the President acknowledged that he "knowingly gave evasive and misleading answers" concerning his relationship with Ms. Lewinsky. That order included a finding that the President thereby violated Arkansas Rule 8.4(d). In his public statement, also released on January 19, 2001, President Clinton said: "I tried to walk a fine line between acting lawfully and testifying falsely, but I now recognize that I did not fully accomplish this goal and that certain of my responses to questions about Ms. Lewinsky were false." Independent Counsel Robert W. Ray announced that same day that, by agreement with President Clinton upon entry of the consent order and issuance of Clinton's public statement, "President Clinton will be discharged from all criminal liability for matters within the remaining jurisdiction of this Office." The President agreed not to seek any reimbursement of his legal fees. *Clinton Accepts Five-Year Suspension to End Disbarment Case, Criminal Probe*, 17 ABA/BNA LAWYER'S MANUAL ON PROFESSIONAL CONDUCT, Current Reports (Jan. 31, 2001).

On October 1, 2001, the U.S. Supreme Court issued a brief order that read: "Bill Clinton, of New York, New York, is suspended from the practice of law in this Court, and a rule will issue, returnable within 40 days, requiring him to show cause why he should not be disbarred from the practice of law in this Court." *In re Discipline of Clinton*, 534 U.S. 806, 122

law. Lawyers routinely handle client funds and make representations to the court. Crimes that reflect adversely on a lawyer's honesty and trustworthiness relate to his or her ability to practice law.

In contrast, other Rules, such as Rule 3.6, governing trial publicity,[5] or Rule 7.2, governing advertising,[6] relate to a lawyer only in her professional capacity. So, if a lawyer/accountant, acting in her capacity as an accountant, seeks clients in a way that is non-misleading but would be improper for a lawyer—*e.g.*, she engages in face-to-face solicitation[7]—she would not be subject to discipline under Rule 7.2 because that provision only relates to lawyers operating in their professional capacity as lawyers.

§ 8.4–2 CATEGORIES OF DISCIPLINABLE CONDUCT

§ 8.4–2(a) Violating or Attempting to Violate a Disciplinary Rule

It is, of course, disciplinable to violate a Disciplinary Rule.[1] The Model Rules add that it is disciplinable to "attempt to violate the Rules."[2]

However, two provisions of the Rules specifically provide that a lawyer is *not* subject to discipline if a lawyer violates them.

First, a portion of Rule 1.5, dealing with fees, advises that, if the lawyer has not regularly represented a client, the lawyer should, within a reasonable time after beginning the representation, communicate to the client the basis of the fee, *"preferably* in

---

S.Ct. 36, 151 L.Ed.2d 254 (2001). This order followed the suspension of his law license in his home state of Arkansas. Initially, the former President announced that he would contest the disbarment. The Supreme Court gave him until November 9, 2001 to say why he should not be permanently barred from appearing before the high court as a lawyer. On that date, the former President, through his lawyer, asked to resign from the Supreme Court bar, rather than fight suspension or disbarment related to the Paula Jones sexual harassment investigation. *President Would Drop High Court Privilege*, Washington Post, Nov. 10, 2001, at p. A3. A few days later, the Court issued an order, *In the Matter of Bill Clinton, D-2270*, 534 U.S. 1016, 122 S.Ct. 584, 151 L.Ed.2d 454 (2001), providing that, "Bill Clinton, of New York, New York, having requested to resign as a member of the Bar of this Court, it is ordered that his name be stricken from the roll of attorneys admitted to the practice of law before this Court. The Rule to Show Cause, issued on October 1, 2001, is discharged."

[5] *Accord* DR 7-107.

[6] DR 2-101.

[7] *Edenfield v. Fane*, 507 U.S. 761, 113 S.Ct. 1792, 123 L.Ed.2d 543 (1993), holding (8 to 1) that the Florida ban on CPA face-to-face solicitation in the business context violated free speech.

[Section 8.4–2]

[1] Rule 8.4(a); DR 1-102(A)(1).

[2] Rule 8.4(a). No corresponding provision existed in the Model Code.

writing. . . ."[3] This particular Rule does not mandate a writing but encourages it.

Of course, lawyers should always put the fee agreement in writing because a writing brings home to the client the significance of what is going on and may reduce misunderstandings. It is sometimes said that an oral contract is not worth the paper it is printed on. Nonetheless, the ABA did not intend to impose a per se violation of the disciplinary rules if the lawyer fails to reduce the fee agreement to a writing.

Second, Rule 6.1, entitled "Voluntary Pro Bono Publico Service" provides a lawyer "should aspire to render at least (50) hours of pro bono publico services per year." The number 50 is in parentheses because that is the ABA recommended minimum. The pro bono references are an aspiration for a lawyer, not a mandate. This Rule specifically provides that the responsibility for pro bono work "is not intended to be enforced through the disciplinary process."[4]

The ABA Model Rules of Professional Conduct (like the ABA Model Code of Professional Responsibility)[5] continue to distinguish between what *must* be done, what *should* be done, and what *may* be done. When the black letter Rules use imperatives such as "shall" or "shall not," violations are disciplinable.[6] Like the Model Code, some provisions of the Model Rules also use the term "may" in order to define areas of permissible lawyer discretion.[7]

Many of the Comments to the Rules also use the term "should." These Comments are comparable to the Ethical Considerations of the Model Code. If a Comment uses the term "should," it does "not add obligations to the Rules but provides guidance for practicing in compliance with the Rules."[8] The Comments also

---

[3]Rule 1.5(b) (emphasis added).

[4]Rule 6.1, Comment 12.

[5]The ABA Model Code explicitly distinguished between Ethical Considerations ("EC") and Disciplinary Rules ("DR"). The Disciplinary Rules, in contrast to the Ethical Considerations, "are mandatory in character," stating "the minimum level of conduct below which no lawyer can fall without being subject to disciplinary action." Model Code, Preliminary Statement; DR 1-102(A)(1) (misconduct to violate a disciplinary rule). The Ethical Considerations in the ABA Model Code were presented as "aspirational" only.

[6]*See* Model Rules, Scope 14. *See also* Rule 8.4(a) (misconduct to violate or attempt to violate the Model Rules).

[7]Model Rules, Scope 14. *See, e.g.,* Rule 1.6(b) (when lawyer "may" reveal client information). *See also* Rule 6.1 ("A lawyer should aspire to render at least (50) hours of pro bono publico services per year."); Rule 1.5(b) (basis of fee should be "preferably in writing").

[8]Model Rules, Scope 14.

explain, elaborate on, and provide interpretative guidance on the Rules, though, of course, "the text of each Rule is authoritative."[9]

Therefore, while the black letter Rules control, one should not conclude that, because prohibited conduct is described in a Comment, it therefore does not violate a more broadly drafted Rule. The conclusion that the conduct in question is prohibited may be derived from the black letter Rule, even though the particular prohibition might be expressed more clearly in a Comment.[10]

§ 8.4-2(b) Violating a Disciplinary Rule Through Another

It is also disciplinable to assist or induce another to violate a Disciplinary Rule.[11] For example, if the lawyer cannot engage a prospective client in a hospital room in a face-to-face encounter in an effort to solicit legal business,[12] Rule 8.4(a) makes it clear that the lawyer may not avoid his responsibilities by hiring a hospital orderly to speak on his behalf.

Consider another, more complicated, example. Rule 4.2 provides that a lawyer may not communicate about the subject of the representation with a person the lawyer knows is represented by his own lawyer. The lawyer must communicate through the opponent's lawyer. However, because this Rule governs lawyers and not their lay clients, "parties to a matter may communicate directly with each other. . . ."[13] This Rule does not prohibit lawyers from advising principals to speak directly with their counterparts.

However, this Rule, in connection with Rule 8.4(a) (lawyer may not violate a Rule "through the acts of another") does preclude a lawyer from "using an intermediary to carry a message from the lawyer to the opposing party. . . ."[14] If lawyer A (on behalf of Party A) makes a settlement offer to the opposing party's lawyer (lawyer B), but lawyer A believes that lawyer B will not communicate that offer to Party B, even then, lawyer A may not com-

---

[9]Rules, Scope 21.

[10]Cf. Committee on Professional Ethics and Conduct of State Bar Association v. Behnke, 276 N.W.2d 838, 840 (Iowa 1979) (violation of an EC, "standing alone," will support disciplinary action; in this case the violation was of EC 5-5).

[11]Rule 8.4(a); DR 1-102(A)(2).

[12]Ohralik v. Ohio State Bar Association, 436 U.S. 447, 98 S.Ct. 1912, 56 L.Ed.2d 444 (1978), In the facts of Ohralik, the state disciplined the lawyer seeking a case for a contingent fee from engaging in a face-to-face meeting with a prospective a cli-

ent. The lawyer solicited Carol McClintock in a hospital room where she lay in traction and sought out Wanda Lou Holbert on the day she came home from the hospital, knowing from his prior inquiries that she had just been released. He employed a concealed tape recorder, apparently to secure evidence of Holbert's oral assent to the representation. 436 U.S. at 467, 98 S.Ct. at 1924.

[13]Rule 4.2, Comment 2.

[14]See The Legislative History of the Model Rules of Professional Conduct 148 (ABA, 1987).

municate directly with Party B to determine whether the offer has been communicated. Nor may lawyer A hire a detective or paralegal to communicate directly with Party B because lawyer A may not violate the Rules of Professional Conduct "through the acts of another."[15]

But lawyer A may advise Party A that Party A may communicate directly with Party B about the offer.[16] However, lawyer A may not script exactly what Party A says, again because lawyer A may not violate the Rules of Professional Conduct "through the acts of another."[17]

Given the general principle that a lawyer may not knowingly assist another to violate the ethics rules or to violate those rules through the acts of another,[18] it is clear that a lawyer is responsible for another lawyer's ethics violation if the first lawyer orders the second to engage in misconduct, or knowingly ratifies the second lawyer's misconduct.[19] The supervisory lawyer is also responsible for the other lawyer's ethical misconduct if the supervisory lawyer fails to take reasonable remedial action to avoid or mitigate the misconduct.[20] For example, "if a supervisory lawyer knows that a subordinate misrepresented a matter to an opposing party in negotiation, the supervisor as well as the subordinate has a duty to correct the resulting misapprehension."[21]

§ 8.4–2(c) Criminal Acts

Not all illegal conduct is disciplinable. The Model Code forbade only those crimes that involved "moral turpitude."[22] The problem with the test of "moral turpitude" is that it is vague and ill-defined. It is not at all evident that the drafters of the Model Code intended to make disciplinable those crimes that are not functionally related to fitness to practice law, particularly because other provisions in the Code imply that such a functional relationship is necessary.[23] Nonetheless, the uncertainness and ambiguity of the "moral turpitude" standard allows, or even invites, a court to discipline attorneys for acts that may be crimes in some states, although the crime is not connected or even relevant to the client-attorney relationship.[24]

Consequently, the Rules adopted more precise language

---

[15] Rule 8.4(a).

[16] ABA Formal Opinion 92-362 (July 6, 1992).

[17] Rule 8.4(a).

[18] Rule 8.4(a); DR 1-102(A)(2).

[19] Rule 5.1(c)(1).

[20] Rule 5.1(c)(2). *Cf.* DR 1-103(A).

[21] Rule 5.1, Comment 5.

[22] DR 1-102(A)(3).

[23] *See* DR 1-102(A)(6), forbidding a lawyer from engaging in "any *other* conduct that adversely reflects on his fitness to practice law." (emphasis added).

[24] *See Grievance Committee of Hartford County Bar v. Broder*, 112 Conn. 263, 152 A. 292 (1930) (extramarital relations with consenting person not a client; held, disciplinable).

because "a lawyer should be professionally answerable only for offenses that indicate lack of those characteristics relevant to law practice."[25] Rule 8.4(b) limits disciplinable crimes to only those that reflect "adversely on the lawyer's honesty, trustworthiness or fitness as a lawyer in other respects." Discipline is inappropriate for violations of "personal morality" such as adultery.[26]

Examples of disciplinable conduct include crimes of fraud or breach of trust; willful (rather than negligent) failure to file an income tax return, or "serious interferences with the administration of justice."[27]

While Rule 8.4(b) requires that the lawyer commit a "criminal" act, it does not require that there be a criminal conviction or even a criminal prosecution.[28] "The rule does not require a criminal conviction; rather, it requires only that the lawyer commit a criminal act that reflects adversely upon the lawyer's honesty, trustworthiness, or fitness to practice"[29]

"Violence" is included in the category of disciplinable crimes,[30] even though violence does not necessarily indicate lack of trustworthiness or dishonesty: a drunken barroom brawl may only indicate a bad temper. Nonetheless, courts have often held

---

[25]Rule 8.4, Comment 2.

[26]Rule 8.4, Comment 2.

[27]Rule 8.4, Comment 2.

See, e.g., In re Tucker, 766 A.2d 510 (D.C.2000) (per curiam), which disbarred a lawyer who received a few hundred dollars in parking tickets, and gave a city employee small sums (e.g., $80 or $70 per occasion) to mark them paid. The lawyer had pled guilty to one count of attempted bribery, a misdemeanor. The amounts involved, however small, related to a crime that involved dishonesty for personal gain and thus merited disbarment.

Office of Disciplinary Counsel v. Klaas, 91 Ohio St.3d 86, 742 N.E.2d 612 (Ohio 2001) (per curiam), a criminal defense lawyer learned that the FBI planned a big drug raid. She secretly told a former client to "clean up his act" and be "squeaky clean." He understood that to mean he should get rid of his drugs for a while. When he was arrested in the raid, he agreed to cooperate with the government. Then, he turned on his lawyer. The lawyer was convicted of an attempt to obstruct justice for her warning, sentenced to 6 months in jail, and fined $1000. The

court in this case also held that her misconduct warranted a one-year suspension from the practice of law with six months of suspension stayed for a probation period during which time the attorney was required to work with a monitor.

[28]*See, e.g., In re Conduct of Morin*, 319 Or. 547, 559, 878 P.2d 393, 399 (1994)(per curiam): "it is not necessary for the accused to be convicted of a crime; clear and convincing evidence meets Bar's burden." *Matter of Riddle*, 700 N.E.2d 788, 793 (Ind.1998): "Criminal charges need not be brought and tried prior to citing of parallel allegations in a disciplinary complaint."

[29]*See, e.g., In re Hassenstab*, 325 Or. 166, 176, 934 P.2d 1110, 1116 (1997) (interpreting DR 1-102(A)(2)). In this case, the criminal proceedings resulted only in a no contest plea to one criminal count of prostitution, but the court found "that the Bar has proved by clear and convincing evidence that, on different occasions, the accused violated three criminal statutes."

[30]Rule 8.4, Comment 2.

that crimes of violence, particularly when the violence is quite serious, are disciplinable.[31]

A Comment advised that a pattern of *repeated* minor offenses could be disciplinable if the pattern indicates "indifference to legal obligation."[32] The drafters give no examples, but repeated violations involving minor offenses may just as likely indicate an indifference only to a *particular* violation. For example, a lawyer may collect a series of parking tickets or traffic tickets, or another lawyer may own a grocery store that repeatedly is open on Sunday, in criminal violation of a local, generally unenforced, "blue law." In both cases, the series of violations are neither breaches of trust nor interferences with the administration of justice. They also do not show any general indifference to legal obligation.

§ 8.4–2(d) Conduct Involving Dishonesty

Conduct, whether or not a crime, that involves dishonesty, fraud, deceit, or misrepresentation, is disciplinable.[33] Noncriminal fraud (for those states that have such an offense) would fall under this rubric. Similarly, violations of fiduciary obligations

---

[31]*See, e.g., Matter of Webb*, 602 P.2d 408 (Alaska 1979) (first degree murder, accessory after the fact).

Attorney Grievance Commission of Maryland v. Painter, 356 Md. 293, 739 A.2d 24 (1999), disbarred a lawyer for multiple incidents of domestic abuse. The opinion describes horrific physical violence toward both the lawyer's wife and children. The lawyer later pled guilty to criminal charges arising out of the incidents. The court, citing cases from California, Indiana and New Jersey, found the abuse to be "morally reprehensible," to be prejudicial to the administration of justice, and to affect adversely the lawyer's ability to practice.

Florida Bar v. McKeever, 766 So.2d 992 (Fla.2000), disbarred an attorney found guilty on five counts of aggravated child abuse involving three boys. The court found no precedent for discipline in the case for such an offense but held that the conduct was "contrary to the oath that every lawyer takes to abstain from offensive personality." 766 So.2d at 994.

[32]Rule 8.4, Comment 2.

[33]Rule 8.4(c); DR 1-102(A)(4).

D.C. Ethics Opinion 323 (2004) discusses "whether attorneys who are employed by a national intelligence agency violate the Rules of Professional Conduct if they engage in fraud, deceit, or misrepresentation in the course of their non-representational official duties." The Opinion notes that intelligence officers acting in their official capacity are required by law, on occasion, to act deceitfully. For example, a lawyer working for the CIA in a clandestine capacity might be required to offer false information about her identity or employment. The Opinion concludes that Rule 8.4 addresses deceitful conduct that "calls into question a lawyer's suitability to practice law." Understood in this light, "the category of conduct proscribed by the Rule does not include misrepresentations made in the course of official conduct as an employee of an agency of the United States if the attorney reasonably believes that the conduct in question is authorized by law."

Undercover Operations. For analysis of undercover operations, see § 4.2-1(b).

(whether or not undertaken in one's capacity as a lawyer) would be disciplinable if they indicate dishonesty.[34]

If the action does not involve dishonesty, deceit, and similar activities, then the lawyer is not subject to discipline under this Rule.[35]

---

[34]*In re Sealed Appellant*, 194 F.3d 666 (5th Cir.1999), involved a lawyer who had backdated a stock certificate to show that it had been deposited by the client in a trust before the date that would make it a fraudulent conveyance. He later lied about the act but his fraud was discovered by analysis of the ink that he had used. The Fifth Circuit affirmed that disbarment was the appropriate sanction, and removed the lawyer from the federal court bar.

Matter of Diggs, 344 S.C. 397, 544 S.E.2d 628 (2001) (per curiam), suspended the respondent for 90 days because he filed a form saying he had attended a CLE seminar when, in fact, he arrived near the end of the seminar. "According to Diggs, he believed at the time he traveled to the CLE that he would be able to claim the hours even though the seminar was over." 344 S.C. at 399, 544 S.E.2d at 629. Diggs argued that the ethics rules relating to misrepresentation "are inapplicable to his disciplinary matter because they concern the representation of clients, and no clients were involved." 344 S.C. at 399, 544 S.E.2d at 630. Later, the court disbarred Mr. Diggs, for other reasons—because he was held in contempt of family court for his knowingly issuing checks from an account that he knew had been closed, his misappropriation of client funds, his disbursements to beneficiaries of an estate that were returned for insufficient funds, his misrepresentations to the probate court regarding estate disbursements he had allegedly made, his failure to comply with an Office of Disciplinary Counsel subpoena, and his failure to cooperate with the attorney appointed to protect the interests of counsel's former clients. *In re Diggs*, 346 S.C. 521, 552 S.E.2d 298

(2001). The court made the disbarment retroactive to the date that he had been suspended in, *In re Diggs*, 343 S.C. 294, 540 S.E.2d 839 (2000).

In re Segal, 430 Mass. 359, 719 N.E.2d 480 (1999), involved a lawyer acquitted of making false statements to a federally-insured bank but later charged by the bar for the same conduct. The lawyer was doing residential closings for a bank that had a policy against lending to people who financed their down payment with a second mortgage. When a buyer said he had just signed a second mortgage, the lawyer said "I can't hear that" and "I am not supposed to know that." The criminal court had decided that closing loans in such circumstances did not involve making a false statement to his bank client, but this court, after concluding that it constituted dealing dishonestly with respect to what he knew to be his client's wishes, imposed a two year suspension.

[35]Commentators have bemoaned what is often seen as a decline in honesty because of a search for higher income. *See, e.g.,* Lisa G. Lerman, *The Slippery Slope From Ambition to Greed to Dishonesty: Lawyers, Money, and Professional Integrity*, 30 HOFSTRA L. REV. 879 (2002), which argues that lawyers have become less inclined to comply with legal ethics and consider the interests of their clients, because they are preoccupied with pursuing money. "A lawyer who is in the grip of a desire to expand his income may be more likely to trample on his client's financial interests, either legally or illegally, honestly or dishonestly." 30 HOFSTRA L. REV. at 881. W. William Hodes, *Truthfulness and Honesty Among American Lawyers: Perception, Reality, and the Professional Reform Initiative*, 53 S.C. L. REV. 527 (2002),

ABA Formal Opinion 337[36] relied on the prohibition against conduct involving dishonesty, fraud, deceit, and misrepresentation to hold that a lawyer's surreptitious tape recording (except in the case of law enforcement that at least is in compliance with statutory and constitutional guidelines) without the consent or prior knowledge of all parties involved is disciplinable. The secret nature of the recording, the Opinion argued, was a form of fraud, even if not a crime under the local jurisdiction. However, ABA Formal Opinion 01-422,[37] the ABA formally withdrew Formal Opinion 337, and concluded that it is not inherently "misleading" for a lawyer to secretly tape record a conversation when local law does not forbid it.

§ 8.4–2(e) Conduct Prejudicial to the Administration of Justice

The final version of the Rules (but *not* the Proposed Final Draft of May 30, 1981) announces that it is disciplinable for a lawyer to "engage in conduct that is prejudicial to the administration of justice."[38] Opponents of this language argued unsuccessfully that this standard—which came from the Model Code[39]—was too vague and loose to be a criterion in a legal code. They argued that there is a basic unfairness in asserting the power to take away one's livelihood, one's ability to practice law, based on a standard so undefined, vague, and amorphous that it varies with the eyes of the beholder.

The disciplinary authorities occasionally discipline a lawyer under this rather loose standard, typically in factual situations that are atypical. *Grievance Administrator v. Fried*[40] provides an illustration of the "prejudicial to the administration of justice" ground for discipline. Two judges in Monroe County had close relatives who practiced there. When parties wanted a reassignment from one or the other of the judges, local lawyers told clients to hire the relevant relative as co-counsel to force the judge's recusal. Disciplinary panels had dismissed the charges, saying this tactic was no different than hiring a lawyer who is known to have been found persuasive by a particular judge, but the Michi-

---

which argues that there is a decline in lawyers' honesty because of the public's sense that lawyers are not trustworthy. David Barnhizer, *Profession Deleted: Using Market And Liability Forces To Regulate The Very Ordinary Business Of Law Practice For Profit,* 17 GEORGETOWN J. LEGAL ETHICS 203 (2004), arguing that "soaring financial expectations" have led to a decline in professionalism.

[36] ABA Formal Opinion 337 (Aug. 10, 1974). This ABA Opinion relied on DR 1-102(A)(4), which is identical to Rule 8.4(c).

[37] ABA Formal Opinion 01-422 (June 24, 2001).

[38] Rule 8.4(d).

[39] DR 1-102(A)(5).

[40] *Grievance Administrator v. Fried,* 456 Mich. 234, 570 N.W.2d 262 (Mich.1997).

gan Supreme Court disagreed. It is one thing to affect a result by having a judge find the lawyer's arguments persuasive, and quite another for a lawyer to traffic in the ability to force recusal. The matter was returned to the disciplinary panels for trial.[41]

The Model Code offered another equally vague and loose catch-all standard: "any other conduct that adversely reflects on his fitness to practice law."[42] The Model Rules, however, refuses to adopt this provision.

§ 8.4–2(e)(1) Racist, Sexist, and Politically Incorrect Speech

If a lawyer makes racist and sexist remarks, that speech is obviously despicable and heinous. But is that speech disciplinable under the Model Rules? Some state ethics rules have language making such speech disciplinable, although such prosecutions raise important free speech concerns.[43] Speech, even hateful speech, is not action, and the First Amendment gives the

---

[41]In *Attorney Grievance Commission v. Childress*, 364 Md. 48, 770 A.2d 685 (2001) (per curiam), the respondent had solicited sex from young girls over the internet. He did not have sexual contact with any of the girls but he was convicted of the federal crime of interstate travel with the intent of doing so, a conviction later reversed. He had violated no Maryland law, but the court found that his conduct violated a Virginia statute against propositioning a girl under the age of 14. The Maryland court held that the attorney engaged (1) in conduct prejudicial to the administration of justice by violating a Virginia statute prohibiting the taking of indecent liberties with children based on a proposal of sexual intercourse, and (2) in conduct prejudicial to administration of justice. This conduct warranted indefinite suspension from the practice of law because predatory internet conduct is of such serious concern that the lawyer had "seriously undermined public confidence in the legal profession." 364 Md. at 65, 770 A.2d at 695. The dissenting justices, arguing that internet sexual predation was conduct "much more dangerous to the public than income tax evasion," would have disbarred the lawyer. 364 Md. at 72, 770 A.2d at 699–700.

In re Ketter, 268 Kan. 146, 992 P.2d 205 (1999), involved a lawyer who was a repeat exhibitionist. He exposed himself to women in several non-practice settings. When admonished by the bar, he promised not to do it again but was unsuccessful in keeping that promise. When a doctor examined the lawyer, his diagnosis was that the lawyer was suffering from "exhibitionism and obsessive compulsive disorder." 268 Kan. at 149, 992 P.2d at 208. The opinion asks, with some care, how, if at all, the court should react in these cases. It decided to suspend discipline pending three years probation during which the lawyer must seek professional help and report his progress to the bar. The court concluded that lewd and lascivious behavior violated the sections of the Kansas Rules of Professional Conduct prohibiting conduct prejudicial to the administration of justice and conduct adversely reflecting on a lawyer's fitness to practice law. Three justices, concurring and dissenting, would have imposed an indefinite suspension from the practice of law.

[42]DR 1-102(A)(5)(b).

[43]These restrictions raise First Amendment problems to the extent that they punish lawyers for what they say or think as opposed to what

Ku Klux Klan and other racists the right to march on the public streets and spread their hate.[44]

The ABA eventually added a Comment to 8.4 which provides that a lawyer who—

> in the course of representing a client, knowingly manifests by *words* or conduct, bias or prejudice based on race, sex, religion, national origin, disability, age, sexual orientation or socioeconomic status, violates paragraph (d) [Rule 8.4(d)] when such actions are prejudicial to the administration of justice. *Legitimate* advocacy respecting the foregoing factors does not violate paragraph (d). A trial judge's finding that peremptory challenges were exercised on a discriminatory basis does not alone establish a violation of this rule.[45]

This Comment is similar to laws that the Supreme Court has invalidated on free speech grounds. It is also similar to college "speech codes," which sought to punish speech that is offensive based on race, sex, sexual orientation, etc., and the lower courts have invalidated these speech codes as well.[46]

This Comment raises various questions. First, there is an important difference between this Comment and the typical speech codes that the lower courts or the U.S. Supreme Court have invalidated. The ABA Comment also bans speech that manifests bias based on "socioeconomic status." So, if a lawyer, in the course of representing a client, objects to the "idle rich," or

---

they do. *See* Ronald D. Rotunda, *Can You Say That?*, 30 TRIAL MAGAZINE 18 (Dec. 1994); Ronald D. Rotunda, *Racist Speech and Attorney Discipline*, 6 THE PROFESSIONAL LAWYER 1 (A.B.A., No. 6, 1995); Ronald D. Rotunda, *What Next? Outlawing Lawyer Jokes?*, WALL STREET JOURNAL, Aug. 8, 1995, at A12, col. 3–5 (Midwest ed.).

[44]*See, e.g., R.A.V. v. City of St. Paul*, 505 U.S. 377, 112 S.Ct. 2538, 120 L.Ed.2d 305 (1992), where the Court overturned a conviction based on a city ordinance that provided that whoever "places on public or private property a symbol, object, appellation, characterization or graffiti, including, but not limited to, a burning cross or a Nazi swastika, which one knows or has reasonable grounds to know arouses anger, alarm, or resentment in others on the basis of race, color, creed, religion or gender commits disorderly conduct and shall be guilty of a misdemeanor."

In this case, R.A.V. and several other teenagers burned a cross inside the privately owned, fenced yard of a black family who lived across the street from where R.A.V. was staying. The Court overturned the conviction and held the ordinance unconstitutional.

See the discussion of this issue in, 5 RONALD D. ROTUNDA & JOHN E. NOWAK, TREATISE ON CONSTITUTIONAL LAW: SUBSTANCE AND PROCEDURE § § 20.37 to 20.40 (Thomson-West, 4th ed. 2008) (6 volumes). W. Bradley Wendel, *Free Speech for Lawyers*, 28 HASTINGS CONSTITUTIONAL L.Q. 305 (2001).

[45]Rule 8.3, Comment 2 (emphasis added).

[46]*See, e.g.*, Robert Sedler, *The Unconstitutionality of Campus Bans on "Racist Speech": The view from Without and Within*, 53 U. PITTSBURGH L. REV. 631 (1992). *See also* Ronald D. Rotunda, *A Brief Comment on Politically Incorrect Speech in the Wake of R.A.V.*, 47 S.M.U. L. REV. 9 (1993); Alex Kozinski & Eugene Volokh, *A Penumbra Too Far*, 106 HARV. L. REV. 1639 (1993).

the "malefactors of great wealth," that lawyer may have a problem under Rule 8.4, Comment 2. One wonders if that is what the drafters really had in mind.

This Comment also allows racist speech and other hateful speech when it is part of "legitimate advocacy." However, the Comment does not define when advocacy is "illegitimate." Assuming that the advocacy does not violate another rule (e.g., the position is not "frivolous" within the meaning of ABA Model Rule 3.1), one would be hard-pressed to know when advocacy is not "legitimate." The Rules elsewhere explain that the lawyer's representation of a client does not constitute an endorsement of the client's views, even if the lawyer accepted the representation willingly and was not court-appointed.[47]

The Comment does not explain why a lawyer's decision to seek to remove a member of a racial minority from the grand jury—an action that violates the U.S. Constitution even if the lawyer who exercises the peremptory challenge is representing a private party in a civil case[48]—is "not a violation of this rule."[49] This Comment appears to give less protection to a lawyer who expresses pure speech complaining about the idle rich than it gives to a lawyer who engages in unconstitutional and racist conduct when choosing a jury.

The position of this Comment may reflect a fact of life regarding peremptory challenges, a fact of life that the Comment does not explain although the situation is explainable. Consider, for example, the situation where, in the course a criminal trial, the prosecutor exercises a peremptory challenge against a juror, and the defense counsel responds with a *Batson* challenge[50] objecting to the juror's exclusion on the grounds that the opposing lawyer had exercised the challenge for reasons that are unconstitutional (such as excluding the juror on grounds of his or her race to sex).

---

[47]Rule 1.2(b). *Cf. In re Green*, 11 P.3d 1078 (Colo.2000)(per curiam). A lawyer had authored letters and motions to a trial judge accusing him of being racist. The state supreme court held that the First Amendment precludes professional discipline for an attorney's criticism of a judge, unless the criticism involves both falsehood and "actual malice;" in this case, the attorney's statements that the trial judge was a "racist and bigot" with a "bent of mind" were opinions based upon fully disclosed and uncontested facts, and thus, attorney could not be disciplined for making those statements.

[48]*Edmonson v. Leesville Concrete Co., Inc.*, 500 U.S. 614, 111 S.Ct. 2077, 114 L.Ed.2d 660 (1991).

[49]Rule 8.4, Comment 3.

[50]In *Batson v. Kentucky*, 476 U.S. 79, 106 S.Ct. 1712, 90 L.Ed.2d 69 (1986), the Court held that the Equal Protection Clause forbids a prosecutor from challenging potential jurors solely on account of their race or on the assumption that black jurors as a group will be unable to impartially consider the State's case against a black defendant. The Court went on to hold that the defendant, in order to establish a prima facie case of purposeful discrimination in selection of the

Under the law, the judge is then supposed to call upon the other lawyer to give a neutral (non-racial or non-sexual) reason why he or she moved to exclude the juror. If the judge is not satisfied by the explanation, he or she then seats the juror and the selection process continues, followed by the criminal defendant's acquittal or conviction.

The prosecutor, who cannot appeal in either case, is unable to respond to the defense lawyer's claim that the prosecutor acted for racist or sexist reasons. Under these circumstances, the trial judge's ruling is not a clear indicator of racist or sexist attitudes. In the nature of things, any prosecutor who has served any reasonable length of time will have lost out on many at-trial motions, as would anyone serving as defense counsel for any length

---

petit jury, must first show that he is a member of a cognizable racial group, that the prosecutor has exercised peremptory challenges to remove from the venire members of the defendant's race, and that the facts and any other relevant circumstances raise an inference that the prosecutor used that practice to exclude the veniremen from the petit jury on account of their race. Later, the Court held that a male has standing to object to the exclusion of females from the jury. *Taylor v. Louisiana*, 419 U.S. 522, 524, 95 S.Ct. 692, 695, 42 L.Ed.2d 690 (1975).

Subsequently, in *Powers v. Ohio*, 499 U.S. 400, 111 S.Ct. 1364, 113 L.Ed.2d 411 (1991), the Court ruled that, under the equal protection clause, a criminal defendant may object to race-based exclusion of jurors effected through peremptory challenges whether or not the defendant and the excluded jurors share the same race. Then, in *Georgia v. McCollum*, 505 U.S. 42, 112 S.Ct. 2348, 120 L.Ed.2d 33 (1992), the Court held that the equal protection clause prohibits a *defendant* from engaging in purposeful discrimination on ground of race; that a defendant's exercise of peremptory challenges was state action for purposes of equal protection clause; and that the state had standing to object to the defendant's peremptory challenge. That same year the Court held that there is state action when a *private* litigant uses a peremptory challenge to exclude a juror on account

of race in a *civil* case. *Edmonson v. Leesville Concrete Co., Inc.*, 500 U.S. 614, 111 S.Ct. 2077, 114 L.Ed.2d 660 (1991), *on remand*, 943 F.2d 551 (5th Cir.1991).

Felkner v. Jackson, 562 U.S. __, 131 S.Ct. 1305, __L.Ed.2d __ (2011) (per curiam). The jury convicted defendant of numerous sexual offenses stemming from his attack on a 72-year woman who lived in his apartment complex. The prosecutor struck two of the three black jurors and defendant raised a *Batson* claim when the prosecutor struck the second juror. The trial court rejected the claim after the prosecutor offered race-neutral explanations. Juror S stated that, between his 16th and 30th birthday, California police frequently stopped him because, in his view, of his race and age. The prosecutor did not want any juror who might harbor any animosity against the police. The prosecutor stated that he struck Juror J because she had a master's degree in social work, and had interned at the county jail, and the prosecutor he does not like "social workers" on the jury. The California trial, appellate, and supreme courts, and federal district court (on habeas review) all rejected Jackson's *Batson* claim. The 9th Circuit reversed in a three-paragraph unpublished opinion. The U.S. Supreme Court unanimously reversed, saying that the 9th Circuit opinion "is as inexplicable as it is unexplained. It is reversed."

though—as discussed below—some of its general provisions are applicable.[1]

The Code provided that a lawyer-legislator may accept private clients but is prohibited from using his public position to obtain a "special advantage in legislative matters for himself or for a client" only in those cases "where he knows or *it is obvious* that such action is not in the public interest."[2]

This section is not so much a meaningful prohibition as it is a license, because of the difficulty of meeting any test using the phrase: "it is obvious." Thus, there is no *per se* prohibition against a lawyer accepting a retainer from a private client who is likely to be affected by proposed legislation.[3] The requirement of "special advantage" means "a direct and peculiar advantage." The "not in the public interest" standard means legislation "clearly inimical to the best interests of the public as a whole."[4]

However, this license does not mean that a lawyer-legislator may ethically receive anything of value from a private client *in exchange for* introducing or voting for legislation. That transaction amounts to a bribe and is directly prohibited by the Model Code.[5] The Model Code also prohibited the lawyer-legislator (or similar person) from accepting anything of value from anyone if the lawyer "knows or it is *obvious* that the offer is for the purpose of influencing his action as a public official."[6] This prohibition applied whether or not the lawyer fulfilled his part of the bargain, *i.e.*, whether the lawyer in fact used, or attempted to use, his influence corruptly, in violation of DR 8-101(A)(3). It also applied if the bargain was only implicit.

In re D'Auria[7] held that it is improper for a judge handling worker's compensation matters to accept numerous "free" lunches from lawyers or insurance companies who had cases then pending before the judge. There was no explicit evidence proving the corrupt intent of those who offered the "free" lunch, but the facts and setting probably convinced the court that the purpose of the offer was "obvious." As economists would say, "There is no such

---

[Section 8.4–3]

[1] *Cf.* Kathleen Clark, *The Ethics of Representing Elected Representatives*, 61 LAW & CONTEMPORARY PROBLEMS 31 (1998).

[2] DR 8-101(A)(1) (emphasis added).

[3] ABA Informal Opinion 1182 (Dec. 5, 1971).

[4] ABA Informal Opinion 1182 (Dec. 5, 1971).

[5] DR 8-101(A)(3). *Cf.* Rules 3.5(a); 8.4(b).

[6] DR 8-101(A)(3) (emphasis added).

[7] *In re D'Auria*, 67 N.J. 22, 24, 334 A.2d 332, 333 (1975).

thing as a free lunch." Where the factual background is less compelling than the facts of *D'Auria*, the result is different.[8]

§ 8.4–3(b) Lawyer-Legislators Under the Model Rules

Though the Rules have no direct counterpart to DR 8-101(A)(3), a fact situation that meets the stiff requirements of that Disciplinary Rule also probably meets the general prohibitions of Rule 8.4(c) or (d), prohibiting dishonesty and conduct prejudicial to the administration of justice. Just as the lawyer-official may not accept anything of value offered to influence her own actions as a public official, neither may a lawyer seek to influence a public official (or juror) improperly.[9]

A lawyer obviously may not use his public position in order to gain a corrupt advantage for himself or his client.[10] The basic question is whether the effort to influence the tribunal was corrupt.

For example, assume that a lawyer-legislator appears before the state commerce commission to urge a rate increase on behalf of a private client. This lawyer-legislator is also on the state house committee that oversees the state commerce commission and sets the administrators' salaries. Such circumstantial facts alone do not show anything improper. The lawyer-legislator also must have actually engaged in an overt attempt to exert improper influence over the state commerce commission.[11]

---

[8]*Cf.* ABA Informal Opinion 1182 (Dec. 5, 1971) (no per se violation of DR 8-101(A)(3) when facts only show that a lawyer-legislator represented in legal matters a client who also was affected by contemplated legislation).

[9]Rule 3.5(a); *Cf.* EC 7-35; DR 9-101(C).

[10]Rule 3.5(a); DR 8-101(A)(2).

[11]ABA Informal Opinion 1182 (Dec. 5, 1971). *See also State ex rel. Nebraska State Bar Association v. Holscher*, 193 Neb. 729, 738, 230 N.W.2d 75, 80 (1975).

for that case and for future cases. Additionally, any disciplinary action taken in State Y can be referred to State A for additional discipline. This result is reinforced by language in the 2002 version of Rule 8.5: "A lawyer not admitted in this jurisdiction is also subject to the disciplinary authority of this jurisdiction if the lawyer provides or offers to provide any legal services in this jurisdiction."[3]

The rationale for the extraterritorial application of ethics rules is easy to understand. The purpose of lawyer discipline is not to punish (although the lawyer may be deprived of her livelihood) but rather to "seek to determine the fitness of an officer of the court to continue in that capacity and to protect the courts and the public from the official ministration of persons unfit to practice."[4]

Given this rationale, if the lawyer engages in improper conduct—even if she engages in the conduct while not acting as a lawyer (e.g., lying to secure a real estate license[5]), and even if the improper conduct occurs outside of the jurisdiction of State A, that conduct still reflects on the ability of that lawyer to practice in State A. The lawyer's admission to practice in State A (even though State A is not the site of her improper act) gives State A the jurisdiction to discipline the lawyer.[6]

The Model Code had no specific provision governing this

1977). *Compare Sheller v. Superior Court*, 158 Cal. App. 4th 1697, 71 Cal. Rptr. 3d 207 (2d Dist. 2008)(holding that trial court may revoke an out-of-state attorney's pro hac vice status, but may not reprimand out-of-state attorney).

[3]Rule 8.5(a). *In re Carl M. Weideman, III*, 2009 WL 1227910 *15 (2d Cir. 2009), quoting this Treatise.

[4]*In re Echeles*, 430 F.2d 347, 349 (7th Cir.1970).

See also The ABA Standards for Imposing Lawyer Sanctions, Standard 1.1 (ABA 1991):

"The purpose of lawyer discipline proceedings is to protect the public and the administration of justice from lawyers who have not discharged, will not discharge, or are unlikely properly to discharge their professional duties to clients, the public, the legal system, and the legal profession."

[5]The ABA Standards for Imposing Lawyer Sanctions, Standard 1.1 (ABA 1991), Commentary, states:

"Lawyers who are not actively practicing law, but who are serving in such roles as corporate officers, public officials, or law professors, do not lose their association with the legal profession because of their primary occupation. The public quite properly expects that anyone who is admitted to the practice of law, regardless of daily occupational activities, will conform to the minimum ethical standards of the legal profession. If the lawyer fails to meet these standards, appropriate sanctions should be imposed."

[6]*See, e.g., In re Carl M. Weideman, III*, 2009 WL 1227910 *15 (2d Cir. 2009), quoting this Treatise. *State v. Pounds*, 525 S.W.2d 547 (Tex.Civ. App.1975) (discipline of nonresident lawyer). *See also, e.g., Selling v. Radford*, 243 U.S. 46, 37 S.Ct. 377, 61 L.Ed. 585 (1917).

Second Circuit Grievance Panel, quoting this Ethics Treatise *In re Weideman*, 327 Fed. Appx. 215, 230–31 (2d Cir. 2009).

jurisdictional question, though it was implicit in the definition of misconduct,[7] which, by its own terms, provided no jurisdictional limitation. The 2002 version of Model Rule 8.5 explicitly codifies the present law: "A lawyer admitted to practice in this jurisdiction is subject to the disciplinary authority of this jurisdiction, regardless of where the lawyer's conduct occurs."[8]

§ 8.5-1(b) Choice of Law Issues

If a lawyer is admitted in State *A*, that state can discipline the lawyer for improper conduct, regardless of where the conduct occurred.[9] A lawyer may be admitted in two different jurisdictions, State *A*, and State *B*. If this lawyer engages in an act (either in State *A*, or *B*, or elsewhere) that is disciplinable, State *A* may discipline that lawyer for engaging in conduct in State *B*, even though State *B* punishes the same conduct less severely (*e.g.*, private admonition, versus suspension for one year, versus disbarment).[10] State *A* will no doubt contend that it has higher standards than State *B*. The situation is analogous to the case where two states adopt the multistate bar examination but one State sets a lower passing rate than the other.

Now consider the case where State *A* seeks to punish the conduct that occurred in State *B*, but the conduct did not violate the rules of State *B*. Choice of law problems are inevitable. If a lawyer practices in two jurisdictions, it is conceivable that conduct *forbidden* in one jurisdiction is ethically *compelled* in another. For example, State *A* may demand disclosure of client confidences in a situation where State *B* may forbid it.

The ABA Model Code had no provisions that dealt specifically with the choice of law problem, and the Model Rules as enacted in 1983 also had no provision on this issue. But in 1993, the ABA adopted Rule 8.5(b). The goal of this Rule was to insure that any particular conduct of a lawyer should be subject to only one set of rules.[11] Both jurisdictions may impose discipline, but they should both be using the same set of rules against which they measure the conduct. Disciplinary authorities should avoid proceeding

---

[7]DR 1-102.

[8]Rule 8.5(a).

[9]Rule 8.5(a). *See* Arvid E. Roach II, *The Virtues of Clarity: The ABA's New Choice of Law Rule for Legal Ethics*, 36 So.Tex.L.Rev. 907 (1995); Ronald D. Rotunda, *West Virginia Provides Model for Legal Discipline Over State Lines*, 7 LEGAL OPINION LETTER 1 (Washington Legal Foundation, No. 15, May 16, 1997).

[10]Some states, for example, allow for permanent disbarment; others do not. Ronald D. Rotunda, *The Case Against Permanent Disbarment*, 5 THE PROFESSIONAL LAWYER 22 (Feb. 1994); Ronald D. Rotunda & Mary M. Devlin, *Permanent Disbarment: A Market Oriented Proposal*, 9 THE PROFESSIONAL LAWYER 2 (1997).

[11]1993 Model Rule 8.5, Comment 3. *See* H. Geoffrey Moulton, Jr., *Federalism and Choice of Law in the Regulation of Legal Ethics*, 82 MINN. L. REV. 73 (1997) for a careful discussion of these issues.

against a lawyer on the basis of two inconsistent rules.[12] The choice of law issue is: which jurisdiction's ethics rules should apply to a lawyer admitted in more than one jurisdiction.

In general, if the conduct at issue takes place before a court, the disciplinary authority should apply only the rules of the jurisdiction where that court sits (unless the rules of that court provide otherwise). Thus, let us assume that a lawyer is admitted generally in State *A*, and is admitted *pro hac vice*[13] in a case heard in State *B*. Under the Model Rules, if that lawyer then violates the rules of the court in State *B*, State *A* should apply the ethics rules of State *B*, which are the rules applicable to that case.[14]

Prior to the 2002 revisions, Rule 8.5 provided that, for all other conduct, if the lawyer is licensed to practice in one jurisdiction only, the disciplinary authority should apply only the rules of that jurisdiction. If the lawyer is licensed to practice in more than one jurisdiction, the applicable rules should be the rules of the jurisdiction where the lawyer (as an individual, not the lawyer's firm) *principally practices*. The Rule contained an exception to this general rule in the case where the particular conduct "clearly has its predominate effect in another jurisdiction," in which case the rules of that other jurisdiction should apply.[15]

In 2000, the ABA created a Commission on Multijurisdictional Practice of Law to study changes in regulating the practice of law across jurisdictional lines. The drafters of the 2002 Model Rules studied Rule 8.5, made recommendations, and deferred consideration of such issues to the MJP Commission, which was responsible for presenting an entire package of proposals on multijurisdictional issues for adoption by the ABA. In 2002, the MJP Commission presented its report on multijurisdictional practice of law to the House of Delegates.[16] In August 2002, the ABA adopted changes to Rule 8.5 on disciplinary jurisdiction.

The MJP Commission believed that the 1993 Rule 8.5's focus on where the lawyer was licensed and where the lawyer "principally practiced" was unclear and did not sufficiently recognize

---

[12] 1993 Model Rule 8.5, Comment 5. *See* Restatement of the Law Governing Lawyers, Third, § 5, Comment *h* (Official Draft 2000). The North Dakota Supreme Court in *In re Overboe*, 745 N.W.2d 852 (Minn. 2008) held that a lawyer licensed in North Dakota and Minnesota who had commingled funds in Minnesota but lied about it in North Dakota was subject to Minnesota law for his commingling conduct and North Dakota law for his misrepresentations to the North Dakota bar.

[13] One time only admission for purposes of a particular proceeding.

[14] Rule 8.5(b)(1).

[15] Former Rule 8.5(b)(2) & former Comment 4, prior to their revision in 2002.

[16] Information about the MJP Commission may be found at its website. *See* http://www.abanet.org. cpr/mjp-home.html.

jurisdictions' interest in enforcing compliance with their rules of professional conduct when lawyers engage in multijurisdictional practice. Thus, the Commission proposed, and the ABA adopted, a new test for situations that do not involve a lawyer's representations before a tribunal. Under new Rule 8.5(b), adopted in 2002, the applicable factors in matters *not* pending before a tribunal now are: (1) *the place where the conduct* occurred, and (2) the *place of predominant effect* of the conduct in question. Thus, the rules of the state where the conduct occurred will apply *unless* the predominant effect of the legal work is in another state. If the predominant effect is in another jurisdiction, the rules of that jurisdiction apply to regulate the lawyer's conduct.[17]

The MJP Commission conceded that this test may not be as simple as the old one, but it was more predictable than traditional choice of law principles. A test that focused on the licensure of the lawyer no longer made sense given the new provisions regulating temporary practice of law out of state under new Rule 5.5.

§ 8.5–1(c) Reciprocal Discipline

Reciprocal discipline is the imposition of a disciplinary sanction for conduct for which a lawyer has been disciplined in another jurisdiction.[18] Typically, the rules governing lawyers provide that when one jurisdiction suspends or disbars a lawyer, that lawyer

---

[17]**Internet Advertising and Choice of Law.** Daniel Backer, *Choice of Law in Online Legal Ethics: Changing a Vague Standard for Attorney Advertising on the Internet*, 70 FORDHAM L. REV. 2409 (2002), which discusses "predominant effect" test. He argues that this test is problematic in the context of the Internet, which is akin to a world-wide Yellow Pages. Anyone, anywhere in the world, can access a website. "[I]t is difficult to discern where the predominant effect of Internet activity is felt." 70 FORDHAM L. REV. at 2411 (footnote omitted). This article proposes that the predominant effect test should not apply to lawyers' conduct in marketing over the Internet. Instead, the lawyer, for Internet advertising, should "conform to the rules of the jurisdiction in which he 'principally practices.'" 70 FORDHAM L. REV. at 2432 (footnote omitted).

See also William E. Hornsby, Jr., *Ad Rules Infinitum: The Need for Alternatives To State-Based Ethics Governing Legal Services Marketing*, 36 U. RICH. L. REV. 49 (2002): "The inherent state-based regulation, the inconsistencies among states, and the high standards combine to make it difficult, if not impossible, for the Twenty-first Century multijurisdictional law firm to fully comply." 36 U. Rich. L. Rev. 49, 50.

J.T. Westermeier, *Ethics and the Internet*, 17 GEORGETOWN J. LEGAL ETHICS 267 (2004): "there is a growing recognition that the legal ethics rules may be inhibiting competition and consumer choice respecting Internet-delivered legal services." 17 GEORGETOWN J. LEGAL ETHICS 267, 311. This article argues for uniform national standards.

[18]ABA Standards for Imposing Lawyer Sanctions, § 2.9. The American Bar Association's Center for Professional Responsibility operates the National Lawyer Regulatory Data Bank.

must report the discipline to every other jurisdiction in which the lawyer is admitted. In addition, the ABA keeps a National Lawyer Regulatory Data Bank in order to facilitate the imposition of reciprocal discipline, so that disciplinary counsel or other appropriate authority in each state can report all cases of public discipline to the ABA.[19] Then, jurisdictions will know of the other jurisdiction's discipline in case the disciplined lawyer does not self-report. These other jurisdictions may then impose reciprocal discipline.[20] A jurisdiction can impose reciprocal discipline without a hearing, but the court should provide the lawyer with an opportunity to raise a due process challenge or to show that a sanction different from the sanction imposed in the other jurisdiction is warranted.

These other jurisdictions may refuse to accept the findings of the first jurisdiction, on the grounds that the procedures were unfair.[21] For example, the federal rule is that—even though admission to practice before a federal court is derivative from membership in a state bar—state disbarment does not result in automatic disbarment by the federal court. The state action is entitled to respect, but it is not conclusively binding on the federal courts.[22] States follow the same principle.

In addition, even if one jurisdiction accepts the other jurisdiction's decision that an act occurred, the common rule is that the other jurisdiction need not automatically impose identical disciplinary measures. The other jurisdiction retains the discretion to impose greater, lesser or no reciprocal discipline.[23] For

---

[19]See http://www.abanet.org/cpr/regulation/databank.html (information about the databank).

[20]See, e.g., In re Discipline of Clinton, 534 U.S. 806, 122 S.Ct. 36, 151 L.Ed.2d 254 (2001).

[21]In re Ruffalo, 390 U.S. 544, 88 S.Ct. 1222, 20 L.Ed.2d 117 (1968). The Sixth Circuit disbarred a lawyer from practice in that court based on reciprocal discipline. The Supreme Court granted certiorari and reversed. The Court held that when a lawyer in a state disbarment proceedings had no notice that his employment of a certain person would be considered a disbarment offense until after both he and that person had testified at length on all material facts pertaining to that phase of case, the absence of fair no-

tice as to the reach of the grievance procedure and the precise nature of the charges deprived that lawyer of procedural due process, even though he was thereafter given several months to respond to that charge.

[22]Theard v. United States, 354 U.S. 278, 281–82, 77 S.Ct. 1274, 1276, 1 L.Ed.2d 1342 (1957); In re Ruffalo, 390 U.S. 544, 547, 88 S.Ct. 1222, 1224, 20 L.Ed.2d 117 (1968).

[23]See, e.g., In re Gardner, 650 A.2d 693 (D.C.1994), holding that reciprocal discipline will be imposed for disciplinary violations in another state unless attorney can show by clear and convincing evidence that a specified exception to reciprocal discipline applied.

example, in the case of *In Matter of Iulo*,[24] the lawyer had been disbarred in New Jersey for misapplying client funds. The applicant was later admitted to the Pennsylvania bar, and the issue was whether he should be disbarred as a result of the New Jersey action. The Pennsylvania court said no, because Pennsylvania seeks to rehabilitate lawyers, while New Jersey seeks to exclude them from practice. A court, using principles of reciprocal discipline, may honor factual findings made elsewhere but may also decide that the ethical violation does not require the imposition of identical sanctions.[25]

In 2002, the ABA House of Delegates amended Rules 6 and 22 of the Model Rules for Lawyer Disciplinary Enforcement.[26] These amendments were based upon the MJP Commission's recommendations and they coordinated the adoption of Rule 5.5 on out-of-state practice and Rule 8.5 on choice of professional responsibility rules. The MJP Commission strongly encourages the use of reciprocal discipline and hopes that its use will ultimately improve the regulation of lawyers who practice across jurisdictions.

§ 8.5–1(d) Suspended and Disbarred Lawyers

A lawyer who is suspended from the practice of law is still subject to the relevant provisions of the Rules of Professional Conduct. As one court explained, "a lawyer whose license is suspended is still an active member of the bar and, although not in good standing, is subject to the Rules."[27] This is a long-standing principle.[28]

---

[24] *In Matter of Iulo*, 564 Pa. 205, 213–14, 766 A.2d 335, 339 (2001).

[25] *See, e.g., In Matter of Iulo*, 564 Pa. 205, 213–14, 766 A.2d 335, 339 (2001).

Lesser Discipline. *See, e.g., State ex rel. Oklahoma Bar Association v. Patterson*, 2001 Ok. 51, 28 P.3d 551 (2001), holding that public censure is the appropriate sanction for a lawyer who practiced law while under suspension even though the Tenth Circuit disbarred him for that misconduct.

Greater Discipline. *See, e.g., The Florida Bar v. Karahalis*, 780 So.2d 27 (Fla.2001), which disbarred a lawyer who paid $12,000 to a Congressman to help transfer his uncle to a different federal prison that was closer to his family. Massachusetts,

where the bribery occurred, suspended the lawyer for four years, but Florida concluded that the lawyer should lose his Florida license because Florida's ethics rules treat bribery as an especially serious failing. The two dissenting justices argued that the court should have followed the lead of the Massachusetts Supreme Judicial Court and that the action for which this Court disbarred Karahalis occurred in Massachusetts in 1985, over 15 years earlier.

[26] *See* ABA CENTER FOR PROFESSIONALISM, ANNOTATED MODEL RULES OF PROFESSIONAL CONDUCT 625 (ABA, 5th ed. 2003).

[27] E.g., *In re Oliver*, 97 Utah 1, 89 P.2d 229 (1939); *State ex rel. Nebraska State Bar Ass'n v. Butterfield*, 172 Neb. 645, 111 N.W.2d 543 (1961); *Kirven v.*

Disbarment severs the lawyer's status and privileges. In contrast, suspension temporarily forces the lawyer to withdraw from the exercise of powers, obligations, and privileges of a member of the bar. "A suspended lawyer is therefore under the same obligation to comply with the Canons of Professional Ethics as is a lawyer in the active practice."[29] Thus, a court disbarred a suspended lawyer who, while engaging in *pro se* litigation against his ex-wife, raised a "completely frivolous" defense, and thus violated Rule 3.1.[30]

The disciplinary authorities also have jurisdiction over a disbarred Lawyer. For example, in one case, the Grievance Commission authorized filing a complaint against a disbarred lawyer, because he held himself out as a lawyer after his disbarment and committed other acts of misconduct. The Attorney Discipline Board dismissed the complaint on the ground that it lacked personal jurisdiction. The state supreme court reversed and held that even a disbarred attorney is subject to formal disciplinary complaint.[31]

§ 8.5–2 STATUTE OF LIMITATIONS

Neither the Code nor the Rules incorporate any statute of limitations for disciplinary actions. Because the purpose of discipline is to protect the public rather than punish the attorney[1] the time

---

Secretary of Bd. of Com'rs on Grievances and Discipline, 271 S.C. 194, 246 S.E.2d 857 (1978); *Matter of Wilkinson*, 251 Kan. 546, 834 P.2d 1356 (1992); *The Florida Bar v. Ross*, 732 So. 2d 1037 (Fla. 1998); *In re C de Baca*, 11 P.3d 426, 429-30 (Colo. 2000), cert. denied, 532 U.S. 921, 121 S. Ct. 1359, 149 L. Ed. 2d 288 (2001); *In re Chavez*, 2000-NMSC-015, 129 N.M. 35, 1 P.3d 417 (2000); *In re Morrissey*, 305 F.3d 211 (4th Cir. 2002), where the Federal District Court for the Eastern District of Virginia disbarred Morrissey, a lawyer licensed to practice in Virginia, for violations of the Virginia Code of Professional Responsibility occurring while his license was suspended. *Barrett v. Virginia State Bar ex rel. Second Dist. Committee*, 277 Va. 412, 414, 675 S.E.2d 827, 829 (2009).

[28]*State ex rel. Nebraska State Bar Ass'n v. Butterfield*, 172 Neb. 645, 649, 111 N.W.2d 543, 546 (1961):

The conduct of the respondent, in advertising in the public press his availability to prepare income tax returns, is therefore violative of Canon 27 of the Canons of Professional Ethics adopted by this court.

[29]*State ex rel. Nebraska State Bar Ass'n v. Butterfield*, 172 Neb. 645, 649, 111 N.W.2d 543, 546 (1961).

[30]*Barrett v. Virginia State Bar ex rel. Second Dist. Committee*, 277 Va. 412, 418–19, 675 S.E.2d 827, 831–32:

[F]or Barrett to assert persistently and repeatedly in the Circuit Court of Grayson County and in the Court of Appeals of Virginia that he is no longer required to support his children is completely frivolous, in light of the facts and the law of this case. Accordingly, we will affirm the Panel's order revoking Barrett's license to practice law in this Commonwealth. The appellant shall pay to the appellee thirty dollars damages.

[31]*Grievance Adm'r v. Hibler*, 457 Mich. 258, 577 N.W.2d 449 (1998).

[Section 8.5–2]

[1]*In re Echeles*, 430 F.2d 347, 349

when the misconduct occurred is relevant only to the extent that it bears on the lawyer's present fitness to practice law.

If the lawyer is accused of conduct that also is a civil tort or criminal wrong, the mere fact that the statute of limitations has run in either the civil or criminal case does not preclude disciplinary action. "Lawyer discipline and disability proceedings should not be subject to any statute of limitations."[2] If a charge against a lawyer is stale, the court might decide that it should not be considered, because an unreasonable delay in the presentation of a charge might make it impossible for the lawyer to procure witnesses or other evidence, but the statute of limitations itself is no defense to such a proceeding.[3]

(7th Cir.1970).

[2] ABA Standards for Lawyer Discipline and Disability Proceedings § 4.6 (1979).

[3] In re Smith, 73 Kan. 743, 745,

85 P. 584, 586 (1906). See also Anne Arundel County Bar Association, Inc. v. Collins, 272 Md. 578, 325 A.2d 724 (1974).

Index

A

G

GENERALLY KNOWN INFORMATION
Conflicts of interest, § 1.9-3

GENTILE DECISION
Publicity and comment, §§ 3.6-1 to 3.6-3

GIFTS FROM CLIENTS
Conflicts of interest, R 1.8(c); § 1.8-4

GOVERNMENT AGENCY LAWYERS
Generally, §§ 1.13-7(d) to 1.13-7(f)
Confidentiality, § 1.6-8; 1.13-7(f)
Conflicts of interest
Imputed disqualification, §§ 1.10-1(b); 1.11-3(e)(1), 1.11-4(b)
Successive employments, R 1.11; §§ 12-1 to 12-4.2
Disclosures, § 1.13-7(f)
Entire government rule, § 1.13-7(g)
Private clients, simultaneously representing, §§ 1.13-7(e), 1.13-7(f)
Representing government, generally, R 1.13 **Comment 9**
Restrictive covenants and contracts, § 5.6-2(c)
Screening, §§ 1.11-3(e)(1) to 1.11-3(e)(4)
Simultaneously representing private clients, §§ 1.13-7(d), 1.13-7(f)
Specific agency rule, § 1.13-7(e)

GROUNDLESS CLAIMS OR ARGUMENTS
Frivolous Claims or Arguments, this index

GUARDIANS
Disabled persons, R 1.14(b); § 1.14-1

H

HALF-TRUTHS
Disclosure, R 4.1; §§ 4.1-1 to 4.1-3

HARASSMENT
Rejecting cases, § 1.2-1(b)
Third party relations, R 4.4; § 4.4-1(a)

HARDBALL
Public image of lawyers, § 1-7

HISTORY
Generally, §§ 1-1(a) et seq.
Advertising, §§ 7.0-1 to 7.0-5
American Law Institute, § 1-3(b)
Candor and truthfulness, §§ 3.3-5 to 3.4-4(g)
Canons of Ethics, § 1-1(c)
Code of Professional Responsibility, § 1-1(d)
Construction with other laws, § 1-5
Hoffman resolutions, § 1-1(a)